Lecture Notes in Computer Science 11622

Commenced Publication in 1973
Founding and Former Series Editors:
Gerhard Goos, Juris Hartmanis, and Jan van Leeuwen

Sanjay Misra · Osvaldo Gervasi ·
Beniamino Murgante · Elena Stankova ·
Vladimir Korkhov · Carmelo Torre ·
Ana Maria A. C. Rocha ·
David Taniar · Bernady O. Apduhan ·
Eufemia Tarantino (Eds.)

Computational Science and Its Applications – ICCSA 2019

19th International Conference
Saint Petersburg, Russia, July 1–4, 2019
Proceedings, Part IV

Springer

Editors
Sanjay Misra
Covenant University
Ota, Nigeria

Osvaldo Gervasi
University of Perugia
Perugia, Italy

Beniamino Murgante
University of Basilicata
Potenza, Italy

Elena Stankova
Saint Petersburg State University
Saint Petersburg, Russia

Vladimir Korkhov
Saint Petersburg State University
Saint Petersburg, Russia

Carmelo Torre
Polytechnic University of Bari
Bari, Italy

Ana Maria A. C. Rocha
University of Minho
Braga, Portugal

David Taniar
Monash University
Clayton, VIC, Australia

Bernady O. Apduhan
Kyushu Sangyo University
Fukuoka, Japan

Eufemia Tarantino
Polytechnic University of Bari
Bari, Italy

ISSN 0302-9743 ISSN 1611-3349 (electronic)
Lecture Notes in Computer Science
ISBN 978-3-030-24304-3 ISBN 978-3-030-24305-0 (eBook)
https://doi.org/10.1007/978-3-030-24305-0

LNCS Sublibrary: SL1 – Theoretical Computer Science and General Issues

This Springer imprint is published by the registered company Springer Nature Switzerland AG
The registered company address is: Gewerbestrasse 11, 6330 Cham, Switzerland

Preface

These six volumes (LNCS volumes 11619–11624) consist of the peer-reviewed papers from the 2019 International Conference on Computational Science and Its Applications (ICCSA 2019) held in St. Petersburg, Russia during July 1–4, 2019, in collaboration with the St. Petersburg University, St. Petersburg, Russia.

ICCSA 2019 was a successful event in the International Conferences on Computational Science and Its Applications (ICCSA) series, previously held in Melbourne, Australia (2018), Trieste, Italy (2017), Beijing, China (2016), Banff, Canada (2015), Guimaraes, Portugal (2014), Ho Chi Minh City, Vietnam (2013), Salvador, Brazil (2012), Santander, Spain (2011), Fukuoka, Japan (2010), Suwon, South Korea (2009), Perugia, Italy (2008), Kuala Lumpur, Malaysia (2007), Glasgow, UK (2006), Singapore (2005), Assisi, Italy (2004), Montreal, Canada (2003), and (as ICCS) Amsterdam, The Netherlands (2002) and San Francisco, USA (2001).

Computational science is a main pillar of most of the current research, industrial and commercial activities, and plays a unique role in exploiting ICT innovative technologies. The ICCSA conference series have been providing a venue to researchers and industry practitioners to discuss new ideas, to share complex problems and their solutions, and to shape new trends in computational science.

Apart from the general track, ICCSA 2019 also included 33 workshops, in various areas of computational sciences, ranging from computational science technologies, to specific areas of computational sciences, such as software engineering, security, artificial intelligence, and blockchain technologies. We accepted 64 papers distributed in the five general tracks, 259 in workshops and ten short papers. We would like to show our appreciations to the workshop chairs and co-chairs.

The success of the ICCSA conference series, in general, and ICCSA 2019, in particular, is due to the support of many people: authors, presenters, participants, keynote speakers, workshop chairs, Organizing Committee members, student volunteers, Program Committee members, Advisory Committee members, international liaison chairs, reviewers and people in other various roles. We would like to thank them all.

We also thank our publisher, Springer, for accepting to publish the proceedings, for sponsoring part of the best papers awards and for their kind assistance and cooperation during the editing process.

We cordially invite you to visit the ICCSA website http://www.iccsa.org where you can find all relevant information about this interesting and exciting event.

July 2019

Osvaldo Gervasi
Beniamino Murgante
Sanjay Misra

Welcome to St. Petersburg

Welcome to St. Petersburg, the Venice of the North, the city of three revolutions, creation of czar Peter the Great, the most European city in Russia. ICCSA 2019 was hosted by St. Petersburg State University, during July 1–4, 2019.

St. Petersburg is the second largest city in Russia after Moscow. It is the former capital of Russia and has a lot of attractions related to this role in the past: imperial palaces and parks both in the city center and suburbs, respectable buildings of nobles and state institutions, multitude of rivers and canals with more than 300 bridges of various forms and sizes. Extraordinary history and rich cultural traditions of both imperial Russia and the Soviet Union attracted and inspired many examples of world's greatest architecture, literature, music, and visual art, some of which can be found in the famous Hermitage and State Russian Museum located in the heart of the city. Late June and early July is the season of white nights where the sun sets only for a few hours, and the nighttime is covered with mysterious twilight.

What to do in the city:

- Enjoy the white nights, see the open bridges during the night and cargo ships passing by from Ladoga Lake to the Gulf of Finland and back. Dvortsovy bridge is open at about 1am. Be sure to stay on the correct side of the river when the bridges open!
- Visit Hermitage (Winter palace) and State Russian Museum to see great examples of international and Russian art, and the Kunstkammer, the oldest museum of St. Petersburg founded by Peter the Great.
- Travel to St. Petersburg suburbs Peterhof and Tsarskoe Selo to see imperial palaces and splendid parks, famous Peterhof fountains.
- Eat Russian food: borsch (beetroot soup), pelmeni and vareniki (meat and sweet dumplings), bliny (pancakes), vinegret (beetroot salad), drink kvas and maybe some vodka.
- Walk around and inside the Peter and Paul Fortress, the place where the city began in 1703.
- Visit the Mariinsky Theater for famous Russian ballet and opera.
- Have a boat tour along the Neva River and canals to look at the city from the water.
- Walk along Nevsky Prospect, the main street of the city.
- Climb St. Isaac's Cathedral colonnade to enjoy great city views.
- Go down to the Metro, the city's underground train network with some Soviet-style museum-like stations.
- Pay a visit to the recently renovated Summer Garden, the oldest park of St. Petersburg.
- Visit a new modern open space on the New Holland Island to see modern art exhibitions, performances and just to relax and enjoy sitting on the grass with an ice cream or lemonade during a hot summer day.

St. Petersburg State University is the oldest university in Russia, an actively developing, world-class center of research and education. The university dates back to 1724, when Peter the Great founded the Academy of Sciences and Arts as well as the first Academic University and the university preparatory school in Russia. At present there are over 5,000 academic staff members and more than 30,000 students, receiving education in more than 400 educational programs at 25 faculties and institutes.

The venue of ICCSA is the Faculty of Economics located on Tavricheskaya Street, other faculties and university buildings are distributed all over the city with the main campus located on Vasilievsky Island and the natural science faculties (Mathematics and Mechanics, Applied Mathematics and Control Processes, Physics, Chemistry) located on the campus about 40 kilometers away from the city center in Peterhof.

Elena Stankova
Vladimir Korkhov
Nataliia Kulabukhova

Organization

ICCSA 2019 was organized by St. Petersburg University (Russia), University of Perugia (Italy), University of Basilicata (Italy), Monash University (Australia), Kyushu Sangyo University (Japan), University of Minho, (Portugal).

Honorary General Chairs

Antonio Laganà	University of Perugia, Italy
Norio Shiratori	Tohoku University, Japan
Kenneth C. J. Tan	Sardina Systems, Estonia

General Chairs

Osvaldo Gervasi	University of Perugia, Italy
Elena Stankova	St. Petersburg University, Russia
Bernady O. Apduhan	Kyushu Sangyo University, Japan

Program Committee Chairs

Beniamino Murgante	University of Basilicata, Italy
David Taniar	Monash University, Australia
Vladimir Korkov	St. Petersburg University, Russia
Ana Maria A. C. Rocha	University of Minho, Portugal

International Advisory Committee

Jemal Abawajy	Deakin University, Australia
Dharma P. Agarwal	University of Cincinnati, USA
Rajkumar Buyya	Melbourne University, Australia
Claudia Bauzer Medeiros	University of Campinas, Brazil
Manfred M. Fisher	Vienna University of Economics and Business, Austria
Marina L. Gavrilova	University of Calgary, Canada
Yee Leung	Chinese University of Hong Kong, SAR China

International Liaison Chairs

Ana Carla P. Bitencourt	Universidade Federal do Reconcavo da Bahia, Brazil
Giuseppe Borruso	University of Trieste, Italy
Alfredo Cuzzocrea	ICAR-CNR and University of Calabria, Italy
Maria Irene Falcão	University of Minho, Portugal
Robert C. H. Hsu	Chung Hua University, Taiwan
Tai-Hoon Kim	Hannam University, South Korea
Sanjay Misra	Covenant University, Nigeria

Takashi Naka	Kyushu Sangyo University, Japan
Rafael D. C. Santos	National Institute for Space Research, Brazil
Maribel Yasmina Santos	University of Minho, Portugal

Workshop and Session Organizing Chairs

Beniamino Murgante	University of Basilicata, Italy
Sanjay Misra	Covenant University, Nigeria
Jorge Gustavo Rocha	University of Minho, Portugal

Award Chair

Wenny Rahayu	La Trobe University, Australia

Publicity Committee Chairs

Elmer Dadios	De La Salle University, Philippines
Hong Quang Nguyen	International University (VNU-HCM), Vietnam
Daisuke Takahashi	Tsukuba University, Japan
Shangwang Wang	Beijing University of Posts and Telecommunications, China

Workshop Organizers

Advanced Transport Tools and Methods (A2TM 2019)

Massimiliano Petri	University of Pisa, Italy
Antonio Pratelli	University of Pisa, Italy

Advanced Computational Approaches in Fractals, Wavelet, Entropy and Data Mining Applications (AAFTWTETDT 2019)

Yeliz Karaca	University of Massachusetts Medical School, USA
Yu-Dong Zhang	University of Leicester, UK
Majaz Moonis	University of Massachusettes Medical School, USA

Advances in Artificial Intelligence Learning Technologies: Blended Learning, STEM, Computational Thinking and Coding (AAILT 2019)

Alfredo Milani	University of Perugia, Italy
Sergio Tasso	University of Perugia, Italy
Valentina Poggioni	University of Perugia, Italy

Affective Computing and Emotion Recognition (ACER-EMORE 2019)

Alfredo Milani	University of Perugia, Italy
Valentina Franzoni	University of Perugia, Italy
Giulio Biondi	University of Florence, Itay

Advances in Information Systems and Technologies for Emergency Management, Risk Assessment and Mitigation Based on the Resilience Concepts (ASTER 2019)

Maurizio Pollino	ENEA, Italy
Marco Vona	University of Basilicata, Italy
Beniamino Murgante	University of Basilicata, Italy

Blockchain and Distributed Ledgers: Technologies and Application (BDLTA 2019)

Vladimir Korkhov	St. Petersburg State University, Russia
Elena Stankova	St. Petersburg State University, Russia

Bio and Neuro-inspired Computing and Applications (BIONCA 2019)

Nadia Nedjah	State University of Rio de Janeiro, Brazil
Luiza de Macedo Mourell	State University of Rio de Janeiro, Brazil

Computer Aided Modeling, Simulation, and Analysis (CAMSA 2018)

Jie Shen	University of Michigan, USA
Hao Chen	Shanghai University of Engineering Science, China
Youguo He	Jiangsu University, China

Computational and Applied Statistics (CAS 2019)

Ana Cristina Braga	University of Minho, Portugal

Computational Mathematics, Statistics, and Information Management (CMSIM 2019)

M. Filomena Teodoro	Portuguese Naval Academy and Lisbon University, Portugal

Computational Optimization and Applications (COA 2019)

Ana Maria Rocha	University of Minho, Portugal
Humberto Rocha	University of Coimbra, Portugal

Computational Astrochemistry (CompAstro 2019)

Marzio Rosi	University of Perugia, Italy
Dimitrios Skouteris	Master-up, Perugia, Italy
Fanny Vazart	Université Grenoble Alpes, France
Albert Rimola	Universitat Autònoma de Barcelona, Spain

Cities, Technologies, and Planning (CTP 2019)

Beniamino Murgante	University of Basilicata, Italy
Giuseppe Borruso	University of Trieste, Italy

Econometrics and Multidimensional Evaluation in the Urban Environment (EMEUE 2019)

Carmelo M. Torre — Polytechnic of Bari, Italy
Pierluigi Morano — Polytechnic of Bari, Italy
Maria Cerreta — University of Naples Federico II, Italy
Paola Perchinunno — University of Bari, Italy
Francesco Tajani — University of Rome La Sapienza, Italy

Future Computing System Technologies and Applications (FISTA 2019)

Bernady O. Apduhan — Kyushu Sangyo University, Japan
Rafael Santos — National Institute for Space Research, Brazil

Geographical Analysis, Urban Modeling, Spatial Statistics (GEO-AND-MOD 2019)

Beniamino Murgante — University of Basilicata, Italy
Giuseppe Borruso — University of Trieste, Italy
Hartmut Asche — University of Potsdam, Germany

Geomatics for Resource Monitoring and Control (GRMC 2019)

Eufemia Tarantino — Polytechnic of Bari, Italy
Rosa Lasaponara — Italian Research Council, IMAA-CNR, Italy
Benedetto Figorito — ARPA Puglia, Italy
Umberto Fratino — Polytechnic of Bari, Italy

International Symposium on Software Quality (ISSQ 2019)

Sanjay Misra — Covenant University, Nigeria

Land Use Monitoring for Sustainability (LUMS 2019)

Carmelo M. Torre — Polytechnic of Bari, Italy
Alessandro Bonifazi — Polytechnic of Bari, Italy
Pasquale Balena — Polytechnic of Bari, Italy
Beniamino Murgante — University of Basilicata, Italy
Eric Gielen — Polytechnic University of Valencia, Spain

Machine Learning for Space and Earth Observation Data (ML-SEOD 2019)

Rafael Santos — Brazilian National Institute for Space Research, Brazil
Karine Reis Ferreira — National Institute for Space Research, Brazil

Mobile-Computing, Sensing, and Actuation in Cyber Physical Systems (MSA4CPS 2019)

Saad Qaisar — National University of Sciences and Technology, Pakistan
Moonseong Kim — Seoul Theological University, South Korea

Quantum Chemical Modeling of Solids with Computers: From Plane Waves to Local Structures (QuaCheSol 2019)

Andrei Tchougréeff	Russia Academy of Sciences, Russia
Richard Dronskowski	RWTH Aachen University, Germany
Taku Onishi	Mie University and Tromsoe University, Japan

Scientific Computing Infrastructure (SCI 2019)

Vladimir Korkhov	St. Petersburg State University, Russia
Elena Stankova	St. Petersburg State University, Russia
Nataliia Kulabukhova	St. Petersburg State University, Russia

Computational Studies for Energy and Comfort in Building (SECoB 2019)

Senhorinha Teixeira	University of Minho, Portugal
Angela Silva	Viana do Castelo Polytechnic Institute, Portugal
Ana Maria Rocha	University of Minho, Portugal

Software Engineering Processes and Applications (SEPA 2019)

Sanjay Misra	Covenant University, Nigeria

Smart Factory Convergence (SFC 2019)

Jongpil Jeong	Sungkyunkwan University, South Korea

Smart City and Water. Resource and Risk (Smart_Water 2019)

Giuseppe Borruso	University of Trieste, Italy
Ginevra Balletto	University of Cagliari, Italy
Gianfranco Becciu	Polytechnic University of Milan, Italy
Chiara Garau	University of Cagliari, Italy
Beniamino Murgante	University of Basilicata, Italy
Francesco Viola	University of Cagliari, Italy

Sustainability Performance Assessment: Models, Approaches, and Applications Toward Interdisciplinary and Integrated Solutions (SPA 2019)

Francesco Scorza	University of Basilicata, Italy
Valentin Grecu	Lucia Blaga University on Sibiu, Romania
Jolanta Dvarioniene	Kaunas University, Lithuania
Sabrina Lai	University of Cagliari, Italy

Theoretical and Computational Chemistry and Its Applications (TCCMA 2019)

Noelia Faginas Lago	University of Perugia, Italy
Andrea Lombardi	University of Perugia, Italy

Tools and Techniques in Software Development Processes (TTSDP 2019)

Sanjay Misra	Covenant University, Nigeria

Virtual Reality and Applications (VRA 2019)

Osvaldo Gervasi	University of Perugia, Italy
Sergio Tasso	University of Perugia, Italy

Collective, Massive and Evolutionary Systems (WCES 2019)

Alfredo Milani	University of Perugia, Italy
Valentina Franzoni	University of Rome La Sapienza, Italy
Rajdeep Niyogi	Indian Institute of Technology at Roorkee, India
Stefano Marcugini	University of Perugia, Italy

Parallel and Distributed Data Mining (WPDM 2019)

Massimo Cafaro	University of Salento, Italy
Italo Epicoco	University of Salento, Italy
Marco Pulimeno	University of Salento, Italy
Giovanni Aloisio	University of Salento, Italy

Program Committee

Kenneth Adamson	University of Ulster, UK
Vera Afreixo	University of Aveiro, Portugal
Filipe Alvelos	University of Minho, Portugal
Remadevi Arjun	National Institute of Technology Karnataka, India
Hartmut Asche	University of Potsdam, Germany
Ginevra Balletto	University of Cagliari, Italy
Michela Bertolotto	University College Dublin, Ireland
Sandro Bimonte	CEMAGREF, TSCF, France
Rod Blais	University of Calgary, Canada
Ivan Blečić	University of Sassari, Italy
Giuseppe Borruso	University of Trieste, Italy
Ana Cristina Braga	University of Minho, Portugal
Massimo Cafaro	University of Salento, Italy
Yves Caniou	Lyon University, France
José A. Cardoso e Cunha	Universidade Nova de Lisboa, Portugal
Leocadio G. Casado	University of Almeria, Spain
Carlo Cattani	University of Salerno, Italy
Mete Celik	Erciyes University, Turkey
Hyunseung Choo	Sungkyunkwan University, South Korea
Min Young Chung	Sungkyunkwan University, South Korea
Florbela Maria da Cruz Domingues Correia	Polytechnic Institute of Viana do Castelo, Portugal
Gilberto Corso Pereira	Federal University of Bahia, Brazil
Alessandro Costantini	INFN, Italy
Carla Dal Sasso Freitas	Universidade Federal do Rio Grande do Sul, Brazil
Pradesh Debba	The Council for Scientific and Industrial Research (CSIR), South Africa
Hendrik Decker	Instituto Tecnológico de Informática, Spain

Frank Devai	London South Bank University, UK
Rodolphe Devillers	Memorial University of Newfoundland, Canada
Joana Matos Dias	University of Coimbra, Portugal
Paolino Di Felice	University of L'Aquila, Italy
Prabu Dorairaj	NetApp, India/USA
M. Irene Falcao	University of Minho, Portugal
Cherry Liu Fang	U.S. DOE Ames Laboratory, USA
Florbela P. Fernandes	Polytechnic Institute of Bragança, Portugal
Jose-Jesus Fernandez	National Centre for Biotechnology, CSIS, Spain
Paula Odete Fernandes	Polytechnic Institute of Bragança, Portugal
Adelaide de Fátima Baptista Valente Freitas	University of Aveiro, Portugal
Manuel Carlos Figueiredo	University of Minho, Portugal
Valentina Franzoni	University of Rome La Sapienza, Italy
Maria Celia Furtado Rocha	PRODEB–PósCultura/UFBA, Brazil
Chiara Garau	University of Cagliari, Italy
Paulino Jose Garcia Nieto	University of Oviedo, Spain
Jerome Gensel	LSR-IMAG, France
Maria Giaoutzi	National Technical University, Athens, Greece
Arminda Manuela Andrade Pereira Gonçalves	University of Minho, Portugal
Andrzej M. Goscinski	Deakin University, Australia
Sevin Gümgüm	Izmir University of Economics, Turkey
Alex Hagen-Zanker	University of Cambridge, UK
Shanmugasundaram Hariharan	B.S. Abdur Rahman University, India
Eligius M. T. Hendrix	University of Malaga/Wageningen University, Spain/The Netherlands
Hisamoto Hiyoshi	Gunma University, Japan
Mustafa Inceoglu	EGE University, Turkey
Jongpil Jeong	Sungkyunkwan University, South Korea
Peter Jimack	University of Leeds, UK
Qun Jin	Waseda University, Japan
A. S. M. Kayes	La Trobe University, Australia
Farid Karimipour	Vienna University of Technology, Austria
Baris Kazar	Oracle Corp., USA
Maulana Adhinugraha Kiki	Telkom University, Indonesia
DongSeong Kim	University of Canterbury, New Zealand
Taihoon Kim	Hannam University, South Korea
Ivana Kolingerova	University of West Bohemia, Czech Republic
Nataliia Kulabukhova	St. Petersburg University, Russia
Vladimir Korkhov	St. Petersburg University, Russia
Rosa Lasaponara	National Research Council, Italy
Maurizio Lazzari	National Research Council, Italy
Cheng Siong Lee	Monash University, Australia
Sangyoun Lee	Yonsei University, South Korea

Jongchan Lee	Kunsan National University, South Korea
Chendong Li	University of Connecticut, USA
Gang Li	Deakin University, Australia
Fang Liu	AMES Laboratories, USA
Xin Liu	University of Calgary, Canada
Andrea Lombardi	University of Perugia, Italy
Savino Longo	University of Bari, Italy
Tinghuai Ma	NanJing University of Information Science and Technology, China
Ernesto Marcheggiani	Katholieke Universiteit Leuven, Belgium
Antonino Marvuglia	Research Centre Henri Tudor, Luxembourg
Nicola Masini	National Research Council, Italy
Eric Medvet	University of Trieste,Italy
Nirvana Meratnia	University of Twente, The Netherlands
Noelia Faginas Lago	University of Perugia,Italy
Giuseppe Modica	University of Reggio Calabria, Italy
Josè Luis Montaña	University of Cantabria, Spain
Maria Filipa Mourão	IP from Viana do Castelo, Portugal
Louiza de Macedo Mourelle	State University of Rio de Janeiro, Brazil
Nadia Nedjah	State University of Rio de Janeiro,Brazil
Laszlo Neumann	University of Girona, Spain
Kok-Leong Ong	Deakin University, Australia
Belen Palop	Universidad de Valladolid, Spain
Marcin Paprzycki	Polish Academy of Sciences, Poland
Eric Pardede	La Trobe University, Australia
Kwangjin Park	Wonkwang University, South Korea
Ana Isabel Pereira	Polytechnic Institute of Bragança, Portugal
Massimiliano Petri	University of Pisa, Italy
Maurizio Pollino	Italian National Agency for New Technologies, Energy and Sustainable Economic Development, Italy
Alenka Poplin	University of Hamburg, Germany
Vidyasagar Potdar	Curtin University of Technology, Australia
David C. Prosperi	Florida Atlantic University, USA
Wenny Rahayu	La Trobe University, Australia
Jerzy Respondek	Silesian University of Technology Poland
Humberto Rocha	INESC-Coimbra, Portugal
Jon Rokne	University of Calgary, Canada
Octavio Roncero	CSIC, Spain
Maytham Safar	Kuwait University, Kuwait
Chiara Saracino	A.O. Ospedale Niguarda Ca' Granda - Milano, Italy
Haiduke Sarafian	The Pennsylvania State University, USA
Francesco Scorza	University of Basilicata, Italy
Marco Paulo Seabra dos Reis	University of Coimbra, Portugal
Jie Shen	University of Michigan, USA

Qi Shi	Liverpool John Moores University, UK
Dale Shires	U.S. Army Research Laboratory, USA
Inês Soares	University of Coimbra, Portugal
Elena Stankova	St. Petersburg University, Russia
Takuo Suganuma	Tohoku University, Japan
Eufemia Tarantino	Polytechnic of Bari, Italy
Sergio Tasso	University of Perugia, Italy
Ana Paula Teixeira	University of Trás-os-Montes and Alto Douro, Portugal
Senhorinha Teixeira	University of Minho, Portugal
M. Filomena Teodoro	Portuguese Naval Academy and University of Lisbon, Portugal
Parimala Thulasiraman	University of Manitoba, Canada
Carmelo Torre	Polytechnic of Bari, Italy
Javier Martinez Torres	Centro Universitario de la Defensa Zaragoza, Spain
Giuseppe A. Trunfio	University of Sassari, Italy
Pablo Vanegas	University of Cuenca, Equador
Marco Vizzari	University of Perugia, Italy
Varun Vohra	Merck Inc., USA
Koichi Wada	University of Tsukuba, Japan
Krzysztof Walkowiak	Wroclaw University of Technology, Poland
Zequn Wang	Intelligent Automation Inc., USA
Robert Weibel	University of Zurich, Switzerland
Frank Westad	Norwegian University of Science and Technology, Norway
Roland Wismüller	Universität Siegen, Germany
Mudasser Wyne	SOET National University, USA
Chung-Huang Yang	National Kaohsiung Normal University, Taiwan
Xin-She Yang	National Physical Laboratory, UK
Salim Zabir	France Telecom Japan Co., Japan
Haifeng Zhao	University of California, Davis, USA
Fabiana Zollo	University of Venice Cà Foscari, Italy
Albert Y. Zomaya	University of Sydney, Australia

Additional Reviewers

Adewumi Oluwasegun	Covenant University, Nigeria
Afreixo Vera	University of Aveiro, Portugal
Agrawal Akshat	International Institute of Information Technology Bangalore, India
Aguilar Antonio	University of Barcelona, Spain
Ahmad Rashid	Microwave and Antenna Lab, School of Engineering, South Korea
Ahmed Waseem	Federal University of Technology, Nigeria
Alamri Sultan	Taibah University, Medina, Saudi Arabia
Alfa Abraham	Kogi State College of Education, Nigeria
Alvelos Filipe	University of Minho, Portugal

Amato Federico	University of Basilicata, Italy
Amin Benatia Mohamed	Groupe Cesi, Francia
Andrianov Serge	Institute for Informatics of Tatarstan Academy of Sciences, Russia
Apduhan Bernady	Kyushu Sangyo University, Japan
Aquilanti Vincenzo	University of Perugia, Italy
Arjun Remadevi	National Institute of Technology Karnataka, India
Arogundade Oluwasefunmi	Federal University of Agriculture, Nigeria
Ascenzi Daniela	University of Trento, Italy
Ayeni Foluso	Southern University and A&M College, USA
Azubuike Ezenwoke	Covenant University, Nigeria
Balacco Gabriella	Polytechnic of Bari, Italy
Balena Pasquale	Polytechnic of Bari, Italy
Balletto Ginevra	University of Cagliari, Italy
Barrile Vincenzo	Mediterranean University of Reggio Calabria, Italy
Bartolomei Massimiliano	Spanish National Research Council, Spain
Behera Ranjan Kumar	Indian Institute of Technology Patna, India
Biondi Giulio	University of Florence, Italy
Bist Ankur Singh	KIET Ghaziabad, India
Blecic Ivan	University of Cagliari, Italy
Bogdanov Alexander	St. Petersburg State University, Russia
Borgogno Mondino Enrico Corrado	University of Turin, Italy
Borruso Giuseppe	University of Trieste, Italy
Bostenaru Maria	Ion Mincu University of Architecture and Urbanism, Romania
Braga Ana Cristina	University of Minho, Portugal
Cafaro Massimo	University of Salento, Italy
Capolupo Alessandra	University of Naples Federico II, Italy
Carvalho-Silva Valter	Universidade Estadual de Goiás, Brazil
Cerreta Maria	University Federico II of Naples, Italy
Chan Sheung Wai	Hong Kong Baptist Hospital, SAR China
Cho Chulhee	Seoul Guarantee Insurance Company Ltd., South Korea
Choi Jae-Young	Sungkyunkwan University, South Korea
Correia Anacleto	Base Naval de Lisboa, Portugal
Correia Elisete	University of Trás-Os-Montes e Alto Douro, Portugal
Correia Florbela Maria da Cruz Domingues	Instituto Politécnico de Viana do Castelo, Portugal
Costa e Silva Eliana	Polytechnic of Porto, Portugal
Costa Lino	Universidade do Minho, Portugal
Costantini Alessandro	Istituto Nazionale di Fisica Nucleare, Italy
Crawford Broderick	Pontificia Universidad Católica de Valparaíso, Chile
Cutini Valerio	University of Pisa, Italy
D'Acierno Luca	University of Naples Federico II, Italy
Danese Maria	Italian National Research Council, Italy
Dantas Coutinho Nayara	University of Perugia, Italy
Degtyarev Alexander	St. Petersburg State University, Russia

Dereli Dursun Ahu	UNSW Sydney, Australia
Devai Frank	London South Bank University, UK
Di Bari Gabriele	University of Florence, Italy
Dias Joana	University of Coimbra, Portugal
Diaz Diana	National University of Colombia, Colombia
Elfadaly Abdelaziz	University of Basilicata, Italy
Enriquez Palma Pedro Alberto	Universidad de la Rioja, Spain
Epicoco Italo	University of Salento, Italy
Esposito Giuseppina	Sapienza University of Rome, Italy
Faginas-Lago M. Noelia	University of Perugia, Italy
Fajardo Jorge	Universidad Politécnica Salesiana (UPS), Ecuador
Falcinelli Stefano	University of Perugia, Italy
Farina Alessandro	University of Pisa, Italy
Fattoruso Grazia	ENEA, Italy
Fernandes Florbela	Escola Superior de Tecnologia e Gestão de Bragancca, Portugal
Fernandes Paula	Escola Superior de Tecnologia e Gestão, Portugal
Fernández Ledesma Javier Darío	Universidad Pontificia Bolivariana, Bolivia
Ferreira Ana C.	University of Lisbon, Portugal
Ferrão Maria	Universidade da Beira Interior, Portugal
Figueiredo Manuel Carlos	Universidade do Minho, Portugal
Florez Hector	Universidad Distrital Francisco Jose de Caldas, Colombia
Franzoni Valentina	University of Perugia, Italy
Freitau Adelaide de Fátima Baptista Valente	University of Aveiro, Portugal
Friday Agbo	University of Eastern Finland, Finland
Frunzete Madalin	Polytechnic University of Bucharest, Romania
Fusco Giovanni	Laboratoire ESPACE, CNRS, France
Gabrani Goldie	Bml Munjal University, India
Gankevich Ivan	St. Petersburg State University, Russia
Garau Chiara	University of Cagliari, Italy
Garcia Ernesto	University of the Basque Country, Spain
Gavrilova Marina	University of Calgary, Canada
Gervasi Osvaldo	University of Perugia, Italy
Gilner Ewa	Silesian University of Technology, Poland
Gioia Andrea	University of Bari, Italy
Giorgi Giacomo	University of Perugia, Italy
Gonçalves Arminda Manuela	University of Minho, Portugal
Gorbachev Yuriy	Geolink Technologies, Russia
Gotoh Yusuke	Kyoto University, Japan
Goyal Rinkaj	Guru Gobind Singh Indraprastha University, India
Gümgüm Sevin	Izmir Economy University, Turkey

Gülen Kemal Güven	Istanbul Ticaret University, Turkey
Hegedus Peter	University of Szeged, Hungary
Hendrix Eligius M. T.	University of Malaga, Spain
Iacobellis Vito	Polytechnic of Bari, Italy
Iakushkin Oleg	St. Petersburg State University, Russia
Kadry Seifedine	Beirut Arab University, Lebanon
Kim JeongAh	George Fox University, USA
Kim Moonseong	Korean Intellectual Property Office, South Korea
Kolingerova Ivana	University of West Bohemia, Czech Republic
Koo Jahwan	Sungkyunkwan University, South Korea
Korkhov Vladimir	St. Petersburg State University, Russia
Kulabukhova Nataliia	St. Peterburg State University, Russia
Ladu Mara	University of Cagliari, Italy
Laganà Antonio	Master-up srl, Italy
Leon Marcelo	Universidad Estatal Peninsula de Santa Elena – UPSE, Ecuador
Lima Rui	University of Minho, Portugal
Lombardi Andrea	University of Perugia, Italy
Longo Savino	University of Bari, Italy
Maciel de Castro Jessica	Universidade Federal da Paraíba, Brazil
Magni Riccardo	Pragma Engineering S.r.L., Italy
Mandanici Emanuele	University of Bologna, Italy
Mangiameli Michele	University of Catania, Italy
Marcellini Moreno	Ecole normale supérieure de Lyon, France
Marghany Maged	Universiti Teknologi Malaysia, Malaysia
Marques Jorge	Universidade de Coimbra, Portugal
Martellozzo Federico	University of Florence, Italy
Mengoni Paolo	University of Florence, Italy
Migliore Marco	University of Cassino e del Lazio Meridionale, Italy
Milani Alfredo	University of Perugia, Italy
Milesi Alessandra	Istituto Auxologico Italiano, Italy
Mishra Biswajeeban	University of Szeged, Hungary
Molaei Qelichi Mohamad	University of Tehran, Iran
Monteiro Vitor	University of Minho, Portugal
Moraes João Luís Cardoso	University of Porto, Portugal
Moura Ricardo	Universidade Nova de Lisboa, Portugal
Mourao Maria	Universidade do Minho, Portugal
Murgante Beniamino	University of Basilicata, Italy
Natário Isabel Cristina Maciel	Universidade Nova de Lisboa, Portugal
Nedjah Nadia	Rio de Janeiro State University, Brazil
Nocera Silvio	University of Naples Federico II, Italy
Odun-Ayo Isaac	Covenant University, Nigeria
Okewu Emmanuel	University of Lagos, Nigeria
Oliveira Irene	University of Trás-Os-Montes e Alto Douro, Portugal
Oluranti Jonathan	Covenant University, Nigeria

Osho Oluwafemi	Federal University of Technology Minna, Nigeria
Ozturk Savas	The Scientific and Technological Research Council of Turkey, Turkey
Panetta J. B.	University of Georgia, USA
Pardede Eric	La Trobe University, Australia
Perchinunno Paola	University of Bari, Italy
Pereira Ana	Instituto Politécnico de Bragança, Portugal
Peschechera Giuseppe	University of Bari, Italy
Petri Massimiliano	University of Pisa, Italy
Petrovic Marjana	University of Zagreb, Croatia
Pham Quoc Trung	Ho Chi Minh City University of Technology, Vietnam
Pinto Telmo	University of Minho, Portugal
Plekhanov Evgeny	Russian Academy of Economics, Russia
Poggioni Valentina	University of Perugia, Italy
Polidoro Maria João	University of Lisbon, Portugal
Pollino Maurizio	ENEA, Italy
Popoola Segun	Covenant University, Nigeria
Pratelli Antonio	University of Pisa, Italy
Pulimeno Marco	University of Salento, Italy
Rasool Hamid	National University of Sciences and Technology, Pakistan
Reis Marco	Universidade de Coimbra, Portugal
Respondek Jerzy	Silesian University of Technology, Poland
Riaz Nida	National University of Sciences and Technology, Pakistan
Rimola Albert	Autonomous University of Barcelona, Spain
Rocha Ana Maria	University of Minho, Portugal
Rocha Humberto	University of Coimbra, Portugal
Rosi Marzio	University of Perugia, Italy
Santos Rafael	National Institute for Space Research, Brazil
Santucci Valentino	University Stranieri of Perugia, Italy
Saponaro Mirko	Polytechnic of Bari, Italy
Sarafian Haiduke	Pennsylvania State University, USA
Scorza Francesco	University of Basilicata, Italy
Sedova Olya	St. Petersburg State University, Russia
Semanjski Ivana	Ghent University, Belgium
Sharma Jeetu	Mody University of Science and Technology, India
Sharma Purnima	University of Lucknow, India
Shchegoleva Nadezhda	Petersburg State Electrotechnical University, Russia
Shen Jie	University of Michigan, USA
Shoaib Muhammad	Sungkyunkwan University, South Korea
Shou Huahao	Zhejiang University of Technology, China
Silva-Fortes Carina	ESTeSL-IPL, Portugal
Silva Ângela Maria	Escola Superior de Ciências Empresariais, Portugal
Singh Upasana	The University of Manchester, UK
Singh V. B.	University of Delhi, India

Skouteris Dimitrios	Master-up, Perugia, Italy
Soares Inês	INESCC and IPATIMUP, Portugal
Soares Michel	Universidade Federal de Sergipe, Brazil
Sosnin Petr	Ulyanovsk State Technical University, Russia
Sousa Ines	University of Minho, Portugal
Stankova Elena	St. Petersburg State University, Russia
Stritih Uros	University of Ljubljana, Slovenia
Tanaka Kazuaki	Kyushu Institute of Technology, Japan
Tarantino Eufemia	Polytechnic of Bari, Italy
Tasso Sergio	University of Perugia, Italy
Teixeira Senhorinha	University of Minho, Portugal
Tengku Adil	La Trobe University, Australia
Teodoro M. Filomena	Lisbon University, Portugal
Torre Carmelo Maria	Polytechnic of Bari, Italy
Totaro Vincenzo	Polytechnic of Bari, Italy
Tripathi Aprna	GLA University, India
Vancsics Béla	University of Szeged, Hungary
Vasyunin Dmitry	University of Amsterdam, The Netherlands
Vig Rekha	The Northcap University, India
Walkowiak Krzysztof	Wroclaw University of Technology, Poland
Wanderley Fernando	New University of Lisbon, Portugal
Wang Chao	University of Science and Technology of China, China
Westad Frank	CAMO Software AS, USA
Yamazaki Takeshi	University of Tokyo, Japan
Zahra Noore	University of Guilan, India
Zollo Fabiana	University of Venice Ca' Foscari, Italy
Zullo Francesco	University of L'Aquila, Italy
Žemlička Michal	Charles University in Prague, Czech Republic
Živković Ljiljana	Republic Agency for Spatial Planning, Serbia

Sponsoring Organizations

ICCSA 2019 would not have been possible without tremendous support of many organizations and institutions, for which all organizers and participants of ICCSA 2019 express their sincere gratitude:

Springer Nature Switzerland AG, Germany
(http://www.springer.com)

St. Petersburg University, Russia
(http://english.spbu.ru/)

University of Perugia, Italy
(http://www.unipg.it)

University of Basilicata, Italy
(http://www.unibas.it)

Monash University, Australia
(http://monash.edu)

Kyushu Sangyo University, Japan
(www.kyusan-u.ac.jp)

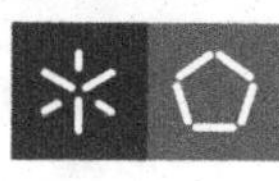

Universidade do Minho
Escola de Engenharia

Universidade do Minho, Portugal
(http://www.uminho.pt)

Contents – Part IV

Machine Learning for Space and Earth Observation Data (ML-SEOD 2019)

Econometrics and Multidimensional Evaluation in the Urban Environment (EMEUE 2019)

Weight Coefficients in the Appraisal System Approach

Pierluigi Morano[1], Francesco Tajani[2], Francesca Salvo[3(✉)], and Manuela De Ruggiero[3]

[1] Department of Civil Engineering Sciences and Architecture, Polytechnic University of Bari, Bari, Italy
[2] Department of Architecture and Design, Sapienza University of Rome, Rome, Italy
[3] Department of Environmental and Chemical Engineering, University of Calabria, Rende, Italy
francesca.salvo@unical.it

Abstract. Among the market oriented appraisal methods, an interesting possibility is represented by the application of the Appraisal System Approach, whose reliability is linked to the availability of an adequate number of comparison data needful to allow the mathematical resolution of the system itself.

The present contribution intends to investigate the possibility of applying the Appraisal System Approach also in case of special appraisal (dissimilar data or not equally reliable ones), using coefficients that can weight the comparables differently in comparison functions due to the different similarities in property characteristics or pricing reliability

Keywords: Appraisal system approach · Similarity degree · Prices reliability

1 Introduction

The possibility to apply the Appraisal System Approach (ASA) is due to the availability of an adequate number of comparables, proportionate to the amount of the unknowns and to allow the mathematical resolution of the system itself.

The number of surveys required for the application of the procedure must also be determined by taking into account that some system equations are sometimes not usable for appraisal because they are redundant.

While a determined or oversized system should lead to logically and practically consistent results, the same cannot be said about an underdeveloped system for which, while there is a possibility to trace a mathematically correct solution through the generalized reverse technique, nothing can be said about the goodness of the solution and its valuation significance.

It is clear then that as much higher the number of data available is, closer to the "true" the results will be.

An opportunity is to broaden the survey sample by introducing dissimilar comparison properties or data that are not always equally reliable, using coefficients that can weight the comparables differently in comparison functions due to the different similarities in property characteristics or pricing reliability.

S. Misra et al. (Eds.): ICCSA 2019, LNCS 11622, pp. 3–12, 2019.
https://doi.org/10.1007/978-3-030-24305-0_1

In this work we first show the traditional application of the appraisal system approach (par. 3.1), in the light of the literature background inherent to atypical markets (par. 2). Then, we describe the proposed approach named WASA - Weighted Appraisal System Approach (par. 3.2) and the construction of the similarity coefficients and reliability ones (par. 3.2.1). After showing the WASA implementation (par. 3.2.3), the methodology has been applied to a case study (par. 4).

2 Literature Review

The International Valuation Standards (IVS) indicates as internationally recognized appraising methods the Market Oriented Approach, the Income Approach, the Cost Approach. When real estate market is active and all necessary market data are available, you may choose the best method for solving the case scenario based on the appraisal purpose and data availability (prices, incomes and costs).

Real estate appraisal methods intend to control as much as possible subjectivity in property valuation.

In this perspective, the Appraisal System Approach [1] is able to appraise property values and hedonic prices in a really automatic way, without any individual personal contribution, just occurring the solution of a linear equations system.

The main limit of this method is the necessity to have an adequate number of comparables, in order to have almost a determined system.

The problem is that the Appraisal System is a theoretical approach structured on the hypothesis of perfect competition market, while in real markets properties transactions are far from this assumption, approaching the conditions of monopolistic competition. More, in some atypical markets data are not available, so ASA system can't be applied.

The issue of limited data quantities in calculating market values and hedonic prices is well known in the real estate literature.

Many studies have been done about lack of data when calculating property price indexes [2–7].

However, these methodologies have some drawbacks, because they are statistical methods (with all their relative limitations) instead of proper appraising tools. Although it is evident the need to perform significance tests, it is important to underline that a statistically correct result may be not always significant by an appraisal point of view.

Therefore, alternative models may be more suitable to use, because they are based on linear equations systems [8].

Another possibility relates to the possibility to use similarity and reliability coefficients [9] in order to increase the number of properties in the comparables sample, introducing also dissimilar properties.

Some studies have been done about measurements of rationality about similarity and reliability degree in appraisal methodologies based on adjustments [10], investigating also the possibility to use the mono-parametric method in atypical markets thanks to reliability coefficients [11].

3 Methodology

3.1 Appraisal System Approach (ASA)

The appraisal system is a methodological approach able to determine a property value and features' hedonic prices on the basis of the solution of a linear equation system.

The ASA is set up starting from the generic appraisal function, for which the price of a property depends on its real estate characteristics, so:

$$P_j = f(x_{j1}, x_{j2}, \cdots, x_{jn}); \tag{1}$$

$$P_j = p_1 x_{j1} + p_2 x_{j2} + \cdots + p_n x_{jn}; \tag{2}$$

where x_{ji} (with i = 1..n) values represent the amount of the i real estate characteristics and p_i represent the related hedonic prices.

The price changes presented by two different j and k properties are consequence and function of the differences between the amounts of the related real estate characteristics:

$$P_k = p_1 x_{k1} + p_2 x_{k2} + \cdots + p_n x_{kn}, \tag{3}$$

so that,

$$P_j - P_k = p_1(x_{j1} - x_{k1}) + p_2(x_{j2} - x_{k2}) + \cdots + p_n(x_{jn} - x_{kn}). \tag{4}$$

therefore, it can be stated that equals properties are priced the same.

The comparable function (4) can be written also for the comparison between the subject and the generic comparable property of the comparables samples as:

$$P_j - V = p_1(x_{j1} - x_{01}) + p_2(x_{j2} - x_{02}) + \cdots + p_n(x_{jn} - x_{on}), \tag{5}$$

where x_{0i} (with i = 1..n) values represent the amount of the subject's real estate characteristics and V is the appraised market value of the subject.

The appraisal system is based on equations related to the comparisons between the property being appraised and every single real estate property of a comparables sample.

The appraisal system implements a set of m pairwise comparisons function related to the comparisons between the property being appraised and every single j real estate property of a comparables sample (j = 1..m):

$$\begin{cases} P_1 = V + \sum_{i=1}^{n} (x_{1i} - x_{0i}) \cdot p_i \\ P_2 = V + \sum_{i=1}^{n} (x_{2i} - x_{0i}) \cdot p_i \\ \ldots = \ldots \\ \ldots = \ldots \\ P_m = V + \sum_{i=1}^{n} (x_{mi} - x_{0i}) \cdot p_i \end{cases} \tag{6}$$

where P_j are the known sales prices.

In matrix form the (6) becomes:

$$P = D \cdot p, \tag{7}$$

in which:
- p is the appraisal vector and P the known sales prices vector:

$$p = \begin{bmatrix} V \\ p_1 \\ p_2 \\ \dots \\ p_n \end{bmatrix}; \quad P = \begin{bmatrix} P_1 \\ P_2 \\ \dots \\ \dots \\ P_n \end{bmatrix}; \tag{7}$$

- D is the differences matrix

$$D = \begin{bmatrix} 1 & d_{11} & d_{12} & \dots & d_{1n} \\ 1 & d_{21} & d_{22} & \dots & d_{2n} \\ \dots & & & & \\ 1 & d_{m1} & d_{m2} & \dots & d_{mn} \end{bmatrix}, \tag{8}$$

where $d_{ji} = x_{ji} - x_{0i}$.

The resolution of the system is performed through the application of the least squares method when the system is determined:

$$p = D^{-1} \cdot P, \tag{9}$$

otherwise it is performed through the application of the Moore-Penrose technique:
- if m < n + 1 then

$$p = D^T \cdot \left(D \cdot D^T\right)^{-1} \cdot P; \tag{10}$$

- if m > n + 1 then

$$p = \left(D^T \cdot D\right)^{-1} \cdot D^T \cdot P. \tag{11}$$

3.2 Weighted Appraisal System Approach (WASA)

As we have already said, the ASA approach well works in the hypothesis of perfect competition markets, when a lot of data are available, where transactions are transparent and more other idealistic conditions. The real estate markets are far from this, usually approaching to the monopolistic competition. The ASA approach continues to well work also in real markets but only when you have so much data you can implement the linear equation system using equally reliable comparables.

In atypical markets, and moreover when lack of data, the appraisal system approach can lead to uncertain results. The idea is to formally rewrite the system using measurements of similarity and reliability as weight coefficients, in order to differently weight the comparables functions in relation to respective similarity and reliability degree.

Similarity and Reliability in Sample Comparables

The central question of the application of market oriented methods is the need to identify a comparison sample of properties similar to the subject. A first consideration is due to "the similarity degree" of the properties in the sample. A second consideration relates to prices data which, although corresponding to the definition of market value, may also be affected by contingent circumstances and present a different "reliability degree" for the purposes of valuation [10].

A similarity coefficient provides a measure of the degree of similarity between the comparables, giving values between 0 and 1, the first corresponding to observations with no common elements, the second relating to the surveys that perfectly meet the criterion used to measure the similarity. The similarity coefficients usually reported in literature can be divided into symmetrical coefficients and asymmetrical ones. While using symmetrical coefficients, null values are interpreted as the absence of the corresponding characteristic (for example, the absence of the garage), and therefore the null data have the same comparative value of the others; in the case of asymmetric coefficients, the null value indicates the absence of information (for example, it was not possible to measure the surface of the garage). A further distinction is between binary coefficients and semi-quantitative or quantitative coefficients: the former are useful in situations where it is sufficient to establish the presence or absence of the characteristic, the latter are functional to interpret and numerically compare observations of quantitative data. Quantitative coefficients are not numerous because, in the presence quantitative data, it is usually preferred the use of distance measures which return a null value for identical observations and a variable value for different observations. The similarity measures can be obtained as 1 minus the distance coefficients. The distance coefficients are usually symmetrical and treat the 0 value as an actual measurement instead of a lack of information.

In the real estate sector, the observations consist of quantitative and semi-quantitative data, so that it is possible to measure the similarity degree through symmetrical distance measurements.

Therefore, a measure able to detect the similarity of individual properties in the real estate sample has its foundation in the "closeness" between the amounts of property characteristics: greater comparability means greater proximity of the amounts of the real estate characteristics, less comparability means more distant amounts. The measure of the "degree of similarity" of comparable properties may, therefore, be expressed as a function of the difference between the amounts of the i-th feature of the comparable and those of the subject.

This difference can be expressed in terms of absolute value in the following way:

$$gs_a^{j^*} = \frac{\sum_{j=1}^{m} \sum_{i=1}^{n} \left| \frac{X_{ij} - X_{i0}}{\bar{X}_i} \right| - \sum_{i=1}^{n} \left| \frac{X_{ij} - X_{i0}}{\bar{X}_i} \right|}{(m-1) \cdot \sum_{j=1}^{m} \sum_{i=1}^{n} \left| \frac{X_{ij} - X_{i0}}{\bar{X}_i} \right|}, \tag{12}$$

where $gs_a^{j^*}$ is the indicator of the degree of similarity of a j* generic property of comparison and $\bar{x}_i$ is the average of the considered characteristic [9].

The difference between the amount of the i-th feature of the comparable and that corresponding to the subject can also be expressed in terms of square standardized distances, as follows:

$$gs_q^{j^*} = \frac{\sum_{j=1}^{m} \sum_{i=1}^{n} \left| \frac{X_{ij} - X_{i0}}{\bar{X}_i} \right|^2 - \sum_{i=1}^{n} \left| \frac{X_{ij} - X_{i0}}{\bar{X}_i} \right|^2}{(m-1) \cdot \sum_{j=1}^{m} \sum_{i=1}^{n} \left| \frac{X_{ij} - X_{i0}}{\bar{X}_i} \right|^2}, \tag{13}$$

where $gs_q^{j^*}$ is the degree of similarity of a generic property of comparison j [9].

The need to assess the degree of reliability is related to the presence of any abnormal market prices for comparables. The anomaly exists if the following assumptions hold: (a) prices were collected in the same market segment of the subject; (b) prices are recent and obey the definition of market value, (c) prices were obtained following a consistent methodology and gathered from common and comparable sources. The methodological condition concerns the possibility for the evaluator to exclude, by a feedback, anomalous prices, and related properties from the comparable sample when the corresponding correct prices exceed the threshold of divergence. Under these assumptions and in accordance with the methodological condition, the measurement of the degree of reliability of the test operates within the range of divergence and, possibly, in the neighborhood of the extreme threshold.

The measure of the "degree of reliability" in each property of comparison, in relation to the sale price, is determined by the following formula:

$$ga^{j^*} = \frac{\left(1 - \left| \frac{P_{cj^*} - \bar{P}_{cj}}{\bar{P}_{cj}} \right| \right)^{m+1}}{\sum_{j=1}^{m} \left(1 - \left| \frac{P_{cj^*} - \bar{P}_{cj}}{\bar{P}_{cj}} \right| \right)^{m+1}} \tag{14}$$

where P_{cj^*} is the sale price of the j*sale and $\bar{P}_{cj}$ is the average sale price [10].

The variation function has an almost linear trend taking values between 0 and 1/(m–1): the greater the difference between the correct price and the correct price of the comparable average of the sample, the lower the reliability of the corresponding correct price.

WASA Implementation

According to the fact that reliability coefficients relate to prices and similarity ones to property characteristics, the ASA may be rewritten as:

$$\begin{cases} ga^{1^*}(P_1 - V) = \sum_{i=1}^{n} gs_q^{1^*}(X_{1i} - X_{0i}) \cdot p_i \\ ga^{2^*}(P_2 - V) = \sum_{i=1}^{n} gs_q^{2^*}(X_{2i} - X_{0i}) \cdot p_i \\ \ldots = \ldots \\ \ldots = \ldots \\ ga^{m^*}(P_m - V) = \sum_{i=1}^{n} gs_q^{m^*}(X_{mi} - X_{0i}) \cdot p_i \end{cases} \tag{15}$$

where using square coefficients, or

$$\begin{cases} ga^{1^*}(P_1 - V) = \sum_{i=1}^{n} gs_a^{1^*}(X_{1i} - X_{0i}) \cdot p_i \\ ga^{2^*}(P_2 - V) = \sum_{i=1}^{n} gs_a^{2^*}(X_{2i} - X_{0i}) \cdot p_i \\ \ldots = \ldots \\ \ldots = \ldots \\ ga^{m^*}(P_m - V) = \sum_{i=1}^{n} gs_a^{m^*}(X_{mi} - X_{0i}) \cdot p_i \end{cases} \tag{16}$$

where using absolute coefficients.

In matrix form we have:

- the unknown vector p

$$p = \begin{bmatrix} V \\ p_1 \\ p_2 \\ \ldots \\ p_n \end{bmatrix} \tag{17}$$

- the differences matrix D

$$D = \begin{bmatrix} ga^{1^*} & gs_q^{1^*}(x_{11} - x_{01}) & \ldots & gs_q^{1^*}(x_{1n} - x_{0n}) \\ ga^{2^*} & gs_q^{2^*}(x_{21} - x_{01}) & \ldots & gs_q^{2^*}(x_{2i} - x_{0n}) \\ \ldots & \ldots & & \ldots \\ ga^{m^*} & gs_q^{m^*}(x_{mn} - x_{0n}) & \ldots & gs_q^{m^*}(x_{mi} - x_{0n}) \end{bmatrix} \tag{18}$$

- the sales prices vector P

$$P = \begin{bmatrix} ga^{1^*} \cdot P_1 \\ ga^{2^*} \cdot P_2 \\ \ldots \\ \ldots \\ ga^{m^*} \cdot P_m \end{bmatrix} \tag{19}$$

Nothing changes about system solution, so that least squares method is used when the system is determined, otherwise it is performed through the application of the Moore-Penrose technique.

Case study and Results

The methodology proposed in this paper has been tested on a sample of properties located in the city of Cosenza, Italy.

The methodology has been applied to a sample of 9 comparables, real estate properties that have been sold in the last year (2017); real estate data have been acquired from the Observatory of Real Estate Market, an Italian real estate market observatory instituted by University of Calabria.

All data relate to segment of the used market for condominiums in multistory buildings. Properties are physically, technically, economically and functionally similar, the use is exclusively the housing one, and motivations of purchase and sale are usually attributable to transfer. The shape of the market is restricted due to monopolistic competition, in which franchise agents are the most common form of intermediation.

From the survey forms associated with each real estate datum, information about real estate features deemed relevant in the mechanism of price formation in the study area were acquired. More specifically, the variables considered in the sample are:

Sale Price (SPR): measured in €, indicates the true price paid in the real estate transaction updated to the appraisal time;

Principal surface (SUP): measured in square meters, is the amount of the principal surface;

Balconies surface (SUB): measured in square meters, is the amount of the balconies surface;

Garage surface (SUG): measured in square meters, is the amount of the garage surface;

Restrooms (RES): n° measured, indicates the number of toilets;

Floor Level (LEV): indicates the apartment floor level, measured with an ordinal scale;

Energy class level (ECL): it is possible to assign a score ranging from a minimum of 1 to a maximum of 8 corresponding to the standard energy classification of buildings (from A + to G);

Maintenance and conservation status (MSC): measured with a scale score, was attributed 0 to indicate a state of poor maintenance, 1 for mediocre maintenance, 2 for adequate maintenance, 3 for a discrete state, 4 if the maintenance status is good, 5 if the maintenance condition is excellent.

In Table 1 collected data are reported; in Table 2 sample statistics are reported.

The methodology has been tested considering every single property as a subject of unknown sale price, appraising its value both with the ASA and the WASA and comparing it with the real known sale price.

Table 1. Data table

Sale price and characteristics	A	B	C	D	E	F	G	H	I
SPR (€)	200.000,00	160.000,00	147.000,00	150.000,00	167.000,00	200.000,00	175.000,00	140.000,00	190.000,00
SUP (sqm)	140	140	130	95	107	136	115	128	120
SUB (sqm)	20	25	15	15	25	32	12	20	15
SUG (sqm)	20	0	0	22	30	0	0	25	35
REST (n°)	2	2	2	1	2	2	2	1	2
LEV (n°)	3	1	3	4	1	3	4	5	3
ECL (score)	1	2	2	3	2	3	4	1	3
MSC (score)	3	1	2	3	2	3	3	0	3

Table 2. Sample statistics

Sale price and characteristics	Average or frequency
SPR (€)	150.888,89
SUP (sqm)	123,88
SUB (sqm)	20,50
SUG (sqm)	12,13
REST (1,2)	2-7
LEV (1,2,3,4,5)	2-0-4-2-1
ECL (1,2,3,4)	2-3-3-1
MSC (0,1,2,3)	1-1-2-5

Observing Table 3 you can notice that values appraised with WASA are more stable than those calculated with the ASA. In fact, ASA values sometimes are extremely far from reality, not only from a numerical point of view, but above all in terms of appraisal significance.

Table 3. Divergence between appraised values and sale prices

Subject	Appraised values		Sale prices	Divergence between appraised values and sale prices	
	WASA	ASA		WASA divergence	ASA divergence
A	182.565,44	162.672,73	200.000,00	0,10	0,23
B	188.740,68	87.800,74	160.000,00	0,18	0,82
C	169.699,75	168.434,06	147.000,00	0,15	0,15
D	178.178,35	381.850,29	150.000,00	0,19	1,55
E	184.807,58	727,53	167.000,00	0,11	228,54
F	187.289,65	268.572,04	200.000,00	0,07	0,34
G	129.203,24	146.764,52	175.000,00	0,35	0,19
H	142.732,22	–91.850,29	140.000,00	0,02	–2,52
I	185.106,55	237.999,95	190.000,00	0,03	0,25

The question is far more complex in terms of hedonic prices, which are really variable both in the WASA and ASA, although this variability is more contained in when using the weight coefficients respect to the traditional approach.

4 Conclusion

The possibility to apply the Appraisal System Approach (ASA) is due to the availability of an adequate number of comparables, proportionate to the amount of the unknowns and to allow the mathematical resolution of the system itself. Also when you have a sufficient data sample, it is not said that the system leads to probative results in terms of appraisal significance. A good opportunity is to use weight coefficients able to take into account the dissimilarities and anomalies present in the sample, useful on the one hand to avoid the exclusion of some comparable from the sample, on the other to improve the quality of the obtained results.

It is clear that the results of the WASA approach cannot be accepted in deterministic terms but interpreted in probabilistic ones, as also the ASA approach requires, but the use of the proposed methodology can extend the applicability fields of the ASA, and it can be proposed as a useful tool to implement Automated Valuation Methods such the computer assisted ones (CAMA).

References

1. Simonotti, M.: Metodi di stima immobiliare. Dario Flaccovio Editore, Palermo (2006)
2. Geltner, D., Pollakowski, H.: A Set of Indexes for Trading Commercial Real Estate Based on the Real Capital Analytics Transaction Prices Database, MIT Center for Real Estate (2007)
3. Bayley, M.J., Muth, R.F., Nourse, H.O.: A regression model for real estate price index construction. J. Am. Stat. Assoc. **58**, 933–942 (1963)
4. Case, K.E., Shiller, R.J.: Prices of single-family homes since 1970: new indexes for four cities. N. Engl. Econ. Rev. **5**, 45–56 (1987)
5. Case, K.E., Shiller, R.J.: The efficiency of the market for single family homes. Am. Econ. Rev. **79**, 125–137 (1989)
6. Pace, R.K.: Performing large scale spatial autoregressions. Econ. Lett. **54**, 283–291 (1997)
7. Pace, R.K., Berry, R., Clapp, J., Rodriguez, M.: Spatiotemporal autoregressive models of neighborhood effects. J. Real Estate Finance Econ. **17**(1), 15–33 (1998)
8. Carini, M., Ciuna, M., De Ruggiero, M., Salvo, F., Simonotti, M.: Repeat assessed values model for housing price index. Real Estate Manag. Valuation **25**(4), 25–39 (2017)
9. Colwell, P.F., Cannaday, R.E., Wu, C.: The analytical foundations of adjustment grid methods. J. Am. Real Estate Urban Econ. Assoc. **11**(1), 11–29 (1983)
10. Simonotti, M., Salvo, F., Ciuna, M., De Ruggiero, M.: Measurements of rationality for a scientific approach to the market-oriented methods. J. Real Estate Lit. **24**, 403–427 (2016)
11. Ciuna, M., De Ruggiero, M., Manganelli, B., Salvo, F., Simonotti, M.: Automated valuation methods in atypical real estate markets using the mono-parametric approach. In: Gervasi, O., et al. (eds.) ICCSA 2017. LNCS, vol. 10406, pp. 200–209. Springer, Cham (2017). https://doi.org/10.1007/978-3-319-62398-6_14

A Multivariate Econometric Analysis for the Forecasting of the Interdependences Between the Housing Prices and the Socio-economic Factors in the City of Barcelona (Spain)

Pierluigi Morano[1], Francesco Tajani[2(✉)], Maria Rosaria Guarini[2], Felicia Di Liddo[2], and Debora Anelli[2]

[1] Department of Civil Engineering Sciences and Architecture, Polytechnic University of Bari, 70125 Bari, Italy

[2] Department of Architecture and Design, "Sapienza" University of Rome, 00196 Rome, Italy

francesco.tajani@uniroma1.it

Abstract. The extreme volatility that has characterized the real estate market in recent years constitutes an important issue for researchers and experts, stimulating the development and the test of evaluation models able to predict future trends and to monitor the consequences of scenario evolutions that are different from those initially expected. With reference to the metropolitan area of Barcelona (Spain), the methodology implemented in this paper has allowed to make explicit the functional relationships between the residential properties prices and the socio-economic variables selected by the model (number of loans, unemployment level, market rent). The analysis carried out is "dynamic", i.e. it refers to a quarterly time series database covering a period of sixty-seven periods (1st quarter 2001-3rd quarter of 2017). The results obtained have shown the forecasted potentialities of the tool used, as support *(i)* for the investment decisions of private operators, *(ii)* for the fiscal decisions of central governments, *(iii)* for the selection of the most convenient urban transformation initiatives from local administrations.

Keywords: Econometric analysis · Spanish residential market · Socio-economic factors · Property values · Market rent

1 Introduction

In the last years, characterized by a situation of latent economic crisis, the non-performing bank loans have strongly increased. In the same category of the non-performing loans, the EU has reported the "unlikely to pay" (UTP) loans and the "bad debts" to be accounted in the banks' balance sheets. Therefore, there is a widespread need to promote transparency and reliability on the estimated values and on the times for the credit recovery, not only for the repayment of the debts, but also in order to ensure more effective mortgage loans [7].

S. Misra et al. (Eds.): ICCSA 2019, LNCS 11622, pp. 13–22, 2019.
https://doi.org/10.1007/978-3-030-24305-0_2

In this sense, the Italian government has provided laws in terms of consumer default management, in relation to the transfer of the property, and in terms of bankruptcy regulations, in order to speed up the judicial procedures, that are particularly long - 1100 days in Italy - compared to other European countries - 410 in Germany and 550 in Spain.

With reference to the market value assessment of properties as guarantee of credit exposures and bad debts, the operators share the need, on the one hand, to obtain prudential valuations, by determining values that are sustainable in the long-term, and, on the other hand, to formulate value judgments that preclude the risk of a sell-off of the properties, preserving the guarantee value and effectively interpreting the conditions of the reference market [1, 4, 12].

The topic of the present research concerns the framework outlined. The work has analyzed the functional relationships between the housing selling prices and the main socio-economic variables relating to the metropolitan area of Barcelona (Spain), for which it has been possible to collect the corresponding time series, sufficiently representative of the evolutions of the characteristics identified. The output obtained is a model of simple interpretation, characterized by a high statistical performance and by the consistency with the expected empirical phenomena, and it represents a useful support for the forecasting of future market price trends, due to the different evolutions of the socio-economic factors in the analyzed context [2, 3, 6, 9, 10].

The research has been structured as follows. In the Sect. 2 the case study has been presented: the time series of the variables considered have been described and the main descriptive statistics have been illustrated. In the Sect. 3 the methodology implemented has been explained, highlighting the advantages of the algorithm used in a dynamic analysis compared to a classic Vector Autoregression (VAR). In Sect. 4 the application of the proposed method has been illustrated: the equations obtained have been specified, the best performing model from a statistical, practical and empirical point of view has been identified. In Sect. 5 the functional relationships of the chosen model have been interpreted and the predictive potentialities of the methodology used have been tested. Finally, the conclusions of the work have been discussed.

2 Case Study

The study sample considered for the present research consists of the time series of the main socio-economic factors collected for the metropolitan area of the city of Barcelona (Spain).

Taking into account the Spanish sources consulted on line, the time series of the variables refer to a period of approximately seventeen years, on a quarterly basis, from the first quarter of 2001 to the third quarter of the year 2017. In particular, the variables considered in the model have been as follows:

- unit selling prices of residential properties, expressed in €/m^2 [Y], which represents the dependent variable of the model. The average value of this variable for the sample measured in the Barcelona metropolitan area is equal to 2,167.38 €/m^2, with the minimum recorded value equal to 1,235.76 €/m^2 (first quarter of the year 2001) and the maximum value 3,280.06 €/m^2 (second quarter of the year 2007);

- number of total transactions of residential properties [*T*] observed in the relevant territorial context. In the study sample, an average value of 13,320 has been recorded, in a range between 4,948 (first quarter of the year 2013) and 28,812 transactions (second quarter of the year 2005);
- total number of residences [*N*] in the metropolitan area of Barcelona, grew by about 15% between the first quarter of the year 2001 (in which there were 2,280,334 residences) and the third quarter of the year 2017 (with a number of residences equal to 2,627,671);
- total population [*P*] in the metropolitan area of Barcelona. For this variable an increase in the analysis period of around 16% has been recorded (=4,804,606 in the first quarter of the year 2001 and 5,576,037 in the third quarter of the year 2017);
- total number of firms [*I*] in the territorial context of the metropolitan area of Barcelona. For this variable, the average number of firms for the selected study sample is equal to 438,518, oscillating from a minimum value of 374,027 (first quarter of the year 2001) to the maximum recorded value of 477,942 (first quarter of the year 2008);
- total number of "new" mortgages for housing purchases [*M*]. On average, over the analyzed period, a number of mortgages in each quarter has been detected equal to 25,733, with the minimum number recorded equal to 5,709 (fourth quarter of the year 2013) and the maximum number equal to 58,879 (first quarter of the year 2006);
- number of unemployed people [*D*] in the metropolitan area of Barcelona. The average number of unemployed people has been equal to 361,306, in a range between the minimum value of 193,467 (second quarter of the year 2007) and the maximum value of 492,288 (first quarter of the year 2013);
- number of employment contracts [*C*]. On average, the number of employment contracts signed during the period considered has been 156,713. The minimum value observed has been equal to 116,913 (first quarter of the year 2009) and the maximum value has been equal to 206,569 (second quarter of the year 2017);
- housing market rent [*L*], expressed in €/m^2 * month. The average value is equal to 11 €/m^2 * month, whereas the values recorded in the chosen period range from a minimum value of 8.85 €/m^2 * month (first quarter of the year 2014) to a maximum value of 13.24 €/m^2 * month (second quarter of the year 2017);
- average selling prices of the buildable soils located in the area of Barcelona metropolitan area [*S*]. The average value observed for the sample has been equal to 314.95 €/m^2, with a minimum value equal to 193.65 €/m^2 (third quarter of the year 2013) and a maximum value equal to 455.53 €/m^2 (fourth quarter of the year 2006).

In Table 1 the main descriptive statistics of the variables considered for the case study have been summarized.

Table 1. Main descriptive statistics of the variables considered in the study sample

Variable	Mean	Standard deviation	Max value	Min value
Unit selling price [€/m^2]	2,167.38	590.63	3,280.06	1,235.76
Number of total transactions of residential properties [n]	13,320.73	6,783.89	28,812	4,948
Total number of residences [n.]	2,513,672	116,166	2,627,671	2,280,334
Total population [n.]	5,346,839	239,760	5,576,037	4,804,606
Total number of firms [n.]	438,518	28,165	477,942	374,027
Total number of "new" mortgages for housing purchases [n.]	25,733	16,954	58,879	5,709
Number of unemployed people [n.]	361,306	101,190	492,288	193,467
Number of employment contracts [n.]	156,713	24,775	206,569	116,913
Housing market rent [€/m^2 * month]	11	1.37	13.24	8.85
Average selling prices of the buildable soils [€/m^2]	314.95	77.83	455.53	193.65

3 The Methodology

The methodology implemented for the dynamic analysis is *Evolutionary Polynomial Regression* (EPR). This is a data-driven hybrid method that combines polynomial structures together with evolutionary search in order to obtain symbolical expressions with exponents of polynomial form by means a simple genetic algorithm engine [5].

In particular, EPR searches for symbolic structures in the first stage by the genetic algorithm and estimates constant values in the second stage by solving a Least Squares linear problem, thus assuming a biunique relationship between a structure and its parameters. The general symbolic expression returned by EPR is reported in Eq. (1):

$$y = \sum_{j=1}^{m} F(X, f(X), a_j) + a_0 \tag{1}$$

where y is the estimated output of the process, a_j is an adjustable parameter determined by the method, F is a function constructed by the process, $\mathbf{X}$ is the matrix of the input variables, f is a function defined by the user, m is the length (number of terms) of the expression (bias excluded).

In the case of dynamic analysis, with reference to the study database in the present work, the dependent variable is the unit selling price at time t (Y_t), whereas the matrix $\mathbf{X}$ of the input variables includes the unit selling prices with the relative "lags" - $Y_{t-1},\ldots, Y_{t-p}$, where p is the maximum eligible lag considered by the user - and the selected input variables, also with the related "lags" - $X_{i,t},\ldots, X_{i,t-p}$, where $i = 1,\ldots, k$ represents a specific variable among the k factors identified in the preliminary phase, and p is the maximum eligible lag considered appropriate for the analysis by the user.

Moreover, in order to obtain the maximum explanatory performance of the final function, EPR provides that each variable of the matrix **X** can be raised to a specific and appropriate exponent, within a range pre-established by the user and iteratively modified until the achievement of the statistically more reliable solution.

The choice of the best models is performed through the calculation of the Coefficient of Determination (COD) for each equation, defined in Eq. (2):

$$COD = 1 - \frac{N-1}{N} \cdot \frac{\sum_{N} (y_{estimated} - y_{detected})^2}{\sum_{N} (y_{detected} - mean(y_{detected}))^2} \quad (2)$$

where $y_{estimated}$ are the values of the dependent variable estimated by the methodology, $y_{detected}$ are the collected values of the dependent variable, N is the sample size in analysis. The fitting of a model is higher when the COD is close to the unit value.

The implementation of a multi-objective genetic algorithm represents the fundamental advantage of the proposed methodology, as optimization strategy based on the Pareto dominance criterion. These objectives are conflictual, and aim at *(i)* the maximization of model accuracy, through the satisfaction of appropriate statistical criteria of verification of each equation; *(ii)* the maximization of model's parsimony, through the minimization of the number of terms (a_j) of the equation; *(iii)* the reduction of the complexity of the model, through the minimization of the number of the input variables (**X**) of the final equation. Therefore, the method allows to obtain, at the end of the modeling phase, a set of model solutions (i.e. the Pareto front of optimal models) for the three objectives considered.

In the case of dynamic analysis on time series, a further advantage of the implementation of the multi-objective genetic algorithm is represented by the identification of the best "lag" of each considered input variable, and consequently the best combination of the possible eligible lags of the variables in the model, in order to optimize the three objectives described above.

This ability of the methodology undoubtedly constitutes an important innovative feature, taking into account that in a classic multivariate econometric technique - for example, a VAR - it is the user that iteratively combines the variables with different lags, up to the model characterized by the best statistical reliability due to several tests (verification of the *t*-value for each parameter of the coefficient matrix, Portmanteau test to verify the reliability of the linear model, Jarque-Bera test to verify the residual normality, analysis of the autocorrelations among the residuals, etc.) [8].

Finally, the compositional logic with which the genetic algorithm operates (combination of several variables within the same additive term and admissibility of the exponents for each term) allows to overcome the constraint of the preliminary univariate analysis for the equations of a VAR (graphic analysis, unit root (ADF) test, etc.). The econometric technique allows, in this way, to gather a consistent range of solutions for the user, different from each other for COD and for complexity of the algebraic form, among which it is possible to select the most appropriate solution according to the specific needs, the knowledge of the phenomenon in analysis and the type of experimental data used [11].

4 Application of the Methodology

4.1 The Model

The methodology is implemented considering the additive function F and no function *f* selected among those allowed by the application software (logarithmic, semi-logarithmic, exponential, etc.). Each additive monomial term is assumed as a combination of the inputs (Y_{t-1}, ..., Y_{t-p}, $X_{i,t}$, ..., $X_{i,t-p}$) raised to the proper exponents. In particular, due to the limited number of the time series sequence, the analysis is carried out considering the autoregressive variable of input, exclusively the one associated with a single delay (Y_{t-1}), whereas for the other input variables an eligible delay of 12 (p = 12) has been assumed.

Candidate exponents belong to the set (−3; −2; −1; −0.5; 0; 0.5; 1; 2; 3). The genetic algorithm therefore, considers all the possible combinations according to the delay of the input parameters (variable from t to t-12 for each characteristic considered), of the selected exponent, of the variables number within the same additive term: the result is a wide range of solutions that define the Pareto frontier for the conflicting objectives imposed by the methodology, among which the best compromise between performance statistics, simplicity of the model algebraic form and the empirical reliability of the relationship between candidate inputs and the dependent variable should be identified.

The maximum number m of additive terms in final expressions set by the user in the preliminary phase, is equal to four. Finally, in order to eliminate the distortive effects that could be generated by the different numerical entities of the time series, a normalization of each historical series, compared to the highest numerical value detected for each variable, has been developed.

The implementation of the EPR methodology has generated several models, the main of which in Table 2 are set out. The equations show different direct and inverse functional relationships between the output variable of the model (selling prices at time t) and the selected inputs variables with their "delays".

All the models generated show a high level of statistical accuracy, with a COD that exceeds 85% in all cases. Among the main models included in Table 2, it should be observed that Eq. (3) presents a functional form characterized by additive terms of simple empirical interpretation than to the subsequent models, for which the functional links statistical improvement becomes not very significant.

Table 2. Equations obtained by the implementation of EPR

Eq. (n)	Model
(3)	$Y_t = +0.078128 \cdot L_{t-4}^{0.5} - 0.030354 \cdot L_{t-2}^{0.5} +$ $- 0.17738 \cdot M_{t-8}^{0.5} \cdot D_{t-8}^{0.5} + 1.0015 \cdot Y_{t-1} + 0.030369$
(4)	$Y_t = +0.017995 \cdot L_{t-11}^{0.5} - 0.024501 \cdot C_{t-6}^{0.5} -$ $+ 0.15475 \cdot M_{t-8} \cdot D_t \cdot D_{t-8} + 0.995544 \cdot Y_{t-1} + 0.034703$

(*continued*)

Table 2. (*continued*)

Eq. (n)	Model
(5)	$Y_t = -0.027627 \cdot C_{t-6} - 0.15812 \cdot M_{t-8} \cdot D_t \cdot D_{t-8} + $ $+ 0.15475 \cdot T_t \cdot T_{t-7} L_{t-11} + 0.98777 \cdot Y_{t-1} + 0.040871$
(6)	$Y_t = -0.030139 \cdot C_{t-6}^{0.5} \cdot S_t^{0.5} - 0.16632 \cdot M_{t-8} \cdot D_t \cdot D_{t-8} + $ $+ 0.16971 \cdot T_t \cdot T_{t-7} \cdot L_{t-11}^2 + 0.99263 \cdot Y_{t-1} + 0.037143$
(7)	$Y_t = -0.14719 \cdot I_{t-2}^2 \cdot M_{t-8}^{0.5} \cdot D_{t-8}^{0.5} + -0.030532 \cdot T_{t-6}^{0.5} \cdot L_{t-2} + $ $+ 0.15319 \cdot T_t^{0.5} \cdot T_{t-3}^{0.5} \cdot L_{t-4} \cdot S_{t-11}^{0.5} + 0.99079 \cdot Y_{t-1} + 0.038832$
(8)	$Y_t = -0.15532 \cdot I_{t-2}^2 \cdot M_{t-8}^{0.5} \cdot D_{t-8}^{0.5} + -0.032974 \cdot T_{t-6}^{0.5} \cdot C_{t-4} \cdot L_{t-2}^{0.5} + $ $+ 0.16108 \cdot T_t^{0.5} \cdot T_{t-3}^{0.5} \cdot L_{t-4} \cdot S_{t-11}^{0.5} + 0.98989 \cdot Y_{t-1} + 0.039316$

Therefore, Eq. (3) has been considered as the best model in terms of statistical performance and interpretive simplicity of functional relationships. Figure 1 shows the time series trends of the Y_t detected and of the Y_t estimated by Eq. (3). The graphical representation points out the statistical goodness of the results: an almost exact match of the values is widely verified between the two curves in the considered time period.

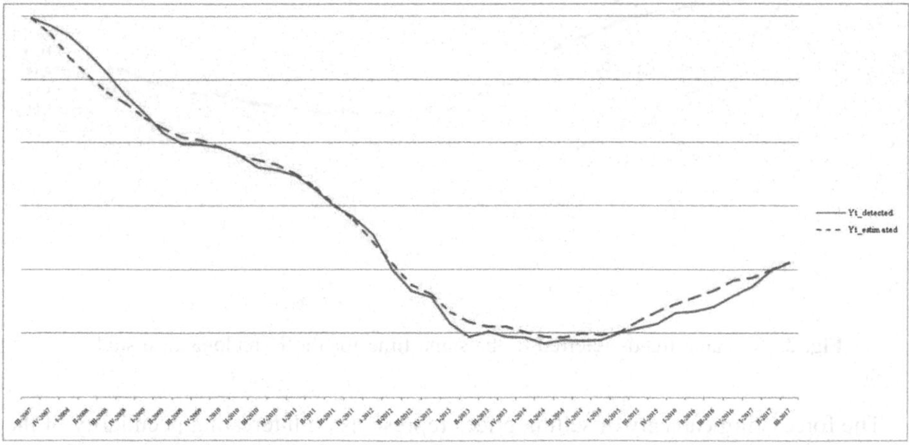

Fig. 1. Y_t detected (continuous line) and Y_t estimated (broken line) for the Barcelona case study

4.2 Interpretation of the Selected Model

The model of Eq. (3) selects only five variables as the most representative in the formation of selling prices at time *t*, and the related mathematical expression allows the immediate verification of the functional links between the selling prices at the time *t* (Y_t) and the following input parameters: selling prices at time *t-1* (Y_{t-1}) through a direct functional correlation; the housing market rent with a delay of four quarters (L_{t-4}), through a direct functional relationship; the housing market rent relate to the time t-2

($L_{t\text{-}2}$), with an inverse functional link; the total number of "new" mortgages for housing purchases with regard to time t-8 ($M_{t\text{-}8}$) and the number of unemployed people at time t −8 ($D_{t\text{-}8}$), combined into a single term, functionally connected to the variable Y_t through an inverse correlation.

The graph in Fig. 2 allows the qualitative representation of the functional correlations between the output variable Y_t and the input variables $L_{t\text{-}4}$, $L_{t\text{-}2}$, $M_{t\text{-}8}$ and $D_{t\text{-}8}$: the trends represented show that at negative phases for the total number of "new" mortgages for housing purchases and the level of unemployment followed increasing phases for selling prices in the metropolitan area of Barcelona after eight quarters (two years), whereas the positive trend for the housing market rents brings forward by four quarters (one year) the growing phase of residential selling prices.

The inverse relationship between the variable $L_{t\text{-}2}$ and the output variable, explained in Eq. (3), does not appear to match the two variables graphic trends, which instead seem to be characterized by fairly consistent trends.

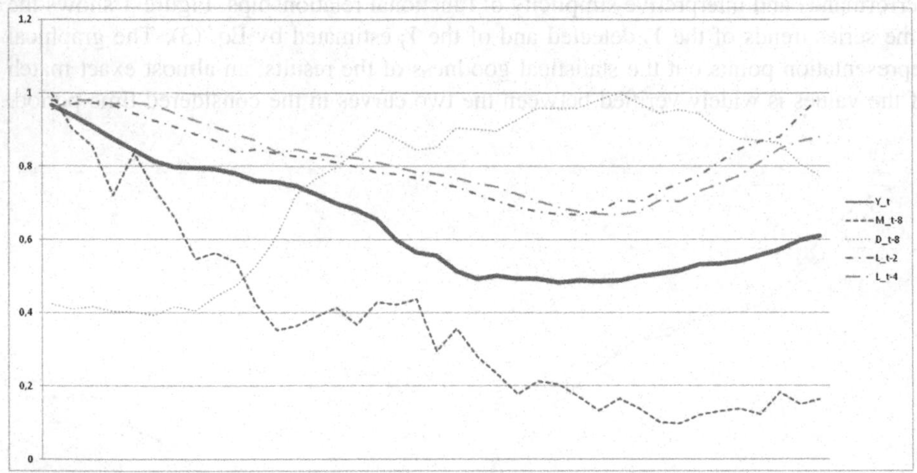

Fig. 2. Variable trends referred to the same time for the Barcelona case study

The forecasting capacity of selling prices represents an interesting peculiarity of the model obtained. In fact, since the selling prices at time *t* are linked to the number of mortgages and the level of unemployment at the time *t*.8, it is possible to exclusively assume different developments over time of the housing market rents and, consequently, to forecast future housing price quotations in the metropolitan area of Barcelona.

Figure 3 describes a sensitivity analysis of the selling prices, after the third quarter of 2017, and considering constant changes in the future market rents in a range [−9%; +9%]. First of all, the results obtained confirm the empirical evidence of a positive correlation between the selling prices and the housing market rent over time: this relationship is evident starting from the convergence point that occurs in the first quarter of 2019, after which positive variations in the housing market rents determine an increase in selling prices, whereas negative changes in housing market rents adversely affect the trend in residential prices. Finally, in the two years considered, the maximum selling price gap between a "very" positive trend in leases (+9%) and a "very" negative trend (−9%) is still not very significant, being equal to about 4%.

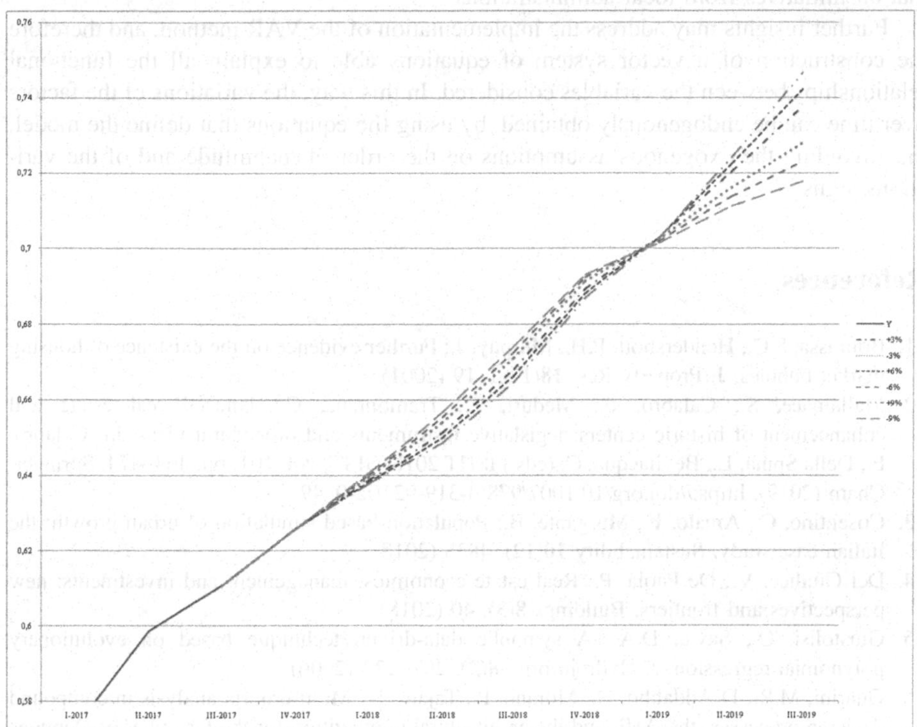

Fig. 3. Possible evolutions in the selling prices due to different variations in the housing market rent in Barcelona

5 Conclusions

In the present research the functional relationships between the residential properties selling prices and the main socio-economic variables related to the metropolitan area of Barcelona (Spain) have been analyzed. In particular, the dynamic analysis has referred to a quarterly time series database covering a period of sixty-seven periods (1st quarter 2001-3rd quarter of 2017). The methodology implemented, named EPR, has allowed to select the most significant correlations, and to generate a model characterized by a high statistical reliability and, at the same time, by a simplicity in the empirical interpretation of the functional relationships.

An important peculiarity of the model is the possibility to be used for forecasting purposes: in particular, as the historical data for the number of mortgages and the level of unemployment are sufficiently available, it is possible to assess the evolution of the selling prices over a period of two years, for different possible variations of the housing market rents. In this sense, the methodology used, applied to the case of the city of Barcelona but implementable in any territorial context, represents a fundamental support *(i)* for the investment decisions of private operators, *(ii)* for the fiscal decisions of central governments, *(iii)* for the selection of the most convenient urban transformation initiatives from local administrations.

Further insights may address the implementation of the VAR method, and therefore the construction of a vector system of equations able to explain all the functional relationships between the variables considered. In this way, the variations of the factors over time can be endogenously obtained, by using the equations that define the model, thus avoiding the exogenous assumptions on the order of magnitude and of the variations signs.

References

1. Bourassa, S.C., Hendershott, P.H., Murphy, J.: Further evidence on the existence of housing market bubbles. J. Property Res. **18**(1), 1–19 (2001)
2. Mallamace, S., Calabrò, F., Meduri, T., Tramontana, C.: Unused real estate and enhancement of historic centers: legislative instruments and procedural ideas. In: Calabrò, F., Della Spina, L., Bevilacqua, C. (eds.) ISHT 2018. SIST, vol. 101, pp. 464–474. Springer, Cham (2019). https://doi.org/10.1007/978-3-319-92102-0_49
3. Cosentino, C., Amato, F., Murgante, B.: Population-based simulation of urban growth: the Italian case study. Sustainability **10**(12), 4838 (2018)
4. Del Giudice, V., De Paola, P.: Real estate economics, management and investments: new perspectives and frontiers. Buildings **8**(3), 40 (2018)
5. Giustolisi, O., Savic, D.A.: A symbolic data-driven technique based on evolutionary polynomial regression. J. Hydroinform. **8**(3), 207–222 (2006)
6. Guarini, M.R., D'Addabbo, N., Morano, P., Tajani, F.: Multi-criteria analysis in compound decision processes: the AHP and the architectural competition for the Chamber of Deputies in Rome (Italy). Buildings **7**(2), 38 (2017)
7. Levy, D.S., Lee, C.K.C.: The influence of family members on housing purchase decisions. J. Property Investment Finan. **22**(4), 320–338 (2004)
8. Manganelli, B., Morano, P., Tajani, F.: House prices and rents: the Italian experience. WSEAS Trans. Bus. Econ. **11**, 219–226 (2014)
9. Rosato, P., Breil, M., Giupponi, C., Berto, R.: Assessing the impact of urban improvement on housing values: a hedonic pricing and multi-attribute analysis model for the historic Centre of Venice. Buildings **7**(4), 112 (2017)
10. Scorza, F., Pilogallo, A., Las Casas, G.: Investigating tourism attractiveness in inland areas: ecosystem services, open data and smart specializations. In: Calabrò, F., Della Spina, L., Bevilacqua, C. (eds.) ISHT 2018. SIST, vol. 100, pp. 30–38. Springer, Cham (2019). https://doi.org/10.1007/978-3-319-92099-3_4
11. Tajani, F., Morano, P., Torre, C.M., Di Liddo, F.: An analysis of the influence of property tax on housing prices in the Apulia region (Italy). Buildings **7**(3), 67 (2017)
12. Vargas-Silva, C.: Monetary policy and the US housing market: a VAR analysis imposing sign restrictions. J. Macroecon. **30**(3), 977–990 (2008)

Incidence of Different Types of Urban Green Spaces on Property Prices. A Case Study in the Flaminio District of Rome (Italy)

Pierluigi Morano[1(✉)], Maria Rosaria Guarini[2], Francesco Tajani[2], Felicia Di Liddo[2], and Debora Anelli[2]

[1] Department of Civil Engineering Sciences and Architecture, Polytechnic University of Bari, 70125 Bari, Italy
pierluigi.morano@poliba.it

[2] Department of Architecture and Design, "Sapienza" University of Rome, 00196 Rome, Italy

Abstract. Although the presence of an urban green areas seems to be an important factor in housing decisions, there are few empirical research on the incidence of different types of urban green spaces on housing prices. With reference to a study sample of apartments located in the Flaminio district of the city of Rome (Italy), an innovative data-driven technique has been implemented. In this way, it was possible to identify, among the main explanatory variables selected by the model as the most influential in real estate price formation phenomena, those relating to green areas and analyzing the marginal contribution of each of them on selling prices. The implemented methodology has allowed to obtain a model characterized by high statistical reliability, by a simplicity and high coherence in the empirical interpretation of the functional relationships between the influencing factors selected and the housing prices. The results clearly indicate that green space is not a homogeneous environmental amenity, rather it is a series of distinct elements that has a different impact on housing prices.

Keywords: Housing prices · Urban green spaces · Private green areas · Genetic algorithm

1 Introduction

In the last decades of the 21st century, urban growth has exceeded the capacity of cities to provide essential services and goods to the inhabitants. The unsustainability of this growth prompts the public administrations on the need for urban models able to deal with the growing demands for urban quality and basic ecosystem services [17, 24]. Public properties represent most of the ecosystem services but, as such, they require proper management skills by public administrations.

In the USA and China, national and local models have been implemented to promote urban forestry as a tool for sustainable urban development. In the Cape Verde city (Africa), green reserves have been increased in and around cities through new trees. Since 1990, the Food and Agriculture Organization of the United Nations

S. Misra et al. (Eds.): ICCSA 2019, LNCS 11622, pp. 23–34, 2019.
https://doi.org/10.1007/978-3-030-24305-0_3

(FAO) has been supporting the dissemination and development of strategic planning capable of supporting urban forestry policies. Recently, the Urban and Peri-urban Forestry Guidelines spreads by the FAO during the 3rd Habitat Conference in Quito (Ecuador) aimed at providing a global reference framework to integrate and connect urban green infrastructures in order to increase a sustainable urban development [25]. These experiences outline that the investments by communities and governments in the protection and restoration of urban forest and green spaces can provide a real contribution to a healthy and resilient urban environment [9, 11].

This situation requires efforts that aim at maintaining or restoring green areas for their importance in the cities' life quality [3, 30]. Urban green areas satisfy some functions and generate various benefits for dwellers [13]. Over the last few decades, numerous studies carried out corroborate the assumption that there is a significant impact of urban green areas on real estate prices [27, 31]. Crompton [5] provides a valuable overview of literature concerning this issue. Among 30 studies analyzed, he highlighted that there were only five that did not support the park proximity as a fundamental factor that raises property prices. Moreover, since 1964 Knetsch, in the USA, had studied this issue [32], finding that benefits of an attractive location may contribute to the growth in the property value. In the 1971 Hendon [14] did not find a uniform influence in the neighborhood of recreational areas on real estate prices. The discussion about green spaces often concerns their homogeneity with distinctions in some cases made with regard to the ownership [4] or the conservation status [16].

Most of the current state of the art on the subject deals with large-scale distinctions on green space such as nature reserves or agricultural fields [13, 20]. Others distinguish the green areas based on size and/or proximity [1]. Only in few cases, the effect that can vary depending on its type, accessibility, diversity, and extra recreation facilities [6, 7, 19, 22] has been studied. There is also some demonstration that scarcity of urban green in the city with high density of development can affect the urban green premium [15, 29]. Nonetheless, the proximity to a park causes negative externalities and decreases property values such as fire risk exposure or poor management, and vulnerability to crime [28].

The analysis of the existing literature allows to identify the following categories of general benefits of urban green areas [23]:

- *environmental*, such as ecological benefits, pollution reduction, cooling urban areas, ensuring biodiversity and wildlife safeguard;
- *economic*, including saving energy, influence on water balance, maximizing the tourist attractiveness of urban areas and increasing the value of properties;
- *social*, as a place of entertainment and recreation, improvement of health and physical and mental condition, strengthening social relationships, crime reduction.

Some of the benefits listed above can have market effects. Regarding a hedonic pricing framework, Sarkar et al. [26] identify five most important reasons that point out the ability of the proximity to urban green spaces to increase residential satisfaction, as well as to influence housing choices and housing prices: (*i*) generation of recreation possibilities, (*ii*) strengthening community relationships and increasing social capital; (*iii*) health and stress relief, (*iv*) natural filtration against pollution and (*v*) protection of urban heat islands.

2 Aim

Although the presence of an urban green space seems to be an important factor in housing decisions there are few empirical research on the incidence of different types of urban green spaces on the housing prices.

The aim of this research is to analyze and quantify in a systematic way the incidence of different types of urban green spaces on housing prices in a central district of Rome.

The functional relationships between property prices and the variables considered in this study have been defined through the implementation of a genetic algorithm called *Evolutionary Polynomial Regression* (EPR) in order to select functions that simultaneously maximize the accuracy of the data and the parsimony of the final mathematical relations.

The analysis is applied to the Flaminio district of the city of Rome (Italy). The study sample consists of 132 residential properties recently purchased, for which the selling prices and the main influencing factors have been detected.

The work is structured as follows. Section 3 describes the case study and specifies the (dependent and independent) variables considered in the model. Section 4 shows the methodology implemented (EPR), the main criteria used to assess the reliability of the returned models are explained and the methods of application are outlined. Section 5 describes the implementation of EPR to the case study and the results obtained in terms of specific statistic performances and empirical reliability of the functional relationships returned by the methodology. Finally, in Sect. 6 the conclusions of the work are discussed.

3 Case Study

The study sample consists of 132 residential properties sold in the last two months of 2018 in the Flaminio district of Rome. The choice of the study area is related to the presence of a wide variety of building tissues and, most of all, a close connection between some building typologies and types of green area. It is possible to identify the following five different building tissue:

- Low-density buildings of the Ex Olympic village built for the 1960 Olympics in Rome. The space in which they are located consists of large public green areas corresponding to the denomination of "Configured Gardens" according to the current urban planning regulations of the municipality of Rome. This configuration is defined by the variable *existence of public green areas* (Gp) among the indicators chosen for the classification of green typologies;
- Residential complexes such as "Villa Riccio", built in 1919, consisting of several buildings in a private enclosed space. The ground between the buildings includes areas for garden represented by the variable called *existence of green areas accessible only to residents* (Gc);

- Social housing complexes ("ICP Flaminio I and II") respectively built in 1905 and in 1925. The first complex is located between Via Flamina and Viale Tiziano. The second complex, located between Lungotevere Flaminio and Viale del Vignola, presents large courtyards with a sequence of semi-public green spaces also included in the variable *existence of green areas accessible only to residents* (Gc) above mentioned;
- High-density buildings realized in 1940 between Via Guido Reni and Ponte Milvio with a few cases in which, inside the courtyard, there is a garden used by residents and taken over by the variable already mentioned as *existence of green areas accessible only to residents* (Gc);
- Historic building dating back to 1883. It consists of houses without green areas in the courtyards for which the variable *existence of green areas accessible only to residents* (Gc) takes zero value.

In Fig. 1 it is possible to notice the distribution of the study sample within the district. In particular, the two different skimmers underline the buildings for which the presence of green areas is related to the explanatory variables of the *existence of green areas accessible only to residents* (Gc) and of the *existence of public green areas* (Gp) above mentioned.

For each property of the study sample, the selling price (dependent variable) and the intrinsic and extrinsic factors (independent variables) most influential on the price have been recorded. As confirmed by the real estate agents operating in the district, the factors identified for this work represent the characteristics considered by buyers and sellers in the phases of negotiation of residential properties. The following three main categories describe the independent variables of the research.

- *Intrinsic characteristics of the property*:
  - the total surface (S) of the property, expressed in square meters of gross floor area;
  - the floor of the property in the building (Lp);
  - the quality of the maintenance conditions of the property (St), taken as a qualitative variable and differentiated, through a synthetic evaluation, by the categories "to be restructured", "fit for habitation" and "restructured" which is assigned, respectively, value "1" for a property to be restructured, value "3" for habitable buildings and value "5" for restructured properties;
  - the existence of at least one view on a tree-lined avenue (Av) for the property, evaluated as a dummy variable, where the value "1" detects the respective presence and the value "0" the absence;
  - the existence of a view on the Lungotevere Flaminio (At) for the property, analyzed as a dummy variable, for which the value "1" defines the presence of this condition and the value "0" the absence.
  - *Technological characteristics of the building in which the property is located*:
    - the existence of the lift inside the building where the residential unit is located (A), considered as a dummy variable, where the value "1" shows the presence of this service and the value "0" detects the absence;

- the existence of the covered or uncovered parking space (Pa) related to the property, assessed as a dummy variable with the value "1" that highlights its presence and the value "0" that detects the absence.

- *Extrinsic characteristics of the building in which the property is located*:
  - the distance from the nearest subway (Dm), expressed in kilometers it takes to walk to it;
  - the existence of green areas accessible only to residents (Gc). In the model this variable is detected as a dummy variable: the presence of this type of green area is indicated with the value "1", whereas the absence with the value "0";
  - the existence of public green areas (Gp), considered in the proposed model as a dummy variable: the value "1" denotes the presence of the above areas, whereas the value "0" detects the respective absence.

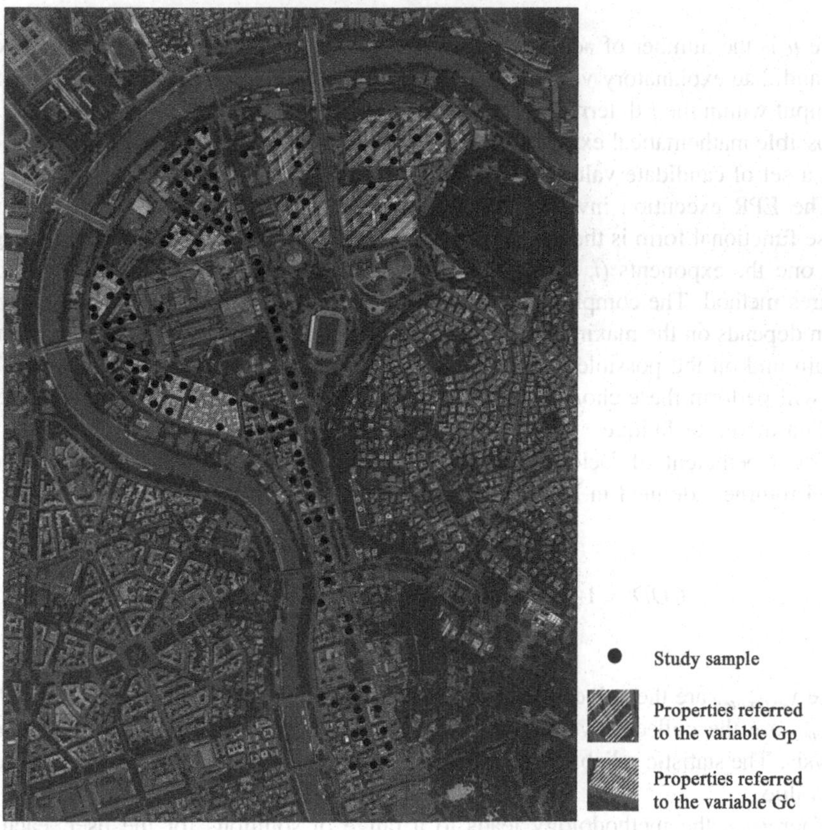

Fig. 1. Distribution of the study sample

4 Methodology

The econometric methodology applied in the present research is the *Evolutionary Polynomial Regression* which integrates the best features of numerical regression [10] with genetic programming [33]. The method proposed is based on a numerical and symbolic regression methods whit polynomial structures [12]. In particular, the technique, starting from experimental data, represents a versatile symbolic regression tool able to search for possible models in polynomial form. Each term that appears is composed of the combinations, with a different degree of complexity, of the input variables selected by the user. Equation (1) is a general non-linear functional structure of the methodology:

$$Y = a_0 + \sum_{i-l}^{n} [a_i \cdot (X_l)^{(i,l)} \cdot \ldots \cdot (X_j)^{(i,j)} \cdot f((X_l)^{(i,j+l)} \cdot \ldots \cdot (X_j)^{(i,2j)})] \tag{1}$$

where n is the number of additive terms, a_i are numerical parameters to be valued, X_i are candidate explanatory variables, (i, l) - with $l = (1, \ldots, 2j)$ - is the exponent of the l-th input within the i-th term in Eq. (1), f is a function selected by the user among a set of possible mathematical expressions. The exponents (i, l) are also selected by the user from a set of candidate values (real numbers).

The EPR execution involves the selection and generation of a series of models whose functional form is the best combination of the input variables Xi, identifying for each one the exponents (i, l) and the numerical coefficients a_i, evaluated by a Least Squares method. The complexity and the number of models that the methodology can return depends on the maximum number of terms that the mathematical expression can contain and on the possible exponents through which the variables are elevated. The user will perform these choices during the preliminary phase of the implementation of the data-driven technique.

The Coefficient of Determination (COD) is indicative of the accuracy of each model returned, defined in Eq. (2):

$$COD = 1 - \frac{N-1}{N} \cdot \frac{\sum_N (y_{estimated} - y_{detected})^2}{\sum_N (y_{detected} - mean(y_{detected}))^2} \tag{2}$$

where $y_{estimated}$ are the values of the dependent variable estimated by the methodology, $y_{detected}$ are the collected values of the dependent variable, N is the sample size in analysis. The statistic reliability of each model is greater when the COD is close to the unit value.

Therefore, the methodology leads to a range of solutions for the user, each one characterized by a more or less complex algebraic form and by a different level of statistical accuracy in terms of COD. The user selects and chooses the most appropriate solution according to the specific needs linked to the purpose of the analysis, the knowledge of the phenomenon and the type and quantity of experimental data used.

5 Application of the Method

The EPR methodology is implemented considering the structure of the generic model identified in Eq. (1) without function f selected and with the dependent variable P (selling price) as the natural logarithm of it ($Y = ln(P)$) [18]. Each additive monomial term of the mathematical expression is assumed as a combination of the inputs - the explanatory variables Xi - raised to the proper numerical exponents. In particular, in order to have a wide range of models, the candidate exponents belong to the set (0; 0.5; 1; 2) and the maximum number n of additive terms in final expressions is assumed to be seven.

The implementation of the econometric method has generated several solutions, each one characterized by a different number of additive terms, combination of the variables and a different level of COD. Table 1 shows the main models provided by the EPR technique and, then, chosen by the user.

Table 1. Equations obtained by the implementation of EPR

Eq. (n)	Model	COD [%]
(3)	$Y = -0.032455 \cdot Dm^2 + 0.18437 \cdot S^{0.5} + 0.16134 \cdot Lp^{0.5} + 10.9939$	85.52
(4)	$Y = -0.11758 \cdot Dm + 0.17635 \cdot S^{0.5} + 0.30376 \cdot At^{0.5} \cdot Av^{0.5} + 0.16911 \cdot Lp^{0.5} + 11.1426$	86.94
(5)	$Y = -0.034534 \cdot Dm^2 + 0.18224 \cdot S^{0.5} + 0.14626 \cdot St \cdot Pa^{0.5} \cdot Gc^{0.5} + 0.07516 \cdot Lp^{0.5} \cdot St^{0.5} + 11.0644$	88.34
(6)	$Y = -0.033504 \cdot Dm^2 + 0.1761 \cdot S^{0.5} + 0.30689 \cdot At^{0.5} \cdot Av^{0.5} - +0.1792 \cdot A^{0.5} \cdot Gp^{0.5} + 0.85067 \cdot Lp^{0.5} - 0.19259 \cdot Lp + 10.5385$	89.48
(7)	$Y = -0.035082 \cdot Dm^2 + 0.17403 \cdot S^{0.5} + 0.059122 \cdot At^{0.5} \cdot Av^{0.5} \cdot Dm^2 + 0 \cdot St + -0.18802 \cdot A^{0.5} \cdot Gp^{0.5} + 0.8494 \cdot Lp^{0.5} - 0.1928 \cdot Lp + 10.5706$	89.62
(8)	$Y = -0.035281 \cdot Dm^2 + 0.17336 \cdot S^{0.5} + 0.004466 \cdot At^{0.5} \cdot Av^{0.5} \cdot S^{0.5} \cdot Dm^2 + -0.19455 \cdot A^{0.5} \cdot Gp^{0.5} + 0.8526 \cdot Lp^{0.5} - 0.1938 \cdot Lp + 0 \cdot Lp^2 \cdot St^2 \cdot Pa^2 \cdot Gc^{0.5} + 10.5777$	89.76
(9)	$Y = -0.39624 \cdot Dm + 0.13269 \cdot S^{0.5} + 0.023317 \cdot S^{0.5} \cdot Dm + 0.21289 \cdot St^{0.5} \cdot Pa^{0.5} \cdot Gc^2 \cdot Av^{0.5} + 0 \cdot A^{0.5} \cdot Gp^2 \cdot S + 0.033674 \cdot A^2 \cdot At^{0.5} \cdot Av \cdot Dm^2 + 0.078459 \cdot Lp^{0.5} \cdot St^{0.5} + 11.7277$	89.83

The models are characterized by a progressively complex algebraic form and a higher statistical accuracy (COD). Each solution has direct and indirect functional links between the dependent variable of the model (selling price) and the independent variables chosen for the analysis. In particular, the model of Eq. (9) has been identified as the best because (*i*) it is defined by a mathematical expression of simple interpretation, not much more complicated than the previous models, (*ii*) it is characterized by a COD equal to 89.83% attesting an excellent statistical reliability of the model, (*iii*) its polynomial form includes most of the explanatory variables chosen, allowing to analyze the contribution of each one in the phenomena of selling price formation.

The variables selected by the methodology as the most influential on property prices in the market in question are: the distance from the nearest metro station (Dm), the total surface of the property (S), the conservative state of the building (St), the presence of the parking space (Pa), the presence within the residential complex of which the property is part of a garden (Gc), the view of the property on a tree-lined

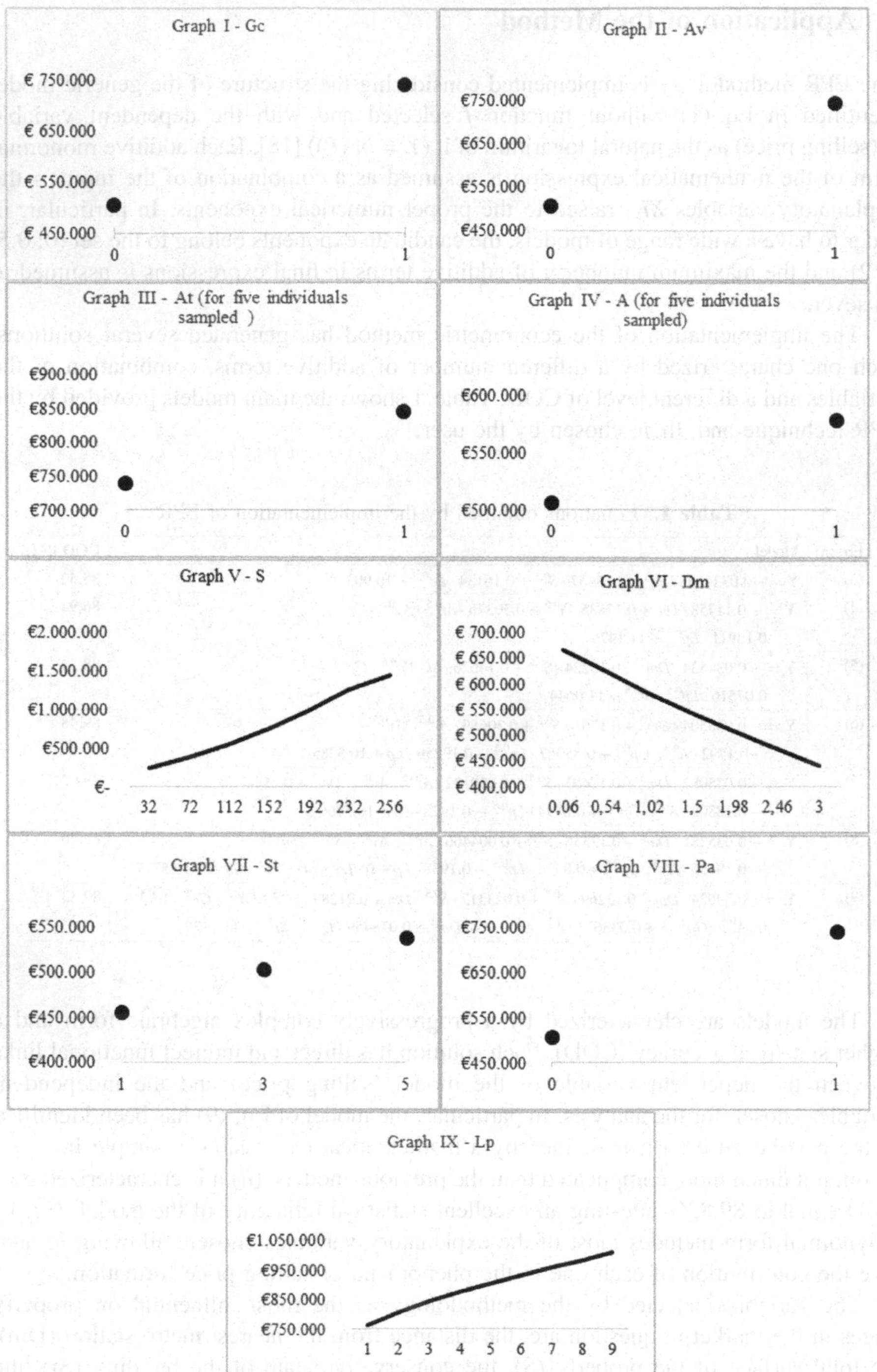

Fig. 2. Functional relationships between the influencing factors selected by the model and the housing prices

avenue (Av), the presence of the elevator (A), the presence of the public garden (Gp), the view of the property on the Lungotevere (At) and the level of the floor (Lp). With regard to the aim of the research related to analyze and to quantify in a systematic way the incidence of different types of urban green spaces on housing prices in a central district of Rome, it should be noted that the model chosen includes all four variables selected for this analysis concerning green spaces.

The expression of the model does not allow to immediately verify the empirical consistency of the signs of the coefficients of the independent variables for none of the selected characteristics, since there are no variables that individually appear in the additive terms. In order to interpret the functional relationships between the dependent variable Y and the independent variables, it is necessary to use a mathematical exogenous approach that allows to quantitatively express the influence of each factor selected by the model of Eq. (9) on the housing prices. In particular, the variation of the *i-th* variable in the range of admissible values in the sample taken is analyzed by assuming the mean values for the quantitative variables (Dm, S, Lp) or measured by a scale of scores (St) and the value 1 for the dummy variables (Pa, Gc, Av, A, Gp, At).

In this respect, it is important to pay attention to any alternative situations for the variables belonging to the same category that cannot simultaneously be equal to 1. Figure 2 shows the functional relationships obtained.

The functional relationships obtained confirm the expected empirical phenomena. Firstly, regarding the variables chosen for the green areas, there is a direct functional relationship between the variable *existence of green areas accessible only to residents* (Gc) and the housing prices. This contingence is verified in the only situation in which the property is equipped of parking space and a view on a tree-lined avenue (Pa = 1 and Av = 1), being the Gc variable combined within the same term with Pa and Av. In the condition in which the green space in the courtyard (Gc), the parking space (Pa) and the view on a tree-lined avenue (Av) are simultaneously factors of the property, the increase in prices is equal to +46.19%.

The same percentage (+46.19%) of increase in selling prices is shown for the properties with a *view on the tree-lined avenue* (Av = 1) when, also in this case – as they appear in the same term of the model - the simultaneous presence of the parking space (Pa = 1) and the garden in the courtyard (Gc = 1) is attested.

The remaining variables related to the green space typology, *existence of public green areas* (Gp) and *existence of a view on the Lungotevere Flaminio* (At), require considerations that are more detailed. The first variable (Gp) appears in a single term of the model, whose numerical coefficient is equal to zero and, therefore, this extrinsic factor is not influential in the phenomena of housing price formation in the market and for the reference sample.

The characteristic *existence of a view on the Lungotevere Flaminio* (At), instead, compares in the model of Eq. (9), in the same additive term with the variables *existence of the lift inside the building* (A), *distance from the nearest subway* (Dm) and *existence of at least one view on a tree-lined avenue* (Av). This feature is appreciated by the market analyzed exclusively for a limited number of properties in the sample (equal to 5 properties) for which, due to the angular position taken, there is the presence of the two features At and Av. Therefore, although for the total study sample, excluding the five properties mentioned, there is the incompatibility of the characteristic Av with the characteristic At, as the impossibility of the contextual presence of the two views in the same property is evident, the incidence of the variable *existence of a view on the Lungotevere Flaminio* on the housing prices is only analyzed with reference to the five properties mentioned above (graph III).

For the variable *existence of the lift inside the building* (A) a similar situation occurs. In fact, although the model of Eq. (9) returns a functional relationship that provides for the significance of the contribution of variable A on property prices, the presence in the algebraic expression of the variable A is verified, in the term with numerical coefficient 0 and characterized by the presence of the variables At and Av that, as shown above, simultaneously occur only for five properties of the sample.

In Fig. 2 the graph V shows a direct relationship between the *total surface* (S) variable and the housing prices and, specifically, there is a percentage of increase in housing prices equal to an average of +7%.

The inverse relationship between the variable *distance from the nearest subway* (Dm) and the housing prices highlights the empirical evidence of a negative influence on the selling prices of the buildings placed at a greater distance from the nearest metro stop, equal to −0.85%.

For the variable *quality of the maintenance conditions of the property* (St), the direct relationship with the housing prices shows a greater appreciation of the market for properties in excellent condition compared to those in good conditions (+29.23%) and, in the same way, for apartments that have a good state of preservation compared to those in poor state of repair (+19.31%). Furthermore, the analysis reflects a direct relationship between the housing prices and the variable *existence of the covered or uncovered parking space* (Pa) in the only situation in which the property has a *garden in the courtyard* (Gc = 1) and a *view on a tree-lined avenue* (Av = 1). In this condition, the increase in prices recorded following the presence of the parking space is equal to +46.19%.

Finally, for the variable *floor of the property in the building* (Lp), the model of Eq. (9) shows an average variation in the selling prices of +3.60% for each increase in the floor.

6 Conclusions

The growing importance attributed to the natural open spaces within the consolidated contexts of the cities has led to the start of works of environmental recovery in degraded areas [8, 21] and to the reconversion of "urban voids" in areas intended for public and/or private green areas. Along these lines, there is a need for public administrations and public authorities to prepare and adopt policy tools for the correct planning, regulation and programming of urban green space management interventions, in order to guarantee a synchronous growth of the city and its green heritage [2].

This research is linked to the issue outlined. In particular, in the work the aim has been to analyze and quantify in a systematic way the incidence of different types of urban green spaces on the housing prices. With reference to a study sample of apartments located in the Flaminio district of the city of Rome (Italy), an innovative data-driven technique has been implemented. In this way, it has been possible to identify, among the explanatory variables selected by the model as the most influential in the property price formation phenomena, the factors relating to green areas and to analyze the marginal contribution of each of them on the selling prices.

The implemented methodology has allowed to obtain a model characterized by high statistical reliability, by a simplicity and high coherence in the empirical interpretation of the functional relationships between the influencing factors selected and the housing prices.

Further insights may address the application of the methodology used in this work in other Italian and international contexts. It could also be interesting to propose the same analysis for another district of the city of Rome, characterized by urban green space typologies similar to those analyzed in this research. Subsequently, the comparison of the results could give rise to inspiring considerations. Another development could concern the extension of the categories of urban green spaces considered, including, for example, among the independent explanatory variables, urban parks or equipped green areas, in order to analyze the contribution of these types of green spaces in the processes of property price formation.

References

1. Abbott, J.K., Klaiber, H.A.: Is all space created equal? Uncovering the relationship between competing land uses in subdivisions. Ecol. Econ. **70**(2), 296–307 (2010)
2. Amato, F., Tonini, M., Murgante, B., Kaneski, M.: Fuzzy definition of rural urban interface: an application based on land use change scenarios in Portugal. Environ. Model Softw. **104**, 171–187 (2018)
3. Barbante, E., Calvo, E., Sanesi, G., Selleri, B., Verlič, A., Vilhar, U.E.D.S.: Urban and periurban forests: management, monitoring and ecosystem services. Emonfur Life + project experiences, p. 279 (2014)
4. Cheshire, P., Sheppard, S.: On the price of land and the value of amenities. Economica **62** (246), 247–267 (1995)
5. Crompton, J.L.: The impact of parks on property values: a review of the empirical evidence. J. Leis. Res. **33**(1), 1–31 (2001)
6. Crompton, J.L.: The impact of parks on property values: empirical evidence from the past two decades in the United States. Manag. Leis. **10**(4), 203–218 (2005)
7. Czembrowski, P., Kronenberg, J.: Hedonic pricing and different urban green space types and sizes: insights into the discussion on valuing ecosystem services. Landsc. Urban Plan. **146**, 11–19 (2016)
8. Del Giudice, V., De Paola, P., Torrieri, F.: An integrated choice model for the evaluation of urban sustainable renewal scenarios. Adv. Mater. Res. **1030–1032**, 2399–2406 (2014)
9. Della Spina, L., Calabrò, F.: Decision support model for conservation, reuse and valorization of the historic cultural heritage. In: Gervasi, O., et al. (eds.) ICCSA 2018. LNCS, vol. 10962, pp. 3–17. Springer, Cham (2018). https://doi.org/10.1007/978-3-319-95168-3_1
10. Draper, N.R., Smith, H.: Applied Regression Analysis. Wiley, Hoboken (2014)
11. Food and Agricolture Organization of the United Nations (FAO): COFO Side Event on "Urban Forests for Sustainable Cities", Rome (2016)
12. Giustolisi, O., Savic, D.A.: A symbolic data-driven technique based on evolutionary polynomial regression. J. Hydroinform. **8**(3), 207–222 (2006)
13. Grey, G.W., Deneke, F.J.: Urban Forestry. Wiley, Hoboken (1978)

14. Hendon, W.S.: The park as a determinant of property values. Am. J. Econ. Sociol. **30**(3), 289–300 (1971)
15. Herath, S., Choumert, J., Maier, G.: The value of the greenbelt in Vienna: a spatial hedonic analysis. Ann. Reg. Sci. **54**(2), 349–374 (2015)
16. Irwin, E.G., Bockstael, N.E.: The problem of identifying land use spillovers: measuring the effects of open space on residential property values. Am. J. Agric. Econ. **83**(3), 698–704 (2001)
17. Istituto Superiore per la Protezione e la Ricerca Ambientale (ISPRA): Definizione del metodo per la classificazione e quantificazione dei servizi ecosistemici in Italia, http://www.isprambiente.gov.it/files/biodiversita/SERVIZI_ECOSISTEMICI.pdf
18. Lynch, A.K., Rasmussen, D.W.: Proximity, neighbourhood and the efficacy of exclusion. Urban Stud. **41**(2), 285–298 (2004)
19. McCord, J., McCord, M., McCluskey, W., Davis, P.T., McIlhatton, D., Haran, M.: Effect of public green space on residential property values in Belfast metropolitan area. J. Financ. Manag. Prop. Constr. **19**(2), 117–137 (2014)
20. Morancho, A.B.: A hedonic valuation of urban green areas. Landsc. Urban Plan. **66**(1), 35–41 (2003)
21. Morano, P., Locurcio, M., Tajani, F., Guarini, M.R.: Urban Redevelopment: A Multi-criteria Valuation Model Optimized through the Fuzzy Logic. In: Murgante, B., et al. (eds.) ICCSA 2014. LNCS, vol. 8581, pp. 161–175. Springer, Cham (2014). https://doi.org/10.1007/978-3-319-09150-1_13
22. Panduro, T.E., Veie, K.L.: Classification and valuation of urban green space. A hedonic house price valuation. Lands. Urban Plan. **120**, 119–128 (2013)
23. Sadeghian, M., Vardanyan, Z.: The benefits of urban parks, a review of urban research. J. Nov. Appl. Sci. **2**(8), 231–237 (2013)
24. Saganeiti, L., Favale, A., Pilogallo, A., Scorza, F., Murgante, B.: Assessing urban fragmentation at regional scale using Sprinkling indexes. Sustainability **10**(9), 3274 (2018)
25. Salbitano, F., Borelli, S., Conigliaro, M., Chen, Y.: Guidelines on urban and peri-urban forestry. FAO Forestry Paper No. 178, Rome (2016)
26. Sarkar, C., et al.: Exploring associations between urban green, street design and walking: results from the greater London boroughs. Landsc. Urban Plan. **143**, 112–125 (2015)
27. Trojanek, R., Gluszak, M., Tanas, J.: The effect of urban green spaces on house prices in Warsaw. Int. J. Strat. Prop. Manag. **22**(5), 358–371 (2018)
28. Troy, A., Grove, J.M., Grove, J.M.: Property values, parks, and crime: a hedonic analysis in Baltimore, MD. Landsc. Urban Plan. **87**(3), 233–245 (2008)
29. Votsis, A.: Planning for green infrastructure: the spatial effects of parks, forests, and fields on Helsinki's apartment prices. Ecol. Econ. **132**, 279–289 (2017)
30. Zhou, X., Parves Rana, M.: Social benefits of urban green space: a conceptual framework of valuation and accessibility measurements. Manag. Environ. Qual.: Int. J. **23**(2), 173–189 (2012)
31. Kim, H., Lee, G.E., Lee, J., Choi, Y.: Understanding the local impact of urban park plans and park typology on housing price: a case study of the Busan metropolitan region. Korea Landsc. Urban Plan. **184**, 1–11 (2019)
32. Knetsch, J.L.: The influence of reservoir projects on land values. Am. J. Agric. Econ. **46**(1), 231–243 (1964)
33. Koza, J.R.: Genetic Programming: on the Programming of Computers by Means of Natural Selection. MIT Press, Cambridge (1992)

Multilayer Perceptron and Particle Swarm Optimization Applied to Traffic Flow Prediction on Smart Cities

Lucas Rodrigues Frank[1], Yan Mendes Ferreira[1], Eduardo Pagani Julio[1], Francisco Henrique C. Ferreira[1], Bruno José Dembogurski[2], and Edelberto Franco Silva[1](✉)

[1] Federal University of Juiz de Fora, Juiz de Fora, Brazil
{lucasrodrigues,yanmendes,eduardo.pagani,francisco.henrique, edelberto}@ice.ufjf.br

[2] Federal Rural University of Rio de Janeiro, Seropédica, Rio de Janeiro, Brazil
brunodembogurski@ufrrj.br

Abstract. Smart cities can increase the live quality of its citizens and Intelligent Transportation Systems is a key topic in this area. When the population density living in the same region increases more and more, the cities suffer from problems as constant traffic jams. Thinking this way, in this paper are present the uses of computational intelligence techniques and analyses to aid in traffic dimensioning solutions. To do this, prediction models and heuristics are the best way to create a more autonomous and intelligent environment. In this work, an application is introduced applying machine learning and an optimization technique to empower a smart ecosystem. To validate it, an evaluation using Multi-Layer Perceptron together with Particle Swarm Optimization was performed, comparing it with the state-of-the-art. All evaluations were done using real data traffic with a free traffic flow scenario. Applying the Particle Swarm Optimization to optimize the activation functions' parameters, we obtained 3.1% average MAPE for Logistic activation function and a MAPE of 3.4% for ReLU activation function.

Keywords: Smart cities · Machine learning · Traffic flow prediction · Intelligent Transportation Systems · Particle Swarm Optimization

1 Introduction

New urban development policies are increasingly directing its focus towards the Internet and broadband network as enablers of a variety of electronic services (e-services). These new concepts and solutions are turning cities into centers for innovation in many areas such as mobility, health, security, socio-environmental, economic and many others [2].

Therefore new problems and challenges are presented when considering how cities and their surroundings can evolve to include smart objects and smart applications, thus accelerating Future Internet research which includes the aforementioned innovations.

S. Misra et al. (Eds.): ICCSA 2019, LNCS 11622, pp. 35–47, 2019.
https://doi.org/10.1007/978-3-030-24305-0_4

Here, the main focus is traffic management, a segment of Intelligent Transportation Systems (ITS) [5,8,12] that tackles traffic dimensioning and orientation.

Considering this topic, the major objective is to provide accurate traffic predictions. This can be achieved through different models aiming for an autonomous and intelligent environment [8]. Usually, these prediction models are used to create simulations of an entire city, but they are not limited to this single purpose. Smaller environments, e.g a university campus, can be modeled as well as introducing new challenges, such as heterogeneous traffic [2,3,16].

The SmartCampus UFJF project aims to create an intelligent campus environment for its users. In order to achieve this goal, many campus' services are being integrated, updated and new ones are being developed. One of these new initiatives seeks a better understanding of vehicle traffic in the campus area, generating new data that can be used to improve the quality of life expectations of all campus users and to support decision making.

To provide a clear understanding of the problem description of the campus environment is necessary. The campus interconnects two key neighborhoods of the Juiz de Fora - Minas Gerais, Brazil - city, allowing free citizen and vehicle traffic through its premises. Thus, traffic volume is not limited to its students, professors, and staff, but also by those who use the campus as a place to practice leisure or exercising activities and those who just pass by. This creates a heterogeneous field, where drivers have different objectives within the campus - mainly academic, leisure and passerby. These contrasting profiles make the prediction task a real challenge when considering the huge traffic volume variation that occurs during the day. This variance is intrinsically linked to the drivers' profile and their schedules - *e.g.* beginning of academic activities and morning commuters going to work.

The main contribution of this work is to use a computational technique to improve the configuration of a neural network model. Specifically, to find the best values of activation functions parameters. After to evaluate and validate the improvements, the model is used in conjunct with predictive techniques in the context of traffic volume estimation, culminating in an application called *SmartTraffic*^{pso}. The evaluations are done using real data traffic in a real free traffic flow scenario.

The rest of this paper is organized as follows. Initially, the related work in Sect. 2 is discussed. Section 3 presents this work architectural proposal and describes its workflow. Moreover, in Sect. 4, the experimental results are presented. Finally, Sect. 5 summarizes the paper and outlines future research directions.

2 Related Work

In this section, ITS and PSO (Particle Swarm Optimization) related papers will be discussed, focusing on traffic prediction and parameters optimization. For this reason, each one will be discussed separately and then a comparison will be made between this works proposal and the ones in the literature.

To complete our study about the state-of-the-art and initiatives applied to ITS two works are present using PSO benefits. The first one is [17] is our best-known application of a metaheuristic to improve a neural network model. In this paper were propose two mechanisms to increase the models' performance. Firstly, the use of Deep Learning which is a recent technique that implies using a neural network with multiple layers. Based on this, the Deep Learning help to solve a problem of predicting the number of occupants in a given location at 15, 30 and 60 min from the current time via wifi data collected. In order to reach the goal, a computational intelligent method, or metaheuristic, called Particle Swarm Optimization (PSO) were proposed to be used to improve the prediction model. PSO as a good iterative population-based method to create particles that represent solutions, in order to achieve the best possible solution a fitness function is used. These particles use mathematical formulations to move in the search space, this one being the number of layers and the number of neurons they seek to optimize. After the results, they concluded that the PSO was successful in reducing model training time from 77% to 85%.

In [7], a combination of SVR and PSO is proposed to improve the results of a vehicle traffic prediction problem. The authors conducted a comparison among its performance with other methods, such as multiple linear regressions and neural networks. In this case, the PSO seeks to optimize the input parameters of the SVR, which are: penalty C, radius and kernel function. The evaluation metric used as fitness function was the Root Mean Square Error (RMSE). At the end of, was possible to conclude that the combination of PSO and SVR had a positive impact, doing a better performance in almost 10% compared to the other models. It is necessary to be clear the limitation of scenario and models compared by the authors, where the use of traffic flow was not based on an open database, and the models compared was not the main on the state-of-the-art today. Because of it, our proposal will be compared with the main work from [8].

The work [8], mentioned from now on by Huang *et al.*, poses as one of the state-of-the-art solutions for traffic flow prediction. The authors propose a Deep Learning Architecture which is achieved by training a Deep Belief Network (DBN) - that can be seen as a stack of Restricted Boltzmann Machines (RBMs) -. The RBM is an unsupervised pattern learning Artificial Neural Network (ANN) that learns through a greedy layerwise training. To fine tune the model's parameters, a supervised regression layer is added on top of the DBN. Using the premise that traffic is a correlated network, the idea of multi-task regression was exploited in the supervised learning process.

The authors implement different traffic flow forecast approaches and compare to their own architecture, outperforming all the others. Despite utilizing a sigmoid regression layer, the authors point to the possibility of replacing it with other regression algorithms such as Support Vector Regression (SVR).

In [13], the authors also applied a deep learning strategy and reinforced the use of historical data to predict traffic flow. Its model is based on Stacked Autoencoders (SAE): A deep neural network that aims to reproduce the input layer into the output layer by adjusting the weights of the synapses. They train the network in a greedy fashion. The unsupervised learning algorithm parameters are then fine-tuned with a sigmoid regression layer.

The model presented in [6] propose the use of the Gated Recurrent Units (GRU). That is a modification of the Long Short Term Memory (LSTM) neural network, whose main characteristic is the storage of information. Thus, allowing the consideration of previous entries when processing new data, enabling it to work better with time series.

While the LSTM has been used as a predictive model for traffic flow in previous works such as [15,19], GRU has not been used for this purpose until then. These two models are evaluated, comparing the results with an AutoRegressive Integrated Moving Average (ARIMA) model, concluding that both models outperformed the ARIMA model and that in 84% of the tests the model GRU outperformed the LSTM.

It is valid to mention that the authors do not assess the scalability of the proposed model and all tests are conducted utilizing a very small amount of data (4 weeks). Since the work proposed in this paper aims to empower a smart ecosystem, scalability is key, therefore this solution was not implemented and evaluated.

The previously mentioned papers evaluate their architectures with free-flowing highways, which is a less challenging task. Differently, [4] propose an architecture composed by a spin-off implementation of a SVR, suited for online applications called On-line SVR (Ol-SVR) [14]. In this investigation, the authors propose an architecture that works both in typical and atypical scenarios (e.g. vehicular crashes, work zone, holidays, etc). In their work, other solutions from the literature were implemented and compared, showing that their proposal presents a solid option for both scenarios, even though it was outperformed in some evaluations.

All mentioned papers utilize the dataset PeMS - introduced in Subsect. 4.1 - to evaluate their proposal. The first three utilize data collected on highways, both recent and historical - *i.e.* traffic volume of past weeks on the same weekday -, while the latter utilizes both typical and atypical traffic scenarios for their evaluation, but only recent data is inputted in the prediction process. The approaches found in the literature are summarized in Table 1 and compared to the one presented in this paper.

3 Proposal

The SmartCampus project is an initiative to create an intelligent and autonomous university campus. Its results are not restricted to campus environments and can be used on other scenarios, like a big smart city. To achieve that, a series of smaller initiatives are being proposed and implemented as services and applications that will be available in an integrated API.

Table 1. Related work comparison.

Work	Architecture	Optimization	Historical	Atypical traffic
[8]	DBN + SVR		X	
[13]	SAE + SR		X	
[6]	GRU		X	
[14]	Ol-SVR			X
[7]	SVR	X (PSO)	X	
SmartTraffic^{pso}	MLP	X (PSO)	X	X

SmartTraffic and its evolutions, *SmartTraffic^{pso}*, is the initiatives' pilot, whose main objective is to provide live traffic volume estimation, serving as a support for future applications - *e.g.* estimating parking spots availability - and supporting the administration in the decision-making process, such as estimating traffic volume in a public event on the campus.

The data can come from different sources, *e.g.* security software and cameras for security environment, traffic cameras to traffic flow monitor. On the traffic flow monitor side, is possible to register all vehicles license plates that pass through its cameras. It is worth mentioning that, among other transformations, the plates are hashed in the Extract-Transform-Load (ETL) process to the database and only quantitative analysis are conducted. Other sources of data flow can be simulated too. As the case of our evaluation, when a real traffic flow data will be used.

Figure 1 synthesizes the proposal. The SmartCampus project provides encapsulated services as endpoints of an API and the workflow adopted in the implementation of *SmartTraffic^{pso}* application is presented. Foremost, it exposes the utilized predictor and then discusses the steps in this pipeline in the following subsections.

3.1 Model Specification

Time series models are well-known problem solvers for traffic flow prediction. From simpler and traditional models, as the ARIMA [20], to more complex and non-linear [9], the time series approach is well-taken in the literature. As opposed to that, another noteworthy line of research utilizes data-driven algorithms such as ANNs [11] or Local Weighted Learning [18] to solve traffic flow prediction problems.

This work proposal, beyond to optimize its activation functions' parameters, an application of neural network on traffic flow prediction. Our application is part of an smart city ecossystem, and is called *SmartTraffic^{pso}*. In our experiments was created a model composed by triple layers Multilayer Perceptron (MLP) ANN.

The MLP is an ANN where all neurons in a layer are connected to all other neurons in adjacent layers. It contains an input layer, a number of hidden layers

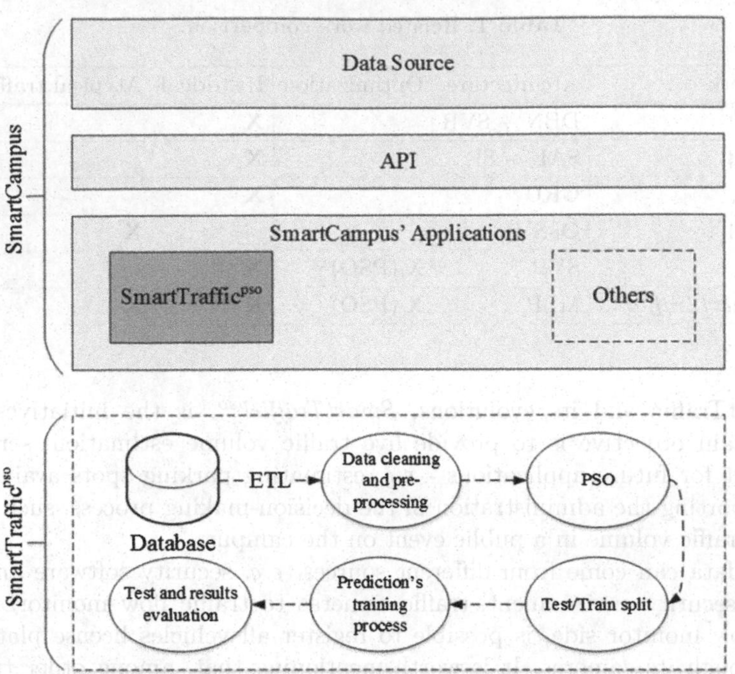

Fig. 1. Global view of SmartCampus project and *SmartTraffic*^{pso}'s pipeline.

- three in this particular architecture - and an output layer. Since the result is a one dimension answer, *i.e.* the traffic flow forecast, the output layer contains only one neuron. The model is described in Eq. 1.

$$f(t+1) = \sum_{i=2}^{4} W_i \cdot g(W_{i-1}^T \cdot x_{i-1} + b_{i-1}) + b_i \tag{1}$$

Where: W_i and W_{i-1} is the set of weights of the ith and $i-1^{th}$ layer, respectively. b_i and b_{i-1} are the bias added to the $i+1^{th}$ and i^{th} layer, respectively. Furthermore, $g(x)$ is the activation function and, finally, x_{i-1} is the set of neurons of the $i-1^{th}$ layer.

The input layer fed to the network, defined in Eq. 2, are past observations, *i.e.* the traffic volume. Moreover, since a cyclic pattern was observed, the model does not use only recent observations but also historic observations, *i.e.* the traffic volume of the same weekday and time of day in previous weeks. The use of historical data shows an improvement in results as seen in the work of [1,8,13].

$$\begin{aligned} x_1 = &\{\#V_t,\ \#V_{t-1},\ \ldots,\ \#V_{t-P}\} \cup \\ &\{\#V_{t+1-(1\ week)},\ \#V_{t+1-(2\ weeks)},\ \ldots,\ \#V_{t+1-(Q\ weeks)}\} \end{aligned} \tag{2}$$

Where V_t is the traffic volume at the tth time stamp, P is the number of recent observations taken into account and Q is the number of historical observations considered.

The network learns through backpropagation [21]. In this paper, two distinct neuron activation functions are evaluated: logistic function (Logi), defined in Eq. 3, and REctified Linear Unit (ReLU), defined in Eq. 4. Those were chosen due to their popularity in the literature and their very different behavior. The solver for the weight optimization process of choice was the stochastic gradient descent [10].

$$g(x) = \frac{1}{1 + e^{-x}} \tag{3}$$

$$g(x) = max(0, x) \tag{4}$$

In order to guarantee reproducibility and to compare this works proposal with [8], the *scikit-learn*[1] implementations of the RBM and SVR was chosen and *keras*[2] to implement a MLP regressor.

As were mentioned, the PSO a metaheuristic and was applied to improve the implementation of the neural network model using MLP. With PSO is possible to the best combination of parameter values for the activation functions, *i.e.* in our case, ReLU and Logi. As can be seen on Algorithm 1, the PSO algorithm works by having a population/swarm of candidate solutions, called particles. To find the best fitness, these particles are moved around in the search space. Its movements are guided by their own best-known position in the search space as well as the entire swarm's best-known position. The process is repeated iteratively to find the best/satisfactory solution. Seen the algorithm can be clear how the population size would find the best values of parameters.

For particle movement, we need to define an initial velocity and position for each particle randomly. And so, from this initial velocity, we can calculate new positions and velocities for the particle [17]. The formulas for new position and velocity can be found in Eqs. 5 and 6, respectively. In Eq. 6 *pbest* is the particle best position and *gbest* is the particle best position in the population.

$${x_i}^{t+1} = {x_i}^{t} + {v_i}^{t+1} \tag{5}$$

$${v_i}^{t+1} = w.{v_i}^{t} + c_1.rand.(pbest - {x_i}^{t}) + c_2.rand.(gbest - {x_i}^{t}). \tag{6}$$

In our proposal, we want to optimize the number of neurons, a learning rate and the alpha parameter (for the logistic function). For the PSO to work correctly, we had to limit the search space to minimize training time and neural network convergence. Therefore, the limit values for each of the parameters are: n_MAX = 140, n_MIN = 60, learning_rate_MAX = 0.0009, learning_rate_MIN = 0.0001, alpha_MAX = 52, alpha_MIN = 2. It is also necessary to define the

[1] http://scikit-learn.org/.

[2] https://keras.io/.

acceleration coefficients c_1 and c_2, and the coefficient of inertia w, both aim to assist in the movement of the particles and were assigned the value 2 for the first two and 0.7 for the latter.

Finally, we define the size of the population and the maximum number of iterations over the population, being 20 for both.

Algorithm 1. PSO

```
Input  : numberIteration, populationSize
Output: numberNeurons, learningRate, alpha
particlePop ← list of particles;
for i ← 0 up to i < populationSize do
    create a particle p;
    initialize p with random parameters within their correspondet intervalls;
    p.pBest ← fitness function calculated after neural network test for particle
      p;
    add particle p in particlePop;
end for
gBest ← best particle in particlePop;
while numberIteration do
    for each particle p in particlePop do
        p ← calculate new velocity;
        p ← calculate new position;
        error ← fitness function calculated after running new parameters in
          neural network for particle p;
        if error < p.pBest then
            p.pBest ← error
            p.positionBest ← p.position
            if error < gBest.pBest then
                gBest ← p;
            end if
        end if
    end for
    numberIteration ← numberIteration − 1;
end while
```

3.2 Data Cleaning and Pre-processing

During peaks in traffic, the software would register multiple entries for a single vehicle. Specifically, it would move slow enough for the system to trigger another snapshot. All observations of the same vehicle within a 1-min range were removed and only the first entry was maintained.

Some entries would not have a license plate tied to it. Since the provided dataset only had raw data and no study of the vehicle detection software was conducted, two options were available on how to deal with this limitation. It could be a fault in the image processing algorithm, where it would not read the plate, but it was indeed a vehicle and should be kept as a piece of valid information or it was a capture of something other than a vehicle - *e.g.* bike or pedestrian - and should be removed. The latter was the chosen option.

After cleaning these sets, the traffic volume was aggregated in a time window and normalized. The normalization is applied to both datasets whereas the other processes are applied only to the university dataset.

3.3 Test/Train Split

For both scenarios, a train-test split of 2/3 and 1/3, respectively, was conducted. It is noteworthy that in Huang et al. [8] original paper, the authors used 10 months of the dataset to train their model and only 2 months to test it. Even though the test set represents 17% of the dataset size, the experiments presented here utilize 33% to minimize overfitting effects and, therefore, there is a marginal difference between the results obtained in this work and [8].

3.4 Test and Evaluation Results

Along with P and Q introduced in Sect. 3.1, the number of neurons N in the hidden layer compose the parameters of the proposed architecture. The same parameters are used by Huang *et al.* [8]. However, N represents the number of components in the DBN's stack.

To focus only on the parameters we seek to optimize, we did several initial tests where the parameters followed the following ranges: P ranging from 10 to 15 with a gap of 1, Q ranging from 0 to 5 and N ranging from 80 to 120 with 10 as a gap. After filtering the obtained results, we separated the best parameters P and Q to be fixed, to save time and to improve the results already found.

The train-test split used was 70% and 30%, respectively.

4 Evaluation

In this section, the model previously presented is validated and compared with the results presented in [8] in a scenario using the PeMS benchmark dataset. It is valid to mention that this work focus on comparing the results with Huang et al. [8] approach since it was the technique that obtained the best results in the literature, considering the state-of-the-art review done during this work. The metric used to compare the models' performance is the Mean Absolute Percentage Error (MAPE), defined by Eq. 7.

$$MAPE = \frac{1}{n}\sum_{t=1}^{n}\left|\frac{\hat{y}_t - y_t}{\hat{y}_t}\right| \tag{7}$$

Finally, the performance of the proposed model is evaluated utilizing two different activation functions, as described in Subsect. 3.1, comparing the results obtained.

All tests were run in a machine which has the following configuration: Intel Core i5-7400 CPU @ 3.00GHz $\times$ 4 processor, 8GB of RAM and on a 64-bit Windows 10 operational system. The programming language of choice was Python 3.6.5.

4.1 PeMS

Scenario Description. The PeMS[3] is a well-known benchmark dataset for traffic-related problems. It consists of an open repository of data collected by a network of sensors. Its sensors are spread across the state of California that register traffic-related information such as vehicle volume in a highway.

In order to reproduce the test scenario from [8], a dataset with the same characteristics used by them was extracted, *i.e.* 12 months from the fifty most busy roads in the year of 2011.

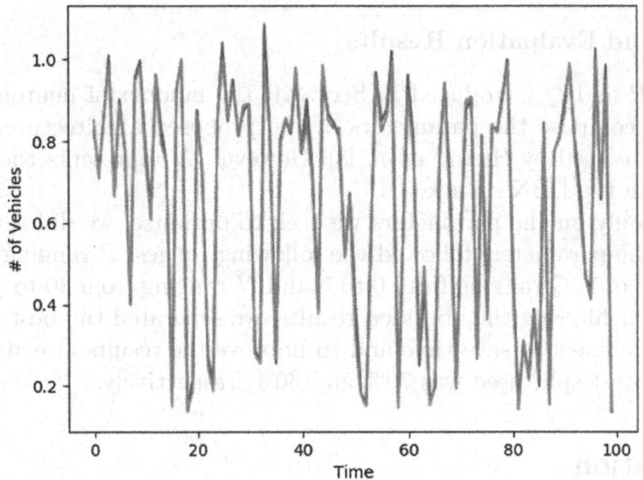

Fig. 2. Prediction curve of the *SmartTraffic*^{pso} for Logistic activation function. The blue line represents the true value and the orange one the model's forecast.

Results. In comparison, the Huang *et al.* approach obtained an average MAPE of 15.81% and its best performance resulted in a 13.18% MAPE. Even though there are implementation and parametrization differences, the results obtained on the same dataset are comparable by, approximately, 1% for the best model.

[3] http://pems.dot.ca.gov.

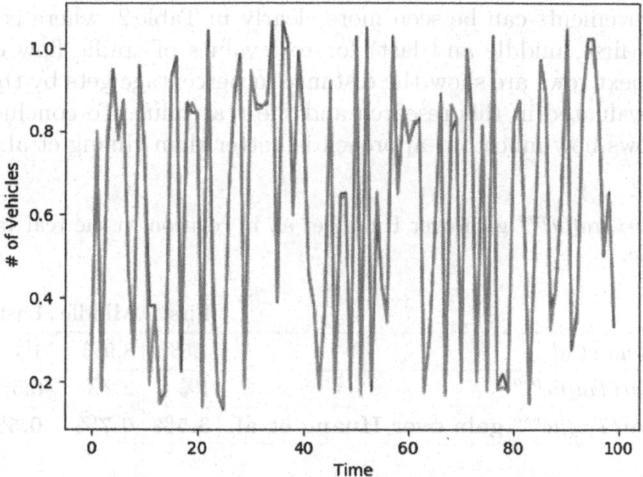

Fig. 3. Prediction curve of the *SmartTraffic*^{pso} for ReLU activation function. The blue line represents the true value and the orange one the model's forecast.

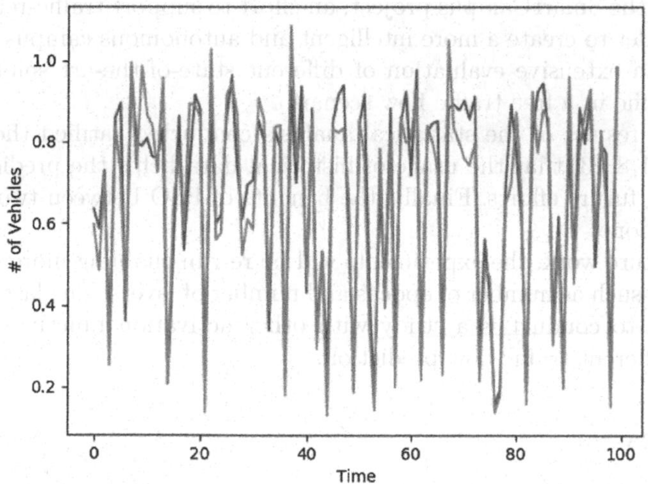

Fig. 4. Prediction curve of the Huang et al. approach. The blue line represents the true value and the orange one the model's forecast.

The MAPE metric evaluation effort the *SmartTraffic*^{pso} consistently outperforms Huang *et al.*'s approach. This can be verified by the best performing model, which had the following configuration: $P = 11$, $Q = 3$, $N = 90$ and it scored a 3.1% average MAPE for Logistic activation function and a MAPE of 3.4%. for ReLU activation function. The plots of said model is shown in Figs. 2 and 3. To conclude our analysis of the approaches performance, Fig. 4 is present.

Our improvements can be seen more clearly in Table 2, where is possible to see 3 points (first, middle and last) for real values of traffic flow on the first row. On the next rows are show the distance in percentage gets by the two main approaches evaluated in this research and the real value. To conclude, the last table line shows how much our approach is better than Huang et al.

Table 2. *SmartTraffic*^{pso} gain over Huang et al. in relation to the real value and the predicted value.

	First	Middle	Last
Huang et al.	4.5%	8.9%	1%
SmartTraffic^{pso}	1%	2.2%	0.5%
SmartTraffic^{pso} **gain over Huang et al.**	**3.5%**	**6.7%**	**0.5%**

5 Conclusion

This paper presented the SmartTraffic and one of its application, one of the pilot initiatives of the SmartCampus project, an effort to support traffic-related applications in order to create a more intelligent and autonomous campus. Moreover, it presents an extensive evaluation of different state-of-the-art solutions using real data traffic in a free traffic flow scenario.

Also, the results of the statistical analysis conducted ratified the evidences pointed by [1,8,13] that the usage of historical data helps the prediction accuracy, guiding future efforts. Finally, the benefits of PSO between two activation functions is done.

As for future work, the experiments will be re-run enabling more parameters optimization such as number of epochs and number of layers. The last interesting investigation to conduct is a study with other activation functions and other scenarios, different traffic flow prediction.

References

1. Abadi, A., Rajabioun, T., Ioannou, P.A.: Traffic flow prediction for road transportation networks with limited traffic data. IEEE Trans. Intell. Transp. Syst. **16**(2), 653–662 (2015)
2. Abuarqoub, A., et al.: A survey on internet of thing enabled smart campus applications. In: Proceedings of the International Conference on Future Networks and Distributed Systems, p. 38. ACM (2017)
3. Alghamdi, A., Shetty, S.: Survey toward a smart campus using the Internet of Things. In: 2016 IEEE 4th International Conference on Future Internet of Things and Cloud (FiCloud), pp. 235–239. IEEE (2016)
4. Castro-Neto, M., Jeong, Y.S., Jeong, M.K., Han, L.D.: Online-SVR for short-term traffic flow prediction under typical and atypical traffic conditions. Expert Syst. Appl. **36**(3), 6164–6173 (2009)

5. Dalal, K., Dahiya, P.: State-of-the-art in VANETs: the core of intelligent transportation system. IUP J. Electr. Electron. Eng. **10**(1), 27 (2017)
6. Fu, R., Zhang, Z., Li, L.: Using LSTM and GRU neural network methods for traffic flow prediction. In: 2016 31st Youth Academic Annual Conference of Chinese Association of Automation (YAC), pp. 324–328, November 2016. https://doi.org/10.1109/YAC.2016.7804912
7. Hu, J., Gao, P., Yao, Y., Xie, X.: Traffic flow forecasting with particle swarm optimization and support vector regression. In: 17th International IEEE Conference on Intelligent Transportation Systems (ITSC), pp. 2267–2268. IEEE (2014)
8. Huang, W., Song, G., Hong, H., Xie, K.: Deep architecture for traffic flow prediction: deep belief networks with multitask learning. IEEE Trans. Intell. Transp. Syst. **15**(5), 2191–2201 (2014)
9. Ishak, S., Al-Deek, H.: Performance evaluation of short-term time-series traffic prediction model. J. Transp. Eng. **128**(6), 490–498 (2002)
10. Kingma, D.P., Ba, J.: Adam: a method for stochastic optimization. arXiv preprint arXiv:1412.6980 (2014)
11. Kumar, K., Parida, M., Katiyar, V.: Short term traffic flow prediction for a non urban highway using artificial neural network. Procedia - Soc. Behav. Sci. **104**, 755–764 (2013)
12. Loce, R.P., Bala, R., Trivedi, M.: Computer Vision and Imaging in Intelligent Transportation Systems. Wiley, Hoboken (2017)
13. Lv, Y., Duan, Y., Kang, W., Li, Z., Wang, F.Y.: Traffic flow prediction with big data: a deep learning approach. IEEE Trans. Intell. Transp. Syst. **16**(2), 865–873 (2015)
14. Ma, J., Theiler, J., Perkins, S.: Accurate on-line support vector regression. Neural Comput. **15**(11), 2683–2703 (2003)
15. Ma, X., Tao, Z., Wang, Y., Yu, H., Wang, Y.: Long short-term memory neural network for traffic speed prediction using remote microwave sensor data. Transp. Res. Part C: Emerg. Technol. **54**, 187–197 (2015)
16. Nati, M., Gluhak, A., Abangar, H., Headley, W.: SmartCampus: a user-centric testbed for Internet of Things experimentation. In: 2013 16th International Symposium on Wireless Personal Multimedia Communications (WPMC), pp. 1–6, June 2013
17. Qolomany, B., Maabreh, M., Al-Fuqaha, A., Gupta, A., Benhaddou, D.: Parameters optimization of deep learning models using particle swarm optimization. In: 2017 13th International Wireless Communications and Mobile Computing Conference (IWCMC), pp. 1285–1290. IEEE (2017)
18. Shuai, M., Xie, K., Pu, W., Song, G., Ma, X.: An online approach based on locally weighted learning for short-term traffic flow prediction. In: Proceedings of the 16th ACM SIGSPATIAL International Conference on Advances in Geographic Information Systems, p. 45. ACM (2008)
19. Tian, Y., Pan, L.: Predicting short-term traffic flow by long short-term memory recurrent neural network. In: 2015 IEEE International Conference on Smart City/SocialCom/SustainCom (SmartCity), pp. 153–158. IEEE (2015)
20. Van Der Voort, M., Dougherty, M., Watson, S.: Combining Kohonen maps with arima time series models to forecast traffic flow. Transp. Res. Part C: Emerg. Technol. **4**(5), 307–318 (1996)
21. Werbos, P.J.: Backpropagation through time: what it does and how to do it. Proc. IEEE **78**(10), 1550–1560 (1990)

The Linguistic Skills of Foreign Students in the Italian School System

Lucia Mongelli[1] and Paola Perchinunno[2(✉)]

[1] Istat, Territorial Office for Abruzzo, Marche and Puglia, Piazza Aldo Moro 61, 70122 Bari, Italy
mongelli@istat.it

[2] Department of Economics, Management and Business Law, University of Bari "Aldo Moro", Largo Abbazia Santa Scolastica 53, 70124 Bari, Italy
paola.perchinunno@uniba.it

Abstract. The relative stability of migration has led to the strong presence of immigrant children in the school. For some decades the Italian school has been faced up with the growing participation of students of foreign origin, although small compared to other countries. In this panorama we will have many young foreigners in the next few years with a degree obtained in Italy. This work aims to analyze the linguistic skills of foreigners on the basis of data collected by the Integration of second generations survey conducted in 2015 by the Italian National Statistical Institute (ISTAT).

Keywords: Migration background · Foreigners · Language skills

1 Introduction

Italy was born as a country of emigrants with the great migratory waves of the last century, but at that time, the internal movements, which led to the urbanization of the great industrial areas of the North, led to a linguistic reshuffle that produced the spread of the national language [1].

In addition to the traditional endogenous plurilingualism that had characterized our language, by the coexistence of Italian and dialects, there is also an exogenous plurilingualism, or neo-multilingualism [2].

The presence of immigrant languages brought Italians in contact with so many cultures and idioms for the first time. Mainly the school has contributed to the socialization of foreign children with Italian children. For foreign students the school is the first place where takes place the matching between the world and the culture of the host country, and this is the first moment they capture the cultural differences of their family. At school, the learning of Italian language is combined with the learning of origin language, as an integral part of schooling, of primary socialization and identity making [3].

The contribution is the result of joint reflections by the authors, with the following contributions attributed to P. Perchinunno (chapters 1,5,6), and to L. Mongelli (chapters 2.3.4).

S. Misra et al. (Eds.): ICCSA 2019, LNCS 11622, pp. 48–61, 2019.
https://doi.org/10.1007/978-3-030-24305-0_5

In the literature, especially in North America, is stated that language learning continues to occur in the transition from one generation to another [4]. The second and third generations, born from immigration, "become more and more similar" to the native or autochthonous population (or deriving from previous migrations) [5], with the need to integrate as quickly as possible with the culture and society of the host country, learning to live according to the rules of the host society [6].

The second generation in the narrow sense, referring to the Recommendation of the Council of Europe in 1984, consists of children of immigrants:

- born in the host country;
- emigrated with their parents;
- who have reached their parents following family reunification or, in any case, after a period of emigration of one or both parents [7].

But, looking at the Italian reality, very different cases match with this category:

- teenagers and children who were born and raised in Italy, are completing the Italian schooling, but they cannot be Italian in the statistics, according to the ius soli (right tied to the place of birth), because the law (n. 91 of 1992) states that citizenship can only be claimed from maturity age and subject to restrictive conditions;
- children of mixed or nomadic couples, considered in full respects by the school system as children of foreign origin as carriers of cultural heterogeneity;
- adolescents joined after completing a broad socialization process in their origin country, or at least reaching their parents after an emigration period of one or both parents.

Furthermore, speaking of immigrant children, we should consider the categories of young immigrants also in reference to the age in which the young moved [8] and, therefore, we will talk about:

- generation 1.75 minor who moves abroad in the preschool age (0-5 years), and carries out the entire academic career in the destination country;
- generation 1.5 child who started primary school in the origin country, but completed school education abroad;
- 1.25 minor generation migrating between the ages of 13 and 17.

They are children and young people in primary education (in the family) and in secondary (at school) [9]. The new ITAGEN2 survey in the school year. 2005/2006 [10, 11].

In 2015, Istat conducted a survey on the integration of second generations co-financed by the European Union and the Ministry of the Interior to apply to the European Fund for the integration of third-country nationals (EIF) to analyze the various aspects of the integration of children with a migration background and different aspects including migration history, school integration, social relations, the family, the use of the Italian language, a sense of belonging and projects for the future [12].

2 The Master Profile of the Interviewed Students

2.1 Percentage Distribution by Citizenship and Country of Birth

The students with foreign citizenship included in the school system are around 815 thousand, equal to 9.2% of the school population as a whole (a percentage higher than that of foreigners relationship to the general population of 8.3%).

The Italian school model is structurally evolving, since some years the migratory origin students represent the dynamic component of Italian school system which contributes with its growth, to contain the decrease of the total school population: in the last five-year period 2011/12–2015/16 foreign students increased by 7.8%, while Italian students decreased by 2.3%. Furthermore, the migration phenomenon is assuming stabilizing characteristics, both for the characteristics of families migratory projects (boys are here without their will), and for the growing rate of immigrant children born in Italy, almost 60% of foreigners students (for all orders and grades), and now outnumber the children of migrants who arrived here after birth [13].

The Istat Integration of second generations survey, foreseen by the 2014–2016 National Statistical Program, is a sampling survey and involved 821 municipalities, it was held in approximately 1,400 secondary schools of first and second degree with at least 5 students of foreign citizenship. The students interviewed are:

- children of mixed couples,
- immigrant children of foreign citizenship (all types of Rumbaut),
- children adopted abroad (international adoptions),
- foreign immigrant children in Italy who have acquired Italian citizenship,
- foreign citizenship children born in Italy from foreign parents,
- children born in Italy from foreign parents who have acquired Italian citizenship,
- children born in Italy from Italian parents since birth.

In 2015, foreign secondary school enrollments amounted to 148 thousand in the first classes and 157 thousand in the second ones. Over 68 thousand students were interviewed, among them just less than half with foreign citizenship, as shown in Table 1 below. The foreign presence among the students interviewed is of 47.2% and concerning males is of 45.9

Table 1. Percentage distribution of respondents according to citizenship, by gender.

Sex	Citizenship		
	Italian	Foreign	Total
Males	54.1	45.9	100.0
Females	52.8	47.2	100.0
Total	**53.5**	**46.5**	**100.0**

Source: ISTAT. Integration of the second generations 2015. Our elaborations

Among the interviewed students born in Italy, as shown in Table 2, the 20% are children of parents with foreign citizenship, while the 2.1% are Italians born abroad, for international adoptions or children of mixed couples with a biography often comparable to that of second generations [14].

Table 2. Percentage distribution of respondents by citizenship and country of birth.

Country of birth	Citizenship		
	Italian	Foreign	Total
Italy	80.0	20.0	100.0
Abroad	2.1	97.9	100.0
Total	**53.5**	**46.5**	**100.0**

Source: ISTAT. Integration of the second generations 2015. Our elaborations

But next this general data, it is essential to look also at the of birth place of students with non-Italian citizenship present in the national territory. Unlike other European countries, immigration in Italy is characterized by the strong diversification of the countries of origin, even with concentration on some nationalities (Romania, Morocco, Albania, China), immigrants represent over 190 different citizenships [15, 16].

Foreign students interviewed, though the concentration in 6 prevalent nationalities: Romania, Albania, Morocco and the People's Republic of China, historic emigration areas towards Italy, and Moldova and Ukraine, new emigration areas, (in total about 20%), represent 162 different nationalities as shown in Table 3. The interviewed students of Romanian citizenship are the most numerous group in the Italian school with

Table 3. Percentage distribution of respondents born abroad, by country of birth.

Country of birth	%
Romania	8.6
Albania	4.1
Morocco	2.3
Moldova	2.0
Ukraine	1.6
Republic of China	1.0
Ecuador	0.9
Republic of Macedonia	0.8
Poland	0.7
Pakistan	0.7
India	0.7
Perù	0.7
Philippines	0.7
150 more countries	75.1

Source: ISTAT. Integration of the second generations 2015. Our elaborations

8.6%, followed by the Albanian students with the 4th, 1%, the Moroccans with 2.3%, the Moldovans with 2.0% and the Ukrainians with 1.6%. A massive presence is represented by Asian nationalities. Among these the most numerous is undoubtedly the Chinese one with 1.0%.

2.2 Percentage Distribution by Migratory Generation

The interviewed students arrived in Italy mainly with their mother, respectively 56.3% those with Italian citizenship and 48.0% those with foreign citizenship or with their father almost 25% of Italians and almost 38% of foreigners (Fig. 1). 4.2% is represented by unaccompanied minors without assistance and representation of parents or other legally responsible adults, plus Italian students (5.4%) of foreign ones, and taken in charge of educational projects carried out in Italy or adopted [17]. Between 3.8 and 4.6% of respondents arrived in Italy with brothers, sisters or other relatives.

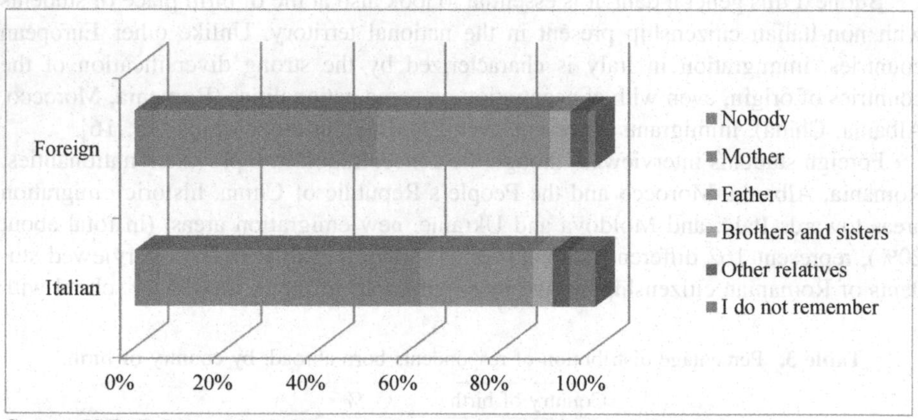

Source: ISTAT. Integration of the second generations 2015. Our elaborations.

Fig. 1. Percentage distribution of respondents born abroad according to the person with whom they came to Italy and citizenship.

Considering the results of the survey and its characteristics of statistical representativeness, we can arrange the 815 thousand students with foreign citizenship who live in Italy in four groups:

- born in Italy, in fact comparable for linguistic skills to Italian speakers;
- born abroad and entered Italy before the age of 6 and not entered the school system;
- born abroad and entered Italy from 6 years to 11 and who started primary school in the country of origin;
- born abroad and entered Italy at the age of 11 and over and who have been included in the study course in their country of origin for some time.

The interviewed boys with foreign citizenship born in Italy are 30.4%, the second generations, the so-called foreigners but not immigrants; while foreigners entering Italy at age 11 and over, defined as foreigners and even immigrants, are almost 20% of students, as shown in Table 4. In the middle there are different situations, namely those born abroad and entered Italy before the age of 6 and from 6 to 11 years, the so-called generation 1.5, about 50% [18], by experience, migration project, economic level and family culture, which largely determine the percentage of academic success.

Table 4. Percentage distribution of foreign respondents according to migratory generation and type of school.

Migration generation	Secondary school		
	1st degree	2nd degree	Total
Born in Italy	43.1	18.4	30.4
Born abroad and entered Italy before the age of 6	23.7	23.3	23.5
Born abroad and entered Italy from 6 to 11 years	22.0	30.1	26.2
Born abroad and entered Italy at age 11 and over	11.2	28.2	19.9
Total	**100.0**	**100.0**	**100.0**

Source: ISTAT. Integration of the second generations 2015. Our elaborations

3 Italian Language Skills for Foreign Students

The relative stability of migration project has determined the strong presence of immigrant children in the school. The learning of Italian language is fundamental, not only for scholastic success, but also in the context of scholastic and social integration strategies and it is the basic condition to understand and to be understood, to participate and to feel part of the community, scholastic and not [19].

The language for the study, distinct from the linguistic elaboration necessary in face-to-face communication (language to communicate) and required in school situations, has been recognized as the determining point, vehicular language, of the teaching-learning of Italian language [20]. As shown in Fig. 2, the Italian language is

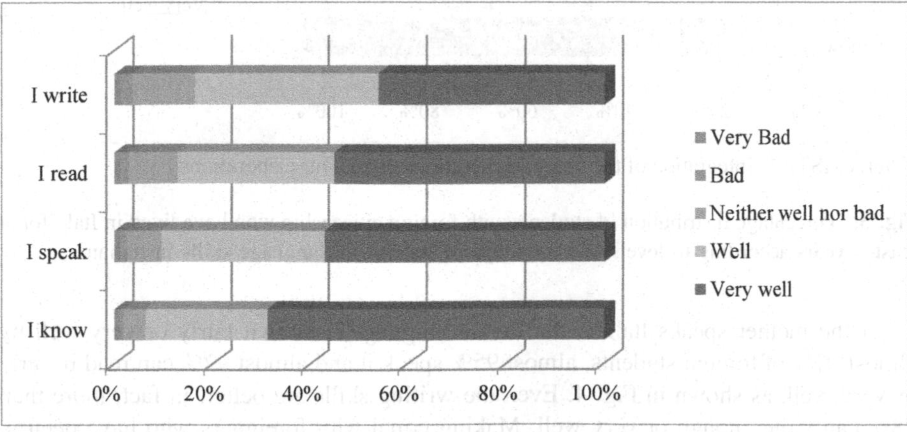

Source: ISTAT. Integration of the second generations 2015. Our elaborations

Fig. 2. Percentage distribution of students with foreign citizenship according to Italian knowledge levels, for language skills in Italian.

known fairly or very well by almost 94% of foreign students: 90.5% speak it quite well or very well, while more than 87% successfully read and study textbooks.

From the top, more than 16% of foreign students has difficulties in mastering the specific complexities of written Italian language (for self-assessment), which is indispensable for successfully studying the various subjects. The Italian language skills of students with foreign citizenship change if they have lived in Italy for at least 5 years, as shown in Fig. 3.

Among the foreign students who have been living in Italy for at least 5 years, over 97% understand the Italian language, almost 96% speak it and more than 92% can read it fairly or very well. Skills in writing also improve with just over 10% who write badly or very badly. To describe the relationship with Italian language by second generations and foreigners we often speak of filial language, as opposed to mother tongue, to emphasize that children are often the ones who bring Italian into their home. While on the one hand, the presence of children in immigrant families is a very important factor in linguistic integration, as it leads many parents to force to learn Italian better [21], and if the parent speaks Italian in Italian, children's linguistic competence grows significantly and aligns with students who have lived longer in Italy. In this context, children and parents play the role of mediators between the language-culture of origin, mother tongue, and the Italian one.

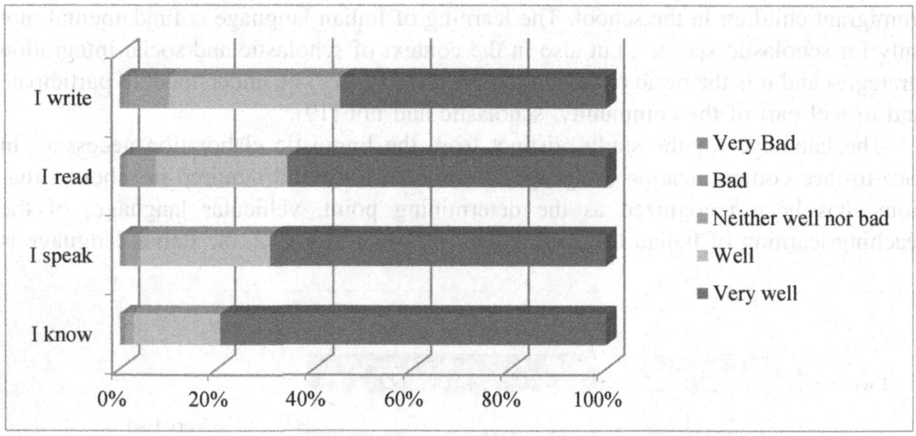

Fig. 3. Percentage distribution of students with foreign citizenship who have lived in Italy for at least 5 years according to levels of knowledge of Italian, for language skills in Italian.

If the mother speaks Italian, the Italian language is known fairly or very well by almost 97% of foreign students, almost 95% speak it and almost 92% can read it fairly or very well, as shown in Fig. 4. Even the writing skills are better, in fact, more than 88% can write enough or very well. Making equal with foreigners who have been in Italy for longer, we will have less than 1% know, speak, read and write Italian very badly.

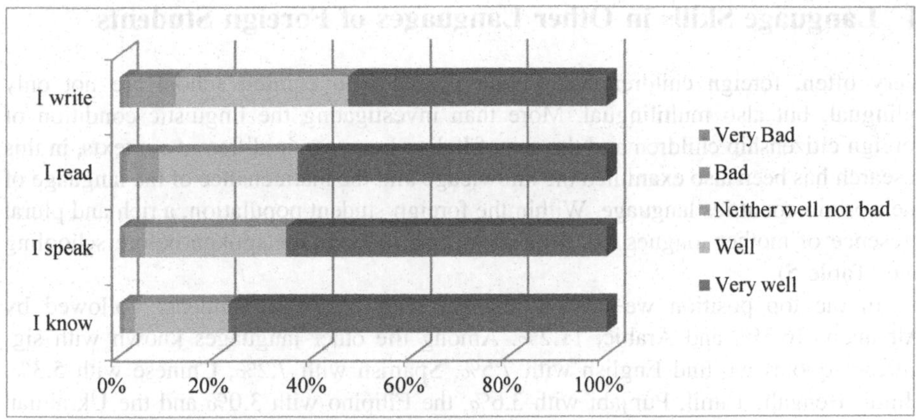

Source: ISTAT. Integration of the second generations 2015. Our elaborations

Fig. 4. Percentage distribution of students with foreign citizenship who speak Italian with mothers according to levels of Italian knowledge, for language skills in Italian.

If, on the other hand, the father speaks Italian, 95% of foreign students know Italian well enough or very well, just over 94% speak it and almost 92% can read it (Fig. 5). Even writing skills are aligned with the values of students who have lived in Italy for more than 5 years with more than 89% who can write enough or very well.

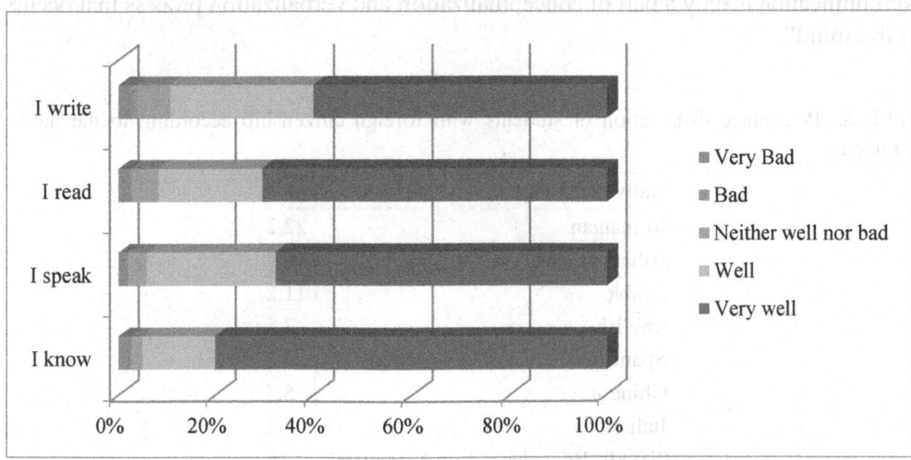

Source: ISTAT. Integration of the second generations 2015. Our elaborations

Fig. 5. Percentage distribution of students with foreign citizenship who speak Italian with fathers according to levels of Italian knowledge, for language skills in Italian.

4 Language Skills in Other Languages of Foreign Students

Very often, foreign children and young people who coming school are not only bilingual, but also multilingual. More than investigating the linguistic condition of foreign citizenship children and the use of Italian language in different contexts, in this research has been also examined the knowledge and the maintenance of the language of their origin countries language. Within the foreign student population, a rich and plural presence of mother tongues has been confirmed, a language spoken before schooling age (Table 5).

In the top position we have Romanian with 22.2% of students, followed by Albanian, 16.3%, and Arabic, 11.2%. Among the other languages known with significant quotas we find English with 7.5%, Spanish with 7.2%, Chinese with 5.3%, Hindi; Bengali; Tamil; Punjabi with 3.6%, the Filipino with 3.0% and the Ukrainian with 2.9%. 5.3% of foreign students recognize Italian as their mother tongue. Language is an articulated system of codes and symbols continuously changing and evolving because it is in continuous contact with both the other languages spoken or known, and with the environment within it is naturally used [22].

For Italian school it is not only important teaching Italian but also understanding in which language the foreign student thinks, to identify the linguistic possibilities that some mother tongues have towards Italian metaphors or allegories, as well as in the comprehension of complex mathematical or scientific abstractions [23].

It is essential to understand in which language the child thinks and what is the degree of completeness in the mastery of his mother tongue. In fact, according to the studies of Cummins [24] and Balboni [25], "what appears" on the surface "in linguistic communication is only a part of conceptualization and verbalization process that occurs in the mind".

Table 5. Percentage distribution of students with foreign citizenship according to the native language.

Native language	%
Romanian	22.2
Albanian	16.3
Arabic	11.2
English	7.5
Spanish	7.2
Chinese	5.3
Italian	5.3
"Hindi; Bengalese; Tamil; Punjabi"	3.6
Filipino (Tagalog)	3.0
Ukrainian	2.9
10 other languages	15.5

Source: ISTAT. Integration of the second generations 2015. Our elaborations

Competence in a language (mother, foreign or second) reflects on the whole linguistic and conceptual individual repertory. It follows that the lack of mastery of any mother tongue in terms of completeness and complexity can create to the foreign boy often unacceptable obstacles to understanding of abstractions, even simple, typical of the Italian language. He is therefore dramatically excluded from the language of the study and consequently from scholastic success [20].

The most positive linguistic environment is one in which the language is used naturally for communication. Considering however that the family is the main agent for maintaining the mother tongue, we examine the knowledge degree of the language parents other than Italian by the students. Figure 6 shows the results of the level of knowledge of the mother's language. Just over 87% of students know it well or very well, just over 82% speak it, 64% read it and almost 56% can write it.

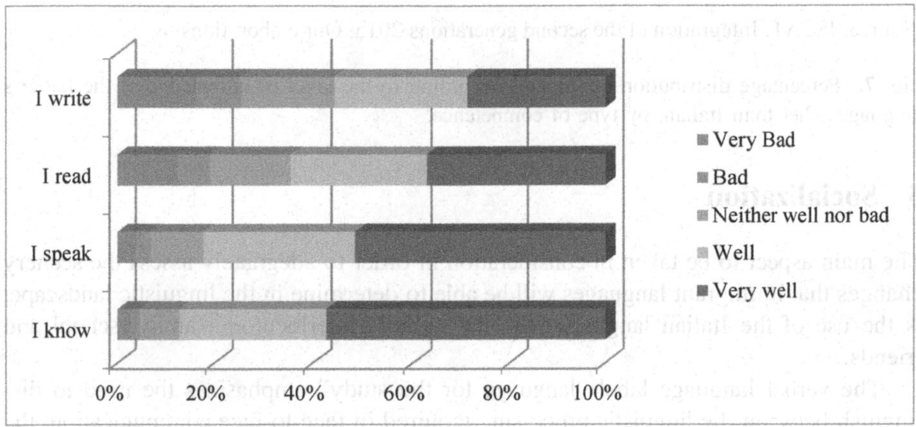

Source: ISTAT. Integration of the second generations 2015. Our elaborations

Fig. 6. Percentage distribution of students according to the level of knowledge of the mother's language other than Italian, by type of competence.

We will discover a different scenery if we analyze the student's knowledge of his father's language other than Italian. More than 54% know it quite or very well, almost 46% speak it, the law almost 43% and 35.5% write it, as shown in Fig. 7.

So, the foreign student brings with him a wealth of knowledge (linguistic, cultural, relational, etc.) which, depending on the context and the interlocutor, can express in one of the different languages he knows.

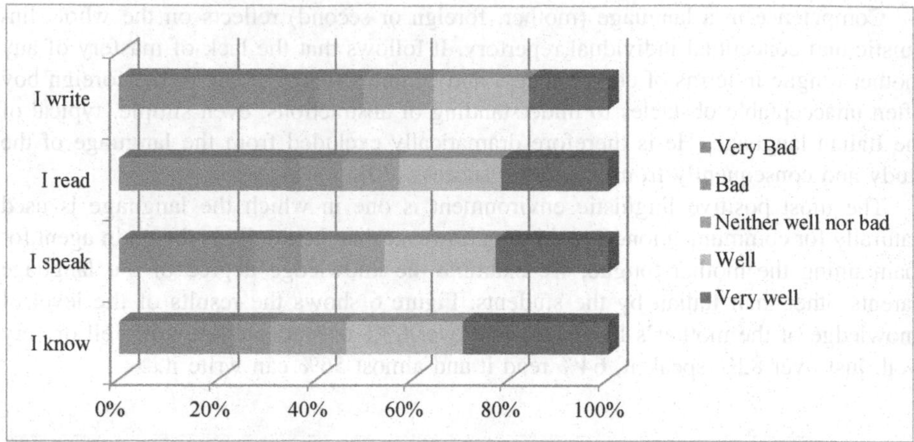

Source: ISTAT. Integration of the second generations 2015. Our elaborations

Fig. 7. Percentage distribution of students according to the level of knowledge of the father's language other than Italian, by type of competence.

5 Socialization

The main aspect to be taken in consideration in order to adeguately assess the scenery changes that immigrant languages will be able to determine in the linguistic landscape, is the use of the Italian language with the various interlocutors, family, school and friends.

The verbal language label "language for the study" emphasizes the need to distinguish between the linguistic processing required in face-to-face communication, the so-called language for communicating and the language required in school situations.

Face-to-face communication uses different elements (tone, rhythm, pauses, look, facial expressions, gestures, etc.), while in school situations, a type of formal communication prevails. A goal of linguistic education is, therefore, the development of communicative competence [26].

The relative majority of foreign students declare that they speak mainly Italian in the scholastic context, which however is not the only occasion for foreign students to learn language. As Table 6 shows, we will have 91.5% of foreign students speak Italian with teachers, 80% with classmates, 57.2% who use it with friends and acquaintances and almost 20% in family.

Many students, children of immigrant, especially second-generation immigrants, sometimes speak Italian with the local audio dial-ups of regional dialects, 5.2% do it in the family and with friends and acquaintances, much less in the school environment: with their classmates school, 3.8%, and with teachers, less than 1%.

In the family almost 30% of students very often use a foreign language and 34.5% use both Italian and foreign languages indifferently.

While, with friends and acquaintances, 19.5% of students indifferently use both Italian and foreign languages.

Table 6. Percentage distribution of students with foreign citizenship according to the language used by type of interlocutors.

With which language you speak	Interlocutors			
	In family	With schoolmates	With friends/acquaintances	With teachers
Almost always in Italian	18.8	80.0	57.2	91.5
Almost always in the dialect of the region where I live	5.2	3.8	5.3	0.8
Almost always in another (foreign) language	29.7	0.7	5.8	0.4
Almost always in Italian and in the dialect of the region where I live	3.8	8.7	8.2	2.7
Almost always in Italian and in another language (foreign)	34.5	3.7	19.5	1.7
Almost always in the dialect of the region where I live and in another (foreign) language	5.5	0.6	1.5	0.4
Not responding	2.5	2.5	2.5	2.5
Total	**100.0**	**100.0**	**100.0**	**100.0**

Source: ISTAT. Integration of the second generations 2015. Our elaborations

The conquest of the Italian-language as a primary language by foreign students has determined the coexistence between mother tongue, adoptive language and dialect, opening new expressive spaces to be lived not as a defect, but as an extra variety, for friendship, playful and creative use [2].

The socialization with the companions and friends also starts from the recreational activities that the students with foreign citizenship realize. 55.8% say they use Italian to watch TV and almost 68% to read comics, books, newspapers and magazines, as shown in Table 7.

Table 7. Percentage distribution of students with foreign citizenship according to the language used, by type of recreational activity.

Language used	Play activity	
	Watch television programs	Read comics, books, magazines, newspapers
Especially in Italian	55.8	67.6
A little in Italian a little in another language	34.0	20.1
Especially in another language	6.3	3.7
I don't watch TV, I don't read comics, books, newspapers, etc.	3.9	8.5
Total	**100.0**	**100.0**

Source: ISTAT. Integration of the second generations 2015. Our elaborations

Of the total number of students, 34% watch TV programs in Italian a little in another language, while 6.3% do it in another language; more than 20% read comics, books, newspapers, and magazines a little in Italian a little in another language, while 3.7% always do it in another language. They declare not to watch TV, not to read comics, books, newspapers and magazines, respectively 3.9% and 8.5% of the boys interviewed.

6 Conclusions

The survey shows that 20% of students, mostly Romanians and Albanians, are students born in Italy but children of parents with non-Italian citizenship.

The majority of students with foreign citizenship came to Italy for the first time accompanied by their mother; they know, speak and read Italian very well, a little less they know how to write. These language skills improve if the students have been in Italy for several years or one of the parents knows Italian. Furthermore, variables linked to the mastery of the language have a strong impact on the academic success of foreign students [27].

Another characteristic of non-Italian mother tongue students is bilingualism, or speaking a language at school and another at home; in fact the non-Italian-speaking student learns Italian to study but also by studying and interacting with teachers and schoolmates so that the socialization process using the Italian language is very good.

Finally, it is clear that having a command of the language favors insertion and good integration, this allows to satisfy primary needs of life and also to get full participation in the activities of our society by interacting adequately.

The foreigner and his linguistic and cultural baggage must be seen as an advantage as a basis on which to develop the potential, also in favor of Italian students; it can also represent an ideal base for plurilingualism and multiculturalism [28, 29] so that the presence of foreign students can really be an opportunity and an opportunity for change for the whole school, a school that could make the most of richness of diversities.

References

1. Ambrosini, M.: Sociologia delle migrazioni. Il Mulino, Bologna (2005)
2. Palermo, M., Barni, M.: Multilinguismo in Italia: nuove minoranze, lingue dell'immigrazione (con M. Barni). In: Maraschio, N., De Martino, D., Stanchina, N. (a cura di): Esperienze di multilinguismo in atto. Atti del Convegno di Firenze, 21–23 maggio 2009, Firenze, Accademia della Crusca (2010)
3. Palermo, M.: Il Neopluringuismo e i futuri assetti dell'Italiano in "Italiano a Stranieri", n. 21, Edizioni Edilingua (2016)
4. Alba, R., Nee, V.: Rethinking assimilation theory for a new era of immigration. Int. Migr. Rev. **31**(4), 826–874 (1997)
5. Brubaker, R.: The return of assimilation? Changing perspectives on immigration and its sequels in France, Germany and the United States. Ethnic Racial Stud. **24**(4), 531 (2001)

6. Portes, A.: For the second generation, one step at a time. In: Jacoby, T. (ed.) Reinventing the Melting Pot. Basic Books, New York (2004)
7. Dizionario della diversità: Le parole dell'immigrazione, del razzismo e della xenofobia. Liberal Libri, Firenze (1998)
8. Rumbaut, R.G.: Assimilation and its discontents: between rhetoric and reality. Int. Migr. Rev. **31**(4), 923 (1997)
9. Barban, N., Conti, C., Gabrielli, D., Gabrielli, G., Guarneri, A.: I nuovi italiani di tanti colori, X Conferenza Nazionale di Statistica (2010)
10. Casacchia, O., Natale, L., Paterno, A., Terzera, L. (a cura di): Studiare insieme, crescere insieme? Un'indagine sulle seconde generazioni in dieci regioni italiane. Franco Angeli, Milano (2008)
11. Dalla Zuanna, G., Farina P., Strozza S.: Nuovi italiani. I giovani immigrati cambieranno il nostro paese? Il Mulino, Bologna (2009)
12. ISTAT. Ministero dell'Interno, Unione Europea. Diversità linguistiche tra i cittadini stranieri. Anno 2011–2012 (2014)
13. MIUR. La via italiana per la scuola interculturale e l'integrazione degli alunni stranieri. Documento ministeriale, ottobre 2017
14. Tognetti, Bordogna M.: Ricongiungere la famiglia altrove. FrancoAngeli, Milano (2005)
15. Palermo, M.: I nuovi italiani e il nuovo italiano. Treccani (2016)
16. ISTAT (2017). Bilancio demografico al 1° gennaio 2017. http://dati.istat.it/
17. Favaro, G.: Un viaggio nel viaggio. Bambini adottati e dinamiche dell'integrazione. In: L'inserimento scolastico dei minori stranieri adottati. Studi e Ricerche. Collana della Commissione per le adozioni internazionali. Istituto degli Innocenti (2003)
18. Rumbaut, R.G., Portes, A.: Ethnicities: Children of Immigrants in America. University of California Press, Berkeley (2001)
19. MIUR. Gli alunni stranieri nel sistema scolastico italiano 2015/2016. Statistica e Studi (2017)
20. Luise, M.C.: Italiano come lingua seconda. Elementi di didattica. Utet, Torino (2006)
21. Palermo, M., Diadori, P., Troncarelli, D.: Insegnare l'italiano come seconda lingua. Carocci, Roma (2015)
22. Ambrosi, S.: Teoria e prassi dell'italiano L2 come lingua per lo studio. Laboratorio Itals. Supplemento alla Rivista EL.LE., Novembre 2012
23. Stefanel S.: Gli stranieri e la scuola Italiana. Educazione & Scuola (2013)
24. Cummins, J.: Language proficiency, biliteracy and French immersion. Can. J. Educ. **8**, 117 (1983)
25. Balboni, P.E.: Le sfide di Babele, Torino, UTET Liberia (2002)
26. Balboni, P.E., Caon, F.: La Comunicazione Interculturale. Marsilio, Venezia (2015)
27. Folgheraiter, K., Tressoldi, P.E.: Apprendimento scolastico degli alunni stranieri: Quali fattori lo favoriscono? Psicologia dell'Educazione e della Formazione, vol. 3 (2003)
28. Bagna, C., Barni, M., Vedovelli, M.: Italiano in contatto con lingue immigrate: nuovi modelli e metodi per il neoplurilinguismo in Italia. In: Consani, C., Desideri, P. (a cura di): Minoranze linguistiche. Prospettive, strumenti, territori, Roma, Carocci (2007)
29. Bagna, C., Barni, M.: La lingua italiana nella comunicazione pubblica/sociale internazionale. Studi Italiani di Linguistica Teorica e Applicata, XXXVI (2007)

Industrial Development and Environmental Sustainability: A Multivariate Statistical Analysis

Paola Perchinunno[1(✉)], Massimo Bilancia[2], and Francesco Rotondo[3]

[1] Department of Economics, Management and Business Law, University of Bari Aldo Moro, Bari, Italy
paola.perchinunno@uniba.it

[2] Ionic Department in Legal and Economic System of Mediterranean: Society, Environment, Culture, University of Bari Aldo Moro, Bari, Italy
massimo.bilancia@uniba.it

[3] Department of Civil Engineering and Architecture, Polytechnic of Bari, Bari, Italy
francesco.rotondo@poliba.it

Abstract. As the world rapidly develops it becomes increasingly urbanized, and it is thus necessary to focus on achieving sustainability results within cities. Getting this goal requires not only to imagine sustainable cities and implementation strategies, but also to assess progress towards sustainable urban development. The present paper is aimed at evaluating urban sustainability through the analysis of the relationship between industrial production consequences and human activities. The case study presented concerns the city of Taranto, located in Southern Italy and characterized by the difficult relationship between the largest steel industry in Europe and a unique natural environment of great biological value. The presence of data in an adequate time scale allows the development of a holistic approach to the assessment of the policies of territorial governance in progress. Data from multiple sources are analyzed using multivariate statistical methods able to summarize the information to assess the first results of ongoing policies.

Keywords: Socio-economic development · Sustainable development · Urban planning strategies · Multivariate statistical methods · Corporate social responsibility · Development policy

1 Introduction

In environmental and economic sciences, environmental sustainability is the condition of a development able to satisfy the needs of the present generation without compromising the ability of future generations to realize their own. The concept of environmental sustainability has undergone a profound evolution, starting from a centered vision. Thus, above all, concerning ecological aspects it has reached a more global meaning, taking into account the social and economic

The authors collaborated in equal parts to the writing of the present essay.

S. Misra et al. (Eds.): ICCSA 2019, LNCS 11622, pp. 62–77, 2019.
https://doi.org/10.1007/978-3-030-24305-0_6

dimension as well as the environment [1,2]. In short, the concept of sustainable development is based on an ethical and political principle, implying that the economic and social dynamics of modern economies are compatible with the improvement of living conditions and the ability of natural resources to reproduce indefinitely [3].

From an urban point of view, it is therefore necessary to start to imagine cities and implementation policies aimed at "sustainable urban development". Urban regeneration is a process helping to limit the urban sprawl phenomenon in order to make cities attractive, livable, vibrant, for the most varied types of people. An urban regeneration that sets these goals involves a connection between three key concepts, urban form, sustainability and livability.

Examples of sustainable cities [4] provide a series of targeted actions to improve some indicators. The presence of urban green in the cities is today a fundamental element in the fight against pollution and the elimination of fine dust, also essential in making cities attractive and comfortable. In order to protect the territory, ongoing efforts are aimed at reducing the net land consumption by concentrating on urban regeneration. In addition, it is even more essential to waste less water, reducing the losses of the aqueducts within the physiological threshold: this involves dispersing two thirds of water less than the current level. Finally, for sustainable mobility the use of cars and motorbikes for urban travel must be limited to what is strictly necessary.

The case of the city of Taranto, located in Southern Italy and home to the largest steel plant in Europe (well known as ex Ilva, now property of the International group ArcelorMittal) is under observation of national and international news after the seizure of the plants in the summer of 2012. Since then it has triggered an alert process on environmental issues and the right to health, as well as the sustainability of factories and the right to work [5–8].

The present paper is therefore aimed at evaluating the urban sustainability of the city of Taranto. The abundance of data available in an adequate time scale allows the development of a holistic approach to the assessment of the policies of territorial governance in progress. The numerous data available, concerning aspects related to the territory and the environment, are analyzed through multivariate statistical methods to synthesize the multiple information to evaluate the relationships between the various components. Furthermore, the use of clustering based on indicators leads to identifying continuous aggregations by the imposition of spatial constraints [9,10]. The presence of heterogeneous data renders, through regional and provincial representations, a holistic approach possible and useful to the evaluation of territorial governance policies. The proposed approach is intended to be sensitive to the integration of social, economic and environmental considerations with land use planning to improve natural and non-urban environments [11].

2 Methodological Framework

2.1 The Source of the Data

In 2016, in line with the process undertaken by Eurostat and other statistical institutes, the Italian National Statistical Institute (Istat) launched the experimentation of "Tailored to the Municipalities" statistical information system based on the integration of a plurality of sources, integrating the data of Istat and those of other National Statistical System Entities (Sistan), in which experimental sources are evaluated alongside other more consolidated, resulting in the "Measures of well-being and planning at municipal level" project.

The objective is to provide an integrated information framework of a set of indicators available at the municipal level, useful for planning and management tasks of Local Authorities. From this point of view, it is important that data can promote knowledge of the social, economic, demographic and environmental conditions of the territory, as well as that it can provide measures reflecting the levels achieved in terms of well-being of local communities. The realization of this system is part of the "Memorandum of Understanding" between Istat, the National Association of Italian Municipalities (ANCI) and the Union of Italian Provinces (UPI), which provides for "the development of databases and integrated information harmonized detailed territorial data". Among the experimental sources, there is the database created within the ARCH.I.M.E.DE project, dealing with the construction and updating of databases for territorial analysis within the Integrated System of Istat Microdata.

The "Tailored to the municipalities" system is strongly consistent with the classification of fair and sustainable welfare indicators, specifically with regard to the BES domains that have been populated with municipal data: Education, Work, Economic well-being, Politics and Institutions, Research and Innovation. It is also useful to the construction of indicators in the Single Programming Document of Local Authorities: Population and families, Culture, communication and leisure, Territory and environment, established economy, infrastructure and mobility.

2.2 Methods to Identify Territorial Clusters

The majority of methods currently available for the identification of territorial clusters are based on the use of a circular window that is moved in space, and a suitable clustering test is thus conducted locally. The precursor of such methods can be found in the GAM - Geographical Analysis Machine algorithm [12], which considers a grid of points within the region studied: in correspondence to each of these points, taken as centres, a circular region with a fixed radius is drawn, usually chosen according to a certain threshold percentage of the number of expected events within the circle. The test is performed by comparing the number of cases observed with the number of cases expected within each window in order to decide whether the latter is significantly higher: if statistical significance is reached, the corresponding circular window is shown on the map. The basic data structure assumes that the region under study can be subdivided into a certain number of areas with no points in common, and that under the null hypothesis the number of cases observed in each can be described by a Poisson distribution with an expected value equal to the number of expected cases.

The GAM algorithm has been criticized for a number of reasons. It should be noted that at the end of the procedure a high number of superimposed clusters (circular windows) will have almost certainly been identified: this occurs inasmuch as tests relating to two distinct circular windows, nevertheless, have areas in common and thus cannot be considered independent since they will be based, at least in part, on the same data. This affects the level of overall real significance and the nominal significance level of each local test should be amended, so that the latter may be maintained at the desired level.

To overcome such problems a new methodology was proposed in [13,14], on the basis of which only the most likely cluster of a certain region is taken into account (thus avoiding conducting a multitude of tests): this approach is available through SaTScan software (http://www.satscan.org). Naturally, many modifications are possible and proposed in literature, such as various methods that differ slightly in the shape of the window to be moved over the region under study: the FlexScan method [15], the ULS - Upper Level Scan Statistic method [16] and the AMOEBA method [17].

In order to describe the SaTScan method, we begin from the assumption that the region under study can be divided into sub-areas having no points in common, and that there exists exactly one subset Z (constituted by the union of one or more areas) and two independent Poisson processes defined on Z and Z^c, respectively designated with X_Z and X_{Z^c}, whose intensity functions are:

$$\lambda_Z(x) = p\mu(x) \quad \text{and} \quad \lambda_{Z^c}(x) = q\mu(x) \tag{1}$$

where p and q describe the individual probability of occurrence, inside the areas Z and Z^c, respectively. The background intensity function has a significance that varies depending on the particular application considered: for example, in investigation of an epidemiological nature, it models the spatial distribution of the population at risk. Null hypothesis testing $H_0 : p = q$ that the probability of occurrence in the internal area considered is not higher than the external is solved using the following likelihood ratio:

$$\begin{aligned} \Lambda_Z &= \frac{\max_{p>q} L(Z,p,q)}{\max_{p=q} L(Z,p,q)} \propto \\ &\propto \left(\frac{y_Z}{\mu(Z)}\right)^{y_Z} \left(\frac{y_G - y_Z}{\mu(G) - \mu(Z)}\right)^{y_G - y_Z} I\left(\frac{y_Z}{\mu(Z)} > \frac{y_G - y_Z}{\mu(G) - \mu(Z)}\right) \end{aligned} \tag{2}$$

where $I(\cdot)$ denotes the indicator function and y_Z and y_G are the number of observed events within the area Z and the entire region G under study respectively, while $\mu(Z)$ and $\mu(G)$ are usually approximated through the size of the population "at risk" within Z and within the region under study, respectively.

The advantage of this approach is that the most likely cluster is identified by the highest value of the likelihood ratio seen as a function of Z, say $\Lambda = \max_Z \Lambda_Z$, where Z is a suitable collection of subset of G, or at least a collection of putative spatial clusters. In addition, once the statistical significance of the clusters defined in area Z that maximises the likelihood ratio has been evaluated, other secondary clusters that do not overlap with the main cluster can be significant [18].

In applications, just as with the GAM algorithm, each zone Z is a circular window with a radius not greater than a threshold determined in advance, with its centre at a point forming part of a grid defined for the region under examination. In addition, the distribution of test statistic Λ cannot be determined analytically under the null hypothesis, but its relative p-values can be easily calculated through the Monte Carlo method.

An alternative method to SaTscan is DBScan (Density Based Spatial Clustering of Application with Noise) a density-based spatial clustering method [19]. The basic idea is to group together points that are close to each other based on a distance measurement (usually the Euclidean distance) and a minimum number of points. The DBScan algorithm basically requires two parameters to identify clusters of different shape: $MinPts$, that is minimum number of points to form a dense region and ϵ, the minimum distance between two points. The latter means that if the distance between two points is lower or equal to ϵ these points are considered neighbors. The choice of these two parameters is crucial, because it determines if a group is a core, i.e. a group with at least $MinPts$ points that are far from the center of a distance less than ϵ and that can be reached by a core already present in the cluster, or is a simple noise, that is, a point that cannot be part of any cluster.

In order to limit the subjectivity of the choice of a value to be assigned to ϵ, usually detected by a heuristic procedure, a new algorithm was developed, called Segmented DBScan (Seg-DBScan), a modified version of DBScan, in which the clusters are aggregated considering different levels of the value of ϵ [20]. Therefore, to define the levels of ϵ, a value of $MinPts$ is set a priori and the distribution of the maximum radius of the cores is analyzed. Subsequently, a histogram of the distribution is constructed and ϵ is selected in such a way as to highlight the histogram peaks that indicate the proximity of the cores of a cluster. As suggested in literature, we can establish the value of $MinPts$ at 4, and a certain number of levels of ϵ equal to the number of the highest peaks of the histogram. The final phase of the algorithm is to join the clusters obtained. The fusion of two C_1 and C_2 clusters characterized by different density levels ϵ_1 and ϵ_2 is obtained if for any couple of points $A \in C_1, B \in C_2$:

$$\min_{A,B} \operatorname{dist}(A, B) < \max\{\epsilon_1, \epsilon_2\} \tag{3}$$

With this new algorithm, the parameter ϵ is no longer established a priori. The function connecting the two points A and B of coordinates $A(x_A, y_A)$ with weight w_A and $B(x_B, y_B)$ with weight w_B $(0 < w_A, w_B < 1)$ is a weighted distance in these terms which is obtained by dividing the Euclidean distance with respect to the harmonic mean of integer order $t > 0$ of weights w_A and w_B (for large t):

$$d_w(A,B) = \frac{\sqrt{(x_A - x_B)^2 + (y_A - y_B)^2}}{\sqrt[t]{\left(\frac{w_A^{-t} + w_B^{-t}}{2}\right)^{-1}}} \tag{4}$$

3 Statistical Analysis of Environmental Indicators: Taranto and Environmental Requalification Policies

3.1 The City of Taranto

Taranto is a typical post-industrial city which drastically witnessed the decrease in the number of residents, becoming a shrinking city. Founded by the Spartans, 706 BC, over its long history it experienced an initial moment of impetuous development when it was in fact considered the "capital" of the so-called Magna Graecia. The writings of the Greek philosopher Archita testify that the advantage that could derive from the central position of the city in the Mediterranean allowed Taranto to become increasingly densely populated, exceeding 200,000 inhabitants and extending well beyond the core of housing built in the phase of its foundation. The strategic position of the florid Spartan colony was such as to allow all types of goods transportable by sea to leave and arrive from its port (see Fig. 1).

The constant growth of the city of the two seas was arrested by the rise of the Romans. From the defeat suffered, the *tarantini* did not have the strength to recover and the decline of the *magnogreca* metropolis was unavoidable. Only with Italy's unification Taranto had the opportunity to recover, because it was chosen as a naval base of strategic importance. In particular, the start of the construction of the maritime military Arsenal gave a significant boost to the new growth of Taranto [21,22]. A rapid economic growth was due to the naval industry allowing the creation of a fair number of manufacturing and commercial activities. In thirty years, from 1881 to 1911, the population of the city of Taranto doubled, from 31,630 inhabitants to 65,238[1]. In the following decades, with the subsequent greater militarization of the city during the two world wars, this process of demographic expansion intensified. The construction of a giant iron and steel plant in the 1960s gave a further impetus that led the city to grow to reach about 244,000 residents when, at the beginning of the eighties, the steel production plants were doubled.

The urban structure of the city is formed by the historical nucleus, which expanded in the course of the twentieth century towards Lecce and Brindisi, characterized by a compact form and located on the opposite side, with respect to the large industrial area, of the Mar Piccolo. This compact and dense urban area is flanked by at least three equally densely populated nucleuses. The first

[1] Source: Istat data, censuses of 1881 and 1911. Data taken from the Istat website (www.istat.it). Web page visited as of 04/02/2019.

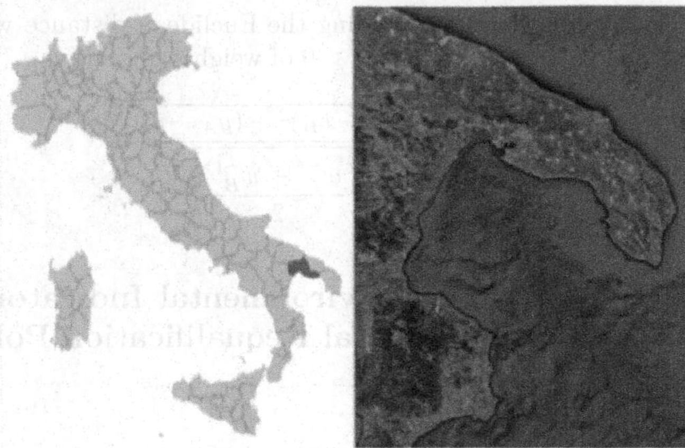

Fig. 1. Gulf of Taranto. The city is located in the middle of a large sea area between the tip of Gallipoli in Puglia and the promontory of Crotone in Calabria. It is one of the largest natural gulfs in the middle of the Mediterranean (as well as in Europe).

is about 20 km from the city's center while the others are slightly closer, 10 and 15 km respectively, but they are also closer to the industrial zone where the largest steel industry in Europe is still active (today owned by the Indian group ArcelorMittal) and an important oil refinery (ENI) is present. These plants represents the two most important sources of urban and provincial pollution. This partially dispersed settlement structure and the location of two populous neighborhoods near the industrial area helps to amplify the effects of pollution of industrial origin.

3.2 Environmental Indicators by Province

Starting from the latest data available on the system "Tailored to the Municipalities" (referring to the year 2016) we will analyze the indicators concerning environmental issues in order to define the levels achieved in terms of the well-being of local communities. We summarize (Table 1) the data relating to the Province of Taranto, in such a way as to compare them to regional data of and territorial data, as well as to national distribution. The environmental indicators considered are the following:

1. *Dispersion from the municipal water supply*: total water losses in municipal drinking water distribution networks (percentage value on total volume fed into the network).
2. *Separate collection of urban waste*: urban waste subject to separate collection per 100 units of urban waste collected.
3. *Passenger cars with emission standards lower than the Euro 4 class*: number of cars in the Euro 0–3 class circulating per 1000 residents.
4. *Land consumption*: ratio between acres of land consumed and the total of acres of land consumed, not consumed and not classified.

Table 1. Some environmental indicators by geographical area. Years 2015–2016

Indicators of the domain Environment and Territory	Province of Taranto		Apulia		South of Italy		Italy	
	2015	2016	2015	2016	2015	2016	2015	2016
Dispersion from the municipal water supply	41.3	44.1	45.9	40.7	46.2	45.5	41.4	37.5
Separate collection of municipal waste	24.8	29.5	30.1	34.3	38.9	43.3	47.5	52.5
Passenger cars with emission standards lower than the Euro 4 class	55.3	51.9	55.4	51.9	56.9	53.7	44.7	41.4
Land consumption	9.6	9.6	8.4	8.4	6.8	6.8	7.8	7.8

The first indicator analyzed concerns the dispersion from the municipal water supply. In the face of a given requirement for the various uses of water (industrial, agricultural and civil) the actual supply is also determined by the dispersions that occur during the distribution phase through the water network. End users do not get all the water fed into the network. In fact, losses may occur due to age of the plants, unauthorized consumption, abusive withdrawals from the grid, errors in measurement. In 2016 in Italy, the volume of water losses was equal to 37.5% of the total volume introduced into the network, down compared to 2015 (41.4%). In the South and in Apulia, this percentage is higher than the national figure, with values of respectively 45.5% and 40.7% in 2016. The province of Taranto, vice versa, shows an increase from 2015 to 2016 going from 41.3% to 44.1%.

An important contribution to environmental health also derives from the increase in the national percentage of separate collection of urban waste, which passes from 47.5% in 2015 to 52.5% in 2016. In the South, the values are lower (38.9% in 2015 and 43,3% in 2016). In Apulia and the province of Taranto in 2016 this percentage is even lower, with values of 34.3% and 29.5% respectively.

With regard to passenger cars in circulation with emission standards lower than Euro 4, we find that the number of cars in the Euro 0–3 class circulating for 1000 residents decreased between 2015 and 2016, passing from 44.7 to 41 in Italy. Higher values are found in 2016 in the South (53.7), in Apulia and in the province of Taranto (51.9).

Land consumption is a phenomenon associated with the loss of a fundamental environmental resource, due to the occupation of the originally agricultural, natural or semi-natural surface. The phenomenon therefore refers to an increase in artificial land cover, linked to settlement dynamics. It is process mainly due to the construction of new buildings and settlements, to the expansion of cities or the conversion of land within an urban area, and to the infrastructure of the territory [23]. In Italy, the value is equal to 7.8, with higher values in Apulia (8.4) and in the province of Taranto (9.6).

3.3 Identification of Territorial Clusters

From the integration of the four indicators illustrated, through the use of the DBScan model, different clusters are identified at the provincial level, representing the level of environmental wellbeing. Clusters are characterized by the value of the internal average: values close to zero are representative of environmental wellbeing situations while values close to one represent situations of environmental malaise. The Seg-DBScan model identifies 6 clusters (Table 2) wth varying levels of environmental hardship, including 47 provinces in total.

Table 2. Numerical composition and description of cluster values obtained with the Seg-DBscan method.

Cluster	Number of provinces	Internal mean
1	5	0.12
2	7	0.31
3	16	0.48
4	4	0.73
5	6	0.87
6	9	0.93

From the graphical representation (Fig. 2) it emerges that the clusters belong to well-specified territorial areas, in which the dark areas are significant in terms of environmental criticality. In particular, the clusters obtained represent the following conditions:

- Cluster 1: territorial area of environmental well-being, with values of the internal average close to zero. It outlines the north-eastern part of Italy, including the regions of Trentino-Alto Adige, Veneto, Friuli-Venezia Giulia and a small part of Lombardy.
- Cluster 2: territorial area of environmental well-being, with values of the internal average of 0.31. It almost entirely delineates one of the two Italian islands, Sardinia.
- Cluster 3: territorial area with an environmental situation in the average (values equal to 0.48). It outlines the part of Central Italy and in particular the regions: Emilia Romagna, Marche, Umbria and Tuscany.
- Cluster 4 territorial area with quite critical environmental situation (average values equal to 0.73). Specifically outlines a region of Southern Italy, Puglia (which includes the municipality of Taranto).
- Cluster 5 territorial area with critical environmental situation (average values equal to 0.87). It outlines the central part of Italy including Campania and part of Lazio;
- Cluster 6 territorial area with very critical environmental situation (average values equal to 0.93). It outlines the southern part of Italy including Campania, Sicily and part of Calabria.

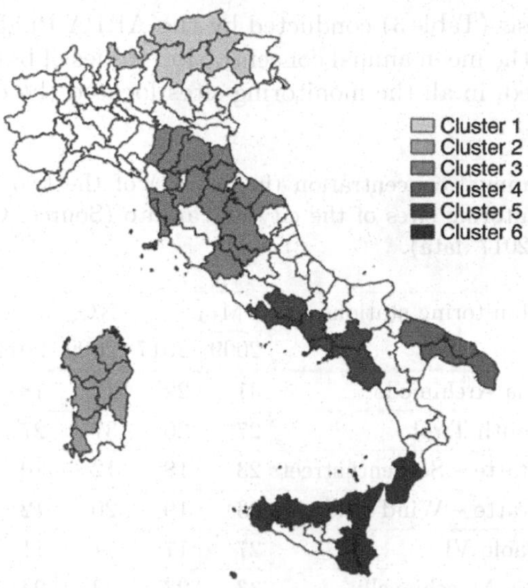

Fig. 2. Graphical representation of the cluster values of the Italian provinces obtained with the Seg-DBscan method.

3.4 Air Quality in Taranto and Environmental Policies

Air quality monitoring is conducted by the Regional Agency for Environmental Protection (ARPA) of Puglia through the Regional Network for Air Quality Monitoring (RRQA), consisting of 53 fixed stations (of which 41 are public owned and 12 are private). The relevant legislation is Legislative Decree 155/2010 (implementation of the EU Directive 2008/50/EC) which came into force on 13th August 2010 and was amended by Legislative Decree 250 of 24th December 2012.

PM_{10} is the set of particles with an aerodynamic diameter of less than 10 μm (10^{-6} m). These particles, originating from both anthropic and natural sources, have the characteristic of remaining "airborne": their settling time is in fact long enough to be considered as "durable" components of the atmosphere itself. Due to its small size, PM_{10} can penetrate the human respiratory system, thus generating health impacts whose severity depends, in addition to quantity, on the type of particles. Legislative Decree 155/10 sets two limit values for PM_{10}: the annual and the daily average must not exceed 40 $\mu g/m^3$ and 50 $\mu g/m^3$, respectively, more than 35 times during the calendar year.

Nitrogen oxides, indicated with the NO_x symbol, are formed above all in high temperature combustion processes and are a by-product of industrial processes and discharges of internal combustion engines. The limits set by Legislative Decree 155/10 for NO_2 are the hourly average of 200 $\mu g/m^3$, that must not be exceeded more than 18 times during the year, and the annual average of 40 $\mu g/m^3$.

The data analysis (Table 3) conducted by the ARPA Puglia [24] shows how, from 2009 to 2017, the mean annual concentration values of both PM_{10} and nitric oxide have decreased, in all the monitoring sites located the city of Taranto.

Table 3. Average annual concentration (in $\mu g/m^3$) of the two main air pollutant, detected by the monitoring sites of the city of Taranto (Source: Our elaborations on ARPA Puglia 2009–2017 data).

Monitoring stations	PM_{10}		NO_2	
	2009	2017	2009	2017
Via Archimede	31	22	17	18
South Tirol	27	20	37	27
Statte – Sorgenti street	23	18	12	10
Statte – Wind Bridge	23	19	20	12
Paolo VI	27	17	11	11
Via Macchiavelli	33	27	33	24

In particular, analyzing the PM_{10} results in the 6 monitoring sites, it is clear that in all of them there has been a clear and significant decline, with a reduction, compared to the 2009 figure, of around 37% in the Paolo VI district and 29% in the Via Archimede. Also with regard to the concentration of nitrogen oxides there is a decrease in all the monitoring sites, with the exception of the one located in Via Archimede (which presents values from 17 in 2009 to 18 in 2017) and that placed in the Paolo VI district in which the value is stationary. Particularly significant is the reduction of nitric oxide in the Municipality of Statte (Wind bridge) with a decrease of 40% compared to 2009.

From the data of the "Assessment of the Damage to Health of the Ilva of Taranto Plan" drawn up in 2017 by three organisms of the Puglia Region (ARPA, ARES Regional Health Agency and ASL Local Health Company of Taranto), it emerges that "measures of environmental concentrations of contaminants of interest to the inhalation risk does not exceed, for the years considered (2013, 2014, 2015 and 2016) the levels set by the rule" [25]. This improvement, compared to the levels of previous years, may be due, in addition to the reduction in industrial production in recent years (steel production has been limited by the intervention of the Judiciary), to a series of rehabilitation measures implemented starting from September 2012 and aimed at limiting the industrial emission load in the so-called "Wind Days", days of high windiness, in which the urban agglomeration located to the leeward of the industrial pole suffers of high levels of air pollution. The data confirm that the measures taken so far have made it possible to maintain the air quality of Taranto within the regulatory limits.

Nevertheless, in light of what emerged from the monitoring of atmospheric depositions coming from the industrial production of the steelworks, a criticality emerged as a consequence of high values of dioxins, in particular in the Tamburi district. In fact, when the wind blows, the steelworks dust covers the Tamburi district. The solution to this problem will be obtained with the coverage of mineral parks. The huge spaces where the mineral is stacked waiting to be used in the production of steel will be covered by 2023, according to the schedule of interventions provided by the new owner of the steel company ArcelorMittal. An impressive job for which the new owners plan to spend at least 265 million euros, as indicated in the Industrial Plan.

In addition to the suspension of industrial activities during the most ventilated days and their reduction after 2012 following the intervention of the judiciary, further measures have been established to mitigate environmental hardship in the city of Taranto and in the municipalities of the province closest to the settlement (Statte and Massafra) through extensive urban forestry works, and the demolition of about 240 houses closer to the steel mill in the Tamburi district.

The “Foresta Urbana Phitoremediation” intervention consists in the realization of a natural barrier to be created in the spaces that will be freed as a result of the demolition of the houses near the plant, in order to create a green area for the urban space, to be carried out after reclamation operations.

This is one of the interventions planned and underway in the city of Taranto following the approval in Parliament of the Special Law for Taranto, which aims to resolve critical environmental, socio-economic and urban redevelopment situations concerning the city and the area of Taranto[2].

4 Conclusions

In the literature, a broad range of different appraisal processes is described under the heading of sustainability assessment [26–29]. The description and quantification of phenomena relevant to sustainable development requires the systematic use of indicators. The integrated analysis, starting from the complexity of the information acquired, is a tool to support planning, identifying the critical issues and environmental problems present in a territory.

The present work is aimed at evaluating urban sustainability through the analysis of the relationship between the consequences of industrial production and human activities. Through a holistic approach the data available are analyzed using multivariate statistical methods able to summarize the information to assess the first results of ongoing policies. The state of the environment outlined in this study through the synthetic indicators elaborated from the available provincial and municipal data, has shown that in Italy, among the provinces analyzed, Taranto still shows significant signs of environmental damage.

[2] Law 4 March 2015, n. 20, art. 5 (paragraph 1). The law provides for the activation of a permanent institutional table for the Taranto area (PIT), set up at the Prime Minister’s Office - Mission structure for the coordination of the reconstruction and development processes of the territories hit by the earthquake of 6 April 2009, development interventions in the area of Taranto and Managing Authority of the National Operational Program Cultural, natural and tourism attractors (decree president council ministry, 1 June 2014 and 23 June 2016) in charge of defining the operational content of the planning tool and coordinating its implementation.

The use of Seg-DBScan method has identified areas characterized by environmental discomfort, that can be considered at risk and need to be monitored. Areas included in the same cluster share the same dangerous level of pollutants and need to be carefully managed.

Urban policies of environmental, social and economic requalification established by the state and the city of Taranto are multiple and consistent with the indications in literature on successful cases in similar situations. Analogous cases such as Manchester, Birmingham in the UK or Pittsburgh in the USA [30], show factors that can contribute to complex urban regeneration policies are manifold. According to Stewart [31] these successful cases have been characterized by:

- Processes of industrial conversion that have allowed communication industries to localize where factories were once located.
- New employment opportunities in science, research and development, advanced design and physical regeneration of formerly inaccessible central areas.
- Combination of features integrating commercial, dining and recreation activities with quality residential accommodation.
- Labor costs and housing units far below London prices.
- Efficiency of transportation links and the absence of urban congestion.
- High quality of living in urban spaces close to great natural parks.

Among these, for cities or regions characterized by significant environmental problems, the improvement of the quality of urban spaces [32] and conspicuous greening policies are the basic conditions for achieving significant results also in the economic and social sectors [33,34].

In the case of Taranto as in that of other de-industrialized cities, such as Pittsburgh [35], the awareness of the levels of pollution present and that of the health consequences entailed was equally important. The goal of revealing the level of atmospheric pollution produced by the steelworks, and making the decision-makers and inhabitants aware of the positioning of their territory through a synthetic and comprehensible comparison with the other Italian provinces, appears to be the most significant result of this study.

Indeed, through a multi-criteria analysis, the positioning of the province of Taranto in comparison with the others, is synthetically revealed in a single synthetic indicator. The regeneration policies already underway, briefly described in the previous paragraph, such as urban forestation, appears to be the next stage to be achieved, in order to attract new productive activities, new investments and other economic actors to favor not only the regeneration of physical spaces but also social and economic ones, involving local communities and rebuilding a sense of belonging and community [36].

Policies for sustainable development require the adoption of a system of descriptors capable of integrating the environmental dimension with the social, economic and institutional dimension. The adoption of an integrated system of sustainable descriptors would allow both the predominantly economistic approach to assess the growth of the economic and production system, as well as the predominantly environmentalist approach to assess the degree of sustainability of the system. In fact, the experience of various countries shows that the adoption of an integrated system of descriptors is a qualifying point both in the development of the political strategies aimed at development, and in the evaluation of their effects [32]. Experience also shows that the descriptor system, in order to prove itself a useful and effective tool for carefully delimiting areas of the same species or nature, must take into account the economic, environmental and social specificities of the areas to which they refer.

References

1. James, P., Magee, L., Scerri, A., Steger, M.B.: Urban Sustainability in Theory and Practice: Circles of Sustainability. Routledge, London (2015)
2. Brodhag, C., Taliere, S.: Sustainable development strategies: tools for policy coherence. Nat. Resour. Forum **30**(2), 136–145 (2006). https://doi.org/10.1111/j.1477-8947.2006.00166.x
3. Cerin, P.: Bringing economic opportunity into line with environmental influence: a discussion on the Coase theorem and the Porter and van der Linde hypothesis. Ecol. Econ. **56**(2), 209–225 (2006). https://doi.org/10.1016/j.ecolecon.2005.01.016
4. Cohen, M.A.: Systematic review of urban sustainability assessment literature. Sustainability **9**(11), 2048 (2017). https://doi.org/10.3390/su9112048
5. Viviano, G., Ziemacki, G., Settimo, G., et al.: Air quality assessment in an urban-industrial area: the Taranto case study. Epidemiologia e prevenzione **29**(5–6 Suppl.), 45–9 (2005)
6. Iavarone, I., Castellano, G., Martinelli, W., et al.: Ecological and human biomonitoring in Taranto, an Italian contaminated site. Epidemiology **20**(6), S171–S172 (2009). https://doi.org/10.1097/01.ede.0000362582.58695.f6
7. Vigotti, M.A., Cavone, D., Bruni, A., Minerba, S., Conversano, M.: Analisi di mortalità in un sito con sorgenti localizzate: il caso di Taranto. In: Comba, P., Bianchi, F., Iavarone, I., Pirastu, R. (eds.) Impatto sulla salute dei siti inquinati: metodi e strumenti per la ricerca e le valutazioni, Rapporti ISTISAN (07/50), pp. 155–165, Roma, Istituto Superiore di Sanità (2007)
8. Marinaccio, A., Belli, S., Binazzi, A., et al. Residential proximity to industrial sites in the area of Taranto (Southern Italy). A case-control cancer incidence study. Annali dell'Istituto Superiore di Sanità **47**(2), 192–199. https://doi.org/10.4415/ANN_11_02_11
9. Cinelli, M., Stuart, R., Coles, K.: Analysis of the potentials of multi criteria decision analysis methods to conduct sustainability assessment. Ecol. Indic. **46**, 138–148 (2014). https://doi.org/10.1016/j.ecolind.2014.06.011
10. Kissinger, M., Rees, W.E., Timmer, V.: Interregional sustainability: governance and policy in an ecologically interdependent world. Environ. Sci. Policy **14**(8), 965–976 (2011). https://doi.org/10.1016/j.envsci.2011.05.007
11. Davidson, K.M., Kellett, J., Wilson, L., Pullen, S.: Assessing urban sustainability from a social democratic perspective: a thematic approach. Local Environ. **17**(1), 57–73 (2012). https://doi.org/10.1080/13549839.2011.631990
12. Openshaw, S., Charlton, M., Wymer, C., Craft, A.W.: A Mark I geographical analysis machine for the automated analysis of point data. Int. J. Geogr. Inf. Syst. **1**(4), 335–358 (1987). https://doi.org/10.1080/02693798708927821

13. Kulldorff, M.A.: A spatial scan statistics. Commun. Stat. Theory Methods **26**(6), 1481–1496 (1997). https://doi.org/10.1080/03610929708831995
14. Kulldorff, M., Nagarwalla, N.: Spatial disease clusters: detection and inference. Stat. Med. **14**(8), 799–810 (1995). https://doi.org/10.1002/sim.4780140809
15. Tango, T., Takahashi, K.: A flexibly shaped spatial scan statistic for detecting clusters. Int. J. Health Geogr. **4**, 11 (2005). https://doi.org/10.1186/1476-072X-4-11
16. Patil, G.P., Taillie, C.: Upper level set scan statistic for detecting arbitrarily shaped hotspots. Environ. Ecol. Stat. **11**(2), 183–197 (2004)
17. Aldstadt, J., Getis, A.: Using AMOEBA to create spatial weights matrix and identify spatial clusters. Geogr. Anal. **38**(4), 327–343 (2006). https://doi.org/10.1111/j.1538-4632.2006.00689.x
18. Waller, L.A., Gotway, C.A.: Applied Spatial Statistics for Public Health Data. Wiley, New York (2004)
19. Ester, M., Kriegel, H.P., Sander, J., Xu, X.: A density-based algorithm for discovering clusters in large spatial databases with noise. In: Proceedings of 2nd International Conference on Knowledge Discovery and Data Mining (KDD 1996), Portland, pp. 226–231 (1996)
20. Montrone, S., Perchinunno, P., L'Abbate, S., Ligorio, C.: Comparing SaTScan and Seg-DBSCAN methods in spatial phenomena. In: Spatial Data Methods for Environmental and Ecological Processes, 1–2 Settembre 2011, Foggia-IT (2011)
21. Cervellera, A.: Arsenalotti. Archita Editore, Taranto (2010)
22. Colli, A., Montecchini, V., Conversano, D., Greco, N.: Progetto di due sobborghi in ampliazione della città di Taranto, approvato con Regio Decreto del 18/09/1865 (1865). http://www.rapu.it/ricerca/scheda_piano.php?id_piano=689. Accessed 07 Feb 2019
23. Van-Camp, L., Bujabarral, B., Gentile, A.R., et al.: Reports of the technical working groups established under the thematic strategy for soil protection. EUR 21319 EN/1, Office for Official Publications of the European Communities, Luxemburg (2004)
24. ARPA Puglia Centro Regionale Aria: Relazione annuale sulla Qualità dell'Aria in Puglia (2017). http://www.arpa.puglia.it/web/guest/rapporti_annuali_qa. Accessed 05 Feb 2019
25. ARPA Puglia, AReSS Puglia: ASL di Taranto: Rapporto di Valutazione del Danno Sanitario Stabilimento ILVA di Taranto ai sensi del Decreto Interministeriale 24 aprile 2013 (2017). http://www.va.minambiente.it/it-IT/ps/Procedure/VdsILVA. Accessed 28 Jan 2019
26. Singh, R.K., Murty, H.R., Gupta, S.K., Dikshit, A.K.: An overview of sustainability assessment methodologies. Ecol. Indic. **9**(2), 89–112 (2011). https://doi.org/10.1016/j.ecolind.2008.05.011
27. Sala, S., Farioli, F., Zamagni, A.: Progress in sustainability science: lessons learnt from current methodologies for sustainability assessment: Part 1. Int. J. Life Cycle Assess. **18**(9), 1653–1672 (2013). https://doi.org/10.1007/s11367-012-0508-6
28. Devuyst, D., Hens, L., de Lannoy, W.: How Green is the City? Sustainability Assessment and the Management of Urban Environments. Columbia University Press, New York (2001)
29. Pinter, L., Hardi, P., Martinuzzi, A., Hall, J.: Bellagio STAMP: principles for sustainability assessment and measurement. Ecol. Indic. **17**, 20–28 (2012). https://doi.org/10.1016/j.ecolind.2011.07.001
30. Jacobs, B.: Strategy and Partnership in Cities and Regions: Economic Development and Urban Regeneration in Pittsburgh. Birmingham and Rotterdam. Palgrave McMillan, London (2000)

31. Stewart, M.: Collaboration in multi-actor governance. In: Haus, M., Heinelt, H., Stewart, M. (eds.) Urban Governance and Democracy: Leadership and Community Involvement, pp. 149–167. Routledge, London (2005)
32. Sala, S., Ciuffo, B., Nijkamp, P.: A systemic framework for sustainability assessment. Ecol. Econ. **119**, 314–325 (2015). https://doi.org/10.1016/j.ecolecon.2015.09.015
33. Ness, E., Piirsalu, U., Anderberg, S., Olsson, L.: Categorising tools for sustainability assessment. Ecol. Econ. **60**(3), 498–508 (2007). https://doi.org/10.1016/j.ecolecon.2006.07.023
34. Bohringer, C., Jochem, P.: Measuring the immeasurable - a survey of sustainability indices. Ecol. Econ. **63**(1), 1–8 (2007). https://doi.org/10.1016/j.ecolecon.2007.03.008
35. Detrick, S.: The post industrial revitalization of Pittsburgh: myths and evidence. Community Dev. J. **34**(1), 4–12 (1999). https://doi.org/10.1093/cdj/34.1.4
36. Tsenkova, S.: Urban Regeneration: Learning from the British Experience. Faculty of Environmental Design University of Calgary, University of Calgary Press (2002)

University Dropout Rates: Factors and Motivations that Influence the Choices of the Students

Francesca Traetta[1], Vito Ricci[1], and Paola Perchinunno[2(✉)]

[1] University Statistics Staff of the General Management, University of Bari, Piazza Umberto I, 70121 Bari, Italy
{francesca.traetta, vito.ricci}@uniba.it

[2] DEMDI, University of Bari, Via C. Rosalba 53, 70100 Bari, Italy
paola.perchinunno@uniba.it

Abstract. One of the most significant indicators for assessing the quality of university study paths is the percentage of dropouts between the first and second year. The reference literature and the results that emerged from numerous specific investigations into the abandonment of the university system show that this is a crucial "joint" in the path of the students. The aim of this work is to analyze the evolution of the phenomenon in Italy, trying to bring out the factors and the motivations that influence the choices of the students, such as, for example, an incorrect orientation activity at the entrance, the need to quickly confront each other with the world of work, a supervening consciousness of not being able to deal with a specific course of study.

Keywords: Dropout rate · University study paths · Performance indicators · Student profiles

1 Introduction

To assess the quality of the study paths, one of the most significant indicators is the drop-out rate between the first and second year, understood as a percentage variation between the number of students enrolled in the second year and that of "pure" students in the previous year.

The reference literature on the topic and the results that emerged from numerous specific surveys on the abandonment of the university system show that this is a crucial "junction" in the path of the students, where the great majority of the dropouts or the decision to change the course of study is concentrated [1–3].

The motivations that push a student to abandon the studies can be different, starting from an incorrect orientation activity at the entrance, to the will or need to quickly confront the world of work, to an unexpected awareness of not being able to face a particular course of study rather than a different one. Indeed, abandonment is not

The contribution is the result of joint reflections by the authors, with the following contributions attributed to V. Ricci (Chaps. 4 and 5), to P. Perchinunno (Chaps. 1 and 2), and to F. Traetta (Chap. 3).

S. Misra et al. (Eds.): ICCSA 2019, LNCS 11622, pp. 78–92, 2019.
https://doi.org/10.1007/978-3-030-24305-0_7

necessarily a definitive condition; those who have abandoned can clearly decide to retrace their steps and resume their studies after a certain period of time; just as he may decide to enroll again in a different course of study at his university or at another university.

According to Eurostat data, in 2016 more than 3 million young Europeans gave up their degree. In the ranking of EU countries with the highest number of university dropouts, Eurostat assigns first place to France (with a third of the total number of study disclaimers), followed by Italy with a drop-out rate of 15.8% and third place from the United Kingdom, with 12%. According to Eurostat, various reasons motivate the renunciation of studies. For 24% of students, aged between 20 and 35, abandonment is motivated by the desire to enter the world of work.

International literature has long focused on these analyzes. In particular, Smith and Naylor [4] studied, with respect to the United Kingdom, the possible determinants of the risk of abandoning studies by a cohort of students, observing that the possible causes are: the pre-university education, the degree subject and characteristics of the Department. For Murray [5], domestic or financial problems also affect abandonment, while for other authors, the profile of the student who tends to abandon their studies is dependent only on the subject studied [6].

The objective of this work is to analyze the trend of drop-out rates in Italy, focusing specifically on the reality of the University of Bari A. Moro, following in detail the path of the students who leave and trying to find out what the factors that have the greatest influence on this choice through a logistic regression model and segmentation trees (classification and regression trees).

2 The Dropout Rate in Italy

2.1 The Dropout Rate Among First and Second Year

At the national aggregate level, the National Agency for the Evaluation of the University System (ANVUR) monitors the performance of the university system using the data of the National Student Registry (ANS) also in relation to the situation regarding dropouts.

In particular, the analysis focuses on the following indices:

1. University drop-out rate between the first and second year between the first and second year of the course (it concerns students who, in the transition to the second year, leave the system, no longer enrolled in any course);
2. Mobility between the first and second year of the course (course changes and university transfers): it is observed if the continuation of the studies, year after year, takes place in the same course of matriculation or in another course, in the same or in other university.

From the data of the last ANVUR 2018 Report on the State of the University System, it emerges that in the bachelor courses the percentage of dropouts between the first and second year in the 2015/16 cohort is 12.2%. Significantly lower drop-out rates are recorded Long Cycle Master courses (Bachelor + master), at 7.5% in the 2015/16 cohort, and in Master courses, which reach 5.9%.

As shown in Fig. 1, the drop-out rates are decidedly down compared to the cohorts of the previous academic years, showing a reduction of 4% points for the bachelor degrees from 2006/07 to 2015/16 and 2% points for the others.

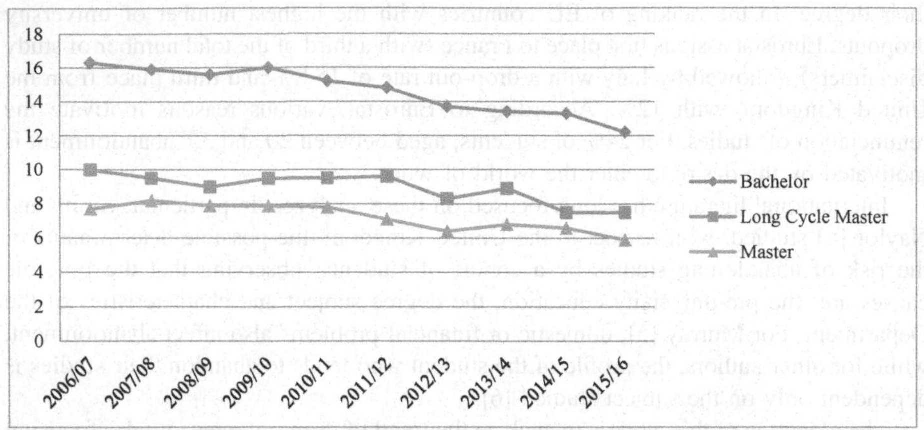

Source: National Register of Students of MIUR-Cineca.

Fig. 1. University dropout rate between I and II year, by type of course (cohorts 2006/07–2015/16)

The tendency to reduce the drop-out rates just highlighted also characterizes the data broken down by scientific area. Distinguishing the CUN course by area of study, a general improvement emerges in recent years; in the few cases where there is an increase in the drop-out rate it is limited and refers to relatively low initial levels.

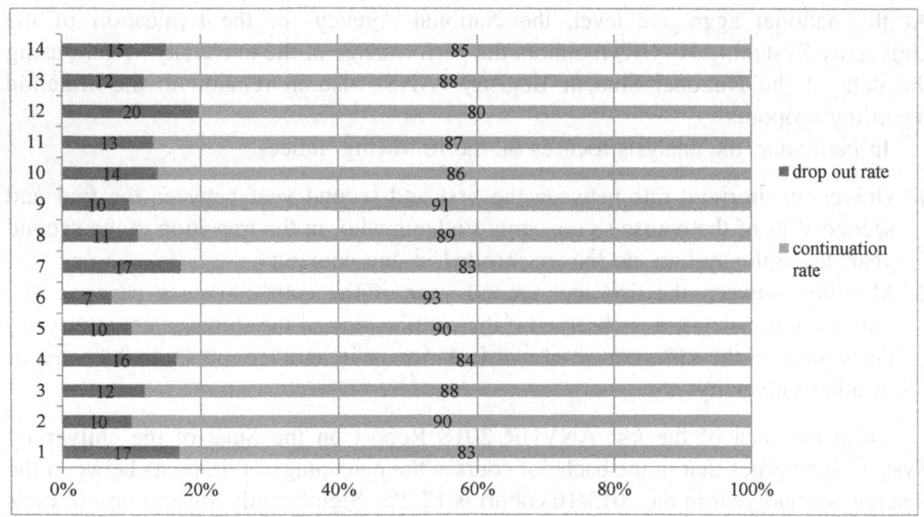

Source: National Register of Students of MIUR-Cineca.

Fig. 2. University dropout rate between I and II year, by CUN area (2015/16 cohort)

For the last cohort of enrolled analyzed (ay 2015/16), the dropout rate is relatively high in Area 12 (Legal Sciences) with 19.8%, and Area 7 (Agricultural and Veterinary Sciences) with 17.1% (Fig. 2).

Further differences are found at the geographical level with at least 3% points of difference between the universities of the North and those of the South; in fact, bachelor degrees have a drop-out rate of 14.3% in the South compared to 10.7% in the North. Same thing for those with a Long Cycle Master degree, with a rate ranging from 9.5% for South universities to 6% for North universities (Fig. 3).

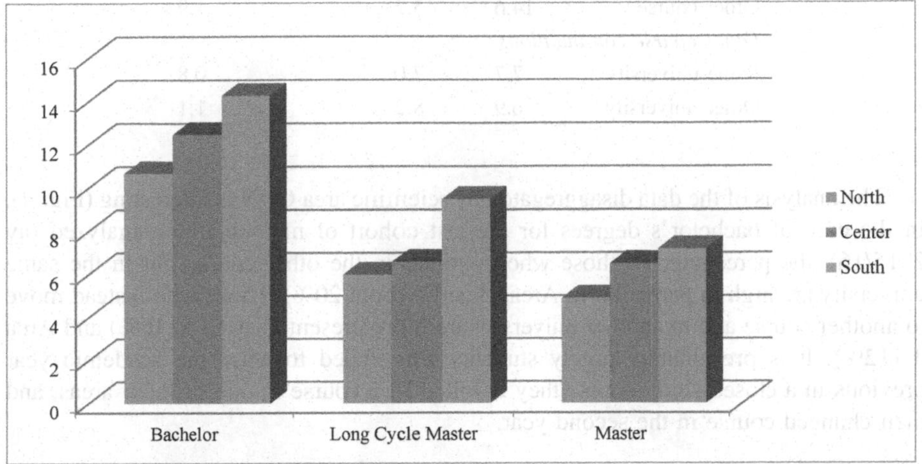

Source: National Register of Students of MIUR-Cineca.

Fig. 3. University dropout rate between the first and second year, by geographical area (cohort 2015/16)

2.2 Mobility Between the First and Second Year of the Course

Considering those who continue the course of study it is however interesting to understand if the students between the first and second year continue to attend the same course (linear continuation) or change course, passing to another course in the same university or passing from one course to another university. In the bachelor and Long Cycle Master degrees the continuation involves 73.2% and 77.4% respectively, while the study course changes between I and II involve approximately 15% of the registered students (Table 1).

Source: our elaboration on National Register of Students of MIUR-Cineca.

Among those who change course at the Bachelor's and Long Cycle Master's degree, about half carry out a transfer to another university; in the bachelor degree the course changes within the same university prevail slightly (7.7%), while for the Long Cycle Master courses transfers to another university are more frequent (8.2%). In the Master's degree courses these latter values are much more contained and regard negligible percentages.

Table 1. Outcome in the transition between the first and second year of the course, by type of course and type of continuation

	Bachelor	Long Cycle Master	Master
Enrolled	239,727	34,908	108,647
Result between I and II year			
Dropout	12.2	7.4	6.2
Continuations	87.8	92.6	93.8
Continuations			
Same course	73.2	77.4	91.9
Other course	14.6	15.2	1.9
Other course continuations			
Same university	7.7	7.0	0.8
Other university	6.9	8.2	1.1

The analysis of the data disaggregated by scientific area CUN is interesting (Fig. 4). In the case of bachelor's degrees for the last cohort of matriculations analyzed (ay 2015/16), the percentage of those who continue in the other course but in the same university are high in particular in Areas 3 and 4 (both 20%). Those who instead move to another course and to another university are more present in Area 5 (16%) and Area 3 (12%). It is presumably largely students who failed to enter the academic year previous in a closed-study course they enrolled in a course in one of these areas, and then changed course in the second year.

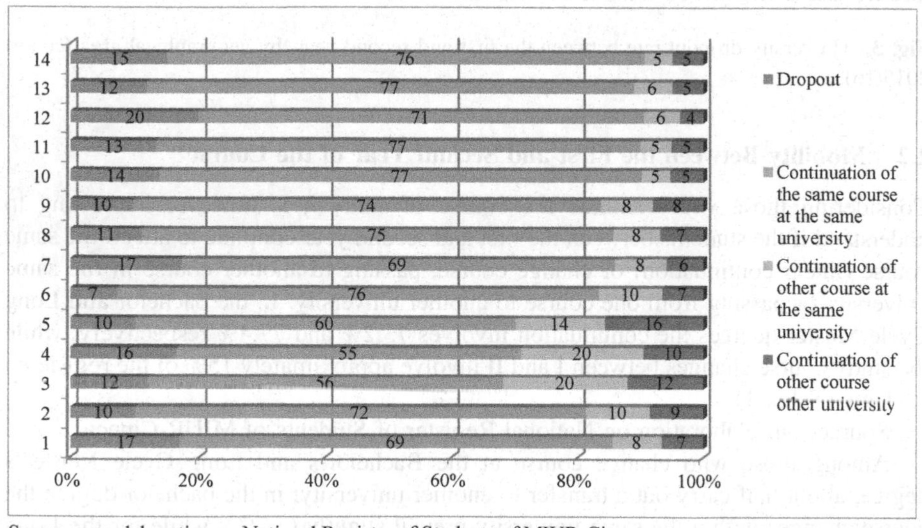

Source: our elaboration on National Register of Students of MIUR-Cineca.

Fig. 4. Outcome in the transition between the first and second year of the course, for bachelor's degrees and Area CUN. Year 2015/16

In the master's and Long Cycle Master's courses the changes are much more contained and no significant differences emerge between the different CUN Areas.

Source: our elaboration on National Register of Students of MIUR-Cineca.

3 Statistical Analysis of the Dropout Rate of the Students of the University of Bari A. Moro

3.1 Sources and Methods

For a correct understanding of the phenomena covered by this treatment it is useful to analyze data's sources and the methodology related to the calculation of the indices.

The University of Bari Aldo Moro is one of the largest Italian universities, based in Puglia, Southern Italy. Currently the University of Bari is ranked tenth among the Italian Universities and second among the Southern Universities (after the Federico II University of Naples) for the number of student population. Data on the university student population were detected from the National Registry Students (ANS) in March 2019.

In particular, the indicators considered in this section are the following:

1. University drop-out rate between the first and second year of the course (it concerns students who, in the transition to the second year, leave the University of Bari, being no longer enrolled in any course of the same);
2. Mobility between the first and second year of the course (course changes): it is observed if the continuation of the studies, year after year, takes place in the same course of matriculation or in another course, in the same class of degree or in another class.

Therefore it is necessary to specify that in this paragraph the university dropout rate refers to those who do not enroll in the second year in the same university thus including not only those who leave their university studies, even those who move to another university. Therefore they must not be compared with the university dropout rates of the previous paragraph but with the sum of the dropouts plus transfers to another university.

In the last academic years the university population amounted to around 45,000 units; the students enrolled in the 2015/16 academic year are approximately 11,000 and refer to Bachelor's, Long Cycle Master's and Master's degree courses.

3.2 University Dropout Rates Between I and II Year

Our analysis refers only to the university dropouts between the first and second year of the bachelor's and Long Cycle Master's degrees, as the abandonment of only the master's degrees concern negligible percentage of students. Moreover, as already mentioned, the drop-out rate between the 1st and 2nd year considered in this work refers to those who do not enroll in the same university, considering as abandonment even those who enroll in another university.

With regard to the dropout rate, there are clear differences between the different types of study course (Table 2). In fact, it differs by more than 5% points between bachelor's and Long Cycle Master's degrees (respectively 21.8% and 16.4%).

Quite high is the percentage of students who between the first and second year of study change course, especially with regard to those who change undergraduate classes (9.7% bachelor's and 11.6% Long Cycle Master's degree).

Table 2. Outcome in the transition between the first and second year of the course, by type of course and type of continuation of the enrolled students a.a. 2015/16

	Bachelor		Long Cycle Master		Total	
Continuations in the same course	3,924	65.8	964	69.8	4,888	66.5
Course changes between the 1st and 2nd year of the same class	158	2.7	31	2.2	189	2.6
Course changes between the first and second year of another class	579	9.7	160	11.6	739	10.1
Dropout between the first and second year and transfers to another University*	1,302	21.8	226	16.4	1,528	20.8
Enrolled total	**5,963**	**100.0**	**1,381**	**100.0**	**7,344**	**100.0**

* Students who have not renewed their enrollment for the academic year 2016/17 in the University of Bari.

Source: National Register of Students of MIUR-Cineca.

Analyzing the university drop-out rates of the bachelor's degrees for the scientific area of the course of study (CUN area), it emerges as for the cohort of matriculations analyzed (academic year 2015/16), the percentage of dropouts is relatively high in Area 04 (Sciences of Earth) with 39.5% and Area 12 (Legal Sciences) with 36.5% of dropouts. This latter figure appears to be in line with what has been analyzed at national level (Table 3).

Even for Long Cycle Master's degrees (Table 4) the highest percentages of drop-out rates per CUN area are found in Area 12 (Legal Sciences) with 20.7% drop-outs and in Area 07 (agricultural sciences and veterinary) with 20%.

In the specific case of study it appears to analyze also the variation of the abandonment rate according to other explanatory variables such as:

- gender (male or female);
- type of secondary school diploma (high school or vocational school);
- diploma grade (from 60 to 100 cents).
- number of formative credits (credit iformativi universitari, CFU) achieved in 2016.

The influence of the sex variable on the university dropout rate study path is interesting. From the data analyzed on the 2015/16 pure enrollment cohort at the University of Bari, it emerges that men are more likely to abandon the path undertaken with differences of more than 5% points (Fig. 5). In fact, as far as bachelor's degrees are concerned, we will have 25.8% of male students and 19% of females, while for Long Cycle Master's degrees we will have 19.1% for males and 14.8% for women.

Table 3. Outcome in the transition between the first and second year of the course, for bachelor's degrees and Area CUN. Year 2015/16

CUNArea	Dropout	Course changes in the same class	Course changes with another class
01 - Mathematical and computer science	22.8	2.8	5.1
02 - Physical sciences	27.3	3.0	15.2
03 - Chemical sciences	17.7	0.0	37.2
04 - Earth Sciences	39.5	1.4	26.2
05 - Biological sciences	18.8	11.3	25.9
06 - Medical sciences	6.6	4.7	15.7
07 - Agricultural and veterinary sciences	28.4	8.5	12.2
10 - Antiquity, philological-literary and historical-artistic sciences	21.3	1.4	5.0
11 - Historical, philosophical, pedagogical and psychological sciences	13.6	0.4	4.8
12 - Legal sciences	36.5	1.7	7.8
13 - Economics and statistics	25.2	1.0	4.3
14 - Political and social sciences	24.7	0.2	7.3
Total	**21.8**	**2.7**	**9.7**

Source: National Register of Students of MIUR-Cineca.

The type of high school diploma also influences the drop-out rates (Fig. 6): those who leave the studies come mainly from professional Institutes (35% Bachelor and 48% Long Cycle Master) and technical Institutes (respectively 26.7% and 35, 3%).

Table 4. Result of transition between the first and second year of the course, for Long Cycle Master's degrees and Area CUN. Year 2015/16

CUNArea	Dropout	Course changes in the same class	Course changes with another class
03 - Chemical sciences	12.5	0.0	12.5
05 - Biological sciences	16.3	6.0	32.1
06 - Medical sciences	2.3	1.7	0.6
07 - Agricultural and veterinary sciences	20.0	0.0	13.3
11 - Historical, philosophical, pedagogical and psychological sciences	1.6	0.0	3.3
12 - Legal science	20.7	0.9	5.4
Total	**16.4**	**2.2**	**11.6**

Source: National Register of Students of MIUR-Cineca.

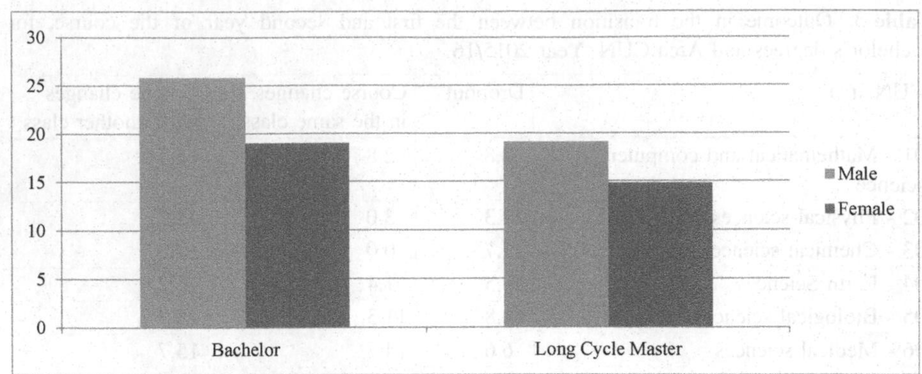

Source: National Register of Students of MIUR-Cineca.

Fig. 5. Dropout rate between the first and second year for the course of study and gender

Even more evident is the link between the diploma grade and the drop-out rate (Fig. 7): in fact, the lower the diploma grade, the more the drop-out rate increases (going from 8% for 100 and praise) to 33% for the class of vote below 69/100).

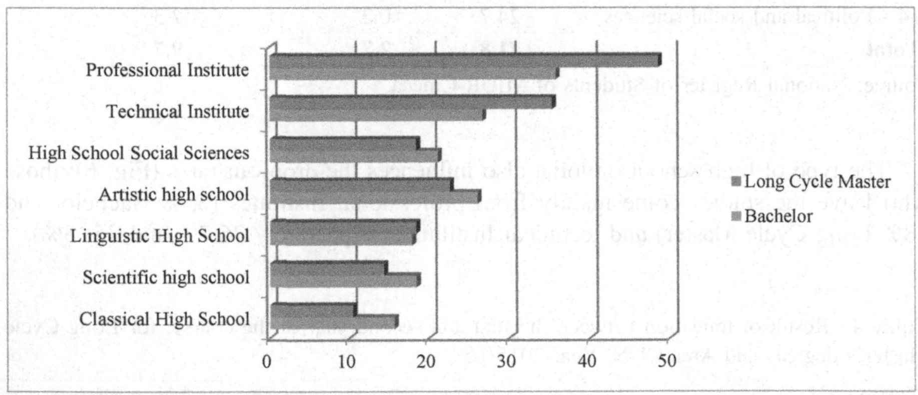

Source: National Register of Students of MIUR-Cineca.

Fig. 6. Drop-out rate between the first and second year for high school diploma and study course

Table 5 shows that students achieving less than 12 CFU in the first year of staying at university have a drop out rate of 61.7% (54.1% for long cycle master and 63% for bachelor), while those having more than 12 CFU present a very low risk of abandon, about 5%.

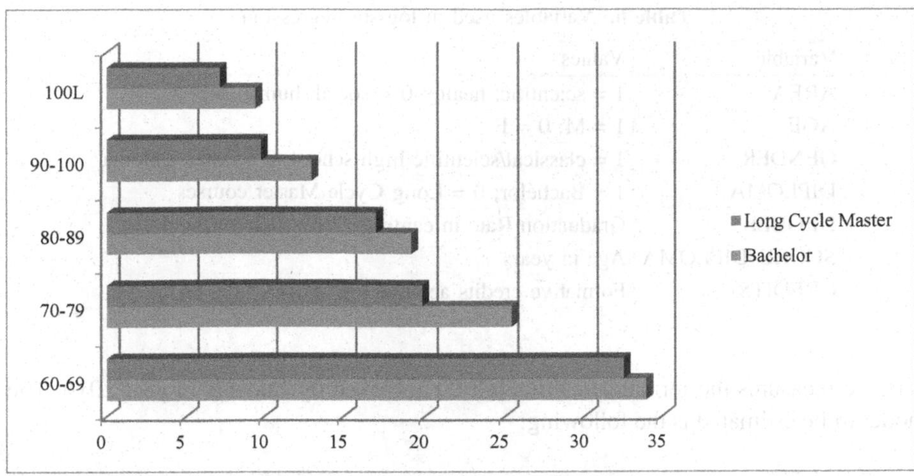

Source: National Register of Students of MIUR-Cineca.

Fig. 7. Drop-out rates between the I and II year high school graduation classes and study course

Table 5. Drop-out rates between the I and II year according CFU achieved in the first year of enrollment

CFU	Drop out
0–12	61.7
13–24	16.1
25–36	5.7
36–48	1.4
49–60	0,4
>60	0,4
Total	**21.8**

4 The Profiles of Students Who Drop Out

The risk of abandonment can be measured using qualitative variables, by constructing logit-type dependency models, in order to identify the most significant determinants of groups of students with a different potential risk of abandoning their studies.

Therefore, the logistic regression model was used to identify which variables, among those detected, most influence the risk of abandonment. The response variable "DROPOUT" is of dichotomous type, equal to 1 if the student has abandoned and to 0 otherwise. The regressors introduced in the model are those reported in Table 6.

The AREA variable distinguishes the medical-scientific area courses from the socio-humanistic area, DIPLOMA the type of diploma achieved by the student, depending on whether he is of high school or other type, the DEGREE variable distinguishes the type of university path undertaken (Bachelor's or Long Cycle Master's degree). The CREDITS

Table 6. Variables used in logistic regression

Variable	Values
AREA	1 = scientific, health; 0 = social, humanistic
AGE	1 = M; 0 = F
GENDER	1 = classical/scientific high school; 0 = other diploma
DIPLOMA	1 = Bachelor; 0 = Long Cycle Master courses
DEGREE	Graduation Rate in cents
SCORE_DIPLOMA	Age in years
CREDITS	Formative credits achieved in 2016

variable measures the formative credits (CFU) achieved by students in year 2016. The model to be estimated is the following:

$$logit(\pi_i) = \log\left(\frac{\pi_i}{1-\pi_i}\right) = \beta_0 + \beta_1 AREA_i + \beta_1 GENDER_i + \beta_2 DIPLOMA + \beta_3 DEGREE_i + \beta_4 SCORE\_DIPLOMA_i + \beta_5 AGE_i + \beta_6 CREDITS_i$$

Where $\pi_i = Prob(DROPOUT = 1|\boldsymbol{X})$ and X is the vector of the regressors and indicates the probability of abandonment. The software R was used to estimate the model parameters and the results are presented in Table 7.

Table 7. Estimate of the logit model parameters

Covariate	Estimate	Std. Error	Z value	Pr(>|z|)	Sig.
(Intercept)	−0.500116	0.407417	−1.228	0.21962	
AREA	−0.384218	0.083418	−4.606	4.11E−06	***
AGE	0.031005	0.012125	2.557	0.01056	*
GENDER	0.337606	0.081022	4.167	3.09E−05	***
DIPLOMA	−0.217468	0.082036	−2.651	0.00803	**
DEGREE	0.115641	0.107503	1.076	0.28206	
SCORE_DIPLOMA	0.010002	0.003642	2.746	0.00603	**
CREDITS	−0.127246	0.003477	−36.596	<2,00E−16	***

Sig. codes: 0 '***' 0,001 '**' 0,01 '*' 0,05 '.' 0,1 ' ' 1

From the estimation of the parameters of the proposed model it emerges how the risk of dropout has a very significant influence in the order: CREDITS, AREA, GENDER, SCORE_DIPLOMA and DIPLOMA. In particular, we have that the probability of abounding in the examined collective decreases with the increase of the diploma grade and the amount of credits achieved, the same increases among those who have attended a higher secondary education institution other than high school and among male students. The contribution in explanatory terms of the other AGE regressors does not seem rather important (p-value = 0.01056) and above all DEGREE; we can conclude that the age has a fairly small influence, while there are important differences in the drop-out rate between the different areas to which the study courses are linked and the different types of them. The most important covariate seems to be CREDITS, meaning that students which pass exams during their first year of enrollment have a very small probability to abandon the university, while inactive students have a serious risk of dropping out. The results obtained on the examined collective appear to be in line with those of other studies of the same genus [7]. We point out that the covariate CREDITS can be measured only a posteriori, if the logistic regression would be used a priori to predict and measure for each student his own risk of drop out this variable can't be employed, an only the other variables in Table 5 have to be used in prediction. For this reason, we propose also an alternative model, excluding the covariate CREDITS and the results are presented in Table 8.

Table 8. Estimate of the logit model parameters (excluding CREDITS covariate)

Covariate	Estimate	Std. error	Z value	Pr(>|z|)	Sig.
(Intercept)	1,5261	0,3051	5,003	5,65E−07	***
AREA	−0,0432	0,0635	−0,681	0,496114	
AGE	0,0151	0,0083	1,814	0,069627	.
GENDER	0,2381	0,0622	3,829	0,000128	***
DIPLOMA	−0,5290	0,0631	−8,386	<2,00E−16	***
DEGREE	0,0609	0,0839	0,726	0,467558	
SCORE_DIPLOMA	−0,0382	0,0027	−14,154	<2,00E−16	***

Sig. codes: 0 '***' 0,001 '**' 0,01 '*' 0,05 '.' 0,1 ' ' 1

Excluding CREDITS changes something in estimates of logistic model parameters: AREA become no significative, AGE lost part of its significativeness, while DIPLOMA and SCORE_DIPLOMA increases their influence in the drop out risk. The pseudo R^2 falls from 0.44 to 0.05.

Another statistical technique used in the literature for the study of abandonment risk is the segmentation trees (CRT = classification and regression trees) [8]; is a methodology having the objective of obtaining a segmentation of a set of statistical units by identifying rules or paths that exploit the relationship existing between a class of belonging and the variables detected for each unit. This tool also makes it possible to identify the profile of the subjects most at risk of drop outs. Also in this case the R software was used for processing. The most important variables for segmentation purposes were CREDITS, AREA, DIPLOMA and GENDER, as already emerged from the logistic regression. Hierarchical segmentation is shown in Fig. 8. The first discriminating variable is the number of credits achieved during the first year of enrollment grade: the dropout rate is reduced to 5% among those who have achieved more than 12 CFU, while it is very high (63%) in the cluster of those that have achieved less than the threshold identified by the statistical software. Within this group, the second discriminating variable is linked to the area of the course: students enrolled in clinical area have a smaller drop out rate (38.2%), while those enrolled in social area register the highest rate (70%). In this cluster, those who have achieved a non-high school maturity the drop-out rate is 74.6% with a significative difference according to the gender (78.7% male vs 71.5% female).

Using the information obtained from the CRT and those obtained with the exploratory analysis and logistic regression in the preceding paragraphs, we can affirm that in the cohort of the pure registrations of the University of Bari in the academic year 2015-16 the subjects at greatest risk of abandonment were male students, with a maturity of non-high school classical or scientific (technical, professional, master's degree, linguistic, artistic) and above all with less than 12 CFU achieved during the first year on staying at university. The results obtained with the CRT present many points of contact with a previous study conducted always among the matriculated students of the University of Bari who used segmentation trees [9].

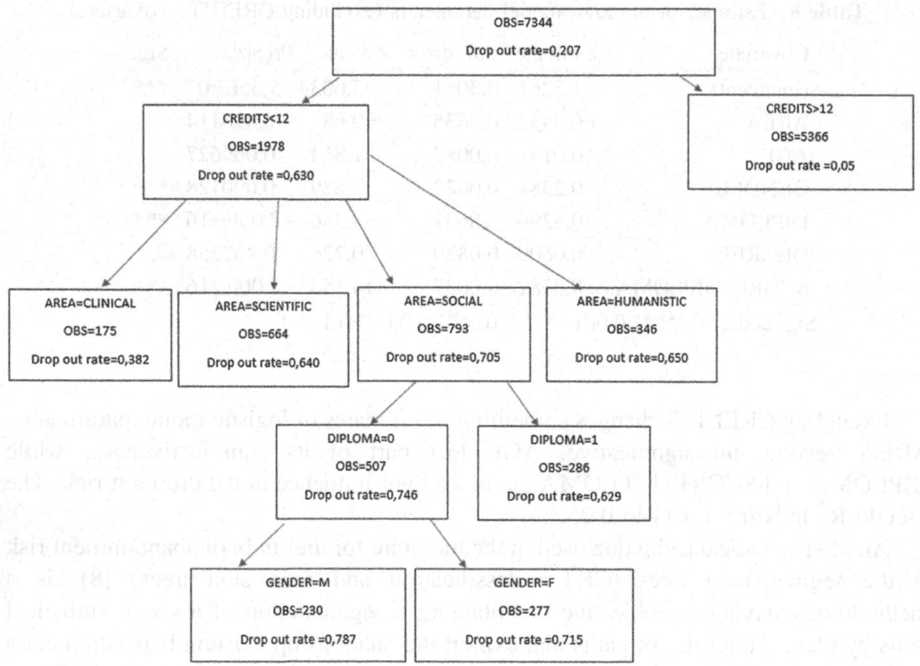

Fig. 8. Tree of classification of the risk of dropout in the cohort of students enrolled in the academic year 2015–16

5 Final Remarks

The abandonment of studies by a considerable number of students has long been indicated as one of the main "pathologies" of the Italian higher education system. The objective of reducing the size of the phenomenon and its negative impact on the productivity of the system and on the profitability of the investment in education by the public sector and private individuals (students and their families) is one of the qualifying elements of the reform of the educational offer and, more generally, of system reforms carried out in Italy since the 2000s.

The literature shows that the main motivation for abandonment is failure in studies, with the consequent fall in individual motivation and loss of confidence in personal abilities. Other negative circumstances are the discontinuity of the training path and the non-frequency of places of study, which can reduce the possibility of mobilizing resources and devising strategies to combat difficulties and delays.

The analysis carried out on the students of the University of Bari Aldo Moro indicates that the risk of leaving school is greater for inactive (less than 12 CFU achieved), male students, with non-brilliant scholastic study paths (grade of maturity lower than 70/100) and that come mainly from professional or technical institutes. Preparation gaps, insufficient knowledge of the university environment, poor mastery of effective study methodologies are in fact elements that can negatively affect students' careers.

It is advisable to adequately monitor these conditions both at entry and during the course of studies, especially in their initial phase which is strategic to define the chances of success or failure. The University of Bari has launched numerous initiatives to reduce the drop-out rate and course changes in the transition between the first and second year, both in the phase of orientation at the entrance, with initiatives aimed at students of the 4th and 5th years of middle school superior (Open Day, Week of orientation and awareness orientation, etc.), both with tutoring activities in itinere, addressed to students of the first year of the course, supported by teaching tutors.

However, the difficult conditions of the labor market, which may also have a direct negative influence on enrollment and continuation of studies, particularly on young people facing difficult individual or family economic conditions, which can make the choices forced to renounce pursuing one's own training project.

Ultimately, therefore, guidance, counseling and possibly support at the entrance appear essential, as well as accompanying and support interventions during the studies, through tutoring services and other tailor-made interventions aimed at reducing the rate of university dropout. However, financial support (scholarships and accommodation for students in poor economic conditions) is also necessary to minimize the number of cases of study interruption.

References

1. Tinto, V.: Dropout from higher education: a theoretical synthesis of recent research. Rev. Educ. Res. **45**, 89–125 (1975)
2. Paura, L., Arhipova, I.: Cause analysis of students' dropout rate in higher education study program. Procedia - Soc. Behav. Sci. **109**, 1282–1286 (2014)
3. Johnson, J.L.: Commuter college students: what factors determine who will persist or who will drop out? Coll. Stud. J. **31**(3), 323–332 (1997)
4. Smith, J.P., Naylor, R.A.: Dropping out of university: a statistical analysis of the probability of withdrawal for UK university students. J. R. Stat. Soc. Ser. A **164**, 389–405 (2001)

5. Murray, M.: Factors affecting graduation and student dropout rates at the University of KwaZulu-Natal. S. Afr. J. Sci. **110**(11/12), 1–6 (2014)
6. Araque, F., Roldán, C., Salguero, A.: Factors influencing university drop out rates. Comput. Educ. **53**(3), 563–574 (2009)
7. Chiandotto, B., Giusti, C.: L'abbandono degli studi universitari. in Crocetta C. (a cura di) Modelli statistici per l'analisi della transizione università-lavoro. CLEUP, Padova (2005)
8. Loh, W.Y.: Classification and regression trees. WIREs Data Min. Knowl. Discov. **1**, 14–23 (2011). https://www.stat.wisc.edu/~loh/treeprogs/guide/wires11.pdf
9. Cazzolle, M., D'Uggento, A.M., Ricci, V.: Analisi retrospettiva di un collettivo di immatricolati presso l'Università degli Studi di Bari Aldo Moro tramite alberi di segmentazione binaria. In: Viola, D. (ed.) Valutazione e qualità degli atenei. Modelli, metodi e indicatori statistici, Bari (2011)

Bottom-Up Processes for Culture-Led Urban Regeneration Scenarios

Lucia Della Spina(✉), Claudia Giorno, and Ruggiero Galati Casmiro

Mediterranea University, Salita Melissari, 89124 Reggio Calabria, Italy
lucia.dellaspina@unirc.it, claudgiorno@gmail.com, ruggiero.galatic@gmail.com

Abstract. The research explored the potentialities of an integrated approach to identify the preferable culture-led urban regeneration scenarios for Catanzaro (Italy). Through a process of knowledge of the urban contest it was possible to identify and analyse transformation also through shared values, as constitutive elements of the vision of the place; through these, it was possible to interact and understand the transformations in progress by developing an intervention strategy that can guide and support a process of culture-led regeneration. The Multi-Criteria and multi-group assessment was carried out through the Analytic Network Process (ANP) method, which allow to support the design of shared and transparent planning and design choices, according to a bottom-up approach. The decision-making process, in its different phases and results, allows making explicit the components that significantly influence the local transformations and that could guide the interaction between the different involved stakeholders towards a shared common vision.

Keywords: Urban regeneration · Culture-led regeneration scenarios · Multi-Criteria Decision Aid (MCDA) · Multi-Stakeholder Decision Analysis (MSDA) · Analytic Network Process (ANP) · Scenario analysis · Multidimensional indicators

1 Introduction

The themes of urban regeneration, social innovation, the redefinition of the role of the public, and local administrations in particular, are connected to each other and to the great challenge that cities around the world are facing in these years: how to give responses to the needs of its citizens with increasingly scarce resources in the face of ever greater challenges. The activation and success of these paths require a combination of conditions, including the cultural endowment and productive vocations of the territories, the development of shared projects and the implementation of enlightened visions/actions, public or private.

The most widespread practices of incorporating culture into the urban regeneration processes are relatively recent, and that activities are seen as catalysts of regeneration and change. The projects are often intended as a symbol of urban regeneration, more

S. Misra et al. (Eds.): ICCSA 2019, LNCS 11622, pp. 93–107, 2019.
https://doi.org/10.1007/978-3-030-24305-0_8

specifically there is the need for different factors to make these projects work, among which the support of the community is a key factor [1–3]. The culture-led regeneration represents the most current and innovative reference model, where the culture becomes the instrument to link the different social, economic and urban components into a single synergistic process, involving the communities in the representation of their own identity.

The culture-led regeneration practices focus on revaluating those cultural resources that represent uniqueness, social vitality and the identity of places as tools for local sustainability and cohesion [2, 4].

The recovery of urban spaces, through the change of their original intended use, represents today one of the (few) levers available to cities to reinvigorate the social fabric and stimulate the emergence of new interactions, in order to generate possible innovative solutions to the multiple challenges in front of which they are found. In this logic, even iconic but disused places, become an active part of an urban ecosystem, aimed at stimulating contamination between different sectors of the economy and the urban social sphere and generating new connections between organized groups of citizens. These places acquire new value for the cities as they intercept networks of active relationships and become containers for projects that civil society is able to express through organized and stable actions. From this point of view, the communities have built their "living space" within these spaces and make them centres of innovation from the bottom-up, often with an open and inclusive approach. Without these communities, any redevelopment project of this type is bound to fail. Without a clear vocation or a long-term design, but above all without the energies that different actors can 'inject' into these spaces, the possibility of making them out of the attractors and generators (of what is new and potentially useful for cities) is missed.

The theme of urban regeneration through the restructuring and re-use of public spaces is a broad and debated topic and therefore it is not surprising that researchers from different disciplines (economics, urban geography, sociology, etc.) have shown, in studying these phenomena and the resources, that local administrators have invested in pursuing policies focused precisely on creativity and culture.

These policies, commonly known as creative or culture-led (or "driven by creativity/culture"), include all those actions undertaken by public subjects (or participated by the public) and aimed at creating the contextual conditions in support of culture and creativity such as lever for the economic and social development of a territory [5–9].

In this sense, there are several cities which, starting from the 1980s, as a response to the crisis, have begun a process of urban regeneration and the re-launching of the economy of a city with a purely industrial past through culture and creativity [7–9].

Recently, culture and creativity, intended as levers for urban regeneration, have been connected to the theme of social innovation, as a creative process, largely of a collective nature, aimed at the realization of goods and services that improve the level of well-being of a community in terms, for example, of education, welfare and social inclusion [9, 10].

From the point of view of social aspects, in fact, the redevelopment of abandoned areas can bring new life to districts or even entire cities, through either a re-appropriation or a rethinking of one's own identity through culture, or an improvement in living conditions thanks to activities of micro-enterprises or social innovation organizations, such as the birth of social and/or cultural enterprises hosted within incubators or creative hubs.

The theme of urban regeneration, therefore, represents a very current phenomenon and of great interest for local administrations, but also very complex.

Under these circumstances, the evaluation of urban transformation scenarios is therefore a complex decision problem where different aspects need to be considered simultaneously. So it is of particular importance to provide the decision makers with integrated evaluation tools able to consider the multiplicity of objectives and values when dealing with urban regeneration processes and to include the opinions and the needs of the different stakeholders involved [11].

Evaluation can be defined as a set of activities oriented to the appropriate organisation of the information necessary to make a choice, so that each actor involved in the decision-making process is able to take a balanced decision [12].

In this perspective, a Multi-Criteria Decision Aid (MCDA) approach represents a useful and effective instrument to understand the structure of the decision-making problem and the multiple and different dimensions that characterise it. Thus, it is possible to face conflicts that do not have unique solutions, but are characterised by variety and uncertainty [13], activating a process of dialogue and communication, not only between technicians, but between all those involved directly or indirectly by the plan choices. Therefore, MCDA can facilitate the decision-making process because it is frequently necessary to face situations in which several solutions are available, but different conflicting criteria must be considered.

The evaluative approach was built using the evaluation deliberative methods and a Multi-Stakeholder Decision Analysis (MSDA) to guide the interaction between the different stakeholders involved towards a shared common vision. This allow for identify the preferable culture-led urban regeneration scenario and to elaborate a strategic potential actions for the scenario implementation.

2 The Case Study

The proposed application concerns the urban area of historic centre of Catanzaro (Italy), capital city of the Calabria Region, known as the "City between the two seas" playing a significant connective and strategic function (Fig. 1), as it is located between the Ionian and Tyrrhenian coasts of the peninsula. It is an important administrative, commercial and cultural centre, with considerable administrative functions at the regional level.

The goal is to create a useful approach to policy makers for the elaboration of a strategy of culture-led regeneration structured through a multidimensional decision-making process and to build future alternative scenarios and actions through both bottom-up processes and top-down processes [14, 15].

Given the limited availability of economic resources, it is crucial to select a set of actions able to promote urban regeneration and development over time.

The knowledge framework has been set to understand the transformation processes in the context of study, in order to identify the significant components, which should

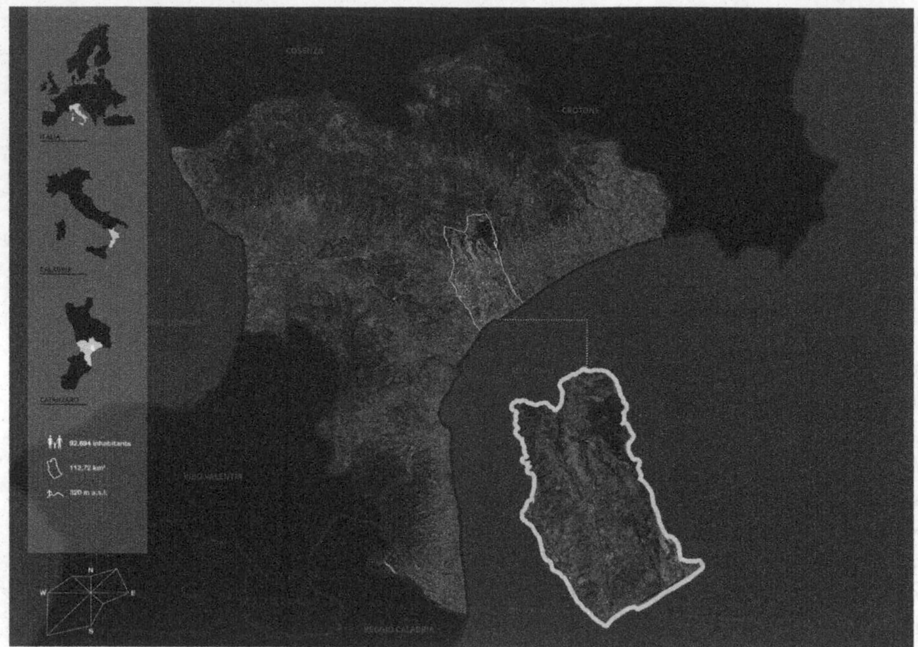

Fig. 1. The study area: Catanzaro (Italy)

characterise the regeneration process and select the actions to be included in the alternative scenarios.

3 Methodological Approach

In the early phases of the methodology used, some preliminary preparatory analysis were conducted, with the aim of analysing the transformations that occurred over time in the urban area of study.

The process of knowledge, through a bottom-up approach, has centred around the study of social, cultural, economic, and urban dynamics in the urban area over the last three decades (Table 1), with the aim of identifying those corrective or improvement actions for the development of future transformations, useful for developing the scenarios alternative of culture-led regeneration.

In Urban Agenda study for the city of Catanzaro, local actors and the authorities operating in the area have identified, through an Institutional Analysis [15, 16] some visions during a process of participation, integrating common knowledge and expert knowledge. The map of the stakeholders was elaborated and articulated considering the following categories: Promoters (institutions of the Municipality of Catanzaro); Operators (associations, economic activities); and Users (inhabitants, tourists, visitors, both actual and potential). This group of people was subjected to a series of questions related to the future vision of the city and the urban changes desired. The different

Table 1. Indicator categories for social, cultural, urban and economic criteria

Criteria	Indicators	Unit of measure
Social criteria	Total residents	n.
	Residents by age groups	n.
	Residents by age groups	n.
	Residents by educational qualification	n.
	Single person households	n.
	2–5 person households	n.
	>5 person households	n.
	% or number of residents in low-income households	% or n.
	% or number of resident foreign residents	% or n.
Cultural criteria	N. of associations	n./10000 inhab.
	N. of social centres/community centre	n.
	% or number of non-profit organization	% or n.
	N. of events or projects supported by volunteers	n./year
	N. of people employed in creative sector/tourism sector	n.
	N. of people employed in the third sector	n.
	N. of employees in supporting institutions for culture	n.
	N. Historical buildings	
	N. Religious buildings	n.
Urban criteria	N. School buildings	n.
	N. or % of well-preserved buildings	n. or %
	N. or % of buildings in poor condition	n. or %
	N. or % of historic building with minor problems	
	N. or % of buildings in ruin	n. or %
	N. or % of improper housing	n. or %
	% of used/partially used historic building	%
	% of unused historic building	%
	N. of historic properties designated as cultural heritage	n.
	N. of restoration and adaptation works undertaken on historic buildings/sites	n.
	% of re-functionalized historic buildings	n./year
	Area of facades of historic buildings rehabilitated	sqm
	% of citizens satisfied with historic buildings quality	%
	% or number of visitors available to make a contribution to heritage restoration	% or n.
Economic criteria	Average price of properties	€/sqm
	Average rent value for residential properties	€/sqm
	Average rent value for commercial-use properties/offices	€/sqm
	N. or % of new residences	n. or %
	N. or % of social housing units	n. or %

(*continued*)

Table 1. (*continued*)

Criteria	Indicators	Unit of measure
	N. or % of office spaces	n. or %
	N. or % of commercial units	n. or %
	N. of new constructions/rehabilitations	n./year
	% of ownership houses/commercial units	%
	% of rented houses/commercial units	%
	Housing/properties vacancy rate	%
	% of real estate owned by public bodies	%
	% of real estate owned by private properties	%
	Increase in taxes related from the tourist tax	€/year %
	N. of artisans registered	n.
	N. of new cooperative enterprises	n./10000 inhab.
	Youth employment rate/Employment rate	%
	N. of people daily working in the historic centre	n./day
	N. or % of jobs in hotels, restaurants, shops, cultural projects, etc. (temporary or permanent, direct and indirect)	n. or %
	N. of creativity jobs supported by digital sectors	n.
	N. of new businesses	n.
	N. or % of new jobs related to typical local production/distribution	n. or %
	N. of businesses in historic centre	n./year
	Average income	€/year
	Average monthly salary	€/month

information gathered and processed allowed us to identify the significant components, select the actions to be included in the alternative scenarios [15, 16].

In a first phase, some keywords emerged from the analysis of the data of the cognitive framework, the needs identified on the site, the situation (in terms of the strengths and weaknesses), and of the potentiality in the context of study. Then, these keywords have been translated into potential actions able to trigger and promote, if supported, real urban regeneration processes guided by culture. Finally, these actions have been elaborated and aggregated (according to four categories of environmental, social, economic and urban criteria) in a strategic map:

- Building Network: Building a network of citizens and visitors.
- Creating Projects: Promotion of creative activities for the territory and facilitate the exchange of ideas and projects.
- Multicultural Integration: Encourage multicultural integration to increase sociality and build meaningful relationships.
- Cultural Promotion: Promote cultural growth and make it accessible to all.
- Sharing: Promote the sharing of knowledge and skills.

- Promotion and Communication: Improve the promotion and hospitality strategy.
- Creating Job: Increase job opportunities and new jobs for economic and social growth; Promoting local agricultural and craft activities.
- Reusing Spaces and Place: Recover and refurbish abandoned and disused spaces and places to give new value and restore the sense of belonging to the unused urban heritage.
- Differentiating the tourist offer throughout the year.
- Improve accessibility.

From the strategic map of the actions it was possible to implement four different urban regeneration alternative scenarios:

1. **Catanzaro as a Smart City**. The goal of this scenario consists in providing a new identity to the area based on the concept of smart city.
2. **Catanzaro as a Cultural, Creative Community Hub**. This scenario is based on the creation of new cultural services for the area, including enhancement of the small economic activities in the area and on the creation of a new urban park.
3. **Catanzaro as Startup**. This project focuses on the creation of innovative business activities in the area.
4. **Catanzaro as Sharing City**. The objective of this project is mainly related to the enhancement of the public spaces in the area, with special attention to innovative shared solution for living and working.

Through the process of knowledge have been identified three suitable central areas for the development of the regeneration program culture-led urban (Fig. 2). These areas characterized by a series of criticalities but also owning considerable transformative potentials. In particular, these areas have all potential triggering of virtuous processes of value building and active co-involvement of the community [16–18]. These areas are to be found in Catanzaro's disused pubblic heritage, they represent areas run-down areas, abandoned industrial buildings and historic disused buildings:

- **Catanzaro Sala**: station hall and surrounding urban area degraded.
- **Gasometro**: degraded urban park with presence unused industrial archaeology goods.
- **Mattonificio**: abandoned industrial park.

In this research have been explored the potentialities of an integrated approach to identify the preferable culture-led urban regeneration scenarios for Catanzaro city (Italy). Through a process of knowledge of the urban contest it was possible to identify and analyse transformation also through shared values, as constitutive elements of the vision of the place. That makes it possible to interact and interpret the transformations in progress by developing an intervention alternative strategies that can guide and support a process of culture-led regeneration.

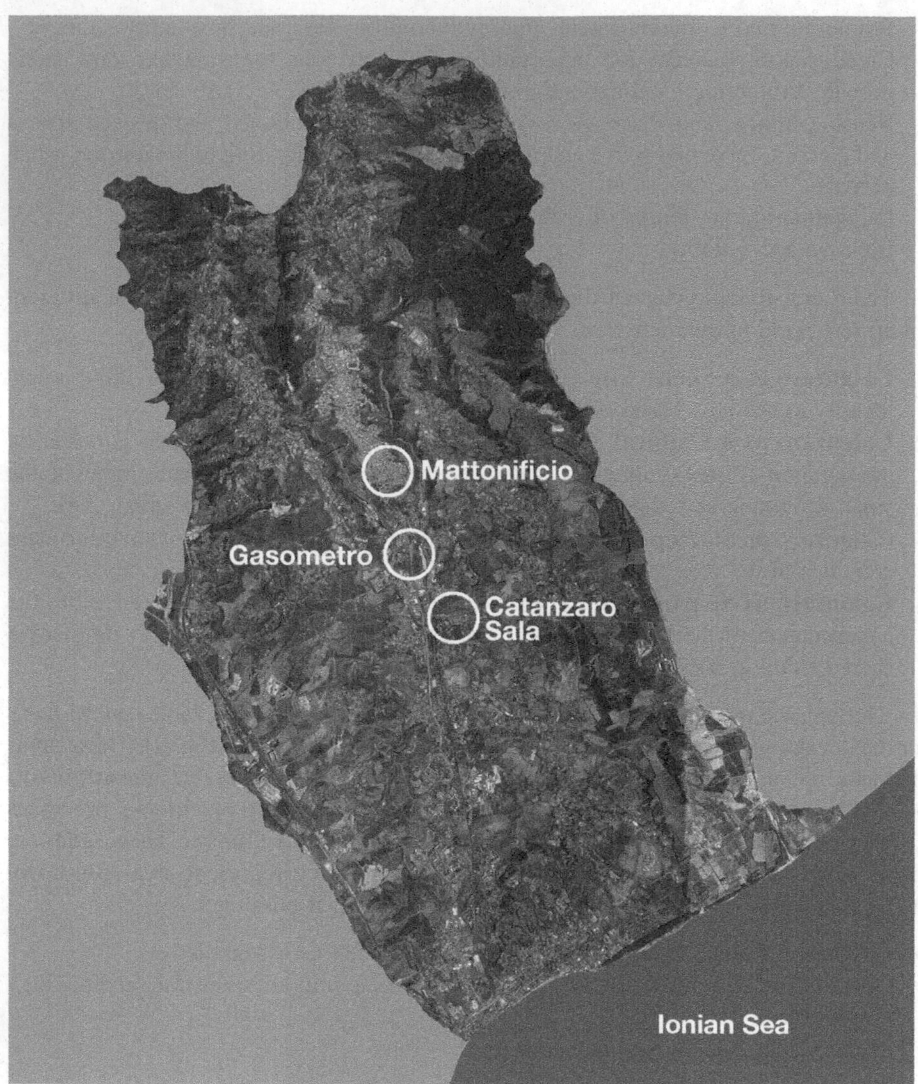

Fig. 2. The three urban areas, aim of culture-led urban regeneration

The Multi-Criteria and multi-group assessment was carried out through the Analytic Network Process (ANP) method, which allows to support the design of shared and transparent planning and design choices, according to a bottom-up approach. The decision-making process, in its different phases and results, allows making explicit the components that significantly influence the local transformations and that could guide the interaction between the different involved stakeholders towards a shared common vision.

Moreover in a preliminary phase, we have subject the future alternatives to:

- Verification of conformity and the best grade of coherence with the prescriptions Municipal Urban Plan [10].
- Verification of the economic and financial feasibility, in order to find the alternative that best preserves the balance between "public benefit" and "private benefit" [19].

However, in this paper, we will illustrate only the Analytic Network Process (ANP) method, which allow to support and assist Decision Makers, Urban planners and Designers in the planning of a strategy of culture-led regeneration structured through a multidimensional decision-making process, in order to build future alternative scenarios and actions through both bottom-up processes and top-down processes [14, 16].

4 Analytic Network Process

For the evaluation of the alternative scenarios for Catanzaro, has been applied the Analytic Network Process (ANP), a Multi-Criteria evaluation method created by T. L. Saaty [20–22] in order to overcome the linear structure of the traditional evaluation methods and to articulate a more dynamic framework, able to consider the complex interactions that characterize the reality. The ANP is a method of supporting decisions that, in addition to the possibility of considering different types of data (quantitative and qualitative), offers the opportunity to assign various weights to the identified criteria, to manage the conflicts between objectives and to deduce the priorities between alternative options. In the ANP method, each decision problem is structured as a network of the elements organized in groups according to multiple reports of the influences. This configuration enables us to find a structure able to incorporate interdependence relationships and feedback. Considering the existence of feedback, in fact, not only alternatives may depend on the criteria, as in a usual hierarchy, but also the criteria may depend on the alternatives and by other elements significant for the decision-making problem [16, 23]. In addition, the method also enables the stakeholders and their points of view to be included in the network.

The information elaborated in the previous knowledge framework was organised into an evaluation matrix consisting of the following categories: objective, criteria, indicators and alternative scenarios. The Multi-Criteria and multi-group evaluation was elaborated by implementing the ANP method [24, 25], with the support of the Super Decision software: the scenarios are compared in pairs in respect to the clusters (criteria) containing the nodes (indicators), which were selected in the previous knowledge framework (Figs. 3 and 4).

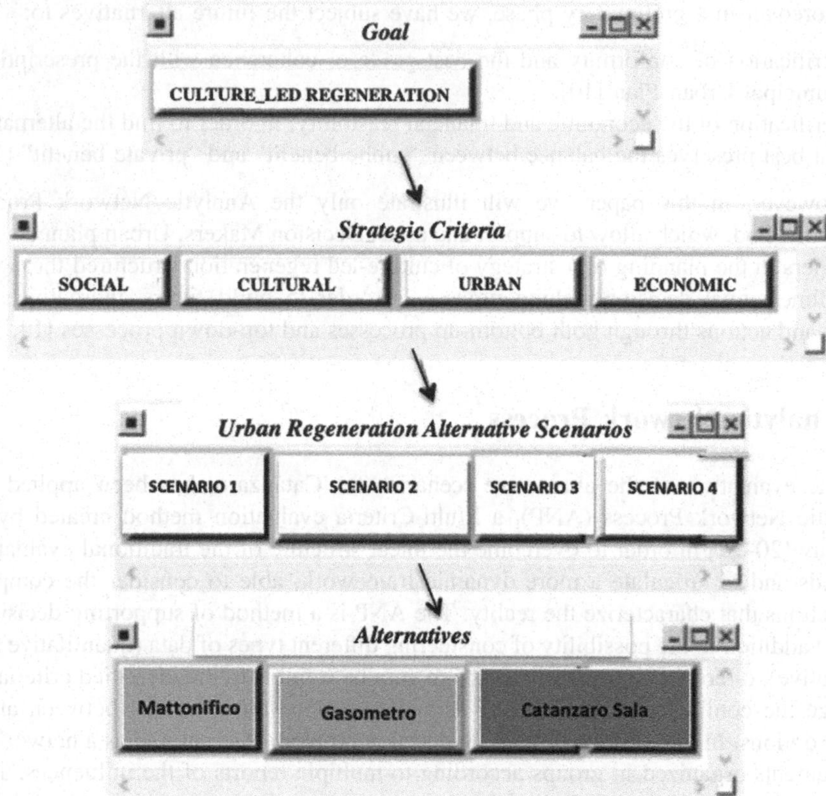

Fig. 3. The structure of ANP model provided by Super Decisions software.

The evaluation process, starting from the map of shared values, identifies the potential actions for the implementation of the preferable scenario for each area and finally return the ranking of the scenarios. Therefore, the most sustainable scenario able to realize the culture-led regeneration strategy is the Scenario 1: **Gasometro-Cultural, Creative Community Hub** with the result of the 39.4%, followed by Scenario 2: **Mattonificio-Smart City** with 31.1% and Scenario 3: **Catanzaro Sala-Sharing City** with 29.5%.

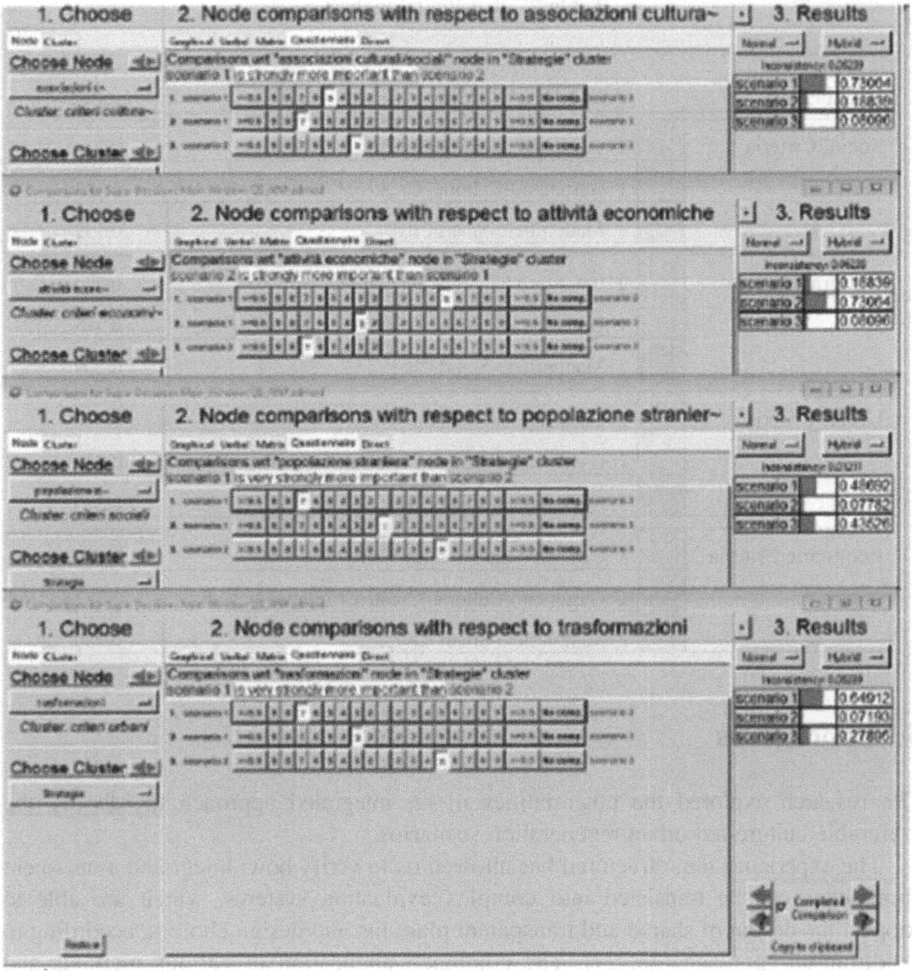

Fig. 4. The ANP supported by the Super Decision software

In order to verify the robustness of the ranking with respect to the selected criteria, a sensitivity analysis was performed (Table 2). It is possible to see how the **Gasometro-Cultural, Creative Community Hub** scenario represents the alternative able to reach the highest scores compared to most of the criteria. Moreover, that scenario satisfies some criteria such as restoration, recovery and re-functioning of the ancient industrial buildings, enhancement, agricultural activity and cultural handcraft, the improvement of the conditions of the reception of the territory, promote recreational activities, increase employment opportunities, enhance the elements characterizing the landscape.

Table 2. Sensitivity analysis

CRITERIA	ALTERNATIVE	Score
Social Criteria	2° Catanzaro Sala-Sharing City	0.234
	1° Gasometro-Cultural, Creative Community Hub	0.323
	3° Mattonificio-Smart City	0.132
Cultural Criteria	2° Catanzaro Sala-Sharing City	0.220
	1° Gasometro-Cultural, Creative Community Hub	0.315
	3° Mattonificio-Smart City	0.209
Urban Criteria	2° Catanzaro Sala-Sharing City	0.320
	1° Gasometro-Cultural, Creative Community Hub	0.328
	3° Mattonificio-Smart City	0.245
Economic Criteria	3° Catanzaro Sala-Sharing City	0.254
	1° Gasometro-Cultural, Creative Community Hub	0.332
	2° Mattonificio-Smart City	0.286

5 Conclusions

The research explored the potentialities of an integrated approach to identify the preferable culture-led urban regeneration scenarios.

The experience thus structured has allowed us to verify how: integrated assessment approaches can be translated into complex evaluation systems, which are able to support the design of shared and transparent planning and design choices, according to a bottom-up approach [26, 27]. The combined application of various methods and techniques, also coming from disciplines not necessarily within the evaluation, enable us to tackle complex decision making, which is characterized by multiple variables and a high level of uncertainty.

In such decision-making contexts, it is necessary to configure an incremental and cyclical process of evaluation, characterized by continuous feedback and constant interactions, useful for delineating a conscious and shared project of transformation and enhancement. In the course of experimentation, the application of an integrated and multi-methodological approach has allowed to take into account the features of the Urban Area under study, the various multidimensional components, the tangible and intangible relations system, and the relative perception of the stakeholders, identifying the weights and identifying the various priorities, selecting actions attentive to context, able to reflect the evolutions of an interactive and dynamic dialogue between the communities, local know-how and experts [28]. At the same time, it is possible to identify some critical issues that are due in some cases to specificities of the context, and in others to the application of the evaluation techniques. The collection of the data requires a careful selection of reliable and updated sources, as well as the availability of the stakeholders identified to collaborate in decision making and to become protagonists in building decisions. A positive issue regards the evaluation with the ANP method, which has allowed an effective interaction between various fields of knowledge and points of view. The use of the ANP approach in an assembly of stakeholders allowed making explicit the preferences and activate an incremental evaluation that enables us increasingly to address the conflicts and to build converging coalitions towards shared visions.

Through a flexible and adaptive methodology path, combining complex evaluation techniques and stakeholder involvement techniques, it is possible to build urban regeneration strategies and promote good governance processes, capable of enhancing the local deliberative democracy by activating effective collaboration between promoters, operators and users [29].

The choices' effectiveness is related to the ability to integrate various sector policies, but also from the consensus that will be devised for intervention alternatives [30]. The success of the path will also depend on the degree of integration that can be achieved through concertation/participation/coordination processes that are in line with sustainable development strategies. This factor implies a large capacity for the coordination of public institutions and the promotion of "good" initiatives with the involvement of private and private-social stakeholders. With the support of integrated assessment approaches, it is possible to start a systemic and active form of preparation for change; they enable building shared actions in a long-term vision in order to develop and build public decision-making effectively.

Acknowledgements. The authors are gratefully to all stakeholder who kindly participated at network.

Author Contributions. Conceptualization, methodological approach and software: Lucia Della Spina; collection, elaboration of the data, cognitive framework: Claudia Giorno, Ruggiero Galati Casmiro; writing-review, editing and supervision: Lucia Della Spina.

References

1. Evans, G., Shaw, P.: The Contribution of Culture to Regeneration in the UK: A Review of Evidence, vol. 4. DCMS, London (2004)
2. Evans, G.: Measure for measure: evaluating the evidence of culture's contribution to regeneration. Urban Stud. **42**, 959–983 (2005)
3. Evans, G.: Cultural Planning: An Urban Renaissance?. Routledge, London (2001)
4. Mangialardo, A., Micelli, E.: Social capital and public policies for commons: bottom up processes in public real estate property valorisation. Procedia - Soc. Behav. Sci. **223**, 175–180 (2016)
5. Garcia, B.: Cultural policy and urban regeneration in Western European cities: lessons from experience, prospects for the future. Local Econ. **19**, 312–326 (2004)
6. Mommaas, H.: Cultural clusters and post-industrial city: towards the remapping of urban cultural policy. Urban Stud. **41**(3), 507–532 (2004)
7. Grandi, R.: Le città creative. Il Mulino **6**, 1037–1044 (2010)

8. Bianchini, F., Parkinson, M. (eds.): Cultural Policy and Urban Regeneration: The West European experience. Manchester University Press, Manchester (1993)
9. Sgaragli, F. (ed.): Enabling social innovation ecosystems for community-led territorial development. Fondazione G. Brodolini, Roma (2014)
10. Mallamace, S., Calabrò, F., Meduri, T., Tramontana, C.: Unused real estate and enhancement of historic centers: legislative instruments and procedural ideas. In: Calabrò, F., Della Spina, L., Bevilacqua, C. (eds.) ISHT 2018. SIST, vol. 101, pp. 464–474. Springer, Cham (2019). https://doi.org/10.1007/978-3-319-92102-0_49
11. Cassalia, G., Tramontana, C., Calabrò, F.: Evaluation approach to the integrated valorization of territorial resources: the case study of the Tyrrhenian area of the metropolitan city of Reggio Calabria. In: Calabrò, F., Della Spina, L., Bevilacqua, C. (eds.) ISHT 2018. SIST, vol. 101, pp. 3–12. Springer, Cham (2019). https://doi.org/10.1007/978-3-319-92102-0_1
12. Nijkamp, P., Rietveld, P., Voogd, H.: Multicriteria Evaluation in Physical Planning. Elsevier, Amsterdam (1990)
13. Fusco Girard, L., Cerreta, M., De Toro, P.: Integrated assessment for sustainable choices. Scienze Regionali **13**, 111–142 (2014)
14. Nesticò, A., Sica, F.: The sustainability of urban renewal projects: a model for economic multi-criteria analysis. J. Prop. Invest. Finance **35**(4), 397–409 (2017). https://doi.org/10.1108/JPIF-01-2017-0003
15. Della Spina, L.: A multi-level integrated approach to designing complex urban scenarios in support of strategic planning and urban regeneration. In: Calabrò, F., Della Spina, L., Bevilacqua, C. (eds.) ISHT 2018. SIST, vol. 100, pp. 226–237. Springer, Cham (2019). https://doi.org/10.1007/978-3-319-92099-3_27
16. Della Spina, L.: The integrated evaluation as a driving tool for cultural-heritage enhancement strategies. In: Bisello, A., Vettorato, D., Laconte, P., Costa, S. (eds.) SSPCR 2017. GET, pp. 589–600. Springer, Cham (2018). https://doi.org/10.1007/978-3-319-75774-2_40
17. Giuffrida, S., Trovato, M.R.: A semiotic approach to the landscape accounting and assessment. An application to the urban-coastal areas. In: Salampasis, M., Theodoridis, A., Bournaris, T. (eds.) 8th International Conference on Information and Communication Technologies in Agriculture, Food and Environment, HAICTA 2017, Chania, Crete Island, Greece, 21–24 September 2017, vol. 2030, pp. 696–708, CEUR Workshop Proceedings (2017). ISSN 16130073
18. Della Spina, L.: Scenarios for a sustainable valorisation of cultural landscape as driver of local development. In: Calabrò, F., Della Spina, L., Bevilacqua, C. (eds.) ISHT 2018. SIST, vol. 100, pp. 113–122. Springer, Cham (2019). https://doi.org/10.1007/978-3-319-92099-3_14
19. Tajani, F., Morano, P., Di Liddo, F., Locurcio, M.: Un'interpretazione innovativa dei criteri di valutazione della DCFA nel partenariato pubblico-privato per la valorizzazione del patrimonio immobiliare pubblico. LaborEst n. 17 (2018)
20. Saaty, T.L.: The Analytic Hierarchy Process, Planning, Priority Setting, Resource Allocation. McGraw-Hill, New York (1980)
21. Saaty, T.L.: Fundamentals of the Analytic Hierarchy Process. RWS Publications, Pittsburgh (2000)
22. Saaty, T.A., Vargas, L.G.: Decision Making with the Analytic Process. Springer, New York (2006). https://doi.org/10.1007/0-387-33987-6
23. Della Spina, L., Ventura, C., Viglianisi, A.: A multicriteria assessment model for selecting strategic projects in urban areas. In: Gervasi, O., et al. (eds.) ICCSA 2016. LNCS, vol. 9788, pp. 414–427. Springer, Cham (2016). https://doi.org/10.1007/978-3-319-42111-7_32
24. Saaty, T.L.: Decision Making with Dependence and Feedback: The Analytic Network Process. RWS Publications, Pittsburgh (1996)

25. Saaty, T.L.: Theory and Applications of the Analytic Network Process. RWS Publications, Pittsburgh (2005)
26. Concilio, G.: Bricolaging knowledge and practices in spatial strategy-making. In: Cerreta, M., Concilio, G., Monno, V. (eds.) Making Strategies in Spatial Planning. Urban and Landscape Perspectives, vol. 9, pp. 281–303. Springer, Dordrecht (2010). https://doi.org/10.1007/978-90-481-3106-8_16
27. Della Spina, L., Scrivo, R., Ventura, C., Viglianisi, A.: Urban renewal: negotiation procedures and evaluation models. In: Gervasi, O., et al. (eds.) ICCSA 2015. LNCS, vol. 9157, pp. 88–103. Springer, Cham (2015). https://doi.org/10.1007/978-3-319-21470-2_7
28. Calabrò, F., Della Spina, L.: Innovative tools for the effectiveness and efficiency of administrative action of the metropolitan cities: the strategic operational programme. In: Advanced Engineering Forum, vol. 11, pp. 3–10. Trans Tech Publications, Switzerland (2014). https://doi.org/10.4028/www.scientific.net/AEF.11.3
29. Calabrò, F., Della Spina, L., Sturiale, L.: Cultural planning: a model of governance of the landscape and cultural resources in development strategies in rural contexts. In: Proceedings of the XVII—IPSAPA Interdisciplinary Scientific Conference, vol. 5, pp. 177–188. Rezekne Higher Educ Inst-Rezeknes Augstskola, Lettonia (2013)
30. Nijkamp, P., Fusco Girard, L.: Le valutazioni per lo sviluppo sostenibile della città e del territorio. Franco Angeli, Milano (1997)

How Urban Resilience Can Change Cities: A System Dynamics Model Approach

Giulia Datola(✉), Marta Bottero, and Elena De Angelis

Interuniversity Department of Regional and Urban Studies and Planning, Politecnico di Torino, Turin, Italy
{giulia.datola, marta.bottero, elena.deangelis}@polito.it

Abstract. Urban resilience is an emerging approach to planning in cities. In last few decades, this concept has been also used as fundamental principle to set up urban development strategies. Urban resilience is a multi-dimensional and dynamic phenomenon and applied to urban planning it leads to cities being considered as complex socio-economic systems. The reason why few cities take appropriate action to enhance their resilience lies in the difficulty of evaluating this process in terms of time. This paper aims to overcome the difficulties which afflict the concept of urban resilience when involved in urban planning, using a System Dynamics Model (SDM) as an evaluation tool to assess how urban resilience can change cities over time, addressing their complexity. This evaluation model is applied to simulate two different urban scenarios for a real case study in the city of Turin (Italy).

Keywords: Urban resilience · Decision-making · System Dynamics Model · Resilient cities · Causality · Strategic planning

1 Introduction

Over the last two decades the concept of resilience has increasingly became recognized as having important role in urban system and more recently it is also employed as an essential principle to set upstrategies for city development [1, 2]. This attention is also due to the fact that a lot of cities across the world are more than ever exposed to a great variety of risks and hazard. These risks include all city dimensions, from the environmental, which is strictly connected to extreme events, to the social and economic [2–5].

Considering the application of this principle to developing urban strategies, urban resilience is not coincided as the return to normality [6]. It is intended as the ability to absorb, adapt and respond to changes in an urban system [7], including various contemporary urban issues, such as sustainability, governance and economic development. For these reasons urban resilience is becoming not only an objective to achieve, but also a necessity to face with the uncertainty, instability and fragility afflicting cities today [3–5, 8].

When applied in planning, urban resilience changes the procedure to define the goal of strategies. It aims to reduce the stresses and hazards which afflicts cities [2–5].

S. Misra et al. (Eds.): ICCSA 2019, LNCS 11622, pp. 108–122, 2019.
https://doi.org/10.1007/978-3-030-24305-0_9

However, few cities around the world take appropriate action to enhance their resilience. This fact is due to the difficulties concerning its concept. Indeed, urban resilience is a multi-dimensional process rather than a static concept and all urban system dimensions should be included [1, 2, 7–9]. Therefore, its definition and the measure of its implication in urban system is difficult.

Designing policies and strategies to built urban resilience underlines the necessity of understanding the dynamics and complexities of urban systems. It also encourages attempts to explain how these dynamics evolve across temporal and spatial scales [2, 10–13].

Planning with the concept of urban resilience has to consider dynamics and feedbacks across a temporal and spatial scale, so it becomes necessary to use projection techniques for anticipating potential future changes and dynamics in the urban system [2]. Considering this complexity and the aim of using urban resilience as a planning tool, it is fundamental to try to propose an evaluation approach which is able to assess the different strategies by analyzing their dynamic behavior over time and to predict how they could change cities across time and spatial scale [10–14]. The main aim is supporting decision makers in the definition and selection of development strategies [9, 12]. This research will adopt a multi-disciplinary approach to urban resilience based on the theory of evolutionary resilience [6]. From this perspective, resilience is not considered as a return to normality, but rather as the ability of socio-ecological systems to change, adapt and transform in response to stresses and strains [7]. This evolutionary understanding of resilience has been articulated using the metaphor of the famous panarchy model of Holling [15, 16]. Under these circumstances, the evaluation of urban transformation scenarios is therefore a complex decision-making problem where different aspects need to be considered simultaneously [2, 10, 12, 13, 17].

Mention has to be made of the fact that, even if the idea of urban resilience is becoming increasingly important for the assessment of urban transformation scenarios, the applications of this concept for supporting real world decision making processes are lacking or very limited [17–23].

Based on the abovementioned assumptions, the proposed paper aims to investigate the problems related to urban resilience, with particular reference to urban strategy development. It tries to elaborate the evaluation framework [17–25] and apply a System Dynamics Model to simulate changes of the city over time, due to the urban resilience scenario [9–13].

In this paper, a System Dynamics Model has been developed and in order to explore and analyze the main elements fostering or hampering resilience [12]. The model has been used to investigate the impact of actions and strategies for resilience improvement on the dynamic evolution of urban system [13, 26–29].

2 Methodology

2.1 Definition and Background

System Dynamics Models (SDMs) are a theoretical and a computer-aided approach applied to dynamic and complex systems defined by mutual interdependence and feedbacks between variables [30]. They are originated by System Dynamics approach (SD).

SD was introduced by Forrester [31–33] at the end of '50s with the aim to solve the problem of insufficient understanding of the strategic processes related to complex systems [34].

SD is considered an effective tool to analyze and describe complex and dynamic systems through the identification of the interdependent relationships between variables [9, 35]. This approach can help to understand the impacts of various factors on defined objectives in a system and provide useful information for decision makers [26, 35].

Forrester's SD methodology provides the guiding principles to develop a computer model which describes complex and dynamic system through the use of feedback loops, stocks and flows (Fig. 2).

System Dynamics Models (SDM) are useful to describe, model, simulate and analyze dynamically complex issues and/or systems in terms of processes, information, organizational boundaries and strategies [35]. It is based on feedback concepts to handle non-linearity, multi-loop and time-lag characteristics of complex dynamic systems.

SDM is an operative approach to help reveal the temporal behavior of complex systems [27] and it can be applied to model and simulate such as complex dynamic systems to understand the dynamics of systems and design management policy for sustainable development [28, 29]. In the last few decades, an increasing amount of SDM application has been recognized in literature [36]. SDMs are currently used for almost any dynamic and complex system that involves a high degree of uncertainty. Important application domains are transportation [26, 37, 38], land use [39, 40], environment management [41], waste management [41], project management [42, 43] and also sustainable urban development [10, 11, 13, 14, 42, 44].

However, there are few existing studies that have used the SDM for simulating and evaluating urban resilience [12], so this is one of the first application.

2.2 Proprieties

A System Dynamics Model is both qualitative/conceptual and quantitative/numerical (Figs. 1 and 2) [9].

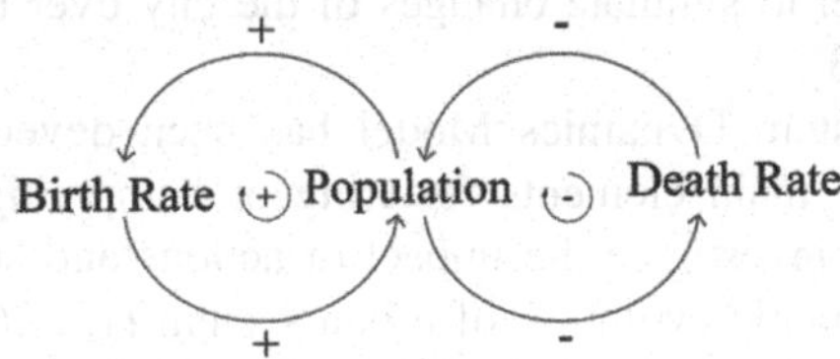

Fig. 1. Population Causal Loop diagram of a population dynamic (Source: [14])

Qualitative modeling can improve the understanding of system functioning [9]. Conceptual modeling is represented by a causal loop diagram [35]. Figure 1 shows a simple single stock model of population where the flow is only due to birth and death [35].

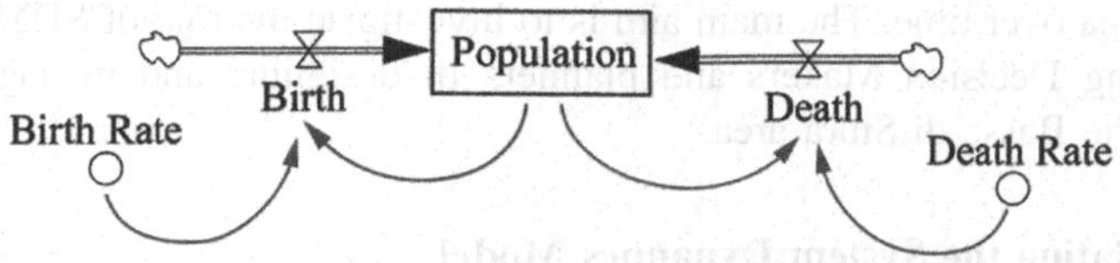

Fig. 2. Stock and flow diagram of a population dynamic (Source: [14], reworked by authors)

Causal loop is a graphic tool used to identify the variables of the system and define the causal effect relationships between them, as shown in Fig. 1. This tool diagrammatically represents the basic mechanism of the system to capture the hypothesis about the causes of its dynamic behavior over time [10, 35]. As Fig. 1 shows, the relationships between the variables can be either positive or negative [35].

Conceptual modelling also makes it possible to better understand the functioning of the system [26, 27].

Quantitative modelling describes the complex system through the stocks and flows model (Fig. 2) [9, 10, 26].

Stock is the first basic building block in SDM. Stocks represent the variables which characterize and describe the condition of the system at any particular time [9, 26, 41, 42]. The second building block in SDM is the Flow. This element tells how stocks change over time [34]. Flows can affect the stocks via inflow or outflow and also interlink the stocks within a system [35]. The third element of SDM is the conveyors, which defines the external inputs to the model. Those variable are related to either externally specified conditions, or to actions/policies [12].

Bases on differential equations, stocks and flows diagram allow the investigation and visualization the effects of different actions within the simulation model over time [10, 11, 43, 44].

3 Application

3.1 Case Study

The case study analysed in this paper aims to define urban resilience strategies for the Basse di Stura area in the city of Turin (Northern Italy). This area is very problematic and its management is complicated. Basse di Stura area is located near the Stura River. Currently, it is a brownfield area, characterized by polluted soil and abandoned buildings exposed to several hazards. Moreover, it is also characterized by complex social and economic conditions, also due to the lack of services [45]. For these reasons, the municipality aims at finding concrete answers to the economic, social, environmental and built environmental needs for this area [45]. In this paper SDM (STELLA®, ISEE Systems Inc.) has been used to investigate and simulate the impacts of two different scenarios, in order to investigate how urban resilience could affect and change the area over time. The main aim is to investigate the role of SDM in assisting and supporting Decision Makers and planners in designing and managing resilient strategy for the Basse di Stura area.

3.2 Articulating the System Dynamics Model

According to the literature [9, 31, 35], System Dynamics Model is generally built in three general steps: (1) Articulation of the problem or conceptualization, (2) Dynamic hypothesis formulation, (3) Testing and analysis. Figure 3 shows the process followed to structure the decision problem for this specific case study, based on the review of SDM application in urban development field [9–11, 13, 29].

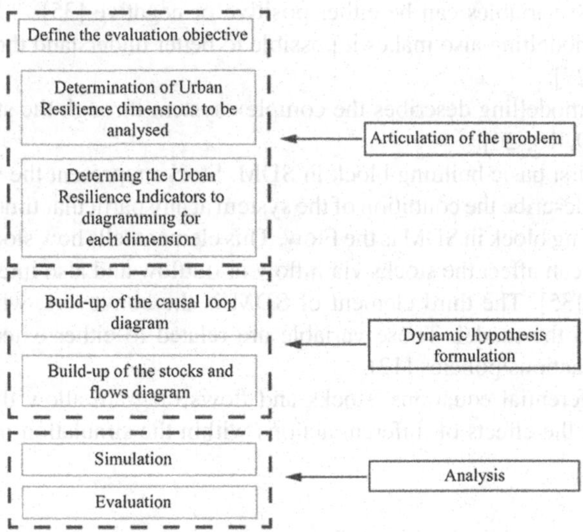

Fig. 3. Structure of decision problem process for the application of SDM (Source: Authors Processing)

3.3 Identifying the Variables of the Model

After the definition of the evaluation objective, in this paper the first step refers to the identification of the urban resilience indicators to be included in the SDM.

For this purpose, a focus group with experts and Decision Makers was organized in order to set up the multidimensional set of variables to be included in the model. As suggested by the literature [2, 17–21, 46], these variables were used both to understand the initial condition of the context and to support planners and Decision Makers in developing strategy and actions to enhance resilience.

It was proposed to the experts and Decision Makers to follow the guideline questions [47] (Table 1) to better identify the appropriate elements from the existing literature of urban resilience indicators [7, 17–21, 25].

Table 1. Questions to be considered (Source: [47])

Who?	Whose Resilience is prioritized? Who is included (and excluded) from the urban system?
What?	What perturbations should the urban system be resilient to? What networks and sectors are included in the urban system?
When?	Is the focus on rapid-onset disturbance or slow-honest changes? Is the focus on short-term resilience or long-term resilience? Is the focus on the resilience of the present or future generation?
Where?	Where are the spatial boundaries of the urban system?
Why?	What is the goal of building urban resilience? What are the underlying motivations for building urban resilience? Is the focus on process or outcome?

Table 2. Urban resilience variables for the SDM (Source: Authors processing)

Dimension	Variables	Description
Economy	New businesses	Number of new businesses created in the area
	Number of jobs	Total number of jobs: existent and news jobs created
Society	Population composition	Percentage of the population differentiation, based on age, sex and ethnicity
	Mixitè index	Index that describes the functional mix of the area
	Health and safety of inhabitants	General condition of health and safety in this area
Built environment	Regeneration	Recovered surfaces
	New construction	New construction land area
	Buildings exposed to hazards	Number of existing buildings exposed to different hazards (example: fire and collapse)
Environment	Permeable surface	Surface of permeable areas
	Soil consumption	Conversion of permeable areas into built areas
	Brownfield	Surface of brownfield area
Governance	Risk reduction	Integration of risk – based planning in the policies for the area
	Funding availability	Municipal budget spent on public services, social protection, investments
	Multi-stakeholders decision planning and decision making	Stakeholders participation in the identification of strategy objectives and actions
	Recovery and restoration	Integration of recovery and restoration in the action plan

Following the questions shown in Table 1, it was possible to identify the key issues on which to intervene (Why? What? Who?) and reasoning about the actions which could be undertaken (Where? When?).

The result of this reasoning process is a multidimensional set of 15 indicators fitted for the case study, which includes the social, economic, environmental and governance dimensions (Table 2).

3.4 Resilient Scenario

Starting from the analysis of Basse di Stura conditions [45] and the identification of the key issues with the support of the guideline questions (Table 1), a preliminary scenario based on urban resilience principle was set up.

The proposed scenario is a medium-long term plan of action (15 years) and it is mainly based on these objectives:

1. Reducing the number of existing buildings exposed to different type of hazards;
2. Reclaiming the brownfield areas;
3. Reducing soil consumption, to try to improve the permeable surface, considering the proximity of the area to the river and also its environmental potentiality;
4. Improving the socio-economic conditions, encouraging the creation of new businesses.

The founding principles of this strategy are the integration of risk reduction, multi-stakeholder decision planning and the recovery and restoration intervention into the strategic plan [23, 24].

The paper considers two different scenarios for the development of the SDM. The inertial scenario thus represents the current plan with no specific actions on the area. The second is the resilient scenario which seeks for the implementation of the transformation of the area, emphasizing the importance of integrating risk reduction, environmental attention and multi-stakeholder participation in the plan actions.

3.5 Causal Loop Diagram

When different variables were identified, it was possible to move to the SDM application. The first phase was to build up the causal loop diagram, as shown in Fig. 4.

To draw the causal loop diagram of the identified variables (Fig. 4) another expert focus group was organized, in which the basis of the cognitive mapping was recalled [48, 49]. In fact, the experts were asked to identify the reciprocal relationships between the chosen multidimensional indicators, considering their expected influence [12]. For example, Fig. 4 shows that "Soil Consumption" has a negative feedback on "Permeable Surface".

Figure 4 represents the identification of the causal relationships between the social, economic, environmental and governance variables, which effects the urban resilience and its performance, referring to the "Basse di Stura" case study.

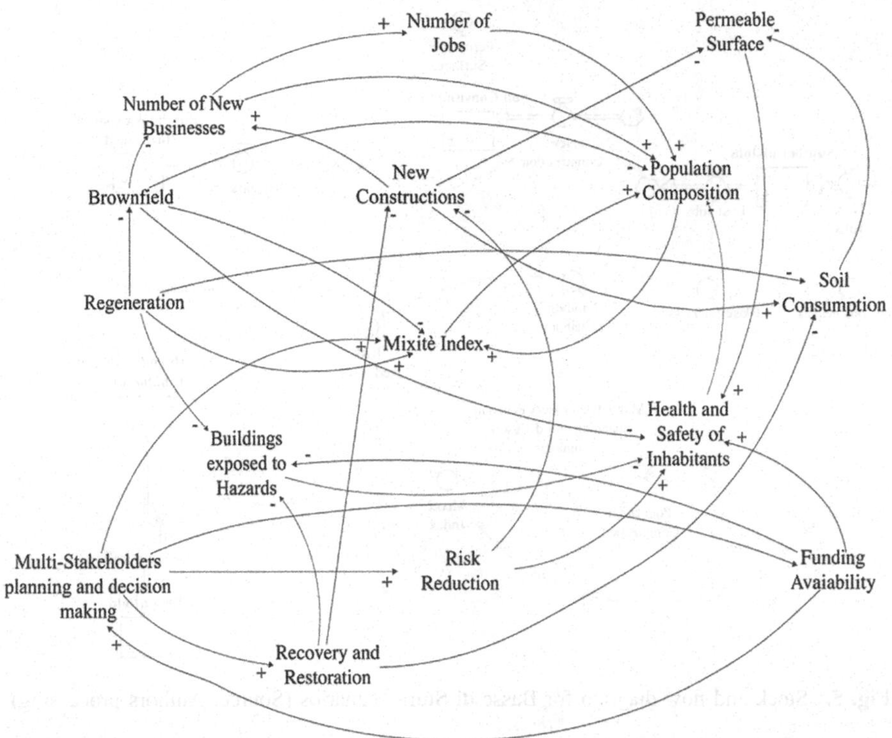

Fig. 4. Causal loop diagram of resilience variables for Basse di Stura scenarios (Source: Authors Processing)

3.6 Stock and Flow Diagram

The conceptual model was used as the basis for stock and flow diagram development. As seen in Fig. 5, some variables have been defined as stock variables and other as flows [14]. However, the strategy principles were translated into the conveyors, because these variables are related to either externally specified conditions, or to actions/policies [12, 35].

The variables identified as stocks are: (1) Brownfield, (2) Health and Safety of the Inhabitants, (3) Buildings exposed to hazards, (4) Soil consumption and (5) Number of Jobs. This choice was made both considering the mutual interdependence between the indicators and the main objectives of the resilient scenario.

Differential equations have been developed for the SDM simulation (Figs. 6, 7 and 8). As an example, we can consider the following equation:

$$\text{Soil Consumption}(t) = \text{soil consumption}(t - dt) + (\text{new construction}) * dt \quad (1)$$

According to this equation, the soil consumption simulation is given by the current soil consumption at the year 0 (Fig. 6) plus the new construction surface.

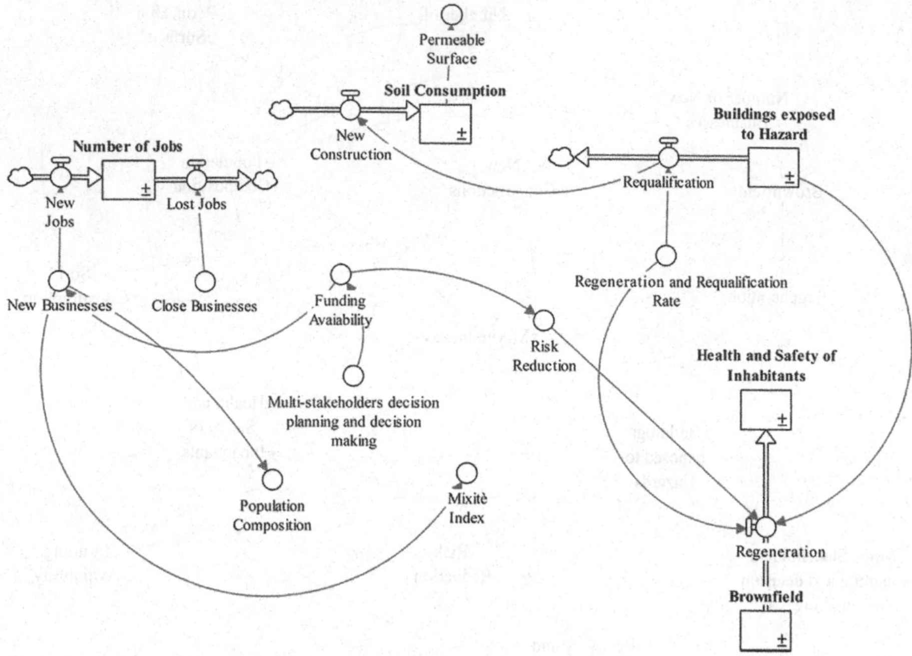

Fig. 5. Stock and flow diagram for Basse di Stura scenarios (Source: Authors processing)

Analogously, other specific equations were developed for the application of the SDM.

It is necessary to reiterate that the aim of this paper is to simulate through the SDM the possible effects over time of scenario inputs and their possible influence in enhancing urban resilience [12].

3.7 Scenarios Simulation and Analysis

The two different scenarios are simulated using SDM (STELLA®, ISEE Systems Inc.), starting from the stock and flow diagram (Fig. 5) which accounts the complexity and dynamic interactions among the multidimensional variables.

The SDM was built to analyze and compare the two different scenarios (inertial and resilient), relying on the prediction of their possible evolution and effects on urban system over time [10, 13, 14].

The main objective of this application was to experiment the use of SDM to evaluate evolution and changes of future transformation scenarios.

In this case, simulations were performed as a "what if" analysis [50] starting form a baseline conditions. The "what if" analysis supports in measuring how changes in a set of independent variables may influence depend variables in a simulation model [12, 35]. Figures 6, 7 and 8 show the results of SDM simulation.

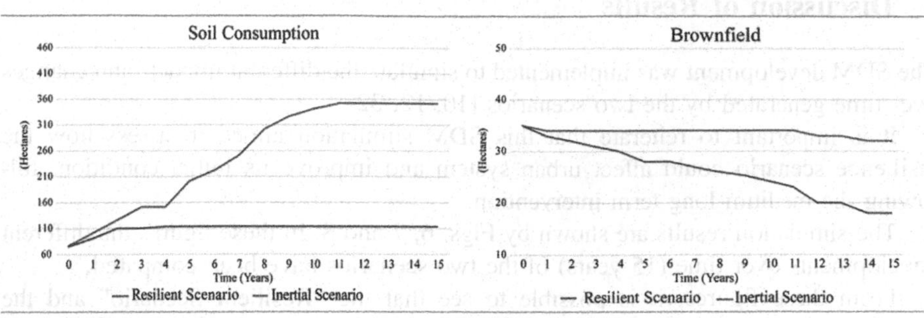

Fig. 6. SDM simulation of environmental variables, scenarios comparison (Source: Authors processing)

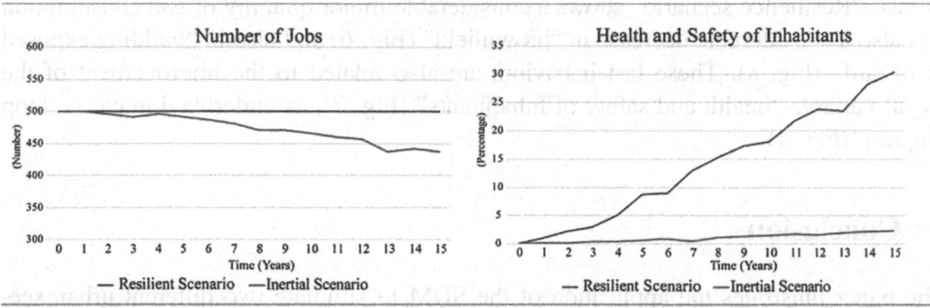

Fig. 7. SDM simulation of economic and social variables, scenarios comparison (Source: Authors processing)

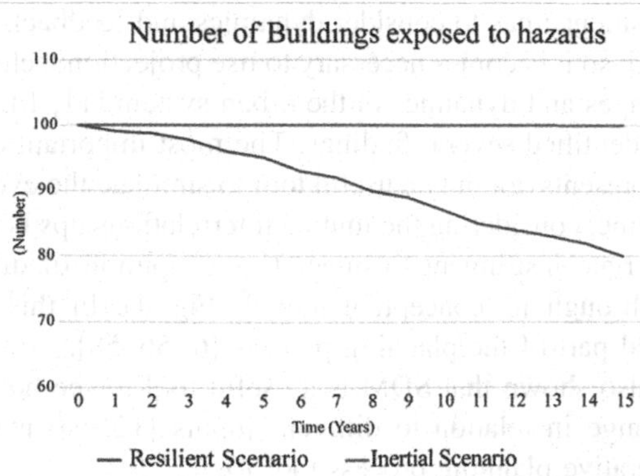

Fig. 8. SDM simulation of built environment variable, scenarios comparison (Source: Author processing)

4 Discussion of Results

The SDM development was implemented to simulate the different impacts and changes over time generated by the two scenarios [10, 12, 32].

It is important to reiterate that this SDM simulation aimed to assess how the resilience scenario could affect urban system and improve its initial condition, following the medium-long term intervention.

The simulation results are shown by Figs. 6, 7 and 8. In these figures the different developments over time (15 years) of the two scenarios have been compared.

From these figures, it is possible to see that the "Resilient Scenario" and the "Inertial Scenario" have significant differences in performance in "soil consumption" and "brownfield" (Fig. 6), "health and safety of inhabitants" (Fig. 7) and "number of buildings exposed to hazard" (Fig. 8). It seems that the resilient scenario could have a positive impact over time in these dimensions, in accordance with its initial objectives. In fact, "Resilience scenario" shows a considerable minor quantity of soil consumption and also a considerable decrease in "brownfield" (Fig. 6) and also in "building exposed to hazard" (Fig. 8). These last behaviors are also related to the improvement of the social variable "health and safety of Inhabitants" (Fig. 7), as underlined in causal loop diagram (Fig. 4).

5 Conclusion

The paper illustrates the application of the SDM to simulate two different urban scenarios, in order to assess how urban resilience applied in planning strategy could affect and change urban system over time.

This application aims to verify the effectiveness of SDM in evaluation of urban resilience strategy [12]. The main objective is to try to answer to the need of measure this multidimensional process by its effects over time [2, 9, 51]. In fact, planning with the concept of urban resilience has to consider dynamics and feedbacks across a temporal and spatial scale [51], so it becomes necessary to use projection techniques to anticipate potential future changes and dynamics in the urban system [11, 14, 17, 52–55].

This study has identified several findings. The most important can be summarized as follows. SDM represents not only a useful tool to simulate the evolutionary behavior of the system over time, considering the mutual interrelationships between its variables, it is also an appropriate instrument to integrate the opinion of different experts and Decision Makers, through its conceptual model (Fig. 4). In this way, participation should be an integral part of the planning process [6, 56–58].

The paper has also shown that SDM is a useful tool to see how the effects of the scenarios could change in relation to different inputs [12], so it should also use as participative and iterative planning process tool [9, 12, 14].

Although the strengths of these important findings, one limitation of this study is the lack of the simulation of the impacts on spatial scale, referred to urban resilience [2, 10, 12, 19]. For this reason, it will be interesting to integrate SDM with GIS to evaluate the effects of urban resilience strategies not only over time but also in spatial scale [10]. It should be an interesting research field in order to introduce and integrated tool which could show processes and impacts in a unique map, to better understand the changes also by Decision Makers.

Taken together, the results of this application demonstrate that SDM is an effective tool for evaluating urban resilience over time, considering its multidimensionality and dynamic behavior.

The application also demonstrates that SDM can be used as tool to set up the strategy and chose the action to be undertaken [59–61], taking into account the opinion and the needs of the different stakeholders [56].

Acknowledgment. Part of the work illustrated in the present paper has been developed in the research project titled VALIUM (Valuation for Integrated Urban Management) that has been supported from the Department of Regional and Urban Studies and Planning - DIST of the Politecnico di Torino (I call 2017).

References

1. Meerow, S., Newell, J.P., Stults, M.: Defining urban resilience: a review. Landsc. Urban Plan. **147**, 38–49 (2016). https://doi.org/10.1016/j.landurbplan.2015.11.011
2. Sharifi, A., Yamagata, Y.: Resilience-oriented urban planning. In: Yamagata, Y., Sharifi, A. (eds.) Resilience-Oriented Urban Planning. LNE, vol. 65, pp. 3–27. Springer, Cham (2018). https://doi.org/10.1007/978-3-319-75798-8_1
3. WEF: The Global Risk Report 2018 13th Edition. http://www3.weforum.org/docs/WEF_GRR18_Report.pdf. Accessed 12 Mar 2019
4. UNISDR: Hyogo Framework for Action 2005–2015: Building the resilience of nations and communities to disasters (2005). https://www.unisdr.org/2005/wcdr/intergover/official-doc/L-docs/Hyogo-framework-for-action-english.pdf
5. UNISR: Sendai Framework for Disaster Risk Reduction 2015–2030 (2015). https://www.preventionweb.net/files/43291_sendaiframeworkfordrren.pdf
6. Folke, C., Carpenter, S.R., Walker, B., Scheffer, M., Chapin, T., Rockström, J.: Resilience thinking: integrating resilience, adaptability and transformability. Ecol. Soc. **15**(4) (2010). http://www.ecologyandsociety.org/vol15/iss4/art20/
7. Desouza, K.C., Flanery, T.H.: Designing, planning, and managing resilient cities: a conceptual framework. Cities **25**, 89–99 (2013). https://doi.org/10.1016/j.cities.2013.06.003
8. Ahern, J.: From fail-safe to safe-to-fail: sustainability and resilience in the new urban world. Landsc. Urban Plan. **100**(4), 341–343 (2011). https://doi.org/10.1016/j.landurbplan.2011.02.021
9. Pluchinotta, I., Pagano, A., Giordano, R., Tsoukiàs, A.: A system dynamics model for supporting decision-makers in irrigation water management. J. Environ. Manag. **222**, 815–824 (2018). https://doi.org/10.1016/j.jenvman.2018.06.083
10. Guan, D., Gao, W., Su, W., Li, H., Hokao, K.: Modeling and dynamic assessment of urban economy-resource-environment system with a coupled system dynamic – geographic information system model. Ecol. Indic. **11**, 1333–1344 (2011). https://doi.org/10.1016/j.ecolind.2011.02.007
11. Park, M., Kim, Y., Lee, H., Han, S., Hwang, S., Choi, M.J.: Modelling the dynamics of urban development projects: focusing on self-sufficient city development. Math. Comput. Model. **57**, 2082–2093 (2013). https://doi.org/10.1016/j.mcm.2011.05.058

12. Pagano, A., Pluchinotta, I., Giordano, R., Vurro, M.: Drinking water supply in resilient cities: notes from L'aquila earthquake case study. Sustain. Cities Soc. **28**, 435–449 (2017). https://doi.org/10.1016/j.scs.2016.09.005
13. Wu, D., Shuang, N.: Dynamic assessment of urban economy-environment-energy system using system dynamics model: a case study in Bejing. Environ. Res. **164**, 70–84 (2018). https://doi.org/10.1016/j.envres.2018.01.029
14. Tan, Y., Jiao, L., Shuai, C., Shen, L.: A system dynamics model for simulating urban sustainability performance: a China case study. J. Clean. Prod. **199**, 1107–1115 (2018). https://doi.org/10.1016/j.jclepro.2018.07.154
15. Holling, C.S.: Resilience and stability of ecological systems. Ann. Rev. Ecol. Syst. **4**, 1–23 (1973). https://doi.org/10.1146/annurev.es.04.110173.000245
16. Holling, C.S.: Engineering resilience versus ecological resilience. Schulze, P. (ed.) Engineering within Ecological Constraints, Washington, DC, USA. The National Academies Press (1996)
17. Sharifi, A., Yamagata, Y.: Principles and criteria for assessing urban energy resilience: a literature review. Renew. Sustain. Energy Rev. **60**, 1654–1677 (2016). https://doi.org/10.1016/j.rser.2016.03.028
18. Sharifi, A.: A critical review of selected tools for assessing community resilience. Ecol. Indic. **69**, 629–647 (2016). https://doi.org/10.1016/j.ecolind.2016.05.023
19. Sharifi, A., Yamagata, Y.: Urban resilience assessment: multiple dimensions, criteria, and indicators. In: Yamagata, Y., Maruyama, H. (eds.) Urban Resilience. ASTSA, pp. 259–276. Springer, Cham (2016). https://doi.org/10.1007/978-3-319-39812-9_13
20. Suarez, M., Gomez-Baggethum, E., Benayas, J., Tilbury, D.: Toward an urban resilience index: a case study in 50 Spanish cities. Sustainability **8**, 774 (2016). https://doi.org/10.3390/su8080774
21. Sellberg, M., Wilkinson, M.C., Peterson, G.D.: Resilience assessment: a useful approach to navigate urban sustainability challenges. Ecol. Soc. **20**(1), 43 (2015). http://dx.doi.org/10.5751/ES-07258-200143
22. Cutter, S.L., Ash, K.D., Emrich, C.T.: The geographies of community disasterresilience. Glob. Environ. Chang **29**, 65–77 (2014). https://doi.org/10.1016/j.gloenvcha.2014.08.005
23. Lazaveric, E., Kekivic, Z., Antonic, B.: In search of the principles of resilient urban design: implentability of the principles in the case of the city in Serbia. Energy Build. **158**, 1130–1138 (2018). https://doi.org/10.1016/j.enbuild.2017.11.005
24. Wilkinson, C.: Social-ecological resilience: insights and issues for planning theory. Plan. Theory **11**(2), 148–169 (2012). https://doi.org/10.1177/1473095211426274
25. Figueiredo, L., Honiden, T., Schumann, A.: Indicators for Resilient Cities, OECD Regional Development Working Papers, 2018/02. OECD Publishing, Paris (2018). http://dx.doi.org/10.1787/6f1f6065-en
26. Yao, H., Shen, L., Tan, Y., Hao, J.: Simulating the impacts of policy scenarios on the sustainability performance of infrastructure projects. Autom. Constr. **20**(8), 1060–1069 (2011). https://doi.org/10.1016/j.autcon.2011.04.007
27. Neuwirth, C., Peck, A., Simonovic, S.P.: Modeling structural change in spatial system dynamics: a Daisyworld example. Environ. Model. Softw. **65**, 30–40 (2015). http://dx.doi.org/10.1016/j.envsoft.2014.11.026
28. Chen, M.C., Ho, T.P., Jan, C.G.: A system dynamics model of sustainable urban development: assessing air purification policies at Taipei City. Asian Pac. Plan. Rev. **4**(1), 29–52 (2006)
29. Zhang, X., Wu, Y., Shen, L., Skitmore, M.: A prototype system dynamic model for assessing the sustainability of construction projects. Int. J. Proj. Manag. **32**(1), 66–76 (2014)

30. Vennix, J.A.M.: Group model-building: tackling messy problems. Syst. Dyn. Rev. **15**(4), 379–401 (1996). https://doi.org/10.1016/j.ijproman.2013.01.009
31. Forrester, J.W.: Industrial Dynamics. The MIT Press, Cambridge (1961)
32. Forrester, J.W.: Principles of Systems. Productivity, Portland (1968)
33. Forrester, J.W.: Lessons from system dynamics modelling. Syst. Dyn. Rev. **3**(2) (1961)
34. Thompson, B.P., Bank, L.C.: Use of system dynamics as a decision-making tool in building design and operation. Build. Environ. **45**(4), 1006–1015 (2010). https://doi.org/10.1016/j.buildenv.2009.10.008
35. Bala, B.K., Arshad, F.M., Noh, K.M.: System Dynamics: Modelling and Simulation. Springer, Singapore (2017). https://doi.org/10.1007/978-981-10-2045-2
36. Kunc, M., Mortenson, M.J., Vidgen, R.: A computational literature review of the field of System Dynamics from 1974 to 2017. J. Simul. **12**(2), 115–127 (2018). https://doi.org/10.1080/17477778.2018.1468950
37. Egilmez, G., Tatari, O.: A dynamic modeling approach to highway sustainability: strategies to reduce overall impact. Transp. Res. Pol. Pract. **46**(7), 1086–1096 (2012). https://doi.org/10.1016/j.tra.2012.04.011
38. Shepherd, S.P.: A review of system dynamics models applied in transportation. Transp. B.: Transp. Dyn. **2**(2), 83–105 (2014). https://doi.org/10.1080/21680566.2014.916236
39. Yu, C.H., Chen, C.H., Lin, C.F., Liaw, S.L.: Development of a system dynamics model for sustainable land use management. J. Chin. Inst. Eng. **26**(5), 607–618 (2003). https://doi.org/10.1016/j.habitatint.2008.02.004
40. Shen, Q., Chen, Q., Tang, B.S., Yeung, S., Hu, Y., Cheung, G.: A system dynamics model for the sustainable land use planning and development. Habitat Int. **33**(1), 15–25 (2009). https://doi.org/10.1016/j.habitatint.2008.02.004
41. Yuan, H., Chini, A.R., Lu, Y., Shen, L.: A dynamic model for assessing the effects of management strategies on the reduction of construction and demolition waste. Waste Manag **32**(3), 521–531 (2012). https://doi.org/10.1016/j.wasman.2011.11.006
42. Güneralp, B., Seto, K.C.: Environmental impacts of urban growth from an integrated dynamic perspective: a case study of Shenzhen. South China. Global Environ. Change **18**(4), 720–735 (2008). https://doi.org/10.1016/j.gloenvcha.2008.07.004
43. Sterman, J.D.: Business Dynamics: Systems Thinking and Modeling for a Complex World (2000)
44. Manetsch, T.J., Park, G.L.: Systems analysis and simulation with applications to economic and social systems. Department of Electrical Engineering and System Science, Michigan State University, USA (1982)
45. Bottero, M.C., Caprioli, C., Berta, M.: Urban problems and patterns of change: the analysis of a downgraded industrial area in Turin. In: Mondini, G., Oppio, A., Stanghellini, S., Bottero, M., Abastante, F. (eds.) Values and Functions for Future Cities. Green Energy and Technology (2019, in press)
46. Cutter, S.L., Burton, C.G., Emrich, C.T.: Disaster resilience indicators for benchmarking baseline conditions. J. Homel. Secur. Emerg. Manag. 7–14 (2010). https://doi.org/10.2202/1547-7355.1732
47. Meerow, S., Newell, J.P.: Urban resilience for whom, what, when, where, and why? Urban Geogr. (2016). https://doi.org/10.1080/02723638.2016.1206395
48. Bottero, M., Datola, G., Monaco, R.: Exploring the resilience of urban systems using fuzzy cognitive maps. In: Gervasi, O., et al. (eds.) ICCSA 2017. LNCS, vol. 10406, pp. 338–353. Springer, Cham (2017). https://doi.org/10.1007/978-3-319-62398-6_24

49. Bottero, M., Datola, G., Monaco, R.: The use of fuzzy cognitive maps for evaluating the reuse project of military barracks in Northern Italy. In: Calabrò, F., Della Spina, L., Bevilacqua, C. (eds.) ISHT 2018. SIST, vol. 100, pp. 691–699. Springer, Cham (2019). https://doi.org/10.1007/978-3-319-92099-3_77
50. Ozemi, U., Ozemi, S.L.: Ecological models based on people knowledge: a multy – step fuzzy cognitive mapping approach. Ecol. Model. **176**, 55 (2004). https://doi.org/10.1016/j.ecolmodel.2003.10.027
51. Batty, M.: Resilient cities, networks, and distruption: editorial. Environ. Plan. B: Urban Anal. City Sci. **40**(4), 571–573 (2013). https://doi.org/10.1068/b4004ed
52. D'Alpaos, C.: Methodological approaches to the valuation of investments in biogas production plants: Incentives vs. market prices in Italy. Valori e Valutazioni **19**, 53–64 (2017)
53. Canesi, R., D'Alpaos, C., Marella, G.: Forced sale values vs. market values in Italy. J. R. Estate Lit. **24**(2), 377–401 (2016)
54. D'Alpaos, C., Bragolusi, P.: Buildings energy retrofit valuation approaches: state of the art and future perspectives. Valori e Valutazioni **20**, 79–94 (2018)
55. Bertolini, M., D'Alpaos, C., Moretto, M.: Do Smart Grids boost investments in domestic PV plants? Evid. Ital. Electr. Mark. Energy **149**, 890–902 (2018)
56. Bottero, M., Mondini, G., Datola, G. Decision-making tools for urban regeneration processes: from stakeholders analysis to stated preference methods. Tema. J. Land Use Mob. Environ. **10**(2), 193–212 (2017). http://dx.doi.org/10.6092/1970-9870/5163
57. Norris, F.H., Stevens, S.P., Pfefferbaum, B., Wyche, K.F., Pfefferbaum, R.L.: Community resilience as a metaphor, theory, set of capacities, and strategy for disaster readiness. Am. J. Commun. Psychol. **41**(1–2), 127–150 (2008). https://doi.org/10.1007/s10464-007-9156-6
58. Peyroux, E.: Discourse of urban resilience and "inclusive development" in the Joannesburg Growth and Development Strategy 2040. Eur. J. Dev. Res. **27**(4), 560–573 (2015). https://doi.org/10.1057/ejdr.2015.52
59. Fastenrath, S., Coenen, L., Davidson, K.: Urban resilience in action: the resilient Melbourne strategy as transformative urban innovation policy? Sustainability **11**, 693–703 (2019). https://doi.org/10.3390/su11030693
60. Brunetta, G., Salizzoni, E., Bottero, M., Monaco, R., Assumma, V.: Measuring Resilience fot territorial enhancement: an experimentation in Trentino. Journal Valori e Valutazioni **20**, 69–78 (2018)
61. Becchio, C., Bottero, M.C., Corgnati, S.P., Dell'Anna, F.: Decision making for sustainable urban energy planning: an integrated evaluation framework of alternative solutions for a NZED (Net Zero-Energy District) in Turin. Land Use Policy **78**, 803–817 (2018)

Automatic Estimate of Depreciated Reproduction Cost for Optimizing the Real Estate Management Through BIM

Benedetto Manganelli(✉), Mauro De Luca Picione, and Sabina Tataranna

School of Engineering, University of Basilicata, Viale dell'Ateneo Lucano, 85100 Potenza, Italy
{benedetto.manganelli, sabina.tataranna}@unibas.it, m.delucapicione@gmail.com

Abstract. Building Information Modeling (BIM) can be defined synthetically as a digital model of a real estate that collects data from the different disciplines that contribute to its realization. In civil engineering, it represents an innovative approach to the construction and management of a building. Cost assessment is a fundamental activity both in the construction phase but especially in the economic management of real estate assets. The use of the BIM makes possible to carry out a rapid and precise estimate of the costs of production, reconstruction or maintenance during the entire life cycle of the building. This work aims to implement the depreciation of real estate assets within a BIM model in order to develop an easy tool to support the economic decisions of those involved in real estate asset management. In particular, the possibility of observing in real time the dynamics of depreciation of the building, placing it in relation, on the one hand, with the dynamics of the land rent and, on the other, with the costs of restoration, can become essential in the choices about times and ways of maintenance, building renovation or eventual razing. The first simulations well confirm the reasons for the research, which is placed in the same direction identified by relevant legislation aimed at the definition of the Real Estate Due Diligence and the digital dossier of the building.

Keywords: Building Information Modeling · Cost value · Depreciation · Economic management

1 Introduction

Building Information Modeling (BIM) represents the most important innovation within the AEC sector (Architectural, Engineering & Construction) [1]. The operators of this sector appreciate the effectiveness of a system that centralizes data and allows continuous and total sharing.

BIM offers the possibility of modeling and managing digital information describing a construction project, from its conception to the end of its life cycle. The BIM methodology, through the search for total sharing, collaboration and communication among all stakeholders, allows the creation of a virtual prototype of the object (whether

S. Misra et al. (Eds.): ICCSA 2019, LNCS 11622, pp. 123–131, 2019.
https://doi.org/10.1007/978-3-030-24305-0_10

it is still to be built or already built) in order to make the building process very efficient both in the implementation and management phases.

The advantages generated by the use of the BIM methodology can be summarized as follows:

- increased sharing, collaboration and communication among all stakeholders, from the client to the user, from technicians to workers and so on;
- possibility of creating a virtual prototype of the object designed before having built it;
- reduction of risks and contingencies on the construction site through the use of software that checks for interference between structural and architectural elements, and systems;
- making analyzes and simulations regarding, for example, the energy or seismic behavior of the building;
- reduction of costs and times;
- optimization of work management.

One of the potentials offered by BIM and on which research has been investing for a long time is to improve the sustainability of the project. Higher levels of sustainability - related to the aspects of structural integrity [2, 3], techniques, construction process and cost - are in fact achievable with the use of tools such as the BIM, which is able to support decisions in choosing the best design solutions or management models [4]. BIM can therefore be used to inform decisions from the earliest stages of building design or restructuring [5].

The integration of data relating to the life cycle cost (LCC) of building components in the BIM platform is fundamental for this purpose [6, 7].

For example, the BIM-integrated approach allows the identification of specific design hotspots that can be displayed on the building model for communicating LCA results and the visual design guide [8–10].

The evaluation of the most advantageous life cycle cost (LCCA Life Cycle Cost Analysis) is one of the support techniques for real estate investment decisions [11]. The analysis involves the comparison between different Life Cycle Costs (LCCs) related to different options regarding the construction and management of the building.

In general, property maintenance involves the enhancement of performance characteristics of the building system, thus an increase of the income capacity and the consequent increase in the property market value.

The convenience of maintenance is therefore a function of the final market value of the building which, in turn, depends on factors that act on urban rent [12]. These factors are characterized by a high uncertainty; we think of urban changes or any changes in the social or economic context, as well as innovations introduced by technological progress in the building production and the consequent new functional and aesthetic requirements. If, on the one hand, forecasting the dynamics of future property values is a complex and uncertain operation, on the other hand, the convenience of the maintenance intervention may also depend on its cost and optimal periodicity, the forecast of which is based on more certain elements.

There are in fact past experiences and databases deriving from the latter, which provide, albeit with some limitations, pointers on the probability of the respective measures.

With regard to the optimal periodicity of maintenance, emphasis must be placed on the concept of standard maintenance or acceptable current limit of the building or its subsystem and on the depreciation concept.

In fact, there is a very strong relationship between depreciation and maintenance. Well-maintained properties show much lower depreciation rates than properties that are subject to poor maintenance.

The graph in Fig. 1 reworks the one proposed by Neto and Bezelga [13]; it provides a useful representation of the difference between the various depreciation factors and their classification. Specially, it is clearly shown that maintenance and refurbishment activities are essential to extend the useful life of the building. In fact, it can be noted that, due to the continuous growth of quality standards (functional obsolescence), the initial quality level, even in the absence of income decay and physical wear, will be below the minimum acceptable one, which therefore defines the threshold of demolition. Even when the building is subject to regular maintenance (curve 1 of Fig. 1), in the absence of modernization interventions, the amount of incurable income decay and physical wear reduce the quality of the building over time and determine an anticipation of the exceeding the demolition threshold, thus producing a reduction in the useful life of the building.

On these premises the research aimed to investigate the possibility of using the BIM methodology in estimating the depreciation of the construction cost, and then assessing the reliability and applicability of the BIM to build a support tool for those involved in asset management estate. The model and the software application that implements it can thus be used in order to evaluate the convenience and optimal periodicity of an extraordinary maintenance intervention on the building or on a part of it.

It should also be noted that the valuation of depreciation has growing importance in the fiscal sphere, when companies (public or private) have the need to enter the balance sheet value of their real estate asset.

2 Notes on Depreciation

In general, depreciation is the loss of value of an asset, caused by various factors all linked to the passage of time (physical wear, functional obsolescence, economic obsolescence). The distinction between economic depreciation and depreciation of the cost is fundamental and preliminary to the estimation approach: the first represents the loss of the market value of the property corresponding to the decrease in time of its utility; the second corresponds to the deduction to be made to the cost of construction or replacement of the building and therefore regardless of the real estate market and its fundamental determinants (supply and demand).

In this work we refer to the depreciation of the cost or to its economic result: the depreciated reproduction cost. The cost value, resulting from the sum of the expenses to be incurred for the production of a building, is in this case better specified as a "reproduction" cost. It is defined as the sum of the expenses to be incurred for the exact duplication of the property, hypothesizing that it should be rebuilt using the same materials and the same production techniques of the time in which it was built. When this is not possible, the value refers to the replacement cost, in other words the sum of

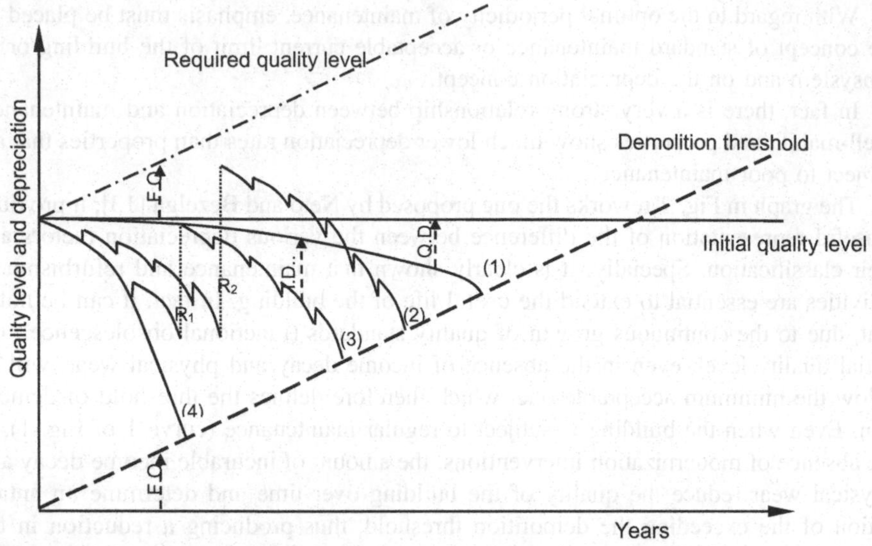

Key:
F.O. = Functional Obsolescence
I.D. = Incurable Income Decay
Q.D.= Quality Decay, due to incurable income decay and physical wear;
(1) = Evolution with very frequent maintenance;
(2) = Evolution with periodic maintenance with redevelopment and modernization (R2);
(3) = Evolution with periodic maintenance with redevelopment (R1) but without modernization;
(4) = Evolution with no maintenance.

Fig. 1. Depreciation evolution due to different factors and for different maintenance hypotheses.

the expenses to be incurred for the construction of a building similar to the existing one as far as possible, to be built with technical and functional characteristics similar to the reference one, using new materials and production techniques, which technological progress has made available.

This cost (new) must then be depreciated to take into account the time elapsed. If we talk about the cost of reproduction and not of construction, the value of the land on which the building stands must then be added to the value of what is built. Take into account that depreciation is a phenomenon that relates exclusively to the built, the value of the land is instead closely linked to the phenomenon of rent and therefore its variation over time is to be linked to the variables that generate the rent.

The estimate of the depreciation of the construction cost is dealt with by applying the model already illustrated in Manganelli [14].

This is an original approach based on the decomposition of the building in its essential functional elements and on the definition of parameters (such as, for example, the duration of life in service, the optimal periodicity and the cost of maintenance) that characterize these elements. The model addresses the estimative problem of depreciation in a rational manner and gives a complete analytical formulation, estimating the depreciation of the individual functional elements through the analytical examination of the factors that determine it.

In this work the depreciation model was implemented in a BIM approach, exploiting the ability of the methodology to manage data.

3 The Model

This research has developed an algorithm implemented in a software capable of developing analysis and estimation of depreciation within a BIM model.

The BIM model of the test building was built with Autodesk Revit software, while the depreciation estimation module was developed through the Dynamo application (Autodesk Inc.) that uses a simple visual programming language.

Dynamo can work as independent software or as a plug-in. Here it was used as a plug-in for Revit.

Dynamo's architecture is based on only two elements: nodes and wires (Fig. 2).

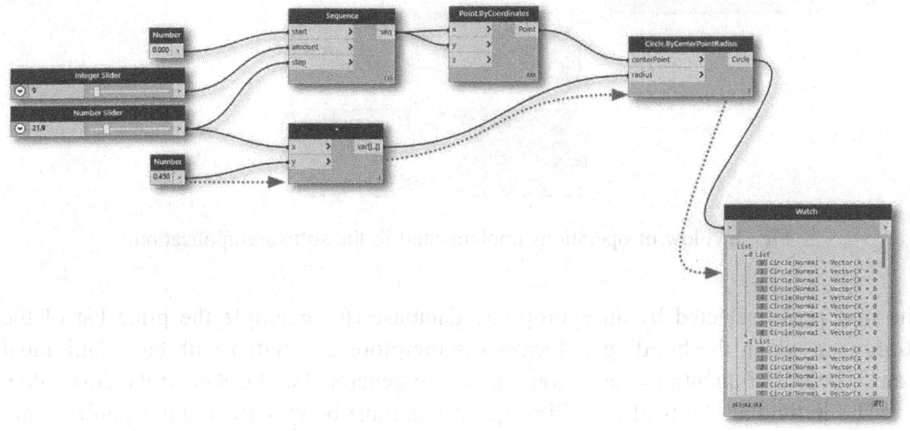

Fig. 2. Sequence of nodes and wires in Dynamo.

Visual programming allows the designer to pay attention only to the information flow even without specific knowledge of the programming language. It is based on the concepts of boxes (nodes) and arrows (wires), where the former are conceived as elements that perform a function and are interconnected by the seconds representing their relations.

In order to automate the estimation of depreciation, the flow of the phases was constructed; in practice the different steps of the estimate are defined in logical sequences then implemented in the packet (Fig. 3).

The input consists of a series of information, partly contained in the BIM model of the building and partly provided as new data.

The BIM model of the building allows the identification of all the workings of the construction process. The measurement obtained using the appropriate scale (surface, volume, weight, etc.) must be connected to each of these items. This data is clearly present in the BIM model and can easily be extracted from it. Through external input,

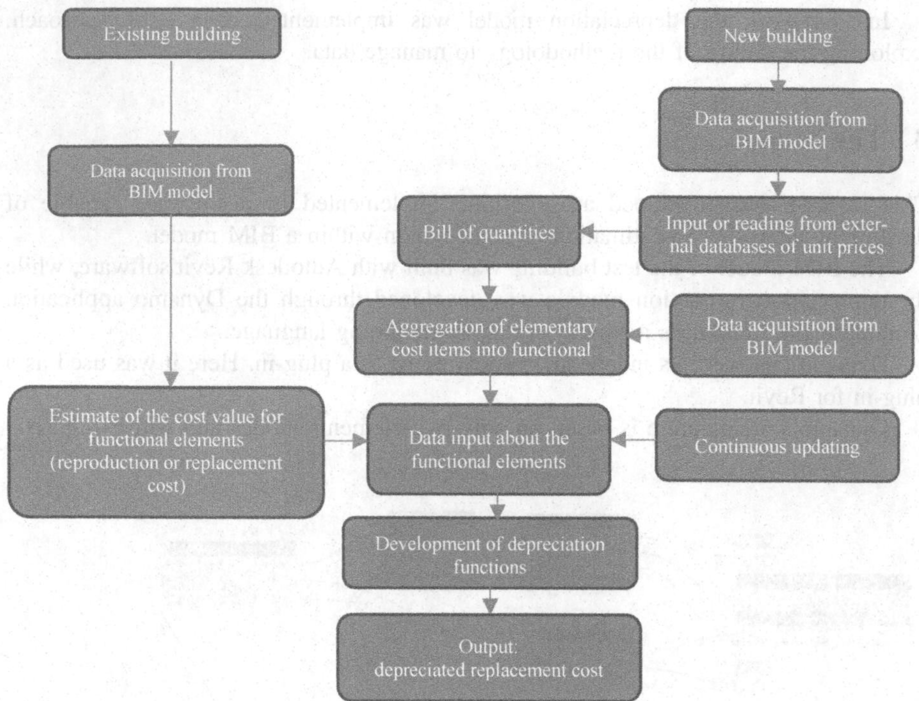

Fig. 3. Flow of operations implemented in the software application.

the unit price, selected by an appropriate database (for example the price list of the Region in which the building is located) is therefore associated with each individual item. The bill of quantities can automatically be generated and obtained the cost value.

The individual items of the bill of quantities must be classified and organized into functional elements. This classification, which is obviously of a higher order than that based on materials and workmanship, groups the latter into elements that perform technologically compatible functions necessary to obtain pre-established services. For example, structures, systems and finishes are macro-categories of this classification; in turn, these can be divided into further and more detailed categories of functional elements (e.g. water system, electrical system, etc.).

This classification is fundamental for estimating the depreciated reproduction cost. The depreciation functions are in fact distinct for each identifiable functional element [15]. Although the equations describing the different depreciation factors are the same in form, they assume different configurations for each functional element in relation to the inputs that characterize them [16, 17]. It is in fact required that the following additional information (second phase) be specified for each functional element:

- age at the time of estimation = estimate year -year of construction (*n*);
- year of the replacement intervention (if carried out);
- year of the extraordinary maintenance intervention (if carried out);
- optimal frequency of maintenance (*s*);

- maintenance costs (*m*), expressed as a percentage of the construction cost as new (*Co*);
- useful life of the element - service life (*v*);
- recovery value at the end of the useful life (*Vr*);
- interest rate (*i*).

The estimate of depreciation involves the separate analysis of the three main factors:

- *Pure age*: it is determined by the progressive reduction of the life in service of the asset.
- *Income decay*: it is related to the lower utility of an asset already in use, compared to the corresponding new one; it is therefore consequent to the expenses to be incurred for extraordinary maintenance interventions capable of restoring its initial efficiency.
- *Functional obsolescence*: it is related to potential variations that occur in the design system, in the materials used or to the poor compliance with new quality standards, but also simply to the introduction of innovative technological systems that have lower operating costs and/or greater efficiency.

Pure age and income decay are two aspects of a single phenomenon: physical wear. The calculation of depreciation due to these two factors (respectively$\Delta Cage$ and $\Delta Cincome$) is developed with the following functions:

$$\Delta C_{age} = (C_0 - V_r)\frac{(1-i)^n - 1}{(1-i)^v - 1} \quad (1)$$

$$\Delta C_{income} = C_0 \cdot m\frac{(1-i)^n - 1}{(1-i)^s - 1} \quad (2)$$

As regards functional obsolescence, given the difficulties generated by the numerous variables involved in the calculation, we proceed to its evaluation in an empirical way. In practice, its effects can be considered by introducing the concept of useful economic life, understood as the period in which that element is used because it constitutes the least expensive solution with respect to its intended use. Therefore, functional obsolescence involves the zeroing of the economic value of the element before the end of its service life. This determines, for the calculation of depreciation by physical wear, the use of the useful economic life (estimated on the basis of experience) instead of useful service life. For most of the elements that make up buildings, functional obsolescence is negligible; it assumes particular importance only for the systems.

Once the depreciation is determined, by subtracting it from the costnew the accumulated depreciation or the final output of the application is determined.

4 The Software

Two versions of the application have been created:

1. extended version, called "*depreciation gb*" (glass box);
2. compact version, called "*depreciation bb*" (black box).

The extended version consists of 131 nodes and 192 arrows; the nodes are collected in 24 groups:

- 6 input groups (with 21 nodes);
- 14 processing groups (with 88 nodes);
- 3 partial outputs groups (with 18 nodes);
- 1 final output group (with 4 nodes).

This version allows precise and punctual control over the operation of the application as it is possible to view and identify any errors.

The compact version was designed for a more practical use, as it is less dispersive than the extended one, presenting a number of nodes reduced to the essential (or better, hidden to the user). In practice there are 23 knots and 23 arrows; the nodes are collected in 8 groups:

- 6 input groups (with 21 nodes);
- 1 partial output group (with 1 custom node);
- 1 final output group (with 1 custom node).

To build it, custom nodes have been used, which allow to enclose within them all the desired nodes, in this specific case the processing and output nodes, leaving visible only the nodes that require user input.

5 Conclusions

BIM allows the collection, sharing and management of information and at the same time their integration in the virtual model of the building. The information is fundamental and necessary to conduct a set of analyses: for example, to simulate the behavior of the building in the design phase, to improve its safety in the construction phase and to allow a deeper knowledge in the management phase.

This research has shown the possibility, starting from the information present in the model and using appropriate tools, to carry out the estimation of the depreciation of the construction or reconstruction cost and automate it to make it dynamically updatable. The automatic estimation of depreciation is possible thanks to the development of a software module that extracts the information associated with each functional element of the work, processes it and returns the depreciated cost, reporting this information in the BIM model. The application was created using visual programming and Dynamo open source software.

The application performs very well the function for which it was designed, but it needs a greater implementation and experimentation; on these operations the future development of the research will concentrate.

References

1. Olatunji, O.A., Sher, W.: Perspectives on modelling BIM-enabled estimating practices. Australas. J. Constr. Econ. Build. **14**(4), 32–53 (2014)
2. Oti, A.H., Tizani, W., Abanda, F.H., Jaly-Zada, A., Taha, J.H.M.: Structural sustainability appraisal in BIM. Autom. Constr. **69**, 44–58 (2016)
3. Vitiello, U., Ciotta, V., Salzano, A., Asprone, D., Manfredi, G., Cosenza, E.: BIM-based approach for the cost-optimization of seismic retrofit strategies on existing buildings. Autom. Constr. **98**, 90–101 (2019)
4. Carvalho, J.P., Bragança, L., Mateus, R.: Optimising building sustainability assessment using BIM. Autom. Constr. **102**, 170–182 (2019)
5. Chong, H.Y., Lee, C.Y., Wang, X.: A mixed review of the adoption of Building Information Modelling (BIM) for sustainability. J. Clean. Prod. **142**, 4114–4126 (2017)
6. Bueno, C., Fabricio, M.M.: Comparative analysis between a complete LCA study and results from a BIM-LCAplug-in. Autom. Constr. **90**, 188–200 (2018)
7. Soust-Verdaguer, B., Llatas, C., García-Martínez, A.: Critical review of bim-based LCA method to buildings. Energy Build. **136**, 110–120 (2017)
8. Röck, M., Hollberg, A., Habert, G., Passer, A.: LCA and BIM: visualization of environmental potentials in building construction at early design stages. Build. Environ. **140**, 153–161 (2018)
9. Najjar, M., Figueiredo, K., Palumbo, M., Haddad, A.: Integration of BIM and LCA: evaluating the environmental impacts of building materials at an early stage of designing a typical office building. J. Build. Eng. **14**, 115–126 (2017)
10. Kehily, D., Underwood, J.: Embedding life cycle costing in 5D BIM. J. Inf. Technol. Constr. **22**, 145–167 (2017)
11. Santos, R., Costa, A.A., Silvestre, J.D., Pyl, L.: Integration of LCA and LCC analysis within a BIM-based environment. Autom. Constr. **103**, 127–149 (2019)
12. Manganelli, B.: Maintenance, building depreciation and land rent. In: 3rd International Conference on Civil Engineering, Architecture and Building Materials, CEABM 2013, Applied Mechanics and Materials, vol. 357–360, pp. 2207–2214 (2013)
13. Neto, F.S., Bezelga, A.A.: Custo e rentabilidadedasintervenções. L.N.E.C, Lisboa (1985)
14. Manganelli, B.: Il deprezzamento degli immobili urbani. Franco Angeli, Milano (2011)
15. Vona, M., Harabaglia, P., Mastroberti, M., Manganelli, B.: About the economic life prediction for existing RC buildings. In: Bakker, J., Frangopol, D.M., van Breugel, K. (eds.) Life-Cycle of Engineering Systems: Emphasis on Sustainable Civil Infrastructure - 5th International Symposium on Life-Cycle Engineering, IALCCE 2016, pp. 2091–2098. CRC Press/Balkema (2017)
16. Del Giudice, V., Manganelli, B., De Paola, P.: Depreciation methods for firm's assets. In: Gervasi, O., et al. (eds.) ICCSA 2016. LNCS, vol. 9788, pp. 214–227. Springer, Cham (2016). https://doi.org/10.1007/978-3-319-42111-7_17
17. Manganelli, B.: Economic life prediction of concrete structure. In: 4th International Conference on Structures and Building Materials, ICSBM 2014, Advanced Materials Research, vol. 919–921, pp. 1447–1450 (2014)

Social Value of Nature Amenities: WTP for the Use of Public Seasides

Pasquale Balena[2], Alessandro Bonifazi[1], and Carmelo Maria Torre[1(✉)]

[1] Department of Civil Engineering Sciences and Architecture, Polytechnic University of Bari, 70125 Bari, Italy
carmelomaria.torre@poliba.it

[2] Department of Civil, Environmental, Land, Building Engineering and Chemistry, Polytechnic University of Bari, 70125 Bari, Italy

Abstract. The value of seaside tourism, its economic dimension, are generated above all by the competitiveness of the coast, especially in sandy beaches, surrounded by valuable landscape contexts, and well connected in terms of services, accessibility, accessibility, and degree of "amenities".

Some parts of the coastal strips are less accessible, due to naturalistic reasons (Sites of community importance, marine parks, protected areas), geomorphological (risk-related problems) and infrastructural (barriers such as the railway line, or the high waterfront); others, on the other hand, enjoy good accessibility, are close to bathing services. In addition to accessibility and support services, the most relevant "physical" indicator is that relating to the ability to accommodate bathers, ensuring the sustainability of the effects on the environment, and social equity. This latter aspect represents a peculiarity of the Italian system of coastal management, as the edge of the coastline is public property, by Constitutional Law, and granted to entrepreneurs through the payment of a fee. The very low value of this Italian form of taxation, however, does not repay the use of natural resources, and often conflicts with European directives (in this case the Bolkenstein Directive) which obliges member states to make a selection among requests for granting the public beach, based on environmental and socio-economic criteria.

Keywords: Social value of nature amenities · WTP for the use of public seasides

1 Introduction

Management of coastal areas in the area of European Community states arena represents one of the more complex activity, for which most of the Member States tried and still try to develop and implement several common strategies, involving economy, research, development and environmental protection. There are many directives and programs that involve coastal areas. The sea is the places of most environmental and ecological services. The data collection of ecological indicators regarding european marine environments, is still on development.

S. Misra et al. (Eds.): ICCSA 2019, LNCS 11622, pp. 132–144, 2019.
https://doi.org/10.1007/978-3-030-24305-0_11

The progressive involvement of the private actor in management of the seaside usually shows a complex procedure, due to the need to shift, even partially from the public domain of marine areas to the private management. In Italy, in fact all the coastline is public, but the license of use of the beach can be accorded with private entrepreneurs. This national rule is on charge on the Italian Marine Regions, that are fifteen on twenty. Regions develop their action plan, that takes in account the peculiarities of each own environmental marine context. Therefore there is a quite complex framework that considers the State, the Region, the Municipalities, having each one of them their proper legislative framework.

The paper explain some relevant aspect of the approach that municipalities have to use in the region of Apulia, where the see represent in various way a main item in the public accounting.

In order to develop regional directives to regulate the licence use at the local level, and by according a set of criteria, the Apulia Regional Government provides the Regional Coastal Plan (RCP) with guidelines for all marine municipalities aiming to produce a "City Coastal Plan" (CCP).

RCP, in the elaborate "Implementation technical standards and general guidelines for the preparation of City Coastal Plan", defines in detail the contents of the CCPs, with reference to the relationships between specific territorial objects, artefacts and works, public uses of the sea and of the coast.

The regional guidelines are

The set of rules of the RCP, establishes the aims of the Municipal Coastal Plan defining it as an "instrument of planning, management, control and monitoring of the coastal municipal territory in terms of landscape protection, environmental protection, guarantee of the right of citizens to access and free use of the natural public heritage, as well as the discipline for its environmentally compatible use. It covers the related public interests:

- the development of the tourism sector, due to its socio-economic implications;
- enjoyment of the asset by the community;
- the protection of the natural environment and the recovery of stretches of coastline that

  they are in a state of degradation, or morphological instability".

In the interpretation given in the RCP, the main objective of the CCP is to pursue economic and social development of coastal areas through the affirmation of the quality and sustainability of the same, outlining defense and government strategies, in the observation that the state current of the coastline is generally affected by a unordered evolution, the effect more than a summation of interventions without any reciprocal connection that of the product of a system logic based on a correct relationship between built environment and natural environment.

The PCC must build a knowledge – base that, according with the national law, is reversed in the National Geographic Information System of Public Domain, to constitute a new, updated system for managing public terrestrial properties.

The last, but not least scope of the CCP is the assessment of the payment due by entrepreneurs for the license of using the coastal line.

The Italian Government establishes a national rate system for marine uses licence that is periodically the rate for square meter, according to a set of categories of marine use. Therefore, since many years the only new decision, is regarding the payment of use licence.

The way of give the use licence highlight show the measure of collaboration between Public Authority and Private entrepreneurs currently represents the unawareness of the municipalities to enjoy of an effective procedure for the convergence of collective interest with the use of public properties.

On one hand the public give the use of coastline also for a major inability to manage all the seaside. On the other hand, the public locates a set of constrains of use for the more environmentally sensible part of the coastline, especially as regards the coastal erosion, the hydrogeological balance and the geomorphological equilibrium and finally the respect of natural areas. The consequence is that the willingness to pay (WTP) is absolutely not the measure for establish a correct fee for a public licence of use of the coastline.

Furthermore, a better the cooperation between the public administration and private investors favors indirectly the sharing of appropriate organizational skills in the transformation and management of the public property assets.

The last, but not least main oddity of the tax-system is that the value is referring at only two level of tourist attractivity of the coast: the yearly fee is 1,38 euros per square meters for all the existing beaches in Italy, classified as normal-touristic attractive, and 2,76 euros per square meters for those beaches classified as "high-touristic attractive". As a consequence, municipalities by the redaction of CCP have to select the coastline sectors, and to classify their belonging to the "normal attractivity" or the "high attractivity".

The paper explains what is the general reasoning that can produce a correct assessment of the beach [1], and depicts a future scenario in case of improvement of the evaluation system of public looking at the methods. The paper is subdivided in several paragraph: in the first is described the context that suggested to the author to experiment the method. In the second the method is explained as regards the scientific framework and the use of the method. Finally, the application the method to the case of study is described in detail.

2 Facts and Data

The case of study regards the application of the City Coastal Plan in a small coastal Municipality of Apulia, the City of RodiGarganico. The territory is extend for about 9.9 km along the north-Gargano coast and appears as a stripe on the map. On 01/01/2018 the Municipality had 6355 residents, of which 1860 women and 138 foreigners. The territory is characterized by some geographical features, representing at the same time a constraint and a stimulus to its economic development.

The municipal territory consists, in fact, of a portion of the northern coast of "Gargano peninsula", connected to a hinterland of limited depth towards the interior, which extends in parallel to the coast itself. Its perimeter seen on the map is reminiscent of an inverted trapezoid, whose northern side represents the coastline, and those to the south continue inland.

The center of Rodi garganico is located at 46 m on the level of the sea, and divides in the middle the municipal territory into two parts, with different morphological characteristics: the Eastside Coast, more impervious and characterized by historical crops, and that of the Westside Coast, more flat and marked by olive-trees and arable crops (Fig. 1).

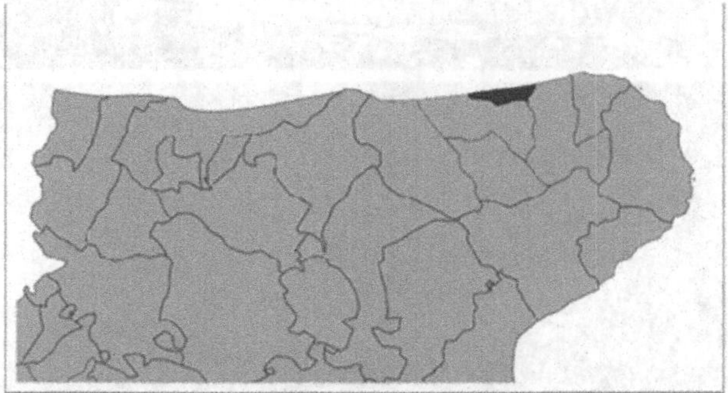

Fig. 1. The position of Rodi Garganico (the darker area in the map) in the North of Apulia

The coastal dynamics of Rodi is affected by the marine meteorological changes and the alternation between phases of advancement of the coast, due to deposition of sand, and the retreat due to marine erosion. In the following figures you can see the variations in depth of beaches and beaches, due to the dynamics mentioned above. In particular, the most significant dynamics are those relating to the east coast, whose dynamics is strongly conditioned by the dynamics related to the port basin, and to the operations of management of the same. It is worth emphasizing that the coastal dynamics has been in constant evolution, and in recent times has "followed the destiny" of the operations carried out in the port basin (dredging, on the seabed, nourishment etc.) alternating phases of retreat and progress. In recent years the retreat has stopped, when the coast has thinned to the point of becoming a sea-side extrusion modelled on the slope on which the state road "SS Garganica" passes. The presence of road works and the seafront at least apparently does not allow further setbacks, but the evolution of the coast is complex (Figs. 2 and 3).

Fig. 2. The ten kms of coast, "cut" in the middle on the promontory where the City of Rodi Garganico and the touristic harbor are laying

Fig. 3. The evolution of the coast near the harbor from 1997 to 2016

Some studies on the suitability of bathing shows that in the whole of 9,260 meters of coastline, 8140 can be usable, and 110 meters unusable. Generally speaking, it should also be considered that many recreational tourist activities take place on the beach or near the beach, outside the area that is conceived to the private entrepreneurs. The development on the coast is related to local condition, more than the general one. But the national law remarks that Municipalities can consider as yearly use fee 2,643€/ m^2 for High Value Coasts (HVC) and 1,322 €/m^2 for Normal Value Coast (HVC).

Due to a problem of lacking funds, the municipality was waiting excessively to redact the Coastal Plan, until when the Apulian Region, according to the law, assigned to a special Public Servant, expert in the matter, the duty to develop a Coastal Plan for the City of Rodi Garganico, and the expert involved a research team of the Polytechnic University of Bari.

During the redaction of the CCP, the team considered interesting to develop a test for identifying the differences between some segment of the coast, according to given criteria, in order to better understand the advantages/disadvantages of simplify due to the National classification of usable seaside. The choice was to subdivide the three coastal section (Westside, City Harbor and Eastside) in sub sections, an to use a spatial multicriteria assessment.

3 Methodological Approach

Multi-criteria assessment represents a methodological approach in problem solving regarding the identification of the best choice among alternatives according to several task/criteria, that in some cases has a practical utility in assessing the sustainability of plans and projects [2–5]. Traditionally, the evaluation of plans and projects preludes to the comparison between different solutions, according a general economic judgment of convenience, in order to understand which solution produces greater complex social use value. The estimation of complex social values is usually multidimensional, and therefore is framed in methodologies that take into account different points of view, which can refer to objectives of equity, environmental protection and increase in economic well-being.

In the field of evaluation of plans and projects, the solutions frequently represent alternative hypotheses (e.g. solutions for reusing a building, solutions among the others for using an area, different location solutions for an activity, etc.) and the criteria are generally of convenience, feasibility, environmental impact [6, 7].

In our case the answer should solve a localization problems: problems related to different localization hypotheses of a given secondary urbanization work, in the face of more possible alternatives provided as, in our case the intended allowed use by planning instrument, which identifies several areas within which it is possible to choose. In other words we can speak of “problems of intended use”: problems relating to identify some areas proportionate according to the plan, for which different locations are possible within a municipal area [8, 9].

The first theoretical step of multiple criteria evaluation is to build a logical model that expresses a “generalized concept” of preference.

By “preference” we mean a relationship between two or more alternative solutions of a problem capable of expressing an *order of priority* among them. This relationship expresses a *criterion of choice*.

This modeling is based on the existence of a binary relationship between a group *non-ordered pairs of solutions* (like ai, aj) of a set {A} that allow to *compare* each other the alternatives of possible alternative solutions, that will be selected according to the development of a ranking.

In the classical formulation the model is presented as follows: Given the solutions a_1, a_2 belonging to the set of alternatives {A} we have:

(1) a_1 P a_2 (preference) it is possible to compare a_1 and a_2, and it is possible to state that a_1 is preferable to a_2 in an absolute manner, because a_1 is preferable to a_2, and the opposite do not make sense;
(2) a_1 I a_2 AND a_2 I a_1(indifference) it is possible to compare a1 and a2, but it is not possible to state that a_1 is preferable to a_2, or that a_2 is preferable to a_1
(3) a_1 I a_2 (incomparability) it is not possible to compare a_1 and a_2

The comparison between two solutions a_1, a_2 will be carried out consequently comparing the values of u(a_1) and u(a_2), where “u” is the utility function with respect to a criterion.

Multicriteria methods are based on different way of comparing before each couple of alternative according each criterion, and after making an aggregation in a single preference ranking, that represents the combination of the others.

In our case we have 8 alternatives and 5 criteria. If the criteria of our set do not have the same importance it is necessary to develop a further step, that is the “*weighting*”.

The method adopted in this case is not the operation of weighting, but the operation of *discriminating*. The discrimination among alternative can be applied in different ways. In this case the evaluation was based on a scale varying from 1 to 5 corresponding to the simplest scale of judgments (“low”, “medium-low”, “medium”, “medium-high” and “high”), associated with a utility function which measures the advantage obtained in relation to the assigned score. The scale of judgments of the criteria foresees therefore five levels of preferability, for five evaluation criteria. If an alternative prevails over all others for all criteria its non-standardized score would be 5, (the sum of five “win” comparison) and the concordance index would be 1.

The utility function has a variable trend from one criterion to another, so in some criteria the score difference is more discriminatory, in others less discriminatory, depending on the trends (concave = less discriminatory, convex = more discriminatory, linear = uniformly discriminatory and “s” = less discriminatory to extreme values). The relevance of the choices with respect to the criteria was also defined through the allocation of weights. The following figures show the tables with the trends of the advantage of the choice (value of the utility) as the scores vary.

Given that the extreme values always remain constant (score0 = utility0; score1 = utility1) regardless of the functions, these are the trends of the laws of variation of utility functions:

- “S” shaped: emphasizes the minimum and maximum values of utility function:fx increases more than the score x if x is higher than the intermediate value of the interval and fy decreases more than the score y is lower than the intermediate value of the interval

- linear shaped: respects the perfect proportionality between scores x and y and value of the utility function fx and fy
- demi-concave shaped: brings the value of the utility function fx of the score x upper than x
- demi-convex shaped: brings the value fx and fy of the utility function of a given scores x and y downer than x and y (Fig. 4)

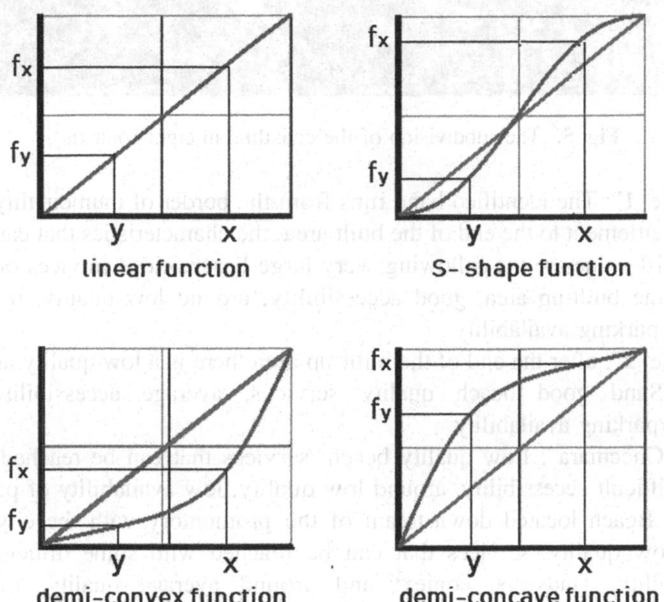

Fig. 4. The discrimination of value in different shaped functions

As already wrote, the choice to weight the importance of criteria by the use of various discriminating rule seems more effective than the traditional one, relating score and functions discriminant character, both in positive and in negative trends.

The considered five criteria are described as follows:

- "Beach depth": the physical depth of the beach (regardless of the depth of the use licensed beach, it is more important a wider and deeper beach than a less wide and shallow one)
- "Services": the greater or lesser presence of services for bathers
- "Accessibility": the greater or lesser presence of access services, vehicular and pedestrian traffic, public transport service stops
- "Parking": the presence of organized parking lots or parking lots along the roads
- "Landscape": the presence of major elements of environmental and/or landscape attractiveness (both natural and architectural and urban)

The alternatives correspond with the subdivision of coastal line in Fig. 5. The coast sectors shift from West to East, identified as follows.

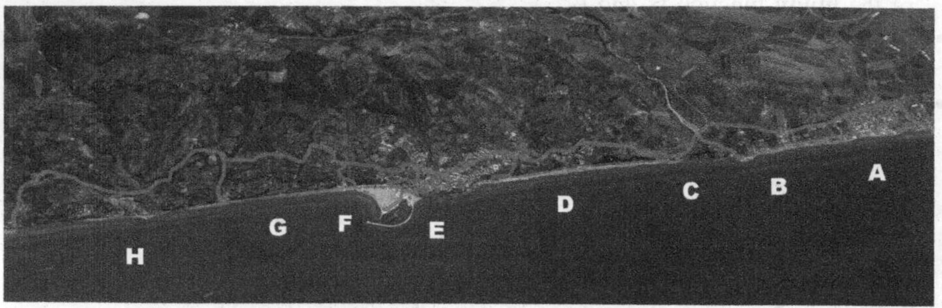

Fig. 5. The subdivision of the coastline in eight contexts

(a) “Ponente_1”: The identified band runs from the border of municipality, hosting a tourist settlement to the end of the built area. the characteristics that can determine the tourist value are the following: very large beach, close services on the beach and in the built-up area, good accessibility, around low quality, medium-high parking/parking availability
(b) “Ponente_2”: after the end of the built-up area there is a low quality area, a small beach Sand good beach quality services, average accessibility, average parking/parking availability
(c) “Punta Cucchiara”: Low quality beach, services that can be reached with difficulty, difficult accessibility, around low quality, low availability of parking
(d) “Ripa”: Beach located downstream of the promontory with the city; medium-sized, low quality, services that can be reached with some difficulty, limited accessibility, landscape context and around average quality, low parking availability
(e) “City – Port”: includes the cliff, a small beach and the port area: services that can be reached on average, accessibility strongly limited by the current regulations for geomorphological risk; landscape context and around of high quality, medium-low availability of parking.
(f) “Levante_1”: it is the area of beach subject to progress due to the effects generated by the presence of the port area, due to the supply of sand due to the presence of the port. whose depth decreases moving away from the harbor basin
(g) “Levante_2”: the second part of the beach, facing east, is less affected by the effects of the harbor area, with dynamics that seem to alternate erosion and progress, although this band does not seem like the further east, where there are problems with erosion.
(h) “Molino - PietreNere”: the area includes the terminal part of the eastern coast of RodiGarganico. It is characterized by a minimum depth of beach, high-quality services but accessible with difficulty, parking difficulties, a landscape remarkable around.

At the end the method is a synthesis between the Concordance analysis, and a fuzzy weighted combination[10].

The test has been carried out with a variation of parameter, with different degree of discrimination. Once the alternative are set and the score have been attributed, the multicriteria approach could be applied. The utility functions have been shaped (see Fig. 6). The next figure shows the most discriminating and the less one pairwise comparison (Fig. 7).

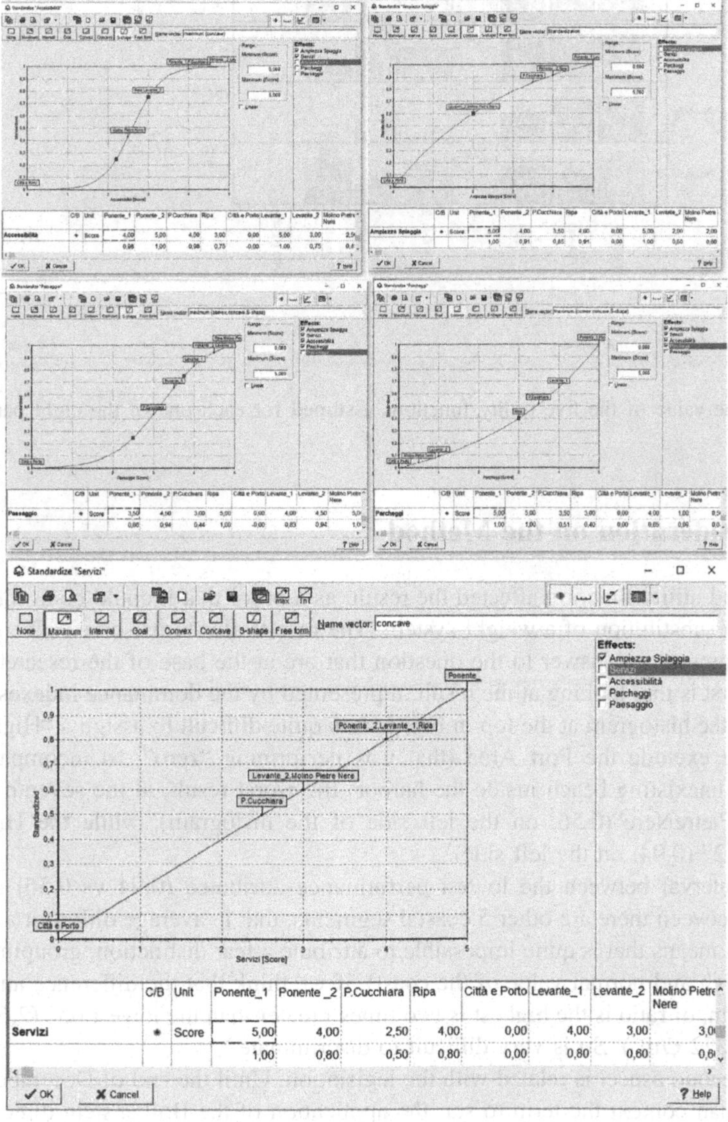

Fig. 6. The graphs show five utility functions corresponding to the criteria, and in evidence the only one that is linear.

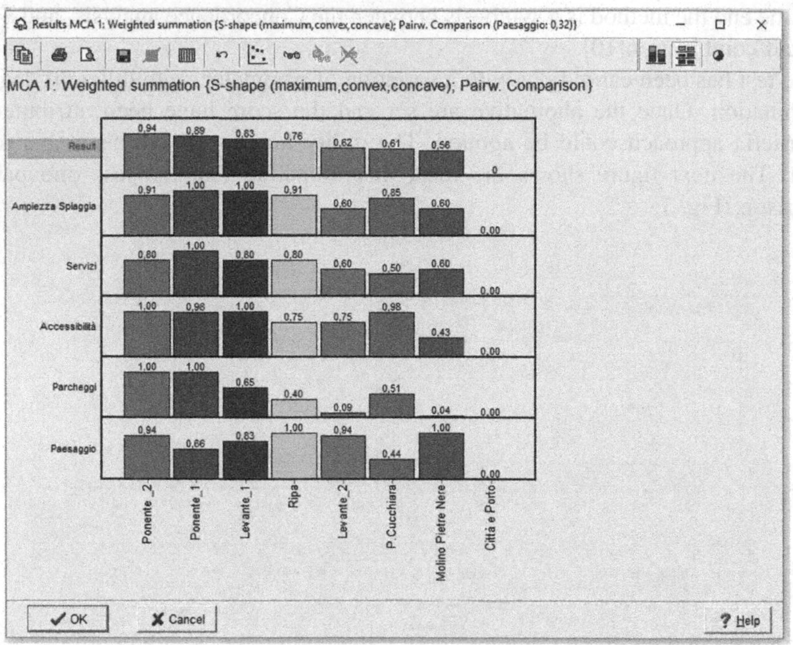

Fig. 7. The value of the five utility functions assumed for each one of the eight parts of the coastline

4 Consideration on the Method

The shaped utility function affected the result, as a proof that it could be as alternative method in substitution of a weight system. The result offer to us some reflections that should represent an answer to the question that are at the base of the research.

The first is that looking at the result, represented by the dominance indexes that are visible at the histogram at the top in Fig. 6, it is quite difficult to assign a “High value” fee. If we exclude the Port Area (that was performing “zero”, as incomparable as regards a unexisting beach inside the harbor) the worst result, at the seventh place is “Molino-PietreNere”(0,56, on the left side of the histogram), while the Highest is “Ponente 2” (0,94, on the left side).

The interval between the lowest performance attributed (0,94 vs 0,56) accounts 0,38. In between there are other 5 coastal segments, that in average differ for a score of 0,06. This means that is quite impossible to attribute a fear distinction, grouping in two cluster (high and normal value of the coast), if we think that the difference among the fees in term, of ratio is the highest is two times greater than the lowest one (2,643 €/m^2 against 1,322 €/m^2). So is very difficult to discriminate.

The second aspect is related with the legislation. Until the end of December, 2018, in the Italian context the term to star the application of the Bolkenstein directive was the first of January, 2020. In the Economic National Plan for the year 2019 the Italian Government refuse to apply immediately the Bolkenstein Directive, and delayed the application until the end of 2034 (more or less fifteen years). This means that our assessment, is destinated to be an experiment for a long timet even if the test shows that is better and more fear to apply a multiscale method to attribute the fee for the use license of the beach in the Public Domain, due to the difficulty to establish a break even point to pass from the normal fee to the high fee.

5 Concluding Remarks

In this paper the focus is related with the correct assessment of the social use value of some part of public environmental heritage[10, 11], and in a special way, the marine seaside. The occasion to think about the question has been given to us just in the case of the application of a regional law of Apulia, that oblige the municipalities to redact a City Coastal Plan (CCP), and to assign a level of taxation of private entrepreneurial use of the public beach, just considering only to two different level: "Normal" and "High". The research started from the hypothesis of change the current regime.

Such values create some non-sense in the perspective to connect the willingness to pay with the public benefit (by tax) of conceding the use of some public property, to have a equilibrate compensation of the use-value of public domain. But we should not forget that, the application of the obligation to assign by bid the use licence, in Italy is shifted further in the future: the application of the obligation of Bolkenstein Directive will be used in Italy in a far future. In a not so unlikely future scenario, when EU could [12] decide an infringement procedure for applying a penalty, maybe the assessment method that is explained in this paper, could be reconsidered not only in theory.

References

1. Torre, C.M., Selicato, M.: The support of multidimensional approaches in integrate monitoring for SEA: a case of study. Earth Syst. Dyn. **4**, 51–61 (2013)
2. Attardi, R., Cerreta, M., Sannicandro, V., Torre, C.M.: Non-compensatory composite indicators for the evaluation of urban planning policy: the land-use policy efficiency index (LUPEI). Eur. J. Oper. Res. **264**(2), 491–507 (2018)
3. Saaty, T.: The Analytic Hierarchy Process: Planning, Priority Setting, Resource Allocation. McGraw-Hill, New York (1985)
4. Torre, C.M., Morano, P., Tajani, F.: Saving soil for sustainable land use. Sustainability **9**(3), 350 (2017)
5. Maria Cerreta, M., Poli, G.: Landscape services assessment: a hybrid multi-criteria spatial decision support system (MC-SDSS). Sustainability **9**(8), 1311 (2017)
6. López Chofre, I., Gielen, E., Jiménez, J.S.P.: Approach to urban metabolism of Almassora municipality, Spain, as a tool for creating a sustainable city. WIT Trans. Built Environ. **179**, 209–219 (2018)
7. Burkhard, B., Kroll, F., Nedkov, S., Müller, F.: Mapping ecosystem service supply, demand and budgets. Ecol. Ind. **21**, 17–29 (2012)
8. Tajani, F., Morano, P.: Concession and lease or sale? A model for the enhancement of public properties in disuse or underutilized. WSEAS Trans. Bus. Econ. **11**, 787–800 (2014)

9. Murgante, B., Borruso, G., Lapucci, A.: Sustainable development: concepts and methods for its application in urban and environmental planning. In: Murgante, B., Borruso, G., Lapucci, A. (eds.) Geocomputation, Sustainability and Environmental Planning. Studies in Computational Intelligence, vol. 348, pp. 1–15. Springer, Heidelberg (2010). https://doi.org/10.1007/978-3-642-19733-8_1
10. Attardi, R., Cerreta, M., Franciosa, A., Gravagnuolo, A.: Valuing cultural landscape services: a multidimensional and multi-group SDSS for scenario simulations. In: Murgante, B., et al. (eds.) ICCSA 2014. LNCS, vol. 8581, pp. 398–413. Springer, Cham (2014). https://doi.org/10.1007/978-3-319-09150-1_29
11. Costanza, R., et al.: The value of the world's ecosystem services and natural capital. Nature **387**, 253–260 (1997)
12. Bolkenstein, F.: The future of European tax policy. EC Tax Rev. **11**, 19 (2002)

International Rankings: A Tool for Comparing Universities Through the Construction of Weighted Indicators

Paola Perchinunno[1(✉)] and Vito Ricci[2]

[1] DEMDI, University of Bari, Via C. Rosalba 53, 70100 Bari, Italy
paola.perchinunno@uniba.it

[2] University Statistics Staff of the General Management, University of Bari, Piazza Umberto I, 70121 Bari, Italy
vito.ricci@uniba.it

Abstract. International rankings are an important communication tool that allows the comparison of Universities according to combinations of different parameters, appropriately weighted. The causes of the widespread diffusion of this information tool are to be found in the process of internationalization of the university system and in the massive increase in the demand and supply of diversified university education. The purpose of the rankings is to allow external subjects to have synthetic and comparable information, for immediate reading, on a university institution. However, often the information rate of the ranking is not combined with a careful examination of the performance indicators that distinguish it and its weighting. The aim of this study is to deepen the methodological aspects of the main global rankings, highlighting the strengths and weaknesses of these tools, while comparing statistical positions to those of the universities that occupy the top place in the rankings.

Keywords: International ranking · Evaluation · Performance · Weighting · Indicators

1 Introduction

In the process of globalization of universities, international rankings have an increasing impact on higher education institutions [1]. International rankings proof to be an important communication tool allowing the comparison of the universities according to combinations of suitably weighted parameters.

The causes of the widespread diffusion of this information tool are to be found in the conspicuous increase in demand and offer of university training in a highly competitive international scenario. The purpose of the rankings is to allow external subjects to have synthetic and comparable information, for immediate reading, on a university institution.

The contribution is the result of joint reflections by the authors, with the following contributions attributed to V. Ricci (chapters 1 and 2), to P. Perchinunno (chapters 3 and 4).

S. Misra et al. (Eds.): ICCSA 2019, LNCS 11622, pp. 145–155, 2019.
https://doi.org/10.1007/978-3-030-24305-0_12

In recent years, the activities related to the international rankings of universities have assumed a growing strategic value due to their undoubted impact both towards foreign students, government agencies, evaluation and communication. In addition, they are used by universities to select partners with whom to conclude cooperation agreements and by some national agencies to give funding or grants to students and/or teachers [2–9].

The criteria and parameters used for the construction of the ranking mainly concern the institutional dimension (number of teachers, staff and students, both national and international), scientific research (number of publications, citations), the reputational survey (Academic reputation and Employer reputation), the economic-financial aspects (income, funds) and the performance of the universities.

The aim of this study is to deepen the methodological aspects of the rankings, highlighting the strengths and weaknesses of these tools. In addition, we will focus on some of the international rankings, synthetically analyzing the indicators considered and the relationship between the positions of some universities using similarity indexes.

2 Main International Ranking

2.1 Introduction

The rankings, according to the type of information analyzed, can be classified into:

1. Global rankings: Times Higher Education World University Rankings (THE), QS World University Rankings, Center for World Rankings (CWUR), Round University Ranking (RUR), Academic Ranking of World Universities (ARWU) and U-Multirank;
2. Search rankings: CWTS Leiden Ranking, Scimago Institution Rankings, Performance Ranking of Scientific Papers for World Universities (Taiwan ranking), University ranking by academic performance (URAP) and Best Global Universities Rankings.

We will focus only on the main global rankings, which consider indicators related to aspects of teaching and research, trying to compare their strengths and their criticalities with respect to the methodologies used and the combinations of appropriately weighted parameters.

2.2 Times Higher Education World University Rankings (THE)

Times Higher Education's mission is to help create the conditions and culture that universities need to succeed, by providing data and insights from the world's top universities. The data for the World University Ranking are: Performance data Universities, Reputation data Academics and Bibliometric data Elsevier. The Times Higher Education World University Rankings 2018 list the top 1,000 universities in the world, making it our biggest international league table to date.

Times Higher Education Ranking uses 13 carefully calibrated performance indicators, provide the most comprehensive and balanced comparisons, and are grouped into 5 areas (Table 1): teaching (the learning environment); research (volume, income and reputation); citations (research influence); international outlook (staff, students and research); and industry income (knowledge transfer). For all indicators except for the Academic Reputation Survey, it is the cumulative probability function using a version of Z-scoring.

Also important is the ranking based on the eleven subjects that diversify the placements on the basis of the different thematic areas of interest in which the universities operate: Arts and Humanities, Social Sciences, Business and Economics, Life Sciences, Physical Sciences, Engineering and Technology, Computer Science, Social Sciences, Law, Education, Psychology, Clinical, Pre-clinical and Health.

Table 1. Performance indicators and weight of times higher education World University Rankings

Areas	Weight	Indicators	Weight
Teaching	30%	Reputation survey	15%
		Staff-to-student ratio	4.5%
		Doctorate-to-bachelor's ration	2.25%
		Doctorates-awarded-to-academic-staff ratio	6%
		Institutional income	2.25%
Research	30%	Reputation survey	18%
		Research income	6%
		Research productivity	6%
Citations	30%	Field Weighted Citations	30%
Industry income	2.5%	Industry research income to academic staff	2.5%
International outlook	7.5%	Proportion of international students	2.5%
		Proportion of international staff	2.5%
		International collaboration	2.5%

Source: elaborations by the authors.

This ranking appears to be balanced both in the choice of indicators and in the weighting system, guaranteeing an overall assessment based on a fairly complete profile of the single universities. However, there is a greater focus on research aspects that, overall (Research and Citations), account for 60% of the total assessment.

2.3 Qs World University Ranking

QS World University Ranking is based mainly on 6 main metrics: Academic Reputation, Employer Reputation, Faculty/Student Ratio, Citations per Faculty, International Faculty Ratio and International Student Ratio. All the indicators are normalized (z-score) so as to vary between 1 and 100; then they are aggregated with weighted average using the ones shown in the following table to obtain the overall score on the basis of which the ranking is achieved (Table 2).

This ranking is strongly influenced by the presence of indicators with very high weights compared to the others. In particular, Academic Reputation and Employer

Table 2. Performance indicators and weight of Qs World University Ranking

Indicators	Weight	Description
Academic reputation	40%	Opinions of over 80,000 experts regarding teaching and research quality at the world's universities based on Academic Survey
Employer reputation	10%	Opinions of over 40,000 employers that indicate those institutions from which they source the most competent, innovative, effective graduates based on QS Employer Survey
Faculty/student ratio	20%	Teacher/student ratios
Citations per faculty	20'%	Total number of citations received in all papers produced by an institution across a five-year period for the number of faculty members at that institution (Elsevier's Scopus database).
International faculty ratio	5%	Percentage of foreign teachers in the total number of teachers
International student ratio	5%	Percentage of foreigners enrolled in the total number of students

Source: elaborations by the authors.

reputation have a significant influence (50%) on the final result, as they assume a significantly higher weight compared to other metrics and are strongly characterized by subjective evaluations of the interviewees rather than by indicators of objective quality.

2.4 Center for World University Rankings (CWUR)

The rankings of CWUR measure the quality of education and training of students as well as the prestige of the faculty and the quality of their research, based on verifiable data and robust indicators. CWUR uses seven indicators to rank the world's top 1000 universities: Quality of Education, Alumni Employment, Quality of Faculty, Research Output, Quality of Publications, Influence and Citations (Table 3).

Table 3. Performance indicators and weight of Center for World University Rankings

Indicators	Weight	Description
Quality of education	15%	Number of a university's alumni who have won major international awards, prizes, and medals relative to the university's size
Alumni employment	15%	Number of a university's alumni who have held CEO positions at the world's top companies relative to the university's size
Quality of faculty	15%	Number of academics who have won major international awards, prizes, and medals
Research output	15%	Total number of research papers
Quality publications	15%	Number of research papers appearing in top-tier journals
Influence	15%	Number of research papers appearing in highly-influential journals
Citations	10%	Number of highly-cited research papers

Source: elaborations by the authors.

This ranking also appears to be well-balanced in the choice of indicators and in the weighting system, ensuring a comprehensive assessment of the different aspects that characterize the quality of a university institution.

2.5 Round University Ranking (RUR)

Round University Ranking (RUR) is published by Rankings Agency and based in Moscow, Russia. The RUR provides comparison of 930 universities according to 20 indicators distributed into 4 areas with equal weights in the measured groups: Teaching, Research, International diversity and Financial sustainability (Table 4). The main types of information to create a ranking are: Bibliometric data obtained from Web of Science Core Collection, Scopus, Google Scholar, etc.; Statistics which include the indicators provided by the universities; Reputational data which collected from specially conducted surveys. In addition to the overall ranking, RUR includes 30 rankings on 6 subject areas: Humanities, Life Sciences, Medical Sciences, Natural Sciences, Social Sciences, Engineering.

This ranking considers in a perfectly balanced way all the aspects useful for a good evaluation of the universities distributing the weighting system between Teaching and Research (40% for each).

Table 4. Performance indicators and weight of Round University Ranking

Areas	Weight	Indicators	Sub weight
Teaching	40%	Academic staff per students	8%
		Academic staff per bachelor degrees awarded	8%
		Doctoral degrees awarded per academic staff	8%
		Doctoral degrees awarded per bachelor degrees awarded	8%
		World teaching reputation	8%
Research	40%	Citations per academic and research staff	8%
		Doctoral degrees per admitted PhD	8%
		Normalized citation impact	8%
		Papers per academic and research staff	8%
		World research reputation	8%
International diversity	10%	Share of international academic staff	2%
		Share of international students	2%
		Share of international co-authored papers	2%
		Reputation outwith the region	2%
		International level	2%
Financial sustainability	10%	Institutional income per academic staff	2%
		Institutional income per students	2%
		Papers per research income	2%
		Research income per academic and research staff	2%
		Research income per institutional income	2%

Source: elaborations by the authors.

3 Comparison Ranking: Limits and Opportunities

3.1 Comparison Between Indicators and Weight Systems

After describing the characteristics and methodologies of the four systems we report a summary of the indicators considered in each of them and their weight systems. In particular, each indicator has a different number of indicators: 13 indicators for THE, 6 indicators for QS, 7 indicators for CWUR and 20 indicators for RUR (Table 5).

Some rankings are mainly based on research or teaching indicators, while others place great emphasis on public opinion surveys. It is evident that the THE and CWUR rankings are characterized by a strong relevance of the indicators linked to aspects of Research, while the RUR ranking is better balanced in the Research/Teaching report. The QS ranking, as already highlighted in the previous paragraph, however, is strongly unbalanced on the aspects related to the reputation of the single universities surveyed.

Table 5. Number of indicators and weight of the different ranking

	Number of indicators				Weight			
	THE	QS	CWUR	RUR	THE	QS	CWUR	RUR
Teaching	5	1	2	5	30%	20%	30%	40%
Research	3		3	5	30%		45%	40%
Citations	1	1	1		30%	20%	10%	
Industry income	1				2,5%			
International outlook	3	2		5	7,5%	10%		10%
Academic reputation		1				40%		
Employer reputation		1				10%		
Financial sustainability				5				10%
Alumni employment			1				15%	
Total	13	6	7	20	100%	100%	100%	100%

Source: elaborations by the authors.

3.2 Comparison of Rankings and Placements

The relationship between global rankings is then analyzed. Of the 17,500 Universities present in the world only 1,000 universities are included in the evaluation of the ranking. In 2018, the TOP 20 universities grouped by nationality see the prevalence of American universities, followed by those of the British. Only eight are European Universities and the rest of the continents are rarely represented [see the discussion by other international authors: 10, 11]. This presence is probably also influenced by the choice of indicators that are best suited to a type of "US" academic reality rather than a "European" one (Fig. 1).

To illustrate the difference between the various rankings, we report the ranking of the top 20 universities in alphabetical order (Table 6).

The various rankings are compared using two measures: Spearman's rank correlation coefficient and Spearman's footrule. The first is a nonparametric measure of rank

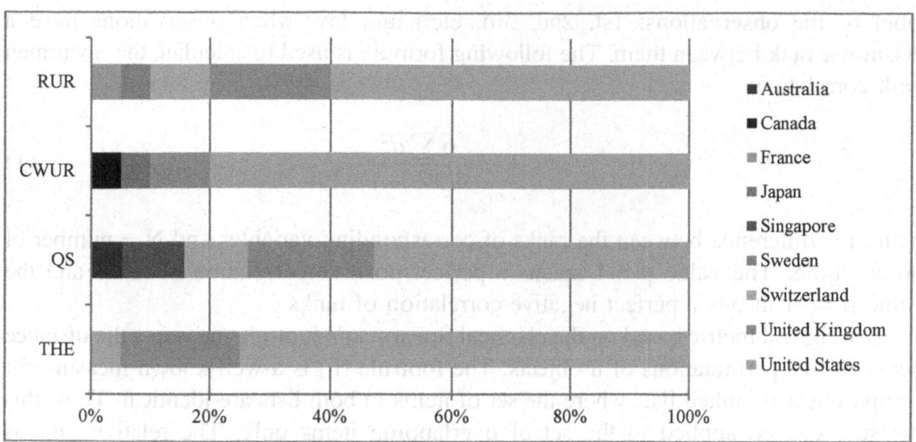

Fig. 1. Classifications of the top 20 university in 2018 by nationality

Table 6. Classifications of the Top 20 universities in 2018 by ranking

	THE	QS	CWUR	RUR
California Institute of Technology	3	4	9	2
Columbia University	14	18	8	8
Cornell University	19	14	14	20
ETH Zurich	10	10	28	15
Harvard University	6	3	1	1
Johns Hopkins University, Baltimore	13	17	16	21
Massachusetts Institute of Technology	5	1	3	6
Northwestern University	20	28	23	19
Princeton University	7	13	7	10
Stanford University	4	2	2	5
University College London	16	7	21	17
University of California, Berkeley	18	27	6	48
University of California, Los Angeles	15	27	15	23
University of Cambridge	2	5	4	9
University of Chicago	9	9	10	3
University of Edinburgh	27	23	34	37
University of Michigan	21	21	18	22
University of Oxford	1	6	5	7
University of Pennsylvania	11	19	13	12
Yale University	12	16	11	14

Source: elaborations by the authors.

correlation that assesses how well the relationship between two variables can be described using a monotonic function [12]. Intuitively, the Spearman's index between two ranks will be high when observations have a similar rank (i.e. relative position label of the observations: 1st, 2nd, 3rd, etc.) and low when observations have a dissimilar rank between them. The following formula is used to calculate the Spearman rank correlation:

$$\rho = 1 - \frac{6\sum d_i^2}{N(N^2 - 1)} \quad (1)$$

with di = difference between the ranks of corresponding variables and N = number of observations. The value ρ = 1 means a perfect positive correlation of ranks and the value ρ = −1 means a perfect negative correlation of ranks.

A weighted metric based on the classical Spearman's footrule measures the distance between two permutations of n objects. The footrule (F) is a well-known measure for comparing two ranked lists where the set of items in both lists are identical. Thus, this measure can be applied to the set of overlapping items only. The relative rank is assigned to each item in both lists. For example, if originally both lists contained 10 elements, but only three of them, a, b and c appeared in both lists, and in list A these elements were ranked 7, 2 and 8, in the list used for computing the footrule, a will be ranked second, b first and c third [13]. The result of the re-rankings is two permutations σ_1 and σ_2 on 1…Z where |Z| is the number of overlapping publications. Spearman's footrule on these transformations [14, 15] is computed as:

$$Fr^{|Z|}(\sigma_1, \sigma_2) = \sum\nolimits_{i=1}^{|Z|} |\sigma_1(i), \sigma_2(i)| \quad (2)$$

When the two rankings are identical on the set Z, $Fr^{|Z|}$ is zero, and its maximum value is $\frac{1}{2}|Z|^2$ if |Z| is even, and $\frac{1}{2}(|Z|+1)(|Z|-1)$ if |Z| is odd. When the result is divided by its maximum value, $Fr^{|Z|}$ will be between 0 and 1, independent of the size of the overlap. Thus, we compute the Normalized Spearman's footrule, NFr, for |Z| > 1:

$$NFr = \frac{Fr(|Z|)}{maxFr(|Z|)} \quad (3)$$

NFr ranges between 0 and 1; it attains the value 0 when the relative ranking of the publications in the set Z is identical. Since we are interested in similarity measures, we define F as:

$$F = 1 - NFr \quad (4)$$

Applying the similarity matrix between the four rankings, we obtain lower values for Spearman's rank correlation coefficient compared to Spearman's footrule (Table 7).

In particular, in the case of Spearman's rank correlation coefficient, which can take values between −1 and +1, positive values are always found. The two most similar rankings are THE ranking and RUR ranking, with a value of ρ = 0.668. On the other hand, similar rankings are QS and CWUR rankings with a value of ρ = 0.259.

As for the Normalized Spearman's footrule which assumes values between zero and one, the relationship between the rankings appears very evident with peaks between THE and QS (F = 0.710) and lower values between QS and CWUR (F = 0.669).

Table 7. Spearman's rank correlation coefficient and Normalized Spearman's Footrule

	THE	QS	CWUR	RUR
	Spearman's rank correlation coefficient ρ			
THE	1,000			
QS	0,607	1,000		
CWUR	0,566	0,259	1,000	
RUR	0,668	0,623	0,605	1,000
	Normalized Spearman's Footrule F			
THE	1,000			
QS	0,710	1,000		
CWUR	0,689	0,639	1,000	
RUR	0,719	0,709	0,669	1,000

From the data analyzed we can, therefore, state that despite the various international rankings being based on different indicators, there is a positive relationship between the different positions of the universities with lower values in the relationship between Qs and CWUR. This factor is justified because the QS ranking is strongly unbalanced on the reputational aspect rather than on objective indicators related to research and teaching, while CWUR is the only ranking that assesses the quality of teaching and research output, without relying on surveys.

4 Conclusions

The rankings on the universities are built on the basis of sets of indicators chosen by the promoters of the rankings. These parameters are typically drawn from public data collections (the number of publications, the number of citations, etc.) or on the basis of data provided directly by the universities being assessed.

The construction of a rating is hardly ever based on a single parameter, but more often results from a combination of parameters, appropriately weighted. The methods of construction and attribution of scores are rarely the object of final user attention. In fact, the information rate that distinguishes the ranking of universities is not combined with the careful examination of the methodological notes that illustrate the criteria for constructing the ranking.

World university rankings are subject to some controversy: subjectivity in the choice of indicators, arbitrary attribution of weights, excessive consideration of the reputational factor, variability in the definition of the classification of results between ordinal/numerical representation and the effective quality of university education [16–21].

Another interesting factor in the international literature is the lack of attention paid to the effects, direct and indirect, that these tools have on students and their university choices. In addition to the need for validity in the rankings they need to be considered as valid and stable [22, 23].

The results reported in this study are undoubtedly encouraging and show how the universities are increasingly willing to become involved to achieve good levels of ranking. The calculated indicators show a strong relationship between the rankings, highlighting how the Top 20 universities occupy high positions in all the classifications analyzed.

As emerges from the international literature [24], however, an awareness campaign would be opportune, aimed at a better communication of the results deriving from the rankings and a review of the indicators and weight systems, which are often not univocally applicable to the specificity of the European universities but strictly linked to the profiles of US universities.

References

1. Altbach, P.G.: The globalization of college and university rankings. Change Mag. High. Learn. **44**(1), 26–31 (2012)
2. Altbach, P.G.: The dilemmas of ranking. Int. High. Educ. **42**, 2–3 (2006)
3. Bastedo, M.N., Bowman, N.A.: College rankings as an interorganizational dependency: establishing the foundation for strategic and institutional accounts. Res. High. Educ. **52**(1), 3–23 (2011)
4. Hazelkorn, E.: Rankings and the battle for world-class excellence: institutional strategies and policy choices. High. Educ. Manage. Policy **21**(1), 55–76 (2009)
5. Hazelkorn, E.: Reflections on a decade of global rankings: what we've learned and outstanding issues. Eur. J. Educ. **49**(1), 12–28 (2014)
6. Huisman, J., Currie, J.: Accountability in higher education: bridge over troubled water? High. Educ. **48**(4), 529–551 (2004)
7. Marginson, S., van der Wende, M.: To rank or to be ranked: the impact of global rankings in higher education. J. Stud. Int. Educ. **11**(3/4), 306–329 (2007)
8. Salmi, J., Saroyan, A.: League tables as policy instruments: uses and misuses. High. Educ. Manage. Policy **19**(2), 31–68 (2007)
9. Williams, R.: Methodology, meaning and usefulness of rankings. Aust. Univ. Rev. **50**(2), 51–58 (2008)
10. Marginson, S.: University rankings and social science. Eur. J. Educ. **49**(1), 45–59 (2014)
11. Billaut, J., Bouyssou, D., Vinke, P.: Should we believe the Shanghai ranking? an MCDM view. Scientometrics **84**(1), 237–263 (2010)
12. Schmid, F., Schmidt, R.: Multivariate extensions of spearman's rho and related statistics. Stat. Prob. Lett. **77**(4), 407–416 (2007)
13. Aguillo, I.F., Bar-Ilan, J., Levene, M., Ortega, J.L.: Comparing university rankings. Scientometrics **85**, 243–256 (2010)
14. Diaconis, P., Graham, R.L.: Spearman's footrule as a measure of disarray. J. Roy. Stat. Soc. Ser. B (Methodol.) **39**, 262–268 (1977)
15. Dwork, C., Kumar, R., Naor, M., Sivakumar, D.: Rank aggregation methods for the Web. In: Proceedings of the 10th World Wide Web Conference, May 2001, Hong-Kong, pp. 613–622 (2001)
16. Dill, D.D., Soo, M.: Academic quality, league tables and public policy: a cross national analysis of university ranking systems. High. Educ. **49**, 499–533 (2005)

17. Frey, B.S., Rost, K.: Do rankings reflect research quality? J. Appl. Econ. **13**(1), 1–38 (2010)
18. Proulx, R.: Higher education ranking and leagues tables: lessons learned from benchmarking. High. Educ. Europe **32**(1), 71–82 (2007)
19. Saisana, M., d'Hombres, B., Saltelli, A.: Rickety numbers: volatility of university rankings and policy implications. Res. Policy **40**(1), 165–177 (2011)
20. Taylor, P., Braddock, R.: International university ranking systems and the idea of university excellence. J. High. Educ. Policy Manage. **29**(3), 245–260 (2007)
21. Tofallis, C.: A different approach to university rankings. High. Educ. **63**(1), 1–18 (2012)
22. Federkeil, G.: Some aspects of ranking methodology. The CHE ranking of German universities. High. Educ. Europe **27**(4), 389–397 (2002)
23. Fidler, B., Parsons, C.: World university ranking methodologies: stability and variability. High. Educ. Rev. **40**(3), 15–34 (2008)
24. Meredith, M.: Why do universities compete in the ratings game? an empirical analysis of the effects of the U.S. news & world report college rankings. Res. High. Educ. **45**(5), 443–461 (2004)

A Multi-dimensional Decision-Making Process for Regenerative Landscapes: A New Harbour for Naples (Italy)

Maria Cerreta(✉), Giuliano Poli, Stefania Regalbuto, and Chiara Mazzarella

Department of Architecture, University of Naples Federico II, Via Toledo 402, 80134 Naples, Italy
{maria.cerreta,giuliano.poli,stefania.regalbuto, chiara.mazzarella}@unina.it

Abstract. The paper aims at testing an evaluative methodology for choosing the best-fit alternative of sustainable development for a complex urban context, stressing advantages and limitations in using Analytic Network Process (ANP) multi-criteria method to rank sustainability indicators, that have been conceived as the criteria - in meaning of control parameters - through which alternatives comparison has been carried out.

The proposed methodology highlighted the relationships between the Sustainable Development Goals (SDG) and the place-based issues in order to define a first step to operationalize the United Nation guidelines, adopting a cross-scale, multi-dimensional and goal-focused approach.

The methodology has been tested on the area of interest which is localized in the eastern part of the Gulf of Naples, in Italy, and falls within the VI District of the City, including "San Giovanni a Teduccio" neighbourhood.

The impact assessment that the design of new harbour will have on surrounding urban districts and the city, in social, economic and environmental terms, is the main issue underpinning the decision-making problem structuring.

Sustainability indicators have been selected from different sources recognized from literature and national and international databases. Thus, each indicator has been categorized, processed and assessed for the focus area by comparing the current scenario with two alternatives development strategies for landscape regeneration.

Keywords: Sustainability indicators · Analytic Network Process (ANP) · Multi-Criteria Decision Aid (MCDA)

1 Introduction

The 17 Sustainable Development Goals (SDGs) and 169 targets of 2030 Agenda for Sustainable Development inform decision-makers, stakeholders and specialists on consistent and generally accepted sustainability issues which needed to be considered when the assessment of best-fit development strategies for complex urban contexts are at stake [1, 2].

S. Misra et al. (Eds.): ICCSA 2019, LNCS 11622, pp. 156–170, 2019.
https://doi.org/10.1007/978-3-030-24305-0_13

While the SDGs depict a global to-do list and plan for the success of all human beings, the purpose of Agenda 2030 at regional scope involves balancing economic, social and environmental dimensions of development [3].

The challenges of the new paradigms of sustainability, afforded by the Landscape Sustainability Science (LSS) [4] and regenerative landscapes framework [5], deal with the research of "place-based" knowledge systems and developmental change methodologies in order to outclass the deterministic approach in favour of stochastic and holistic ones.

The Landscape Sustainability Science (LSS) is concerned with a practical field of application of sustainability theoretical principles. It has been defined as "place-based" and "use-inspired" science, which aims to understand and implement the dynamic relationships that exist between landscape and human activities, through the use of spatially explicit methods [6].

Within a cross-scale perspective for operationalizing sustainability targets, the regenerative development has been considered as developmental change methodology which is able to support the paradigm shift including the principles of LSS and regenerative design. Leveraging on interdependencies among different knowledge domains and interdisciplinary issues, the above-mentioned framework works on multiple scopes to assess development strategies [5, 7].

According to this theoretical background, two main issues addressed by the paper are concerned with:

1. How is the operationalization of the SDGs targets achieved in order to conceive more sustainable development strategies in urban planning and design?
2. Which indicators have to be selected and categorized as proxy parameters to put in practice the sustainability definition?

Moreover, a third question connected to the above-mentioned issues relates to the choice of suitable multi-criteria methods to compare the indicators each other and perform the alternatives' priorities.

When faced with strategies of economic development for the harbour and surrounded complex urban systems, it is necessary to evaluate alternatives in multidimensional terms, considering the interaction of multiple criteria within the decision-making problem structuring [8].

In this perspective, Multiple Criteria Decision Analysis (MCDA) provides a set of theory and methods that give support to structure and solve complex issues encountered in different disciplines and fields of human activity, in which incommensurate and conflicting criteria subsist [9].

Concurrently, the trade-off between economics and ecology is widely known in the Post-Normal Science field as well as many authors have been focusing on the complexity of performing objective evaluations when environmental conflicts are strong [10–13].

The paper aims at testing an evaluative methodology, established in the literature, for choosing the best-fit alternative of development for a complex urban context, stressing advantages and limitations in using Analytic Network Process (ANP) method to rank indicators, that have been treated as the criteria through which the comparison of the alternatives has been carried out.

The proposed methodology has been tested on the area of interest which covers the eastern part of the Gulf of Naples and falls within the VI District of the City, including the neighbourhood of "San Giovanni a Teduccio".

The overall outcome of the paper highlighted that, through procedural rationality and control systems based on place-based indicators, the multi-level strategies can be tested and calibrated in terms of long-term sustainability and resilience.

In summary, the first part of the paper (Sect. 2) shows the purpose of research and methodological approach; the second one (Sect. 3) identifies the case study for which the methodology has been elaborated; the third one (Sect. 4) analyses the results obtained with the evaluation model tools, and the last part (Sect. 5) concerns with discussion and conclusions about the issues afforded.

2 Purpose of Research and Methodological Approach

The purpose of research aims at evaluating scenarios of urban transformation through sustainability indicators and MCDA methods in order to support Decision-Makers in choosing a suitable set of actions and guidelines to activate urban and territorial regeneration processes.

The Organization for Economic Co-operation and Development (OECD) has provided, over the years, guidelines for the activation of Local Agenda 21 processes promoted by the United Nations conference in Rio de Janeiro in 1992. In particular, the methodology proposed by OECD for pursuing sustainable development strategies concerns with the use of analytical tools that are able to facilitate understanding and evaluation of complex issues. These tools relate to indicators, which can be defined, in their broadest sense, as those parameters that are useful to describe the multi-dimensional phenomenon in quantitative or qualitative terms [14, 15].

According to Persada et al. 2018, evaluation indicators can be processed considering [16]:

- Main goals of the evaluation framework;
- Results of stakeholders assessment and public opinion;
- Different targets of sustainable development;
- Different data sources.

In line with these issues, the multi-dimensional approach applied in this research aims at transposing the SDGs targets into place-based indicators in order to conceive Sustainability Indicators to implement for complex landscapes interpretation and evaluation.

As shown in Fig. 1, the methodological workflow has been structured into the following 4 steps:

1. Theoretical background. The first step is concerned with the drivers of research and theory-driven models which are focused on operationalization of sustainability definitions;
2. Decision-Making Problem Structuring. In this phase, the main goal and issues to be afforded are defined, and the evaluation tools are selected;

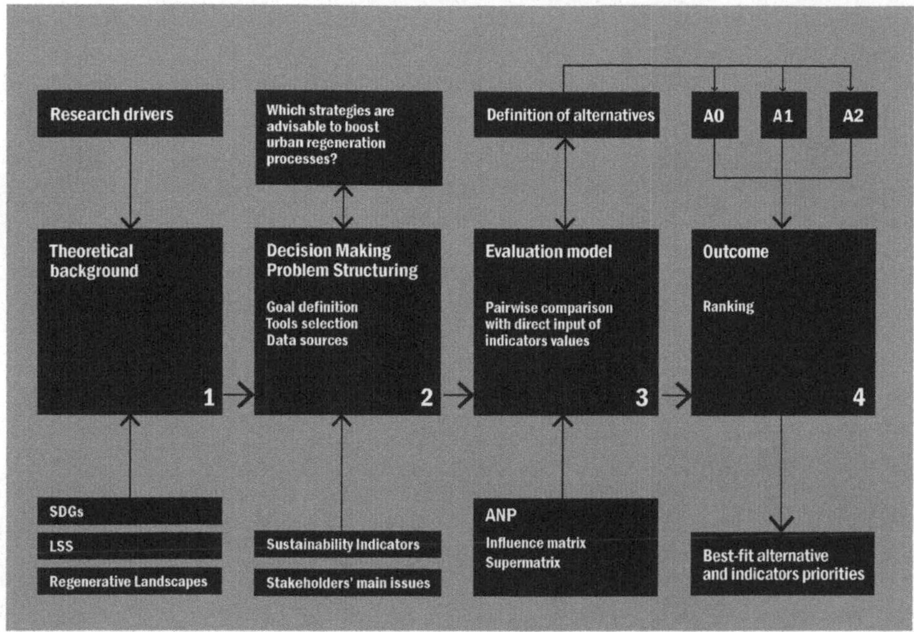

Fig. 1. The methodological workflow

3. Evaluation model. The problem structuring at the previous task leads to the choice of MCDA method and modelling of the decision-making process;
4. Outcome. The last step involves ranking the alternatives, acquiring the priorities and assessing the best-fit scenario.

The methodology has been elaborated and tested on the case study which will be presented and described in the next section (Sect. 3).

3 Case Study

The area of interest is located in the eastern part of the Gulf of Naples and falls within the VI District of the City, including the neighbourhood of San Giovanni a Teduccio. Figure 2 frames the focus area, which extends over the coast of the Tyrrhenian Sea between the residential district and the Port System Authority zone.

Nowadays it is constituted by numerous residential properties and abandoned industrial buildings. The inhabitants are 11,159 and population density is approximately 6,841.9/Kmq. The unemployment rate is 36.5%, while the young unemployment rate is 69.4%. The place is concerned with the changing pattern of land uses, taking into account the strong decrease in demand for industrial activities.

The administrative boundaries are regulated by policy systems both of the Metropolitan City of Naples and the Port System Authority of the Central Tyrrhenian Sea (AdSP), which are the main stakeholders in force.

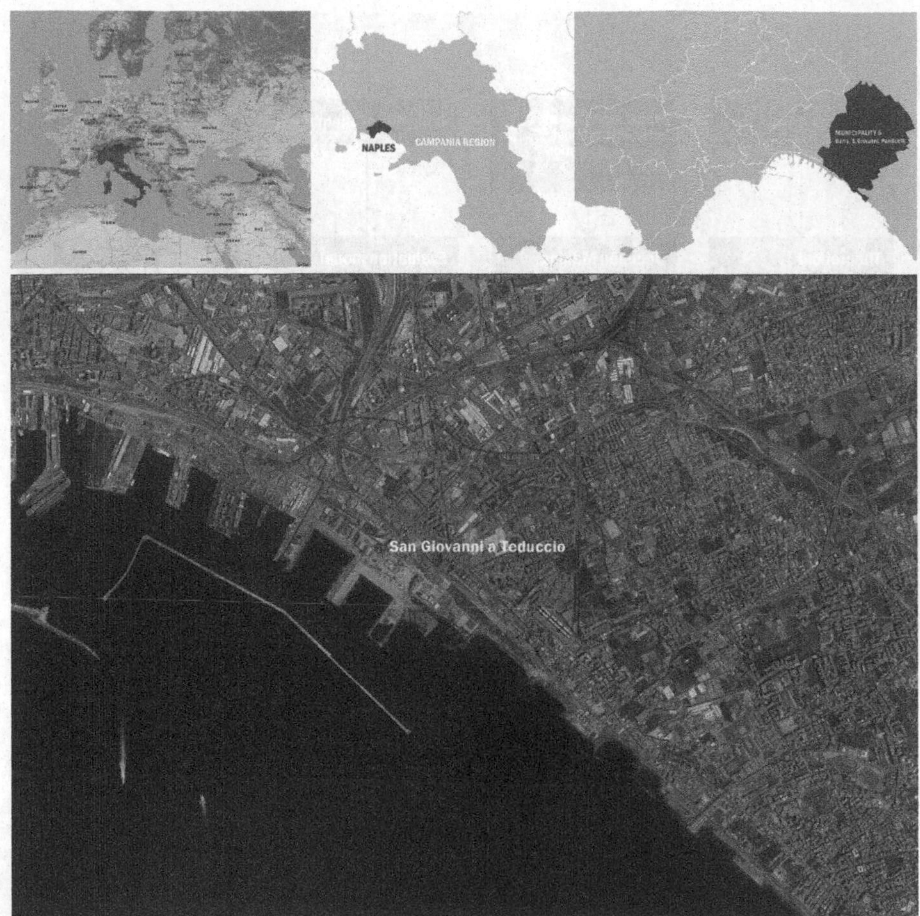

Fig. 2. The focus area in San Giovanni a Teduccio neighbourhood, within the VI District of Naples, Italy

The coastal area of San Giovanni a Teduccio is currently marked by a large number of abandoned industrial buildings and brownfields, strengthening the previous caesura between port and city.

The selection of focus area has been determined according to the coverage of information, data and issues highlighted by the working team of Master's Degree Course Level II in "Sustainable planning and design of port areas", coordinated by prof. Maria Cerreta, during their thesis elaboration for the academic year 2016–2017.

4 Decision-Making Problem Structuring with ANP

The general question underlying the structure of the decision-making problem is the following:

– Which alternative urban regeneration processes of the East Naples harbour is preferable to activate for the neighbourhood of "San Giovanni a Teduccio"?

Starting from the main issue, the decision-making problem has been structured according to ANP method and with the support of "Super Decisions" software v.3 [17]. ANP is a Multiple Criteria Decision Aid (MCDA) method that allows outclassing the rigidity of the Analytic Hierarchy Process (AHP), taking into account inner and outer dependencies among sets of criteria [18, 19].

By defining the sets or clusters - i.e. goal, criteria and alternatives - which contain subsets or nodes - i.e. the inner elements characterizing criteria - the global priorities of alternatives can be obtained with the pairwise comparison technique.

In the case study, five domains - corresponding to: Economic Growth and Development (EGD), Traffic Accessibility (TA), Urban Metabolism (UM), Society and Culture (SC), and Urban Landscape Quality (ULQ) - have been conceived as clusters of the network; while sixteen sustainability indicators, distributed into each five clusters, represent the nodes of network, as shown in Fig. 3.

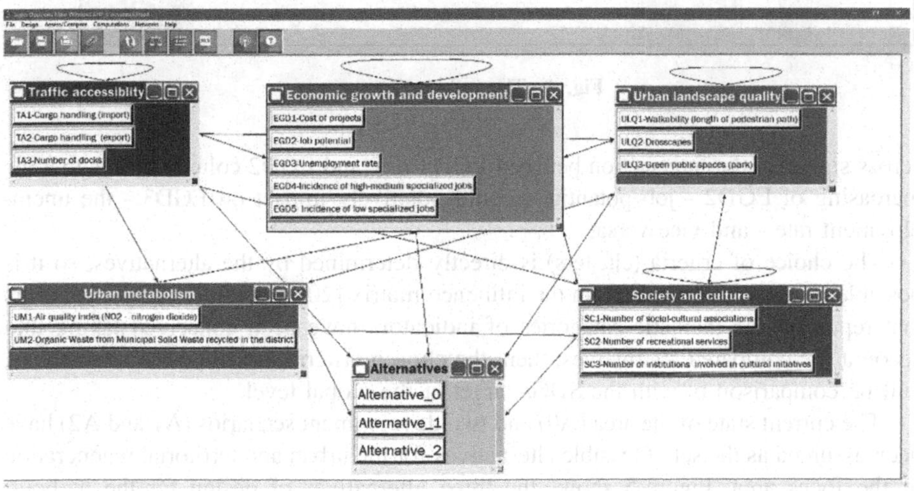

Fig. 3. The graphical network (screenshot from Super Decisions software v.3)

When the problem has been formulated and clusters and nodes defined, it has been possible to complete the influence matrix.

The influence matrix, represented in Fig. 4, shows the dependencies among the elements of the network recording them with a cross. Specifically, the cross inside the coloured clusters highlights the inner relationships among the nodes. In an example,

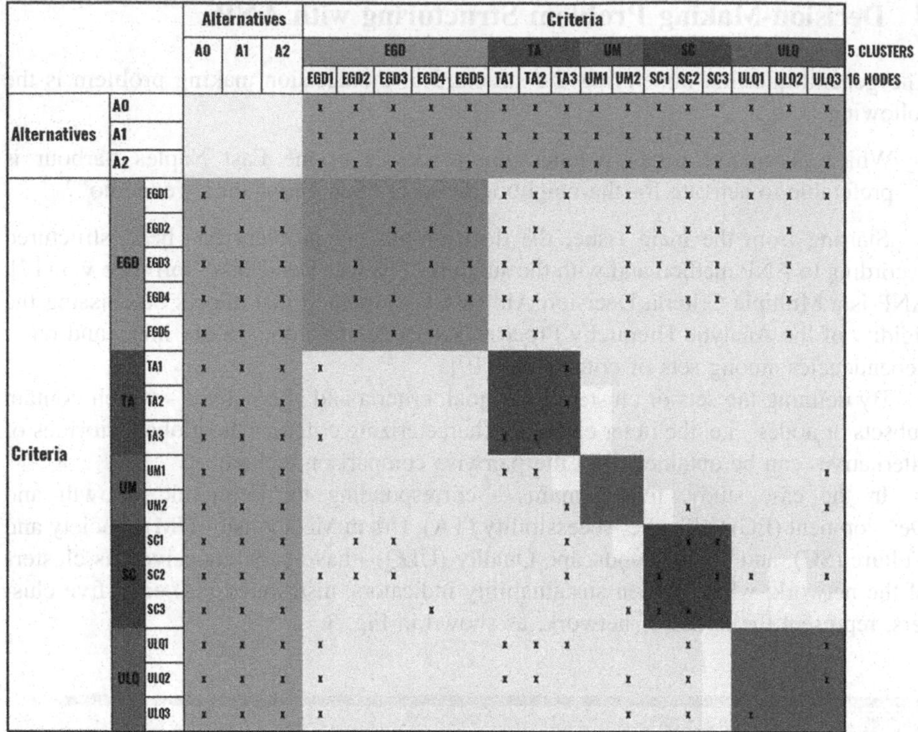

		Alternatives			Criteria																
		A0	A1	A2	EGD					TA			UM		SC			ULQ			5 CLUSTERS
					EGD1	EGD2	EGD3	EGD4	EGD5	TA1	TA2	TA3	UM1	UM2	SC1	SC2	SC3	ULQ1	ULQ2	ULQ3	16 NODES
Alternatives	A0				x	x	x	x	x	x	x	x	x	x	x	x	x	x	x	x	
	A1				x	x	x	x	x	x	x	x	x	x	x	x	x	x	x	x	
	A2				x	x	x	x	x	x	x	x	x	x	x	x	x	x	x	x	
Criteria EGD	EGD1	x	x	x						x	x	x		x		x		x	x	x	
	EGD2	x	x	x			x	x	x	x	x			x	x	x	x		x		
	EGD3	x	x	x		x		x	x	x	x			x	x	x	x		x		
	EGD4	x	x	x		x	x		x	x	x			x		x	x		x		
	EGD5	x	x	x		x	x	x		x	x			x		x			x		
TA	TA1	x	x	x	x							x									
	TA2	x	x	x	x							x									
	TA3	x	x	x	x					x	x										
UM	UM1	x	x	x						x	x									x	
	UM2	x	x	x								x				x				x	
SC	SC1	x	x	x		x	x					x				x	x				
	SC2	x	x	x	x	x	x					x			x		x	x		x	
	SC3	x	x	x				x						x	x	x					
ULQ	ULQ1	x	x	x	x					x	x	x				x				x	
	ULQ2	x	x	x	x					x	x			x		x				x	
	ULQ3	x	x	x	x									x		x		x			

Fig. 4. The influence matrix

across signed at the intersection between EGD3 row and EGD2 column means that the increasing of EGD2 - job potential - could positively impact on EGD3 - the unemployment rate - and vice versa.

The choice of criteria (clusters) is directly determined by the alternatives, so it is possible to exclude the goal from the influence matrix [20]. Therefore, the five clusters that represent the thematic categories of indicators have been conceived taking into account the compared alternatives; then, the chosen criteria, based on the alternatives, will be comparison of with the SDGs target at the global level.

The current state of the area (A0) and two development scenarios (A1 and A2) have been assumed as the set of feasible alternatives for the urban and territorial regeneration of the focus area. Figure 5 shows the three alternatives of design for the harbour. A detailed description of the alternatives follows on.

The current layout of "San Giovanni a Teduccio" focus area, identified as A0 alternative and representing No-intervention alternative, has been conceived as the control scenario in order to analyze two scenarios of transformation.

Due to the changing pattern of land uses triggered by the strong decrease in demand for industrial activities, "San Giovanni a Teduccio" neighbourhood is currently marked by a large number of abandoned industrial buildings, brownfields and drosscapes.

Despite its location and connections guaranteed by two railway stations, the district has a peripheral character strengthened by inadequate accessibility to the coastal area and scarce presence of green urban areas. Nevertheless, along last years, new activities and functions have been implemented, improving the cultural supply and sense of place, as the first step towards urban regeneration processes.

A1 alternative provides for a tourist harbour with recreational, commercial, nautical and sport facilities, extending on 145,000 square meters. Five typologies of interventions have been defined in order to pursue the transformation of the area:

1. new layout for yachting facilities including 850 berths and one dockyard;
2. restoration of warehouses within industrial archaeology site and allocation of new functions related to commercial, manufacturing and nautical facilities;
3. construction of new "building as a bridge" to facilitate the pedestrian accessibility for the harbour;
4. design of new green areas and urban public spaces;
5. refurbishment of existing roads and implementation of the road network for vehicles accessibility to the harbour.

This alternative has been commissioned by Naples Municipality and is part of a larger process of the urban periphery regeneration.

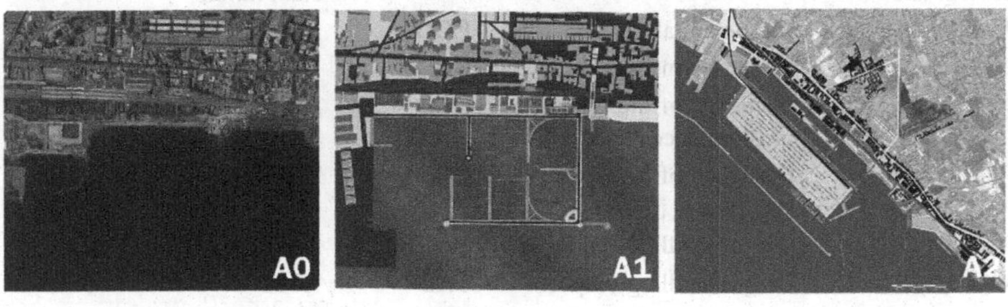

Fig. 5. The three alternatives: the current scenario (A0), the tourist harbour (A1) and the commercial terminal with urban waterfront regeneration (A2)

A2 alternative provides for multiple interventions related to three major thematic categories: the commercial port, the urban waterfront and the innovation dock.

Designing a channel among the existing coastline and terminal container is intended to redefine the urban waterfront configuration. The waterway is conceived as filtering area, connecting and dividing port from the city at once. Three categories of interventions have been defined in order to pursue "San Giovanni a Teduccio" regeneration:

1. new layout for maritime trade: extension of the terminal container, equipped with new rail freight infrastructure in addition to backing areas for the commercial function among which the distripark;
2. new layout for urban waterfront: waterway marked by commercial activities and urban loisir activities;
3. innovative manufacturing hubs placed in two urban landmarks with commercial and research functions.

The "Alternative 2" has been developed within the above mentioned Master's Degree Course by the students Silvia Sivo, Gennaro Salzano, Teresa Scandale, Stefania Regalbuto, Irina Di Ruocco, Vincenzo Lobasso, Salvatore Polverino.

The main stakeholders involved in the area management processes are: Municipality of Naples, Campania Region, Port System Authority of the Central Tyrrhenian Sea (AdSP), University of Naples Federico II, the power plant "Tirreno Power", and the construction company "Porto Fiorito".

4.1 Sustainability Indicators as Tools for Evaluating the Best-Fit Scenario

In the context of the above-mentioned evaluation methodology, a place-based set of indicators, which are useful for the focus area knowledge and the decision-making problem structuring, has been defined in Table 1.

Table 1. The sustainability indicators

Domain (Cluster)	Indicator (Node)	Indicator code	Data source	Relation to SDGs
Economic Growth and Development	Costs	EGD1	Authors elaboration	9
	Job potential	EGD2	ISTAT	9
	Unemployment rate	EGD3	ISTAT	9
	Incidence of high-medium specialized jobs	EGD4	ISTAT	9
	Incidence of low specialized jobs	EGD5	ISTAT	9
Traffic Accessibility	Cargo handling (import)	TA1	AdSP	9
	Cargo handling (export)	TA2	AdSP	9
	Number of docks	TA3	AdSP	9
Urban Metabolism	Air Quality Index (AQI)	UM1	ISPRA	12
	Organic Municipal Solid Waste recycled in the district	UM2	Authors elaboration	12
Society and Culture	Number of social-cultural associations	SC1	OpenStreetMap	11
	Number of recreational services	SC2	OpenStreetMap	11
	Number of high schools involved in cultural initiatives	SC3	Authors elaboration	11
Urban Landscape Quality	Walkability (length of pedestrian path)	ULQ1	OpenStreetMap	11
	Drosscapes	ULQ2	Authors elaboration	11
	Green public spaces	ULQ3	OpenStreetMap	11

Properly identified on the basis of theoretical guidelines proposed by SDGs, the selected indicators have been gathered and categorized into five domains (clusters) which have been determined along with the local stakeholders within the thematic focus group held at the Master's Degree course:

1. **E**conomic **G**rowth and **D**evelopment;
2. Traffic **A**ccessibility;
3. Urban **M**etabolism;
4. **S**ociety and **C**ulture;
5. Urban **L**andscape **Q**uality.

The sixteen selected indicators, clustered into the above five thematic classes, have been assumed as pivotal in choosing the best-fit strategy for the sustainable regeneration of "San Giovanni a Teduccio" harbour.

Each class, indeed, has been correlated to one of three SDGs selected from the seventeen goals of 2030 Agenda.

The Sustainable Development Goal 9 underlying the strategic relevance of "industries, innovation and infrastructure" in increasing productivity, improving health and education, has been considered alongside "Economic Growth and Development" and "Traffic Accessibility" cluster. The "Urban Metabolism" domain is instead put in relation to SDG 12 dealing with "responsible consumption".

Aiming to minimizing economic, environmental and social costs and maximizing economic competitiveness at once, the goal calls upon to define development plans taking into account the entire supply chain. Lastly, the clusters concerned with "Society and Culture" and "Urban Landscape Quality" are put in relation to SDG 11 "sustainable cities and communities", leveraging on increasing public transport, creating green public spaces, with the purpose of making cities safer and more sustainable.

4.2 Indicators Sources

The indicators have been built starting from databases of national and international relevance and from the scientific literature.

In particular, LEED and ITACA, which are two databases from which six indicators have been derived, are systems structured to assess sustainability.

LEED (Leadership in Energy and Environmental Design) is a certification of sustainability that was developed by U.S. Green Building Council, first just for buildings and later for cities and communities, including differentiated formulations for any kind of building and for urban areas, to provide a worldwide consistent way to measure and communicate performance [21].

ITACA protocol (UNI/PdR 13:2015) is an Italian evaluation tool that derives from the international evaluation model, raised to face the need of Regions to provide professional, public and private bodies with a certified tool for the sustainability assessment of buildings and urban areas. "ITACA Protocollo a Scala Urbana" was developed internationally by iiSBE (International Initiative for a Sustainable Built Environment) [22].

In this study, indicators EGD3, UM1 and UM2 have been carried out from LEED recommendation; while EGD2, ULQ1 and ULQ3 indicators have been derived from ITACA protocol.

The selection of sustainability indicators has been carried out starting from the identification of some macro-issues that characterize the area of interest, and then assumed as thematic categories/domains.

4.3 Outcomes

In this study, the ANP multi-criteria method has been chosen since it is capable to grasp and assess the relationships among different phenomena affecting the decision-making process' stages. ANP has been employed for decision-making problem structuring and definition of best-fit scenario addressed to the harbour development for the regeneration of "San Giovanni a Teduccio" neighbourhood.

ANP is, indeed, one of the alternative-based methods which are able to take into account inner and outer dependencies among multiple criteria, therefore the interrelations between the economic, social, environmental and cultural dimensions. The sustainable development alternatives for the focus area have been analyzed using the proposed Sustainability Indicators set.

As shown in Table 2, quantitative values have been processed in relation to 12 of 16 indicators, and subsequently placed as direct input into Super Decisions software in order to perform the pairwise comparison; the judgments for other four indicators - EGD3, EGD4, EGD5 and SC3 - have been inferred qualitatively instead.

The Inconsistency Ratio (IR), which refers to the stability of judgement attribution, has been processed and reported for each indicator in Table 2. All the judgments of pairwise comparison are consistent since the IR is always minor than 0.1 [23].

The limit super-matrix in Fig. 6 provides the priorities vector of each element of the decision network.

It is possible to observe that the most relevant issues are expressed by the values of the indicators within the cluster "Society and Culture". Specifically, the highest priority has been attributed to indicator "SC2" – referring to the number of recreational services – with 0.1 as eigenvector value. Also "SC1" – referring to the number of social-cultural associations in the same cluster – reaches 0.07 value.

High values have been obtained also for "Economic Growth and Development" cluster, where the most relevant issues concern with indicator "EGD2" – referring to the job potential and reaching 0.07 value – and "EGD3" – related to the unemployment rate – with the same value.

Conversely, the indicators within the cluster "Traffic Accessibility" and "Urban Metabolism" have low values, varying into the range 0–0.03.

From the observation of the values graph, the results show that the best-fit scenario for the focus area is A2 with 66.9% of priority, normalized by the cluster "alternatives". Meanwhile, A0 and A1 reach almost the same value, that is approximately the 16%; it means pursuing A1, or remaining at the current state (A0), is not suitable in terms of multi-dimensional sustainability.

Table 2. Indicators values and Inconsistency Ratio (IR) of the judgements

Indicator	A0	A1	A2	Measure unit	IR
EGD1	0	77,627,660	653,000,000	€	0
EGD2	14.6	15.1	21,1	%	0
EGD3	13.2	A1 is strongly more preferable than A0	A1 is very strongly more preferable than A0	%	0.062
EGD4	19.9	A1 is moderately more important than A0	A2 is strongly more preferable than A1	%	0.037
EGD5	24.9	A1 is equally as preferable as A0	A2 is very strongly more preferable than A0	%	0.01
TA1	536,917	536,917	1,200,000	TEU	0
TA2	499,631	499,631	1,116,666	TEU	0
TA3	200	828	500	n.	0
UM1	40.9	40.9	150.3	mg/Nm3	0
UM2	0	0	390	ton/year	0
SC1	8	8	10	n.	0
SC2	10	10	18	n.	0
SC3	8	A1 is equally as preferable as A0	A2 is moderately as preferable as A0	n.	0
ULQ1	2.23	1.32	5.29	km	0
ULQ2	62.03	27.05	1.91	he	0
ULQ3	3.66	4.36	9.70	he	0

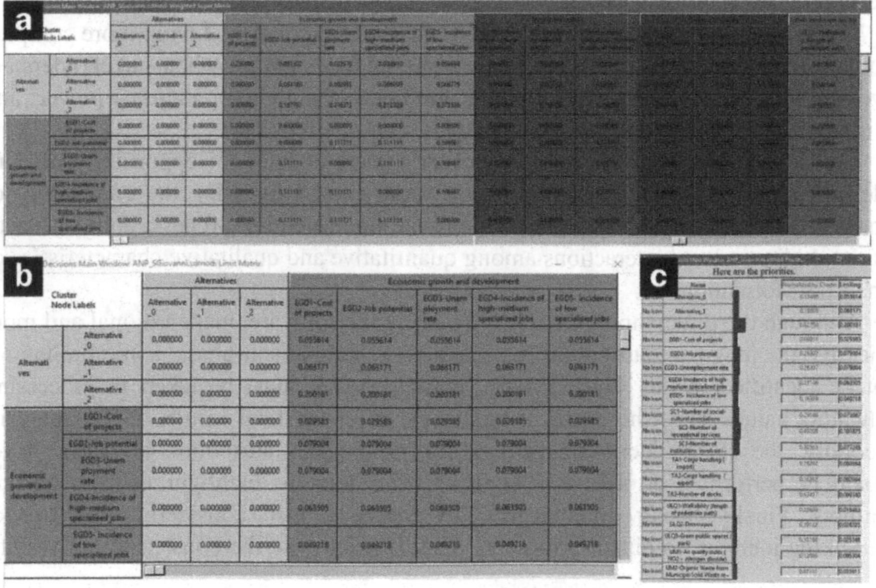

Fig. 6. Screenshot from super decisions software v.3 showing the weighted super-matrix (a), the limit super-matrix (b), and the priorities (c)

5 Discussion and Conclusion

In order to aid Decision Makers in choosing the best-fit sustainable development strategies for a complex urban context, the SDGs, as programmatic guidelines for balancing economic, social and environmental dimension of development, can be assumed.

According to place-based and use-inspired features of LSS, the cross-scale regenerative development provided the theoretical framework by which the proposed methodology has been developed [24–26]. With the purpose of operationalizing the SDGs targets, a Problem Structuring Method (PSM) [27], requiring a selection of indicators and Multi-Criteria Decision Aids (MCDA), has been proposed.

Moreover, assuming port-cities as complex systems, ANP method has been chosen since it allows to grasp the existing relationship among criteria, which have been arranged as proxies for sustainability domains [28].

The decision-making problem structuring in complex urban context requires a selection of indicators and Multi-Criteria Decision Aiding (MCDA) methods which are suitable for supporting the Decision Maker in choosing the preferable alternative among a feasible set [29].

Sustainability indicators set as part of a knowledge-based system has been set up, in order to improve the logical processes through which Decision Makers take choices regarding the urban transformation [30].

In this research, the organizational structure of data allowed the management of significant quantities of information with different features; meanwhile, the selection of suitable indicators has been a crucial point in the elaboration of the decision-making process, since that make rational and objective "ex-ante" evaluation, along with an alternative-based process [31].

The main drawbacks related to the ANP method are concerned with: more complex problem modelling; time-consuming questionnaire and surveys, when stakeholders are involved into decisional problem solving; the need of high computational power; and results which could be difficult to understand and communicate.

The advantages in using this multi-criteria method refer to: opportunity of considering interdependencies among criteria; capacity of expressing the complexity of urban systems and implementation of the dynamic evaluation process; ability to activate multidimensional interactions among quantitative and qualitative characteristics of urban transformations.

Although the direct input of data, allowed by the software, make rational and more objective the judgment attribution in the pairwise comparison phase, some limitations can be identified in this study. Firstly, particular care must be taken in processing indicators values since the errors at this stage affect the final results of the analysis. Secondly, the stakeholders engagement for preferences attribution at cluster level should be performed in order to weight the five domains highlighting trade-off and conflicts. Finally, using different MCDA methods, also considering the use of outranking methods to obtain priorities, is advisable to test the consistency of results.

This study is intended as a first step to stress the evaluation methodology in decisional arenas with local stakeholders, by implementing it with the integration of multi-group assessments and spatially explicit multi-criteria approach.

References

1. United Nations General Assembly: Transforming our world: The 2030 agenda for sustainable development. United Nations, Department of Economic and Social Affairs, New York (2015)
2. Bebbington, J., Russell, S., Thomson, I.: Accounting and sustainable development: reflections and propositions. Crit. Perspect. Account. **48**, 21–34 (2017)
3. Rosati, F., Faria, L.G.: Addressing the SDGs in sustainability reports: the relationship with institutional factors. J. Cleaner Prod. **215**, 1312–1326 (2019)
4. Wu, J.: Landscape sustainability science: ecosystem services and human well-being in changing landscapes. Landscape Ecol. **28**, 999–1023 (2013)
5. Gibbons, L., Cloutier, S., Coseo, P., Barakat, A.: Regenerative development as an integrative paradigm and methodology for landscape sustainability. Sustainability **10**, 1910 (2018)
6. Huang, L., Wu, J., Yan, L.: Defining and measuring urban sustainability: a review of indicators. Landscape Ecol. **30**(7), 1175–1193 (2015)
7. Benne, B., Mang, P.: Working regeneratively across scales—insights from nature applied to the built environment. J. Cleaner Prod. **109**, 42–52 (2015)
8. Cerreta, M., Panaro, S., Poli, G.: A knowledge-based approach for the implementation of a SDSS in the Partenio Regional Park (Italy). In: Gervasi, O., et al. (eds.) ICCSA 2016. LNCS, vol. 9789, pp. 111–124. Springer, Cham (2016). https://doi.org/10.1007/978-3-319-42089-9_8
9. Wiecek, M.M., Ehrgott, M., Fadel, G., Figueira, J.R.: Multiple criteria decision making for engineering. Omega Int. J. Manage. Sci. **36**, 337–339 (2008)
10. Torre, C.M., Morano, P., Tajani, F.: Post-normal rationality in assessment of environmental damage and environmental risk. In: Gervasi, O., et al. (eds.) ICCSA 2018. LNCS, vol. 10962, pp. 490–501. Springer, Cham (2018). https://doi.org/10.1007/978-3-319-95168-3_33
11. Iojă, I.C., Hossu, C.A., Niţă, M.R., Onose, D.A., Badiu, D.L., Manolache, S.: Indicators for environmental conflict monitoring in Natura 2000 sites. Procedia Environ. Sci. **32**, 4–11 (2016)
12. Funtowicz, S.O., Ravetz, J.R.: Uncertainty and Quality in Science for Policy. Kluwer, Dordrecht (1990)
13. Las Casas, G., Scorza, F., Murgante, B.: New urban agenda and open challenges for urban and regional planning. In: Calabrò, F., Della Spina, L., Bevilacqua, C. (eds.) ISHT 2018. SIST, vol. 100, pp. 282–288. Springer, Cham (2019). https://doi.org/10.1007/978-3-319-92099-3_33
14. United Nations (UN): Indicators of Sustainable Development. Guidelines and Methodologies. In: United Nations (ed.) Economic and Social Affairs, New York (2007)
15. Garnåsjordet, A., et al.: Sustainable development indicators: from statistics to policy. Environ. Policy Gov. **22**, 322–336 (2012)
16. Persada, C., Sitorus, S., Djakapermana, R.: Policy model of sustainable infrastructure development (case study: Bandarlampung City, Indonesia). In: IOP Conference Series: Earth and Environmental Science, vol. 124, p. 1. IOP Publishing Ltd (2018)
17. www.superdecisions.com

18. Saaty, T.L.: The Analytic Hierarchy Process. McGraw-Hill, New York (1980). Clemmons, R. (2006)
19. Saaty, T.L.: Theory and Applications of the Analytic Network Process: Decision Making With Benefits, Opportunities, Costs, and Risks. RWS publications, Pittsburgh (2005)
20. Ishizaka, A., Nemery, P.: Multi-criteria Decision Analysis: Methods and Software. Wiley, Chichester (2013)
21. USGB Council: Leadership in Energy and Environmental Design (LEED). Building Design and Construction, version, 4 (2008)
22. Gruppo di lavoro interregionale "Protocollo Scala Urbana": Protocollo ITACA a Scala Urbana (2016)
23. Saaty, T.L.: The analytic network process. Decision Making with the Analytic Network Process. International Series in Operations Research and Management Science, vol. 95, pp. 1–26. Springer, Boston (2006). https://doi.org/10.1007/0-387-33987-6_1
24. Nassauer, J.I., Opdam, P.: Design in science: extending the landscape ecology paradigm. Landscape Ecol. **23**, 633–644 (2008)
25. DuPlessis, C.: Towards a regenerative paradigm for the built environment. Build. Res. Inf. **40**, 7–22 (2012)
26. DuPlessis, C., Brandon, P.: An ecological paradigm as basis for a regenerative sustainability paradigm for the built environment. J. Cleaner Prod. **109**, 53–61 (2015)
27. Lami, I.M., Abastante, F., Bottero, M., Masala, E., Pensa, S.: Integrating multicriteria evaluation and data visualization as a problem structuring approach to support territorial transformation projects. EURO J. Decis. Processes **2**(3–4), 281–312 (2014)
28. Cerreta, M., Cannatella, D., Poli, G., Sposito, S.: Climate change and transformability scenario evaluation for Venice (Italy) port-city through ANP method. In: Gervasi, O., et al. (eds.) ICCSA 2015. LNCS, vol. 9158, pp. 50–63. Springer, Cham (2015). https://doi.org/10.1007/978-3-319-21410-8_4
29. Kumar, A., et al.: A review of multi criteria decision making (MCDM) towards sustainable renewable energy development. Renew. Sustain. Energy Rev. **69**, 596–609 (2017)
30. Lehtonen, M., Sébastien, L., Bauler, T.: The multiple roles of sustainability indicators in informational governance: between intended use and unanticipated influence. Curr. Opin. Environ. Sustain. **18**, 1–9 (2016)
31. Xu, H., Xue, B.: Key indicators for the resilience of complex urban public spaces. J. Build. Eng. **12**, 306–313 (2017)

Geomatics for Resource Monitoring and Control (GRMC 2019)

Comparison of Satellite and Geomorphic Indices for Flooded Areas Detection in a Mediterranean River Basin

Vincenzo Totaro(✉), Giuseppe Peschechera, Andrea Gioia, Vito Iacobellis, and Umberto Fratino

Politecnico di Bari, Via Orabona 4, Bari 70125, Italy
{vincenzo.totaro,giuseppe.peschechera,andrea.gioia,vito.iacobellis,umberto.fratino}@poliba.it

Abstract. Flood-hazard map delineation is an important task in planning land management activities. This evaluation is usually based on coupled hydraulic/hydrological models, which often require time consuming and expensive measurement campaigns in order to estimate the necessary distributed physical information for their implementation (e.g. digital elevation models, land cover and geological maps); moreover, the observed effects of flood events are needed for their calibration and validation. The obtained flooded maps can allow to perform geomorphic DEM-based procedure, which is a valid tool useful for the rapid identification and mapping of flood-prone areas; in addition remote sensing is a reliable and widespread source of input data for the application of hydrological and hydraulic models: particular interest generate the attitude of the Landsat-8 OLISR data in the definition of the effective flooded area. The goal of this work is to compare performances of remote sensing and DEM-based techniques for the definition of flood-prone areas, using as reference map that obtained by a two-dimensional hydraulic simulation. An objective comparison between these two approaches has been carried out(using linear binary classifiers method and ROC curves) on the case study of Lato river basin, located in the Puglia region, Southern Italy; the satellite indices showed good performances even if the selected geomorphic descriptors still remain the most performing in reproducing the inundated areas.

Keywords: Geomorphological descriptors · Flooded areas · Satellite indices · Hydraulic model

1 Introduction

Natural disasters, such as floods and droughts, have devastating social, environmental and economic implications for many areas of the world. With the aim to reduce and mitigate the effects of such phenomena, in the latest few years flood-hazard map delineation is assuming a growing interest.

S. Misra et al. (Eds.): ICCSA 2019, LNCS 11622, pp. 173–185, 2019.
https://doi.org/10.1007/978-3-030-24305-0_14

The evaluation of floodable areas is usually carried out by applying coupled hydrological and hydraulic models: the former are used for the definition of a flood event (e.g. [1–10]), the latter are exploited for performing flood propagation (e.g. [11–16]); this approach, in more cases, involves lot of human and informatic resources for its parametrization; moreover it needs time consuming and expensive measurement campaigns for the estimation of the required inputs distributed information and observed data useful for calibration and validation.

In order to satisfy the increasing requirements of end users (like Basin Authorities, Civil Protection agencies) and the needs of recent legislation on flood risk protection (e.g. Floods Directive 2007/60/EC), a necessary upgrade of theoretical approaches used for mapping the hydraulic hazard level of the territory is needed with the purpose to mitigate and contain the catastrophic effects of the inundations, which are becoming more frequent in recent decades. Moreover, the increasing availability of high-resolution topographical data (i.e. digital terrain models - DTMs) due to new technologies for the measurement of surface elevation (i.e. Light Detection And Ranging - LiDAR) gives strong impulse to the increasing development of new DTM-based techniques (e.g. [17, 18]) able to provide a rapid and reliable identification of flood susceptibility maps (e.g. [19–21]) using only geomorphological information, in areas characterized by poor hydrological information..

Recently, in addition to these consolidated methodologies, the evolution of surface phenomena can be monitored also using remote sensing techniques [22–33], providing good performances in investigating indices [21, 34] useful for the rapid identification of inundated areas.

Interesting developments of such methodologies can be conducted considering multiple case studies on a wide area for the evaluation at regional scale (e.g. [35]) or extending the proposed approach to other fields of application (e.g. [36, 37]).

In this study satellite and geomorphic indices for flooded areas detection are compared on the Lato river basin located in Puglia Region (southern Italy), in order to evaluate their reliability in representing reference maps of inundated area, estimated using a classical approach of a combined hydrological and hydraulic model.

2 Case Study

The proposed analysis is focused on the Lato river which, flowing into the Gulf of Taranto (Ionian Sea), receives the runoff contributions of Castellaneta and Laterza municipalities, located in the Taranto province (Fig. 1). His length is about 5 km and his basin area has an extension of about 670 km^2. The analysis was performed on a flood event that occurred downstream of the Lato river in the days of 6/7 October 2013.

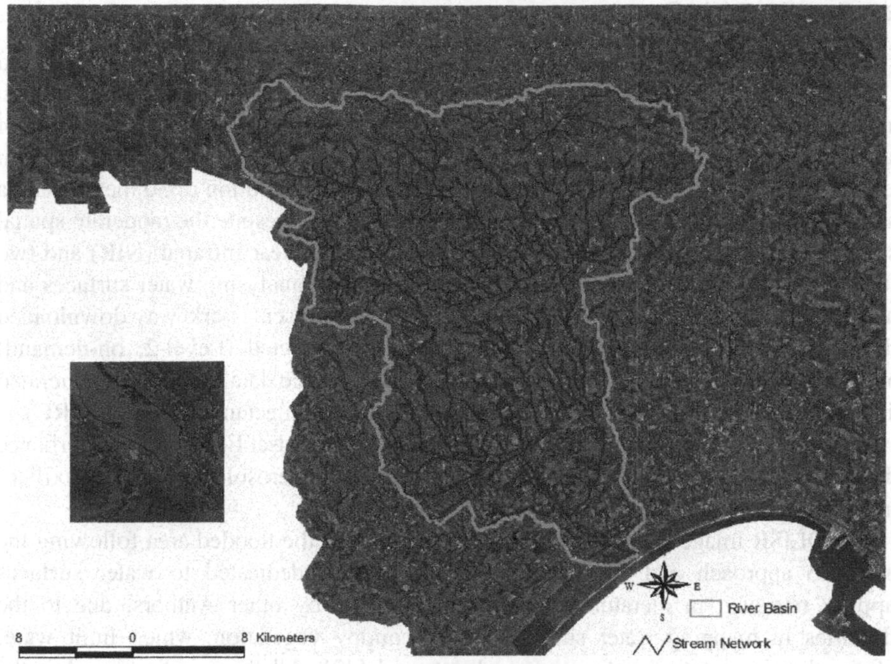

Fig. 1. Study area. Coordinate System UTM WGS 84 zone 33 N.

3 Methodologies

In this section the following topics are illustrated:

- the definition of flooded area (used as reference map) by exploiting hydrologic/hydraulic models;
- flood-prone areas evaluation, using satellite and geomorphic descriptors;
- the selection of the most appropriate basin descriptor through binary classifiers and Receiver Operating Characteristic method.

3.1 Hydrologic/Hydraulic Modeling

Flooded area generated by the investigated meteorological event has been delineated by coupling a two-dimensional hydraulic model (FLO 2D [38]) with the CN-SCS hydrological model (USDA-SCA [39]) for the estimation of the flood hydrograph. In particular the numerical simulation was conducted over the computational grid within the selected Digital Terrain Model and the flood event was reproduced introducing the simulated hydrograph as boundary condition. The hydraulic modeling has been calibrated using flooded areas (with return periods of 30 and 200 years) extracted from the database of the Basin Authority of Puglia for the investigated study area (e.g. http://www.adb.puglia.it/public/news.php).

3.2 Satellite Basin Descriptors

In this study a single post flooding Landsat 8 Operational Land Imager (OLI) acquired on 10th October 2013 (LC081880322013101001T) was used. The Landsat 8 mission was developed inherited the properties of the previous Landsat products in terms of spatial, spectral, and temporal (16 days) resolutions. The sensor OLI consists of eight spectral bands (bands 1–7 and 9) with a moderate spatial resolution of 30 meters, and a panchromatic band (Pan) with a higher resolution (15 m). Despite the moderate spatial resolution of the sensor, it is provided of one band in the Near Infrared (NIR) and two in the Short Wave Infrared (SWIR) which are useful for analysing water surfaces and plant water content [32, 40]. The image used in the present work was downloaded radiometrically, geometrically and atmospherically corrected (Level-2, on-demand) from the USGS website. The Landsat-8 Surface Reflectance data (L8SR) are generated using the radiative transfer model Landsat 8 Surface Reflectance Code (LaSRC), a novel algorithm that performs better than the previous (Landsat Ecosystem Disturbance Adaptive Processing System) due to the use of the coastal aerosol band and of auxiliary climate data from MODIS [41].

The OLISR image was used for the identification of the flooded area following the band-ratio approach and testing different SR indices dedicated to water surfaces mapping retrieved in literature. Moreover, as shows by other Authors, due to the difficulties in mapping water surfaces under canopy vegetation, which limit water surface, three vegetation indices were also tested [42]. All these indices exploit the information from the visible and the infrared (both NIR and SWIR) regions. The list of the adopted indices is provided in Table 1.

The Simple Ratio (SR) is the simplest ratio-based vegetation index based on the ratio between the reflectance recorded in the NIR and Red bands usually used to distinguish green leaves from other objects in the scene for example, soil and water [43]. The Normalized Difference Vegetation Index (NDVI) is one of the widely index used for measure of healthy, green vegetation [44]. It is obtained as normalized difference between the NIR and red reflectance and therefore results functionally, but not linearly, equivalent to the SR. The NDVI has a finite validity range (from –1 to +1) while the SR is always positive with an infinite range (0 to infinity), which can be a practical disadvantage as compared to NDVI. However, is demonstrated that also the NDVI tends to saturate for dense vegetation. For optimizing the vegetation signal in areas of high leaf area index, was developed the Enhanced vegetation index (EVI). Moreover, due to the use of the blue reflectance region, it corrects the soil background signals and reduces atmospheric influences [45]. All these vegetation indices are usually used for vegetation monitoring and classification, while in this work were used for mapping floods.

The Normalized Difference Water Index (NDWI) was introduced by McFeeters to enhance water features maximizing its reflectance in the visible domain (by using green wavelengths) and minimizing the reflectance of NIR [46]. However, due to the similar reflectance pattern of built-up land and water in the green band, water features extracted include false positives from built-up land, which overestimates the area of extracted water. Hence a modified NDWI (MNDWI) was developed, in which the SWIR band was used to replace the NIR band in the NDWI in order to enhance open water features (which are characterized by higher absorption in the SWIR region than in NIR) while efficiently suppressing, and even removing, built-up land, vegetation and soil noise. For this reason, it is more suitable for enhancing and extracting water features in contexts dominated by built-up land areas [47]. Another modification of the NDWI was used in the present study, the Land Surface Water Index (LSWI). It uses the NIR and the SWIR regions of the electromagnetic spectrum and, thanks to the strong light absorption by liquid water in the SWIR, it is sensitive to the total amount of liquid water in vegetation and its soil background. It is worth to mention that the index has different nomenclatures: Gao [48] called it NDWI while Wilson et al. called it Normalized Difference Moisture Index (NDMI) [49].

Lastly, we tested the Automated Water Extraction Index (AWEI). The AWEI was developed to improve water extraction accuracy in the presence of various sorts of environmental noise that other classification methods often fail to classify correctly (including shadow and dark surfaces) and at the same time offers a stable threshold value [50].

Table 1. List of multispectral indices used for the identification of the flooded area.

Index	References
$SR = \frac{\rho_{NIR}}{\rho_{Red}}$	[43]
$\text{NDVI} = \frac{\rho_{red} - \rho_{NIR}}{\rho_{red} + \rho_{NIR}}$	[51]
$EVI = 2.5 \times \frac{\rho_{NIR} - \rho_{Red}}{\rho_{NIR} + 6\rho_{Red} - 7.5\rho_{Blue} + 0.5}$	[45]
$\text{NDWI} = \frac{\rho_{green} - \rho_{NIR}}{\rho_{green} + \rho_{NIR}}$	[46]
$\text{MNDWI}^{*} = \frac{\rho_{green} - \rho_{SWIR}}{\rho_{green} + \rho_{SWIR}}$	[47]
$\text{AWEI} = 4 \times (\rho_{Green} - \rho_{SWIR1}) - (0.25\rho_{NIR} + 2.75\rho_{SWIR2})$	[50]

*Two indices calculated for respectively SWIR-1and SWIR-2

3.3 Morphological Basin Descriptors

Geomorphic indices are useful tools for evaluating flood-prone areas in a very fast way; they can reflect the behaviors of inundated areas. In this context previous evaluation have been already carried out on the same investigated case study (e.g. [21]); in this paper an integration analysis including the application of the Receiver Operating Characteristic (ROC) approach is introduced. For sake of brevity only the best performant indices are explained, but the reader can find a complete description in [21]:

- *elevation to the nearest stream, H [m]:* this index computes the elevation difference between a considered cell on the river basin and that hydrologically connected on the stream network.
- $ln(h_r/H)$ (Gemomorphic Flood Index, GFI): this index relates, for each point on the river basin, the water depth h_r with the synthetic descriptor H, where h_r can be defined as:

$$h_r \cong bA_r^n \tag{1}$$

with A_r [m^2] upslope contributing area calculated at the hydrologically connected point on the stream network, b a scale factor usually set equal to 10^{-2} and n a dimensionless exponent set equal to 0.3.

3.4 Linear Binary Classifiers and ROC Curves Methods

The methodology for performing calibration of indices, using linear binary classifiers and ROC methods, has been explained by a step-by-step procedure in [52]. It requires to scale and normalize the descriptor maps considering values ranging between –1 and 1. Then, applying a moving threshold with an assigned step (10^{-3} in this case), binary (0–1) maps are obtained. Using this approach, each cell on the investigated domain may be classified as True Positive (TP), False Positive (FP), True Negative (TN) and False Negative (FN), by a comparison with reference binary map. In order to define the threshold with the lowest rate of errors, the following Objective Function (OB) is computed for each selected threshold:

$$OB = r_{fp} + \left(1 - r_{tp}\right) \tag{2}$$

where r_{fp} and r_{tp} are:

$$r_{tp} = \frac{TP}{TP + FN} \tag{3}$$

$$r_{fp} = \frac{FP}{FP + TN} \tag{4}$$

The best index is that with the lowest value of the objective function, while flooded maps can be obtained applying the corresponding normalized threshold τ_{norm} to the index map.

The ROC approach [53] is a useful tool for testing the performances of the investigated indices, relating r_{tp} and r_{fp}. The measure of the goodness of fit, for each considered index, is obtained calculating the Area Under Curve (AUC) on the selected investigated domain.

4 Results and Discussion

The application of linear binary classifier and ROC tests has been conducted on satellite indices described in the Sect. 3.2, leading to the results shown in Table 2 and Fig. 2.

The minimum values of the objective function range between 0.375 and 0.401, showing similar performances. A more detailed analysis can be performed looking at the true positive (r_{tp}) and false positive rate (r_{fp}), defined as in (3) and (4) respectively and reported in Table 2, and observing the related calibrated flooded maps, reported in Fig. 3. Reference flooded map is reported in the top left of the Fig. 3.

Table 2. Results of the linear binary classifier test and Area Under Curve evaluation for the investigated satellite descriptors.

	τ_{norm}	r_{fp}	r_{tp}	*min*(OB)	AUC
SR	−0.883	0.088	0.713	0.375	0.895
NDVI	0.153	0.089	0.714	0.375	0.895
EVI	0.144	0.079	0.700	0.378	0.894
NDWI	−0.333	0.107	0.736	0.371	0.898
MNDWI SWIR 1	−0.451	0.096	0.748	0.348	0.878
MNDWI SWIR 2	−0.022	0.070	0.676	0.394	0.865
AWEI	0.350	0.026	0.625	0.401	0.836

Following the criterion of choosing the index characterized by the lowest value of the objective function, the best performant index is the MNDWI SWIR 1, but it can be interesting to carry out a more detailed analysis. In fact, the AWEI index has the lowest rate of false positive, as it can be confirmed by looking at the Fig. 3: the AWEI flooded map has really a small percentage of inundated cells outside the real flooded area, revealing an interesting performance in the false positive detection. However, this advantage disappears if we look at the true positive rate, which assumes the lowest value respect to the other descriptors. In this case, the best ability in recognizing inundated cells is performed by the MNDWI SWIR 1 index.

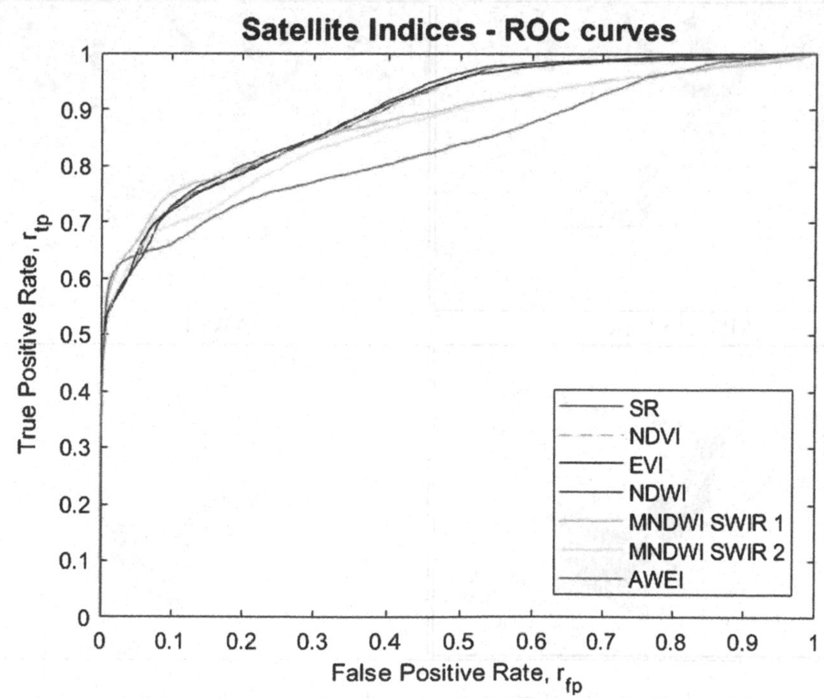

Fig. 2. ROC curves for satellite indices

The best compromise between the true positive (r_{tp}) and false positive rate (r_{fp}) is achieved by minimizing the objective function.

Similitudes between satellite indices shown in Table 2 can also be observed looking at the Fig. 2, where the Receiver Operating Characteristic curves are shown. In fact, the curves are pretty similar, and the AWEI is the index with lowest performance, whose curve reflects, moreover, its ability in detecting the false positive.

Figure 3 shows the comparison between the flooded area reference map (on the top left) retrieved by using the hydraulic modelling and those estimated using the surface reflectance indices. All the indices are not suitable to retrieve the mainstream, due to

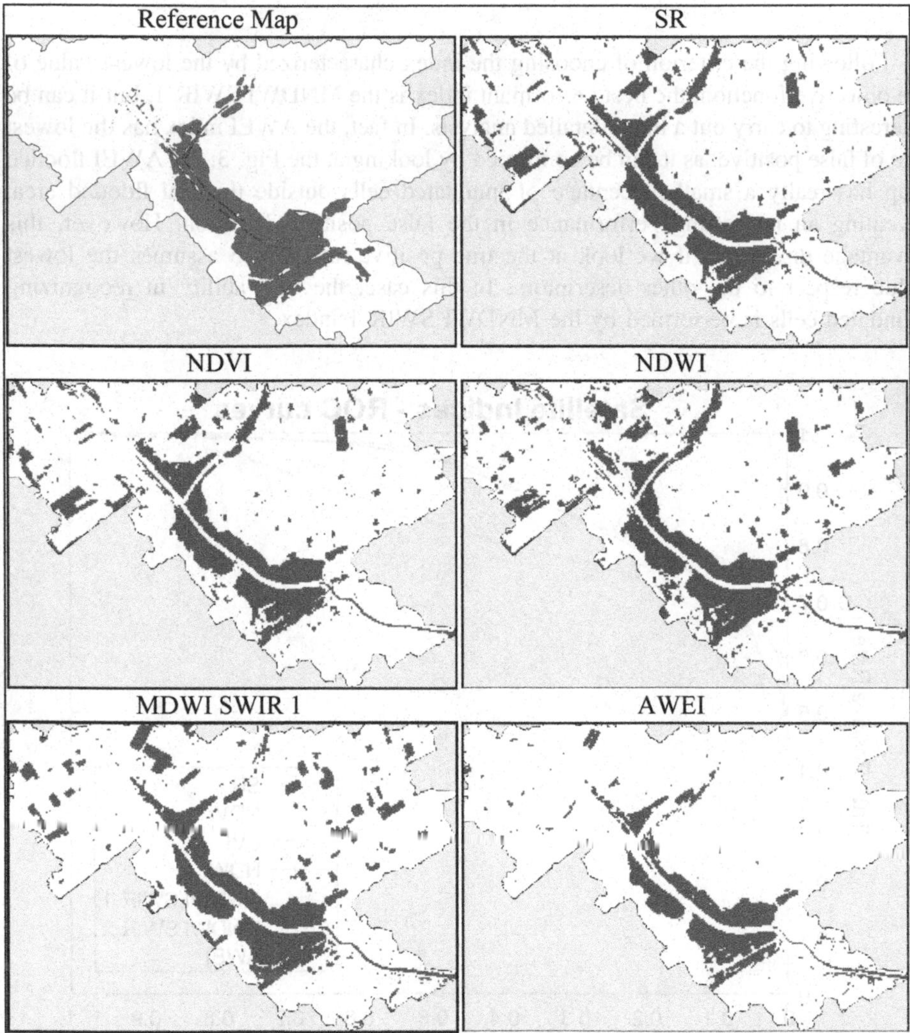

Fig. 3. Comparisonbetween the reference map and flooded areas obtained through calibration procedure applied to some satellite descriptors.

the presence of the riparian vegetation. The vegetation indices (SR, NDVI, EVI), based on Red and NIR bands, can reproduce the same area, with an overestimation of false flooded areas. Only the AWEI index reduces the cases of false flooding estimation, even if it underestimates the extension of the true flooded area.

Results of the linear binary classifiers test for the geomorphic indices H and GFI, indicated as the most performants in a previous research(21), are already reported in this study. In particular, looking at the ROC curves showed in Fig. 4, it is possible to observe similar performances for the selected indices, whose AUC and OB values are reported in Table 3. Moreover, it is quite evident how geomorphic descriptors are suitable to reproduce floodable areas really better than satellite indices, avoiding false positive values far from the real flood-prone zone. More in detail, while false positive rate is low for both indices, it is very important to note the ability of the H descriptor in detecting true positive cells. In particular, their physical link with the river network is a strong element for justifying its excellent performances.

Table 3. Results of linear binary classifier test and Area Under Curve evaluation for the selected geomorphic descriptors

	τ_{norm}	r_{fp}	r_{tp}	*min*(OB)	AUC
H	−0.975	0.051	0.941	0.110	0.981
GFI	−0.231	0.057	0.746	0.211	0.970

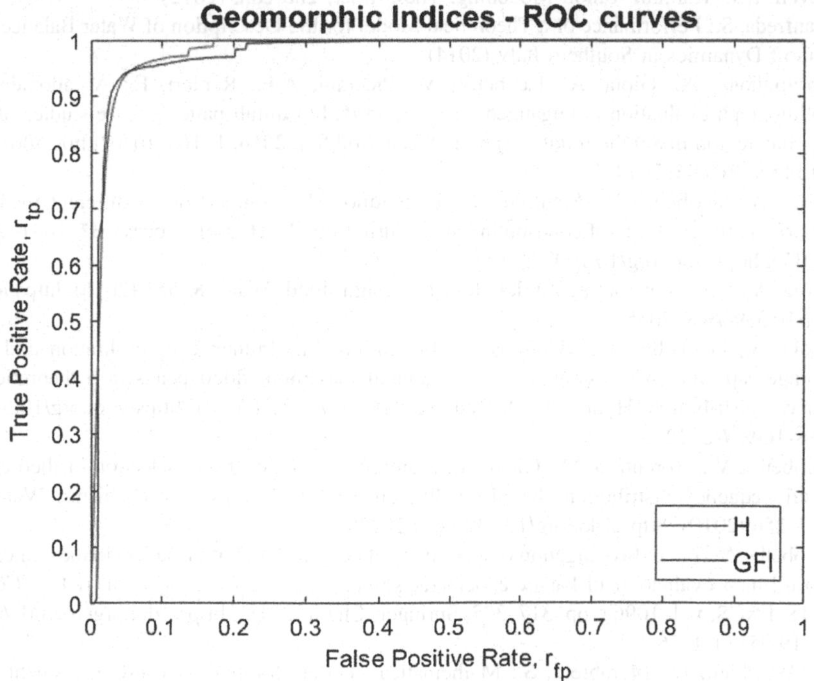

Fig. 4. ROC curves for geomorphic indices

5 Conclusions

In this paper an investigation on the ability of satellite indices in detecting flood-prone areas has been carried out. Despite the lag-time between the observed flood event and the first available satellite image (about three days), the results of the linear binary classifiers approach and Receiver Operating Characteristic curves methodology are very promising; in particular the existing lag-time may influence the capacity in detecting true positive flooded areas. Notwithstanding the good performances showed by the satellite indices on the investigated study area, the selected geomorphic descriptors (H and GFI) still remain the most performing in reproducing the inundated areas. The increasing availability of satellite products can help the scientific community in the development of new techniques for a rapid flood-prone areas identification. However, further investigations on the possibility of using these images should be conducted, for an aware knowledge in the context of hydraulic applications.

References

1. Feldman, A.D.: Hydrologic modeling system HEC-HMS. Technical reference manual (2000)
2. Fiorentino, M., Gioia, A., Iacobellis, V., Manfreda, S.: Analysis on flood generation processes by means of a continuous simulation model. In: Advances in Geosciences, pp. 231–236. Copernicus GmbH (2006). https://doi.org/10.5194/adgeo-7-231-2006
3. Beven, K.J.: Rainfall-Runoff Modelling: The Primer, 2nd edn. (2012)
4. Manfreda, S.: Performance of a Theoretical Model for the Description of Water Balance and Runoff Dynamics in Southern Italy (2014)
5. Gorgoglione, A., Gioia, A., Iacobellis, V., Piccinni, A.F., Ranieri, E.: A rationale for pollutograph evaluation in ungauged areas, using daily rainfall patterns: case studies of the Apulian region in Southern Italy. Appl. Environ. Soil Sci. **2016**, 1–16 (2016). https://doi.org/10.1155/2016/9327614
6. Gioia, A., Iacobellis, V., Manfreda, S., Fiorentino, M.: Comparison of different methods describing the peak runoff contributing areas during floods. Hydrol. Process. **31**, 2041–2049 (2017). https://doi.org/10.1002/hyp.11169
7. Gioia, A.: Reservoir routing on double-peak design flood. Water **8**, 553 (2016). https://doi.org/10.3390/w8120553
8. Gioia, A., Iacobellis, V., Manfreda, S., Fiorentino, M.: Influence of infiltration and soil storage capacity on the skewness of the annual maximum flood peaks in a theoretically derived distribution. Hydrol. Earth Syst. Sci. **16**, 937–951 (2012). https://doi.org/10.5194/hess-16-937-2012
9. Iacobellis, V., Fiorentino, M., Gioia, A., Manfreda, S.: Best fit and selection of theoretical flood frequency distributions based on different runoff generation mechanisms. Water **2**, 239–256 (2010). https://doi.org/10.3390/w2020239
10. Iacobellis, V., et al.: Investigation of a flood event occurred on Lama Balice, in the context of hazard map evaluation in karstic-ephemeral streams. In: Gervasi, O., et al. (eds.) ICCSA 2018. LNCS, vol. 10964, pp. 317–333. Springer, Cham (2018). https://doi.org/10.1007/978-3-319-95174-4_26
11. De Wrachien, D., Mambretti, S.: Mathematical models for flood hazard assessment. Int. J. SAFE. **1**, 353–362 (2011). https://doi.org/10.2495/SAFE-V1-N4-353-362

12. Iacobellis, V., Castorani, A., Di Santo, A.R., Gioia, A.: Rationale for flood prediction in karst endorheic areas. J. Arid Environ. **112**, 98–108 (2015). https://doi.org/10.1016/j.jaridenv.2014.05.018
13. Bates, P.D., Anderson, M.G., Price, D.A., Hardy, R.J., Smith, C.N.: Analysis and development of hydraulic models for floodplain flow. In: Floodplain Processes, pp. 215–254 (1996)
14. Jain, S.K., Singh, R.D., Jain, M.K., Lohani, A.K.: Delineation of flood-prone areas using remote sensing techniques. Water Resour. Manage **19**, 333–347 (2005). https://doi.org/10.1007/s11269-005-3281-5
15. Fluet-Chouinard, E., Lehner, B., Rebelo, L.-M., Papa, F., Hamilton, S.K.: Development of a global inundation map at high spatial resolution from topographic downscaling of coarse-scale remote sensing data. Remote Sens. Environ. **158**, 348–361 (2015). https://doi.org/10.1016/j.rse.2014.10.015
16. Manfreda, S., et al.: Flood-prone areas assessment using linear binary classifiers based on flood maps obtained from 1D and 2D hydraulic models. Nat. Hazards J. Int. Soc. Prev. Mitig. Nat. Hazards **79**, 735–754 (2015)
17. Nardi, F., Vivoni, E., Grimaldi, S.: Investigating a floodplain scaling relation using a hydrogeomorphic delineation method. Water Resour. Res. **42** (2006). https://doi.org/10.1029/2005WR004155
18. Marks, K., Bates, P.: Integration of high-resolution topographic data with floodplain flow models. Hydrol. Process. **14**, 2109–2122 (2000)
19. Degiorgis, M., Gnecco, G., Gorni, S., Roth, G., Sanguineti, M., Taramasso, A.C.: Classifiers for the detection of flood-prone areas using remote sensed elevation data. J. Hydrol. **470–471**, 302–315 (2012). https://doi.org/10.1016/j.jhydrol.2012.09.006
20. De Risi, R., Jalayer, F., De Paola, F., Giugni, M.: Probabilistic delineation of flood-prone areas based on a digital elevation model and the extent of historical flooding: the case of Ouagadougou. Bol. Geol. Min. **125**, 329–340 (2014)
21. Totaro, V., Gioia, A., Novelli, A., Caradonna, G.: The use of geomorphological descriptors and landsat-8 spectral indices data for flood areas evaluation: a case study of Lato river basin. In: Gervasi, O., et al. (eds.) ICCSA 2017. LNCS, vol. 10407, pp. 30–44. Springer, Cham (2017). https://doi.org/10.1007/978-3-319-62401-3_3
22. Mattia, F., et al.: Time series of COSMO-SkyMed data for landcover classification and surface parameter retrieval over agricultural sites. In: 2012 IEEE International Geoscience and Remote Sensing Symposium, pp. 6511–6514 (2012). https://doi.org/10.1109/IGARSS.2012.6352738
23. Balenzano, A., et al.: On the use of multi-temporal series of COSMO-SkyMed data for LANDcover classification and surface parameter retrieval over agricultural sites. In: 2011 IEEE International Geoscience and Remote Sensing Symposium, pp. 142–145 (2011). https://doi.org/10.1109/IGARSS.2011.6048918
24. Balenzano, A., et al.: A ground network for SAR-derived soil moisture product calibration, validation and exploitation in Southern Italy. In: 2014 IEEE Geoscience and Remote Sensing Symposium, pp. 3382–3385 (2014). https://doi.org/10.1109/IGARSS.2014.6947206
25. Olang, L.O., Kundu, P., Bauer, T., Fürst, J.: Analysis of spatio-temporal land cover changes for hydrological impact assessment within the Nyando River Basin of Kenya. Environ. Monit. Assess. **179**, 389–401 (2011). https://doi.org/10.1007/s10661-010-1743-6
26. Balacco, G., Figorito, B., Tarantino, E., Gioia, A., Iacobellis, V.: Space–time LAI variability in Northern Puglia (Italy) from SPOT VGT data. Environ. Monit. Assess. **187**, 434 (2015). https://doi.org/10.1007/s10661-015-4603-6
27. Crocetto, N., Tarantino, E.: A class-oriented Strategy for features extraction from multidate ASTER imagery. Remote Sens. **1**, 1171–1189 (2009). https://doi.org/10.3390/rs1041171

28. Saradjian, M.R., Hosseini, M.: Soil moisture estimation by using multipolarization SAR image. Adv. Space Res. **48**, 278–286 (2011). https://doi.org/10.1016/j.asr.2011.03.029
29. Iacobellis, V., Gioia, A., Milella, P., Satalino, G., Balenzano, A., Mattia, F.: Inter-comparison of hydrological model simulations with time series of SAR-derived soil moisture maps. Euro. J. Remote Sens. **46**, 739–757 (2013). https://doi.org/10.5721/EuJRS20134644
30. Tarantino, E.: Monitoring spatial and temporal distribution of sea surface temperature with TIR sensor data. Ital. J. Remote Sens. **44**(1), 97–107 (2012)
31. Aquilino, M., Novelli, A., Tarantino, E., Iacobellis, V., Gentile, F.: Evaluating the potential of GeoEye data in retrieving LAI at watershed scale. In: Presented at the Remote Sensing of the Ocean, Sea Ice, Coastal Waters, and Large Water Regions 1 October 2014 (2014). https://doi.org/10.1117/12.2067185
32. Peschechera, G., Novelli, A., Caradonna, G., Fratino, U.: Calibration of the CLAIR model by using landsat 8 surface reflectance higher-level data and MODIS leaf area index products. In: Gervasi, O., et al. (eds.) ICCSA 2017. LNCS, vol. 10407, pp. 16–29. Springer, Cham (2017). https://doi.org/10.1007/978-3-319-62401-3_2
33. Peschechera, G., Fratino, U.: Calibration of CLAIR model by means of Sentinel-2 LAI data for analysing wheat crops through landsat-8 surface reflectance data. In: Gervasi, O., et al. (eds.) ICCSA 2018. LNCS, vol. 10964, pp. 294–304. Springer, Cham (2018). https://doi.org/10.1007/978-3-319-95174-4_24
34. Gioia, A., Totaro, V., Bonelli, R., Esposito, A.A.M.G., Balacco, G., Iacobellis, V.: Flood susceptibility evaluation on ephemeral streams of Southern Italy: a case study of Lama Balice. In: Gervasi, O., et al. (eds.) ICCSA 2018. LNCS, vol. 10964, pp. 334–348. Springer, Cham (2018). https://doi.org/10.1007/978-3-319-95174-4_27
35. Fiorentino, M., Gioia, A., Iacobellis, V., Manfreda, S.: Regional analysis of runoff thresholds behaviour in Southern Italy based on theoretically derived distributions. In: Advances in Geosciences, pp. 139–144. Copernicus GmbH (2011). https://doi.org/10.5194/adgeo-26-139-2011
36. Valentino, S., Costa, P.J., Humberto, V., Giuseppina, U., Fabio, F.: Structural degradation assessment of RC buildings: calibration and comparison of semeiotic-based methodology for decision support system. J. Perform. Constructed Facil. **33**, 04018109 (2019). https://doi.org/10.1061/(ASCE)CF.1943-5509.0001249
37. Valentino, S., Giuseppina, U., Fabio, F.: User reporting-based semeiotic assessment of existing building stock at the regional scale. J. Perform. Constructed Facil. **32**, 04018079 (2018). https://doi.org/10.1061/(ASCE)CF.1943-5509.0001227
38. O'Brien, J.S., Julien, P.Y., Fullerton, W.T.: Two-dimensional water flood and mudflow simulation. J. Hydraul. Eng. **119**, 244–261 (1993). https://doi.org/10.1061/(ASCE)0733-9429(1993)119:2(244)
39. Service, U.S.S.C.: SCS National Engineering Handbook, Section 4: Hydrology (1972)
40. Chen, D., Huang, J., Jackson, T.J.: Vegetation water content estimation for corn and soybeans using spectral indices derived from MODIS near- and short-wave infrared bands. Remote Sens. Environ. **98**, 225–236 (2005). https://doi.org/10.1016/j.rse.2005.07.008
41. Vermote, E., Justice, C., Claverie, M., Franch, B.: Preliminary analysis of the performance of the Landsat 8/OLI land surface reflectance product. Remote Sens. Environ. **185**, 46–56 (2016). https://doi.org/10.1016/j.rse.2016.04.008
42. Malinowski, R., Groom, G., Schwanghart, W., Heckrath, G.: Detection and delineation of localized flooding from WorldView-2 multispectral data. Remote Sens. **7**, 14853–14875 (2015). https://doi.org/10.3390/rs71114853
43. Birth, G.S., McVey, G.R.: Measuring the color of growing turf with a reflectance spectrophotometer 1. Agron. J. **60**, 640–643 (1968). https://doi.org/10.2134/agronj1968.00021962006000060016x

44. Rouse, J.W.: Monitoring vegetation systems in the Great Plains with ERTS. Presented at the 1 January (1974)
45. Huete, A., Didan, K., Miura, T., Rodriguez, E.P., Gao, X., Ferreira, L.G.: Overview of the radiometric and biophysical performance of the MODIS vegetation indices. Remote Sens. Environ. **83**, 195–213 (2002). https://doi.org/10.1016/S0034-4257(02)00096-2
46. McFeeters, S.K.: The use of the normalized difference water index (NDWI) in the delineation of open water features. Int. J. Remote Sens. **17**, 1425–1432 (1996). https://doi.org/10.1080/01431169608948714
47. Xu, H.: Modification of normalised difference water index (NDWI) to enhance open water features in remotely sensed imagery. Int. J. Remote Sens. **27**, 3025–3033 (2006). https://doi.org/10.1080/01431160600589179
48. Gao, B.: NDWI—a normalized difference water index for remote sensing of vegetation liquid water from space. Remote Sens. Environ. **58**, 257–266 (1996). https://doi.org/10.1016/S0034-4257(96)00067-3
49. Wilson, E.H., Sader, S.A.: Detection of forest harvest type using multiple dates of Landsat TM imagery. Remote Sens. Environ. **80**, 385–396 (2002). https://doi.org/10.1016/S0034-4257(01)00318-2
50. Feyisa, G.L., Meilby, H., Fensholt, R., Proud, S.R.: Automated water extraction index: a new technique for surface water mapping using Landsat imagery. Remote Sens. Environ. **140**, 23–35 (2014). https://doi.org/10.1016/j.rse.2013.08.029
51. Rouse Jr., J.W., Haas, R.H., Schell, J.A., Deering, D.W.: Monitoring Vegetation Systems in the Great Plains with Erts, vol. 351, pp. 309. NASA Special Publication (1974)
52. Balacco, G., Totaro, V., Gioia, A., Piccinni, A.F.: Evaluation of geomorphic descriptors thresholds for flood prone areas detection on ephemeral streams in the metropolitan area of Bari (Italy). In: Misra, S., et al. (eds.) ICCSA 2019. LNCS, vol. 11622, pp. 239–254. Springer, Cham (2019)
53. Fawcett, T.: An introduction to ROC analysis. Pattern Recogn. Lett. **27**, 861–874 (2006). https://doi.org/10.1016/j.patrec.2005.10.010

Supporting Insurance Strategies in Agriculture by Remote Sensing: A Possible Approach at Regional Level

Enrico Borgogno-Mondino[1(✉)], Filippo Sarvia[1], and Mario A. Gomarasca[2]

[1] DISAFA, University of Torino, L.go Braccini 2, 10095 Grugliasco, Italy
enrico.borgogno@unito.it
[2] CNR-IREA, Via a. Corti, 12, 20133 Milan, Italy

Abstract. Climate variability is one of the greatest risks for farmers. The ongoing increase of natural calamities suggests that insurance strategies have to be more dynamic than previously. In this work a remote sensing based service prototype is presented aimed at supporting insurance companies with the aim of defining an operative tool to objectively calibrate insurance annual fares, tending to cost reduction able to attract more potential customers. Methodology was applied to the whole Piemonte region (NW Italy) that is greatly devoted to agriculture. MODIS MOD13Q1-v6 image time series were used for this purpose. MODIS data were used to figure out the ongoing climate change trends at regional scale, looking at the NDVI time series ranging from 2000 to 2018; the average phenological behaviour of the main agriculture classes in the area (CORINE Land Cover classes Level 3, CLC2012) was considered looking at the yearly average NDVI value trend in the analysed period. This analysis was intended to describe the yearly tuning of the average insurance risk factor and fares in respect of the reference year (2000). A patch level investigation comparing the NDVI average value of a single CLC2012 patch with its reference class was differently used to map local differences of crops performance, aimed at locally tuning insurance risk and fares around the average one as resulting from the previous step. Proposed methodology proved to be able to describe the average temporal evolution of crop classes performances and to locally tune, at single field and crop type level, the agronomic performances of insured areas.

Keywords: Crop insurance · MODIS NDVI · Remote sensing-based services

1 Introduction

Crops may be classified as "subsistence crops" if they will support producers (personally or their livestock), or "income crops" if they will be sold for profit. The latter, which will be sold immediately after the harvest, have a financial potential that depends on the yearly growing season, when plants are constantly exposed to various types of threats, included weather conditions. Ordinary agricultural management model cannot be maintained in the long term because of the recent climate change, inducing higher temperatures, anomalous rainfall trends and lower water reserves [1]. Climate change

S. Misra et al. (Eds.): ICCSA 2019, LNCS 11622, pp. 186–199, 2019.
https://doi.org/10.1007/978-3-030-24305-0_15

impacts on ecosystems have been extensively analyzed [2–4]. However, only recently climate change effects on crop development production have been documented [5–7]. Climate change can damage crops leading a significant impact on human activities with particular concern for those countries where Gross Domestic Product (GDP) is largely dependent on agriculture [8, 9]. Crop monitoring at country and international level is therefore needed to quantify yield exposure to adversity. Insurance companies are currently looking at remote sensing from satellite missions as a promising tool to support their strategies in the agriculture sector. Remote sensing, based on long time series of images, has been thought to satisfy two types of requirements: one related to the ex-post estimation of damages from extreme weather events e.g. droughts, floods and hail [10, 11]; another related to the ex-ante quantification and mapping of risk related to a potential reduction of crop production determined by long term climate change trends. Italy has been ready to tackle the issue of risk management in agriculture, introducing since the 1970s with the National Solidarity Fund (FSN), the principle of solidarity for companies suffering damages caused by natural disasters. The goal of the FSN is to promote prevention and measures in the areas affected by natural disasters, with the aim of promoting the economic and productive recovery of the damaged companies. In the insurance sector the remote sensing is expected to map spatial and temporal differences to better and more consciously calibrate the insurance premiums, longing for their reduction and the consequent easier approach from farmers. Presently, insurance companies must operate a ground survey to evaluate each compensation request; in a not too far future, remote sensing systems should explore circumstantially the entire territorial context highlighting anomalies, thus targeting appraisals to quantify possible losses. Economic and management strategies supported by this new type information will increase competitiveness and business income of insurance companies. Satellite-based remote sensing effectively responds to requirements of large-scale mapping of vegetation [12, 13]. Natural disasters related economy, e.g. insurance strategies, greatly long for low cost tools for risk assessment, possibly fitting all situations around the world [14–16]. Global datasets, like satellite images archives, often available for free, can represent a valid support to assess large areas, especially if used jointly with georeferenced ground data needed to correctly address deductions [17]. Governments and international donors currently promote 'Climate Insurance', generic term to indicate a series of financial checks aimed at tuning payments following meteorological events. The G7 (Group of Seven) '*InsuResilience*' initiative is meant to significantly increase the insurance cover of low income people against negative impact of extreme weather events induced by climate change within the next 5 years. This initiative is intended to provide funds to governments with the aim of stabilizing and fostering the recovery of a large part of the affected population. For example, for the climate conference in Paris *InsuResilience* pledged 400 million USD [18], and the portfolio of the Global Index Insurance Facility is 148 million USD [19]. The estimate of the global volume of agriculture insurance premiums is approximately around 5 billion USD for emerging markets. Moreover, the World Bank estimates that 44% of insurance premiums in agriculture consist of subsidies [20].

A yearly amount of subsidies of two billion dollars for agricultural insurance are supposed to interest emerging markets. Insurance programs presenting technological innovation, are considered promising for reducing poverty and improving climate risk management and resilience in developing countries where smallholder agriculture dominates. These programs may be defined as 'index insurance' and tend to link payouts to environmental proxies rather than occurred losses [21]. Governments and donors are showing great interest about this type of insurance programs and a large number of pilot studies are promoted worldwide [22–24]. In the Italian agriculture context, risk prevention insurances policies are mainly managed collectively, at district level, through the so called "*agricultural defense consortia*". Consortia contracts with insurance companies mainly to cover yield losses of their associated. Italian Government contributes to a part of the premium paid by the farmer. In particular the Ministry of Agriculture decree n. 28405/17 regulates contributions to agricultural insurance premiums defining a yearly plan. The plan aims at extending insurance coverages by means of facilitated policies covering crop, facilities and livestock damages from adverse climatic conditions. Annex 1 of the above mentioned decree defines crops, corporate structures and types of insurable cattle. Crops such as corn, wheat and grass fall into this list. Insurance policies can also cover production losses permitting different insurance choices in respect of both type and quantity of crops. Definition of insurance parameters can be found in Annex 5 of the 28405/17 decree, but can be summarized as it follows.

Revenue policies are contracts that cover the loss of revenue from the insured production. Loss is intended as a combination of yield reduction due to both seasonal adversities and market price reduction with the following definitions: - *yield reduction* is the difference between the actual yield at the time of harvest and the insured yield. The latter can be assumed equal to: (a) the average production of the previous three years; (b) the average production of the previous five years excluding the years with the lowest and highest production; (c) the actual obtainable production of the insurance year, if lower; - *price reduction* is the difference between market reference price, as determined by the Institute of Services for the Agricultural Market (ISMEA), in respect of the third quarter of the year of collection of the insured product, and the price determined by law; - *effective yield* is the one determined with reference to the time of harvest from the period of the insurance company that took charge of the risk.

Indexed policies are insurance contracts that cover the loss of production insured for damage in quantity and quality as a result of adverse weather conditions, identified by a positive or negative variance from a biological and/or meteorological index. The relative damage will be recognized based on the actual difference with respect to the value of the aforesaid index. The following indices can be considered: - *meteorological index* identifies a meteorological event recorded based on a predefined parameter, such as the sum of average daily temperatures and/or cumulated precipitations, referring to a determined period of cultivation development, potentially harmful for agricultural production in a specific production area; - *biological index* identifies a biotic event registered on a predefined parameter, such as for example the lost biomass referred to a determined period of cultivation development, potentially harmful for the agricultural production in a specific production area; - *adverse climatic trend index* is used to take care about the ongoing climatic trend as described by some selected parameters like rainfall and/or cumulated temperatures (in the cultivation period or in part of it) which deviate significantly from the optimal trend for a certain crop in a given phenological phase generating negative effects on production that can be measured by biological indices. In this work free satellite data from NASA (National Aeronautics and Space Administration) MODIS (Moderate Resolution Imaging Spectro-radiometer) sensor, on board of the TERRA satellite [5, 25, 26], have been used to draw a possible operational tool to calibrate agricultural insurance strategies with revenue policies in the Piemonte region (NW Italy), with special concern about indexed policies. Even if the proposed methodology have been tested in Piemonte, it is thought with a global perspective, that it can be easily adapted to any other part of the world.

2 Materials and Methods

2.1 Study Area

The study area is located in the Piemonte region (NW Italy, Fig. 1). It sizes 25388 km^2 and well fits size requirements for moderate resolution satellite imagery. It well represents the northern Italian agricultural context with a typically temperate climate having a continental character, where NW Alps gradually determines a temperature reduction while altitude rises.

2.2 Available Data

A NDVI (*Normalized Difference Vegetation Index*, [27]) image time series composed of 432 images covering the period 2000–2018, was generated from the MOD13Q1-v6 dataset available from the NASA LPDAAC collection [28]. Data were obtained in TIF format, WGS84 geographic reference frame from the AppEEARS system [29].

The MOD13Q1 Version 6 product provides a Vegetation Index (VI) value at a per pixel basis. Native grid is 4800 $\times$ 4800 pixels having a GSD (Ground Sampling Distance) of 250 m. The MOD13Q1 algorithm selects, at pixel level, the best VI value from all the acquisitions available in a period of 16 days. Criteria defining the "best" value are: low cloud coverage, low viewing angle and the highest NDVI/EVI value. Pixel reliability (PR) and CDOY layers, supplied within the MOD13Q1-v6, were considered to refine NDVI time series. Pixel Reliability layer (PR) defines the overall quality of the NDVI value of each pixel, giving information about its status, as explained in Table 1.

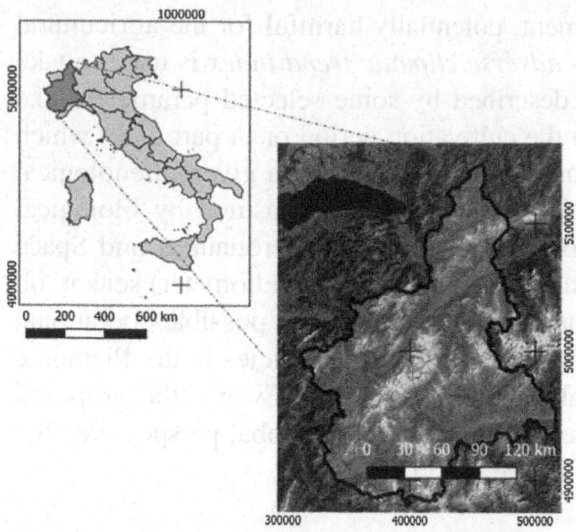

Fig. 1. The study area is located in Piemonte, NW Italy (Reference frame: WGS 84 UTM 32 N).

Composite day of the year layer (CDOY) contains, for each pixel of the image, the day of the year in which reflectances used in the VIs computation were acquired; this information is needed to properly build NDVI time series (TS) placing NDVI values at the right dates for each pixel.

According to Leprieur [30] NDVI is a vegetation index designed for describing vegetation canopy biophysical properties, and according to Turvey [31] it can be adopted in when dealing with VI in the crop insurance context.

Table 1. MOD13Q1/A1 pixel reliability

Rant Key	Summary QA	Description
–1	Fill/No Data	Not Processed
0	Good Data	Use with confidence
1	Marginal data	Useful, but look at other QA information
2	Snow/Ice	Target covered with snow/ice
3	Cloudy	Target not visible, cover with cloud

NDVI is computed according to Eq. 1:

$$NDVI = (\rho_{NIR} - \rho_{RED})/(\rho_{NIR} + \rho_{RED}) \quad (1)$$

where ρ_{NIR} and ρ_{RED} are the NIR and RED at-the ground reflectance, respectively, at that pixel location. Many studies proved that NDVI is a good predictor of crops production and that can be somehow useful to calibrate insurance premiums in agriculture [32, 33]. The CORINE Land Cover dataset, release 2012, level 3 (hereinafter CLC2012), was used to map cultivated areas over Piemonte. CLC is thought at European level specifically for detection and monitoring of land cover/use, with particular focus on environmental protection requirements. CLC inventory started in 1985 (reference year 1990) and updates have been produced for the 2000, 2006, 2012, and 2018 years. CLC consists of 44 land cover classes organized in 4 hierarchical meaning levels. Technical features of the CLC2012 dataset are reported in Table 2. Agricultural classes from CLC2012 considered for this work are reported in Table 3.

An administrative boundaries vector map (hereinafter called AB, 1:100000 map scale, 2012 updated), mapping municipalities (1181) over the whole Piemonte Region, was used to compute statistics of cultivated areas at municipality level. It was obtained for free from the Regional Geoportal.

Table 2. CLC2012 technical features

Technical feature	Value
Satellite data source	IRS P6 LISS III and RapidEye
Time consistency	2011–2012
Geometric accuracy (satellite data)	$\leq$ 25 m
Geometric accuracy (CLC)	Better than 100 m
Thematic accuracy	$\geq$ 85%
Minimum mapping unit/width	25 ha/100 m
Access to the data	free
Number of countries involved	39

Table 3. Agricultural classes according to CLC 20122.

Level 2	Level 3	Content of the classes
2.1	2.1.1.	Non-irrigated arable land
	2.1.3.	Rice fields
2.2	2.2.1.	Vineyards
	2.2.2.	Fruit trees and berry plantations
2.3	2.3.1.	Pastures
2.4	2.4.2.	Complex cultivation patterns
	2.4.3.	Land principally occupied by agriculture, with significant areas of natural vegetation

MODIS NDVI Time Series Analysis

The whole Piemonte Region resulted to be imaged by 432 NDVI maps, 16 days regularly distributed. PR layers, supplied in the same number of NDVI maps, were used for a first selection of "good" observations (PR = 0 or 1) along the NDVI temporal profile of each pixel. All other observations were excluded from computation. This determined that native regularly spaced NDVI time series were turned into irregularly spaced one. Remaining observations were therefore interpolated by spline with tension (value = 10) with reference to the correspondent DOY, from the associated DOY layer, obtaining a new 5 days spaced NDVI profile (time series was densified from 23 to 73 image per year). A further refinement was achieved only for vegetated pixels that were found within the image by testing that the yearly NDVI maximum value was over 0.5. The refinement was intended to remove anomalous, but "good", NDVI values along the expected phenological trend of vegetated areas (e.g. late snow, soil flooding, etc.). Consequently, the previously interpolated NDVI image time series was filtered using an FFT (Fast Fourier Transform) approach on year basis. The yearly NDVI temporal profile of each pixel was transformed into the frequency domain. The three most powerful frequency components were retained, while all the other ones were filtered out. Consequently, a reverse FFT was applied to return back to the NDVI domain determining the final NDVI profile that was analysed. For each of the available years and for each image vegetated pixel, the annual mean NDVI value was computed between the Starting of the Season, SOS, and the End of the Season, EOS [34, 35]. SOS and EOS were placed along the pixel NDVI profile in the moment when the local NDVI value became higher (SOS) and lower (EOS) of 0.4, forcing research within the middle of February and the middle of November. For not-vegetated pixel (yearly NDVI maximum < 0.5) the yearly NDVI mean local value was calculated simply excluding bad observations (PR $\neq$ 0) with no further refinement. A new stack of 19 NDVI maps $NDVI_{\mu}(x,y,t)$ was therefore obtained (t = 2000–2018) by averaging at year level, the filtered/interpolated pixel NDVI temporal profile.

NDVI Statistics at Municipality Level for Cultivated Areas

CLC2012 and AB vector maps were intersected by ordinary Geoprocessing tools available in QGIS 2.18.4 to get crossed information needed to investigate crops yearly performances as detectable by NDVI annual mean value at municipality and agricultural class level. A new regional tessellation scheme was therefore obtained, generating 7017 patches from the original 2997 ones (from CLC2012 Level 3 map). Zonal statistics from the above mentioned *NDVI(x,y,t)* maps were computed, making possible to yearly qualify each patch in respect of the average vegetative behaviour that its agricultural part expressed. According to the 19 *NDVI(x,y,t)* maps, the annual mean NDVI value of each agricultural CLC2012 Level 3 class was computed and the time trend approximated with a 1st order polynomial by Ordinary Least Squares (OLS) estimation. Resulting time-dependent lines were assumed as driving rules to derive an insurance risk factor (hereinafter called "discount rate", $k_i(t)$) useful to tune the average insurance premium in respect of the reference year, that, for this work, was decided to be the first one (2000). The discount rate (hereinafter called K) was computed according to Eq. 2.

$$k_i(t) = \left(\frac{\alpha_i + \beta_i}{\alpha_i \cdot t + \beta_i}\right) \cdot 100 \quad (2)$$

where α_i and β_i are the trend line coefficients estimated by OLS according to the NDVI annual mean values of the CLC2012-Level 3 for the *i-th* class; *t* is the progressive year count from the starting one (2000 is t = 1). A k value higher than 100 means that the insurance premium has to be augmented in respect of the reference one (at the year 2000); on the contrary, a k value lower than 100 mean that the premium must be reduced accordingly. The underlying criterion is that an increase of the annual average NDVI value of a certain agricultural class determines a reduction of the risk related to crop production, making possible a refinement of premiums required to farmers. A further step was done trying to relate premiums not only to the average annual NDVI value of the agricultural CLC2012 Level 3 classes where a certain insured crop can be included, but also in respect of the local conditions. For this purpose authors computed annual NDVI patches' anomalies (PA_i) according to Eq. 3.

$$PA_i(t) = \frac{\mu_i(t)}{\mu_{c_j}(t)} \quad (3)$$

where $\mu_{i(t)}$ is the average NDVI of the *i-th* patch and $\mu_{c_j}(t)$ the NDVI average value of the c_j class that the patch *i-th* belongs to, at the *t* year. For each of the investigated years a map of PA(t) was therefore generated to make possible to locally tune (at patch level) the average class premium in the considered year. Patches having PA > 1 indicates that the insurance premium for fields falling in that patch can be somehow reduced in respect of the average one for that class in that year; PA < 1 means that the insurance premium for fields falling in that patch has to be somehow increased in respect of the average one for that class in that year, since expected yield could be lower the class average one.

3 Results and Discussion

A first investigation concerned the qualification of the area in terms of main land use classes (according to CLC2012 Level 2 classification). Results of this analysis are reported in Table 4 showing that about the 35% of Piemonte region is specifically devoted to agriculture, making the area a good benchmark to test new insurance strategies.

Table 4. Distribution of land cover classes in Piemonte (CLC2012 L3 dataset).

Coverage class	Number class	Area (ha)	Area (%)
Permanent crops	2.2	77313	2
Inland waters	5.1	30878	1
Pastures	2.3	37451	1
Arableland	2.1	697702	20
Heterogeneous agricultural areas	2.4	441183	13
Open areas with little or no vegetation	3.3	218068	6
Scrub and/or herbaceous vegetation associations	3.2	424397	12
Forest	3.1	1417750	41
Industrial, commercial and transport units	1.2	25631	1
Urban fabric	1.1	84307	2
Other	–	8358	1
Total	–	3463038	100

Concerning MOD13Q1 NDVI time series processing, to perceptively demonstrate the effectiveness of the adopted data filtering strategy based on the selective application of the FFT, a profile of a sample vegetated pixel is reported in Fig. 2 with reference to the 2000 year.

Concerning time trend of class annual average NDVI values, according to the CLC2012 Level 3 classification, results of Table 5 were obtained. After removal of evident outliers related to the 2007 and 2013 years, NDVI trends were modelled by a class specific 1st order polynomial, whose coefficients are reported in Table 6 together with the correspondent coefficient of determination (R^2).

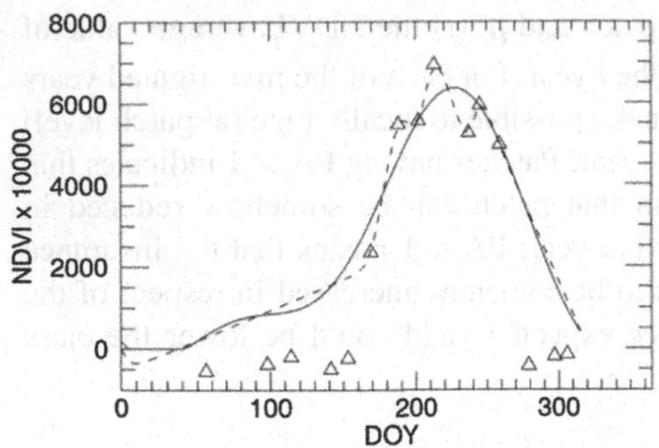

Fig. 2. Black line represents the FFT filtered NDVI profile of a sample pixel (year 2000). Dotted line represents the spline function interpolating "good" observations (Pixel Reliability = 0 or 1). Triangles represent raw data before filtering. DOY is the Day of the Year ranging between 0 and 365.

According to Table 6 all classes proved to suffer from a positive trend of NDVI values in the considered period, suggesting that climate conditions are moving towards a more favourable conditions for agriculture in the area (i.e. a decreasing of the risk associated to yield reduction). The strongest correlation between time and NDVI average class value was found for class 243, the only one containing a natural vegetation component, that, since not managed, mostly emphasizes the effects of medium term climate effects. This suggests that, probably, when testing such features, natural vegetation can represent a better witness of ongoing phenomena. Vineyards (class 221) showed the most significant positive trend with a good correlation, too. Pastures (class 231) scored the second highest R^2 value confirming that, natural and semi-natural vegetation are better indicators of climate changes.

Table 5. NDVI annual mean values for the agricultural CLC2012-Level 3 classes in the area.

Year	CLC2012 – Level 3 classes						
	211	213	221	222	231	242	243
2000	0.54	0.46	0.58	0.64	0.68	0.59	0.65
2001	0.54	0.45	0.58	0.63	0.67	0.59	0.65
2002	0.57	0.47	0.62	0.67	0.7	0.62	0.67
2003	0.5	0.42	0.54	0.61	0.65	0.56	0.63
2004	0.53	0.46	0.57	0.63	0.66	0.57	0.64
2005	0.56	0.47	0.6	0.65	0.68	0.61	0.66
2006	0.55	0.45	0.59	0.64	0.67	0.59	0.65
2007	–	–	–	–	–	–	–
2008	0.56	0.47	0.6	0.66	0.68	0.61	0.66
2009	0.53	0.45	0.6	0.64	0.68	0.59	0.66
2010	0.56	0.46	0.62	0.66	0.7	0.61	0.67
2011	0.53	0.45	0.58	0.59	0.67	0.57	0.65
2012	0.55	0.45	0.61	0.66	0.68	0.6	0.66
2013	–	–	–	–	–	–	–
2014	0.59	0.49	0.64	0.67	0.72	0.64	0.69
2015	0.57	0.47	0.63	0.67	0.71	0.62	0.69
2016	0.57	0.46	0.61	0.65	0.7	0.61	0.68
2017	0.54	0.45	0.57	0.62	0.67	0.58	0.65
2018	0.58	0.5	0.64	0.68	0.71	0.63	0.69

It is worth to remind that not all the variations in NDVI values can be assumed as significant, since: (a) in literature, it was proved that averagely the accuracy in NDVI computation from remotely sensed data is about 0.02 NDVI points [36]; (b) NDVI class mean value assumed as index of yearly crop performance variations should have to be compared with the correspondent NDVI class standard deviation. Authors are working to improve these remaining weaknesses in the proposed methodology.

Table 6. Gain (α), offset (β) and coefficient of determination (R^2) values of the 1st order polynomial approximating the time trend of the annual average class NDVI values. Underlined values are discussed in the text.

CLC2012 class code	α	β	R^2
211	0.0016	0.5360	0.2
213	0.0009	0.4522	0.1
221	<u>0.0023</u>	0.5762	0.26
222	0.0011	0.6352	0.07
231	0.0017	0.6675	0.27
242	0.0017	0.5830	0.2
243	0.0019	0.6425	<u>0.39</u>

Table 7. Discount rate values computed for the agricultural CLC2012 Level3 classes along the time series.

CLC2012 level 3							
Year	Discount rate (%, reference = year2000)						
	211	213	221	222	231	242	243
2000	100	100	100	100	100	100	100
2001	99.7	99.8	99.6	99.8	99.7	99.7	99.7
2002	99.4	99.6	99.2	99.7	99.5	99.4	99.4
2003	99.1	99.4	98.8	99.5	99.2	99.1	99.1
2004	98.8	99.2	98.4	99.3	99	98.8	98.8
2005	98.5	99	98	99.2	98.7	98.5	98.5
2006	98.2	98.8	97.6	99	98.5	98.2	98.2
2007	97.9	98.6	97.3	98.8	98.3	98	97.9
2008	97.6	98.4	96.9	98.7	98	97.7	97.7
2009	97.4	98.2	96.5	98.5	97.8	97.4	97.4
2010	97.1	98	96.1	98.3	97.5	97.1	97.1
2011	96.8	97.8	95.8	98.2	97.3	96.8	96.8
2012	96.5	97.6	95.4	98	97	96.6	96.5
2013	96.2	97.4	95	97.8	96.8	96.3	96.2
2014	96	97.2	94.7	97.7	96.6	96	96
2015	95.7	97	94.3	97.5	96.3	95.7	95.7
2016	95.4	96.8	94	97.3	96.1	95.5	95.4
2017	95.1	96.6	93.6	97.2	95.9	95.2	95.1
2018	94.9	96.4	93.3	97	95.6	94.9	94.9

To translate the modelled trends into computation of insurance premiums, the annual discount rate values were calculated for all the CLC2012 Level 3 classes with reference to the 2000 year. Results are reported in Table 7 and graphically represented in Fig. 3. It can be noticed that expectation is that insurance premium average costs, in 19 years, would have had to be reduced from the 3% up to the 7% of the 2000 average cost. Maximum expected reduction was related to vineyards (221), minimum to fruit trees and berry plantations (222).

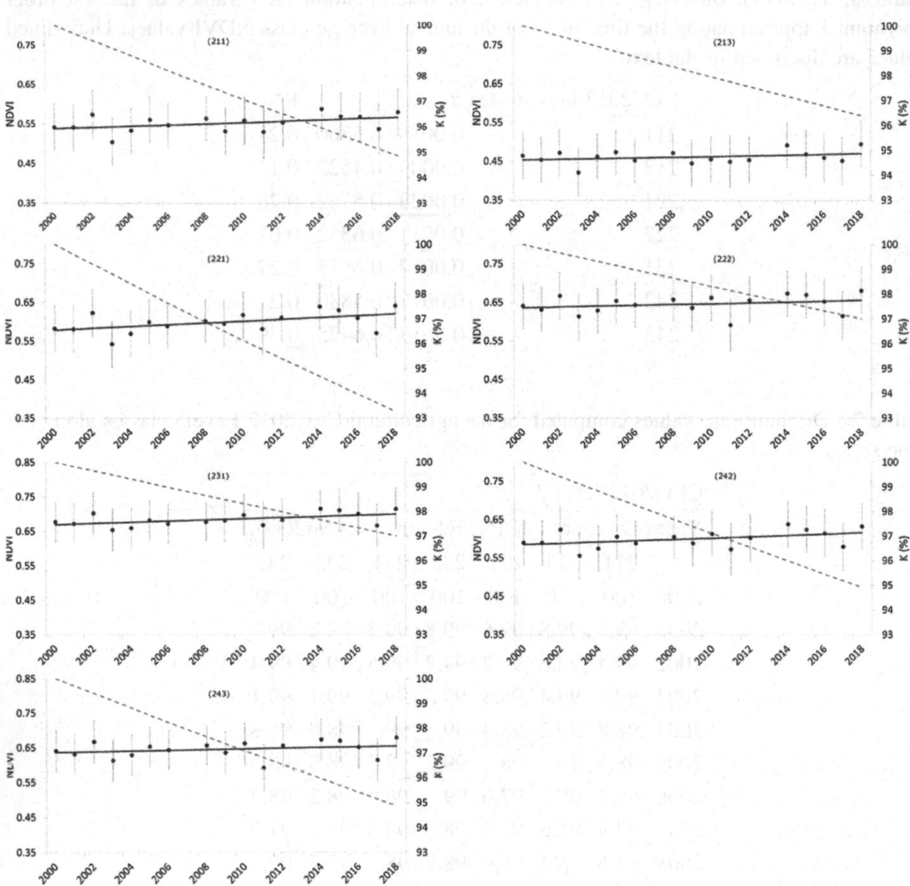

Fig. 3. Time trends of NDVI annual mean values (continuous line) and of the discount rate (dotted line) averaged over the agricultural CLC2012 Level 3 classes (reported in each graph).

According to Eq. 3, for each of the analyzed years, a map of PA(t) was generated at patch level (Fig. 4), permitting to locate, in the whole region, where cultivated areas were supposed to perform over, or under, the expected average class NDVI (i.e. expected yield). This further information, translated to the insurance operational compart, could permit to better calibrate, around the class average premium, the one specifically designed for the field for which a farmer is paying its fee. The difference

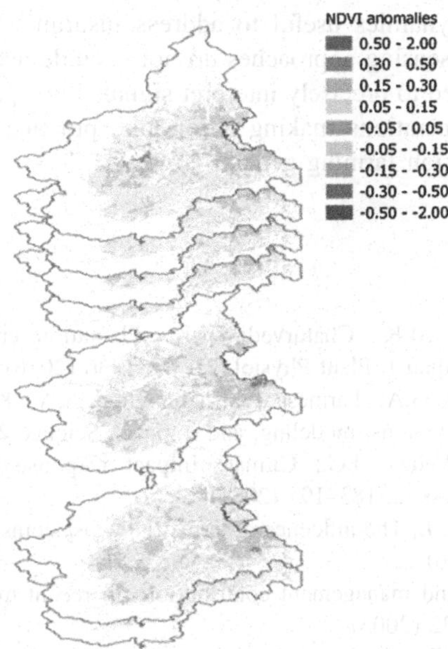

Fig. 4. Map of NDVI anomalies computed according to the CLC2012 level 3 classes for the period 2000–2018 (Geographic Reference system is WGS-84, EPSG: 4326).

1.0–PA(t) determines values lower than 0 for those areas that tend to behave better than their own class mean.

4 Conclusions

In the crop insurance sector remote sensing is expected to support premiums definition, longing for such a reduction that could attract more farmers. Presently, insurance companies must operate a ground survey to evaluate each compensation request; in a not too far future, remote sensing systems should circumstantially explore the entire territorial context locating those anomalies useful to better target appraisals to quantify losses. Economical and management strategies, supported by this new type of information, is expected to increase competitiveness and business income of insurance companies. Optical images from MODIS sensor, obtainable for free, in spite of their reduced geometric resolution, proved to effectively support investigation of climate change effects onto crops in the medium period. NDVI time series showed that crop performances, supposed to be directly related to the average annual vigour, could be reasonably described through a linear increasing trend, whose strength depends on the investigated crop type. In general it was observed that low managed crops (from the water supplying point of view), like vineyards and orchards, are more conditioned by changing climate conditions.

It is surprising that even in highly fragmented agricultural areas like the Italian ones, derivable information from a long NDVI time series can operationally support interpretation of crops dynamics useful to address insurance policies. It should be remembered that remote sensing approaches do not exclude accurate ground surveys, that, oppositely, are needed to precisely interpret signals in respect of occurring events and crop management operations making agronomic practices simplest, fastest and most effective, in a precision farming general context.

References

1. Hebbar, K.B., Berwal, M.K., Chaturvedi, V.K.: Plantation crops: climatic risks and adaptation strategies. Indian J. Plant Physiol. **21**, 428–436 (2016)
2. Easterling, D.R., Meehl, G.A., Parmesan, C., Changnon, S.A., Karl, T.R., Mearns, L.O.: Climate extremes: observations, modeling, and impacts. Science **289**, 2068–2074 (2000)
3. Füssel, H.-M., van Minnen, J.G.: Climate impact response functions for terrestrial ecosystems. Integr. Assess. **2**, 183–197 (2001)
4. Meir, P., Cox, P., Grace, J.: The influence of terrestrial ecosystems on climate. Trends Ecol. Evol. **21**, 254–260 (2006)
5. Lobell, D.B.: Climate and management contributions to recent trends in U.S. agricultural yields. Science **299**, 1032 (2003)
6. Chmielewski, F.-M., Müller, A., Bruns, E.: Climate changes and trends in phenology of fruit trees and field crops in Germany, 1961–2000. Agric. Forest Meteorol. **121**, 69–78 (2004)
7. Sbaouelgi, J.: Impact of climate change on date production in Tunisia. Environ. Model. Assess. **23**, 597–607 (2018)
8. Dell'Acqua, F., Iannelli, G., Torres, M., Martina, M.: A novel strategy for very-large-scale cash-crop mapping in the context of weather-related risk assessment, combining global satellite multispectral datasets, environmental constraints, and in situ acquisition of geospatial data. Sensors **18**, 591 (2018)
9. Martinelli, L.A., Naylor, R., Vitousek, P.M., Moutinho, P.: Agriculture in Brazil: impacts, costs, and opportunities for a sustainable future. Curr. Opin. Environ. Sustain. **2**, 431–438 (2010)
10. Church, S.P., Dunn, M., Babin, N., Mase, A.S., Haigh, T., Prokopy, L.S.: Do advisors perceive climate change as an agricultural risk? An in-depth examination of Midwestern US Ag advisors' views on drought, climate change, and risk management. Agric. Hum. Values **35**, 349–365 (2018)
11. Hill, R.V., et al.: Ex ante and ex post effects of hybrid index insurance in Bangladesh. J. Dev. Econ. **136**, 1–17 (2019)
12. Xie, Y., Sha, Z., Yu, M.: Remote sensing imagery in vegetation mapping: a review. J. Plant Ecol. **1**, 9–23 (2008)
13. Inglada, J., et al.: Assessment of an operational system for crop type map production using high temporal and spatial resolution satellite optical imagery. Remote Sens. **7**, 12356–12379 (2015)
14. Gurenko, E.N.: Climate Change and Insurance: Disaster Risk Financing in Developing Countries. Routledge, London (2015)
15. Joyette, A.R.T., Nurse, L.A., Pulwarty, R.S.: Disaster risk insurance and catastrophe models in risk-prone small Caribbean islands. Disasters **39**, 467–492 (2015)
16. Jongman, B., et al.: Increasing stress on disaster-risk finance due to large floods. Nat. Clim. Change **4**, 264–268 (2014)

17. Brown, J.C., Kastens, J.H., Coutinho, A.C., de Castro Victoria, D., Bishop, C.R.: Classifying multiyear agricultural land use data from Mato Grosso using time-series MODIS vegetation index data. Remote Sens. Environ. **130**, 39–50 (2013)
18. Climate Risk Insurance for Strengthening Climate Resilience of Poor People in Vulnerable Countries: A Background Paper on Challenges, Ambitions and Perspectives (2015)
19. Global Index Insurance Facility: Achievements Report, (2016)
20. Mahul, O., Stutley, C.J.: Government support to agricultural insurance: challenges and options for developing countries. The World Bank (2010)
21. Müller, B., Johnson, L., Kreuer, D.: Maladaptive outcomes of climate insurance in agriculture. Glob. Environ. Change **46**, 23–33 (2017)
22. Karlan, D., Osei, R., Osei-Akoto, I., Udry, C.: Agricultural decisions after relaxing credit and risk constraints. Q. J. Econ. **129**, 597–652 (2014)
23. Greatrex, H., et al.: Scaling up Index Insurance for Smallholder Farmers, p. 32 (2015)
24. Jensen, N., Barrett, C.: Agricultural Index Insurance for Development. Applied Economic Perspectives and Policy (2016). https://doi.org/10.1093/aepp/ppw022
25. Wardlow, B.D., Egbert, S.L.: Large-area crop mapping using time-series MODIS 250 m NDVI data: an assessment for the U.S. Central Great Plains. Remote Sens. Environ. **112**, 1096–1116 (2008)
26. Ozdogan, M.: The spatial distribution of crop types from MODIS data: temporal unmixing using independent component analysis. Remote Sens. Environ. **114**, 1190–1204 (2010)
27. Rouse Jr., J.W., Hass, R.H., Schell, J.A., Harland, J.C.: Monitoring the Vernal Advancement of Retrogradation of Natural Vegetation (1994)
28. Solano, R., Didan, K., Jacobson, A., Huete, A.: MODIS vegetation index user's guide (MOD13 series), pp. 1–38. Vegetation Index and Phenology Lab, The University of Arizona (2010)
29. Didan, K.: MOD13Q1 MODIS/Terra vegetation indices 16-day L3 global 250 m SIN grid V006. NASA EOSDIS Land Processes DAAC (2015)
30. Leprieur, C., Verstraete, M.M., Pinty, B.: Evaluation of the performance of various vegetation indices to retrieve vegetation cover from AVHRR data. Remote Sens. Rev. **10**, 265–284 (1994)
31. Turvey, G., Marshall I.H.: Buckling and Postbuckling of Composite Plates (2012)
32. Haghverdi, A., Washington-Allen, R.A., Leib, B.G.: Prediction of cotton lint yield from phenology of crop indices using artificial neural networks. Comput. Electron. Agric. **152**, 186–197 (2018)
33. Zambrano, F., Vrieling, A., Nelson, A., Meroni, M., Tadesse, T.: Prediction of drought-induced reduction of agricultural productivity in Chile from MODIS, rainfall estimates, and climate oscillation indices. Remote Sens. Environ. **219**, 15–30 (2018)
34. Testa, S., Soudani, K., Boschetti, L., Mondino, E.B.: MODIS-derived EVI, NDVI and WDRVI time series to estimate phenological metrics in French deciduous forests. Int. J. Appl. Earth Obs. Geoinf. **64**, 132–144 (2018)
35. Testa, S., Mondino, E.C.B., Pedroli, C.: Correcting MODIS 16-day composite NDVI time-series with actual acquisition dates. Eur. J. Remote Sens. **47**, 285–305 (2014)
36. Borgogno-Mondino, E., Lessio, A., Gomarasca, M.A.: A fast operative method for NDVI uncertainty estimation and its role in vegetation analysis. Eur. J. Remote Sens. **49**, 137–156 (2016)

Geomatics for Environmental Monitoring, Analysis and Forecast

Valery G. Gitis and Alexander B. Derendyaev(✉)

Institute for Information, Transmission Problems RAS (Kharkevich Institute), Moscow, Russia
gitis@iitp.ru, wintsa@gmail.com

Abstract. We suggest geomatic technology for monitoring natural processes, which is implemented on three web GIS platforms: (1) http://distcomp.ru/geo/arctic/—monitoring the hydroecological situation in the Arctic, (2) http://distcomp.ru/geo/2/, http://distcomp.ru/geo/3/—analysis of seismic fields and (3) http://distcomp.ru/geo/prognosis/—automatic prediction of earthquakes. Platforms combine two levels of geodata analysis. The first level supports automatic data processing and simple analysis tools that are suitable for any Internet user. The second level is designed for detailed data analysis performed by a specialist. Thus, users of the platform have the opportunity to receive preliminary information about the processes in the environment and conduct research.

Keywords: Web-based GIS platform · Arctic · Seismic fields · Automatic forecasting of earthquakes · Machine learning · Method of the minimum area of alarm

1 Introduction

Monitoring of natural and man-made processes is used for regular observation, assessment, and prediction of the state of the environment. The solution to these problems is connected with the analysis of large volumes of heterogeneous spatial and spatio-temporal data. The characteristics of such data require the use of specialized methods and technologies that are implemented in web GIS.

The main set of GIS operations for monitoring and analyzing natural processes were considered in [1]. Currently, a web GIS is usually used for visual analysis of meteorological fields. For example, the https://www.windy.com and https://www.ventusky.com/ systems provide up-to-date and predictive information for a large number of meteorological processes, as well as relevant information about the infrastructure. Both GIS have high-quality interactive 4D visualization of temporal processes with animation elements. The presence of animated cartography and interactive graphics, the possibility of joint visualization of several processes, user-friendly interface contribute to the understanding of the meteorological situation.

The work was supported by Russian Foundation for Basic Research, project No. 17-07- 00494.

S. Misra et al. (Eds.): ICCSA 2019, LNCS 11622, pp. 200–215, 2019.
https://doi.org/10.1007/978-3-030-24305-0_16

When developing technology, we proceeded from the fact that monitoring data in many cases should be used to predict hazardous phenomena. Therefore, it is desirable that the monitoring system supports not only convenient data visualization but also analytical functions. Information obtained from the system can be divided into two groups. The first group includes information that can be obtained from initial observations automatically using predefined data processing methods. The second group includes information for which an extraordinary complex analysis of data is required. We believe that any Internet users, including employees of federal and regional services and administrations, as well as research staff, can be interested in the first group of information. The second group of information is requested by problem domain specialists performing scientific research. The first group of users requires automatic loading, processing, visual representation of results and a simplified interface. The second group of users requires a set of tools needed for joint data analysis, as well as an ability to download and integrate additional data from remote servers and local network. In systems for seismic hazard analysis and earthquake prediction, it is advisable to combine both levels of data analysis. The first level should support monitoring of seismic fields and the forecast of earthquakes, providing automatic loading and processing of data and providing the operator with simple analysis tools in combination with a visual representation of the results. The second level is designed for detailed analysis of hypotheses, which an expert can formulate at the first level.

The idea of two-level analysis of geographic data is universal. It has proven itself in the ESRI solution [2], in which editing and administration of maps are performed using ArcGIS Online, and in-depth data analysis is supported using ArcGIS Desktop [3].

The monitoring platforms implemented in this technology combine automatic data analysis, accessible to any Internet user, with detailed analysis performed by a specialist. Thus, platforms are convenient for all users. They receive preliminary information about the processes in the environment and have the opportunity to conduct research. Platforms consist of two web GIS. The first GIS automatically loads and processes the source data, provides the user with analytical tools with intuitive operations and a simplified interface, starts calculations on a remote server and prepares a GIS project for the second GIS. The second GIS is a multifunctional system focused on the analysis of spatio-temporal processes, which is performed by a specialist.

In Sects. 2, 3 and 4 we present three geomatic technologies. They are implemented on the following network platforms: (1) http://distcomp.ru/geo/arctic/ is the platform for monitoring of hydroecological processes in the Arctic, (2) http://distcomp.ru/geo/2/ and http://distcomp.ru/geo/3/ are the platforms for analysis of seismic fields and (3) http://distcomp.ru/geo/prognosis/ is the platform for automatic prediction of earthquakes.

2 The Technology of Monitoring and Analysis of the Hydroecological Situation in the Arctic

Natural and anthropogenic processes in the Arctic substantially affect the nature of the entire Earth [4, 5], and high sensitivity of the Arctic to the increase in the average temperature here plays a unique role. Warming in the Arctic leads to ice cover reduction, causes reflection of solar rays, and, therefore heating of the whole Earth. Discharge of cold fresh water as a result of ice melting reduces seawater salinity in the near-Arctic regions, which causes changes in oceanic currents. Melting of permafrost and reduction of the ice cover can lead to discharged large methane volumes to the Earth's atmosphere, therefore promoting global warming [6].

The Arctic is notably rich in hydrocarbon, mineral and biological resources, which makes it a region of growing economic activity for their exploration. Hydrocarbons are mined on the Arctic shelf, rare earth minerals are drilled on the coasts, and the marine environment is widely used for fishing and transit. Economic activity, storage of industrial waste and various emergencies can significantly affect the ecology of the Arctic. It is clear that the anthropogenic impact on natural processes in the Arctic will only increase in the future. Note that the peculiarity of the Arctic environment is its long-term recovery after adverse anthropogenic influences [7]. The above factors show why the Arctic is today one of the most important objects for monitoring natural and anthropogenic processes.

Arctic monitoring technology is implemented on a network platform (http://distcomp.ru/geo/arctic), which consists of two web GIS [8, 9]. The first GIS, GIS GeoMonitor, is built in a client-server architecture with a thin client. It supports automatic loading and processing of data, a visual representation of spatio-temporal processes, marine vehicles and earthquake epicenters, measurement of hydrometeorological fields and point data attributes, and also forms a GIS project and starts modeling hydrocarbon spills on a remote server.

GIS GeoTime 3 is realized in a thick Java-based client-server architecture (http://www.geo.iitp.ru/GT3/). It is a big multi-functional system focused on the analysis of spatio-temporal environmental processes and earthquake forecasting research. It is launched from the GIS GeoMonitor page with the data that is used for analysis. Tools of GeoTime 3 makes it possible to supplement the GIS project with tile maps and 2D, 3D, 4D point, vector and grid data from remote and local servers. GIS Geo-Time 3 supports the joint processing of all these types of data. The leading interactive operations supporting visual analysis are the following: presentation of data in the form of maps, cuts, plots, diagrams, and tables; animation visualization of one or more spatio-temporal processes; measurement of distances, areas and reading the attributes; evaluation of statistics for points and polygons.

The platform provides users with access to the analysis of three types of spatial and spatio-temporal data: re-analysis of historical data, operational observations, and forecast. The information resources of the platform include: (1) Reanalysis data of ERA-Interim for 1979–2015 (ECMWF); (2) Data of operative mid-term (0–120 h) forecast of the GFS and NCEP/NOAA meteorological fields (Roshydromet), (3) Data on movements of vessels (the North Sea Route Administration); (4) Data of operative forecast of vessels icing rate (Pacific Marine Environmental Research Laboratory); (5) Operative ice cover maps of the Arctic Ocean (the Arctic and Antarctic Research Institute); (6) Forecast data of hydrocarbon spill modeling (State Oceanographic Institute); (7) Earthquake catalogs (International Seismological Centre); (8) Google Maps tiled maps.

On the start page of the platform, there is access to three applications. The first application incorporates the climatic fields of the Arctic Zone for the last 37 years.

For this purpose, it employs the ERA-Interim. The fields of climatic parameters are calculated from the following hydrometeorological characteristics: (1) Temperature of the underlying surface, K; (2) Air temperature at a height of 2 m, K; (3) Near-surface pressure, hPa; (4) Integrity of ice cover (ratio between the ice-covered area and the total area of the cell of the gridded field); (5) Divergence of the field of the wind speed at a height of 10 m; (6) Rotation of the field of the wind speed at a height of 10 m. The last two characteristics are calculated from meridional and zonal components of the wind speed (in m/s). The fields of the mentioned parameters are presented in the interval of latitudes from 55° to 85° N, on the grid of 0.75° × 0.75° × 30 days.

The data refer to the following three time intervals: T_1 = 01.01.1979–01.01.1998, T_2 = 01.01.2006–01.01.2015 and T_3 = 01.01.1979–01.01.2015. For each month and for each of the above hydrometeorological characteristics, GIS GeoMonitor presents field maps for the following four climatic indicators: (1) Average monthly values in intervals T_1 and T_2; (2) Mean square deviations of values in intervalsT_1 and T_2; (3) Values of significance of changes in the mean values of characteristics in intervals T_1 and T_2 (based on the Student statistics); (4) Trends of characteristics in the interval T_3.

As an example, let us consider the analysis of the indicator estimating the significance of changes in the temperature regime of the underlying surface at arctic latitudes. Figure 1 demonstrates the GIS GeoMonitor screenshots with the maps of significance of changes in average monthly temperatures of the underlying surface for odd months (January, March, May, July, September, and November) of intervals T_1 (1979–1998) and T_2 (2006–2015), i.e., the Student statistics that equals the difference (normalized to the mean square deviation) between mean values in intervals T_2 and T_1. It can be seen in the maps that temperatures in "winter" months (January and November) of 2006–2015 considerably increased (light gray tones) in comparison with the period of 1979–1998, whereas temperatures in "summer" months (May and July) decreased (dark gray tones). Additionally, it is seen in the maps that temperature changes are spatially inhomogeneous.

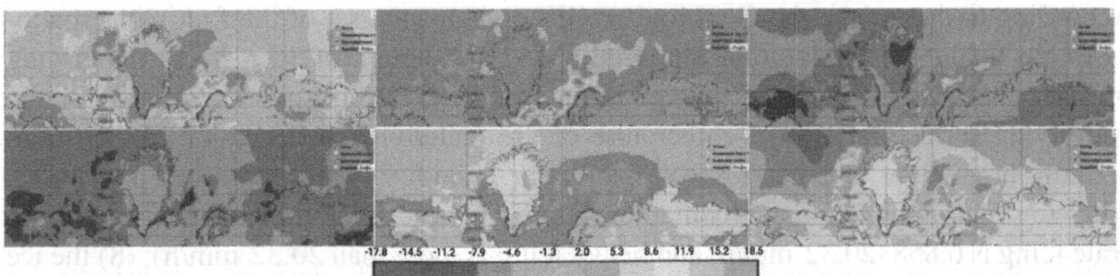

Fig. 1. The maps of the significance of changes in the average monthly temperature between time intervals 2006–2015 and 1979–1998, from left to right and from top to bottom: January, March, May, July, September, November.

Figure 2 shows the screenshot from GIS GeoTime 3 with the ice cohesion map in January as a percentage, averaged over 2006–2016 and a graph of average monthly ice cohesion for the point 70.385° N, 54.489° E.

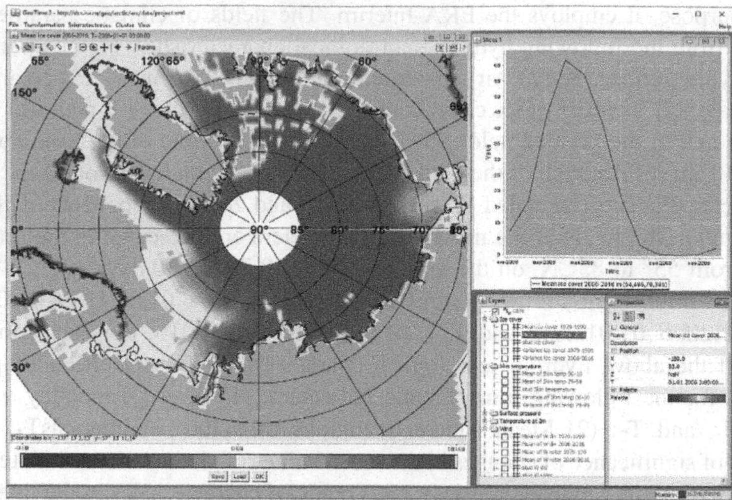

Fig. 2. Ice cohesion in January as a percentage averaged over 2006–2016. The right is a graph of average monthly ice cohesion for the point 70.385° N, 54.489° E.

The second and third applications launch the GIS GeoMonitor with modules to analyze the operational and forecast situation in the Barents and White seas, as well as in the Bering Sea region. Analysis of operative data and forecast of the environmental situation is of significant interest to all participants of sea-based activities. Due to the intensified anthropogenic load in the region, the operative data module contains, apart hydrometeorological characteristics, such data as operative locations and movement directions of vessels, forecasts of their icing rates, and forecast of the evolution of possible emergencies related to hydrocarbon spills.

The data of monitoring of the operative situation in the White and Barents seas are automatically updated. They consist of the observed values of parameters and forecast. According to these data, the GeoMonitor GIS contains the set of the following spatio-temporal fields: (1) Modulus of the wind speed at a height of 10 m from underlying surface, m/s; (2) Intensity of precipitation, mm/h; (3) Atmospheric pressure at the underlying surface, hPa; (4) Temperature of the underlying surface, °C; (5) Air temperature at a height of 2 m, °C; (6) Specific air humidity (water mass in 1 kg of air), g/kg; (7) Icing rate or ice augmentation, mm/h (light icing is 0.1–6.858 mm/h, moderate icing is 6.858–20.32 mm/h, and heavy icing is more than 20.32 mm/h); (8) the ice cohesion.

The interactive user interface of the GIS GeoMonitor allows reading of the attributive data: these data for vessels are the name, type, movement direction, and speed; for earthquake epicenters, these data are the occurrence time, magnitude, and hypocentral depth. An example of the presentation of operational data in the Bering Sea region is shown in Fig. 3.

An authorized user of the GIS GeoMonitor can also perform analysis of oil product distribution after a spill. Analysis of the distribution of hydrocarbon spills proceeds as follows. First, in the GIS GeoMonitor dialog box, the modeling parameters are set by

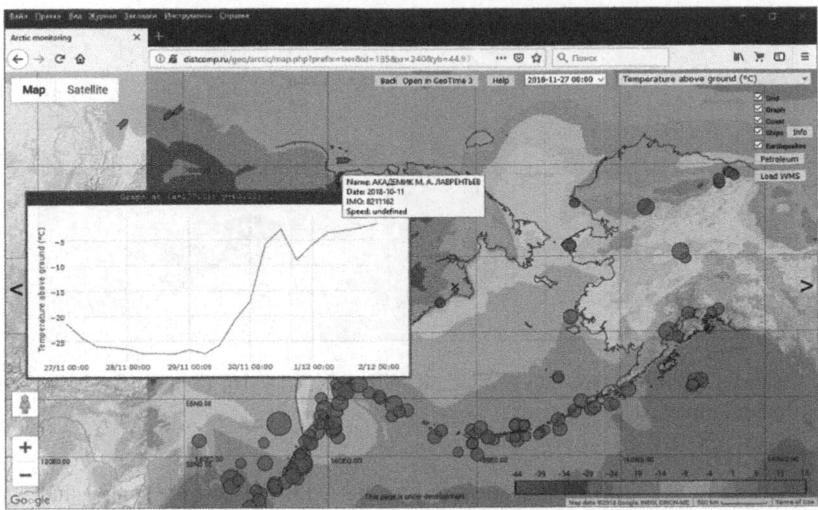

Fig. 3. GeoMonitor working window: a slice of the spatio-temporal air temperature field at the height of 2 m dated 11.27.2008 00:00 and the temperature forecast graph at the point marked with a cross. Earthquake epicenters marked with red circles. (Color figure online)

the operator: the execution time of the prediction of the distribution of oil or oil products, visualization step, type of oil product, time of the accident, coordinates of the spill point, intensity and duration of oil discharge. Further, according to these data, the remote server calculates the coordinates, shape, and thickness of the film for each modeling stage, taking into account the coastline, ice conditions, meteorological forecast and other data on the state of the environment [10]. According to the report on the completion of the next iteration, the GIS GeoMonitor loads the spill spot with differentiation across the thickness of the oil film. After that, the user can display the spatio-temporal oil spill model for each simulation stage on an interactive map.

Predicted positions and shapes of the oil spill at 2, 4, 14, 16, 18, and 19 h after the spill are shown in Fig. 4. The spill point is marked with a cross.

3 The Platform for Monitoring of Seismic Activity Fields

Seismic activity characterizes the intensity of the process of accumulation and release of seismic energy. Long-term seismic activity maps show the spatial distribution of seismic process intensity. Spatial and temporal variations of seismic activity indicate the processes of seismic quietness and activation. It is known that anomalous manifestations of these processes may precede strong earthquakes [11]. Seismic quietness is associated with the process of accumulation of seismic energy in the preparation of an earthquake [12]. The increase in seismic activity reflects changes in the geological environment, which may relate to both the preparation of a strong earthquake and the appearance of post-seismic deformations [13].

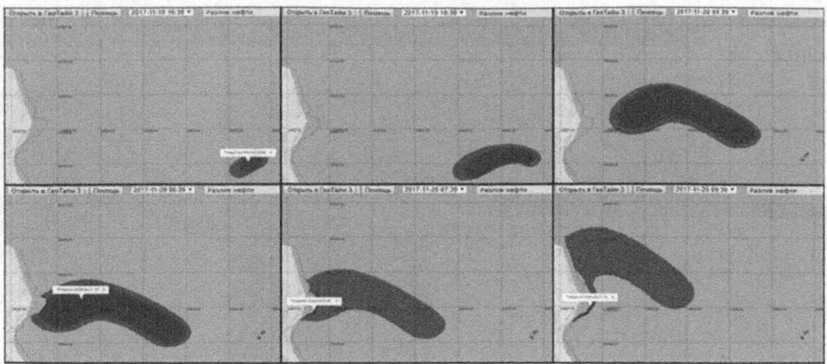

Fig. 4. Predicted positions and shapes of the oil spill at 2, 4, 14, 16, 18, and 19 h after the spill. The spill point is marked with a cross.

The GIS platform represents a seismic process with the help of spatial and spatio-temporal grid-based fields. It consists of two Web GISs. GIS SeismoMap provides automatic loading, processing, and analysis of seismic data, and GIS GeoTime 3 supports a comprehensive analysis of the seismic process.

GIS SeismoMap is realized in a thin client-server architecture. It calculates seismic grid fields, represents the results in the geographical context of the Google Maps API, and it is intended for both professionals and a wide range of Internet users. GIS SeismoMap daily downloads regional catalogs of earthquakes for 24 seismically active regions. GIS calculates two types of fields: spatial (2D) fields characterizing the background regime of the seismic process, and spatio-temporal (3D) fields characterizing the behavior of the seismic process on the test time interval. The background seismic regime is represented by 2D grid fields, the values of which are averaged over the interval of 540 weeks. These include the field of averages of b-value, the field of seismic activity, the field of root-mean-square deviations of seismic activity, the field of quantiles of seismic activity distribution. The test seismic regime is represented by the following 3D grid fields: the field of test seismic activity with a time step of 7 days the values of which are estimated over the intervals 100 day, the field of variation (anomaly) of the test seismic activity, the values of which are equal to the normalized difference of the test and background activity (the field of the seismic activity change points), the field, the values of which are equal to those quantile distribution of background seismicity, those correspond to the values of the test activity, and the field of the ratios of the current values of seismic activity to the background ones. The GIS SeismoMap user interface supports the visualization of 2D and 3D seismic fields and earthquake epicenters, reading of earthquake attributes and plotting of time series graphs in interactively selectable points. The fields of the density of epicenters, seismic activity, and b-value were calculated using the method of local kernel regression [14]. Student's t-statistic is used to assess the field of seismic activity anomalies. It is defined for each grid node as the ratio of the difference of average values of the current (196 days) and background (3650 days) intervals to the standard deviation of this difference. Positive t-statistics values correspond to higher values on the test interval.

Screenshots of three time slices of quantiles of the background seismic activity corresponding to the values of test seismic activity are shown in Fig. 5. The earthquake epicenters are in the interval of 60 days from the date of the slice. The first two slices show a significant decrease in seismic activity in the depicted circle. The third slice shows in this circle an earthquake with a magnitude of $M = 6.5$, the depth of the epicenter $H = 35$ km, which occurred on 05.09.2018.

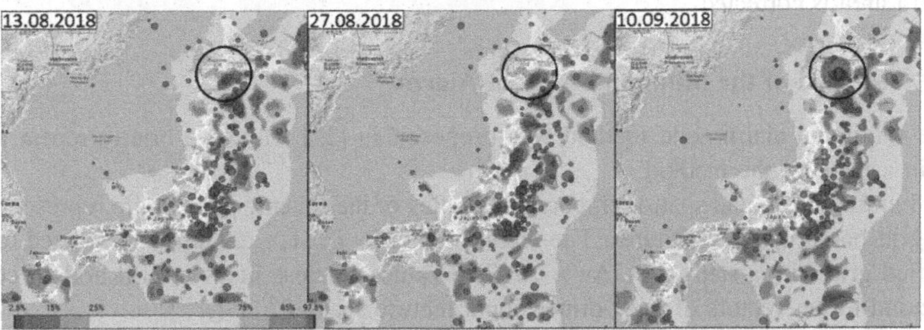

Fig. 5. Time slices of quantiles of the background seismic activity corresponding to the values of test seismic activity. The earthquake epicenters are in the interval of 60 days from the date of the slice.

4 Earthquake Forecasting

4.1 Platform

Earthquakes occur when the stress in rocks of the earth's crust exceeds the ultimate strength. This causes movements within the earth's crust. This phenomenon accompanies the sudden release of energy in the Earth's lithosphere that creates seismic waves, which causes great social and economic damage. Spatio-temporal forecast consists of estimating the location, time and magnitude of the future earthquake [15, 16]. To find the prediction rule, machine learning methods are used, for example, the Bayesian approach assuming that the prediction features are independent [17], the well-known M8 algorithm [18], artificial neural networks [19]. The complexity of the problem is determined mainly by two factors: insufficient knowledge on the mathematical models of earthquake preparation processes, as well as incompleteness of observations about the seismotectonic processes. At the same time, the existing knowledge and available data allow for the use of modern information technologies in order to promote systematic analysis of seismic processes and forecasting the earthquakes [20, 21]. The seismic and geodynamic monitoring data necessary for this purpose are published in real time on a number of remote servers.

The earthquake forecasting platform (http://distcomp.ru/geo/prognosis) is constructed using the same technology as the above-mentioned systems. It consists of two Web GI Systems: GeoPrognosis and GeoTime 3. GIS GeoPrognosis is built in a client-server architecture with a thin client. It operates regularly with constant step Δt. At the moment of forecasting t the system performs the following actions: loads new input data, converts the input data to grid-based fields, calculates the feature fields, calculate the forecast field, which is a function of the feature fields, calculates the alarm area, tests the forecast outcome for the interval $(t - \Delta t, t)$, computes the forecast statistics, and forms a GIS project for launching the GIS GeoTime 3. Thus, for any forecast point in time t, the work of the platform can be divided into two intervals: the interval for feature field processing and training from start time to t, and the forecast interval from t to $t + \Delta t$. At each step, the training time of the forecast field increases by Δt and the alarm area is corrected.

4.2 Method of the Minimum Area of Alarm

The minimum alarm zone method was proposed in [22]. Here we briefly repeat the main aspects of the method.

Let the spatial and spatio-temporal properties of the seismic process are represented by grid-based fields of features. The feature fields $\mathbf{F}_i$, $i = 1, \ldots, I$, are interpolated to a unified grid with a step $\Delta x \times \Delta y \times \Delta t$. The values of these fields at grid node n correspond to the vectors of the I-dimensional feature space $\mathbf{f}^{(n)} = \{f_i^{(n)}\}$.

A forecast field $\mathbf{\Phi}$ is a function of the feature fields. It is trained using retrospective data that contains a sample set of target earthquakes $q = 1, \ldots, Q$ with the magnitudes $M \geq M^*$ and a set of grid feature fields $\mathbf{F}_i$, $i = 1, \ldots, I$, which describe spatial (quasi-stationary) and spatio-temporal (dynamic) properties of the seismotectonic process.

The method of the minimum area of alarm uses the following data model.

1. Strong earthquakes are preceded by anomalous (improbable) values of the feature fields.
2. The feature fields are constructed in such a way that for anomalies, the values of some of them are close to maximum or minimum. To simplify the explanation in this section, we assume that the anomalies refer only to the *largest* values of the feature fields.
3. If the $\mathbf{f}^{(q)}$ is an anomaly vector, preceding the target event q, then any vector $\mathbf{f}$ with the components $f_i \geq f_i^{(q)}$ for all $i = 1, \ldots, I$ can also precede a similar target event (*monotonicity condition*).

The vectors for which $\mathbf{f} \geq \mathbf{f}^{(q)}$ componentwise we will call *the base vectors of the feature space*. The nodes of the grid of the forecast field with the values $\varphi \geq \varphi^{(q)}$ we will call *the base nodes of the forecast field*.

From the assumptions it follows that the earthquake forecast can be carried out using the simplest threshold decision rule. If the value of the forecast field $\varphi^{(n)} \geq \theta$, then spatio-temporal *alarm cylinders* are created at all base nodes of the forecast field with the values $\varphi \geq \varphi^{(n)}$. The alarm cylinder of the grid node n with the coordinates $(x^{(n)}, y^{(n)}, t^{(n)})$ has center of base in the node $(x^{(n)}, y^{(n)}, t^{(n)})$, the base radius R and the element $[(x^{(n)}, y^{(n)}, t^{(n)}), (x^{(n)}, y^{(n)}, t^{(n)} + \mathrm{T})]$. From this it follows that for a given value of the threshold θ an earthquake with the epicenter coordinates (x^*, y^*, t^*) will be detected if and only if the cylinder with the center of the base (x^*, y^*, t^*), radius R and the element $[(x^*, y^*, t^* - \mathrm{T}), (x^*, y^*, t^*)]$, contains at least one grid node with the value $\varphi^{(n)} \geq \theta$. This cylinder will be called a *precursor cylinder*.

The alarm field detects an earthquake if its epicenter falls within an area consisting of a combination of alarm cylinders (*alarm area*). The quality of the forecast field at threshold θ is determined by two values: (1) the ratio of a number of correctly detected events $Q^*(\theta)$, to all Q target events: $U(\theta) = Q^*(\theta)/Q$ (*probability of detection*) and (2) the ratio of a number of grid nodes $L^*(\theta)$ of the alarm area, to a number of grid nodes L of all area under study: $V(\theta) = L^*(\theta)/L$ (*volume of alarm*).

The basis of our machine learning method is nonparametric new one-class classification algorithm. It has two peculiar properties compared to standard ones [23, 24]. The first relates to the data model. The model postulates two properties of anomalous objects: (1) anomalous objects are unlikely, and some of their properties take values close to the maximum (or minimum) among the sample, and (2) the vectors of the space of features, which are componentwise larger (or smaller) of the vector corresponding to the anomalous object, can also be anomalous objects. This model allows one to build a classification rule from a set of anomalous objects. In this case, normal objects are considered statistically through the probability of detecting anomalous objects by a random forecast. The second difference is that the algorithm allows constructing a forecast function that optimizes the probability of detecting anomalous objects in the training sample if the probability of a random forecast is not more than predetermined.

For training, we have a sample of occurred target earthquakes and a set of feature fields.

At the first step, the algorithm should move from a sample set of target earthquakes to a sample set of target earthquake precursors. A *precursor* of the earthquake q is the vector $\mathbf{f}^{(q)}$ of a feature space which has the minimum volume of alarm $v^{(q)} = L^{(q)}/L$ among all vectors corresponding to the grid nodes of the cylinder of precursor of the event q, where L is the number of all grid nodes of the analyzed area, $L^{(q)}$ is the number of nodes in the grid of the alarm areas generated by the base points of the vector $\mathbf{f}^{(q)}$.

There are three the most important versions of the algorithm.

The first version of the algorithm is to construct the forecast field so that as the threshold θ decreases, the training earthquakes are detected in sequence in which the corresponding alarm volumes increase $v^{(Q)} \leq v^{(Q-1)} \leq \ldots \leq v^{(2)} \leq v^{(1)}$ (this version is selected for testing). The version consists of the following steps.

To create a training sample $\{\mathbf{f}^{(q)}, v^{(q)}\}$, where $\mathbf{f}^{(q)}$ is the precursor of the earthquake q, $v^{(q)}$ is the corresponding alarm volume.

To order the precursors $\mathbf{f}^{(q)}$, $q = 1, \ldots, Q$, by increasing the alarm volume: $v^{(Q)} \leq v^{(Q-1)} \leq \ldots \leq v^{(q)} \leq \ldots \leq v^{(2)} \leq v^{(1)}$.

To assign to the nodes of the grid of the forecast field $\mathbf{\Phi}$ a value of 0.

To replace the value of 0 by Q at the nodes of the grid of the forecast field, for which the monotonicity condition, $f_i^{(n)} \geq f_i^{(Q)}$ for all $i = 1,\ldots, I$, is satisfied in the feature space; to replace the value of 0 by $Q - 1$ at the nodes of the grid of the forecast field, for which the monotonicity condition, $f_i^{(n)} \geq f_i^{(Q-1)}$ for all $i = 1, \ldots, I$ is satisfied in feature space, and then, successively, in the same way, to replace the values 0 by $Q + 1 - q$.

Obviously, the choice of the order of the earthquake precursors at the 2nd step of the algorithm determines the dependence $U(V)$ obtained from the forecast field. The 2nd version of the algorithm makes it possible to optimize the forecast field so that when the next target earthquake is detected, the alarm volume increases by a minimum value. To do this, one should arrange the precursors so that when changing from event detection $q + 1$ to event q, the increase in alarm volume is minimal. Here, at each transition from the previously selected event $q + 1$ to q, a small search through the remaining q events is required. The 3rd version of the algorithm allows one to optimize the forecast field so that it detects the maximum number of target earthquakes with a total alarm volume of less than or equal to the predetermined value. In this case, you need to perform a full search of the selected number of events.

4.3 Testing

The method of minimum area of alarm was tested on the platform of automatic earthquake forecast (http://distcomp.ru/geo/prognosis). The system tests the data with a constant step Δt. On each step (at time t) the raster fields of features are computed, the alarm area is trained based on data before the time t, and the system tests for time since t till $t + \Delta t$ if the alarm area covers an epicenter of the target earthquake. Then at time $t + \Delta t$ the training time is increased by Δt, the alarm zone is updated and the test is repeated.

Testing of the forecast method should provide an opportunity to compare different methods of solving the problem on the same indicators of the forecast quality. In this method, we use two quality indicators: the probability of detecting the target events from the test interval $U = Q^*/Q$ and the volume of alarm $V = L^*/L$. The number of target events Q is determined by a set of test samples, the number of target events detected Q^* is determined by the results of the forecast, the analysis area and its size L is selected at the beginning of the test, the size of the alarm zone L^* is determined by the training data.

In the following test experiments, the area of analysis was chosen such that in any circle with radius R = 100 km for the period 1984–1993 at least 300 earthquake epicenters with a magnitude of at least minimum magnitude of completeness in earthquake catalog were recorded. This condition allows one to select a seismically active area for analysis but does not ensure its seismic homogeneity. Therefore, the indicator of the volume of alarm obtained during testing should be considered only in the context of the selected area of analysis. At the same time, the choice of the field of analysis according to a formal rule makes it possible to compare the results of the forecast obtained using various methods and according to different data.

One way to assess the quality of a forecast is to compare a regular forecast obtained by the algorithm under analysis (*regular forecast*) with a random one. We will assume that the forecast is random if the values of the forecast field are selected from a segment in accordance with a uniform distribution. Obviously, for this probabilistic model, the alarm volume V_r is equal to the probability of a random prediction U_r. It follows from this that comparing the probability of a regular forecast U with the probability of a random forecast U_r for the same alarm volumes $V = V_r$ is equivalent to comparing U with the corresponding alarm volume V. If, at the same time, a sample of target events were cleaned of aftershocks and foreshocks, then by proposing the independence of target events and using the binomial distribution model for them, we could build a confidence interval for estimating U.

In the number of articles, the results of a regular forecast are compared with the results of a forecast by a stationary field. In papers [16, 24, 25], the regular forecast is compared with the forecast by the 2D field of seismic activity (or earthquake epicenter density). The result of the comparison makes it possible to evaluate the efficiency of a regular forecast in relation to the forecast by the field F, which is based only on the spatial heterogeneity of the seismic process. Comparison of results can be done in two ways. In one method the probabilities of regular prediction of Q target earthquakes are compared with the results of predicting the same earthquakes by a stationary field F (for example, F is a 2D field of the earthquake epicenter density). Another method uses the Gutenberg-Richter model [26].

Testing was performed for two regions: the Mediterranean and California. The Mediterranean region: 10°–30° E, 34°–47° N. Input data: earthquakes for the period from 27.05.1983 till 14.02.2018 with magnitudes $M \geq 2.7$ and depths of hypocenters $H \leq 160$ km from the International Seismological Centre catalog [27]. Target earthquakes: magnitudes $M \geq 6.0$ and hypocenter depths $H \leq 60$ km. California region: 126°–114° W, 32°–43° N. Input data: earthquakes for the period of 01.01.1983–15.02.2018 with magnitudes $M \geq 2.0$ and depths of hypocenters $H \leq 160$ km from the NEIC USGS catalog [28]. For the forecast, the target earthquakes with magnitudes $M \geq 5.7$ have been selected.

The following 6 fields of features were analyzed for forecasting:

- $\mathbf{F_1}$ is 3D field of the density of all considering earthquakes in the region.
- $\mathbf{F_2}$ is 3D field of mean magnitudes among all considering earthquakes in the region.

The estimation of 3D fields of $\mathbf{F_1}$ and $\mathbf{F_2}$ is performed with the method of local kernel regression. The kernel function for the *n*-th earthquake has the form $K_n = [\mathrm{ch}^2(r_n/R)^2\ \mathrm{ch}^2(t_n/T)]^{-1}$, where $r_n < R\varepsilon$, $t_n < T\varepsilon$ are the distance and time interval between the *n*-th epicenter of the earthquake and the node of the 3D grid of the field, $\varepsilon = 2$, $R = 50$ km, $T = 100$ days for $\mathbf{F_1}$ and $R = 100$ km, $T = 730$ days for $\mathbf{F_2}$.

- $\mathbf{F_3}$ is 3D field of negative temporal anomalies of the density of earthquakes.
- $\mathbf{F_4}$ is 3D field of positive temporal anomalies of the density of earthquakes.
- $\mathbf{F_5}$ is 3D field of positive temporal anomalies of mean earthquake magnitude.

To estimate the field of $\mathbf{F_3}$, $\mathbf{F_4}$, $\mathbf{F_5}$, the Student's *t*-statistic was used, which is defined for each grid node as the ratio of the difference of average values of the current (196 days) and background (3650 days) intervals to the standard deviation of this difference. Positive t-statistics values correspond to higher values on the test interval.

- $\mathbf{F_6}$ is 2D field of the density of earthquake epicenters: kernel smoothing in the interval 1988-2008 the parameter $R = 50$ km.

The grid fields for the Mediterranean were calculated in a grid step $\Delta x \times \Delta y \times \Delta t = 0.2° \times 0.13° \times 49$ days. The forecast field was trained from 1998 until the next step of the forecast after 2008. The radius of the alarm cylinder is $R = 20$ km and the element is $T = 50$ days. Testing is performed in the interval of 2008–2019. There are 11 target earthquakes in the analysis area. We used the method of stepwise selection to find the most informative fields of features. The algorithm selected the $\mathbf{F}_3$ and $\mathbf{F}_6$ fields to construct the alarm field.

We compare the earthquake prediction probabilities obtained using different fields of features in Table 1: U_1 is the forecast probability using the earthquake density field 2D (**F**$_6$), U_2 is the probability using 3D field of negative earthquake density anomalies (**F**$_3$), $\mu(V)$ is the probability of forecast by 2D field of earthquake epicenters density, obtained using the Gutenberg-Richter model, and U_3 is the probability using **F**$_3$ and **F**$_6$ fields. We can see that the highest probability of a successful forecast occurs when the fields **F**$_3$and **F**$_6$ are used together. When $V = 0.2$ ($U_r = 0.2$), the ratios for the prediction probability obtained with **F**$_3$ and **F**$_6$ fields to the prediction probabilities obtained with 2D earthquake density field (**F**$_6$) and for the field calculated using the Gutenberg-Richter ratio, are equal respectively $U_3(0.2)/U_1(0.2) = 0.91/0.64 = 1.49$ and $U_3(0.2)/\mu(0.2) = 0.91/0.41 = 2.2$.

Table 1. Comparison of the probabilities of earthquake forecast for the Mediterranean.

V_{learn}: alarm volumes for learning interval	0.01		0.05		0.1		0.15		0.20	
Test indicators	V_{test}	U_{test}	V_{test}	U_{test}	V_{test}	U_{test}	V_{test}	U_{test}	V_{test}	U_{test}
Field F$_6$	0.00	0.00	0.03	0.09	0.10	0.09	0.15	0.45	0.20	0.64
Field F$_3$	0.00	0.00	0.02	0.09	0.20	0.36	0.29	0.45	0.35	0.64
$\mu(V)$: probability for the field F$_6$ obtained by the model	–	0.00	–	0.1	–	0.26	–	0.35	–	0.41
Fields F$_3$ and F$_6$	0.03	0.00	0.08	0.36	0.15	0.45	0.24	0.55	0.32	0.91

Table 1 shows the values of two types of alarm volumes: V_{learn} is the alarm volume received in accordance with the training data, and V_{test} is the alarm volume corresponding to the alarm volume V_{lean}, but observed on the test data. You can see that when testing in almost all cases, except for testing the 2D-field **F**$_6$, the volumes of V_{test} are greater than V_{lean}. This is explained by the fact that the number of recorded earthquakes in a region changes over time (Fig. 6). The number of earthquakes is influenced by the development of a seismic network and natural changes in the seismic process. Figure 6 shows that the number of earthquakes increases significantly in the test interval. An increase in the density of earthquake epicenters leads to an increase in the field values of the **F**$_3$ function, which ultimately leads to an increase in the volume of anxiety during testing.

The grid fields for California were calculated in a grid step $\Delta x \times \Delta y \times \Delta t = 0.125° \times 0.11° \times 49$ days. The radius of the alarm cylinder is $R = 14$ km and the element is $T = 100$ days. Testing of the earthquake forecast was performed for the interval 2009–2018. There were 9 target earthquakes. The algorithm selected tree fields of features for the construction of the alarm field: **F**$_4$, **F**$_5$, and **F**$_6$.

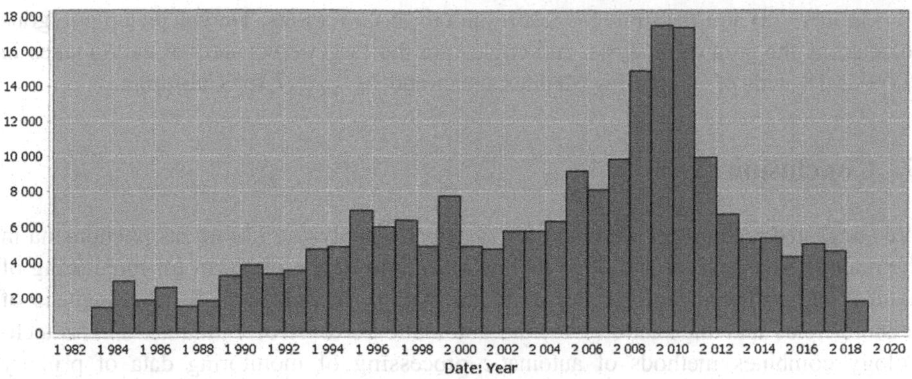

Fig. 6. Histogram of the number of earthquakes with a magnitude greater than 2.7 and a depth of hypocenters less than 160 km.

Table 2 shows the probabilities of earthquake forecast for California.

Table 2. Probabilities of earthquake forecast for California.

Volume of alarm V_{learn}	Volume of alarm V_{test}	Number of correct forecasts	Forecast probability U
0.01	0.01	1	0.11
0.05	0.06	4	0.44
0.1	0.13	4	0.44
0.15	0.13	4	0.44
0.2	0.25	8	0.89

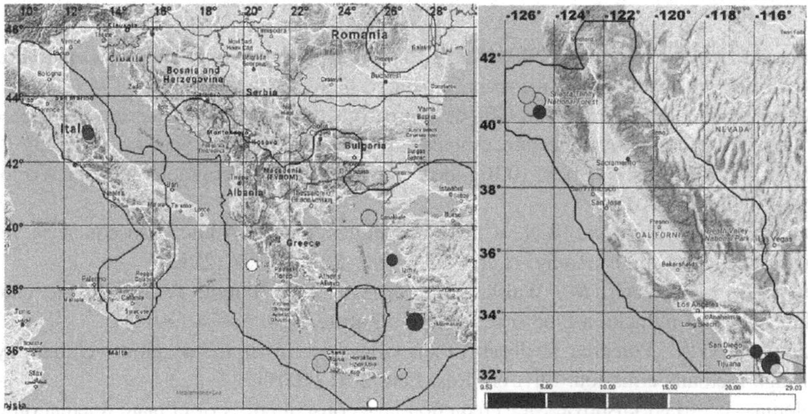

Fig. 7. Areas of analysis and tested target epicenters of earthquakes in 2009–2018: (a) the Mediterranean, (b) California. Shades of grey indicate the minimum volume of alarm with which the epicenter was forecasted. The darkness of grey decreases in accordance with the volume of the alarm: 0.05, 0.1, 0.15, 0.2. White color indicates that an earthquake is not forecasted with an alarm volume of less than 0.2.

Figures 7(a) and (b) show the test results for both regions. They depicted polygons selected as the area of analysis, and circles are the target epicenters of earthquakes in 2009–2018 with $M \geq 6.0$ for Mediterranean and $M \geq 5.7$ for California.

5 Conclusion

We suggested technology designed for systematic analyzing hazardous phenomena in the natural environment and three its implementations: the platform for monitoring of natural and anthropogenic processes in the Arctic, the platform for the analysis of seismic fields and the platform for the automatic forecast of earthquakes. The technology combines methods of automatic processing of monitoring data of primary observations, fairly simple methods of visual data analysis and analytical tools for the comprehensive study of spatio-temporal processes and prediction of hazardous phenomena. The technology has two advantages: (1) simplicity of configuration for a new problem area and (2) a combination of interactive easy analysis supported by intuitive operations and a simplified user interface with a detailed, comprehensive analysis of spatio-temporal processes intended for specialists.

Earthquake prediction platform uses the method of the minimum area of alarm. Test results showed satisfactory forecast quality. In addition, after the launch of the automatic earthquake prediction platform in February 2018, a Greek earthquake of 25.10.2018 with a magnitude of 6.6–6.8 was predicted. The epicenter of the earthquake got into the alarm zone 26.09.2018. At the same time, these results are preliminary. Indeed, testing was conducted only for three regions and for the simplest seismological characteristics. Therefore, we believe that the results show only the effectiveness of the method and the operability of the forecast platform.

References

1. Tsou, M.H.: Integrating Web-based GIS and image processing tools for environmental monitoring and natural resource management. J. Geogr. Syst. **6**(2), 155–174 (2004)
2. Dangermond, J.: Geodesign and GIS–designing our futures. In: Peer Reviewed Proceedings of Digital Landscape Architecture, Anhalt University of Applied Science, Germany (2010)
3. Harder, C.: The ArcGIS Book: 10 Big Ideas about Applying Geography to Your World. Esri Press, Redlands (2015)
4. Kattsov, V.M., Porfir'ev, B.N.: Climatic changes in the Arctic: consequences for the environment and the economy. Arct. Ecol. Econ. **2**(6), 66–78 (2012)
5. Overland, J.E., Wang, M., Walsh, J.E., Stroeve, J.C.: Future Arctic climate changes: adaptation and mitigation time scales. Earth's Future **2**(2), 68–74 (2014)
6. Anisimov, O.A.: Potential feedback of thawing permafrost to the global climate system through methane emission. Environ. Res. Lett. **2**(4) (2007)
7. Zelenina, L.I., Fed'kushova, S.I.: Prediction and consequences of climate fluctuation of the Arctic region. Arktikai Sever **5**, 1–5 (2012). (In Russian)
8. Gitis, V., Derendyaev, A., Weinstock, A.: Web-based GIS technologies for monitoring and analysis of spatio-temporal processes. Int. J. Web Inf. Syst. **12**(1), 102–124 (2016)

9. Gitis, V.G., et al.: Technology of monitoring and analysis of the hydrometeorological situation in the Arctic. J. Commun. Technol. Electron. **63**(6), 691–705 (2018)
10. Zatzepa, S.N., et al.: Modelling of oil spills in sea for planning on guaranteeing of ecological safety by realization of oil and gas plans. Part 1: methodology. ProblemyArktikiiAntarktiki **4** (106), 27–39 (2015)
11. Huang, Q., Sobolev, G.A., Nagao, T.: Characteristics of the seismic quiescence and activation patterns before the M = 7.2 Kobe earthquake, January 17,1995. Tectonophysics **337**(1–2), 99–116 (2001)
12. Kagan, Y.Y., Jackson, D.D.: New seismic gap hypothesis: five years after. J. Geophys. Res. Solid Earth **100**(B3), 3943–3959 (1995)
13. Chen, C.C., et al.: The 1999 Chi-Chi, Taiwan, earthquake as a typical example of seismic activation and quiescence. Geophys. Res. Lett. **32**(22) (2005). https://doi.org/10.1029/2005GL023991
14. Gitis, V.G., Derendyaev, A.B., Pirogov, S.A., Spokoiny, V.G., Yurkov, E.F.: Earthquake prediction using the fields estimated by an adaptive algorithm. In: Proceedings of the 7th International Conference on Web Intelligence, Mining and Semantics, Article No. 30 (2017)
15. Keilis-Borok, V., Soloviev, A.A. (eds.): Nonlinear Dynamics of the Lithosphere and Earthquake Prediction. Springer, Heidelberg (2013)
16. Kossobokov, V., Shebalin, P.: Earthquake prediction. In: Keilis-Borok, V.I., Soloviev, A.A. (eds.) Nonlinear Dynamics of the Lithosphere and Earthquake Prediction. SSSYN, pp. 141–207. Springer, Heidelberg (2003). https://doi.org/10.1007/978-3-662-05298-3_4
17. Zavyalov, A.D.: Extended Forecast of Earthquakes: Fundamentals, Methodology, Realization. Nauka, Moscow (2006). (in Russian)
18. Kossobokov, V.G.: User manual for M8. In: Healy, J.H., Keilis-Borok, V.I., Lee, W.H.K. (eds.) Algorithms for Earthquake Statistics and Prediction, vol. 6, pp. 167–222 (1997)
19. Bhatia, A., Pasari, S., Mehta, A.: Earthquake forecasting using artificial neural networks. In: International Archives of the Photogrammetry, Remote Sensing & Spatial Information Sciences (2018)
20. Rhoades, D.A.: Application of the EEPAS model to forecasting earthquakes of moderate magnitude in southern California. Seismol. Res. Lett. **78**(1), 110–115 (2007)
21. Bishop, C.M.: Machine Learning and Pattern Recognition. Information Science and Statistics. Springer, Heidelberg (2006)
22. Gitis, V.G., Derendyaev, A.B.: Earthquake prediction learning using the least alarm method. J. Commun. Technol. Electron. **63**(6), 680–690 (2018)
23. Khan, S.S., Madden, M.G.: A survey of recent trends in one class classification. In: Coyle, L., Freyne, J. (eds.) AICS 2009. LNCS (LNAI), vol. 6206, pp. 188–197. Springer, Heidelberg (2010). https://doi.org/10.1007/978-3-642-17080-5_21
24. Molchan, G.M.: Earthquake prediction as a decision-making problem. Pure. appl. Geophys. **149**(1), 233–247 (1997)
25. Kossobokov, V.G., Romashkova, L.L., Keilis-Borok, V.I., Healy, J.H.: Testing earthquake prediction algorithms: statistically significant advance prediction of the largest earthquakes in the Circum-Pacific, 1992–1997. Phys. Earth Planet. Inter. **111**(3–4), 187–196 (1999)
26. Gutenberg, B., Richter, C.: Frequency of earthquakes in California. Bull. Seismol. Soc. Am. **34**(4), 185–188 (1944)
27. International Seismological Centre: Internatl. Seismol. Cent., Thatcham, United Kingdom (2015). http://www.isc.ac.uk
28. Masse, R.P., Needham, R.E.: NEIC-The National Earthquake Information Center. Earthquakes Volcanoes (USGS) **21**(1), 4–44 (1989)

Free and Open Source GIS Technologies for the Assessment of Tsunami Hazards in the Ionic Sea

Michele Mangiameli(✉), Giuseppe Mussumeci, and Salvatore Oliva

Dipartimento di Ingegneria Civile ed Architettura,
University of Catania, Catania, Italy
{michele.mangiameli,
giuseppe.mussumeci}@dica.unict.it,
oliva.salvatore.ct@gmail.com

Abstract. It has been largely proven that Geographic Information Systems (GIS) provide a valuable tool as Decision Support System (DDS) for the assessment and management of environmental hazards. In this work we used the GIS technologies to simulate scenarios associated to possible tsunamis in the Ionian Sea, involving the territory of Acireale (Catania), in East Sicily (Italy). In particular, we implemented a literature model for the propagation of tsunamis using free and open source GIS technologies. Our GIS modelling has been used to identify the inhabited areas and the loose of efficiency of roads possibly interested by the tsunami. For this reasons, the approach can be an efficient DSS for civil protection purposes, providing a prompt answer for the identification and management of people's risk condition.

Keywords: GIS technology · Tsunami hazard · DSS

1 Introduction

The Italian territory is particularly affected by calamitous events, such as earthquakes, landslides or forest fires, etc. The triggering causes of most events can be considered of anthropic nature, linked to a not careful use of the environment, but also due to the geomorphological characteristic of the Italian territory which is characterized by a great variability of geological, geomorphological, tectonic and climatic features. The element at risk include people, the environment (air, soil, water) and goods (movable and immovable property).

In view of the possible disaster scenarios that can affect Italy, the National Civil Protection Service was established by law 225 of 24 February 1992.

The primary purpose of this law is, in fact, to defend people and to guarantee, by all means, the maintenance of a "civil" level of life. In second instance, it serves the purpose of safeguarding the other elements of risk, such as cultural heritage or property. This is done through forecasting, prevention, rescue and emergency relief activities.

The Department of Civil Protection gives guidelines for the preparation of forecasting and prevention programs, then local authorities, in particular the Provinces and Municipalities, put them into practice with forecasting activities and prevention

S. Misra et al. (Eds.): ICCSA 2019, LNCS 11622, pp. 216–224, 2019.
https://doi.org/10.1007/978-3-030-24305-0_17

interventions. Each institution should have a Civil Protection Plan whose purpose is to safeguard people and elements at risk, through the use of strategies and resources aimed at minimizing the presumed damage.

In order to prepare and integrate in an effective and functional way the different activities that can intervene in risk reduction, it is necessary to prearrange a general methodological framework able to explain the effect on risk reduction. In the literature, however, there are different definitions of risk depending on the specific field of analysis, with different aims and purposes that are difficult to direct towards Civil Protection activities. Furthermore, at present, neither a uniform conceptual-scientific model is available for all risk classes, nor quantitative evaluation criteria, especially due to the objective difficulty in identifying some factors that contribute to the definition of risk. It is therefore important to deepen the concept of risk and understand the factors it depends on.

For civil protection purposes, the risk is represented by the possibility that a natural phenomenon or one induced by human activities may cause harmful effects on the population, housing and productive settlements and infrastructure, within a particular area, in a given period of time.

The risk can be therefore translatable into the formula:

$$\boldsymbol{R} = \boldsymbol{H} \times \boldsymbol{V} \times \boldsymbol{E}$$

where

H = Hazard, i.e. the probability that a phenomenon of a certain intensity occurs in a certain period of time, in a given area.
V = Vulnerability, i.e. the propensity of an element (people, buildings, infrastructures, economic activities) to suffer damage as a result of the stresses induced by an event of a certain intensity.
E = Exposure or Exposed Value; i.e. the number of units or "value" of each element at risk present in a given area, such as human lives or settlements.

Therefore, to concretely assess a risk, it is not sufficient to estimate the degree of danger, but it is also necessary to carefully estimate the value of the exposure, that is the assets present in the territory that may be involved in an event and their vulnerability (Fig. 1).

GIS is a consolidated technology for risk analysis. Indeed GIS tools have been developed for different kind of environmental applications, including flooding [3] and volcanic eruptions [4]. Moreover, GIS have been also used within integrated software applications that, thanks to the direct connection with a spatial database, allow real-time emergency management in case of natural disasters [5–8].

In this work a GIS application was developed for the management of tsunami risk in the eastern part of Sicily and in particular in the coastal coast of the territory of the municipality of Acireale.

The GIS application was developed using free and open source software and considering historical data in order to provide accurate risk scenarios.

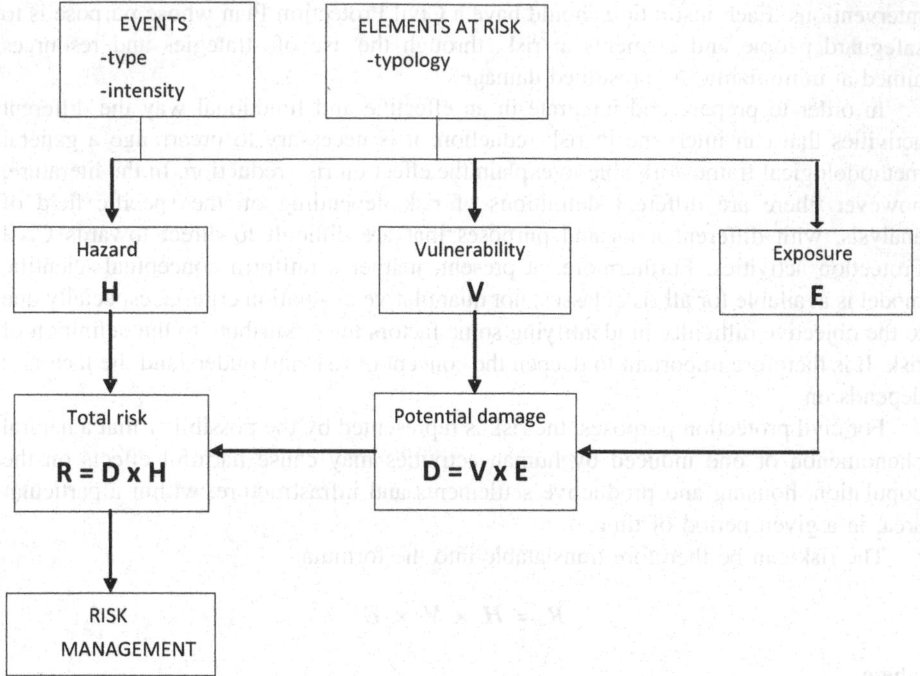

Fig. 1. Methodological scheme proposed for risk analysis

2 Tsunami Risk in Italy

Tsunamis are natural phenomena that can be caused by various environmental factors, such as underwater landslides, strong earthquakes with epicenter in the sea, etc. When earthquakes occur at sea, large masses of water are shifted violently from the bottom upwards, in correspondence with the friction zone or subduction of the tectonic plates. Tsunamis are in fact characterized by very long wave sequences in which the distance between one wave and the other can reach even a hundred kilometers.

In general the speed of a wave decreases rapidly as the depth of the water decreases. However, while in the shallow waters the first wave slows down, the second, which is even a hundred kilometers from the first, still travels at the initial speed. The result is that the distance between the waves decreases rapidly and the displaced water mass accumulates, forming waves that rise dramatically. The wave of the tsunami that was only a few centimeters high in the ocean can rise, reaching in some cases 30–40 m. The waves destroy everything in front of them causing death and destruction.

The Mediterranean presents a significant risk of tsunami, not only due to the seismicity of the entire area, but also to the presence of numerous emerged and submerged volcanic buildings. The risk due to tsunamis can be assessed on the basis of historical knowledge. In the Mediterranean Sea, unlike the oceans, the masses of water involved are smaller, so if a tsunami is produced, it will not have the same strength and intensity as one that develops in an ocean. However, through simulations, it has been noticed that the anomalous wave propagation times in the Mediterranean are very short and most of the possible tsunami source zones are very close to the coast. Consequently the main problem is that of being able to give the alarm in a very short time (e.g. within the first 10 min) and this explains why the alert system for the Mediterranean area must be faster and more effective than the one adopted in the Ocean Pacific.

The Mediterranean countries' commitment to a tsunami warning system is part of the ICG/NEAMTWS Intergovernmental Coordination Group (Intergovernmental Coordination Group/North Eastern Atlantic & Med Tsunami Warning System) coordinated by UNESCO. Italy, represented by the Department of Civil Protection, participates, along with the national scientific research institutes INGV and ISPRA, for the construction of the CAT (Tsunami Warning Centre) which operates 24 h per day. The CAT, experimentally activated in 2014 and operational since 1 January 2017, serves as an international alert node capable of alerting the Civil Protection authorities of the other Mediterranean basin states that have joined the NEAMTWS program.

In history, the tsunamis that affected the Mediterranean coasts were 127; of these, around 90 occurred in the central Mediterranean area, i.e. in Italy, eastern Greece, Albania, Croatia and Algeria.

In Italy, tsunamis have historically originated in the Tyrrhenian area and in the Ionian area. The latter was triggered by seismic events in the Greek Aegean islands and by events in the Calabrian coast and in the Crotone area.

The eastern coast of Sicily was affected by anomalous waves that affected the Val di Noto in 1693, Messina in 1908 and the Tyrrhenian coast of Sicily, with high waves up to 10.9 m in 2002 due to a landslide in Stromboli. Also the Sicilian Ionian coast has been affected by several tsunamis. Among all the documented events, the one related to the earthquake-tsunami of Messina in 1908 reports reliable data on a tsunami that has simultaneously affected the coast of Catania [1, 2].

Therefore, considering the location of the epicenter of the earthquakes prior to 1908 and especially the events generated along the Ibleo-Maltese slope (1693–1818) we can hypothesize a wave height between 3 and 15 m.

3 Case Study: Acireale (Sicily)

The City of Acireale was largely built on a plateau, characterized by rocks of lava origin and by various faults, called "Timpa", which, with its ~ 150 m, puts it almost overlooking the Ionian sea. The Timpa represents the northern continuation of the Ibleo-Maltese Escarpment of the Etna region that in the past triggered devastating earthquakes with the consequent development of anomalous waves that affected the entire Ionian coast. In addition, the territory is characterized by the presence of numerous active faults that have caused considerable damage to things and people in history.

The coast (where different hamlets are located) is characterized by a cliff of lava origin, while the remaining part of the municipal territory falls into an hilly area. The inhabited area is essentially composed of the urban center built on the plateau and of twenty hamlets distributed partly along the coast and in the hilly areas. The hamlets are: Aciplatani, Balatelle, Guardia, Mangano, Pennisi, Piano d'Api, Pozzillo, Santa Caterina, Santa Maria La Scala, Santa Tecla, Santa Maria Ammalati, Santa Maria delle Grazie, Santa Maria La Stella, San Giovanni Bosco, Scillichenti, Stazzo, San Cosmo, Baracche, Capomulini, and Fiandaca.

The marine hamlets, that are Pozzillo, Stazzo, Santa Maria La Scala, Santa Tecla and Capo Mulini, are equipped with small ports with moorings.

The municipal territory is served not only by the State Road S.S.114, but also by provincial, municipal and local roads, and by the Messina-Catania A18 motorway. Therefore the territory can be interested by different risks: seismic, hydrogeological, geomorphological and hydraulic, volcanic, and also by tsunami events on the coast that would affect the population centers that overlook the Ionian Sea. From South to North, these are: Capo Mulini, Santa Maria La Scala, Santa Tecla, Stazzo and Pozzillo.

4 GIS for the Assessment and Management of Tsunami Hazards

GIS is a consolidated technology to dynamically manage geographic data and to obtain a real Decision Support System (DSS) to provide primary care to the affected population and to overcome emergencies. GIS are a valuable tool to manage a large amount of real time data acquired from monitoring and alerting sensors [5].

GIS applications have been used for the management of risk phenomena and e.g. the loss of efficiency of the infrastructures affected by the calamitous event [6–8].

In this work a GIS application was created to simulate risk scenarios related to a tsunami, and to develop possible intervention actions in the inundated areas, including the loss of efficiency of road infrastructures.

The bibliographical research has allowed us to hypothesize an applicative scenario characterized by a wave height measured in the shoreline of 5 and 7 m [1, 2, 9–11].

Our GIS application provides as output the areas affected by a possible anomalous wave propagation phenomenon with the hypothesized characteristics.

The workflow includes:

- Choosing of a geo-referenced Digital Elevation Model (DEM) with a good geometric resolution;
- Creating a grid with the same geometric resolution as the DEM for the two wave heights assumed by the literature data;

- Executing the difference between the DEM raster and the hypothesized height grids in order to obtain a raster where the negative pixels represent portions of the territory that will surely be flooded by a possible wave propagation;
- Converting the obtained raster data to a vector in order to compare a possible flooding area with the existing anthropic elements.

For this purpose, a WGS84 geo-referenced orthophoto and a 20-m DEM were loaded as a WMS service and used as basic cartography in the GIS environment.

Two raster grids were created, with a square mesh and a 20 m side, comparable with the DEM in terms of radiometric resolution. To each pixel of the two grids we associated the two assumed values of wave height, 5 and 7 m (Fig. 2). Subsequently, using the raster calculator tool in the GIS environment, the raster grids with the wave heights were removed from the DEM obtaining the portions of the territory that will surely be flooded.

Fig. 2. Areas affected by a tsunami with a wave of 5 (left) and 7 (right) meters along the Acese coast

Through the raster to vector tool, we converted the resulting raster of the wave into a vector to analyze the possible consequences on the territory due to the propagation of the hypothesized waves.

Then, through the intersect function, the vector relative to the simulated wave was intersected to the vector of building.

The resulting vector reported the potential structures affected by the anomalous wave propagation (Fig. 3).

Fig. 3. (left) Potential structures involved by an anomalous wave equal to 5 (left) and 7 (right) meters: buildings completely submerged (in red); buildings damaged, but not completely submerged (in blue); buildings not affected by the anomalous waves (in green). (Color figure online)

The same procedure was used to analyze the road infrastructures inundated by the tsunamis. So the vector layer of the road graph was intersected with the vector layers related to wave propagation with a height of 5 and 7 m (Fig. 4).

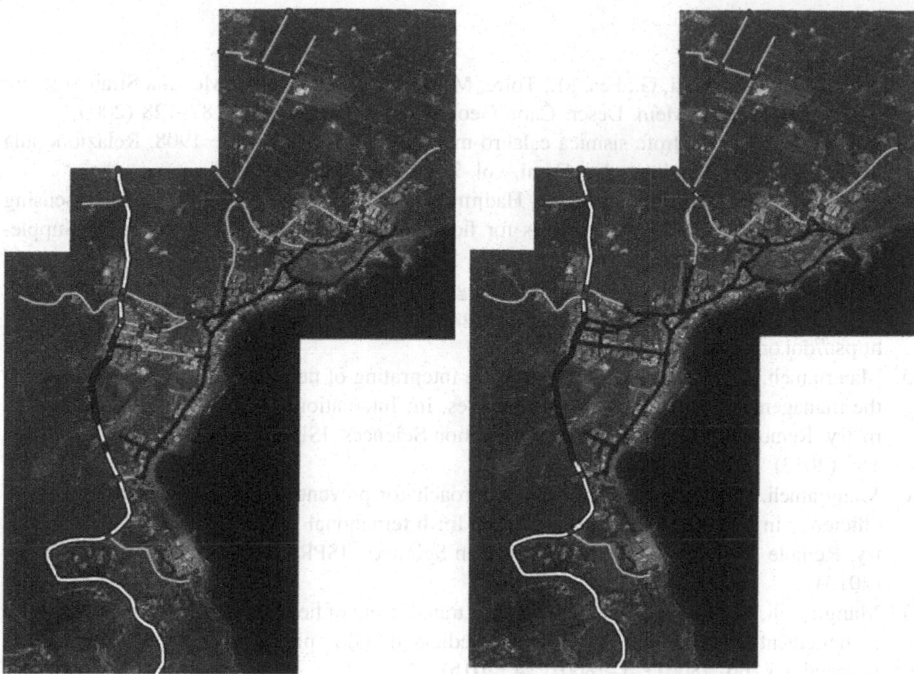

Fig. 4. Road arches (in red) made non-trafficable by an anomalous wave equal to 5 (left) and 7 (right) meters. (Color figure online)

5 Conclusions

In this work a GIS application for tsunami risk assessment was presented, providing a valid simulation tool for identifying possible areas flooded by an anomalous wave.

The area under study was the city of Acireale (Catania, Italy), in the Ionian Sea. Thanks to data obtained from bibliographic research, two possible wave heights have been identified, e.g. 5 and 7 m.

The results of the GIS simulations have highlighted how the Acireale-Stazzo and Acireale-Scillichenti vehicular flow on the SP2 would be interrupted due to the propagation of anomalous waves both of 5 m and 7 m. Furthermore, the completely submerged buildings in which it would be impossible to take refuge were highlighted in the two cases.

The GIS application developed represents a valid Decision Support System (DSS) that could be used by public institutions to plan the management of risk in case of tsunami emergencies.

References

1. Aversa, M., Bussoletti, G., Fea, M., Torre, M.: The seaquakes in the Messina Strait area. In: Proceeding ISPRA: Mem. Descr. Carta Geol. d'It. XCvi (2014), pp. 87–128 (2009)
2. Baratta, M.: La catastrofe sismica calabro-messinese del 28 dicembre 1908. Relazione alla Società Geografica Italiana, Ed. Forni, vol. 2, 458 pp., Roma (1910)
3. Franci, F., Bitelli, G., Mandanici, E., Hadjimitsis, D., Agapiou, A.: Satellite remote sensing and GIS-based multi-criteria analysis for flood hazard mapping. Nat. Hazards **83**(Supplement 1), 31–51 (2016)
4. Bartolini, S., Cappello, A., Martí, J., Del Negro, C.: QVAST: a new Quantum GIS plugin for estimating volcanic susceptibility. Nat. Hazards Earth Syst. Sci. **13**, 3031–3042 (2013). https://doi.org/10.5194/nhess-13-3031-2013
5. Mangiameli, M., Mussumeci, G.: Real time integrating of field data into a GIS platform for the management of hydrological emergencies. In: International Archives of the Photogrammetry, Remote Sensing and Spatial Information Sciences- ISPRS Archives, vol. 40, pp. 153–158 (2013)
6. Mangiameli, M., Mussumeci, G.: GIS approach for preventive evaluation of roads loss of efficiency in hydrogeological emergencies. In: International Archives of the Photogrammetry, Remote Sensing and Spatial Information Sciences- ISPRS Archives, vol. 40, pp. 79–87 (2013)
7. Mangiameli, M., Mussumeci, G.: Real time transferring of field data into a spatial DBMS for management of emergencies with a dedicated GIS platform. In: AIP Conference Proceedings, pp. 780012_1–780012_4 (2015)
8. Mangiameli, M., Mussumeci, G.: A spatial DB model to simulate the road network efficiency in hydrogeological emergency. In: AIP Conference Proceedings, vol. 1702, p. 180017 (2015). https://doi.org/10.1063/1.4938966
9. Maramai, A., Brizuela, B., Graziani, L.: The Euro-Mediterranean tsunami catalogue. Ann. Geophys. **57**, 4 (2014)
10. Platania, G.: Il maremoto dello Stretto di Messina del 28 dicembre 1908. Bollettino della Società Sismologica Italiana **13**, 369–458 (1909)
11. Platania, G.: I fenomeni marittimi che accompagnarono il terremoto di Messina del 28 dicembre 1908. Rivista Geografica Italiana **XVI**, 154–161 (1909)

Comparative Analysis of Different UAV-Based Photogrammetric Processes to Improve Product Accuracies

Mirko Saponaro[1(✉)], Alessandra Capolupo[2], Eufemia Tarantino[1], and Umberto Fratino[1]

[1] Politecnico di Bari, via Orabona 4, 70125 Bari, Italy
mirko.saponaro@poliba.it

[2] Plinivs Research Center – LUPT, University of Naples Federico II, Via Toledo, 402, 80134 Naples, NA, Italy

Abstract. Producing geographic information has become increasingly widespread over the last few years thanks to the development of new sensors, tools and algorithms, easily to be implemented and user friendly. Nevertheless, the accuracy of photogrammetric outcomes, obtained by automated software instructions and the use of un-calibrated cheap sensors, is often unsatisfying. As a consequence, the results accuracy and the potentialities and repeatability of those procedures have to be improved, defining the best workflow to be adopted. In literature, different approaches related to the correct and efficient reduction of geometric errors are available, although, to date, comprehensive method has not yet been defined.

This research work is aimed to detect an optimized workflow on the base of the comparison the accuracies achieved by applying different 3D reconstruction procedures of the cultural heritage. The process was subdivided in two steps: the former is related to a processing test, executed by analyzing four image-datasets acquired with a prosumer UAV equipped with a non-metric camera and a low-accuracy GNSS/INS receiver; the latter is based on an high-accuracy ground-truth survey, performed to evaluate the lever-arm and the camera self-calibration parameters, which are fundamental for reducing the errors propagation in the final accuracy. Thus, different 3D models were generated, modifying the processed image datasets and the spatial and numerical distribution of the Ground Control Points (GCPs). The root-mean-square error (RMSE) values on the Control Points (CPs), compensated differently in the Bundle Block Adjustment process, were assessed for each processing. Promising results were achieved in order to validate an optimal photogrammetric workflow.

Keywords: UAV · Direct Georeferencing · Lever-arm · Self-calibration

1 Introduction

The technological advances of sensors and algorithms and the introduction of new tools, such as Unmanned Aerial Vehicles (UAVs), in the field of survey have strongly improved the outcomes accuracy produced by photogrammetric technique.

S. Misra et al. (Eds.): ICCSA 2019, LNCS 11622, pp. 225–238, 2019.
https://doi.org/10.1007/978-3-030-24305-0_18

The combination of UAVs ability to overflow areas hard to access and to reduce operational time and cost with the improvements to Structure from Motion (SfM) and Multi-View Stereo (MVS) algorithms making photogrammetry more competitive than the traditional survey systems on the small and medium-sized areas [1]. Nevertheless, James et al. [2] highlighted that a homogeneous quality of the outcomes is still tough to reach and, therefore, as proposed by Manfreda et al. [1], the whole workflow should be subjected to a critical inspection for detecting the best approach among the several possible methods. Although, in literature, there are traces of procedures to be adopted for reducing correctly and efficiently the geometric errors, an exhaustive method has not yet been validated [3, 4].

Currently, the most widespread UAVs are equipped with L1 single-frequency and/or C/A code GNSS receivers, assisted with low-cost Inertial Measurement Unit (IMU) and non-metric cameras. Consequently, that low-equipment is not able to guarantee the achievement of standard accuracy requirements. This is complicated by the lack of information on the used processing algorithms and the clear definition of the relationships among parameters. Indeed, for instance, most of the available SfM software operate as a black-box, in which several parameters are preset [5] or, as in the case of the environments chosen to calibrate the camera mounted on UAVs, discussed in several papers [2, 6]. That last step is essential since camera lenses often introduce significant non-linear geometric distortions into the images, compromising their overall accuracy. Therefore, it is generally concerted that, unless an accurate pre-calibration is performed onsite, a robust self-calibration procedure is indispensable in order to compensate the inherent instability of the consumer cameras mounted on-board [7]. Thus, the synchronization between camera and navigation system, the determination of the exposure time of each image and, above all, of the lever-arm offset between the Perspective Center (PC) camera position and the GNSS Antenna Phase Center (APC) are required [8]. This constant displacement vector is rarely introduced in the processing software to compensate the lever-arm offset, affecting the final accuracy.

Apart from the camera, the on-board GNSS receiver is the other crucial tool mounted on the UAV. It is essential both for planning and driving the aircraft, and Direct Georeferencing (DG) of images during the SfM processing. The DG is a crucial step towards the automating all the procedure, however, as demonstrated in several papers [6, 9–11], their results are not satisfactory results compared to Indirect Georeferencing (IG). For that reason, the topographic UAV-based processing is generally performed using some known points, defined Ground Control Points (GCPs). The output accuracy of that method depends on the number and accuracy of GCPs involved in the metric reconstruction. Clearly, operational cost and time increase proportionally to the GCPs acquired during the field campaigns [12, 13], and, consequently, optimizing the survey activities would hence improve the reliability and repeatability of UAV-derived products [5].

The present work is aimed to define the best workflow in order to maximize the accuracy of the photogrammetric outcomes, comparing some 3D models of cultural heritage produced applying several approaches. Basic processing methods was screened to identify the most effective strategy for a reliable evaluation of camera calibration and lever-arm offset. Then a scheme of systematic errors related to the number of GCPs used and their spatial distribution was constructed.

2 Material and Method

A comprehensive UAV-based photogrammetric workflow was tested in order to improve the interior and exterior orientation parameters, and to reduce the error during computing process.

The process was split in two steps. The former based on the analysis of four images datasets acquired by applying a prosumer UAV equipped with a non-metric camera and a low-accuracy GNSS/INS receiver. The density of the obtained points clouds was gradually reduced, by selecting the points on the base of three cleaning criteria, described more in depth in the following paragraphs. The latter, based on an high-accuracy ground-truth survey, was carried out to evaluate the lever-arm and the camera self-calibration parameters. Particularly, the error must be mathematically modelled since these lens distortions and displacement vector are systematic effects.

The last phase is aimed to pull out on different 3D models. Combining the effects of image datasets with GCPs spatial and numerical distribution, systematic errors and the accuracy variation, reported as the root-mean-square-error (RMSE), on the Control Points (CPs), compensated differently in the relative phase of the Bundle Block Adjustment (BA), were then assessed.

2.1 Study Area, Data and Technology

The experiment was carried out in a farmhouse called ‘Casale di Pacciano’, located in the countryside of Bisceglie, 40 km far away from Bari (Puglia Region, Southern Italy). The farmhouse, dated back to the 11th century (Fig. 1), was already examined by the Polytechnic University of Bari in previous work [14].

Fig. 1. The test site and GCPs distributed in the area

It was over flown during two flight campaigns, performed using a prosumer quadcopter DJI Inspire 1, programmed through the iOS app DJI Ground Station Pro. The UAV was equipped with a non-metric camera DJI ZenMuse X3, characterized by a focal length of 3.61 mm and a pixel size of 1.56 µm. Moreover, it was also equipped with an economical GNSS/INS receiver, which the average accuracy of 2.54 m along the axes.

The two missions were planned in order to acquire images converging two opposite sides of the building. The former was managed at the constant altitude of 30 m Above Ground Level (AGL) in order to obtain an Average Ground Sample Distance (GSD) equal to 0.013 m/pix. The camera was set in a nadir-position. The latter was performed at a altitude of 20 m AGL, inclining the camera at 45°. In this case a GSD equal to 0.009 m/pix was expected. The image overlap was set to 90% in both longitudinal and lateral direction of the flight.

Three datasets were generated (Table 1): the "NAD" dataset composed only by nadiral images; the "NAD+45°" source of data consisted by all the images acquired during the two missions; the "NAD+CON" dataset characterized by 11 selected convergent images taken during the second flight. UAV flights patterns with different heights and additional cross strip introduce additional depth information and support efficient calibration of low-cost cameras [3].

Table 1. Imagery dataset features

Dataset	n° images	Camera inclination	Altitude AGL [m]	GSD [m/pix]	Image size	Pixel size [µm]	Focal length [mm]	Image quality
NAD	75	90°	30	0.013	4000 × 3000	1.56	3.61	0.8528
NAD+CON	86	90°/45°	30/20	0.013/0.009	4000 × 3000	1.56	3.61	0.8525
NAD+45°	194	90°/45°	30/20	0.013/0.009	4000 × 3000	1.56	3.61	0.8515

Each acquired image was correlated with the information related to their position on the moment of shooting.

The metric reconstruction was improved using 8 GCPs, homogeneously distributed along the border and the central side of the study area (Fig. 1). Their coordinates were accurately detected through the application of the Global Navigation Satellite System (GNSS) Leica Viva GS14 receivers, performing measurements in Real Time Kinematic (RTK) relying on a baseline between the static master station and the "Margherita di Savoia" permanent reference station of the National Dynamic Network (RDN2008). Their features are described in Table 2. The metric reconstruction was implemented in Agisoft PhotoScan environment (version 1.4.1).

2.2 Workspace Setting and Calibration System

A reasonable calibration of the system and a workspace setting was fixed. The quality of images was checked in order to detect and remove images, not suitable for the photogrammetric processing purposes. PhotoScan software provides a useful tool that independently analyses each image, estimating for it a quality value between 0 (low) and 1 (high). Table 1 shows the average values of the image quality, which are

Table 2. GCP coordinates features

GCP label	Easting [m]	Northing [m]	Geodetic height [m]	Accuracy E [m]	Accuracy N [m]	Accuracy H [m]
GNSS001	623202.809	4563587.783	68.551	0.001825	0.001714	0.008375
GNSS002	623227.598	4563583.821	66.682	0.004196	0.003988	0.019079
GNSS003	623220.777	4563599.963	66.107	0.004158	0.003709	0.017090
GNSS004	623216.743	4563605.399	66.104	0.004167	0.003744	0.016646
GNSS005	623235.381	4563588.782	67.835	0.004266	0.003889	0.017085
GNSS006	623233.660	4563606.238	65.799	0.004588	0.004079	0.016514
GNSS008	623239.901	4563582.427	67.771	0.004447	0.004246	0.013493
GNSS011	623260.574	4563621.193	65.373	0.004414	0.004113	0.012621

higher than the threshold 0.5, and, consequently, no of them should be removed. Moreover, the images didn't show any evident distortions or blur effects.

The reference system WGS84 (EPSG::4326) was defined for the imagery qualified by the geo-tags, while for the detected GCPs the reference system RDN2008/UTM zone 33N (NE) (EPSG::6708) was set. In Accuracy Image (m) parameter a value of 3 m was chosen as conservative setting, although knowing the actual value equal to 2.54 m. The precision of this value is linked to the receiver rate of position measurements per second (Hz) and accordingly to the mean speed of the aircraft [8]. However, despite the imagery are acquired in hovering and the precision can be considered robust, a conservative value is recommended. At the same time, since there are no manufacturing information, in Accuracy Image (deg) the default value of 10° is retained, so as to incorporate within it the negative effects caused by the low accuracy of the IMU-onboard. The Precision Marker (m) parameter was set a mean value of 0.02 m: that parameter represents the mean precision of GCPs coordinates in object space. As regards the calibration of the image coordinates in the software workspace, a more realistic Marker Precision (pix) value of 0.5 pix was set, i.e. the actual ability of the operator to identify the target in the image. The accuracy of the tie points is kept at the default value of 1 pix [3]. The images sharpness influences the tie points positioning. A subpixel value of this parameter prevents the photogrammetric block from being distorted, but at the same time it cut the points re-projections number. The Tie points accuracy, Precision Marker (pix) and Precision Marker (m) parameters are used to construct the variance-covariance matrix within the stochastic model, thus primary for the BA optimization.

An additional dataset characterized by the union of the nadiral image dataset with the calibration file, named NAD+CALIBR, was generated using the Agisoft Lens tool in the laboratory. The camera calibration of the other datasets was obtained during the cameras alignment step.

It is important to set the GPS/INS Offset in order to obtain the lever-arm values corrections measured in the laboratory. Precisely, the displacement vector (X, Y, Z) measured is equal to (0.005, 0.10, 0.25) m with precision of about 0.01 m, and IMU values calibration (yaw, pitch, roll) is put equal to 0° with an accuracy equal to 2°. These values were optimized in the consecutive phases.

Once the workspace was set up, the Camera Alignment step was run with 'high' accuracy option, setting the Limit of Key Points and Tie Points equal to 0. Once the cameras alignment the of all processes was completed and interior and exterior orientation and camera calibration parameters were defined, the cleaning clouds process started by utilizing three picking criteria of the Gradual Selection tool [3]. The first criterion utilized, named Reconstruction Uncertainty, allows removing points with low base-to-height ratios. Namely, tie points situated in the margins of the surveyed area generally have a higher degree of reconstruction uncertainty than those in the model centre, due to the low lateral overlapping of the images. Removal of such points don't affect the accuracy of optimization, but beneficially lightens the model.

The second criterion utilized, called Projection Accuracy, allows identifying less reliable tie points. In this work case, poor quality matches are indicated by a parameter value equal to 10 which means, that those points have an uncertainty 10 times higher than the points of minimum uncertainty.

The third criterion, the Re-projection Error, is applied to remove erroneous points with big residuals. Effectively, this parameter involves the largest direct influence on the root-mean-square-error (RMSE) of the GCPs and CPs, and it improve conspicuously the orientation parameters.

As suggested by Mayer et al. [3], the obtained points cloud was subjected to a Gradual Selection treatment, as reported in Table 3. The clouds are cleaned out from inaccurate points for the accuracy optimization, whereupon 8 GCPs are identified in the images.

Table 3. n° of tie points reduction in Gradual Selection processes in 1st step

Dataset	Initial n° tie points	Reconstruction Uncertainty [Value 10]	Projection Accuracy [Value 3]	Reprojection Error [Value 0.40]
NAD	282202 →	147874 →	101343 →	88538
NAD+CON	319609 →	152800 →	104516 →	93021
NAD+45°	741240 →	228767 →	161548 →	142373
NAD +CALIBR	292000 →	155994 →	105777 →	68491

The Bundle Block Adjustment (BA) procedures were launched through the Optimize Cameras process, which were used to adjust the coordinates of estimated points, camera parameters and lever-arm values minimizing the sum of re-projection errors and reference coordinate misalignment error [3]. Nevertheless, it is able to compensate only the linear model misalignment, and not the non-linear components.

The applied operations yielded estimates of the calibration parameters of the camera and of the lever-arm vector for each processed dataset.

2.3 3D Model Generation Workflow

Subsequently, the datasets were carried out using three Chunks. The alignment of cameras in 'high' precision mode was started, in order to generate the three sparse points clouds. The procedure applied was equal to that one described in the first step, the clouds were treated in Gradual Selection, reducing the size and re-projection errors related to the uncertainty and ambiguity of the points (Table 4).

Table 4. n° of tie points reduction in Gradual Selection processes in 2nd step

Dataset	Initial n° tie points	Reconstruction Uncertainty [Value 10]	Projection Accuracy [Value 3]	Reprojection Error [Value 0.40]
NAD	281896 →	147477 →	101040 →	88107
NAD+CON	319456 →	152718 →	104337 →	92670
NAD+45°	741274 →	228569 →	161429 →	142086

In order to understand the influence of the number of GCPs used and their spatial distribution for the optimization of the accuracy of the UAV-based products, the 8 GCPs reported in Table 2 and Fig. 1 were again introduced in the three Chunks.

Number of GCPs. Nine copies were generated for each Chunk, in a total of 27 sparse points cloud in the workspace. The nine clouds for Chunk have been georeferenced by implementing from a maximum of 8 GCPs to 0 GCPs, thus considering also the case of DG. The implemented GCPs were chosen according to the common criterion which start from the more external points up to the more central ones of the reconstructed 3D model [3]. The remaining number of non-implemented ground points in each process are consequently defined as CPs.

Once the casuistry was defined, the BA was run applying the Optimize Cameras process, which it is strictly conditioned by the fixed georeferencing.

GCPs Spatial Distribution. Starting from the three basic Chunks, for each of these, additional copies were generated: the influence of the spatial distribution of GCPs varies according to the number of those implemented [12]. At the beginning, 7 clouds of points were generated for each Chunk, with a number of GCPs ranging from 1 to 7, adopting an opposite strategy of choice than the previous case, i.e. from central GCPs to those on borderlines. Further for each Chunk, other 7 clouds have been generated but adopting another GCPs strategy of choosing, i.e. balancing homogeneously the distribution. The workspaces were organized with a total of 42 Chunk: the Optimize Cameras procedure was started.

3 Results and Discussion

3.1 Camera Calibration and Lever-Arm

Figure 2 shows the differences among the different calibrations estimated in the four processes described in Sect. 2.2. In particular, Fig. 2a reports the differences of trends among the estimated values in the different processes for each parameter. In order to make indicative the representation, the value of the focal length F was set as the percentage of the difference from the initial theoretical value, while the other parameters were represented using their actual estimated values. The figure shows that there are no substantial differences among the estimates since their trends are analogous. The outcomes obtained from the Chunks NAD+45° and NAD+CON reveal a similar behaviour, pointing out the opportunity to reduce the acquisition and processing time. The comparison of the Standard Deviation (SD) values, resulting from each parameter estimation, is reported in Fig. 2b. The SDs of the NAD+45° dataset (the blue lines) show a more robust results compared to the others. The values regarding the Chunk NAD+CALIBR are not reported in the figure since they are identified as outliers because of their non-conforming values. This demonstrated that the pre-calibration procedure performed in the laboratory has low reliability.

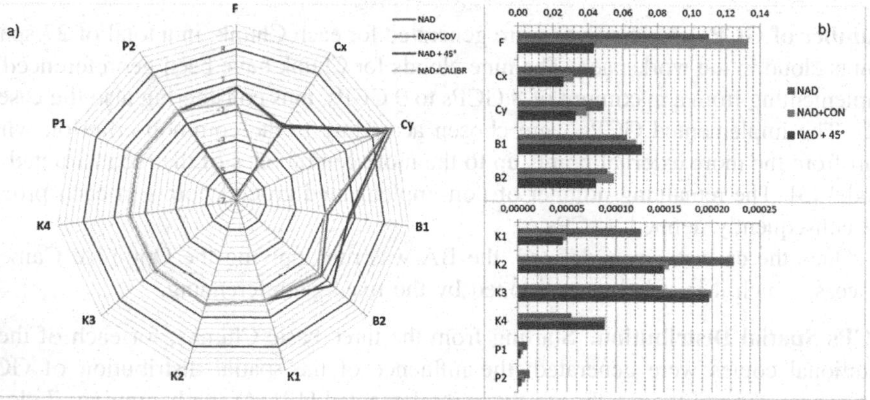

Fig. 2. (a) Graphical comparison of camera calibration parameters. In F that mean the focal length, the value represents a percentage difference from the initial theoretical value. Cx and Cy describe the offset of the main point. K1-K2-K3-K4 are related to the radial distortion coefficients while P1 and P2 to the tangential distortion coefficients. The B1-B2 parameters mean the affinity value and the non-orthogonality coefficient. (b) SD values resulting from the computing

In order to identify the most suitable processing for extracting the optimal values of the camera calibration parameters, the variance-covariance matrices have been extrapolated (Fig. 3). Comparing the covariances among the Chunks, a percentage reduction of the correlation in the Chunk NAD+45° is traced. Covariance is an reliable index to estimate camera calibration since its reduction indicates the estimation errors of each parameter are independence. Like in the previous case, the NAD+CON model shows results that are directly comparable with the previous one. Therefore, the parameters estimated in NAD+45° are selected.

Once defined camera calibration parameters, the values of the lever-arm were detected in order to mitigate the interior and relative exterior orientation errors of the cameras. Although the values of lever-arm appear comparable, except for the Chunk NAD+CALIBR because of the high RMSE of GCPs, as shown in Fig. 4, the lever-arm parameters obtained from NAD model were chosen, since the other Chunks were characterized by a higher re-projection errors (pix).

NAD	F	Cx	Cy	B1	B2	K1	K2	K3	K4	P1	P2
F	1	0.04	0.03	0.05	0.01	0.92	0.88	0.59	0.55	0.02	0.1
Cx		1	0.04	0.06	0.03	0.03	0.03	0.02	0.02	0.67	0.09
Cy			1	0.09	0.13	0.06	0.03	0.02	0.01	0.07	0.62
B1				1	0.05	0.08	0.05	0	0.01	0.13	0.13
B2					1	0	0.01	0.01	0.02	0.01	0.16
K1						1	0.95	0.77	0.71	0	0.11
K2							1	0.9	0.86	0	0.1
K3			symm.					1	0.99	0.02	0.07
K4									1	0.01	0.06
P1										1	0.18
P2											1

NAD+CON	F	Cx	Cy	B1	B2	K1	K2	K3	K4	P1	P2
F	1	0.02	0.2	0.14	0.04	0.09	0.23	0.12	0.13	0.05	0.19
Cx		1	0.03	0.01	0.09	0.03	0.01	0.02	0.03	0.12	0.02
Cy			1	0.03	0.02	0.01	0.04	0.01	0.02	0.01	0.21
B1				1	0.07	0.07	0.02	0.05	0.06	0.09	0.1
B2					1	0.01	0.01	0.01	0.01	0.09	0.03
K1						1	0.9	0.86	0.79	0.06	0.07
K2							1	0.98	0.95	0	0.04
K3			symm.					1	0.99	0.01	0.02
K4									1	0.01	0.02
P1										1	0.13
P2											1

NAD+45°	F	Cx	Cy	B1	B2	K1	K2	K3	K4	P1	P2
F	1	0.01	0.2	0.15	0.11	0.16	0.22	0.19	0.18	0.05	0.07
Cx		1	0.09	0.03	0.33	0.01	0	0.01	0.02	0.53	0.06
Cy			1	0.03	0.02	0.02	0.02	0.02	0.02	0.05	0.49
B1				1	0.03	0.08	0.01	0.04	0.05	0.05	0
B2					1	0	0.01	0	0.01	0.12	0.03
K1						1	0.96	0.9	0.85	0	0.08
K2							1	0.98	0.95	0.02	0.03
K3			symm.					1	0.99	0.02	0.02
K4									1	0.02	0.01
P1										1	0.02
P2											1

Fig. 3. Variance-Covariance matrices extrapolated from the Calibration Camera stochastic models of each processing. Values between 0 and ±1 that indicate relatively no-correlation or full correlation.

GPS/INS Offset – *Lever-Arm*							
NAD	*Initial [m]*	*Adjusted [m]*	*Accuracy [m]*	NAD+CON	*Initial [m]*	*Adjusted [m]*	*Accuracy [m]*
X [m]	0.0050	0.0023	0.0100	X [m]	0.0050	0.0022	0.0100
Y [m]	0.1000	0.0998	0.0100	Y [m]	0.1000	0.0998	0.0100
Z [m]	0.2500	0.2505	0.0100	Z [m]	0.2500	0.2487	0.0100
Yaw [°]	0	0.8377	2	Yaw [°]	0	0.5442	2
Pitch [°]	0	5.7062	2	Pitch [°]	0	0.7121	2
Roll [°]	0	1.7367	2	Roll [°]	0	1.3552	2
NAD+45°	*Initial [m]*	*Adjusted [m]*	*Accuracy [m]*	NAD+CALIBR	*Initial [m]*	*Adjusted [m]*	*Accuracy [m]*
X [m]	0.0050	0.0027	0.0100	X [m]	0.0050	0.0023	0.0100
Y [m]	0.1000	0.0994	0.0100	Y [m]	0.1000	0.0997	0.0100
Z [m]	0.2500	0.2485	0.0100	Z [m]	0.2500	0.2490	0.0100
Yaw [°]	0	0.2391	2	Yaw [°]	0	0.8182	2
Pitch [°]	0	-21.3456	2	Pitch [°]	0	5.8299	2
Roll [°]	0	0.7601	2	Roll [°]	0	1.7480	2

Fig. 4. In the first table are presented the comparable RMSE values about the 4 Chunk. At the second table the different estimated GPS/INS Offsets extrapolated from PhotoScan.

3.2 Positional Accuracy Assessment

Number of GCPs Impact. Table 5 shows the RMSE values related to the 27 datasets processing, obtained varying the number of GCPs used in the BA procedures and, consequently, in georeference phase. The RMSE values define the overall trend of systematic errors recorded in the GCPs and in the remaining CPs along the three axes. 8 and 0 GCPs were used in the IG and DG procedure, respectively. As described in Sect. 2.1, the low accuracy of the sensors mounted on board the UAV does not allow the achievement of high positional accuracy in the DG. DG procedure shows important deviations along the Y axis. This highlighted the lack of reliability of the data recorded by the on-board receiver. The lack of raw position data acquired by the on board receiver does not allow, however, to investigate the causes and, thus, their estimation cannot be improved. In order to go beyond this problem, It is necessary to include an efficient amount of GCPs in the data processing workflow in order to increase the accuracy of geospatial products.

Overall, the three datasets show a similar behavior respect to the number of GCPs implemented. There is a reduction in RMSE values in the transition from a number of GCPs used from 2 to 3, with a RMSE value of 5.7 cm in the NAD+CON dataset. The following steps confirm the order of magnitude achieved with slight centimetric improvements. By focusing on the differences between the three processed datasets, some considerations emerge. The NAD+45° dataset returns a better RMSE value by implementing only one GCP. The subsequent values reveal a worsening of the estimates compared to the other datasets due to the relative increase in the errors of re-projection of the points. A rather similar trend is recorded on the NAD and NAD+CON datasets until the implemented of 6 GCPs. Beyond that limit, NAD+CON is affected by the points' re-projection errors equally to NAD+45°. The value of absolute geometric accuracy achieved by NAD with 7 GCPs implemented is comparable to the value of GSD, defined in Sect. 2.1.

Table 5. RMSE values achieved by varying the number of GCPs implemented

	n° GCPs	RMSE [NAD]				RMSE [NAD+CON]				RMSE [NAD+45°]			
		X (m)	Y (m)	Z (m)	XYZ (m)	X (m)	Y (m)	Z (m)	XYZ (m)	X (m)	Y (m)	Z (m)	XYZ (m)
GCP	0	–	–	–	–	–	–	–	–	–	–	–	–
CP		1.053	3.372	1.532	3.8500	1.373	3.406	1.310	3.8995	1.846	3.140	1.202	3,8358
GCP	1	0.000	0.000	0.000	0.0003	0.000	0.000	0.000	0.0004	0.000	0.000	0.001	0.0012
CP		0.519	0.428	1.759	1.8830	0.494	0.648	1.530	1.7332	0.511	1.387	0.907	1.7337
GCP	2	0.007	0.013	0.021	0.0254	0.000	0.000	0.002	0.0020	0.000	0.000	0.003	0.0026
CP		0.054	0.073	0.803	0.8084	0.032	0.074	0.830	0.8339	0.056	0.126	0.926	0.9366
GCP	3	0.012	0.028	0.033	0.0450	0.006	0.005	0.010	0.0127	0.007	0.013	0.003	0.0150
CP		0.024	0.017	0.064	0.0706	0.022	0.025	0.046	0.0570	0.057	0.069	0.073	0.1154
GCP	4	0.013	0.020	0.064	0.0688	0.018	0.015	0.036	0.0428	0.018	0.012	0.058	0.0616
CP		0.025	0.019	0.039	0.0495	0.023	0.031	0.019	0.0426	0.057	0.079	0.030	0.1020
GCP	5	0.012	0.017	0.058	0.0613	0.017	0.013	0.035	0.0408	0.019	0.011	0.052	0.0566
CP		0.030	0.021	0.040	0.0545	0.027	0.035	0.015	0.0471	0.063	0.092	0.033	0.1157
GCP	6	0.019	0.019	0.059	0.0651	0.019	0.012	0.030	0.0378	0.047	0.050	0.051	0.0858
CP		0.023	0.016	0.002	0.0276	0.017	0.041	0.016	0.0467	0.030	0.048	0.011	0.0575
GCP	7	0.023	0.019	0.055	0.0622	0.019	0.021	0.033	0.0430	0.044	0.052	0.047	0.0825
CP		0.009	0.007	0.005	0.0123	0.010	0.008	0.027	0.0298	0.002	0.002	0.020	0.0205
GCP	8	0.021	0.017	0.051	0.0581	0.018	0.019	0.031	0.0410	0.041	0.048	0.044	0.0771
CP		–	–	–	–	–	–	–	–	–	–	–	–

GCPs Spatial Distribution Impact. The spatial location of the GCPs on the image block was also taken into account. Figure 5a shows the interpolated trend lines by examining the RMSE values of the CPs obtained from the three GCPs spatial configurations, in response to changes in their number. The trend lines, concerning the RMSE variations of GCP points, are also shown in order to obtain a complete overview of the geometric accuracy achieved in each model. Trend lines mitigate the effects of the different spatial distribution of points, defining a general trend in accuracy. Overall, the trends of the values of CPs confirm the previous results even if, they show some appreciable improvements for the NAD+CON and NAD+45° datasets. This means that a different spatial distribution of the implemented GCPs affects re-projection errors and the achievable accuracy. On the other hand, a compensation of about 2–4 cm of the errors of the GCPs, in the NAD+CON modelling, represent a reasonable correctness of the internal and external orientation of the model. Finally, Figs. 5b–c–d show the statistical treatment for each model, so as to examine the best distribution strategy of GCPs. The third selected spatial distribution returns better accuracy values. In particular, as discussed by Rangel et al. [12], the best results are obtained with a gradual GCPs distribution in order to obtain a homogeneous density of the points in the area, maintaining a reasonable distance among the points. Promising results are also generated from the first spatial distribution, including marginal GCPs and central CPs, according to the literature [12, 13].

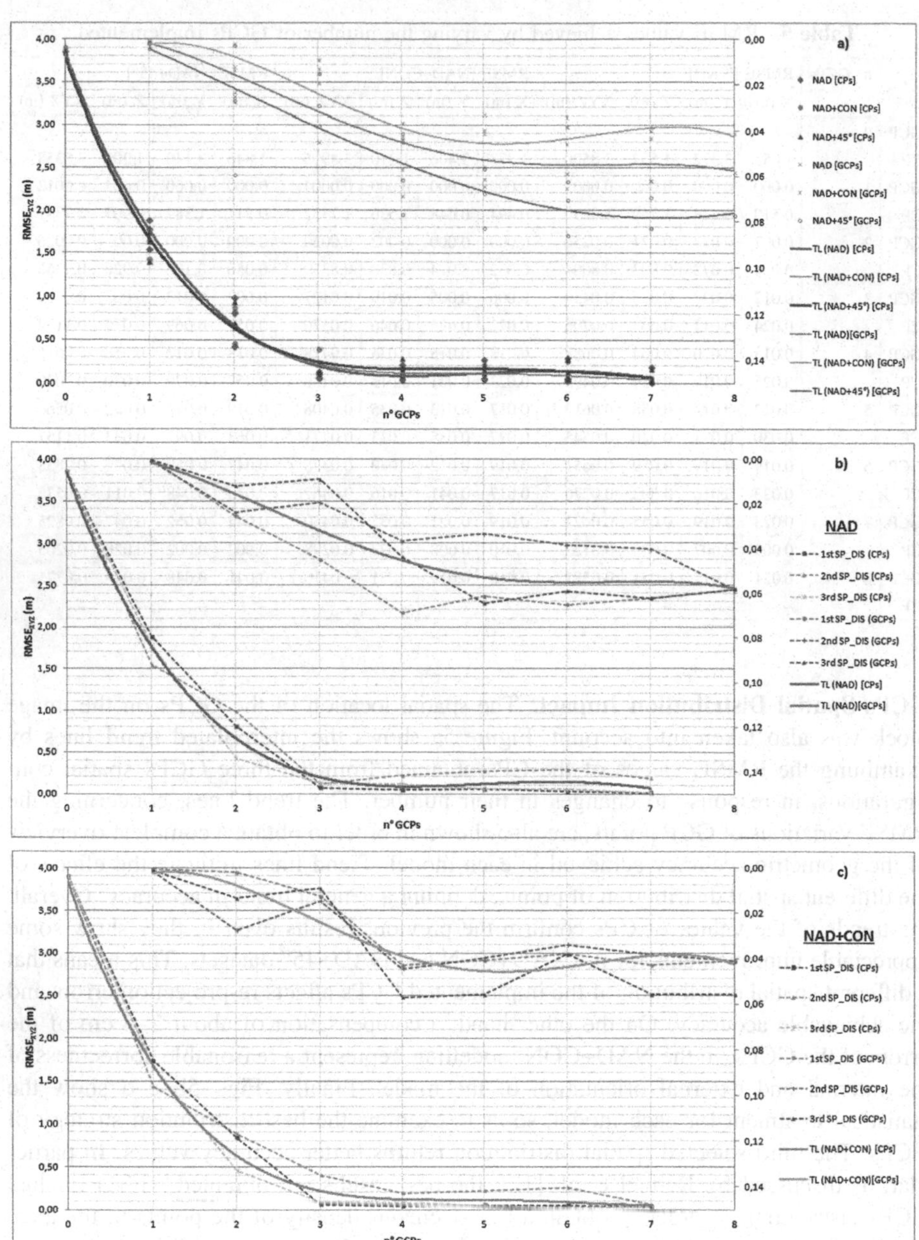

Fig. 5. Impact of GCPs spatial distribution. (a) Trend lines interpolated on 3 different spatial distributions of GCPs by varying the number of these latter. (b) NAD dataset developments and trend line by varying the spatial distribution. (c) NAD+CON dataset developments and trend line by varying the spatial distribution. (d) NAD+45° dataset developments and trend line by varying the spatial distribution.

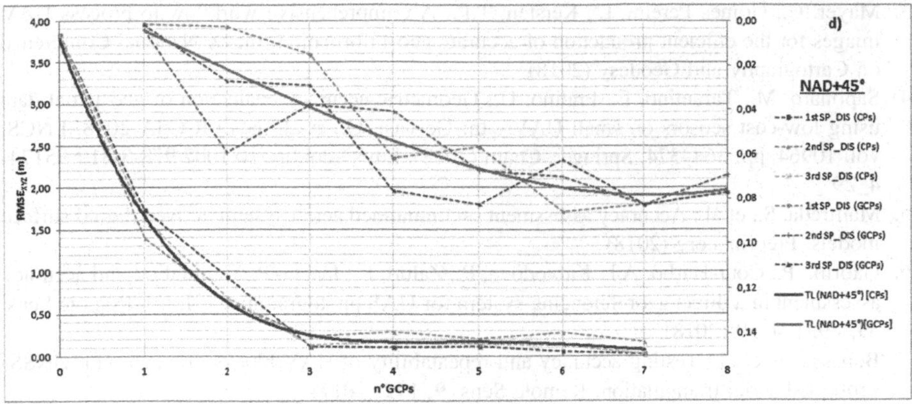

Fig. 5. (*continued*)

4 Conclusion

The current research activity is aimed to identify the most effective comprehensive workflow to increase the accuracy of the photogrammetric outcomes as much as possible. Therefore, this work demonstrated that a reliable camera calibration and lever-arm vector estimation avoid errors propagation in the final product accuracy and its repeatability. Moreover, UAV flights performed at different heights, camera inclinations and additional cross strip introduce additional depth information and support efficient calibration of low-cost cameras. Sparse points clouds obtained have to be treated identifying tie points with low-quality matching and high re-projection errors, and therefore removed prior to BA process. Subsequently, the influence of the final accuracy of the number and spatial distribution of the GCPs was detected. In the meanwhile, appreciable differences in accuracy were investigated by examining combined image datasets.

Results generated by the dataset of nadiral images, assisted only by 11 convergent images, look interesting. Obvious gaps were highlighted about the DG, noting instead the need of only 3 GCPs for a high quality geo-referencing. Moreover, homogeneous distribution of GCPs improves the metric reconstruction accuracy.

Future applications should be aimed to make more efficient the photogrammetric processing. A possible future application will automate the research of the optimal spatial and numerical distribution of the GCPs.

References

1. Manfreda, S., et al.: On the use of unmanned aerial systems for environmental monitoring. Remote Sens. **10**, 641 (2018)
2. James, M.R., Robson, S., d'Oleire-Oltmanns, S., Niethammer, U.: Optimising UAV topographic surveys processed with structure-from-motion: ground control quality, quantity and bundle adjustment. Geomorphology **280**, 51–66 (2017)

3. Mayer, C., Gomes Pereira, L., Kersten, T.P.: A comprehensive workflow to process UAV images for the efficient production of accurate geo-information. In: IX National Conference on Cartography and Geodesy (2018)
4. Saponaro, M., Tarantino, E., Fratino, U.: Geometric accuracy evaluation of geospatial data using low-cost sensors on small UAVs. In: Gervasi, O., et al. (eds.) ICCSA 2018. LNCS, vol. 10964, pp. 364–374. Springer, Cham (2018). https://doi.org/10.1007/978-3-319-95174-4_29
5. Manfreda, S., et al.: Accuracy assessment on unmanned aerial system derived digital surface models. Preprints.org (2018)
6. Gabrlik, P., Cour-Harbo, A.l., Kalvodova, P., Zalud, L., Janata, P.: Calibration and accuracy assessment in a direct georeferencing system for UAS photogrammetry. Int. J. Remote Sens. **39**, 4931–4959 (2018)
7. Benassi, F., et al.: Testing accuracy and repeatability of UAV blocks oriented with GNSS-supported aerial triangulation. Remote Sens. **9**, 172 (2017)
8. Padró, J.-C., Muñoz, F.-J., Planas, J., Pons, X.: Comparison of four UAV georeferencing methods for environmental monitoring purposes focusing on the combined use with airborne and satellite remote sensing platforms. Int. J. Appl. Earth Obs. Geoinf. **75**, 130–140 (2019)
9. Daakir, M., et al.: Lightweight UAV with on-board photogrammetry and single-frequency GPS positioning for metrology applications. ISPRS J. Photogram. Remote Sens. **127**, 115–126 (2017)
10. Grayson, B., Penna, N.T., Mills, J.P., Grant, D.S.: GPS precise point positioning for UAV photogrammetry. Photogram. Rec. **33**, 427–447 (2018)
11. Hu, J., et al.: A brief review on the positioning technologies for unmanned aerial vehicles. In: IEEE International Conference on Unmanned Systems (ICUS), pp. 527–532 (2017)
12. Rangel, J.M.G., Gonçalves, G.R., Pérez, J.A.: The impact of number and spatial distribution of GCPs on the positional accuracy of geospatial products derived from low-cost UASs. Int. J. Remote Sens. **39**, 7154–7171 (2018)
13. Sanz-Ablanedo, E., Chandler, J.H., Rodríguez-Pérez, J.R., Ordóñez, C.: Accuracy of Unmanned Aerial Vehicle (UAV) and SfM photogrammetry survey as a function of the number and location of ground control points used. Remote Sens. **10**, 1606 (2018)
14. Caradonna, G., Tarantino, E., Scaioni, M., Figorito, B.: Multi-image 3D reconstruction: a photogrammetric and structure from motion comparative analysis. In: Gervasi, O., et al. (eds.) ICCSA 2018. LNCS, vol. 10964, pp. 305–316. Springer, Cham (2018). https://doi.org/10.1007/978-3-319-95174-4_25

Evaluation of Geomorphic Descriptors Thresholds for Flood Prone Areas Detection on Ephemeral Streams in the Metropolitan Area of Bari (Italy)

Gabriella Balacco, Vincenzo Totaro(✉), Andrea Gioia, and Alberto Ferruccio Piccinni

Politecnico di Bari, Via E. Orabona, 470125 Bari, Italy
{gabriella.balacco, vincenzo.totaro, andrea.gioia, albertoferruccio.piccinni}@poliba.it

Abstract. Using geomorphic descriptors is a fast and reliable approach for mapping flood-prone areas exploiting Digital Elevation Models and their tools. However, calibration and validation procedures require a flooded map obtained by 1D/2D hydraulic simulation, which usually needs lots of information (available, for example, from remote sensing techniques) and important computational efforts. This approach is usually performed by calibration on a single event, using linear binary classifiers method and Receiver Operating Characteristics curves, in order to define an optimal threshold corresponding to a selected flooded map. On the other hand, the availability of flood-risk maps, provided by public or private institutions, is an important source of data for applying this procedure on a wide and hydrologically homogeneous area, in order to analyze some similitudes. In this study some interesting case studies located in Puglia region (Southern Italy) are investigated, using flooded maps for return periods of 30, 200 and 500 years provided by Basin Authority of Puglia; the aim of the proposed work is to compare the known flooded map areas with those obtained using several geomorphologic index on four case studies located in the metropolitan area of Bari (Puglia).

Keywords: Geomorphological descriptors · Flood-prone areas · DTM-based approach

1 Introduction

Puglia region (Southern Italy) is characterized by numerous shallow karst ephemeral/episodic streams locally known as "Lame". The deep fractured limestone that characterizes the western part of the middle of Puglia (called "Alta Murgia") ensures a high infiltration capacity and consequently this territory is characterized by the absence of a real and distinguishable drainage networks, except for several natural incisions. However, during extreme rainfall events, these streams are interested by significant flow rates that induce damages for assets and people.

S. Misra et al. (Eds.): ICCSA 2019, LNCS 11622, pp. 239–254, 2019.
https://doi.org/10.1007/978-3-030-24305-0_19

In the last years the increase of flood risk [1], as well as the observed changes in rainfall and flood frequency have generated the need of adapting traditional statistical tools for extreme events investigation and management [2–4]. Moreover, the increasing urbanization coupled with a decrement of vegetated areas may lead to the reduction of soil infiltration capacity with the consequent increasing of the frequency and significance of floods. Given the magnitude of the related consequences, the importance of accurate hazard evaluation and management is crucial not only in this field (e.g. [5]). In this way, decision-makers are aware of the need of developing appropriate actions useful to make safe people and assets from flood risk.

Several methodologies have been recently proposed for the investigation of the effects of a flood event (e.g. [6–13]) in the context of flood-prone areas delineation (e.g. [14–24]); these approaches need of hydrological and hydraulic data input, often scarcely available but essential for a reliable assessment.

In this direction, novel approaches, thanks to satellite products or earth observation images able to monitor spatial and temporal evolution of a territory, provide distributed information for hydraulic and/or hydrological applications (e.g. [25–31]), such as land use maps (e.g. [32–36]), stream network [37, 38], soil moisture condition (e.g. [39]) used for calibration/validation of hydrological models (e.g. [40, 41]) or building dataset (e.g. [42]). One of the most promising approaches is based on the basin geomorphology that permits to obtain useful data for determining the flood exposure.

Technical literature reported interesting results about the mutual relationship between floods and floodplain characteristics, that led to the proposition of simple methodologies which exploit geomorphic properties of river basins. (e.g. [43–47]).

Analyses reported in this work are carried out using a DEM-based methodology like that proposed by Samela et al. [22] and already tested by Gioia et al. [48] on a well-known ephemeral stream of central Puglia region. First results highlighted that this methodology is able to correlate the morphology of a basin with a certain extent of the floodplain, even if some of these descriptors are more suitable than others.

Regional analyses aim to extend at-site information to a wider area in order to make predictions for unmeasured locations [49, 50]. This is a relevant quality of these methods, because they can be very useful for large scale monitoring operations in several fields (e.g. [51]). Moving into this framework, we applied geomorphic descriptors on four case studies located in the metropolitan area of Bari (Puglia), looking for analogies or homogeneity in results.

2 Cases Study

Four case studies located in the metropolitan area of Bari (Puglia-Southern Italy) have been considered in this work. Their calibration domains are shown in Fig. 1.

Figure 2 shows the study areas inside a red outline, while stream networks are reported with a green line. Three different shades of blue have been used for representing the flooding maps corresponding to three design events characterized respectively by return periods of 30, 200 and 500 years. For the sake of clarity they have been extracted from the database of the Basin Authority of Puglia (http://webgis.adb.puglia.it/gis/map_default.phtml).

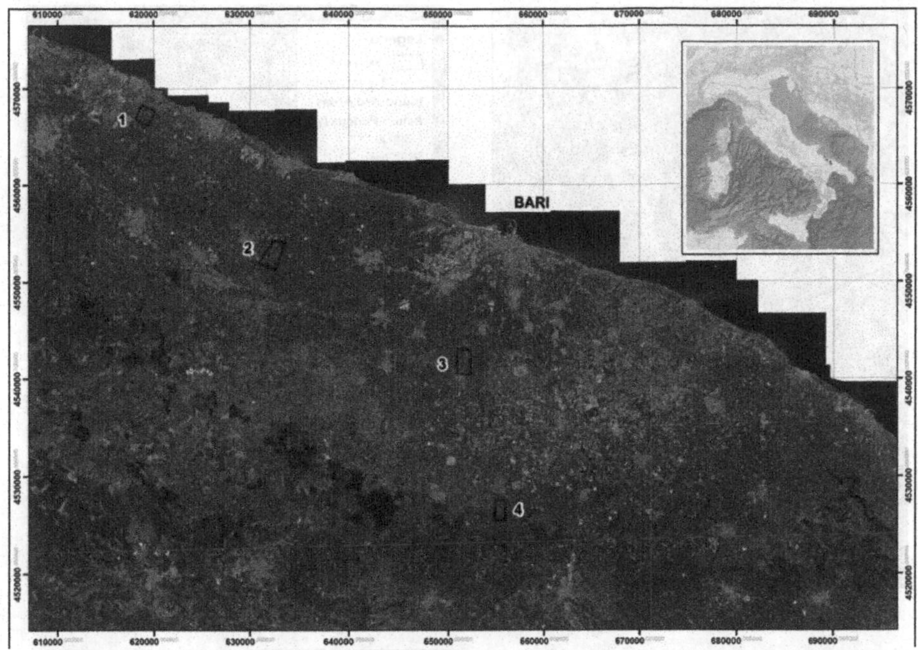

Fig. 1. Localization of the four study areas (in red) (Color figure online)

2.1 Study Area 1

Study area 1 is a part of a lama that originates in the municipality of Trani and, oriented in a SW-NE direction, slopes towards the sea crossing this territory. The stream extends for a length of approximately 5 km, with an estimated average slope of about 1.87%. The basin has an area of about 16 km^2 with altitudes ranging between 0 and 143 m.a.s.l.

This lama has a shallow morphological configuration crossing cultivated land with a total absence of incisions.

2.2 Study Area 2

Study area 2 is a part of the Martina lama (also known with the name of Cupa lama). It originates in Terlizzi at an elevation of about 210 m.a.s.l., where the stream network is not very recognizable and there is not a main riverbed. However, the main riverbed gradually becomes more pronounced proceeding downstream, assuming appreciable geomorphological significance already at the border of Molfetta. The outlet of this stream is located near the north-eastern area of Molfetta city.

The main reach of Martina lama extends for a length of approximately 17.6 km, with an estimated average slope of about 1.25%. The basin area, calculated at the mouth, reaches 25 km^2 with variable altitudes ranging between 0 and 224 m.a.s.l.

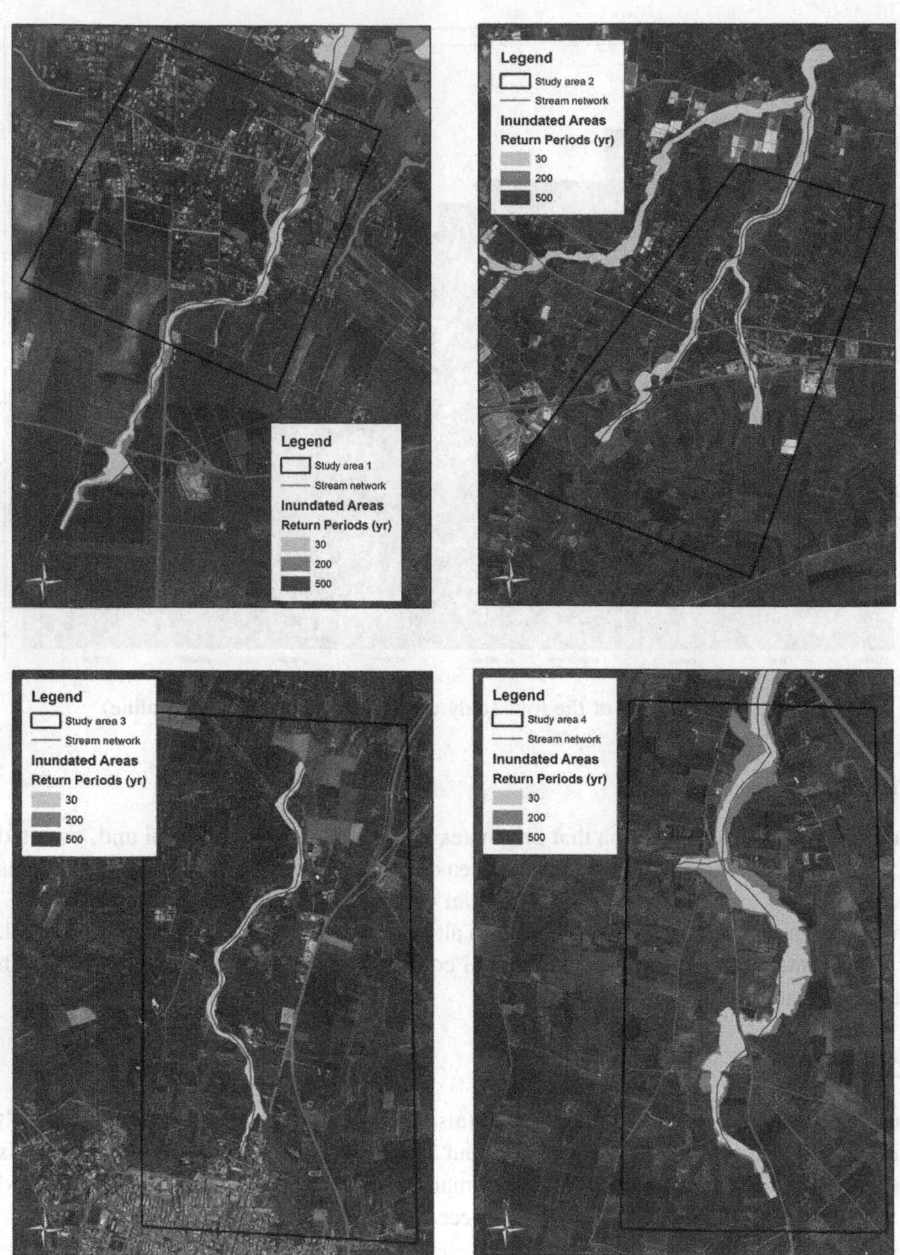

Fig. 2. Study areas.

2.3 Study Area 3

The study area identified as 3 concerns a portion of the hydrographic network of the Lamasinata lama, which is among the most important ephemeral streams of the metropolitan area of Bari. It originates between Palo del Colle and Bitetto and flowing through the land between Modugno and Bitritto reaches the industrial area of Bari. It flows approximately near the beach of S. Francesco-S. Cataldo, where it is still visible and is known as "canalone", built at the beginning of the twentieth century. The Lamasinata lama is characterized by a drainage area of about 370 km^2.

2.4 Study Area 4

This study area concerns a portion of the hydrographic network of Picone lama, which is the most important ephemeral stream that crosses the metropolitan area of Bari. It arises from the confluence of the Baronale stream, that flows through Adelfia, Loseto, Valenzano and Ceglie territories, and a second stream that originates from Sannicandro and flows through Loseto, Bitritto and Ceglie territories. The Picone lama, flowing in a SW-NE direction, reaches the city of Bari and finally flows into the sea together with Lamberti lama.

It has a drainage area of 292 km^2 and three different slope zones: a first section, very steep, with elevations above the 425 m.a.s.l.; follows a second zone, with elevations ranging between 425 and 325 m.a.s.l. characterized by a lower slope that connects to the final one, even less steep, which develops near the town of Bari.

There are historical evidences about floods occurred on the Picone lama as early as 1500; such events led the Duchess Isabella Sforza d'Aragona to undertake the construction of a channel outside the walls of the city, in order to canalize water during floods. However, in 1567 a flood destroyed these works, making the mouth of the lama even more unhealthy.

Since then many floods have occurred in Bari, due to significant rainfall events occurred on the Picone lama river basin, until in the early '900s a channel was built, to partially protect the city [52] by floods.

3 Methodologies

In the following the synthetic and composite geomorphological descriptors adopted for the evaluation of flood-prone areas, and the binary classifiers method, which allows to determine the best-performing descriptors are summarized. Receiver Operative Characteristics are mentioned in the last part of this section.

3.1 Morphological Descriptors of Basin

Geomorphic DEM-based descriptors are useful tools for appreciating the role of morphology on the evaluation of the susceptibility of areas to floods.

The model has been applied using a digital terrain model (DTM) with 8 m of resolution that was extracted from the territorial information system of Puglia Region (http://www.sit.puglia.it/).

There are different indices for evaluating flood prone areas, but the amount of data managed during the conducted analyses had led to describe only the four with the best performances.

Synthetic Descriptors

- *distance from the nearest stream, D [m]:* length of path connecting a cell on the grid with that hydrologically related on the drainage network;
- *elevation to the nearest stream, H [m]:* it is similar to D, but this index computes the elevation difference between the same points.

Composite Descriptors

- $ln(h_l/H)$: water depth h_l is an intrinsic cell quantity that can be defined as

$$h_l \cong bA_l^n \tag{1}$$

  where A_l [m^2] is the upslope contributing area for the selected cell, b is a scale factor usually set equal to 10^{-2} and n is a coefficient set equal to 0.3 [53].
- $ln(h_r/H)$ *Geomorphic Flood Index (GF)*: in this case, the upslope contributing area A_r [m^2] for the selected cell is related to that hydrologically connected on the stream network.

The ability of traditional indices in mapping flood prone areas has been tested using linear binary classifiers method [47]. The step-by-step procedure can be summarized as follows:

1. scaling and normalizing each map in the range between −1 and 1;
2. binary maps (*MOD*) are obtained applying a variable threshold to each normalized map with a step of 0.001. For each cell, the identifier 1 is assigned if flooded, 0 otherwise;
3. for each threshold step, a comparison with reference map (*REF*) has been done cell by cell, defining:
   - True Positive (TP): MOD(cell) and REF(cell) are both equal to 1;
   - False Positive (FP): MOD(cell) is 1 but REF(cell) is 0;
   - False Negative (FN): MOD(cell) is 0 and REF(cell) is 1;
   - True Negative (TN): MOD(cell) and REF(cell) are both equal to 0;

4. *true positive* and *false positive rate* are defined for each threshold as:

$$r_{tp} = \frac{TP}{TP + FN} \tag{2}$$

$$r_{fp} = \frac{FP}{FP + TN} \tag{3}$$

5. the best threshold (τ_{norm}) is defined minimizing the following objective function *OB:*

$$OB = r_{fp} + (1 - r_{tp}) \tag{4}$$

6. further considerations have been conducted plotting the whole series of r_{tp} and r_{fp} (i.e. the Receiver Operating Characteristics). Area under this curve is another tool which can give other useful information on the index performances.

4 Results and Discussion

The application of the procedure above described in Sect. 3, leads to the results reported in Tables 1, 2, 3 and 4. The ROC curves for a 200 years event are reported too in Figs. 3, 4, 5 and 6. In Fig. 7 flooded areas for a 200 years event and for H descriptors are shown.

Table 1. Results of the linear binary classification test for the Area 1

	Indices	τ_{norm}	r_{fp}	r_{tp}	*min*(OB)	AUC
30 years	D	−0.869	0.256	0.909	0.347	0.906
	H	−0.898	0.125	0.845	0.280	0.938
	GFI	−0.523	0.184	0.923	0.261	0.943
	ln(h_l/H)	−0.535	0.196	0.895	0.302	0.930
200 years	D	−0.886	0.191	0.795	0.396	0.862
	H	−0.862	0.137	0.812	0.325	0.888
	GFI	−0.523	0.145	0.845	0.301	0.893
	ln(h_l/H)	−0.543	0.173	0.805	0.368	0.885
500 years	D	−0.886	0.182	0.799	0.383	0.866
	H	−0.862	0.127	0.814	0.313	0.889
	GFI	−0.523	0.135	0.844	0.291	0.893
	ln(h_l/H)	−0.544	0.165	0.804	0.361	0.887

Table 2. Results of the linear binary classification test for the Area 2

	Indices	τ_{norm}	r_{fp}	r_{tp}	*min*(OB)	AUC
30 years	D	−0.821	0.191	0.866	0.325	0.919
	H	−0.790	0.162	0.917	0.245	0.938
	GFI	−0.444	0.128	0.887	0.241	0.933
	ln(h_l/H)	−0.503	0.160	0.866	0.294	0.923
200 years	D	−0.794	0.225	0.874	0.351	0.906
	H	−0.790	0.147	0.867	0.280	0.923
	GFI	−0.475	0.144	0.861	0.284	0.913
	ln(h_l/H)	−0.516	0.164	0.829	0.335	0.901
500 years	D	−0.794	0.206	0.869	0.337	0.909
	H	−0.773	0.150	0.867	0.283	0.919
	GFI	−0.474	0.126	0.834	0.292	0.907
	ln(h_l/H)	−0.526	0.163	0.812	0.351	0.891

Table 3. Results of the linear binary classification test for the Area 3

	Indices	τ_{norm}	r_{fp}	r_{tp}	*min*(OB)	AUC
30 years	D	−0.913	0.138	0.903	0.235	0.946
	H	−0.859	0.152	0.957	0.194	0.948
	GFI	−0.366	0.122	0.950	0.172	0.958
	ln(h_l/H)	−0.447	0.144	0.919	0.225	0.943
200 years	D	−0.898	0.160	0.925	0.235	0.944
	H	−0.849	0.157	0.943	0.214	0.942
	GFI	−0.390	0.130	0.942	0.188	0.954
	ln(h_l/H)	−0.447	0.138	0.889	0.249	0.935
500 years	D	−0.887	0.154	0.773	0.381	0.876
	H	−0.806	0.166	0.829	0.337	0.902
	GFI	−0.411	0.114	0.754	0.360	0.885
	ln(h_l/H)	−0.506	0.156	0.812	0.344	0.903

The first observation arises by looking at the shape of flooded areas (Fig. 2): in fact, a simple visual inspection of areas 2 and 4 shows that they are very similar for the three investigated return periods; this reflects on the performances of the indexes, which are similar (but not equal) in terms of minimum of the objective function. More in detail, if we look at the objective function, H is always the best performant descriptors, except in few cases (where GFI is slightly better).

Table 4. Results of the linear binary classification test for the Area 4

	Indices	τ_{norm}	r_{fp}	r_{tp}	*min*(OB)	AUC
30 years	D	−0.765	0.208	0.803	0.405	0.890
	H	−0.845	0.129	0.861	0.268	0.934
	GFI	−0.506	0.124	0.848	0.276	0.930
	$\ln(h_l/H)$	−0.570	0.213	0.930	0.283	0.929
200 years	D	−0.725	0.240	0.838	0.402	0.887
	H	−0.829	0.112	0.884	0.229	0.952
	GFI	−0.524	0.106	0.871	0.235	0.948
	$\ln(h_l/H)$	−0.574	0.188	0.931	0.257	0.944
500 years	D	−0.709	0.252	0.856	0.396	0.890
	H	−0.829	0.099	0.876	0.223	0.955
	GFI	−0.539	0.108	0.877	0.231	0.951
	$\ln(h_l/H)$	−0.574	0.175	0.923	0.252	0.946

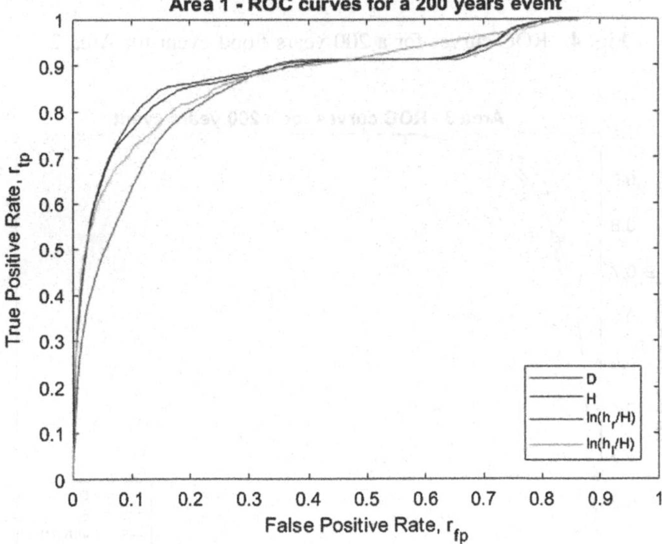

Fig. 3. ROC curves for a 200 years flood event for Area 1

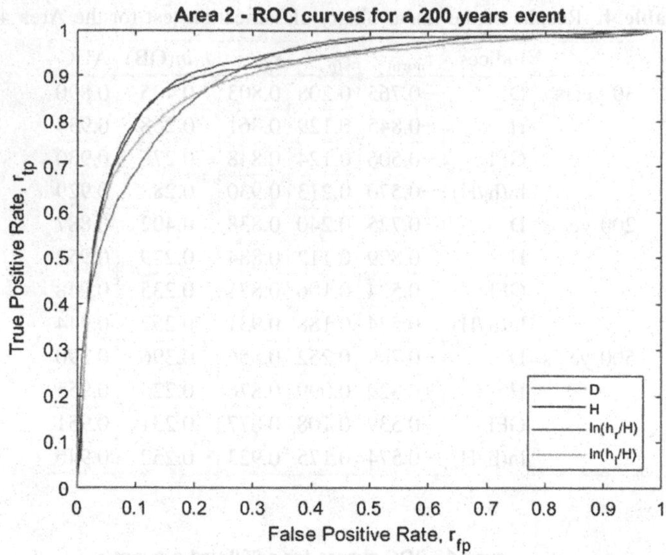

Fig. 4. ROC curves for a 200 years flood event for Area 2

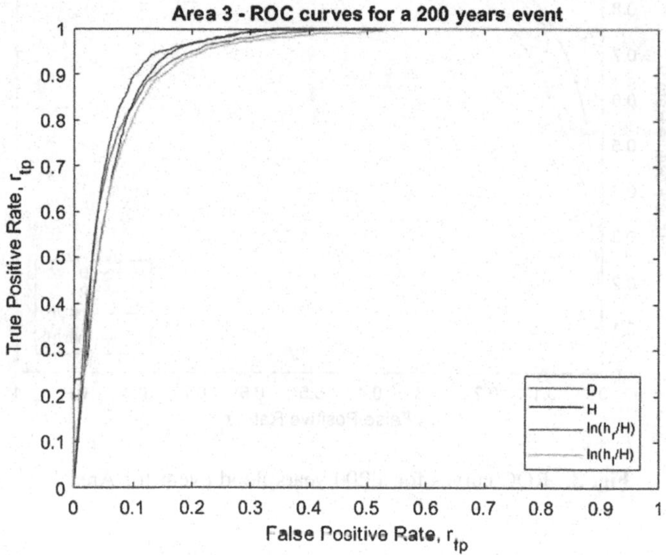

Fig. 5. ROC curves for a 200 years flood event for Area 3

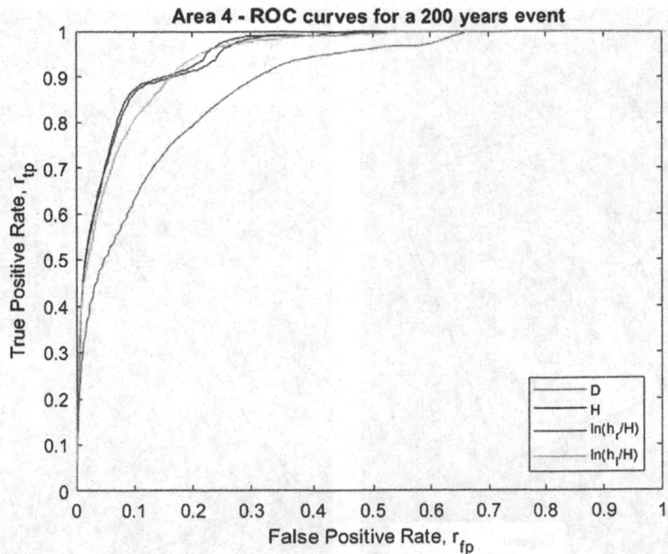

Fig. 6. ROC curves for a 200 years flood event for Area 4

Areas 1 and 3 are affected by a modification in the structure of flooded area: in fact, looking at the Fig. 2, in area 1 a secondary stream is activated for a return period greater than 200 years. The main consequence is that an increasing in the minimum of the objective function. Secondary streams are also activated for a return period of 500 years, generating a not significant lost in performances bot in the minimum of the OB and in the AUC: this can be related to a homogeneous distribution of morphology in the river stream.

An interesting observation arises from the previous tables, and it concerns with the GFI false positive rate which is, except in a few cases, that with the lowest value. This can reveal an ability of this descriptor to represent a good indicator for flood-prone areas delineation. A more complex situation for the true positive rate can be reported too.

Finally, it can be useful to remark that the particular distribution of flooded areas (which are similar for the three return periods analyzed) reflects on the values of the normalized thresholds: in fact, a reduced difference with the increasing of return period has been found. This is coherent with the theoretical framework which underlies this approach.

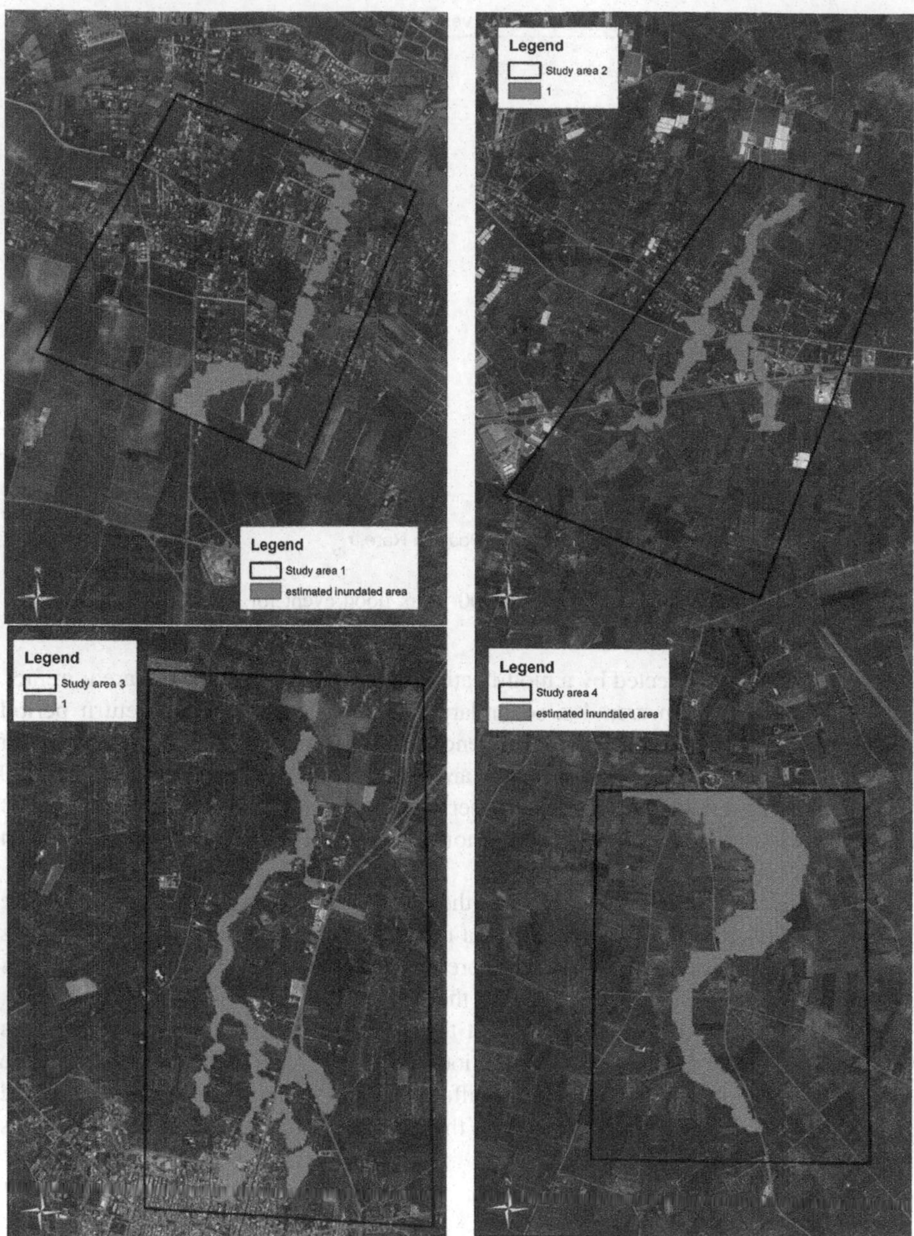

Fig. 7. Area exposed to flood inundation identified by the descriptor H for a 200 years event

5 Conclusions

The application of geomorphic descriptors to four ephemeral streams located in a small area in the district of Bari (southern Italy) has been shown in this work. The hydraulic complexity of this kind of streams and the singularity of the morphology in surrounding areas are the two main factor that, in our opinion, may influence the spatial distribution of flooded areas. The first observation that arises is the substantial analogy of geomorphological descriptors performances in the cases of similar reference flooded areas, while there is a different behavior when secondary streams are activated. The most important role, in this case, can be played by the local morphology, which can lead to a redistribution of flood that cannot be recognized by descriptors. Their ability in detecting flooded areas can be influenced, moreover, by a compromise between a wide flooded area and the value of the thresholds. However, the performances of the investigated indicators are globally good. This study can confirm the importance of the availability of fast and rapid tools for a preliminary definition of flood risk maps at regional scale.

It is interesting to point out that the DTM resolution may influence this kind of analyses; in this context an interesting detection of extended study areas and the DTM resolution effects on the descriptor performances, may be conducted in future works.

Extending case studies to other ephemeral streams located in different study areas can be an important step for understanding not only their behavior with DTM based methods, but also for improving the degree of knowledge of these steams.

References

1. Milly, P.C.D., Wetherald, R.T., Dunne, K.A., Delworth, T.L.: Increasing risk of great floods in a changing climate. Nature **415**(6871), 514 (2002)
2. Salas, J.D., Obeysekera, J.: Revisiting the concepts of return period and risk for nonstationary hydrologic extreme events. J. Hydrol. Eng. **19**(3), 554–568 (2013)
3. De Paola, F., Giugni, M., Pugliese, F., Annis, A., Nardi, F.: GEV parameter estimation and stationary vs. non-stationary analysis of extreme rainfall in African test cities. Hydrology **5**(2), 28 (2018)
4. Obeysekera, J., Salas, J.D.: Quantifying the uncertainty of design floods under nonstationary conditions. J. Hydrol. Eng. **19**(7), 1438–1446 (2013)
5. Sangiorgio, V., Uva, G., Fatiguso, F.: Optimized AHP to overcome limits in weight calculation: building performance application. J. Constr. Eng. Manage. **144**(2), 04017101 (2017)
6. Ignacio, J.A.F., Cruz, G.T., Nardi, F., Henry, S.: Assessing the effectiveness of a social vulnerability index in predicting heterogeneity in the impacts of natural hazards: case study of the Tropical Storm Washi flood in the Philippines. Vienna Yearb. Popul. Res. **13**(1), 91–130 (2015)
7. Feldman, A.D.: Hydrologic Engineering Center (U.S.), Hydrologic Modeling System HEC-HMS, US Army Corps of Engineers, Hydrologic Engineering Center (2000)
8. Fiorentino, M., Gioia, A., Iacobellis, V., Manfreda, S.: Analysis on flood generation processes by means of a continuous simulation model. Adv. Geosci. **7**, 231–236 (2006). ISSN 1680-7340

9. Merz, R., Blöschl, G.: Flood frequency hydrology: 1. Temporal, spatial, and causal expansion of information. Water Resour. Res. **44**, W08432 (2008). https://doi.org/10.1029/2007WR006744
10. Iacobellis, V., Fiorentino, M., Gioia, A., Manfreda, S.: Best fit selection of theoretical flood frequency distributions based on different runoff generation mechanisms. Water **2**(2, 1), 239–256 (2010)
11. Beven, K.: Rainfall-Runoff Modelling. The Primer, 2nd edn. Wiley-Blackwell, Chichester (2012)
12. Gioia, A., Manfreda, S., Iacobellis, V., Fiorentino, M.: Performance of a theoretical model for the description of water balance and runoff dynamics in southern Italy. J. Hydrol. Eng. **19**(6), 1113–1123 (2014)
13. Di Modugno, M., et al.: Build-up/wash-off monitoring and assessment for sustainable management of first flush in an urban area. Sustainability **7**, 5050–5070 (2015)
14. Gioia, A., Iacobellis, V., Manfreda, S., Fiorentino, M.: Comparison of different methods describing the peak runoff contributing areas during floods. Hydrol. Process. **31**(11), 2041–2049 (2017)
15. De Wrachien, D., Mambretti, S.: Mathematical models for flood hazard assessment. Int. J. Saf. Secur. Eng. **1**(4), 353–362 (2011)
16. Iacobellis, V., Castorani, A., Di Santo, A.R., Gioia, A.: Rationale for flood prediction in karst endorheic areas. J. Arid Environ. **112**(PA), 98–108 (2015)
17. Bates, P., Anderson, M., Price, D., Hardy, R., Smith, C.: Analysis and development of hydraulic models for floodplain flows. In: Anderson, M.G., Walling, D.E., Bates, P.D. (eds.) Floodplain Processes. Wiley, New York (1996)
18. Aronica, G., Hankin, B., Beven, K.J.: Uncertainty and equifinality in calibrating distributed roughness coefficients in a flood propagation model with limited data. Adv. Water Resour. **22**(4), 349–365 (1998)
19. Jain, S.K., Singh, R.D., Jain, M.K., Lohani, A.K.: Delineation of flood-prone areas using remote sensing techniques. Water Resour. Manage. **19**(4), 333–347 (2005)
20. Fluet-Chouinard, E., Lehner, B., Rebelo, L.M., Papa, F., Hamilton, S.K.: Development of a global inundation map at high spatial resolution from topographic downscaling of coarse-scale remote sensing data. Remote Sens. Environ. **158**, 348–361 (2015)
21. Peña, F., Nardi, F.: Floodplain terrain analysis for coarse resolution 2D flood modeling. Hydrology **5**(4), 52 (2018)
22. Manfreda, S., et al.: Flood-prone areas assessment using linear binary classifiers based on flood maps obtained from 1D and 2D hydraulic models. Nat. Hazards **79**(2), 735–754 (2015)
23. Iacobellis, V., et al.: Investigation of a flood event occurred on lama Balice, in the context of hazard map evaluation in karstic-ephemeral streams. In: Gervasi, O., et al. (eds.) ICCSA 2018. LNCS, vol. 10964, pp. 317–333. Springer, Cham (2018). https://doi.org/10.1007/978-3-319-95174-4_26
24. Totaro, V., Gioia, A., Novelli, A., Caradonna, G.: The use of geomorphological descriptors and Landsat 8 spectral indices data for flood areas evaluation: a case study of Lato river basin. In: Gervasi, O., et al. (eds.) ICCSA 2017. LNCS, vol. 10407, pp. 30–44. Springer, Cham (2017). https://doi.org/10.1007/978-3-319-62401-3_3
25. Totaro, V., Peschechera, G., Gioia, A., Iacobellis, V., Fratino, U., Tarantino, E.: Comparison of satellite and geomorphic indices for flooded areas detection in a Mediterranean river basin (in preparation)
26. Bates, P.D., Horritt, M.S., Smith, C.N., Mason, D.C.: Integrating remote sensing observations of flood hydrology and hydraulic modelling. Hydrol. Process. **11**, 1777–1795 (1997)

27. Horritt, M.S., Mason, D.C., Luckman, A.J.: Flood boundary delineation from synthetic aperture radar imagery using a statistical active contour model. Int. J. Remote Sens. **22**(13), 2489–2507 (2001)
28. Mattia, F., et al.: Time series of COSMO-SkyMed data for landcover classification and surface parameter retrieval over agricultural sites. In: Proceedings of the IEEE 2012 International Geoscience and Remote Sensing Symposium, pp. 6511–6514 (2012). ISBN 978-1-4673-1159-5
29. Balenzano, A., et al.: On the use of multi-temporal series of COSMO-SkyMed data for landcover classification and surface parameter retrieval over agricultural sites. In: Proceedings of the 2011 IEEE International Geoscience and Remote Sensing Symposium, 24–29 July 2011, Vancouver, Canada, pp. 142–145 (2011)
30. Balenzano, A., et al.: A ground network for SAR-derived soil moisture product calibration, validation and exploitation in southern Italy. In: Proceedings of the IEEE 2014 International Geoscience and Remote Sensing Symposium, IGARSS 2014 (2014)
31. Tarantino, E., Novelli, A., Laterza, M., Gioia, A.: Testing high spatial resolution WorldView-2 imagery for retrieving the leaf area index. In: Third International Conference on Remote Sensing and Geoinformation of the Environment (RSCy2015), vol. 9535, p. 95351N. International Society for Optics and Photonics (2015)
32. Trombetta, A., Iacobellis, V., Tarantino, E., Gentile, F.: Calibration of the AquaCrop model for winter wheat using MODIS LAI images. Agric. Water Manag. **164**(Part 2), 304–316 (2016)
33. Olang, L.O., Kundu, P., Bauer, T., Fürst, J.: Analysis of spatio-temporal land cover changes for hydrological impact assessment within the Nyando River Basin of Kenya. Environ. Monit. Assess. **179**, 389–401 (2011)
34. Pattison, I., Lane, S.N.: The link between land-use management and fluvial flood risk: a chaotic conception? Prog. Phys. Geogr. **36**, 72–92 (2011)
35. Balacco, G., Figorito, B., Tarantino, E., Gioia, A., Iacobellis, V.: Space-time LAI variability in Northern Puglia (Italy) from SPOT VGT data. Environ. Monit. Assess. **187**, 434 (2015)
36. Caprioli, M., Tarantino, E.: Identification of land cover alterations in the Alta Murgia National Park (Italy) with VHR satellite imagery. Int. J. Sustain. Dev. Plan. **1**(3), 261–270 (2006)
37. Crocetto, N., Tarantino, E.: A class-oriented strategy for features extraction from multidate ASTER imagery. Remote Sens. **1**(4), 1171–1189 (2009)
38. Fidelibus, M.D., Balacco, G., Gioia, A., Iacobellis, V., Spilotro, G.: Mass transport triggered by heavy rainfall: the role of endorheic basins and epikarst in a regional karst aquifer. Hydrol. Process. **31**(2), 394–408 (2017)
39. Figorito, B., Tarantino, E., Balacco, G., Fratino, U.: An object-based method for mapping ephemeral river areas from WorldView-2 satellite data. In: Remote Sensing for Agriculture, Ecosystems, and Hydrology XIV, vol. 8531, p. 85310B. International Society for Optics and Photonics (2012)
40. Saradjian, M.R., Hosseini, M.: Soil moisture estimation by using multipolarization SAR image. Adv. Space Res. **48**(2), 278–286 (2011)
41. Iacobellis, V., Gioia, A., Milella, P., Satalino, G., Balenzano, A., Mattia, F.: Inter-comparison of hydrological model simulations with time series of SAR-derived soil moisture maps. Eur. J. Remote Sens. **46**(1), 739–757 (2013)
42. Peschechera, G., Fratino, U.: Calibration of CLAIR model by means of Sentinel-2 LAI data for analysing wheat crops through Landsat-8 surface reflectance data. In: Gervasi, O., et al. (eds.) ICCSA 2018. LNCS, vol. 10964, pp. 294–304. Springer, Cham (2018). https://doi.org/10.1007/978-3-319-95174-4_24

43. Gioia, A., Iacobellis, V., Manfreda, S., Fiorentino, M.: Influence of infiltration and soil storage capacity on the skewness of the annual maximum flood peaks in a theoretically derived distribution. Hydrol. Earth Syst. Sci. **16**, 937–951 (2012)
44. Williams, W.A., Jensen, M.E., Winne, J.C., Redmond, R.L.: An automated technique for delineating and characterizing valley-bottom settings. Environ. Monit. Assess. **64**(1), 105–114 (2000)
45. Gallant, J.C., Dowling, T.I.: A multiresolution index of valley bottom flatness for mapping depositional areas. Water Resour. Res. **39**(12), 1347 (2003). https://doi.org/10.1029/2002WR001426
46. Nardi, F., Vivoni, E.R., Grimaldi, S.: Investigating a floodplain scaling relation using a hydrogeomorphic delineation method. Water Resour. Res. **42**, W09409 (2006). https://doi.org/10.1029/2005WR004155
47. Manfreda, S., Di Leo, M., Sole, A.: Detection of flood prone areas using digital elevation models. J. Hydrol. Eng. **16**(10), 781–790 (2011)
48. Samela, C., Manfreda, S., Paola, F.D., Giugni, M., Sole, A., Fiorentino, M.: DEM-based approaches for the delineation of flood-prone areas in an ungauged basin in Africa. J. Hydrol. Eng. **21**(2), 06015010 (2015)
49. Gioia, A., Totaro, V., Bonelli, R., Esposito, A.A.M.G., Balacco, G., Iacobellis, V.: Flood susceptibility evaluation on ephemeral streams of Southern Italy: a case study of lama Balice. In: Gervasi, O., et al. (eds.) ICCSA 2018. LNCS, vol. 10964, pp. 334–348. Springer, Cham (2018). https://doi.org/10.1007/978-3-319-95174-4_27
50. Cunnane, C.: Methods and merits of regional flood frequency analysis. J. Hydrol. **100**(1–3), 269–290 (1988)
51. Fiorentino, M., Gioia, A., Iacobellis, V., Manfreda, S.: Regional analysis of runoff thresholds behaviour in Southern Italy based on theoretically derived distributions. Adv. Geosci. **26**, 139–144 (2011)
52. Sangiorgio, V., Uva, G., Fatiguso, F.: User reporting–based semeiotic assessment of existing building stock at the regional scale. J. Perform. Constr. Facil. **32**(6), 04018079 (2018)
53. Mossa, M.: The floods in Bari: what history should have taught. J. Hydraul. Res. **45**(5), 579–594 (2007)

On BIQUE Procedures Applied to GPS Pseudorange Measurements

Nicola Crocetto[1], Salvatore Ponte[1], and Eufemia Tarantino[2(✉)]

[1] Dipartimento di Ingegneria, Università della Campania "Luigi Vanvitelli", Via Roma 29, 81031 Aversa, CE, Italy
{nicola.crocetto,salvatore.ponte}@unicampania.it
[2] DICATECH – Politecnico di Bari, Via Orabona 4, Bari, Italy
eufemia.tarantino@poliba.it

Abstract. Best-Invariant-Quadratic-Unbiased-Estimation (BIQUE) of the variance factors is used in this work to evaluate the adequacy, or goodness, of different stochastic models affecting GPS pseudorange measurements (assumed uncorrelated), using the linear Gauss-Markov functional model. Four different stochastic models of the observations are tested, verifying that incorrect results of the BIQUE estimates (i.e. negative variance components) imply large inaccuracies of GPS-derived user positions. Results on real measurement campaigns show that the SNR (Signal to Noise Ratio) is effective in reducing the GPS position errors, by using models with SNR and SNR squared. BIQUE estimations with negative variance components allowed us to reject one of the four chosen stochastic models. No significant differences have been noted using slightly different (high) values of the redundancy r of the observations ($r = 20$ and $r = 28$). We use formulas in which the BIQUE methodology does not require the evaluation of least-squares (LS) residuals. Therefore, the BIQUE of the variance and covariance components could be performed in pre-adjustment, without the necessity of cumbersome LS adjustments during each iteration.

Keywords: BIQUE · VCE · Variance-covariance component estimation · Variance factors · Stochastic models · GPS pseudorange measurements · Functional models · Gauss-Markov

1 Introduction

Estimation of the variance and covariance components for GPS pseudorange measurements, i.e. adoption of a suitable stochastic model of the observations, is a crucial step to assess the accuracy of GPS-derived user coordinates. In the last two decades, many methodologies for VCE (Variance-Covariance Estimation) have been presented in the statistical and geodetic literatures (Moghtased-Azar et al. 2014; Junhuan et al. 2011). Among them, BIQUE (Best Invariant Quadratic Unbiased Estimation) techniques, in the framework of least-squares adjustment, can be basically categorized with respect to the adopted stochastic and functional models (with or without unknown

S. Ponte—Member, IEEE.

S. Misra et al. (Eds.): ICCSA 2019, LNCS 11622, pp. 255–268, 2019.
https://doi.org/10.1007/978-3-030-24305-0_20

parameters). Iterative formulas have already been developed and they have different expressions, depending on the selected models.

This work presents BIQUE methods to evaluate the effectiveness, or validity, of different stochastic models applied to some GPS observables (in particular, pseudorange measurements, assumed uncorrelated), verifying that incorrect results of the BIQUE estimates (i.e. negative variance components) imply bad choices of the stochastic models, and therefore large inaccuracies of GPS-derived user positions.

Let us suppose that the $(n, 1)$ random GPS pseudorange measurements vector $\boldsymbol{l}$ is normally distributed and that the observations are uncorrelated. Denoting the k unknown variance and covariance components σ_i^2 and σ_{ij}, respectively, we define the $(k, 1)$ vector $\boldsymbol{\sigma} = (\sigma_1, \ldots, \sigma_k)^{\mathrm{T}}$ (T denotes transposition).

Regarding the stochastic model, we model the definite positive (n, n) covariance matrix $\boldsymbol{\Sigma}_l$ of the observables as a linear combination of the unknown vector $\boldsymbol{\sigma}$:

$$\boldsymbol{\Sigma}_l = \sum_1^k \sigma_i \mathbf{Q}_i \tag{1.1}$$

with assigned (n, n) symmetrical cofactor matrices $\mathbf{Q}_i$.

The observation weight matrix is:

$$\mathbf{P} = \boldsymbol{\Sigma}_l^{-1} \tag{1.2}$$

In Appendix A we will derive the relations for the BIQUE of $\boldsymbol{\sigma}$ in the functional model of condition only. This model will be the starting point for the general BIQUE of the variance-covariance components.

Generally, it must be noted that formulating the condition equations (see Appendix A, Eq. A.1) of the functional model of condition only can be very difficult. As far as GPS pseudorange measurements are concerned, the well-known GPS navigation equations and the Gauss-Markov functional model are used. In the case of GPS pseudorange observations, in next section we will apply the general formulations (derived in Appendix B) in the case of Gauss-Markov functional model.

The paper is structured as follows: after introducing the general linear stochastic model, we apply (Sect. 2) the BIQUE estimation to the Gauss-Markov functional model, which is the model adopted for GPS pseudorange measurements (Li et al. 2011). In Sect. 3 we will show numerical results of the least-squares adjustment of GPS observables (pseudorange) by considering different stochastic models and testing the effectiveness of the model via the BIQUE procedure. Section 4 contains concluding remarks. In Sect. 5 (Appendix A) we derive formally the BIQUE estimation equations under the hypothesis of a condition adjustment functional model, whereas in Sect. 6 (Appendix B) we show a generalized methodology for BIQUE.

2 BIQUE of the GPS Pseudorange Variance Factors (Gauss-Markov Model)

As it will be shown in Appendix B, the methodology for the BIQUE VCE of the observed GPS pseudoranges (for which we adopt the Gauss-Markov functional model) implies the iterative resolution of the system:

$$\mathbf{H}\hat{\sigma} = \mathbf{f} \tag{2.1}$$

where:

$$\mathbf{H} = \{h_{ij} = tr(\mathbf{MQ}_i\mathbf{MQ}_j)\} \tag{2.2}$$

$$\mathbf{f} = \{\mathrm{f}_i = l^{\mathrm{T}}\mathbf{MQ}_i\mathbf{M}l\} \tag{2.3}$$

$$\mathbf{M} = \mathbf{PQ}_{\hat{\mathbf{v}}}\mathbf{P} = \mathbf{PR} \tag{2.4}$$

and $\mathbf{M}$ is a symmetric matrix defined in Appendix B (Eq. B.1).

We will show in Appendix B (Eq. (B.12)) that it is not necessary to perform a least-squares adjustment, which could imply great computational cost. Therefore, it is possible to avoid the evaluation of the least-squares (LS) residuals $\hat{\mathbf{v}}$, and (B.12) reduces to (2.3). Moreover, in our case of Gauss-Markov functional model, the expression of the cofactor matrix $\mathbf{Q}_{\hat{\mathbf{v}}}$ of the least-squares residuals, used in (2.4), turns out to be:

$$\mathbf{Q}_{\hat{\mathbf{v}}} = \mathbf{P}^{-1} - \mathbf{A}(\mathbf{A}^{\mathrm{T}}\mathbf{PA})^{-1}\mathbf{A}^{\mathrm{T}} \tag{2.5}$$

where $\mathbf{A}$ is the known (n, u) design matrix of the linearized pseudorange equations (Rahemi et al. 2014), with rank$(\mathbf{A}) = u \leq n$. Therefore, (2.4) becomes:

$$\mathbf{M} = \mathbf{PQ}_{\hat{\mathbf{v}}}\mathbf{P} = \mathbf{PR} = \mathbf{P} - \mathbf{PA}(\mathbf{A}^{\mathrm{T}}\mathbf{PA})^{-1}\mathbf{A}^{\mathrm{T}}\mathbf{P} \tag{2.6}$$

Since the matrix $\mathbf{M}$, defined in Eq. (2.6) and required in (2.2) and (2.3), contains the weight matrix $\mathbf{P}$ of the pseudorange observations and hence the covariance matrix $\boldsymbol{\Sigma}_l$ (that is, the vector $\boldsymbol{\sigma}$ of variance-covariance components) it is necessary to implement an iterative numerical procedure. Starting with a reasonable vector $\hat{\boldsymbol{\sigma}}^{(0)}$ of a priori variance-covariance components, a first estimation $\hat{\boldsymbol{\sigma}}^{(1)}$ is carried out. The resulting values of the components are then multiplied by the corresponding cofactor matrices, obtaining improved matrices $\mathbf{Q}_i^{(1)} = \hat{\boldsymbol{\sigma}}^{(1)}\hat{\boldsymbol{\sigma}}^{(0)}\mathbf{Q}_i$, from which the updated covariance matrix $\boldsymbol{\Sigma}_l^{(1)} = \sum_1^k \mathbf{Q}_i^{(1)}$ is computed. This new covariance matrix represents the input of the subsequent iteration. The procedure is repeated until the estimates will reproduce themselves (in the case of process convergence), namely until $\hat{\boldsymbol{\sigma}}^{(v)}$ converges to the vector $(1,\ldots,1)^{\mathrm{T}}$. Supposing convergence after ν iterations, the final values of the variance-covariance components are expressed as:

$$\hat{\sigma}_i = \prod_{\alpha=0}^{\nu} \hat{\sigma}_i^{(\alpha)}, i = 1,\ldots,k \tag{2.7}$$

The sum of the elements h_{ij} of the matrix **H**, defined in (2.2), equals the total redundancy r (Crocetto et al. 2000):

$$\sum_{i,j=1}^{k} h_{ij} = r \tag{2.8}$$

Furthermore (Crocetto et al. 2000), the k elements of the vector **f** (see (2.3)) add up to the total quadratic form of the weighted least-squares residuals of the observations:

$$\sum_{1}^{k} \mathrm{f}_i = \boldsymbol{l}^{\mathrm{T}}\mathbf{M}\boldsymbol{l} \tag{2.9}$$

From (2.8) and (2.9), we can observe that the total quadratic form $\boldsymbol{l}^{\mathrm{T}}\mathbf{M}\boldsymbol{l}$ is somewhat spread among the f_i, as well as the total redundancy over the elements of **H**.

3 Case Study: GPS Pseudorange Measurements

The BIQUE technique will be applied to the estimation of the phase center coordinates of a GPS receiver antenna and of the receiver clock offset by means of redundant pseudorange measurements. The test antenna was placed in a point of the regional GNSS network (located in southern Italy).

We have assumed four stochastic models for the measured pseudoranges (assumed uncorrelated), to carry out a correct LS adjustment, as follows:

(SA): constant variance (σ_ρ^2) of all pseudorange measurements;

(SB): constant term with additive term depending on the measured pseudorange value;

(SC): constant term with additive term inversely proportional to the measurement Signal-to-Noise Ratio (SNR), derived from the receiver;

(SD): constant term with additive term inversely proportional to the SNR squared.

In formulas:

$$\text{(SA)} \qquad \sigma_\rho^2 = cost = \sigma_{01}^2 \quad \Leftrightarrow \quad \boldsymbol{\Sigma}_l = \sigma_{01}^2 \mathbf{Q}_1 \tag{3.1}$$

$$\text{with} \qquad \mathbf{Q}_1 = \mathbf{I} \tag{3.2}$$

$$\text{(SB)} \quad \sigma_\rho^2 = \sigma_{01}^2 + (\sigma_{02}\rho)^2 \quad \Leftrightarrow \quad \mathbf{\Sigma}_l = \sigma_{01}^2\mathbf{Q}_1 + \sigma_{02}^2\mathbf{Q}_2 \tag{3.3}$$

$$\text{with} \quad \mathbf{Q}_1 = \mathbf{I} \text{ and } \mathbf{Q}_2 = diag\left[\rho_i^2\right] \tag{3.4}$$

$$\text{(SC)} \quad \sigma_\rho^2 = \sigma_{01}^2 + \left(\frac{\sigma_{02}}{\text{SNR}}\right)^2 \quad \Leftrightarrow \quad \mathbf{\Sigma}_l = \sigma_{01}^2\mathbf{Q}_1 + \sigma_{02}^2\mathbf{Q}_2 \tag{3.5}$$

$$\text{with} \quad \mathbf{Q}_1 = \mathbf{I} \text{ and } \mathbf{Q}_2 = diag\left[\left(\frac{1}{\text{SNR}_i}\right)^2\right] \tag{3.6}$$

$$\text{(SD)} \quad \sigma_\rho^2 = \sigma_{01}^2 + \left(\frac{\sigma_{02}}{\text{SNR}^2}\right)^2 \quad \Leftrightarrow \quad \mathbf{\Sigma}_l = \sigma_{01}^2\mathbf{Q}_1 + \sigma_{02}^2\mathbf{Q}_2 \tag{3.7}$$

$$\text{with} \quad \mathbf{Q}_1 = \mathbf{I} \text{ and } \mathbf{Q}_2 = diag\left[\left(\frac{1}{\text{SNR}_i^2}\right)^2\right] \tag{3.8}$$

where σ_ρ^2 is the variance of the pseudorange ρ, σ_{01}^2 is the first constant part of σ_ρ^2, and σ_{02}^2 is the second variance factor.

The satellite's clock offset and coordinates are derived from a precise ephemerides file in the SP3 format (Standard Product 3, Hilla 2007). The pseudorange measurements are derived from the C/A (Coarse/Acquisition) code embedded in the transmitted signal and are input in the format RINEX 3.01 (Receiver Independent Exchange) (IGS 2013). As for the SNR, the values retrieved from the RINEX files have range from 0 to 80.

Two measurement campaigns have been performed. In the first session, data obtained by dual-frequency receivers were gathered. Ephemeris data of eight satellites were considered, with four 15-min measurement epochs, between 16:00 h and 16:45 h on Oct. 10, 2018. The total number of observations is n = 32, and the global redundancy r is equal to 28. In a second measurement session, 24 observations were collected (in three measurement epochs), with $r = 20$.

Table 1. BIQUE values with the selected stochastic models and $r = 20$.

Stochastic model	$\hat{\sigma}_{01}$ (m)	$\hat{\sigma}_{02}$ (m)
(SA)	8.9	
(SB)	Negative	Negative
(SC)	2.7	445
(SD)	1.8	25096

Tables 1 and 2 report the results of the BIQUE estimates with the chosen stochastic models SA, SB, SC, SD, for two values of r (20 and 28).

Since the BIQUE values for model (SB) are found to be negative, the stochastic model (SB) is not correct. This is because the pseudorange values lay in a small interval, therefore the elements of the matrix $\mathbf{Q}_2 = \text{diag}\left[\rho_i^2\right]$ (see Eq. (3.4)) are not

Table 2. BIQUE values with the selected stochastic models and $r = 28$.

Stochastic model	$\hat{\sigma}_{01}$ (m)	$\hat{\sigma}_{02}$ (m)
(SA)	8.4	
(SB)	Negative	Negative
(SC)	2.3	428
(SD)	2.1	23661

significantly different. Consequently, a stochastic model with two unknown variance components turns out to be not significant. Caspary (1985) suggests, in case of negative VCE, the reduction of the number of unknown variance-covariance components. In this work we explore, as an alternative, the possibilities of different stochastic models.

The variance component estimates in models (SC) and (SD) are positive, being the SNR values significantly different.

The receiver coordinates evaluated with the models (SA), (SC), (SD) were compared to very accurate values derived from phase measurements and by linking the GPS position to the IGS (International-GPS-Service-Geodynamics) network. Results of the estimated GPS coordinates are reported in Table 3.

Table 3. Estimated coordinate differences with the selected stochastic models, $r = 20$. Δs is the root sum squared (RSS) of the errors ΔX, ΔY, ΔZ.

Stochastic model	ΔX (m)	ΔY (m)	ΔZ (m)	Δs (m)
(SA)	6.9	−4.8	6.3	10.5
(SC)	−4.2	2.1	3.0	5.6
(SD)	2.8	3.4	−2.1	4.9

Models (SC) and (SD) improve the accuracy of the estimated coordinates with respect to model (SA). As can be deduced from Table 3, model (SD) best describes the pseudorange stochastic errors.

Results show that a suitable stochastic improves significantly the estimation accuracy, and the BIQUE methodology allows us to evaluate the adequacy of a selected model.

A fundamental hypothesis for effective application of VCE with BIQUE techniques is the absence of blunders in the observations. Gross measurement errors could cause the estimation of too great values of the variances, impairing the efficacy of the procedure and of the subsequent LS adjustment. A preliminary detection test of outliers with reasonable values of the variance factors (based on the experience of the experimenters) should therefore be performed in advance.

4 Conclusions

In this work we have performed VCE within the framework of the condition functional model, showing the BIQUE estimation equations (Appendix A) and generalizing the obtained results to all the functional models (Appendix B). As an example of the BIQUE methodology, we applied our theoretical results to GPS pseudorange measurements, using the linear Gauss-Markov functional model and testing four different stochastic models of the observations. The SNR flag retrieved from the RINEX files of GPS pseudorange measurement turned out to be effective in reducing the GPS position errors, by using models (SC) and (SD), with SNR and SNR squared respectively. Comparing the results obtained with two different redundancy values (r respectively equal to 20 and 28), we point out that large redundancies are necessary for good estimates, but no significant differences in the results have been noted when using slightly different (high) values of r. In both measurement campaigns, however, stochastic model (SB) turned out to be inadequate, providing negative values of the variance and covariance components, even with high redundancy values. This allowed us to reject model (SB).

It is worth stressing that Eq. (2.3) of our BIQUE technique does not require the evaluation of the least-squares residuals. Consequently, no cumbersome LS adjustments are necessary during each iteration, and the BIQUE methodology can be performed in pre-adjustment. This significantly reduces the computational effort, implying that the iterative BIQUE methodologies could easily be implemented in real-time data processing.

Furthermore, the BIQUE technique does not impose any constraint on the variance components, not forcing them to be positive. This could lead, in case of inadequate or erroneous stochastic modeling and/or observation groups with low redundancy, to negative values of the estimated variance components. The anomalous behavior of the BIQUE estimation turns out to be an advantage, rather than a weakness, because a VCE procedure with negative variances implies a bad choice of the stochastic model. BIQUE methodologies play therefore a significant role, allowing us to gain insight into the assessment of the goodness of the selected stochastic models.

5 Appendix A – BIQUE Estimation in Condition Functional Model

The condition (functional) adjustment model is the system of $r < n$ condition equations:

$$\mathbf{A}\mathbf{v} = \mathbf{w} = \mathbf{d} - \mathbf{A}\boldsymbol{l} \tag{A.1}$$

where $\mathbf{A}$ is a known (r, n) design matrix with rank$(\mathbf{A}) = r < n$, $\mathbf{v}$ is the $(n, 1)$ vector of the n observation errors, $\mathbf{w}$ is the $(r, 1)$ random normal misclosure vector which is determined by the observations, $\boldsymbol{l}$ is the $(n, 1)$ random vector of the observations which we will assume normally distributed, $\mathbf{d}$ is the $(r, 1)$ deterministic vector.

As stochastic model, we consider the general linear model (1.1).

As it is well known, for the LS solution of the (A.1) the following relations hold:

$$\begin{aligned}\hat{\mathbf{v}} &= \boldsymbol{\Sigma}_l\mathbf{A}^{\mathrm{T}}\left(\mathbf{A}\boldsymbol{\Sigma}_l\mathbf{A}^{\mathrm{T}}\right)^{-1}\mathbf{w} = \mathbf{P}^{-1}\mathbf{A}^{\mathrm{T}}\left(\mathbf{A}\mathbf{P}^{-1}\mathbf{A}^{\mathrm{T}}\right)^{-1}\mathbf{w} \\ \mathbf{Q}_{\hat{\mathbf{v}}} &= \boldsymbol{\Sigma}_l\mathbf{A}^{\mathrm{T}}\left(\mathbf{A}\boldsymbol{\Sigma}_l\mathbf{A}^{\mathrm{T}}\right)^{-1}\mathbf{A}\boldsymbol{\Sigma}_l = \mathbf{P}^{-1}\mathbf{A}^{\mathrm{T}}\left(\mathbf{A}\mathbf{P}^{-1}\mathbf{A}^{\mathrm{T}}\right)^{-1}\mathbf{A}\mathbf{P}^{-1}\end{aligned} \tag{A.2}$$

where $\boldsymbol{\Sigma}_l$ and $\mathbf{P}$ are given by Eqs. (1.1) and (1.2) respectively, $\hat{\mathbf{v}}$ is the vector of least-squares residuals and $\mathbf{Q}_{\hat{\mathbf{v}}}$ is the corresponding cofactor (variance-covariance) matrix.

$$\mathbf{p}^{\mathrm{T}}\boldsymbol{\sigma} = \sum_{1}^{k} p_i\,\sigma_i \tag{A.3}$$

where p_i are known coefficients.

The estimation is performed through a quadratic form of the misclosure vector $\mathbf{w}$:

$$q_w = \mathbf{w}^{\mathrm{T}}\mathbf{B}\mathbf{w} = \mathbf{p}^{\mathrm{T}}\hat{\boldsymbol{\sigma}} \tag{A.4}$$

where $\mathbf{B}$ is an arbitrary symmetric (r, r) matrix.

The criterion of unbiasedness implies:

$$E(q_w) = E\left(\mathbf{w}^{\mathrm{T}}\mathbf{B}\mathbf{w}\right) = \mathbf{p}^{\mathrm{T}}\boldsymbol{\sigma} \tag{A.5}$$

In addition, the minimum-variance criterion implies:

$$var(q_w) = \sigma^2_{q_w} = var\left(\mathbf{w}^{\mathrm{T}}\mathbf{B}\mathbf{w}\right) = min \tag{A.6}$$

We recall that if $\mathbf{x}$ is a $(n, 1)$ random vector with expectation $E(\mathbf{x}) = \mathbf{0}$ and covariance matrix $\boldsymbol{\Sigma} = E(\mathbf{x}\mathbf{x}^{\mathrm{T}})$, then for the expectation of the quadratic form $q = \mathbf{x}^{\mathrm{T}}\mathbf{B}\mathbf{x}$ we have (Caspary 1987; Sjöberg 1984):

$$E(q) = tr(\mathbf{B}\boldsymbol{\Sigma}). \tag{A.7}$$

where $tr(\,)$ denotes the trace of a square matrix; furthermore, if $\mathbf{x}$ is normally distributed, the variance of q is given by (Caspary 1987; Sjöberg 1984):

$$\sigma^2_q = 2tr(\mathbf{B}\boldsymbol{\Sigma}\mathbf{B}\boldsymbol{\Sigma}) \tag{A.8}$$

The misclosure vector $\mathbf{w}$ has expectation zero (in absence of bias on the observations), hence the unbiasedness and minimum variance criteria imply:

$$\begin{aligned} tr(\mathbf{B}\boldsymbol{\Sigma}_{\mathbf{w}}) &= \mathbf{p}^{\mathrm{T}}\boldsymbol{\sigma} \\ tr(\mathbf{B}\boldsymbol{\Sigma}_{\mathbf{w}}\mathbf{B}\boldsymbol{\Sigma}_{\mathbf{w}}) &= min \end{aligned} \tag{A.9}$$

For $\boldsymbol{\Sigma}_{\mathbf{w}}$, the (r, r) covariance matrix of $\mathbf{w}$, using the error propagation law to (A.1) and inserting (1.1), we have:

$$\boldsymbol{\Sigma}_{\mathbf{w}} = \mathbf{A}\sum\nolimits_{\mathbf{v}}\mathbf{A}^{\mathrm{T}} = \mathbf{A}\sum\nolimits_{l}\mathbf{A}^{\mathrm{T}} = \mathbf{A}\left(\sum\nolimits_{1}^{k}\sigma_i\mathbf{Q}_i\right)\mathbf{A}^{\mathrm{T}} = \sum\nolimits_{1}^{k}\sigma_i\mathbf{A}\mathbf{Q}_i\mathbf{A}^{\mathrm{T}} = \sum\nolimits_{1}^{k}\sigma_i\tilde{\mathbf{Q}}_i \tag{A.10}$$

where:

$$\tilde{\mathbf{Q}}_i = \mathbf{A}\mathbf{Q}_i\mathbf{A}^{\mathrm{T}} \tag{A.11}$$

From the first of (A.9) and (A.10), we have:

$$tr(\mathbf{B}\Sigma_{\mathbf{w}}) = tr\left(\mathbf{B}\sum_{1}^{k}\sigma_i\tilde{\mathbf{Q}}_i\right) = \sum_{1}^{k}p_i\sigma_i \Leftrightarrow tr\left(\mathbf{B}\tilde{\mathbf{Q}}_i\right) = p_i(i = 1,\ldots.k)$$

Consequently, for the unbiasedness and minimum variance criteria we obtain:

$$\begin{gathered} tr\left(\mathbf{B}\tilde{\mathbf{Q}}_j\right) = p_j(j = 1,\ldots.k) \\ tr(\mathbf{B}\Sigma_{\mathbf{w}}\mathbf{B}\Sigma_{\mathbf{w}}) = min \end{gathered} \tag{A.12}$$

Hence the Lagrange function of the problem is expressed as:

$$L = tr(\mathbf{B}\Sigma_{\mathbf{w}}\mathbf{B}\Sigma_{\mathbf{w}}) - 2\sum_{1}^{k}\lambda_j\left[tr\left(\mathbf{B}\tilde{\mathbf{Q}}_j\right) - p_j\right] \tag{A.13}$$

where $\boldsymbol{\lambda} = (\lambda_1,\ldots..,\lambda_k)^{\mathrm{T}}$ is a k-vector of Lagrange multipliers. The solution is found by equating the partial derivatives of L with respect to $\mathbf{B}$ and $\boldsymbol{\lambda}$ to zero.

In order to do that, we recall that if $\mathbf{A}$, $\mathbf{B}$ and $\mathbf{C}$ are (n,n) matrices, the matrices of partial derivatives of the scalar functions $tr(\mathbf{AB})$ and $tr(\mathbf{ABAC})$ with respect to the elements of $\mathbf{A}$ are respectively (Caspary 1987):

$$\begin{gathered} \tfrac{\partial}{\partial \mathbf{A}}tr(\mathbf{AB}) = \mathbf{B}^{\mathrm{T}} \\ \tfrac{\partial}{\partial \mathbf{A}}tr(\mathbf{ABAC}) = (\mathbf{BAC} + \mathbf{CAB})^{\mathrm{T}} \end{gathered} \tag{A.14}$$

Because the matrices $\tilde{\mathbf{Q}}_i$ are symmetrical, the use of (A.14) yields:

$$\frac{\partial L}{\partial \mathbf{B}} = 2\Sigma_{\mathbf{w}}\mathbf{B}\Sigma_{\mathbf{w}} - 2\sum_{1}^{k}\lambda_j\tilde{\mathbf{Q}}_j$$

and leads to the set of equations:

$$\begin{gathered} tr\left(\mathbf{B}\tilde{\mathbf{Q}}_j\right) = p_j(j = 1,\ldots.k) \\ \Sigma_{\mathbf{w}}\mathbf{B}\Sigma_{\mathbf{w}} - \sum_{1}^{k}\lambda_j\tilde{\mathbf{Q}}_j = 0 \end{gathered} \tag{A.15}$$

An auxiliary matrix $\mathbf{M}$ is introduced to solve Eqs. (A.15) for $\mathbf{B}$:

$$\mathbf{M} = \mathbf{N}^{-1} \tag{A.16}$$

with:

$$\mathbf{N} = \boldsymbol{\Sigma}_{\mathbf{w}} = \mathbf{A}\boldsymbol{\Sigma}_{l}\mathbf{A}^{\mathrm{T}} \tag{A.17}$$

and is selected to meet the conditions:

$$\mathbf{M}\boldsymbol{\Sigma}_{\mathbf{w}}\mathbf{B}\boldsymbol{\Sigma}_{\mathbf{w}}\mathbf{M} = \mathbf{N}^{-1}\mathbf{N}\mathbf{B}\mathbf{N}^{-1}\mathbf{N} = \mathbf{B}$$

Pre- and post-multiplication of the second equation of (A.15) with $\mathbf{M} = \mathbf{N}^{-1}$ yields:

$$\mathbf{B} = \sum\nolimits_{1}^{k} \lambda_{j}\mathbf{N}^{-1}\tilde{\mathbf{Q}}_{j}\mathbf{N}^{-1} \tag{A.18}$$

Inserting (A.18) in the first of (A.15) we have:

$$tr(\mathbf{B}\tilde{\mathbf{Q}}_{i}) = \sum\nolimits_{i=1}^{k} \lambda_{j} tr(\mathbf{N}^{-1}\tilde{\mathbf{Q}}_{i}\mathbf{N}^{-1}\tilde{\mathbf{Q}}_{j}) = p_{j}(j = 1, \ldots .k) \tag{A.19}$$

Let $\mathbf{H}$ be the (k, k) matrix composed of the elements:

$$h_{ij} = tr(\mathbf{N}^{-1}\tilde{\mathbf{Q}}_{i}\mathbf{N}^{-1}\tilde{\mathbf{Q}}_{j})\,(i, j = 1, \ldots .k) \tag{A.20}$$

then Eq. (A.19) can be written in the concise form:

$$\mathbf{H}\lambda = \mathbf{p} \tag{A.21}$$

with the k-vectors $\boldsymbol{\lambda}$ and $\mathbf{p}$ defined as above.

Noting that the matrix $\mathbf{H}$ could turn out to be singular (i.e. non-full rank), a generalized solution of the (A.21) for $\boldsymbol{\lambda}$ requires the (Moore-Penrose) pseudoinverse $\mathbf{H}^{+}$ defined by:

$$\mathbf{H}\mathbf{H}^{+}\mathbf{H} = \mathbf{H},\;\; \mathbf{H}^{+}\mathbf{H}\mathbf{H}^{+} = \mathbf{H}^{+},\;\; (\mathbf{H}\mathbf{H}^{+})^{\mathrm{T}} = \mathbf{H}\mathbf{H}^{+},\;\; (\mathbf{H}^{+}\mathbf{H})^{\mathrm{T}} = \mathbf{H}^{+}\mathbf{H} \tag{A.22}$$

Therefore:

$$\boldsymbol{\lambda} = \mathbf{H}^{+}\mathbf{p} \Leftrightarrow \lambda_{i} = \mathbf{g}_{i}^{\mathrm{T}}\mathbf{p} = \mathbf{p}^{\mathrm{T}}\mathbf{g}_{i} \tag{A.23}$$

where $\mathbf{g}_{i}$ is the i–th column of the matrix $\mathbf{H}^{+}$. Substitution into Eq. (A.18) yields:

$$\mathbf{B} = \sum\nolimits_{1}^{k} \mathbf{p}^{\mathrm{T}}\mathbf{g}_{i}\mathbf{N}^{-1}\tilde{\mathbf{Q}}_{i}\mathbf{N}^{-1} \tag{A.24}$$

and results in the estimation for $\mathbf{p}^{\mathrm{T}}\boldsymbol{\sigma}$:

$$q_w = \mathbf{p}^{\mathrm{T}}\hat{\sigma} = \mathbf{w}^{\mathrm{T}}\mathbf{B}\mathbf{w} = \mathbf{w}^{\mathrm{T}}\sum\nolimits_1^k \mathbf{p}^{\mathrm{T}}\mathbf{g}_i\mathbf{N}^{-1}\tilde{\mathbf{Q}}_i\mathbf{N}^{-1}\mathbf{w} \tag{A.25}$$

Defining the k–vector $\mathbf{f}$ as:

$$\mathbf{f} = \left\{\mathrm{f}_i = \mathbf{w}^{\mathrm{T}}\mathbf{N}^{-1}\tilde{\mathbf{Q}}_i\mathbf{N}^{-1}\mathbf{w}\right\} \tag{A.26}$$

the Eq. (A.25) can be put in a more suitable form:

$$q_w = \mathbf{w}^{\mathrm{T}}\mathbf{B}\mathbf{w} = \sum\nolimits_1^k \mathbf{p}^{\mathrm{T}}\mathbf{g}_i\mathrm{f}_i = \mathbf{p}^{\mathrm{T}}\mathbf{H}^{+}\mathbf{f} = \mathbf{p}^{\mathrm{T}}\hat{\boldsymbol{\sigma}} \tag{A.27}$$

from which the final result is obtained as:

$$\hat{\sigma} = \mathbf{H}^{+}\mathbf{f} \tag{A.28}$$

Thus, the **locally** best invariant quadratic unbiased estimates $\hat{\sigma}_i^2$ and $\hat{\sigma}_{ij}$ of the variances and covariances are solutions of the system

$$\mathbf{H}\hat{\sigma} = \mathbf{f} \tag{A.29}$$

with:

$$\mathbf{N} = \mathbf{A}\boldsymbol{\Sigma}_l\mathbf{A}^{\mathrm{T}} \tag{A.30}$$

$$\tilde{\mathbf{Q}}_i = \mathbf{A}\mathbf{Q}_i\mathbf{A}^{\mathrm{T}} \tag{A.31}$$

$$\mathbf{H} = \left\{h_{ij} = tr\left(\mathbf{N}^{-1}\tilde{\mathbf{Q}}_i\mathbf{N}^{-1}\tilde{\mathbf{Q}}_j\right)\right\} \tag{A.32}$$

$$\mathbf{f} = \left\{\mathrm{f}_i = \mathbf{w}^{\mathrm{T}}\mathbf{N}^{-1}\tilde{\mathbf{Q}}_i\mathbf{N}^{-1}\mathbf{w}\right\} \tag{A.33}$$

We note that with the previous relations (A.29)–(A.33) the evaluation of the LS residuals is not required. Hence, with the functional model of condition only, the BIQUE VCE can be performed in pre-adjustment; furthermore, in this functional model there are no unknown parameters and a possible datum defect has no influence on the overall procedure.

It is worth noting that $\mathbf{N}$, defined in Eq. (A.30) and used in (A.32) and (A.33), contains the covariance matrix $\boldsymbol{\Sigma}_l$, i.e. the vector $\boldsymbol{\sigma}$. Therefore, it is mandatory to implement an iterative numerical approach, like the one depicted in Sect. 2.

A further observation concerns the Eqs. (A.1) of the functional model of condition only, which in some cases can be very difficult to write. Other functional models (with unknown parameters) turn out to be generally easier to formulate, and therefore are more frequently used. As a result, it is useful to elaborate a BIQUE VCE procedure which could be used in any functional model, given the stochastic model (1.1). This will be shown in Appendix B.

6 Appendix B – A Generalized Procedure for BIQUE VCE

In this section we show a generalization of the BIQUE procedure for all functional models. For this purpose, we introduce an (n, n) symmetric matrix $\mathbf{M}$:

$$\mathbf{M} = \mathbf{A}^{\mathrm{T}}\mathbf{N}^{-1}\mathbf{A} \tag{B.1}$$

As for the elements h_{ij}, inserting (A.30) into (A.31) and from (B.1), we have:

$$\begin{aligned} h_{ij} &= tr\left(\mathbf{N}^{-1}\tilde{\mathbf{Q}}_i\mathbf{N}^{-1}\tilde{\mathbf{Q}}_j\right) = tr\left(\mathbf{N}^{-1}\mathbf{A}\mathbf{Q}_i\mathbf{A}^{\mathrm{T}}\mathbf{N}^{-1}\mathbf{A}\mathbf{Q}_j\mathbf{A}^{\mathrm{T}}\right) \\ &= tr\left[\left(\mathbf{A}^{\mathrm{T}}\mathbf{N}^{-1}\mathbf{A}\right)\mathbf{Q}_i\left(\mathbf{A}^{\mathrm{T}}\mathbf{N}^{-1}\mathbf{A}\right)\mathbf{Q}_j\right] = tr\left(\mathbf{M}\mathbf{Q}_i\mathbf{M}\mathbf{Q}_j\right) \end{aligned} \tag{B.2}$$

and the elements f_i are expressed by using $\mathbf{w} = \mathbf{A}\hat{\mathbf{v}}$, inserting (A.30) into (A.32), and recalling (B.1):

$$\mathrm{f}_i = \mathbf{w}^{\mathrm{T}}\mathbf{N}^{-1}\tilde{\mathbf{Q}}_i\mathbf{N}^{-1}\mathbf{w} = \hat{\mathbf{v}}^{\mathrm{T}}(\mathbf{A}^{\mathrm{T}}\mathbf{N}^{-1}\mathbf{A})\mathbf{Q}_i(\mathbf{A}^{\mathrm{T}}\mathbf{N}^{-1}\mathbf{A})\hat{\mathbf{v}} \tag{B.3}$$

Between the observation vector $\boldsymbol{l}$ and the least-squares residuals vector $\hat{\mathbf{v}}$ the following relation holds:

$$\hat{\mathbf{v}} = -\mathbf{R}\boldsymbol{l} \tag{B.4}$$

where the redundancy matrix $\mathbf{R}$ is equal to:

$$\mathbf{R} = \mathbf{Q}_{\hat{\mathbf{v}}}\mathbf{P} = \boldsymbol{\Sigma}_l\mathbf{A}^{\mathrm{T}}\mathbf{N}^{-1}\mathbf{A} \tag{B.5}$$

and is idempotent, with:

$$rank(\mathbf{R}) = tr(\mathbf{R}) = r \tag{B.6}$$

From (B.1), (B.4), (B.5) and (A.29) we easily deduce the relations:

$$\mathbf{M}\hat{\mathbf{v}} = \mathbf{P}\hat{\mathbf{v}} = -\mathbf{M}\boldsymbol{l} \tag{B.7}$$

which, introduced into (B.3), yield

$$\mathrm{f}_i = \boldsymbol{l}^{\mathrm{T}}\mathbf{M}\mathbf{Q}_i\mathbf{M}\boldsymbol{l} = \hat{\mathbf{v}}^{\mathrm{T}}\mathbf{M}\mathbf{Q}_i\mathbf{M}\hat{\mathbf{v}} = \hat{\mathbf{v}}^{\mathrm{T}}\mathbf{P}\mathbf{Q}_i\mathbf{P}\hat{\mathbf{v}} \tag{B.8}$$

From (A.29) and the second of (A.2) we note that the matrix $\mathbf{M}$ (B.1) can be arranged in the compact general form:

$$\mathbf{M} = \mathbf{P}\mathbf{Q}_{\hat{\mathbf{v}}}\mathbf{P} \tag{B.9}$$

and it can be fully characterized by inserting the expression of $\mathbf{Q}_{\hat{\mathbf{v}}}$ related to the chosen functional model.

Therefore, assuming the linear stochastic model (1.1), the generalized BIQUE VCE consists in solving iteratively the system:

$$\mathbf{H}\hat{\boldsymbol{\sigma}} = \mathbf{f} \tag{B.10}$$

where:

$$\mathbf{H} = \left\{h_{ij} = tr\left(\mathbf{M}\mathbf{Q}_i\mathbf{M}\mathbf{Q}_j\right)\right\} \tag{B.11}$$

$$\mathbf{f} = \left\{\mathrm{f}_i = \boldsymbol{l}^{\mathrm{T}}\mathbf{M}\mathbf{Q}_i\mathbf{M}\boldsymbol{l} = \hat{\mathbf{v}}^{\mathrm{T}}\mathbf{M}\mathbf{Q}_i\mathbf{M}\hat{\mathbf{v}} = \hat{\mathbf{v}}^{\mathrm{T}}\mathbf{P}\mathbf{Q}_i\mathbf{P}\hat{\mathbf{v}}\right\} \tag{B.12}$$

$$\mathbf{M} = \mathbf{P}\mathbf{Q}_{\hat{\mathbf{v}}}\mathbf{P} \tag{B.13}$$

It is easy to verify that the formulas of the h_{ij} and f_i provided by other authors (Koch 1986; Ou 1989; Rao 1973; Sjöberg 1983; Yu 1992) are particular cases of the generalized expressions (B.10)–(B.13).

References

Caspary, W.F.: Concepts of network and deformation analysis. School of Surveying, pp. 97–111. The University of New South Wales, Kensington, N.S.W., Australia (1987)

Crocetto, N., Gatti, M., Russo, P.: Simplified formulae for the BIQUE estimation of variance components in disjunctive observation groups. J. Geodesy **74**, 447–457 (2000)

Hilla, S.: The Extended Standard Product 3 Orbit Format (SP3-c). NGS (2007). http://gnsser.com/Information/ViewDetails/346. Accessed 18 Mar 2019

International GNSS Service (IGS): RINEX-The Receiver Independent Exchange Format, Version 3.02, April 3, 2013. RINEX Working Group and Radio Technical Commission for Maritime Services Special Committee 104 (RTCM-SC104), 88 pp. (2013). https://kb.igs.org/hc/en-us/article_attachments/115007665107/rinex302.pdf. Accessed 18 Mar 2019

Junhuan, P., Yun, S., Shuhui, L., Honglei, Y.: MINQUE of variance-covariance components in linear gauss-markov models. J. Surv. Eng. **137**(4), 129–139 (2011)

Koch, K.R.: Maximum likelihood estimate of variance components. Bull. Géodésique **60**, 329–338 (1986)

Li, B., Shen, Y., Luo, L.: Efficient estimation of variance and covariance components: a case study for GPS stochastic model evaluation. IEEE Trans. Geosci. Remote Sens. **49**(1), 203–210 (2011)

Moghtased-Azar, K., Tehranchi, R., Amiri-Simkooei, A.R.: An alternative method for non-negative estimation of variance components. J. Geodesy **88**, 427–439 (2014)

Rahemi, N., Mosavi, M.R., Abedi, A.A., Mirzakuchaki, S.: Accurate solution of navigation equations in GPS receivers for very high velocities using pseudorange measurements. Adv. Aerosp. Eng. (2014). Article ID 435891. http://dx.doi.org/10.1155/2014/435891. Accessed 10 Mar 2019

Rao, C.R.: Linear Statistical Inference and its Applications. Wiley, New York (1973)
Sjöberg, L.E.: Unbiased estimation of variance-covariance components in condition adjustment with unknowns – a MINQUE approach. ZfV **108**(9), 382–387 (1983)
Sjöberg, L.E.: Non negative variance components estimation in the Gauss-Helmert adjustment model. Manuscripta Geodaetica **9**, 247–280 (1984)
Ou, Z.: Estimation of variance and covariance components. Bull. Géodésique **63**, 139–148 (1989)
Yu, Z.: A generalization theory of estimation of variance-covariance components. Manuscripta Geodaetica **17**, 295–301 (1992)

UAV Survey of Bridges and Viaduct: Workflow and Application

Vincenzo Barrile, Gabriele Candela(✉), Antonino Fotia, and Ernesto Bernardo

Mediterranea University, 89128 Reggio Calabria, RC, Italy
{vincenzo.barrile,gabriele.candela,antonino.fotia, ernesto.bernardo}@unirc.it

Abstract. In this paper a workflow for bridges and viaducts aerial survey through Unmanned Aerial Vehicle (UAV) is presented.

Actual methodologies for bridge inspection and survey are described focusing on the use of UAV and 3d photogrammetry as a game changer to speed-up the process for the extraction of relevant data. In this context, a workflow for the complete survey of bridges, from data gathering, elaboration, presentation of results and automatic extraction of geometrical data is presented. The presented workflow was applied to a highway viaduct "Annunziata" located in a seismic risk zone in the city of Reggio Calabria. The application of this workflow allows a complete 3d reconstruction of the viaduct, with the extraction of the structure's geometry for future analysis and remote inspection using a web-based platform.

Keywords: Aerial survey · Photogrammetry · UAV

1 Introduction

Infrastructure maintenance and monitoring, with particular attention to bridges and viaducts, is an actual problem that western country has to face. These critical infrastructures are highly exposed to seismic risks. The first document and regulation about the maintenance activity to be performed on infrastructure and bridge's "Retrofitting guidelines for Highway Bridges" was emitted in the US Federal Highway Administration (FHWA) in 1983; while the first research program, financed by FHWA, to investigate and evaluate the seismic risk assessment of bridges started in 1992. The output of that research was released on 1995, "Seismic Retrofit Manual for Highway Bridges" and updated until today in the "Seismic Retrofitting Manual for Highway Structures: Part 1 Bridges" (Buckle et al. 2006) Seismic Retrofitting Manual for Highway Structures: Part 2 Retaining structures, slopes, tunnels, culverts and roadways" (Power et al. 2004).

In Europe the Eurocode 8 part 2 contains a document for "Design of structure for earthquake resistance: Bridges" (Holst et al. 2011) and the evaluation of seismic risks, but the code for assessment and retrofitting of structures limits their analysis only on existing buildings (Eurocode 8 part 3 "Assessment and retrofitting of buildings" (Holst et al. 2011). In Italy, designs regulations are contained in "Norme tecniche per le Costruzioni" NTC2018 (Ministero delle Infrastrutture e dei Trasporti 2018). Moreover,

S. Misra et al. (Eds.): ICCSA 2019, LNCS 11622, pp. 269–284, 2019.
https://doi.org/10.1007/978-3-030-24305-0_21

"Civil protection Department" (DPC) has activated research in collaboration with Italian University about "Evaluation and reduction of seismic risk of existing bridges". The main objective is to develop a procedure to evaluate the structural condition of the existing bridge in order to reduce the risks.

In Italy "Union of Italian Province" (UPI) has developed a recent report (Unione Province Italiane 2018) about the actual condition of Italian infrastructure focusing on Bridges and Viaducts that have exceeded their life cycle (almost 50 years). The report was the result of the investigation requested by the Italian Minister for Transportation (MIT) after the collapse of Morandi Bridge in Genova (2018). Italian provinces have to manage almost 100.000 km of roads with 30.000 bridges, viaducts and tunnels. The status of these bridges is reassumed in the next graph (Fig. 1):

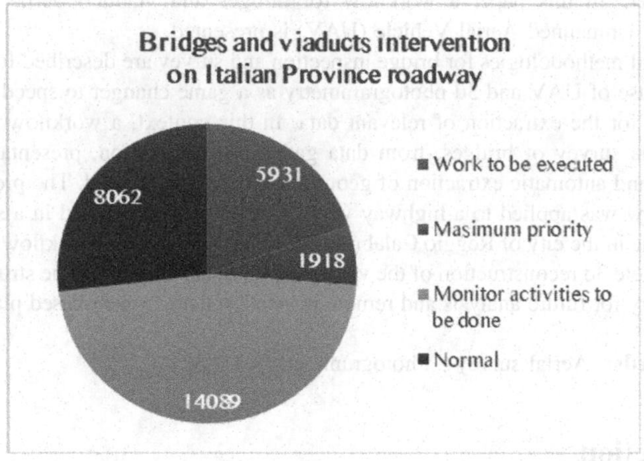

Fig. 1. Status and distribution of Italian Province bridges and viaduct

The estimated cost for the monitoring of 14.000 bridges is about 566 million and estimated costs of intervention for actual bridges is 2.7 billion. This count excludes the intervention on the regional and national highway, managed by public or joint venture (public-private) company Autostrade per l'Italia (ASPI) (4200 bridges and viaducts) and Anas (13.000 bridges and viaduct). Each of this company has its own monitoring system and standard operation manual to ensure maintenance and control. Actual methodology for monitor and control of bridges are presented in the next paragraph. The major damages on bridges and viaducts due to external forces such as seismic loads can be divided according to super and substructure: major damages and cause of collapse are in fact concentrated on deck and piers (Pinto et al. 2009): deck doesn't have anti-seismic resistance function and major cause of collapse are essentially due to hammering between adjacent span and losses of support. Piers, responsible for supporting the deck and resists to different forces, can collapse due to flexural ductility defects, shear resistance and inadequate design of beam/pier joint. Adequate monitoring and survey techniques are necessary to understand the structural health of the construction.

1.1 Infrastructure Survey Techniques

Structure from motion coupled with the use of UAV represent the latest and significant advance in digital surveying, thanks to the possibility to acquire information in a cheap and fast way, and their non-invasive characteristics guarantee the acquisition without any contact with the object/area to be surveyed. The use of photogrammetry in surveying and monitoring spread in recent years and is growing rapidly, thanks to the numerous advantages compared with more traditional survey techniques. The choice of the survey technique to be used by the surveyor is related to the expected results and different factors such as: (i) data accuracy and precision needed, (ii) intended usage of the captured data, (iii) constraints such as time and budget for the operation and (iv) expertise and availability of both hardware and software for data acquiring and processing. Compared with traditional techniques, such as Total Stations, GPS (Global Positioning System), LIght Detection And Ranging (LIDAR), airborne laser scanning (ALS) and terrestrial laser scanning (TLS), photogrammetric algorithms coupled with UAV survey can offer truly 3d information with reduced labor cost and capital expenditure (Mader et al. 2015). Moreover with careful use of ground control points (GCP) this technique can rival other digital survey methods for spatial accuracy, and with the use of more precise onboard Global Navigation Satellite System (GNSS) navigation (e.g. Real Time Kinematic GNSS) the spatial accuracy can be improved to centimeter precision without GCP (Gerke and Przybilla 2016; Cryderman et al. 2014) (Table 1).

Table 1. Survey techniques comparison

Survey method and equipment	Type	Spatial extent (km)	Spatial resolution (pt m^2)	Data acquisition rate (point/hour)	3d point accuracy (m)
Visual inspection	Direct	0,1	-	-	-
Total Station	Direct	0,1 – 1	0,1 – 5	Hundreds	<0,01
dGPS	Direct	2,4 – 1	0,1 – 5	Thousands	0,005
Lidar (ALS)	Remote	5 – 100	0,2 – 10	Millions	0,2
Lidar (TLS)	Remote	0,01 – 5	100 – 10.000	Millions	0,05
Photogrammetry	Remote	5,0 – 50	0,5 – 10	Ten of thousands	0,5
SFM - MVS	Remote	0,01 – 1	1 – 10.000	Millions	0,01–0,2

With careful application, the delivered results in terms of accuracy can be compared to the best achieved with any other topographic surveying method, both direct or indirect (Marcus and Fonstad 2008). From the other side, limitations are represented by the dependency on external ambient light condition (Marcus and Fonstad 2008; Gienko and Terry 2014), the high computational power needed to elaborate data and the impossibility to elaborate live data on field in order to understand attributes that the point cloud will have. Moreover, software used for point cloud analysis and elaboration actually is in its infancy.

1.2 Photogrammetric Algorithms for 3d Reconstruction: SFM-MVS

Photogrammetric principles and algorithms allow, as discussed, the reconstruction of the 3d scene starting from different images acquired respecting stereographic criteria. Quality of photogrammetric reconstruction is influenced by Sensor size, resolution, photo acquisition parameters, image format acquisition, stabilization. The well-known computer vision algorithm *Structure from Motion (SFM)* (Micheletti et al. 2015) is the most reliable and utilized algorithms for the generation of a valuable 3d model from 2d imagery. *SFM* algorithms identify matching features in a collection of overlapping digital images and calculate the camera location and orientation from the differential position of multiple matched features. Based on these calculations overlapping imagery can be used to reconstruct a "sparse" 3d point cloud model of the acquired scene. Later the model is refined to a much finer resolution using *Multi-Stereo-View* methods, producing high-quality, dense, 3D point clouds of a scene/area with minimal financial cost. The use of this computer vision algorithms to become relevant in geoscience thanks to the emergence of affordable commercial user-friendly software coupled with rapid developments of UAVs platform.

2 Methods: Aerial Survey Using UAV

The combination of Unmanned Aerial Vehicle (UAV) and computer vision algorithms presented makes this combined solution the perfect *inspection platform* for infrastructure surveying, bridge and viaducts inspection and monitoring. The first level of application can be represented by photographic dataset acquired according to structure segmentation. A more precise level of acquisition involves the 3d reconstruction and virtual asset inspection using Virtual Reality. The main advantages related to the use of these technologies are summarized in (i) the possibility of reaching inaccessible zones in reduced time and (ii) gather high detail of structural components with camera zoom (iii) use of remote piloting (Behoind Visual Line Of Sight operation) (iv) setting-up standard and automatic flight plan for data gathering associated with different scenarios and (v) ensure regular service during inspection process and (vi) repeatability of inspection process during time. Moreover, with tailored camera and systems (vii) non-invasive deformation monitoring it's applicable (Yoon et al. 2018), (viii) creation of dynamic database and (ix) creation of 3d model for a virtual tour and remote collaborative inspection. Applying computer vision images analysis (x) automatic finding of defects and deterioration and (xi) extraction of geometrical characteristics to perform structural analysis.

From the other side different challenges and open point in the ***acquisition phase*** must be faced: (i) environment complexity (presence of obstacles, vegetation near the structure) for flight, (ii) presence of river near the infrastructure, (iii) complex structure, thins parts and occlusion requires manual flight or dedicated UAV for confined space inspection, (iv) weak or not reliable GPS signal under the bridge.

Moreover, the main challenges in ***data analysis*** are represented by (i) 3d point cloud segmentation, (ii) extraction of key information according to tasks, (iii) visualization and sharing of acquired data and models (iv) no possibility to verify the quality of the data during the acquisition process.

As discussed before, the use of UAV technology in infrastructure surveying recently spread from 2013. Different applications and case studies have been presented in last 5 years (Ham et al. 2016; Khaloo et al. 2018; Hackl et al. 2018; Chen et al. 2018; Morgenthal and Hallermann 2014; Escobar-Wolf et al. 2018; Lovelace 2015). However, due to the different disciplines involved in this application and to the recent and new technology used, there is not a standard methodology and workflow for data acquisition and analysis.

The use of this technology it's not yet available as a standard inspection platform and it's task dependent. Moreover, the competence needed for acquisition and data analysis involves the different field of science and requires different knowledge in aeronautics, civil engineering, electronics, computer vision and 3d graphics. The technician involved it's only a pilot but should have different specialization. Acquisition techniques depend on different factors such as Level of Detail required, payload and sensors, and data analysis and extraction of crucial characteristics from a large dataset (e.g. 3d point clouds or terabyte of images) are not yet standardized. In this paragraph a methodology for the standardization of the bridges inspection process through UAV survey is presented (Fig. 2):

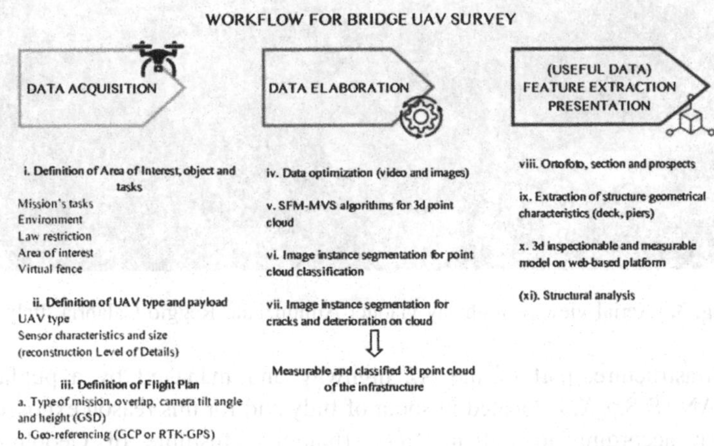

Fig. 2. Workflow for UAV photogrammetry bridge survey

Three main phases for the bridge survey and 3d reconstruction using UAV can be identified: first planning and acquisition phase according to the area, structure and task specification. The main issue is represented by the setup of the flight acquisition plan. In the second phase, the acquired data (e.g. photo or video) are elaborated to extract a measurable and classified 3d point cloud of the infrastructure. In the third phase, the extraction of the relevant characteristics is performed with the use of a web-based platform to visualize and analyse the results, allowing the possibility to perform virtual inspection of the scene and extract key information for future analysis.

3 Annunziata Viaduct: Case Study

3.1 Annunziata Viaduct, A2 Highway Reggio Calabria

The methodology for survey with UAV and extraction of geometrical features was applied to a highway bridge located on the A2 "Autostrada del Mediterraneo" in the city of Reggio Calabria, Italy (Fig. 3). The viaduct, built on 1970 upon the "Annunziata" river, is a *simply supported*, *beam* viaduct made of pre-stressed *reinforced concrete* with 9 *short-spans* of 29 m, and a total length of 254 m (in curve). Curvature radius is 150 m and the medium height of the bridge is 25 m a.s.l. The viaduct has a simple structure and static schema. No vegetation or other obstacles are present around the object, so free and pre-programmed flight are possible without issues.

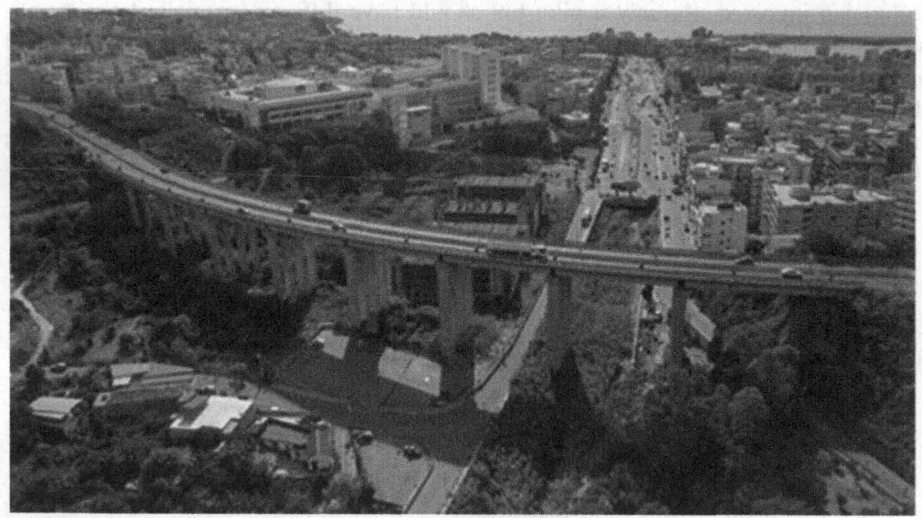

Fig. 3. Aerial view of highway viaduct Annunziata, Reggio Calabria, Italy

The infrastructure, part of the A2 highway and managed by a public-private company, ANAS S.p.A, is located in south of Italy and for this reason exposed to high seismic risk according to Italian INGV (National Institute of Geophysics and Volcanology). The strategic position makes this viaduct fundamental for the entire highway, linking north and south part of the city, allowing circulation of vehicle and truck outside of the city. In case of collapse the entire highway will be interrupted with high risk and consequence on vehicle circulation and on emergency response. The viaduct deck is composed by standard module of 29 m with 4 beams and 3 crosses in pre-stressed reinforced concrete (Fig. 4).

The two decks (one per each direction) are sustained by a couple of piers with a common foundation (Fig. 5a, b). Piers are made of rectangular section of 2.50 m × 1.60 m and pier cap dimensions are 8 m × 3 m.

Fig. 4. Deck structure

(a)

(b)

Fig. 5. (a) Bridge structure and deck from left side, (b) piers foundation

Several superficial cracks are present on the structure (Fig. 6), as sign of lack of maintenance operations. Moreover, water infiltration from deck to piers, due to lack of adequate gutter, represents a serious issue for structure.

(a)

(b)

Fig. 6. Superficial cracks on piers (a, b)

The airspace around the viaduct is classified by ENAC (Ente Nazionale Aviazione Civile) as CTR (Controlled Traffic Region) and non-critical operation are allowed for UAV with operating take-off mass less than 25 kg, up to maximum height of 70 m above ground level (AGL). Regulation in Italy are defined in "Regolamento Mezzi Aerei a Pilotaggio Remoto" by ENAC. The national regulations have integrated the EASA Drone Regulatory Framework, active in the European Union (Fig. 7).

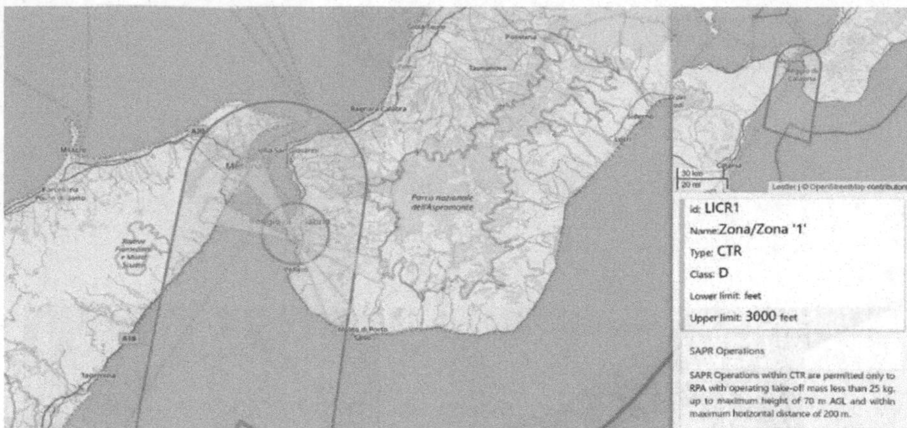

Fig. 7. Controlled space for UAV operation in the survey area

Visual line of sight (VLOS) flight is allowed at a maximum distance of 200 m, with manual or automatic flight. In the area of interest, to avoid collisions and delimitate the operating zone, a virtual geo-fence was created to allows UAV operations in the limited space area to accomplish local regulation. With the software limitation, the UAV can fly only inside the virtual area (Fig. 8). The airspace around the viaduct is occupied by low altitude buildings and two cranes in the right side, and vegetation in the right side. The operation has taken into consideration the presence of these obstacles. The viaduct height is 25 m a.gl. and the maximum flight height is 70 m a.g.l.

Fig. 8. Geo-fence around Annunziata Viaduct for delimitation of aerial space for survey

3.2 Annunziata Viaduct Data Acquisition

The aerial survey of the Annunziata Viaduct was executed in the early morning with cloudy weather to avoid direct sunlight in the acquired images and optimizing the dataset for 3d reconstruction process. The workflow explained in the previous paragraph was applied in order to plan the survey, the acquisition and elaboration process. The survey was performed by an authorized UAV pilot for non-critical operation.

Definition of Mission's Objective, Area and Tasks. The mission objective was the complete acquisition of the Annunziata viaduct with centimetre accuracy and the extraction of the geometrical feature of the structure.

Definition of UAV Type and Payload. The aerial survey was performed using a commercial quadrotor UAV from DJI (DJI, Shenzen, China), Mavic Pro, whose specs are summarized in the following table (Table 2):

Table 2. DJI Mavic Pro characteristics

DJI Mavic Pro Specs	
Dimensions	83 × 83 × 198 mm
Weight	734 g
Flight autonomy	27 m
Battery type. capacity	LiPo 3S – 3830 mAh
Operating temperature	0°–40° C
GNSS system	GPS/GLONASS
Flight accuracy	Vertical +/– 0,1 m Horizontal +/– 0,3 m

This low-cost UAV has onboard GPS and waypoint navigation with front collision sensors, allowing the possibility to execute automatic waypoint missions. The combination of these characteristics makes this platform compliant with local regulation and suitable for viaduct survey operation.

Mavic Pro UAV has a fixed payload with Sony camera sensor. Camera characteristics are reported in Table 3.

Table 3. Payload camera sensor

Payload camera specs	
Sensor	Sony 1/2.3″ CMOS
Lens	28 mm f/2.2
Real focal length	5 mm
Real sensor width	6.17 mm
Field Of View (FOV)	78.8°
Electronic Shutter Speed	8 s–1/8000 s
ISO range	100–1600
Image resolution	12.35 MP
Geotagging	Internal built-in GPS

Definition of the Flight Plan. The first acquisition plan was set-up to obtain a low detail 3d model in order to use it as input for a more detailed acquisition plan in the 3d space. The acquisition plan in a two-dimensional environment was set-up and executed using Pix4d (Pix4d Inc. Lausanne).

The first mission for the area acquisition was set up using 6 different circular mission (to cover the entire area) at 50 m a.s.l. capturing images every 5° (for a total of 72 photos per circle) as summarized in the next table (Fig. 9 and Table 4):

Table 4. Circular mission for area acquisition

Mission	Type	Height (agl)	Time of flight	Camera Yaw	Area (m)
Mission 1	Circular	52 m	5 m: 26 s	45°	89 × 86
Mission 2	Circular	52 m	5 m: 31 s	45°	89 × 86
Mission 3	Circular	52 m	5 m: 29 s	45°	89 × 68
Mission 4	Circular	52 m	5 m: 37 s	45°	82 × 68
Mission 5	Circular	52 m	5 m: 37 s	45°	82 × 68
Mission 6	Circular	52 m	4 m: 19 s	30°	55 × 59

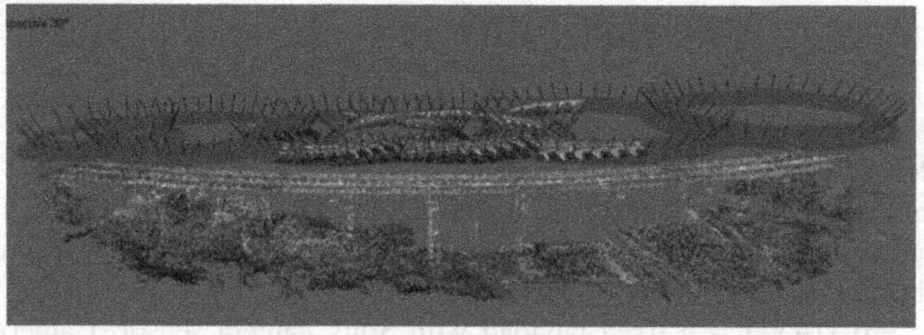

Fig. 9. Sparse point cloud of circular mission elaborated with SFM algorithm

To reconstruct the scaled and georeferenced 3d model a GNSS survey of the area where performed acquiring different Ground Control Point (GCP) on WGS84 reference system, evenly distributed on the area (Table 5):

The processed 3d model, reconstructed with SFM-MVS algorithm, was imported in the UGCS software (Universal Ground Control Software) (SPH Engineering, Latvia) and used to plan a specific mission for detailed and automatic acquisition of the area (Fig. 10).

Two different side missions for 3d model acquisition were executed to ensure (i) 80% overlap between images and a (ii) Ground Sampling Distance (GSD) less than 1 (cm/pix). Mission parameters are defined in Fig. 11, flight pattern for 3d flight execution are presented in Fig. 12:

The use of 3d planning tool allows operation's repeatability to perform regular inspection and acquisition on a defined time-basis.

Table 5. Acquired ground control point

Point n.	Latitude	Longitude	Altitude
5	38.123166	15.664129	48.039
6	38.123097	15.664128	48.224
7	38.123097	15.664129	70.557
8	38.121631	15.663419	68.445
9	38.123412	15.663525	54.120
10	38.123737	15.664095	58.325

Fig. 10. 3d model imported in UGCS plan software

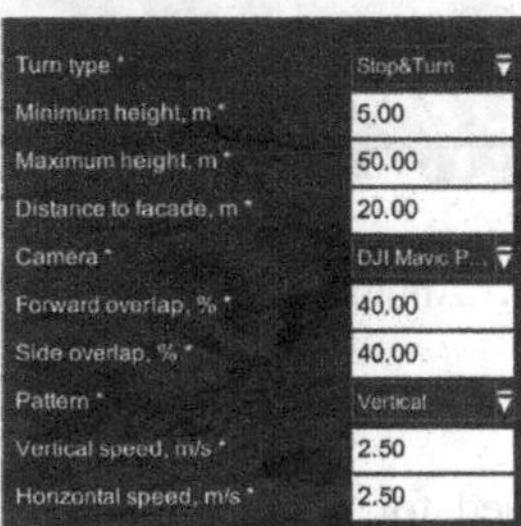

Turn type *
Stop&Turn
Minimum height, m *
5.00
Maximum height, m *
50.00
Distance to facade, m *
20.00
Camera *
DJI Mavic P...
Forward overlap, % *
40.00
Side overlap, % *
40.00
Pattern *
Vertical
Vertical speed, m/s *
2.50
Horizontal speed, m/s *
2.50

Fig. 11. Flight parameter for side acquisition

(a) (b)

Fig. 12. 3d side scanning of viaduct

4 Results

The obtained photographic dataset (1039 photos, 2,5 GB) was elaborated using Agisoft Metashape (Agisoft LLC, Russia) using SFM-MVS reconstruction process. Previously, the images obtained have been optimized to improve the contrasts and the light/shadow ratio to highlights details. After the elaboration process, the reconstructed sparse point cloud obtained consists of 46.000 points, and dense point cloud obtained was composed of 32 billion points. In Fig. 13 the obtained 3d model of the highway bridge is represented:

Fig. 13. Annunziata Viaduct 3d model

The obtained model was used for the extraction of the relevant geometric information of the structure, and to perform a virtual and collaborative inspection with an online platform.

Extraction of Structure Geometrical Characteristics. To extract relevant information from the surveyed model a methodology for semi-automatic extraction of geometry is presented. The use of this procedure allows to extract shapes from the structural parts, and automatically insert this data into a pre-defined spreadsheet. The classified structural parts are then transformed from point cloud into a 3d mesh object using Screened Poisson Surface Reconstruction (Kazhdan and Hoppe 2013). The entire workflow of the developed methodology is synthetized in Fig. 14: after the photogrammetric survey using Drone (1), and the creation of mesh as previously described (2), the ad-hoc instruments integrated with a simplified User Interface (UI) automatic transcribe data into a spreadsheet (point 3) using Rhinoceros and Grasshopper (McNeel, North America); point 4 is a file for data swap used to avoid non-compatibility of extraction algorithms with Visual Basic Marco and point 5 allows the transcription of information for analysis on the spread-sheet file.

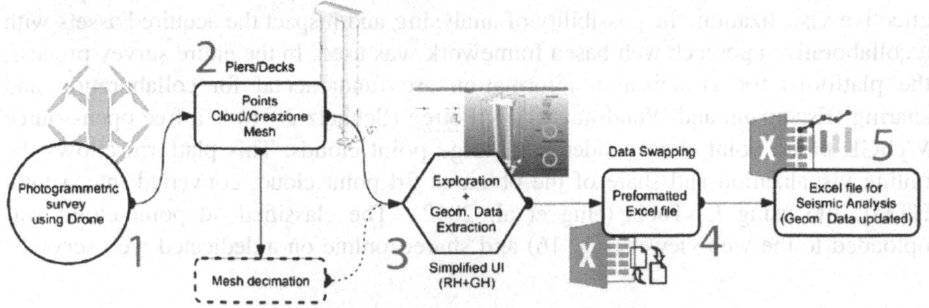

Fig. 14. Extraction of geometrical features

All the components are programmed ad-hoc. The basic principle used is the definition of two cut-plane XY and YZ to define the structure resistant section. The bounding box, as volumetric element around the object, was created to intersect cut-plan inside the box and the object. Subsequentially the cut-planes are setting up in XY and YZ. The user can define the position of the cutting plan in % compared with height, offset distance from cutting-plane and a total number of cutting plane as shown in Fig. 15:

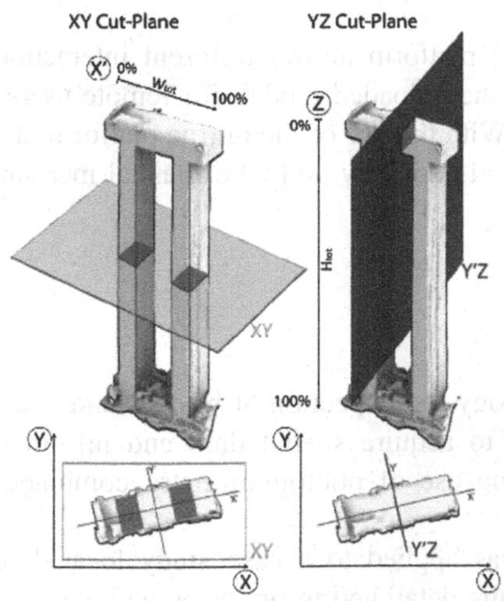

Fig. 15. XY and YZ plane to extract geometrical feature of piers

A preventive verification of the planarity and closure of the polyline is executed. If the polyline it's not close, the algorithm will approximate the closure. The developed module was used both on piers and deck to extract the geometry and automatically insert on the spreadsheet.

3D Inspection and Measurable Model on a Web-Based Platform. The reconstructed 3d point clouds are huge data and information difficult to manage and share (Wimmer and Scheiblauer 2006; Scheiblauer et al. 2014). To enable a simple and effective visualization, the possibility of analysing and inspect the acquired assets with a collaborative approach web-based framework was used. In the entire survey process, the platforms for visualization information are fundamental for collaboration and sharing (Eschmann and Wundsam 2017). Potree (Schuetz 2016) is a free open-source WebGL based point cloud renderer for large point clouds. This platform allows the online visualization and share of the obtained 3d point cloud, converted into a light HTML file using LasTools (Hug et al. 2012). The classified 3d point cloud was uploaded to the web viewer (Fig. 16) and shared online on a dedicated web server.

Fig. 16. Web-interface for visualization and collaborative inspection

Moreover, the online platform allows different interaction and measurements to gather information from the uploaded model, for remote users and inspector access to the surveyed 3d model. With the use of the online platform, it's also possible to verify the automatically extracted geometry and take manual measurements of the structural parts.

5 Conclusions

In this paper a methodology for inspection of bridges and viaduct is presented. Survey and modern techniques to acquire spatial data and information are discussed with particular attention to the use of photogrammetry combined with UAV to acquire spatial data.

The methodology was applied to a case study located on a highway bridge in Reggio Calabria, to acquire detail and information with centimetre accuracy. Finally, a platform to present and share surveyed model between client and different stakeholder's is discussed. The obtained results compared with blueprint confirms the survey's quality and the possibility to automatically extract the geometrical feature for future structural analysis. Moreover, the obtained 3d model was uploaded on a web platform to allows remote inspection.

References

Buckle, I., Friedland, I., Mander, J., Geoffrey, M., Nutt, R., Power, M.: Seismic Retrofitting Manual for Highway Structures: Part 1 – Bridges. Fhwa, January 2006

Chen, S., Truong-Hong, L., Laefer, D., Mangina, E.: Automated Bridge Deck Evaluation through UAV Derived Point Cloud, September 2018

Cryderman, C., Mah, S.B., Shufletoski, A.: Evaluation of UAV photogrammetric accuracy for mapping and earthworks computations. Geomatica **68**(4), 309–317 (2014)

Eschmann, C., Wundsam, T.: Web-based georeferenced 3D inspection and monitoring of bridges with unmanned aircraft systems. J. Surv. Eng. **143**(3), 04017003 (2017)

Escobar-Wolf, R., Oommen, T., Brooks, C.N., Dobson, R.J., Ahlborn, T.M.: Unmanned Aerial Vehicle (UAV)-based assessment of concrete bridge deck delamination using thermal and visible camera sensors: a preliminary analysis. Res. Nondestruct. Eval. **29**(4), 183–198 (2018)

Gerke, M., Przybilla, H.-J.: Accuracy analysis of photogrammetric UAV image blocks: influence of onboard RTK-GNSS and cross flight patterns. Photogramm. Fernerkund. Geoinformation **2016**(1), 17–30 (2016)

Gienko, G.A., Terry, J.P.: Three-dimensional modeling of coastal boulders using multi-view image measurements. Earth Surf. Process. Landf. **39**, 853–864 (2014)

Hackl, J., Adey, B.T., Woźniak, M., Schümperlin, O.: Use of Unmanned Aerial Vehicle photogrammetry to obtain topographical information to improve bridge risk assessment. J. Infrastruct. Syst. **24**(1), 04017041 (2018)

Ham, Y., Han, K.K., Lin, J.J., Golparvar-Fard, M.: Visual monitoring of civil infrastructure systems via camera-equipped Unmanned Aerial Vehicles (UAVs): a review of related works. Vis. Eng. **4**(1), 1–8 (2016)

Holst, J.M.F.G., et al.: Eurocode 8 Part 3: Assessment and retrofitting of buildings. J. Constr. Steel Res. **54**(2), 18–20 (2011)

Hug, C., Krzystek, P., Fuchs, W.: Advanced Lidar data processing with Lastools. In: International Society for Photogrammtry and Remote Sensing (ISPRS), pp. 12–23, July 2012

Kazhdan, M., Hoppe, H.: Screened poisson surface reconstruction. ACM Trans. Graph. **32**(3), 1–13 (2013)

Khaloo, A., Lattanzi, D., Cunningham, K., Dell'Andrea, R., Riley, M.: Unmanned Aerial Vehicle inspection of the Placer River Trail Bridge through image-based 3D modelling. Struct. Infrastruct. Eng. **14**(1), 124–136 (2018)

Lovelace, B.: Unmanned Aerial Vehicle Bridge Inspection Demonstration Project, p. 214, July 2015

Mader, D., Blaskow, R., Westfeld, P., Maas, H.G.: UAV-based acquisition of 3D point cloud - a comparison of a low-cost laser scanner and SFM-tools. Int. Arch. Photogramm. Remote. Sens. Spat. Inf. Sci.-ISPRS Arch. **40**(3W3), 335–341 (2015)

Marcus, W., Fonstad, M.: Optical remote mapping of rivers at sub-meter resolutions and watershed extents. Earth Surf. Process. Landf. **33**, 1491–1501 (2008)

Micheletti, N., Chandler, J.H., Lane, S.N.: Structure from motion (SFM) photogrammetry, vol. 2, pp. 1–12 (2015)

Ministero delle Infrastrutture e dei Trasporti: Aggiornamento delle "Norme Tecniche per le Costruzioni" - NTC 2018, pp. 1–198 (2018)

Morgenthal, G., Hallermann, N.: Quality assessment of Unmanned Acrial Vehicle (UAV) based visual inspection of structures. Adv. Struct. Eng. **17**(3), 289–302 (2014)

Pinto, P.E., Franchin, P., Lupoi, A.: Valutazione e consolidamento dei ponti esistenti in zona sismica, p. 7 (2009)

Power, M., et al.: Seismic Retrofitting Manual for Highway Structures: Part 2 - Retaining Structures, Slopes, Tunnels, Culverts and Roadways. Mceer, 370 p., August 2004

Scheiblauer, C., et al.: Interactions with Gigantic Point Clouds (2014)

Schuetz, M.: Potree: Rendering Large Point Clouds in Web Browsers, p. 84 (2016)

Unione Province Italiane: Nota stampa Ponti: i risultati del monitoraggio delle Province, 0–3 (2018)

Wimmer, M., Scheiblauer, C.: Instant points: fast rendering of unprocessed point clouds. In: Proceedings Symposium on Point-Based Graphics 2006, pp. 129–136 (2006)

Yoon, H., Shin, J., Spencer, B.F.: Structural displacement measurement using an unmanned aerial system. Comput. Aided Civ. Infrastruct. Eng. **33**(3), 183–192 (2018)

The Geological Risk in the Historic Centers

Alessandro Reina(✉), Maristella Loi, and Davide Pellegrini

Polytechnic University of Bari, Via Orabona n.4, 70125 Bari, Italy
{alessandro.reina,maristella.loi}@poliba.it

Abstract. The objective of the present study concerned the determination of the geological risk of the historical center. Risk assessment is a complex issue that aims to assess different aspects of disaster damage. Traditionally, risk analysis is based on a series of historical and site data to verify the probability that an event occurs in a certain place with a certain intensity at a certain time (Orlando et al. 2005a, b). The main limitation of this method is the complexity of the mathematical models necessary to represent reality and therefore it is not always possible to make realistic assumptions about possible future scenarios. Furthermore, the interest is concentrated only on disaster scenarios deriving from a type of geological risk: either floods, or seismicity, etc.

Therefore, a new approach is needed that takes into account all aspects of geological risk as a product of danger and vulnerability, and that will serve to define the response capacity of a territorial disaster system.

A weighted combination of vulnerability and danger has finally allowed to determine the geological risk, whose planning applications urban planning and Civil Protection were examined in detail in the concluding chapters. The evaluation phase is carried out through the Analysis Hierarchy Process method.

The aim of the research is to test procedures of analysis and techniques of geological risk assessment that take into account the complexity of the geological system and the state of the building heritage.

In this work, completely independent of the vulnerability, we proceed to the definition of the danger as the sum of the geomorphological, hydraulic and seismic one.

The result is a mapping of the areas studied (information base) elaborated in a GIS environment consisting of "layers of information layers of danger" interpolated with "layers of information layers on the structural history of the building", descriptive of the state of the building heritage.

The approach is tested in a case study estimating all geological risks in the Municipality of Polignano a Mare (Puglia, Italy).

This contribution showed that the proposed method would allow the development of a methodology that ensures replicability applicable to the various centers in Puglia.

Keywords: Historical heritage · Geological risks · GIS

S. Misra et al. (Eds.): ICCSA 2019, LNCS 11622, pp. 285–296, 2019.
https://doi.org/10.1007/978-3-030-24305-0_22

1 Introduction

The historic centers of Puglia, represent a cultural and historical heritage, which are known, because well documented, the architectural characteristics and the settlement transformations that characterize them. Little or nothing is known about the security conditions of the historical building heritage. The lack of structural investigations, of data on building typologies and of their relationships with the geomorphological, stratigraphic, seismic and hydrogeological conditions on which the historical settlement insists, can lead to the degradation and insecurity of the citizens with the consequent slowing of the modern tourist evolution which is involving most of the historic centers of Puglia.

With this study, for first time, a qualitative-quantitative method is proposed for the evaluation of the risk conditions of the historical centers: the objective of this study was to identify a scientific method able to identify and evaluate the degree of geological risk of the historical centers, by virtue of the conditions, of danger and of the state of vulnerability, of the buildings that make up the historical nucleus.

The objective of the present study concerned the determination of the geological risk of the historical center of the City of Polignano a Mare (Fig. 1).

This objective was pursued by evaluating two parameters deliberately independent of each other: the vulnerability and the dangerousness of the area under study.

This represents the strong point of the experimental path elaborated as it allows the applicability of the method to different types of scenarios simply replacing, if needed, the variables that contribute to their determination.

The territory in question is bounded towards the sea by a high coast with banks, with elevations between 10 m and 25 m.

The coast is articulated by an uninterrupted series of indentations and ledges, to places with small rocks a short distance from the shore. The stretches of ripa with greater difference in height are characterized by the presence of caves and caves most often placed at sea level.

From a morphogenetic point of view, the cliff is a current form resulting mainly from the demolition of the sea and the collapses, presumably of higher Pleistocene age.

The geological structure of the old town of Polignano a mare is very simple: it is characterized by outcropping rocks consisting of calcareniticlithotypes, often fractured and otherwise resistant to mechanical erosion that rest in unconformity on stratified, karst and fractured carbonate rocks of the Cretaceous (Fig. 2).

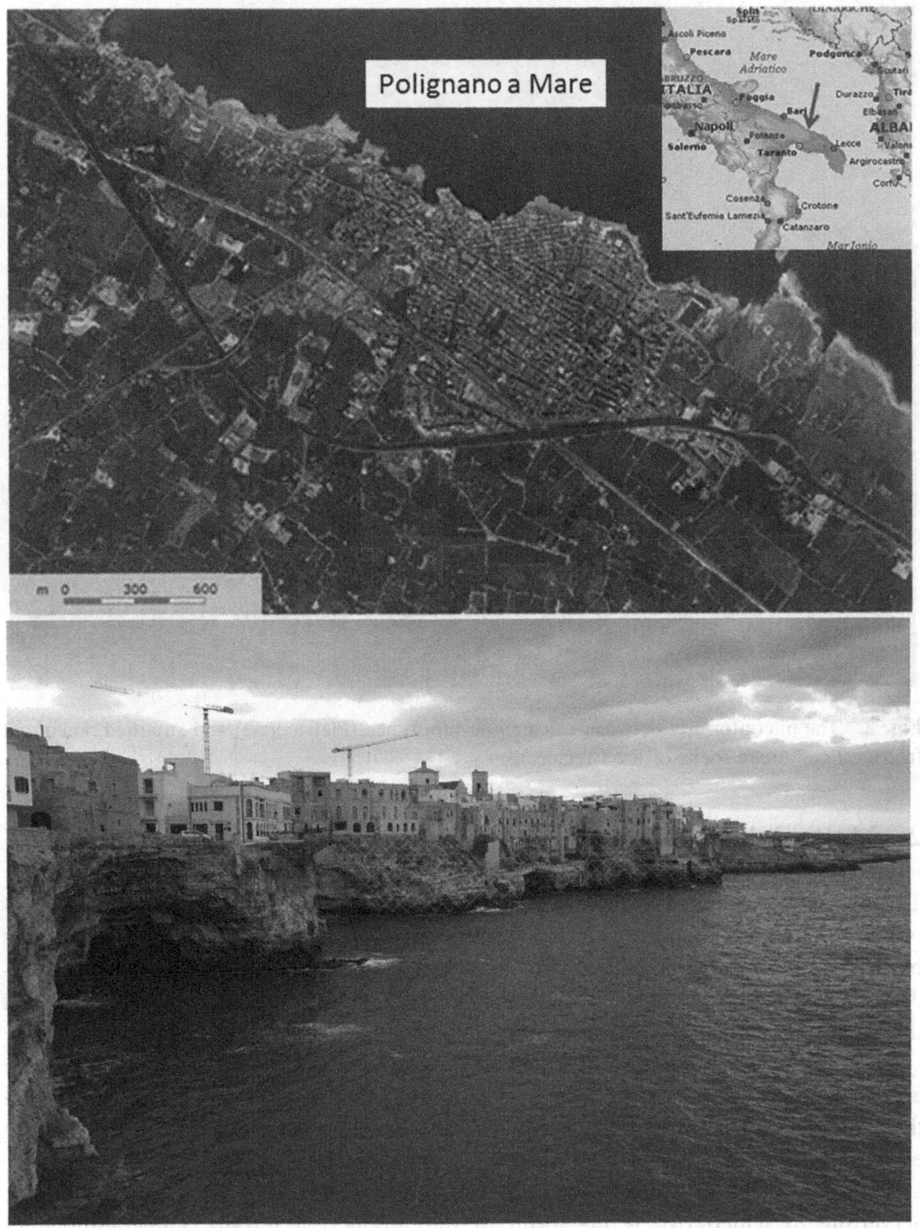

Fig. 1. Location of the city of Polignano a Mare

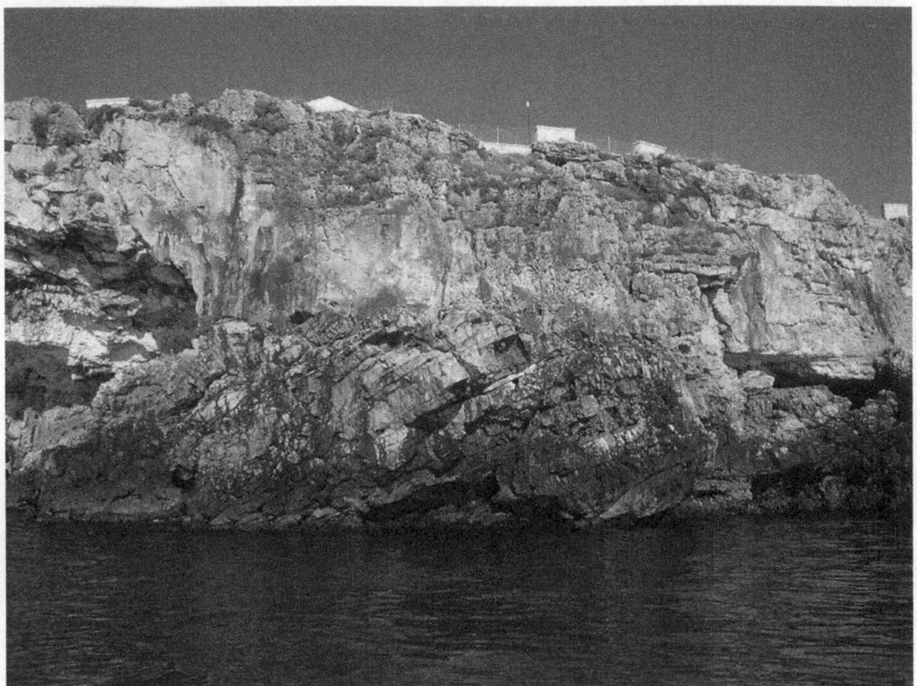

Fig. 2. The unconformity between calcarenitic lithotypes (Pleistocene) and stratified, karst and fractured carbonate rocks of the Cretaceous

2 Methodology

The research is oriented to the definition of a valid method for risk assessment, elaborated through the joint analysis of the architectural and structural characteristics of the built (construction methods, materials etc.) and of the geological dangerousness conditions of the territory considering for example the areas floods, those in landslide and the presence of underground cavities.

It is necessary to establish in which way and to what extent these aspects influence and are influenced by a hypothetical catastrophic event in order to be able to reassure the systemic vulnerability and consequently the damages resulting from a catastrophic event.

Traditionally, ever since a definition of risk was proposed by the UNDRO in 1979, according to which risk is the result of the product of hazard, vulnerability and exposure scores. Therefore, by submitting a model of the receiving system to the expected stress, the possible scenarios are defined and the material damages that follow are identified. The use of these models is certainly useful for the construction of risk scenarios, but it presents at least a double order of problems: the complexity of implementing mathematical models capable of representing phenomenal reality; the impossibility of considering some aspects related to the scenarios produced by catastrophic events.

The emergence of a systemic notion of reality, the discovery of the interrelations that link living beings to each other and to their habitat, have made the notion of the isolability of the single elements of study waver (Menoni 1996).

The joint processing of data relating to the study of danger and vulnerability, through the composition of matrices, defines a scale of risk values (output), to which correspond detailed maps indicative of the degree of safety compared with the degree of vulnerability building (exposure factor and ability to respond to the calamitous event). In the first instance, these assessments will contribute to defining the priority safety measures.

The evaluation phase is carried out through the Analysis Hierarchy Process method (Giangrande 2001), which allows to determine the benefits/costs ratio of a project when it is not possible to evaluate the advantages and disadvantages that would derive from its realization in purely monetary terms (Saaty 1988, 1990; Figueira et al. 2005).

The multi-criteria analysis lends itself to our study as it represents a technique capable of simultaneously taking into account a multiplicity of aspects specific to the problem being faced, both qualitative and quantitative, bringing out the different points of view of the actors involved. It allows, therefore, to determine the relationship between the geological risk and the resilience of an area of historical value, when it is not possible to determine the degree of security with only sector information, i.e. relative to the sole danger or vulnerability only.

The evaluation process first of all involves the construction of a dominance hierarchy, a reticular structure articulated on one or more levels representative of the objectives. The first level contains the general objective of the evaluation (geological risk). Each primary level could be subdivided into lower levels identifying more specific objectives (seismic risk, hydrogeological risk, volcanic risk etc.). The actions to be evaluated (danger and vulnerability) are located at the base of the hierarchy and are directly linked to the more specific objectives (terminal objectives). A hierarchy, in addition to the objectives and actions, may contain other elements of the decision-making process: among these, the actors of the process (the exposure based on the degree of use, the use of the property, etc.) must be included.

The result is a mapping of the areas studied (information base) elaborated in a GIS environment consisting of "layers of information layers of danger" interpolated with "layers of information layers on the structural history of the building", descriptive of the building status of the historical centers.

3 Results and Discussion

Polignano a Mare is a town in the metropolitan city of Bari in Puglia with a resident population as of 1 January 2016 of 18˙023 inhabitants (Istat data).

Located on the Adriatic side of the Murgian plateau, in an intermediate position between the plain of Bari (to NO) and that of Fasano (SE), the Polignano's territory occupies an area of just over 65 km^2 characterized by an almost triangular shape that leads to border with the territories of Mola di Bari, Conversano, CastellanaGrotte and Monopoli.

Its population increases up to 5 times during the summer period as it has a strong tourist value.

The coastline develops in a NO-SE direction of about 16 km: proceeding from north to south, after a couple of kilometers of low coast, the coast continues with a crag stretch whose height varies between 5 m and 10 m, interspersed with narrow and long coves, more or less wide coves and natural caves. The crag reaches heights close to 24 m at the inhabited area (Fig. 3).

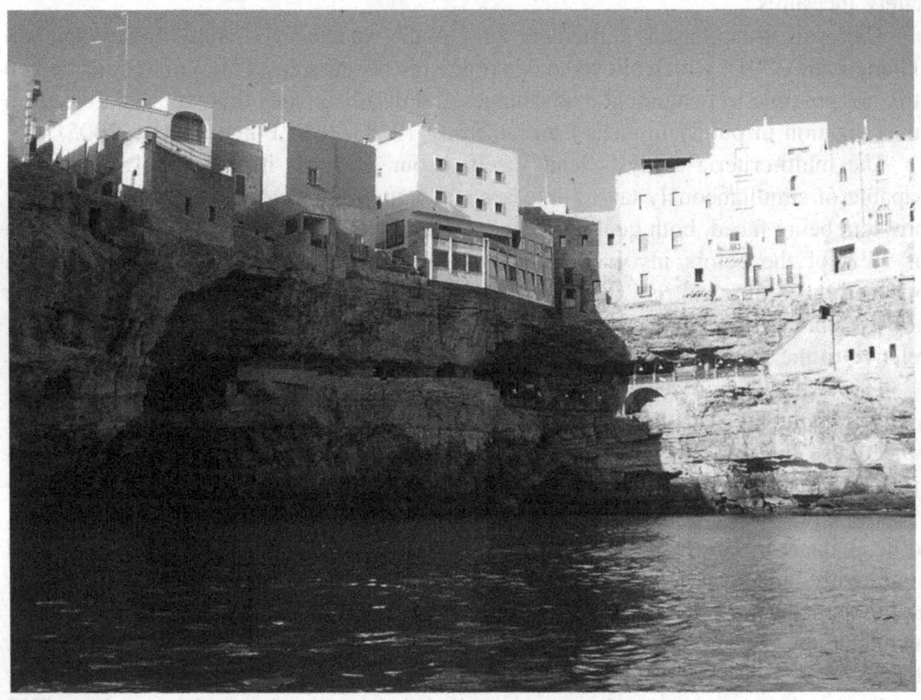

Fig. 3. The cliff of Polignano a Mare

This town was chosen as a case study as the strong tourist value attracts many visitors and therefore lends itself very effectively to the need for a risk assessment, to which the users of the historic center may be exposed.

The historic center of Polignano a Mare has occupied an offshoot of the coast characterized by a cliff between the Monachile Lama, the Bastion of Santo Stefano and the GrottaPalazzese. It has a perimeter that can be estimated around 750 m linear and an area of approximately 32,500 m^2.

All the buildings have been identified by combining the buildings in aggregate and distinguishing them with a progressive number (Fig. 4). For each merger a form has been compiled which defined the construction methods, the structural conditions as well as the use and functionality. All the data contained in the forms have been merged thanks to the use of the GIS to an information database.

Fig. 4. In red identification and numbering of the buildings considered (Color figure online)

In this work the vulnerability is indicated, as the intrinsic capacity of a given element (building or aggregate buildings) to suffer damage due to a significant event, whose entities appear to be a function of the intensity of the phenomenon itself.

Therefore, in order to determine the vulnerability, an analysis of the state of the building heritage (buildings for the vast majority of masonry structures) was necessary, accompanied by an assessment of the exposure, or of the set of relations that are established between the building and the user.

After having carried out the analysis of the state of the building heritage falling within the historical center of Polignano a Mare and after evaluating the exposure of the elements it is possible to combine the two aspects in order to obtain an overall assessment of the vulnerability.

Combining the three classes used to define the state of the buildings with the three exposure classes, nine vulnerability classes are obtained (Fig. 5). The vulnerability map is shown in Fig. 6.

The geomorphological danger of the municipality of Polignano a Mare is the presence of a cliff that characterizes a coastline with a strong regressive tendency (due to erosion) along which we observe the spread of sea caves (Fig. 7).

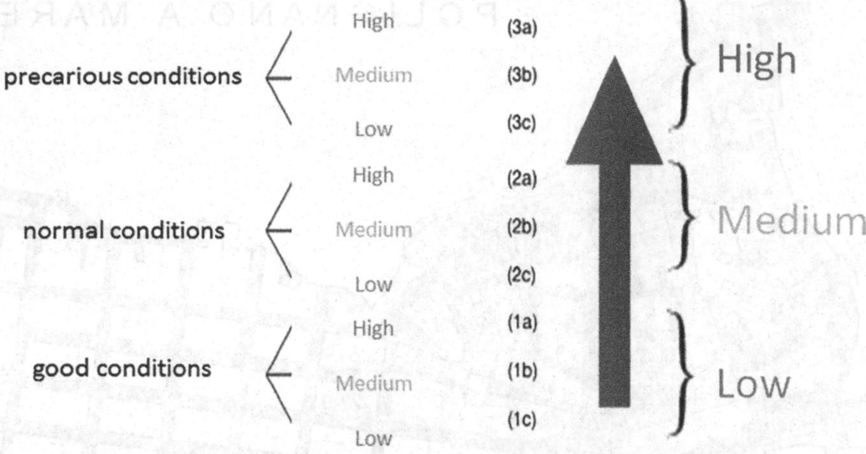

Fig. 5. The nine classes obtained for vulnerability

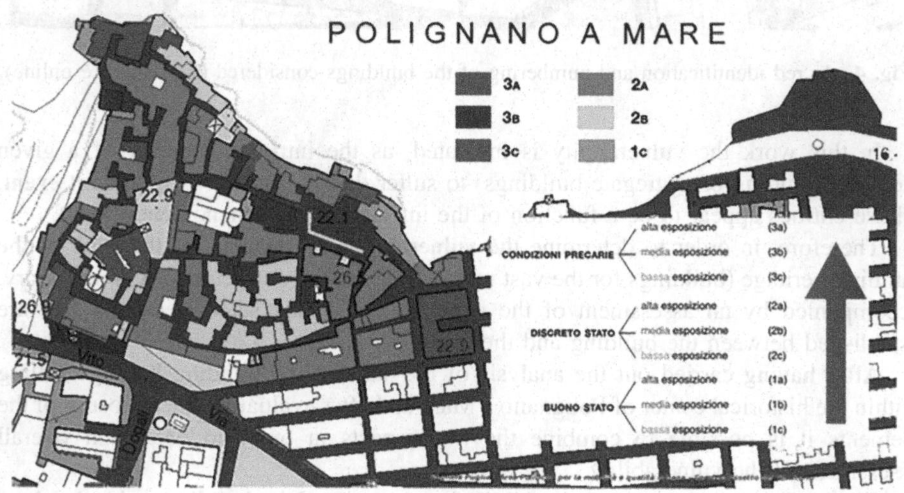

Fig. 6. Vulnerability map

Hazards have been defined depending on the distance from the caves and from the coast. In addition, the perimeter of the areas of hydraulic hazard taken from the hydrogeological planning plan of the district authority of Southern Italy is indicated (Fig. 8).

Belonging to the 4th seismic zone (very low seismicity) and the absence of obvious significant variations in the local seismic response did not lead to further distinctions of a specific nature.

The combination of the 3 hazard classes with the 3 vulnerability classes initially generated 9 risk classes.

Fig. 7. The cliff coast with the widespread presence of sea caves

One of the choices characterizing the experimental path concerned the definition of a hierarchy for the 9 classes: having chosen to assign the same "dignity" to both vulnerability and danger, the following hierarchical scale was obtained, in turn reorganized into 3 different degrees of risk.

To define the danger of each building in the area using the QGIS software, the building was located within the digital map (Fig. 10).

We can talk about geological risk when in a certain area there are dangerous conditions and these interfere with situations of overt vulnerability.

More generally, it can therefore be argued that the geological risk is the set of situations affecting people and assets deriving from the action of slope dynamics, water courses, avalanches and all those processes that, in a real way or potential, they can destabilize the conditions of territorial balance.

From the experimental point of view, the geological risk characterization is fundamentally based on the construction of a matrix able to combine vulnerability analysis with danger analysis.

The combination of the 3 danger classes with the 3 vulnerability classes initially generated 9 risk classes.

One of the choices characterizing the experimental path concerned the definition of a hierarchy for the 9 classes: having chosen to assign the same "dignity" to both vulnerability and danger, the following hierarchical scale was obtained, in turn reorganized into 3 different degrees of risk (Fig. 11).

Fig. 8. In blue the perimeter of the areas of hydraulic hazard (Color figure online)

Fig. 9. The last event of flooding in Polignano a Mare

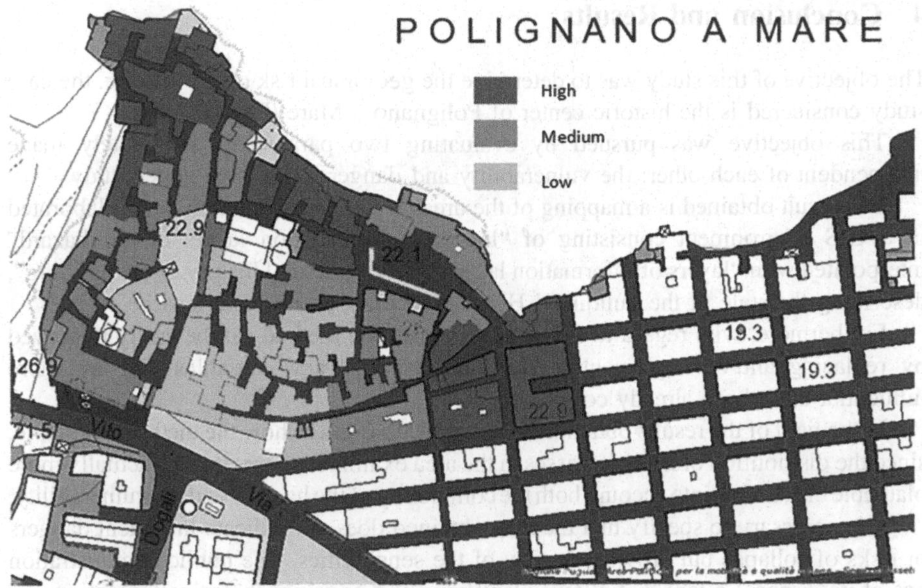

Fig. 10. Dangerousness map

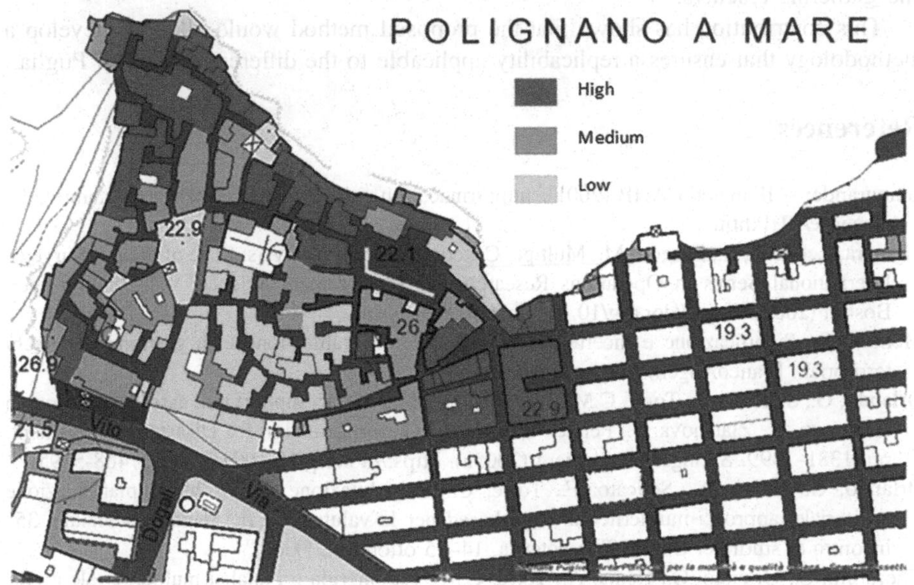

Fig. 11. Risk map

4 Conclusion and Results

The objective of this study was to determine the geological risk of the historic. the case study considered is the historic center of Polignano a Mare (Puglia, Italy).

This objective was pursued by evaluating two parameters deliberately made independent of each other: the vulnerability and danger of the area under study.

The result obtained is a mapping of the areas studied (information base) elaborated in a GIS environment consisting of "layers of information layers of the hazard" interpolated with "layers of information layers on the structural history of the building", describing the state of the buildings' Heritage of the Centers historians.

Furthermore, with regard to the same scenario, the method can be easily improved by replacing and/or implementing the analysis with new variables that are more influential than those already considered.

In the light of the results obtained it is possible to observe how the method is reliable, since the distribution of the risk classes in the area examined represents the actually more plausible one, taking into account both the complexity of the hazards and the vulnerability.

It is necessary to specify that the map obtained does not indicate imminent dangers or risks of collapse but provides a view of the sensitivities. The public administration has at its disposal a tool that allows identifying the priorities in mitigation actions.

An application is aimed at civil protection: it is possible to identify the most sensitive points and therefore the most effective escape routes and waiting areas, shelter and gathering rescuers.

This contribution has shown that the proposed method would allow to develop a methodology that ensures a replicability applicable to the different centers of Puglia.

References

Giangrande: – Il metodo AHP (2001). http://rmac.arch.uniroma3.it/Master/lezioni/giangrande/dispense/AHP.htm

Figueira, J., Greco, S., Ehrgott, M.: Multiple Criteria Decision Analysis: State of the Art Surveys. International Series in Operations Research and Management Science, vol. 78. Springer, Boston (2005). https://doi.org/10.1007/b100605

Menoni, S.: Pianificazione e incertezza. Elementi per la valutazione e la gestione dei rischi territoriali. FrancoAngeli, Milano (1996)

Orlando, G., Selicato, F., Torre, C.M.: The use of GIS as tool to support risk assessment. In: van Oosterom, P., Zlatanova, S., Fendel, E.M. (eds.) Geo-information for Disaster Management, pp. 1381–1399. Springer, Heidelberg (2005a). https://doi.org/10.1007/3-540-27468-5_95

Orlando, G., Reina, A., Selicato, F., Torre, C.M.: Valutazione del rischio e pianificazione territoriale: approcci multicriteriali e gis-based per la valutazione del danno potenziale, 35° incontro di studi del Co.S.E.T. a potenza, 14–15 ottobre (2005b)

Cherubini, C., Orlando, G., Reina, A., Torre, C.M.: La sinergia tra analisi multicriteriale e GIS nella valutazione del rischio da esondazione: il bacino della lama Baronale-Picone, Provincia di Bari, Giornale di Geologia Applicata, vol. 3, pp. 109–113 (2006)

Saaty, T.L.: Multicriteria Decision Making - The Analytic Hierarchy Process. Planning, Priority Setting, Resource Allocation. RWS Publishing, Pittsburgh (1988)

Saaty, T.L.: Decision Making for Leaders – The Analytic Hierarchy Process for Decisions in a Complex World. RWS Publishing, Pittsburgh (1990)

A Crowd-Sensing System for Geomatics Applications

Lorenzo Boccia[1], Alessandra Capolupo[2(✉)], Giuseppina Esposito[1], Giuseppe Mansueto[1], and Eufemia Tarantino[3]

[1] Department of Architecture, University of Naples Federico II, Via Forno Vecchio, 12, 80134 Naples (NA), Italy

[2] Plinivs Research Center - LUPT, University of Naples Federico II, Via Toledo, 402, 80134 Naples (NA), Italy
alessandra.capolupo@unina.it

[3] DICATECh, Politecnico di Bari, Via E. Orabona 4, 70125 Bari, Italy

Abstract. Risk prevention is recognized as one of the most critical aspects of the policies of environmental monitoring. Because of the limited resources and the large amount of structures used for erosion control and slope protection, the Civil Protection and the Italian Forestry Carabinieri are not able to supervise them directly, with enough frequency. The present work is aimed to develop an innovative technique for periodically monitoring those structures, combining Mobile Crowd-Sensing (MCS) technology with photogrammetry and GIS. The experiments were performed in the Nature Reserve of Tirone (a protected natural area located inside the Vesuvius National Park in Naples) by analysing the metric reconstruction of two structures (a small weir and a log crib wall), before and after an accident, artificially generated for simulating a hydrogeological event or an act of vandalism, in order to evaluate GCPs influence. The procedure was split into four main phases: periodic acquisition of sets of photos with common smartphones and their transmission via the Internet; elaboration of the threedimensional model starting from a subset of selected pictures; comparison between the generated and the previous model; database update and programming of the subsequent monitoring. The accuracy of photogrammetric reconstructions was evaluated comparing the reconstruction with and without Ground Control Points (GCPs). The results show the models extracted without GCPs are satisfactory, since they allow to retrieve dimensional information of the examined constructions and to detect any instability. Models, generated using GCPs, are more detailed, but the processing and operational time is strongly higher.

Keywords: Crowd sensing · Photogrammetry · Structures monitoring

1 Introduction

The Italian Statistical Institute (ISTAT) classifies the national territory into 35.2% of mountains, 41.6% of hills and only 23.2% of plains. In such a morphologically complex territory, a large hydrogeological instability ensues [1]. Disastrous events such as ones occurred in Liguria Region in 2011 and 2014, in Messina and Giampilieri in 2009, in Sarno in 1998, in Amalfi coast in 1954, causing more than 500 life losses and

S. Misra et al. (Eds.): ICCSA 2019, LNCS 11622, pp. 297–312, 2019.
https://doi.org/10.1007/978-3-030-24305-0_23

huge damages to the built environment. [2] expressed the Risk (R) as the convolution of Hazard intensity (H), Exposure (E) and vulnerability (V) (Eq. 1):

$$R = H * E * V \tag{1}$$

Currently, risk assessment and management is an essential operational field to tackle and monitor hydrological instability, even if a promising result may be achieved only thanks to a permanent and constant activity. All of this implies that the permanent management of the mountain and hill territory, where are a large amount of structures used for the erosion control or slope stabilization, built using both traditional techniques and bioengineering approaches, is necessary in addition to the management of watercourses and the main landuse. Some small structures, such as small weirs, retaining walls, live fascines, brush layering and palisades, small stream diversions etc., are individually characterized by a little importance; on the contrary, when they are grouped and considered together, they represent fundamental elements able to protect the territory. An inventory plan of these constructions, commonly built without a real project and not subjected to any maintained plan, is missed and, therefore, often, they are not subjected to any monitoring by Basin Authorities, Regions and Civil Protection. Moreover, many of them are also located in areas difficult to access and to notice. These situations exceeds 10000 units, although our estimate exceeds 50000 situations on the Italian national territory. In the past, the State Forestry Corps, a police force responsible for governing and controlling the agro-forestry area, now called Carabinieri Forestali, exercise a monitoring and control action. The use of the mountains and hills for agro-livestock activities was itself a monitoring action. Because of the progressive urbanization, the reduction of the Carabinieri Forestry and the new assigned tasks, the problem of technical monitoring becomes even more important. In the forestry field, the satellite imagery and/or drone technology has not brought the same advantages as in other areas due to the presence of vegetation. Monitoring have to be carried out by explorers. Furthermore, monitoring is qualitative and the decision-making action in the event of changes in the state of the places belongs to the explorers. The scout must have a considerable technical skill and know the single construction. The interest in modern monitoring, on the contrary, is focused in reducing the operational time and the involvement of technicians, leaving them the ultimate choice and the ultimate responsibilities but not the operational tasks, assigned to less qualified staff. Not a high accuracy is required for those kind of structures, therefore that metric reconstruction should be satisfactory. Nowadays, the awareness of citizens is more sensitive and open-minded regarding the environment and the protection of the territory; moreover, many of them are also available to share information and data (Crowd). In the meanwhile, new methodolo- 3 gies are available, such as smartphones equipped with high resolution cameras and a built-in Global Position System (GPS). Also the 4G network, available since 2013 in most of the nations, is an essential prerequisite to largely widespread the smartphone use in surveying. The latest generation photogrammetry is undoubtedly much faster than in the past and authors such as [3–6] try urban buildings and artifact reconstructions, without ground control points.

According to these premises the research is aimed to demonstrate the possibility to create an integrated technology, suitable for delegating to surveyors not nspecialized, the scout action. Evaluating how to obtain an elaboration suitable to emphasize any critical issues and reduce the intervention of the high profile technicians only during the decision-making moment, on the basis of sufficiently detailed and sufficiently accurate quantitative information, is in additional purpose of the current research activity. The high skilled technician, thanks to this support, should be able to take a binary decision regarding the monitoring rescheduling or related the necessary to send a specialized engineer on the field to supervise the structures [7].

2 Materials and Method

2.1 Study Area and Selection of the Structures to Be Investigated

The experiment was conducted in Tirone-Alto Vesuvio Reserve, in the area of the Vesuvius National Park in the Province of Naples (southern Italy), characterized by the presence of small hydraulic-forestry structures, built using both traditional techniques and naturalistic engineering techniques. During a first survey, two study cases, representing a widespread constructions typology in the Campania Region that can be investigated by applying the crowd sensing, were selected: a log crib wall and a small weir. More than 2000 of these structures are scattered throughout Campania Region [8].

Fig. 1. Study case in the Tirone Alto-Vesuvio Reserve (Vesuvius Natural Park. Napoli, Italy): (a) structure 2 - log crib wall, (b) structure 5 – small weir to prevent gulling and land sliding in a occasional stream.

The former (Fig. 1a) is a grid of wooden trunks (a log crib wall), able to support a small slope of about 5 m and about 15 m in height and in plan, respectively. The frequency of its maintenance is typically fixed to ten-years. The latter (Fig. 1b) is a small weir (properly a step) long about 5 m and height about 1.50 m. The outflanking due to stream diversions, the breaking of the crest and the sediment accumulation upstream are the typical failures of these constructions. Verifying both the maintenance status and the functionality of the construction is the final purpose.

2.2 Operational Workflow

All the applied procedure is summarized in the workflow, described in Fig. 2. It consists of five steps:

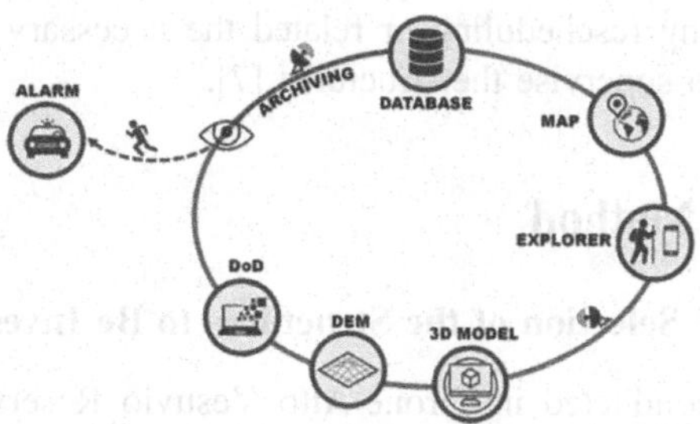

Fig. 2. Proposed workflow

1. creating a digital database (DB) of the structures of the territory to be monitored;
2. generating maps of georeferenced flags;
3. surveying the camp by applying selected operators or volunteers, called by us "scout";
4. Carrying out photogrammetric and GIS elaboration through specialized operators (3D model, DEM, DoD);
5. evaluating the risk: reporting alarm and/or updating of database.

The database (DB) has to be developed on an online platform and progressively updated and integrated with new information and objects. The complete geographic information has to be collected and organized for each structure. The DB must report the date of last inspection and that one of subsequent survey, the authorized scouts, risk level classification, the historical series of acquired image sets, photogrammetric reconstructions, DEM etc. The database produces periodically a set of viewpoints (flags), that will be sent to a group of scouts. Each scout receives all the information related to the target that he should survey.

The scout acquires the images of the target by applying an own Smartphone. In our case, we used a Smartphone, an Iphone 7 Plus. The scout has to follow the specific 5 guidelines with the support of a certified App and tutorials. The surveys must be carried out during the day, possibly avoiding time slots in which shadows are too sharp. The device must be keep vertical with the A-GPS turned on. Collecting an adequate number of images, characterized by the overlap of 60% and 80%, longitudinally and transversally direction, respectively, in order to assure that every point appears in three images at least [9]. In perspective, a dedicated App will implement various functions, like as the zoom block, the vibrations for the nonverticality of the sensor, the real time check of defocused and blurry images, and the measure of the distance between camera positions. SfM (Structure from Motion) software's is necessary to collect the images during the movement [10]. When the images of the target are acquired by a camera, the app should also inform the scout, though an acoustic signals, if its motion is too fast [11].

Subsequently, the acquired data will be sent via 4G or Wi-fi to a powerful calculation station. Photogrammetric elaboration will be performed by a specialist with a dedicated photogrammetric software. The procedure was described in depth in [12, 13]. Once the virtual inspection of the metric reconstruction and the measure of any defect points have been completed, any degradation situations and the estimation of the accumulated materials will be investigated through the comparison between the baseline and the successive 3D models.

The 3D model will be obtained thanks to through the metric reconstruction. The outcome of this step is the generation of a high resolution Digital Elevation Model (DEM). The comparison between the two DEMs, overlapping them, highlights all the dimensional anomalies and allows to quantify the differences. The outcome of that procedure is the Dem of Differences (DoD) [14]. This operation is pretty laborious since the models generated by the photogrammetric reconstructions without (GCPs Ground Control Points) cannot be geo-located with sub-metric precision, and, therefore, the DEMs reposition should be performed. This step allows to emphasize and objectively quantify some issues, such as an excessive deposition, erosion of weir material, undercutting, debris upstream or downstream of a weir, etc. The final step is related to the evaluation of the operation capability of the specialist to identify and quantify the action need without using instrumental measures. Just few technicians are skilled for such kind of decisions. These skilled technicians are involved only in this phase. Their decision will be supported by the 3D models and the DoD. In any case, all acquired and processed images are archived into the database in view of the next monitoring campaign. The alarming situations are signalled and checked with inspections and interventions or notifications.

2.3 Crowd Sensing Operations

For each case study, about 100 photographs were taken using a iPhone7 Plus, equipped with a 12 MP wide-angle camera - pixel size of 1.22 microns and a focal length of 3.99 mm. At a shooting distance shorter than 15 m, the Ground Sample 6 Distance (GSD) is better than 5 mm. The autofocus zoom effect and all pre-calibrated settings were deactivated. The operator, moving himself sideways with single steps from a short distance (5-8 m), acquired three sets of about 30 photos: the former keeping the camera at chest height (1.2 m), the latter at eye level (1.7 m) and, the last slightly inclining the camera (tilt of about 15°) at the height of about 2 m (Fig. 3). On the second site, a damage or a vandalism act was simulated. The purpose is to validate the methodology in case of changes in the state of a forestry structure (Fig. 4). 3D model reconstructions of each structure, were obtained with the software Agisoft PhotoScan. The initial step is the alignment of the input photos. The algorithms of PhotoScan automatically identify the tie points in each photo and build the Sparse Points Cloud and realign the photos. Really, since the GCPs coordinates are in ETRS 89, when these GCPs are used, the photos are reoriented in ETRS 89 ETRF2000. The GCPs, if used, were localized manually in each photos (Figs. 5, 6 and 7 and Tables 1 and 2).

In order to assess the accuracy of the photogrammetric reconstructions, a series of paper targets (black and white circle of 80 mm in diameter) were positioned along the areas of interest and their coordinates were measured. The survey of Ground Control

Fig. 3. Example of image acquisition: H is the height of camera sensor and d is the distance between the operator and the structure 2.

Fig. 4. Simulated damage in front to Structure 5.

Fig. 5. Three-dimensional reconstruction of Structure 2 with the GCPs

Fig. 6. Three-dimensional reconstruction of Structure 5 with the picture alignment

Fig. 7. Workflow reconstruction of structure 5: (a) Loading Photos with target, (b) Reconstruction of a Sparse Point Cloud, (c) Reconstruction of Dense Point Cloud, (d) Build 3D Mesh (the GCPs are blue flags and in this case are used only for dimensional control of the results) (Color figure online)

Table 1. Number of points elaborated for a three-dimensional reconstruction

Structure 2	No. of photos	Sparse points	Dense points
With GCPs	38	2.6×10^4	1.2×10^6
Without GCPs	38	2.3×10^4	1.2×10^6

Table 2. Number of points elaborated for a three-dimensional reconstruction

Structure 5	No. of photos	Sparse points	Dense points	DEM resolution (mm/pixel)
With GCPs	42	2.4×10^4	1.2×10^7	3.96
Without GCPs	40	2.5×10^4	1.2×10^7	4.88
Without GCPs	48	2.3×10^4	1.4×10^7	4.43

Points (GCPs) was carried out using a Geomax GPS Zenith 35, connected via 4G to the Campania Region's permanent network of stations to obtain, in real time, the signal corrections (Differential Global Positioning System in RTK DGPS). In forestry field, this DGPS configuration is susceptible to reflections and disturbance to GPS signal (due to weak 4G connection, presence of tall vegetation), so it was decided to use also a Geodimeter 600 PRO total station. Since it was desired to obtain coordinates of the GCPs in ETRS89 ETRF 2000 system, the surveys, carried out using the total station, were calculated by orienting the station applying the inverse intersection (Snellius Pothenot), manually solved on three DGPS points, using points where the GPS had provided good accuracies. Furthermore, it was decided to compare photogrammetric 3D reconstruction with and without GCPs for each site. As suggested by [15] the accuracy was evaluated by computing the scatterplot between the measured and the estimated values (Fig. 8).

Fig. 8. (a) Target, (b) Measurement of the GCPs by Structure 2 using DGPS, (c) Measurement of the coordinates of GCPs by Structure 5 using dGPS, (d) Measurement of GCPs by Structure 2 with the Total Station

3 Results

In order to evaluate the reconstruction accuracy, 13 mutual Euclidian distances among the GCPs coordinates were calculated. Subsequently, in each reconstruction with GCPs, the same distances were measured with the "Scale Bar" tool of the Software Agisoft: the paper target were directly detected on the 3D model and a yellow line joined the selected points. Figure 9 shows the decimated mesh of structure 2: the scale bars in part A were more accurate than the scale bars of the part B.

The two reconstructions without GCPs and targets were opportunely scaled using one reference distance as input, in order to obtain the same effect that is possible inserting in the photo scene a Range Pole. For the first structure, the reference distance is 1.46 m between the GCPs 1003 and 1004, and for the second structure is 1.40 m between GCPs 2018–2020. After this operation, a new mesh was created and the distances (reported in the table) were measured. Figure 10 shows the same reference scale bar in two pictures, one with targets and the other without them. In the second case, the recognition of the reference points is more difficult. Figure 10c shows the scale bars obtained for the second structure after the simulated damage. After the simulated damage, the point 2021 was covered by the woods and, in this case, was impossible to measure the Euclidean distances. The results of measurements and their comparison in term of difference and percentage difference were listed in Tables 3, 4, 5, 6 and 7. Moreover, in order to evaluate outcomes accuracy also the average (μ), the Root Mean Square Error (RMSE) (Tables 3, 4, 5 and 6), scatterplots and coefficient of correlation (Fig. 11).

The best results were obtained from the model reconstruction with the aid of GCPs, with a standard deviation of 0.02 for the first structure and 0.04 for the second structure. As expected, the standard deviations of the differences obtained from the comparison with the reconstructions without GCPs and the Euclidean distances are highest (0.13 for the structure 2 and 0.09 for the structure 5). The distance measured on the 3D model of the structure 5 after the damage compared with the Euclidian distance gives an excellent result in term of standard deviation ($\sigma = 0.05$). These results demonstrate that the methodology is consistent with the aim of the paper. For these structures, actually commonly monitored without any measure but only on the base of the experience, an accuracy of the order of 0.1 m is largely satisfactory. The scatterplot and the coefficient of correlation of each group composed by estimated and measured points show a very high values: R^2 is higher than 0.99.

The Digital Elevation Models (DEMs) of the site 5 - before and after damage - were generated in Agisoft PhotoScan. The first and the second DEMs was georeferenced using ArcMap and overlap. DEMs are shown in Figs. 11 and 12. The colour scale ranges from red (inferior altitude) to green (superior altitude). The DoD was generated by subtracting the DEM before and after the damage. Figure 13 illustrates the DoD: the red areas represent the negative differences in altitude and the yellow areas indicates the

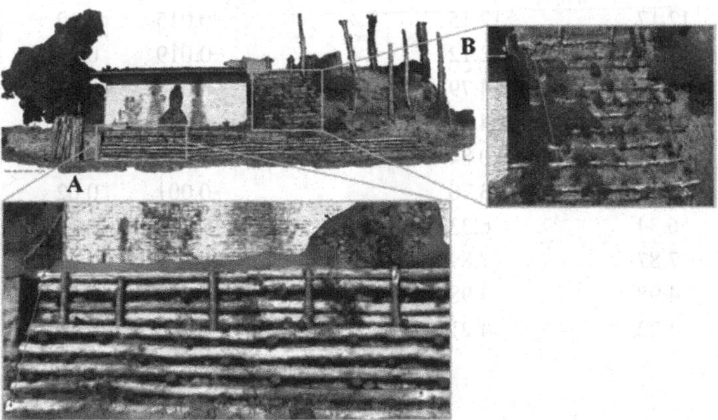

Fig. 9. Zoom of the 3D model of the Structure 2: (A) (B). Detail of the scale bar used to measure and the distance between three GCPs (1001. 1002. 1003) for the comparison with the measures with the total station.

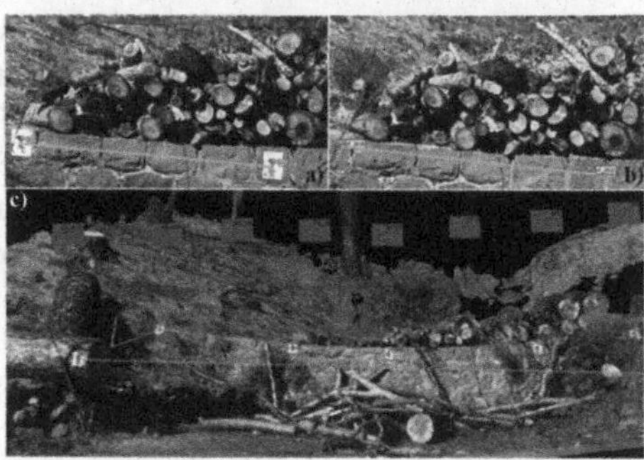

Fig. 10. Scale Bar between GCPs 2018 and 2020 of Structure 5 in (a) photo with Target, (b) photo without Target, (c) 3D Model post-damage.

positive difference. The blue areas reflect the absence of surface reconstruction. The areas in green are characterized by negligible differences in terms of altitude. The DoD emphasizes the failure when submitted to the attention of an expert of the forestry service.

Table 3. Euclidean distance between point A and point B of structure 2, calculated using the coordinates: measured (second column) and estimated from the reconstruction of the 3D model with Target Ground Control Points (third column). Difference between measured distance and the estimated distance (fourth column) and percentage difference (fifth column). SD: Standard Deviation, μ: average, RMSE: Root Mean Square Error

ID point	Measured distance (m)	Measured distance with GCPs (m)	Difference (m)	Percentage difference (%)
1001–1002	1.84	1.85	0.008	0.43
1001–1003	5.05	5.02	−0.023	0.46
1001–1004	5.01	5.00	−0.018	0.37
1001–1005	12.17	12.15	−0.015	0.12
1001–1006	12.13	12.12	−0.019	0.16
1002–1003	4.81	4.79	−0.018	0.37
1007–1008	4.33	4.27	−0.060	1.39
1008–1009	0.84	0.84	0.00004	0.005
1010–1011	3.70	3.70	−0.001	0.02
1010–1012	6.34	6.33	−0.006	0.10
1010–1014	7.87	7.89	0.021	0.27
1011–1012	4.98	4.98	−0.004	0.07
1014–1015	4.22	4.21	−0.007	0.16
SD			**0.02**	
μ			**0.01**	
RMSE			**0.02**	

Table 4. Euclidean distance between point A and point B of structure 2, calculated using the coordinates: measured (second column) and estimated from the reconstruction of the 3D model without Target Ground Control Points (third column). Difference between the measured distance and the estimated distance (fourth column) and percentage difference (fifth column). SD: Standard Deviation, μ: average, RMSE: Root Mean Square Error

ID point	Measured distance (m)	Measured distance without GCPs (m)	Difference (m)	Percentage difference (%)
1001–1002	1.84	1.78	0.057	3.12
1001–1003	5.05	4.88	0.163	3.24
1001–1004	5.01	4.82	0.191	3.81
1001–1005	12.17	11.72	0.447	3.67
1001–1006	12.13	11.74	0.389	3.21
1002–1003	4.81	4.65	0.154	3.20
1007–1008	4.33	4.21	0.117	2.70
1008–1009	0.84	0.82	0.028	3.32
1010–1011	3.70	3.60	0.098	2.64
1010–1012	6.34	6.08	0.257	4.05
1010–1014	7.87	7.47	0.396	5.03
1011–1012	4.98	4.80	0.183	3.68
1014–1015	4.22	3.99	0.232	5.51
SD			**0.13**	
μ			**0.01**	
RMSE			**0.02**	

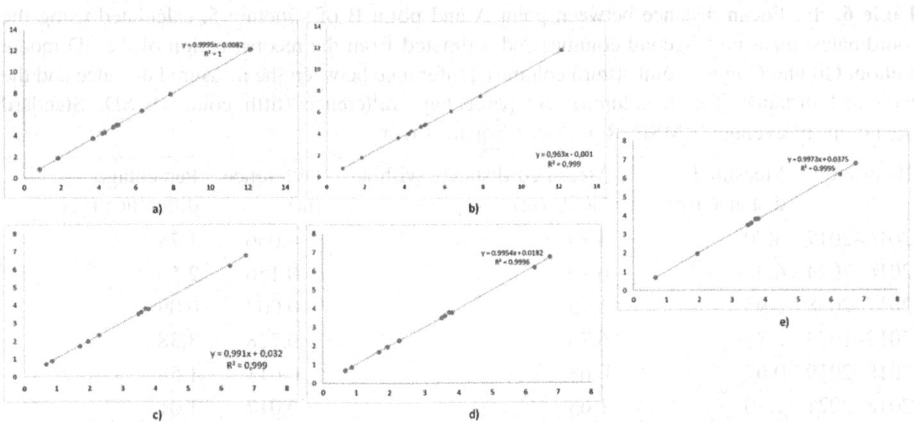

Fig. 11. Scatterplot between measured and estimated values. (a) Scatterplot corresponding to Table 3, (b) Scatterplot corresponding to Table 4, (c) Scatterplot corresponding to Table 5, (d) Scatterplot corresponding to Table 6, (e) Scatterplot corresponding to Table 7.

Table 5. - Euclidean distance between point A and point B of structure 5, calculated using the coordinates: measured (second column) and estimated from the reconstruction of the 3D model with Target Ground Control Points (third column). Difference between the measured distance and the estimated distance (fourth column) and percentage difference (fifth column). SD: Standard Deviation, μ: average, RMSE: Root Mean Square Error

ID point	Measured distance (m)	Measured distance without GCPs (m)	Difference (m)	Percentage difference (%)
2016–2017	3.70	3.79	0.085	2.31
2016–2024	6.27	6.19	−0.081	1.29
2017–2018	1.95	1.95	0.003	0.17
2017–2023	6.75	6.76	0.012	0.18
2018–2019	0.67	0.68	0.009	1.40
2018–2021	1.70	1.68	−0.017	1.03
2018–2022	3.48	3.49	0.006	0.18
2019–2022	3.57	3.59	0.018	0.50
2020–2021	0.86	0.86	−0.007	0.78
2021–2022	2.28	2.30	0.023	1.00
2023–2024	3.79	3.77	−0.021	0.54
2016–2017	3.70	3.79	0.085	2.31
2016–2024	6.27	6.19	−0.081	1.29
SD			**0.05**	
μ			**0.03**	
RMSE			**0.05**	

Table 6. Euclidean distance between point A and point B of structure 5, calculated using the coordinates: measured (second column) and estimated from the reconstruction of the 3D model without Ground Control Points (third column). Difference between the measured distance and the estimated distance (fourth column) and percentage difference (fifth column). SD: Standard Deviation, μ: average, RMSE: Root Mean Square Error

ID point	Measured distance (m)	Measured distance without GCPs (m)	Difference (m)	Percentage difference (%)
2016–2017	3.70	3.79	0.066	1.78
2016–2024	6.27	6.19	−0.156	2.50
2017–2018	1.95	1.95	−0.002	0.09
2017–2023	6.75	6.76	−0.228	3.38
2018–2019	0.67	0.68	0.011	1.58
2018–2021	1.70	1.68	−0.017	1.01
2018–2022	3.48	3.49	−0.058	1.67
2019–2022	3.57	3.59	−0.065	1.81
2020–2021	0.86	0.86	0.010	1.21
2021–2022	2.28	2.30	−0.027	1.21
2023–2024	3.79	3.77	−0.200	5.27
SD			**0.09**	
μ			**– 0.06**	
RMSE			**0.011**	

Table 7. Euclidean distance between point A and point B of structure 5, calculated using the coordinates: measured (second column) and estimated from the reconstruction of the 3D model with target and without Ground Control Points (third column). After the simulation of a damage. Difference between the measured distance and the estimated distance (fourth column) and percentage difference (fifth column). SD: Standard Deviation, μ: average, RMSE: Root Mean Square Error

ID point	Measured distance (m)	Measured distance without GCPs (m)	Difference (m)	Percentage difference (%)
2016–2017	3.70	3.82	0.119	3.22
2016–2024	6.27	6.22	−0.051	0.81
2017–2018	1.95	1.96	0.007	0.35
2017–2023	6.75	6.79	0.037	0.55
2018–2019	0.67	0.68	0.006	0.89
2018–2021	1.70			
2018–2022	3.48	3.50	0.019	0.55
2019–2022	3.57	3.60	0.032	0.89
2020–2021	0.86			
2021–2022	2.28			
2023–2024	3.79	3.83	0.035	0.93
SD			**0.05**	
μ			**− 0.03**	
RMSE			**0.05**	

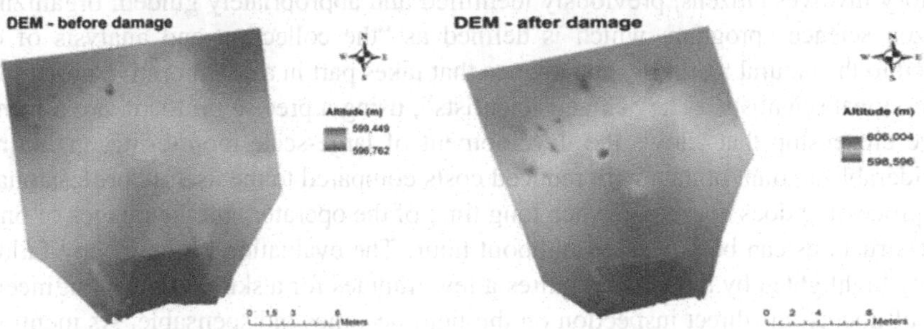

Fig. 12. Digital elevation models: (a) before the damage, (b) after the damage.

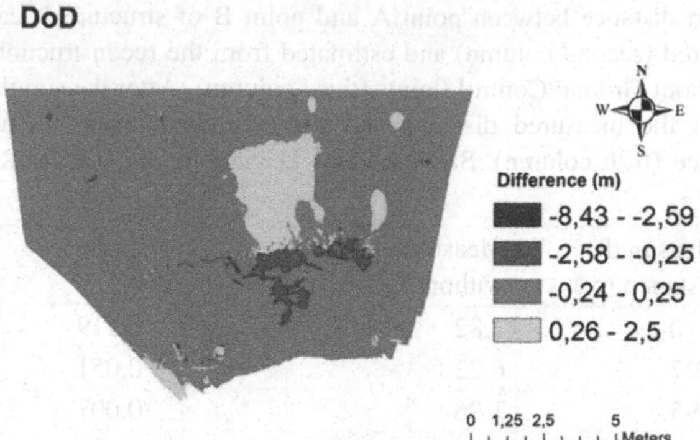

Fig. 13. DoD between the digital elevation model before the damage and the digital elevation model after the damage.

4 Conclusions

The paper is focused on the investigation of small structures in forestry or in mountain areas. Indeed, the paper is aimed to identify a procedure for monitoring the structures for erosion control and slope stabilization, often located in remote locations, without the involvement of professional engineers on the site in order to optimize the use of human high skilled resources. Subsequently, also the quantification of the conditions were conducted. 14 The experiment showed that the methodology is suitable for reaching the objectives of the research. The monitoring of these structures on the territory involves citizens, previously identified and appropriately guided, organizing a "citizen science" program, which is defined as "the collection and analysis of data related to the natural world by an audience that takes part in a collaborative project with professional scientists". The "citizen scientists", using a precise protocol, are a form of active citizenship that allows the development of large-scale monitoring, gathering a considerable amount of data with reduced costs compared to the use of "professionals". The processing does not require such long time of the operator and the images of one or more structures can be processed in about hour. The evaluation phase of any failures, clearly highlighted by the DoD, requires a few minutes for a skilled Forest engineer. In case of doubts, the direct inspection on the field becomes indispensable. As mentioned above, this technique is not proposed for infrastructural constructions, such as bridges or dams. On the contrary, It is well applicable to constructions for which the risk is little or the exposed value is punctually limited or the vulnerability is limited. These constructions are usually poorly monitored, although their failures or lack of maintenance increase the hydrogeology instability of the territory. A quantitative measurement system, such as the one tested, albeit inaccurate, is much more reliable than qualitative assessments based on the memory of the constructions and situations seen years before. The precision of the measurements is not a fundamental parameter in this case; on the contrary, the accuracy that allows the comparison with previous conditions is essential. It was shown that the proposed methodology achieved decimetric accuracy, sufficient in the forest environment. The successive step consists in the development of an App suitable to disable the zoom and the special effects (like the HDR option), stop the steps and click with sounds, activate the GPS, control the vertical position of the camera, etc., during the acquisition phase. This technique would lead the creation of a 3D database of constructions, largely spread overall the territory, which would progressively be enriched, allowing the planned and orderly management of the thousands of small widespread structures, destined for oblivion.

Acknowledgement. This study was financed by the I.Z.S.Me/C.I.R.AM "Campania trasparente".

References

1. ISTAT annuario statistico italiano 2017, pp. 5–55. ISBN 978-88-458-1933-9. https://www.istat.it/it/files/2017/12/Asi-2017.pdf. Accessed 20 Mar 2019
2. Varnes, D.J.: Landslide hazard zonation: a review of principles and practice (1984). ISBN 92-3-101895-7. https://unesdoc.unesco.org/ark:/48223/pf0000063038
3. Angelats, E., Parés, M.E., Kumar, P.: Feasibility of smartphone based photogrammetric point clouds for the generation of accessibility maps. In: 2018 ISPRS TC II Mid-term Symposium "Towards Photogrammetry 2020". The International Archives of the Photogrammetry, Remote Sensing and Spatial Information Sciences, vol. XLII-2, Riva del Garda, Italy, 4–7 June 2018
4. Caradonna, G., Tarantino, E., Scaioni, M., Figorito, B.: Multi-image 3D reconstruction: a photogrammetric and structure from motion comparative analysis. In: Gervasi, O., et al. (eds.) ICCSA 2018, Part V. LNCS, vol. 10964, pp. 305–316. Springer, Cham (2018). https://doi.org/10.1007/978-3-319-95174-4_25
5. Nocerino, E., Poiesi, F., Remondino, F., Van Gool, L.: Point clouds from smartphones. GIM Int. **32**(3), 18–21 (2018)
6. Masiero, A., Fissore, F., Pirotti, F., Guarnieri, A., Vettore, A.: Toward the use of smartphones for mobile mapping. Geo-Spatial Inf. Sci. **19**(3), 210–221 (2016). https://doi.org/10.1080/10095020.2016.1234684
7. Di grazia, F., Cantelli, L., Fabbri, S., Grumiero, B.: Citizen – photographers help environmental monitoring thanks to a photogrammetric approach, Geophysical Research Abstracts, vol. 20, EGU2018-18099, 2018 EGU General Assembly 2018 (2018)
8. Triglia, A., Iadanza, C., Bussettini, M., Lastoria, B.: Dissesto idrogeologico in Italia: pericolosità ed indicatori di rischio – Edizione 2018. Ispra, Rapporti 287/2018 (2018)
9. Micheletti, N., Chandler, J.H., Lane, S.N.: Investigating the geomorphological potential of freely available and accessible structure-from-motion photogrammetry using a smartphone. Earth Surf. Process. Landf. **40**, 473–486 (2015)
10. Schönberger, J.L., Frahm, J.M.: Structure-from-motion revisited. In: IEEE Conference on Computer Vision and Pattern Recognition, pp. 4104–4113 (2016)
11. Nocerino, E., et al.: 3D reconstruction with a collaborative approach based on smartphones and a cloud-based server. In: 2017 5th International Workshop LowCost 3D – Sensors, Algorithms, Applications. The International Archives of the Photogrammetry, Remote Sensing and Spatial Information Sciences, vol. XLII-2/W8, Hamburg, Germany, 28–29 November 2017

12. Capolupo, A., Pindozzi, S., Okello, C., Fiorentino, N., Boccia, L.: Photogrammetry for environmental monitoring: the use of drones and hydrological models for detection of soil contaminated by copper. Sci. Total Environ. **514**, 298–306 (2015). https://doi.org/10.1016/j.scitotenv.2015.01.109. ISSN: 0048-9697
13. Capolupo, A., Pindozzi, S., Okello, C., Boccia, L.: Indirect field technology for detecting areas object of illegal spills harmful to human health: application of drones, photogrammetry and hydrological models. Geospatial Health **8**, 699–707 (2014). https://doi.org/10.4081/gh.2014.298. ISSN: 1970-7096
14. Capolupo, A., Cervelli, E., Pindozzi, S., Boccia, L.: Assessing volumetric and geomorphologic changes of terraces in Amalfi Coast using photogrammetric technique. In: International Conference AIIA, Bari, Italy, 5–8 July 2017
15. Capolupo, A., Kooistra, L., Boccia, L.: A novel approach for detecting agricultural terraced landscapes from historical and contemporaneous photogrammetric aerial photos. Int. J. Appl. Earth Obs. Geoinf. **73**, 800–810 (2018)

Old Methods and New Technologies: A Multidisciplinary Approach to Archaeological Research in Sant'Arsenio (Salerno, Italy)

Nicodemo Abate(✉), Angelo Aromando(✉), and Rosa Lasaponara(✉)

Consiglio Nazionale delle Ricerche – Istituto di Metodologie per l'Analisi Ambientale, C.da S. Loja, 85050 Tito Scalo (PZ), Italy
{nicodemo.abate,angelo.aromando, rosa.lasaponara}@imaa.cnr.it

Abstract. This contribution is part of a project for the identification, research and protection of archaeological evidence in the village of Sant'Arsenio (SA), through the use of new technologies applied to archaeological research. In particular, the activity combines typical Remote Sensing tools (satellite data and UAVs), with a preference for open source software and open access databases, and common archaeological research practices (study of ancient and modern bibliographic sources, field survey, topographic analysis, etc.). Sant'Arsenio is a small town in the western part of Vallo di Diano, a large plain surrounded by mountains, between 450 and 480 m above sea level, located on the border between Campania and Basilicata. Information about the archaeological potential of the Sant'Arsenio appear to be relatively scarce compared to those available for the surrounding municipalities (Polla, Atena Lucana, Teggiano, Sala Consilina). This lack is due to the absence of systematic studies and planned archaeological research activities in the municipality. This paper presents the data collected between the end of 2018 and the beginning of 2019 by IMAA-CNR (Istituto di Metodologie per l'Analisi Ambientale del Consiglio Nazionale delle Ricerche). In particular, the satellite data (Sentinel-2), assisted by archaeological research, allowed to identify some anomalies of archaeological interest.

Keywords: Remote Sensing · Cultural Heritage · Open data

1 Introduction

This paper is part of a project developed by Consiglio Nazionale delle Ricerche – Istituto di Metodologie per l'Analisi Ambientale (CNR-IMAA), about the use of Remote Sensing and new technologies for research, monitoring and protection of national and international Cultural Heritage.

The municipality of Sant'Arsenio (Salerno, Italy) is the object of this work as subject of an agreement between the CNR-IMAA and the municipality itself.

S. Misra et al. (Eds.): ICCSA 2019, LNCS 11622, pp. 313–326, 2019.
https://doi.org/10.1007/978-3-030-24305-0_24

The aim of the study is to combine archaeological research with new non-invasive technologies (Remote Sensing) and, above all, open data, such as the Sentinel-2 images of the Copernicus program, to expand the knowledge of a specific place and protect any evidence, for a conscious urban development.

Sentinel-2 images are optimal for archaeological research, as evidenced by several works published in recent years [1–3]. The ability to download free data at a good resolution is essential in archaeology. Moreover, the archaeological data for the municipality of Sant'Arsenio are scarce and the Sentinel-2 images have quickly provided an overview of a large territory, allowing us to isolate areas of interest (AOIs) for further research as will be seen in the following pages.

2 Materials and Methods

Research in Sant'Arsenio concerns the use of the traditional archaeological method associated with the use of Remote Sensing techniques.

To identify a range of potentially AOIs, an overlap was made between the bibliographic/archaeological sources (geo-referenced and transposed into a GIS platform), Sentinel-2A multispectral satellite data [1], acquired through the Copernicus platform (https://scihub.copernicus.eu), IGM cartography (1: 25.000), multi-temporal images present on the National Geoportal Viewer (http://www.pcn.minambiente.it/viewer/) and Google Earth [2].

2.1 Methodology

Sentinel-2 data are fundamental to increase the knowledge of the study area. In fact, the images are free and see beyond the visible spectrum (*see* Table 1). Furthermore, Sentinel-2 data have a good resolution in the RGB and NIR bands (10 m) [3].

Table 1. Spectral bands of Sentinel-2A images.

Bands	Central wavelength (nm)	Spatial resolution
Band 1 – Coastal aerosol	0.443	60 m
Band 2 – Blue	0.490	10 m
Band 3 – Green	0.560	10 m
Band 4 – Red	0.665	10 m
Band 5 – Vegetation Red Edge	0.705	20 m
Band 6 – Vegetation Red Edge	0.740	20 m
Band 7 – Vegetation Red Edge	0.783	20 m
Band 8 – NIR	0.842	10 m
Band 8A – Vegetation Red Edge	0.865	20 m
Band 9 – Water vapour	0.945	60 m
Band 10 – SWIR – Cirrus	1.375	60 m
Band 11 – SWIR	1.610	20 m
Band 12 – SWIR	2.190	20 m

Multispectral images are useful in archaeological studies to easily recognize and categorize surfaces and their spectral response (spectral signatures), analyzing variations during the time of vegetation, soil, humidity, etc. The images allow to identify possible archaeological evidences, thanks to the integration with other sources [4].

Archaeologists use the analysis of multispectral images to identify buried or hidden structures, observing different indices (combination of bands) and anomalies in vegetation and soil (crop-marks, soil-marks) [5].

The images used for the study of Sant'Arsenio come from the Copernicus platform, with a percentage of clouds less than 10% per image and an acquisition period from 05/23/2016 to 10/25/2018.

The open source software ESA SNAP (http://step.esa.int/main/download/) processed all the images.

We have created an automated process to generate indices and images, thanks to SNAP's "graph building" function, speeding up all operations.

The workflow is simple and operations on Sentinel images follow this order: Read, Resampling (on Red Band or 10 m), Subset (reduces the file size), BandMaths (*see* Table 2), BandMarge (joins the Sentinel bands with indices), Write.

Table 2. Indices used for the identification of possible archaeological areas (referred to Sentinel-2 bands).

Index	Equation	Reference
Burned Area Index (BAI)	$\frac{1}{(0.1-B4)^2+(0.06-B8)^2}$	[6]
Difference Vegetation Index (DVI)	$B8 - B4$	[7]
Enhanced Vegetation Index (EVI)	$2.5 \times \frac{(B8-B4)}{(B8+6\times B4-7.5\times B2+1)}$	[8]
Green Difference Vegetation Index (GDVI)	$B8 - B3$	[9]
Green Normalized Difference Vegetation Index (GNDVI)	$\frac{(B8-B3)}{(B8+B3)}$	[9]
Green Ratio Vegetation Index (GRVI)	$\frac{B8}{B3}$	[9]
Normalized Difference VegetationIndex (NDVI)	$\frac{(B8-B4)}{(B8+B4)}$	[10]
Normalized Archaeological Index (NAI)	$\frac{(B7-B5)}{(B7+B5)}$	[3]
Modified Chlorophyll Absorption in Reflectance Index	$((B5 - B4) - 0.2 \times (B5 - B3)) \times \left(\frac{B5}{B4}\right)$	[11]
Normalized Difference Water Index (NDWI)	$\frac{(B8-B11)}{(B8+B11)}$	[12]

We have used the software to "trace" the spectral signature of the different pixels and make a physical and optical distinction between them [13–15].

We have used the Qgis Software for the last phase of processing and for the interpretation, loading into a single project the entire dataset from Sentinel-2 (bands, images and indices), IGM cartography, historical photos from WMS National Service and ancillary data acquired during the preliminary research phase.

In one case, aerial shots (UAV - DJI Phantom 3 Professional), photogrammetry software (Agisoft Photoscan) and data processing software (Cloud Compare, MeshLab) were used to expand the knowledge of one of the identified sites.

Approximately 99 aerial shots were acquired in 25 min of flight. The entire set of images was processed using the Agisoft Photoscan software and the point clouds (sparse and dense), the polygon mesh and the textured model were created. Each data is geo-referenced thanks to the metadata contained within the pictures. Cloud Compare and MeshLab software provided DEMs, contour lines, orthophotos and other useful data.

2.2 The History of Sant'Arsenio Through Archaeological Sources and Data, from Prehistory to the Late Medieval Period

Sant'Arsenio is a small town near Salerno, located on the western slope of the Vallo di Diano, a wide valley, between 450 and 480 m above sea level (*see* Fig. 1).

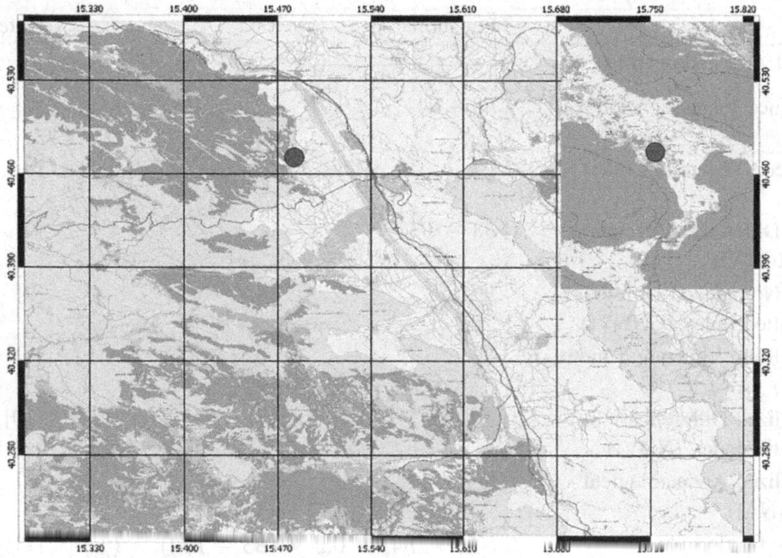

Fig. 1. Sant'Arsenio (Salerno, Italy).

The valley - which extends longitudinally - is located on the border between Campania and Basilicata. It is a natural link between the territory of Salerno and Lucania.

The valley dates back to the beginning of the Pleistocene and appeared as a large lake basin. Around 200,000 years ago, it became a large swamp, then modified - in historical times - by land reclamation and canalization work, starting from the "Roman period", for urban development and agricultural land use [16].

Excavations and archaeological research have shown traces of frequentation within the caves of Pertosa, Zachito, Castelcivita, of Ausino and Polla, with rare cases of *sub divo* evidences in the cases of Buccino, Atena Lucana and Sala Consilina [17].

The Bronze Age represents, for the area, a clear change within the settlement forms and economic vitality [18, 19].

The Iron Age (950 BC) is a very important moment for the Vallo di Diano. Villanovan culture groups penetrate the valley and occupy the heights.

For the archaic period (6th century BC) and the classical period (5th-4th century BC), data are scarce due to systematic archaeological operations.

Most of the information in our possession comes from the excavation of some sepulchral contexts. The 6th century shows similar characteristics to the previous one, as shown by the funeral goods and artifacts found during the excavation of the necropolis of Sala Consilina and Atena Lucana [20].

The presence of roads and passes through the Apennines greatly favors connections with areas such as the Val d'Agri, the Ionian Cost of Basilicata and the Tyrrhenian Cost, through the Sella di Corticato (Teggiano) and Monte Pruno (Roscigno) passes. In these places, a fortified site has been identified and excavated, probably datable to the 6th century BC [21].

For the Roman period, although still incomplete, the archaeological investigations and documentary sources (texts and epigraphs) are able to clearly delineate the situation of the Vallo di Diano.

One of the first points of contact between Rome and the populations of the Vallo happens, certainly, in the 3rd century. BC (272), with an alliance. This agreement ends at the end of the 3rd century, with the Annibalic wars, when the Lucanians of the Apennines supported Hannibal, paying - subsequently - the duty of defeat with heavy dispossession of territory in favor of the *ager publicus populi Romani* [22, 23].

The importance of the centers along the Capua-Regio route must certainly have increased at this time. Atena Lucana, Polla, Sala Consilina and Teggiano show a remarkable and constant urban growth up to the Augustan age, confirmed by inscriptions and inscriptions [24].

The late republican age and the imperial age saw the formation of a class of middle landowners who left the place, between 3rd and 4th centuries AD, to a landowner aristocracy [25].

During the medieval period the Vallo continues to play the role of crossroads for goods and people. This is very clear inside a letter of Cassiodorus (485–580 ca.) (*Variae, 8, 33*) of 527 AD when the author describes an important annual fair in a place identified as San Giovanni in Fonte, where the ruins of an early Christian baptistery are kept [26].

The Municipality of Sant'Arsenio is located on the western side of the Vallo di Diano, below the Alburni Mountains, in a natural basin formed by the heights, called, from south to north, Costa Masturso, Costa di S. Maria, the Cerri, Serra the Compra e Cornaleto.

It is widely believed that the origins of the town are to be found in the centuries of the Middle Ages and that the "importance" of the center in the economy of the territory remains marginal until the passage of the village to the Abbey of Cava de' Tirreni (12th century).

The most ancient evidences identified in the place are those found by the S.t.A.r.S. (Sant'Arsenio Survey) and V.A.L.L.O. (Valorizzazione Archeologica di un Lago non Lago Onnicomprensivo) projects, directed by Prof. A. Guidi (University of Rome 3), by Prof. A. Cazzella (University of Rome La Sapienza), coordinated in the field by dr. F. Nomi (University of Rome 3), in the years 2012, 2013 and 2014 [18, 19].

The work of the archaeologists has deepened the knowledge about the occupational dynamics, with materials and remains of inhabited areas from the Eneolithic (3800 BC) to the Bronze Age (1700 BC) and fragments of cups or olla dating back to the 8th-6th century BC, in an area famous for the discovery of tombs from the Archaic period and possible traces of settlement from the Roman period.

The remains preserved on the Cornaleto (593 m above sea level) could be dated to the Middle Bronze Age and could be part of a defensive system of masonry and terracing.

The excavations took place between 2013 and 2014, with the aim of understanding the extent and nature of the evidence identified in the previous year during the survey phase. Above the Cornaleto three excavation trenches were opened (A3 on the top and two A1, A4 at a lower altitude).

Materials dating back to the protohistoric phase also emerged during the surveys carried out on the heights of the Alburni (Collina di S. Vito, the Cerri, Costa di S. Maria).

Some fragments of figurative ceramics and a crater date back to the time of the Magna Graecia colonies, mentioned by the Sestieri [27].

Some sources mention a Roman settlement, just north of the hill of S. Vito, and a boundary stone in the place, although - as often happens in the places of our peninsula - the overlap of the settlements in later times complicates the understanding of place.

The news on the town of Sant'Arsenio are, certainly, more conspicuous for the medieval and post-medieval centuries.

The foundation of the primitive settlement dates back to the early medieval period; precisely, between the Greek Gothic war and the Lombard conquest of southern Italy [28], by some Byzantine settlers, in the 6th/early 7th century AD, near the locality called Serrone [29].

Otherwise, other hypotheses see the foundation of the village dating back to the 9th–10th century AD, a period in which the southern part of the peninsula is crossed by a multitude of Italian-Greek religious who, starting from Sicily and Calabria, move towards the north to found new monasteries [30–32].

With the collapse of the Lombard power in southern Italy, the construction of the Norman Kingdom of Sicily and the rise of Roger II (1145) who, in a climate of strong political instability, local lordships and religious congregations expand their properties. The history of the Vallo di Diano, in this period (12th century) is closely linked to the Abbey of Cava de' Tirreni and the development of the *Ordo Cavensis*. In fact, information in our possession comes from the Cavense Archive and from the homonymous code [33].

The document provided the Abbey of Cava with concessions mainly in the civil sphere (exploitation of pastures, forests, men etc.) with the donation of the Church of

Santa Maria, the village of Sant'Arsenio and all the men and income connected to it. The donation appears rather punctual in the description of the boundaries of the territory of the church of Santa Maria [34].

The first mention of a church and a monastery of Sant'Arsenio is about a decade after the donation of Santa Maria, in a pontifical privilege of Eugene III of 1149 [30].

About twenty years later (1186), there is explicit mention of the church of Sant'Arsenio, with information about the presence of a prior, Cipriano, in a donation made by Andreas [35].

It is not to be excluded that the management of the monastery was entrusted to Greek monks at least until 1186 when for the first time the prior Cipriano was appointed, sent directly by Cava. The village of Sant'Arsenio is still mentioned within some imperial documents which confirm its ownership to the Cavensian abbots (1221–1231).

The last twenty years of the thirteenth century represents a turning point in the management policy of its dependencies by the Abbey of Cava. With the crisis of the great monastic possessions and the devastation brought to Vallo di Diano by the Vespro war (1282–1302) priorates, farmhouses and appliances pass or are destroyed.

In 1310–1320 Roberto d'Angiò, on behalf of his father Carlo II, started an investigation to ascertain the ability to pay of the houses, following the war events, revealing a very impoverished reality for Sant'Arsenio. In 1381–1382 the abbot of Cava, Antonio, imposed on his vassals the oath of loyalty, given in the name of the community of Sant'Arsenio by the judge Cirone of Gargano. In 1394, Pope Boniface IX raised Cava as the seat of the diocese, giving the Cavense abbots the episcopal jurisdiction and including the church of Sant'Arsenio in the dowry. Between the 14th and 15th centuries the village of Sant'Arsenio appears to be flourishing with about 200 fires, vegetable gardens, cultivated lands, mills, ovens and various pastures [30].

3 Results: An Agreement Between Literary Sources, Materials and Technology

The information in our possession about the archaeological potential of the territory of Sant'Arsenio appears relatively poor if compared to those available for the municipalities in the district (Polla, Atena Lucana, Teggiano, Sala Consilina).

This lack is to be attributed to the absence of systematic studies and archaeological research activities in the area.

The place presents, from a strictly archaeological point of view, pros and cons.

Like most small towns in Campania, in fact, it is a multi-layered village. Some "historic" places have maintained unchanged toponyms and connotations and they are still identifiable today (a clear example is represented by the places called Fontanella, Lamato, Secchio, Foce, Serra La Compra and Costa Santa Maria). Furthermore, life continued uninterruptedly from the medieval period to the present and urbanization seems to have only partially involved the surrounding fields and the western highlands.

The information reported in the bibliography of the last century has exposed for Sant'Arsenio a fairly variegated picture with archaic necropolis and Roman elements placed in the plain, near the present cemetery, and an occupation of the heights during the middle ages, which has given life to the current historic center and the expansion of the village, later, inside the Vallo di Diano.

The data reported in the previous pages show a complex and articulated situation from an archaeological point of view, to which an abundance of sources is associated with a lack of material elements.

The analysis of Sentinel-2 images, visible and non-visible, has allowed us to identify some areas that, according to the sources, with archaeological data and with an anthropological *ratio*, seem to be of interest for the Cultural Heritage (*see* Fig. 2).

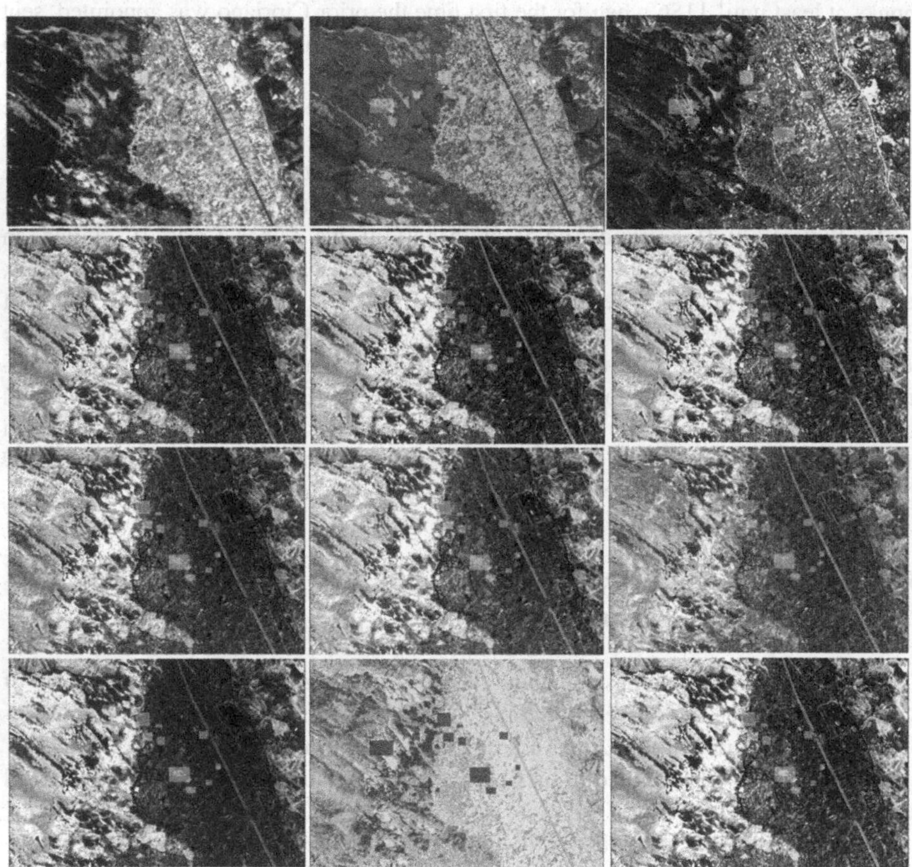

Fig. 2. From the top left corner to the bottom right corner: RGB, NIR-RG, BAI, DVI, EVI, MCARI, GDVI, GNDVI, NDWI, GRVI, NDVI, NDI.

The different indices used, shown in Table 2, in agreement with the present bibliography, show variations in vegetation and plowed fields.

The AOIs, for which further study is proposed in the future, are located within or on the borders of the municipality of Sant'Arsenio.

To the West/North-West, on the heights, some "spectral" anomalies have highlighted possible archaeological sites on the San Vito hill (*see* Fig. 3, n. 19) and of the Cornaleto (*see* Fig. 3, n. 14), supported from the multi-temporal images present within the National Geoportal; on the top of Serra la Compra (*see* Fig. 3, n. 15; *see* Fig. 4); behind Monte Carmelo in a place called Il Lago (*see* Fig. 3, nn. 1, 2, 16; *see* Fig. 5).

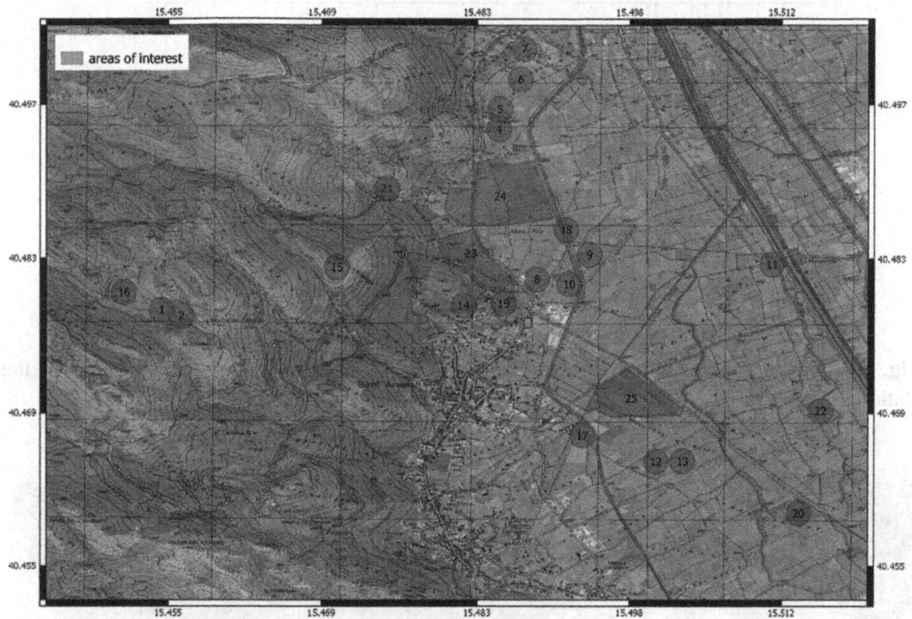

Fig. 3. Areas of interest.

On the height of Serra la Compra, the anomaly found - identified as a possible site of prehistoric age, similar to that found on the Cornaleto - appears as a patch of abundant vegetation, which detaches clearly from the barren landscape of the surrounding area. This evidence is clearly visible within the Sentinel-2 images, on a multitemporal scale, within the various indices and in the analysis of the spectral signatures of the examined pixels, in accordance with what established by the modern bibliography [36].

The survey improved knowledge of the site on Mount Carmel, in a place called Il Lago.

The site is a large rectangular structure and, from Sentinel-2 images, looks like a church. Furthermore, not far from this structure, an anomaly orthogonal to the road is clearly visible.

A thorough investigation was conducted for these anomalies thanks to the use of a drone [37] and 3D photogrammetry [38–40].

The analysis allowed us to understand the nature of the buildings. These are not religious buildings but could be old buildings useful for water management (*see* Fig. 6).

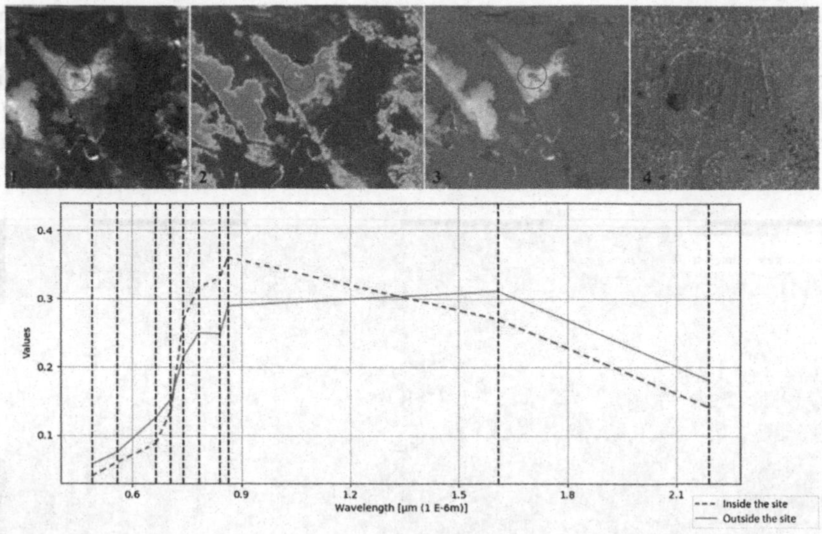

Fig. 4. Serra la Compra through the use of Sentinel 2 satellite images and image from the National Geoportal (1. RGB; 2. NDVI; 3. NIR-RG; 4 RGB from NG).

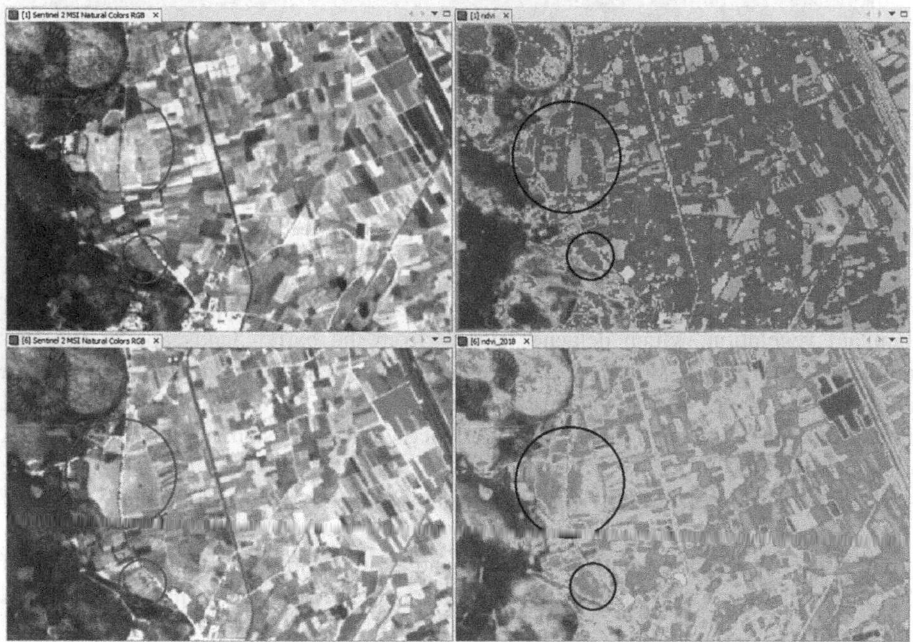

Fig. 5. AOIs north of the town (Sentinel 2 images: RGB and NDVI).

Fig. 6. Results obtained through the use of a UAV on Mount Carmelo.

To the north towards Polla, the bibliography speaks of a possible necropolis of the Archaic period and a Roman settlement. Hypothetically, it is possible that the sites mentioned may be located in Contrada Parisi and Contrada Priore, in the area known as Pozzo (*see* Fig. 3, nn. 23–24), for which a fairly large anomaly is reported.

Slightly to the west, along the course of the river, there are evidences that could be of archaeological interest (*see* Fig. 3, n. 21); while other spots to consider are located in the locality called Foce and in Petrosa, near the border with the municipality of Polla (*see* Fig. 3, nn. 4–7).

In the East some anomalies lead to the signaling of some places that could prove interesting - traces of ancient canalizations interrupted by large circular anomalies - arranged along the medieval border of the municipality of Sant'Arsenio in the Lamato locality and Fossa locality, close to the current road "Via fosso del Mulino" (*see* Fig. 3, nn. 11–13, 17, 20, 22, 25).

4 Conclusions

Although in a preliminary way, the synergy between archaeological research and data acquired through Remote Sensing appears to be useful for the study, knowledge, research and protection of visible and non-visible structures. In particular, the use of data and software freely provided by the European Space Agency (ESA) through the Copernicus program and the "sentinels" greatly facilitates the retrieval of information and its processing.

The Sentinel-2 images, in fact, have the advantage of providing a fairly good resolution for preliminary analysis (10 m) and are systematically acquired, allowing data to be processed on a time series.

The multispectrality made available by Sentinel-2 also allows the user to be able to range over the non-visible, using the individual bands (B4, B8) to observe the particular spectral response of some elements or to combine them to obtain additional information from the various indices. In the case of archeology, profits turned out to be the indices listed above; in particular, the analysis of those related to the state of health of vegetation and humidity was significant (EVI, NDVI, NDWI).

Although the territory of Sant'Arsenio is not optimal for the use of satellite images with a resolution of over ten meters, the comparative analysis of archaeological data and multispectral images Sentinel-2A allowed the identification of different areas of interest archaeological.

This study is a proof of how a multidisciplinary approach is now the very essence of research. The cognitive potential of the archaeological method is, in fact, exponentially increased thanks to the contribution of Remote Sensing. The practical demonstration is that provided by the example of the sites identified on the heights of Serra La Compra and in Locality Lago, practically never identified by the human eye but clearly visible within the satellite images.

Furthermore, the satellite data allows to give strength to only advanced ideas thanks to the archaeological studies as in the cases of the anomalies identified north of the municipality, where the existence of an archaic necropolis/Roman settlement is assumed.

References

1. Zanni, S., De Rosa, A.: Remote sensing analyses on Sentinel-2 images: looking for Roman roads in Srem region (Serbia). Geosciences **9**(1), 25 (2016)
2. Tapete, D., Cigna, F.: Appraisal of opportunities and perspectives for the systematic condition assessment of heritage sites with Copernicus Sentinel-2 high-resolution multispectral imagery. Remote Sens. **10**(4), 561 (2018)
3. Agapiou, A., Alexakis, D.D., Sarris, A., Hadjimitsis, D.G.: Evaluating the potentials of Sentinel-2 for archaeological perspective. Remote Sens. **6**(3), 2176–2194 (2014)
4. Lasaponara, R., Masini, N.: Pattern recognition and classification using VHR data for archaeological research. In: Lasaponara, R., Masini, N. (eds.) Satellite Remote Sensing: A New Tool for Archaeology. Remote Sensing and Digital Image Processing, vol. 16, pp. 65–85. Springer, Dordrecht (2012). https://doi.org/10.1007/978-90-481-8801-7_3
5. De Guio, A.: Cropping for a better future: vegetation indices in archaeology. In: Chavarria Arnau, A., Reynolds, A. (eds.) Detecting and Understanding Historic Landscapes, Mantova, Italy, pp. 109–152 (2015)
6. Chuvieco, E., Martin, M.P., Palacios, A.: Assessment of different spectral indices in the red-near-infrared spectral domain for burned land discrimination. Int. J. Remote Sens. **23**(23), 5103–5110 (2010)
7. Tucker, C.J.: Red and photographic infrared linear combinations for monitoring vegetation. Remote Sens. Environ. **8**, 127–150 (1979)
8. Huete, A.R., Liu, H.Q., Batchily, K., van Leeuwen, W.: A comparison of vegetation indices over a global set of TM images for EOS-MODIS. Remote Sens. Environ. **59**, 440–451 (1997)
9. Gitelson, A.A., Merzlyak, M.N.: Remote sensing of chlorophyll concentration in higher plant leaves. Adv. Space Res. **22**, 689–692 (1998)
10. Rouse, J.W., Haas, R.H., Schell, J.A., Deering, D.W., Harlan, J.C.: Monitoring the Vernal Advancements and Retrogradation (Greenwave Effect) of Nature Vegetation. NASA, Greenbelt (1974)

11. Agapiou, A., Lysandrou, V., Hadjimitsis, D.G.: Optical remote sensing potentials for looting detection. Geosciences **7**(4), 98 (2017)
12. Serrano, L., Ustin, S.L., Roberts, D.A., Gamon, J.A., Peñuelas, J.: Deriving water content of Chaparral vegetation from AVIRIS data. Remote Sens. Environ. **74**(3), 570–581 (2000)
13. Agapiou, A., Lysandrou, V., Lasaponara, R., Masini, N.: Study of the variations of archaeological marks at neolithic site of Lucera, Italy using high-resolution multispectral datasets. Remote Sens. **8**(9), 723 (2016)
14. Bennett, R., Welham, K., Hill, R.A., Ford, A.: The application of vegetation indices for the prospection of archaeological features in grass-dominated environments: application of vegetation indices in grass-dominated environments. Archaeol. Prospect. **19**(3), 209–218 (2012)
15. Moriarty, C., Cowley, D.C., Wade, T., Nichol, C.J.: Deploying multispectral remote sensing for multi-temporal analysis of archaeological crop stress at Ravenshall, Fife, Scotland. Archaeol. Prospect. **26**, 33–46 (2019)
16. Di Maio, G., Santangelo, N., Santo, A.: Inquadramento geologico e dati preliminari sui riempimenti. In: Pellegrini, E. (ed.) Risultati delle ricerche alla grotta del Pino (Sassano, Salerno): 1997–1998, pp. 137–143. Bullettino di Paletnologia Italiana, Roma (2001)
17. D'Agostino, B.: Storia del Vallo di Diano, I. L'età antica. Laveglia editore, Salerno (1981)
18. Fiore, I., Nomi, F., Truffi, M.: I resti faunistici dell'abitato appenninico del Cornaleto (Sant'Arsenio, SA). In: 50° Riunione Scientifica dell'Istituto Italiano di Preistoria e Protostoria del cibo (Roma, ottobre 2015), Roma, pp. 1–11 (2017)
19. Guidi, A., Nomi, F.: Centri d'altura della media età del bronzo nel Vallo di Diano e nelle aree limitrofe. Nuove evidenze dal progetto V.A.L.L.O. In: Cicala, L., Pecciarelli, M. (eds.) Centri fortificati indigeni della Calabria dalla protostoria all'età ellenistica (Napoli, gennaio 2014), pp. 479–783. Naus, Napoli (2017)
20. Balio Modesti, G.: Il periodo arcaico. In: D'Agostino, B. (ed.) Storia del Vallo di Diano. I. L'età antica, pp. 85–122. Laveglia editore, Salerno (1981)
21. Greco, E.: Magna Grecia (Guida Archeologica Laterza). Laterza, Roma-Bari (2008)
22. Fraschetti, A.: L'età romana. Le vicende storiche. In: D'Agostino, B. (ed.) Storia del Vallo di Diano. I. L'età antica, pp. 201–215. Laveglia editore, Salerno (1981)
23. Del Luongo, S.: La Lucania tardoantica nella Tabula Peutingeriana alla luce delle fonti gromatiche. Les Mélanges de l'École française de Rome – Antiquité, Roma, vol. 129(2) (2017)
24. Bracco, V.: I materiali epigrafici. In: D'Agostino, B. (ed.) Storia del Vallo di Diano. I. L'età antica, pp. 181–197. Laveglia editore, Salerno (1981)
25. Coarelli, F.: Il Vallo di Diano in età romana. I dati dell'archeologia. In: D'Agostino, B. (ed.) Storia del Vallo di Diano. I. L'età antica, pp. 217–249. Laveglia editore, Salerno (1981)
26. Greco, E.: Problemi topografici nel Vallo di Diano tra VI e IV sec. a.C. In: D'Agostino, B. (ed.) Storia del Vallo di Diano. I. L'età antica, pp. 125–148. Laveglia editore, Salerno (1981)
27. Sestieri, C.: Appunti su una classe di vasi italici. Archeol. Cl. **3**, 129–137 (1951)
28. Gilberti, L.: Il Comune di Sant'Arsenio. Contributo alla storia municape dell'Italia meridionale. Tip. degli Artigianelli, Napoli (1923)
29. Pica, L.: La nuova chiesa in Sant'Arsenio e la Valle del Tanagro (Salerno). Cantelmi, Salerno (1971)
30. Ebner, P.: Chiesa, baroni e popolo nel Cilento, vol. 2, pp. 570–579. Edizioni di storia e letteratura, Roma (1982)
31. Abate, N., Mammato, A.: Nuovi dati sul monachesimo in Costiera Amalfitana (X-XI secolo). In: Marazzi, F., Raimondo, C. (eds.) Monasteri Italogreci (secoli VII-XI). Una lettura archeologica, Atti del Convegno Internazionale svoltosi a Squillace (CZ), 23–24 marzo 2018, pp. 75–88. Volturnia edizioni, Cerro al Volturno (2018)

32. Marchionibus, M.R.: Monasteri bizantini in Cilento e Vallo di Diano: tra storia e monumenti. In: Marazzi, F., Raimondo, C. (eds.) Monasteri Italogreci (secoli VII-XI). Una lettura archeologica, Atti del Convegno Internazionale svoltosi a Squillace (CZ), 23–24 marzo 2018, pp. 57–74. Volturnia edizioni, Cerro al Volturno (2018)
33. Ambrogi, M.: Sant'Arsenio tra Medioevo ed età Moderna. Storia, arte e caratteri urbani di un antico casale dello Stato di Diano, pp. 35–48. Lapelosa Printing, Sala Consilina (2006)
34. Visentin, B.: Il Monastero di Sant'Arsenio e la presenza cavense nel Vallo di Diano (Secc. XI-XV). In: Visentin, B. (ed.) Atti del Convegno La Badia di Cava e il Vallo di Diano - Sant'Arsenio (SA), 20 Novembre 2010, pp. 83–99. Edizioni Laveglia-Carlone, Salerno (2012)
35. Vitolo, G.: Dalla pieve rurale alla chiesa ricettizia. Istituzioni ecclesiastiche e vita religosa dall'alto Medioevo al Cinquecento pre-tridentino. In: Cilento, N. (ed.) Storia del Vallo di Diano, II, p. 146. Laveglia, Salerno (1982)
36. Lasaponara, R., Masini, N.: Detection of archaeological crop marks by using satellite QuickBird. J. Archaeol. Sci. **34**(2), 214–221 (2007)
37. Nex, F., Redmondino, F.: UAV for 3D mapping applications: a review. Appl. Geomat. **6**, 1–15 (2014)
38. Chianramdo, F., Lingua, A., Rianudo, F., Spano, A.: Archaeological site monitoring: UAV photogrammetry can be an answer. International Archives of the Photogrammetry, Remote Sensing and Spatial Information Sciences, Melbourne, vol. XXXIXB5, pp. 583–588 (2012)
39. Remondino, F., Barazzetti, L., Nex, F., Scaioni, M., Sarazzi, D.: UAV photogrammetry for mapping and 3D modeling – current status and future perspectives. In: 2011 ISPRS Zurich 2011 Workshop. International Archives of the Photogrammetry, Remote Sensing and Spatial Information Sciences, vol. XXXVIII-1/C22, pp. 25–31. ISPRS, Zurich (2011)
40. Remondino, F., El-Hakim, S.: Image-based 3D modelling: a review. Photogramm. Rec. **21** (115), 269–291 (2006)

International Symposium on Software Quality (ISSQ 2019)

Can Software Metrics Be Unified?

Yusuf U. Mshelia(✉) and Simon T. Apeh

Department of Computer Engineering, Faculty of Engineering, University of Benin, PMB 1154, Benin-City, Nigeria
mshelia@ieee.org, apeh@uniben.edu

Abstract. Software metrics produce discrete values as output from input source code as an indication of software quality. Many software have automated software metrics with different tools that are producing varying result. Measurement of software metrics cannot be said to be precise, repeatable and reproducible. This is consequent of varying definitions, design and implementation of the same software metrics, varying result, assessment and analysis of the same metrics from relative and personalized approaches to varying benchmarks, non-uniform definition of implementation contexts, software measurement terminologies and lack of standard reference and calibration with respect to the measure of "level of confidence" in software measurement. Several studies have proposed the unification of software metrics without necessarily looking at the underlying causes of these widely observed inconsistencies across existing metrics and their automated tools. This work identified pitfalls ways to minimize variances in the implementation of software measurements across contexts. From this stage of an ongoing research, we are determining the possibility of objectively unifying software metrics by closing the gap in observed sources of expressed variance and adoption of metrological approaches to software measurement.

Keywords: Metrics variance · Software metrics · Metrology

1 Introduction

Software metrics as a tool used in software quality assessment has gained increasing importance within its different areas of application. Metrics in software measurement has generally drawn its definition within a specific context-area of application. This forms a significant constraint in the inclusive application of software metrics from a globally-defined standard point of view. Software metrics from source code are generally used in fault and software quality predictions.

Fenton and Neil [1] reported the existence of thousands of software metrics that supposedly measures some form of metric, attribute, artefact or quality in software. In addition, more than 5000 software metrics are reported [2] in classifying metrics for assessing for maintainability of object-oriented systems. These numerous software metrics are identified to produce several inconsistences. These inconsistencies from the creation, design, implementation and automation of software metrics have introduced the following concerns:

1. Varying definitions, design and implementation of the same software metrics founded on different theories [3].

S. Misra et al. (Eds.): ICCSA 2019, LNCS 11622, pp. 329–339, 2019.
https://doi.org/10.1007/978-3-030-24305-0_25

2. Varying result, assessment and analysis of the same metrics founded on relative and personalized approaches to benchmarks and interpretation [4].
3. Non-uniform definition of implementation contexts, terminologies and metrics.
4. Measurement of metrics cannot be said to be precise, repeatable and reproducible comprehensively in a different context from which is was originally designed [5].
5. Lack of standard reference and calibration with respect to the measure of "level of confidence" [5].

As an approach to measurement of software artifacts, relative definition of metrics, application and interpretation have been the trend in the definition of software metrics. Unlike the field that studies the science and technology of measurement - metrology, software metrics suffers from insufficient approaches that checks measures of software metrics with the required rigor and standard. Other fields have benefited from metrological approaches to measurement, especially in the measurement of physical objects in physics, chemistry, manufacturing, etc. Software however, is inundated with having to measure intangible non-physical objects without a standard etalon.

As a key to delivering a uniform standard in the definitions, methods, processes and implementation, pitfalls must be identified and duly avoided with best practices and to minimize variances in the implementation of software measurements across contexts.

This work identified sources of variations as observed in literature and experiments and proposed some variance reduction techniques. It further clarifies the systems of measurement in software metrics and metrology. This research paper presents observed challenges in software measurement that has contributed to varying values of the same name metric and ways to achieve uniform standard in software measurement.

The next section presents sources of variance as expressed in literature and observed from experience and literature. Section 3 discusses techniques in reducing variations in metrics results. Software metrics system of measurement is compared to measurement as in metrology in Sect. 4. Finally, from the understanding of the previous sections, we discussed the connections with respect to the contribution of metrics variance in unifying the software metrics in Sect. 5.

2 Sources of Expressed Variance in Software Metrics

2.1 Literature

As generally seen in literature, informed basis for specific work of unifying software metrics at different levels are inconsistency, disparity and non-uniformity in software measurement processes, models, systems, techniques and tools. The need for a consistent terminology and nomenclature of software measures was the focus of Rana et al. [6], Abran et al. [7] and García et al. [8] and an effort towards catalog format for software metrics Bouwers et al. [9]. A metrics collection tool (MECOT) was designed as a class-based metrics collector for accumulating different metrics into a repository [10]. Furthermore, other works have contributed to unifying methods and frameworks in implementing software metrics [11–21]. Furthermore, recommendations in standardizing software metrics within the framework of metrology have been proposed. Of fundamental significance in this area are works by Abran [22] and Flater et al. [5].

As an approach to unifying software metrics, an approach in establishing suite of metrics are also proposed as in the cognitive complexity metrics of Object Oriented Programs [23]. In identifying bugs in files, a work by Huo and Li [24] proposed a deep model called LS-CNN (Long Short-term memory based on Convolutional Neural Network) to enhance the unified features for bug localization by exploiting the sequential nature of source code, where a particular network structure is designed to combine CNN (Convolutional Neural Network) and LSTM (Long Short-Term Memory) that captures sequential semantics as well as structural information from source code. Another that outlined perceptions and challenges in defect prediction is by Wan et al. [25]. Code smells with respect to bad programming practice are reported as a contributor metric quality variance [26, 27]. The reporting of bugs was described to lead to high irregular patterns as the repository size is increasing with enormous rate, resulting in uncertainty and irregularities [28, 29]. Irrelevant features exist in source-codes that has motivated the work on the framework that validates the source code metrics and identify a suitable set of source code metrics with the aim to reduce irrelevant features and improve the performance of the fault prediction model.

The results of software metrics as expressed in the study of software metrics has posed challenges that largely varies in output, application and context. We define variance in this context as the difference in the way the implementations of metrics have contributed to the independent definitions, results applications and interpretations. Consequently, the following are causes to some of these differences:

2.2 Correlation Analysis of Software Metrics Suites

The analysis of Project L^3 [30], established that the relationship in the output values computed by the tools vary between a positively strong and negative correlation to negatively strong and weak correlation to perfectly positive and negative correlations. In addition, there exists no correlation at all to some degree for all the project classes for which results were attempted to be correlated.

A reason identified for such a wide gap in the degree of correlation across the metrics tools used in the experiment is that not all the tools analyzed the same number of metrics. Example from strongly negative results and no relationship are sourced in the fact at the tools have a non-uniform number of variables the tools independently measure.

2.3 Definition of Counted Reference Point

Counting is the most prevalent technique used in the software quality measurement. In software metrics, nearly every quantity that is not actually a physical quantity is determined through counting [5]. Table 1 below enumerates the “base measures and their measurement units” from parts 2–4 of ISO 9126, a standard for the evaluation of software quality with instructive units. It therefore summarized that almost 3/4 of the measures are counts of something other than bytes, time, or money.

Table 1. Derived Categorization of ISO 9126 quality metrics by types of units of measurement from [5]

Std part	Total	Time	Money	Bytes	Other count	Weighted score
2.(External)	38	10		2	26	
3.(Internal)	34	2		1	31	
4.(In use)	10	4	1		4	1
Total	82	16	1	3	61	1

The measurement of counted metrics may have an ambiguous definition in the implementation of metric tools which ripples to relative or self-defined analysis and interpretation. Line of Code (LOC) metric for example is an ambiguous metrics in that what makes it precise is the reference and pointer to what it is counting. Because LOC can take the forms of Logical LOC, Physical LOC, Blank LOC, Comment LOC. The difference in all these is the reference of what is counts. The variations have different applications as commented LOC will not be necessary in understanding software size, however, it will go a long way in deciding the comprehension or understandability of the source code.

In particular instances of measurements by count within the source code, there is no reference as to if blank lines are part of the count of a physical line of code or not, since most code editors generate a serial count irrespective of what is coded.

2.4 Naming Metrics and Their Definitions

Despite all the efforts and new developments in research and international standardization during the last decade, software measurement is currently in the phase in which terminology, principles, and methods are still being defined, consolidated, and agreed. In particular, there is no consensus yet on the concepts and terminology used in this field. For instance, software measurement researchers and practitioners have not reached an agreement on the precise meaning of some terms commonly used, such as 'measurement', 'measure', 'metric', 'measurable attribute', etc. Even worse, inconsistencies between the different research measurement proposals often occur [8]. Rana et al. [6] also reported that one of the limitations to develop a generic software quality prediction approach is inconsistency found in naming software product measures. In some cases, the same measure has been given different labels whereas in other cases same label has been used for different measures and classified these two anomalies as Type I and Type II inconsistencies respectively.

As metrics are created, the naming structure does not provide for exclusivity to titles or names of the metrics. This causes the recreation of the same named metrics of a different theory or implementation targeting to measure different artefact. Of the 568 software metrics surveyed by de AG Saraiva et al. [2] for analyzing metrics, many were found with inconsistencies in the names of metrics because there were metrics with the same names but different meaning. There were also metrics with different names, however with similar meanings.

Furthermore, from the definition of fundamental forms within the framework of the counting source statement in [31], multiple other forms[1,2] of LOC have been identified to bear components of the already identified forms in addition to some added components or even entirely not built on executable lines of code but on the general content of source code.

2.5 Exclusions from Optimization Techniques

Optimization of source code is aimed at to eliminating dead code, avoiding recursion, avoiding floating-point operations to the possible extent, avoiding large library routines and removal of loop-invariant statements. However, the use of correct optimization level of the compiler provides different optimization levels from 0 to 3 as the highest which can be set based on the need.

As a result, the optimization of software metrics tools can choose to exclude some portions of the source code in count situations especially if a lot of code reuse is involved. The optimization that is abstracted from the programmer and handled by the compiler can produce different results based on the compiler need perception in assigning what levels of optimization is needed.

2.6 Implementing Algorithm and Optimization Techniques

Being that every computational system is a representation of an underlying theory of the algorithm. These theories may have some different intermediate representations of algorithms for achieving the same result. Therefore, the data structure of such algorithmic statements may take different transformations that within some contexts could take just a statement to accomplish whereas within another context some transformation and result will take multiple statements.

Therefore, if a created metrics is not utterly explicit in the definition of its theory and to its intermediate steps, the chance of implementing the same metrics may have or adopt different algorithms especially when the programmer has multiple approaches as an alternative. As a result, the different approaches will consequently yield different result especially in counts of logical statements.

Again, optimization either by automatic optimizers or programmers can change the structure of either the metrics analyzer or an optimized algorithm used in source code to be assessed.

2.7 Metrics Aggregation Techniques

Source-code metrics are usually defined on a micro-level of method, class, package, etc., and should therefore be aggregated in order to provide insights in the evolution at the macro-level (system) [32]. Popular aggregation techniques like the standard summary statistical measures as mean, median, or sum. Their main advantage is universality

[1] http://www.locmetrics.com/index.html.

[2] https://en.wikipedia.org/wiki/Source_lines_of_code.

(metrics-independence): whatever metrics are considered; the measures should be calculated in the same way. However, as the distribution of many interesting software metrics is skewed, the interpretation of such measures becomes unreliable [33].

In the same line, the results of metrics vary with respect to the aggregation used in the analysis of metrics results. From nature of the relation between various aggregation techniques between Gini, Theil, Atkinson, and Hoover indices (I), correlation between I_{Theil} and I_{Kolm}, as well as between $I_{Atkinson}$ and I_{Kolm} increases as the system size increases, while correlation between mean and I_{Kolm} fluctuates without clear relation to system size.

3 Variance Reduction Techniques

3.1 Homogeneity of Standard Names and Definitions

Resulting from lack of a common terminology and inconsistencies between the different standards, the existing situation may seriously risk the effectiveness and potential benefits of software standardization efforts. A consistent software measurement terminology may provide an important communication vehicle to companies when interoperating with others [8].

Currently, the International Organization for Standards (ISO) is updating the definition of software engineering terminologies as a foundation to upgrade software measurement terminologies. Furthermore, there is need for increased referential materials to terminologies, approaches and frameworks for measurement.

The International Vocabulary of Basic and General Terms in Metrology (called VIM) [34] provides general standard terminology in measurement science or metrology. However, because of the uniqueness of some specific fields of measurements, other some areas have customized the VIM definitions within the context of the specific area. For the purpose of a concise definition of measurement concepts that is peculiar to software metrics, there is also a corresponding need for a precise work as in the Eurachem Guide [35], a collection of terminology in analytical measurement.

3.2 Counts and Reference Points

As shown in Table 1, counting is the most prevalent technique used in the software quality measurement, there is need in precise and explicit pointer to what to measure and what not. In the definition of counts, there must be no ambiguity or else, it will be subject too relative and subjective opinions and applications. In software metrics, nearly every quantity that is not actually a physical quantity is determined through counting.

3.3 Metrics Optimization Buffering

Realizing that metrics algorithm implemented independent of external modification will to a degree be consistent across different platforms and within the same context. Hence, if an optimization buffer or avoidance is adopted, results can be uniform.

3.4 Symmetry with Metrology

Metrology, defined by International Bureau of Weights and Measures (IBWM) is the science of measurement, embracing both experimental and theoretical determinations at any level of uncertainty in any field of science and technology. Measurement as in software metrics are quite different from that of metrology. Since metrology has an established structure for instituting measurement standards, software metrics can benefit from the it like other areas of measurement in physics and chemistry.

4 Software Metrics System Vs. Metrology

Generally, measurements are used to make comparisons, to make decisions, or simply to ascertain facts about an object of measurement.

Measurement of software metrics are measures of quality of software – a non-physical, non-tangible property or attribute of the software. Causal relationships that are widely observed to exist between real properties of the objects of measurement and measured quantity values are expressed in the form of physical laws which are strongly supported by empirical evidence. If a set of analogous laws about nontrivial properties of software existed, software engineering could have "widely accepted measurements traceable to solid principles, rigorously defined quantities, and base and derived units".

Equally, the discovery of measurement laws might just depend on first making the right measurements of the right properties. It is idealized that the primary difference between software measurement and physical measurement is the maturity of the

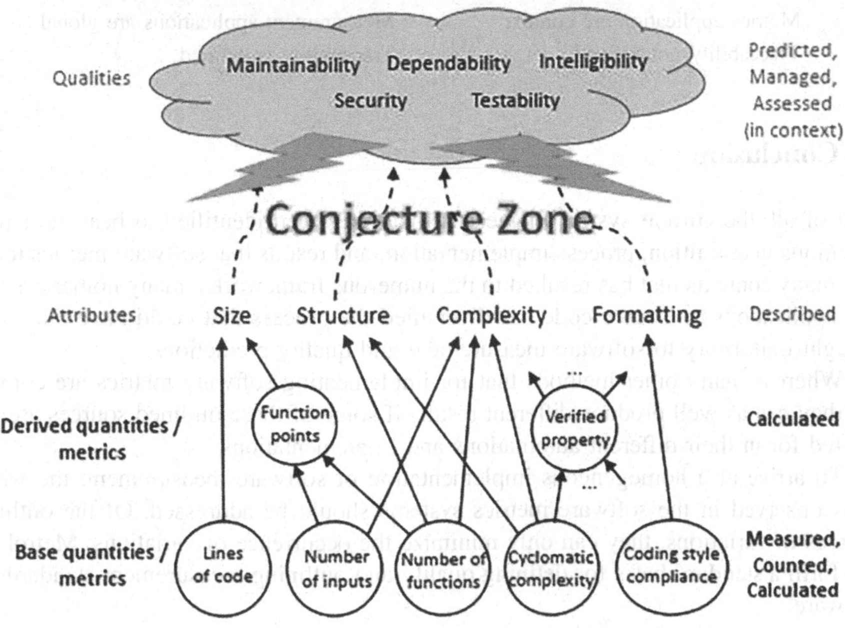

Fig. 1. Relating quality to quantity from Flater et al. [5]

measurement discipline. To the extent that software measurement is analogous to physical measurement, applying the established methods ought to shortcut the centuries-long process of refinement that evolved the capability to perform reliable physical measurements [5].

In further explanation of metrology framework for software measurement, vocabulary definitions in processes of that characterize *repeatability vs. reproducibility, measurand vs. realized quantity, instantaneous vs. cumulative quantity* were defined.

Figure 1 above shows the relationship between quality as an object of measurement as in software to quantity as in metrology. In order to realize this feat, specific areas in software metrics and metrology must be aligned. Areas of the differences that should be addressed to align to metrology in order to achieve the beauty of measurement standard, calibration, units and scaling are *traceability* and *measure of uncertainty*. This is largely lacking in the software metrics systems of quality assessment.

Other difference between the software metrics and metrology are outline in Table 2 below.

Table 2. Comparing software measurement to metrology

S/N	Software metrics systems	Metrology
1	Measures quality	Measures quantity
2	Objects of measurement are non-physical	Objects of measurement are physical
3	Undefined measure of uncertainty	Defined measure of uncertainty
4	No standard unit of measurement, calibration and scaling	Available standard unit of measurement, calibration and scaling
5	Metrics application are context	Measurement applications are global
6	Traceability not defined	Traceability is defined

5 Conclusion

First of all, the current system of measurement has been identified to bear numerous variations in definition, process implementation, and results that software metrics tools. The many contexts that has resulted to the numerous frameworks, many nomenclatures and applications on source code has diversified the process that could have otherwise brought uniformity to software measurement and quality predictions.

Whereas many other methods that for implementing software metrics are coming up, they can as well produce different results if some of these outlined sources are not catered for in their different automations and implementations.

To arrive at a homogeneous implementation of software measurement, the variations observed in the software metrics systems should be addressed. Of the outlined sources of variations, they can only minimize the occurrence of variations. Metrology can form a standard basis for defining quality and outlining measurement standards in software.

The researchers reported variations in software metrics systems as expressed in the literature, and other causes and proposed recommendations on how to reduce these variations. In addition to the reported sources of variations, if ambiguous definition of counted reference, naming variations and metrics algorithm optimization of analyzers re addressed, variations will largely be reduced. However, even when applied standard unit, calibration and scaling will not come from these. Consequently, software metrology is identified as an established field whose structure when applied to software metrics, will unifying formalized standards in software measurement.

What is next? Points of symmetry between software measurement and metrology within the constraint of traceability is the next phase of this work.

References

1. Fenton, N.E., Neil, M.: Software metrics: roadmap. In: Proceedings of the Conference on the Future of Software Engineering, pp. 357–370 (2000)
2. de AG Saraiva, J., De França, M.S., Soares, S.C., Fernando Filho, J., de Souza, R.M.: Classifying metrics for assessing object-oriented software maintainability: a family of metrics' catalogs. J. Syst. Softw. **103**, 85–101 (2015)
3. Mshelia, Y.U., Apeh, S.T., Edoghogho, O.: A comparative assessment of software metrics tools. In: 2017 International Conference on Computing Networking and Informatics (ICCNI), pp. 1–9 (2017)
4. Olaye, E.: Benchmarking software quality using traditional software metrics on web-based systems, Ph.D., Computer Engineering, University of Benin, Benin-city (2017)
5. Flater, D.W., et al.: A rational foundation for software metrology (2016)
6. Rana, Z.A., Awais, M.M., Shamail, S.: Nomenclature unification of software product measures. IET Softw. **5**, 83–102 (2011)
7. Abran, A., Sellami, A., Suryn, W.: Metrology, measurement and metrics in software engineering. In: Proceedings of the 5th International Workshop on Enterprise Networking and Computing in Healthcare Industry (IEEE Cat. No. 03EX717), pp. 2–11 (2003)
8. García, F., et al.: Towards a consistent terminology for software measurement. Inf. Softw. Technol. **48**, 631–644 (2006)
9. Bouwers, E., van Deursen, A., Visser, J.: Towards a catalog format for software metrics. In: Proceedings of the 5th International Workshop on Emerging Trends in Software Metrics, pp. 44–47 (2014)
10. Mshelia, Y.U.: MECOT: a software quality metrics collection tool. J. Syst. Integr. **10**, 21–35 (2019)
11. Alawneh, L., Debbabi, M., Hassaine, F., Jarraya, Y., Soeanu, A.: A unified approach for verification and validation of systems and software engineering models. In: 13th Annual IEEE International Symposium and Workshop on Engineering of Computer-Based Systems (ECBS 2006), pp. 10, 418 (2006)
12. Lochmann, K., Goeb, A.: A unifying model for software quality. In: Proceedings of the 8th International Workshop on Software Quality, pp. 3–10 (2011)
13. Mercier, S., Abran, A., Lavoie, M., Champagne, R.: Unified software method: towards a method of measurement of the necessary changes to software in maintenance (2006)
14. Bartolomei, T.T., Garcia, A., Sant'Anna, C., Figueiredo, E.: Towards a unified coupling framework for measuring aspect-oriented programs. In: Proceedings of the 3rd International Workshop on Software Quality Assurance, pp. 46–53 (2006)

15. Cavano, J.P., McCall, J.A.: A framework for the measurement of software quality. In: ACM SIGMETRICS Performance Evaluation Review, pp. 133–139 (1978)
16. Abran, A., Bourque, P., Dupuis, R.: The SWEBOK initiative and software measurement intentions. In: Proceedings of the 12th International Workshop on Software Measurement (IWSM 2002), pp. 168–178 (2002)
17. Jacquet, J.-P., Abran, A.: From software metrics to software measurement methods: a process model. In: Proceedings of IEEE International Symposium on Software Engineering Standards, pp. 128–135 (1997)
18. Kelemen, Z.D., Trienekens, J., Kusters, R., Balla, K.: A process based unification of process-oriented software quality approaches. In: 2009 Fourth IEEE International Conference on Global Software Engineering, pp. 285–288 (2009)
19. Akingbehin, K., Maxim, B.: A three-layer model for software engineering metrics. In: Seventh ACIS International Conference on Software Engineering, Artificial Intelligence, Networking, and Parallel/Distributed Computing (SNPD 2006), pp. 17–20 (2006)
20. Symons, C., Abran, A., Ebert, C., Vogelezang, F.: Measurement of software size: advances made by the COSMIC community. In: 2016 Joint Conference of the International Workshop on Software Measurement and the International Conference on Software Process and Product Measurement (IWSM-MENSURA), pp. 75–86 (2016)
21. Dumke, R.R., Braungarten, R., Kunz, M., Schmietendorf, A., Wille, C.: Strategies and appropriateness of software measurement frameworks. In: Proceedings of the International Conference on Software Process and Product Measurement (MENSURA 2006), pp. 150–170 (2006)
22. Abran, A.: Software metrics need to mature into software metrology (recommendations). In: NIST Workshop on Advancing Measurements and Testing for Information Technology (IT), Maryland, USA (1998)
23. Misra, S., Adewumi, A., Fernandez-Sanz, L., Damasevicius, R.: A suite of object oriented cognitive complexity metrics. IEEE Access **6**, 8782–8796 (2018)
24. Huo, X., Li, M.: Enhancing the unified features to locate buggy files by exploiting the sequential nature of source code. In: IJCAI, pp. 1909–1915 (2017)
25. Wan, Z., Xia, X., Hassan, A.E., Lo, D., Yin, J., Yang, X.: Perceptions, expectations, and challenges in defect prediction. IEEE Trans. Softw. Eng. (2018)
26. Gupta, A., Suri, B., Kumar, V., Misra, S., Blažauskas, T., Damaševičius, R.: Software code smell prediction model using Shannon, Rényi and Tsallis Entropies. Entropy **20**, 372 (2018)
27. Gupta, A., Suri, B., Misra, S.: A systematic literature review: code bad smells in Java source code. In: Gervasi, O., et al. (eds.) ICCSA 2017. LNCS, vol. 10408, pp. 665–682. Springer, Cham (2017). https://doi.org/10.1007/978-3-319-62404-4_49
28. Kumari, M., Misra, A., Misra, S., Fernandez Sanz, L., Damasevicius, R., Singh, V.B.: Quantitative quality evaluation of software products by considering summary and comments entropy of a reported bug. Entropy **21**, 91 (2019)
29. Singh, V.B., Misra, S., Sharma, M.: Bug severity assessment in cross project context and identifying training candidates. J. Inf. Knowl. Manag. (JIKM) **16**, 1–30 (2017)
30. Mshelia, Y.U., Apeh, S.T., Olaye, E.: Parametric correlation and variance in constituent software metrics tools of project L^3. J. Data Anal. **11**, 125–137 (2016)
31. Park, R.E.: Software size measurement: a framework for counting source statements, Carnegie-Mellon Univ Pittsburgh PA Software Engineering Inst. (1992)
32. Vasilescu, B., Serebrenik, A., van den Brand, M.: You can't control the unfamiliar: a study on the relations between aggregation techniques for software metrics. In: 2011 27th IEEE International Conference on Software Maintenance (ICSM), pp. 313–322 (2011)

33. Vasa, R., Lumpe, M., Branch, P., Nierstrasz, O.: Comparative analysis of evolving software systems using the Gini coefficient. In: 2009 IEEE International Conference on Software Maintenance, pp. 179–188 (2009)
34. Vim, I.: International vocabulary of basic and general terms in metrology (VIM), International Organization, vol. 2004, pp. 9–14 (2004)
35. Barwick, V., Prichard, E.: Eurachem guide: terminology in analytical measurement–Introduction to VIM 3. Disponible à l'adresse www.eurachem.org (2011)

An Empirical Study on the Role of Macro-Meso-Micro Measures in Citation Networks

Rishabh Narang[1], Sanjay Misra[2], and Rinkaj Goyal[1(✉)]

[1] University School of Information, Communication and Technology, GGS Indraprastha University, Dwarka, New Delhi, India
rnradon17@gmail.com, rinkajgoyal@gmail.com
[2] Covenant University, Ota, Nigeria
sanjay.misra@covenantuniversity.edu.ng

Abstract. Due to the growing number of articles published every year as the research output, it is imperative to analyze their impact on future and current research. In this cito-analytical study, we use two publicly available citation datasets, i.e., arXiv's High-Energy Physics Citation Theory Network and Cora Citation Network. This study employs different macro-meso-micro level indicators such as K-cores, centrality measures, and clustering coefficient in identifying relevant network characteristics and establishing their inter-relationships to determine impactful research. While the meso-level feature identifies the type of citation network, the micro-level indicators (centrality measures) help in recognizing the individual node (research paper) strength and macro-level statistics comments upon the global network characteristics. The current exposition empirically demonstrates the relevance of using macro-meso-micro level statistics together as the unit in determining influential and significant research output. While previous researchers have independently used these metrics in other academic networks, we, however, showed their importance and inter-relationship using an integrationist approach in citation networks.

Keywords: Scientometrics · Social media analytics · Citation networks · Impact analysis

1 Introduction

In recent years, pattern exploration in the scholarly and scientific literature community to examine the knowledge flows, knowledge networks, and research impact has gathered a considerable interest and curiosity from the researcher's community [44]. Due to the rapid growth of the number of articles being published globally, information scientists have started analyzing such academic networks by focusing on collaborations, citations, and co - citation networks using Social Network Analysis (SNA) techniques [7,18,33,34].

This work was supported by the FRGS [Grant number: FRGS-2018-60-1115], Guru Gobind Singh Indraprastha University, New Delhi.

S. Misra et al. (Eds.): ICCSA 2019, LNCS 11622, pp. 340–356, 2019.
https://doi.org/10.1007/978-3-030-24305-0_26

These techniques take the complex network of academic activities (Citation Network, Co-authorship Network, Repository Analysis, etc.) into consideration to conceptualize relevant theories and develop models using relational processes or structural outcomes of some key concepts.

In academia, the citations are an integral part of the process of referencing and acknowledging the information gathered from books, papers, or web sites. Researchers' use citations as one of the metrics to determine the popularity and importance of an article. Citation network is a complex directed graph in which the articles are defined as nodes of the graph and the new paper citing the studies of old papers form a directed edge between them. In an attempt to evaluate how specific areas have evolved and matured, different efforts have been made to analyze the emergence of principal authors and the types of papers that are currently influencing the field [8].

Studies that examine the trends in scientific citations using graph-theoretic and SNA techniques are called 'cito-analytical' studies or 'citations analysis'. Previous studies have investigated academic citation networks to describe their diverse patterns, clustering of nodes, structural cohesiveness, and macro, meso, micro-level network properties to determine the structure of such networks as a function of the detail level [16,27,36].

Prior studies in this area either focus on macro-level statistics to investigate the network's overall structure or on micro-level indicators to obtain the vertex importance for co-citation or co authorship networks (Table 1). We, however, in this study empirically identify the importance of macro-meso-micro indicators (a Social Network Analysis characteristic) in the field of cito-analytics.

Table 1. Previous studies dealing with macro-meso-micro features of social network analysis.

S.No	Study	Measures
1	Luukkonen et al. [25]	Macro (Frequency Distribution)
2	Glänzel et al. [15]	Macro (Frequency Distribution and Empirical Density)
3	Guardio et al. [17]	Macro and Meso (Degree Distribution, Clustering)
4	Yan and Ding [42]	Meso (Clustering)
5	Bibi et al. [4]	Micro (Centrality)
6	Zare et al. [43]	Micro (Centrality)
7	Bollen et al. [5]	Micro (Centrality)

2 Method and Materials

2.1 Networks Following Power-Law

In the field of statistical analysis, power-law provides a functional relationship between the two metrics in consideration. A relative change in one metric resonates as a proportional relative change in the other metric. This change is independent of the initial size of those metrics. Thus, in other words, one metric varies as a power of the other. During the network evolvement, the dis-proportionality of the vertices increases because of the formation of new links over the nodes which already have a large number of edges. This thereby results in a heavy-tailed degree distribution graph of the network. Any network following such characteristics is termed as a scale-free network [2]. The term scale-free network refers that magnifying on any part of the distribution of the network would not change its shape because of the presence of a few highly connected vertices and a large number of weakly connected nodes.

2.2 Influencing Factors for Cito-Analytical Studies

Freeman [11] developed centrality measures based upon the betweenness properties of the nodes in the network. He further introduced four types of centralities: closeness, betweenness, degree, and eigenvector to be used in the domain of social networks. In citation networks, we use the same centrality measure to determine the structural importance and impact of the articles in the network.

Closeness Centrality. It determines the direct or indirect closeness of a node with respect to all other nodes in the network [24]. The value of closeness centrality for a node v is defined as the sum of the reciprocal of distances to the node v to all other nodes in the network.

$$C_c(v) = \Sigma \frac{1}{d_{v,t}} \tag{1}$$

where $d_{v,t}$ denotes the shortest distance between node v and t.

Betweenness Centrality. Betweenness centrality quantifies how much a node controls the communication between all pairs of vertices in the network by acting as a bridge between the two randomly chosen vertice's shortest path [19,24]. It is calculated as the ratio of the number of shortest paths passing through the given vertex to the total number of shortest paths.

$$C_b\left(v\right) \;=\; \Sigma_{i\; \neq v \neq j} \frac{\sigma_{ij}\left(v\right)}{\sigma_{ij}}, \tag{2}$$

where $\sigma_{ij}(v)$ is the number of those paths that intersect node v, and σ_{ij} is total number of shortest paths from node i to node j in graph G.

Degree Centrality. Degree Centrality defines the number of ties a node has with its immediate neighboring nodes in the network, i.e., the number of edges that are adjacent to the given vertex [19,24]. Degree centrality is computed as

$$C_d\left(v\right) \;=\; \frac{k_v}{n-1} = \Sigma_{j \in G}\, \frac{a_{vj}}{n-1} \tag{3}$$

where k_v is the degree of the node, n is the total number of the nodes in the network, and a_{vj} is the number of nodes j that are adjacent to node v.

PageRank. PageRank algorithm is the part of Google search engine to rank web sites based upon the direction of the links. Brin and Page [6] proposed it as an alternative of Eigenvector Centrality, which works only with undirected networks.

PageRank has constantly been used for cito-analytical studies to determine the importance of cited nodes by measuring the impact of citing vertices like authors, articles, journals, etc. [39]. PageRank algorithm measures the popularity and importance of a scholar from a citation perspective by computing the ranking of the authors depending upon the network of the incoming links.

2.3 Dataset and Description

In this paper, we consider two publicly available cito-analytic data sets: arXiv's High-Energy Physics Citation Theory Network [12,22] and Cora Citation Network [1,21,37]. We used datasets of sufficient sizes for conclusion stability. These datasets have more nodes and edges in comparison to DBLP dataset used in other studies. These are directed networks with each node representing a scientific paper ID. In the given set U consisting of node ID, the citing relation is given as $R \subseteq U \times U$, $uRv \equiv v\ cites\ u$ which provides a citation network $N = (U, R)$ [3]. Alternatively, the directed edge $(A \rightarrow B)$ denotes that publication A cites publication B. The basic description of the two data sets is as follows:

1. **arXiv's High-Energy Physics Citation Theory Network:**–The data set contains citations from e-print arXiv and covers the period of papers from January 1993 to April 2003 (124 months). arXiv was launched on August 14, 1991, and thus represents essentially the complete history of its HEP-TH section. The dataset consists of 27,770 articles (nodes) with a total of 352,807 citations (edges).
2. **Cora Citation Network:**– This consists of computer science papers and references gathered through crawling and automatic parsing of the bibliographies of the papers. This data set includes 23,166 nodes and 91,500 edges.

Henceforth, these datasets will be referred as Network-1 and Network-2 respectively.

3 Results and Discussions

Table 2 illustrates the work flow behind the cito-analytical study that is followed.

3.1 Macro-Level Statistics

We compute the macro-level statistics to determine the global network characteristics of each network (data set). Table 3 describes the network metrics such as the number of nodes (scientific papers), edges (citations), average degree connectivity (average of the nearest neighbor of nodes with degree k), and network density (proportion of the direct links in the network with respect to the total ties possible) of each network. We further use Degree Distribution, Gini Coefficient, Lorenz Curve, Giant Component Size, and K-cores to identify the global properties of the considered networks.

Table 2. Research methodology for cito-analytical study.

Property	Method	Indicator type
Verify real-world network	(a) Clustering Coefficient	(a) Meso-level
Verify scale-free network	(a) Degree Distribution	(a) Macro-level
	(b) Frequency Distribution on Centrality Measures	(b) Micro-level
Evaluate network distribution and reachability of nodes	(a) Lorenz Curve and Gini Coefficient	(a) Macro-level
Identify key paper in the network	(a) K-Cores	(a) Macro-level
	(b) Centrality Measures	(b) Micro-level
Measure the redundancy of metrics used for ranking articles	(a) Kendall's Concordance Based Correlation Coefficient for Centrality Metrics	(a) Micro-level

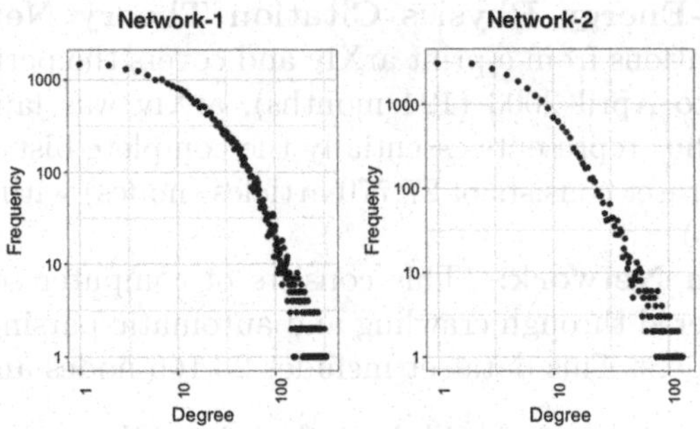

Fig. 1. Degree distribution

Degree Distribution. Since degree distribution tells us about how often an event of a given size occurs, we focus on the relationship between the activity of two users citing each others article. Figure 1 represents that the networks used in this study are scale-free networks because degree distribution exhibits a power-law characteristic (see Sect. 2.1). The fraction of $P(k)$ of nodes having k connections with other nodes of the network is defined as $P(k) \sim k^{-\gamma_\kappa}$, where $-\gamma_\kappa$ is the scale-free degree exponent of the network [29].

Lorenz Curve and Gini Coefficient. Corrado Gini [14] proposed a coefficient (Gini Coefficient) to measure statistical depression, which is commonly used to calculate inequality of wealth and income distribution in economics sector.

However, it can also be used to measure other distributions as well, including quantification of social, or scientific collaboration in researchers network [38]. The coefficient (G) is calculated as the area between the Lorenz Curve of the given distribution and a straight line drawn at a 45° angle from the origin ($G = A/(A+B)$, where A is the area between the straight line drawn at a 45° angle from the origin and Lorenz Curve, and B is the area under the Lorenz Curve). Gini coefficient lies in between 0 to 1 and with a low value tending towards 0 indicates a more equal distribution while a high value tending towards 1 illustrates a more unequal distribution among the parts.

We calculate the Gini Coefficient by plotting a Lorenz Curve (Fig. 2) between the fraction of actors (nodes) and their edges. The coefficient value obtained for Network-1 is 0.570 or 57% and that for Network-2 is 0.521 that is 52.1%. Following this value, we observe that the latter network is slightly more equally distributed amongst the two since the value of Gini Coefficient for Network-2 is less than Network-1 (0.570 and 0.521 for Network-1 and Network-2 respectively).

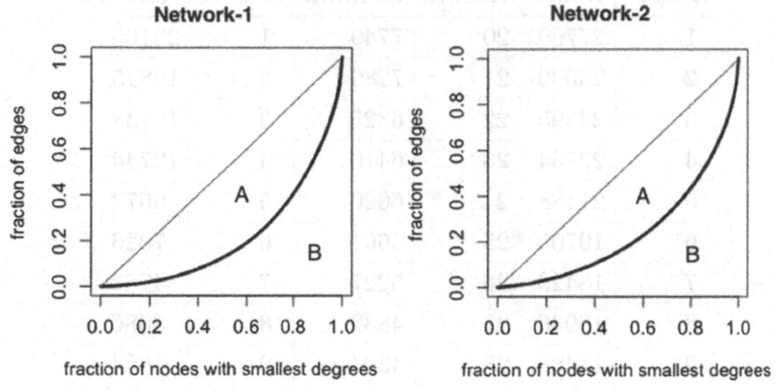

Fig. 2. Lorenz curve

Table 3. Macro-level statistics.

Dataset	Total nodes	Total edges	Average degree connectivity	Network density	Giant component size
Network-1	27770	352807	0.000174	0.000457	7464
Network-2	23166	91500	0.00116	0.000170	3991

Giant Component Size. The largest strongly connected component of a directed graph is the largest association of nodes in the network in which all the nodes are reachable by following the direction of the edges [32]. It can be used to represent the main core of research activities [10]. Therefore, we measure the portion of the network that subjects to be the part of the main core. The GCC of the Network-1 contains 7464 nodes (refer Table 3) that compute to be 26.89% of the total nodes of the network, while for Network-2 is 17.92% of the total actors of the network; thus depicting that a small portion of the network is strongly connected.

K-Cores. For the directed citation networks used in this study, we use another measure, K- Core. Seidman first proposed it for unweighted graphs and since then it has found widespread in the analysis of real networks in social sciences [35,41]. K-core measure identifies the number of times an author is cited. This aids in generating the cores of key articles leading to the impact analysis in the network. Each node present in the k-core has a degree no less than k. To calculate the number of authors in each core, we consider the values of k ranging from 1 to the maximum degree of the node that is 37 in case of Network-1 and 15 for Network-2. For the directed cito-analytic dataset, the K-Core measures the innermost core of the highly cited authors in the network [40]. Table 4 depicts the number of authors in each core k for the Network-1 and Network-2 respectively.

Table 4. Total nodes present in each kth core of Network-1 and Network-2

Network-1				Network-2	
K-Core	Nodes	K-Core	Network	K-Core	Network
1	27769	20	7749	1	23166
2	26099	21	7289	2	19815
3	24395	22	6825	3	16138
4	22764	23	6410	4	12744
5	21188	24	6020	5	9673
6	19705	25	5661	6	7026
7	18429	26	5227	7	4787
8	16936	27	4832	8	3086
9	15488	28	4394	9	1684
10	14406	29	4011	10	1089
11	13303	30	3515	11	535
12	12215	31	2938	12	96
13	11366	32	2406	13	32
14	10668	33	1728	14	30
15	10003	34	1364	15	27
16	9500	35	112		
17	9002	36	108		
18	8601	37	52		
19	8175				

3.2 Meso-Level Features

Meso-level features use clustering as a central mechanism to identify the structural characteristics of the network. Table 5 shows the meso-level features such as the average clustering coefficient and transitivity. The value of the average global clustering coefficient is close to 0 that is 0.312 and 0.265 for both Network-1 and Network-2 respectively. The global clustering coefficient lies between 0 to 1 where value closer to 1 depicts that the network is fully connected and not a real network, while a real-world network has the value significantly less than 1 [30]. It is measured as:

$$C = \frac{3 \times Number\ of\ triangles}{Number\ of\ connected\ triples\ of\ vertices} \tag{4}$$

This measure can be applied to both directed and undirected networks, and refers to the concept of "fraction of transitive triples" used in sociology [41].

Table 5. Meso-level feature

Dataset	Average clustering coefficient	Transitivity
Network-1	0.312	0.132
Network-2	0.265	0.127

3.3 Micro-level Indicators

After employing the macro-level statistics and meso-level measures, we further investigate the micro-level indicators of both the networks to analyze the individual node's power for their network impact analysis. The four centrality measures described in Sect. 2.2 are computed for determining the influencing nodes of the network. Figures 3 and 4 depict the frequency distributions of Closeness, Degree, Betweenness and PageRank Centralities for Network-1 and Network-2 respectively. The vertical axis depicts the frequency corresponding to the metric values on the horizontal axis. The frequency distribution of Degree, Betweenness, and PageRank Centralities for both the datasets again follow a power law where the majority of the articles have a low value of centrality while a very small amount of articles possess a higher value (refer Sect. 2.1). While the Closeness Centrality frequency distribution follows a normal curve.

Thereafter, using the same micro-level parameter, i.e. centrality measures, we examine the key articles of influence. Table 6 and 7 describes top 30 article IDs based on different centrality measures and citation counts. While centrality measures give the important nodes responsible for information flow as described in Sect. 2.2, citation count allows us to determine the impact of an article according to the number of times it has been cited by other researchers. To determine the key article for impact analysis, we can not focus solely on a single metric. Table 6 and 7 both show some inconsistency with respect to the rankings of centrality measures and citation count. The most cited article in Network-1 with article ID 9711200 does not even come under the top 30 ranking articles based upon Closeness and Betweenness Centrality. It has a relatively lower rank (rank 5) under the PageRank metric for computing the influencing node. Whereas, few articles such

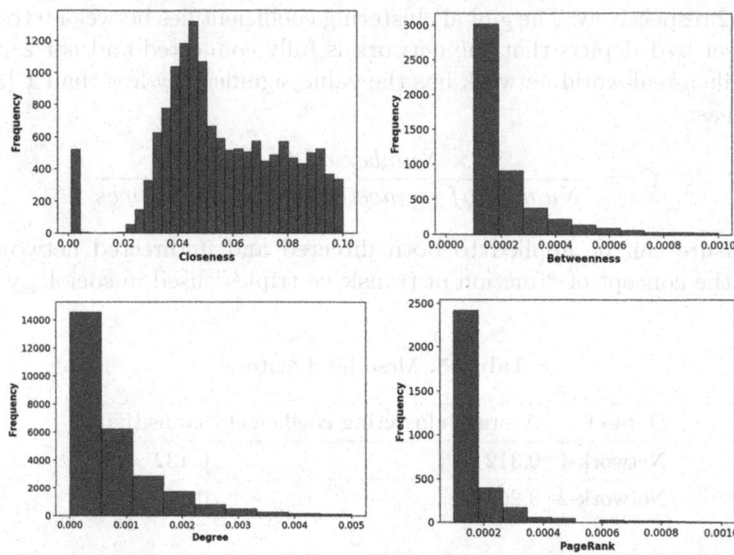

Fig. 3. Frequency distribution based on closeness centrality, betweenness centrality, degree centrality and PageRank for Network-1

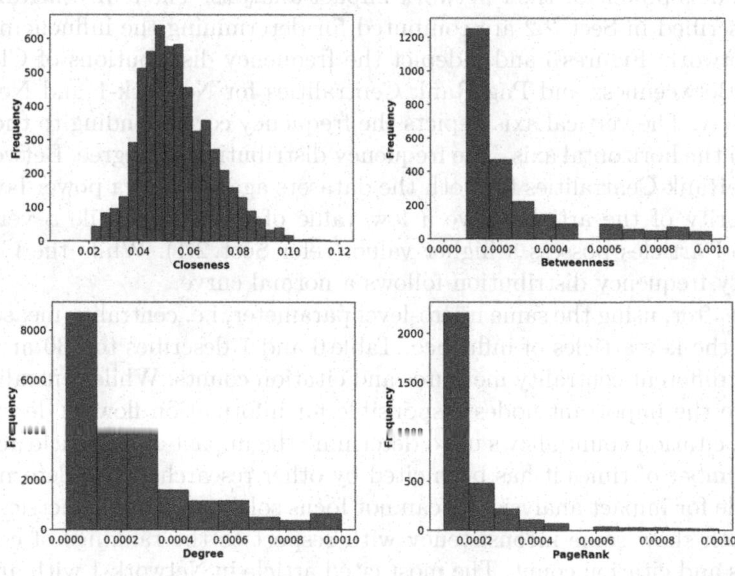

Fig. 4. Frequency distribution based on closeness centrality, betweenness centrality, degree centrality and PageRank for Network-2

Table 6. Network-1's top 30 article ids based on different centrality measures and citation count

Rank	CC based[a] Article ID	DC based[b] Article ID	BWC based[c] Article ID	PR based[d] Article ID	Most cited Article ID
1	9407087	9711200	9905111	9407087	9711200
2	9503124	9802150	9810008	9503124	9802150
3	9510017	9802109	206223	9510017	9802109
4	9401139	9905111	9509140	9402044	9407087
5	9402002	9407087	9803001	9711200	9610043
6	9410167	9908142	9912210	9410167	9510017
7	9408099	9610043	9902121	9408099	9908142
8	9408074	9510017	9607239	9207016	9503124
9	9510135	9503124	206182	9402002	9906064
10	9402032	9906064	9907085	9610043	9408099
11	9207016	9408099	9904179	9205068	9905111
12	9301042	9510209	9904036	9510135	9510209
13	9305185	9711162	9903033	9201015	9711162
14	9304154	9510135	111093	9205027	9510135
15	9501068	9410167	3136	9304154	9410167
16	9504090	9611050	9905046	9802150	9611050
17	9412184	9601029	204158	9401139	9601029
18	9510209	9602022	9906064	9504090	9602022
19	9205027	9803131	206196	9802109	9603142
20	9610043	9603142	9605009	208020	9803131
21	9602022	9603167	9908105	9305185	9603167
22	9512059	9711165	9908142	9207053	9711165
23	9207053	9412184	302221	9307049	9611230
24	9512077	9401139	110123	9204102	9409089
25	9302103	9611230	108172	9510209	9412184
26	9411149	9602052	9611016	9501068	9703166
27	9510169	9703166	204004	9906064	9401139
28	9402044	9608024	110234	9402032	9411149
29	9602052	9710046	9711200	9301042	9602052
30	9511030	9409089	9906151	9403198	9510169

[a] Closeness Centrality
[b] Degree Centrality
[c] Betweenness Centrality
[d] PageRank

Table 7. Network-2's top 30 article ids based on different centrality measures and citation count

Rank	CC[a] based Article ID	DC[b] based Article ID	BWC[c] based Article ID	PR[d] based Article ID	Most Cited Article ID	Rank	CC[a] based Article ID	DC[b] based Article ID	BWC[c] based Article ID	PR[d] based Article ID	Most cited Article ID
1	1435	660	1435	1219	660	16	2955	1475	1044	1589	1475
2	1219	1435	1561	660	1435	17	1257	190	513	4301	300
3	1248	322	5399	1435	322	18	2689	1452	647	1044	1546
4	290	681	923	689	681	19	654	113	2442	1452	113
5	482	3005	1546	1248	3005	20	1076	491	278	7691	1219
6	11320	124	3427	262	124	21	1218	1219	152	407	491
7	742	352	224	1218	352	22	2442	3717	4074	124	3717
8	352	647	1012	1690	647	23	1710	1640	3342	6108	554
9	4187	1546	1465	3941	1248	24	681	399	1886	3333	399
10	3005	1248	367	681	262	25	7212	554	6613	399	331
11	5399	262	1437	5585	1044	26	689	532	159	647	1481
12	1589	1044	9053	322	1646	27	8953	1924	4004	168	144
13	1452	1646	2637	278	1407	28	576	331	8966	2660	1182
14	2552	1407	2582	2988	190	29	1407	1481	17151	4392	532
15	4392	300	1640	2827	1452	30	6725	497	7922	3778	278

as article ID 1435 in Network-2 (Table 7) are consecutively high ranked attaining a position of 1, 2, 1, 3 and 2 in Closeness, Degree, Betweenness, PageRank and Most Cited Article ID metrics respectively. Paper with high degree centrality is important as it suggests that there is an exchange of information with a large number of different papers. Similarly, articles with high closeness centrality rank imply that there is an information flow in the nearby neighbors of the connected component of the node under consideration. Moreover, nodes with high betweenness centrality value have more control over the flow of information as the majority of the information passes through that bridge node. Consecutively, since PageRank centrality takes link's direction into account, it suggests that the information can flow only in one direction that is from the cited paper to the article citing it. Hence, the node with the high PageRank centrality means that there are many articles pointing to it or a paper with a high PageRank is pointing to it thereby the node has an influence extending into the wider network, delimiting the direct connections [9].

Various metrics such as different centrality measures have been studied rigorously for the identification of the important nodes within a complex network [11,31]. Amongst these metrics, K-Cores decomposition (refer Sect. 3.1) is considered as one of the well-established measures to identify the node's influencing power in a network. Kitsak et al. [20] argued that K-Core is a better metric to

Table 8. Centrality metric rankings of all the Article ID's present in the Kth core of Network-1

Article ID in Kth core	Rank in CC[a]	Rank in DC[b]	Rank in BWC[c]	Rank in PR[d]	Article ID in Kth Core	Rank in CC[a]	Rank in DC[b]	Rank in BWC[c]	Rank in PR[d]
110242	10205	147	12950	746	202157	10421	649	4544	2465
201081	10233	132	5332	839	202186	10399	662	757	2745
112044	10255	93	298	649	202190	10485	2448	9923	4786
202021	10235	7213	314	559	203018	10478	4443	245	4123
202109	10368	130	458	978	203080	10464	1807	7929	4156
202153	10426	787	5709	2595	203082	10448	918	382	3943
202179	10431	429	2483	2549	203231	14948	829	5228	3801
203028	12015	1037	1680	3788	204002	15041	2300	6078	9372
203093	10496	1376	4573	4481	204026	14220	1867	4045	6156
203124	10450	385	42	3935	204033	14998	1249	171	5433
203134	10498	1113	869	4554	204146	15019	611	1210	2886
203140	14942	737	2388	4994	204234	15079	989	1209	12093
203164	10810	1248	10820	4347	205008	15623	2301	12402	15328
203186	12083	1225	3434	5022	205109	15154	1922	10550	16613
203229	10503	955	2362	4293	205134	15149	1058	5588	10466
203249	14925	1281	4640	4645	205200	14364	550	92	9671
203255	14938	1806	5370	3792	205266	16513	1547	8873	15045
203257	14954	1153	2962	5411	205279	16510	830	3654	5038
204001	14981	2668	4353	9135	205303	16536	1589	8639	17366
204004	9228	597	27	4012	205311	16509	638	2332	4736
204054	14951	333	681	3930	206010	16559	738	3905	11415
204174	15048	1757	4828	9339	206029	16557	990	7267	19814
204196	15035	1645	2232	8314	206062	16573	875	4595	16536
205067	15066	769	3634	12121	207037	16586	1282	4268	14128
205089	15022	391	725	2747	207175	18090	1719	13329	22706
202111	9170	373	564	1971	211178	17717	245	6382	19583

identify the influential vertices in the network as compared to a node having the highest degree in the network. The nodes that are the part of the last core of the network are considered as the most influential vertices. A node even if it has a lower degree centrality value, but is placed strategically in the core of the network can disseminate information at a higher extent. Furthermore, the authors also stated that K-Core is more efficient than some of the other centrality measures which require high computations like closeness and betweenness centrality.

Table 9. Centrality metric rankings of all the Article ID's present in the Kth core of Network-2

Article ID in Kth Core	Rank in CC[a]	Rank in DC[b]	Rank in BWC[c]	Rank in PR[d]	Article ID in Kth Core	Rank in CC[a]	Rank in DC[b]	Rank in BWC[c]	Rank in PR[d]
155	648	86	639	443	2880	1065	107	636	42
223	278	539	1279	7110	3174	1031	67	642	35
273	1221	130	666	231	3529	6750	1038	1095	821
375	11048	665	13952	13952	4112	133	1649	774	1898
399	112	24	583	25	4113	6334	2005	775	2467
917	858	577	776	2939	4897	7434	436	721	497
1125	1166	125	680	65	5555	1601	116	674	71
1472	765	254	736	301	5680	12738	15188	2760	15188
1473	331	48	638	124	7800	7397	1698	753	861
1546	5	9	346	34	7804	6812	2273	759	1230
1770	587	176	754	814	8056	13717	917	15942	15942
1865	920	104	921	222	9202	1708	190	720	237
2376	3065	780	1294	7589	10119	4294	1721	11499	6263
2620	258	489	745	984					

We thus represent the article IDs found in the kth core that is 37 for Network-1 and 15 for Network-2 (refer Tables 8 and 9) and compare the rankings of these articles with the rankings obtained from different centrality metrics.

From Table 4 we observe that the majority of the article ID's present in the last core of both the networks are not the top ranking nodes obtained from the centrality metrics [26]. Hence, to understand the relationship between micro-level statistics using centrality measures and macro-level indicators using K-Cores, we calculate the Kendall's Concordance Based Correlation amongst all the centrality metrics and K-Core Index Value (normalised by the maximum k value [13]). Tables 10 and 11 enlist the values of Kendall's Concordance Based Correlation Coefficient. While previous researchers have used this metric in co-authorship networks to determine the relationship between centrality measures [4], we use it to establish the relationship between Micro-level Indicators (Centrality Measures) and Macro-level Statistics (K-Core Index) in cito-analyical studies. Though besides Kendall's Concordance Based Correlation Coefficient, other similar measures also exist such as Pearson's Product-Moment Correlation Coefficient, and Spearman's Rank-based Correlation Measure [23], however, we use Kendall's Rank Order Correlation Coefficient to discern the importance of micro-macro-level indicators because it has a more intuitive interpretation. Further, the metric gives higher accuracy as compared to Spearman's Rank-based Correlation on smaller samples [28]. The resultant values range between -1 to 1, where values close to 1 indicate strong agreement between the two rankings, while -1 indicates strong disagreement.

Table 10. Kendall's rank-based correlation coefficient values for Network-1

	CC[a]	DC[b]	BWC[c]	PR[d]	KCI[e]
CC[a]		0.365	0.417	0.606	0.332
DC[b]			0.543	0.319	0.863
BWC[c]				0.366	0.503
PR[d]					0.235
KCI[e]					

[e]K-Core Index

Table 11. Kendall's rank-based correlation coefficient values for Network-2

	CC[a]	DC[b]	BWC[c]	PR[d]	KCI[e]
CC[a]		0.472	0.645	0.798	0.415
DC[b]			0.530	0.439	0.852
BWC[c]				0.604	0.465
PR[d]					0.332
KCI[e]					

From Tables 10 and 11 the highest correlation amongst the centrality metrics can be seen in Closeness-PageRank Centrality, while the least correlation exists for Degree-PageRank Centrality for both the datasets. Whereas, comparing the Kendall's Concordance Based Correlation Coefficient amongst the macro-micro metrics, we see that Degree Centrality-K-Core Index has the highest value (0.863 for Network-1 and 0.852 for Network-2). This suggests that Degree Centrality and K-Core Index Value have a high relationship tendency. Higher Kendall's Correlation Coefficient measure in terms of ranking of nodes provides a greater similarity in the order of ranking as can be observed in Closeness-PageRank Centrality Metrics. When two metrics are highly correlated, the information gain from their perspective becomes redundant while uncorrelated metrics can provide unique insights regarding the network. Thus in order to determine the most impactful articles of the network, it is better to use both macro (K-Core) and micro (Centrality Measures) indicators together.

4 Conclusions

The analysis of academic networks such as co-authorship, co-citation, bibliographic, citation, repository networks using social network analysis (SNA) techniques has recently attracted considerable interests of researchers community. Prior studies in this area show the effectiveness of SNA based approaches in revealing meaningful patterns in these networks. In this study, we empirically show the significance of using macro-meso-micro level statistics together while analysing citation networks. Initially, the type of citation network can be identified by applying meso-level features (clustering) to ascertain that whether the network is a small-world or a real-world network. The type of network can also be verified using macro-level statistics (degree distribution) and the frequency distribution of micro-indicators (centrality measures). Through the empirical analysis of two citation datasets: arXiv's High-Energy Physics Citation Theory Network and Cora Citation Network, we observed that it is essential to consider both macro-level statistics (K-Cores) and micro-level indicators (Centrality Metrics) to find the most impactful nodes of the network. Since the majority of the nodes present in the last k^{th}core of the network which is considered to be the most impactful core of the network are not the top influential vertices according to the different centrality measures, it is imperative to consider both the metrics while finding the influential nodes of the network.

Furthermore, Kendall's Correlation measure reveals that amongst the centrality measures, Closeness-PageRank Centrality Metric has the highest correlation value, while Degree Centrality and K-Core has the maximum correlation when considering the relationship amongst the centrality metrics, or between the centrality measures and K-Cores respectively of the two given networks. Thus, instead of Closeness Centrality which is a computationally high centrality metric, a computationally low centrality measure, i.e., PageRank can be used to calculate the influential nodes in the two citation network.

References

1. Cora citation network dataset - KONECT, September 2016. http://konect.uni-koblenz.de/networks/subelj_cora
2. Barabási, A.L., Albert, R.: Emergence of scaling in random networks. Science **286**(5439), 509–512 (1999)
3. Batagelj, V.: Efficient algorithms for citation network analysis. arXiv preprint cs/0309023 (2003)
4. Bibi, F., Khan, H., Iqbal, T., Farooq, M., Mehmood, I., Nam, Y.: Ranking authors in an academic network using social network measures. Appl. Sci. **8**(10), 1824 (2018)
5. Bollen, J., Van de Sompel, H., Hagberg, A., Chute, R.: A principal component analysis of 39 scientific impact measures. PloS ONE **4**(6), e6022 (2009)
6. Brin, S., Page, L.: The anatomy of a large-scale hypertextual web search engine. Comput. Netw. ISDN Syst. **30**(1–7), 107–117 (1998)
7. Crane, D.: Invisible Colleges: Diffusion of Knowledge in Scientific Communities (1972)
8. Dawson, S., Gašević, D., Siemens, G., Joksimovic, S.: Current state and future trends: a citation network analysis of the learning analytics field. In: Proceedings of the Fourth International Conference on Learning Analytics and Knowledge, pp. 231–240. ACM (2014)
9. Ding, Y., Yan, E., Frazho, A., Caverlee, J.: Pagerank for ranking authors in co-citation networks. J. Am. Soc. Inf. Sci. Technol. **60**(11), 2229–2243 (2009)
10. Fatt, C., Ujum, E., Ratnavelu, K.: The structure of collaboration in the journal of finance. Scientometrics **85**(3), 849–860 (2010)
11. Freeman, L.C.: A set of measures of centrality based on betweenness. Sociometry **40**, 35–41 (1977)
12. Gehrke, J., Ginsparg, P., Kleinberg, J.: Overview of the 2003 KDD cup. ACM SIGKDD Explor. Newsl. **5**(2), 149–151 (2003)
13. Giatsidis, C., et al.: A k-core decomposition framework for graph clustering. arXiv preprint arXiv:1607.02096 (2016)
14. Gini, C.: Variabilità e mutabilità. In: Pizetti, E., Salvemini, T. (ed.) Reprinted in Memorie di metodologica statistica. Libreria Eredi Virgilio Veschi, Rome (1912)
15. Glänzel, W., Debackere, K., Thijs, B., Schubert, A.: A concise review on the role of author self-citations in information science, bibliometrics and science policy. Scientometrics **67**(2), 263–277 (2006)

16. Gondal, N.: The local and global structure of knowledge production in an emergent research field: an exponential random graph analysis. Soc. Netw. **33**(1), 20–30 (2011)
17. Guardiola, X., Guimera, R., Arenas, A., Diaz-Guilera, A., Streib, D., Amaral, L.: Macro-and micro-structure of trust networks. arXiv preprint cond-mat/0206240 (2002)
18. Jones, B.F., Wuchty, S., Uzzi, B.: Multi-university research teams: shifting impact, geography, and stratification in science. Science **322**(5905), 1259–1262 (2008)
19. Kas, M., Carley, L.R., Carley, K.M.: Monitoring social centrality for peer-to-peer network protection. IEEE Commun. Mag. **51**(12), 155–161 (2013)
20. Kitsak, M., Gallos, L.K., Havlin, S., Liljeros, F., Muchnik, L., Stanley, H.E., Makse, H.A.: Identification of influential spreaders in complex networks. Nat. Phys. **6**(11), 888 (2010)
21. Kunegis, J.: KONECT - the Koblenz network collection. In: Proceedings of International Conference on World Wide Web Companion, pp. 1343–1350 (2013). http://userpages.uni-koblenz.de/~kunegis/paper/kunegis-koblenz-network-collection.pdf
22. Leskovec, J., Kleinberg, J., Faloutsos, C.: Graphs over time: densification laws, shrinking diameters and possible explanations. In: Proceedings of the Eleventh ACM SIGKDD International Conference on Knowledge Discovery in Data Mining, pp. 177–187. ACM (2005)
23. Li, C., Li, Q., Van Mieghem, P., Stanley, H.E., Wang, H.: Correlation between centrality metrics and their application to the opinion model. Eur. Phys. J. B **88**(3), 65 (2015)
24. Liu, B.: Social network analysis. In: Web Data Mining. Data-Centric Systems and Applications. Springer, Heidelberg (2011). https://doi.org/10.1007/978-3-642-19460-3_7
25. Luukkonen, T., Persson, O., Sivertsen, G.: Understanding patterns of international scientific collaboration. Sci. Technol. Hum. Values **17**(1), 101–126 (1992)
26. Malliaros, F.D., Rossi, M.E.G., Vazirgiannis, M.: Locating influential nodes in complex networks. Sci. Rep. **6**, 19307 (2016)
27. Marchiori, M., Possamai, L.: Micro-macro analysis of complex networks. PloS ONE **10**(1), e0116670 (2015)
28. Meghanathan, N.: Evaluation of correlation measures for computationally-light vs. computationally-heavy centrality metrics on real-world graphs. J. Comput. Inf. Technol. **25**(2), 103–132 (2017)
29. Muchnik, L., et al.: Corrigendum: origins of power-law degree distribution in the heterogeneity of human activity in social networks. Sci. Rep. **5**, 15932 (2015)
30. Newman, M.E.: Models of the small world. J. Stat. Phys. **101**(3–4), 819–841 (2000)
31. Newman, M.E.: The structure and function of complex networks. SIAM Rev. **45**(2), 167–256 (2003)
32. Newman, M.E.: Coauthorship networks and patterns of scientific collaboration. Proc. Natl. Acad. Sci. **101**(suppl 1), 5200–5205 (2004)
33. Parreira, M.R., Machado, K.B., Logares, R., Diniz-Filho, J.A.F., Nabout, J.C.: The roles of geographic distance and socioeconomic factors on international collaboration among ecologists. Scientometrics **113**(3), 1539–1550 (2017)
34. Popp, J., Balogh, P., Oláh, J., Kot, S., Harangi Rákos, M., Lengyel, P.: Social network analysis of scientific articles published by food policy. Sustainability **10**(3), 577 (2018)
35. Seidman, S.B.: Network structure and minimum degree. Soc. Netw. **5**(3), 269–287 (1983)

36. Small, H., Griffith, B.C.: The structure of scientific literatures I: identifying and graphing specialties. Sci. Stud. **4**(1), 17–40 (1974)
37. Šubelj, L., Bajec, M.: Model of complex networks based on citation dynamics. In: Proceedings of the WWW Workshop on Large Scale Network Analysis, pp. 527–530 (2013)
38. Subramanian, S.V., Kawachi, I.: Income inequality and health: what have we learned so far? Epidemiol. Rev. **26**(1), 78–91 (2004)
39. Waltman, L., Yan, E.: PageRank-related methods for analyzing citation networks. In: Ding, Y., Rousseau, R., Wolfram, D. (eds.) Measuring Scholarly Impact, pp. 83–100. Springer, Cham (2014). https://doi.org/10.1007/978-3-319-10377-8_4
40. Wang, S., Rohe, K., et al.: Discussion of "coauthorship and citation networks for statisticians". Ann. Appl. Stat. **10**(4), 1820–1826 (2016)
41. Wasserman, S., Faust, K.: Social Network Analysis: Methods and Applications, vol. 8. Cambridge University Press, Cambridge (1994)
42. Yan, E., Ding, Y.: Scholarly network similarities: how bibliographic coupling networks, citation networks, cocitation networks, topical networks, coauthorship networks, and coword networks relate to each other. J. Am. Soc. Inf. Sci. Technol. **63**(7), 1313–1326 (2012)
43. Zare-Farashbandi, F., Geraei, E., Siamaki, S.: Study of co-authorship network of papers in the journal of research in medical sciences using social network analysis. J. Res. Med. Sci. Off. J. Isfahan Univ. Med. Sci. **19**(1), 41 (2014)
44. Zhao, D., Strotmann, A.: Analysis and visualization of citation networks. Synth. Lect. Inf. Concepts Retrieval Serv. **7**(1), 1–207 (2015)

Tailoring PMI and OGC Portfolio Frameworks

Ana Lima[1,2(✉)], Gabriela Fernandes[2], and Ricardo J. Machado[1,2]

[1] CCG/ZGDV Institute, 4800-058 Guimarães, Portugal
ana.lima@ccg.pt, rmac@dsi.uminho.pt

[2] ALGORITMI Research Centre, Universidade do Minho, 4800-058 Guimarães, Portugal
g.fernandes@dps.uminho.pt

Abstract. The strategy definition in organizations and its implementation by projects has been difficult to achieve. Project portfolio management processes provide the linkage between the organization's strategic objectives and their programs and projects. It is worthless to have the latest technology and resources to develop projects, if there are no organized processes and focus on strategic interests. The organizations need to develop processes, tools, and techniques that support their business, to act at the required level, but keeping in mind that these processes and tools need to evolve over time. Therefore, for a better understanding of the processes and use of artefacts from 'project portfolio management', this paper aims to develop an information technology 'project portfolio management' framework based on 'project portfolio management' processes from PMI and artefacts from OGC (Axelos, until 2013). For a better understanding of the process, inputs and outputs artefacts, the framework is modelled using the BPMN-Business Process Modelling and is done a traceability map, of an example artefact, using UML State Machine Model.

Keywords: Project portfolio management · PMI · OGC · BPMN · Axelos

1 Introduction

The term "Portfolio" began to be used by organizations in the area of finance, defining a selection of investments made by an individual or organization, with the objective of reducing investment risk [1]. An organization's investment project portfolio represents its current strategy in that it represents its structure, processes and products [2]. Due to globalization, organizations tend to consider innovation and product development projects as crucial to the longevity of their organizations [3, 4].

Organizations need to develop processes, tools, and techniques that support their business, to act at the required level, but keeping in mind that these processes and tools need to evolve over time [5]. There are different techniques and tools that can be used in estimating, evaluating, and selecting projects for a portfolio. However, many of these techniques and tools are not widely applied, because of its complexity, requiring many input data, or simply because of their high degree of difficulty in understanding and use by decision makers [6].

S. Misra et al. (Eds.): ICCSA 2019, LNCS 11622, pp. 357–371, 2019.
https://doi.org/10.1007/978-3-030-24305-0_27

Senior management in Information Technology (IT) organizations, despite their evolution, have tended to ignore the perspective of the portfolio, focusing only on the individual management of projects [7].

For 'project portfolio management' (PfM) guidance some frameworks focused on prioritization, selection or monitoring of projects have been developed [6, 8–11].

The PfM Standard from PMI (designate in this paper as, PMI PfM framework) presents the collected knowledge of PfM through a set of processes [12], and PfM Standard from OGC (designate in this paper as, OGC PfM framework) presents the collected knowledge of PfM through as a set of practices [13]. These processes and practices have emerged as an approach to support decision making in organizations.

In the context of this paper, an IT PfM framework is proposed for PfM based on these two most recognized standards for 'project portfolio management': "The Standard for Portfolio Management" from the Project Management Institute (PMI), version 2013 [12] and "Management of Portfolios (MoP)" from Axelos, the Office of Government Commerce (OGC) until 2013, version 2011 [13]. Recently, the PMI released a new version (fourth edition) of "Standard for Portfolio Management" [12], however the researchers already had conclude most of their research and therefore the third version of PMI PfM framework was maintained.

The PMI PfM framework is considered to be the most complete framework currently available for PfM [14, 15], while the OGC PfM framework is particularly relevant for IT PfM [16]. PMI has a better defined structure of PfM processes [17], and the OGC standard for PfM has a greater detail on how to implement PfM practices from the artefacts [18], therefore the IT PfM framework proposed is based on PMI processes and OGC artefacts. For a better understanding of process, and inputs and outputs artefacts, the IT PfM framework is modelled using the *Business Process Modeling Notation* (BPMN) [19].

This paper is organized as follows. Section 2 presents the specification of the dependency analysis between OGC artefacts and PMI processes using BPMN model. Section 3 shows, as an example, the traceability map of, the most used and most updated artefact by all PMI PfM processes, the OGC. A [27.1] Portfolio Delivery Plan – Schedule, using the Unified Modeling Machine (UML) State Machine Model. Finally, conclusions and some highlights for further research are presented.

2 Dependency Between PMI PfM Processes and OGC PfM Artefacts

For the development of a more detailed IT PfM framework was done a merge between the PMI and OGC PfM frameworks, more specifically between the processes defined by PMI and the defined artefacts from OGC, with the objective of helping professionals to execute the PfM processes more efficiently through a complete set of artefacts.

This research's work, based on the researchers' extensive professional experience in PfM and in an in-depth analysis and discussion of the concepts and definitions of each artefact from PMI and OGC PfM frameworks, establishes a mapping between the artefacts from OGC PfM framework and PMI PfM framework.

Therefore, the tailored IT PfM framework proposed adopts the processes from the PMI PfM framework and, through the mapping of artefacts from the PMI PfM framework to OGC PfM framework, a complete artefact's structure from OGC PfM framework is used [20].

Table 1 presets the mapping between all the PMI portfolio processes and OGC PfM artefacts. As an example, the researchers analyze the PMI process {PP1} DPSP 'Develop Portfolio Strategic Plan' [17], through their interaction with artefacts from the OGC PfM framework [20].

2.1 Elementary Dependency Analysis

In Table 1, {PP1} DPSP 'Develop Portfolio Strategic Plan' process from PMI PfM framework receives information through the OGC PfM artefacts ("IN", "I/O" and "OUT"): A[1] 'Strategic Objectives', A[2] 'Organizational Environmental Analysis', A [3] 'Individual Stakeholder Engagement and Communication Plans', A[4] 'Organizational Management Strategy and Risk', A[5] 'Governance Structures', A [6] 'Portfolio Risk Management Strategy', A[7] 'Financial Metrics and Investment Criteria', A[12] 'Portfolio's Categorization', A[13] 'Portfolio's Governance', A[14] 'Portfolio Strategy', A[21] 'Portfolio Stakeholder Engagement and Communication Plan', A[22] 'Portfolio Resource Schedule', A[23] 'Resource Forecast', A[25] 'Standards and Templates to guide programme and project Planners', A[26] 'Lessons Learned', A[27.2] 'PDP. Resources' (PDP represents 'Portfolio Delivery Plan', sub-group, Resources), A[27.3] 'PDP.Cost' (PDP represents 'Portfolio Delivery Plan', sub-group, Cost) and A[27.4] 'PDP.Risk' (PDP represents 'Portfolio Delivery Plan', sub-group, Risk) [20].

The relationships between processes and artefacts are represented in the matrix of Table 1, where an "IN" means input artefact, "OUT" for output artefact, and "I/O" for input and output artefact.

After {PP1} DPSP 'Develop Portfolio Strategic Plan' process is executed, it sends or generates information to the following OGC PfM artefacts: A[27.1] 'PDP. Schedule', A[8] 'Portfolio' and A[14] 'Portfolio Strategy'. All PMI PfM processes in the depicted mapping, in Table 1, are positioned in the respective knowledge area from PMI PfM framework (as an example, the {PP1} DPSP 'Develop Portfolio Strategic Plan', is located in the lane of the '*Portfolio Strategic Management*' knowledge area). All the PMI PfM processes are organized by five knowledge areas [17].

The tailored IT PfM framework proposed is developed under the knowledge areas from PMI PfM framework, with two objectives: (1) to clarify the sequence of processes to be executed for each area of knowledge; and, (2) to perceive if professionals can perform only a set of processes without any dependence on other processes, for example, the professional can only perform the processes of the area of knowledge, '*Portfolio Risk Management*'.

A knowledge area includes PMI PfM processes (see Table 2), which are linked to the respective inputs and outputs (artefacts and processes).

The tailored IT PfM framework, with processes from PMI PfM framework and OGC PfM artefacts, and a possible order of execution of the processes by area of knowledge is presented, in detail by using the Business Process Model and Notation (BPMN), as an example see Fig. 1.

Table 1. The mapping between all the PMI portfolio processes and OGC PfM artefacts

Portfolio Process (PMI) / Artefacts (OGC)		PMI-Defining Process Group								PMI-Aligning Process Group						PMI-Authorizing and Controlling Process Group				
		PSM (PP 1) DPSP S,M,C,I	PSM (PP 2) DPC S,M,C,I	PSM (PP 3) DPR S,M,C,I	PGM (PP 4) DPMP S,M,C,I	PGM (PP 5) DP S,M,C,I	PPM (PP 6) DPPMP S,M,C,I	PCM (PP 7) DPCMP M,C,I	PRM (PP 8) DPRMP S,M,C,I	PSM (PP 9) MSC M,C,I	PGM (PP 10) OP S,M,C,I	PPM (PP 11) MSD S,M,C,I	PPM (PP 12) MPV S,M,C,I	PCM (PP 13) MPI M,C,I	PRM (PP 14) MPR M,C,I	PGM (PP 15) AP S,M,C,I	PGM (PP 16) PPO S,M,C,I	Number of Artefacts	INPUT Number of Artefacts	OUTPUT Number of Artefacts
OGC ARTEFACTS — OGC.A[1] Strategic Objectives	OGC.A[1.1] Market Sizing	IN													IN			2	2	0
	OGC.A[1.2] Innovation	IN													IN			2	2	0
	OGC.A[1.3] Human Resources	IN													IN			2	2	0
	OGC.A[1.4] Financial Resources	IN													IN			2	2	0
	OGC.A[1.5] Physical Resources	IN													IN			2	2	0
	OGC.A[1.6] Productivity	IN													IN			2	2	0
	OGC.A[1.7] Social Responsability	IN													IN			2	2	0
	OGC.A[1.8] Profit Requirements	IN													IN			2	2	0
OGC.A[2] Organizational Environmental Analysis	OGC.A[2.1] SWOT analysis	IN	IN		IN		IN		IN						IN			6	6	0
	OGC.A[2.2] PESTLE analysis	IN	IN		IN		IN		IN						IN			6	6	0
	OGC.A[2.3] Porter's five forces analysis	IN	IN		IN		IN		IN						IN			6	6	0
OGC.A[3] Individual Stakeholder Engagement and Communication Plans		IN			IN		IN	IN	I/O						OUT			7	5	2
OGC.A[4] Organizational Management Strategy and Risk		IN			IN		IN	IN	I/O						OUT			7	5	2
OGC.A[5] Governance Structures		IN			IN		IN	IN	I/O						OUT			7	5	2
OGC.A[6] Portfolio Risk Management Strategy		IN	I/O		I/O	IN	I/O	I/O	I/O	I/O	I/O		OUT	I/O	I/O	OUT	I/O	24	12	12
OGC.A[7] Financial Metrics and Investment Criteria		IN	I/O		I/O	IN	I/O	I/O	I/O	I/O	I/O		OUT	I/O	I/O	I/O	I/O	26	13	12
OGC.A[8] Portfolio		OUT		IN		I/O		IN			I/O	I/O	OUT	IN	IN	I/O	I/O	16	9	7
OGC.A[9] Portfolio Maps				I/O	IN	I/O		IN		I/O	I/O		IN				IN	12	8	4
OGC.A[10] Portfolio reports								IN			I/O	I/O	I/O	I/O	I/O	I/O	I/O	15	8	7
OGC.A[11] Portfolio Scope			OUT	OUT	IN	IN				OUT	IN						IN	7	4	3
OGC.A[12] Portfolio's Categorization		IN	I/O		I/O	IN	I/O	I/O	I/O	I/O	I/O		OUT	I/O	I/O	OUT	I/O	24	12	12
OGC.A[13] Portfolio's Governance		IN	I/O		I/O	IN	I/O	I/O	I/O	I/O	I/O	OUT	OUT	I/O	I/O	OUT	I/O	25	12	13
OGC.A[14] Portfolio Strategy		I/O	I/O	IN	I/O	IN	I/O	I/O	I/O	I/O	I/O		I/O	I/O	I/O	OUT	I/O	27	14	13
OGC.A[15] Benefits Forecast											IN			IN	IN			3	3	0
OGC.A[16] Portfolio-level Benefits Realisation Plan											IN			IN	IN			3	3	0
OGC.A[17] Portfolio's Business Case																		0	0	0
OGC.A[18] Financial Plan											IN			IN	IN	I/O	I/O	7	5	2
OGC.A[19] Portfolio's Performance								IN			IN	OUT	I/O	IN			I/O	8	5	3
OGC.A[20] Portfolio-level Performance Metrics								IN			IN	OUT	I/O	IN			I/O	8	5	3
OGC.A[21] Portfolio Stakeholder Engagement and Communication Plan		IN	I/O		I/O	IN	I/O	I/O	I/O	I/O	I/O		OUT	I/O	I/O	OUT	I/O	24	12	12
OGC.A[22] Portfolio Resource Schedule		IN	I/O		I/O	IN	I/O	I/O	I/O	I/O	I/O	I/O	I/O	I/O	I/O	I/O	I/O	28	15	13
OGC.A[23] Resource Forecast		IN	I/O		I/O	IN	I/O	I/O	I/O	I/O	I/O	I/O	I/O	I/O	I/O	I/O	I/O	28	15	13
OGC.A[24] Portfolio Skills Register																		0	0	0
OGC.A[25] Standards and Templates to guide programme and project Planners		IN	I/O		I/O	IN	I/O	I/O	I/O	I/O	I/O		OUT	I/O	I/O	OUT	I/O	24	12	12
OGC.A[26] Lessons Learned		IN	I/O		I/O	IN	I/O	I/O	I/O	I/O	I/O		OUT	I/O	I/O	OUT	I/O	24	12	12
OGC.A[27] Portfolio Delivery Plan	OGC.A[27.1] Schedule	OUT	I/O	IN	I/O	I/O	I/O	I/O	I/O	I/O	I/O	I/O	I/O	I/O	I/O	I/O	I/O	30	15	16
	OGC.A[27.2] Resources	IN	I/O		I/O	IN	I/O	I/O	I/O	I/O	I/O		OUT	I/O	I/O	OUT	I/O	24	12	12
	OGC.A[27.3] Cost	IN	I/O		I/O	IN	I/O	I/O	I/O	I/O	I/O		OUT	I/O	I/O	I/O	I/O	26	13	12
	OGC.A[27.4] Risk	IN	I/O		I/O	IN	I/O	I/O	I/O	I/O	I/O		OUT	I/O	I/O	OUT	I/O	24	12	12
[illegible]											IN			IN	IN	I/O	I/O	7	5	2
Number of Artefacts		28	18	6	22	17	20	22	20	16	24	6	19	22	34	18	22			
INPUT Number of Artefacts		27	17	4	22	17	20	22	20	18	24	5	8	22	31	8	22			
OUTPUT Number of Artefacts		3	15	2	14	3	14	14	17	16	17	8	18	15	16	16	20			

Table 2. Alignment between knowledge areas and portfolio processes of PMI PfM framework

Portfolio Management Knowledge Areas (PMKA)	Portfolio Processes (PP)	Acronym
Portfolio Strategic Management (PSM)	Develop Portfolio Strategic Plan	{PP 1} DPSP
Portfolio Strategic Management (PSM)	Develop Portfolio Charter	{PP 2} DPC
Portfolio Strategic Management (PSM)	Define Portfolio Roadmap	{PP 3} DPR
Portfolio Governance Management (PGM)	Develop Portfolio Management Plan	{PP 4} DPMP
Portfolio Governance Management (PGM)	Define Portfolio	{PP 5} DP
Portfolio Performance Management (PPM)	Develop Portfolio Performance Management Plan	{PP 6} DPPMP
Portfolio Communication Management (PCM)	Develop Portfolio Communication Management Plan	{PP 7} DPCMP
Portfolio Risk Management (PRM)	Develop Portfolio Risk Management Plan	{PP 8} DPRMP
Portfolio Strategic Management (PSM)	Manage Strategic Change	{PP 9} MSC
Portfolio Governance Management (PGM)	Optimize Portfolio	{PP 10} OP
Portfolio Performance Management (PPM)	Manage Supply and Demand	{PP 11} MSD
Portfolio Performance Management (PPM)	Manage Portfolio Value	{PP 12} MPV
Portfolio Communication Management (PCM)	Manage Portfolio Information	{PP 13} MPI
Portfolio Risk Management (PRM)	Manage Portfolio Risks	{PP 14} MPR
Portfolio Governance Management (PGM)	Authorize Portfolio	{PP 15} AP
Portfolio Governance Management (PGM)	Provide Portfolio Oversight	{PP 16} PPO

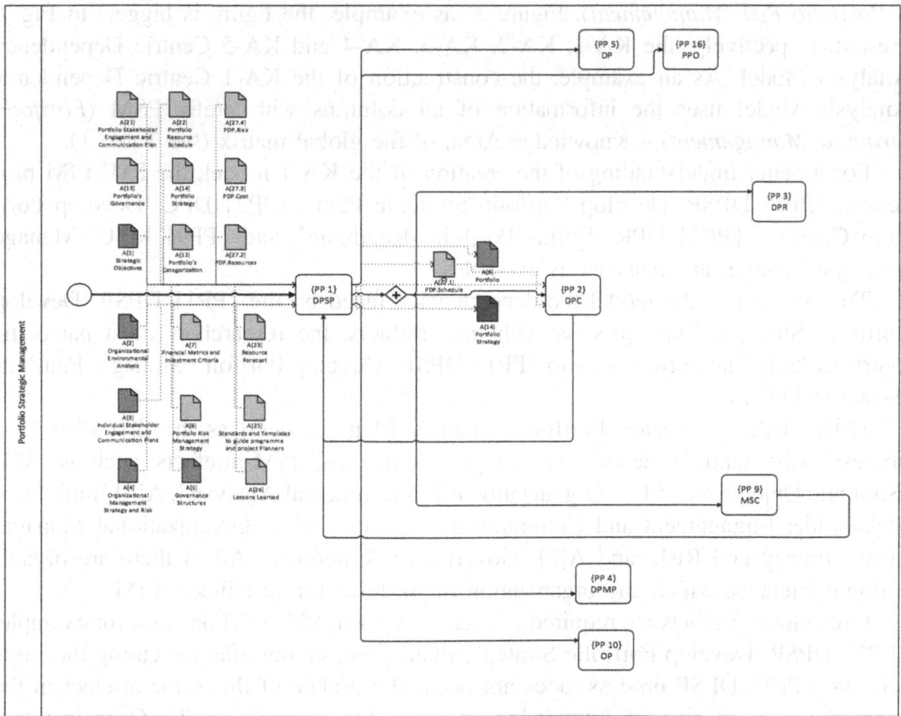

Fig. 1. {PP1} DPSP 'Develop Portfolio Strategic Plan'- centric dependency analysis (Color figure online)

According to the Object Management Group (OMG) [19], the BPMN notation is a process-modelling standard, which purpose is to facilitate the understanding of process diagrams by all stakeholders involved. This notation is used to draw the flowchart drawings that represent the activities or tasks belonging to a business process.

BPMN is a graphical notation explicitly created to represent business processes, identifying activities, dependency control, the tasks, and sub processes [21]. Therefore, the BPMN notation is used for the representation of the Tailoring PMI PfM framework and the OGC PfM framework and their interaction with OGC PfM artefacts.

In Fig. 1, green artefacts represent artefacts not yet used by the PMI PfM processes; grey artefacts represent artefacts created by PMI PfM processes; and red artefacts represent artefacts already created and generated by PMI PfM processes.

2.2 Knowledge Area Centric Dependency Analysis

The objective of using centric dependency analysis in this research work is to show the dependencies between portfolio processes from the PMI PfM framework and artefacts from the OGC PfM framework related to a specific knowledge area from PMI PfM framework. Therefore, five models have been created. They are called KA-n Centric Dependency Analysis Model (where n corresponds to the knowledge area under study, 1 – *Portfolio Strategic Management*, 2 – *Portfolio Governance Management*, 3 – *Portfolio Performance Management*, 4 – *Portfolio Communication Management* and 5 – *Portfolio Risk Management*). Figure 2 (as example, the figure is bigger) to Fig. 6 present, respectively, the KA-1, KA-2, KA-3, KA-4 and KA-5 Centric Dependency Analysis Model. As an example, the construction of the KA-1 Centric Dependency Analysis Model uses the information of all columns with prefix PSM (*Portfolio Strategic Management*) – Knowledge Area, of the global matrix (see Table 1).

For a better understanding of the creation of the KA-1 model, the PMI PfM processes; {PP1} DPSP 'Develop Portfolio Strategic Plan', {PP2} DPC 'Develop Portfolio Charter', {PP3} DPR 'Define Portfolio Roadmap', and {PP9} MSC 'Manage Strategic Change' are analysed as examples.

To represent in the model the dependencies faced by the {PP1} DPSP 'Develop Portfolio Strategic Plan' process with the artefacts, the researchers must parse the matrix column that corresponds to {PP1} DPSP 'Develop Portfolio Strategic Plan', as shown in Fig. 1.

{PP1} DPSP 'Develop Portfolio Strategic Plan' process, as the first PMI PfM process to be handled, needs several inputs from OGC PfM artefacts, such as: A[1] 'Strategic Objectives', A[2] 'Organizational Environmental Analysis', A[3] 'Individual Stakeholder Engagement and Communication Plans', A[4] 'Organizational Management Strategy and Risk' and A[5] 'Governance Structures'. All of them are organizational artefacts, which any organization might have for an efficient PfM.

Green tone artefacts are required to execute a given PMI PfM process, for example, {PP1} DPSP 'Develop Portfolio Strategic Plan' process, but after executing the same process, {PP1} DPSP process, does not occur the update of this same artefact in the process group of area of knowledge covered, for example, A[2] 'Organizational Environmental Analysis'.

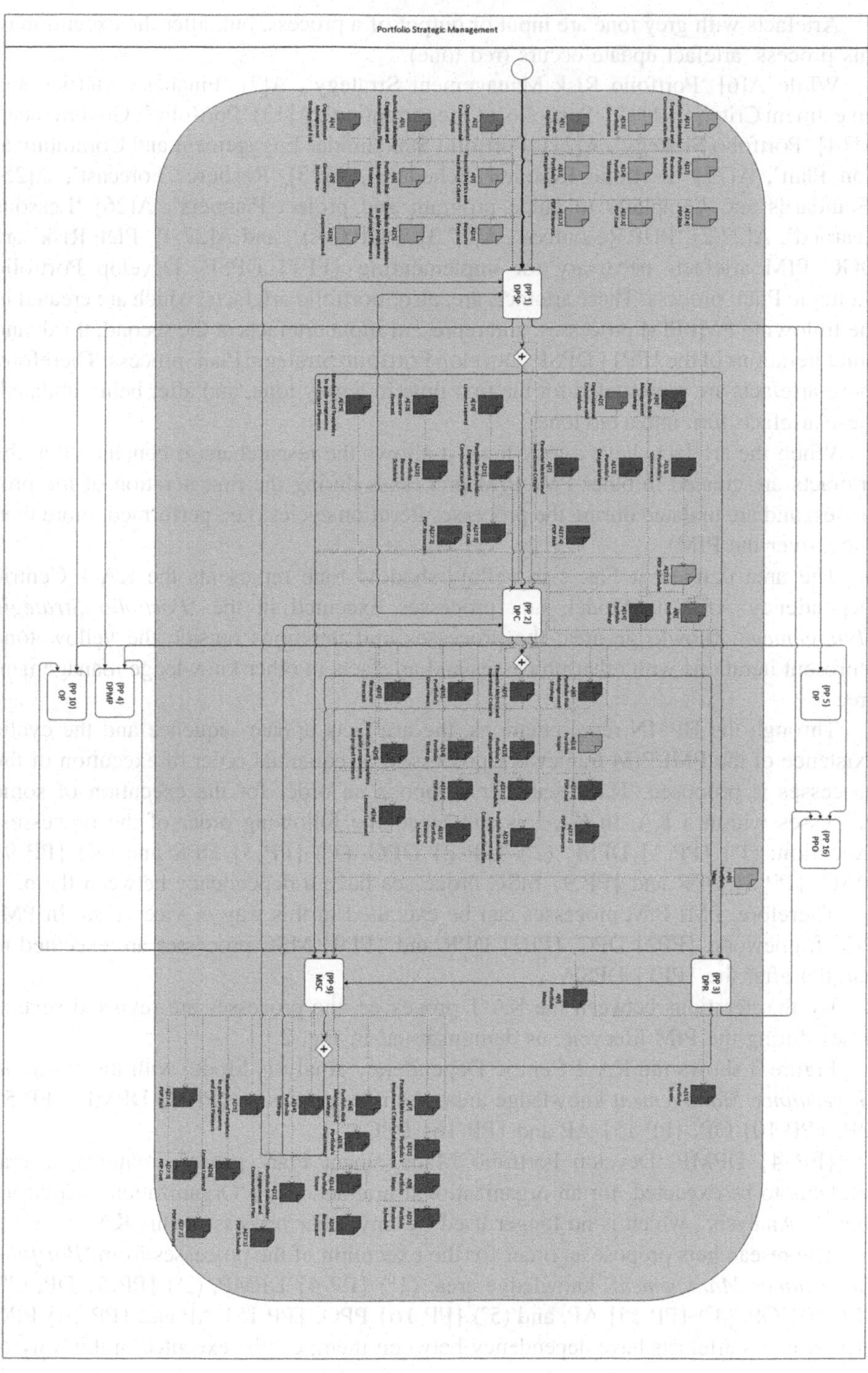

Fig. 2. KA-1 centric dependency analysis model (Color figure online)

Artefacts with grey tone are input or output of a process, but, after the execution of this process, artefact update occurs (red tone).

While A[6] 'Portfolio Risk Management Strategy', A[7] 'Financial Metrics and Investment Criteria', A[12] 'Portfolio's Categorization', A[13] 'Portfolio's Governance', A[14] 'Portfolio Strategy', A[21] 'Portfolio Stakeholder Engagement and Communication Plan', A[22] 'Portfolio Resource Schedule', A[23] 'Resource Forecast', A[25] 'Standards and Templates to guide program and project Planners', A[26] 'Lessons Learned', A[27.2] 'PDP.Resources', A[27.3] 'PDP.Cost', and A[27.4] 'PDP.Risk' are OGC PfM artefacts necessary for implementing {PP1} DPSP 'Develop Portfolio Strategic Plan' process. These artefacts are, also, portfolio artefacts, which are created in the following PMI PfM processes, and represent input artefacts at the second, third, and other iterations of the {PP1} DPSP 'Develop Portfolio Strategic Plan' process. Therefore, these artefacts are represented for the first time in a grey tone, and after being updated, these artefacts turn into a red tone.

When the artefacts have a grey tone, it allows the researchers to conclude that the artefacts are created in other PMI PfM processes during the first iteration of the processes, and are updated during the processes iteration cycles (i.e., performed, more than once, over the PfM).

The area defined at Fig. 2 in yellow shadow tone represents the KA-1 Centric Dependency Analysis Model, i.e., processes executed in the '*Portfolio Strategic Management*' knowledge area; the processes and iterations outside the yellow tone represent iterations with other processes and artefacts in other knowledge management area.

Through the BPMN representations, the artefacts update sequence and the cyclic existence of the PMI PfM framework processes, a sequential order of execution of the processes is proposed. The researchers propose an order for the execution of some processes within a KA. In KA-1 is suggested the following order of the processes' execution: (1°) {PP 1} DPSP, (2°) {PP 2} DPC, (3°) {PP 3} DPR and (4°) {PP 9} MSC. {PP 3} DPR and {PP 9} MSC processes have a dependency between them.

Therefore, PMI PfM processes can be executed in this way or vice versa. In PMI PfM framework, {PP2} DPC, {PP3} DPR and {PP9} MSC processes are executed in parallel after the {PP1} DPSP.

By the iterations between the KA-1 processes, the processes are revisited several times during the PfM lifecycle, as demonstrated in Fig. 2.

Figure 3 shows the KA-2 Centric Dependency Analysis Model with the *Portfolio Governance Management* knowledge area, with the processes {PP 4} DPMP, {PP 5} DP, {PP 10} OP, {PP 15} AP and {PP 16} PPO.

{PP 4} DPMP 'Develop Portfolio Management Plan' process requires several artefacts to be executed, for an organizational artefact, A[2] 'Organizational Environmental Analysis', which is no longer used by any other process of this KA.

The researchers propose an order for the execution of the processes from '*Portfolio Governance Management*' knowledge area: (1°) {PP 4} DPMP, (2°) {PP 5} DP, (3°) {PP 10} OP, (4°) {PP 15} AP, and (5°) {PP 16} PPO. {PP 15} AP and {PP 16} PPO processes, as artefacts have dependency between them; can be executed in this way or vice versa.

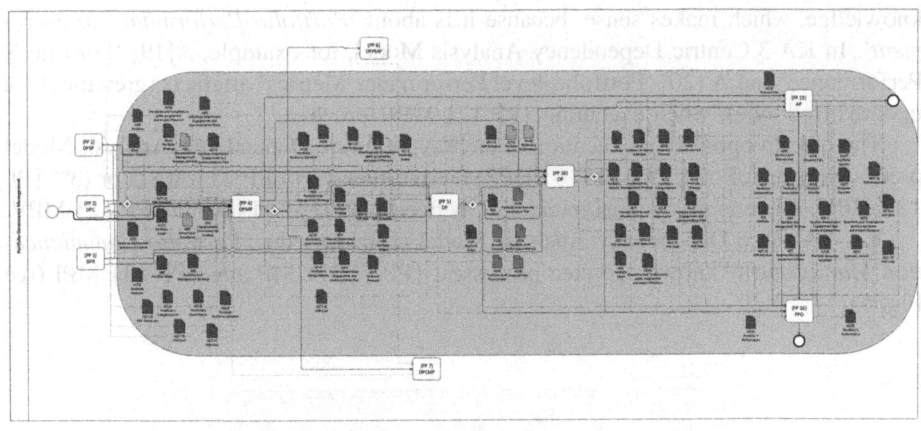

Fig. 3. KA-2 centric dependency analysis model

Figure 4 presents the processes flow of the '*Portfolio Performance Management*' knowledge area, KA-3 Centric Dependency Analysis Model.

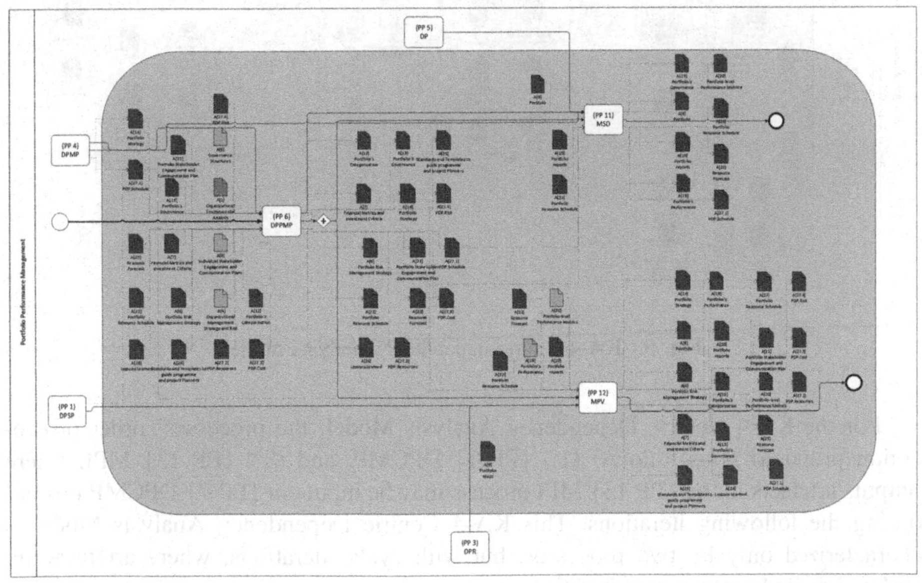

Fig. 4. KA-3 centric dependency analysis model

Three processes are characterized in the KA-3 Centric Dependency Analysis Model: {PP 6} DPPMP, {PP 11} MSD and {PP 12} MPV, which are related through their artefacts. Most of the input and output artefacts represented in Fig. 4 are created in processes of previous areas of knowledge (red tones), the reason why the researchers are able to conclude that this area of knowledge is only used after other areas of knowledge, which makes sense, because it is about '*Portfolio Performance Management*'. In KA-3 Centric Dependency Analysis Model, for example, A[19] 'Portfolio's Performance' and A [20] 'Portfolio-level Performance Metrics' artefacts (grey tone) are updated (red tone), when executing {PP 12} MPV process.

The order proposed for execution of the KA-3 Centric Dependency Analysis Model processes is as follows: (1°) {PP 6} DPPMP, and then (2°) {PP 11} MSD or (3°) {PP 12} MPV. There is no cyclical interaction between {PP 11} MSD and {PP 12} MPV.

KA-4 Centric Dependency Analysis Model represents the '*Portfolio Communication Management'* knowledge area processes, {PP 7}DPCMP and {PP 13} MPI (see Fig. 5).

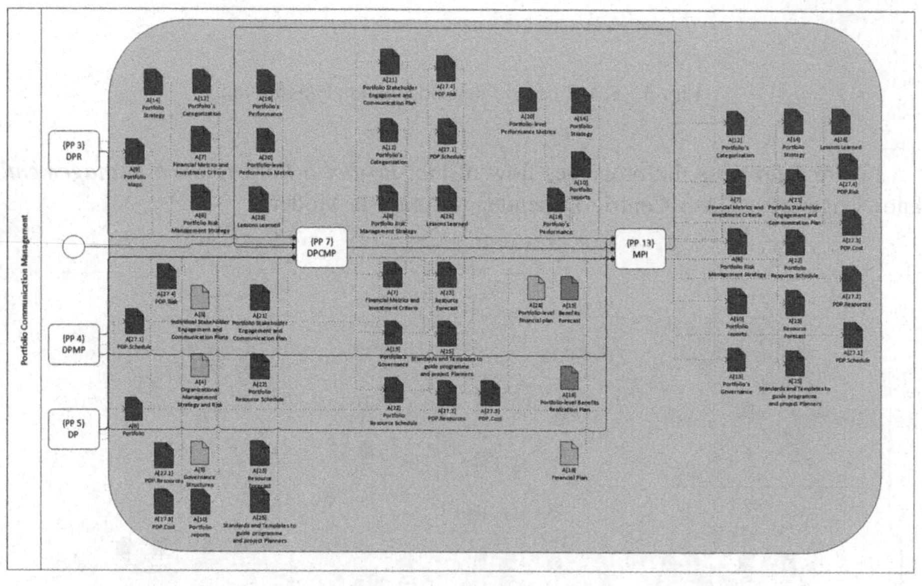

Fig. 5. KA-4 centric dependency analysis model

For the KA-4 Centric Dependency Analysis Model, the processes' order of execution proposed is as follows: (1°) {PP 7} DPCMP, and (2°) {PP 13} MPI, where outputs artefacts in the {PP 13} MPI process may be inputs in {PP 7} DPCMP process during the following iterations. This KA-4 Centric Dependency Analysis Model is characterized only by two processes, but with cyclic iterations, where artefacts are updated according to a new iteration.

Figure 6 presents the KA-5 Centric Dependency Analysis Model, with the two processes of the '*Portfolio Risk Management*' knowledge area, {PP 8} DPRMP and {PP 14} MPR.

KA-5 Centric Dependency Analysis Model is characterized by the input artefacts of the 'portfolio' and 'organizational' among them, A[1] 'Strategic Objectives' and A[2] 'Organizational Environmental Analysis'.

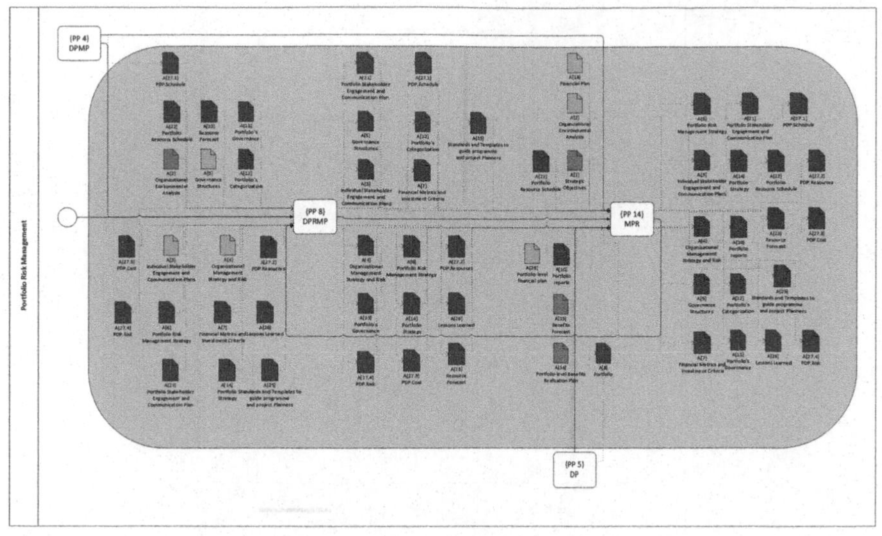

Fig. 6. KA-5 centric dependency analysis model

The order of execution of the KA-5 processes proposed is as follows: (1º) {PP 8} DPRMP, and (2º) {PP 14} MPR, being the iterations cycled between the two processes.

The group of Centric Dependency Analysis Models: KA-1, KA-2, KA-3, KA-4 and KA-5 represents the tailored IT PfM framework, based on the PfM frameworks from PMI and OGC. The use, creation and update of a set of forty OGC PfM artefacts and proposal of an order of execution of the PMI PfM processes allows PfM professionals to perform their jobs systematically.

3 Traceability Map of an Example Artefact Using UML State Machine Model

By the mapping in Table 1, it is noted that the most used and most updated artefact by all PMI PfM processes is A[27.1] 'Portfolio Delivery Plan – Schedule'. Therefore, in order to demonstrate, as an example, the creation and the various updates of this particular artefact A[27.1], throughout the processes and respective knowledge areas, the researchers use the UML State Machine Model (see Fig. 7).

The UML State Machine Model [22] comes from the statecharts [23]. This type of model is used to model the different states of an object during the execution of a process. A state can receive information indicating activities in the input, permanence, and exit of the state (exit/output). The concepts as superstate (or compound states) and substates, present in statecharts, are used in UML state machines model [24].

In Fig. 7, superstate is, for example, '*Portfolio Strategic Management*', with several states 'PSM_1', 'PSM_2', etc. Each state, e.g., PSM_1, represents the transition of the A[27.1] 'Portfolio Delivery Plan – Schedule' artefact for a given process.

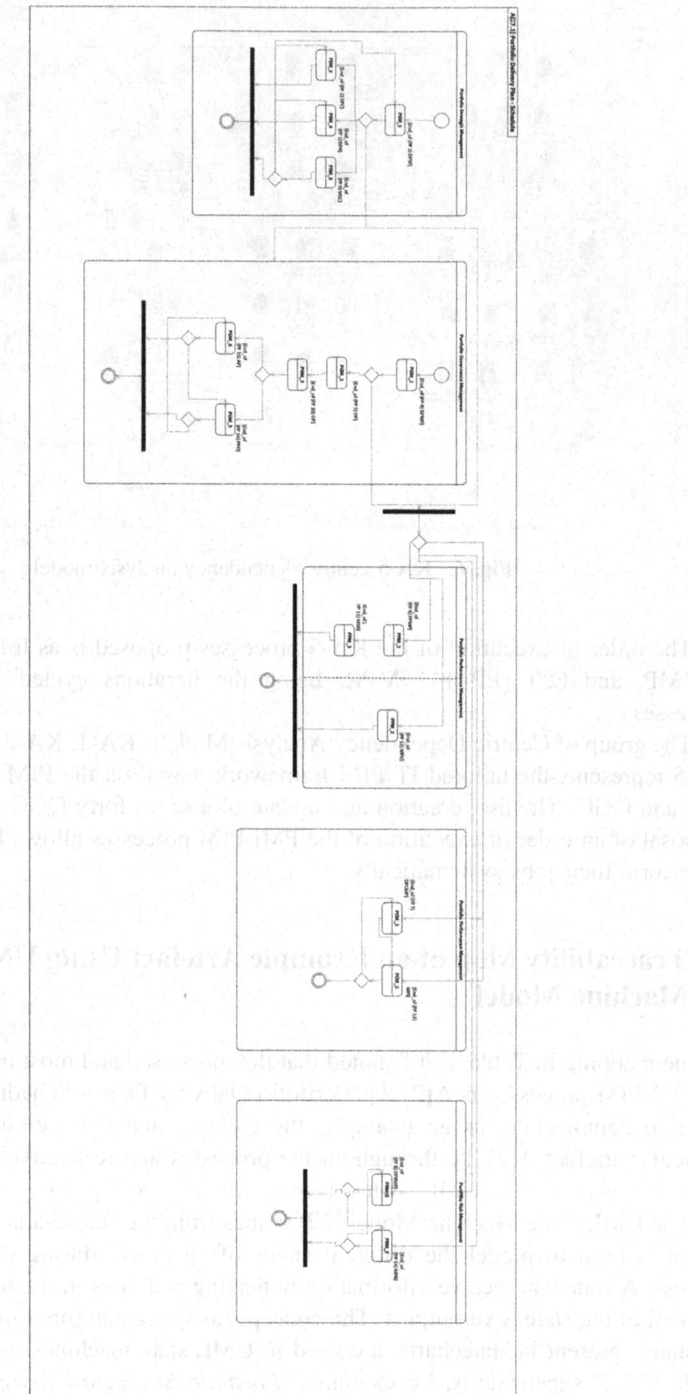

Fig. 7. A[27.1] 'Portfolio Delivery Plan Schedule' artefact using UML State Machine Model

For example, the artefact A[27.1] is input in the process {PP2} DPC, but it is also output in this same process. Therefore, when the process {PP2} DPC is executed, the artefact A[27.1] is modified and a new output of A[27.1] is created.

Portfolio Strategic Management (PSM), *Portfolio Governance Management* (PGM), *Portfolio Performance Management* (PPM), *Portfolio Communication Management* (PCM) and *Portfolio Risk Management* (PRM) knowledge areas are considered the compound states or superstates (see Fig. 7).

Within the '*Portfolio Strategic Management*' compound state or superstate, after passing PSM_1 state, the A[27.1] 'Portfolio Delivery Plan – Schedule' artefact may be executed in the other PSM processes, as can be also used as input artefact in PGM and PPM compound states (represented by a grey line). This artefact may also be input (initialized) in the PGM compound state. After passing the PGM_1 state, A[27.1] 'Portfolio Delivery Plan – Schedule' artefact can input the subsequent processes into the PGM or can input the PPM, PCM or PRM composite states. A [27.1] 'Portfolio Delivery Plan – Schedule' artefact, when showing up in the PPM, PCM or PRM compound states, comes from the PSM or PGM compound states.

In summary, Fig. 7 shows that, A[27.1] 'Portfolio Delivery Plan – Schedule', OGC PfM artefact interacts with sixteen PMI PfM processes, and therefore it is an essential artefact for PfM.

4 Conclusions and Future Work

This paper contributes to individuals and organizations interested in increasing their performance in PfM, by presenting the mapping between OGC PfM artefacts and PMI PfM artefacts and the mapping between PMI PfM processes and OGC PfM artefacts, from the two worldwide recognized PfM frameworks: OGC (now Axelos) and PMI.

Nevertheless, OGC PfM framework has a broader collection of artefacts regarding how PfM processes should be performed. Therefore, this research's work, based on the researchers' extensive professional experience in PfM and in an in-depth analysis and discussion of the concepts and definitions of each artefact from PMI and OGC PfM frameworks, establishes a mapping between the artefacts from OGC PfM framework and PMI PfM framework. The paper increases the understanding of how to execute PfM processes from artefacts, bringing mainly a contribution for practice.

A tailored IT PfM framework, based on processes from the PMI PfM framework and artefacts from the OGC PfM framework is proposed, through a previous mapping between artefacts from the PMI PfM framework and artefacts from the OGC PfM framework.

The tailored IT PfM framework proposed aims to help PfM professionals in understanding "how to" use the PfM processes from PMI PfM framework, and the order of execution of the processes, using a wide range of existing artefacts from OGC PfM framework.

The researchers present the tailored IT PfM framework used BPMN representation. However, due to the complexity and richness of the artefacts, additionally, the researchers, present a representation in UML State Machine of the most used and updated artefact in IT PfM framework, A[27.1] 'Portfolio Delivery Plan – Schedule' artefact. This representation allows showing all the details of the transitions, through the different areas of knowledge and processes.

Therefore, the next step will be to conduct a case study to validate the IT PfM framework at a particular organizational context - information technology projects in a research and development organization. The case study will allow: (1) to validate the processes flow (i.e. processes execution order) and (2) to identify what artefacts will be necessary to discard or to create taking into account the organizational context, refining the IT PfM framework.

Acknowledgements. This work has been supported by FCT – Fundação para a Ciência e Tecnologia within the Project Scope: UID/CEC/00319/2019.

References

1. Markowitz, H.: Portfolio selection. J. Finance **7**(1), 77–91 (1952)
2. Kopmann, J., Kock, A., Killen, C.P., Gemünden, H.G.: The role of project portfolio management in fostering both deliberate and emergent strategy. Int. J. Proj. Manag. **35**(4), 557–570 (2017)
3. Kester, L., Griffin, A., Hultink, E.J., Lauche, K.: Exploring portfolio decision-making processes. J. Prod. Innov. Manag. **28**(5), 641–661 (2011)
4. McNally, R.C., Durmuşoğlu, S.S., Calantone, R.J.: New product portfolio management decisions: antecedents and consequences. J. Prod. Innov. Manag. **30**(2), 245–261 (2013)
5. McCarthy, I.P., Tsinopoulos, C., Allen, P., Rose-Anderssen, C.: New product development as a complex adaptive system of decisions. J. Prod. Innov. Manag. **23**(5), 437–456 (2006)
6. Archer, N., Ghasemzadeh, F.: An integrated framework for project portfolio selection. Int. J. Proj. Manag. **17**(4), 207–216 (1999)
7. Rautiainen, K., Schantz, J., Vahaniitty, J.: Supporting scaling agile with portfolio management: case Paf. com. In: 2011 44th Hawaii International Conference on System Sciences (HICSS), pp. 1–10 (2011)
8. Bitman, W.R., Sharif, N.: A conceptual framework for ranking R&D projects. IEEE Trans. Eng. Manag. **55**(2), 267–278 (2008)
9. Blau, G.E., Pekny, J.F., Varma, V.A., Bunch, P.R.: Managing a portfolio of interdependent new product candidates in the pharmaceutical industry. J. Prod. Innov. Manag. **21**(4), 227–245 (2004)
10. Cooper, R., Edgett, S., Kleinschmidt, E.: Portfolio management in new product development: lessons from the leaders-II. Res. Technol. Manag. **40**(6), 43–52 (1997)
11. Mikkola, J.H.: Portfolio management of R&D projects: implications for innovation management. Technovation **21**(7), 423–435 (2001)
12. Project Management Institute: The Standard for Portfolio Management. Project Management Institute, Newtown Square (2013)
13. Axelos, MoP^{TM} Management of Portfolios, London (2011)
14. McDonald, C., Sarbazhosseini, H.: A state transition approach to conceptualising research: the project portfolio management domain. In: 24th Australasian Conference on Information Systems (ACIS), pp. 1–10 (2013)
15. Young, M., Conboy, K.: Contemporary project portfolio management: reflections on the development of an Australian competency standard for project portfolio management. Int. J. Proj. Manag. **31**(8), 1089–1100 (2013)

16. Williams, B., Young, M., Young, R., Zapata, J.: Project, programme and portfolio maturity: a case study of Australian Federal Government. Int. J. Manag. Proj. Bus. **7**(2), 215–230 (2014)
17. Lima, A., Monteiro, P., Fernandes, G., Machado, Ricardo J.: Dependency analysis between PMI portfolio management processes. In: Gervasi, O., et al. (eds.) ICCSA 2016. LNCS, vol. 9790, pp. 288–300. Springer, Cham (2016). https://doi.org/10.1007/978-3-319-42092-9_22
18. Lima, A., Machado, R.J., Fernandes, G.: Input and output artefacts in portfolio practices from the OGC standard for Management of Portfolios. In: 2017 17th International Conference on Computational Science and Its Applications (ICCSA), pp. 1–8 (2017)
19. OMG, Business Process Model And Notation™ (BPMN™), OMG (2013). http://www.omg.org/spec/BPMN/2.0.2/PDF/. Accessed 25 Aug 2017
20. Lima, A., Fernandes, G., Machado, R.J.: Mapping between PMI and OGC artefacts for project portfolio management. In: International Conference on Intelligent Systems 2018'IS (2018)
21. Lübke, D., Schneider, K.: Visualizing use case sets as BPMN processes. In: Requirements Engineering Visualization, 2008. REV 2008, pp. 21–25 (2008)
22. OMG, OMG unified modeling language, superstructure version, 2015 (2015). http://www.omg.org/spec/UML/2.5/PDF/. Accessed 28 Aug 2017
23. Harel, D.: Statecharts: a visual formalism for complex systems. Sci. Comput. Program. **8**(3), 231–274 (1987)
24. Gross, H.: Component-Based Software Testing with UML. Springer, Heidelberg (1998)

Graph-Based Fault Localization

Béla Vancsics(✉)

Department of Software Engineering, University of Szeged,
Dugonics tér 13, Szeged 6720, Hungary
vancsics@inf.u-szeged.hu

Abstract. The subject of fault localization (FL) is a much-researched area, it has large literature. There are plenty of algorithms that try to identify the location of the bugs using different approaches. Debugging has a large resource requirement, therefore the bug's location's reflective identificaton greatly helps developers and testers to maintain the quality and reliability of the software.

Our goal is to implement a graph-based Fl *GFL* approach that effectively finds the location of the bugs in the source code. In our research we performed an empirical evaluation using the Defects4J and the results were compared with six other algorithms accepted by the literature. The results show that our method finds the errors more effectively than the other presented procedures, thus speeding up the bug fixes.

Keywords: Fault localization · Program spectra · Software testing · Program debugging

1 Introduction

Identifying bugs in the software is not a trivial task, so several methods have been developed to automatically support the fault localization process. That is to detect the error in the code.

We need tests to know if there are bugs in the code. The number of tests, number of methods and code coverage ratio greatly influence the quality and reliability of our program [9,21], also the effectiveness of fault localization methods.

There are a lot of methods that try to predict the location of bugs by some approach ([10,16,32]), but it is not possible to have 100% accuracy in each case. There are different "levels of identification", such as statement, branch or function levels and these can influence the effectiveness of the algorithms. These products a sequence of suspicions between the code elements and the developer checks the source code according to this order.

Examining and validating the effectiveness of the methods is not a trivial issue. There are two types of benchmarks to "compete" with algorithms:

1. the code contains injected errors: Developers intentionally corrupt the code manually or by using some kind of (e.g.: mutation) tool [1,3,31]. Using this

S. Misra et al. (Eds.): ICCSA 2019, LNCS 11622, pp. 372–387, 2019.
https://doi.org/10.1007/978-3-030-24305-0_28

method (or benchmark), the researcher can verify the results of fault localization algorithms on unknown software, because it can be known exactly where the bug is, as it is caused (by the researcher or the tool) In addition, it is an advantage that some "fault groups" (e.g.: incorrect *if* condition) can be produced and analyzed in large quantities.
2. the code contains real bugs: bugs, that are mined from the version tracking (and issue system), are used for evaluation [5,12,17]. The exact location of the patch can be traced back and usually there is a bug fixing test. These types of errors provide a more realistic picture of the effectiveness of the methods.

Studies have shown that there are large discrepancies between result of algorithms if they analyze real errors or injected errors.

In our research we present a new, graph-based FL method that was compared to 6 other metrics [15] using real-bugs [11].

2 Related Work

The fault localization is a much-researched area with extensive literature [17,24,25]. There are a lot of algorithms, all of which are intended to determine the exact location of the bugs. These can be grouped based on their "nature" and the data used [27]:

- Static, Dynamic and Execution Slice-Based Methods (eg. [33])
- Program Spectrum-based Methods (eg. [10,20])
- Statistics-based Methods (eg. [13])
- Program State-based Methods (eg. [22])
- Machine Learning-based Methods (eg. [6,26])
- Model-based Methods (eg. [14])
- Data Mining-based Methods (eg. [7])

One of the largest categories is the Spectrum-Based FL (SBFL). The essence of the method is that the collected execution data can be deduced from the behavior of the program and thus on the possible location of the bug.

One of the most popular SPFL methods is Tarantula [10,34]. It prioritizes the methods using the coverage information and the test results. The algorithm orders the methods based on the ratio of the executed failed tests and the not executed failed tests, as well as the executed passed and do not executed tests.

Renieris and Reiss [18] presented a method which is based on the differences between the demeanor of pass and failed test. The method selects the correct execution according to the distance criterion, which is the most similar to the incorrect run, compares the spectra of the two runs and sets the order based on the "suspicious program elements".

The first failed test does not necessarily have the same information as the second or third and so on. The same applies to pass tests. Wong et al. [28] introduced an algorithm, which gave better results to the SIR[1] C program benchmark than many earlier (eg Tarantula, Liblit05 and SOBER) metrics.

[1] https://sir.csc.ncsu.edu/portal/index.php.

Abreu et al. has used the Ochiai method in their studies ([2–4]). This metric was adapted from molecular biology. It was shown that Ochiai produces better results than Tarantula using the Siemens and the SIR (see Footnote 1) bug dataset.

Wong et al. [23] presented the DStar technique, which was evaluated in 24 programs and compared the results of the algorithm with 38 different techniques. Single-fault and multi-fault programs are used for assessment. Empirical evaluation has shown that DStar is better than all other methods.

There are many comparative studies [3,15,23] that compare the results of different algorithms. To sum up, these studies came to the following conclusions: (1) there is difference inefficiency injected and real bugs (2) Ochiai performed better than Tarantula (3) DStar was better than Ochiai.

3 Overview and Goal

The aim is to create a new graph-based FL method that uses collected per-test, method level coverage information and test result data. In addition, the research includes comparing results with other FL algorithms.

3.1 Method

The process consists of four components (Fig. 1). These steps are necessary to evaluate the effectiveness of the methods.

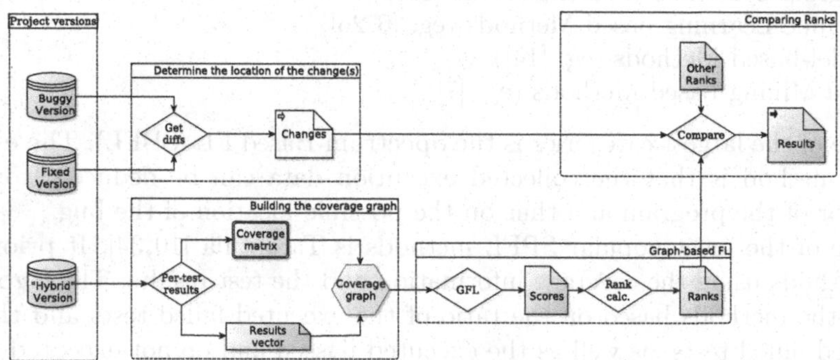

Fig. 1. Overview

(a) **Determination of change set**: We need to know which methods have been changed by the bug-fix. These methods are considered to be faulty, these will be the location of error. This can be extracted by the difference between the buggy and fixed version of the source code.

(b) **Building the graph**: A graph is built from the coverage matrix, where the nodes are the tests (T) and the methods (M). There is an edge between $m \in M$ and $t \in T$, if m is covered by t.

(c) **GFL algorithm**: On the basis of the neighbor-conditions in the graph and the test results, we determine the order of suspicion of the methods. The more efficient the algorithm is, the higher the faulty methods are in the order.
(d) **Comparison**: We examine the different methods about how effectively detect the location of bugs. There are several options: average ranks (project-level or in all bugs) and relationship of metrics to each other.

The differences in efficiency between algorithms are quantified from the results after the fourth step and can be used to infer the effectiveness of the methods.

3.2 Subjects

For evaluation, we need validated, identifiable and fixed bugs. *Defects4J* was used in our research. It is a framework that has collected bug data for real Java projects. High-level's interface provides options to achieve different states of a bug (for example: buggy or fixed version) and it allows to run test cases. The bug DB contains relevant, reproducible and isolated errors [11].

(a) "The bug is related to source code: a developer explicitly labelled the commit of fixed version (V_{fix}) as a bug fixing commit, and the bug fix applies to the source code — bug fixes within the build system, configuration files, documentation, or tests are not included."
(b) "The bug is reproducible: V_{fix} is accompanied by at least one test that passes on V_{fix} but fails on Vbug, and the bug is reproducible using the project's build system and an up-to-date JVM (Java 7)"
(c) "The bug is isolated: the bug fix (i.e., the diff between V_{bug} and V_{fix}) does not include unrelated changes such as features or refactorings."

3.3 Research Questions

Three research questions are formulated about FL-efficiency. These evaluate algorithms in two ways: based on the rankings of the bugs and the relations between the ranks.

- ***RQ1:*** Does *GFL* perform better ranks than other metrics?
  We examine the average rankings of the new FL method. (Does it find the bugs "sooner" than the other methods or not?)
- ***RQ2:*** Does *GFL* give several times better (and less often worse) values than the other metrics?
  We examine how many cases give *GFL* better results than other metrics.
- ***RQ3:*** Does *GFL* result in a relevant improvement?
  We examine how many cases result the *GFL* algorithm in a "quality improvement"

The answers to the questions give an objective picture of the effectiveness of the algorithms.

4 Spectrum-Based Fault Localization

Several FL methods are available in the literature, which can be classified into different groups by their characteristics [25]. For example: Program State-based, Machine Learning-Based, or Program Spectrum-Based Methods.

One of the most popular algorithm-group is Program Spectrum-Based Methods (PSBM), which capture program execution data (such as executable information), and thus monitor the behavior of the program. The list of suspicious elements are determined based on dynamic information provided by tests, however, not only faulty test cases can provide useful information [20], but also pass tests [28]. Studies have shown that algorithms that take into account both successful and unsuccessful tests are more effective than those focusing on unsuccessful tests.

4.1 Coverage and Result Data

One way to store this dynamic information is the coverage matrix whose rows represent the tests (T), and columns show the (source) code elements (for example: method - M). The matrix has 1 value in a given $x_{i,j}$ position if the m_j code element is covered by t_i test, otherwise this value is 0.

With another data structure (with the result vector) the results of the tests are stored (where if the t_i test is fail then it gets 0, otherwise 1): In our research, we worked with method-level granularity, code elements designated methods. These data provide the information they need to build the graph.

$$COV = \begin{bmatrix} x_{1,1} & \dots & x_{1,l} \\ \vdots & \ddots & \vdots \\ x_{k,1} & \dots & x_{k,l} \end{bmatrix}, \ RES = \begin{bmatrix} y_1 \\ \vdots \\ y_k \end{bmatrix} \quad \begin{array}{r} x_{a,b} \in \{0,1\} : \ a \in T \ b \in M \\ x_{i,j} = 1 \text{ if } m_j \text{ is covered by } t_i \\ y_a \in \{0,1\} : \ a \in T \\ y_a = 1 \text{ if } t_i \text{ is pass, else } 0 \end{array}$$

4.2 Metrics

A special case for PSBM is the Executable Statement Hit Spectrum (ESHS) [18]. It collects which methods (or statements or branches) have been executed by the tests. We focused on the method level in this paper.

For a m method, it assigns four values based on the coverage and the result information

(a) m_{ep}: number of passing tests covered by m
(b) m_{fp}: number of failing tests covered by m
(c) m_{np}: number of passing tests not covered by m
(d) m_{nf}: number of failing tests not covered by m

These four values are used by many formula [19,30], thus trying to achieve the best results. In this paper, the GFL algorithm's results were compared with 6 popular metrics.

Barinel [3]: $1 - \frac{m_{ep}}{m_{ep} + m_{ef}}$, DStar [24] : $\frac{m_{ef}^2}{m_{ep} + (m_{ef} + m_{nf}) - m_{ef}}$

Jaccard [8]: $\frac{m_{ef}}{m_{ef} + m_{nf} + m_{ep}}$, Ochiai [2]: $\frac{m_{ef}}{\sqrt{(m_{ef} + m_{nf}) \cdot (m_{ef} + m_{ep})}}$

Op2 [15]: $m_{ef} - \frac{m_{ep}}{m_{ep} + m_{np} + 1}$, Tarantula [10]: $\frac{\frac{m_{ef}}{m_{ef}+m_{nf}}}{\frac{m_{ef}}{m_{ef}+m_{nf}} + \frac{m_{ep}}{m_{ep}+m_{np}}}$

5 Graph-Based FL (GFL)

Our neighbors-based fault localization method differs somewhat from the methods described above. The input data required for the method is the coverage matrix and the result vector, but *GFL* cannot be written with only the four numbers used.

An example can be seen in the Fig. 2 that contains 7 methods and 8 tests. Two of the tests are failed ($t1$ and $t2$), the others are pass.

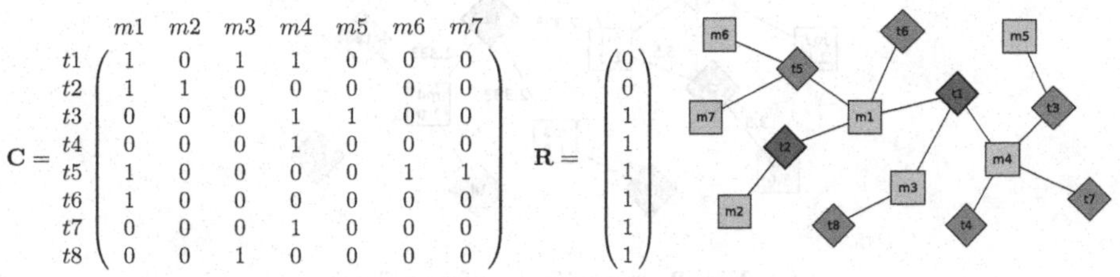

Fig. 2. Coverage matrix, result vector and coverage graph

5.1 Algorithm

As the first step, we build a graph from the coverage matrix. Tests and the methods will be the nodes, and $t_i \mapsto m_j$ edge exists if an m_j ($\in M$) is covered by the t_i ($\in T$), otherwise it does not.

GFL works as though the failed tests would infect the methods that cover them. If a method has many connections with failed tests and the proportion of these tests is high compared to the pass tests it is suspicious. In addition, we examine how the passed-failed test pairs resemble each other and we use it to create the rank.

The process consists of six steps, the result of which will be the scores assigned to the method.

Every method has a start value (score = 1.0). Then we continue the algorithm with the following steps:

1. "Specificity of tests" (Fig. 3): Number of methods and number of covered methods (for $t_i inT$) are devided. If this value is high, it indicates that the failed t_i test only covers a small part of the methods, ie the tests are "method specific". We propagandize these values on the $t_i \mapsto m_j$, it will be the weight of the $t_i \mapsto m_j$ edge.

$$t_i \mapsto m_j = \frac{\|M\|}{\|CM_t\|}$$
$$t_i \in T_F,\ m_j \in M$$
$$T_F = \{t \in T : R_t = 0\}$$
$$CM_t = \{m \in M : C_{t,m} = 1\}$$

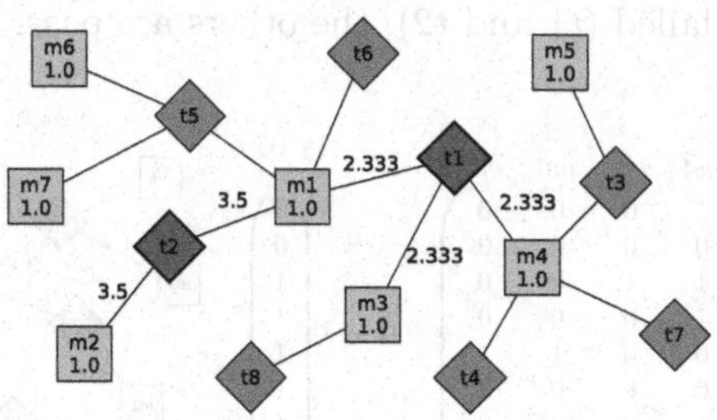

Fig. 3. "Specificity of tests"

2. "Projection" (Fig. 4): These values are projected to the method-edges. It determines the average value of $t_i \mapsto m_j$ edge weight.

$$t_i \mapsto m_j = \frac{t_i \mapsto m_j}{|CPT_{m_i} \cup CFT_{m_i}|}$$
$$T_P = \{t \in T : R_t = 1\}$$
$$CFT_{m_j} = \{t \in T_F : C_{t,m_j} = 1\}$$
$$CPT_{m_j} = \{t \in T_P : C_{t,m_j} = 1\}$$

3. "Aggregation" (Fig. 5): The $t_i \mapsto m_j$ edge weight will be aggregated into the scores of methods.

$$score_{m_j} = \sum_{t \in CFT_{m_j}} t \mapsto m_j$$
$$CFT_{m_j} = \{t \in T_F : C_{t,m_j} = 1\}$$

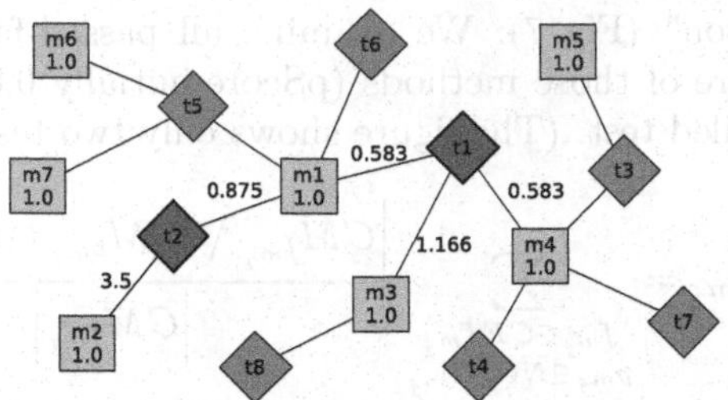

Fig. 4. "Projection"

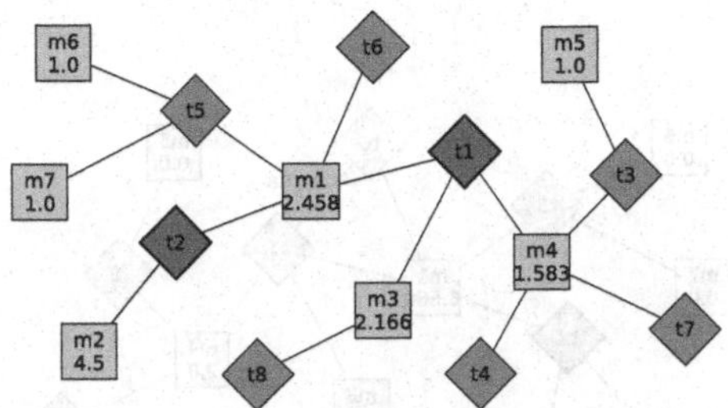

Fig. 5. "Aggregation"

4. "Responsibility" (Fig. 6): We calculate the ratio of the number of failed edge (from m) and the number of total failed edge.

$$score_{m_j} = score_{m_j} \cdot \frac{|CT_{m_j} \cap T_F|}{|FE|}$$

$$CT_{m_j} = \{t \in T : C_{t,m_j} = 1\}$$
$$FE = \{(t, m) : t \in T_F, m \in M,\ C_{m,t} = 1\}$$

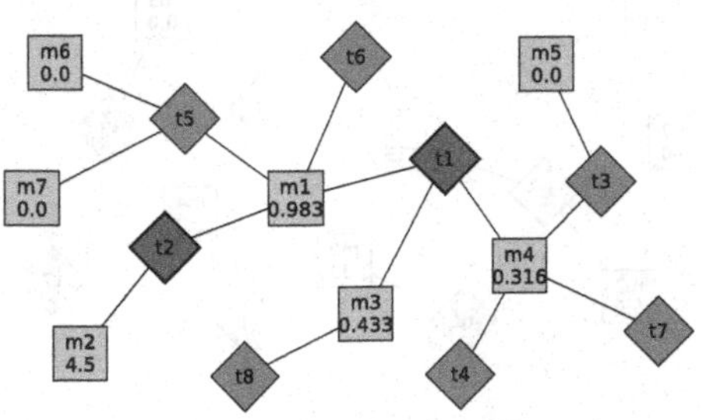

Fig. 6. "Responsibility"

5. “Paired comparison” (Fig. 7): We examine all passed-failed test pairs and increase the pScore of those methods (pScore initially 0.0), which were only covered by the failed test. (The figure shows only two test-pairs)

$$pScore_{m_j} = \sum_{\substack{f_{m_j} \in CFT_{m_j} \\ p_{m_j} \in NCPT_{m_j}}} \frac{\left|CM_{f_{m_j}} \setminus (CM_{p_{m_j}} \cap CM_{f_{m_j}})\right|}{\left|CM_{f_{m_j}}\right|}$$

$$NCPT_{m_j} = \{t \in T_P : C_{m_j,t} = 0\}$$

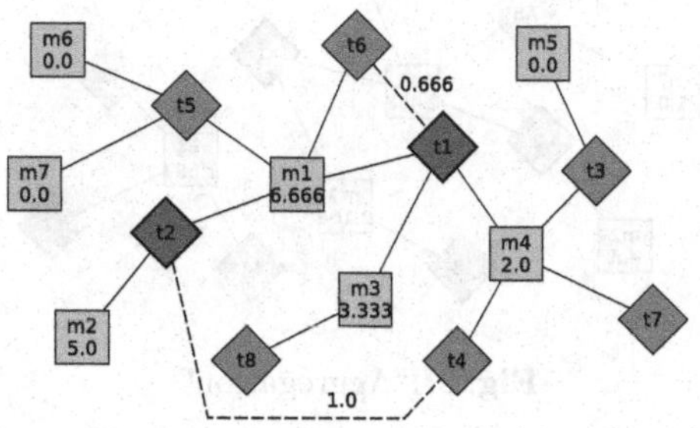

Fig. 7. “Paired comparison”

6. “Averaging” (Fig. 8): The value associated with the method is divided by the number of covered failed tests.

$$pScore_{m_j} = \frac{pScore_{m_j}}{|CFT_{m_j}|}$$

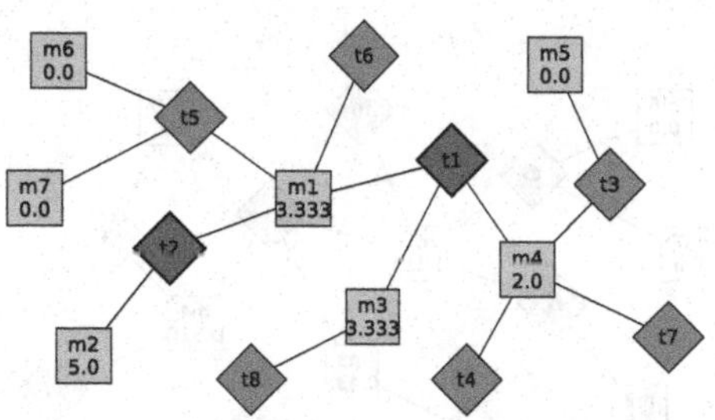

Fig. 8. “Averaging”

The six steps described above can be summarized in the following formula:

$$GFL_{m_j} = \frac{\sum_{t \in CFT_{m_j}} \frac{\frac{|M|}{|CM_t|}}{|CPT_{m_j} \cup CFT_{m_j}|} |CT_{m_j} \cap T_F|}{|FE|} \sum_{\substack{f_{m_j} \in CFT_{m_j} \\ p_{m_j} \in NCPT_{m_j}}} \frac{\left|CM_{f_{m_j}} \setminus (CM_{p_{m_j}} \cap CM_{f_{m_j}})\right|}{\left|CM_{f_{m_j}}\right| |CFT_{m_j}|}$$

The values thus obtained will be the basis of rank-order.

6 Evaluation

Defects4J was used to quantify the fault localization algorithms. With the help of the bytecode instrumentation tool, which is based on *Javassist*, the necessary information about the programs have been collected.

The minimum requirement for *Javassist* is Java 5, so we had to exclude older programs and those where the instrument was unable to perform a successful results (Table 1) [11].

Table 1. Subject programs

Project	KLOC	Tests	Bugs
Commons Lang	22	2 245	52
Commons Math	85	3 602	82
JFreeChart	96	2 205	24
Joda-Time	28	4 130	26
Total	231	12 182	184

Ranks were used as comparison basis, because the scores of metrics for the methods cannot be compared, for example interpretation range of *GFL* is not limited to [0.0, 1.0] intervals. Bug-rank is the position of changed (buggy) method in suspicious order, which calculated based on FL scores. If there are more methods with the same score, they will get their average rank. Fixing the bug can affect more methods, in this case, the lowest value of the method ranks is taken into account. For example: if $m2$ and $m4$ are modified methods then the rank for this bug is 1, because $m2$ has lower rank (rank:1), than $m4$ (rank:4).

Comparisons have been made for each project based on ranking. Tables 2 and 3 show the results. It can be seen that in four cases (Commons Lang: 3,981, Joda-Time: 12,769, JFreeChart: 7,583 and all bugs: 7,416) the GFL gave the best average rank value, and it gets the 2th best result on Commons Math.

Looking at the results, it can be seen that the DStar produces rather extreme ranks. In many cases it gives very good value, but there are also extremely bad results and these have a negative effect on the average rank values. It is interesting that Ochiai gets the second best in complete bug data set, but it

Table 2. Average ranks

	Barinel	DStar	Jaccard	Ochiai	Op2	Tarantula	GFL
Commons Math	7,92	200,90	7,82	8,16	8,83	7,92	7,85
Commons Lang	4,84	168,24	4,37	4,26	4,20	4,84	3,98
Joda-Time	17,90	13,77	16,89	13,89	18,00	17,90	12,77
JFreeChart	12,19	280,5	8,73	8,23	35,65	12,19	7,58
The average of all	9,02	175,61	8,24	7,88	12,32	9,02	7,42

Table 3. Ranks of the average ranks

Project	Barinel	DStar	Jaccard	Ochiai	Op2	Tarantula	GFL
Commons Math	3,5	7	1	5	6	3,5	2
Commons Lang	5,5	7	4	3	2	5,5	1
Joda-Time	5,5	2	4	3	7	5,5	1
JFreeChart	4,5	7	3	2	6	4,5	1
Ranks based on all	4,5	7	3	2	6	4,5	1

produced once the second best result for a single project (and in other cases it was worse).

Another comparative option is to examine the rankings in pairs. There are three "options" for each pairing comparison: M_a is lower than M_b, M_a is equal to M_b, M_a is higher than M_b. M_a is better than M_b, if its rank is lower. For example: Op2 28 times gave smaller rank than Barinel and 109 times gave equal than DStar metric (Tables 4 and 5).

Table 6 shows the results per project received by comparison. It can be seen that for the DStar the number of draws is the lowest and there are more cases when a metric loses more than it wins (for example: DStar - Commons Lang or Jaccard - Joda-Time).

Table 4. Comparison of metric-pairs (number of non-equal ranks)

<	Barinel	DStar	Jaccard	Ochiai	Op2	Tarantula	GFL	**SUM**
Barinel		31	7	8	19	0	11	**76**
DStar	44		41	32	37	44	26	**224**
Jaccard	20	28		4	18	20	7	**97**
Ochiai	26	27	16		17	26	4	**116**
Op2	28	38	25	22		28	18	**159**
Tarantula	0	31	7	8	19		11	**76**
GFL	47	54	42	36	31	47		**257**
SUM	165	209	138	110	141	165	77	

Table 5. Comparison of metric-pairs (number of equal ranks)

=	Barinel	DStar	Jaccard	Ochiai	Op2	Tarantula	GFL	SUM
Barinel		109	157	150	137	184	126	**863**
DStar	109		115	125	109	109	104	**671**
Jaccard	157	115		164	141	157	135	**869**
Ochiai	150	125	164		145	150	144	**878**
Op2	137	109	141	145		137	135	**804**
Tarantula	184	109	157	150	137		126	**863**
GFL	126	104	135	144	135	126		**770**

Table 6. Comparison of metric-pairs: number of "action" (rank)

Project	"Actions"	Barinel	DStar	Jaccard	Ochiai	Op2	Tarantula	GFL
Common Math	Win	27	90	37	33	44	29	103
	Draw	412	323	411	419	385	412	352
	Defeat	51	79	44	40	63	51	37
Commons Lang	Win	20	55	26	36	50	20	67
	Draw	244	186	248	248	236	244	230
	Defeat	48	71	38	28	26	48	15
Joda-Time	Win	6	44	13	23	42	6	42
	Draw	111	96	109	112	98	111	103
	Defeat	39	16	34	21	16	39	11
JFreeChart	Win	21	35	21	24	23	21	45
	Draw	96	66	101	99	85	96	85
	Defeat	27	43	22	21	36	27	14
All	Win	76	224	97	116	159	76	257
	Draw	863	671	869	878	804	863	770
	Defeat	165	209	138	110	141	165	77

Overall, GFL won the most often (257) and lost the least (77). Interestingly, DStar was the second (224) and lost (209) the most often. It can be stated based on Tables 2 and 6 that DStar behaves rather extremely: often wins but also often produces extremely bad rank values, which greatly affects the rank values. The results in the tables clearly show that the graph-based algorithm is fairly balanced and it produces the best ranks.

According to some studies [29], developers examine only top-5 or top-10 suspicious elements during bug fixes. Therefore 3 groups were created: (1) errors' location is 5th or lower in ranking (2) errors' location is between 5th and 10th place (3) errors' location is worse than the 10th place. Table 7 shows what kind of movements happened, that is, the rank of a bug was transferred to another group by the GFL algorithm. It seems that the result of GFL often puts the bug into a "better group" (a total of 58) and rarely makes it into a "worse group" (a total of 10).

Table 7. Rank improvement

	$[\infty, 10) \rightarrow [10, 5)$	$[\infty, 10) \rightarrow [1, 5]$	$[10, 5) \rightarrow [1, 5]$	$\sum$
$Barinel \rightarrow GFL$	2	1	4	7
$DStar \rightarrow GFL$	2	20	4	26
$Jaccard \rightarrow GFL$	1	1	3	5
$Ochia \rightarrow GFL$	2	0	2	4
$Op2 \rightarrow GFL$	1	8	0	9
$Tarantula \rightarrow GFL$	2	1	4	7
	$[10, 5) \rightarrow [\infty, 10)$	$[1, 5] \rightarrow [\infty, 10)$	$[1, 5] \rightarrow [10, 5)$	$\sum$
$Barinel \rightarrow GFL$	0	1	1	2
$DStar \rightarrow GFL$	0	0	4	4
$Jaccard \rightarrow GFL$	0	0	0	0
$Ochia \rightarrow GFL$	0	0	0	0
$Op2 \rightarrow GFL$	0	1	1	2
$Tarantula \rightarrow GFL$	0	1	1	2

Answers to previous questions are based on the results presented above:

RQ1: Results showed that four out of five cases the *GFL* gave the best results. It produced the lowest rank for three projects and aggregate data (Tables 2 and Table 3).

RQ2: The *GFL* won the most often (it was the second in only one project), it lost the least (in every case), it achieved the best result based on all and aggregated results (Table 4-Table 6).

RQ3: In any case, the *GFL* had larger improvements than it had losses. It has resulted in a total of 58 "quality improvements" and it was only 10 times worse than the "original quality group" (Table 7).

Acknowledgment. This study was supported by the project "Integrated program for training new generation of scientists in the fields of computer science", no EFOP-3.6.3-VEKOP-16-2017-0002. The project was supported by the European Union and co-funded by the European Social Fund.

References

1. Abreu, R., Zoeteweij, P., van Gemund, A.J.C.: On the accuracy of spectrum-based fault localization. In: Testing: Academic and Industrial Conference Practice and Research Techniques - MUTATION (TAICPART-MUTATION 2007), pp. 89–98 (2007)
2. Abreu, R., Zoeteweij, P., c. Van Gemund, A.J.: An evaluation of similarity coefficients for software fault localization. In: 2006 12th Pacific Rim International Symposium on Dependable Computing (PRDC 2006), pp. 39–46, December 2006
3. Abreu, R., Zoeteweij, P., Gemund, A.J.C.v.: Spectrum-based multiple fault localization. In: Proceedings of the 2009 IEEE/ACM International Conference on Automated Software Engineering, ASE 2009, pp. 88–99. IEEE Computer Society (2009)
4. Abreu, R., Zoeteweij, P., Golsteijn, R., van Gemund, A.J.: A practical evaluation of spectrum-based fault localization. J. Syst. Softw. **82**(11), 1780–1792 (2009). sI: TAIC PART 2007 and MUTATION 2007
5. B Le, T.D., Lo, D., Le Goues, C., Grunske, L.: A learning-to-rank based fault localization approach using likely invariants. In: Proceedings of the 25th International Symposium on Software Testing and Analysis, ISSTA 2016, pp. 177–188 (2016)
6. Brun, Y., Ernst, M.D.: Finding latent code errors via machine learning over program executions. In: Proceedings. 26th International Conference on Software Engineering, pp. 480–490, May 2004
7. Cellier, P., Ducassé, M., Ferré, S., Ridoux, O.: Formal concept analysis enhances fault localization in software. In: Medina, R., Obiedkov, S. (eds.) ICFCA 2008. LNCS (LNAI), vol. 4933, pp. 273–288. Springer, Heidelberg (2008). https://doi.org/10.1007/978-3-540-78137-0_20
8. Chen, M.Y., Kiciman, E., Fratkin, E., Fox, A., Brewer, E.: Pinpoint: problem determination in large, dynamic internet services. In: Proceedings of the 2002 International Conference on Dependable Systems and Networks, pp. 595–604. IEEE Computer Society, Washington (2002)
9. Horváth, F., et al.: Test suite evaluation using code coverage based metrics. In: 14th Symposium on Programming Languages and Software Tools, SPLST 2015, CEUR-WS (2015)
10. Jones, J.A., Harrold, M.J.: Empirical evaluation of the tarantula automatic fault-localization technique. In: Proceedings of the 20th IEEE/ACM International Conference on Automated Software Engineering, ASE 2005, pp. 273–282. ACM, New York (2005)
11. Just, R., Jalali, D., Ernst, M.D.: Defects4j: a database of existing faults to enable controlled testing studies for java programs. In: Proceedings of the 2014 International Symposium on Software Testing and Analysis, ISSTA 2014, pp. 437–440. ACM, New York (2014)
12. Laghari, G., Murgia, A., Demeyer, S.: Fine-tuning spectrum based fault localisation with frequent method item sets. In: Proceedings of the 31st IEEE/ACM International Conference on Automated Software Engineering, ASE 2016, pp. 274–285. ACM, New York (2016)
13. Liu, C., Fei, L., Yan, X., Han, J., Midkiff, S.P.: Statistical debugging: a hypothesis testing-based approach. IEEE Trans. Softw. Eng. **32**(10), 831–848 (2006)
14. Mateis, C., Stumptner, M., Wotawa, F.: Modeling java programs for diagnosis. In: Proceedings of the 14th European Conference on Artificial Intelligence, pp. 171–175. IOS Press (2000)

15. Naish, L., Lee, H.J., Ramamohanarao, K.: A model for spectra-based software diagnosis. ACM Trans. Softw. Eng. Methodol. **20**(3) (2011)
16. Nessa, S., Abedin, M., Wong, W.E., Khan, L., Qi, Y.: Software fault localization using N-gram analysis. In: Li, Y., Huynh, D.T., Das, S.K., Du, D.-Z. (eds.) WASA 2008. LNCS, vol. 5258, pp. 548–559. Springer, Heidelberg (2008). https://doi.org/10.1007/978-3-540-88582-5_51
17. Pearson, S., et al.: Evaluating and improving fault localization. In: Proceedings of the 39th International Conference on Software Engineering, ICSE 2017, pp. 609–620. IEEE Press, Piscataway (2017)
18. Renieres, M., Reiss, S.P.: Fault localization with nearest neighbor queries. In: 18th IEEE International Conference on Automated Software Engineering, 2003. Proceedings, pp. 30–39, October 2003
19. Sohn, J., Yoo, S.: Fluccs: Using code and change metrics to improve fault localization. In: Proceedings of the 26th ACM SIGSOFT International Symposium on Software Testing and Analysis, ISSTA 2017, pp. 273–283. ACM, New York (2017)
20. Taha, A.B., Thebaut, S.M., Liu, S.S.: An approach to software fault localization and revalidation based on incremental data flow analysis. In: Proceedings of the Thirteenth Annual International Computer Software Applications Conference, pp. 527–534 (1989)
21. Tengeri, D., et al.: Relating code coverage, mutation score and test suite reducibility to defect density. In: 2016 IEEE Ninth International Conference on Software Testing, Verification and Validation Workshops (ICSTW), pp. 174–179 (2016)
22. Wang, T., Roychoudhury, A.: Automated path generation for software fault localization. In: Proceedings of the 20th IEEE/ACM International Conference on Automated Software Engineering, ASE 2005, pp. 347–351. ACM, New York (2005)
23. Wong, W.E., Debroy, V., Gao, R., Li, Y.: The DStar method for effective software fault localization. IEEE Trans. Reliab. **63**(1), 290–308 (2014)
24. Wong, W.E., Debroy, V., Li, Y., Gao, R.: Software fault localization using DStar (D*). In: 2012 IEEE Sixth International Conference on Software Security and Reliability, pp. 21–30 (2012)
25. Wong, W.E., Gao, R., Li, Y., Abreu, R., Wotawa, F.: A survey on software fault localization. IEEE Trans. Softw. Eng. **42**(8), 707–740 (2016)
26. Wong, W.E., Shi, Y., Qi, Y., Golden, R.: Using an RBF neural network to locate program bugs. In: 2008 19th International Symposium on Software Reliability Engineering (ISSRE), pp. 27–36 (2008)
27. Wong, W.E., Debroy, V.: A survey of software fault localization. Department of Computer Science, University of Texas at Dallas, Technical report UTDCS-45 9 (2009)
28. Wong, W.E., Debroy, V., Choi, B.: A family of code coverage-based heuristics for effective fault localization. J. Syst. Softw. **83**(2), 188–208 (2010). Computer Software and Applications
29. Xia, X., Bao, L., Lo, D., Li, S.: "Automated debugging considered harmful" considered harmful: a user study revisiting the usefulness of spectra-based fault localization techniques with professionals using real bugs from large systems. In: 2016 IEEE International Conference on Software Maintenance and Evolution (ICSME), pp. 267–278. IEEE, October 2016
30. Xie, X., Chen, T.Y., Kuo, F.C., Xu, B.: A theoretical analysis of the risk evaluation formulas for spectrum-based fault localization. ACM Trans. Softw. Eng. Methodol. **22**(4), 31:1–31:40 (2013)

31. Xuan, J., Monperrus, M.: Test case purification for improving fault localization. In: Proceedings of the 22nd ACM SIGSOFT International Symposium on Foundations of Software Engineering, FSE 2014, pp. 52–63. ACM, New York (2014)
32. Zeller, A.: Isolating cause-effect chains from computer programs. SIGSOFT Softw. Eng. Notes **27**(6), 1–10 (2002)
33. Zhang, X., He, H., Gupta, N., Gupta, R.: Experimental evaluation of using dynamic slices for fault location. In: Proceedings of the Sixth International Symposium on Automated Analysis-driven Debugging, AADEBUG 2005, pp. 33–42. ACM (2005)
34. Zou, D., Liang, J., Xiong, Y., Ernst, M.D., Zhang, L.: An empirical study of fault localization families and their combinations. IEEE Trans. Softw. Eng. 1–1 (2019). https://doi.org/10.1109/TSE.2019.2892102

Comparison of Test Groups Based on Behavior and Package Hierarchy

Béla Vancsics(✉)

Department of Software Engineering, University of Szeged,
Dugonics tér 13, Szeged 6720, Hungary
vancsics@inf.u-szeged.hu

Abstract. Data collected from the software and the development process is usually part of some kind of underlying structure, hence they could be organized into groups or clusters. This is true of the test cases. There are several concepts for creating groups, one approach is that the tests are grouped by their location, another approach is that they are categorized based on their behavior. For unit tests, ideally, these two approaches would give the same result. However this is not true in reality!

In our empirical study the difference between the two concepts (on Java systems) was examined, also the behaviour groups based on coverage and the location-groups based on package hierarchy were analyzed.

Groups containing tests were examined as well. In addition the difference between package-based groups and behavior-based groups based on coverage matrix was explored. To quantify the results, empirical experiments were performed and the differences were identified with the metrics used in the literature.

Keywords: Code coverage · Clustering · Software evolution

1 Introduction

Knowing about groups of strongly related elements has many benefits in software engineering. These groups reflect the underlying relations in the software such as structure, behavior or other aspects of the designer's intentions. These are often called *clusters* in software engineering research. Clusters can not only be interpreted for software components but in terms of teams, error reports, documents, informal messages, version controlling information, and many others as well. Cluster identification, or simply *clustering*, means finding these groups by automatic means. It has different applications in maintenance, program comprehension, redocumentation, traceability and so on [13,16,18].

Clustering software engineering artifacts has a large literature, and there are quite effective algorithms and tools available for various purposes [2,12,14].

Well-formed groups can help to understand the program, create appropriate unit tests [1], detect bad smell [21], feature detection [9] increase maintenance as well. It is difficult to measure a cluster algorithms' success, because there is no perfect clustering and "standards" making is very costly. There are many clustering

S. Misra et al. (Eds.): ICCSA 2019, LNCS 11622, pp. 388–402, 2019.
https://doi.org/10.1007/978-3-030-24305-0_29

approaches and plenty of algorithms [3]. Out of these, choosing the most suitable for us is a non-trivial question. Clustering software engineering artifacts has large literature, and there are quite effective algorithms available [2,14].

Dynamic information was compared to the static information extracted from the location of the source code. The difference between the two approaches points to places where static and dynamic groups present discrepancies, what is to say the intention of the designer (shown by the location) and the behavior of the coverage shows the divergences. These differences make it difficult to understand the program, impair maintenance and thus increase development (and maintenance) costs.

In our research, we investigated how the groups created on the basis of static and dynamic test information are similar. If there is a high degree of similarity between the two clusters, it means that the location of the test in the structure represents the "function" of the test. In this study several clustering algorithms were used, differences between the results were examined. This way we got a more comprehensive picture of the differences between the two types of structure.

2 Overview and Goals

In this paper, we present results of an empirical study whose goal is to compare different clustering approaches on test cases based on behavior and package hierarchy. Several similarities and approaches were examined to determine the dynamic groups. To quantify the results the clustering metrics recognized by the literature were used.

This research is a step towards a practically usable method, which would give the place of anomalies between structural and behavioral groups and could help the refactoring.

2.1 Method

Figure 1 shows a general overview of the experiment. There are four main parts of the process:

1. Construction of Package-Based Clustering:
   The package clusters are treated as a good approach which indicates the function of the test cases and thus helps developers' and testers' understanding. The appropriate package structure improves maintainability and traceability.
2. Construction of Coverage-Based Clustering:
   On the basis of the coverage information, we examine how similar the test cases are to each other. Elements with similar coverage will have a high chance of belonging to the same group because they are likely to test the same function.
3. Comparison of the two clusterings:
   The similarity between the groups obtained in the previous two steps is quantified. Thus, the difference between them becomes measurable, so the efficiency of the algorithms (in this aspect) can be evaluated quantitatively.

4. Evaluation:
   We examine the results of each algorithm according to different aspects, and investigate whether there is a method that stands out from the others (i.e. the result is most similar to the Package-Based Clustering).

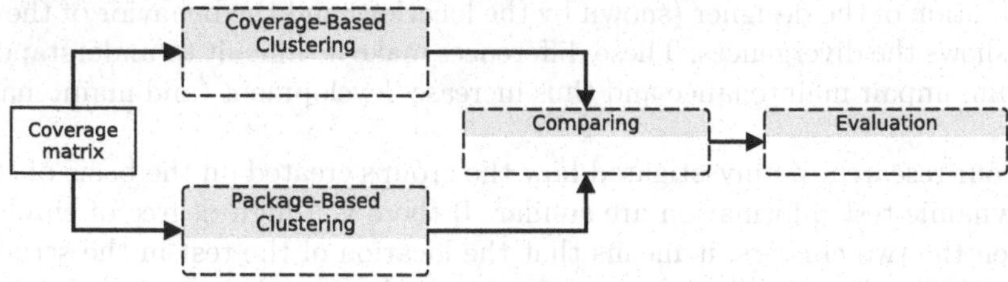

Fig. 1. Overview of the method: it contains four steps of Package-Based Clustering, construction of Coverage-Based Clustering, comparison of two algorithms and evaluation

2.2 Subjects

We conducted the experiment by applying the clustering methods on 7 small to medium sized open source Java systems. All of the subjects' test suites are written in JUnit, the unit testing framework often used for Java systems. Table 1 lists the subject systems along with some of their basic properties.

The granularity we used in our experiments was JUnit test cases, i. e., the basic entities used for clustering are the test cases. Clover tool[1] was used for coverage measurement [20]. It is an open source tool managed by Atlassian (until 2017) which uses source code instrumentation technique. It gives more precise information about source code entities than tools based on bytecode instrumentation (e.g Cobertura and JaCoCo).

Table 1. Subject programs and their basic properties

Program	Version	LOC	Methods	Tests
Checkstyle	6.11.1	114K	2655	1487
Commons-lang	#00fafe77	69K	2796	3326
Commons-math	#2aa4681c	177K	7167	5081
Joda-Time	2.9	85K	3898	4174
Netty	4.0.29	140K	8230	3982
Orientdb	2.0.10	229K	13118	925
Oryx	1.1.0	31K	1562	208

[1] https://atlassian.com/software/clover.

2.3 Research Questions

We may describe the goals of our empirical study more precisely as follows.

RQ1 How close are the "behavior-based" Coverage-Based Clusterings to the Package-Based Clusterings?
How similar are the resulting groups of different algorithms to the package structure?

RQ2 Are there Coverage-Based Clustering configurations that are definitely better (or worse) than others?
Which is the projection-algorithm "pair" that gives a much better (or worse) similarity?

RQ3 How great are the deviation of results within a program?
We look at the size difference between the results of the algorithms.

3 Package-Based Clustering

It is shown how the Package-Based Clustering is created that is based on the physical code structure (Fig. 2). Since we are dealing with Java systems in the present experiment and, in Java, the basic physical entity that represents the system's hierarchical architecture is a *package*, we are using this term in this part.

Our aim with test clustering is to detect groups of tests that are connected together by the "intention" of the developer or tester. This means that their placement within a hierarchical package structure of the system is a natural classification according to their intended role. It helps other developers and testers understand the connection between tests and their subjects. Packages often include subpackages as well.

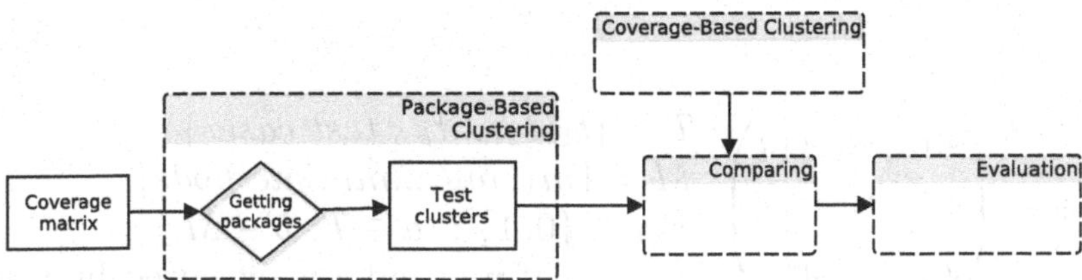

Fig. 2. Package-Based Clustering

Our Package-Based Clustering simply means that we assign the fully qualified name of the innermost containing package to each test, and treat them belonging to the same package members of the same cluster.

There are two important things to note here: first, we do not consider the physical directory and file structure of the source code elements as they appear in the file system (although in Java these usually reflect package structuring).

Second, tests' names are not considered either; the classification if a particular piece of code is a unit test or regular code is determined by the rules of JUnit (such as the special annotations), our unit testing framework.

Some properties of the resulting clusters is shown in Table 2.

Table 2. Properties of package-based test clusters

Program	Number of test cluster	Size of the smallest group	Size of the largest group
Checkstyle	23	5	178
Commons-lang	12	17	1156
Commons-math	61	1	924
Joda-Time	7	1	2969
Netty	35	1	3109
Orientdb	53	1	185
Oryx	23	1	45

4 Coverage-Based Clustering

Coverage-Based Clustering takes into account only the dynamic code coverage relationship between the test cases and the code elements. Using code coverage in software testing is based on simple concepts [8,19]. The coverage matrix is a bit-matrix representing which test cases cover which code elements.

$$A_{cov} = \begin{pmatrix} x_{1,1} & \dots & x_{1,l} \\ \vdots & \ddots & \vdots \\ x_{k,1} & \dots & x_{k,l} \end{pmatrix} \quad \begin{array}{l} T = \{t_1, t_2, ...t_k : test\ cases\} \\ M = \{m_1, m_2, ...m_l : methods\} \\ x_{a,b} \in \{0,1\} : \ a \in T, \ b \in M \\ x_{i,j} = 1 \text{ if method } j \text{ is executed by test } i \end{array}$$

The basic idea behind this approach is that we want to identify groups in the coverage data, which are more closely resembled to the in-group elements than the out-group elements. These regions may indicate that there is a tight correspondence between the associated test cases from a dynamic point of view. For finding similarity, we use "projection-functions" that indicate how similar the two elements are to each other. The basis for clustering will be the similarity matrix thus obtained (Fig. 3).

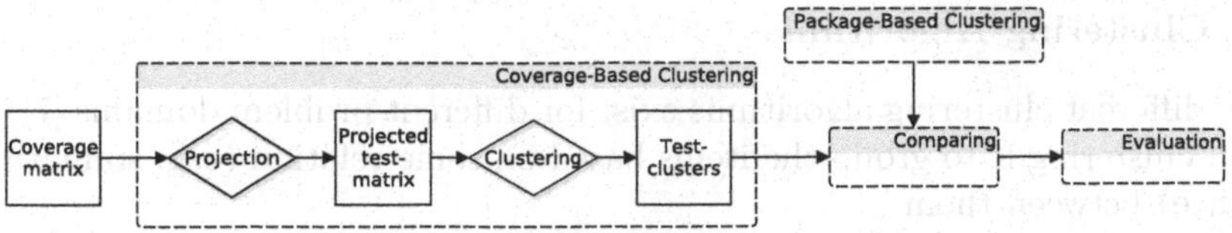

Fig. 3. Coverage-Based Clustering

4.1 Projection

From coverage matrix was produced a "projected" matrices ($A \rightarrow P$) by a (dis)similarity function. Projected matrix captures the similarities among pairs of tests. The larger this value, the more similar the coverage and the more likely they are responsible for the same feature.

The projected matrix specifies how two elements are similar to each other. The higher the value, the more similar the two elements are (based on coverage). These projected matrices are the basics of clustering.

For example: if $t_a \in T$ and $t_b \in T$ and $P_{t_a,t_b} = 0.98$, then tests will most likely cost the same cluster because their coverage is very similar.

Well-known similarity (or distance) functions have been selected to describe the relationship between two elements. These functions give the similarity of two (u and v) boolean (test coverage) vectors, where $c_{i,j}$ is the number of occurrences of $u[k] = i$ and $v[k] = j$ for $k < n$ ($n =$ length of vector) and $i, j \in \{0, 1\}$.

Table 3. Similarity functions

$$\text{\underline{D}ice(u, v)} = \frac{c_{1,0} + c_{0,1}}{2 * c_{1,1} + c_{0,1} + c_{1,0}} \qquad \text{\underline{H}amming(u, v)} = \frac{c_{1,0} + c_{0,1}}{n}$$

$$\text{\underline{J}accard(u, v)} = \frac{c_{1,0} + c_{0,1}}{c_{1,1} + c_{0,1} + c_{1,0}} \qquad \text{\underline{K}ulsinski(u, v)} = \frac{c_{1,0} + c_{0,1} + c_{1,1} + n}{c_{0,1} + c_{1,0} + n}$$

$$\text{\underline{R}ogers-\underline{T}animoto(u, v)} = \frac{R}{c_{1,1} + c_{0,0} + R} \qquad \text{\underline{R}ussell-\underline{R}ao(u, v)} = \frac{n - c_{1,1}}{n}$$

$$\text{\underline{S}okal-\underline{M}ichener(u, v)} = \frac{R}{c_{1,0} + c_{0,1} + R} \qquad \text{\underline{S}okal-\underline{S}neath(u, v)} = \frac{R}{c_{1,1} + R}$$

$$\text{\underline{Y}ule(u, v)} = \frac{R}{c_{1,1} * c_{0,0} + \frac{R}{2}}$$

,where $R = 2 * (c_{1,0} + c_{0,1})$

4.2 Clustering Algorithms

Many different clustering algorithms exist for different problem domains [7]. The aim of clustering is to group the items based on some relation (e. g. similarity or distance) between them.

Classification is similar to clustering nevertheless there is an important difference: classification is supervised while clustering is an unsupervised grouping. The resulting clusters can be overlapping (an item can belong to several groups) or disjoint (an element can only belong to one group). Clustering algorithms can have three important properties (scale invariance, consistency and richness), however, maximum of two properties can be realized for a certain clustering algorithm [10].

The algorithms can be divided into two groups based on whether the number of clusters is a parameter (e. g.: K-means) or is determined by the method (e. g.: Affinity Propagation). In the first case the predefined cluster number has a significant influence on the result, but it is also a drawback because, generally, it is impossible to determine the cluster number in advance. It should also be expected to be determined automatically.

In our research, we only used algorithms that do not need to give the number of clusters.

Affinity Propagation (AP). This algorithm is based on a "passing-message-between-datapoints" strategy. It requires as input a matrix and gives as the output a set of disjointed clusters. Real-valued messages are exchanged between data points until a high-quality set of exemplars and corresponding clusters gradually emerge. The method finds "exemplars" (or data point) that is representative enough of itself and some other data points [6].

The algorithm proceeds by two message passing steps. They will update two matrices.

- The first matrix has values $r(i, j)$ that quantify how well-suited x_j is to serve as the exemplar for x_i, relative to other candidate exemplars for x_i ($x_{i,*}, x_{j,*} \in A'$).
- The second matrix contains values $a(i, j)$ that represent how "proper" it would be for x_i to pick x_j as its exemplar, taking into account other points' preference for x_j as an exemplar.

The algorithm then performs the updates iteratively:

- $r(i,j) \leftarrow s(i,j) - max_{j' \neq j}\{a(i,j') + s(i,j')\}$
- $a(i,j) \leftarrow min\left(0, r(j,j) + \sum_{i' \notin \{i,j\}} max(0, r(i',j))\right), (i \neq k)$
  $a(j,j) \leftarrow \sum_{i' \neq j} max(0, r(i',j))$
- $s(i,j) = -\left\|x_i - x_j\right\|^2$

The iterations are repeated until there is change in the cluster.

Birch Clustering (BC). Balanced Iterative Reducing and Clustering using Hierarchies [11,23](BIRCH) is based on hierarchical clustering approach. It is an efficient and scalable clustering method, based on an in-memory data structure called CF-tree (clustering feature-tree), which serves as an in-memory summary of the data distribution.

The data is represented by the CF nodes. Each node represents a cluster in the cluster hierarchy, intermediate nodes are superclusters and the leaf nodes are the actual clusters. The algorithm needs two parameters: (i) threshold - it is a limit between sample and the existing subclusters (ii) branching factor - it is a limit for the number of subclusters.

In the first step, the method builds a clustering feature (CF) vector that summarizes information for each cluster.

$$CF(C) = (|C|, S_1, S_2), \text{ where } |C| = \text{number of instance in C cluster}$$

$$S_1 = \sum_{X_i \in N} X_i \ , S_2 = \sum_{X_i \in N} |X_i|^2$$

In the second step, the algorithm discovers all leaf in the CF-tree to rebuild a new, smaller tree. It removes the outliers and grouping congested subclusters. In the third step, an agglomerative hierarchical clustering is used to cluster all leafs.

DBSCAN Clustering (DB). Density-Based Spatial Clustering of Applications with Noise [5](DBSCAN) is one of the most common and most cited clustering algorithm.

It is a density-based clustering method which uses the concept of density reachability and density connectivity: given a group of points in some space, it groups together points that are closely connected together.

Let D be a set of data points:

- ϵ-neighborhood of a point: $N_\epsilon(p) = \{q \in D | \text{distance}(p, q) \leq \epsilon\}$
- *Core Point*: $N_\epsilon(p) \geq N_{min}$
- Directly Density-Reachable (DDR): if $p \in N_\epsilon(q)$ and $N_\epsilon(q) \geq N_{min}$ then p is DDR from q
- Density-Reachable (DR): if there is a sequence of points $p = p_1, p_2, ..., p_n, p_1 = q, p_n = q$ such as p_{i+1} is DDR from p_i
- Density-Connected (DC): if there is r such as both, p and q are density-reachable from r then p is DC to q

The clusters are the set of density-connected points that are maximal with respect to density-reachability. Let C be a cluster: $\forall p, q$: if $p \in C$ and q is density-reachable from p then $q \in C$.

DBSCAN has several variations and extensions [7].

Mean Shift Clustering (MS). Mean shift is the center-based clustering algorithm [4]. It is a simple iterative procedure that shifts each data point to the average of data points in its neighborhood [4].

The clustering aims to discover "blobs" in a smooth density of samples. It iteratively shifts each point in the data set until it is the top of its nearest kernel density estimation (KDE) surface peak. The algorithm copies the original data set and it freezes the original points, then copied points are shifted against the frozen data. The point moves closer to the nearest KDE surface peak by iterations.

Gaussian kernel function $K(x_i - x) = e^{-c\|x_i - x\|^2}$ determines the weight of nearby points for re-estimation of the mean.

The weighted mean of the density in the window determined by kernel function is

$$m(x) = \frac{\sum_{x_i \in N(x)} K(x_i - x)x_i}{\sum_{x_i \in N(x)} K(x_i - x)},$$

where $N(x)$ is the neighborhood of initial estimate (x). The algorithm sets $x \leftarrow m(x)$ and the estimation is repeat until $m(x)$ converges.

5 Comparing and Evaluation

The quantification of the results is on three levels (Fig. 4): (1) clustering of the tests (there are only tests in the groups) were examined (2) methods' clustering (the groups contain only methods) and (3) combined (or heterogeneous) clusters. The focus was only on the test clusters.

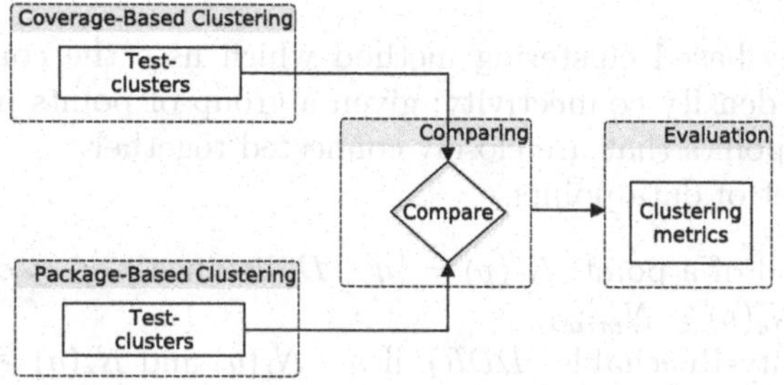

Fig. 4. Overview of comparing and evaluation

Comparing two clusterings C and C means calculating a similarity value $\delta(C, C')$ using some measure δ, which ranges $[0, 1]$, 0 being the least similar and 1 representing identical clustering. Except for the identical clustering, the similarity is difficult to express since two clusterings may differ in many ways: in the cluster numbers, in the content of the clusters, in the amount of relationships within and between clusters, etc. Hence, there might not exist a universal measure for the similarity; each different definition might be suitable from a certain perspective. In the literature, different comparison methods have been advised [7], and we selected six of them in order to see if they show similar or different results. Each metric is interpreted in the test- , method- and heterogeneous clusters.

Evaluating the performance of a clustering algorithm is not trivial, but there are some approaches that are accepted by the scientific literature. In the research, five popular metrics were used to quantify the differences.

5.1 Adjusted and Normalized Mutual Information

The Mutual Information (MI) of two variables is a measure of the mutual dependence between the two variables. Adjusted Mutual Information [22] (AMI) is an adjustment of the MI score to account for chance. (This is necessary because MI is higher for two clusterings with a larger number of clusters, disregarding whether there is actually more information shared or not.) Normalized Mutual Information [17] (NMI) is a normalization of the MI score to scale the results between 0 and 1.

$$MI(C,C') = \sum_{i=1}^{|C|}\sum_{j=1}^{|C'|}\frac{|C_i \cap C'_j|}{N} \cdot log\left(\frac{N \cdot |C_i \cap C'_j|}{|C_j| \cdot |C'_j|}\right)$$

$$H(C) = -\sum_{i=1}^{|C|}\frac{|C_i|}{N} \cdot log\left(\frac{|C_i|}{N}\right), \quad H(C') = -\sum_{j=1}^{|C'|}\frac{|C'_j|}{N} \cdot log\left(\frac{|C'_j|}{N}\right)$$

$$AMI(C,C') = \frac{MI - E[MI]}{max\left(H(C'), H(C')\right) - E[MI]} \qquad NMI(C,C') = \frac{MI(C,C')}{\sqrt{H(C) \cdot H(C')}}$$

5.2 Completeness, Homogeneity and V-measure Scores

A clustering result appeases homogeneity if all of its clusters contain only data points which are members of a single class and it satisfies completeness if all the data points that are members of a given class are elements of the same cluster. [15]. V-measure (v) is an entropy-based measure, which is calculated by the harmonic mean of distinct homogeneity (h) and completeness(c) scores [15].

$$a_{ij} = ||a \in N : a \in C_i \text{ and } a \in C'_j|| \text{ ,where N is data points}$$

$$H(C|C') = -\sum_{k=1}^{|C'|}\sum_{c=1}^{|C|}\frac{a_{ck}}{N} log \frac{a_{ck}}{\sum_{c=1}^{|C|} a_{ck}}, \quad H(C) = -\sum_{c=1}^{|C|}\frac{\sum_{k=1}^{|C'|} a_{ck}}{n} log \frac{\sum_{k=1}^{|C'|} a_{ck}}{n}$$

$$H(C'|C) = -\sum_{c=1}^{|C|}\sum_{k=1}^{|C'|}\frac{a_{ck}}{N} log \frac{a_{ck}}{\sum_{k=1}^{|C'|} a_{ck}}, \quad H(C') = -\sum_{k=1}^{|C'|}\frac{\sum_{c=1}^{|C|} a_{ck}}{n} log \frac{\sum_{c=1}^{|C|} a_{ck}}{n}$$

$$h = \begin{cases} 1 & \text{if } H(C,C') = 0 \\ 1 - \frac{H(C|C')}{H(C)} & \text{else} \end{cases} \qquad c = \begin{cases} 1 & \text{if } H(C',C) = 0 \\ 1 - \frac{H(C'|C)}{H(C')} & \text{else} \end{cases}$$

$$v = \frac{2 \cdot h \cdot c}{h + c}$$

5.3 Results

Different metrics facilitate quantitative comparison of the projection algorithm pairs. In this study, we investigated which projections and algorithms are the best and the worst results in most cases.

Table 4 shows the average metric values and their standard deviation. In most cases, these values are between 0,2 and 0,5 (but interestingly, AMI value is usually lower). In addition, the *homogenity metrics* have high standard deviation, that is to say, the values obtained are in a broad spectrum. In general, *OrientDB* had the highest average values, so the groups of *OrientDB* tests are the most similar to each other. The smallest group matches was observed in the case of *Joda-Time.*

Table 4. Average values and standard deviations

		v	h	NMI	AMI	c
Checkstyle	AVG	0,3064	0,3000	0,3218	0,1886	0,3857
	STD.DEV	0,1454	0,2361	0,1449	0,0779	0,0628
Commons-math	AVG	0,3502	0,4000	0,3866	0,1866	0,4845
	STD.DEV	0,2031	0,3411	0,1917	0,1189	0,1153
Commons-lang	AVG	0,3611	0,4968	0,4066	0,2061	0,4334
	STD.DEV	0,1147	0,3333	0,1214	0,0868	0,1479
Joda-Time	AVG	0,1446	0,3610	0,1821	0,0767	0,1095
	STD.DEV	0,0728	0,3340	0,1132	0,0308	0,0274
Netty	AVG	0,2210	0,4222	0,2613	0,1159	0,2204
	STD.DEV	0,1100	0,3299	0,1323	0,0763	0,133
OrientDB	AVG	0,3984	0,3972	0,4381	0,2293	0,5949
	STD.DEV	0,2251	0,3215	0,1971	0,1543	0,0586
Oryx	AVG	0,2323	0,3017	0,2604	0,1075	0,3034
	STD.DEV	0,0815	0,1983	0,0759	0,0464	0,1768

Tables 5 and 6 show how many times the algorithms and projections produced the best and worst results. It can be seen that in the case of the three metrics (V-measure, homogeneity and NMI) Birch clustering gave the best results in most cases, but in the other two cases this method was not good. Overall, in most cases the Birch gave the best results (17), followed by Mean Shift (8), which performed well in complexity metric. Most of the time, the DBSCAN had the worst results (34), followed by the Mean Shift (10). Interestingly, the Birch never gave the worst values.

In the case of projections, the *Yule* was the best, producing the best results 20 times. It gave the highest metric values almost always and only once appeared in the worst configuration. Surprisingly, there were four projections (*Hamming, Rogers-Tanimoto, Russell-Rao and Sokal-Michener*) that never appeared in the best-performing configuration. Of the projections, the *Hamming* gave the worst results for a total of 12 times (*Rogers-Tanimoto and Sokal-Michener*: 8 - 8).

Table 5. Average scores and standard deviation

	Number of best cases				Number of worst cases			
	AP	BC	DB	MS	AP	BC	DB	MS
v	2	5	0	0	0	0	8	1
h	0	6	0	0	0	0	9	1
NMI	0	6	0	1	0	0	7	2
AMI	3	0	2	2	0	0	9	1
c	1	0	1	5	2	0	1	5
SUM	**6**	**17**	**3**	**8**	**2**	**0**	**34**	**10**

Table 6. The best and the worst projections

	Number of best cases						Number of worst cases					
	v	h	NMI	AMI	c	SUM	v	h	NMI	AMI	c	SUM
D	1	0	0	1	0	**2**	0	0	1	0	1	**2**
H	0	0	0	0	0	**0**	3	3	2	3	1	**12**
J	1	0	3	1	1	**6**	1	1	1	1	1	**5**
K	0	0	0	1	0	**1**	1	1	1	1	1	**5**
RT	0	0	0	0	0	**0**	2	2	1	2	1	**8**
RR	0	0	0	0	0	**0**	0	0	0	0	1	**1**
SM	0	0	0	0	0	**0**	2	2	1	2	1	**8**
SS	0	4	0	0	2	**6**	1	1	1	1	0	**4**
Y	5	3	4	4	4	**20**	0	0	0	0	1	**1**

Table 7 shows the best and the worst metrics (per project), the number of clusters and the algorithm-projection pair. It can be observed that the number of clusters vary across a wide range, which may be very different from the number of packages. The worst results were typically achieved by configurations with very low cluster number (but there is an exception that gave a high number).

The answer for the **RQ1** and **RQ3**: It was found that the programs can be relatively well structured on the basis of behavior, except in the case of *Joda-Time* that has produced poor results (Tables 4 and 7).

Table 7. The best and the worst configurations for projects

		best score			worst score		
		score	$\|C'\|$	algorithm-projection pair	score	$\|C'\|$	algorithm-projection pair
Checkstyle	v	0,6150	639	BC-Y	0,0050	2	DB-H
	h	0,9348	639	BC-Y	0,0025	2	DB-H
	NMI	0,6545	639	BC-Y	0,0311	2	DB-H
	AMI	0,3020	63	DB-J	0,0010	2	DB-H
	c	0,5032	53	DB-Y	0,1733	5	MS-Y
Commons-Math	v	0,6124	2454	BC-J	0,0214	4	DB-RT, DB-SM
	h	0,9919	2835	BC-Y	0,0101	4	DB-RT, DB-SM
	NMI	0,6619	2454	BC-J	0,0671	2	MS-D
	AMI	0,3977	375	AP-D	0,0081	4	DB-RT, DB-SM
	c	0,9176	3	MS-SS	0,1783	2	MS-D
Commons-Lang	v	0,5229	364	AP-Y	0,0154	2	DB-SM, DB-RT
	h	0,9974	1508	BC-SS	0,0079	2	DB-SM, DB-RT
	NMI	0,5718	941	BC-Y	0,0537	2	DB-SM, DB-RT
	AMI	0,3906	93	DB-Y	0,0070	2	DB-SM, DB-RT
	c	0,6975	2	MS-J	0,2492	906	AP-SM, AP-RT
Joda-Time	v	0,2459	368	AP-Y	0,0043	3	DB-H
	h	0,9919	2479	BC-Y	0,0022	3	DB-H
	NMI	0,3655	1753	BC-J	0,0146	3	DB-H
	AMI	0,1279	14	MS-Y	0,0012	3	DB-H
	c	0,1569	14	MS-Y	0,0603	2	MS-RR
Netty	v	0,5215	8	MS-Y	0,0024	2	DB-H
	h	0,9936	1461	BC-SS	0,0012	2	DB-H
	NMI	0,5336	8	MS-Y	0,0263	2	DB-H
	AMI	0,4221	8	MS-Y	0,0009	2	DB-H
	c	0,6616	8	MS-Y	0,0837	2	MS-J
OrientDB	v	0,7065	265	BC-D	0,0386	2	DB-K
	h	0,9592	350	BC-SS	0,0202	2	DB-K
	NMI	0,7297	298	BC-J	0,0940	2	DB-K
	AMI	0,4893	50	AP-K	0,0138	2	DB-K
	c	0,8043	2	MS-SS	0,4383	2	DB-K
Oryx	v	0,7801	79	BC-Y	0,1085	3	DB-SS, MS-J
	h	0,9889	103	BC-SS	0,0592	3	DB-SS, MS-J
	NMI	0,7973	79	BC-Y	0,1953	3	DB-SS, MS-J
	AMI	0,5952	28	AP-Y	0,0343	3	DB-SS, MS-J
	c	0,7149	28	AP-Y	0,4612	10	MS-H

The answer for the **RQ2**: By analyzing Table 7, we can find out how many times the best and the worst values were given by projection-algorithm pairs. Yule projection with Birch (8) and MeanShift (6) gave the best scores in most cases, these were "the best configurations". The Hamming-DBSCAN pair stands out from the worst configurations, and it has the worst metrics 12 times.

All in all, we can find that there are extremely good projection-algorithm pairs whose results are very similar to the structure, but in many cases clusters can vary significantly and this is also apparent in standard deviation. However, by choosing the appropriate methods, the differences can highlight points in the program where transparency and maintainability can be increased by refactoring.

Acknowledgment. This study was supported by the project "Integrated program for training new generation of scientists in the fields of computer science", no EFOP-3.6.3-VEKOP-16-2017-0002. The project was supported by the European Union and co-funded by the European Social Fund.

References

1. Balogh, G., Gergely, T., Beszédes, A., Gyimóthy, T.: Are my unit tests in the right package? In: 2016 IEEE 16th International Working Conference on Source Code Analysis and Manipulation (SCAM), pp. 137–146. IEEE (2016)
2. Barman, S., Gope, H.L., Islam, M.M., Hasan, M.M., Salma, U.: Clustering techniques for software engineering. Indonesian J. Electr. Eng. Comput. Sci. **4**(2), 465–472 (2016)
3. Berkhin, P.: A survey of clustering data mining techniques. In: Kogan, J., Nicholas, C., Teboulle, M. (eds.) Grouping Multidimensional Data. Springer, Heidelberg (2006). https://doi.org/10.1007/3-540-28349-8_2
4. Comaniciu, D., Meer, P.: Mean shift: a robust approach toward feature space analysis. IEEE Trans. Pattern Anal. Mach. Intell. **24**(5), 603–619 (2002)
5. Ester, M., Kriegel, H.P., Sander, J., Xu, X., et al.: A density-based algorithm for discovering clusters in large spatial databases with noise. In: KDD, vol. 96, 226–231 (1996)
6. Frey, B.J., Dueck, D.: Clustering by passing messages between data points. Science **315**(5814), 972–976 (2007)
7. Gan, G., Ma, C., Wu, J.: Data Clustering: Theory, Algorithms, and Applications. Society for Industrial and Applied Mathematics, Philadelphia (2007)
8. Horváth, F., et al.: Test suite evaluation using code coverage based metrics. In: Proceedings of the 14th Symposium on Programming Languages and Software Tools (SPLST2015), pp. 46–60, October 2015
9. Kicsi, A., Vidács, L., Beszédes, A., Kocsis, F., Kovács, I.: Information retrieval based feature analysis for product line adoption in 4gl systems. In: Proceedings of the 17th International Conference on Computational Science and Its Applications - ICCSA 2017, pp. 1–6. IEEE (2017)
10. Kleinberg, J.: An impossibility theorem for clustering. In: NIPS, vol. 15, pp. 463–470 (2002)
11. Lorbeer, B., Kosareva, A., Deva, B., Softić, D., Ruppel, P., Küpper, A.: Variations on the clustering algorithm Birch. Big Data Res. **11**, 44–53 (2017)
12. Lung, C.H., Zaman, M., Nandi, A.: Applications of clustering techniques to software partitioning, recovery and restructuring. J. Syst. Softw. **73**(2), 227–244 (2004)

13. Maletic, J.I., Marcus, A.: Supporting program comprehension using semantic and structural information. In: Proceedings of the 23rd International Conference on Software Engineering, pp. 103–112. IEEE Computer Society (2001)
14. Mitchell, B.: Clustering software systems to identify subsystem structures. Department of Mathematics & Computer Science Drexel University, Philadelphia (2006)
15. Rosenberg, A., Hirschberg, J.: V-measure: A conditional entropy-based external cluster evaluation measure. In: Proceedings of the 2007 Joint Conference on Empirical Methods in Natural Language Processing and Computational Natural Language Learning (EMNLP-CoNLL) (2007)
16. Shtern, M., Tzerpos, V.: Clustering methodologies for software engineering. Adv. Softw. Eng. **2012**, 1 (2012)
17. Strehl, A., Ghosh, J.: Cluster ensembles-a knowledge reuse framework for combining multiple partitions. J. Mach. Learn. Res. **3**, 583–617 (2002)
18. Tabacznyj, C.: Abstract clustering for program comprehension. In: Proceedings of the 4th Irish conference on Formal Methods, pp. 93–108. British Computer Society (2000)
19. Tengeri, D., Beszédes, A., Havas, D., Gyimóthy, T.: Toolset and program repository for code coverage-based test suite analysis and manipulation. In: 2014 IEEE 14th International Working Conference on Source Code Analysis and Manipulation (SCAM), pp. 47–52. IEEE (2014)
20. Tengeri, D., Horváth, F., Beszédes, Á., Gergely, T., Gyimóthy, T.: Negative effects of bytecode instrumentation on Java source code coverage. In: Proceedings of the 23rd IEEE International Conference on Software Analysis, Evolution, and Reengineering (SANER 2016), pp. 225–235, March 2016
21. Van Rompaey, B., Demeyer, S.: Exploring the composition of unit test suites. In: 2008 23rd IEEE/ACM International Conference on Automated Software Engineering-Workshops, ASE Workshops, pp. 11–20. IEEE (2008)
22. Vinh, N.X., Epps, J., Bailey, J.: Information theoretic measures for clusterings comparison: Variants, properties, normalization and correction for chance. J. Mach. Learn. Res. **11**, 2837–2854 (2010)
23. Zhang, T., Ramakrishnan, R., Livny, M.: Birch: an efficient data clustering method for very large databases. In: ACM Sigmod Record, vol. 25, pp. 103–114. ACM (1996)

Virtualization, Containerization, Composition, and Orchestration of Cloud Computing Services

Isaac Odun-Ayo[1(✉)], Victor Geteloma[1], Ibukun Eweoya[1], and Ravin Ahuja[2]

[1] Department of Computer and Information Sciences, Covenant University, Ota, Nigeria
isaac.odun-ayo@covenantuniversity.edu.ng
[2] Delhi College of Engineering, Delhi, India

Abstract. Cloud Computing is a dynamic concept which applies virtualization cum allied techniques to facilitate the provision of services to users. To support provision of resources to users by the service and deployment models, core technologies such as virtualization, containerization and orchestration are used on the cloud. However, the task of having to determine a research focus is challenging and rigorous. A systematic map enables a synthesis of a scheme for categorizing data in a domain that interests researchers. This work conducts a systematic mapping study of virtualization, containerization and orchestration of cloud computing services. The results indicated that articles on virtualization in the area of valuation research and experience papers were 8.56% and 3.28% respectively. In addition, many articles discussed deployment based on validation and solution research with 4.92% and 13.93% respectively. There were more papers published that discussed orchestration in terms of philosophical papers with 2.45%. The lowest publications on models were on the topic of orchestration which was 1.9%. Also, the lowest number of papers on evaluation research was on deployment which was 3.28%. Furthermore, the lowest numbers of articles on validation research were on composition enabler which was 0.82%, while that of solution proposal were on orchestration with 0.82%. The result of this research reveals the gaps that will be beneficial to the trio of researchers, industries, and providers.

Keywords: Cloud computing · Virtualization · Containerization · Composition · Orchestration · Systematic mapping

1 Introduction

Cloud is a parallel and distributed computing system consisting of a collection of interconnected and virtualized computer with a dynamic provisioning and it makes its resources available with reference to standard agreements between all the cloud stakeholders [1]. Virtualization is the core technology being adopted on the cloud. It allows the provision of virtual resources to clients in form of operating system, servers, file, and storage. The importance of virtualization is underscored as it is often considered

S. Misra et al. (Eds.): ICCSA 2019, LNCS 11622, pp. 403–417, 2019.
https://doi.org/10.1007/978-3-030-24305-0_30

the key to the success of cloud computing [2]. However, based on virtualization and multi-tenancy on the cloud, security challenges do exist [3, 4]. Containerization takes virtualization to the next level in terms of architecture and efficiency. The concept of host and guest operating system (OS) is eliminated, including the virtual machines (VM) concept, and making the use of a container to achieve the same task but now on a single host OS.

The cloud automation tools that enhance the activities on the cloud orchestration involves workloads, servers and VM, through a complicated process. The core architecture and applications of the cloud environment have made Cloud computing very effective and regularly enhancing the services [5, 6]. The main cloud consulting services are Software-as-a-Service (SaaS), Platform-as-a-Service (PaaS) and Infrastructure-as-a-Service (IaaS). Cloud SaaS is a solution provided to users that enables them access applications and database on the internet using web browser based on CSP provision. Cloud PaaS provides freedom from the need for underlying infrastructure and allows a user to focus on application design and deployment using the CSP infrastructure. IaaS in the cloud makes storage, network, and compute recourses available to the user based on payment subscription. The cloud user has limited control of the CSPs infrastructure but there is no need spending at all in infrastructure.

The cloud deployment models are private, public, community, and hybrid clouds. Private clouds are hosted and utilized by one organization only and it is adjudged to be of a better security. Public clouds offerings are available through the CSP that do possess large data centers with sophisticated infrastructure spanning different geographical locations. Services are on demand, elastic, and scalable and the resources appear to be infinite. Community cloud are hosted by organizations and institutions involved in similar activities like universities and hospitals. Hybrid cloud combines private and public clouds. The basis is to outsource processes that are not critical to the public cloud while retaining critical processes on private clouds. Although the CSPs are striving to provide very efficient and reliable services despite the trust concerns [7].

A container is a collection of many applications running on one host [8]. Containers are lightweight-virtualization solution with benefits related to size and flexibility, and relevant to PaaS cloud in terms of application packaging and orchestration [9]. The prominent concepts that ensure containerization are: (i) A lightweight portable runtime environment; (ii) The ability for development, testing, and deployment of applications to many servers; (iii) The ability to do an interconnection of containers [10]. An example of the container technology is Docker, which implemented the concept of micro-service model for application development and publishing.

Virtualization is a "sandbox" environment where the computer hardware is abstracted to an operating system called virtual machines; the operating system, the application, and the configurations of a physical server make up the virtual machines [11]. Virtualization aims to enhance how flexible the deployed cloud is and how well it is integrated to new network services in the networks of the operators [12]. While virtualization helps cloud stakeholders to achieve an optimization of their application performance in a pocket friendly way, it can also carry some security risks [13]. Presently, several tools can manage and instantiate containers in the cloud and they include Docker Swarm, Kubernetes, Magnum, Google Container Engine, and Open Stack Neutron [14]. There are two basic approaches to virtualization which are the para-virtualization which requires having the guest operating system (OS) modified, and the full virtualization which is a guarantee for unchanged guest OS [15]. Despite many works published on cloud virtualization, containerization and orchestration, significant shortfalls in understanding of cloud orchestration techniques remain [16].

Generally, embarking on a qualitative research requires identifying specialized areas of interest, which involves searching several conference proceedings, journals, books, digital libraries, and also involves making observations in research environments, attending workshops, seminars and conferences, with the goal of identifying a research topic [17]. During the process of literature review, researchers do discover new research concepts. This allows for collaboration and cross-fertilization of ideas that do motivate the choice of research topic; which is a rigorous task.

This work conducts a systematic mapping study (SMS) of virtualization, containerization, and orchestration in the cloud. SMS provides an avenue for revealing research areas and topics that are not sufficiently covered. An SMS is utilized to categorize such reports based on a unique scheme and structure, and the summaries are presented visually as a map [18]. There is a classification process for sorting relevant articles into a scheme. There is a data extraction process for determining the various categories to be applied and it is usually presented on a spreadsheet. Subsequently, the frequency of publications is used to create a systematic map. The bubbles plots have sizes corresponding to the number of papers in such categories. The analysis of publications in this study was carried out based on three concepts: the topic, contribution, and research concepts. The topic concept is used to extract key aspects of the discussion on virtualization, containerization, and orchestrations. The research facet establishes the type of research conducted in the publications. The contribution facet considers issues like the method or tools applied in the study. Based on reviewed literature, no previous research has explored SMS of cloud virtualization, containerization and orchestration. This paper has created a systematic map pointing to areas lacking in studies in terms of systematic mapping study of virtualization, containerization, and orchestration in the cloud. Therefore, it is obvious that subsequent researches in the industry and the academia can leverage on this work to advance research work in diverse domains.

In this paper, Sect. 2 focuses related work. Section 3 discusses the systematic mapping process, Sect. 4 presents the results and discussion; while Sect. 5 concludes the paper, and suggests future direction of research.

2 Related Work

The work of [19] elaborated on the planning stage of an SMS. Furthermore, it identifies the software patterns as evident during the requirement engineering level of projects, it provides a thorough understanding of the relevance of those patterns in relation to the basic parameters of the development process. The work provided a protocol with required steps to replicate the work by interested researchers, thereby confirming its validity. The academic digital repositories explored in this research are ACM DL, IEEExplore, SCOPUS, and Web of Science. The standards in [18] were employed for this work.

The work of [20] described the protocol for a systematic mapping study (SMS) in relation to domain-specific languages (DSL) which is a point of concentration of the work; this is based on current trends and the direction for future research. The work spans through July 2013 to October 2014, with basic guidelines to perform systematic review, which are: planning, the conduct of the review, and reporting such.

The SMS in [21] analyzed the use of concept maps in Computer Science. It delivers an SMS result that centers on the collection and evaluation of existing research on concept maps in the computing field. Five digital libraries were utilized with backward snowballing and manual approaches employed for the search. The work displayed extensive focus and a thorough investigation of concept maps, based on supports that have to do with how to learn and teach. SCOPUS, ScienceDirect, Compedex, ACM DL, and IEEExplore digital libraries were the resources employed in this work based on the search strings.

In [22], an SMS was employed in the examination of how games related techniques were used in software engineering education, with research trends, shortcomings, and identification of the future direction. The laid down rules in [18] were adhered to for its mapping process based on primary studies that spans 1974 through 2016 that yielded 156 primary studies for the work.

The work in [23] did a mapping of power system model by providing an overview of power system models, which entails the analysis of their modelling features and identification of modelling gaps. A total of 228 surveys were administered to power experts to elicitate information, but only 82 were filled and returned which was utilized for the mapping.

In [24], an SMS of domain-specific languages was carried out with emphasis on the contribution, the type of research, and the context. The search based on reputable search engines spans 2006 to 2012. The SMS concentrated on the process defining research questions, the search conduct, how papers were screened, classified, and then how data was extracted. Opinion papers, experience papers, philosophical or conceptual papers, solution proposal, and validation research materials were consulted.

[25] did an SMS of the literature on ontologies in the legal context. The work based its search on "legal theory" and "legal concepts". Also, the selected studies were categorized based on contributions in terms of language, tool, method, and model; with ontological research was involved.

[26] were of the opinion that the evaluation and the SMS conduct should be noted for updates. The authors conducted an SMS of systematic maps, and discovered that in the large number of the studies conducted, a collection of guidelines were consulted and integrated which lead to different ways in conducting SMS.

The work of [27] is an SMS that gives an overview of empirical research in software cloud-based testing in the process of building a classification scheme. There was an investigation of testing methods; its applications, and peculiarities. The work was primarily based on 69 studies coined out of 75 publications. This yielded a resourceful statistical analysis and eventual quantitative results. From literature examined, no work has focused on SMS of Cloud business and legal implications.

The protocol for systematic mapping study (SMS) of human computer interaction evaluation for ubiquitous applications was explored in [21], with interest in relevant quality characteristics, and methodologies or models to be employed in the evaluation under study. The systematic mapping process was adapted from [26]. The resource databases are Scopus, IEEExplore, ACM Library, Springer, ScienceDirect, and Compedex. From literature, no work has focused on systematic mapping study of cloud virtualization, containerization and orchestration.

3 The Systematic Mapping Process

3.1 Review Stage

An SMS covers a visual presentation of results based on literature review in a related field. This study was based on the guidelines established in [18, 28]. An SMS is a process that can be replicated, it is employed to extract and interprete ready materials relation to a research objective [29]. Firstly, the research questions are defined, where the research scope is enunciated; then a primary studies search to obtain all available papers in the field is done. Having obtained all papers, the next step is to screen all the paper to determine those relevant for inclusion in the study. Thereafter, the keyword process is applied to the abstracts in an attempt to developing a classification scheme. Finally, the process to extract data from the included papers which leads to a systematic map. The design of a systematic map for visualization, containerization, composition and orchestration entails all the steps discussed so far. In context of our selected paper criteria depicted by the prerequisites of the examination's destination and research questions, we have considered 122 papers to be relevant for inclusion out of an initial list of 1,678 papers from 2010 to 2018.

3.2 Definition of Research Questions

The purpose of an SMS is to find out the research type and the volume of research carried out in a research domain. It is necessary to know the publication outlet of the papers. These are the concepts that influence the choice of research questions for the study. The research questions for this study are:

RQ1: What areas of virtualization, containerization, composition and orchestration in relation to the cloud are addressed and how many articles concern the different areas?

RQ2: What types of papers are published in the area and in particular what evaluation and novelty do they constitute?

3.3 Conduct of Research for Primary Studies

This is fundamentally the starting point for any review. It is carried out by an exploration of major digital libraries. However, it is possible to do it manually for journals and conference papers. To get papers for this research, the necessary search was conducted on major academic digital repositories that are accessible online. It was not done on information from books and other printed materials.

This process was actually carried out on a couple of major electronic databases because of the high impact factor of the publications in these digital libraries. The selected repositories used for the search is shown in Table 1.

Table 1. Electronic databases used for systematic mapping study

Electronic database	URL
ACM	http://dl.acm.org/
IEEE	http://ieeexplore.ieee.org/Xplore/
Science Direct	http://www.sciencedirect.com/
Springer	http://www.springerlink.com/

The search string used for this study was designed in terms of population, intervention, outcome and comparison. The search keywords used represent all aspects of the title for this study. The employed search string on the academic digital repositories selected is as follows:

(TITLE (Virtualization) OR TITLE (Containerization) OR TITLE (composition) OR TITLE (Orchestration) OR TITLE (enablers)) AND (TITLE (Cloud) OR KEY (cloud)) AND (LIMIT- TO (SUBJ AREA, "COMP")).

The searches were carried out based on the process and strings above on the digital academic repository to be sure that prominent studies were not excluded. In this work, search for primary studies in terms of cloud and computer science were considered in the established repositories adopted.

3.4 Screening of Papers for Inclusion and Exclusion

The reason to have some criteria to select is to find and include all papers that are relevant to the study. The standard criteria were employed to eliminate publications that are not significant to the study. The criteria were also used to discard papers that do not relate to the research questions. There are abstracts that had the focus of study, but without sufficient details, hence they were excluded. In addition, the study excluded papers on panel discussions, presentation slides, prefaces, editorials, tutorials and summaries because they do not contain abstracts. However, papers were included if it discussed the main focus with adequate details of secondary issues. The main focus of this study is cloud enablers in terms of visualization, containerization, composition and orchestration. Therefore, Table 2 shows the process that ensured the papers were effectively screened base on relevance.

3.5 Key Wording of Abstracts

Key wording of abstract is a core aspect of the systematic mapping process (SMP). It influences the design of the classification scheme. It is usually produced as part of the SMP as shown in Fig. 1 based on the established standard in [18].

Table 2. Inclusion and exclusion criteria

Inclusion criteria	Exclusion criteria
• The paper fully discusses enablers in cloud computing • The paper discusses the enablers in terms of containerization, virtualization, composition and orchestration	• The paper is off context of cloud computing • The abstract does not discuss cloud computing enablers

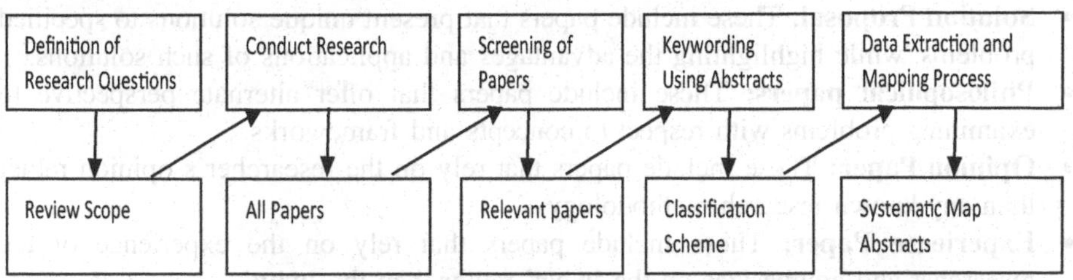

Fig. 1. The systematic mapping process [18]

- Abstract
- Key wording
- Classification scheme
  - Articles
  - Sorting articles into scheme
  - Updating scheme
- Systematic map

Key wording is necessary in reduce the period that is required to produce a classification scheme. Furthermore, keywords does a confirmation of the coverage of classification scheme of prominent publications. This usually involves knowing the context of the study. For this study, keywords from the included publications on virtualization, containerization, composition and orchestration were collected to provide sufficient understanding in terms of the types and contributions of all the articles. Subsequently, the process was applied to the set of categories for the scheme. However, it was sometimes necessary to study what introduced and concluded an article to ensure reliable key wording for the study. Finally, a group of keywords was used to establish the categories used to the map of this study.

In this study on virtualization, containerization, composition and orchestration, three facets were used in producing the results. The first facet is the topic facet which is based on topics from different aspects of the focus of study. The second facet is the contribution facet in terms of metric, method, model, tool and process as discussed in [18]. Although, this is independent of the focus of this study, it was considered very appropriate for the study. The third facet deals with the types of research conducted in tandem with the focus of the study.

3.6 Research Type Facets with Categories and Descriptions

This study adopted the classification approaches in [30], based on the explanations below:

- **Validation research:** The procedure used is unique but not yet implemented, as it is still at the experimental stage.
- **Evaluation research:** The procedure has been implemented and the resultant outcomes are outlined based on pros and con.
- **Solution Proposal:** These include papers that present unique solutions to specified problems, while highlighting the advantages and applications of such solutions.
- **Philosophical papers:** These include papers that offer alternate perspective to examining problems with respect to concepts and frameworks.
- **Opinion Paper:** These include papers that rely on the researcher's opinion rather than any known research methodology.
- **Experience Paper:** These include papers that rely on the experience of the researcher and emphasizes on the 'what' rather than the 'why'.

This classification of research approaches were considered adequate and appropriate for use in the classification scheme of this study. All the included papers were assessed based on the categories and description in the classification of research approaches. The outcome of this process is the research category results used in this study.

3.7 Data Extraction and Mapping Studies

During the classification phase, the relevant articles were sorted in a scheme. The next phase was used to extract data from the included papers. The data extraction process follows after the classifications scheme; which entails categories addition, merging, and removal of irrelevant ones. After the classification process, the procedure to extract data for this study was carried out by calculating the frequencies of each category of publications. The essence is to see which aspect of the selected topics on virtualization, containerization, composition and orchestration were emphasized more in the study. This provides insight into the gaps and enables recommendation for the cloud computing researchers.

Based on the results, a bubble plot was used to present the frequencies of publications thereby creating a systematic map. The systematic map involves a two dimensional x-y scatter plot with bubbles at the meeting point of the categories. The coordinates have bubble sizes that represents the number of articles in such categories at the various meeting points. There are two quadrants in the maps because of the three categories being used in this study. Each quadrant provides visual maps based on the facets of study at the nodes of the topics category with either the contribution or research category. Hence, a simultaneous consideration of diverse facets gets easier. Furthermore, summary statistics got included to the bubble to fine-tune understanding. Overall, the systematic map offers a quick insight into research on virtualization, containerization, composition and orchestration of web services in cloud computing.

4 Results and Discussion

The primary focus of this study on virtualization, containerization, composition, and orchestration is thematic analysis and classification. Although, it may sometimes be necessary to identify the location (venue) of publication. As a result of the analysis, gaps were identified by graphing using the bubble plot, thus showing which research types and topic areas are well covered in terms of publication. It also shows topic areas where there is shortage in research. In this work, high level categories were utilized in the assessment of the references utilized in creating the frequencies of articles and the subsequent systematic map produced. The systematic map on virtualization, containerization, composition and orchestration on the cloud is at Fig. 2.

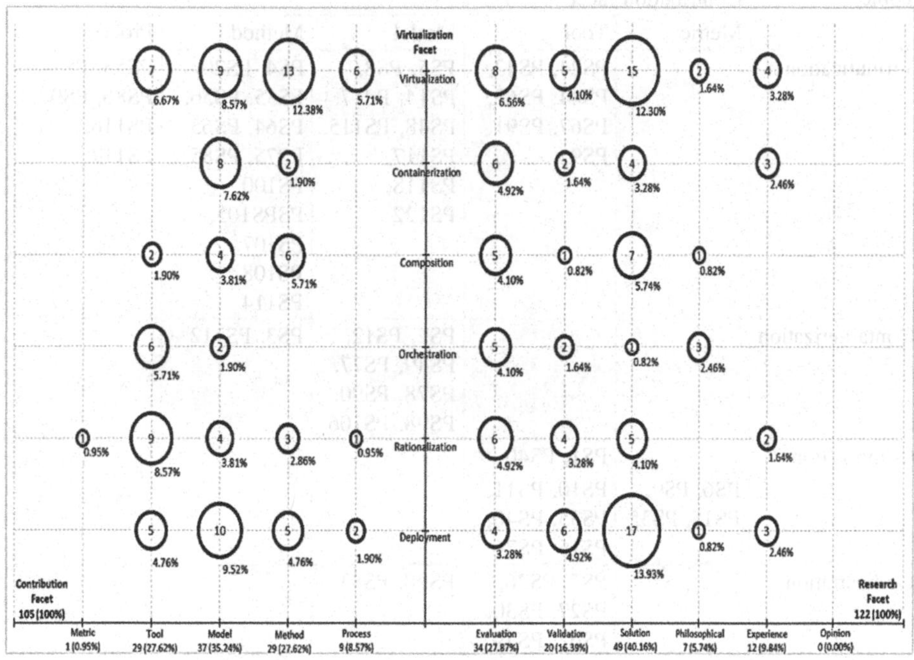

Fig. 2. Bubble map of selected studies

4.1 Topic and Contribution Facet

The topic category is central to this study. The topics that were extracted on virtualization, centralization, composition and orchestration during classification in the area of cloud computing services are:

- Virtualization
- Centralization
- Composition
- Orchestration

- Rationalization
- Deployment.

The left quadrant of Fig. 2 shows the relationship between the topic and contribution facet. The total number of articles included during the data extraction process for the contribution category is 105. The results show that publications that discussed model in respect of virtualization, containerization, composition, orchestration, rationalization and deployment is 35.24% out of 105 papers in this category. Similarly, metric contributed 1%, tool and method had 28% each, and process had 9%. The results are summarized in Table 3.

Table 3. Topics and contribution facet primary studies

Topic	Contribution facet				
	Metric	Tool	Model	Method	Process
Virtualization		PS24, PS43, PS44, PS63, PS67, PS91, PS95	PS5, PS8, PS14, PS17, PS48, PS115, PS117, PS118, PS122	PS4, PS20, PS55, PS56, PS64, PS65, PS75, PS85, PS100, PSPS105, PS107, PS108, PS114	PS53, PS74, PS86, PS97, PS116, PS117
Containerization			PS2, PS12, PS49, PS77, PS78, PS90, PS98, PS106	PS3, PS112	
Composition		PS1, PS40			
	PS6, PS9, PS15, PS35	PS10, PS11, PS35, PS40, PS16, PS76			
Orchestration		PS7, PS26, PS27, PS30, PS62, PS79	PS28, PS83		
Rationalization	PS18	PS18, PS36, PS39, PS42, PS47, PS82, PS87, PS109, PS119	PS93, PS99, PS101, PS110	PS33, PS42, PS58, PS59	PS70
Deployment		PS21, PS23, PS25, PS104, PS120	PS29, PS31, PS38, PS51, PS54, PS88, PS96, PS102, PS103, PS111	PS41, PS60, PS68, PS84, PS121	
Percentage	**0.95%**	**27.62%**	**35.24%**	**27.62%**	**8.57%**

4.2 Topic and Research Facet

The right quadrant of Fig. 2 indicates the relationship between the topic facet and the research type. The total number of papers included during the data extraction process for the research category is 122. The results indicate that solution proposal discussions in relation to the topics of the study was 40% out of the 122 papers in this category. Approximately, evaluation research had 28%, validation had 16%, philosophical had 6%, and experience had 10%. The results are summarized in Table 4.

4.3 Systematic Map of Virtualization, Centralization, Composition and Orchestration

The result of the analysis carried out and presented on Fig. 2, makes it easy to identify which areas had more emphasis based on the frequencies of publications. The results presented the category of the study that has been emphasized more or otherwise. Also, the number in each bubble plot in Fig. 2 indicates the number of publications in the study on virtualization, centralization, composition, orchestration, rationalization and deployment that discussed the contribution and research facets.

Starting with the left quadrant, it is obvious that there are more publications in terms of rationalization in the area of tool with 8.57%. There are more paper published in the area of virtualization, in terms of model, method and process with 8.57%, 12.38%, and 5.71% respectively. There is only one publication in terms of metric on the topic of rationalization which is 0.95%.

Similarly, the right quadrant indicates that there are more publications that discussed virtualization in the area of evaluation research and experience papers with 8.56% and 3.28% respectively. In addition, there are more articles that discussed deployment in the area of validation and solution research with 4.92% and 13.93% respectively. There are more papers published that discussed orchestration in terms of philosophical papers with 2.45%.

On the other hand, the lowest publication on the model discussion is on the topic of orchestration which is 1.9%. Similarly, the lowest number of papers on evaluation research is on deployment which is 3.28%. The lowest numbers of articles on the validation research discussion is on the composition enabler which is 0.82%. The lowest paper published in terms of solution proposal is on orchestration with 0.82%.

There are no publications in the study on virtualization, centralization, composition that discussed metric. There are no articles that discussed tool in the area of containerization. There are no papers published that discussed method as it relates to orchestration. Finally, there are no publications on containerization, composition and orchestration that focused on process.

From the map, the discussion on virtualization and development has the highest number of publications generally. This is of relevance because researchers of all sorts can leverage on this for the advancement of their work. Six categories of studies were provided namely: Virtualization, centralization, composition, orchestration, rationalization, deployment in relation to the focus of study; they can be discussed in terms of tools, models, methods, metrics and processes, evaluation, validation, solution, philosophical and opinion research.

Table 4. Topics and research facet primary studies

Topic	Research facet					
	Evaluation	Validation	Solution	Philosophical	Experience	Opinion
Virtualization	PS5, PS8, PS48, PS53, PS56, PS63, PS64, PS65	PS14, PS17, PS20, PS75, PS85	PS24, PS43, PS44, PS67, PS91, PS95, PS97, PS100, PS107, PS108, PS114, PS115, PS117, PS118, PS122	PS74, PS116	PS4, PS55, PS86, PS105	
Containerization	PS3, PS19, PS22, PS57, PS61, PS73	PS49, PS90	PS2, PS98, PS106, PS112		PS12, PS77, PS78	
Composition	PS10, PS11, PS46, PS69, PS81	PS66	PS1, PS6, PS9, PS15, PS16, PS35, PS40	PS76		
Orchestration	PS27, PS30, PS79, PS83, PS113	PS7, PS26	PS13	PS28, PS45, PS62		
Rationalization	PS39, PS47, PS82, PS87, PS109, PS119	PS18, PS36, PS93, PS110	PS58, PS59, PS70, PS99, PS101		PS33, PS42	
Deployment	PS29, PS31, PS38, PS41,	PS32, PS37, PS52, PS71, PS89, PS92	PS21, PS23, PS25, PS34, PS51, PS54, PS60, PS68, PS84, PS88, PS94, PS96, PS102, PS103, PS111, PS104, PS120	PS72	PS50, PS80, PS121	
Percentage	**27.87%**	**16.39%**	**40.16%**	**5.74%**	**9.84%**	**0%**

5 Conclusion

Recently cloud computing has continued to evolve both in terms of usage and technology. More individuals and organizations are embracing the use of the cloud. The future success of cloud computing must be the perfect combination of cloud technology and end computing enabled by virtualization, containerization, orchestration, and composition.

This paper has created a systematic map of virtualization, containerization, orchestration, and composition on the cloud. the topics of virtualization, centralization, composition, orchestration, rationalization, and deployment were extracted from the included papers based on the focus of this study. The visual appeal of the systematic map makes it quite useful. It is easy to view the categories simultaneously. The map easily generates interest because different aspects can be seen at the same time. In addition, the systematic map helps to summarize results and transfer to those who need it. It is important to state that conducting a systematic mapping study without a follow-up systematic literature review is very unique; also, gaps are easily identified in the topic area and make available areas for further studies.

The results from this study is based on the gaps identified in terms of tools, models, methods, metrics, and processes, in relation to virtualization, containerization, orchestration, and composition on the cloud. In addition, the paper identified gaps in the area evaluation, validation, solution, philosophical and opinion research on virtualization, containerization, orchestration, and composition on the cloud. To the best of our knowledge, studies are lacking in the area of virtualization, centralization, composition on the cloud as it relates to metrics. Also there are no articles that either discussed tool as it relates to containerization or method as it relates to orchestration. Finally, there are no publications on containerization, composition and orchestration that focused on process.

This systematic mapping study has been able to identify some areas where there is minimal focus in terms of virtualization, containerization, orchestration, and composition by virtue of the categories employed for the analysis. The gaps that have been identified are recommended for further studies, as it is expected that it will serve as a broad guide into topics that can be researched on in the area of virtualization, containerization, orchestration, and composition on the cloud. The list of references will be of assistance to interested researchers. Further research could also be carried out to validate this study or resolve contradictory issues.

Acknowledgments. We acknowledge the support and sponsorship provided by Covenant University through the Centre for Research, Innovation, and Discovery (CUCRID).

References

1. Buyya, J., Goscinski, A.: Cloud Computing; Principles and Paradigms, pp. 4–11. Wiley, Hoboken (2011)
2. Jain, R., Paul, S.: Network virtualization and software defined networking for cloud computing: a survey. IEEE Commun. Mag. **51**(11), 24–31 (2013). https://doi.org/10.1109/MCOM.2013.6658648
3. Odun-Ayo, I., Misra, S., Abayomi-Alli, O., Ajayi, O.: Cloud multi-tenancy: issues and developments. In: Companion Proceedings of the 10th International Conference on Utility and Cloud Computing, pp. 209–214 (2017)
4. Odun-Ayo, I., Misra, S., Omoregbe, N., Onibere, E., Bulama, Y., Damasevičius, R.: Cloud-based security driven human resource management system. Front. Artif. Intell. Appl. **295**, 96–106 (2017)
5. Odun-Ayo, I., Ananya, M., Agono, F., Goddy-Worlu, R.: Cloud computing architecture: a critical analysis. In: IEEE Proceedings of the 2018 18th International Conference on Computational Science and Its Applications (ICCSA 2018), pp. 1–7 (2018). https://doi.org/10.1109/iccsa.2018.8439638
6. Odun-Ayo, I., Odede, B., Ahuja, R.: Cloud applications management – issues and developments. In: Gervasi, O., et al. (eds.) ICCSA 2018. LNCS, vol. 10963, pp. 683–694. Springer, Cham (2018). https://doi.org/10.1007/978-3-319-95171-3_54
7. Odun-Ayo, I., Omoregbe, N., Odusami, M., Ajayi, O.: Cloud ownership and reliability – issues and developments. In: Wang, G., Atiquzzaman, M., Yan, Z., Choo, K.-K.R. (eds.) SpaCCS 2017. LNCS, vol. 10658, pp. 231–240. Springer, Cham (2017). https://doi.org/10.1007/978-3-319-72395-2_22

8. Liu, W., Fan, W., Li, P., Li, L.: Survey of big data platform based on cloud computing container technology. In: Barolli, L., Terzo, O. (eds.) CISIS 2017. AISC, vol. 611, pp. 954–963. Springer, Cham (2018). https://doi.org/10.1007/978-3-319-61566-0_90
9. Pahl, C.: Container and clusters for edge cloud architecture – a technology review. Irish centre for cloud computing and commerce, Dublin City University, Ireland (2014)
10. Li, Z., Kihl, M., Lu, Q., Andersson, J.A.: Performance overhead comparison between hypervisor and container-based virtualization. arXiv:11708.01388v1 (cs.dc) (2017)
11. Josyula, V., Oir, M., Page, G.: Cloud computing; Automating the virtualized data centers. CISCO System Inc., Indianapolis (2011)
12. Veeraraghavan, M., Sato, T., Buchanan, M., Rahimi, R., Okamoto, S., Yamanaka, N.: Network function virtualization: a survey. IEICE Trans. Commun. **E100B**(11), 1978–1991 (2017). https://doi.org/10.1587/transcom.2016NNI0001
13. Manohar, N.: A survey of virtualization techniques in cloud computing. In: Chakravarthi, V., Shirur, Y., Prasad, R. (eds.) Proceedings of International Conference on VLSI, Communication, Advanced Devices, Signals & Systems and Networking (VCASAN-2013). LNEE, vol. 258, pp. 461–470. Springer, India (2013). https://doi.org/10.1007/978-81-322-1524-0_54
14. Fazio, M., Clesti, A., Ranjan, R., Chen, L., Liu, C., Villari, M.: Open issues in scheduling microservices in the cloud. IEEE Cloud Comput. **3**(5), 81–88 (2016). https://doi.org/10.1109/MCC.2016.112
15. Brakensick, J., Droge, A., Botteck, M., Hartig, H., Lackorznski, A.: Virtualization as an enabler for security in mobile devices. In: 1st Workshop on Isolation and Integration in Embedded Systems, Glasgow, Scotland, pp. 17–22 (2008) https://doi.org/10.1145/1435458.1435462
16. Weerasiri, D., Barukh, M.C., Benatallah, B., Sheng, Q.Z., Ranjan, R.: A taxonomy and survey of cloud resource orchestration techniques. ACM Comput. Surv. **50**(2) (2017). https://doi.org/10.1145/3054177
17. Odun-Ayo, I., Ajayi, O., Goddy-Worlu, R., Yahaya, J.: A systematic mapping study of cloud resources management and scalability in brokering, scheduling, capacity planning and elasticity. Asian J. Sci. Res. **12**(2), 151–166 (2019). https://doi.org/10.3923/ajsr.2019.151.166
18. Petersen, K., Feldt, R., Mujtaba, S., Mattsson, M.: Systematic mapping studies in software engineering. In: Proceedings of the 12th International Conference on Evaluation and Assessment in Software Engineering, EASE 2008, Italy, pp. 68–77 (2008)
19. Barros-Justo, J.L., Cravero-Leal, A.L., Benitti, F.B., Capilla-Sevilla, R.: Systematic mapping protocol: the impact of using software patterns during requirements engineering activities in real-world settings. Cornell University Library, arXiv:1701.05747v1 [cs.SE] (2017)
20. Kosar, T., Bohra, S., Mernik, M.A.: Protocol of a systematic mapping study for domain-specific languages. J. Inf. Softw. Technol. **21**(C), 77–91 (2016)
21. Santos, V., Souza, E.F., Felizardo, K.R., Vijaykumar, N.L.: Analyzing the use of concept maps in computer science: a systematic mapping study. Inform. Educ. **16**(2), 257–288 (2017). https://doi.org/10.15388/infedu.2017.13
22. Souza, M., Veado, L., Moreira, R.T., Figueiredo, E., Costa, H.: A systematic mapping study on game-related methods for software engineering education. Inf. Softw. Technol. **95**, 201–218 (2018)
23. Fernandez-Blanco, C.R., Careri, F., Kavvadias, K., Hidalgo Gonzalez, I., Zucker, A., Peteves, E.: Systematic mapping of power system models: expert survey, EUR 28875 EN. Publications Office of the European Union, Luxembourg (2017). ISBN 978-92-79-76462-2. https://doi.org/10.2760/422399, JRC10912

24. Mernik, M.: Domain-specific languages: a systematic mapping study. In: Steffen, B., Baier, C., van den Brand, M., Eder, J., Hinchey, M., Margaria, T. (eds.) SOFSEM 2017. LNCS, vol. 10139, pp. 464–472. Springer, Cham (2017). https://doi.org/10.1007/978-3-319-51963-0_36
25. Griffo, C., Almeida, J.P.A., Guizzardi, G.: A systematic mapping of the literature on legal core ontologies. In: Brazilian Conference on Ontologies, ONTOBRAS 15, CEUR Workshop Proceedings, p. 1442 (2015)
26. Petersen, K., Vakkalanka, S., Kuzniarz, L.: Guidelines for conducting systematic mapping studies in software engineering: an update. Inf. Softw. Technol. **64**, 1–18 (2015)
27. Ahmad, A., Brereton, P., Andras, P.: A systematic mapping study of empirical studies on software Cloud testing methods. In: IEEE International Conference on Software Quality, Reliability and Security Companion, pp. 555–562 (2017)
28. Kitchenham, B., Charters, S.: Guidelines for performing systematic literature Reviews in Software Engineering, vol. 2(2) (2007)
29. Muhammad, A.C., Muhammad, A.B.: A systematic mapping study of software architectures for cloud based system. Software System Section, IT University of Copenhagen (2014)
30. Wieringa, R., Maiden, N.A.M., Mead, N.R., Rolland, C.: Requirement engineering paper classification and evaluation criteria: a proposal and a discussion. Requirement Eng. **11**(1), 102–107 (2006)

Code Smells Enabled by Artificial Intelligence: A Systematic Mapping

Moayid Ali Zaidi and Ricardo Colomo-Palacios(✉)

Faculty of Computer Sciences, Østfold University College, Postboks 700, 1757 Halden, Norway
{moayid.a.zaidi,ricardo.colomo-palacios}@hiof.no

Abstract. Code smells are an indicator of poor design in software systems. Artificial intelligence techniques have been applied in several ways to improve soft-ware quality in code smells detection i.e. (detection rules or standards using a combination of object-oriented metrics and Bayesian inference graphs). Literature in the field has identified artificial intelligence techniques and compare different artificial intelligence algorithms, which are used in the detection of code smells. However, to the best of our knowledge, there is not a systematic literature review devoted to study in deep the interaction of these fields. In this paper, authors conduct a systematic mapping to get to know how artificial intelligence inter-acts with code smells. Results show the deep connection of Artificial Intelligence with code smells in a solid way, as well as, providing potential challenges and opportunities for future research.

Keywords: Artificial intelligence · Code smells · Bad smells · Systematic mapping

1 Introduction

The source code of the system is refined by iterations, reconstructed and changed due to many reasons to reflect the modification in requirements, enhance or to improve its features. It is reported that, these type of maintenance activities consume 90% of the total cost of the project [1]. Given the importance of software quality, several practices have been designed to improve its excellence and maintainability. Code smells are assumed to indicate bad design that leads to less maintainable code [2]. Code smells explained by Fowler [3] are symptoms of poor design and implementation choices. He also defines 22 sets of symptoms of code smells. They are also called design anomalies and they refer to design circumstances which affect the maintenance of the software. Code smell detection is seen as a technique to identify refactoring opportunities [4]. These refactoring opportunities include aspects like reducing program error proneness, increasing program comprehensibility, fault- and change-proneness and combating software design degradation, naming just some of the reported aspects [5]. Code smells present the advantage of focusing on aspects that requires deeper analysis [6].

However, the task is normally quite complex and time consuming [7], making software engineering highly dependent on human capital [8]. To avoid over costs and improve overall efficiency, there is a trend nowadays to automate software tasks in the

S. Misra et al. (Eds.): ICCSA 2019, LNCS 11622, pp. 418–427, 2019.
https://doi.org/10.1007/978-3-030-24305-0_31

field [9]. Therefore, several automatic detectors, able to identify instances of code smells in the source code have been produced by the literature [10]. Most of the works are based on the analysis of the structural properties of the source code. Heuristics-Based smell detectors have been proposed as well; it has two steps where metrics are computed first and then these metrics have to separate the smelly and non-smelly classes through thresholds [11]. There have been reports that, these detectors have been performing good in terms of accuracy [12]. Although, most of the detectors require the specific threshold to separate the non-smelly or smelly code and the threshold selection has an impact on the accuracy.

Machine Learning (ML) techniques and methods have been used in the detection of code smells [13] extensively. In this sense, supervised learning (when the model is trained by labeled data) is used and independent attributes are used to predict the dependent attributes using regression and other techniques. A first look at literature shows a set of initiatives in the intersection of these two fields. Where, Kreimer proposed an adaptive detection technique for smells based on metrics [14]. Khomh suggested a Bayesian approach to detect the existences of antipatterns in open source programs [15]. He also presented a proposal based on Bayesian belief networks [16] and Yang applied ML algorithms on code clones [17], naming just some of the most relevant works.

Given the increasing importance of the topic, in this paper, authors present a systematic mapping devoted to investigate the intersection of these two fields. To the best of our knowledge, there is no systematic mapping on artificial intelligence (AI) interacting with code smells. Although, there is a recent effort devoted to study ML techniques for code smell detection [11]. In spite there is a similar goal, our approach is wider in the use of AI as a whole and not only ML aspects, providing with it new insights on the topic.

The remainder of this paper is organized as follows: In Sect. 2, the method used in this study is described. In Sect. 3, the result of the systematic mapping is discussed. Section 4 presents the conclusion and provides recommendations for further research on this topic.

2 Research Method

The purpose of this study is to structure and characterize the state of the practice on the use of AI techniques in code smells. This will be done by means of an analysis of previous works published in the literature to provide an overview of the topic and to help discover potential gaps for future research. Thus, the main research question driving this study is:

What is the state of the practice of the use of AI in code smells?

To do so, our study follows the guidelines by the Petersen [18] for Systematic Mapping literature studies. Figure 1 shows the systematic mapping process flow. Authors followed these steps to conduct the systematic mapping.

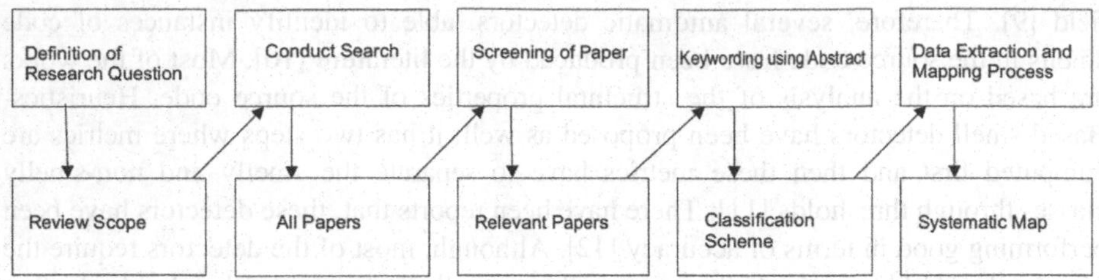

Fig. 1. Systematic mapping process

2.1 Research Questions

In the context of our goal underlined before, research questions are as follows:

RQ1: Which fields inside AI present more impact in Code Smells?
RQ2: Which aspects in Code Smells have been reported as influenced by AI?
RQ3: What are the reported challenges and opportunities in the use of AI in Code Smells?

In the first research question our focus is to detect which fields in artificial intelligence are more active in the code smells, while in the second, we discuss which features in code smells have been reported as affected by AI and finally, the third question investigates potential challenges and opportunities.

2.2 Study Protocol

Authors constructed a search string according to our basic goal and research questions. The string should be simple, in order to provide us several results to cover our exact topic. We use Boolean operator OR for the concatenation of alternative words and spellings, whereas, the AND operator used for the concatenation of major terms [19]. After identifying the keywords, we formulated the string and then we selected different digital libraries and databases on the basis of popularity in the computing field [18]. Although small modifications in the syntax were performed, the general string was:

("Artificial Intelligence") AND ("Code smell" OR "bad smell")

With regards to databases, the following databases were used to find relevant literature on the topic:

- ACM Digital Library (http://dl.acm.org)
- IEEE Explore (https://explore.ieee.com)
- SpringerLink (https://link.springer.com)
- ScienceDirect (https://www.sciencedirect.com/)
- Wiley Online Library (https://onlinelibrary.wiley.com)

These databases were chosen by authors, given that they are among the most relevant sources of articles within the broad field of computing and because they are accessible using institutional accounts.

Zotero was used as a reference management tool, to manage references and to avoid duplications.

The criteria of inclusion and exclusion are used to exclude articles and studies which are not relevant to answer our research questions. Table 1 depicts the inclusion and exclusion criteria we applied in this study:

Table 1. Inclusion and exclusion criteria used in the review

Inclusion criteria	Exclusion criteria
Papers written in English reporting AI techniques for code smells	The paper contains no relevant data to answer the research questions
Available papers that can provide answers to research questions	Paper's full text is not available
Papers published 2014 onwards	Paper is not peer reviewed
	Papers Published before (2014)

For our study, authors followed the process which is shown in Fig. 2. We followed a keywording strategy in this paper. We read the abstract and inspect the keywords and the concept of the paper and identify the context of the research. By doing this, the keywords from different papers are joined to develop a high level of understanding about the nature of the research, as well as, helping us to set up the different categories. When abstract is not able to explain the meaningful keywords then, we also study the introduction part and conclusion part of the paper. When the significant keywords have been chosen, then they are used to create the categories for the map.

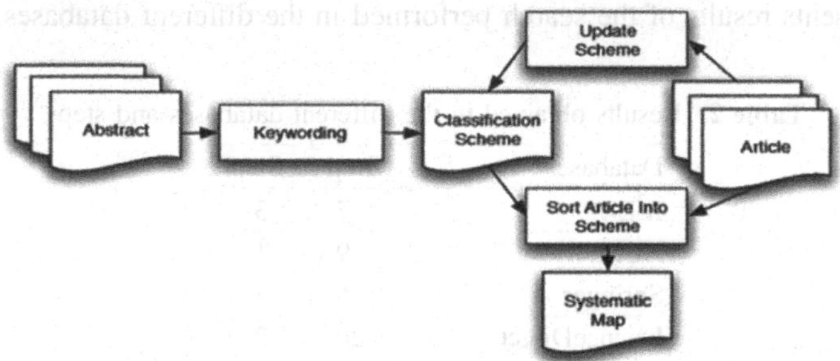

Fig. 2. Classification scheme adopted

In our study, in order to analyze the kind of works present in the literature, we classify papers based on three different aspects: research scope, contribution type and research.

After that the classification took place, we sorted the relevant articles to the scheme. While working on the data extraction, the classification scheme evolved during the process, by merging and adding the categories. We used Excel for the data extraction process. The following categories are adopted.

Firstly, with regards to research scope, categories are as follows:

- Challenges: In this category, the challenges on the topic are discussed.
- Opportunities: This category contains articles with different opportunities for the topic.
- Fields: This category includes different fields used in the paper.
- Aspects: This category includes aspects which are reported.

With regards to contribution type, authors adopted the following categories:

- Process: A process describes the activities, action and their workflow.
- Tool: A software tool is developed to support code smells.
- Model: Representation of information to be used in the topic.
- Technique: It is used to achieve a specific task. It could come, accompanied by a support tool.

The final classification is research type. In this aspect, the following categories are adopted:

- Solution proposal: A solution to the problem is proposed.
- Opinion Paper: Someone expresses personal opinion.
- Experience Paper: What and how something is done in practice.
- Validation Research: The technique not yet been implemented in practice and novel.

3 Results

Table 2 presents results of the search performed in the different databases:

Table 2. Results obtained in the different databases and steps

Database	Step 1	Step 2
IEEE	7	3
ACM	9	1
Springer	75	3
ScienceDirect	20	2
Wiley Online Library	1	1
Total	**112**	**10**

In the column entitled Step 1, authors wrote initial results per database and in Step 2, results after inclusion and exclusion criteria are coded. One can find the significance of the various databases in the search and the key importance of Springer both for Step 1 and Step 2.

Apart from results themselves, it is also worth to present frequencies in each aspect. That is, the Analysis of the outcomes presenting the frequencies of publications for each category. It results in concluding which categories have been highlighted in past research and then, to find gaps and possibilities for future research work. This is in further demonstrated by x-y coordinates scatterplots with bubbles in category intersections. The size of the bubble depends on the number of articles that are pair in each category, corresponding to the bubble coordinates. Figure 3 presents the information in a graphical way:

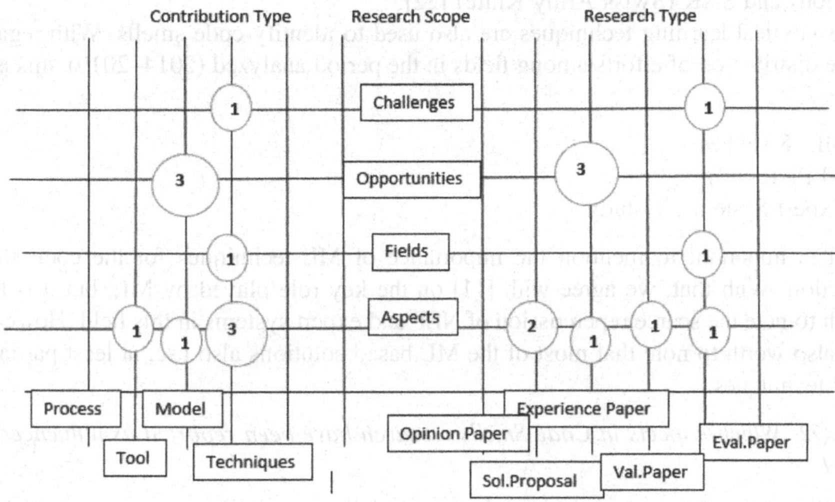

Fig. 3. Bubble plot of the distribution of contributions among the three criteria

The plot clearly shows that, the number of experience papers with different types of opportunities are more than any other category in research type. It also indicates, most of the papers are written on aspects of AI with different techniques and diverse opportunities, with different types of models in contribution type. Other areas have less number of papers so still, there is a need to do more research in those areas.

4 Analysis and Discussion

In this section, research questions are answered by authors by means of the literature review conducted.

RQ1: Which fields inside AI is more active in Code Smells?

Artificial intelligence is a vast term and it includes fields like ML, natural language processing (NLP), vision, expert systems, and robotics. As stated before, there is a very recent study on the use of ML in code smells, however, our idea is quite broader, including AI as a whole. Consistent with previous studies, in our work we found several ML methods which are used to detect code smells, compare different types of code smells tools and suggest different techniques for solving the code smell problem. Bad smells can be predicted using ML algorithms [20] and these techniques are also used to classify the severity of code smells.

The algorithms from ML as well as artificial intelligence helps to detect the smells and improve the performance of detection techniques. These algorithms are used to detect smells in both object-oriented and software-oriented paradigms [21]. In natural language processing applications, the support vector machine (SVM) is used to detect the code smell or anti-pattern i.e. SC (spaghetti code), Blob, FD (functional decomposition) and SAK (Swiss Army Knife) [22].

Analytical learning techniques are also used to identify code smells. With regards to the distribution of efforts among fields in the period analyzed (2014–2019), this is as follows:

- ML: 8 studies
- NLP: 1 study
- Expert Systems: 1 study

It is important to mention the importance of ML techniques for the code smell detection. With that, we agree with [11] on the key role played by ML, but it is also worth to note the scarce repercussion of NLP and expert systems in this field. However, it is also worth to note that most of the ML based solutions also use, at least partially, NLP techniques.

RQ2: Which Aspects in Code Smells research have been reported as influenced by AI?

With the development of ML, the number of proposed approaches are increasing over the years. The propose approaches are decision-based approach, Bayesian belief networks, Support Vector Machine (SVM), and a metrics-based approach to identify feature envy and code smells [23]. Usually, as literature reports, a supervised method is used to detect code smells [24]. ML based and rule-based approaches gained importance and most of the researchers move to work with these approaches because, metrics, rules and classifier algorithm can define to detect smells in a more precise way [25]. NLP has also used for the detection and correction of smells or REST (Representational State Transfer) linguistics antipatterns [21]. Ban also identify the bugs and antipatterns through AI algorithms [26]. Feature envy detection has also been reported by the AI, one of the most common code smell which is exploited by the deep learning. The proposed approach improves the refactoring solutions and features envy detection [23]. Table 3 shows the different machine learning methods on the basis of accuracy on identifying different code smells [27]. The reason behind selecting these code smells is that it has a severe impact on the software quality i.e. God Class, Data Class, Feature Envy and Long Method [22].

Table 3. Comparison of ML methods

ML method	Data Class	God Class	Feature Envy	Long Method
JRip	97.14	**97.86**	96.19	99.52
Random Forest	**98.57**	97.38	96.90	**99.76**
Multilayer Perception	97.86	96.43	**99.67**	93.43
Naïve Bayes	83.81	95.95	89.76	96.43

In Table 3, the results which are bolded, are the highest accuracy in the detection of code smells. For the Data Class, Random Forest achieved 98.57%, for God class JRip achieved 97.86%, for Feature Envy Multilayer Perceptron achieved 99.76% and Random Forest achieved 99.76 for Long Method.

The three main aspects for code smell detection are as follows: (i) performance of a set of classifers over the total number of sample in the dataset, (ii) accurately detect the code smell on the minimum training dataset size, and (iii) different classifers detected the number of code smell over the dataset. All these aspects are analyzed by ML algorithms [23].

RQ3: What are the reported challenges and opportunities in the use of AI in Code Smells?

One of the important challenges which are faced by the ML based detectors is the need to gather a large number of labeled samples to train the classifiers. In fact, more study is needed toward structuring the datasets correctly within the predictors to be used [24]. The disadvantage of using the relational model is that, it only specifies the defective Class, but cannot find the exact problem; so a separate analysis of metrics and metrics error is required to determine the defect [20]. The main focus of the studies are on detection of smells as compared to maintenance. There is also literature reporting the use of version control in code smells [21]. According to Nunez, there are less papers on code smell detection in object-oriented metrics and on object-oriented programming compared to other paradigms [28]. Apart from literature itself, recent studies find that there is a lack of human expertise and validation benchmarking processes [25]. Bafandeh Mayvan underlined that 17% of the publications on the code smell and anti-patterns detection present a lack of maturity [29]. So, authors perform an indirect call for mature works in the topic. Maturity in tools is a common issue in all available solutions in a variety of fields of application and distribution models [30], and maybe both the relative novelty of the topic is not helping to get a mature and standardized versions code smells tools and processes.

5 Conclusions and Future Work

A code smell is an understanding that something has gone wrong in your code. Code smells describe a particular sort of outline failures in the code. The main motivation for this work was to examine how Artificial intelligence interacts with the code smells through systematically mapping literature on the topic. Results show the importance of the intersection of these research fields paving the way to new research efforts. Conclusions on our work also identifies challenges and opportunities in the topic. In addition, the review conducted highlights that ML is the most active field inside AI in code smells while vision, NLP, robotics and expert system attracts less attention. However, and in spite of the low attention, authors want to extend their works towards the use of NLP in Code Smells apart from the use of ML techniques in the detection of code and architectural smells.

References

1. Kessentini, W., Kessentini, M., Sahraoui, H., Bechikh, S., Ouni, A.: A cooperative parallel search-based software engineering approach for code-smells detection. IEEE Trans. Softw. Eng. **40**, 841–861 (2014). https://doi.org/10.1109/TSE.2014.2331057
2. Sjøberg, D.I.K., Yamashita, A., Anda, B.C.D., Mockus, A., Dybå, T.: Quantifying the effect of code smells on maintenance effort. IEEE Trans. Softw. Eng. **39**, 1144–1156 (2013). https://doi.org/10.1109/TSE.2012.89
3. Fowler, M.: Refactoring: Improving the Design of Existing Code. Addison-Wesley Professional, Boston (2018)
4. Hozano, M., Garcia, A., Fonseca, B., Costa, E.: Are you smelling it? Investigating how similar developers detect code smells. Inf. Softw. Technol. **93**, 130–146 (2018). https://doi.org/10.1016/j.infsof.2017.09.002
5. Palomba, F., Bavota, G., Penta, M.D., Fasano, F., Oliveto, R., Lucia, A.D.: On the diffuseness and the impact on maintainability of code smells: a large scale empirical investigation. Empir. Softw. Eng. **23**, 1188–1221 (2018). https://doi.org/10.1007/s10664-017-9535-z
6. Walter, B., Fontana, F.A., Ferme, V.: Code smells and their collocations: a large-scale experiment on open-source systems. J. Syst. Softw. **144**, 1–21 (2018). https://doi.org/10.1016/j.jss.2018.05.057
7. Liu, H., Guo, X., Shao, W.: Monitor-based instant software refactoring. IEEE Trans. Softw. Eng. **39**, 1112–1126 (2013). https://doi.org/10.1109/TSE.2013.4
8. Garcia-Crespo, A., Colomo-Palacios, R., Gomez-Berbis, J.M., Mencke, M.: BMR: benchmarking metrics recommender for personnel issues in software development projects. Int. J. Comput. Intell. Syst. **2**, 257–267 (2009)
9. Colomo-Palacios, R., Fernandes, E., Soto-Acosta, P., Larrucea, X.: A case analysis of enabling continuous software deployment through knowledge management. Int. J. Inf. Manag. **40**, 186–189 (2018). https://doi.org/10.1016/j.ijinfomgt.2017.11.005
10. Palomba, F., Bavota, G., Di Penta, M., Fasano, F., Oliveto, R., De Lucia, A.: A large-scale empirical study on the lifecycle of code smell co-occurrences. Inf. Softw. Technol. **99**, 1–10 (2018). https://doi.org/10.1016/j.infsof.2018.02.004
11. Azeem, M.I., Palomba, F., Shi, L., Wang, Q.: Machine learning techniques for code smell detection: a systematic literature review and meta-analysis. Inf. Softw. Technol. **108**, 115–138 (2019). https://doi.org/10.1016/j.infsof.2018.12.009
12. Fernandes, E., Oliveira, J., Vale, G., Paiva, T., Figueiredo, E.: A review-based comparative study of bad smell detection tools. In: Proceedings of the 20th International Conference on Evaluation and Assessment in Software Engineering - EASE 2016, Limerick, Ireland, pp. 1–12. ACM Press (2016). https://doi.org/10.1145/2915970.2915984
13. Arcelli Fontana, F., Mäntylä, M.V., Zanoni, M., Marino, A.: Comparing and experimenting machine learning techniques for code smell detection. Empir. Softw. Eng. **21**, 1143–1191 (2016). https://doi.org/10.1007/s10664-015-9378-4
14. Kreimer, J.: Adaptive detection of design flaws. Electron. Notes Theor. Comput. Sci. **141**, 117–136 (2005). https://doi.org/10.1016/j.entcs.2005.02.059
15. Khomh, F., Vaucher, S., Guéhéneuc, Y., Sahraoui, H.: A Bayesian approach for the detection of code and design smells. In: 2009 Ninth International Conference on Quality Software, pp. 305–314 (2009). https://doi.org/10.1109/QSIC.2009.47
16. Khomh, F., Vaucher, S., Guéhéneuc, Y.-G., Sahraoui, H.: BDTEX: a GQM-based Bayesian approach for the detection of antipatterns. J. Syst. Softw. **84**, 559–572 (2011). https://doi.org/10.1016/j.jss.2010.11.921

17. Yang, J., Hotta, K., Higo, Y., Igaki, H., Kusumoto, S.: Filtering clones for individual user based on machine learning analysis. In: 2012 6th International Workshop on Software Clones (IWSC), Zurich, Switzerland, pp. 76–77. IEEE (2012). https://doi.org/10.1109/IWSC.2012.6227872
18. Petersen, K., Vakkalanka, S., Kuzniarz, L.: Guidelines for conducting systematic mapping studies in software engineering: an update. Inf. Softw. Technol. **64**, 1–18 (2015). https://doi.org/10.1016/j.infsof.2015.03.007
19. da Mota Silveira Neto, P.A., do Carmo Machado, I., McGregor, J.D., de Almeida, E.S., de Lemos Meira, S.R.: A systematic mapping study of software product lines testing. Inf. Softw. Technol. **53**, 407–423 (2011). https://doi.org/10.1016/j.infsof.2010.12.003
20. Czibula, G., Marian, Z., Czibula, I.G.: Detecting software design defects using relational association rule mining. Knowl. Inf. Syst. **42**, 545–577 (2015). https://doi.org/10.1007/s10115-013-0721-z
21. Sabir, F., Palma, F., Rasool, G., Guéhéneuc, Y.-G., Moha, N.: A systematic literature review on the detection of smells and their evolution in object-oriented and service-oriented systems. Softw. Pract. Exp. **49**, 3–39 (2019). https://doi.org/10.1002/spe.2639
22. Kaur, A., Jain, S., Goel, S.: A support vector machine based approach for code smell detection. In: 2017 International Conference on Machine Learning and Data Science (MLDS), pp. 9–14 (2017). https://doi.org/10.1109/MLDS.2017.8
23. Liu, H., Xu, Z., Zou, Y.: Deep learning based feature envy detection. In: Proceedings of the 33rd ACM/IEEE International Conference on Automated Software Engineering - ASE 2018, Montpellier, France, pp. 385–396. ACM Press (2018). https://doi.org/10.1145/3238147.3238166
24. Nucci, D.D., Palomba, F., Tamburri, D.A., Serebrenik, A., Lucia, A.D.: Detecting code smells using machine learning techniques: are we there yet? In: 2018 IEEE 25th International Conference on Software Analysis, Evolution and Reengineering (SANER), pp. 612–621 (2018). https://doi.org/10.1109/SANER.2018.8330266
25. Alkharabsheh, K., Crespo, Y., Manso, E., Taboada, J.A.: Software Design Smell Detection: a systematic mapping study. Softw. Qual. J. (2018). https://doi.org/10.1007/s11219-018-9424-8
26. Bán, D., Ferenc, R.: Recognizing antipatterns and analyzing their effects on software maintainability. In: Murgante, B., et al. (eds.) ICCSA 2014. LNCS, vol. 8583, pp. 337–352. Springer, Cham (2014). https://doi.org/10.1007/978-3-319-09156-3_25
27. Karađuzović-Hadžiabdić, K., Spahić, R.: Comparison of machine learning methods for code smell detection using reduced features. In: 2018 3rd International Conference on Computer Science and Engineering (UBMK), pp. 670–672 (2018). https://doi.org/10.1109/UBMK.2018.8566561
28. Nuñez-Varela, A.S., Pérez-Gonzalez, H.G., Martínez-Perez, F.E., Soubervielle-Montalvo, C.: Source code metrics: a systematic mapping study. J. Syst. Softw. **128**, 164–197 (2017). https://doi.org/10.1016/j.jss.2017.03.044
29. Bafandeh Mayvan, B., Rasoolzadegan, A., Ghavidel Yazdi, Z.: The state of the art on design patterns: a systematic mapping of the literature. J. Syst. Softw. **125**, 93–118 (2017). https://doi.org/10.1016/j.jss.2016.11.030
30. Colomo-Palacios, R., Fernandes, E., Sabbagh, M., de Amescua Seco, A.: Human and intellectual capital management in the cloud: software vendor perspective. J. Univers. Comput. Sci. **18**, 1544–1557 (2012)

Understanding Test-to-Code Traceability Links: The Need for a Better Visualizing Model

Nadera Aljawabrah[1(✉)], Támas Gergely[1], and Mohammad Kharabsheh[2]

[1] Department of Software Engineering, University of Szeged, Szeged, Hungary
{nadera, gertom}@inf.u-szeged.hu

[2] Department of Computer Information System, The Hashemite University, Zarqa, Jordan
mohkh86@hu.edu.jo

Abstract. Visualization of test-to-code traceability links is a great approach to understand test-to-code relations. It efficiently supports software developers in various software development activities throughout the software development life cycle (SDLC) by browsing, recovering and maintaining, links between various software artifacts. However, only a small portion of research has been done on visualization of test-code relations and its importance in maintenance, comprehension, evolution, and refactoring of a software system. This paper extensively draws attention of the reader/researcher to the usefulness of visualizing test-to-code traceability links and opens up several research questions or research paths for further advanced exploration.

Keywords: Visualization · Test-code relations · Traceability links

1 Introduction

Testing is considered to be an important phase in the software development life cycle (SDLC) in which the unit test plays a significant role in software evolution and maintenance and assists in building a quality product [1]. Visualization is a very effective method which helps testers to quickly understand the structure of code and testing correlation. Though there are many studies that address software visualization, only a few have focused on the visualization of test-code relations. This paper highlights this interesting problem for practitioners and researchers, which may drive more adoption of the test-code relation tools in practice, as well as trigger more study and development on related techniques and tools.

Understanding the relations between test and code is essential for other activities in SDLC, such as: change impact analysis, refactoring and reengineering [1]. In this work, we focus on the visualization of test-code relations from two aspects: visualization of test information and visualization of test-to-code traceability links. All information relevant to the testing process, such as test results, code coverage, and test-related metrics, can be treated as test information. Visualization of test information can be a means of providing valuable information about the adequacy of code testing [2], visualizing software faults [3], and evaluating code coverage of test suites' quality [4].

S. Misra et al. (Eds.): ICCSA 2019, LNCS 11622, pp. 428–441, 2019.
https://doi.org/10.1007/978-3-030-24305-0_32

The area of visualizing test information has been targeted by a number of research teams. For example, visualization of code coverage [5] displays all statements that are executed by test suites and thus facilitates the location of faults in these statements. Another method, described by Cornelissen et al. [6], used a UML sequence diagram to visualize test information. Quite recently, there has been growing interest in visualizing test-related metrics which can be considered as an indication of the quality and the process of testing effort [7, 8]. Test-to-code traceability is useful in many software development tasks such as maintenance, refactoring and regression testing; visualization of these relations is one important methodology to assist the tasks.

Current research on test-to-code traceability links is focused on how to retrieve the links between test and code as well as different approaches that have been suggested and used to recover test-to-code-traceability links. However, in [9] the authors find that there is a lack of visualization support, one of the main challenges in the current test-to-code traceability recovery approaches and tools. This study aims to investigate the existing literature on test-related visualization. We have defined two research questions (RQs) to identify, evaluate and select all quality research evidence relevant to those questions. Our research questions focus on two test-code relation areas: Testing information and test-to-code traceability links.

RQ1 to what extent has a visualization of test-code relations been supported in existing studies?
The motivation of this question is to show whether the researchers and practitioners pay any attention to using visualization in identifying the links between test and code as well as obtaining more information about these links (e.g. how the artifacts are connected, types of relations, etc.).

RQ2 what visualization techniques and tools are available to represent test-code relations?
The purpose of this question is to identify the approaches followed in the literature to represent test-code relations in a visual manner, the most common methods followed in representation, and to obtain an overview about different types of visualization tools used and identify their purposes.

Investigating these questions can provide more information about the areas that have used the visualization and how much they have been supported by researchers and practitioners respectively. To answer these questions we explored many publications in the domain of software visualization, source-code related visualization and, particularly, test-related visualization.

The remainder of this paper is organized in different sections as follows: Background information and some related works are presented in the next section, why we need to visualize test and code relations is discussed in Sect. 3. We present results and discussion of our work in Sect. 4 and we conclude our paper in Sect. 5.

2 Background Information and Related Work

2.1 Software Visualization

Software development is a complex process that combines many tasks such as comprehension, analysis, and maintenance. In this context, software visualization plays a vital role in program understanding and in reducing the complexity of understanding the source code structure. Program comprehension is a very effective part, which provides an initial perception of the software structure and supports the maintainability of the software. Throughout the history of software development, visualization of software artifacts has attracted much attention from research teams and several visualization approaches have been proposed to analyze and explore different aspects of software systems, such as runtime behavior, source code or software evolution [10, 11]. Koschke [10], for example, conducted a survey discussing the use of software visualization in the context of software maintenance, re-engineering, and reverse engineering. The survey collected the perspectives of 82 researchers to identify how far visualization is used in these contexts. The results indicated that the researchers believe in the value of visualization in their work. While Caserta et al. [11] in their survey addressed all visualization techniques used in visualizing the evolution of static aspects of the software (e.g. code lines, classes, software architecture). They listed all visualizing tools developed to display the relations in software inheritance, access, and method calls.

Various visualization-based techniques have been used in software visualization. Graphs are the most frequently used visualization to convey information and describe binary relations (in general), as well as different layout tools, have been developed to draw graphs [12, 16]. Other techniques are also used depending on the context, such as charts, UML diagrams, and trees. Out of these techniques, in recent years, a metaphor has become a key concept where ideas or objects (lower level of abstraction) are used as a representative or symbol of other things (higher level of abstraction) which are different from their actual meaning.

The area of visualizing source code relevant information is widely targeted in literature and it has been accepted as a means to help in software maintenance and understand the evolution of software systems. Visualization methods could be elicited depending on the user's need and the information to be visualized (e.g. metrics, relationships, and dependencies). For example, graph-based representation turned out to be appropriate for visualizing source code evolution. Most of the studies have focused on visualizing source code-related metrics and many approaches are proposed in this regard. Metrics is a numerical/proportional value to describe and measure the quality of software artifacts [12, 13] (e.g. source code quality, testing quality, and documentation quality); therefore, it is called quality metrics. Identification of the metrics to be used depends on the intent of the visualization. The code-related metrics which have been frequently used for visualization purpose are: line of codes (LOC), McCabe complexity [14, 15] and number of methods (NOM) [16, 17]. These metrics support the maintainability of source code. In visualization space, data and metrics are mapped to a set of visual attributes as per the context of visualization.

City metaphor is the most popular metaphor used for visualizing program components [18]. This metaphor supports navigation of the program, interaction with represented elements, and explores the city structure. City metaphor is an effective 3D method to represent software structure that enables the user to be well aware of the position of software objects, thus it can be easily retrieved to the development process. In other words, 3D visualization makes use of the spatial memory of users [19]. Wettel and Lanza [20] presented a 3D city metaphor-based language-independent interactive 3D visualization tool named 'CodeCity'. This tool presents class as building and package as a district of a 'software city'. Two code metrics are used for mapping on visual properties: NOM maps on the height of the building and NOA maps on the width. Their visualization is limited to a higher level of abstraction, i.e. package and class. Quite recently, considerable attention has been paid to use of a 3D games environment in software visualization. CodeMetropolis [21] is a command line which helps the city metaphor to visualize source code at a lower level of abstraction (methods and attributes). It uses a game engine 'Minecraft' [22] to visualize the structure of the source code. A single method is represented as a floor located in a building (class). Code metrics display the distinct attributes of a software system. These attributes are mapped to various properties in visual representation space. For instance, the height of the floor expresses the size of the method in terms of logical lines of code. A developer is a player who can fly and explore the Minecraft word and obtain details about internal classes. Balogh et al. [8] extended CodeMetropolis [21] to include visualization of test-related metrics to support developers to better understand the test suite's quality and its relation to the production code. CodePark [23] is another game environment-based tool, which has been recently developed to visualize source code. In this tool, the source code itself has been directly visualized in 3D space instead of using a metaphor to represent it. A set of code metrics has been used to explore a 3D graphs metaphor to describe the internal structure and relations of large-size programs for quality assessment purposes [24]. Visual properties of program entities (e.g. size, shape, color) represent particular metrics of these entities for mapping in 3D visualization metaphor. Information is presented from two points of view: usage-based pattern and inheritance-based pattern. Depending on these patterns, quality attributes such as the size and complexity of programs can be observed in visual space.

In line with the above-mentioned works, many extensive research works have been conducted on code visualization. These works have been immensely useful to reduce the effort in understanding software architecture and thereby simplify the software maintenance and evolution process [10].

Coding and testing are very important activities in the software development life cycle. They are firmly associated with agile software development where the software is evolved frequently. Visualization supports understanding of the inner workings of source code and the behavior of test suites [6].

However, from the developer's perspective, testing is a time-consuming process. Developers believe that their code is well written and, for the purpose of profit, their interest is mainly focused on delivering the software on time, thus testing is often excluded [1]. Hence, visualizing relevant test information (e.g. test suites, test results) is not sufficiently highlighted. Using visualization with testing can be an effective method to provide valuable information about: the adequacy of code testing, visualizing software faults [25, 26], and evaluation code coverage of test suites' quality. This paper contributes to drawing attention to a visualization of test-code relations and concentrates particularly on two areas: visualization of testing information and visualization of test-to-code traceability links.

2.2 Test-to-Code Traceability Links

Current research on test-to-code traceability links is focused on how to retrieve the links between test and code. Rompaey and Demeyer [27] have compared six traceability recovery strategies in terms of the applicability and the accuracy of each approach. The comparison covers only those approaches relating to requirement traceability and test-to-code traceability. The strategies have been evaluated based on three open-source Java programs. In these approaches, units under test are identified by matching test cases, production code's name, vocabulary (e.g. identifiers, comments), examining method invocation in test cases, looking at the last calls right before assert statement, and capturing changes on test cases and production code in the version control change log. The results show that last call before assert, lexical analysis and co-evolution have high applicability; however, they have low accuracy. While naming convention and fixture element types showed high precision and recall, the best results are provided by combining the high-applicability strategies with the high-accuracy ones.

Qusef et al. [28] proposed a more accurate test-to code traceability recovery tool (SCOTCH+ – Source code and Concept-based Test to Code traceability Hunter). This technique depends on applying dynamic slicing and conceptual coupling to recover the links between test cases and source code, thus identifying class under test (CUT).

Recently, various techniques have been developed to support visualization of traceability links between software system artifacts. In addition, different tools have also been developed to automatically/semi-automatically retrieve traceability links between different software artifacts types (e.g. requirements, source code, and document). Marcus et al. [29] studied traceability links between software artifacts and showed how visualization can be important in recovering, maintaining and browsing links between such artifacts.

Traceability links can be identified according to a specific task required to retrieve these links, (e.g. recovering links for evolution purposes). The most popular types of links retrieved are established among items based on the types of software artifacts, which can be either implicit or explicit [30].

Visualization techniques and tools have been developed depending on the type of data to be visualized and the objectives of visualization (e.g. to understand the dependencies and relationships between software artifacts, how they interact with each other, and help document links between several kinds of software artifacts -e.g. requirements, tests) [31]. In Table 1, a set of traceability techniques and tools are listed. Some tools [33, 34] allow the user to add, browse and delete links or even edit the properties of such links. Another tool is pluggable with an IDE [29] to give a uniform user experience for test-to-code traceability links and software artifacts. Each tool provides one or more visualization techniques which may display links in different ways depending on the information task context. For example, the Multi-Viso Trace tool [33] provides four visualization techniques depending on the context in which the traceability is being applied. The visualization displays a global structure of traceability and a detailed overview of each link.

Table 1. Traceability links visualization techniques and tool

Visualization method/Technique	Links visualized	Link recovery method	Visualization tool
Context-based technique (Sunburst, Matrix Tree, Graph) [33]	Links between software artifacts	Automatic (REREATOS) tool	Multi-Visio Trace
Graph (Chain Graph) [13]	Links between software requirements	Manual	–
List [30]	Links between software artifacts	Automatic	ADAMS re-trace
Requirement Matrix (RTM-E, RTM-NLP) [34]	Requirement dependencies	Automatic + Manual	–
Small color squares [29]	Links between software artifacts	Manual	TraceViz
Sunburst, Net map [35]	Links between requirement artifacts (project goals, task, etc.)	Manual	–
Tree map Hierarchal tree [36]	Links between classes in source code and documents elements	Automatic	–
Tree, Matrix Sunburst, Table [32]	Links between software artifacts	Automatic (REREATOS tool)	D3TraceView

While most of the listed techniques present the links extracted between requirements and different software artifacts (e.g. documents, source code), none of these tools address the ease of visualizing the links between unit tests and code, which lays the foundation of this research.

3 Why Is the Visualization of Test-to-Code Relations Needed?

Test-to-code relations can be treated as traceability links that display how test cases and the code under test can be connected. Test suites are usually used to evaluate software systems and detect the program faults. The larger the programs are, the larger the test cases executed, thus a huge amount of data will be produced which is difficult to be interpreted in textual form. Visualization of test suites is useful to give any reader an obvious view of the testing results as well as to determine the fault occurrence in the source code with the least effort and time. Unit tests are used to determine whether the software being tested works correctly or not for a given input [37]. A test case is considered as an up-to-date document that reflects how parts of the code are changed and how they are supposed to be executed [1]. The benefits of running test cases lie in: improving software quality, reducing maintenance effort and cost [25], and identifying faults in software systems. A unit test plays an important role during regression testing where a unit test is re-executed and evolved in parallel with code changes [38]. However, the development process is an iterative and ongoing process which means new changes and updates continuously appear on the software, thus numerous regression tests have to be run (i.e. increasing the testing cost). Therefore, visualizing established links between units under test and their related test suites helps in reducing generating regression tests and saves much time during software evolution process [28].

Units test and tested code can be connected by different types of relations (e.g. direct tests, calls, indirect uses). These links emphasize the consistency between unit test and tested code (e.g. when a test case fails, the links show which part of the code is related to this failure). Thereby, visualizing test-to-code traceability links provides a better understanding of the inter-relationships between tests and tested code which in turn contributes to maintaining and browsing these relations. In addition, refactoring of the code requires some modifications to the test suite in order to keep it valid after refactoring, thus visualization of recovered relationships between unit test and unit under test could be exploited to support and facilitate the refactoring process [28].

With the increasing size and complexity of software under test and its automated test suites, visualization is needed to analyze code coverage and to provide testers with a wide range of information about the quality, performance, the location of a test suite, its relation with the production code, and which parts of code are covered by test cases [39]. There is a large amount of literature that deals with the visualization of test information and a wide range of tools have been proposed for the task of visualization of testing information as mentioned in the section above. However, to the author's best knowledge, very few publications are available in the literature that addresses the issue of visualizing test-to code-traceability links. Studies on test-to-code traceability links have paid more attention to how to recover links between test and With the increasing size and complexity of software under test and its automated test suites, visualization is needed to analyze code coverage and to provide testers with a wide range of information about the quality, performance, the location of a test suite, its relation with the production code, and which parts of code are covered by test cases [39]. There is a large amount of literature that deals with the visualization of test information and a wide range of tools have been proposed for the task of visualization of testing information as mentioned [40]. However, to the author's best knowledge, very few publications are available in the literature that addresses the issue of visualizing test-to code-traceability links. Studies on test-to-code traceability links have paid more attention to how to recover links between test and code, as well as various approaches have been proposed to retrieve the traceability links between the test units and units under test, as mentioned in Sect. 2. However, none of these methods supports the representation of such links in a visual manner. The focal point of this work is to draw attention to the importance of using a visualization technique to display the links between a code and its related unit test.

4 Results and Discussion

In this section we analyze the collected results according to our research questions:

RQ1: To what extent has a visualization of test-to-code relations been investigated in existing studies?
We performed a detailed review of the literature following citations and references using web-based literature search engines. This effort resulted in gathering a number of publications that listed various approaches on the basis of different techniques relating to visualization topics. Thus from all the gathered publications, relevant literature which is found to be 44 in number, we refined and selected those approaches that satisfy the following criteria in accordance with our research purpose:

1. Those approaches that use visualization techniques to represent software source code.
2. Those approaches that use visualization techniques to represent test-related information.
3. Those approaches that use visualization techniques to represent test-to-code traceability links.

Figure 1 shows the share of the different investigated studies in percentage related to various methods of visualization from a selected sample of research papers. Our investigation shows that 48% of total software testing-related research works talk about visualization of source code. Testing information-based (test-code relations) visualization works amount to 29% and visualization of test-to-code traceability links does not receive any interest in the studied literature. This implies that works on testing related visualization are still practically limited. One possible reason is that writing tests is considered to be a time-consuming and not interesting task. Developers could focus more on the development process and activities which are responsible for testing activities. They trust their code is well written and does not need any tests. Therefore, not visualization in specific but testing, in general, is neglected.

Moreover, despite the importance of test-to-code traceability links in understanding, maintaining and refactoring code, it is not commonly used and its scope is highly neglected in software development.

As mentioned in the previous section, there is a huge requirement to advance test-to-code traceability recovery visualization techniques. The existing approaches have several limitations which make the visualization process somewhat difficult; for instance, most of the links that could be retrieved using the current methods are either redundant links or missing links-there is no way to recover specific links of high importance. Furthermore, identifying links is purely a manual task that needs higher time and effort investment.

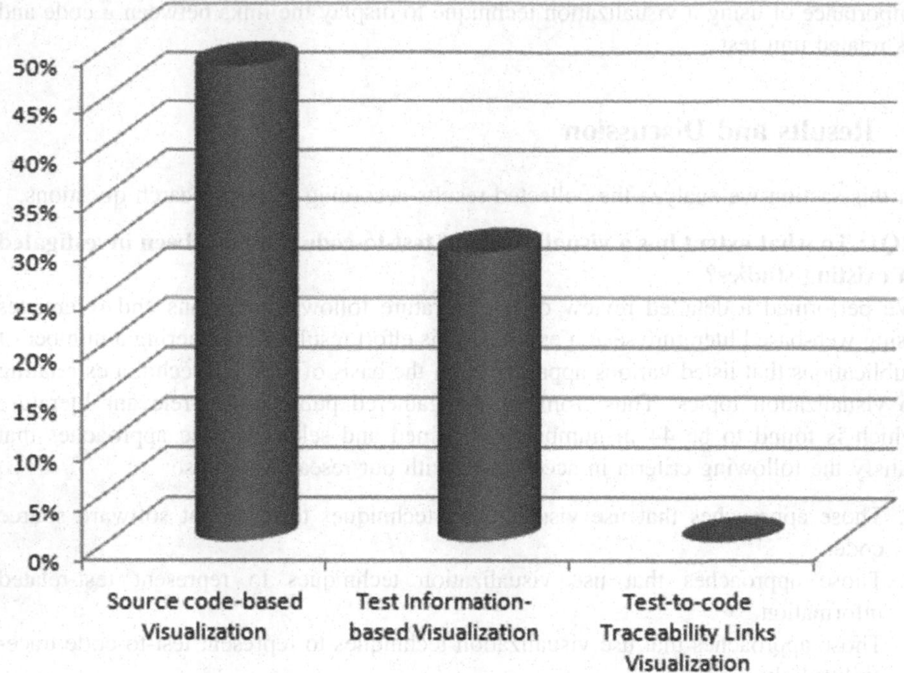

Fig. 1. Analysis of the results depending on **RQ1**

RQ2: What visualization techniques and tools are proposed to represent test-code relations?

A variety of visualization techniques have been developed to visualize different types of testing-related information. Examples of these techniques, as discussed in previous paragraphs, are graph-based, UML diagrams, metaphor. The graph-based visualization technique can be considered as the most popular visualization technique used; however, this may depend on the purpose of the deployment of the visualization technique. Various visualization techniques have many use cases, such as to obtain an overview of the code and test evolution, or improve the understanding of dependencies between code and test, or to support the visualization of testing information [25]. Concerning test-to-code traceability links, there is not much interest in developing approaches to visualize links between test and code. Most of the approaches have been developed to visualize relationships/links between requirements and other software artifacts (source code, design, test cases) such as graphs, traceability matrices, hyperlinks (cross-references) and lists, as shown in Fig. 2 [41]. Based on our investigations, it is clear that further research in the area of visualization of test-to-code traceability links is necessary. Below we provide some open questions that can help to reveal specific topics in this area for further research and try to give some answers as an example. We feel the following questions and directions are the most interesting ones.

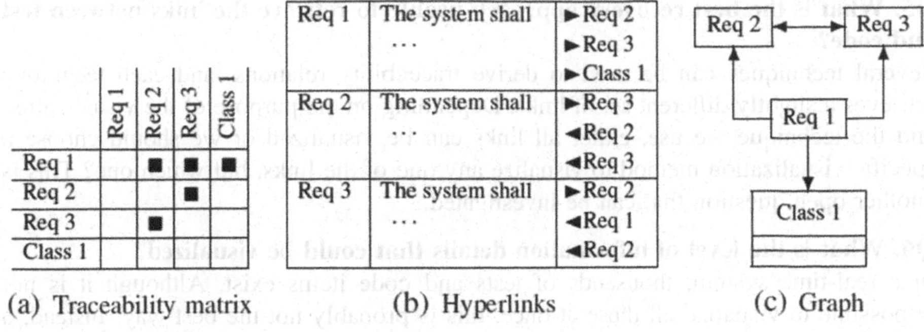

Fig. 2. (from [41]) Visualization techniques

Q.1. What is the purpose of visualization?
Visualization must have a purpose. Defining our goal can help in finding proper visualization techniques to be used and appropriate elements to be presented in it. Purpose can be: understand relations, impact analysis, find problems (e.g. bad smells).

Q.2. What is a suitable visualization technique that can be used to display test-to-code traceability relations and their attributes?
There are several possible ways to visualize test-to-code relations including graphs, matrices, hyperlinks, lists, tree maps, 3D space. Among the available visualization techniques, 'graph-based visualization' and 'traceability matrices' seem to be the most suitable methods for various needs to find traceability links between code and tests. However, the determination of the most suitable method depends on the use case meaning, as the most suitable method may vary from one use case to another. For example, when one tries to check the relations of an item for impact analysis, 'graph representations' and 'hyperlinks' seem to be relevant. On the other hand, if someone needs a broader view to check inconsistencies among the relations, 'graph representation' showing the traceability links inferred using different link-detection techniques in different colors might be a better choice. But a 3D visualization also seems to be appropriate to display attributes of various items and relations.

Q3. What test and code items and properties should be objects and attributes in the visualization?
Relations can be visualized directly as objects in the visualization space (e.g. as lines between objects), or we can only map their properties to the attributes of the connected objects.

Q4. What are the criteria taken into account to choose the best visualization technique?
As an example, the size of a program can be a criterion, and should be taken into account while using any visualization technique. Visualization methods often become too large and thus hard to read and understand in the case of big projects.

Q5. What is the best recovery approach usable to retrieve the links between test and code?
Several techniques can be used to derive traceability relations, and each technique retrieves a slightly different set of links. Depending on the purpose of the visualization and the technique we use, either all links can be visualized or we should choose a specific visualization method to visualize any one of the links, but which one? This is another open question that can be investigated.

Q6. What is the level of information details that could be visualized?
In a real-time system, thousands of tests and code items exist. Although it is not impossible to visualize all these at once, this is probably not the best way. Instead, a selective or hierarchical visualization approach seems to be a better choice. For example, instead of method-level visualization, one can show (test and production) classes or group items based on their relations or some other purposes and visualize the groups only.

5 Conclusion and Future Work

As there are many sources from where the traceability relations can be inferred, one of the most important questions is to decide which source or combination of sources is the best to determine the test-to-code links. It is obvious that, if these sources disagree, this will make it harder to understand what is going on, what was the goal of the developer, how the components are really related and change impact analysis can yield in false results, etc. Fortunately, visualization can aid this task. In this work, we analyzed the scope, advantages, and concerns surrounding the visualization of test-to-code traceability links. Test-to-code traceability links couple test cases to code elements based on the relationship that enables us to understand which code modules are tested by which unit tests. Therefore, visualization of such relations helps in improving the quality of software development, testing or maintenance processes, and lessen bugs. It makes updating the features of existing features of a piece of software or adding new features to it easier. Still, there is a room for research and development for better test-to-code traceability visualization techniques.

Further research then can then aim to make a statistical comparison of these inference methods. Work on addressing the questions mentioned above is in progress and will be presented in future papers.

Our future work is to develop a tool that visualizes and stores traceability links among unit test and its related code and can be integrated with a traceability links recovery tool that extracts links between code and tests. One of the goals of using visualization is to identify the disagreement between traceability links inferred from different sources. This might point out places where something is wrong with the tests and/or the code (at least their relationship) in a specific system.

References

1. Demeyer, S.: Object-oriented reengineering (2008)
2. Tamisier, T., Karski, P., Feltz, F.: Visualization of unit and selective regression software tests. In: Luo, Y. (ed.) CDVE 2013. LNCS, vol. 8091, pp. 227–230. Springer, Heidelberg (2013). https://doi.org/10.1007/978-3-642-40840-3_33
3. D'Ambros, M., Lanza, M., Pinzger, M.: A bug's life visualizing a bug database. In: VISS 2007 – Proceedings of the 4th IEEE International Workshop on Visualizing Software for Understanding and Analysis, pp. 113–120 (2007)
4. Araya, V.P.: Test blueprint: an effective visual support for test coverage. In: 2011 33rd International Conference on Software Engineering (ICSE), pp. 1140–1142 (2011)
5. Jones, J.A., Harrold, M.J., Stasko, J.: Visualization of test information to assist fault localization. In: Proceedings of the 24th International Conference on Software Engineering, ICSE 2002, pp. 467–477 (2002)
6. Cornelissen, B., Van Deursen, A., Moonen, L., Zaidman, A.: Visualizing testsuites to aid in software understanding. In: Proceedings of the European Conference on Software Maintenance and Reengineering, CSMR, pp. 213–222 (2007)
7. Filipe, J., Maciaszek, L.A.: Evaluation of novel approaches to software engineering, July 2013
8. Balogh, G., Gergely, T., Beszedes, A., Gyimothy, T.: Using the city metaphor for visualizing test-related metrics. In: 2016 IEEE 23rd International Conference on Software Analysis, Evolution, and Reengineering, pp. 17–20 (2016)
9. Parizi, R.M., Lee, S.P., Dabbagh, M.: Achievements and challenges in state-of-the-art software traceability between test and code artifacts. IEEE Trans. Reliab. **63**(4), 913–926 (2014)
10. Koschke, R.: Software visualization in software maintenance, reverse engineering, and re-engineering: a research survey. J. Softw. Maint. Evol. Res. Pract. **15**(2), 87–109 (2003)
11. Caserta, P., Zendra, O.: Visualization of the Static aspects of Software: a survey. IEEE Trans. Visual Comput. Graphics **17**(7), 913–933 (2011)
12. Erdemir, U., Tekin, U., Buzluca, F.: E-Quality: a graph based object oriented software quality visualization tool. In: 2011 6th IEEE International Workshop on Visualizing Software for Understanding and Analysis (VISSOFT), pp. 1–8 (2011)
13. Heim, P., Lohmann, S., Lauenroth, K., Ziegler, J.: Graph-based visualization of requirements relationships. In: 2008 3rd International Workshop on Requirements Engineering Visualization, REV 2008 (2008)
14. Wingkvist, A., Ericsson, M., Lincke, R., Löwe, W.: A metrics-based approach to technical documentation quality. In: Proceedings of the 7th International Conference on Quality of Information and Communications Technology, QUATIC 2010, pp. 476–481 (2010)
15. Varet, A., Larrieu, N., Sartre, L.: METRIX: a new tool to evaluate the quality of software source codes. In: AIAA Infotech@ Aerospace (I@ A) Conference, p. Draper Laboratory-, (2013)
16. Marcus, A., Comorski, D., Sergeyev, A.: Supporting the evolution of a software visualization tool through usability studies. In: Proceedings of the IEEE Workshop on Program Comprehension, pp. 307–316 (2005)
17. Boccuzzo, S., Gall, H.C.: Software visualization with audio supported cognitive glyphs. In: IEEE International Conference on Software Maintenance, ICSM, pp. 366–375 (2008)
18. Wettel, R., Lanza, M.: Visualizing software systems as cities. In: VISS 2007 – Proceedings of the 4th IEEE International Workshop on Visualizing Software for Understanding and Analysis, pp. 92–99 (2007)

19. Cockburn, A., McKenzie, B.: Evaluating the effectiveness of spatial memory in 2D and 3D physical and virtual environments. In: Proceedings of the SIGCHI Conference on Human Factors in Computing Systems: Changing Our World, Changing Ourselves - CHI 2002, no. 4, p. 203 (2002)
20. Wettel, R., Lanza, M.: CodeCity. In: Companion 13th International Conference on Software Engineering - ICSE Companion 2008, p. 921 (2008)
21. Balogh, G., Beszédes, A.: CodeMetropolis-code visualisation in MineCraft. In: 2013 IEEE 13th International Working Conference on Source Code Analysis and Manipulation (SCAM) (2013)
22. Minecraft Official Website. http://minecraft.net/
23. Khaloo, P., Maghoumi, M., Taranta, E., Bettner, D., Laviola, J.: Code park: a new 3D code visualization tool (2017)
24. Lewerentz, C., Simon, F.: Metrics-based 3D visualization of large object-oriented programs. In: Proceedings of the 1st International Workshop on Visualizing Software for Understanding and Analysis, pp. 70–77 (2002)
25. Agrawal, H., et al.: Mining system tests to aid software maintenance. Computer (Long. Beach. Calif.) **31**(7), 64–73 (1998)
26. Breugelmans, M., Van Rompaey, B.: TestQ: exploring structural and maintenance characteristics of unit test suites. In: WASDeTT-1 1st International Workshop on Advanced Software Development Tools and Techniques, no. i, pp. 1–16 (2008)
27. Van Rompaey, B., Demeyer, S.: Establishing traceability links between unit test cases and units under test. In: Proceedings of the European Conference on Software Maintenance and Reengineering, CSMR, no. ii, pp. 209–218 (2009)
28. Qusef, A.: Test-to-code traceability: why and how? In: 2013 IEEE Jordan Conference on Applied Electrical Engineering and Computing Technologies, AEECT 2013 (2013)
29. Marcus, A., Xie, X., Poshyvanyk, D.: When and how to visualize traceability links? In: Proceedings of the 3rd International Workshop on Traceability in Emerging Forms of Software Engineering, 8 November, pp. 56–61. ACM (2005)
30. De Lucia, A., Fasano, F., Oliveto, R., Tortora, G.: ADAMS re-trace: a traceability recovery tool. In: Proceedings of the European Conference on Software Maintenance and Reengineering, CSMR, pp. 32–41 (2005)
31. Lago, P., Muccini, H., van Vliet, H.: A scoped approach to traceability management. J. Syst. Softw. **82**(1), 168–182 (2009)
32. Gilberto Filho, A.D., Zisman, A.: D3TraceView: A Traceability Visualization Tool
33. Rodrigues, A., Lencastre, M., De Cysneiros Filho, G.A.A.: Multi-VisioTrace: traceability visualization tool. In: Proceedings of the 2016 10th International Conference on the Quality of Information and Communication Technologies, QUATIC 2016, pp. 61–66 (2017)
34. Di Thommazo, A., Malimpensa, G., De Oliveira, T.R., Olivatto, G., Fabbri, S.C.P.F.: Requirements traceability matrix: automatic generation and visualization. In: Proceedings of the 2012 Brazilian Symposium on Software Engineering, SBES 2012, pp. 101–110 (2012)
35. Merten, T., Jüppner, D., Delater, A.: Improved representation of traceability links in requirements engineering knowledge using Sunburst and Netmap visualizations. In: 2011 4th International Workshop on Managing Requirements Knowledge, MaRK 2011 - Part 19th IEEE International Requirements Engineering Conference, RE 2011, pp. 17–21 (2011)
36. Chen, X., Hosking, J., Grundy, J.: Visualizing traceability links between source code and documentation. In: Proceedings of IEEE Symposium on Visual Languages and Human-Centric Computing - VL/HCC, pp. 119–126 (2012)
37. Fraser, G., Arcuri, A.: Whole test suite generation. IEEE Trans. Softw. Eng. **39**(2), 276–291 (2013)

38. Eagan, J., Harrold, M.J., Jones, J.A., Stasko, J.: Technical note: visually encoding program test information to find faults in software. In: IEEE Symposium on Information Visualization 2001, INFOVIS 2001, pp. 33–36 (2001)
39. Van Rompaey, B., Demeyer, S.: Exploring the composition of unit test suites. In: ARAMIS 2008 - 1st International Workshop on Automated Engineering of Autonomous and Run-Time Evolving Systems, ASE 2008 23rd IEEE/ACM International Conference on Automated Software Engineering, pp. 11–20 (2008)
40. Koochakzadeh, N., Garousi, V.: TeCReVis: a tool for test coverage and test redundancy visualization. In: Bottaci, L., Fraser, G. (eds.) TAIC PART 2010. LNCS, vol. 6303, pp. 129–136. Springer, Heidelberg (2010). https://doi.org/10.1007/978-3-642-15585-7_12
41. Winkler, S., von Pilgrim, J.: A survey of traceability in requirements engineering and model-driven development. Softw. Syst. Model. **9**(4), 529–565 (2010)

Testing in a DevOps Era: Perceptions of Testers in Norwegian Organisations

Daniela Soares Cruzes[1(✉)], Kristin Melsnes[2(✉)], and Sabrina Marczak[3]

[1] SINTEF, Trondheim, Norway
danielac@sintef.no
[2] Bouvet, Oslo, Norway
Kristin.melsnes@bouvet.no
[3] PUCRS, Porto Alegre, Brazil
sabrina.marczak@pucrs.br

Abstract. To better understand the challenges encountered by testers in DevOps development, we have performed an empirical investigation of what are the trends and challenges for the testers in the DevOps environment. We have discussed the quality assurance in the difference focus areas of DevOps: Social Aspects, automation, leanness, sharing, measurement. The results were then themed in five different topics of concern to testers: collaboration, roles and responsibilities, types of tests, automation and monitoring and infrastructure. In Testing, there has been a change on the roles and responsibilities of testers, where there is much more focus on the responsibilities for testing across the teams, instead of a sole responsibility of the tester. Testers are also forced to collaborate more with other stakeholders as operations and business. Testing is brought to another level of automation in DevOps but there is still need for manual tests, that have to be much more risk-based than before. And finally, testing transparency is a must in this process and should involve not only development team but also operations and customers. This paper contributes to the body of knowledge on what are the areas we need to focus for improvement in testing for the DevOps environment. This paper also contributes to practitioners to improve their testing focusing on specific areas that needs attention.

Keywords: DevOps · Testing · Empirical

1 Introduction

DevOps is a term that has been increasing in popularity since 2009. DevOps emerged from continuous software delivery, which captures market opportunities and reduces feedback time. DevOps is a movement stemming from practice seeking to address certain limitations of agile methodology in terms of operational and business readiness. More specifically, this approach aims towards a shorter time to market [6]. Debois [10] opined that the term DevOps is just a stub for more global company collaboration, which, he explains, works as follows: Once priorities have been determined and work can begin, developers pair together with operations people to get the job done. This pairing allows for better knowledge diffusion across the two traditionally separate

S. Misra et al. (Eds.): ICCSA 2019, LNCS 11622, pp. 442–455, 2019.
https://doi.org/10.1007/978-3-030-24305-0_33

teams. Issues such as stability, monitoring and backup can be addressed immediately, rather than being afterthoughts, and operations staff obtain a better understanding of how the application works before it is deployed to production. In addition, feedback is available to all staff: those in operations learn which issues they might expect in production, while developers learn about the production environment. Gottesheim [16] affirms that DevOps aligns business requirements with IT performance, with the goal of adopting practices that allow a fast flow of changes to a production environment, while maintaining a high level of stability, reliability and performance in these systems.

While a central goal of DevOps is to achieve an improved deployment frequency, it is crucial to consider how QA plays a role in helping or hindering that ability. An important driver for DevOps is the need for businesses to quickly enact changes to the market. At the same time, quality must remain high to, for example: (i) attract new and retain existing customers and users and offer professional systems; (ii) avoid downtime; and (iii) provide user-friendly solutions and low support. In this context, software testing is not only 'essential', but is 'critical' for the software application or product survival.

However, throughout the history of software development, testing techniques have struggled to keep up with the ever-changing trends in software development paradigms, and little data exists on software professionals' software testing and quality assurance (QA) practices [18]. In an agile environment, continuous testing is mostly viewed as focusing on testing as early as possible, whereas in DevOps it is seen as a continuous activity, which is also performed in production. Whether developing, testing, or deploying software, DevOps seeks the most efficient mode of delivering an application continuously through the pipeline. This leads to a requirement for significantly more collaboration and effective cross-functional teams, where everyone is responsible for quality. Furthermore, a team works towards less documentation and increased transparency in testing activities.

Angara et al. [1] performed a systematic review of 29 articles concerning factors driving testing in the DevOps setting, to understand the different motivational factors and attempts to identify key technical, cultural and managerial factors behind testing in the DevOps setting. The authors observed that testing in DevOps is closely associated with the automation of test cases. Factors such as agility, scale, metric driven processes, and reduction of complexity and costs appeared in more than 16 review articles. DevOps demands alternative metrics, to achieve better collaboration and communication between various stakeholders of the system. Angara et al. [1] concluded that DevOps testing has not been systematically studied in academic scientific literature. Angara et al. [1] did not find any real-time case studies in the context of DevOps testing frameworks in academic journals. The traditional isolated QA/testing skills may be challenged and play a limited role in DevOps. A QA/tester has to scale beyond regular testing functions, and aid in development and operations teams to satisfy the philosophical objectives of DevOps. DevOps testing requires the design of alternative metrics/measures, which elevate the culture of an organisation, increase collaboration and create a proper benchmarking base.

In this study, we expand on previous work by focusing on QA/testing in DevOps development. We aim to obtain a further understanding of what can be done to improve teamwork between developers and testers in a DevOps testing context. We interviewed testers, with a focus on the following research questions:

- What is new for testing in DevOps?
- Which approaches for testing are utilised in DevOps?
- What are the challenges for testing in DevOps?

The remainder of this paper is organised as follows. Sections 2, 3 and 4 recapitulate the DevOps principles. Section 3 describes the research methodology followed in this research, and Sect. 4 presents the results. In Sect. 5, we discuss the results in light of previous literature, as well as the implications for research and practices concerning DevOps testing. Finally, Sect. 6 concludes this paper.

2 DevOps Principles

In 2016, França et al. [13] described a set of principles, skills and tools to support the practices characterising DevOps based on the DevOps literature. Figure 1 illustrates the principles associated with DevOps, grouped into six categories, which are briefly explained as follows [13]:

- Automation: claimed to be one of the core principles of DevOps, owing the benefits it could promote. It is considered that manual and repetitive tasks can be automated to reduce unnecessary effort and improve software delivery. Hence, automation would improve not only the delivery speed, but also the infrastructure consistency, productivity of teams and repeatability of tasks.
- Quality Assurance: to assure the quality of both development and operations processes as products. This principle supports the implementation of DevOps practices, as it links different stakeholders (development, operations, support and customers) to perform activities in an efficient and reliable manner, as well as to achieve a product and services satisfying established quality standards.
- Leanness: some DevOps practices are based on lean thinking principles [26]. DevOps requires lean processes, as it intends to ensure a continuous flow to develop and deliver software regularly through small and incremental changes, thus fostering constant and fast feedback between the development, testing and operations teams, as well as with customers.
- Sharing: information and knowledge are disseminated among individuals to promote the exchange of personal learning and project information. In this sense, individuals should spread relevant information, for instance regarding how to implement and perform practices recommended in the context of DevOps.
- Measurement: an important principle often instantiated by collecting efficient metrics to support decision-making in the software development and operations lifecycle.
- Social Aspects: despite all technical principles, many DevOps characteristics are associated with social aspects among the software development and operations teams, which is one of the reasons that DevOps is often seen as a cultural shift.

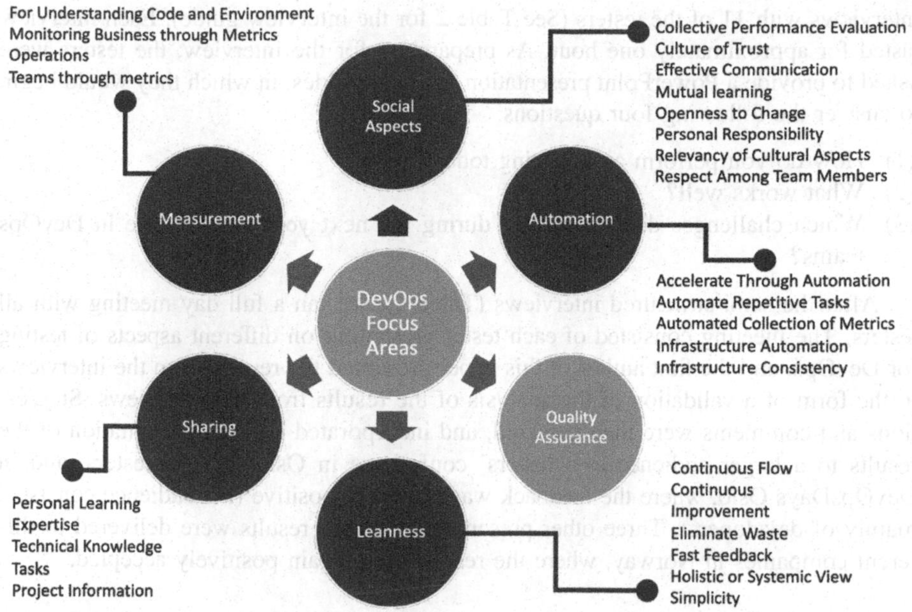

Fig. 1. DevOps principles by França, Junior and Travassos [13]

3 Research Methodology

In the study presented here, we aim to investigate the testing process for DevOps projects. To answer our research questions, we performed various data collection methods. Initially, as there were no scientific papers to be found, we focused on understanding the insights we could glean from various blogs and posts online concerning DevOps Testing. The characteristics of these source are that information is scattered, with each blog focusing on different aspects of DevOps principles, and most focusing only on automation aspects, while others focus on culture or the shift-left needs. These blogs were used to create a interview guide for discussion with testers (Table 1).

The context of this study concerns a consultancy firm providing services in information technology, digital communication and enterprise management to different private and public organisations in Norway. Bouvet have approximately 1300 employees at 14 offices in Norway and Sweden. Furthermore, Bouvet is committed to maintaining long-term client relationships, and is a strategic partner for a number of enterprises through innovation, development and implementation of solutions of critical significance for society.

Bouvet's approach is adapted to the customer, culture, directions and contract. The testers are all experienced testers and are allocated to different projects each year. The testers are allocated to different companies, and therefore they express experiences of different environments. There are 15 testers. For this study, there were multiple discussions with the test leader. In addition, the first author conducted one-on-one interviews with 11 of the testers (See Table 2 for the interview guide). Each interview lasted for approximately one hour. As preparation for the interview, the testers were asked to provide a PowerPoint presentation with four slides, in which they would begin to answer the following four questions:

(1) How do you perform agile testing today?
(2) What works well?
(3) Which challenges do you foresee during the next year in your role in DevOps teams?

After the semi-structured interviews (Table 2), we ran a full day meeting with all testers. The meeting consisted of each tester presenting on different aspects of testing for DevOps, and the first author of this paper presented the results from the interviews in the form of a validation of the analysis of the results from the interviews. Suggestions and comments were then gathered, and incorporated into the presentation of the results to a larger audience at a testers' conference in Oslo for 250 testers, and in DevOpsDays Oslo, where the feedback was also very positive (the audience consisted mainly of developers). Three other presentations of the results were delivered to different companies in Norway, where the results were again positively accepted.

Table 1. Data collection

	Data Collection
Focused interview	Test leader/11 testers
Blogs, magazines and online reports	✓
Meetings with testers	✓
Interviews	✓
Plenary presentations to testers and developers	✓

Table 2. Interview guide

Interview guide1. Would you say that you are performing agile testing today? Can you describe what you do today?
2. What is DevOps Testing for you?
3. What is the difference from agile testing in terms of processes and approaches? How do the different types of tests change, such as unit testing and functional testing?
4. What is different from agile testing in terms of collaboration and communication with ops and developers? Can you describe how communication between dev and ops teams usually occurs within your projects?
5. What kind of information do you usually receive/send to/from the other teams? Could you provide some examples? How often does this communication occur? How long does it take? How do you think this will be different with DevOps testing?
6. Are there meetings in which all teams are invited to participate (product release, etc.)? How do you think these will change with DevOps?
7. In terms of automation, do you think things will change much from what you do today?
8. Do you perform any types of monitoring activities today that help with testing? Do you foresee any possible monitoring activities that will be introduced by DevOps testing?
9. What is the "infrastructure as code" for testing? How do you see this topic?
10. Do you foresee any changes in your role/competence or responsibilities in this new scenario of performing DevOps testing? Are there barriers to DevOps testing, such as individual (skills and competences), team (work in teams), project characteristics (small, big, public, private or fixed contract) or organisational (impossible to change structures) barriers?
11. What are the major enablers in achieving DevOps testing?

4 Results

Table 3 presents a summary of the benefits that testers mentioned by improving testing practices in the DevOps environment. The table also presents the strategies mentioned by testers to improve testing in different areas. In this section, we also summarise the results, based on an analysis of the interviews, and other insights collected concerning the different observations of the testers' discussions on the topic with pratictioners in Norway.

4.1 Collaboration

In agile projects, testers and developers have already been brought much closer together: testers have left 'tester teams' to become part of the 'development team', where testers are allocated to each development team in an agile team. There is already a positive culture of open and effective communication. In DevOps, the testers' perspective is that they are 'forced' to also become closer to operations and business teams. The perception of testers is although that there is more pressure to be closer to business than operations.

To be able to achieve continuous deployment, testers have to be much more closely aligned to what the business is expecting of the deliverables. In some teams, customers have their own representatives in the team. However, it is challenging to gain an understanding from both developers and customers to participate in and execute early testing at short notice. This demands a high level of flexibility, understanding and attendance from the testers' perspective. There is also a requirement to build trust and transparency in the testing process for customers, such as in collaborating with users on test automation. One challenge mentioned regarding the relationship with customers is that they are not always prepared for a tighter communication stream with development, and therefore collaboration is hindered.

In projects worked on by the testers, testers still find that communications between testers and operations (OPS) are ad-hoc. Specifically, when there is a separate operation department, collaboration is even harder. From the perspective of the testers, one of the main reasons for challenge is that the OPS often also has other reward systems and incentives, and is therefore opposed to DevOps goals.

4.2 Roles and Responsibilities

The testers mentioned that there is a requirement for teams to rethink their roles and responsibilities towards QA activities. The focus is more on competences than on roles, but one tester mentioned: *'There is still a need to find a leader/facilitator/advisor for testing, because the whole team approach needs to be better understood'.* The testers mentioned that the following competences are increasingly requested of testers:

- More technical understanding (code; architecture; coding; and infrastructure such as virtualisation and operations);
- More knowledge on test automation;
- Different testing techniques, such as security testing;

Table 3. Benefits of improvements for DevOps and strategies

	Benefits of improvements for DevOps	Strategies used by teams
Collaboration	More collaboration with operations: • Helps on obtaining more knowledge about the system and how it should work • Provides more complete information to the test • Helps testers to find operating errors earlier • Facilitates the handover process • OPS traditionally have more experience with monitoring, logging of activities; testers can learn from them • Better test coverage by everyone thinking about quality • Closer proximity to the production environment	• Collaborate with users on writing test acceptance criteria on user stories • Add testers to review user stories as part of the definition of "prepared" • Give access to automated test results to customers • Explain the team's goals on quality to all stakeholders • Increase testing process transparency to all stakeholders • Tighter the communication with customers regarding testing
Roles and responsibilities	Testers mentioned that the benefits of having developers increasingly involved with different testing activities include: • By involving developers in the specification and test process earlier, testers gain greater knowledge of the business and solution, consequently preventing errors by building better solutions • Bugfix is the most 'boring' task for developers. By contributing to finding deviations early, developers will spend less time on error correction • Creating a culture where 'finding mistakes is positive'. Avoid tab quotes and blame games. Celebrating when we finding errors before the system is in production	• Pair testers with developers and operations for testing activities • Job rotation: testers as developers and developers as testers • Post-mortem analysis of bugs in production • Learning from bugs through statistics • Celebrating bugs • Bug crush day: having a day when everyone in the team is only working on closing bugs • Encourage team members on learning of testing competences ('learning the testing language')

(*continued*)

Table 3. (*continued*)

	Benefits of improvements for DevOps	Strategies used by teams
Types of testes	• The process becomes less test-case oriented more risk-based • Testing becomes more about minimising the risk of critical errors in production, and continuously assessing the impacts on costs related to testing Automation of tasks to prevent human error becomes increasingly essential to the process	• Risk-based acceptance and regression tests (scenario-based and customer-based) • Take risks and evaluate the impact of changes in real time (e.g., A/B testing) • Experimentation of features • Feature toggle • Testing in production
Automation	Manual test will basically complement automated tests: • Dynamic, more unplanned and unpredictable • Focus on tests that requires Knowledge, creativity and special situations that are expensive or not practical to automate, user experiences and shopping patterns are still difficult to automate	• Proper exploratory tests
Monitoring	Considerable improvement is required in this area. However, there is not much experience reported here	• Bug monitoring • Green-light test cases • Measurements of usage of features

- More business and strategic thinking:
  - Risk-based testing;
  - Manual tests that focus on the customer's quality goals;
- Playing the role of advisor/leader/facilitator for testing activities:
  - Following up that testing is performed continuously and has good coverage.
- Learning techniques for testing in production.

The testers also recognise that some 'traditional' behaviours should be discarded, such as '*having a black box testing only mind set*'. Furthermore, some old skills need to be reinvented, such as adapting lean practices of demand management, governance, standardisation and optimisation techniques; and delivering pre-packaged test suites, estimation models and risk-based testing with the aim of decreasing development before deployment time.

Concerning the question of whether there is still a need for someone in the team to be named the tester, the testers opined: '*Testers' skills will still be important: we have our own ability to dig out errors, and we have a great deal of knowledge about techniques that can be used to bring them about*'. Another tester mentioned: '*We must build trust and get the team to trust our knowledge*'.

There is also a need for the team to have an end-to-end responsibility for the product. This means that the entire team is involved in the testing/QA of the delivered content. Testers mentioned that *'developers are generally not used to testing functionality/user experience: they basically do not want additional tasks'*.

The testers also see the need to develop the testing skills of developers, so that there is less of a bottleneck on testing activities in the continuous flow of delivered features. Testers mentioned that they expect that developers will *'perform some functional tests, include tests in the definition of complete and in code reviews, and perform their part of testing'*.

4.3 Types of Tests

In DevOps, the focus shifts from the phases and quadrants of testing [8] to an approach that is focused on filtering bugs. Testing becomes is so integrated into the overall development process that it can be difficult to determine who, where and when testing is performed. The main goal is to prevent and eliminate coding errors before the application has reached production. This also calls for more risk-based testing [11, 12, 22] processes, and less test-case oriented testing. The testing becomes more focused on minimising the risk of critical errors in production, and continuously assessing the impacts on costs related to testing. The automation of tasks to prevent human error becomes increasingly essential in this process. One tester mentioned: *'We need a thought-through streamline test process, and the teams need to have a very clear and defined test process with the steps that each component has to go through before it is released into production'*. Another tester mentioned: *'It's about continuously getting feedback right from the start. And applying the concept of Fail fast, fail often and getting frequent feedback on whether things work or not'*.

The types testing documentation change as well, there is less focus on test case documentation and more on streamlining test specifications. Updating of test scenarios each time something changes is avoided to save time and effort, and there is increased use of exploratory testing and charters showing the areas of testing and types of tests that are performed for each part of the system. One tester mentioned: *'The focus on documentation was previously to build the trust that we have tested what we should have. Now we don't have time for that, and we need to build trust in other ways'*. One approach to this is to have more transparency in the testing process for all stakeholders. One tester mentioned: *'When the team have closer contact with each other documentation lose importance'*.

On the non-functional aspects of the system, security has been more emphasised, and is increasingly demanding as a type of test to be performed and learned. The testers mentioned that this is one of the major obstacles for them to implement DevOps testing. The testers noted that other non-functional requirements are also important, such as scalability, performance and user experience, and that developers are usually mostly focused on testing whether the functionality works.

4.4 Automation

The testers in this study emphasised the importance of understanding that continuous testing is not the same as test automation. Code quality, pipeline automation, application quality and customer experience are all steps towards achieving a higher quality product through continuous delivery. The testers in the interviews emphasised the need for manual testing in most projects. One main message that the testers would like to get across is *'do not ignore the power of manual tests'*.

For the testers, manual testing has its own advantages and disadvantages. In manual testing, the tester can unveil many problems, from user experience issues to critical issues, but it can take a long time to perform and require all of the tester's attention. In manual testing, the testers becomes familiar with the tested application and aware of all its pitfalls. Therefore, by performing manual testing there are more chances to easily explore the system and know exactly where to look for hidden bugs.

One tester mentioned: *'In automation, we robotise the testing. This is very effective for (boring) routine repetitive tasks, interface simulations, combinations of data, loads and so on. However, this are somehow static. Such tests perform again and again what you asked them to do a week ago'*. One tester mentioned that *'teams sometimes forget that automated tests are also code: they require maintenance, they can contain errors and they become outdated'*.

4.5 Monitoring and Infrastructure

Consistent with the observation that testers are still not collaborating as much with operations, testers in this aspect, therefore the testers had less experience to discuss concerning the principles of operations. The main conclusion from this research in this topic is that tools, processes and monitoring data are not yet explored in development. Testers were not able to have an opinion on how monitoring could affect testing.

5 Discussion

5.1 What Are the Main Challenges on Testing in DevOps?

DevOps calls for more efficient testing to satisfy customers and end-users requirements. The challenges mentioned most often were:

- Full automation is a danger to the product;
- A whole-team approach to quality is hard to achieve;
- There is still a requirement for increased maturity of the whole development chain for taking full advantage of DevOps.

DevOps tools can significantly automate and streamline development, but they must be integrated into a complete solution that simplifies the entire process. The right test environment management and test automation tools allow teams to increase their test speed and coverage. However, these tools also still require further maturation. As noted previously, manual testing remains a very important activity for QA for many different reasons. One tester mentioned: *'Automated functional testing at all levels works against valuable input to both the team and the customer. It is a challenge to move the team away from the business knowledge and application knowledge they gain when they participate in manual functional testing. I believe that the understanding of the application and customer business is a big part of the high quality in deliveries we have achieved in our team'.*

As previously mentioned in this paper, it is already a challenge in agile to integrate everyone into the testing process. In DevOps, this is even more pronounced, as it requires even more collaboration and alignment. The cooperation with operations is even more challenging, because traditionally the IT infrastructure personnel are distanced from the reality of the development process. From the perspective of testers, developers are still yet to change their mindset towards testing, to think holistically about the implementation of the features where the definition of 'done' includes the whole quality chain that will ensure the feature is ready for production. Testers also mentioned that it has been challenging to gain an understanding from both developers and customers that there is a need for their participation of the tests as early as possible and many times at a short notice.

The motivation of developers towards testing activities represents an additional challenge. The perception of testers is that developers are not very interested in testing, and that testing is considered to be boring. In Norway, there is also a trend that testers do not have development skills, and most testers are used to doing everything manually. Therefore, testers are not focused on test automation. Many teams are working on the process of improving collaboration between testers and developers to create automated tests.

DevOps requires considerable trust and maturity from the all stakeholders (customers, suppliers etc.), and the testers pointed out the need to understand that this will not always be a fit. The companies/teams that wishes to implement DevOps will have to adapt the approach to their contexts and understand which practices can be adopted in their contexts.

5.2 Bridging Practice and the State-of-the-Art in Testing in DevOps

Table 4 lists the implications of the practice of and research on each of the principles shown in Fig. 1.

Table 4. Implications for research

DevOps principle	Main conclusions	Implications for research
Social aspects	The whole-team approach to QA is essential	Some studies indicate that communication processes tend to have the capacity to mediate interactions and misalignment between developers and testers [2, 4, 24, 27]. More research on collaboration and communication must be conducted to help organisations understand how to improve the whole-team approach and interactions between testers and developers, operations, business and other stakeholders

(*continued*)

Table 4. (*continued*)

DevOps principle	Main conclusions	Implications for research
Automation	Automation is a must, but manual testing still cannot be ignored	Automation is a hot topic in academia, and there is a vast amount of research on this topic. The challenges and approaches are covered well, but there remain many challenges to be covered [14, 15, 21, 23]
Leanness	The process of QA still requires maturation, and all principles of DevOps should be addressed to get QA working well There is a need for a more risk-based testing processes and less test-case oriented testing	More empirical work must to be conducted to understand which approaches work where. We also need to evolve risk-based testing, and achieve wider-spread use in industry [11, 12, 22]. We need a better understanding of how to achieve a better return of investment of DevOps practices and principles depending on the context. In addition, we need frameworks and theories that support the adoption of DevOps by other parts of organisations, such as higher-level managers and sellers or products/projects
Sharing	Working as a cross-functional team is a must Roles and responsibilities in QA are changing, and competences must also change	We have not yet found research papers focusing on understanding how to get teams to work efficiently as cross-functional teams and using roles, responsibilities, competences in the best manner for cross-functional teams in DevOps QA
Measurement	There are blogs on test environment management and performance testing as a code. However, not much material is available on measurements that help teams improve their work in testing	There are discussions in academia about using artificial intelligence to improve the testing of products, but companies are not yet adopting these approaches [5, 19]. In addition, there is the concept of chaos engineering, which can be better explored in DevOps environments [3]

5.3 Limitations

The research reported here has limitations. In terms of reliability of the study, i.e., how dependent are the data and analysis on the researchers involved [25]. First, our study was limited to members of one company. However, the participants are allocated to different projects in different organisations with different characteristics, helping to overcome certain issues concerning the generalisability of our results. There is also the limitation that this study describes the perspective of testers regarding the studied phenomena. To mitigate this limitation, we have performed presentations to developers, and validated the results in that context. We have also used blogs focusing on different roles in different organisations in the results. Finally, the observations and findings were verified with other companies' representatives, to avoid false interpretations and inconsistencies.

Another limitation of our study is that we relied mainly on interviews and observations to derive our results. To mitigate this threat, we discussed and improved the interview protocol iteratively before data collection, besides we have used blogs and academic literature to drive the construction of the interview guide. Concerning the analysis, the researchers coded all interviews individually, and in a second step all authors discussed all the results including the interviewees.

6 Conclusions

In this paper, we have presented the results from a study on testing/QA activities in DevOps. We have also identified challenges, approaches and opportunities in different areas such collaboration, roles and responsibilities, types of tests, automation and monitoring and infrastructure. We could observe that to trigger any improvement in the state of this practice there will be necessary serious efforts in predicting trends, learning stakeholder mindsets, and pinpointing software-testing problem areas. This paper represents a starting point for some of these issues, which require attention from both practitioners and academics as described in the discussion.

As future work we plan to further investigate the trends to DevOps quality assurance and investigate possible new techniques that can be spready adopted by software teams in DevOps development projects.

Acknowledgments. This work was supported by the EMERGE project, funded by the Research Council of Norway under the grant 231679.

References

1. Angara, J., Prasad, S., Sridevi, G.: The factors driving testing in DevOps setting- a systematic literature survey. IJST (2017). ISSN 0974-5645
2. Barney, S., Mohankumar, V., Chatzipetrou, P., Aurum, A., Wohlin, C., Angelis, L.: Software quality across borders: three case studies on company internal alignment. Inf. Softw. Technol. **56**, 20–38 (2014)
3. Basiri, A., et al.: Chaos engineering. IEEE Softw. **33**(3), 35–41 (2016)
4. Bjarnason, E., et al.: Challenges and practices in aligning requirements with verification and validation: a case study of six companies. Empirical Softw. Eng. **19**(6), 1809–1855 (2014)
5. Briand, L.C.: Novel applications of machine learning in software testing. In: QSIC 2008, pp. 3–10 (2008)
6. Claps, G.G., Svensson, R.B., Aurum, A.: On the journey to continuous deployment: technical and social challenges along the way. IST **57**, 21–31 (2015)
7. Collins, E., Macedo, G., Maia, N., Dias-Neto, A.: An industrial experience on the application of distributed testing in an agile software development environment. In: IEEE Seventh International Conference on Global Software Engineering (ICGSE), pp. 190–194 (2012)
8. Crispin, L., Gregory, J.: Agile Testing: A Practical Guide for Testers and Agile Teams. Addison-Wesley Professional, Boston (2009)
9. Cruzes, D.S., Moe, N.B., Dybå, T.: Communication between developers and testers in distributed continuous agile testing. In: ICGSE 2016, pp. 59–68 (2016)

10. Debois, P.: DevOps: a software revolution in the making. Cutter IT J. **24**(8), 3–5 (2011)
11. Felderer, M., Grossmann, J., Schieferdecker, I.: Recent results on classifying risk-based testing approaches. CoRR abs/1801.06812 (2018)
12. Foidl, H., Felderer, M.: Integrating software quality models into risk-based testing. Software Qual. J. **26**(2), 809–847 (2018)
13. França, B.B.N., Jeronimo Jr., H., Travassos, G.H.: Characterizing DevOps by hearing multiple voices. In: SBES 2016, pp. 53–62 (2016)
14. Garousi, V., Mäntylä, M.V.: A systematic literature review of literature reviews in software testing. Inf. Softw. Technol. **80**, 195–216 (2016)
15. Garousi, V., Mäntylä, M.V.: When and what to automate in software testing? A multi-vocal literature review. Inf. Softw. Technol. **76**, 92–117 (2016)
16. Gottesheim, W.: Challenges, benefits and best practices of performance focused DevOps. In: Proceedings of the International Workshop on Large-Scale Testing, Austin, TX, USA, ser. LT 2015, p. 3. ACM, New York (2015)
17. Hussaini, S.W.: Strengthening harmonization of development (dev) and operations (ops) silos in IT environment through systems approach. In: International IEEE Conference on Intelligent Transportation Systems, Barcelona, Spain, pp. 178–183. IEEE, October 2014
18. Kassab, M., DeFranco, J.F., Laplante, P.A.: Software testing: the state of the practice. IEEE Softw. **34**(5), 46–52 (2017)
19. Noorian, M., Bagheri, E., Du, W.: Machine learning-based software testing: towards a classification framework. In: SEKE 2011, pp. 225–229 (2011)
20. Moe, N.B., Cruzes, D.S., Dybå, T., Mikkelsen, E.M.: Continuous software testing in a globally distributed project. In: ICGSE 2015, pp. 130–134 (2015)
21. Rafi, D.M., Moses, K.R.K., Petersen, K., Mäntylä, M.: Benefits and limitations of automated software testing: systematic literature review and practitioner survey. In: AST 2012, pp. 36–42 (2012)
22. Ramler, R., Felderer, M., Leitner, M.: A lightweight approach for estimating probability in risk-based software testing. In: Großmann, J., Felderer, M., Seehusen, F. (eds.) RISK 2016. LNCS, vol. 10224, pp. 115–128. Springer, Cham (2017). https://doi.org/10.1007/978-3-319-57858-3_9
23. Raulamo-Jurvanen, P., Mäntylä, M., Garousi, V.: Choosing the right test automation tool: a grey literature review of practitioner sources. In: EASE 2017, pp. 21–30 (2017)
24. Taipale, O., Smolander, K.: Improving software testing by observing practice. In: ISESE 2006, pp. 262–271 (2006)
25. Whittemore, R., Chase, S.K., Mandle, C.L.: Validity in qualitative research. Qual. Health Res. **11**(4), 117–132 (2001)
26. Womack, J.P., Jones, D.T.: Lean Thinking: Banish Waste and Create Wealth in Your Corporation. Simon and Schuster, New York (2010)
27. Zhang, X., Stafford, T.F., Dhaliwal, J.S., Gillenson, M.L., Moeller, G.: Sources of conflict between developers and testers in software development. Inf. Manage. **51**(1), 13–26 (2014)

Towards an Extensible Architecture for Refactoring Test Code

Rogério Marinke[1], Eduardo Martins Guerra[1], Fábio Fagundes Silveira[2(✉)], Rafael Monico Azevedo[1], Wagner Nascimento[1], Rodrigo Simões de Almeida[1], Bruno Rodrigues Dembosck[1], and Tiago Silva da Silva[2]

[1] National Institute for Space Research, São José dos Campos, Brazil
rmarinke@gmail.com, guerraem@gmail.com, rmonico1@gmail.com, nascimentolwtn@gmail.com, rsalmeidafl@gmail.com, dembosck@gmail.com

[2] Federal University of São Paulo – UNIFESP, São José dos Campos, Brazil
{fsilveira,silvadasilva}@unifesp.br

Abstract. As the software evolves, new codes are written, and many other codes are refactored. Refactoring also involves the test code, to ensure that it continues performed, and adequately verifying the behavior of the software. This work proposes the creation of an extensible architecture named EARTC to perform refactoring safely in test code. The coding of a specific refactoring for the test code is hampered by coupling to the unit testing automation framework so that it becomes desirable to eliminate this coupling from the refactoring code. The architecture proposed in this work implements extension points, which allows refactoring to be performed regardless of the test framework to be used, that is, other refactorings can be added to the architecture without the need to change the test code. Additionally, the architecture enables other testing frameworks to be coupled without interfering with their internal structure. To validate the independence among architecture modules, a Design Structure Matrix was done, which shows that the objectives were achieved. Also, to analyze the results of the proposed architecture in an experiment, a tool called Neutrino was implemented. The results obtained with Neutrino are satisfactory and show that the architecture meets the objectives described for the accomplishment of this work.

Keywords: Neutrino · Refactoring · Test driven development

1 Introduction

One alternative to improve software product quality is to implement automated testing. The automated tests are easily reproducible, maintain the characteristic of being systematic, and control the execution of all the tests. Moreover, they store test artifacts, assist in verifying changes in software behavior and the test code itself after the refactorings [16].

According to Gerlec et al. [9], the changes from software maintenance are part of software evolution. However, it is important to emphasize that although

S. Misra et al. (Eds.): ICCSA 2019, LNCS 11622, pp. 456–471, 2019.
https://doi.org/10.1007/978-3-030-24305-0_34

such maintenance and refactoring are unavoidable, the changes may lead to new defects and contribute to the decline of the software architecture initially designed. In this context, it is essential to know the types of changes requested and the impact of these changes in the structural aspects of architecture and quality.

During the activities of software development is natural to apply the code refactoring process. It happens due to constantly changes in environment as well as in the requirements. On the other side, when considering the development of software using Extreme Programming (XP), refactoring plays a fundamental role in the development process because of the interactions between test code and production code.

According to Fowler and Beck [6] and Beck [4], the code changes made in the internal structure of the software are intended to make the software easier to understand and cheaper to modify without altering its observable behavior. Still, according to these authors, there is a relationship between refactoring and Test-Driven Development (TDD) because, without the unit testing and acceptance activities, it is difficult to ensure that the changes were correctly made as expected.

XP is a software development method where the code is not the most important. Other activities as analysis, documentation, and planning became the XP itself relevant for the community of software development [4,24]. According to Williams et al. [24] and Beck [4], the primary objective of XP is to provide a set of good practices for software development. The most known XP techniques are testing-first programming, refactoring all the time, write short interactions and develop the simplest possible solutions [4,24].

Several XP practices involve pair programming, where usually programmers work together in only one requirement at a time. Beyond, programmers create a unit test for expected behavior. In the XP approach, the code is refactored to achieve the result, and the test previously written is executed again, until the functionality has all test passed with success [24].

TDD was proposed as a practice in agile method XP [12], not initially with this name, and according to Janzen and Saiedian [12] the main objectives in TDD are the relationship with design and analysis, not the testing itself. TDD recommend to write the simplest codes before the production code, and from this point are then made the refactor both in test and production code until all specified functionalities are implemented [12,24]. As a result of this approach, the programmer can execute the tests after they are written [24]. TDD is a practice to aid in developing software and to be used with other practices and methodologies such as agile, waterfall, spiral, incremental or evolutionary [12].

Software maintenance and implementation are crucial problems for the companies, mainly for those that use complex systems, considering that these have systems with many functionalities and many code refactoring are necessary, which should be tested to the maximum after each change to avoid including errors in the software. Thus, the study of new technologies and techniques that help in the minimization of software defects is relevant, once the aspects such as reliability, efforts with maintenance and alterations in the source code may contribute to the organization and allocation of resources, minimization of costs and improvement of the quality and maturity of the software. In this context, it is necessary to improve the researches on the TDD, which have provided different approaches that impact directly on the costs and the quality of projects of development and maintenance of software.

The test code does not have tools for refactoring as the production code has. Although, a refactoring in the test code may improperly change the external behavior of the test. In this direction, this work is an attempt to bridge the gap of automation tools for refactoring of test code, being independent of the test framework adopted in the development project.

The remaining of this paper is structured as follows: Sect. 2 reports the background notions related to refactoring testing. Section 3 describes the *Extensible Architecture for Refactoring Test Code* (EARTC) proposed in this work. Section 4 describes the plugin Neutrino, discusses the results of our research and presents the threats to validity. Finally, Sect. 5 summarizes our findings.

2 Refactoring Code and Tools

2.1 Refactoring Test Code

The primary goal of refactoring the test code is to make it easier to understand, without duplication, and to collaborate with its maintenance [6]. According to Fowler [6], refactoring test code can occur mainly due to two factors: In the first form, refactoring test code occurs naturally as a consequence of the development activity – sometimes this refactoring is also performed to remove duplicates in the test code. The second factor that involves refactoring refers to the inclusion of new functionalities in the production code, so the test code needs to be refactored [6].

It is important to highlight that this approach is to guide the development of functionalities in the simplest possible way and maintains the focus on what needs to be implemented. Another relevant feature of this approach is that whenever there is a need for refactoring in the production code due to a possible change in the scope of functionality, you must first refactor the test code, only to later refactor the production code [6,19]. In addition to that, when refactoring is performed in the production code, the previously implemented test suite will signal if the behavior of the software has changed, helping to maintain the quality [6].

Although refactoring is necessary for software evolution, when codes are refactored, faults can be included during the refactoring. Some of these failures can be avoided or minimized with the detection of code smells. Code smells are symptoms of insufficient implementation, and that may lead to fault proneness [23]. At the same time, the code smells represent a design problem which is also an opportunity to improve the software through the refactoring, highlighting the importance of refactoring the test code [2,6].

According to Van Deursen et al. [23] and Meszaros [15], test code refactorings is different from production code refactoring because there is a distinct set of bad smells involved, and improving test code involves additional test-specific

Table 1. Refactorings techniques for test code [23]

Refactoring	Description
Inline resource	To remove the dependency between a test method and some external resource
Setup external resource	Creates or allocates resources as directories, databases, or files, before testing
Make resource unique	To avoid the use of overlapping resource names use unique identifiers
Reduce data	Minimize the data that is setup in fixtures, it contributes to the documentation, and your tests will be less sensitive to changes
Add assertion explanation	Use message to distinguish between different assertions that occur in the same test
Introduce equality method	Add an implementation for the equals method. Rewrite the tests that use string equality to use this method

refactorings. Moreover, according to these authors, the refactoring test code requires a set of other refactoring techniques that aim to ensure, among other characteristics, the quality and behavior of the test code, as shown in Table 1.

Mens and Tourwe [14] published a survey which described the refactoring activities that are supported and the effect of refactoring on the software process. They concluded the need for formalisms, processes, methods, and tools that address refactoring.

Guerra and Fernandes [10] presented three types of test code refactoring, considering the implementation scope: (i) Refactoring inside a test method – in general, has the source from the need to redefine the test scenario; (ii) Refactoring inside a test class – comes from the need to include/remove tests, fine-tuning the methods of finalizing and initializing the test suite; and (iii) Structural refactoring of test classes – some refactorings that occur in production code related to class structure (e.g., impact on the requirement that the structure of the test codes is also refactored.

2.2 Refactoring Tools

Although some of the works presented in this subsection examine refactoring tools in a wide context, also considering refactoring tools for production code, the selected works are relevant because they highlight some problems also found in refactoring tools for test code.

The use of automated testing suite has become more familiar with the use of tools such as the xUnit framework proposed by Meszaros [15], and this is important to support the TDD. These tests are gradually added to the project during the incremental development and are refactored as the project evolves. In this context, when a production code is refactored, the test suite is performed again to ensure that the behavior has not changed. However, when refactoring is performed on the test code, we do not have a test suite for the tests themselves to ensure that the behavior has not changed. Considering this context, there is a need for refactoring test code tools that provide and verify whether the external behavior of the test has been maintained.

In the work presented by Murphy-Hill et al. [17], refactoring tools usage is observed and some forms of use and features of the tools are evaluated. The experimental method takes data from eight different sources, and their findings also suggest that refactoring tools need further improvements before programmers can use them frequently. The authors concluded that programmers do refactor frequently, but when committing code to version control systems, developers' messages appear not to indicate refactoring activity reliably.

According to Bavota et al. [3], refactoring activities induce faults, mainly as refactorings involving hierarchies. They carried out an empirical study on three Java software systems and automatically detected 15,008 refactoring operations. The authors suggest more accurate code inspection or testing activities when such specific refactorings are performed.

An empirical study was also presented by Gatrell et al. [8]. The work addresses two perspectives: the nature of classes to which refactorings have been applied and the overlap and correspondence between refactorings applied to each class type. In the study, it was used a bespoke tool for extracting a set of fifteen refactorings. They concluded that production and test classes evolve almost independently regarding refactoring.

Passier et al. [18] addressed the problem of breaking the link between the production code and the test code after a refactoring. Moreover, they proposed a tool for Eclipse IDE that maintains tracking of the modifications made to the production code and analyzes the impact of these modifications on the test suite. This way, it provides tips to the developer on how to update the test suite codes. However, the tool proposed by the authors, considering the project specifications, the refactoring track, and the analyzes, is performed after refactoring the production code. This is a different approach as suggested by TDD since in TDD the specification is used at first to write a test in the simplest possible way.

According to Silva et al. [22], when refactoring a production code we must pay attention to avoid inserting unwanted behavior into the software. One way to ensure that the behavior has not changed is the use of automatically generated regression test suites. Moreover, the authors addressed this problem by evaluating the tests cases generated automatically by the Randoop and EvoSuite tools. Authors concluded that the tools generated many obsolete test cases and that the automatically generated tests fail in more than 50% of all injected faults.

Kaur and Singh [13] divided the survey in code refactoring study and described an algorithm to improve the refactoring process. They concluded that the effectiveness of work by comparing the different code maintainability indexes generated by the tool.

In the work carried out by Rizzi et al. [20], the authors investigated the problem of the Cyclic Dependency and proposed a tool to detect smells at the software architectural level. Furthermore, the tool is able to identify and suggest a possible refactoring approach to resolve Cyclic Dependency.

Bladel and Demeyer [5] introduced a tool to support the analysis of whether refactoring in test code does not change the behavior of the test. The tool uses a Test Behavior Tree to represents the behavior of the test code. Their approach considers to be stored the formula, variables, values, and objects detected in the test code. A similar technique is used in some compilers. The tree is constructed for both test codes, before and after refactoring. Although the tool can detect the change of behavior of the test suite, the tool is performed out of the development IDE, making their use more complicated by development teams.

3 The Extensible Architecture for Refactoring Test Code

Coding unit tests can provide higher quality and helps to maintain the production code functionality. However, a refactoring applied to a test code should have known about the framework for which this test code was written. This behavior occurs because there is information in the test code about the test framework, how tests should be implemented, suites, assertions, and how methods are implemented.

This coupling and dependency between the test framework and test code and, consequently, the refactorings intended for the test code, creates a difficulty in the creation of these refactorings, since the test frameworks, such as JUnit, require different implementations depending on the version used. Besides, it is a challenge to implement a general tool that provides specific refactorings for the test code independently of the framework being used. Another difficulty is the implementation and use of specific refactorings for test code, which may involve the detection of bad smells.

In this context, this work proposes the creation of an extensible architecture for refactoring test code in order to uncouple the unit testing framework from IDE and development project. It is contemplated a process and an abstract structure of code which represents tests. The process manipulates this structure, and both are decoupled from the test code framework. This way, it allows test refactorings to be performed independently of the test framework, and those new frameworks like JUnit 5 and TestNG can be added to make use of the existing refactorings in the EARTC. Besides, the EARTC allows that new refactoring methods can be added without any explicit modification in the architecture.

3.1 Overview

The EARTC is considered an intermediate structure and abstract syntax tree, aiming to represent the elements of the unit tests. This structure is called the Abstract Test Code Representation (ATCR) and was based on the model proposed by Guerra [11]. ATCR performs the parser of the test code for the class structure that represents the elements and operations of a test suite. This activity is performed by reading the test code to be refactored and, after that, the parser is transformed into a structure of classes according to the model detailed in Sect. 3.3. Moreover, ATCR is also responsible for writing the new refactored test code file.

Since the proposal goal is to have an extensible architecture in the EARTC, which allows another test frameworks to be added, the ATCR has an abstract interface. That is, ATCR has a part where the operations that can be performed on the elements of a test are abstracted. However, the most important architectural feature is its decoupling of any unit testing framework. Thus, its concrete implementations have details on how these operations will affect each test framework.

It is important to emphasize that refactoring is conceptual, that is, the definition of refactoring does not depend on the programming language to which it was implemented, but only on the elements that are manipulated by it. Therefore, the EARTC may be used as a basis for the construction of others refactoring of the same type, including the use of other programming languages besides Java.

3.2 Functionalities

Guerra and Fernandes [10] developed a specific test code catalog for refactoring. This work uses such a catalog as a basis for deriving the functionalities that make up the EARTC. A list of the architecture functionalities are displayed in Table 2.

In addition to the architectural functionalities described above, the EARTC also are able to detect bad smells [23] according to the catalog proposed by Fowler [6] and adapted by Guerra [11]. The list of test bad smells detected by the EARTC are listed below:

- Eager test - when many behaviors are verified in a single test;
- Assertion Roullete - same behavior is verified, and for all verifications, the expected result is the same. When the test fails it is difficult to detect which exact line of assertion has failed;
- Assertion without explanation - lack of messages that explain to the programmer the reason for the error;
- Composite Assertion - more than one assertion in a single line of code, usually joined by the boolean operators AND and OR;
- Many assertions in the sequence - induce duplication of code and generally do not clearly express the intent of the test;
- Duplication of code at startup or termination - testing methods have the same initialization or termination code; and
- Branching in code - insertion of conditional codes to verify states of other objects. The problem could be solved by using the initialization or finalization methods.

It is important to highlight that the EARTC can perform refactorings in test code written for the Unit3 and Unit4 testing frameworks. Furthermore, as mentioned in the Sect. 3.1, the EARTC is extensible, and any other testing automation framework can be added.

3.3 Internal Architectural

ATCR defines the elements in the test code so that its manipulation by the refactoring implementation code can be done in a decoupled way from the unit testing framework for which the test code was written. The ATCR implementation was made considering the test definitions proposed by Guerra [11]. Thus, the ATCR in its internal organization has as a higher level element: the battery of tests. It contains the list of test suites that is composed of one more test classes. Below the test suite is the test method, which is responsible for running the tests of a functionality individually. A test suite must have at least one test method, i.e., empty test suites are not allowed. Below the test method is the test element, and this element represents a line of code belonging to a testing method. The test element can exist in two forms: actions and assertions. An action is a line of code where a test is prepared or exercised; this way, it is not a test properly, but an action necessary for the execution of it – can be methods or functions. The assertion, in turn, is the verification that the result obtained with action are addressed with the expected behavior. During the verification process

Table 2. Architecture functionalities of the EARTC (adapted from [10])

Refactoring	Description
Add assertion explanation	It adds a string parameter in the assertion method with its explanation
Create template test	It creates a template test to abstract functions like the template method design pattern [7]
Decompose assertion	It substitutes one composite assertion for similar ones. Refactoring inside a test class o Add Fixture - It creates a fixture and uses it as a test target
Extract setup method	It creates a setup() method and moves initialization code to it
Extract tear down method	It creates a teardown() method and moves finalization code to it
Introduce equality method	It substitutes many comparisons in the same object with a comparison method [23]
Join incremental tests	It joins tests that are created incrementally
Join similar tests with different data	It joins all similar tests that use different data in only one. Structural refactoring of test classes
Mirror hierarchy to tests	It mirrors to test classes the same hierarchy of the application classes
Pull down test	It moves a test method down in the hierarchy
Pull up test	It moves a test method up in the hierarchy
Simplify use setting	It substitutes the actions to simpler ones with the same effect on the test target
Split action from assertion	It substitutes an assertion that makes modifications on one action and one assertion
Split test from aggregated class	It separates the verification of the responsibility of an aggregated class into another unit test

(a set of assertions), in this context, an object called fixture will have some of its properties checked against an expected value [11].

In order to reach these requirements, we decided to divide the EARTC into four components:

- Preliminary Test Code Parser (PTCP);
- Preliminary Test Code Representation (PTCR);
- Test Code Parser (TCP); and
- Abstract Test Code Representation (ATCR).

The aiming of PTCP is to provide the source code received for the parsing in a way that is easy to be used by the other EARTC components. For this purpose, the PTCP uses an External Source Code Parser (ESCP) that deals directly with the source code. Thus, the PTCP ends up functioning as an intermediate layer that separates the complexity of the ESCP from the other components of the EARTC.

At the end of the parsing performed by the PTCP, the PTCR is generated, which is where the elements of the source code are represented for their later separation in the elements of the test code. After the encapsulation of the source code elements in the PTCR, it is then used by the TCP to separate the test code elements, which forms the ATCR. Finally, ATCR is then available for use by refactoring, thereby decoupling the code from those of the testing framework for which the test code was written. Figure 1 illustrated the architecture of the EARTC proposed in this paper.

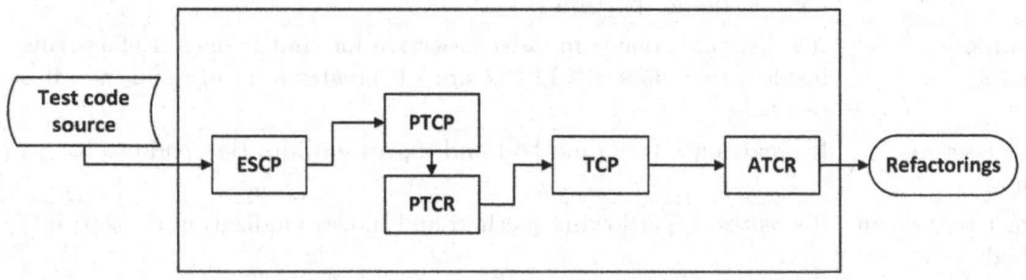

Fig. 1. Architecture of the EARTC proposed in this work.

The parsing process is started with the source code by the PTCP. This component sends the source code for the ESCP, where it will be separated into objects coupled to a specific ESCP. Once the ESCP, its elements, and especially the complexity of its specific functionalities are encapsulated in the PTCP, the resulting PTCR will be available for use in the next step of the process, the TCP. The work of TCP is to separate the components found in the first parsing, in the form of PTCR, in actions and assertions, which form the basis of the ATCR.

It is important to notice that all four components of the EARTC have implementations with abstract and concrete classes and are decoupled from the specific implementations of each component, which allows the architecture to be extended and used by other proposals individually.

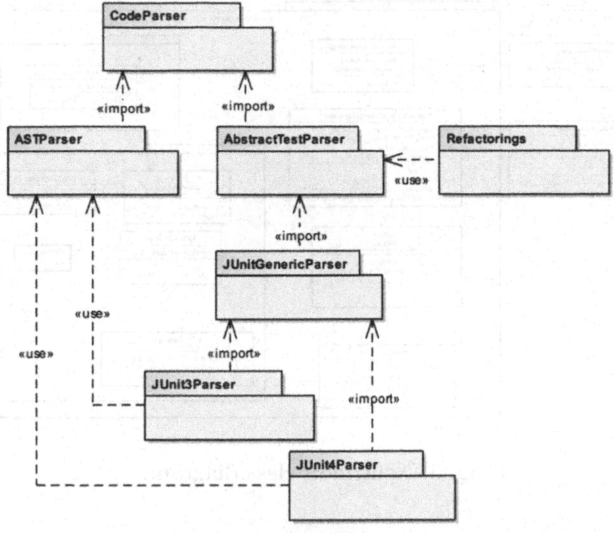

Fig. 2. Parsing classes structure.

3.4 Extension Points

The PTCP module is responsible for the creation of the tree structure form the test source code. However, since the EARTC should be extensible for other test frameworks, PTCP was designed containing abstract classes that should have a reference implementation for the testing framework to be used. In this way, the EARTC contains a package called ASTParser, which makes use of the AST framework contained in the PTCP. Thus, the ASTParser contains the concrete implementations of AST. AST is an API for transforming test source code into a tree structure of AST nodes. These nodes are subclasses of ASTNode, and each subclass is specialized in a Java language element, such as methods, variables, assignments, and so on [1].

Therefore, to allow other testing automation frameworks to be added to the EARTC, the ASTParser module must be extended. Figure 2 depicts the classes structure for parsing.

4 Neutrino: A Tool for Test Code Refactoring

In order to provide a proof of concept for the EARTC, we developed a plugin for the Eclipse IDE, called Neutrino[1]. This plugin is a non-intrusive tool, which means to use Neutrino it is not necessary to modify previously the annotation inserted in the test code, nor performing inheritance or interface implementations.

[1] https://github.com/nascimentolwtn/Neutrino.

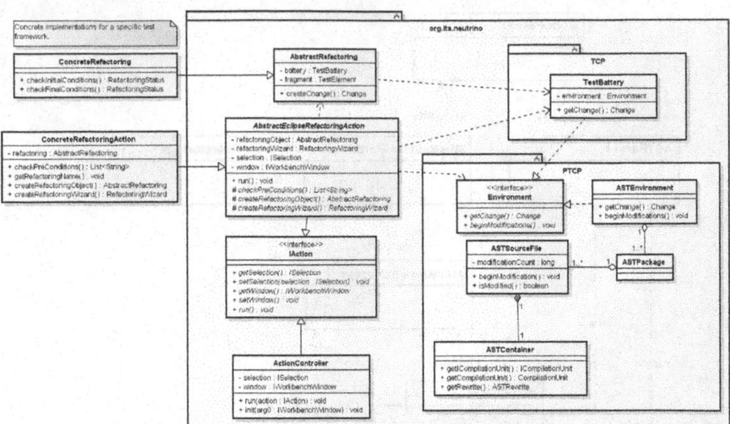

Fig. 3. Neutrino's class diagram.

To refactor the test code, Neutrino executes a set of activities exchanging data between the EARTC modules and the Eclipse IDE. These activities are detailed below. For a better understanding of the activities described here and performed by Neutrino, the class diagram with the main EARTC modules is shown in Fig. 3.

The first activity carried out by Neutrino is to perform a previous check of the IDE conditions, done by the specific container. In this check, it is verified whether the test code refactoring is possible or not. Nonetheless, this check is performed before parsing the test code, which makes this check quite superficial since no element of the test code is available. However, a negative result in this check ends the refactoring job immediately. Thus, this preliminary checking of the IDE conditions is intended to avoid unnecessary parsing execution.

After the first check is completed, the source code parsing must be performed. Since it does not have details related to refactoring, it is executed by the abstract container. After the execution of the PTCP, a PTCR object is then returned. This object will be used as a parameter in the next step, which is the parsing of the test code. In the same way parsing source code, the test code parsing is not dependent on the refactoring that was requested by the user. Therefore, this parsing is executed by the abstract container. This way, there is no coupling with IDE classes, as opposed to parsing the source code. After the test code parsing, an object represented by the ATCR is then generated.

Once the test code has been separated into its component elements, the class responsible for applying the test code refactoring is instantiated. With the instantiated class, it is configured with the ATCR object generated in the test code parsing. Since this task requires knowledge about the requested refactoring, it is executed in the specific refactoring container.

At this moment, the second and final check of the initial conditions is made. This second check of initial conditions is done after parsing the test code so that the elements identified in this step can be used by this check, which does not occur with the previous one. Thus, the second initial condition check is independent of the test code automation framework.

Before the actual application of the changes to the test code, the final preparation of the refactoring object is still done. This step is used to ask the developer for the parameters needed to apply the refactoring, if necessary. Since the purpose of this step is to interact with the user, it is necessary that the user can cancel the application of the refactoring. This step is carried out by the specific container since it varies according to the refactoring and has a coupling to the development IDE. After requesting possible parameters to the user, the refactoring object is finally ready. At this point, the changes are applied to the ATCR, and the changes propagate from refactoring to the source code.

4.1 The Neutrino Refactoring Process

To use the tool is necessary to open the test class to perform refactoring, and choose *(re) run smell detection* from the menu. In this way, Neutrino will parse the code and display the detected bad smells, as depicted in Fig. 4.

The next step is to perform the refactorings in the test code as suggested by Neutrino. This process is performed automatically by the tool, but the developer must choose one kind of refactoring at a time. Figure 5 shows the execution of the *add explanation to assertion* refactoring, from the moment the developer chooses the line of code with a bad smell to be solved until the refactoring of the test code. Other refactorings have similar behavior for their execution. In most cases should be selected the line of code with bad smell, or even positioning the cursor within the test class and choose the desired option in the Eclipse menu.

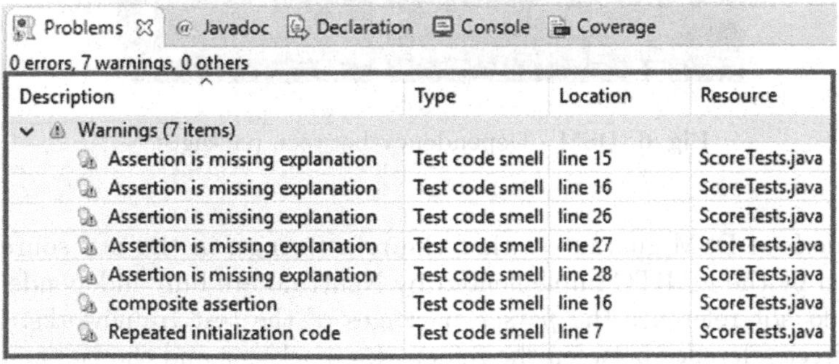

Problems ☒ @ Javadoc Declaration Console Coverage

0 errors, 7 warnings, 0 others

Description	Type	Location	Resource
Warnings (7 items)			
Assertion is missing explanation	Test code smell	line 15	ScoreTests.java
Assertion is missing explanation	Test code smell	line 16	ScoreTests.java
Assertion is missing explanation	Test code smell	line 26	ScoreTests.java
Assertion is missing explanation	Test code smell	line 27	ScoreTests.java
Assertion is missing explanation	Test code smell	line 28	ScoreTests.java
composite assertion	Test code smell	line 16	ScoreTests.java
Repeated initialization code	Test code smell	line 7	ScoreTests.java

Fig. 4. Neutrino bad smells detection.

4.2 Design Structure Matrix

DSM is a strategy for managing dependencies between software modules. Using DSM makes it easy to view the architecture, identify structural problems, and

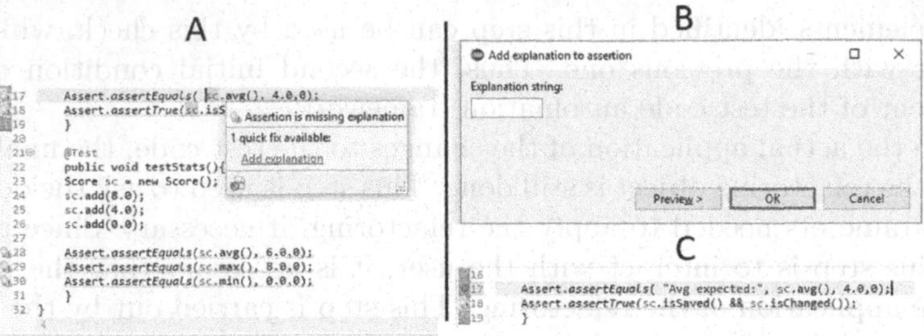

Fig. 5. An example of using Neutrino in eclipse.

check for refactoring results. The DSM is an adjacency matrix with the software modules labeling the horizontal and vertical axes, and indices in the columns and rows to represent the dependency between modules. In the matrix not considered self-dependencies, therefore there are no diagonal markings of the matrix [21].

In the context of this work, to validate the independence between the modules of the EARTC, a DSM was derivated, as described in Figs. 6 and 7.

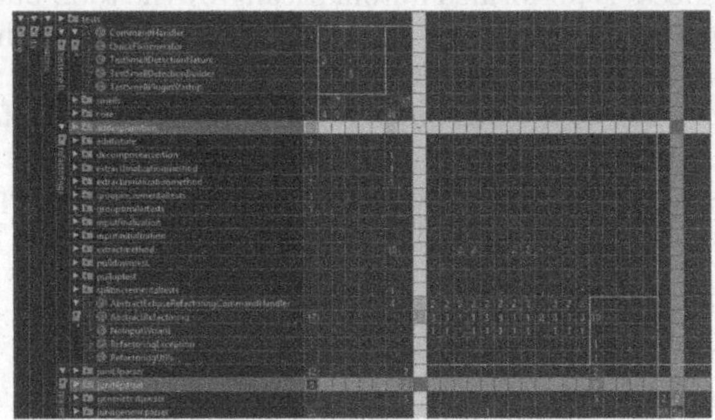

Fig. 6. DSM - Dependency between packages.

The derived DSM guarantees that the refactorings, in the test source code, performed by the EARTC implemented by Neutrino are fully independent, that is, they do not reference the *parser* packages of the test frameworks. If there were a direct reference between the refactoring packages and the *parser* package of the frameworks, refactoring would not work in other test frameworks, as is possible to see in Fig. 6.

The decoupling between test frameworks and EARTC modules can also be observed in the following references:

– there are no references from refactoring methods directly to the test frameworks, such as *junit3parser* and *junit4parser* (Figs. 6 and 7);

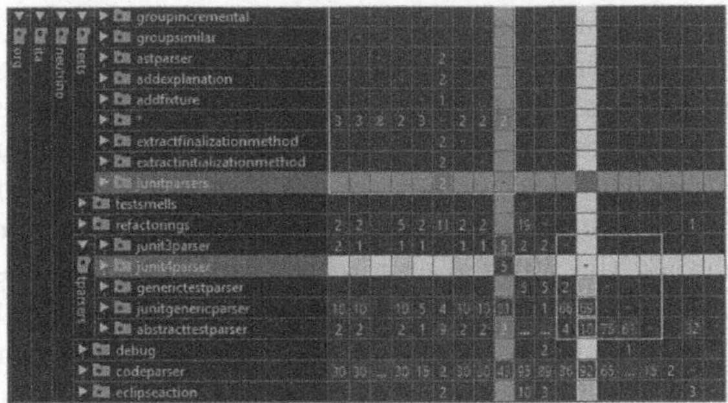

Fig. 7. DSM - Dependency with unit tests.

- Figure 7 indicates that there are 5 references to the *junit4parser* package, which come from the *tests* package. In this package are the parser unit tests. Therefore, this dependence does not influence the decoupling of frameworks.

Thus, these analyses of DSM allow concluding that the modules of the EARTC are wholly decoupled from the test frameworks. This feature makes the EARTC extensible, allowing new test frameworks to be incorporated into the Neutrino framework without the need for architectural change. Besides, as shown in Fig. 6, new refactorings for test code can be added to the EARTC without impacting architectural changes.

5 Conclusion and Future Work

The use of XP methodology has been receiving efforts from the academic community to investigate new methods and techniques to improve software development. In this context, the use of TDD has a relevant role, because it is a technique adopted for many industries with the aim to improve the quality of software products. The use of TDD has a relationship with the refactoring of the test code because the test is written first rather than of production code. However, it is essential to notes the impact of refactoring activity. In other words, it is necessary to check if the behavior of the test code is not changed after the refactoring. It is possible that the behavior of the test code has been changed. Besides, some refactorings might have added bad smells in the source test code impacting to fall of quality of the software.

The use of test automation can shorten software development and testing time by helping to save resources and improve quality. There are many test frameworks used for the industry with the objective the test automation, like JUnit and TestNG. However, these frameworks and other tools available in the literature do not make the detection of bad smells, and also not suggest automatic refactoring in the test code without change the original test behavior.

This work addresses the relevance of refactoring test code during software evolution. Refactoring is a repeated activity in many cycles of software development, and in this context, test codes are also refactored in order to meet changes or needs for the implementation of new functionalities. As cited in Sect. 3, this work proposed an extensible architecture named EARTC for refactoring test code. The EARTC allows refactorings to be performed in the test source code in order to remove any test problems, such as assertion without explanation, many comparisons in the same object, composite assertions, and problems in the hierarchy of class. The EARTC allows new refactorings to be written without needing to change the internal architecture module. Besides, it allows the use of several frameworks for performing a unit test, such as JUnit. The incorporation of other testing frameworks can also be performed using the original architecture of the EARTC. Besides, this work implements a plugin (Neutrino) for the Eclipse IDE in order to validate the EARTC. To use Neutrino it is not necessary to make changes in the test classes, this non-intrusive feature facilitates the use of the tool. The results obtained by Neutrino were satisfactory and are shown in Sect. 4. Moreover, a DSM was derived from the Neutrino project to verify and prove the independence between the internal modules of the EARTC.

As future work, we plan to address the refactoring of test code and the use of mutation test. In this context, to improve the quality of software in the project, an alternative is to analyze the behavior of a test class before and after the insertion of mutation test classes. These analyses will allow verifying the external behavior of the test code after the refactoring.

Acknowledgments. The authors would like to thank CNPq (grant 455080/2014-3) and FAPESP (grant 2014/16236-6) for financial support.

References

1. Arthorne, J., Laffra, C.: Official Eclipse 3.0 FAQ (Eclipse Series). Addison-Wesley Professional, Boston (2004)
2. Bavota, G., Carluccio, B.D., Lucia, A.D., Penta, M.D., Oliveto, R., Strollo, O.: When does a refactoring induce bugs? An empirical study. In: 2012 IEEE 12th International Working Conference on Source Code Analysis and Manipulation, pp. 104–113, September 2012
3. Bavota, G., Qusef, A., Oliveto, R., Lucia, A.D., Binkley, D.: An empirical analysis of the distribution of unit test smells and their impact on software maintenance. In: 2012 28th IEEE International Conference on Software Maintenance (ICSM), pp. 56–65, September 2012
4. Beck, K.: Test-Driven Development: By Example. Addison-Wesley Professional, Boston (2003)
5. Bladel, B.v., Demeyer, S.: Test behaviour detection as a test refactoring safety. In: Proceedings of the 2nd International Workshop on Refactoring, IWoR 2018, pp. 22–25. ACM, New York, NY, USA (2018). https://doi.org/10.1145/3242163.3242168
6. Fowler, M., Beck, K.: Refactoring: Improving the Design of Existing Code. Addison-Wesley Professional, Boston (1999)
7. Gamma, E., Helm, R., Johnson, R., Vlissides, J.: Elements of Reusable Object-Oriented Software. Addison-Wesley Professional, Boston (1994)

8. Gatrell, M., Counsell, S., Swift, S., Hierons, R.M., Liu, X.: Test and production classes of an industrial c# system: a refactoring and fault perspective. In: 2015 41st Euromicro Conference on Software Engineering and Advanced Applications, pp. 35–38, August 2015
9. Gerlec, Č., Rakić, G., Budimac, Z., Heričko, M.: A programming language independent framework for metrics-based software evolution and analysis. Comput. Sci. Inf. Syst. **9**(3), 1155–1186 (2012)
10. Guerra, E.M., Fernandes, C.T.: Refactoring test code safely. In: International Conference on Software Engineering Advances, p. 44, August 2007
11. Guerra, E.M.: Um Estudo sobre Refatoração de Código de Teste. Ph.D. thesis, Instituto Tecnológico de Aeronáutica, São José dos Campos (2005)
12. Janzen, D., Saiedian, H.: Test-driven development concepts, taxonomy, and future direction. Computer **38**(9), 43–50 (2005). https://doi.org/10.1109/MC.2005.314
13. Kaur, G., Singh, B.: Improving the quality of software by refactoring. In: 2017 International Conference on Intelligent Computing and Control Systems (ICICCS), pp. 185–191, June 2017. https://doi.org/10.1109/ICCONS.2017.8250707
14. Mens, T., Tourwe, T.: A survey of software refactoring. IEEE Trans. Softw. Eng. **30**(2), 126–139 (2004)
15. Meszaros, G.: XUnit Test Patterns: Refactoring Test Code. Pearson Education, London (2007)
16. Mosley, D.J., Posey, B.A.: Just Enough Software Test Automation. Prentice Hall Professional, Upper Saddle River (2002)
17. Murphy-Hill, E., Parnin, C., Black, A.P.: How we refactor, and how we know it. IEEE Trans. Softw. Eng. **38**(1), 5–18 (2012)
18. Passier, H., Bijlsma, L., Bockisch, C.: Maintaining unit tests during refactoring. In: Proceedings of the 13th International Conference on Principles and Practices of Programming on the Java Platform: Virtual Machines, Languages, and Tools, pp. 18:1–18:6. ACM (2016)
19. Pipka, J.U.: Refactoring in a "test first"-world. In: Proceedings of Third International Conference eXtreme Programming and Flexible Processes in Software Engineering (2002)
20. Rizzi, L., Fontana, F.A., Roveda, R.: Support for architectural smell refactoring. In: Proceedings of the 2nd International Workshop on Refactoring, IWoR 2018, pp. 7–10. ACM, New York, NY, USA (2018)
21. Sangal, N., Jordan, E., Sinha, V., Jackson, D.: Using dependency models to manage complex software architecture. In: Proceedings of the 20th Annual ACM Conference on Object-Oriented Programming, Systems, Languages, and Applications, vol. 40, pp. 167–176 (2005)
22. Silva, I.P.S.C., Alves, E.L.G., Andrade, W.L.: Analyzing automatic test generation tools for refactoring validation. In: Proceedings of the 12th International Workshop on Automation of Software Testing, AST 2017, pp. 38–44. IEEE Press, Piscataway, NJ, USA (2017)
23. Van Deursen, A., Moonen, L., Van Den Bergh, A., Kok, G.: Refactoring test code. In: Proceedings of the 2nd International Conference on Extreme Programming and Flexible Processes in Software Engineering, pp. 92–95 (2001)
24. Williams, L., Kessler, R.R., Cunningham, W., Jeffries, R.: Strengthening the case for pair programming. IEEE Softw. **17**(4), 19–25 (2000). https://doi.org/10.1109/52.854064

Machine Learning Approach for Reliability Assessment of Open Source Software

Ranjan Kumar Behera[1(✉)], Santanu Kumar Rath[1], Sanjay Misra[2], Marcelo Leon[3], and Adewole Adewumi[2]

[1] National Institute of Technology Rourkela, Rourkela, India
jranjanb.19@gmail.com, skrath235@gmail.com
[2] Covenant University, Ota 1023, Nigeria
{sanjay.misra,adewumi}@covenantuniversity.edu.ng
[3] Universidad Nacional De Loja, Loja, Ecuador
marceloleon11@hotmail.com

Abstract. Some of the quality parameters for any successful open source software may be attributed to affordability, availability of source code, re-distributability, and modifiability etc. Quality of software can be further improvised subsequently by either users or associated developers by constantly monitoring some of the reliability aspects. Since multiple users are allowed to modify the code there is a potential threat for security, which might degrade the reliability of software. Bug tracking systems are often considered to monitor various software faults, detected mostly in open source software projects. Various authors have made research in this direction by applying different techniques in order to improve the reliability of open source software projects. In this work, an various machine learning models have been implemented to examine the reliability of the software. An extensive numerical illustration has also been presented for bug data recorded on bug tracking system. The effectiveness of machine learning models for estimating the level of faults associated with the systems has been verified by comparing it with similar approaches as available in the literature.

Keywords: Software reliability · Open source software · Probabilistic neural network · Goodness of fit · Concave model

1 Introduction

The popularity of the software has been increasing at an exponential rate as it has become an essential part of human life. As the open source software are exposed to public domain, the assessment of failure rate for software is a major concern from developers point of view. Software reliability is an important attribute which determines the quality of the product. It can be defined as the ability of the software to handle both software and hardware faults [1].

S. Misra et al. (Eds.): ICCSA 2019, LNCS 11622, pp. 472–482, 2019.
https://doi.org/10.1007/978-3-030-24305-0_35

Users not only want the higher reliability of the product, they also want the quantitative figure for reliability before buying any software product. Accurate measurement of software reliability is a challenging task as there are several factors that contributes to measuring software reliability. Some of the attributes that influence the reliability of software are dependent on two factors [14]:

- Total number of faults or number of failures associated with the software.
- The way user operates the system, also known as the operational profile. So, every time we develop a software, in turn we also maintain a complete profile for the software and there will be an associated documentation which mentions the operation profile.

There are several problems associated with software reliability assessment:

- Errors which are embedded in the software program may or may not the cause of failure. So, the error may not cause the failure with same degree of frequency.
- The failure rate is observer dependent.

A number of new technology along with methodologies have been emerged to improve the reliability of the software. Several models have been developed in order to improve the scalability and reliability at different phases of software development [2,3]. Waterfall model seems to be simple and elegant for development process as it deals with sequential phases of improvement. Reliability requirement analysis is realized at the software analysis phase only. However, the degree of reliability is strengthening at consecutive stages of the development process by drawing attention through full proof class diagram. The product design aspects are then reduced to executable form in implementation stage Error detection and recovery and robustness has been tested at the testing phase. In this stages the validation and verification process has been performed to check is the product meets both user and software requirement or not. The software is then finally process to minimize the future possibility of damages. From development point of view software can be broadly classified into two types [4]:

- Closed Source Software (CSS)
- Open Source Software (OSS).

CSSs are not distributed in the public domain. These type of software's are having some licensing agreement and can be distributed only as a commercial software. Unlike CSS, Open source software are made available publicly for accessing and modify by the user with few restrictions. They are designed to facilitate the users to have collaborative participation, rapid prototyping, idea exchange, transparency etc. However, they are often prone to security and reliability threats. The development approach to OSS mainly focuses on strengthen the reliability parameters which might provide uninterrupted service within a given period of time. SRGMs are mathematical models to predict the rate of failure. There are many types of SRGMs [5]. These SRGMs are grouped into 2 categories

- Concave Shaped Models
- S-Shaped Models

The best thing about these models is, the fault detection rate decreases as the amount of fault detected increases. Figure 1 presents the concave and s-shaped models, for software reliability growth. In concave shaped models, initially failure rate increases to its peak and after reaching the peak it starts decreasing. So, Concave models indicate that after reaching the peak value failure rate is expected to decrease exponentially. In S-shaped models: initially, when the testers don't have that much knowledge about the software, the fault removal rate will be less but once they get to know about the software there is an increase in fault removal rate. So basically, the fault removal rate depends upon the skills of the tester.

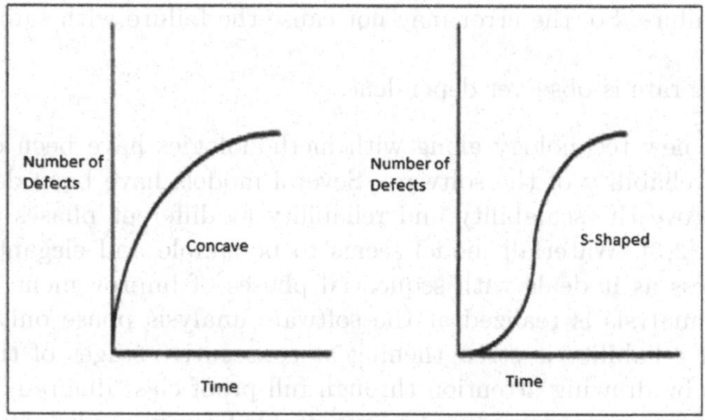

Fig. 1. Concave and S-shaped software reliability growth models

SRGMs don't care about the dependency between various components and consider the entire software as a single entity. So basically, SRGMs are also called as black box models. These models measure the value of reliability in the testing phase and on the basis of reliability value they decide whether to release the software or not [6]. Each SRGM imposes restrictions or assumptions. These assumptions are as follows:

- Once a fault is discovered in the system, it should be fixed immediately.
- Correction of a defect will not cause an introduction of a new defect in the system.
- During the quality assurance test no new code is introduced.
- Each fault is equally probable. They can lie into any severity class such as major, minor or critical.
- The failures are independent of each other.

Sometimes these models are not applicable to wide range of projects due having multiple constraints. Machine learning are found to be promising tools for accessing the reliability of the network. In this paper, various neural models have been applied to validate the reliability parameters of the software. The functionality of the neural model is similar to the ways human brain works. It consists of several processing units known as neurons in layering fashion. Basically it consists of three layers such as input, hidden and output layer. There could be more than hidden layers where complex problem can be solved. Accessing the complex software requires high number of computational units for which we need more hidden layer. This approach leads to extension of several complex neural processing known as deep neural network. In this paper we have accessed the software reliability through several neural network models.

2 Background

In the past, many software reliability models have been proposed to assess the reliability of software. Among these models, the question is which model to select in a particular situation. Musa *et al.* have used various models and shown that some models are producing better results in comparison to others; for an example, the geometric family models are providing better prediction results in comparison to other models [7]. Goel *et al.* stated that the performance of different models depends on the type of dataset if one model is giving a good result for one dataset it may not perform well for another dataset [6]. So, for selecting the best model for a particular project we need to compare the results of various models. But it is also true that there is no way by which we can select a model a priori [8,9]. So, many authors have studied and proposed methods for selecting a model at an early stage of software development [10].

Brocklehurst *et al.* proposed that the model selection process basically depends upon the nature of faults presents in the system [11]. They have stated that the design flaws present in the software are the main reason for the failures. Abdel-Ghaly *et al.* analyzed ten models using five different approaches to measure the predictive quality of these models [12]. They observed that the criteria used for the evaluation of the model, choose a different model to be a good predictor. Khoshgoftaar also uses different criteria for selecting a model and he observed that Akaike Information Criteria (AIC) is the best criteria for selecting any model [13]. Lyu and Nikora also analyzed various software projects and they have developed a tool for selecting a model. In their paper, they have stated that Goodness-of-Fit (GOF) is the best criteria for selecting any particular model [14].

Shukla et al. have collected historical data from different software projects and with the help of this historical data they have proposed a method for selecting the best model for software reliability assessment [15]. But the flaw in this method is how to measure the similarity between different software projects. Stringfellow *et al.* have proposed a method for the selection of appropriate SRGM and it also helps in deciding to which extent we have to perform testing and what would be the appropriate time to release any software [16].

3 Fault Data Recorded in Bug Tracking System

Usually The fault data associated with a OSS are stored in separate file which can be reused for future development process. Bug-tracking systems are the tools that are usually adopted for mining fault data for both proprietary and open source software. Bugzilla and Buglister are widely used bug tracking system for OSS and proprietary software respectively. A number of parameters are associated with the datasets. Out of all the parameters only eight have been considered to predict the fault. Some of the parameters are date of capturing the fault, name of component, name of product, name of platform etc. The fault levels have been categorized into eight different groups. The categorical classification of fault levels is listed in Table 1.

Table 1. The indexed fault levels recorded on bug tracking system

Index number	Fault level
1	Trivial
2	Enhancement
3	Minor
4	Normal
5	Regression
6	Blocker
7	Major
8	Critical

4 Machine Learning Techniques Used

Machine learning algorithms are found to be suitable for classification and prediction task. In this work, we have considered various machine learning models for multi-level classification for fault identification. After the fault prediction, the reliability of the software has been accessed for measuring the feasibility of the software. Following are the list machine learning techniques used in this work

(1) Naive Bayes
(2) Decision Tree Classifier
(3) Random Forest Classifier
(4) Support Vector Machine (SVM)
(5) Artificial Neural Network (ANN)
(6) Probabilistic Neural Network (PNN)

5 Methodology Used

The Methodology used for identification of critical fault is shown in Fig. 2. Following are the steps used for the identification of critical fault present in the system

(i) The data of various OSS products have been collected from Bugzilla website [17].
(ii) The data collected from the website of Bugzilla is raw data, so it can't be directly processed into the models. So first, we have converted that data into fault count on the basis of occurrence.
(iii) After data conversion various machine learning techniques have been applied to the identification of critical fault present in the system.
(iv) Then various performance evaluation parameters such as accuracy, precision, recall and f-score have been calculated to compare the performance of each model.
(v) If the value of these parameters meets the objective then calculate the value of reliability factor and goto step (vii). Function for calculating reliability value is [34]

$$R(\Delta t|t) = e^{-a[e^{-bt}-e^{-b(t+\Delta t)}]} \quad (1)$$

where, a = Expected total number of defects to be eventually detected
b = Defect detection rate
t = Time interval
Δt = The increment of execution time

(vi) Otherwise modify the parameters and repeat the steps (iii) to (v) again.
(vii) If the value of reliability factor is acceptable then release the software otherwise it requires more testing effort.

6 Dataset

The software specification of open source software is associated with both functional and non-functional parameters. The fault data have been collected for four different OSS product namely Firefox, Core, Tomcat and Camino Graveyard [17]. The fault data extracted with the help of bug tracking system are

Table 2. Open source software used for experiment

Sl no.	Product name	Number of failures
1	Camino Graveyard	12502
2	Core	10000
3	Mozilla Firefox	10000
4	Tomcat	11025

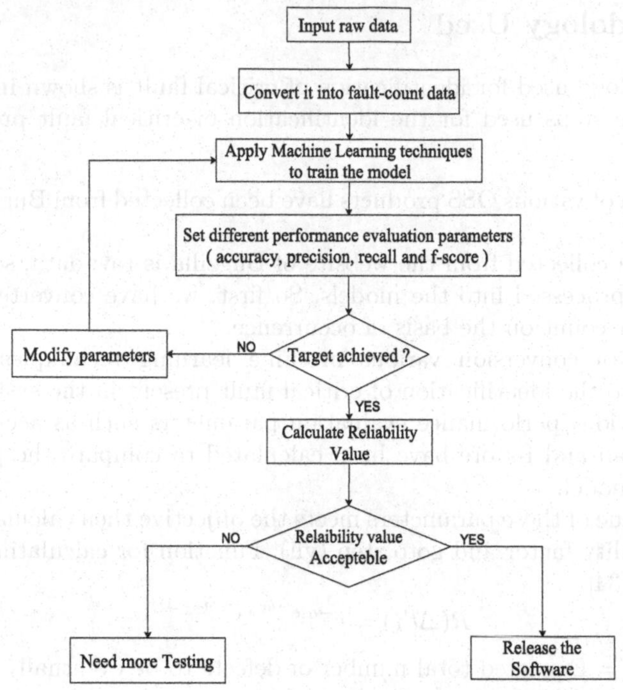

Fig. 2. Methodology used for software reliability assessment

not directly processed in machine learning model as it contains number of undesired features. Datasets have been preprocessed in order to filter and reduce the dimension. The dataset used in this paper is listed in Table 2.

7 Performance Evaluation Criteria

(i) **Precision**: Precision is defined as the total number of true positives divided by the total number of predicted positives [11].

$$Precision = \frac{T_p}{T_p + F_p} \tag{2}$$

(ii) **Recall**: Recall is defined as the total number of true positives divided by the total number of actual positives [11].

$$Recall = \frac{T_p}{T_p + F_n} \tag{3}$$

(iii) **F-score**: F_1 score is calculated by taking the harmonic mean of recall and precision, mathematically it can be defined as [11]

$$F\text{-}score = 2\frac{Precision \times Recall}{Precision + Recall} \tag{4}$$

(iv) **Accuracy**: Accuracy is defined as the total number of correct classifications divided by the total number of observations [11]. Mathematically accuracy can be defined as

$$Accuracy = \frac{T_p + T_n}{T_p + F_p + T_n + F_n} \tag{5}$$

where,

T_n = Observations that are actually negative and predicted negative (true negative).
T_p = Observations that are actually positive and predicted positive (true positive).
F_n = Observations that are actually positive and predicted negative (false negative).
F_p = Observations that are actually negative and predicted positive (false positive).

8 Results and Discussion

Bugzilla bug tracking system is being considered to obtained the raw dataset from different open source software. They have been preprocessed in order to make the dimensionality reduction for eradicating undesired features. Five different machine learning algorithms have been implemented to measure the reliability of the software. Eight fault levels have been considered on the objective variable that have been used in bug tracking system. The description of the fault levels has been presented in Table 1. The fault levels for instances of datasets have been estimated by using various machine learning algorithms. The machine learning models have been evaluated by using various performance parameters like accuracy, precision, recall and f-measure. The result of various models for multilevel classification have been presented in Tables 2, 3, 4 and 5.

Table 3. Performance analysis for Camino Graveyard dataset

Model	Accuracy	Recall	Precision	F-score
Naive Bayes	0.5984	0.5786	0.5984	0.5768
Decision Tree	0.6204	0.6074	0.6204	0.6374
Random Forest Classifier	0.6298	0.6242	0.6328	0.5718
SVM	0.6328	0.6512	0.6158	0.5678
ANN	0.6556	0.6086	0.6186	0.5968
PNN	**0.7016**	**0.6932**	**0.6434**	**0.6537**

It can be observed that the probabilistic based neural network provides better results as compared to other machine learning algorithms in most of the

Table 4. Performance analysis for core dataset

Model	Accuracy	Recall	Precision	F-score
Naive Bayes	0.7836	0.6828	0.7836	0.7972
Decision Tree	0.7933	0.6945	0.7836	0.7351
Random Forest Classifier	0.7944	0.6999	0.7944	0.7445
SVM	0.7984	0.6979	0.7982	0.7485
ANN	0.8104	0.7207	0.8104	0.7948
PNN	**0.8174**	**0.7256**	**0.8234**	**0.7988**

Table 5. Performance analysis for Firefox dataset

Model	Accuracy	Recall	Precision	F-score
Naive Bayes	0.7966	0.7086	0.7861	0.7459
Decision Tree	0.8264	0.7697	0.8164	0.7893
Random Forest Classifier	0.8272	0.7880	0.8172	0.8023
SVM	0.8352	0.7930	0.8271	0.8133
ANN	0.8476	0.6849	0.8376	0.8195
PNN	**0.8536**	**0.7349**	**0.8446**	**0.8235**

datasets. The reliability index for each software has been measured after identification of the critical faults. Probabilistic approach is found to be most suitable for predicting the fault levels. Naive Bayes algorithm has the less performance in all the datasets. The PNN has more than 85% accuracy in case of Firefox dataset where as in case of Tomcat dataset the accuracy is only 65%. Although accuracy is less, it is better than all other machine learning algorithms. The f-score in Tomcat dataset is found to be less for PNN model as it contained more unbalanced instances. However, the PNN model is found to be perform better in term of other parameters like accuracy, precision and recall (Table 6).

Table 6. Performance analysis for Tomcat dataset

Model	Accuracy	Recall	Precision	F-score
Naive Bayes	0.5755	0.5921	0.5355	0.5896
Decision Tree	0.5981	0.5607	0.5481	0.5818
Random Forest Classifier	0.5936	0.5692	0.5491	0.5312
SVM	0.6042	0.5804	0.5942	0.6280
ANN	0.6359	0.5981	0.5459	0.5856
PNN	**0.6559**	**0.6012**	**0.5989**	**0.5646**

9 Conclusion and Future Work

A number of bug tracking system are widely available for extracting the bug information from the open source software. In this work we have considered the Bugzilla bug tracking system for mining the bus from the software. The various characteristics of reliability parameters have been explored after identification of the fault level in order to predict whether the software is feasible for use or not. Machine learning algorithms have been implemented for predicting the fault level of the instances of the software. After the fault prediction the reliability of the software has been measures which help in identifying the best models based on both stability and fitting capabilities. From the experimental results, It has been found that probabilistic neural network is the most suitable algorithm to handle the fault prediction. This work can be extended by implementing deep learning models like Convolutional Neural Network (CNN), Recurrent neural network (RNN) in order to have better accuracy for fault prediction.

References

1. Lyu, M.R. (ed.): Handbook of Software Reliability Engineering. IEEE Computer Society Press, Los Alamitos (1996)
2. Yamada, S.: Software Reliability Modeling: Fundamentals and Applications. Springer, Tokyo/Heidelberg (2014). https://doi.org/10.1007/978-4-431-54565-1
3. Tamura, Y., Matsumoto, M., Yamada, S.: Software reliability model selection based on deep learning. In: Proceedings of the International Conference on Industrial Engineering, Management Science and Application, Korea, 23–26 May 2016, pp. 77–81 (2016)
4. Behera, R.K., Shukla, S., Rath, S.K., Misra, S.: Software reliability assessment using machine learning technique. In: Gervasi, O., et al. (eds.) ICCSA 2018. LNCS, vol. 10964, pp. 403–411. Springer, Cham (2018). https://doi.org/10.1007/978-3-319-95174-4_32
5. Yamada, S., Tamura, Y.: OSS Reliability Measurement and Assessment. Springer, London (2016). https://doi.org/10.1007/978-3-319-31818-9
6. Goel, A.L.: Software reliability models: assumption, limitations, and applicability. IEEE Trans. Softw. Eng. **12**, 1411–1423 (1985)
7. Musa, J.D., Iannino, A., Okumoto, K.: Software Reliability, Measurement, Prediction and Application. McGraw-Hill, New York (1987)
8. Sharma, K., et al.: Selection of optimal software reliability growth models using a distance based method. IEEE Trans. Reliab. **59**(2), 266–276 (2010)
9. Schick, G.H., Wolverton, R.W.: An analysis of competing software reliability models. IEEE Trans. Softw. Eng. **2**, 104–120 (1978)
10. Sukert, A.N.: Empirical validation of three software errors predictions models. IEEE Trans. Reliab. **28**, 199–205 (1979)
11. Brocklehurst, S., Chan, P.Y., Littlewood, B., Snell, J.: Recalibrating software reliability models. IEEE Trans. Softw. Eng. **SE–16**(4), 458–470 (1990)
12. Abdel-Ghaly, A.A., Chan, P.Y., Littlewood, B.: Evaluation of competing software reliability predictions. IEEE Trans. Softw. Eng. **SE–12**(12), 950–967 (1986)
13. Khoshgoftaar, T.M.: On model selection in software reliability. In: 8th Symposium in Computational Statistics (Compstat 1988), pp. 13–14, August 1988

14. Lyu, M., Nikora, A.: CASREA-a computer-aided software reliability estimation tool. In: Proceedings of the Fifth International Workshop on Computer-Aided Software Engineering, Montreal, pp. 264–275 (1992)
15. Shukla, S., Behera, R.K., Misra, S., Rath, S.K.: Software reliability assessment using deep learning technique. In: Chakraverty, S., Goel, A., Misra, S. (eds.) Towards Extensible and Adaptable Methods in Computing, pp. 57–68. Springer, Singapore (2018). https://doi.org/10.1007/978-981-13-2348-5_5
16. Stringfellow, C., et al.: An empirical method for selecting software reliability growth models. Empir. Softw. Eng. J. **7**, 319–343 (2002)
17. The Mozilla Software Foundation: The Mozilla project. https://bugzilla.mozilla.org/

A Requirements Catalog of Mobile Personal Health Records for Prenatal Care

Mariam Bachiri[1], Ali Idri[1(✉)], Leanne M. Redman[2], Jose Luis Fernandez-Aleman[3], and Ambrosio Toval[3]

[1] Software Project Management Research Team, ENSIAS, Mohammed V Universityin Rabat, Rabat, Morocco
{mariam_bachiri, ali.idri}@um5.ac.ma

[2] Reproductive Endocrinology and Women's Health Laboratory Pennington Biomedical Research Center, Louisiana State University, Baton Rouge, USA
leanne.redman@pbrc.edu

[3] Department of Informatics and Systems, Faculty of Computer Science, University of Murcia, Murcia, Spain
{aleman, atoval}@um.es

Abstract. Mobile Personal Health Records (mPHRs) for prenatal care are mobile health applications that allow pregnant women manage, access and share their health data with healthcare providers. In this paper, a requirements catalog was developed, according to standards, guidelines and relevant literature. The catalog covers requirements about Sustainability, Internationalization (i18n), Operability, Reliability, Functional suitability and Performance efficiency. The usefulness of this catalog consists in conducting audit evaluations of prenatal care mPHRs, in addition to helping stakeholders and developers identify potential requirements for their mPHRs.

Keywords: mPHRs · Requirements · Catalog · Prenatal care · Sustainability · ISO/IEC 25010 · i18n

1 Introduction

Mobile health is experiencing a growth trend as consumers request more accessibility to the medical health professionals and transparency in healthcare becomes more important. Moreover, the health, fitness and medical industries have been identified as the top three fields to accelerate the growth of mobile devices [1].

Mobile Personal Health Records (mPHRs) for prenatal care are mobile health applications used by pregnant women, which allow them to access and coordinate their health information using mobile devices and track their pregnancy until the day of delivery [2]. The mPHRs for prenatal care also store personal and health data recorded by the pregnant women, which can also be accessed by their healthcare providers [3].

S. Misra et al. (Eds.): ICCSA 2019, LNCS 11622, pp. 483–495, 2019.
https://doi.org/10.1007/978-3-030-24305-0_36

The mPHRs for prenatal care are currently available in the leading mobile applications stores: Apple App store and Google Play store. In fact, Android and iOS platforms are currently the prominent and adopted mobile operating systems for health apps development [4].

The health data collected using prenatal care mPHRs usually include [2]: (i) Personal information such as name, telephone number, marital status and insurance details; (ii) Physical body information such as height, weight, waist size and blood pressure; (iii) Personal medical history such as blood group, allergies, medication use and family health history; and (iv) Obstetrical history such as last menstrual period, estimated due date, gynecological history and contraception method prior to pregnancy. In addition to the specific functionalities, expected for these kinds of mobile applications, a number of non-functional requirements can be considered, either for development or auditing purposes, which can be gathered in a requirements catalog.

To target a large number of pregnant women, the content of the mPHRs for prenatal care should be conceived with consideration of diverse languages and regions [5]. Thus, requirements for internationalization (i18n) should be determined at early stages of the development lifecycle of prenatal care mPHRs.

According to the findings of our previous study [2], Operability, Performance efficiency, Reliability and Functional suitability are the most influenced quality characteristics, of the ISO/IEC 25010 [6] product quality model, by the requirements of mPHRs for prenatal care. ISO/IEC 25010 defines: Operability is the degree to which the product has attributes that enable it to be understood, learned and attractive to the user, when used under specified conditions. Performance efficiency is the performance relative to the amount of resources used within stated conditions. Reliability is the degree to which a system performs specified functions under specified conditions for a defined period of time. Finally, functional suitability is the degree to which the product provides functions that meet stated needs under specified conditions. Hence, requirements related to these quality characteristics should be delineated.

Moreover, according to the United Nations (UN), sustainability is defined as "the ability to meet the needs of the present without compromising the ability of future generations to satisfy their own needs" [7]. There are five dimensions of sustainability [8]: economic, social and environmental, in addition to two dimensions that have been identified for software sustainability, which are: individual (human) and technical dimensions [9, 10]. Endorsing the sustainability of mPHRs for prenatal care is necessary to expand their adoption by the users. Therefore, requirements about sustainability should be considered.

To the best of our knowledge, a requirement catalog for prenatal care mPHRs has not yet been developed. This paper aims to develop a requirements' catalog for the inherent properties of mPHRs for prenatal care. According to the ISO/IEC 25010 Standard [6], software product properties are divided into inherent properties and assigned properties. Inherent properties determine the capabilities of a software product, and they are permanent features; they can be classified as either functional properties or quality properties. Functional properties determine what the software is able to do, while quality properties show the degree to which the software is able to provide and maintain its specified services. Assigned properties are not considered as quality characteristics of the software, as they can be changed without changing the software [6]. This catalog mainly focuses on i18n, sustainability and the quality characteristics of the ISO/IEC 25010 product quality model: Operability, Reliability, Functional suitability and Performance efficiency for prenatal care mPHRs.

The paper is structured as follows: Sect. 2 presents the related work on developing requirements catalogs for mobile health applications. Section 3 describes the method used to develop the present catalog. Section 4 reports the results of an illustration example on the use of this catalog on an mPHR for prenatal care. Section 5 discusses the findings of this illustration. The conclusion and future work are presented in Sect. 6.

2 Related Work

According to the standard ISO/IEC/IEEE 29148 [11], software requirements specification is defined as "a structured collection of the requirements (functions, performance, design constraints, and attributes) of the software and its external interfaces". Hence, collecting these requirements in the Software Requirements Specification (SRS) document is essential to clearly disclose the requirements to stakeholders and define them accurately to developers.

Previous studies have established requirements catalogs, such as the study of Zapata et al., which proposes a SRS that specifies the usability requirements for mobile health applications, in addition to an audit method [12]. The requirements of this catalog were extracted from recommended standards, popular guidelines and literature. The proposed catalog was designed to be reused and adapted to different projects. Moreover, a study of Ouhbi et al. defined a reusable requirements catalog for blood donation applications with regards to i18n and sustainability [13] . The requirements identified in this catalog were derived from the main related software engineering and e-health standards and literature. Another study of Ouhbi et al. defined a reusable requirements catalog for sustainable connected health applications [14]. This catalog provides requirements that cover the individual, social, environmental, and technical dimensions of sustainability, and can be adapted to specific m-health applications.

Furthermore, Jensen et al. identified reusable technical security requirements for healthcare applications, which were extracted from legislation applicable to the healthcare domain [15].

In our previous work [2], a framework was developed in order to evaluate the software quality of prenatal care mPHRs according to the ISO/IEC 25010 quality standard. The aim of this framework was to study the influence of the common requirements of mPHRs for prenatal care, which were extracted from literature and existing mobile apps on the market, on the software quality characteristics and sub-characteristics of the ISO/IEC 25010. These requirements were classified according to 7 blocks: App's accessibility, the expectant woman's personal details, the expectant woman's physical body information, the expectant woman's personal medical history, the expectant woman's obstetrical and pregnancy information, user's actions, and app's components.

The findings of this study stated that the quality characteristics most influenced by the mPHRs for prenatal care requirements are Functional suitability, Reliability, Operability and Performance efficiency.

3 Method

3.1 Requirements Specification of mPHRs for Prenatal Care

The limited adoption of Personal Health Records (PHRs) by individuals is a real issue [15, 16], due to several reasons such as the use of medical terminologies that are usually difficult to understand by users [17], the lack of multi-language support, in addition to socio-cultural barriers [18, 19]. Moreover, PHRs for pregnancy are an intriguing focus because of the high attention paid to health information by pregnant women [20]. The adoption of mPHRs for prenatal care is also influenced by software quality [2]. Hence the requirements related to i18n, software quality and sustainability should be taken in consideration when developing an mPHR for prenatal care.

In order to identify the requirements of mPHRs for prenatal care to be included in the catalog, the present study relied on : (i) An analysis of the features and functionalities of mPHRs for prenatal care [21]. (ii) Previous studies about the software quality evaluation of mPHRs for prenatal care [2, 22]. (iii) A requirements catalog related to usability [12]. And (iv) Requirements catalogs related to i18n [5, 13] and sustainability [13, 14]. Furthermore, the following standards were used to extract requirements [14]:

- ISO/IEC 25010 standard for system and software product quality requirements and evaluation [6].
- ISO/TR 14292 standard for the definition, scope and context of PHRs [23].
- ISO/TR 20514 standard for the definition, scope and context of Electronic Health Records (EHRs) [24].
- The W3C standards for Web and mobile devices [25].
- ISO/TS 14265 standard for the classification of purposes for processing personal health information [26].
- ISO/TR 18307 standard for interoperability and compatibility in messaging and communication standards – Key characteristics [27].
- ISO/HL7 27931 standard for data exchange in health care environments [28].
- ISO 21090 standard about harmonized data types for information interchange [29].

3.2 Requirements Catalog for Prenatal Care mPHRs

The present requirements catalog is developed according to: (i) The guidelines provided by SIREN (SImple REuse of software requirements), which is an approach based on software engineering standards that can be used to create, select and specify the requirements of a software, in addition to promoting the reuse of requirements. This approach was firstly introduced by Toval et al. [30]. (ii) Recommendations from the IEEE 29148 standard [11], which provides a definition of the normative content of the SRS. This standard contains provisions for the processes and products related to the engineering of requirements for systems and software products and services throughout the life cycle. (iii) Guidelines from the IEEE 1233 guide for the development of the set of requirements, System Requirements Specification that satisfy an expressed need. It also covers the necessary characteristics and qualities of individual requirements and the set of all requirements [31].

The development of the present catalog is focused on providing a complete, consistent and valid set of requirements for prenatal care mPHRs. The generation process of the catalog is divided into four steps, as described in Fig. 1: (i) The identification of sources, which are the relevant studies and standards previously presented. (ii) The extraction of requirements from the identified sources. (iii) The generation of the catalog from the extracted requirements by adopting the SIREN approach. (iv) The maintenance of the catalog by regularly updating it due to changes to the standards used or to the mPHRs for prenatal care. The structure of the catalog is adapted to the general SRS structure from the IEEE 29148:2011 standard [11] as shown in Table 1.

The aim of the present catalog is to cover the mPHRs for prenatal care requirements related to: Sustainability, i18n, Reliability, Performance efficiency, Functional suitability and Operability (named Usability in the IOS/IEC 9126-1 standard [32]). As shown in Table 1, the Functional suitability requirements are in the subsection 3.2, the Usability requirements are in the subsection 3.3, the Performance efficiency requirements are in the subsection 3.4, the Reliability requirements are in the subsection 3.7.1, and finally two subsections have been integrated in the SRS structure: 3.7.6 and 3.7.7 for i18n and Sustainability requirements, respectively, according to [13]. Each requirement identified has a set of predefined attributes that describes it, such as: a unique Project Unique Identification (PUID), source, description, priority, current state, version history, date and rationale.

4 Results

Based on the existing mPHRs for prenatal care for both iOS and Android, previous studies [33, 2] and scientific literature related to pregnancy [34, 35, 36] (Step 1 in Fig. 1), the requirements of mPHRs for prenatal care have been extracted (Step 2 in Fig. 1). Note that the requirements related to i18n and Sustainability have been slightly adapted to mPHRs for prenatal care according to [13] and [5].

The requirements of mPHRs for prenatal care are presented in Table 2.

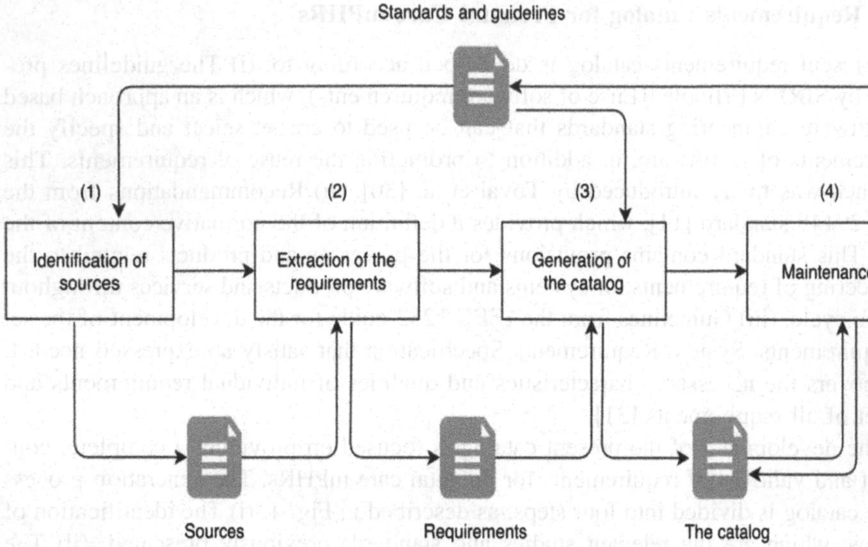

Standards and guidelines

(1) (2) (3) (4)

Identification of sources

Extraction of the requirements

Generation of the catalog

Maintenance

Sources

Requirements

The catalog

Fig. 1. Generation process of the catalog

4.1 Illustration Using an mPHR for Prenatal Care: Pregnancy +

In order to illustrate how to apply the developed catalog to evaluate an mPHR for prenatal care, we selected Pregnancy +, which is the most downloaded, best reviewed and free mPHR in Google Play store. Pregnancy + is available for both Android and iOS mobile operating systems. However, the Android version has been considered in this study since the popularity of Android: in December 2018, Android had a worldwide market share of 75.16 percent, according to [37].

The review score of this app is 4.6 of 5 stars, which is considered as very high, and the number of total installs exceeds ten millions. Note that these information were extracted in March 2019.

A questionnaire including 30 questions has been generated from the developed catalog. This questionnaire has been used in the evaluation of the app "Pregnancy +", and contained only questions related to relevant requirements in the case of this app.

After installing the app "Pregnancy +", the first author conducted the evaluation on the 1st March 2019. The answers to the questions were either: Yes (1 point), No (0 point) or Partially (0.5 point). The questionnaire of this evaluation is presented in Table 3.

The answers to the questionnaire for the evaluation of the "Pregnancy +" app, as shown in Table 3, are as follows: 2 Partially (6.67%), 15 Yes (50%) and 13 No (43.33%). The questions that got "Partially" as an answer are Q21 and Q28. The reason for which Q21 got this answer, is because the app only provides a weight tracker but not a blood pressure tracker. Moreover, for the question Q28, the app includes the baby trackers (contraction timer and kicks counter); however, the app should be upgraded to the premium version so that the user can use these features. Hence the total score of this app is: (2*0.5 + 15*1)/30 = 53.33%, which is considered as a good score, since more than half of the answers are positive. Nevertheless, there is still room for improvement, as it can be deduced from the answers that are not positively validated.

Table 1. Table of contents (IEEE 29148:2011) [11]

1. Introduction
   - 1.1 Purpose
   - 1.2 Scope
   - 1.3 Overview
   - 1.4 Definitions
2. References
3. Specific requirements
   - 3.1 External interface requirements
   - 3.2 Functions
   - 3.3 Usability requirements
   - 3.4 Performance requirements
   - 3.5 Logical database requirements
   - 3.6 Design constraints
   - 3.7 Software system attributes
     - 3.7.1 Reliability
     - 3.7.2 Availability
     - 3.7.3 Security
     - 3.7.4 Maintainability
     - 3.7.5 Portability
     - 3.7.6 i18n
     - 3.7.7 Sustainability
   - 3.8 Supporting information
4. Verification
5. Appendices

5 Discussion

According to the findings of the evaluation that has been conducted on the app “Pregnancy +”, most of the main requirements are included in this app. However, some of the questions that got “No” as an answer remain very important for an mPHR for prenatal care, such as:

- Q2: It should be stated in the description of an mPHR in the app store that it supports multiple languages, even identifying which are them, in order to encourage users around the world to download and use the app.

Table 2. Requirements identified for prenatal care mPHRs

I18n requirements
1) The tool shall be designed for cultural diversity and multilingual use. 1.1) The mPHR shall adapt its content to the user language preferences. 1.2) The mPHR shall be available in several languages, by providing an easy and clear way to switch them. 1.3) The mPHR shall adapt the help, privacy policy and disclaimer sections to the user language preferences. 1.4) The mPHR shall adapt the pregnancy related terminology to user language preferences. 1.5) The mPHR shall display the text with the correct text align depending on the user language preferences. (From left or right) 2) The mPHR shall use pictures to express ideas. 3) The mPHR shall illustrate the content with icons. 4) The mPHR shall use graphs to present the measurements history (e.g blood pressure, weight). 5) The mPHR shall use appropriate formats, units of measurement and currency for an international audience. 5.1) The mPHR shall adapt the number formatting to the user language preferences. 5.2) The mPHR shall adapt the currency to the user geographic location. 5.3) The mPHR shall adapt the units of measurements to user geographic location. 5.4) The mPHR shall adapt the date and time formatting to the user preferences. 5.5) The mPHR shall adapt the phone numbers to user geographic location. 5.6) The mPHR shall adapt the address to user geographic location. 6) The mPHR shall take into account the first day of the week by geographic location. 7) The mPHR shall adjust the advertisements displayed to the user to avoid cultural discrepancies. 8) The mPHR shall allow the user to manage personal information, such as different countries' specific legislation or regulations regarding user ownership of personal information. 8.1) The user should be able to adjust personal information in accordance with different countries' specific legislation or regulations regarding user ownership of personal information. 8.2) The user should be able to control personal information in accordance with different countries' specific legislation or regulations regarding user ownership of personal information. 8.3) The user should be able to process personal information in accordance with different countries' specific legislation or regulations regarding user ownership of personal information.
Sustainability requirements
1) The mPHR shall have a positive individual impact. 1.1) The mPHR shall respect security and privacy of the user. 1.2) The mPHR shall promote personal health and well-being of the user. 2) The mPHR shall have a positive social impact. 2.1) The mPHR shall allow interaction among users (e.g forums). 2.1.1) The mPHR shall connect to social networks. 2.2) The mPHR shall promote social solidarity and share among users. 3) The mPHR shall have a positive environmental impact. 3.1) The mPHR shall reduce transportation means to find obstetrics and gynecology health centers.

(continued)

Table 2. (*continued*)

3.2) The mPHR shall be convenient for frequent use. 3.3) The mPHR shall connect to other resources (e.g the connection to an EHR). 3.3.1) The mPHR shall back up data in data repositories, drivers or cloud systems. 3.3.2) The mPHR shall use device features such as Bluetooth, Global Positioning System (GPS), camera and fingerprint sensor. 3.3.3) The mPHR shall connect with maps applications to display locations. 3.4) The mPHR shall be energy-efficient. 4) The mPHR shall have a positive technical impact. 4.1) The mPHR shall easily adapt with future updates. 4.2) The mPHR shall shut down in idle mode.
Operability requirements
1) Appropriateness recognizability 1.1) The mPHR home page, with respect to colors, layout and content shall be attractive. 1.2) The content in the screens of the mPHR shall be well positioned. 1.3) The main menu in the mPHR shall be well structured. 1.4) The content in the different sections of the mPHR shall be well classified. 1.5) The presentation of the measurements entered in the mPHR shall be understandable. 1.6) The design and the features of the mPHR shall be compliant. 2) Ease of use 2.1) The degree of mastering the mPHR. 2.2) The degree of ease while using the mPHR. 3) User error protection 3.1) The mPHR shall display dialog boxes if the user enters wrong or missed data. 4) User interface aesthetics 4.1) The mPHR's layout shall be attractive and consistent. 4.2) The fonts used in the mPHR shall be attractive. 4.3) The colors used in the different screens of the mPHR shall be attractive. 4.4) The color theme used in the mPHR shall be consistent. 4.5) The colors used, in terms of their adequacy with each functionality/feature, and with the pregnancy theme shall be appropriate. 4.6) The fonts used in the mPHR shall facilitate the legibility. 4.7) The mPHR shall adapt to the screen orientation (horizontal and vertical). 5) Technical learnability 5.1) The mPHR shall be easy to learn. 5.2) The frequency of the support needed from a technical person to use the mPHR. 5.3) The mPHR shall include a Help/Frequently Asked Questions (FAQ) section.
Functional suitability requirements
1) Functional appropriateness 1.1) The mPHR shall include functionalities that are well integrated and complementary for a better prenatal care. 1.2) The degree of inconsistency of the functionalities/ features for prenatal care in the mPHR while executing the requested tasks, whether it gives the expected results or not. 1.3) The section about the weekly progress of pregnancy for the baby and the expectant woman shall be useful for users.

(*continued*)

Table 2. (*continued*)

1.4) The pregnant woman section shall track at least weight and blood pressure, with the possibility to browse the history of the measurements taken. 1.5) The baby section shall include at least a contraction timer and kicks counter with the possibility to browse the history of the values entered. 1.6) The appointments feature shall include the full details about the appointment, a reminder and the possibility to add notes / questions to the doctor. 1.7) The features and functionalities of the mPHR shall be very clear and simple to access and use. 2) Accuracy 2.1) Any measurement entered to the mPHR shall be accurate and valid.
Reliability requirements
1) The mPHR shall keep the measurements, already taken, available and shall provide the possibility to restore and check them any time while using the app. 2) The mPHR shall provide the option to restore the preferences/ settings each time it is used.
Performance efficiency requirements
1) The navigation between hierarchical screens, in terms of response time, shall be consistent in the mPHR. 2) The user shall be able to make a call from the mPHR to a contact from the phone repository in case of an emergency. 3) The user shall be able to connect the mPHR to an external device. 4) The user shall be able to create an instant health report in the mPHR and send it to the stakeholders.

- Q9: Recovering sensitive data stored in an mPHR for prenatal care is mandatory [21]. Hence backing up data is one of the requirements that must be met.
- Q10: The mPHR for prenatal care should shut down in idle mode for security purposes and for saving the device's battery as well.
- Q24: The home page should be attractive and well structured in order to encourage users to use the mPHR.
- Q7: The presence of a community feature in the mPHR for prenatal care is very important, since users can share and ask about information related to their pregnancies [21]. This can be fostered either by implementing forums or linking social networks to the mPHR. The community feature helps pregnant women interact with each other and gain more support.

Table 3. Assessment questionnaire used for "Pregnancy +"

Question ID	Question	Answer
Q1	-Does the mPHR support multiple languages?	Yes
Q2	-Is the number of languages supported stated in the description of the mPHR in the app store?	No
Q3	-Does the mPHR provide the possibility to choose the units of measurements to be used?	Yes
Q4	-Does the mPHR use pictures / illustrations to explain ideas?	Yes
Q5	-Is there a possibility to browse the history of the measurements taken?	Yes
Q6	-Does the mPHR use graphs to illustrate data history?	Yes
Q7	-Does the mPHR promote interaction among users via social networks?	No
Q8	-Is the mPHR connected to an EHR?	No
Q9	-Is the user able to back up its data?	No
Q10	-Does the mPHR shut down in idle mode?	No
Q11	-Is the user able to find nearby healthcare centers?	No
Q12	-Does the mPHR connect to social networks?	No
Q13	-Does the mPHR adapt to both horizontal and vertical orientations?	No
Q14	-Does the mPHR include a Help or FAQ section to help understand it?	Yes
Q15	-Is the color theme consistent?	Yes
Q16	-Is it possible to connect the mPHR to an external device?	No
Q17	-Is it possible to make a call to an emergency contact from the mPHR?	No
Q18	-Are the measurements filled in the trackers stored in the mPHR?	Yes
Q19	-Does the mPHR remember the preferences / settings already set by the user?	Yes
Q20	-Is the user able to access the mPHR without Internet connection?	Yes
Q21	-Does the pregnant woman's trackers section include a weight and blood pressure trackers?	Partially
Q22	-Are the fonts styles used for the text easily legible?	Yes
Q23	-Are the colors used attractive?	Yes
Q24	-Is the home page well structured?	No
Q25	-Is the navigation between the screens consistent and quick?	Yes
Q26	-Is there a possibility to create an instant health report from the data entered in the trackers?	No
Q27	-Does the mPHR connect with maps applications to display locations?	No
Q28	-Does the baby's trackers section include a contraction timer and kicks counter?	Partially
Q29	-Are the various functionalities of the mPHR well integrated?	Yes
Q30	-Did the design suit the purpose of the mPHR?	Yes

6 Conclusion and Future Work

In this study, a requirements catalog has been developed for prenatal care mPHRs, with respect to i18n, Sustainability, Operability, Performance efficiency, Reliability and Functional suitability in order to help developers and stakeholders extract and disclose requirements for these apps. The content of the catalog was conceived based on guidelines, recommendations, standards and previous studies.

This catalog is targeting stakeholders and developers of mPHRs for prenatal care, since it will help them elicit, identify and validate their potential requirements. It can also be beneficial for the development of further mPHRs for prenatal care or improving the existing ones. The catalog can be used for audit purposes as well [5].

As future work, we intend to conduct an audit on a set of mPHRs for prenatal care, in order to analyze their degree of compliance with the requirements of our catalog. The present catalog can also be improved by covering other quality characteristics of the ISO/IEC 25010 quality model such Maintainability and Compatibility [6].

Acknowledgments. This work was conducted within the research project PEER, 7-246 supported by the US Agency for International Development. The authors would like to thank the National Academy of Science, Engineering and Medicine, and USAID for their support.

References

1. Statista.com: mHealth - Statistics & Facts. https://www.statista.com/topics/2263/mhealth/. Accessed 18 Jan 2019
2. Idri, A., Bachiri, M., Fernández-Alemán, J.L.: A framework for evaluating the software product quality of pregnancy monitoring mobile personal health records. J. Med. Syst. **40**, 50 (2016)
3. Kharrazi, H., Chisholm, R., VanNasdale, D., Thompson, B.: Mobile personal health records: An evaluation of features and functionality. Int. J. Med. Inform. **81**, 579–593 (2012)
4. Healthcare Mobile App Development and mHealth Apps in 2017. https://medium.com/@Adoriasoft_Com/healthcare-mobile-app-development-and-mhealth-apps-in-2017-eb307d-4cad36. Accessed 2 Feb 2019
5. Ouhbi, S., Fernández-Alemán, J.L., Carrillo-de-Gea, J.M., Toval, A., Idri, A.: E-health internationalization requirements for audit purposes. Comput. Methods Programs Biomed. **144**, 49–60 (2017)
6. ISO/IEC FCD 25010, Systems and software engineering – System and software product Quality Requirements and Evaluation (SQuaRE)) – System and software quality models (2014)
7. Brundtland Commission: Our common future: report of the world commission on environment and development. Technical report (1987)
8. Becker, C., Chitchyan, R., Duboc, L., Easterbrook, S., Penzenstadler, B., Seyff, N., Venters, C.C.: Sustainability design and software: the karlskrona manifesto. Proc. - Int. Conf. Softw. Eng. **2**, 467–476 (2015)
9. Calero, C., Piattini, M.: Introduction to green in software engineering. In: Calero, C., Piattini, M. (eds.) Green in Software Engineering, pp. 3–27. Springer, Cham (2015). https://doi.org/10.1007/978-3-319-08581-4_1
10. Penzenstadler, B.: Infusing green: requirements engineering for green in and through software systems. In: Workshop on Requirements Engineering for Sustainable Systems, pp. 44–53, Karlskrona (2014)
11. IEEE Standard: IEEE 29148-2011 - ISO/IEC/IEEE International Standard - Systems and software engineering – Life cycle processes –Requirements engineering (2011)
12. Cruz Zapata, B., Fernández-Alemán, J.L., Toval, A., Idri, A.: Reusable software usability specifications for mhealth applications. J. Med. Syst. **42**, 45 (2018)
13. Ouhbi, S., Fernández-Alemán, J.L., Idri, A., Toval, A., Pozo, J.R., El Bajta, M.: A reusable requirements catalog for internationalized and sustainable blood donation Apps, pp. 285–292 (2017)
14. Ouhbi, S., Fernández-Alemán, J.L., Toval, A., Rivera Pozo, J., Idri, A.: Sustainability requirements for connected health applications. J. Softw. Evol. Process. **30**, e1922 (2018)
15. Jensen, J., Tøndel, I.A., Jaatun, M.G., Meland, P.H., Andresen, H.: Reusable security requirements for healthcare applications. In: 2009 International Conference on Availability, Reliability and Security, pp. 380–385. IEEE (2009)
16. Ukoha, E.P., Yee, L.M.: Use of electronic patient portals in pregnancy: an overview. J. Midwifery Womens. Health. **63**, 335–339 (2018)

17. Monkman, H., Kushniruk, A.: Considerations for personal health record procurement. In: Courtney, K.L., Shabestari, O. (eds.) Enabling Health and Healthcare through ICT, pp. 308–313. IOS Press, Amsterdam (2013)
18. Lee, L.-H., Chou, Y.-T., Huang, E.-W., Liou, D.-M.: Design of a personal health record and health knowledge sharing system using IHE-XDS and OWL. J. Med. Syst. **37**, 9921 (2013)
19. Liu, L.S., Shih, P.C., Hayes, G.R.: Barriers to the adoption and use of personal health record systems. In: Proceedings of 2011 iConference - iConference 2011, pp. 363–370 (2011)
20. Day, K., Gu, Y.: Influencing factors for adopting personal health record (PHR). Stud. Health Technol. Inform. **178**, 39–44 (2012)
21. Bachiri, M., Idri, A., Fernández-Alemán, J.L., Toval, A.: Mobile personal health records for pregnancy monitoring functionalities: analysis and potential. Comput. Methods Programs Biomed. **134**, 121–135 (2016)
22. Idri, A., Bachiri, M., Fernandez-Aleman, J.L., Toval, A.: ISO/IEC 25010 based evaluation of free mobile personal health records for pregnancy monitoring. In: 2017 IEEE 41st Annual Computer Software and Applications Conference (COMPSAC), pp. 262–267. IEEE (2017)
23. ISO/TR 14292:2012 - Health informatics – Personal health records – Definition, scope and context (2012)
24. ISO/TR 20514:2005 - Health informatics – Electronic health record – Definition, scope and context (2005)
25. W3C. The web and mobile devices. https://www.w3.org/Mobile/. Accessed 17 Jan 2019
26. ISO/TS 14265:2011 - Health Informatics - Classification of purposes for processing personal health information (2011)
27. ISO/TR 18307:2001 - Health informatics – Interoperability and compatibility in messaging and communication standards – Key characteristics (2001)
28. ISO/HL7 27931:2009 - Data Exchange Standards – An application protocol for electronic data exchange in healthcare environments (2009)
29. ISO 21090:2011 - Health informatics – Harmonized data types for information interchange (2011)
30. Toval, A., Nicolás, J., Moros, B., García, F.: Requirements reuse for improving information systems security: a practitioner's approach. Requir. Eng. **6**, 205–219 (2002)
31. IEEE: IEEE Std 1233, 1998 Edition : IEEE Guide for Developing System Requirements Specifications. IEEE (1998)
32. International Organization for Standardization (ISO): ISO 9126-1: Software engineering – Product quality – Part 1: Quality model, Geneva (2003)
33. Bachiri, M., Idri, A., Fernández-Alemán, J.L., Toval, A.: Mobile personal health records for pregnancy monitoring functionalities: Analysis and potential. Comput. Methods Programs Biomed. **134**, 121–135 (2016)
34. Queensland Maternity and Neonatal Clinical Guidelines program: Queensland Maternity and Neonatal Operational Framework: Maternity Shared Care, Queensland (2011)
35. American Academy of Pediatrics committee on fetus and newborn, American College of Obstetricians and Gynecologists committee on Obstetric practice: Guidelines for perinatal care. American Academy of Pediatrics (2012)
36. (WHO), W.H.O.: Pregnancy, Childbirth, Postpartum, and Newborn Care: A Guide for Essential Practice, Geneva (2006)
37. Statista.com: Mobile operating systems' market share worldwide from January 2012 to December 2018. https://www.statista.com/statistics/272698/global-market-share-held-by-mobile-operating-systems-since-2009/. Accessed 20 Feb 2019

Prediction of SQL Injection Attacks in Web Applications

Chamundeswari Arumugam[1(✉)], Varsha Bhargavi Dwarakanathan[1(✉)], S. Gnanamary[1(✉)], Vishalraj Natarajan Neyveli[1(✉)], Rohit Kanakuppaliyalil Ramesh[1(✉)], Yeshwanthraa Kandhavel[1(✉)], and Sadhanandhan Balakrishnan[2(✉)]

[1] Department of Computer Science and Engineering, SSN College of Engineering, Kalavakkam, Chennai, Tamil Nadu, India
chamundeswaria@ssn.edu.in, {varsha15120, gnanamary15304, vishalraj1612, rohit16086, yeshwanthraa16128}@cse.ssn.edu.in
[2] Indium Software (India) Limited, Chennai, India
Sadhanandh.b@indiumsoft.com

Abstract. As web applications become increasingly complex and connected, it becomes imperative to reduce the vulnerabilities in applications. SQLIA is a part of OWASP vulnerabilities and it is extremely important to prevent them. The proposed system aims to predict the occurrence of SQLIA on a given server, with applications deployed on it, from a given source, at a particular time. This prediction can be done with the help of JMeter tool. Apache JMeter is used to simulate logs data. From this, one can pre-process, extract features, and classify, which is then fed to a model for prediction of SQLIA.

Keywords: SQL injection · Web application · Classification · Prediction

1 Introduction

It is no secret that the world has become increasingly dependent on technology in the past decade. Many factors have led an increasing number of organizations and individuals to rely on web-based applications to provide access to a variety of services. However, insecure software is undermining our security-critical environments such as finance, healthcare, defense, energy, etc. As applications become increasingly complex and connected, the importance of achieving application security increases exponentially. It is imperative to reduce the vulnerabilities in applications and make them impervious to attacks.

Web application vulnerabilities [15] involve a system flaw or weakness in a web-based application. They have been around for years, largely due to not validating or sanitizing form inputs, misconfigured web servers, and application design flaws. Validation checks if the input meets a set of criteria (such as a string contains no standalone single quotation marks). Sanitization [7] modifies the input to ensure that it is valid (such as doubling single quotes).

S. Misra et al. (Eds.): ICCSA 2019, LNCS 11622, pp. 496–505, 2019.
https://doi.org/10.1007/978-3-030-24305-0_37

Many of the servers that store critical data for websites and services use SQL to manage the data in their databases. An SQL Injection Attack (SQLIA) [16] specifically targets this kind of server, using malicious code to get the server to divulge information it normally would not. Successful SQLIA typically occur because a vulnerable application does not properly sanitize inputs provided by the user. Cross Site Scripting (XSS) [8] attack also involves injecting malicious code into a website. Cross-site scripting allows an attacker to execute malicious scripts in another user's browser. One of the most common ways an attacker can deploy a cross-site scripting attack is by injecting malicious code into an input field that would be automatically run when other visitors view the infected page.

The objective of the paper is to predict SQLIA in the web application. Apache JMeter, an open source software was used as a load generator to create log data. From log data, the preprocessing is done to perform feature extraction. With respect to the prediction, the logistic regression model was used. The paper is organized as follows: Sect. 2 describes about the related work of SQLIA while Sect. 3 describes about the proposed system and implementation of this work. Section 4 discuss about the results while Sect. 5 describes about the conclusion.

2 Literature Survey

Scholte et al. [1] present a study of input validation vulnerabilities with the aim of gaining deeper in-sights into how these common web vulnerabilities can be prevented. They focus on the relationship between the specific programming language used to develop web applications and the vulnerabilities that are commonly reported, and found that most SQLIA and XSS vulnerabilities can be prevented using straightforward validation mechanisms based on common data types. Alkhalaf et al. [2] talk about input validation and sanitization. They propose to use the validation and sanitization functions as input to the algorithm, which will perform differential repair. The main aim is to remove redundancy at server side as well as at other checking instances. The repair algorithm takes the validation and sanitization functions as input and aims to repair the semantic difference.

Frajták et al. [3] concentrate on reducing user input validation code in web applications using Pex extension. Pex is a white box testing input generator for .NET applications. This approach reduces the amount of code created by developers. The code that validates the values of method input parameters does not have to be duplicated in JavaScript and this code is updated whenever a change is made to the code of the method that handles client request. Li et al. [4] summarizes all the known vulnerabilities and attacks. They present a survey of recent techniques and approaches for server side securing of web applications. Cho et al. [5] proposed a technique, which verifies input values of Java-based web applications using static byte code instrumentation and runtime input validation. This approach searches for target methods or object constructors in compiled Java class files, and statically inserts byte code modules.

Medeiros et al. [6] discussed the use of static analysis to detect vulnerabilities in web applications. They then use the output and apply data mining techniques to detect and reduce the number of false positives. Solomon et al. [9] applied machine learning predictive analytics to predict and prevent SQLIA in cloud hosted web application. An web proxy application programming interface to accurately predict malicious SQLIA in web request was provided as a web service for protecting back-end database. Jingling et al. [14] proposed a dynamic taint tracking approach to explore SQLI and XSS vulnerabilities in web applications. WOVSQLI [10], one of the SQLIA tool was developed to detect the attack. This tool with SQL word vector and LSTM neural networks was used to detect the SQLIA in web application. A large dataset was used to demonstrate the accuracy of the tool.

A tool to detect SQLIA AMNESIA [12] was implemented for Java-based web applications and tested on five real time application without producing false positive. Haldar et al. [11] proposed a tagging and tracking approach to detect the user input in web application so as to prevent number of attacks. Komiya et al. [13] suggested to adapt machine learning approach for classification and detection of malicious user inputs in web code. Thus, vulnerability prediction is important and this work considers the SQLIA for prediction.

3 Proposed System

For a given system, where a system is considered to be a server and the applications hosted on it, the solution aims to predict the chance of SQLIA to occur, from a particular place, at a particular time. For prediction, raw data is collected from the server logs. The Source IP gives the location from which a particular request is generated. The data and time give information as to when a particular request hits the server. This data from the server's log is pre-processed and the dataset is formed. Therefore, given a server and deployed applications, there is historic data. As the server gets more and more hits, the log data also increases, thus enabling the model to learn better, and in turn predict more accurately in real time.

From an application point-of-view, given a query to an application, it has to go via the server. This again gets recorded in the logs. Now, using request parameters and destination page information, it can also be found out as to what particular application this attack was directed at. The reason this is done is as follows. Consider Application A, as a standalone application may have some vulnerability based on the code. However, A can be deployed on Server X as well as on Server Y. Request to different servers will be different, in the sense that, they can come from different sources, and at different times, and A might be less vulnerable when deployed on X than it might be when deployed on Y. To tackle this problem, the proposed solution represented in Fig. 1, considers both the server and the applications hosted on it at any time as a whole system and then predicts SQLIA. The data saved in the access log is preprocessed and features are extracted. This is followed by classification and prediction.

3.1 Implementation

SQL (Structured Query Language) injection [16] is an important attack methodology that targets the data residing in a database through the firewall that shields it. The attack takes advantage of poor input validation in code and website administration. SQL

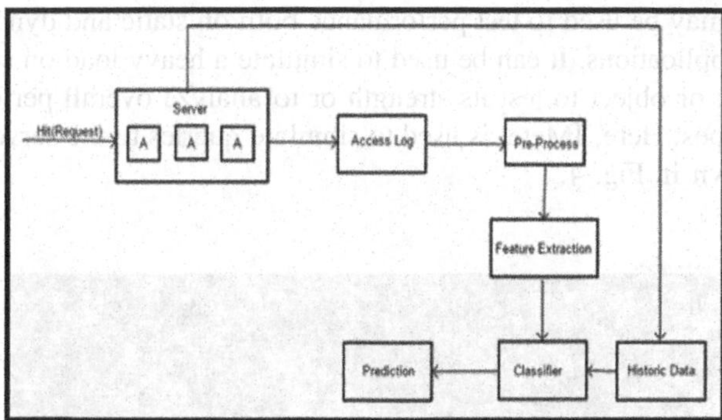

Fig. 1. Proposed system

Injection Attacks occur when an attacker is able to insert a series of SQL statements into a query by manipulating user input data in to a web-based application. The attacker can take advantage of web application programming security flaws, pass unexpected malicious SQL statements, and query through a web application for execution by the back-end database.

For example, consider the PHP code segment-1 as provided in Fig. 2. If the user enters value; DROP TABLE table; as the input, the query becomes as shown in Fig. 3. which is undesirable, as here the user input is directly compiled along with the pre-written SQL query. Hence the user will be able to enter an SQL query required to manipulate the database.

```
$variable = $_POST['input'];
mysql_query("INSERT INTO `table` (`column`) VALUES ('$variable')");
```

Fig. 2. PHP code segment-1

```
INSERT INTO `table` (`column`) VALUES('value'); DROP TABLE table;--')
```

Fig. 3. PHP code segment-2

3.2 Creation of Dataset and Classification

Apache JMeter is an Apache project that can be used as a load testing tool for analyzing and measuring the performance of a variety of services, with a focus on web applications. The Apache JMeter application is a open source software, a Java application designed to load test functional behavior and measure performance. It was originally designed for testing Web Applications but has since expanded to other test functions.

Apache JMeter may be used to test performance both on static and dynamic resources, Web dynamic applications. It can be used to simulate a heavy load on server, group of servers, network or object to test its strength or to analyze overall performance under different load types. Here, JMeter is used to simulate queries to the server and generate log data as shown in Fig. 4.

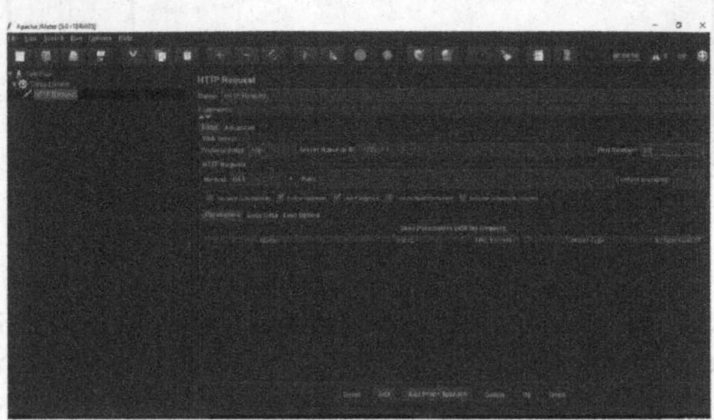

Fig. 4. JMeter tool to generate log data

Any request to the web server is recorded in its logs. This log data contains SourceIP, Date and Time, Request Parameter, and Destination pages. This raw data is used for creation of the dataset. For creation of log data, two PHP web applications have been used as shown in Fig. 5.

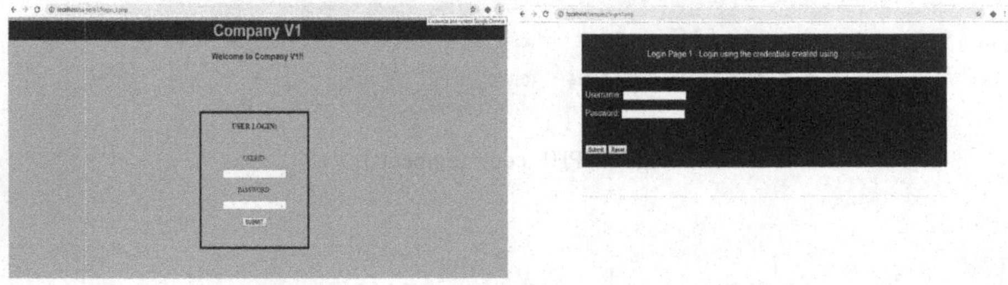

Fig. 5. Two PHP web application to create log data

WAMP server has been used for deployment of these applications. Both applications work on MySQL Database. Here, in order to create a huge training set, log data is simulated manually. These applications were hit with numerous requests via JMeter, in order to create multiple entries in the access log file. Working of JMeter is represented in Fig. 6.

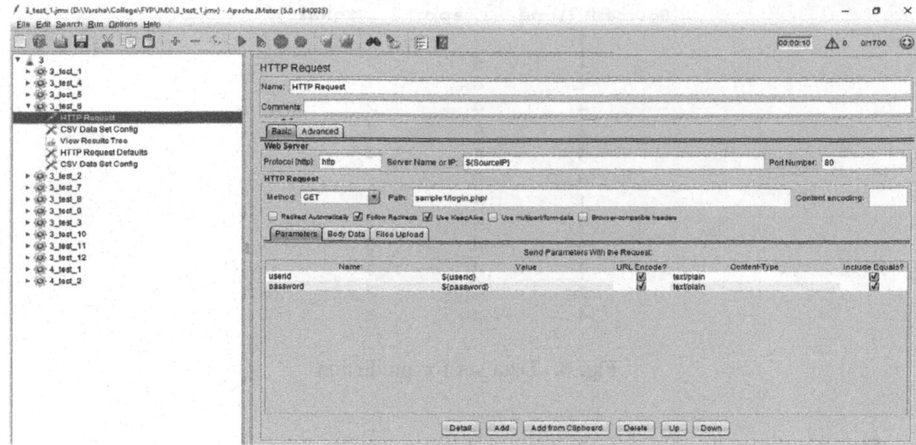

Fig. 6. JMeter working

Requests to these applications are recorded in the Apache Access logs. The access log is stored as a text file. This text file is converted into a csv file. From csv file, the *Source IP, Date, Time, Request parameter* and *Target application* features are extracted it is represented in Fig. 7. SQLIA related key words are extracted from the Request Parameter in order to predict SQLIA.

SourceIP	Time	Request	Sqlia
192.168.0.104	[27/Feb/2019:15:55:33	/sample1/login.php/?userid=Drop+table&password=pass	
192.168.0.103	[27/Feb/2019:15:55:33	/sample1/login.php/?userid=user1&password=pass1	
192.168.0.103	[27/Feb/2019:15:55:33	/sample1/login.php/?userid=user2&password=pass2	
192.168.0.106	[27/Feb/2019:15:55:33	/sample2/?products=-+%27+order+by+5+--+%2F%2F	
192.168.0.104	[27/Feb/2019:15:55:33	/sample1/login.php/?userid=Drop+table&password=pass	
192.168.0.106	[27/Feb/2019:15:55:33	/sample1/login.php/?userid=user8&password=pass8	
192.168.0.106	[27/Feb/2019:15:55:33	/sample2/?products=pillows	
192.168.0.103	[27/Feb/2019:15:55:33	/sample2/?products=-+%27+union+select+1	
192.168.0.106	[27/Feb/2019:15:55:33	/sample2/?products=book+shelf++	
192.168.0.105	[27/Feb/2019:15:55:33	/sample2/login1/?username=user2&password=pass2	

Fig. 7. Feature extraction from access log.

85 SQLIA commands where collected from research and they are used to compare with the SQL command in *Request parameter.* Using this the query is classified as *SQLIA* or not. These data is converted into a Dataset that can be fed into a logistic regression model. The Dataset comprises of features *Source IP, Time, Target application* and *SQLIA* and it is represented in Fig. 8.

SourceIP	Time	app	Sqlia1
2	4	1	1
1	4	1	0
1	4	1	0
4	4	2	1
2	4	1	1
4	4	1	0
4	4	2	0
1	4	2	0
4	4	2	0
3	4	3	0
3	4	3	1
2	4	3	0
4	4	3	1

Fig. 8. Data set for prediction

4 Prediction

Data Prediction refers to an area of statistics that deals with extracting information from data and using it to predict trends and behavior patterns. Here, it is done to predict the chance of SQLIA to occur on a system (Server and applications deployed on it) from a given place, at a particular time. For this prediction, logistic regression is used.

Logistic regression [17] is an classification algorithm, that is used where the response variable is categorical. The idea of logistic regression is to find a relationship between features and probability of particular outcome. Logistic regression works with binary data, where either the event happens (1) or the event does not happen (0). So given some feature it tries to find out whether some event y happens or not. So *y* can be either 0 or 1. In the case where the event happens, *y* is given the value 1. If the event does not happen, then *y* is given the value of 0. Logistic regression uses the sigmoid function, which gives an 'S' shaped curve to model the data. The curve is restricted between 0 and 1, so it is easy to apply when *y* is binary.

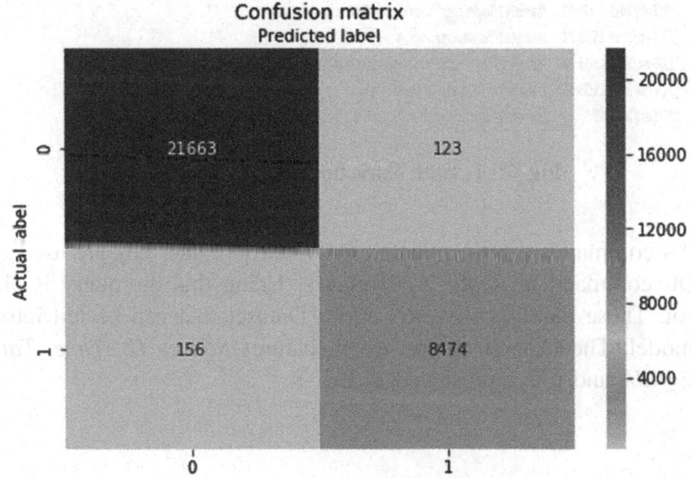

Fig. 9. Confusion matrix

From research, it was found that the following words occur with decreasing order of frequency in SQLIA Queries: Union Select, All, And, where, or, as, from, like, etc. Thus, the model was built and trained according to the key-words found in the request parameter. Out of a data set of about 1,00,000, 70% was used for training, and the rest for testing. Dataset comprising of *Source IP, Time, Target application* and *SQLIA* are fed to the model. For logistic regression, consider *Source IP, Time, Target application*, and *SQLIA* as independent variables and SQLIA as dependent variables. This model gives a 72% accuracy. This can be seen in the confusion matrix and the ROC curve as shown in Figs. 9 and 10.

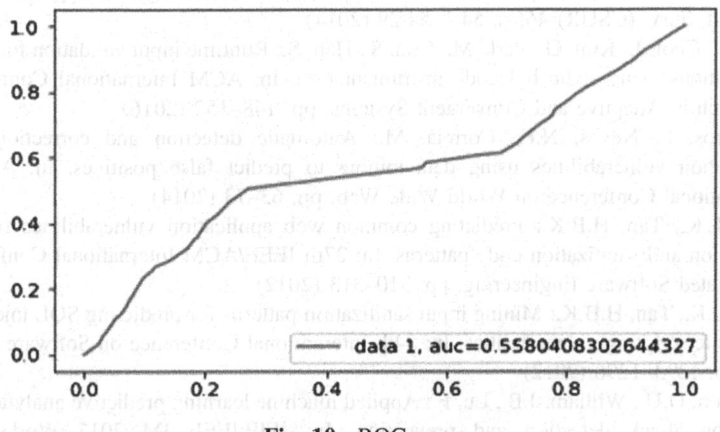

Fig. 10. ROC curve

5 Conclusion

Vulnerabilities prediction is a challenging task and it is addressed in this work. Here the web application was developed and deployed in a server. For the deployed application, the JMeter software was used to generate the log files. The log files was used here and SQL queries statement was taken for prediction. The chance of SQLIA to occur on a deployed web application from a given place, at a particular time was predicted. For this prediction, logistic regression was used on 1,00,000 data points. 70% was used for training, and the rest for testing. The model gives an 72% accuracy to predict SQL injection.

As a future work, a module can be implemented to raise an alarm, when an SQL Injection Attack occurs. Also, from the Source IP, one can backtrack to determine the actual physical location from which the attack is coming. The actual user can also be identified in the process. Deep learning methods and Tree regressors can be implemented for better results.

References

1. Scholte, T., Robertson, W., Balzarotti, D., Kirda., E.: An empirical analysis of input validation mechanisms in web applications and languages. In: 27th Annual ACM Symposium on Applied Computing, pp. 1419–1426 (2012)
2. Alkhalaf, M., Aydin, A., Bultan, T.: Semantic differential repair for input validation and sanitization. In: ACM International Symposium on Software Testing and Analysis, pp. 225–236 (2014)
3. Frajták, K., Bureš, M., Jelínek, I.: Reducing user input validation code in web applications using Pex extension. In: ACM 15th International Conference on Computer Systems and Technologies, pp. 302–308 (2014)
4. Li, X., Xue, Y.: A survey on server-side approaches to securing web applications. ACM Comput. Surv. (CSUR) **46**(4), 54:1–54:29 (2014)
5. Cho, S., Choi, J., Kim, G., Park, M., Cho, S., Han, S.: Runtime input validation for Java web applications using static bytecode instrumentation. In: ACM International Conference on Research in Adaptive and Convergent Systems, pp. 148–152 (2016)
6. Medeiros, I., Neves, N.F., Correia, M.: Automatic detection and correction of web application vulnerabilities using data mining to predict false positives. In: ACM 23rd International Conference on World Wide Web, pp. 63–73 (2014)
7. Shar, L.K., Tan, H.B.K.: Predicting common web application vulnerabilities from input validation and sanitization code patterns. In: 27th IEEE/ACM International Conference on Automated Software Engineering, pp. 310–313 (2012)
8. Shar, L.K., Tan, H.B.K.: Mining input sanitization patterns for predicting SQL injection and cross site scripting vulnerabilities. In: 34th International Conference on Software Engineering, pp. 1293–1296 (2012)
9. Solomon, O.U., William, J.B., Lu, F.: Applied machine learning predictive analytics to SQL injection attack detection and prevention. In: IFIP/IEEE IM 2017 Workshop: 3rd International Workshop on Security for Emerging Distributed Network Technologies, pp. 1087–1090 (2017)
10. Fang, Y., Peng, J., Liu, L., Huang, C.: WOVSQLI: detection of SQL injection behaviors using word vector and LSTM. In: Proceedings of the 2nd International Conference on Cryptography, Security and Privacy, pp. 170–174 (2018)
11. Haldar, V., Chandra, D., Franz, M.: Dynamic taint propagation for Java. In: Annual Computer Security Applications Conference, pp. 09–15 (2005)
12. Halfond, W.G.J., Orso, A.: AMNESIA analysis and monitoring for neutralizing SQL-injection attacks. In: Proceedings of IEEE and ACM International Conference on Automatic Software Engineering, Long Beach, CA, USA, pp. 54–59 (2005)
13. Komiya, R., Paik, I., Hisada, M.: Classification of malicious web code by machine learning. In: 3rd International Conference on Awareness Science and Technology (iCAST), pp. 406–411 (2011)
14. Jingling, Z., Junxin, Q., Liang, Z., Baojiang, C.: Dynamic taint tracking of Web application based on static code analysis. In: 10th International Conference on Innovative Mobile and Internet Services in Ubiquitous Computing, pp. 96–101 (2016)
15. Kumar, S., Mahajan, R., Kumar, N., Khatri, S.K.: A study on web application security and detecting security vulnerabilities. In: 6th International Conference on Reliability, Infocom Technologies and Optimization (ICRITO), pp. 451–455 (2017)

16. Jane, P.Y., Chaudhari, M.S.: SQLIA: detection and prevention techniques: a survey. IOSR J. Comput. Eng. (IOSR-JCE) **2**, 56–60 (2009). Second International Conference on Emerging Trends in Engineering (SICETE)
17. Peng, C.J., Lee, K.L., Ingersoll, G.M.: An introduction to logistic regression analysis and reporting. J. Educ. Res. **96**, 3–14 (2002)

A Chatbot for Goal-Oriented Requirements Modeling

Danilo Arruda[1], Matheus Marinho[1], Eric Souza[2], and Fernando Wanderley[1(✉)]

[1] Universidade Católica de Pernambuco, UNICAP, Recife, Pernambuco, Brazil
darruda.silva2@gmail.com, matheuzmarinho@gmail.com,
fernando.wanderley@unicap.br

[2] Universidade Nova de Lisboa, UNL, Lisboa, Portugal
er.souza@campus.fct.unl.pt

Abstract. Goal-Oriented Requirements Engineering approaches, in which the KAOS framework plays a key role, have been widely used for eliciting software requirements because they provide an easier way of communicating among stakeholders. However, the goal-oriented requirements modeling is not an easy way for novice requirements engineers. These professionals need more support in creating KAOS models. Recent studies have focused on the applicability of Artificial Intelligence techniques (e.g., Natural Language Processing – NLP) to support Requirements Engineering activities. In this sense, this paper aims to describe a way to support requirements elicitation for novice requirements engineers through the use of NLP within a chatbot. The chatbot (*KAOSbot*) acts as a KAOS modeling assistant. To evaluate our hypotheses about perceived efficacy from the novice requirements engineers perspective, we performed a quasi-experiment concerning *KAOSbot's* perceived ease of use, perceived usefulness and intention to use. The results show that *KAOSbot* tool is a promising approach for specifying KAOS models because it was perceived as easy to use, useful, and the participants intend to use it in the future.

Keywords: Goal-Oriented Requirements Engineering · KAOS modeling · Chatbot · Natural Language Processing · Quasi-experiment

1 Introduction

Goal-oriented requirements engineering (GORE) is a paradigm concerned with the use of goals for eliciting, documenting, and modifying requirements [30]. The main motivations of GORE approaches are [8]: (i) greater understanding of the client's objectives; (ii) better communication among project stakeholders; (iii) ability to trace the origin of a software requirement; (iv) conflict management among software requirements. The KAOS framework is the most commonly used GORE approach [8, 28, 32], and makes it possible to build a model of the whole

S. Misra et al. (Eds.): ICCSA 2019, LNCS 11622, pp. 506–519, 2019.
https://doi.org/10.1007/978-3-030-24305-0_38

system, not just the software part of it [21]. However, the goal modeling task is not an easy way for novice requirements engineers [22,30]. As a consequence, it requires more support in the KAOS modeling tasks by less experienced professionals [30].

Recent studies have focused on the applicability of Artificial Intelligence techniques to support Software Engineering activities [5,14]. For example, the needs to extract information from textual documents used as requirements source has motivated a lot of researches on the application of Natural Language Processing (NLP) in requirements engineering area [4,9,11,25].

In this sense, this paper aims to describe a way to support requirements elicitation for novice requirements engineers through the use of NLP within a chatbot. For this, we develop the KAOSbot, a proof-of-concept chatbot for KAOS modeling that acts as modeling assistant for novice requirements engineers. To evaluate our hypotheses about perceived efficacy from the novice requirements engineers perspective, we performed a quasi-experiment to check *the perceived ease of use and the perceived usefulness* for the KAOSbot tool when producing KAOS models. In addition, we also evaluate the participants' intention to use the tool in the future. This quasi-experiment was performed following the best practices of Evidence-Based Software Engineering (EBSE) community. The results show that *KAOSBot* tool is a promising approach for novice requirements engineers specify KAOS models because it was perceived as easy to use, useful, and the participants intend to use it in the future.

The rest of this paper is organized as follows: Sect. 2 discuss about the background theory contained the main concerns for our work: (i) Goal-Oriented Requirements Engineering including KAOS framework, (ii) Natural Language Processing for Requirements Engineering and (iii) Chatbot. Section 3 describes the architecture and operation of KAOSbot. Section 4 presents the evaluation of KAOSbot. Section 5 presents the related works to our paper and Sect. 6 the main conclusions about our work.

2 Background

This section presents a brief overview of the three essential elements of our approach: (i) Goal-Oriented Requirements Engineering, (ii) Natural Language Processing for Requirements Engineering, and (iii) Chatbot.

2.1 Goal-Oriented Requirements Engineering

Goal-Oriented Requirements Engineering (GORE) [29] is a paradigm that concerns in use goals in the various activities of the Requirements Engineering (RE) such as eliciting, elaborating, structuring, specifying, analyzing, negotiating, documenting, and modifying requirements. The KAOS approach [29] is the most commonly used GORE approaches [8,28,32]. The KAOS model helps to fit problem descriptions by allowing requirements engineers to define and manipulate concepts relevant to problem description and improves the domain analysis by providing a systematic approach for discovering and structuring requirements. KAOS also clarifies the responsibilities of all the project stakeholders and facilitates the stakeholder's communication about the requirements by offering a graphical model to discussion [21]. The main advantage of KAOS is its ability to align requirements for business goals. This alignment increases the chances that the new development will add value to business [1].

In KAOS, a goal can be defined as the intent statement that the system must achieve. It is refined into sub-goals that explain HOW that goal should be achieved. Goal refinement ends when a sub-goal is performed by an agent. Then, this sub-goal becomes a requirement or expectation. An agent can be a human (environment agent) or an automated component (system agent). Requirements must be satisfied by a system agent. Expectations must be satisfied by an environment agent.

This work aims to support less experienced requirements engineers on creating KAOS models through a chatbot tool.

2.2 Natural Language Processing for Requirements Engineering

Natural Language Processing (NLP) is a subset of Artificial Intelligence that concerns the development of computer programs related to understanding, writing or speech in a Natural Language (NL). [6] NLP covers a set of techniques for manipulating and analyzing NL in an automated manner [11,13,25]. Text mining is one of the NLP techniques used to derive high-quality information from text, and there are some available tools in the literature to facilitate its processing (e.g., Stanford CoreNLP [16]). Text mining has often been used to improve and automate RE tasks [15]. For example, it is used to detect inconsistencies in requirements [9], and construct domain models from textual documents [13,19].

In this work, we develop a chatbot tool to interact with user in a textual way. In this sense, NLP techniques was used to interpret what the user writes.

2.3 Chatbot

Thanks to advances in artificial intelligence and NLP techniques, conversational systems have been increasingly used [31]. Chatbots are systems that interact with humans to answer questions on a specific domain [26] and they are used in several domains such as customer service, education, and financial advising [31]. Through an interface, people talk by voice or by typing with a computer system in the same way they would chat others people. Because there is no need for installation packages, chatbots are fast and trouble-free to be used in practice [20]. In general, a chatbot can understand the context of a conversation and learn from the chats, improving itself over time by using Machine Learning techniques [2].

We have created a chatbot tool responsible for conducting a conversation with the user to elicit requirements within the context of the KAOS goal-oriented requirements engineering method.

3 KAOSbot

This section describes a proposed solution to facilitate generating KAOS models by less experienced requirements engineers. First, we introduce the approach to elicit goals through a chatbot tool. After, we described the chat flow process (KAOSbot Interface) and the algorithm used to identify the goal concept in natural language sentences written in English (KAOSbot Service).

3.1 The Approach

We have proposed a chatbot-based tool to support goal-oriented requirements elicitation with the KAOS framework. This tool, named KAOSbot, has the role of hold a chat with the user to extract relevant information about a domain in question. Therefore, KAOSbot identifies Goals, Expectations, Requirements, and Agents through NLP techniques.

KAOSbot is composed of two parts: the *graphical interface* and *service*. The *graphical interface* is responsible for conducting the conversation with the user. On another hand, the KAOSbot's *service* is responsible for getting natural language sentences and extracting KAOS concepts in them.

Figure 1 shows a chat example between the human user and the chatbot. The user interacts with the KAOSBot interface through textual messages written in English. The KAOSbot Interface forwards the user's message to the KAOSbot service. Then, the KAOSbot Service identifies and extracts the KAOS concepts from the user's message using NLP techniques. Next, KAOSbot Service returns KAOS concept extracted to the KAOSbot Interface. After receiving the KAOS concept, KAOSbot Interface knows precisely where to represent the concept into the model, through the chat context.

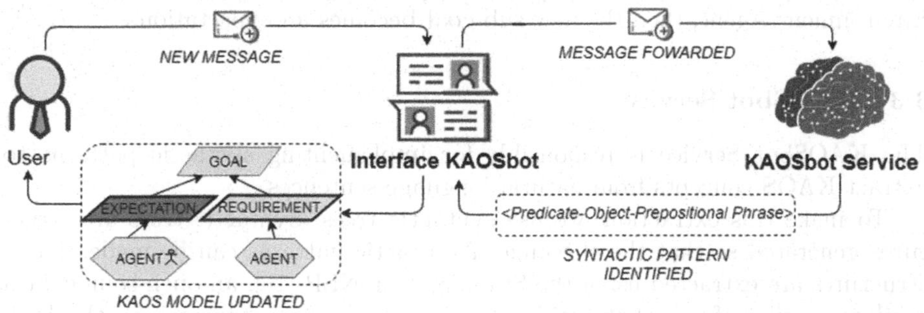

Fig. 1. Approach overview

3.2 KAOSbot Interface

Figure 2 shows the three areas that makes the KAOSbot's graphical interface: legend, modeling, and chat. The legend area shows the graphic representations of

KAOS concepts (Fig. 2-left). The modeling area shows the KAOS model which is being generated (Fig. 2-middle) according to messages typed on chat (Fig. 2-right). Through this chat, KAOSbot extracts useful information related to KAOS concepts and updates the model in the modeling area, providing continuous visual feedback on how current the model is.

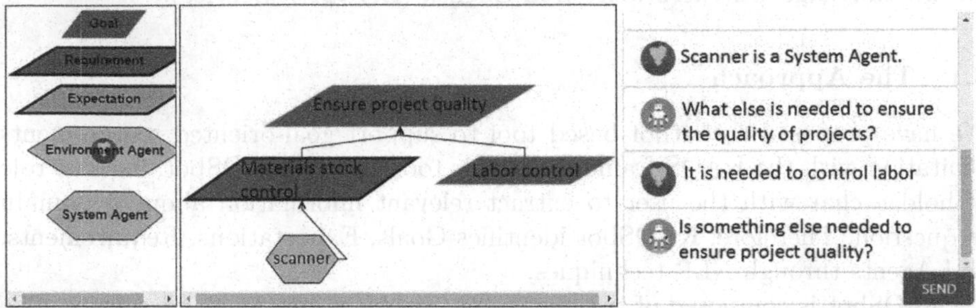

Fig. 2. KAOSbot interface

The KAOSbot conducts a chat flow as shown in Fig. 3. The chatbot starts by asking what the primary goal of the user is. Next, It then wants to know, at an abstract high-level, what goals should be realized for that the primary goal is satisfied. After achieving the primary goal and all its main sub goals, KAOSbot conducts a conversation in order to refine each identified subgoal and extract its requirements and expectations. KAOSbot refines the goals until a new subgoal is performed by an agent. KAOSbot then asks whether the agent responsible for the new subgoal is an Environment Agent or a System Agent. If the agent is a System Agent, then the new subgoal becomes a requirement. If the agent is an Environment Agent, then the new sub goal becomes an expectation.

3.3 KAOSbot Service

The KAOSbot Service is responsible for implementing syntactic patterns to extract KAOS concepts from natural language sentences.

To make this extraction, we use syntactic trees. Syntactic trees are structures generated so that the checking of syntactic patterns can be made. These structures are extracted using the Stanford CoreNLP [16], an open-source Java implementation of a probabilistic natural language parser trained on the Wall Street Journal document collection. KAOSbot uses the version 3.9.1 of the Stanford Parser.

The process of KAOS goal extraction works according to Fig. 4. First, the user's message is transformed into the syntactic tree through the Stanford CoreNLP library. Second, the parsed tree is submitted to the algorithm of identification of syntactic patterns, which verifies the pattern that fits the generated syntactic tree.

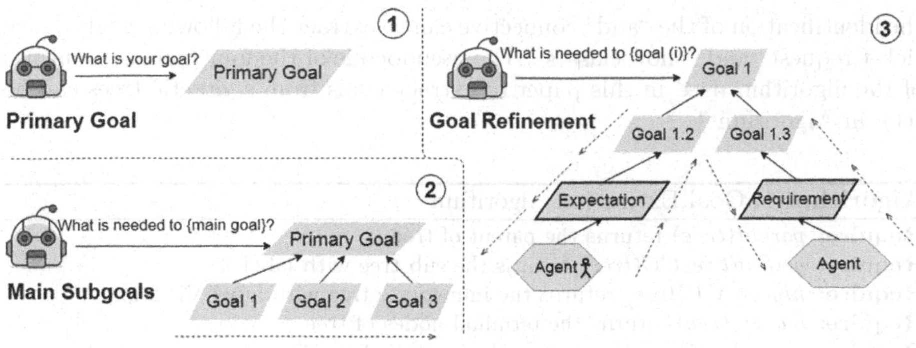

Fig. 3. KAOSbot conversation flow

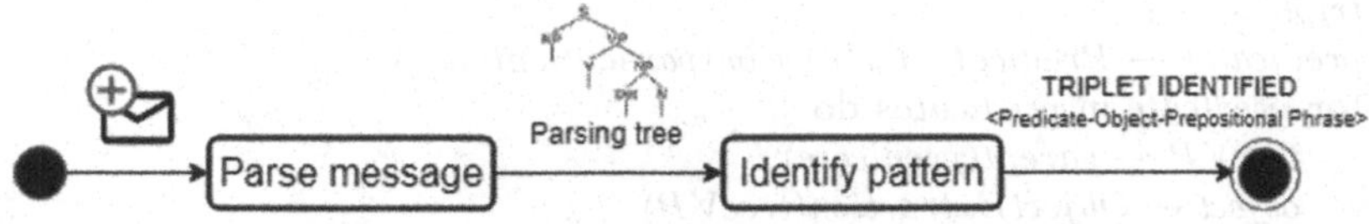

Fig. 4. Processing a NL message to identify goal

The main part of the goal extraction is to identify the corresponding syntactic pattern in the parsing tree. The KAOSbot uses the following patterns: <Predicate-Object-Prepositional Phrase> and <Subject-Predicate-Object-Prepositional Phrase>. The predicate is referred to as the goal of the KAOS model, and performs the action on the entity described by the object. The prepositional phrase contains important information about the action or about the subject of the sentence. When a subject is detected in the sentence, it is considered as the Agent responsible by the Goal (i.e., the predicate). For instance, the triplet extracted from the parsing tree for the sentence "My goal is to ensure the quality of projects" is of the type <Predicate-Object-Prepositional Phrase> and has value <ensure-the quality-of projects>.

We developed the pattern-based grammatical algorithm to extract the goal-related triplets from the Stanford Parser syntactic trees. This algorithm is based on the algorithm presented in [4], which was implemented to extract <Predicate-Object-Prepositional Phrase> triplets from textual documents, extracting and modeling goals. We also used the algorithm presented in [23] to extract <Subject-Predicate-Object> triplets from text as part of a methodology that generates summaries of documents [24]. However, important improvements were made to the context of KAOSbot. For example, (i) the Prepositional Phrase was added to the <Subject-Predicate-Object> triplet because of the important information it carries about the Object of the sentence, becoming <Subject-Predicate-Object-Prepositional Phrase>; and (ii) several goals can now be extracted through the identification of connectives in the user's message. For instance, in the sentence "It is necessary to save ticket request and to show classes", the KAOSbot through the identification of the "and" connective can to extract the following goals: "save ticket request" and "show classes". The pseudocode of the four main subroutines of the algorithm used in this paper to extract goals from syntactic trees can be seen in Algorithm 1.

Algorithm 1. Goal Extraction Algorithm

```
Require: parent(tree) returns the parent of tree
Require: getSubTreeCC(tree) returns the sub tree with label CC
Require: highestVP(tree) returns the immediate tree with label VP found
Require: leaves(tree) returns the terminal nodes of tree
Require: leavesVerb(tree) returns the terminal nodes of tree with label in
   [VB,VBD,VBG,VBN,VBP,VBZ]
  procedure GoalExtraction(parsedSentence)
      triplets ← []
      predicates ← PredicatesExtraction(parsedSentence)
      for predicate in predicates do
          treeVP ← parent(predicate)
          object ← ObjectExtraction(treeVP)
          prepositionalPhrase ← PrepositionalPhraseExtraction(treeVP)
          triplets ← triplets + (predicate, object, prepositionalPhrase)
      return triplets
  procedure PredicatesExtraction(parsedTree)
      treeS ← deepestSentenceTree(parsedTree)
      treeVP ← highestVP(parsedTree)
      predicates ← leavesVerb(treeVP)
      return predicates
  procedure ObjectExtraction(treeVP)
      object ← []
      for childTree in children(treeVP) do
          if label(childTree) in [NP,ADJP] then
              object ← object + leaves(childTree)
      return object
  procedure PrepositionalPhraseExtraction(treeVP)
      pp ← []
      for childTree in children(treeVP) do
          if label(childTree) is PP then
              object ← object + leaves(childTree)
      return pp
```

The main function of the algorithm receives the parsing tree of the user's message as input. The algorithm identifies the predicates containing in sub trees, that is, nodes labeled with verb tags like VB, VBD, VBG, VBN, VBP or VBZ. Then, for each predicate extracted, its parent node is obtained, the treeVP. The treeVP is passed to the functions ObjectExtraction and PrepositionalExtraction in order to get both object and prepositional phrase. The output of main function GoalExtraction is the <Predicate-Object-Prepositional Phrase> triplet filled.

ObjectExtraction takes as input the treeVP subtree. The object is found by seeking in the VP subtree for all leaves of Noun Phrase (NP) or Adjective Phrase (ADJP) sub trees of the treeVP. PrepositionalPhraseExtraction also receives the treeVP as input. However, this function searches for all leaves in PP subtrees of the treeVP. Both object and prepositional phrase can be empty strings if no results are found.

PredicateExtraction identifies the deepest S node from the parsing tree. After, the highest VP tree is obtained to extract their verb leaves nodes, that is, words in the treeVP children which are tagged as VB, VBD, VBG, VBN, VBP or VBZ.

4 A Quasi-experiment

This section describes a **quasi-experiment** to evaluate perceived efficacy (i.e., *perceived ease of use* and *perceived utility*) for the KAOSbot tool when creating KAOS models. In addition, this experiment also evaluates the participants' intention to use the tool in the future. Thus, the research questions for our quasi-experiment are as follows:

RQ1: *Is the KAOSbot tool perceived as easy to use when creating KAOS models?*
RQ2: *Is the KAOSbot tool perceived as useful when creating KAOS models?*
RQ3: *Do participants intend to use the KAOSbot tool in the future?*

4.1 Experiment Design

This section discusses the design of the experiment to evaluate the three research questions. Following the Goal-Question-Metric (GQM) process [3], the goal of this experiment is to **analyze** the perception of the participants **for the purpose of** verifying the perceived efficacy of the tool **with respect to** the perceived ease of use, the perceived usefulness, and intention to use the tool in the future **from the point of view of** novice requirements engineers, **in the context of** undergraduate students in Computer Science.

Context of the Experiment: We focused our evaluation on novice requirements modelers since one of our goals is to provide an easy and useful tool that will help less experienced modelers to specify KAOS models. The participants of the experiment are **29** undergraduate students in Computer Science at the Universidade Católica de Pernambuco (UNICAP), Brazil. They have already completed the *"requirements engineering"* and *"software engineering"* disciplines and are currently in the final year of the course[1]. They were asked to accomplish this experiment as a part of a series of optional lab exercises of the course. All the students were volunteers and were aware of the practical and pedagogical purposes of the experiment, but they did not know the experimental hypotheses nor did they had previous knowledge on KAOSbot. Although we plan to perform other experiments with more experienced participants, Gorschek [10] recommends to first perform initial evaluations in lab environments.

[1] The UNICAP Computer Science course lasts at least 4 years.

Hypotheses Formulation: We formulated three null hypotheses, defined in a one-tailed manner, as we want to analyze the effect of the use of our tool on the variables. Each null hypothesis and its alternative are presented as follows:

H1-0: There is no significant perceived ease of use of the KAOSbot tool during the creation of the KAOS model/**H1-a:** The tool to create KAOS is perceived as ease of use.

H2-0: There is no significant perceived usefulness of the KAOSbot tool during the creation of the KAOS model /**H2-a:** The tool to create KAOS is perceived as useful.

H3-0: There is no significant intention to use the KAOSbot tool in the future /**H3-a:** Participants intend to use the tool in the future.

Selected Variables and Experimental Objects: The independent variable of interest is the use of our method with nominal values. Hence, the experiment uses only one treatment: verify how the KAOSbot tool creates KAOS models. The dependent variables are perception-based, assessing the participants' perceptions of the KAOS modeling performance using the KAOSbot tool. They are based on Technology Acceptance Model (TAM) [7], a widely applied theoretical model which uses empirical support through validations and replications [12] to analyze user acceptance and usage behavior of emerging information technologies [7]. The perceived efficacy [7] of the method can be broken down into two subjective dependent variables:

- **Perceived Ease of Use (PEOU):** Indicates the degree to which the participant believes that learning and using our tool would not require significant effort.
- **Perceived Usefulness (PU):** Indicates the degree to which the participant believes that using our tool will increase her/his job performance within an organizational context.

In addition, we evaluated the following variable:

- **Intention to use (ITU):** Indicates which the participant intends to use our tool.

These three subjective variables were measured using a 5-point Likert scale questionnaire with a set of 12 closed-questions: 6 questions for PEOU, 4 for PU, and 2 for ITU[2]. They were formulated using the opposing statement format. So, each question contains two contradictory statements representing the max and min possible values (5 and 1), where 3 is considered a neutral perception. The aggregated value is the arithmetical mean of the answers to the questions associated with each perception-based variable. We used Cronbach's alpha test [18] to evaluate the reliability of the questionnaire.

[2] The questionnaire can be found at https://bit.ly/2CN0aFd.

Experiment Design: The participants were randomly assigned to two different groups (each using one experimental object). Table 1 summarizes the design of the experiment. In the first two parts of the experiment, the participants watched video classes about KAOS and the KAOSbot tool. The comprehension of the videos class may also affect the perception of the tool. We alleviated the influence of this factor by selecting two representative and illustrative examples of a complexity suitable for application in the 40 min slots available for the execution of the experiments.

Table 1. Experiment design

Groups	Part 1	Part 2	Part 3
A	Introduction to KAOS	KAOSbot (Object1)	Experimental questionnaire
B	Introduction to KAOS	KAOSbot (Object2)	Experimental questionnaire

Analysis Procedure: We chose statistical tests for their robustness and sensitivity to analyze the data collected. Thus, in all the tests we decided to accept a probability of 5% of committing a Type-I-Error [33], rejecting the null hypothesis when it is true. As the number of participants is not large, we tested the normality of the data distribution with the Shapiro-Wilk test [27]. To verify our hypotheses, we used the T-test to one sample when data could assume the normal distribution. However, we applied the Wilcoxon-test when the data could not assume the normal distribution.

Table 2. The descriptive statistics for PEOU, PU, and ITU

Group	PEOU					
	Min.	Max.	Med.	Mean	Std. Dev.	p-value
A	3.67	5	4.33	4.26	0.45	0.95
B	3	5	4.25	4.17	0.57	0.256
A and B	3	5	4.33	4.21	0.52	0.388
PU						
A	3	5	4.5	4.37	0.52	0.393
B	2	5	4	3.95	0.85	0.137
A and B	2	5	4.25	4.14	0.74	0.007
ITU						
A	3	5	4.5	4.30	0.72	0.012
B	2	5	4.5	4.25	0.77	0.008
A and B	2	5	4.5	4.27	0.73	0.000

4.2 Discussion of the Quasi-experiment Results

The use of multiple items to measure the same construct requires the examination of the questionnaire's reliability. We used Cronbach's alpha [18], and the result for the questionnaire was 0.862. This means that the questionnaire is reliable (Cronbach's alpha is higher than 0.7 [18]).

In order to finalize our analysis, we need to check whether, in general (the two groups together), participants perceive the tool as easy to use and useful and that participants intend to use it in the future. For this, we must consider the samples of the groups as a single sample, and check if the final mean is significantly greater than 3 (neutral value). We applied the Shapiro-Wilk test in the single sample (Union of the data of group A and B) to verify if the single sample has a normal distribution (Rows with group *"A and B"* data from Table 2).

The descriptive statistics data (mean and medians higher than 3), apparently, shows that the participants perceived KAOSbot as being easy to use, useful and they intend to use it in the future. However, we must verify this result checking the hypotheses. For this, we applied the Shapiro-Wilk test to check the normality of the distribution for all variables (column *p-value* in Table 2). The results show that PEOU has a normal distribution (PEOU > 0.05) and PU and ITU does not have a normal distribution (PU and ITU < 0.05). Thus, to finalize, we applied the one-sample T-test in PEOU and Wilcoxon-test in PU and ITU data to confirm if the mean is higher than 3 (PEOU = 0.000, PU = 0.000, and ITU = 0.000). As the results of the Wilcoxon-test and one-sample test were lesser than 0.05, **we can accept that KAOSbot tool was perceived as ease to use and useful, confirming hypotheses H1-a and H2-a. In addition, participants intend to use the KAOSbot tool in the future, confirming hypothesis H3-a.** This conclusion is reinforced by the positive answers obtained from the participants through the questionnaire, such as, "*By using the tool, it becomes clearer what are the goals, needs, and desires for the software in question. The tendency is for the resulting model to be closer to the desired model for the software.*"

4.3 Threats to Validity for the Quasi-experiment

Certain issues may threaten the validity of this experiment. About *internal validity*, the main threats are the learning effect, participants' experience, information exchange among participants, and understandability of the documents. The learning effect was mitigated by ensuring that each group of participants worked with only one experimental object. Participants' experience was not an issue as none of them had previous experience with KAOSbot tool. To minimize the information exchange among participants, they were monitored by the experimenters to avoid communication biases while performing the tasks. Understandability of the material was alleviated by performing a pilot study, with the translation of the materials to Portuguese (the participants' native language), and the removal of any doubts during the execution of the experiment by the experimenters. Concerning *external validity*, the main threats are representativeness of the results and the size and complexity of the tasks. The representativeness of the results may be affected by the experimental objects used and the participants' context selected. About the selection of experimental objects, we mitigated this by considering two different experiment objects with a set of artifacts with similar size and complexity. Regarding size and complexity of the tasks, we used small tasks since an experiment requires participants to complete the assigned tasks in a limited amount of time. The main *construct validity* threats respect the measures applied in the data analysis and the reliability of the questionnaire. We mitigated this by using measures that are commonly used in other software engineering experiments, and the variables are based on Technology Acceptance Method (TAM) [7,12]. The reliability of the questionnaire was tested with the Cronbach test [18]. Finally, *conclusion validity* threat is the validity of the statistical tests applied. We chose the most common tests employed in empirical software engineering due to their robustness and sensitivity [17].

5 Related Work

There are several papers about chatbot in the literature [2,20,31]. However, to the best of our knowledge, we only know about [19] dealing with chatbot for software engineering. [19] presents a modeling bot to interpret natural language sentences to generate metamodels. Our approach elicits requirements within the context of the KAOS goal-oriented requirements engineering method. In [4], the authors do not have produced a chatbot, but they present a computational method (NLP-KAOS) that uses NLP and text mining techniques to support requirements engineers in extracting and modeling goals from textual documents. This work also employs NLP and text mining techniques for identifying goals, however our approach focuses on the interaction with novice requirements engineers to facilitate the requirements elicitation through the use of a chatbot tool.

Our approach joins the chatbot concepts used in SOCIO with the text mining algorithms used in NLP-KAOS to extract goals from text documents.

6 Conclusions and Future Works

In this paper, we present an approach to support goal-oriented requirements elicitation for novice requirements engineers through the use of NLP within a chatbot tool. This chatbot is named KAOSbot, because it acts as a KAOS modeling assistant. Then, we show how KAOSbot works and how it was implemented. Finally, we evaluated our approach through a quasi-experiment with respect to the perceived efficacy (i.e., perceived ease of use and perceived utility) for the KAOSbot tool when creating KAOS models. In addition, we also evaluate the participants' intention to use the KAOSbot in the future. The results show that KAOSBot tool is a promising approach for specifying KAOS models because it was perceived as easy to use, useful, and the participants intend to use it in the future.

For future works, we plan to improve our NLP algorithm to make KAOSbot cover more KAOS components such as Obstacles and Operations. Also, we plan to provide accessibility for people with motor limitations through the use of speech for the generation of KAOS models and to aggregate a machine learning system that indicates possible non-functional requirements during the conversation.

References

1. Almisned, F., Keppens, J.: Requirements analysis: evaluating KAOS models. J. Softw. Eng. Appl. **3**(09), 869 (2010)
2. Baby, C.J., Khan, F.A., Swathi, J.: Home automation using IoT and a chatbot using natural language processing. In: 2017 Innovations in Power and Advanced Computing Technologies (i-PACT), pp. 1–6. IEEE (2017)
3. Basili, V.R., Rombach, H.D.: The tame project: towards improvement-oriented software environments. IEEE Trans. Softw. Eng. **14**(6), 758–773 (1988)
4. Casagrande, E., Woldeamlak, S., Woon, W.L., Zeineldin, H.H., Svetinovic, D.: NLP-KAOS for systems goal elicitation: smart metering system case study. IEEE Trans. Softw. Eng. **40**(10), 941–956 (2014)
5. Casamayor, A., Godoy, D., Campo, M.: Mining textual requirements to assist architectural software design: a state of the art review. Artif. Intell. Rev. **38**(3), 173–191 (2012)
6. Chowdhury, G.G.: Natural language processing. Annu. Rev. Inf. Sci. Technol. **37**(1), 51–89 (2003)
7. Davis, F.D.: Perceived usefulness, perceived ease of use, and user acceptance of information technology. MIS Q. **13**, 319–340 (1989)
8. Espada, P., Goulão, M., Araújo, J.: Measuring complexity and completeness of KAOS goal models. In: 2011 First International Workshop on Empirical Requirements Engineering (EmpiRE), pp. 29–32. IEEE (2011)
9. Gervasi, V., Zowghi, D.: Reasoning about inconsistencies in natural language requirements. ACM Trans. Softw. Eng. Methodol. (TOSEM) **14**(3), 277–330 (2005)
10. Gorschek, T., Garre, P., Larsson, S., Wohlin, C.: A model for technology transfer in practice. IEEE Softw. **23**(6), 88–95 (2006)
11. Ibrahim, M., Ahmad, R.: Class diagram extraction from textual requirements using natural language processing (NLP) techniques. In: 2010 Second International Conference on Computer Research and Development, pp. 200–204. IEEE (2010)
12. King, W.R., He, J.: A meta-analysis of the technology acceptance model. Inf. Manag. **43**(6), 740–755 (2006)
13. Kof, L.: From requirements documents to system models: a tool for interactive semi-automatic translation. In: 2010 18th IEEE International Requirements Engineering Conference (RE), pp. 391–392. IEEE (2010)
14. Kurtanović, Z., Maalej, W.: Automatically classifying functional and non-functional requirements using supervised machine learning. In: 2017 IEEE 25th International Requirements Engineering Conference (RE), pp. 490–495. IEEE (2017)
15. Luisa, M., Mariangela, F., Pierluigi, N.I.: Market research for requirements analysis using linguistic tools. Requirements Eng. **9**(1), 40–56 (2004)
16. Manning, C., Surdeanu, M., Bauer, J., Finkel, J., Bethard, S., McClosky, D.: The Stanford CoreNLP natural language processing toolkit. In: Proceedings of 52nd Annual Meeting of the Association for Computational Linguistics: System Demonstrations, pp. 55–60 (2014)

17. Maxwell, K.: Applied Statistics for Software Managers. Prentice Hall, Upper Saddle River (2002)
18. Nunnally, J.C., Bernstein, I.H.: Psychometric Theory. McGraw-Hill, New York (1978)
19. Pérez-Soler, S., Guerra, E., de Lara, J.: Assisted modelling over social networks with socio. In: MODELS (Satellite Events), pp. 561–565 (2017)
20. Rahman, A., Al Mamun, A., Islam, A.: Programming challenges of chatbot: current and future prospective. In: 2017 IEEE Region 10 Humanitarian Technology Conference (R10-HTC), pp. 75–78. IEEE (2017)
21. Respect-IT: A KAOS Tutorial (2007)
22. Rolland, C., Souveyet, C., Achour, C.B.: Guiding goal modeling using scenarios. IEEE Trans. Softw. Eng. **24**(12), 1055–1071 (1998)
23. Rusu, D., Dali, L., Fortuna, B., Grobelnik, M., Mladenic, D.: Triplet extraction from sentences. In: Proceedings of the 10th International Multiconference Information Society-IS, pp. 8–12 (2007)
24. Rusu, D., Fortuna, B., Grobelnik, M., Mladenić, D.: Semantic graphs derived from triplets with application. Informatica **33**(3), 357–362 (2009)
25. Sawyer, P., Rayson, P., Cosh, K.: Shallow knowledge as an aid to deep understanding in early phase requirements engineering. IEEE Trans. Softw. Eng. **31**(11), 969–981 (2005)
26. Shah, A., Jain, B., Agrawal, B., Jain, S., Shim, S.: Problem solving chatbot for data structures. In: 2018 IEEE 8th Annual Computing and Communication Workshop and Conference (CCWC), pp. 184–189. IEEE (2018)
27. Shaphiro, S., Wilk, M.: An analysis of variance test for normality. Biometrika **52**(3), 591–611 (1965)
28. Souza, E., Moreira, A.: Deriving services from KAOS models. In: Proceedings of the 33rd Annual ACM Symposium on Applied Computing, pp. 1308–1315. ACM (2018)
29. Van Lamsweerde, A.: Goal-oriented requirements engineering: a guided tour. In: Proceedings Fifth IEEE International Symposium on Requirements Engineering, pp. 249–262. IEEE (2001)
30. Van Lamsweerde, A.: Goal-oriented requirements enginering: a roundtrip from research to practice [enginering read engineering]. In: Proceedings 12th IEEE International Requirements Engineering Conference, pp. 4–7. IEEE (2004)
31. Vasconcelos, M., Candello, H., Pinhanez, C., dos Santos, T.: Bottester: testing conversational systems with simulated users. In: Proceedings of the XVI Brazilian Symposium on Human Factors in Computing Systems, p. 73. ACM (2017)
32. Wanderley, F., Araujo, J.: Generating goal-oriented models from creative requirements using model driven engineering. In: 2013 International Workshop on Model-Driven Requirements Engineering (MoDRE), pp. 1–9. IEEE (2013)
33. Wohlin, C., Runeson, P., Höst, M., Ohlsson, M.C., Regnell, B., Wesslén, A.: Experimentation in Software Engineering, 1st edn. Springer-Verlag, Heidelberg (2012). https://doi.org/10.1007/978-3-642-29044-2. http://link.springer.com/10.1007/978-3-642-29044-2

Adopting Social Group Optimization Algorithm Using Mutation Testing for Test Suite Generation: SGO-MT

Shweta Rani(✉) and Bharti Suri

USICT, GGS Indraprastha University, Delhi, India
shweta2610@gmail.com, bhartisuri@gmail.com

Abstract. Test case generation is popular among the researchers and doing this manually is an exhaustive and time taking process. Automation can cut its cost and create an effective test suite that is evaluated for its adequacy over a set of faults. These faults can be created by applying mutagenic rules that have been used appropriately for searching the improved test inputs in search-based approaches. Researchers have advised these approaches combining mutation testing are more effective at test generation. This paper proposes a novel test generation algorithm SGO-MT by adopting social group optimization algorithm (SGO) with the goal to reveal maximum faults in the software. SGO follows the concept of learning the traits of humans in a group. It works in two phases: acquiring phase (learning from society) and improving phase (learning from the teacher) that try to enhance the fitness of each individual. In learning from society, each individual test case is influenced by another while in the latter case, test data are evolved with respect to the fittest test case. SGO-MT stops functioning when it achieves its desired objective ie. detection of maximum possible artificial faults.

Keywords: Mutation testing · Social group optimization · Search based mutation testing · Test case generation

1 Introduction

Software quality is an important factor and must be verified before releasing the software to the customer [1,2]. It heavily relies on how and at what extent, testing is performed. To ensure error- free delivery, software is executed with sufficient test cases that should be effective in identifying the faults. For exhaustive testing, artificial faults can be injected using mutation testing that is a prominent area of research [3,5]. These faults are also known as mutants and used to assess the quality of the test set (adequacy score). Quality of a test case is evaluated on the basis of how many faults it can detect. The more faults it recognizes, the more it is said to be effective. However, manually creating the test suite is quite cumbersome and costly. Automation can generate an effective test set and

S. Misra et al. (Eds.): ICCSA 2019, LNCS 11622, pp. 520–528, 2019.
https://doi.org/10.1007/978-3-030-24305-0_39

also cuts the cost of generation. Prior studies [6–10] suggest that search based algorithms perform better for automatic generation of test cases.

Initially studied by Miller and Spooner [11], search based testing algorithms start searching the solution space using a random set of initial population. This population is then evolved over a number of generations till it gets converged. In testing, at convergence, test data must successfully satisfy the coverage criteria ie. branch coverage, statement coverage, mutation coverage, path coverage and so on. Fraser in his studies [12,13] reveal that mutation coverage criteria is superior and generates an exhaustive test suite. In the literature [7,8,10], different population-based algorithms have been adopted. Genetic algorithm, particle swarm optimization, ant colony optimization, bee colony optimization are some of the popular techniques in the area. Researchers [14–21] are still working to simulate the behavior of different species and suggesting new search based algorithms for solving complex problems. Some of the recently developed techniques are lion optimization [15], grey wolf optimization [19], ant lion optimization [20], moth flame optimization [14], spider monkey optimization [17], social group optimization [21].

Search based algorithms have been effectively combined with mutation testing to solve the test suite related problems i.e. test suite generation, optimization, prioritization and selection and can be traced in these surveys [4,22–26]. Most of these algorithms require several input parameters and for optimal performance, these parameters must be chosen carefully. Social group optimization (SGO) is one of the recently proposed optimization algorithms and takes a few parameters and is quite simple to understand. It is originally developed by Satapathy and Naik [21] and simulates human learning behavior. In this paper, we propose a novel test data generation algorithm ie, SGO-MT by combining SGO and mutation testing. However, we could not find any test generation algorithm based on SGO. Despite the ease in understanding, SGO is found to perform well over GA and PSO when applied for fault analysis in dissolved gas analysis system [26] and when used for solving data clustering problems [27].

2 Search Based Algorithms

We study different search algorithms (refer to Table 1). Some of these techniques are popular and some are recently proposed as discussed below.

2.1 Genetic Algorithm (GA)

The principle of GA is laid upon the Darwinian principle of survival of fittest. It was initially conceived by Holland [28]. GA is one of the popular algorithms among the researchers [22,23,29]. The basic process of GA starts with the random initialization of the population which is forwarded for fitness evaluation and is evolved by applying a choice of reproduction operators. Reproduction operators consist of three types of operators ie. selection, crossover and mutation. It selects the best fit individuals for crossover and mutation. Crossover is performed between the two individuals that exchange their properties while mutation makes some changes in the individual to diverse the complete solution. It iteratively quests for a better solution and provides the globally optimal solution at convergence.

2.2 Particle Swarm Optimization (PSO)

It is a swarm-based search technique that mimics the behavior of animals and is inspired by bird flocking and herding [30]. A number of solutions refer to the swarm of particles that fly in searching for the best solution. During the search, they keep updating their location and velocity and find the best solution in their path.

2.3 Ant Colony Optimization (ACO)

Initially proposed by Dorigo [31], the foundation of ACO is based on the food finding behavior of ants. In spite of being blind, ants find the smallest route to the food source by the detection rate of pheromone. It consists of two processes ie. pheromone deposition and evaporation. Each ant deposits the pheromone while trailing a path and this evaporates with the time. In the end, each ant updates the trail along with pheromone that in turns provides the shortest route to the food source.

Table 1. Search Based Algorithms

S. No	Algorithm	Inspired by	Year
1.	GA	Survival of fittest, mimic gene behavior of mating	1992
2.	PSO	Bird flocking	1995
3.	ACO	Ants food locating nature	1996
4.	SMO	Fission and fusion behaviour of spider monkeys	2013
5.	MFO	Navigation method of moth	2015
6.	SGO	Influencing behavior of human in a group	2015
7.	LOA	Prey locating behavior of lion	2016
8.	WOA	Bubble net feeding method of whale	2016

2.4 Moth Flame Optimization (MFO)

In 2015, Mirjalili [14] proposed an optimization algorithm mimicking the navigation method of moths. Moths try to evolve in the night and travel in a straight line at a fixed angle with respect to the moon. Artificial light misguides the Moths and makes it trapped in the spiral motion of light. Moths are basically the agent and fitness is referred to as flame. Each moth in the population repeatedly updates its location and flames according to the best moth and finds the best solution at the end.

2.5 Lion Optimization Algorithm (LOA)

Inspired by the prey locating behavior of lions, Yazdani, and Jolai [15] developed a new lion optimization algorithm (LOA). Previously Rajakumar [32] only proposed the lion's operators for mating and generating new solutions. Lions are wild cat animal and considered to be highly co-operative as well as antagonistic [33]. They are divided into two groups ie. residents (live in a group called pride), nomads (move alone or in pairs). In LOA, the initial population is randomly generated and some of them selected as nomads and rest as residents. They move and hunt to find the prey and attack it fastly. Weak lions die with time and only strong lions (solutions with food) remain alive at the end.

2.6 Spider Monkey Optimization (SMO)

Bansal et al. [17] proposed SMO that follows the idea of fission and fusion to find the food source. In this, a group of spider monkeys with a female leader starts searching the food and if she could not find the sufficient food then she divides the group into small groups that again hunt for food throughout the day. SMO impose limits on how many times a group can be divided. A member of the group can interact with other local member or a member in a different group for finding the food. They interact with each other using sounds, postures and positions.

2.7 Social Group Optimization (SGO)

The foundation of SGO is laid upon the influential behavior of humans [21]. They are great in mimicking the behavior. Each person has some knowledge and improves it with the influence of others knowledge and their behavior. SGO is a population-based algorithm where a group of person is considered as a population. SGO works in two phases ie. improving phase and acquiring phase. In the first phase, the best fit solution tries to improve each individual in the group. On the other hand, knowledge is enhanced by communicating with other members of that group in acquiring phase. In each phase, if the new solution is better then it is kept otherwise rejected. The whole process of acquiring the knowledge is repeated until convergence.

2.8 Whale Optimization Algorithm (WOA)

Inspired by the hunting nature of whale, Mirjalili and Lewis [16] proposed whale optimization algorithm. Whales are the biggest mammals and can be maximum 30 m long and 180t weight. They are social in nature and can live alone or in groups. They search their food by bubble net feeding method [34] in which a group of whales locate the food and catch it tightly by creating a net of bubbles. Whales have similar cells like human and these cells make them intelligent and emotional [35]. These cells help whales to locate the prey and consider it as the best solution. After finding the best solution by exploration and exploitation [16], all others try to evolve towards the best one.

3 Proposed Test Data Generation Approach: SGO-MT

In this section, we propose a novel search based algorithm by applying SGO and mutation testing for test data generation and named it SGO-MT. The flow chart in Fig. 1 illustrates the functioning of SGO-MT. The process starts with random initialization of the population of persons. Here, the population of persons is considered as a set of test cases. Each person has its knowledge to solve any problem. In our case, each test case is known for its fitness along with its value. Fitness is the adequacy score of a test case that is devised by executing it against the mutants. The more it kills the mutants, the higher its fitness is. Then, it works on evolving the test suite by improving it with respect to the best test case and other test cases. Evolution takes place in two phases ie. improving phase and acquiring phase. After repeated evolution, it provides the optimal solution at convergence.

Step 1: Initialize Population
Initially, decide the size of the initial population (N), number of generations (g), number of input variables (I) and limits of each variable (U_L, L_L). For the size of the population (N), randomly generate an initial set of test cases. Each test case consists of values equal to D. The population (P) is represented in the following form.

$$Population(P) = \begin{pmatrix} TC_{1,1} & TC_{1,2} & TC_{1,3} & \ldots & TC_{1,I} \\ . & . & . & & . \\ . & . & . & & . \\ . & . & . & & . \\ TC_{N,1} & TC_{N,2} & TC_{N,3} & \ldots & TC_{N,I} \end{pmatrix}$$

Step 2: Fitness Evaluation
To test the usefulness of the test case, each test case in P is intended for fitness evaluation. Here, fitness is the adequacy score of the test case which is measured by executing it against the mutants [3]. It is also known as mutation score (refer Eq. 1).

$$Fitness\ Score\ (FS) = (Killed\ Mutants/Total\ number\ of\ Mutants)\ * 100; \tag{1}$$

Step 3: Improving Phase:

In this phase, each test case is improved with the influence of the best-fit test case. It applies the concept of learning from a teacher who is considered to be the best in the group. Test data is enhanced using Eq. 2. We accept the new test case if found better. Let *gbest* be the best solution with the highest fitness.

$$P^{i}_{new}(j) = c * P^{i}_{old}(j) + r * (gbest - P^{i}_{old}(j)); \tag{2}$$

Here, P(i, j) is the test case value, $i \varepsilon (1, N)$ and $j \varepsilon (1, I)$. c is self-introspection parameter lies in (0, 1). r is a random number lies in (0, 1).

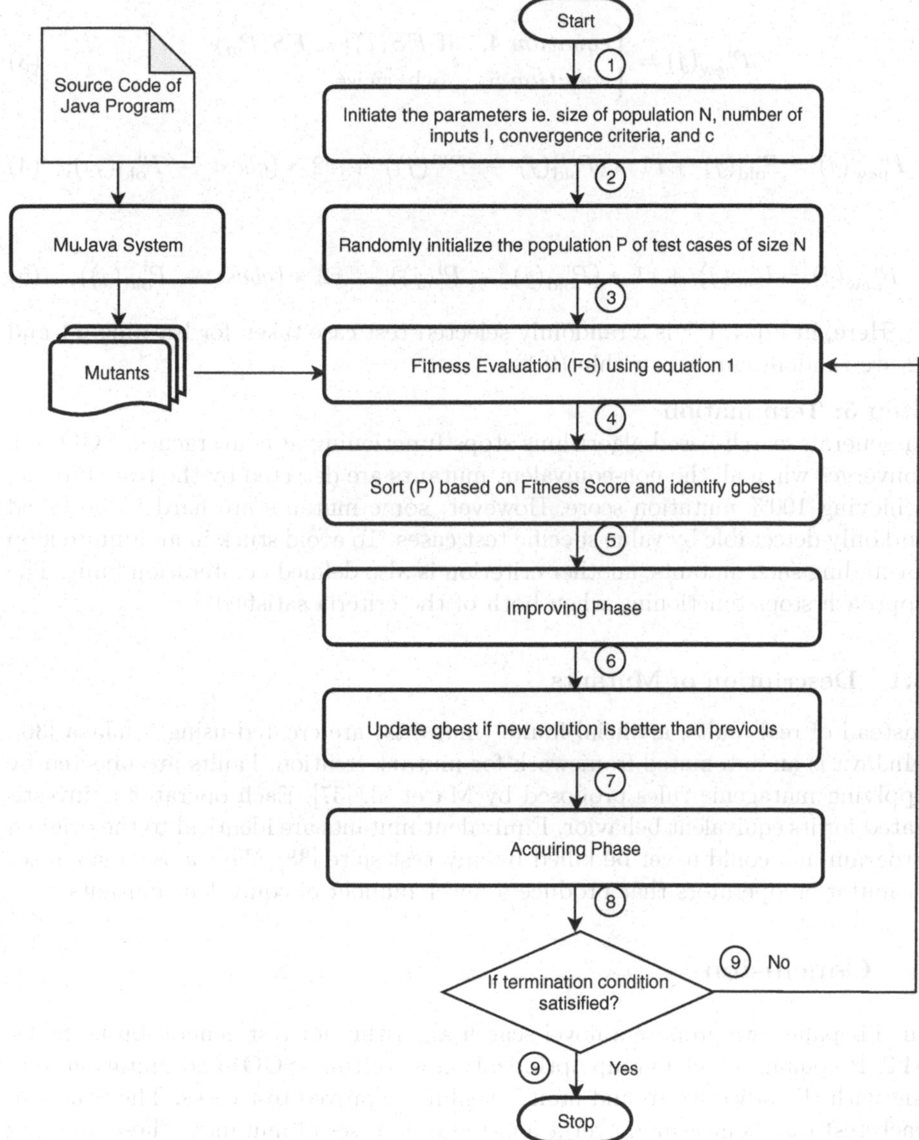

Fig. 1. Flow Chart of the proposed SGO-MT approach for Test Data Generation

Step 4: Acquiring Phase
In a group, each member tries to improve by learning from others. Here, each test case intends to improve its fitness with respect to other test cases in the population. Test data is enhanced using Eq. 3. The new test case is kept in the system if it contributes to the effectiveness of the test suite.

$$P^{i}_{new}(j) = \begin{cases} equation\ 4, & \text{if } FS(P_{i}) < FS(P_{m}) \\ equation\ 5, & \text{otherwise} \end{cases} \quad (3)$$

$$P^{i}_{new}(j) = P^{i}_{old}(j) + r1 * (P^{i}_{old}(j) - P^{m}(j)) + r2 * (gbest - P^{i}_{old}(j)); \quad (4)$$

$$P^{i}_{new}(j) = P^{i}_{old}(j) + r1 * (P^{r}_{old}(j) - P^{i}(j)) + r2 * (gbest - P^{i}_{old}(j)); \quad (5)$$

Here, in Eq. 4, P^{m} is a randomly selected test case taken for learning. r1 and r2 are random numbers within (0,1).

Step 5: Termination
In general, search-based algorithms stops functioning at convergence. SGO-MT converges when all the non-equivalent mutants are detected by the test suite i.e. achieving 100% mutation score. However, some mutants are hard to be killed and only detectable by value specific test cases. To avoid stuck in an infinite loop for finding such mutants, another criterion is also defined i.e. iteration limit. The approach stops functioning when both of the criteria satisfied.

3.1 Description of Mutants

Instead of real faults, artificial faults (mutants) are created using MuJava [36]. MuJava is an automated framework for mutant creation. Faults are injected by applying mutagenic rules proposed by Ma et al. [37]. Each operator is investigated for its equivalent behavior. Equivalent mutants are identical to the original program and could never be killed by any test suite [38]. We choose a small set of mutation operators that produce a fewer number of equivalent mutants.

4 Conclusion

In this paper, we propose a novel search algorithm for test generation ie. SGO-MT. It combines social group optimization algorithm (SGO) and mutation testing with the objective to find fault revealing improved test cases. The fitness of each test case is measured over a non-redundant set of mutants. These mutants are powerful and create a few redundant and equivalent mutants. SGO is inspired by the learning behavior of humans. They learn from society and from the teacher. Learning is associated with the evolution of test cases in SGO-MT and each test case keeps learning till stagnation. In the future, we plan to investigate and compare SGO-MT with other search-based testing algorithms for test data generation.

Acknowledgment. The authors would like to acknowledge Ministry of Electronics and Information Technology, Govt. of India for supporting this research under Visvesvaraya Ph.D. Scheme for Electronics and IT.

References

1. Myers, G.J.: The Art of Software Testing. Wiley, New York (1989)
2. Agarwal, K.K., Singh, Y.: Software Engineering. New Age International Publishers (2007)
3. Jia, Y., Harman, M.: An analysis and survey of the development of mutation testing. IEEE Trans. Softw. Eng. **37**(5), 649–678 (2011)
4. Zhu, Q., Panichella, A., Zaidman, A.: A systematic literature review on how mutation testing supports quality assurance processes. Softw. Test. Verif. Reliab. **28**(6), 1675 (2018)
5. Andrews, J.H., Briand, L.C., Labiche, Y.: Is mutation an appropriate tool for testing experiments? In: Proceedings of the 27th International Conference on Software Engineering, ICSE 2005, pp. 402–411. ACM (2005)
6. Dave, M., Agrawal, R.: Search based techniques and mutation analysis in automatic test case generation: a survey. In: 2015 IEEE International Advance Computing Conference (IACC), pp. 795–799 (2015)
7. McMinn, P.: Search-based software test data generation: a survey: research articles. Softw. Test. Verif. Reliab. **14**(2), 105–156 (2004)
8. McMinn, P.: Search-based software testing: past, present and future. In: Proceedings of the 2011 IEEE Fourth International Conference on Software Testing, Verification and Validation Workshops, ICSTW 2011, pp. 153–163. IEEE Computer Society (2011)
9. Sahin, O., Akay, B.: Comparisons of metaheuristic algorithms and fitness functions on software test data generation. Appl. Soft Comput. **49**, 1202–1214 (2016)
10. Ali, S., Briand, L.C., Hemmati, H., Panesar-Walawege, R.K.: A systematic review of the application and empirical investigation of search-based test case generation. IEEE Trans. Softw. Eng. **36**(6), 742–762 (2010)
11. Miller, W., Spooner, D.L.: Automatic generation of floating-point test data. IEEE Trans. Softw. Eng. **SE–2**(3), 223–226 (1976)
12. Fraser, G., Zeller, A.: Mutation-driven generation of unit tests and oracles. IEEE Trans. Softw. Eng. **38**(2), 278–292 (2012)
13. Fraser, G., Arcuri, A.: Achieving scalable mutation-based generation of whole test suites. Empir. Softw. Eng. **20**(3), 783–812 (2015)
14. Mirjalili, S.: Moth-flame optimization algorithm: a novel nature-inspired heuristic paradigm. Knowl.-Based Syst. **89**, 228–249 (2015)
15. Yazdani, M., Jolai, F.: Lion Optimization Algorithm (LOA): a nature-inspired metaheuristic algorithm. J. Comput. Des. Eng. **3**, 24–36 (2016)
16. Mirjalili, S., Lewis, A.: The Whale Optimization Algorithm. Adv. Eng. Softw. **95**, 51–67 (2016)
17. Bansal, J.C., Sharma, H., Jadon, S.S., Clerc, M.: Spider Monkey Optimization algorithm for numerical optimization. Memetic Comput. **6**(1), 31–47 (2013)
18. Shah-Hosseini, H.: The intelligent water drops algorithm: a nature-inspired swarm-based optimization algorithm. Int. J. Bio-Inspired Comput. **1**(1), 71–79 (2009)
19. Mirjalili, S., Mirjalili, S.M., Lewis, A.: Grey Wolf Optimizer. Adv. Eng. Softw. **69**, 46–61 (2014)
20. Mirjalili, S.: The Ant Lion Optimizer. Adv. Eng. Softw. **83**, 80–98 (2015)
21. Satapathy, S., Naik, A.: Social group optimization (SGO): a new population evolutionary optimization technique. Complex Intell. Syst. **2**, 173–203 (2016)
22. Silva, R.A., de Souza, S.D.R.S., de Souza, P.S.L.: A systematic review on search based mutation testing. Inf. Softw. Technol. **81**, 19–35 (2017)

23. Jatana, N., Suri, B., Rani, S.: Systematic literature review on search based mutation testing. e-Inform. Softw. Eng. J. **11**(1), 59–76 (2017)
24. Rodrigues, D.S., Delamaro, M.E., Correa, C.G., Nunes, F.L.S.: Using genetic algorithms in test data generation: a critical systematic mapping. ACM Comput. Surv. **51**(2), (41)1–(41)23 (2018)
25. Souza, F.C., Papadakis, M., Durelli, V.H.S., Delamaro, M.E.: Test data generation techniques for mutation testing: a systematic mapping. In: Proceedings of 11th Workshop on Experimental Software Engineering Latin Americal Wrokshop (ESELAW) (2014)
26. Fang, J., Zhang, H., Liu, J., Zhao, J., Zhang, Y., Wang, K.: A transformer fault diagnosis model using an optimal hybrid dissolved gas analysis features subset with improved social group optimization-support vector machine classifier. Energies MDPI Open Access J. **11**(8), 1–18 (2018)
27. Naik, A., Satapathy, S.C., Ashour, A.S., Dey, N.: Social group optimization for global optimization of multimodal functions and data clustering problems. Neural Comput. Appl. **30**(1), 271–287 (2016)
28. Holland, J.H.: Adaptation in Natural and Artificial Systems: An Introductory Analysis with Applications to Biology. Control and Artificial Intelligence. MIT Press, Cambridge (1992)
29. Yang, X.S.: Nature Inspired Metaheuristic Algorithms, vol. 504. Luniver Press (2010)
30. Kennedy, J., Eberhard, R.: Particle swarm optimization. In: IEEE International Conference on Neural Networks, vol. 4, pp. 1942–1948 (1995)
31. Dorigo, M., Maniezzo, V., Colorni, A.: The ant system: optimization by a colony of cooperating agents. IEEE Trans. Syst. Man Cybern. **26**(1), 29–41 (1996)
32. Rajakumar, B.: The Lion's Algorithm: a new nature-inspired search algorithm. Procedia Technol. **6**, 126–135 (2012)
33. McComb, K., Pusey, A., Packer, C., Grinnell, J.: Female lions can identify potentially infanticidal males from their roars. Biol. Sci. R. Soc. **252**(1333), 59–64 (1993)
34. Watkins, W.A., Schevill, W.E.: Aerial observation of feeding behavior in four baleen whales: eubalaena glacialis, balaenoptera borealis, megaptera novaeangliae, and balaenoptera physalus. J. Mammal. **60**(1), 155–163 (1979)
35. Hof, P.R., Van Der Gucht, E.: Structure of the cerebral cortex of the humpback whale, Megaptera novaeangliae (Cetacea, Mysticeti, Balaenopteridae). Adv. Integr. Anat. Evol. Biol. Anat. Rec. **290**, 1–31 (2007)
36. Ma, Y.-S., Offutt, J., Kwon, Y.R.: MuJava: an automated class mutation system. Softw. Test. Verif. Reliab. **15**(2), 97–133 (2005)
37. Ma, Y.-S., Offutt, J.: Description of method-level mutation operators for Java. Technical report, Electronics and Telecommunications Research Institute, Korea (2005)
38. Grun, B.J.M., Schuler, D., Zeller, A.: The impact of equivalent mutants. In: 2009 International Conference on Software Testing, Verification, and Validation Workshops, pp. 192–199. IEEE (2009)

Evaluation of Textual Similarity Techniques in Code Level Traceability

Viktor Csuvik[1(✉)], András Kicsi[1], and László Vidács[1,2]

[1] Department of Software Engineering, University of Szeged, Szeged, Hungary
{csuvikv,akicsi,lac}@inf.u-szeged.hu

[2] MTA-SZTE Research Group on Artificial Intelligence, University of Szeged, Szeged, Hungary

Abstract. Automatic recovery of test-to-code traceability links is an important task in many areas of software engineering, like quality assurance and code maintenance. The research community has shown great interest in such a topic and has developed several techniques that already made significant advances in the field. These techniques include text-based learning algorithms, of which corpus is built from the source code of the software components. Several techniques based on information retrieval have been benchmarked, but the capabilities of many learning algorithms have not yet been tested. In this work we examine the textual similarity measures produced by three different machine learning techniques for the recovery of traceability information while also considering various textual representations of the source code. The obtained results are evaluated on 4 open source systems based on naming conventions. We have been able to improve the current textual similarity based state-of-the-art results in the case of each evaluated system.

Keywords: Traceability · Testing · Test-to-code · Machine learning · Text similarity

1 Introduction

True perfection in software engineering does not exist. Software testing, however, constitutes a major aspect in the assurance of quality. Besides simply detecting faults in software, tests are also essential for other areas in software engineering, like Automatic Program Repair (APR), where tests are needed in the patch generation process, or code maintenance. The primary aspect of testing is to provide information on whether the software achieves the general result its stakeholders desire. Testing can provide an independent view of the software and opens new opportunities in calculating the risks. It is known that complete testing is not fully achievable, still writing tests on edge cases and increasing their amount is considered to be a good coding practice. It is not a coincidence that large systems often incorporate vast amounts of tests.

Considering tens of thousands of tests, their maintenance becomes cumbersome and the goal of some tests may even become unknown. In these cases

S. Misra et al. (Eds.): ICCSA 2019, LNCS 11622, pp. 529–543, 2019.
https://doi.org/10.1007/978-3-030-24305-0_40

recovering which test case assesses a specific part of code can prove to be a challenge. Traceability in general stands for the task of tracing software items through a variety of software products. The previously described specific problem is called *test-to-code* traceability. Traceability is a well-researched area with a serious industrial background. While the most widespread problem in this field is domain requirement traceability [3,22], test-to-code traceability also gained attention from the research community [5,15,35].

Using good coding practices [41] can make the task easier and with proper naming conventions [35] very accurate results can be achieved. However, if a developer lacks these skills or proper foresight, the traceability problem becomes non-trivial with many pitfalls. In these cases, automatic recovery approaches should be introduced, which does not require such assumptions from the examined system. While several attempts have already been made to cope with this problem, these techniques are limited since they typically depend on intuitive features. In our previous work [5,15] we provided a method, that automatically links test cases and production classes relying only on conceptual information. In the current paper, we make an attempt to improve our former results by involving new machine learning techniques. We compare these results and also show that combining them outperforms the current semantic information based approaches in the traceability task.

The paper is organized as follows. We present a high-level overview of our research in the following section by depicting the proposed approach to recover test-to-code links and specify our research objectives. Next, we introduce the examined database and its representations upon which the experiments were carried out. Evaluation on four systems and analysis are presented in Sect. 5. Related work is discussed in Sect. 6, and we conclude the paper in the last section.

2 Overview

Test-to-code traceability means finding the links between test cases and production code. More precisely for a test case we want to find certain parts of the code which it was meant to test. For a large system, this task can be challenging, particularly when the development lacks good coding practices [41] like proper naming conventions. Using practices like naming the test classes after the tested production code automatically creates a conceivable link between the test and the tested artifact. It is well known, that with proper naming conventions, retrieving traceability links is a minor task [35]. If we consider, however, a system where the targets of the test cases are unknown to us, other approaches should be applied.

Figure 1 provides an illustration of the comprehensive approach we propose. We consider a software system written in the Java programming language. It contains both test classes and production classes and we aim to recover the relationship between them. We made no assumptions about the names of the software artifacts. From the raw source code, we extract the classes of the system

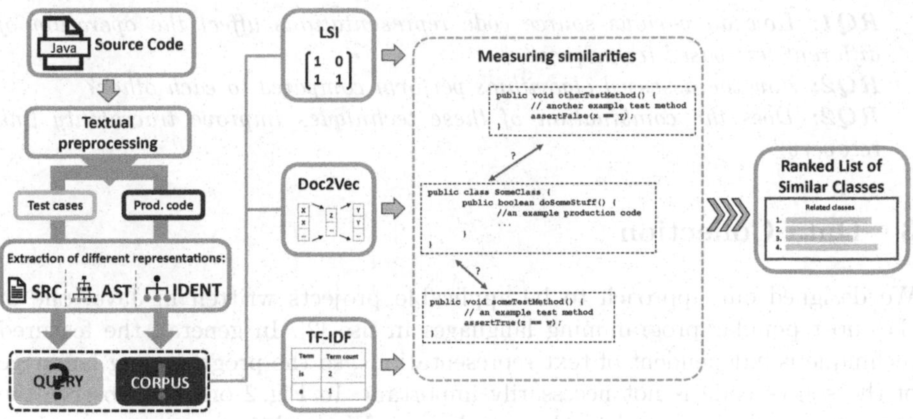

Fig. 1. A high-level illustration of our process.

using the Source Meter[1] static analysis tool and separate test cases and production code. We generate three diverse representations of the source code (SRC, AST, IDENT) which we discuss in Sect. 3 and use machine learning techniques to measure the similarity between code snippets. In the case of Latent Semantic Indexing (LSI) and Term Frequency-Inverse Document Frequency (TF-IDF) methods the models are trained on the production code (corpus) and the test cases are the queries. There is a slight difference in the case of Doc2Vec since the training corpus consists of both the test and production classes. After the models are trained, we measure the similarity between tests and code classes, from which a ranked list is constructed. The basic idea is that test and code classes are *similar* in some sense. Therefore, from the ranked similarity list, we observe the first N production classes, allowing us to consider these techniques as recommendation systems.

We recommend classes for a test case starting from the most similar and also examine the top 2 and top 5 most similar classes. Looking at the outputs in such a way holds a number of benefits. Foremost, if we would consider only the most similar class then those instances when tests assess the proper functioning of several classes rather than only one would be missed. Also, a class usually relies on other classes, consequently a recommendation system can highlight the test and code relationship more thoroughly. Since overly abundant recommendations can result in a high number of false matches which can diminish the usefulness of the information itself, we restricted the consideration to only the 5 most similar classes in each case, keeping the technique as simple as possible. In our current work we used our previously available tools for the generation of LSI-based similarities [5,15].

Summarizing our work, we organize our experiment along three research points, and formulate the following research questions:

[1] https://www.sourcemeter.com/.

RQ1: *How do various source code representations affect the operation of different text-based techniques?*
RQ2: *How the assessed algorithms perform compared to each other?*
RQ2: *Does the combination of these techniques improve traceability link recovery?*

3 Data Collection

We designed our approach to be applicable projects written in Java, one of the most popular programming languages in use [2]. In general, the featured technique is independent of text representations, so the programming language of the source code is not necessarily important. In Fig. 2 one can observe the projects, on which we evaluated our technique. We used the exact same versions of the referenced projects in our previous work [5,15].

COMMONS MATH V. 3.4.1	COMMONS LANG V. 3.4	JFREECHART V. 1.0.19	MONDRIAN V. 3.0.4
Tests: 3493	Tests: 2473	Tests: 2239	Tests: 1546
Methods: 14837	Methods: 6523	Methods: 11594	Methods: 12186
Classes: 2033	Classes: 596	Classes: 953	Classes: 1626

Fig. 2. Size and versions of the examined systems. The area of boxes is proportional to the number of test cases.

The choice of the projects was influenced by several factors: (1) the projects should be publicly available, so we could obtain the source code (2) proper naming convention were followed to some extent (for further information see Sect. 5), and (3) we refer to our previous work, where we used these projects and found they are good representatives for the evaluation. Here we briefly introduce them. Two of the systems strive to have minimal dependencies on other libraries [4] and are modules of the Apache Commons project, these are Commons Lang[2] and Commons Math[3]. Mondrian[4] has a large development history (the development was started in 1997 [26]) and is an open source Online Analytical Processing system, which enables high-performance analysis on massive amounts of data. JFreeChart[5] is a relatively new software, its first release was in 2013. The project is one of the most popular open source charting tools.

From these projects, we obtained three different textual representations to measure similarity. We also described these representations in more detail in our previous work [5]. Similar representations are widely used in other research experiments, such as [38,40]. Here we present brief summary of our representations and through a brief example, we try to better explain them:

[2] https://github.com/apache/commons-lang.
[3] https://github.com/apache/commons-math.
[4] https://github.com/pentaho/mondrian.
[5] https://github.com/jfree/jfreechart.

- **SRC**: In this case, we process the source code as a structured text file. Only splitting [8,12] and stemming are applied. We split the source code along special characters and compound words by the camel case rule. For example, consider the code snippet *int a = 12;* where SRC only splits the text.
- **AST**: Initially, we construct the Abstract Syntax Tree (AST) for a code snippet, then print the type of each node in a pre-order fashion. We employed the publicly available JavaParser[6] tool for AST generation. For the previous example, the representation would be: *VariableDeclarationExpr VariableDeclarator PrimitiveType SimpleName IntegerLiteralExpr.*
- **IDENT**: Like in the previous case, we construct the Abstract Syntax Tree but instead of types we print the only the values and only for the terminal nodes. In the postprocessing phase literals are replaced with placeholders. These printed values are generally the identifiers and constants present in the code. In the previous example, the representation replaces the integer literal, so we get the following sentence: *int a<INT>*.

4 Experiment Design

In this section, we describe the experiments and utilized machine learning methods in detail. Let us consider a straightforward example. In Fig. 3 a simple JUnit test case is presented with its corresponding production code. The code snippet is part of the Commons Lang project. It is easy to see, that the test code chiefly consists of *assert* statements, where the tested methods header is called many times. On the other hand, before the production code, in the comments, the name of the method also often occurs. Notice, that in the IDENT representation the string literals are replaced with placeholders so the method calls will be practically identical in the test case. Although the bodies of the two methods differ, some kind of similarity can be observed. In addition, we measure the similarity between classes, so other methods also contribute to the results. In the upcoming subsections, we explain the techniques used to obtain the similarity between two parts of the source code. We used the Gensim [1] toolkit's implementation for all three machine learning methods.

4.1 Term Frequency–Inverse Document Frequency: TF-IDF

TF-IDF is an information retrieval method, that relies on numerical statistics reflecting how important a word is to a document in a corpus [20]. It is basically a metric and its value increases proportionally to the number of times a word appears in the document but is offset by the frequency of the word in the corpus. One can compute TF-IDF by multiplying a local component (term frequency) with a global component (inverse document frequency) and normalizing the resulting documents to unit length. The formula for a non-normalized weight of term i in document j in a corpus of D documents is displayed in Eq. 1.

[6] https://github.com/javaparser/javaparser.

test.java.org.apache.commons.lang3.StringUtilsSubstringTest

```
@Test
public void testSubstringAfterLast_StringString() {
    assertEquals("baz", StringUtils.substringAfterLast("fooXXbarXXbaz", "XX"));
    assertEquals(null, StringUtils.substringAfterLast(null, null));
    assertEquals(null, StringUtils.substringAfterLast(null, ""));
    assertEquals(null, StringUtils.substringAfterLast(null, "XX"));
    ...
    assertEquals("t", StringUtils.substringAfterLast("foot", "o"));
    assertEquals("", StringUtils.substringAfterLast("abc", "c"));
    assertEquals("", StringUtils.substringAfterLast("", "d"));
    assertEquals("", StringUtils.substringAfterLast("abc", "")); }
```

SIMILARITY?

```
/*StringUtils.substringAfterLast(null, *) = null
 * StringUtils.substringAfterLast("", *) = ""
 * ...
 * StringUtils.substringAfterLast("a", "z") = ""
 * ... */
public static String substringAfterLast(final String str, final String separator) {
    if (isEmpty(str)) { return str; }
    if (isEmpty(separator)) { return EMPTY; }
    final int pos = str.lastIndexOf(separator);
    if (pos==INDEX_NOT_FOUND || pos==str.length() - separator.length()) { return EMPTY; }
    return str.substring(pos + separator.length());
}
```

main.java.org.apache.commons.lang3.StringUtils

Fig. 3. An example test case from Commons Lang and the associated production class.

One of the simplest ranking functions is computed by summing the weights for each query term, but many more sophisticated ranking functions also exist [11, 28].

$$weight_{ij} = \left(frequency_{ij} * log_2 \frac{D}{DocumentFrequency_i}\right) \tag{1}$$

4.2 Document Embeddings: Doc2Vec

Doc2Vec is originated from Word2Vec, which was introduced by Google's developers in [25]. Word2Vec encodes words into vectors containing real numbers with a neural network, these are called word embeddings. The basic idea is the following: for a given surrounding, the model predicts the current word (CBOW model) or the prediction goes in the opposite direction (Skip-gram model). The trick is that the hidden layer of the shallow neural network used has fewer neurons than the input and output layers, forcing the model to learn a compact representation. The weight in the hidden layers will provide the word embeddings and the number of neurons will be the dimension of the embedding. Doc2Vec differs only in small details: it can encode whole documents by adding a unique identifier of the document to the input layer. This way a word can have multiple embeddings in different documents (which is more realistic in some cases, e.g.: blue, bear). Utilizing the embeddings, we can compute the similarity between documents. We used the 3COSMUL metric proposed in [21], displayed in Eq. 2 to measure similarity between the vectors.

$$arg \max_{b* \in V} \left(\frac{cos(b*, b)cos(b*, a*)}{cos(b*, a) + \epsilon}\right) \tag{2}$$

4.3 Latent Semantic Indexing: LSI

LSI is a technique in natural language processing of analyzing the relationships between documents. During the learning procedure, a matrix is constructed, which contains word counts. The elements inside the matrix are typically weighted with the TF-IDF values, but note that the base process differs from the previous one. The main idea of LSI is that the matrix is transformed into a lower dimension using singular value decomposition and in the resulting matrix the conceptually more similar elements get more similar representations. The most similar documents to a query can easily be found as the query also represents a multidimensional matrix with which a suitable distance method can rank each document by similarity.

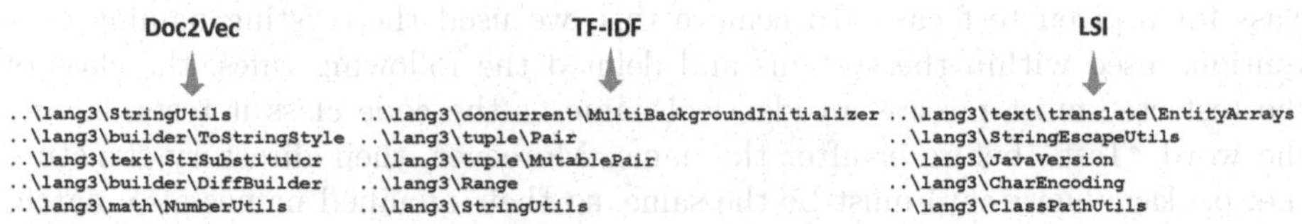

Fig. 4. Ranked lists produced by different approaches for the *StringUtilsSubstringTest* test class.

4.4 Result Refinement with a Combined Technique

After test and code classes had been separated and the code representations had been obtained, we trained the three models separately and investigated the similarities. In Fig. 4 we show the ranked lists of the three alternative methods trained on the IDENT representation. For a given test class (*StringUtilsSubstringTest*) only the Doc2Vec method classified the desired code class (*StringUtils*) as the most similar (while of course in a different case another one of the methods could provide the desired class). Additionally note, that TF-IDF put the *StringUtils* class in the fifth place, while LSI didn't rank it among the top-5 most similar classes (it was in the 11th place of the ranked list). This example demonstrates that the ranked list of each technique can contain useful information, the desired code class appears close to the top of every list. Thus it can be possible to refine the obtained results one technique provides with the list of other techniques. We defined a simple algorithm to achieve this goal, which is shown in Listing 1. We filter the ranked list obtained from the first method with the seconds ranked list. Since the ranked lists contain every code class, we limit them to the top 100 most similar classes, this way the featured algorithm will drop out classes from the first if those are not present on the second ranked list. Note, that this refinement procedure cannot introduce new classes to the first ranked list, only removes them.

```
    # ranked_list_i: ranked list from the i-th technique,
      which contains the top 100 most similar classes
result = []
for code_class in ranked_list_1:
    if code_class in ranked_list_2:
        result.append(code_class)
```

Listing 1. Algorithm used to refine the obtained similarity lists.

5 Experiments and Analysis

In this section, we evaluate and discuss the featured text-based models and source code representations. To evaluate our method, we should know whether the proposed machine learning techniques recommend the correct production class for a given test case. To achieve this, we used the existing naming conventions used within the systems and defined the following rules: the class of the test case must possess an identical name as the code class it tests, having the word "Test" before or after the name. Moreover, their directory structure (i.e. package hierarchy) must be the same, so their qualified names also match. For example, if the tested production code class is [CodeClass] than the test should be named [CodeClass*Test*] or [*Test*CodeClass] and their package hierarchy should also match to be considered a correct pair. We calculated precision - the proportion of correctly detected test-code pairs as can be seen in Eq. 3, where the upper part of the fraction denotes how many tests we could retrieve, while the bottom is the number of test cases that match the naming convention. This evaluation strategy is well suited for the listed systems since they are fairly well covered by proper naming conventions.

$$precision = \frac{|relevantTest \cap retrievedTest|}{|retrievedTest|} \tag{3}$$

As detailed in the previous sections, we experimented with three different source code representations and three text-based similarity techniques. We already know, that Doc2Vec and LSI are capable of recovering traceability links, although we do not know how LSI performs on different source code representations. Figure 5 provides a comprehensive collection of the results obtained. From this diagram, it's clear at first glance, that the IDENT representation surpassed all others and AST performed poorly. In some cases, the SRC representation produced quite promising results (e.g.: with TF-IDF at the Commons Math project), but in general, it achieved much lower precision than IDENT. We experienced similar behavior in our previous work, so this confirms our preceding assumption that IDENT is the most suitable representation for test-to-code traceability, since other techniques also performed at lower precision using other representations. Because IDENT seems to be prevalent in finding traceability links correctly, we are going to focus on it in the upcoming discussions.

Answer to RQ1: Based on the results of each evaluated algorithm, we found the IDENT representation to be the most appropriate for finding traceability links correctly.

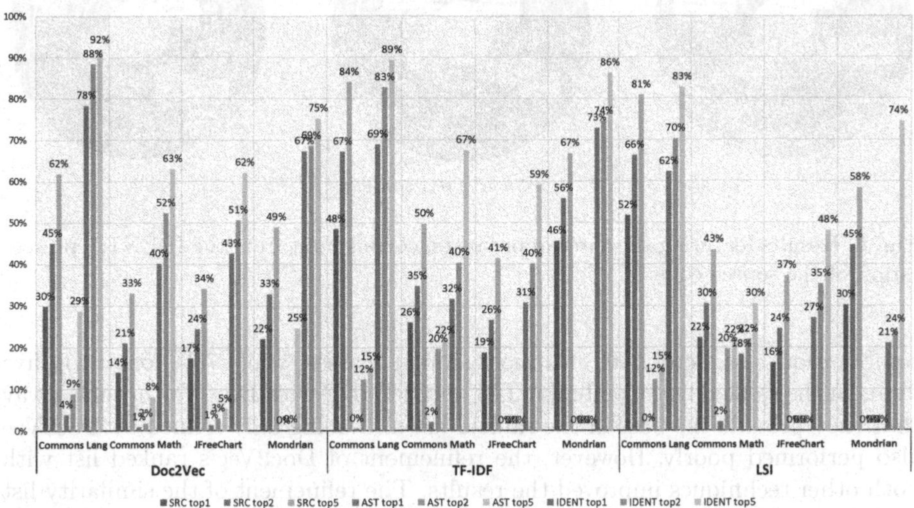

Fig. 5. Results featuring the corpus built from different representations of the source code provided by each technique evaluated.

By examining the results in more detail, we can see, that the precision of Doc2Vec in most cases rises above the rest. Figure 6 presents the results of the featured techniques trained on the IDENT representation. The figure showcases the results we gathered with the most similar classes. It is visible that LSI performed the lowest on the examined systems. TF-IDF's case is a bit unusual since it outperformed the Doc2Vec technique on the Mondrian project with 73% precision rate. The results from other systems also seem quite promising. Therefore from our experiments, Doc2Vec seemed to be the best approach in the test-to-code traceability task, although in some cases other text-based approaches may overperform it. The results of Doc2Vec, in general, are quite convincing, but the obtained matches could still be refined. Because TF-IDF found better results in the Mondrian project than Doc2Vec, combining (for more detail about combination refer to Sect. 5) these methods seems to be a rational idea.

Answer to RQ2: According to the data gathered, we find that in most cases Doc2Vec achieves the best results, although in exceptional cases other text-based techniques can still outperform it.

We investigated the combination possibilities among all the examined techniques. The relation between them is asymmetric, since the first methods ranked list refines the second ones. We found that combining LSI just with TF-IDF only seems to damage the results in both directions, the average precision using this

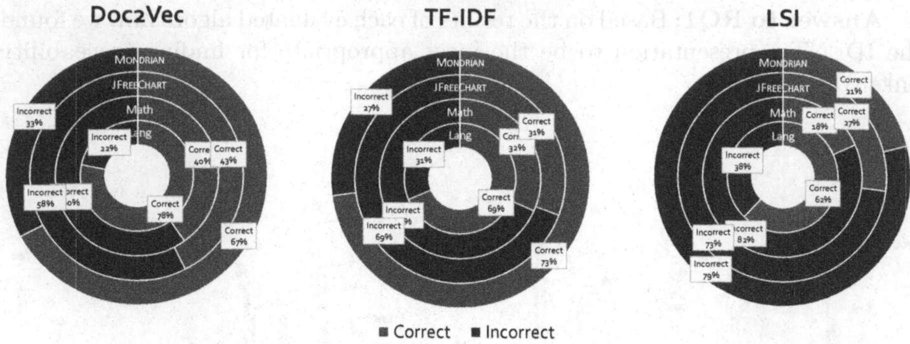

Fig. 6. Results featuring the three approaches, corpus built from the IDENT representation of the source code.

combination was merely 50% for most similar classes, while 70% for to top five items in the ranked list. Combining LSI and TF-IDF with Doc2Vec in such a way that they provide the base of the ranked list and being only refined by Doc2Vec also performed poorly. However, the refinement of Doc2Vec's ranked list with both other techniques improved the results. The refinement of the similarity list with LSI resulted in more than 2.5% improvement compared to Doc2Vec as a standalone technique. Although TF-IDF also improved the values, the improvement was just under 2%. Due to space limitations and to stick to the results that seem more important we do not display these results in detail. We also experimented with the combination of all three techniques: the main similarity list was provided by Doc2Vec and refined by TF-IDF and LSI. When we combined Doc2Vec with both of the other methods, the obtained results were even better than in the other cases. Table 1 presents the results of Doc2Vec as a standalone technique, and as a combination with other approaches. If we compare these results an advantage in the latter method's precision can be recognized. If only the most similar code class is considered, Doc2Vec's average precision was 57%, while with the combined technique we achieved nearly 60%. The most prominent improvement can be identified at Commons Math (roughly 8%), but it is evident that the precision values of every system have increased.

Answer to RQ3: Based on the results, we can clearly see that the combination of techniques has improved the performance in test-to-code traceability link recovery.

While the produced model seems to outperform Doc2Vec in every aspect, Mondrian still remains an outlier. As we saw before, TF-IDF resulted in an outstanding 72.8% precision value, while Doc2Vec merely achieved 67.2%. The deviation is also present if we consider the top 2 or top 5 most similar classes (74%/68% and 86%/75% respectively). While the combined approach improved the outcome of the basic Doc2Vec model, it did not reach the precision of TF-IDF in this single case. Even this considered, on average the combined approach improved the results compared to Doc2Vec by almost 4% (Fig. 7).

Table 1. Results obtained from Doc2Vec as a standalone technique and as a mixed approach.

Top$_N$ results	Doc2Vec			Doc2Vec-TFIDF-LSI		
	1	2	5	1	2	5
Commons Lang	**78.3%**	88.4%	91.8%	**78.3%**	88.4%	93.1%
Commons Math	**40.1%**	52.3%	62.9%	**48.2%**	58.0%	68.2%
JFreeChart	**42.5%**	50.6%	62.0%	**45.3%**	55.2%	67.3%
Mondrian	**67.2%**	68.5%	75.1%	**67.6%**	70.2%	80.7%

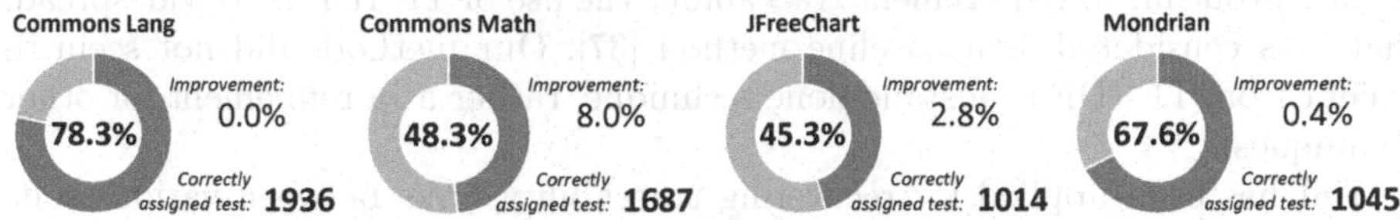

Fig. 7. Result values of the combined Doc2Vec method, trained on the IDENT representation of the source code.

6 Related Work

Traceability in software engineering research typically refers to the discovery of traceability links from requirements or related natural text documentation towards the source code [3,22]. Even as test-to-code traceability is not the most fashionable topic among link recovery tasks, there are several well-known methods that aim to cope with this problem [35]. Test related traceability examples also can be found [5,13,15,31,35], however no known perfect solution exists to the problem. In the research community serious attempts have been made at combating the problem via plugins in the development environment [29] or via static or dynamic analysis [36]. The current state-of-the-art techniques [30] rely on a combination of diverse methods. In this work, we also took advantage of various textual similarity techniques, and the combination of these resulted in a promising recovery precision.

Recommendation systems are also not new to software engineering [18,33,34], presenting a prioritized list of most likely solutions seems to be a more resilient approach even in traceability research [5,15].

Word2Vec [25] gained a lot of attention in recent years and became a very popular approach in natural language processing. With this method, calculating similarity between text elements became a mainstream process [9,19,23,27,38,40,43,44]. Textual similarity is useful for example in the clone detection problem [40]. Doc2Vec [24] is an extension of the Word2Vec method dealing with whole documents rather than single words. Although not enjoying the immense popularity of Word2Vec, it is still prominent to the scientific community [6,7,39,46]. In requirement traceability, researchers also made use of word embeddings to recover appropriate links [9,44,45]. Our current approach differs from these in many aspects. To begin with, we make use of three different similarity concepts, not just one. Next, we compute document embeddings in one step, while in other approaches this is usually achieved in several steps. Finally, our models were trained only on source code (or on some representation which was obtained from the source code) and there was no natural language based corpus.

Using TF-IDF for traceability is not a novelty in the software engineering domain, however, most of the researchers cope with the requirement traceability problem. For example, this technique was used in [42] to trace textual requirement elements to related textual defect reports, or in [10] for the after-the-fact tracing problem. In requirement traceability the use of TF-IDF is so widespread, that it is considered as a baseline method [37]. Our methods did not seem to benefit from TF-IDF as a standalone technique, rather as a refinement for other techniques.

LSI has been applied for recovering traceability links between various software artifacts, even in feature extraction experiments [16]. LSI is already known to be capable of producing good quality results combined with structural information [14,17]. Besides feature extraction, LSI as a standalone technique can be applied to the test-to-code traceability task as well [5,15].

Although natural language based methods are not the most effective standalone techniques, state-of-the-art test-to-code traceability methods like the method provided by Qusef et al. [30,32] incorporate textual analysis for more precise recovery. In these papers, the authors named their method SCOTCH and have proposed several improvements to it. Although their purpose is similar to ours, a fundamental difference is that they used dynamic slicing and focus on the last assert statement inside a test case. Their approach also relies on class name similarity, while we encoded code snippets without any assumptions on naming conventions. These methods use LSI for textual similarity evaluation, while previous evaluations of word embeddings for this purpose are unknown.

7 Conclusions

Test-to-code traceability helps to find production code for a given test case. Our assumption was that the related test and code classes are similar to each other in some sense. We employed three different similarity concepts, based on Doc2Vec, LSI and TF-IDF. Since these methods are intended for natural language texts, we experimented with three different source code representations. Analyzing the obtained data, we derived the conclusion that from simple source code representations, IDENT performs more desirable in test traceability. We compared the obtained results from the three textual similarity techniques and found that the Doc2Vec based similarity performs better in the recovery task than other approaches. Finally, we refined Doc2Vec's ranked similarity list with the recommendation of the other approaches. With this experiment we have successfully improved the performance of Doc2Vec for every project, therefore introducing a successful mixed approach for the textual matching of tests and their production code.

Acknowledgements. This work was supported by the UNKP-18-2 New National Excellence Program and the European Union, co-financed by the European Social Fund (EFOP-3.6.3-VEKOP-16-2017-00002). The Ministry of Human Capacities, Hungary grant 20391-3/2018/FEKUSTRAT is also acknowledged.

References

1. Gensim: Gensim webpage. https://radimrehurek.com/gensim/. Accessed 2019
2. TIOBE programming community index. https://www.tiobe.com/tiobe-index. Accessed 2019
3. Antoniol, G., Canfora, G., Casazza, G., De Lucia, A., Merlo, E.: Recovering traceability links between code and documentation. IEEE Trans. Softw. Eng. **28**(10), 970–983 (2002)
4. Apache Commons webpage (2019). http://commons.apache.org/
5. Csuvik, V., Kicsi, A., Vidács, L.: Source code level word embeddings in aiding semantic test-to-code traceability. In: 10th International Workshop at the 41st International Conference on Software Engineering (ICSE) - SST 2019. IEEE (2019)
6. Dai, A.M., Olah, C., Le, Q.V.: Document Embedding with Paragraph Vectors, July 2015
7. DeFronzo, R.A., et al.: Combination of empagliflozin and linagliptin as second-line therapy in subjects with type 2 diabetes inadequately controlled on metformin. Diab. Care **38**(3), 384–393 (2015)
8. Dit, B., Guerrouj, L., Poshyvanyk, D., Antoniol, G.: Can better identifier splitting techniques help feature location? In: 2011 IEEE 19th International Conference on Program Comprehension (ICPC), ICPC 2011, pp. 11–20. IEEE, Washington, DC (2011)
9. Guo, J., Cheng, J., Cleland-Huang, J.: Semantically enhanced software traceability using deep learning techniques. In: Proceedings - 2017 IEEE/ACM 39th International Conference on Software Engineering, ICSE 2017, pp. 3–14. IEEE, May 2017
10. Hayes, J.H., Dekhtyar, A., Sundaram, S.K.: Improving after-the-fact tracing and mapping: supporting software quality predictions. IEEE Softw. **22**(6), 30–37 (2005)
11. Hiemstra, D.: A probabilistic justification for using tf - idf term weighting in information retrieval. Int. J. Digit. Libr. **3**(2), 131–139 (2000)
12. Hill, E., Binkley, D., Lawrie, D., Pollock, L., Vijay-Shanker, K.: An empirical study of identifier splitting techniques. Empirical Softw. Eng. **19**(6), 1754–1780 (2014)
13. Kaushik, N., Tahvildari, L., Moore, M.: Reconstructing traceability between bugs and test cases: an experimental study. In: 2011 18th Working Conference on Reverse Engineering, pp. 411–414. IEEE, October 2011
14. Kicsi, A., et al.: Feature analysis using information retrieval, community detection and structural analysis methods in product line adoption. J. Syst. Softw. (2019)
15. Kicsi, A., Tóth, L., Vidács, L.: Exploring the benefits of utilizing conceptual information in test-to-code traceability. In: Proceedings of the 6th International Workshop on Realizing Artificial Intelligence Synergies in Software Engineering, pp. 8–14 (2018)
16. Kicsi, A., Vidács, L., Beszédes, A., Kocsis, F., Kovács, I.: Information retrieval based feature analysis for product line adoption in 4GL systems. In: Proceedins of the 17th International Conference on Computational Science and Its Applications - ICCSA 2017, pp. 1–6. IEEE (2017)

17. Kicsi, A., Vidács, L., Csuvik, V., Horváth, F., Beszédes, Á., Kocsis, F.: Supporting product line adoption by combining syntactic and textual feature extraction. In: Capilla, R., Gallina, B., Cetina, C. (eds.) ICSR 2018. LNCS, vol. 10826, pp. 148–163. Springer, Cham (2018). https://doi.org/10.1007/978-3-319-90421-4_10
18. Kochhar, P.S., Xia, X., Lo, D., Li, S.: Practitioners' expectations on automated fault localization. In: Proceedings of the 25th International Symposium on Software Testing and Analysis - ISSTA 2016, pp. 165–176. ACM Press, New York (2016)
19. Le, Q.V., Mikolov, T.: Distributed representations of sentences and documents. Technical report (2014)
20. Lefebvre-Ulrikson, W., Da Costa, G., Rigutti, L., Blum, I.: Data Mining. New York (2016)
21. Levy, O., Goldberg, Y.: Linguistic regularities in sparse and explicit word representations. Technical report (2014)
22. Marcus, A., Maletic, J.I., Sergeyev, A.: Recovery of traceability links between software documentation and source code. Int. J. Softw. Eng. Knowl. Eng., 811–836 (2005)
23. Mathieu, N., Hamou-Lhadj, A.: Word embeddings for the software engineering domain. In: Proceedings of the 15th International Conference on Mining Software Repositories - MSR 2018, pp. 38–41 (2018)
24. Mikolov, T., Sutskever, I., Chen, K., Corrado, G., Dean, J.: Distributed representations of words and phrases and their compositionality. Technical report (2013)
25. Mikolov, T., Sutskever, I., Chen, K., Corrado, G., Dean, J.: Distributed representations of words and phrases and their compositionality. In: Proceedings of the 26th International Conference on Neural Information Processing Systems, NIPS 2013, vol. 2, pp. 3111–3119, December 2013
26. Mondrian webpage (2019). http://www.theusrus.de/Mondrian/
27. Nguyen, T.D., Nguyen, A.T., Phan, H.D., Nguyen, T.N.: Exploring API embedding for API usages and applications. In: Proceedings - 2017 IEEE/ACM 39th International Conference on Software Engineering, ICSE 2017, pp. 438–449. IEEE, May 2017
28. Paik, J.H.: A novel TF-IDF weighting scheme for effective ranking. In: Proceedings of the 36th international ACM SIGIR Conference on Research and Development in Information Retrieval - SIGIR 2013, p. 343. ACM Press, New York (2013)
29. Bouillon, P., Krinke, J., Meyer, N., Steimann, F.: EzUnit: a framework for associating failed unit tests with potential programming errors. In: Concas, G., Damiani, E., Scotto, M., Succi, G. (eds.) XP 2007. LNCS, vol. 4536, pp. 101–104. Springer, Heidelberg (2007). https://doi.org/10.1007/978-3-540-73101-6_14
30. Qusef, A., Bavota, G., Oliveto, R., De Lucia, A., Binkley, D.: Recovering test-to-code traceability using slicing and textual analysis. J. Syst. Softw. **88**, 147–168 (2014)
31. Qusef, A., Bavota, G., Oliveto, R., De Lucia, A., Binkley, D.: SCOTCH: test-to-code traceability using slicing and conceptual coupling. In: IEEE International Conference on Software Maintenance, ICSM, pp. 63–72. IEEE (2011)
32. Qusef, A., Bavota, G., Oliveto, R., Lucia, A.D., Binkley, D.: Evaluating test-to-code traceability recovery methods through controlled experiments. J. Softw. Evol. Process **25**(11), 1167–1191 (2013)
33. Robillard, M., Walker, R., Zimmermann, T.: Recommendation systems for software engineering. IEEE Softw. **27**(4), 80–86 (2010)
34. Robillard, M.P., Maalej, W., Walker, R.J., Zimmermann, T. (eds.): Recommendation Systems in Software Engineering. Springer, Heidelberg (2014). https://doi.org/10.1007/978-3-642-45135-5

35. Rompaey, B.V., Demeyer, S.: Establishing traceability links between unit test cases and units under test. In: European Conference on Software Maintenance and Reengineering, CSMR, pp. 209–218. IEEE (2009)
36. Sneed, H.: Reverse engineering of test cases for selective regression testing. In: European Conference on Software Maintenance and Reengineering, CSMR 2004, pp. 69–74. IEEE (2004)
37. Sundaram, S.K., Hayes, J.H., Dekhtyar, A.: Baselines in requirements tracing. In: ACM SIGSOFT Software Engineering Notes, vol. 30, p. 1. ACM Press, New York (2005)
38. Tufano, M., Watson, C., Bavota, G., Di Penta, M., White, M., Poshyvanyk, D.: Deep learning similarities from different representations of source code. In: Proceedings of the 15th International Conference on Mining Software Repositories - MSR 2018, vol. 18, pp. 542–553 (2018)
39. Wang, S., Tang, J., Aggarwal, C., Liu, H.: Linked document embedding for classification. In: Proceedings of the 25th ACM International on Conference on Information and Knowledge Management - CIKM 2016, pp. 115–124. ACM Press, New York (2016)
40. White, M., Tufano, M., Vendome, C., Poshyvanyk, D.: Deep learning code fragments for code clone detection. In: Proceedings of the 31st IEEE/ACM International Conference on Automated Software Engineering - ASE 2016, pp. 87–98 (2016)
41. Wilson, G., et al.: Best practices for scientific computing. PLoS Biol. **12**(1), e1001745 (2014)
42. Yadla, S., Hayes, J.H., Dekhtyar, A.: Tracing requirements to defect reports: an application of information retrieval techniques. Innovations Syst. Softw. Eng. **1**(2), 116–124 (2005)
43. Yang, X., Lo, D., Xia, X., Bao, L., Sun, J.: Combining word embedding with information retrieval to recommend similar bug reports. In: Proceedings - International Symposium on Software Reliability Engineering, ISSRE, pp. 127–137. IEEE, October 2016
44. Ye, X., Shen, H., Ma, X., Bunescu, R., Liu, C.: From word embeddings to document similarities for improved information retrieval in software engineering. In: Proceedings of the 38th International Conference on Software Engineering - ICSE 2016, pp. 404–415. ACM Press, New York (2016)
45. Zhao, T., Cao, Q., Sun, Q.: An improved approach to traceability recovery based on word embeddings. In: Proceedings - Asia-Pacific Software Engineering Conference, APSEC, vol. 2017-Decem, pp. 81–89. IEEE, December 2018
46. Zhu, Z., Hu, J.: Context aware document embedding, July 2017

Reducing Efforts in Web Services Refactoring

Guillermo Rodriguez[1(✉)], Leonardo Fernández Esteberena[2], Cristian Mateos[1], and Sanjay Misra[3]

[1] ISISTAN-UNICEN-CONICET, Tandil, Argentina
{guillermo.rodriguez,cristian.mateos}@isistan.unicen.edu.ar
[2] Globant, Tandil, Argentina
[3] Covenant University, Ota, Nigeria
ssopam@gmail.com

Abstract. In Service-Oriented Computing, systems provide a service interface described by a computer-readable language called Web Services Description Language (WSDL), but document descriptions often exhibit design problems as systems expand. Moreover, a major problem in this type of applications is its growth; as size and complexity of applications increase, the probability of duplicity of code also increases. This issue could have a negative impact on quality attributes, such as performance, maintainability and evolution, among others, providing developers with some clues to detect refactoring opportunities. Conducting a detection process of these opportunities could be a daunting task; however, this work proposes a methodology to conduct manual refactoring of service descriptions of legacy systems. The methodology allows software developers to collect metrics of time effort and space reduction. The metrics indicate a 75% reduction in services and 63% of the lines of code on average. Additionally, a statistical analysis carried out with the obtained metrics yielded as result that the number of services refactored according to the size of its refactoring group is adjusted to a logarithmic function. We also analyzed how refactoring time increases with the size of services. The results indicate that our methodology could be applied in similar case-studies based on legacy systems.

Keywords: Software refactoring · Web Services · Web service description language · Statistical analysis

1 Introduction

In the context of Service Oriented Computing (SOC), a widespread implementation of services is the use of Web Services [1]. Web services enable interactivity among software components. The communication transmits distributed data and information between those components via standard Web protocols [2]. A Web Service is a piece of software designed to enable interoperability in machine-to-machine interactions, making use of different technologies and protocols such as

S. Misra et al. (Eds.): ICCSA 2019, LNCS 11622, pp. 544–559, 2019.
https://doi.org/10.1007/978-3-030-24305-0_41

SOAP, HTTP and XML along with other standards. To exhibit their functionality, Web Services provide an interface described by the Web Services Description Language (WSDL) [3].

However, from a technical perspective, software developers need to dedicate significant effort to discovering sets of suitable services, interpreting them, developing software that overcomes their inherent data and process mismatches, and finally composing them into a complex process [4]. Furthermore, a common difficulty that arises with the use of WSDL documents is that they are prone to develop design problems as the system expands, forcing them to increase development effort for adding new functionalities [5]. Another challenge of WSDL documents is how to integrate service based tools and contents, mobile applications and cloud computing services into the legacy systems [6].

To deal with those issues, refactoring seems to be the most suitable strategy to apply. By refactoring the code, the internal structure of the system can be improved but the system behavior is not altered. Ideally, developers should allocate time in their development iterations to fix refactoring issues, particularly those that are critical for maintenance or harm the system architecture [7].

In this work we propose a novel methodology to conduct a refactoring process of legacy service-oriented applications wrapped by means of WSDL documents. We have previously developed a tool to conduct a semi-automated detection of refactoring opportunities [8]. Our aim is to provide metrics that quantify in general terms of WSDL documents before and after the refactoring, and the effort required to achieve this process manually. Additionally, a statistical analysis carried out with the obtained metrics yielded as result that the number of services refactored according to the size of its refactoring group is adjusted to a logarithmic function. We also analyzed how refactoring time increases with the functional size of services.

The remaining of this paper is organized as follows. Section 2 describes the background. Section 3 presents the related work. Section 4 presents the proposed approach to conduct the refactoring process. The empirical evaluation of the approach is explained and summarized in Sect. 5. Finally, conclusions and future lines of research are stated in Sect. 6.

2 Background

Service-Oriented Computing paradigm promotes the efficient development and deployment of an application in terms of cost and time. To flexibly enable the composition of applications Web Services are utilized as building blocks [9]. In this context, web services are usually described by means of WSDL documents. This language is an XML format that allows software developers to describe service functionality and communication protocols to be accessed through the Internet [10]. The main conceptual elements in WSDL documents are Types, Messages, PortTypes, Bindings and Services, among others. Types contain the definitions of the types of data that will be used in/out the service. To specify types, an XML schema is utilized. Each data type defines an element with a complexType inside it, which lists a series of elements of basic types (built-in).

Messages define the contents of a message abstractly by using data types defined in *wsdl: types*. Each message consists of one or more parts that will make use of an element or complexType, referencing them with the element and type message attributes respectively. There will be as many *wsdl:message* tags as necessary.

A PortType is a set of abstract operations that indicate which abstract messages are received and sent. WSDL supports several operational patters including one-way (receives a message), request-response (receives a message, then sends one in response), request-response (sends a message, then receives one in response) and notification.

To define operations, their messages are detailed by means of the *wsdl:operation tag*. The fact that they are request-response operations are specified implicitly by firstly placing the *wsdl:input* tag and then *wsdl:output*. Bindings provide the format and protocol details for the messages and operations of a PortType. For example, the operations might be accessed by means of the protocol SOAP, and then a specific SOAP binding is declared in the document [11]. Finally, Services are a set of related ports under the same name. Each port defines a particular and concrete endpoint of the communication, linking a binding with a location address.

3 Related Work

Software evolvability is an important quality attribute, however, sometimes it is hard to achieve specially in long-living systems that are in continuous change. Moreover, some authors have concentrated on supporting evolvability in SOA systems by improving web services descriptions [12]. Mateos et al. have introduced an Eclipse plug-in to assist software developers in obtaining WSDL documents from the code, minimizing the number of anti-patterns [13]. Webster et al. have presented an approach to try to resolve the conflict which is specified when the service provider needs evolve its interface to respond to new requirements, without affecting consumers of that service [14]. In [10], the authors have presented a novel structural-semantic approach to help developers in retrieving and selecting services. The approach is based on a comprehensive structural scheme for service Interface Compatibility analysis, and WordNet as the semantic support to assess identifiers of operations and parameters.

The authors in [15] have revealed a lack of systematic guidance on the refactoring process for existing monolithic applications. However, there is a wide range of semi-automated techniques to support the refactoring process. In [16], the authors propose a semi-automatic approach for migrating applications to a PaaS environment, avoiding cloud restrictions through user-defined refactorings. In [17], the authors have generated insights into service-oriented evolution qualities, and provided a modifiability comparison of the two popular service-based architectural styles by qualitatively mapping principles and patterns of Service-Oriented Architecture (SOA) and Microservices onto tactics.

Although there is a considerable number of research works that have addressed the refactoring process of service-oriented applications, our research work proposes a novel methodology beyond a systematic guidance that also provides an statistical analysis of refactoring time as a function of the size of services.

4 Our Approach

The general steps of the proposed methodology are explained by means of an activity diagram (Fig. 1). The methodology begins with the initial classification and then a iterative procedure takes control until all original services are grouped into a refactored service. Each iteration is responsible for refactoring a service and consists of the following steps: Detection, Design and Specification. At the end of each iteration a question is made: Are there original services not included in the refactored services? If so, another iteration must be started from the Detection step otherwise the refactoring is done.

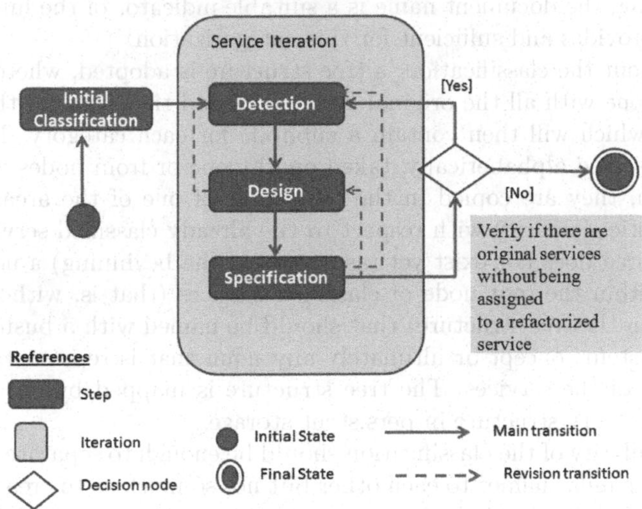

Fig. 1. Our proposed methodology.

Note that the methodology shows which step should be passed at the end of the previous step using the main transitions, but also Fig. 1 indicates revision transitions that are taken during the development of a step to go back when any of the previous decisions should be improved. The following sub-sections shed some light on each of the steps of the proposed methodology.

4.1 Initial Classification

Initially, WSDL documents are received with no defined organization. Starting to generate refactoring groups in this situation would involve browsing all the documents and internally exploring a considerable number of operations, with no notion of its functionalities. To deal with this issue, a first initial classification is done. This allows for:

- Having a first contact with the system, familiarizing in general with the types of services provided and sometimes suggesting how they relate each other.
- Creating an organizational structure that divides services into areas of possible clustering. In many cases an internal search in a classification area is enough to select a refactoring group.
- Even in several cases where the formation of a group requires the detailed exploration of more than one classification area (in taxonomic terms) it is possible that the structure act as an index, speeding up any search process.

The classification is not intended to accurately delineate groups for refactoring; this task demands effort and will be executed during service iterations. On the contrary, it must be general and brief. Since each WSDL document contains one service tag, the document name is a suitable indicator of the functionalities the service provides and sufficient for this categorization.

To carry out the classification, a tree structure is adopted, where two nodes are created: one with all the original documents and the other for the classified documents, which will then contain a subnode for each category. The original services are sorted alphabetically, taken one by one or from nodes with similar names. Then, they are copied in the (sub)node of one of the areas according to the semantic similarity with respect to the already classified services of each area. If the area does not exist yet (as occurs at the beginning) a new subnode is created within the root node of classified services (that is, without creating more depth in the tree structure) that should be named with a business area or process, a system concept or ultimately any noun that is representative of the functionality of the services. The tree structure is mapped by our supporting tools to a directory structure in persistent storage.

The granularity of the classification should be enough to separate most of the services with similar names to each other but not so much as to create subnodes that allocate only two or three documents. Besides, it is recommendable to avoid incurring details that could only be resolved by exploring the content of the WSDL documents by the developer. For these two reasons, it is suggested to create a category named "Other" for the services that are particular to enter into other classifications or that cannot be classified without a WSDL document perusal.

After classifying all the documents, each subnode is browsed and its content is reviewed, making local changes to services that are considered poorly classified and being aware of the features provided, without accessing the content of the documents. This first task should not take more than one hour (of useful working time) and the resulting artifact is a set of nodes, or directories, representing functional areas of the system, which contain all the original WSDL documents.

4.2 Service Iteration

After the initial classification, a series of iterations for refactoring the services are conducted, each one creates a service in the new system that supplies the functionalities of a group of original services. The iteration is divided into three steps: detection, design and specification, which must be performed preferably without major interruptions, so as not to hinder the process and avoid revisions that would increase the total necessary time. Although the steps are commonly performed in order, it is not a completely linear process: in several circumstances it becomes necessary to return temporarily to a previous step to make some revisions and changes.

Detection. The first step in our methodology is to find a group of services that can be unified. The discovery of refactored services is not necessarily achieved at the end of this step. In several cases, for example, decisions as to whether the original services will comprise a single refactored service or several services, whether any of them should be left out or in, whether it is better to unify them or not, they are just made in the step of design and occasionally modified even during the specification step. The aim of this first step is to find a set of potentially candidate groupable services.

Firstly, the category directories of the initial classification are used as input (they will have been modified if one or more refactoring iterations have passed) and one directory is chosen. The choice may be at random, however, in case there have been previous iterations, it is useful to prioritize areas related to the recent refactorings to take advantage of the developer's familiarity and his recall capabilities.

Within the chosen category, WSDL documents are opened and candidates for unification are sought for evaluating the content of the documents. Once a group of well-defined candidates is selected, possible members in the category "Other" (if it exists) and in other categories considered to be closely related are revised, looking for names that suggest a relationship and opening more candidate documents for evaluation. The detection ends when a group of unified services is considered done and there is no other service to add to this group. The evaluation criteria for the selection of candidate services are:

- The services provide the same functionality: sometimes, functionality provided are quite similar, but sometimes it is necessary to elucidate if the functionality is at least partially overlapping. One way to determine this is to look at the names of the services and operations that define and ask: could the functionality of candidates be supplied by combining or intelligently using operations of other candidates, at least partially?
- The domain of the services is the same: in most cases the services which must be grouped, work on the same data set. The natural place to find out is in dataTypes defined by types. It is highly likely that candidate services will have definitions of dataTypes with equivalent names, but more important is that they have within their definitions various elements with common names

and types. Another possibility is that there are many elements with the same names in more than one service, but distributed between definitions of different data types. This is also another reason to think that services work on the same domain and that the design of dataTypes could be generalized.
- The ultimate goal of service provision is the same: even when services have disjoint functionalities, these services must be candidates if the fundamental reason of their existence for the user is the same. Finding clues about this requires looking beyond the immediate meaning of the names of operations and visualizes in which context the user will make use of the service. A useful question is: at the time of use, would the user naturally find all the operations of the services if they were included in a service with a more general name? If the answer is yes and the granularity is fine enough, unification must be considered.
- The services belong to the same business area or domain: there are few cases in which a service refactored is not defined by original services belonging to the same category. This issue is the main reason why the initial classification accelerates the Detection step, but at this stage all the content of the documents can be used (operations names, dataTypes, message content, etc.) to find new relations between services. DataTypes are especially useful in opportunities where the service name obfuscates its functionality but the names of the elements in the dataTypes reveal a relationship at concept level.

Not all criteria must be met to establish services as candidates, nor is it strictly necessary to check the criteria one by one separately. Instead, WSDL documents are browsed and a consideration is made of whether the services comply with them to a greater or lesser extent before making the decision that a group for refactoring has actually been detected. In case of doubt whether a service should be part of the group or not, it is better to include it: the original services that will integrate the refactored service can be decided with design considerations in the subsequent steps. On the other hand, if it is decided that the selected group is wrong, it should be discarded and start the detection step again.

Finally, a service can be labeled with a different category to another during the Detection step and if it is necessary a new category can be created. Detection requires more research and time effort than the initial classification, but it is basically the continuation of the same, carried out at the same time as gaining detailed knowledge of the system through the other stages of the iterations. The result of the Detection step is the set of services to be unified.

Design. Once a group of candidate services is defined, it is necessary to determine how the service will be actually refactored. The Design step aims to solve the main problems of integration of the original services and to give shape to the refactored service. In particular, this step consists of the decisions about how operations and dataTypes will be generalized. The two main activities and the criteria for each are:

- The generalization of operations, so that a minimum set of operations covers all the original features. It is not vital that the functions given are exactly same as the refactored service allows for performing all the previous actions with such ease. Also, it is not a problem that the refactor system provides a bit more functionality than before, as long as a new definition of an operation does not necessarily imply a substantial drift in the quality of service.
- The generalization of dataTypes, with the main objective of minimizing the size of description documents. In this case, the size refers to the number of definitions of dataTypes, the number of messages and the number of lines of code. Additionally, this activity takes into account to a lesser extent the modifiability of messages content. This contributes to the centralization and to locate changes in the parameters of operations, in addition to improve readability for subsequent changes and for future refactorings. In any case, the priority is always to give the ability to reuse dataTypes with the main aim to reduce the number of lines of code.

The approach starts with the activity that is considered to be less complex for the candidates and then follow with the others, adapting it to the first perspective of the solution.

In practice, the recommendation is to start with dataTypes, especially for large groups, because these groups have a multitude of operations whose delimitation is not clear: the dataTypes give a real look at the information that the user will need to provide in order to use the operation. This issue makes a guide to group operations with data requirements to decide whether the operations need to be defined separately. For many services centered on queries to a database this approach arises naturally; the general design will rotate around the information that must be received and sent. In addition it is common to use dataTypes with the same name as the operations in the case of the SOAP protocol, so rethink the dataTypes often provide enough information to reorganize operations later.

Alternatively, when the services have similar benefits or the same subsequent goals, it is possible to start off by setting the final group of operations and then define dataTypes for the objects involved in each new operation, ignoring previous dataTypes except to collect the elements contained. This approach was used less frequently in practice, but it is almost mandatory for cases where the data domain of candidates is not the same.

The goal of the Design step is to create a general concept for service as briefly as possible, to be expanded and refined during the specification. The design experience of each developer will propose different alternatives on how to achieve this, some may be more suitable than others in terms of conceptual integrity but, beyond that, any solution is acceptable as long as it meets the aforementioned criteria in the two activities. However, to begin with, the following approach to a solution is suggested: to browse all candidate documents, to identify repeated entities (referring primarily to operations and types) and answer the following questions:

- Is it one entity included within another? For dataTypes this means that the elements of a definition are a subset of the elements of another definition.

Operations should be analyzed semantically if one of them can be used to obtain the same (or the same ones and more) end effects than the other. If so, the entity that solves only the particular case must be eliminated.
- Could two entities be daughters of another entity in an inheritance tree? If true, both entities must be eliminated and the general case must be defined.

Moreover, in the case of dataTypes, it is also important to consider whether they define all abstract objects that are individually required. Sometimes, elements of several abstract concepts are merged into the same dataType. It is desirable as long as the objects have no more than one dependency from different origins, because that would force them to repeat their elements. For example, the data of an Order can be next to those of the Invoice within a dataType used by an operation, but on the other hand, the data of the Invoice are repeated next to those of the Delivery inside another dataType used by a second operation. This situation is undesirable from the viewpoint of modifiability, minimization of lines of code and intelligibility; a possible solution is to define the complexType of the invoice to be used by the other two elements. Situations may involve more complex relationships, but the solution can always be achieved by identifying involved objects that need to be reused or used individually and create a definition for each object.

The proposed solution must include all services that will be unified and therefore some services candidates can be disregarded if they fail to fit the design or are considered to work better for outside of this refactored service. Additionally, it is possible to deal with considerable difficulty to find a general design that show the necessity of dividing the group of candidate services into more than one service refactored. In that case, the group more studied and defined is taken to continue with the current step. If, on the other hand, the solution allows spectrum of services, it is possible to go back to the Detection step to search for more potentially compatible candidates before proceeding. Once a viable solution has been found and the documents that will be part of the refactored service has been selected, they are taken to a separate node, which later will be named with the new service name.

The result of the stage is the set of original services that will define the refactored service on the one hand, and the design concept on the other. At this stage, this set (e.g. mapped to a WSDL document folder) goes to the next step: Specification.

Specification. The last step is to specify the service, this means defining the refactored service in written format, with enough detail so that the materialization can be derived easily. For that, software developers should declare all dataTypes, messages, portTypes and operations that the refactored service will have and all its operations must be explained concisely. This level of detail forces the details and occasionally highlights unforeseen design conflicts, due to particularities in the relationships between operations, messages and dataTypes of the services. The sub-steps are listed as follows:

- To declare the service. As a consideration to contribute to the readability and understanding of the Web Services of the system, it is preferred using names related to processes, concepts or business nouns (as specified in the Oracle standard [10]).
- To declare operations based on the concept proposed at the design step. For the name of the operations, the use of verbs is highly recommended.
- To declare the dataTypes taking into account the data that is necessary for the messages of each operation: first declaring the dataTypes raised in the solution of the previous step and then ensuring to have the dataTypes that will be needed to send and receive the information associated with each operation. At this point, protocols and patterns will be used, respecting the style of the original system but making sure to simplify it.
- To declare the messages, make sure to cover the supported protocols but minimizing the number declared. For example, the use of SOAP protocols is allowed, SOAP 1.2, HTTP-GET and HTTP-POST, but this requires only two variations in the messages: SOAP (containing a single dataType that bears the name of the operation) and HTTP. Additionally, it is important to reuse the messages when the same dataType is required for more than one operation.
- To declare the portTypes, which in practice are always one per supported protocol.
- To define the operation of operations in natural language. It is preferable that explanations are short and preferably rigorous.

The final result after applying our methodology is a document that specifies the refactored service, with all the information necessary for its materialization from the group of original services.

5 Experimental Results

Our proposed methodology was applied on a case-study that contains a total of 252 operations in 211 services, each defined by a WSDL document. By applying our methodology, that number was reduced to 140 defined operations in 52 services. It is assumed that any changes produced by this refactoring should also impact accordingly on the components that interact with the web services, both on the server or on the client sides; however, this analysis is out of the scope of this work. Web services refactorings maintain the original style and support the initial set of functionalities.

In order to quantify the results achieved and the effort required by and for manual refactoring, a set of metrics related to both working time and features of WSDL documents before and after the refactoring were taken into account.

5.1 Analysis of Metrics

To evaluate the impact of applying our methodology, Table 1 shows the results of the metrics before and after the refactoring process. The last column calculates the percentage of gain achieved.

Table 1. Obtained reductions after refactoring.

	Original system	Refactored system	Reduction
Services	211	52	75.36%
Operations	252	140	44.44%
DataTypes	1144	616	46.15%
Messages	1512	458	69.71%
PortTypes	633	104	83.57%
Lines of Code	38912	14201	63.50%

Figure 2 shows that refactoring significantly reduced the size of the elements of WSDL documents, such as services, operations, dataTypes, messages, portTypes and lines of code. For example, the number of services and operations fell by 75% and 44% respectively. Figure 3 shows the mean and standard deviation of reduction of each WSDL element analyzed.

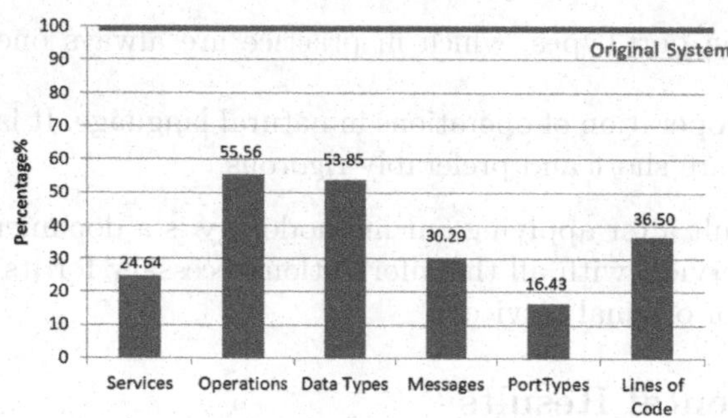

Fig. 2. Refactored system as percentages of original system.

Figure 4 shows a histogram with the absolute number of refactored services (axis X) that are composed of different number of original services (axis Y) and the best adjustment function found using the Origin software[1]. The number of services refactored according to the size of its refactoring group is adjusted to a logarithmic function:

$$y = a - (b * ln(x + c))$$

In this case, $a = 6.4$; $b = 2.3$ and $c = -0.995$ with a determination coefficient of adjusted of $R^2 = 0.93$.

The dataset size is insufficient to perform a generalization and the coefficient of determination may be due to over-adjustment. However, the residual distances of data to the logarithmic function seem to have a random distribution,

[1] http://www.originlab.com/.

so the high coefficient R^2 shows the curve is representative for this particular refactoring. The analysis also goes according to the intuitive perception that as refactoring progresses, it is increasingly difficult to recognize large refactoring groups.

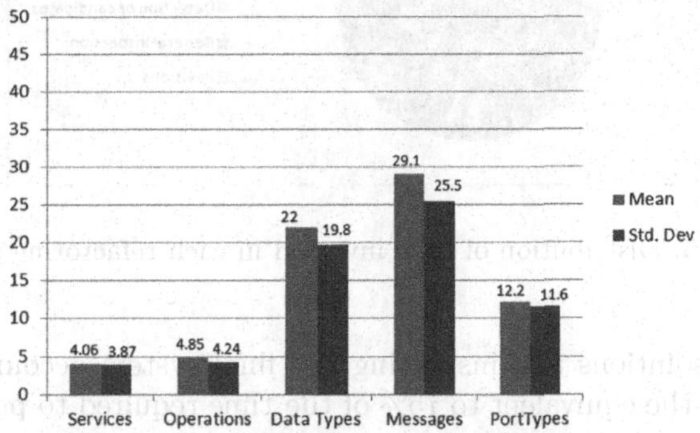

Fig. 3. Mean and standard deviation of refactoring groups.

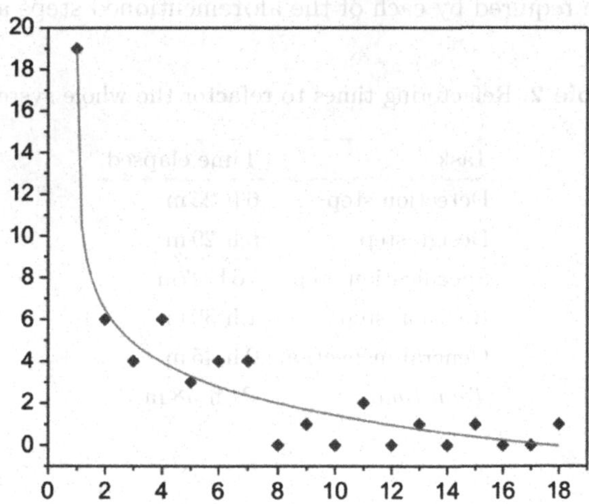

Fig. 4. Histogram of distribution of refactored services by number of members.

Figure 5 depicts the percentage of time to perform each task of our methodology. Approximately, 50% of the time was spent making the specification itself and 5% of the total time was used in revisions on how the specification was performed, this means that 57% of the total time is directly invested in the specification of services. Searching for candidates services for refactoring,

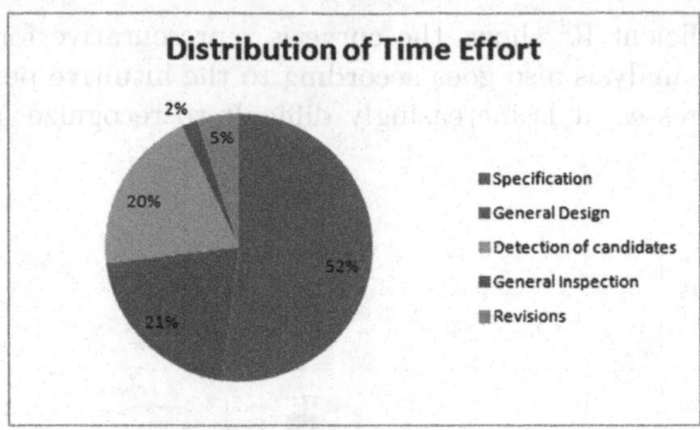

Fig. 5. Distribution of time invested in each refactoring step.

posing general solutions and inspecting the final system accounted for 43% of the time, this is the equivalent to 75% of the time required to perform the specification.

Table 2 shows the total time required by each step of the methodology when conducting the case-study: Detection step 20%, Design step 21%, Specification step 52%, Revision step 5%, General Inspection 2%. Moreover, Table 3 shows on average the time required by each of the aforementioned steps at service level.

Table 2. Refactoring times to refactor the whole system.

Task	Time elapsed
Detection step	6 h 25 m
Design step	6 h 29 m
Specification step	16 h 27m
Revision step	1 h 30 m
General inspection	0 h 45 m
Total time	*31* h *38* m

5.2 Discussion

It is also worth noting how the refactoring times increase with the size of the services. Figure 6 (right) shows the time required to refactor a service seems to have a weak correlation with the number of lines of code in the initial refactoring group ($R^2 = 0.31$), but Fig. 6 (left) implies an expected greater relationship with the final code lines ($R^2 = 0.54$).

This means that refactoring groups, even if they are large, can take a short time if they can be reduced to a few lines of code. Figure 5 also shows that, in general, refactoring times for services with few lines of code are consistently low: less than 30 or 40 min for almost all groups with 1000 lines of code or less, but it

Table 3. Refactoring times at service level.

Task	Mean	Std. Dev
Detection step	5 m 52 s	5 m 22 s
Design step	7 m 22 s	11 m 27 s
Specification step	19 m 0 s	20 m 11 s
Total time	*32* m *20* s	*33* m *01* s

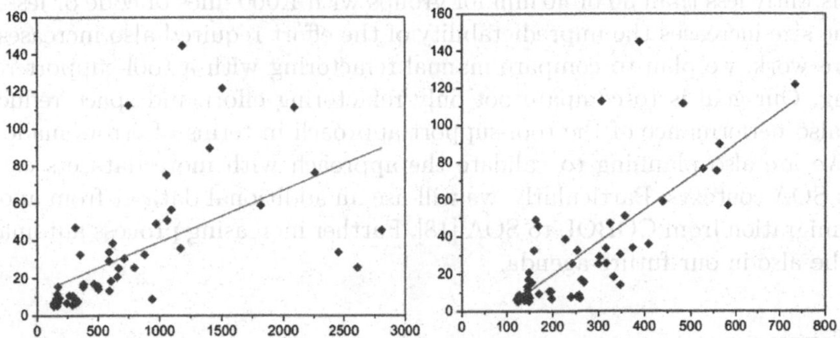

Fig. 6. Left: Refactoring time (Y) according to Line of Code of the original services (X) – Right: Refactoring time (Y) according to Lines of code of the final service (X).

is much more difficult predict how long it will take to refactor a group with much more lines of code. Some of them are especially problematic and may require a much larger redesign to accommodate all of their original services.

To sum up, by using our methodology we simplified the 211 original services with 254 operations with 38,912 lines of code to a specification that defines 52 refactored services that contain a total of 140 operations with 14,201 lines of code; in total, it took 31 hours and 38 min of useful work for the implementation of the refactoring methodology. In other words, the results shows a reduction of 75.35% in the number of services, 44.88% in the number of operations, and in 63.5% in the lines of code.

6 Conclusions

In this work, we proposed a novel methodology to tackle the refactoring of the description of web services belonging to real legacy systems. To evaluate the methodology and the required effort were defined metrics that were monitored throughout the methodology and which may be relevant when comparing this refactoring with other systems. Furthermore, these metrics are intended to act as reference when comparing the manually refactoring of the same system with the assistance of automation tools.

The relationship between the decrease in services, operations, data types, messages, portTypes and lines of code was consistent with what would be expected of the relationships between the elements of WSDL and the patterns of our case-study. Clusters of original services in services refactorings show a logarithmic distribution described as the number of services refactored according to the size of the groups (the larger size, the fewer occurrences). This finding confirms our hypothesis that as refactoring progresses, it is increasingly difficult to recognize large refactoring groups. The time required to refactor each service is consistently less than 30 or 40 min for groups with 1,000 lines of code or less, but as the size increases the unpredictability of the effort required also increases. As future work, we plan to compare manual refactoring with a tool-support refactoring. Our goal is to compare not only refactoring effort and space reduction but also performance of the tool-support approach in terms of errors made.

We are also planning to validate the approach with more datasets coming from SOA contexts. Particularly, we will use an additional dataset from another real migration from COBOL to SOA [18]. Further increasing process automation will be also in our future agenda.

References

1. Schekkerman, J.: What you all need to know about services orientation! structuring the enterprise around services. The Differences between Hype, Hope and Reality. Institute for Enterprise Architecture Developments (2006). Accessed 3 July 2017
2. Lojka, T., Bundzel, M., Zolotová, I.: Service-oriented Architecture and Cloud Manufacturing. Acta Polytech. Hung. **13**(6) (2016)
3. Fowler, M.: Refactoring: Improving the Design of Existing Code. Pearson Education India (1999)
4. Pedrinaci, C., Domingue, J.: Toward the next wave of services: linked services for the web of data. J. UCS **16**(13), 1694–1719 (2010)
5. Rodríguez, G., Soria, Á., Teyseyre, A., Berdun, L., Campo, M.: Unsupervised learning for detecting refactoring opportunities in service-oriented applications. In: Hartmann, S., Ma, H. (eds.) DEXA 2016. LNCS, vol. 9828, pp. 335–342. Springer, Cham (2016). https://doi.org/10.1007/978-3-319-44406-2_27
6. Garcia-Penalvo, F.J., Alier, M., Lytras, M.D.: Some reflections about service oriented architectures, cloud computing applications, services and interoperability. J. Univ. Comput. Sci. **18**(11), 1405–1409 (2012)
7. Erickson, J., Siau, K.: Web services, service-oriented computing, and service-oriented architecture: separating hype from reality. In: Principle Advancements in Database Management Technologies: New Applications and Frameworks, p. 176 (2009)
8. Rodriguez, G., Teyseyre, A., Soria, A., Berdun, L.: A visualization tool to detect refactoring opportunities in SOA applications. In: XLIII Latin American Conference on Informatics. IEEE (2017)
9. Ezenwoke, A., Misra, S., Adigun, M.O.: An approach for e-commerce on-demand service-oriented product line development. Acta Polytech. Hung. **10**(2), 69–87 (2013)
10. Garriga, M., et al.: A structural-semantic web service selection approach to improve retrievability of web services. Inf. Syst. Front. **20**(6), 1319–1344 (2018)

11. Which style of WSDL should I use? 24 May 2005. https://www.ibm.com/developerworks/library/ws-whichwsdl/. Accessed 3 July 2017
12. Rodriguez, J.M., Crasso, M., Mateos, C., Zunino, A.: Best practices for describing, consuming, and discovering web services: a comprehensive toolset. Softw. Pract. Exp. **43**(6), 613–639 (2013)
13. Mateos, C., Rodriguez, J., Zunino, A.: A tool to improve code-first web services discoverability through text mining techniques. Softw. Pract. Exp. **45**(7), 925–948 (2015)
14. Webster, D., Townend, P., Xu, J.: Interface refactoring in performance-constrained web services. In: 2012 IEEE 15th International Symposium on Object/Component/Service-Oriented Real-Time Distributed Computing (ISORC), pp. 111–118. IEEE (2012)
15. Fritzsch, J., Bogner, J., Zimmermann, A., Wagner, S.: From monolith to microservices: a classification of refactoring approaches. In: Bruel, J.-M., Mazzara, M., Meyer, B. (eds.) DEVOPS 2018. LNCS, vol. 11350, pp. 128–141. Springer, Cham (2019). https://doi.org/10.1007/978-3-030-06019-0_10
16. Borges, M., Barros, E., Maia, P.H.: Cloud restriction solver: a refactoring-based approach to migrate applications to the cloud. Inf. Softw. Technol. **95**, 346–365 (2018)
17. Bogner, J., Wagner, S., Zimmermann, A.: Using architectural modifiability tactics to examine evolution qualities of Service-and Microservice-Based Systems. SICS Softw.-Intensive Cyber-Phys. Syst., 1–9 (2019)
18. Mateos, C., Zunino, A., Flores, A., Misra, S.: COBOL systems migration to SOA: assessing antipatterns and complexity. Inf. Technol. Control (2019, in press)

Machine Learning for Space and Earth Observation Data (ML-SEOD 2019)

Potential of Using Sentinel-1 Data to Distinguish Targets in Remote Sensing Images

Mikhaela Aloísia Jéssie Santos Pletsch[1(✉)], Thales Sehn Körting[1], Willian Vieira de Oliveira[1], Ieda Del'Arco Sanches[1], Victor Velázquez Fernandez[2], Fábio Furlan Gama[1], and Maria Isabel Sobral Escada[1]

[1] National Institute for Space Research, Av. dos Astronautas, 1.758 - Jardim da Granja, São José dos Campos, SP 12227-010, Brazil
{mikhaela.pletsch,thales.korting,willian.oliveira,ieda.sanches, fabio.furlan,isabel}@inpe.br

[2] School of Arts, Sciences and Humanities, University of São Paulo, Av. Arlindo Béttio, 1000 - Ermelino Matarazzo, São Paulo, SP 03828-000, Brazil
vvf@usp.br

http://www.inpe.br/, http://www.each.usp.br/

Abstract. Copernicus is the World's largest single Earth Observation (EO) programme, whose satellite constellations are planned to be launched between 2014 and 2025. Among the constellations, Sentinel-1 (S-1) is a C-band SAR able to support land cover mapping. Although optical data are commonly used for land cover monitoring, the low availability of cloud-free scenes along the year hinders the mapping process. In such a way, S-1 presents an important source of data, able of providing all-weather and day-and-night imagery of EO. In this study, we investigate the potential of using S-1 data to distinguish targets in Remote Sensing images in three different Brazilian biomes, Amazon, Cerrado, and Atlantic Forest. Based on that, we proposed a methodology to classify SAR images, which was validated considering a different area from the ones used for sampling purposes. The results showed that through S-1 data, it is possible to detect mainly water and urban area targets, with overall accuracy of 0.90, evidencing that our approach is reproducible in other regions.

Keywords: Radar · Sentinel · Land cover mapping · Satellite imagery · Pattern analysis

Supported by the National Council for Scientific and Technological Development (CNPq), process 140377/2018-2, and the São Paulo Research Foundation (FAPESP), grant 2017/24086-2.

S. Misra et al. (Eds.): ICCSA 2019, LNCS 11622, pp. 563–576, 2019.
https://doi.org/10.1007/978-3-030-24305-0_42

1 Introduction

A set of satellite constellations, called Sentinels, is being developed in order to fulfill Global Monitoring for Environmental Security (GMES) service needs [3,24]. Such constellations are planned to be launched between 2014 and 2025 [3], ensuring a significant data continuity, which is fundamental for Earth Observation (EO) studies [4]. Among them, Sentinel-1 (S-1) is a polar-orbiting satellite constellation, whose first spacecraft was launched in 2014 and the second in 2016. Designed to carry a C-band Synthetic Aperture Radar (C-SAR), S-1 presents the possibility to monitor land cover [3,4,24].

Optical data sources are commonly used for land cover monitoring, such as the Landsat Series [5,14,35,36], however, accurate mapping of extensive areas based on this kind of data is an arduous task, due to the low availability of cloud-free scenes along the year [34]. For this reason, S-1 is an alternative data source, considering its potential of providing day-and-night and all-weather imagery [24]. Therefore, S-1 presents an important source of data, although it is not as used as optical data. Aiming to explore SAR Remote Sensing (RS) signal pattern and support other studies in the thematic, in this paper, we investigate the potential of using S-1 data to distinguish a variety of land cover classes, called here as targets, in RS images in different Brazilian biomes, namely: *Natural Vegetation* (NVA) and *Water* from Amazon biome; *Eucalyptus Plantations* (EP), *Pasture*, *Soil*, *Turfgrass* and *Natural Vegetation* (NVC) from Cerrado biome; and *Urban Areas* from Atlantic Forest biome.

After an exploratory data analysis, we analyzed the signal behaviour and categorized the dataset in three classes: *Water*, *Urban Areas* and *Others*. Based on that, we proposed a methodology to classify SAR images, which was validated considering a different area from the ones used for sampling purposes, Colônia Crater, in the extreme southern of the São Paulo metropolitan region. The results may provide a better comprehension about RS signal pattern, enabling the assessment and monitoring of land cover changes in future studies, as well as temporal data fusion of both radar and optical data.

2 Material and Methods

2.1 Study Area

Brazilian Biomes. Although there are different concepts, a biome is considered an uniform environment [9,44], which can take into account a range of factors. Brazil presents six main biomes, Amazon, Cerrado, Atlantic Forest, Caatinga, Pantanal, and Pampa. Among them, Amazon, Cerrado and Atlantic Forest are considered the three main Brazilian biomes for Carbon sequestration [27] (Fig. 1).

Amazon is the worlds largest rainforest. Two-thirds of its basin is localized in Brazil, which represents about 5 million km^2 [12]. Although it congregates a great biodiversity, it faces a range of threats, such as deforestation [13] and fire processes [2].

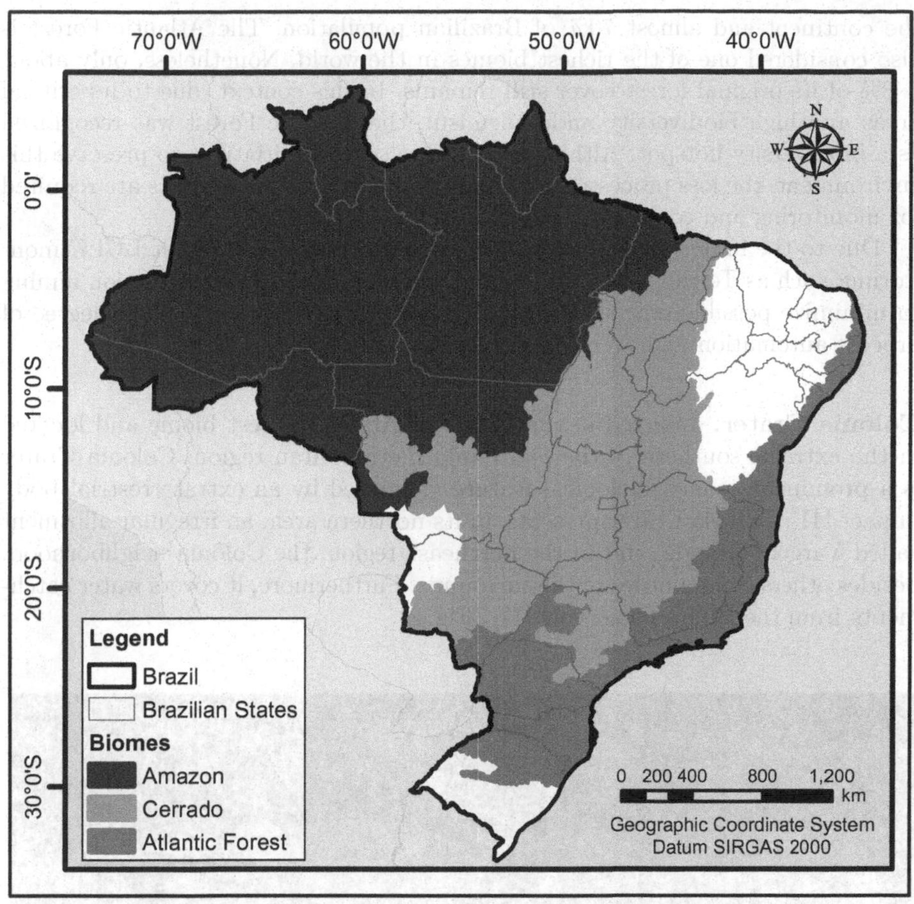

Fig. 1. Brazilian Amazon, Cerrado and Atlantic Forest Biomes.

Comprehending more than 20 million km^2 [16], the Cerrado biome is the second largest biome in South America and it presents the richest biodiversity among the tropical savannas [35]. Even though, only 6% of Brazilian savannas are located in areas of integral protection [14]. If compared with efforts performed in order to monitor and manage Land Use and Land Cover (LULC) changes in the Amazon, Cerrado biome has been overlooked [5,38]. Moreover, this biome has become one of the top grain and beef-producing regions in the world [29]. In such a way, both points of view unravels the importance of preserving this rich biome not only due to its biodiversity but also for its role in global food production. In this context, the lack of conservation approaches associated with the high level of land conversion to agriculture performs the major environmental problem faced by Cerrado [37].

The original area of the Atlantic Forest ranged from 1 to 1.5 million km^2 along 15 Brazilian States, housing three of the most populated urban centers on the continent and almost 70% of Brazilian population. The Atlantic Forest is also considered one of the richest biomes in the world. Nonetheless, only about 7–8% of its original forest cover still remains. In this context, due to its critical areas and high biodiversity and endemism, the Atlantic Forest was recognized as a biodiversity hotspot. Although there are several initiatives to preserve this environment, the loss processes are highly complex and more efforts are required for monitoring and controlling LULC in the area [21, 39].

Due to the importance of these biomes, some initiatives aim at LULC monitoring, such as Terra Class Cerrado [26], which includes manual edition aiming to minimize possible errors, and MapBiomas Project [25], with high degree of process automation and overall accuracy around 80%.

Colônia Crater. Inserted in the Brazilian Atlantic Forest biome and located in the extreme southern of the São Paulo metropolitan region, Colônia Crater is a prominent geomorphological feature generated by an extraterrestrial body impact [41]. Colônia Crater presents, in its northern area, an irregular allotment called Vargem Grande, and in the northeast region, the Colônia neighborhood, besides others communities in the surrounds. Furthermore, it covers water catchments from the Billings reservoir [42] (Fig. 2).

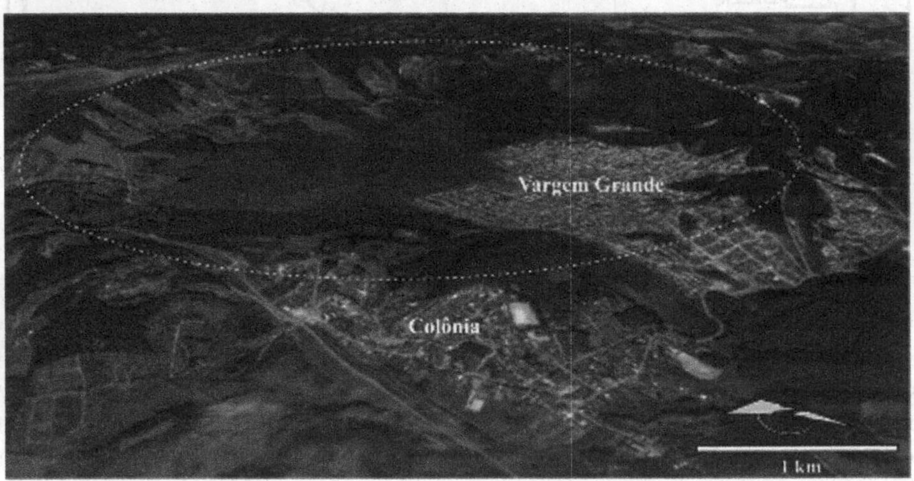

Fig. 2. Colônia Crater from an oblique view. Extracted from [40].

2.2 Exploratory S-1 Data Analysis and Processing

For this exploratory analysis, eight targets were selected along the Amazon, Cerrado and Atlantic Forest biomes (Table 1). The sampling data of *Natural Vegetation* (NVA) and *Water* of a river were manually extracted from a portion of Itamaraty municipality in the Amazon biome. The region is characterized by constant high temperature, which coldest month is of 18 °C or higher [19]. Data of *Eucalyptus Plantations* (EP), *Pasture*, *Soil*, *Turfgrass* and *Natural Vegetation* (NVC) from the Cerrado biome were based on [33] field campaign conducted in Campo Verde – MT, Brazil (May 9–13, 2016). The area is characterized by an average temperature of 22.3 °C, and rainfall of 1726 mm [33]. According to the authors, *Soil* refers to uncultivated areas, such as bare soil, soil with weeds, or with crop residues from the previous harvest. Finally, *Urban Areas* target sampling was extracted from the Bela Vista district limits in the central region of the São Paulo municipality.

Table 1. Analyzed targets.

Target	Data source (biome)
Eucalyptus Plantations (EP)	Cerrado
Natural Vegetation (NVA)	Amazon
Natural Vegetation (NVC)	Cerrado
Pasture	Cerrado
Soil	Cerrado
Turfgrass	Cerrado
Water	Cerrado
Urban Areas	Atlantic Forest

Scenes from Sentinel-1, Level-1 Single Look Complex (SLC) were selected according to its temporal proximity to the field campaign conducted by [33]. Operating in C-band (central frequency of 5.404 GHz), Sentinel-1 products are distributed by ESA (European Space Agency) and can be accessed freely (scihub.copernicus.eu/). Among the four exclusive modes that Sentinel-1 Synthetic Aperture Radar (SAR) instrument can acquire, we used the Interferometric Wide Swath (IW). With a swath width of 250 km on the ground at 5 m by 20 m spatial resolution, the provided imagery are dual-polarisation (vertical transmit and vertical receive - VV, and vertical transmit and horizontal receive - VH) [11].

The processing of SLC product was performed on the Sentinel Application Platform, SNAP (Fig. 3). After splitting the images into subswaths, the process was divided in two. In order to obtain the backscatter coefficient (Sigma0), the data were radiometric calibrated. Then, we removed eventual gaps, multi-looked the data (look = 4), corrected the orbit and the terrain, removed thermal noise, and applied Speckle Filter (Refined Lee, 5 × 5). After that, the data were decomposed using eigenvalue decomposition, proposed by [7], engendering the polarimetric parameters VV and VH. Meanwhile, a similar process based on polarimetric tools was applied to obtain the complex data of entropy (measure of the randomness of the scaterring mechanism) and alpha angle (dominant

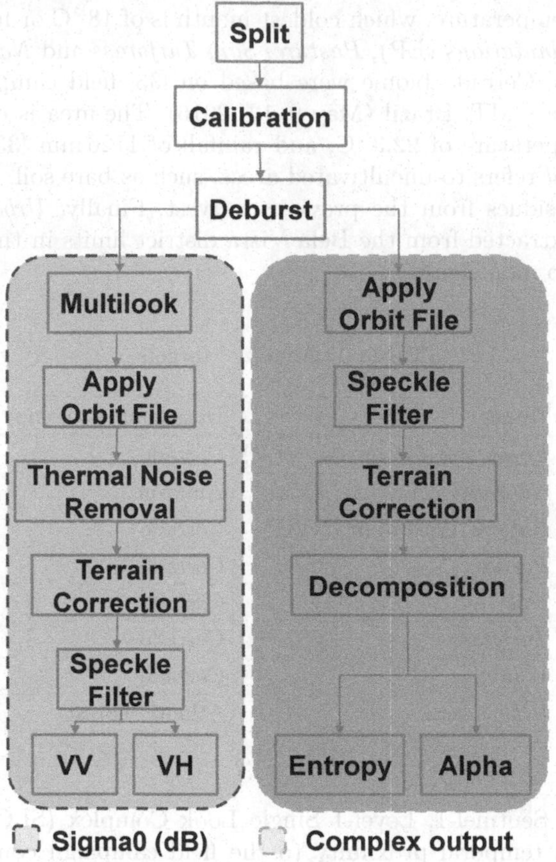

Fig. 3. Methodology flowchart.

scaterring mechanism). Different variables were used, once it is an important step in image classification [1].

After that, SAR signal pattern was analyzed through boxplots in order to statistically characterize the behaviour of targets in images. According to the boxplots analysis, targets with similar behaviour were grouped in the class named *Others*.

2.3 Development of the Methodology to Classify SAR Images

For each class resulted from the previous stage, 1,000 randomly samples were selected in order to develop a methodology to classify SAR images. For that, we used the workbench for machine learning WEKA (Waikato Environment for Knowledge Analysis) [15].

Firstly, the data were classified using the data mining algorithm J48, an implementation of the C4.5 algorithm [30]. This algorithm is widely used, and it has been commonly applied in order to analyze novel approaches [32], once it enables fast comparisons. Furthermore, C4.5 is considered to have one of the best relations of error rate and speed [22]. The results were evaluated based on a stratified k-fold cross validation [18], which splits the training data into $k = 10$ equal-sized partitions. After that, based on the classification model generated by C4.5 algorithm, the methodology to classify SAR images was applied.

2.4 Accuracy Assessment

An image of the Colônia Crater region was classified by means of the developed methodology in order to assess its accuracy. After that, the classified data results were analyzed based on a reference datased from the MapBiomas Project [25].

Areas smaller than 0.2 ha were filtered in both, classified and reference data, due to the difference in spatial resolution and noise interference. Moreover, in order to harmonize the data, the legend from the reference data was adapted according to the targets used to compose the methodology (listed in Table 1). The final accuracy assessment was performed through a Cohen's Kappa coefficient [8]; the Producer's Accuracy, which is a complement of the omission error; and, the User's Accuracy, which corresponds to the commission error. The detailment of the classification result based on the proposed methodology and the reference dataset from MapBiomas Project is then presented in a confusion matrix.

3 Result and Discussion

3.1 SAR Remote Sensing Signal Pattern

For VV polarimetric parameter (Fig. 4A), it is possible to notice that NVA presented higher values than EP, NVC and *Pasture*. Furthermore, the two last aforementioned targets were similar. *Turfgrass* and *Water* presented also similar distributions. Finally, *Urban Areas* presented high variability if compared to the other targets, as can be observed by the wide range [0.00; 2.00 dB], and interquartile range intervals [0.25; 1.00 dB].

According to the VH polarimetric parameter (Fig. 4B), NVA presented higher values than EP, NVC was similar to *Pasture*, and *Turfgrass* and *Water* presented similar distribution. *Soil* values distribution is asymmetrical and surprisingly wide. As identified in VV, the range of values in *Urban Areas* is also ample in VH parameter. Entropy values distribution (Fig. 4C) shows that *Turfgrass*, *Urban Areas* and *Water* could be better distinguished from other targets, and again the range of distribution for *Urban Areas* is wider. For the polarimetric parameter of Alpha (Fig. 4D), *Urban Areas* and *Water* could be better identified, with ample values distribution and low values, respectively.

Although it is not consolidated yet, [6] identified in an agricultural perspective that the polarimetric parameter VV is not well correlated with canopy height. Besides that, according to [43], VV may be sensitive to surface and volume scaterring, nonetheless, theorical modelling indicated also double bounce

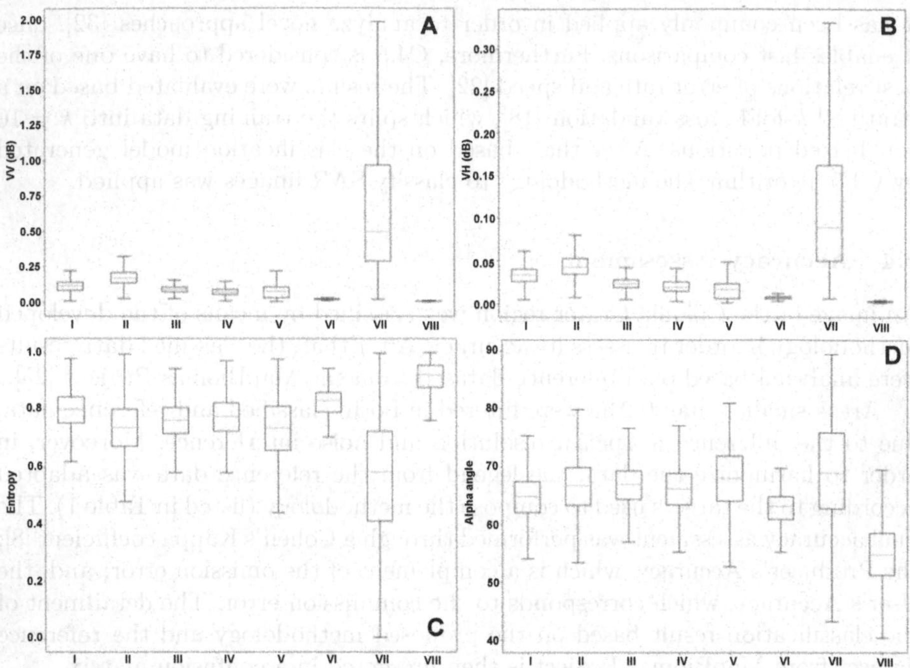

Fig. 4. Results according to polarimetric parameters. A. VV (dB); B. VH (dB); C. Entropy; D. Alpha angle. I. *Eucalyptus Plantations* (EP); II. *Natural Vegetation from Amazon* (NVA); III. *Natural Vegetation from Cerrado* (NVC); IV. *Pasture*; V. *Soil*; VI. *Turfgrass*; VII. *Urban Areas*; VIII. *Water*.

term. In the present work, it was not possible to correlate the parameter VV with canopy height. However, we identified that NVA presented higher values, as well as *Urban Areas*, probably due to volume and double bounce scaterring, respectively. Moreover, the polarimetric parameter VH could distinguish targets in a similar way as VV.

According to [6,17], cross polarizations (i.e. VH) are sensitive to crop growth. As such, this parameter may be able to better distinguish and monitor for instance crops through multitemporal and auxiliary data [31]. Another approach also based on a multitemporal perspective is regarding the potential of Sentinel-1, polarizations VV and VH, for burned area mapping [20]. The process was performed based on change detection, statistical analysis, and unsupervised classification. According to the authors, due to the fire occurrence, there is an increasing of the backscattering, making the burned areas present lighter pixels than the rest of the image. Polarimetric parameters also could be integrated to optical data in order to improve classification accuracy. For instance, HH and HV amplitudes from PALSAR-2 combined with spectral bands from Landsat-OLI improved the classification process in 6% in northern Brazilian Amazon, indicating the potential of hybrid models to classify LULC [28].

Entropy and Alpha angle are effective to distinguish certain land covers, such as low vegetated and agricultural areas [45]. However, in the present study, such polarimetric parameters were found to be effective mainly for *Water* target. Soil values distribution along the analyzed parameters was asymmetrical and surprisingly wide, probably due to its land cover heterogeneity, according to the reference data used in this research.

In this manner, according to SAR remote sensing signal patterns, *Urban Areas* and *Water* were the most distinguished targets by S-1 in the analyzed regions. The remaining six targets presented similar behaviour, and consequently were grouped in the class *Others*.

3.2 Methodology Assessment

A total of 3,000 samples from *Urban Areas*, *Water* and *Others* targets were classified using the C4.5 algorithm. The C4.5 tree presented 24 leaves and the size was 47 (Fig. 5). The classification model represented by the decision tree is relatively simple, once more complex classification tasks can grow massively, with more than 100 nodes. Considering that it is hard to comprehend large decision trees, the developed methodology's extension is an advantage. If required, it is also possible to use more generic rules through the simplification of the tree. For that, it is necessary to respect the condition that every outcome must be able to be tracked along the path of the root of the tree [30].

For the first order numbers (0, 1, 2), the main parameters selected by the methodology were VV and VH (Fig. 5). Entropy is included just in order number 3, and Alpha in number 4. Entropy and Alpha also are the only parameters presented in the last order, 8, which indicates that both are used in refined classifications in the developed approach. Furthermore, the target *Water* was classified in the order number 0, and from 1 to 8, the targets *Urban Area* and *Others* are classified, evidencing the difficulty of its segregation, probably due to its land cover characteristics.

As a result of the cross validation process, more than 91% of the data were correctly classified with Kappa statistic of 0.87. Moreover, the Precision ranged from 0.837 to 0.991, Recall from 0.822 and 0.998, and F-measure from 0.867 and 0.995 (Table 2).

Table 2. Detailed accuracy from the cross validation step.

Class	Precision	Recall	F-Measure
Urban Areas	0.917	0.822	0.867
Water	0.991	0.998	0.995
Others	0.837	0.918	0.876
Average	0.915	0.913	0.912

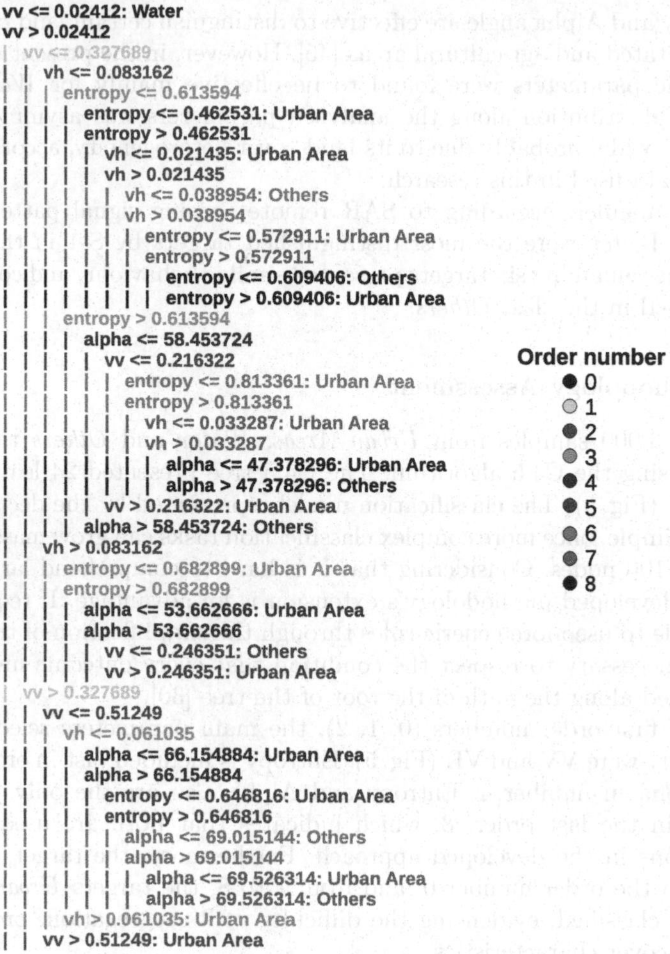

```
vv <= 0.02412: Water
vv > 0.02412
|   vv <= 0.327689
|   |   vh <= 0.083162
|   |   |   entropy <= 0.613594
|   |   |   |   entropy <= 0.462531: Urban Area
|   |   |   |   entropy > 0.462531
|   |   |   |   |   vh <= 0.021435: Urban Area
|   |   |   |   |   vh > 0.021435
|   |   |   |   |   |   vh <= 0.038954: Others
|   |   |   |   |   |   vh > 0.038954
|   |   |   |   |   |   |   entropy <= 0.572911: Urban Area
|   |   |   |   |   |   |   entropy > 0.572911
|   |   |   |   |   |   |   |   entropy <= 0.609406: Others
|   |   |   |   |   |   |   |   entropy > 0.609406: Urban Area
|   |   |   entropy > 0.613594
|   |   |   |   alpha <= 58.453724
|   |   |   |   |   vv <= 0.216322
|   |   |   |   |   |   entropy <= 0.813361: Urban Area
|   |   |   |   |   |   entropy > 0.813361
|   |   |   |   |   |   |   vh <= 0.033287: Urban Area
|   |   |   |   |   |   |   vh > 0.033287
|   |   |   |   |   |   |   |   alpha <= 47.378296: Urban Area
|   |   |   |   |   |   |   |   alpha > 47.378296: Others
|   |   |   |   |   vv > 0.216322: Urban Area
|   |   |   |   alpha > 58.453724: Others
|   |   vh > 0.083162
|   |   |   entropy <= 0.682899: Urban Area
|   |   |   entropy > 0.682899
|   |   |   |   alpha <= 53.662666: Urban Area
|   |   |   |   alpha > 53.662666
|   |   |   |   |   vv <= 0.246351: Others
|   |   |   |   |   vv > 0.246351: Urban Area
|   vv > 0.327689
|   |   vv <= 0.51249
|   |   |   vh <= 0.061035
|   |   |   |   alpha <= 66.154884: Urban Area
|   |   |   |   alpha > 66.154884
|   |   |   |   |   entropy <= 0.646816: Urban Area
|   |   |   |   |   entropy > 0.646816
|   |   |   |   |   |   alpha <= 69.015144: Others
|   |   |   |   |   |   alpha > 69.015144
|   |   |   |   |   |   |   alpha <= 69.526314: Urban Area
|   |   |   |   |   |   |   alpha > 69.526314: Others
|   |   |   vh > 0.061035: Urban Area
|   |   vv > 0.51249: Urban Area
```

Order number
0
1
2
3
4
5
6
7
8

Fig. 5. Developed methodology tree.

Aiming to assess the developed methodology, it was applied to classify an image of the Colônia Crater region, a totally different area from those used to acquire training data. The overall accuracy was of 0.90. The misclassified data are spread along the area, but mainly in the *Urban Areas* of the southern region (Fig. 6).

The confusion matrix indicates that the most accurate classes are *Others*, *Water*, and *Urban Areas*, respectively (Table 3). The target *Water* was not representative in the area, with less than 18.00 ha. Although this target did not suffered a severe omission error ($PA = 92\%$), the commission error was the second highest among the results, which was confused with *Others* by the classifier ($UA = 68\%$).

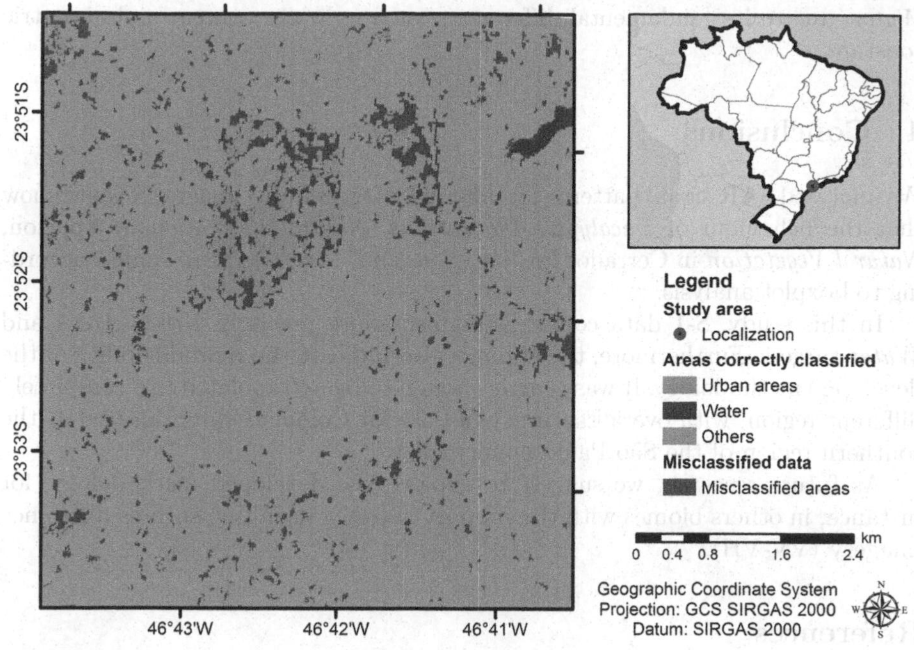

Fig. 6. Developed methodology accuracy.

Table 3. Confusion matrix. Classification result based on the proposed methodology (Sentinel-1 data), and the reference dataset (MapBiomas Project). Producer's accuracy - PA; User's accuracy - UA.

		MapBiomas (ha)			Row total (ha)	UA
		Water	*Urban Areas*	*Others*		
Sentinel-1 (ha)	*Water*	16.259	0.000	7.518	23.777	68%
	Urban areas	0.000	145.655	239.404	385.059	38%
	Others	1.470	192.174	3843.292	1036.936	95%
Column total (ha)		17.729	337.829	4090.214	**4445.772**	
PA		92%	43%	94%		

Expressively more *Urban Areas* targets were misclassified with *Others* than correctly classified, presenting thus the lowest UA (38%), and PA of 43%. As already found by [10,23], low building areas can be misclassified with targets such as vegetation/forest and bare land. *Others* was misclassified mainly by *Urban Areas*, followed by *Water*, but presented the highest accuracy among the targets, once it is the most extensive area and is generic enough to incorporate different targets. Furthermore, there was no confusion between *Urban Areas* and

Water, due to its fundamental differences, such as water content and dielectric constant.

4 Conclusions

We analysed SAR signal patterns for different targets in RS images. Results show that the behaviour of *Eucalyptus Plantations*, *Natural Vegetation* in Amazon, *Natural Vegetation* in Cerrado, *Pasture*, *Soil*, and *Turfgrass* were similar according to boxplot analysis.

In this study, S-1 data could distinguish more precisely *Urban Areas* and *Water* targets. Furthermore, the findings also indicate the reproducibility of the developed methodology. It was generic enough to be extrapolated to a completely different region, with overall accuracy of 0.90 for Colônia Crater, located at the southern region of the São Paulo municipality.

As future research, we suggest to explore the developed methodology, for instance, in others biomes with the support of other variables, such as difference imagery (VV-VH).

References

1. Abdikan, S., Sanli, F.B., Ustuner, M., Calò, F.: Land cover mapping using sentinel-1 sar data. In: The International Archives of Photogrammetry, Remote Sensing and Spatial Information Sciences, vol. 41, p. 757 (2016)
2. Aragão, L.E.O.C., Anderson, L.O., Lima, A., Arai, E.: Fires in Amazonia. In: Nagy, L., Forsberg, B.R., Artaxo, P. (eds.) Interactions Between Biosphere, Atmosphere and Human Land Use in the Amazon Basin. ES, vol. 227, pp. 301–329. Springer, Heidelberg (2016). https://doi.org/10.1007/978-3-662-49902-3_13
3. Aschbacher, J., Milagro-Pérez, M.P.: The European Earth monitoring (GMES) programme: status and perspectives. Remote Sens. Environ. **120**(2012), 3–8 (2012). https://doi.org/10.1016/j.rse.2011.08.028
4. Berger, M., Moreno, J., Johannessen, J.A., Levelt, P.F., Hanssen, R.F.: ESA's sentinel missions in support of Earth system science. Remote Sens. Environ. **120**, 84–90 (2012). https://doi.org/10.1016/j.rse.2011.07.023
5. Beuchle, R., et al.: Land cover changes in the Brazilian Cerrado and Caatinga biomes from 1990 to 2010 based on a systematic remote sensing sampling approach. Appl. Geogr. **58**, 116–127 (2015). https://doi.org/10.1016/J.APGEOG.2015.01.017. https://www.sciencedirect.com/science/article/pii/S0143622815000284
6. Canisius, F., et al.: Tracking crop phenological development using multi-temporal polarimetric Radarsat-2 data. Remote Sens. Environ. **210**, 508–518 (2018). https://doi.org/10.1016/j.rse.2017.07.031
7. Cloude, S., Pottier, E.: An entropy based classification scheme for land applications of polarimetric SAR. IEEE Trans. Geosci. Remote Sens. **35**(1), 68–78 (1997). https://doi.org/10.1109/36.551935
8. Congalton, R.G., Green, K.: Assessing the Accuracy of Remotely Sensed Data: Principles and Practices. CRC Press, Boca Raton (2008)
9. Coutinho, L.M.: O conceito de bioma. Acta botanica brasílica **20**(1), 13–23 (2006)

10. Dostálová, A., Hollaus, M., Milenković, M., Wagner, W.: Forest area derivation from sentinel-1 data. In: ISPRS Annals of the Photogrammetry, Remote Sensing and Spatial Information Sciences, vol. 3, p. 227 (2016)
11. ESA: Sentinel-1 sar user guide (2014). https://sentinel.esa.int/web/sentinel/user-guides/sentinel-1-sar
12. FAO, ITTO: The State of Forests in the Amazon Basin, Congo Basin and Southeast Asia. Technical report, FAO, Food and Agriculture Organization of the United Nations and ITTO, International Tropical Timber Organization, Rome (2011)
13. Fearnside, P.M.: Deforestation in Brazilian Amazonia: history, rates, and consequences. Conserv. Biol. **19**(3), 680–688 (2005)
14. Françoso, R.D., Brandão, R., Nogueira, C.C., Salmona, Y.B., Machado, R.B., Colli, G.R.: Habitat loss and the effectiveness of protected areas in the Cerrado Biodiversity Hotspot. Natureza e Conservacao **13**(1), 35–40 (2015). https://doi.org/10.1016/j.ncon.2015.04.001
15. Frank, E., Hall, M.A., Witten, I.H.: The WEKA Workbench. Online Appendix for "Data Mining: Practical Machine Learning Tools and Techniques", 4th edn. Morgan Kaufmann (2016)
16. IBGE: Mapa de biomas (2004). ftp://ftp.ibge.gov.br/Cartas_e_Mapas/Mapas_Murais/
17. Jiao, X., et al.: Object-oriented crop mapping and monitoring using multi-temporal polarimetric RADARSAT-2 data. ISPRS J. Photogrammetry Remote Sens. **96**, 38–46 (2014). https://doi.org/10.1016/j.isprsjprs.2014.06.014. Elsevier
18. Kohavi, R., et al.: A study of cross-validation and bootstrap for accuracy estimation and model selection. In: International Joint Conference on Artificial Intelligence - IJCAI, Montreal, Canada, vol. 14, no. 2, pp. 1137–1145 (1995)
19. Kottek, M., Grieser, J., Beck, C., Rudolf, B., Rubel, F.: World map of the köppen-geiger climate classification updated. Meteorologische Zeitschrift **15**(3), 259–263 (2006)
20. Lasaponara, R., Tucci, B.: Identification of burned areas and severity using SAR sentinel-1. IEEE Geosci. Remote Sens. Lett. (2019)
21. Leal, C.G., de Gusmão Câmara, I.: The Atlantic Forest of South America: Biodiversity Status, Threats, and Outlook, vol. 1. Island Press, Washington, DC (2003)
22. Lim, T.S., Loh, W.Y., Shih, Y.S.: A comparison of prediction accuracy, complexity, and training time of thirty-three old and new classification algorithms. Mach. Learn. **40**(3), 203–228 (2000)
23. Makinde, E., Oyelade, O.: Land cover mapping using sentinel-1 SAR satellite imagery of Lagos state for 2017. In: Multidisciplinary Digital Publishing Institute Proceedings, vol. 2, p. 1399 (2018)
24. Malenovskỳ, Z., et al.: Sentinels for science: potential of sentinel-1,-2, and-3 missions for scientific observations of ocean, cryosphere, and land. Remote Sens. Environ. **120**, 91–101 (2012)
25. MapBiomas, P.: MapBiomas: Collection 3 (2018). http://mapbiomas.org/
26. Ministério do Meio Ambiente (MMA): Mapeamento do uso e cobertura do cerrado: Projeto terra class cerrado 2013. Technical report, 67, MMA (2015)
27. Nunes Carvalho, J.L., Avanzi, J.C., Naves Silva, M.L., Mello, C.R.D., Pellegrino Cerri, C.E.: Potencial de sequestro de carbono em diferentes biomas do brasil. Revista Brasileira de Ciência do Solo **34**(2) (2010)
28. Pavanelli, J.A.P., Santos, J.R.d., Galvão, L.S., Xaud, M., Xaud, H.A.M.: Palsar-2/alos-2 and oli/landsat-8 data integration for land use and land cover mapping in northern brazilian amazon. Boletim de Ciências Geodésicas **24**(2), 250–269 (2018)

29. Pereira, P.A.A., Martha, G.B., Santana, C.A., Alves, E.: The development of Brazilian agriculture: future technological challenges and opportunities. Agric. Food Secur. **1**(1), 4 (2012)
30. Quinlan, J.R.: C4.5: Programs for Machine Learning. Elsevier (2014)
31. Rüetschi, M., Schaepman, M., Small, D.: Using multitemporal sentinel-1 c-band backscatter to monitor phenology and classify deciduous and coniferous forests in Northern Switzerland. Remote Sens. **10**(1), 55 (2017)
32. Ruggieri, S.: Efficient c4.5 [classification algorithm]. IEEE Trans. Knowl. Data Eng. **14**(2), 438–444 (2002)
33. Sanches, I.D., et al.: Campo verde database: seeking to improve agricultural remote sensing of tropical areas. IEEE Geosci. Remote Sens. Lett. **15**(3), 369–373 (2018). https://doi.org/10.1109/LGRS.2017.2789120
34. Sano, E.E., Ferreira, L.G., Asner, G.P., Steinke, E.T.: Spatial and temporal probabilities of obtaining cloud-free Landsat images over the Brazilian tropical savanna. Int. J. Remote Sens. **28**(12), 2739–2752 (2007). https://doi.org/10.1080/01431160600981517
35. Sano, E.E., Rosa, R., Brito, J.L.S., Ferreira, L.G.: Land cover mapping of the tropical savanna region in Brazil. Environmen. Monit. Assess. **166**(1–4), 113–124 (2010). https://doi.org/10.1007/s10661-009-0988-4
36. Sano, E.E., Rosa, R., Brito, J.L.S., Ferreira, L.G.: Mapeamento de cobertura vegetal do bioma Cerrado: estratégias e resultados, 1st edn. Embrapa Cerrados, Planaltina (2007)
37. Silva, J., Farinas, M., Felfili, J., Klink, C.: Spatial heterogeneity, land use and conservation in the cerrado region of Brazil. J. Biogeogr. **33**(3), 536–548 (2006)
38. Strassburg, B.B.N., et al.: Moment of truth for the Cerrado hotspot. Nature Ecol. Evol. **1**(4), 0099 (2017). https://doi.org/10.1038/s41559-017-0099
39. Tabarelli, M., Pinto, L.P., Silva, J.M.C., Hirota, M.M., Bedê, L.C.: Desafios e oportunidades para a conservação da biodiversidade na mata atlântica brasileira. Megadiversidade **1**(1), 132–138 (2005)
40. Velázquez, V.F., Colonna, J., Sallun, A.E.M., Sobrinho, J.M.A., Sallun Filho, W., Paiva, P.C.: The colônia impact crater: geological heritage and natural patrimony in the southern metropolitan region of São Paulo, Brazil. Geoheritage **6**(4), 283–290 (2014)
41. Velázquez, V.F., et al.: Evidence of shock metamorphism effects in allochthonous breccia deposits from the colônia crater, São paulo. Brazil. Int. J. Geosci. **4**(01), 274 (2013)
42. Velázquez, V.F., et al.: The current situation of protection and conservation of the colônia impact crater, São paulo, Brazil. Geojournal Tourism Geosites **IX**(1), 7–20 (2016)
43. Veloso, A., et al.: Understanding the temporal behavior of crops using Sentinel-1 and Sentinel-2-like data for agricultural applications. Remote Sens. Environ. **199**, 415–426 (2017). https://doi.org/10.1016/j.rse.2017.07.015
44. Walter, H.: Vegetação e zonas climáticas: tratado de ecologia global. In: Vegetaçao e zonas climáticas: tratado de ecologia global. EPU (1986)
45. Whyte, A., Ferentinos, K.P., Petropoulos, G.P.: A new synergistic approach for monitoring wetlands using Sentinels-1 and 2 data with object-based machine learning algorithms. Environ. Model. Softw. **104**, 40–54 (2018). https://doi.org/10.1016/j.envsoft.2018.01.023

Evaluating Classification Models in a Burned Areas' Detection Approach

Olga Oliveira Bittencourt, Fabiano Morelli, Cícero Alves dos Santos Júnior, and Rafael Santos(✉)

INPE – National Institute for Space Research, Av. dos Astronautas, 1758, São José dos Campos, SP 12227-010, Brazil
{olga.bittencourt,rafael.santos}@inpe.br

Abstract. We present a study to improve automation and accuracy on a Woody Savannah burned areas' classification process through the use of Machine Learning (ML) classification models. The reference method for this is to extract polygons from images through segmentation and identify changes in polygons extracted from images taken from the same area but in different times through manual labeling. However, not all differences correspond to burned areas: there are also deforestation, change in crops, and clouds. Our objective is to identify the changed areas caused by fire. We propose an approach that employs polygons' attributes for classification and evaluation in order to identify changes caused by fire. This paper presents the more relevant classifier models to the problem, highlighting Random Forest and an Ensemble model, that achieved better results. The developed approach is validated over a study area in the Brazilian Woody Savannah against reference data derived from classifications manually done by experts. The results indicate enhancement of the methods used so far, and will eventually be applied to more data from different areas and biomes.

Keywords: Burned areas · Classification models · Remote sensing data

1 Introduction

Woody Savannah (commonly referred to as Cerrado in Brazil) is a biodiversity rich region and one of the most threatened biomes in the country. It occupies around 204 million hectares, 24% of the Brazilian territory, and it is estimated that it lost almost half of its original vegetation cover. Deforestation and vegetation fires are the main reasons for this process. More than 30,000 vegetation fires per year have been recorded in this biome in the last 15 years. Several studies cover the fire-related aspects and their economic, social and environmental impacts [3,6,9,16].

To understand the effects and impacts of fire on the Woody Savannah it is important to regularly monitor fire occurrences and to have accurate data products. The Brazilian National Institute for Space Research (INPE) maintains a

S. Misra et al. (Eds.): ICCSA 2019, LNCS 11622, pp. 577–591, 2019.
https://doi.org/10.1007/978-3-030-24305-0_43

program of Burns and Forest Fires Monitoring [5] based in Earth Observation satellites. It continually analyzes aspects related to the fire occurrences in vegetation areas in the Woody Savannah biome as well as in the rest of Brazil and part of Latin America. As part of this project, some data products are available, such as daily monitoring of active fires, fire risk prediction and periodic fine particulate matter ($PM_{2.5}$) emission estimates, and, more recently, burned surface's estimation. These products are used, for example, by alert services and for public policy subsidies (e.g. application of the Brazilian Forest Code). They are also used to contribute to the reduction of greenhouse gas emissions targets assumed by the Brazilian Government in the Climate Convention [13].

Using satellite data to define burned areas in a fast, continuous and reliable method is a real challenge. Our reference method extracts polygons that represent changed areas and compare changes between different times. However, some of these polygons are deforestations, crops, and clouds. Then, we currently use a method that employs manual evaluation to classify these polygons in burned and non burned polygons. The last published official result of burned areas estimation in the Woody Savannah, in 2017, was published using this manual evaluation. The results are very good but the work is expensive. Considering the need of more automation in the process our aim is to develop an study to improve automation and accuracy on burned areas' classification process through the use of machine learning (ML) classification models. Since there is no generic model for the problem of classifying burned data in a continuous monitoring with controlled accuracy, we employed the solid expertise acquired by the INPE during the last decades of continuous monitoring. We decided to explore features, classifiers and their combinations to improve our approach.

In this article, we present a classification approach through ML that combines distinct vegetation indexes and related features and it is able to distinguish between burned and non burned areas. The proposed approach is validated over a study area in the Brazilian Woody Savannah against reference data derived from classifications done by experts. The results indicates enhancement on the methods used so far, and will eventually be applied to more data from different areas and biomes.

This paper is organized in the following sections: Sect. 2 shows how remote sensing is used to monitor burned areas. Section 3 explains what data is used for classification of areas of interest into burned and non burned areas and presents INPE's burned areas mapping process with the proposed attributes to improve the classification process. Section 4 presents the experiments for some classification models and discuss the results. Section 5 presents the conclusions and future work.

2 Burned Areas Mapping by Remote Sensing Monitoring

The use of remote sensing images collected in different wavelengths is the most efficient way to monitor fires in places with great territorial extension or areas of difficult access. Furthermore they frequently provides recent information. In Brazil, for example, it is the most efficient fire monitoring means, with the lowest cost. In recent years, new generations of satellites (e.g. Landsat 8, Sentinel-2 and China–Brazil Earth Resources (CBERS-4)) were developed to provide better resolution images and more precise georeferencing. Features and advances made possible by these new satellites generation may be found in [8].

Inside the automatic mapping of burned areas literature, there are few studies applying the new advances of medium resolution data. Liu et al. [9] developed an algorithm to continuous monitoring of annually burned areas using the harmonic model in Landsat time series rather than two image comparisons, as we do. Pereira et al. [16] presents an approach for automatically mapping of burned areas. Their study has good accuracy results in using a One-Class Support Vector Machine (SVM) Trained by Active Fire. Like them, we compare two images, but our work did not process images, it is focused on evaluating polygons attributes generated in a remote sensing extraction data.

There are many recent studies on applying machine learning techniques on distinct research fields. Plazas et al. [19] employed ML classifiers in another problem: the Cacao production classification and had better precision with Random Forest classifier. Some works employ successfully ensemble approaches such as text information retrieval [1] and Polikar [20] that presents details and advantages of using combined classifiers.

In [2] we proposed a semiautomatic approach to classify burned areas through the use of neural networks. Previous results decreased the number of polygons wrongly classified and showed the viability of using Neural Networks in the classification process. Mithal et al. [14] employ machine learning approaches in the problem of burned areas mapping. They present a three-step approach to map burned areas in tropical areas which compares data from two low resolution (500m) successive images from Moderate Resolution Imaging Spectroradiometer (MODIS), feeds it into a proprietary algorithm to classify these data and makes final processing for burned areas. According to the authors, although it has many errors in indicating correct burned areas, it is a promising global approach brings a more comprehensive assessment of tropical fires. The general idea of our whole process is similar and the main difference is that our work is focused on building robust classifiers to evaluate supposed burned polygons to work every two weeks with high reliability for medium resolution images (30 m).

Previous results show the difficulty of choosing one specific model to answer our burn classification problem. To contribute to understanding this problem, our work is related to the effort to develop automated approaches to classify burned areas. We treat this problem by separating it into two parts: one that looks for all the changes that occurred with the suspicion of burning and another that classifies these data. We use the high reliability of finding changes and combine with the comprehensiveness of machine learning techniques to classify burned areas in a continuous and periodical way with high accuracy.

3 Burned Areas Mapping Process at INPE

INPE's monitoring is developed in two independent ways, using different satellite images' resolutions. Low-resolution images (with pixels larger than 300 m) are used to generate daily data products. Medium-resolution images (with pixel' sizes around 30 m) are used for less frequent but more accurate studies. With these distinct views, it is possible to monitor forest fires detected by satellites and to analyze related information, such as estimation of burned area and the prediction of the risk of fire on vegetation. These products can be used to prevent, monitor, combat and create actions to reduce the damage caused by fire, analyze the impacts of burning and estimate the emission of pollutants.

A challenge for monitoring extensive territories is to combine efficiency, quickness and reliability. If it generates a high number of false detections (to classify non burned polygons as burned polygons) it arises, e.g., the risk of waste effort on non-priority areas. If it loses the highest number of burned areas, it arises, for example, the risk of does not know real events. In a reality of fire use culture [18], areas with difficult access, few combat resources and a great number of active fires, it needs to have the smallest error tax as possible, mainly in the burned areas set. Furthermore, to be officially published without manual validation in each polygon, it is at maximum of 5% of false burns error tax.

The INPE's burned areas mapping process finds which areas have changed in a comparison of two different acquisition moments. An algorithm [12] automatically defines areas that have changed from the previous image with high reliability in detect changed areas. The changes detected are caused by many factors and some of them are burns. This is our interest set: changed areas caused by fire. Thus, a further evaluation process is essential to classify burned and non burned areas. The aim of this study is to develop an automatic approach to separate this changed areas set with reliability at around 95%.

Figure 1(a) illustrates a composition of RGB colors of an image fragment on September 24th. Three areas are highlighted. An area with clowns, an area with forest cover and a burning area with visible active fires. Figure 1(b) shows a similar fragment on October 10th, next Landsat's passage. The black lines in the image highlight the polygons detected with changed areas.

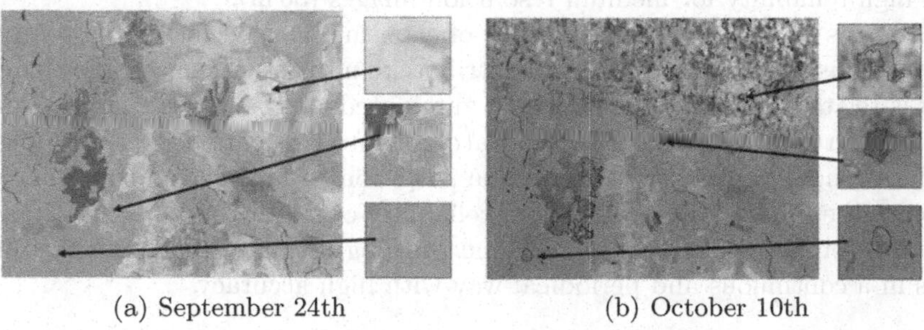

(a) September 24th (b) October 10th

Fig. 1. Fragments of an example RGB composition in two consecutive dates

3.1 Data

The INPE's Fire Monitoring Program uses images from Landsat satellites. The Landsat Program [23] stands out among Earth observation satellites that provide medium resolution orbital images of the same area every 16 days since the 1980s. It provides environmental data with all corrections processed, such as spectral band values and spectral vegetation indexes.

Landsat imagery is separated by path and row. The red parallelogram in Fig. 2, the study area of this work, illustrates a fragment of an image position of path 220 and row 065, part of the Woody Savannah biome in the states of Maranhão and Piauí, in Brazilian territory. Light gray highlights indicate Woody Savannah delimitation and dark gray indicates protected areas. Each single pixel in the image corresponds to a square cell of 30 m × 30 m on the terrain and each complete image represents a coverage area of 18,500 × 18,500 ha.

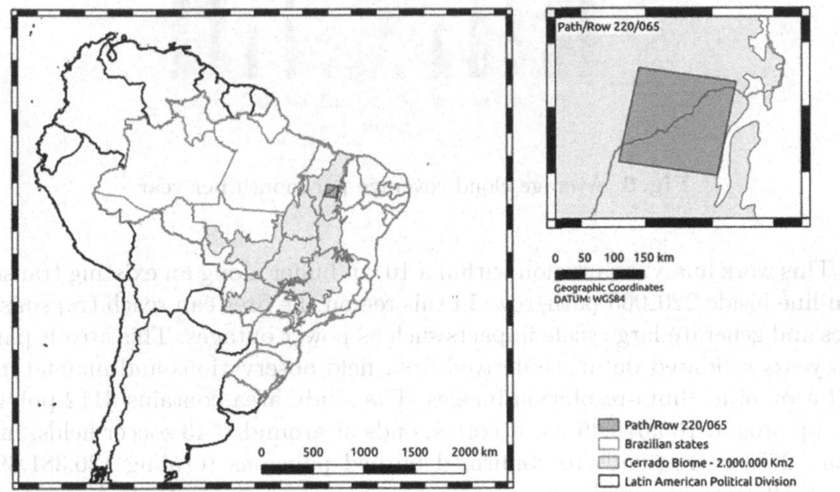

Fig. 2. Fragment of Brazilian territory illustrating Woody Savannah biome and highlighting Landsat 220_065 path/row

Our approach is based on comparing images from the same orbit-point to different dates, with the standard difference being a 16-day. The ones that present interference like noise or many clouds are discarded and an image prior to this one is used, with 32, 48 or at most 64 days difference. At intervals greater than this, the vegetation recovers and it is not possible to detect the changes. The whole images set is composed of 18 images of the 220_065 path/row of the years 2017 and 2018, with data ranging from April to October. The resulting database is composed of polygons extracted by the burned areas mapping algorithm [12].

The Woody Savannah has two well defined seasons: rainy and dry. Figure 3 illustrates the average monthly percentage of clouds for the available images in these two years. This value is generated by Landsat Programs and indicates the area occupied by clouds in the each image. From November to March it's a rainy season and images frequently contain high clouds percentage. In these months, the use of successive images is low and the number of real burnings is small. From May to August it's a dry season with low rainy level and small clouds percentage. April is considered a transition between the rainy to the dry season and, September and October are transitions between dry and rainy season.

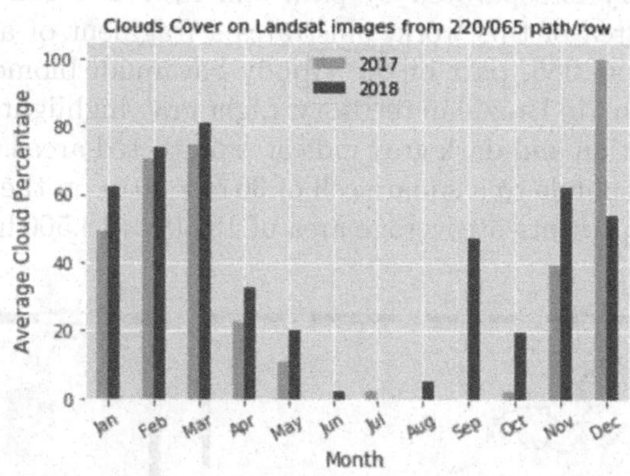

Fig. 3. Average cloud coverage per month per year

This work analyzes a region within a 10 km buffer along an existing transmission line inside 220_065 path/row. In this region the fires can reach transmission lines and generate large scale impacts such as power outages. This area is part of two years validated database derived from field observations and manual interpretation of medium-resolution images. The study area contains 4112 polygons add up around 166,679.46 ha. It corresponds at around 1543 soccer fields. Inside them, 2753 corresponds to confirmed burned polygons totaling 126,381.69 ha and 1359 areas changed due to other factors, which we call non burned polygons and sum 40,297.77 ha. Each polygon is associated with a set of attributes. Figure 4 illustrates the number of polygons and the area occupied by changed areas by month in each year.

In this study, b4 is an anagram to data from Landsat band 4, b5 corresponds to data from Landsat band 5 and so on. As each original Landsat image contains the reflectance spectra for each pixel in a digital image, the polygons are composed by a set of pixels. The set of attributes of each polygon is composed by the average of each Landsat band from b2 to b7 and other vegetation indexes.

3.2 Preprocessing

The first step to apply the machine learning approach to classify burned data is to understand the knowledge database: data and their set of attributes. The strategy is to have a small set of relevant attributes to reduce the volume of analyzed data and the processing time while maintaining a low error rate.

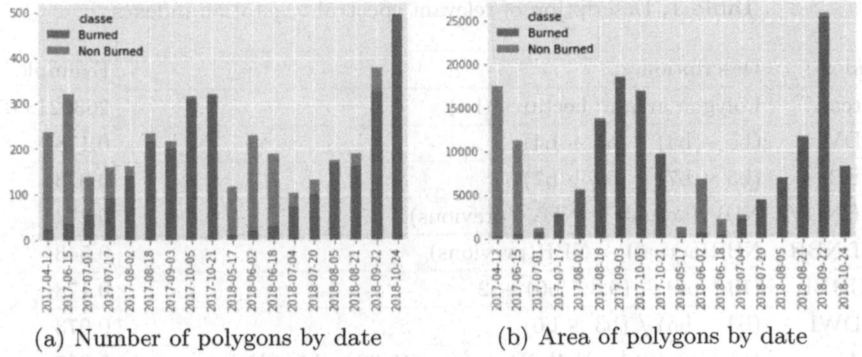

(a) Number of polygons by date (b) Area of polygons by date

Fig. 4. Distribution of burned and non burned areas (number of polygons and occupied area)

The knowledge database is composed by area characteristics, spectral bands values, and spectral vegetation indexes. Each polygon inside this set was manually evaluated by expert and is classified in burned and non burned polygons. Figure 5 shows an overview of spectral bands data from b2 to b7 through the boxplot charts. It allow us a general idea on the differentiation of burned and non burned data sets. Except for b7, the sets are symmetric. The graphs have some outliers, common to the process data. They should not be discarded to avoid some tendency results. We highlight bands b4, b5 and b6 as the best differentiators among burned and non burned datasets.

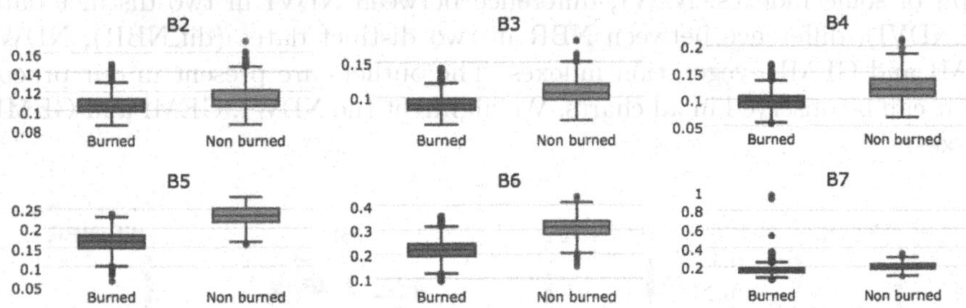

Fig. 5. Boxplot charts of spectral bands b2, b3, b4, b5, b6 and b7

Based on the best differentiators of bands (b4, b5, and b6), we tested spectral vegetation indexes that used at least one of these indexes. We used: Normalized Difference Vegetation Index (NDVI) [21], Normalized Burn Ratio (NBR) [7], Mid-Infrared Burn Index (MIRBI) [22], Normalized Difference Water Index (NDWI) [11], Burn Area Index (BAI) [4], Char Soil Index (CSI) [10], and Global Environment Monitoring Index (GEMI) [17]. A summary of the vegetation indexes applied in this approach can be found in Table 1.

Table 1. Description of relevant spectral vegetation indexes

Index	Description	Example
Area	Polygon area in hectares (ha)	263021.807
NDVI	(b5 − b4) / (b5 + b4)	0.178
NBR	(b5 − b7) / (b5 + b7)	0.073
dif_NDVI	NDVI(actual) − NDVI(previous)	0.274
dif_NBR	NBR(actual) − NBR(previous)	0.543
MIRBI	(10 * b7) − (9.8 * b6) + 2	0.178
NDWI	(b3 − b6) / (b3 + b6)	0.073
BAI	(1/((pow((0.1 − b4),2)) + (pow((0.06 − b5),2))))	0.067
CSI	b2/b6	0.056
GEMI	(n * (1 − 0.25 * n) * (b5 − 0.125) / (1 − b5)) where n is	0.274
	n = (2 * (pow(b7,2) − pow(b5,2)) + 1.5 * b7 + 0.5 * b5)/(b7 + b5 + 0.5)	
GEMIL	Apply b6 in the place of b7 on GEMI index definition	0.543

Each index brings a different combination of bands and highlights some specific characteristics of the vegetation cover change. We verified the most relevant ones for our classification process and present here the smallest set able to characterize our burned data. We also made a change in the GEMI index, calling it GEMIL, since instead of using b5 and b7, it uses b5 and b6 data, which is spectrally close and better differentiated our target set. Figure 6 shows the boxplot graph of some indexes: NDVI, difference between NDVI in two distinct dates (dif_NDVI), difference between NBR in two distinct dates (dif_NBR), NDWI, GEMI and GEMIL vegetation indexes. The outliers are present in our process and it can be observed in all charts. We highlight the NDWI, GEMI and GEMIL indexes.

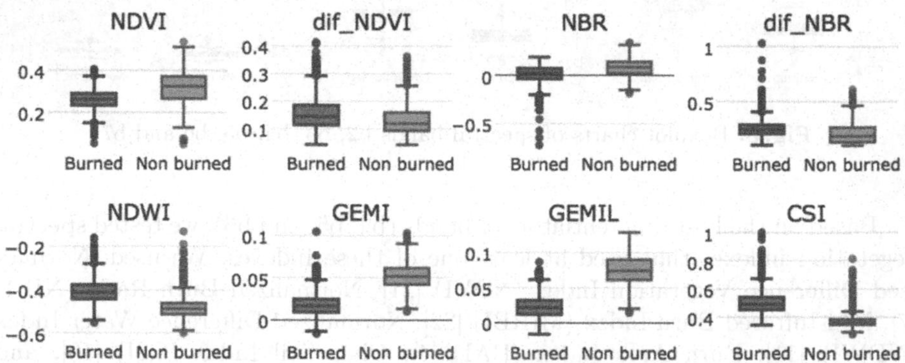

Fig. 6. Boxplot charts of vegetation indexes

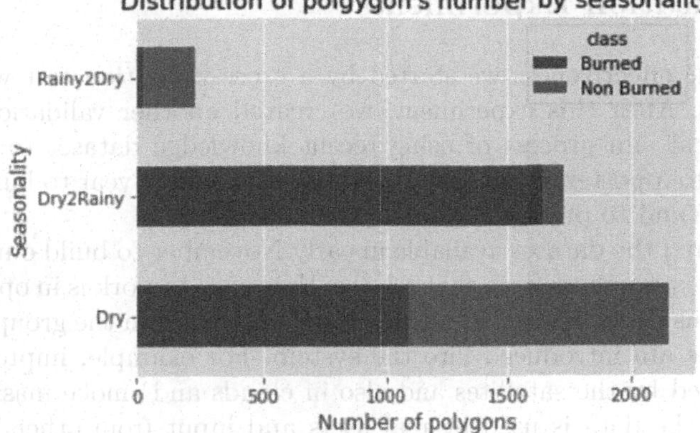

Fig. 7. Seasonality of Burned and Non burned polygons

The rains seasonality was added to database based on the month acquisition image. The spectral response of a burned area and its recovery are influenced by the season in which it occurs. For example, fire that strikes vegetation in the transition from a rainy season to a dry season brings a different spectral response to the fire that strikes vegetation in a dry season. The result, illustrated in Fig. 7, is a set of four binary attributes: Rainy(that doesn't contain polygons in this study case), Dry, Rainy2Dry, and Dry2Rainy that describes the seasonality.

Attributes area, MIRBI and, BAI were processed arithmetic operations, such as the application of log operation with subsequent division by 10, to decrease the range of attributes values. Figure 8 shows the original set and the resulting data set after fit processing. The processed data preserves the original distribution characteristics, decreases the outliers effect and allows a better interpretation of the set.

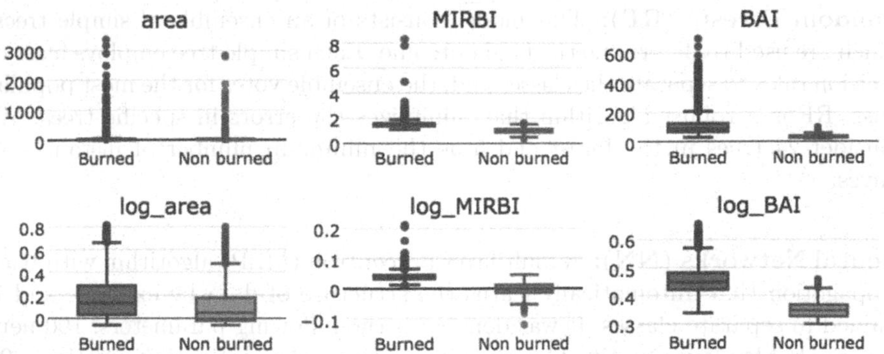

Fig. 8. Boxplot of original and processed attributes area, MIRBI and BAI

4 Classification Experiments

To explore the effectiveness we started by a cross-validation test with 30% of the whole set. After this experiment, we created another validation test that simulates a real aim process of using recent knowledge dataset to predict the classification to a posterior data. We used the whole 2017 year to build a knowledge database and to predict the whole 2018 dataset.

We recovered the dataset available in early November to build our knowledge base and run experiments from that release. However, as work is in operation and with continuous development, as advances are made within the group's research, some advances are introduced into the system. For example, improvements in the data offered by the satellites and also in clouds and smoke masks. In addition, because the data is used by real users and input from other information systems, some omission or detection errors are reported. In this way, the data is reprocessed, re-evaluated and sometimes the official results are updated in the official system and made available to the user.

4.1 Classification Models

We performed experiments at Scikit-learn environment [15]. The training sets are the same for all models and the result is the average of the values in these 10 tests. Individual cross-validations results and parameters are detailed to each algorithm in the next subsections.

K-Nearest Neighbors (kNN): A kNN is a data classification algorithm that employs the influence of the majority of labeled nearest neighbors to perform the classification. It determines what group a data point is in by looking at the data points around it. The best parameters used in the experiments are: 3 neighbors, Euclidean metric and Distance weight.

Random Forests (RF): This model consists of an ensemble of simple trees, which are used to determine the final outcome. Each simple tree employs a set of decision rules to separate the classes and, the ensemble votes for the most popular class. RF is a robust algorithm that minimizes the errors in specific trees. We consider 24 trees in the forest and 5 as the minimum number of instances in leaves.

Neural Networks (NN): A multilayer perceptron (MLP) algorithm with back propagation that automatically learns the structure of data by example and is trained to separate classes. It was done with the following parameters: 100 neurons per hidden layer, rectified linear unit function as the activation function, 300 as the maximum number of iterations and 0,00010 as the penalty (regularization term) parameter.

Support Vector Machines (SVM): A SVM is a discriminative classifier that employs the best hyperplane to separate two target classes in the space. The parameters used to set the experiments are: Cost: 100; Regression loss epsilon: 0,5; kernel Linear; Numerical tolerance: 0,01 and Iteration limit: 1000.

Ensemble of Classification Models (ST): It consists of an ensemble of Random Forest and Neural Networks previous trained models into a single meta-model. We used a Stacking [24] algorithm to combine our better two distinct paradigms with a Logistic Regression model to minimize individual error rates.

4.2 Experiment 1: Test the the Whole Dataset

The dataset is composed by 4112 polygons that correspond to more than 160,000 ha. The cross-validation algorithm separated 70% to training dataset and 30% to test dataset. Then, 2878 were used to train and 1234 were used to test the models. This test was done 10 times, the result is the average of the values and the training set is the same on the five tested models.

To compare resulting details, we combined the individual confusion matrix in a side by side way that can be seen in Table 2. In the rest of this work we use the acronym B to indicate the number of burned areas and NB to indicate the number of non burned areas.

Table 2. Average cross-validation confusion matrix of each classifier model

		Predictions									
		kNN		SVM		RF		NN		ST	
		B	NB	B	NB	B	NB	B	NB	B	NB
Reference	B	823	8	818	13	823	8	821	10	825	6
	NB	8	395	23	380	3	400	12	391	4	399

The average errors set have similar results with small values, both in false positives or false burns (NB polygons classified as B polygons) and false negatives or lost burns (B polygons classifieds as NB polygons). Specifically, SVM presents a higher number of lost burns and the smallest number of false burns. ST and RF presents the small error sets, but the results are statistically similar.

The statistical metric accuracy is the proportion of correctly classified examples in relation to the total number of samples classified. Overall accuracies are larger than 0.96 and they are statistically similar. SVM accuracy is 0.97, NN accuracy is 0.98 and kNN, RF and ST accuracies are 0.99. These high accuracies results indicates the viability of our dataset and our approach to classify burned data.

4.3 Experiment 2: Using the 2017 Dataset to Classify the 2018 Dataset

In this experiment, 2105 areas belong to the 2017 year and 2007 areas belong to the 2018 year. The training set (data from the 2017 year) is composed by 1370 burned polygons, 637 non burned polygons and it is the same on the five tested models. The set is not balanced, but it represents the real dataset and it is important to deal with this characteristic of class imbalance. Table 3 presents the individual resulting confusion matrix to each model.

Table 3. Individual resulting confusion matrix of each classifier model

		Predictions									
		kNN		SVM		RF		NN		ST	
		B	NB	B	NB	B	NB	B	NB	B	NB
Reference	B	1353	17	1356	14	1339	31	1355	18	1351	19
	NB	34	603	65	572	14	623	35	602	23	613

As results in the first experiment, SVM classifier presents the larger number of false burns (NB polygons classified as B polygons). kNN and NN have similar quantity of false burns and RF and ST presented the better results. Inside lost burns (B polygons classified as NB polygons), RF presented the larger values. Other classifiers presented similar results.

Our set is not balanced, neither in the number of polygons nor in the total extension. It is important to check F1, precision and recall metrics to best overview and understand our results. Table 4 presents statistics evaluation metrics accuracy, precision, recall and F1 calculated for each model. The precision is the proportion of true positives among instances classified as positive. In our case, e.g., the number of confirmed B polygons inside all predicted B polygons. Recall is the proportion of recovered true positives among all positive instances in the data. In our case, e.g., the number of recovered B polygons inside all real B polygons. F1 is a weighted harmonic mean to detach a balance between precision and recall.

As previous tests, in this experiment overall metrics are greater than 0.95. The accuracies are greater than 0.96 and the F1 values indicates the models deals well with this uneven class distribution. The error set size is very small, both in lost burns and false burns. SVM presents a higher number of lost burns and the smallest number of false burns, but the difference is numerically very small. Better results were obtained by RF, NN and ST and experiments showed that the classifier models are suitable for classifying burned polygons.

Given the above goods results, we chose two classifiers to inspect another result of some classifiers model, the probability of the observed object to be part of a specific class. Some family of classifiers, as RF, NN and ST, use this value (that ranges from 0 to 1) to divide their results into the classes, employing

Table 4. Evaluation results considering the average over classes

Classifier	Accuracy	Precision	Recall	F1
kNN	0.97	0.98	0.99	0.98
SVM	0.96	0.95	0.99	0.97
RF	0.98	0.99	0.98	0.98
NN	0.97	0.97	0.99	0.98
ST	0.98	0.98	0.98	0.98

0.5 value as the division limit. In our case, we inspected the probability of each object to be similar to the set of burned data. The aim was to verify if the errors (lost burns and false burns) are accumulated in the mean values to deal with doubt values and to decrease the error set. Figure 9 illustrates the probabilities distributions of RF and ST models.

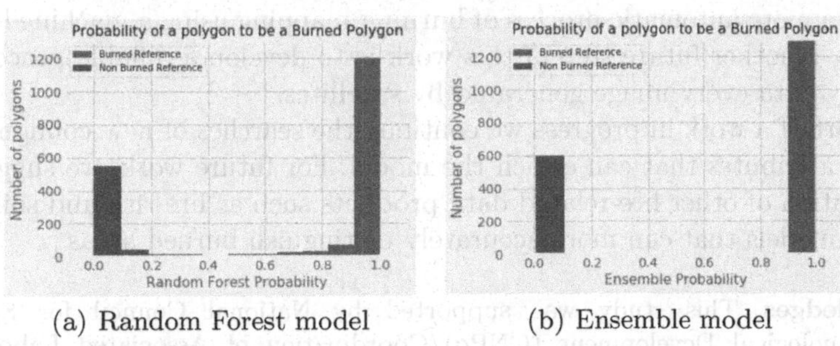

(a) Random Forest model (b) Ensemble model

Fig. 9. Probability resulting distribution in RF and ST models (Color figure online)

Figure 9(a) presents distribution probability of RF model and Fig. 9(b) presents distribution probability of ST model. In red, real B polygons are represented and in green, real NB polygons are represented. Both sets have the majority of results concentrated smaller than 0.1 and greater than 0.9. RF resulting data is a few more spread out than ST resulting data. The set of errors is very small and it not is possible to observe if resulting data presents classification errors closer to the center of the set (0.5) than the ST. This study continues with other areas to increase the reliability of the approach.

The errors and doubts will be evaluated by experts in a posterior moment. We know the expert validation is a error susceptible and a highly expensive process. However, it is important an expert to solve the doubts because he uses knowledge to verify the specific data and the round area to better understand the indication. Therefore, we will use this reevaluated data to insert data into knowledge base to build a more robust approach.

5 Conclusions and Future Work

We developed a more generic and automated model to classify burned data that is robust enough to deal with previously unknown data. We proposed a small and more complete set of features to build a knowledge base to be used in a machine learning approach to classify burned and non burned areas.

We used our previous approach [2] to evolving from three months model to a more accurate model. Since there is no complete model that describes whether it is burned, we proposed more relevant features. After this we studied distinct classifiers using a labeled dataset that is the real classifications made by experts. As each different algorithm creates a different model, we have analyzed various types of classifiers to explore the performance of each one. We chose an Ensemble model to combine better characteristics of Random Forest and Neural Network models. These tests present precision and recall near the value of 0.95.

We are working on testing the adaptability of this model to other areas or the need to develop other local area specific knowledge base. Preliminary results show that is possible to use this knowledge approach to classify distinct areas and to create a more automatic process of burning mapping using a machine learning approach. Another future step of this work is to develop a reliable process able to classify data every image generated by satellites.

As part of a work in progress we continue the searches of new configurations and new attributes that can enrich the model. For future work, we suggest the incorporation of other fire-related data products such as fire risk and soil use to generate models that can more accurately distinguish burned areas.

Acknowledges. This study was supported by National Council for Scientific and Technological Development (CNPq)/Coordination of Associated Laboratories (CLA/INPE) (no.300587/2017-1).

References

1. Che Alhadi, A., Deraman, A., Abdul Jalil, M.M., Wan Yussof, W.N.J., Mohamed, A.A.: An ensemble similarity model for short text retrieval. In: Gervasi, O., et al. (eds.) ICCSA 2017. LNCS, vol. 10404, pp. 20–29. Springer, Cham (2017). https://doi.org/10.1007/978-3-319-62392-4_2
2. de Andrade, R.N., Bittencourt, O., Morelli, F., Santos, R.: Classificação semi-automática de áreas queimadas com o uso de redes neurais. In: XVIII Brazilian Symposium on Geoinformatics - GeoInfo 2017, pp. 92–97 (2017)
3. Bowman, D., et al.: Fire in the earth system. Science **324** (2009)
4. Chuvieco, E., Martín, M.: Cartografía de grandes incendios forestales en la península ibérica a partir de imágenes noaa-avhrr. Serie Geográfica **7** (1998)
5. Instituto Nacional de Pesquisas Espaciais (INPE): Programa de monitoramento de queimadas. http://www.inpe.br/queimadas/portal. Accessed 28 Jan 2018
6. Katagis, T., Gitas, I., Toukiloglou, P., Veraverbeke, S., Goossens, R.: Trend analysis of medium- and coarse-resolution time series image data for burned area mapping in a mediterranean ecosystem. Int. J. Wildland Fire (2014)

7. Key, C., Benson, N.: Landscape assessment: ground measure of severity, the composite burn index; and remote sensing of severity, the normalized burn ratio. In: FIREMON: Fire Effects Monitoring and Inventory System, pp. 1–51 (2006)
8. Li, J., Roy, D.: A global analysis of sentinel-2A, sentinel-2B and landsat-8 data revisit intervals and implications for terrestrial monitoring. Remote Sens. **9** (2017)
9. Liu, J., Heiskanen, J., Maeda, E.E., Pellikka, P.K.: Burned area detection based on Landsat time series in savannas of Southern Burkina Faso. Int. J. Appl. Earth Obs. Geoinf. **64**, 210–220 (2018)
10. Smith, A.M.S., Drake, N., Wooster, M.J., Hudak, A.T., Holden, Z.A., Gibbons, C.J.: Production of Landsat ETM+ reference imagery of burned areas within Southern African Savannahs: comparison of methods and application to MODIS. Int. J. Remote Sens. **28**, 2753–2775 (2007)
11. McFeeters, S.: The use of normalized difference water index (NDWI) in the delineation of open water features. Int. J. Remote Sens. **17**, 1425–1432 (1996)
12. Melchiori, A.E., Setzer, A.W., Morelli, F., Libonati, R., Cândido, P.d.A., Jesús, S.C.d.: A Landsat-TM/OLI Algorithm for Burned Areas in the Brazilian Cerrado: Preliminary Results, pp. 1302–1311. Imprensa da Universidade de Coimbra (2014)
13. Ministério do Planejamento, Orçamento e Gestão (MPOG): Plano plurianual 2016–2019: Desenvolvimento, produtividade e inclusão social. http://www.planejamento.gov.br/assuntos/planeja/plano-plurianual/relatorio-objetivos.pdf. Accessed 12 Sept 2017
14. Mithal, V., Nayak, G., Khandelwal, A., Kumar, V., Nemani, R., Oza, N.C.: Mapping burned areas in tropical forests using a novel machine learning framework. Remote Sens. **10** (2018)
15. Pedregosa, F., et al.: Scikit-learn: machine learning in Python. J. Mach. Learn. Res. **12**, 2825–2830 (2011)
16. Pereira, A.A., et al.: Burned area mapping in the Brazilian savanna using a one-class support vector machine trained by active fires. Remote Sens. **9**(11) (2017)
17. Pinty, B., Verstraete, M.: GEMI: a non-linear index to monitor global vegetation from satellites. Vegetation **101**, 15–20 (1992)
18. Pivello, V.: The use of fire in the cerrado and amazonian rainforests of Brazil: past and present. Fire Ecol. **7**, 24–39 (2011)
19. Plazas, J.E., López, I.D., Corrales, J.C.: A tool for classification of cacao production in colombia based on multiple classifier systems. In: Gervasi, O., et al. (eds.) ICCSA 2017. LNCS, vol. 10405, pp. 60–69. Springer, Cham (2017). https://doi.org/10.1007/978-3-319-62395-5_5
20. Polikar, R.: Ensemble based systems in decision making. IEEE Circuits Syst. Mag. **6**, 21–45 (2006)
21. Rouse Jr., J.W., Haas, R.H., Schell, J.A., Deering, D.W.: Monitoring vegetation systems in the Great Plains with ERTS. NASA Spec. Publ. **351**, 309 (1974)
22. Trigg, S., Flasse, S.: An evaluation of different bi-spectral spaces for discriminating burned shrub-savannah. Int. J. Remote Sens. **22**, 2641–2647 (2001)
23. U.S. Geological Survey (USGS): Usgs science data lifecycle. https://earthexplorer.usgs.gov. Accessed 18 Oct 2018
24. Wolpert, D.H.: Stacked generalization. Neural Netw. **5**(2), 241–259 (1992)

Mobile-Computing, Sensing, and Actuation in Cyber Physical Systems (MSA4CPS 2019)

Evaluating HTTP Adaptive Streaming Algorithms Under Parallel TCP Connections

Saad Qaisar, Syed Hamid Rasool, and Abdul Basit(✉)

National University of Sciences and Technology,
Sector H-9 Islamabad, Islamabad, Pakistan
{saad.qaisar,14mseesrasool,basit.khan}@seecs.edu.pk

Abstract. Online video streaming services have been gaining rapid growth, and that has led to an increase in Internet traffic and have matched with traditional television video services in terms of content consumption. HTTP Adaptive streaming service has been adopted as the medium for video delivery over the Internet with its variants, HTTP Adaptive Streaming (HLS) and Dynamic Adaptive Streaming over HTTP (MPEG-DASH) supporting all playback devices.

In video streaming domain, the performance is measured in terms of the Quality of Experience (QoE) provided to the user and has been known to be influenced by the bitrate adaptation methodology. The objective scores of QoE are related to the bitrate quality delivered while keeping video stalls and rebuffering to a minimum. These include classes of buffer based and network throughput based adaptive switching mechanisms to optimize the QoE. In our work, we evaluate the performance of both these classes of algorithms over parallel HTTP connections at the client, a proven method to increase network throughput to resultantly increase the bitrate quality over an emulated WAN environment, controlled by actual traces conducted during an extensive measurement study over a distributed global DASH measurement cluster.

Keywords: Video streaming · SD-WANs · QoS

1 Introduction

Video streaming services have not stopped growing in recent years, and that has led to an increase in Internet traffic, probably due to the growth of devices with access to the network, such as phones and tablets. Today, services such as YouTube or Netflix, among others dominate much of the world as can be seen in the "Global Internet Phenomena", a report carried out by Sandvine [1] with periods of maximum download activity of up to 25% of total traffic for YouTube in Europe during July 2015. According to Akamai State of the Internet report 2016, the median connection speed in Pakistan is 2.0 Mbps as compared with a global average of 5.6 Mbps and 12.2 Mbps originating from US. Pakistan is not the only target however, still 35% of all global connections are still less than 4 Mbps. Video streaming has come a long way since its inception in the early 90s.

S. Misra et al. (Eds.): ICCSA 2019, LNCS 11622, pp. 595–610, 2019.
https://doi.org/10.1007/978-3-030-24305-0_44

Nowadays the predominant technique for transmitting live and on-demand video is adaptive streaming using HTTP segments, the reasons that allowed it were its simple deployment and management since the HTTP infrastructure (proxies, caches and content delivery networks, CDN) was already deployed. With HTTP being also a standard protocol for the Internet.

The video streaming methods have been evolving over time, the use of the UDP protocol [11] for the delivery of live video and reliable transport protocols such as TCP [12] for the delivery of videos on demand has been decreasing. Currently, the transmission of both live video and video on demand (VoD) is done mainly through HTTP, over the TCP protocol. The main reason for the use of HTTP is the possibility of reusing its infrastructure, since it is friendly with NAT devices, which allow exchanging packets between two networks that assign mutually incompatible addresses, and also allows passing through most firewalls through port 80. Also, since the HTTP flow is directed by the client, it supports all the adaptation logic, reducing persistent server-application connections.

Adaptive Streaming is a technique used for the distribution of multimedia flow and was born as a major advance regarding the progressive discharge of the flow in order to optimize the user experience by distributing the best possible bitrate based on the user's available bandwidth final. To do this, a video is encoded in different bitrates and segmented into pieces of a few seconds, allowing each segment to be available for the different bit rates.

Dynamic Adaptive Streaming over HTTP (DASH) [14] is a standard for adaptive streaming over HTTP developed by MPEG that became an international standard in November 2011 and was published as ISO/IEC 23009-1: 2012 in April 2012 [25]. A second edition was published in May 2014 as ISO/IEC 23009-1: 2014.

The streaming model that defines MPEG-DASH offers control exclusively to the client, who requests the information through the HTTP protocol to the server [18].

The objective of our work is to improve the Quality of Experience of end users video sessions in terms of average bitrate quality and rebuffering events on real world measured traces of video streaming sessions by applying parallel HTTP connections through an emulated DASH HTTP video player.

The rest of the paper is as follows. We introduce various streaming protocols in Sect. 2 including, traditional and HTTP. In Sect. 3, we provide the system model of QoE and MPEG-DASH. In Sect. 4, we provide details on the measurement study of DASH flows and in Sect. 5, we explain the emulation tests conducted including the parallel streaming architecture. Section 6 provides discussion of the results followed by the conclusion.

2 Related Work

HTTP adaptive streaming has been an area of great interest that grew after the publication of first version of DASH ISO specifications in 2012 by the MPEG group. The loose specifications allowed the choice of adaptive streaming algorithm to be in the hands of the video player developers to allow innovation and optimization in the bitrate adaptation controller logic.

The note worthy works using alternate approach includes the use of server-side bitrate switching [9,16,27], TCP changes to avoid bursts [2]. Our focus will be on the client-side problem for two key reasons. First, client-side solutions are immediately deployable in contrast to other solutions that require support from in-network devices [6], server-side software changes [7,28], or modifications to lower-layer transport protocols [16]. Direct interaction with content providers is also not required as some studies have been done in conjuction with the content providers live network [11,12,14,21]. Secondly, the client is often well placed to detect performance issues and respond to dynamics in network connection [22].

For the client side which is our focus, several techniques have been proposed since and several techniques and algorithms have been developed. They are largely grouped into broad classes, buffer based algorithms and bandwidth based algorithms, as they primarily influenced by either the amount of remaining buffer value or the currently observed network connection bandwidth to control the bitrate quality set [19,26]. There are also newer studies that have incorporated both these parameters and applied optimization solvers to provide the solution.

Prior works have also shown that sudden changes in available network capacity confuse existing ABR algorithms, causing the algorithms to either overestimate or underestimate the available network capacity [10,15]. The overestimation leads to unnecessary rebuffers [23]. In our work, we take separately both the throughput based algorithms as well as buffer based algorithms and measure their performance under low bandwidth conditions.

The underestimation not only fills throughput as well as buffer based approach, the buffer with video chunks of lower quality, but also leads to the ON-OFF traffic pattern in video traffic: when the playback buffer is full, the client pauses the download until there is space. In the presence of competing TCP flows, the ON-OFF pattern can trigger a bad interaction between TCP and the ABR algorithm, causing a further underestimate of capacity and a downward spiral in video quality [13]. When competing with other video players, overlapping ON-OFF periods can con-fuse capacity estimation, leading to fluctuating video quality and unfair link share among players [1]. It has also been established that the streaming algorithms that request aggressively for higher bitrates, tend to get more bandwidth out of the network.

A related work uses parallel connections to download video files, which were not in DASH format, in different representations as a whole and use the download time improvement to claim better performance [3]. However, the video downloaded was not segmented and hence, the video quality could not be adapted. Another study downloaded segments in parallel [24] and while their they can be applied to DASH streaming logic, their work fetched segments in parallel from different sections in the video to aid seeking and skipping ahead in videos using some look ahead content that is pre-downloaded using their parallel technique. The last similar study was performed through parallel streaming using multiple server technique in which the same video content was placed on different servers. Their technique is called MD-DASH (multiple descriptor DASH) [7] and requires customization to the original DASH manifest file format and is hence, non-compliant with the ISO-BMFF standard.

To the best of our knowledge, parallel video streaming using the standard DASH architecture has not been tested, evaluated or compared with the existing state of the art adaptive bitrate switching algorithm to measure the performance gains that can be achieved for video streaming sessions.

3 System Model

Video quality is a key benchmark for any streaming service, be it traditional broadcast, cassettes, DVDs or Internet video. It has been evaluated by various subjective and objective metrics. We provide the models for the currently used metrics for HTTP streaming after describing all the options. We will also model the typical MPEG-DASH playback model after its protocol architecture.

3.1 DASH Model

We will now model the overall MPEG-DASH system architecture [20]. In order to enable DASH streaming, the video file has to be encoded in multiple bit rates and resolutions and then each of the file is then segmented into small chunks. As per DASH specification, the segment size can be set from 2–10 s.

Here is the abstract model of the DASH video player in Fig. 1.

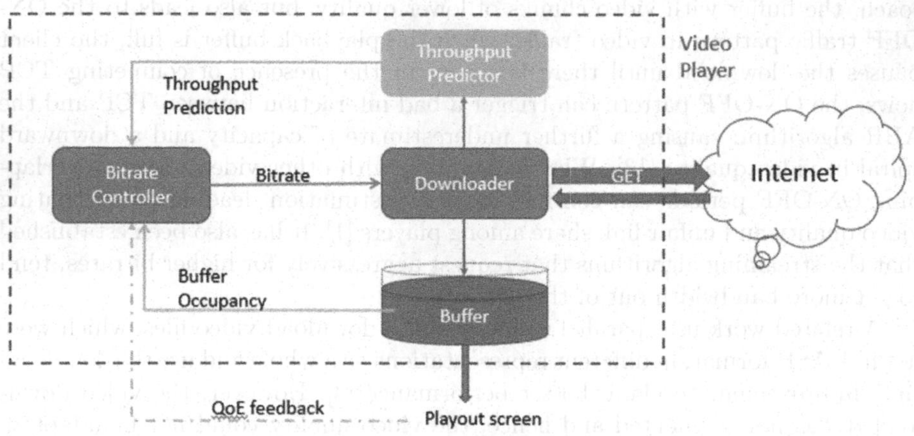

Fig. 1. Abstract model of DASH player.

On the client side, the selection logic is performed by the bitrate controller [25]. The controller takes into account, the feedback of the network throughput and amount of video content stored in buffer and makes the decision by setting the bitrate of the next segment after taking into account the history of previous segment rates. This logic decoupled from the main MPEG-DASH protocol fixed standard, i.e. the ISO-BMFF format [20] of the manifest (mpd) file of the DASH encoded video and the playback engine, allows to develop custom framework in order to improve video streaming performance by researchers and video service owners.

3.2 DASH Specifications

When the video is prepared into DASH format, the final produced highest resolution video (mezannine file) is split into segments (chunks) of 2–10 s of duration. This number is consistent for a DASH video. The next step is the transcoding of video into multiple representations with a set bitrate and resolution (e.g. 1080p at 3000 kbps, 720p at 2000 kbps, 240p at 300 kbps). The complete metadata of the file: duration of the video; duration of segment; file path of each segment.

The MPD file is the strict standard which is a component of all MPEG-DASH video. In the below Fig. 2, the complete architecture of DASH is presented.

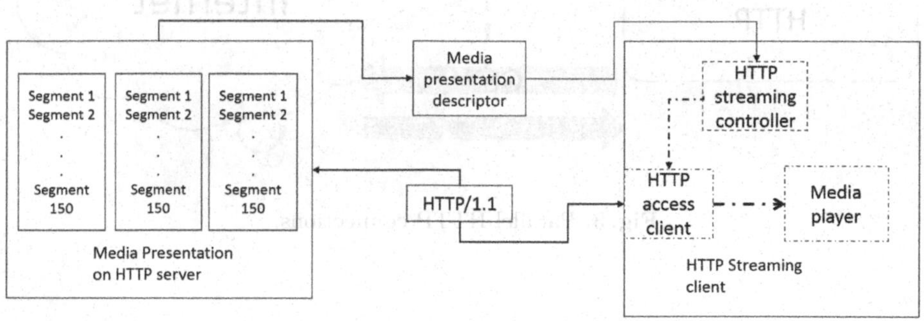

Fig. 2. MPEG-DASH architecture.

In the above diagram, the specifications of DASH client and DASH web server are detailed. The important aspect of the diagram is that the solid blocks are required to be fixed as per standard, while the dotted blocks are up to the implementation of DASH by the users. The fixed blocks include the segmentation and transcoding of file in different representations as shown in the segment blocks as well the descriptor file in accordance. The dotted blocks represent the bitrate controller, HTTP client (directed by the streaming controller) and the media player. This enables both innovation in terms of engineering as well as design as each DASH client is visually different from each other as presented in YouTube, Netflix as well as most of the other large media content providers on the Internet since DASH is now widely adopted.

4 Protocol Details

In our study, we apply a unique approach to improve DASH performance through establishing multiple HTTP connections to the video server fetching data in parallel. The fetching of data in parallel has been useful for multiple applications running over the Internet - the Internet Download Manager (IDM) uses this technique to speed file downloads while modern FTP clients, like FileZilla also use them in order to perform data transfers. This parallel technique is visualized below (Fig. 3).

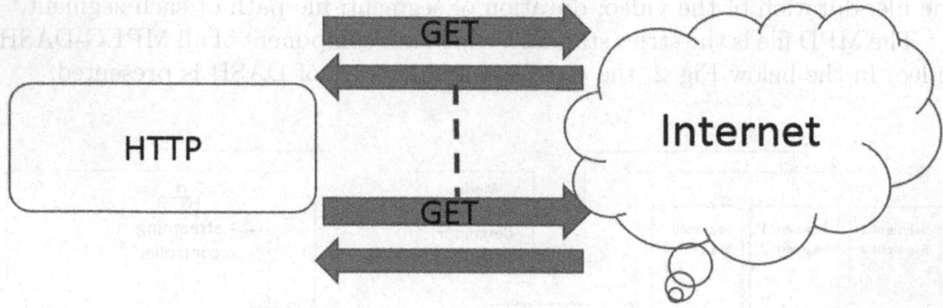

Fig. 3. Parallel HTTP connections.

4.1 Parallel Streaming Algorithm

After establishing parallel connections by setting a predefined number, we proceeded to create a dynamic algorithm for this purpose. We use the information provided in the DASH manifest file to obtain the size of all segments for various resolutions and tune the throughput based adaptive bitrate algorithm to suit for dynamic parallel HTTP throughput based algorithm.

Parallel ABR algorithm
Selection of the batch size, T (default T=2)
Initialization of T by obtaining size of the segment z (in bytes) through HTTP HEAD request.

z[n] is less than β_L
T[n] = 1single connection
z[n] is greater than β_H
T[n] = 88 parallel connections
z[n] is greater than 1.15z[n-1]
T[n] = min(T[n-1]++,5)increase connections
z[n] is less than 0.85z[n-1]
T[n] = max(T[n-1]–,1)decrease connections

Select next segment rate, *R[n]*
1) Estimate bandwidth by equating to the measured throughput

$$x'[n] = x[n-1]$$

2) Calculate the moving average of the last K segments

$$y = \sum_{k=1}^{K} x_k[n]$$

3) Select R' by calculating the weighted average

$$R'[n] = \gamma x'[n].(1-\gamma)y$$

4) Quantize R' to the the set of available bitrates to determine the next rate

$$R[n] = Q(R'[n])$$

Initially after running controlled experiments with parallel connections we observed that, for some reason we were not able to gain any performance advantage through varying the amount of parallel connections dynamically as opposed to setting a fix number of parallel connections. Upon careful observation of the dynamics of HTTP parallel connections, we found that when sequential one-by-one segment download occurs, we can track the download time of each segment (and hence the download rate) and predict the best bitrate for the next one. This approach works well for the state of art throughput based algorithms, but we cannot use it with parallel downloads, unfortunately.

For simplification we can think that every batch will be downloaded in batch_size parallel connections. We use last batch download size, last batch download time and average size (in bytes) of last batch segments. The algorithm then adjusts the batch size after the each batch download to increase next average batch download rate. Once this is set, it is incorporated into the main throughput based algorithm which selects the next bitrate. Our parallel algorithm determines the batch_size for the next segment. It is interesting to note that although our parallel algorithm greatly affects the results of the throughput based controller, it is completely transparent and does not affect the algorithm, instead the performance is improved due to the resulting improvement in bandwidth which is used in the calculations.

5 Measurement Study

The motivation of our work is to improve the video QoE for lower bandwidth regions. For this purpose, we performed extensive measurements to calculate the video quality as experienced by endpoints in a third world country with poor overall Internet speed, as evident from stats in the Sandvine global Internet report.

5.1 Neubot

Neubot is an open source tool for network collection and measurement. The operation of Neubot is that when the software is installed on the client, it automatically runs several tests after each 30 min interval: download speedtest, upload speedtest, bittorrent test and dashtest [4]. It connects to the central neubot server where it is redirected to one of 124 server placed in one of 40 different geographical locations across the world and one of the four types of tests at random. Since we are interested in measuring video streaming performance, we modified the software actions to enforce it to run dashtest only after every 20 min through a Python script running continuously in the Windows background for a number of months.

5.2 Measurement Setup

The study was conducted on two different Internet providers. Since we had to minimize affect of externalities, we conducted all experiments on wired connections. First one was performed over the educational backbone Internet provider, PERN. The second variant was performed over the home connection from a large fixed broadband ISP located in Islamabad.

5.3 Measurement Results

Overall, we conducted almost 20,000 separate video sessions during the period from January to July 2017. Out of these, 14000 came from the backbone network and Here are some of the notable overall stats of the data collected. The below Table 1 shows the key statistical figures from the two settings.

Table 1. Statistical overview of the measurement study.

ISP	Backbone	Commercial	Combined
No of video sessions	13789	6029	19818
No of downloaded segments	210073	91462	301535
No of different servers	86	119	119
No of rebuffering events	2483	846	3372
No of incomplete sessions	574	140	714
Avg download speed (kbps)	1046	1136	1074
Avg bitrate quality (kbps)	803	816	807

5.4 Analysis

The following is the distribution of the frequency plot that we obtained for the readings. It is evident that for single HTTP connections in low bandwidth setting, the throughput is poor relative to the capacity of the network link. This behavior is also a result of less aggressive approach in selection of bitrate as discussed in a previous study (Fig. 4).

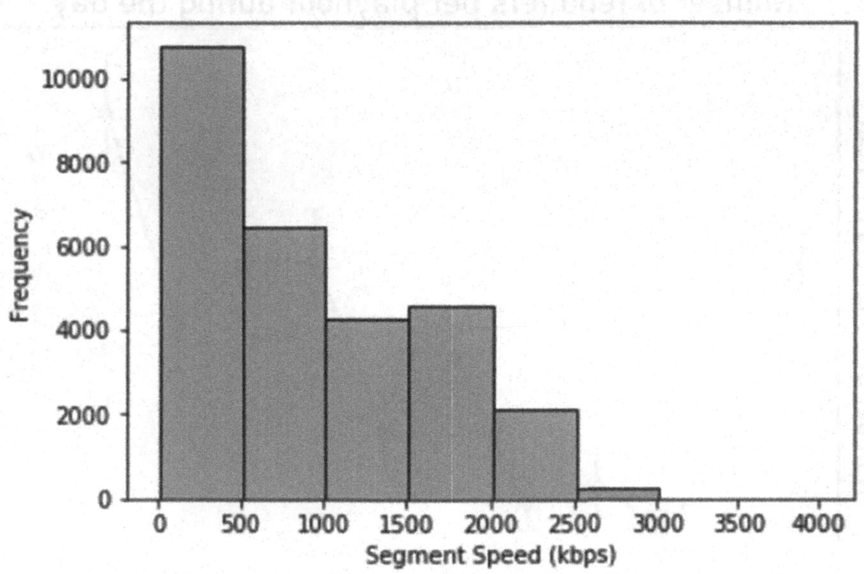

Fig. 4. Frequency plot of segment download speeds.

We also observed a high amount of rebuffering events that occured over the course of our study, over 3000 sessions experienced rebuffering events while over 700 sessions failed to complete due to network failure during the playback process. Below is a plot that represents the number of buffering events over the course of 24 h period. The average download time for every segment was 1.6 s which is lower than 2 which meant that a large proportion of video sessions were smoothly played out.

The last and perhaps the most significant observation from the statistics were the average download speed and average bitrate quality. Considering that the two Internet providers had 3 Mbps and 4 Mbps links and we conducted the experiments throughout the 24 h mark to neutralize any effect on any background traffic activity that might affect the application performance. The average speeds determined were a meager 1046 kbps and 1136 kbps for the backbone and commercial ISP respectively. This leaves a huge gap for potential improvements through parallel connections as only a third of the capacity is being utilized on average.

6 Video Streaming Experiment

After evaluating the state of Internet video performance, we proceeded to conduct controlled experiments to improve the Quality of Experience (Fig. 5).

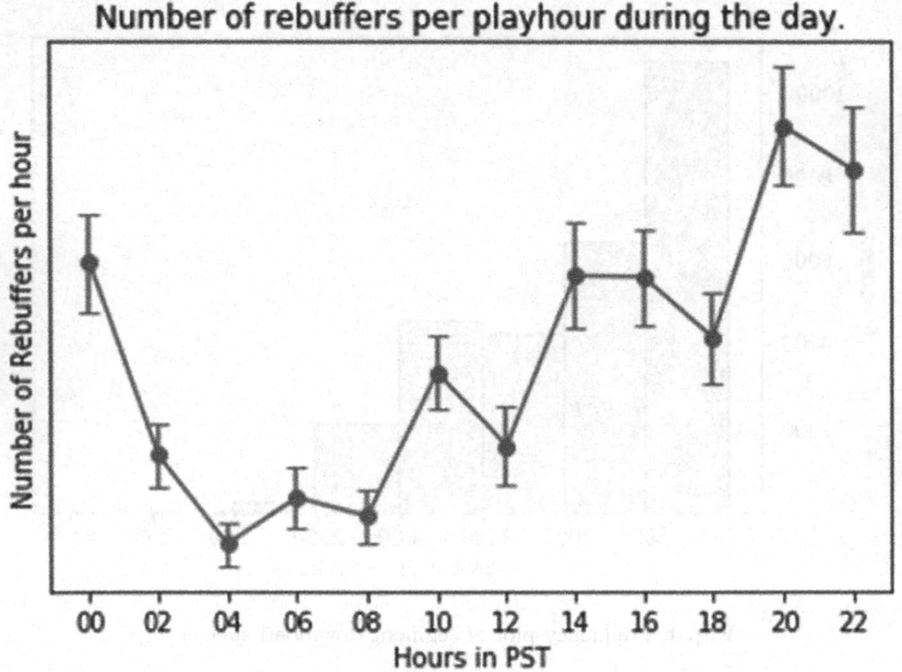

Fig. 5. Rebuffering events occurrance per hour.

6.1 DASH Encoding

We start by encoding the standard Big Buck Bunny video into 5 different representations. The process is performed by an open source utility FFMpeg which is available for both Linux and Windows platforms. The following Table 2 represents the resolutions and bitrates to which we chunked and encoded into the ISO-BMFF format of the DASH manifest file.

Table 2. Video representations.

Resolution	360 × 240	480 × 360	640 × 480	1024 × 720	1920 × 1080
Bitrate (kbps)	350	600	1000	2000	3000

6.2 Experiment Setup

To conduct testing of our parallel algorithm, we used an open source DASH emulator framework named AStream. The player framework is built using Python and uses various HTTP libraries to download and parse through the DASH manifest file to obtain all resolution and bitrate information. The player then emulates playback by downloading the video segments and selecting the next bitrate through 1 of the 2 state of the art throughput based and a buffer based adaptive switching algorithm.

The client and server instances are virtual machines placed and orchestrated on a centrally controlled academic cloud, named GENI. The GENI project [5] enables research studies with the facility of spinning up Linux and BSD instances and allows them to remotely access the machines to run experiments and execute scripts. The same topology can be replicated on a single PC using a hypervisor, such as KVM, VirtualBox or VMWare Player to connect 2 VMs. The setup can also be created by connecting 2 physical computers or servers together by LAN cable or even through networking of 2 docker containers running on Linux host Operating system.

The server is running Apache web server and the DASH encoded Big Buck Bunny video, a common evaluation video [17], segments have been placed on it along with the manifest file. On the client side, a Net shaper module has been added to emulate a WAN connection between the client and server so that the network conditions obtained through our measurement study is replicated. Dummynet [8] is used to control the latency and bandwidth of the emulated WAN connection. From literature, the ping latency is set to 80 ms while the throughput is taken through random samples from the 19000 data points of our study.

6.3 Parallel Streaming Results

We modify the code in the AStream emulator to take advantage of a system utility named aria2 which facilitates provision for parallel HTTP downloading according to our parallel streaming algorithm explained in Sect. 3. We integrate aria2 functions that split the file into multiple chunks and fetch them in parallel.

The following results were obtained when we applied our algorithm in the single connection scenario (default state of the art), and with 2, 3 and 4 parallel connections as labelled by N equals 1, 2, 3, 4 in the figure. We observed that due to being small files, there was a loss of improvement after increasing the connections greater than 4 as the segments are further split into smaller files causing greater overhead than the performance advantage gain.

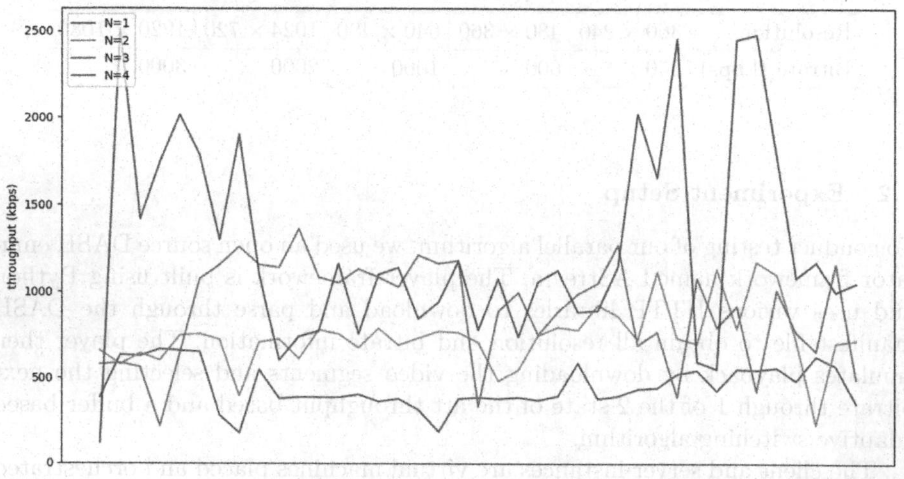

Fig. 6. Download speed of parallel video streaming.

The results show that parallel HTTP connections provide a considerable performance improvements over the single HTTP connection when evaluated for a state of the art throughput based ABR algorithm. The trend observed is that the throughput generally increases with increasing the number of parallel connections. Some interesting observations are made from the plot, when higher bitrates are selected, the file size becomes larger and the parallel connections tend to benefit further as seen from the peaks in case of 3 and 4 parallel connections.

The result of multiple runs in terms of the average throughput segment downloading speed has improved to more than double as in the case of the default single HTTP connection in case of the same throughput based ABR algorithm (Fig. 6).

The following Fig. 7 represents the bitrate quality selected for both single and dynamic parallel connections for both throughput based and buffer based algorithms.

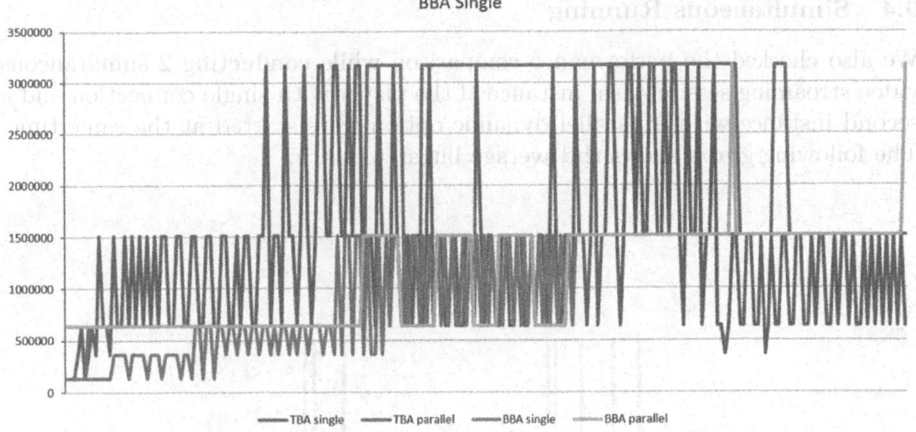

Fig. 7. Bitrate quality of parallel video streaming.

For the same experiment, the below bar chart represents the average speed during the runs to show the clear difference between the video quality improvement (Fig. 8).

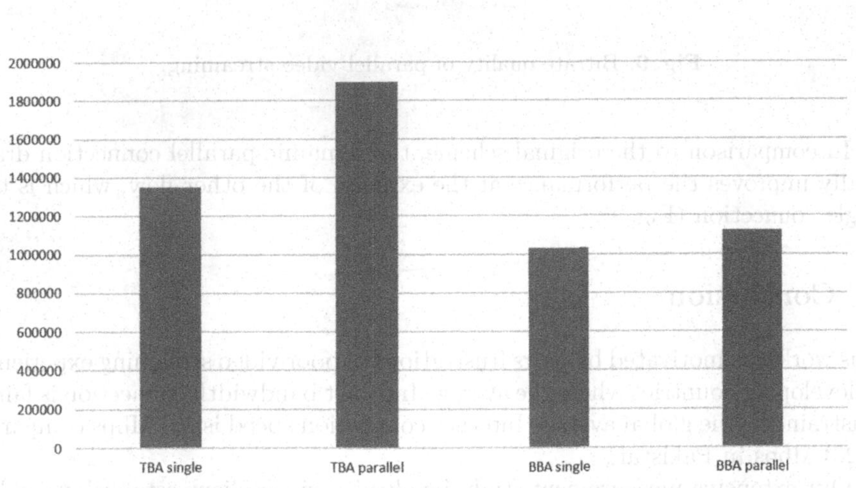

Fig. 8. Bitrate quality of parallel video streaming.

6.4 Simultaneous Running

We also checked the performance comparison while conducting 2 simultaneous video streaming sessions. An instance of the player with single connection and a second instance with a parallel dynamic option were started at the same time. The following graph shows the average bitrate quality:

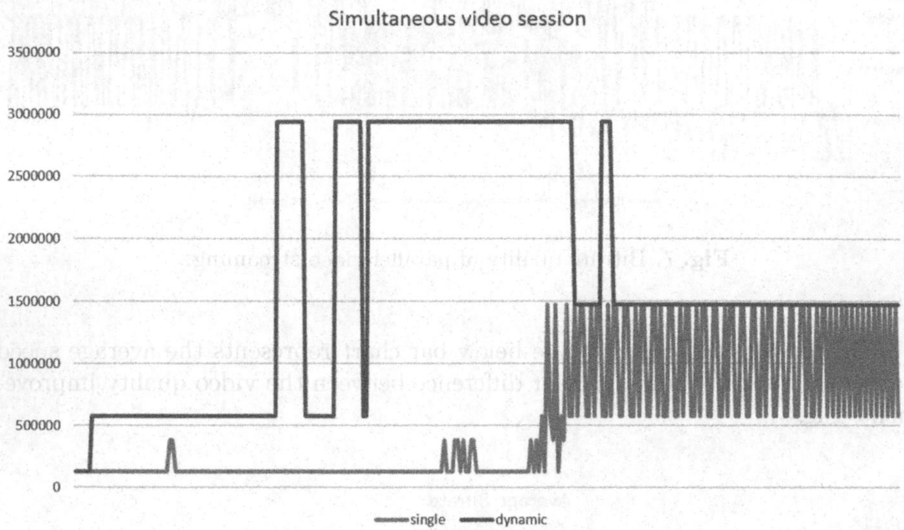

Fig. 9. Bitrate quality of parallel video streaming.

In comparison to the original scheme, the dynamic parallel connection drastically improves the performance at the expense of the other flow, which is the single connection (Fig. 9).

7 Conclusion

This work was motivated by users frustrations of poor video streaming experience in developing countries where the average Internet bandwidth connection is fairly constrained. The global average Internet connection speed is 5.6 Mbps compared to 2.0 Mbps in Pakistan.

Our extensive measurement study involved a video client establishing video sessions with 119 servers located in different geographical locations over a course of 6 months and collecting statistics of almost 20,000 video sessions out of which some of them were prone to buffering events and some even failure.

As we found out the margins for improvement through our measurement study, our test bed results validated our thoughts after observing up to twice the segment downloading throughput rates as a result of utilizing multiple connections for the same state of the art adaptive streaming algorithm.

References

1. Akhshabi, S., Anantakrishnan, L., Begen, A.C., Dovrolis, C.: What happens when HTTP adaptive streaming players compete for bandwidth? In: Proceedings of the 22nd International Workshop on Network and Operating System Support for Digital Audio and Video, pp. 9–14. ACM (2012)
2. Ameur, C.B.: TCP protocol optimization for HTTP adaptive streaming. Ph.D. thesis, Rennes 1 (2015)
3. Ansari, M., Ghaderi, M.: Parallel HTTP for video streaming in wireless networks. In: IEEE 24th International Symposium on Modeling, Analysis and Simulation of Computer and Telecommunication Systems (MASCOTS), pp. 337–342. IEEE (2016)
4. Basso, S., Servetti, A., Masala, E., De Martin, J.C.: Measuring dash streaming performance from the end users perspective using neubot. In: Proceedings of the 5th ACM Multimedia Systems Conference, pp. 1–6. ACM (2014)
5. Berman, M., et al.: GENI: a federated testbed for innovative network experiments. Comput. Netw. **61**, 5–23 (2014)
6. Bhat, D., Rizk, A., Zink, M., Steinmetz, R.: SABR: network-assisted content distribution for QoE-driven ABR video streaming. ACM Trans. Multimed. Comput. Commun. Appl. (TOMM) **14**(2s), 32 (2018)
7. Bruneau-Queyreix, J., Negru, D., Batalla, J.M., Borcoci, E.: Multiple description-DASH: pragmatic video streaming maximizing end-users' quality of experience. In: IEEE International Conference on Communications (ICC), pp. 1–7. IEEE (2016)
8. Carbone, M., Rizzo, L.: Dummynet revisited. ACM SIGCOMM Comput. Commun. Rev. **40**(2), 12–20 (2010)
9. Concolato, C., Le Feuvre, J., Denoual, F., Nassor, E., Ouedraogo, N., Taquet, J.: Adaptive streaming of HEVC tiled videos using MPEG-DASH. IEEE Trans. Circuits Syst. Video Technol. **28**, 1981–1992 (2017)
10. De Cicco, L., Caldaralo, V., Palmisano, V., Mascolo, S.: Elastic: a client-side controller for dynamic adaptive streaming over HTTP (DASH). In: 20th International Packet Video Workshop (PV), pp. 1–8. IEEE (2013)
11. Hoßfeld, T., Schatz, R., Biersack, E., Plissonneau, L.: Internet video delivery in YouTube: from traffic measurements to quality of experience. In: Biersack, E., Callegari, C., Matijasevic, M. (eds.) Data Traffic Monitoring and Analysis. LNCS, vol. 7754, pp. 264–301. Springer, Heidelberg (2013). https://doi.org/10.1007/978-3-642-36784-7_11
12. Hoßfeld, T., Seufert, M., Sieber, C., Zinner, T., Tran-Gia, P.: Identifying QoE optimal adaptation of HTTP adaptive streaming based on subjective studies. Comput. Netw. **81**, 320–332 (2015)
13. Huang, T.-Y., Handigol, N., Heller, B., McKeown, N., Johari, R.: Confused, timid, and unstable: picking a video streaming rate is hard. In: Proceedings of the 2012 Internet Measurement Conference, pp. 225–238. ACM (2012)
14. Huang, T.-Y., Johari, R., McKeown, N., Trunnell, M., Watson, M.: A buffer-based approach to rate adaptation: evidence from a large video streaming service. ACM SIGCOMM Comput. Commun. Rev. **44**(4), 187–198 (2015)
15. Jiang, J., Sekar, V., Zhang, H.: Improving fairness, efficiency, and stability in HTTP-based adaptive video streaming with festive. IEEE/ACM Trans. Networking (TON) **22**(1), 326–340 (2014)
16. Kua, J., Armitage, G., Branch, P.: A survey of rate adaptation techniques for dynamic adaptive streaming over HTTP. IEEE Commun. Surv. Tutor. **19**(3), 1842–1866 (2017)

17. Lederer, S., Mueller, C., Timmerer, C., Concolato, C., Le Feuvre, J., Fliegel, K.: Distributed DASH dataset. In: Proceedings of the 4th ACM Multimedia Systems Conference, pp. 131–135. ACM (2013)
18. Lederer, S., Müller, C., Timmerer, C.: Dynamic adaptive streaming over HTTP dataset. In: Proceedings of the 3rd Multimedia Systems Conference, pp. 89–94. ACM (2012)
19. Li, Z., et al.: Probe and adapt: rate adaptation for HTTP video streaming at scale. IEEE J. Sel. Areas Commun. **32**(4), 719–733 (2014)
20. Mpeg, I.: Information technology-dynamic adaptive streaming over HTTP (DASH)-part 1: media presentation description and segment formats. Technical report, ISO/IEC MPEG (2012)
21. Plissonneau, L., Biersack, E.: A longitudinal view of HTTP video streaming performance. In: Proceedings of the 3rd Multimedia Systems Conference, pp. 203–214. ACM (2012)
22. Rainer, B., Lederer, S., Müller, C., Timmerer, C.: A seamless web integration of adaptive HTTP streaming. In: Proceedings of the 20th European Signal Processing Conference (EUSIPCO), pp. 1519–1523. IEEE (2012)
23. Sieber, C., Blenk, A., Hinteregger, M., Kellerer, W.: The cost of aggressive HTTP adaptive streaming: quantifying YouTube's redundant traffic. In: IFIP/IEEE International Symposium on Integrated Network Management (IM), pp. 1261–1267. IEEE (2015)
24. Smanchat, S., Sangkul, K., Tham, J.Y.: Enabling parallel streaming of multiple video sections by segment scheduling. In: Proceedings of the 13th International Conference on Advances in Mobile Computing and Multimedia, pp. 221–226. ACM (2015)
25. Stockhammer, T.: Dynamic adaptive streaming over HTTP-: standards and design principles. In: Proceedings of the Second Annual ACM Conference on Multimedia Systems, pp. 133–144. ACM (2011)
26. Wang, C., Rizk, A., Zink, M.: SQUAD: a spectrum-based quality adaptation for dynamic adaptive streaming over HTTP. In: Proceedings of the 7th International Conference on Multimedia Systems, p. 1. ACM (2016)
27. Zhang, S., Li, B., Li, B.: Presto: towards fair and efficient HTTP adaptive streaming from multiple servers. In: IEEE International Conference on Communications (ICC), pp. 6849–6854. IEEE (2015)
28. Zhou, C., Lin, C.-W., Guo, Z.: mDASH: a Markov decision-based rate adaptation approach for dynamic HTTP streaming. IEEE Trans. Multimedia **18**(4), 738–751 (2016)

Software Defined Machine Learning Based Anomaly Detection in Fog Based IoT Network

Qaisar Shafi(✉), Saad Qaisar(✉), and Abdul Basit(✉)

School of Electrical Engineering and Computer Science (SEECS), National University of Sciences and Technology (NUST), Islamabad, Pakistan
{qaisar.shafi,saad.qaisar,basit.khan}@seecs.edu.pk

Abstract. Adaptation of intelligent devices with smart connectivity has tremendously increased the Internet of Things (IoT) traffic. For the security of IoTs massive applications, anomaly detection in these large number of devices is resource intensive task. This anomaly detection neither can be done in a cloud where analytical applications run nor in IoT device due to its limited computation capability. The Software Defined Networking (SDN) promises better management of network due to centralized control. In this paper, we proposed a software-defined machine learning (ML) based anomaly detection framework that provides network control in two scenarios, first is cloud infrastructure, and other is collocated fog(network edge) infrastructure. We compare our work in terms of delay in cloud against a collocated fog (processing) node; furthermore, we have also evaluated both scenarios with respect to packet error rate and throughput. Moreover, we discuss that these factors are critical in attack detection and mitigation. In the end, we conclude that in machine learning based anomaly detection, fog nodes provide better computational (attack detection) results in comparison with a cloud infrastructure.

Keywords: SDN · DDoS · Machine learning · Internet of Things · Fog · Cloud

1 Introduction

Connected devices are next-generation networks that interact without human interaction. These devices produce massive data that require pre-processing before use by an analytical application that employs machine learning techniques for enhanced results [1]. Cloud based infrastructure is best fit in this scenario. Moreover, edge computing and Softwarization of network and its numerous applications are also gaining the interest of researchers [2]. These smart systems have applications in transport, grids, health-care, surveillance and many more we can name [4]. Fog based infrastructure [4,21] are considered to be best to do computation at the edge of the network to lodge latency. The Software Defined

S. Misra et al. (Eds.): ICCSA 2019, LNCS 11622, pp. 611–621, 2019.
https://doi.org/10.1007/978-3-030-24305-0_45

Networking (SDN) promises better management of network due to centralized control [5]. In securing application and anomaly detection, computational systems are considering SDN as their candidate that separate control plan from data plan [3].

The massive application of IoT networks also increase the security vulnerabilities in these applications. Intrusion Detection and Prevention System (IDPS) must operate in real-time, delay in mitigation of attack process can block IoT traffic. Anomaly and attack detection systems in combination with machine learning(ML) techniques provide best attack detection results, but this task is resource intensive as well. Collocated fog nodes process the IoT data (anomaly detection) before going towards cloud where already analytical application are running and also avoid processing at IoT device which is already computationally limited. In this paper, we proposed two network perspective methods of machine learning based anomaly detection techniques. First we present, that detection mechanism is located on the cloud that is represented by an intercontinental link/slow or delayed link because is at a distance. In this arrangement the cloud is providing anomaly detection services. In the second scenario, the fog layer is collocated that has a fast link from IoT network and providing anomaly detection services at the network edge.

We evaluated our proposed scheme in terms of a delay from cloud versus collocated fog computational node. Moreover, the packet error rate and throughput are also evaluated to validate our proposed methodology for attack detection. Moreover, we discuss that these factors are critical in attack detection and mitigation. For ML-based anomaly detection we make use of the novel approach of detecting low-intensity and high-intensity DDoS attacks proposed in [6]. The main focus of the work is on network parameters to analyze the cloud and fog computational platforms for effective anomaly detection.

1.1 Research Contributions

Referring to the above discussion, the main contribution of this research is briefed as:

- We devised a system for intrusion detection/prevention (IDPS) for IoT network and provide comparative parameters for computation at cloud versus at network edge (fog).
- For effective anomaly detection (computation), we train machine learning classifiers that provide results in an automated way.
- We implemented, evaluated and analyzed both scenarios (cloud vs. fog) in number of network factors.

The remaining paper is structured as follows. Related work in Sect. 2, followed by main proposed architecture in Sect. 3. Main setup, implementation and result discussion in Sect. 4. In the end, we conclude the work in Sect. 5.

2 Background and Related Work

In this section, we will discuss the background of the proposed work. Intrusion Detection and Prevention System (IDPS) must operate in real-time; delay in mitigation of attack process can chock IoT traffic. Entropy-based schemes are in considering for attack detection due to limitations of volume centric based schemes for detection of passive and active attacks [7]. Entropy- based schemes provides measure for better classification of attacks [8,9]. Using entropy based schemes detects attacks due to the change in the distribution of traffic across network [10]. Multiple features are also utilized to detect notorious attacks. For example, change in the rate of occurrence of destination address points to Distributed denial of service (DDoS). The core idea behind machine learning based anomaly detection and detection of DDoS attacks at the network edge are motivated by the work presented in [1]. Machine learning based techniques are widely used in intrusion detection and anomalous detection methods. The detailed survey is presented in [11]. The SDN and machine learning techniques are coupled and used in many research areas including traffic classification, security, routing and quality of service. The detail work is presented in [12]. The mininet based evaluation of SDN networks is presented in [13]. This work analyzed resources capability and utilization of SDN resources. The work in [14] analyzed throughput and packet loss in different SDN scenario and they also used multiple platforms. Mininet has been using in the development of many SDN based systems. The work is presented in [15] for development of the framework for custom network topology using mininet [16]. Also presented mininet as SDN based testing platforms. The work in [17] also used mininet for prototyping and emulating SDN based networks.

3 Proposed Network (Attack Detection) Architecture

This is section we present the complete system model and architecture of the proposed scheme. Figure 1 represents the two proposed scenario of the system. The lower portion of the figure shows the IoT network connected by a switch. The figure upper portion describe shows the SDN controller is far-apart and it has machine learning based anomaly detection module running in it that will be described in a later section. The main purpose of this fig is to show that the cloud is at distance and it can be represented by an intercontinental link that is slow or delayed link. In this figure, the whole ML-based anomaly detection mechanism will be carried out in cloud which is obviously at some distance as shown using intercontinental link.

The Fig. 1 lower portion illustrates the second scenario of the work in which the ML-based anomaly detector mechanism is collocated with fog node. It means that detection of anomalies is done at the network edge so it is represented by a fast link as shown in the figure. The attacker is trying to launch an attack (DDoS) on IoT network, the proposed system will detect and mitigate the attack in both above arrangements and more effective results will be compared in later

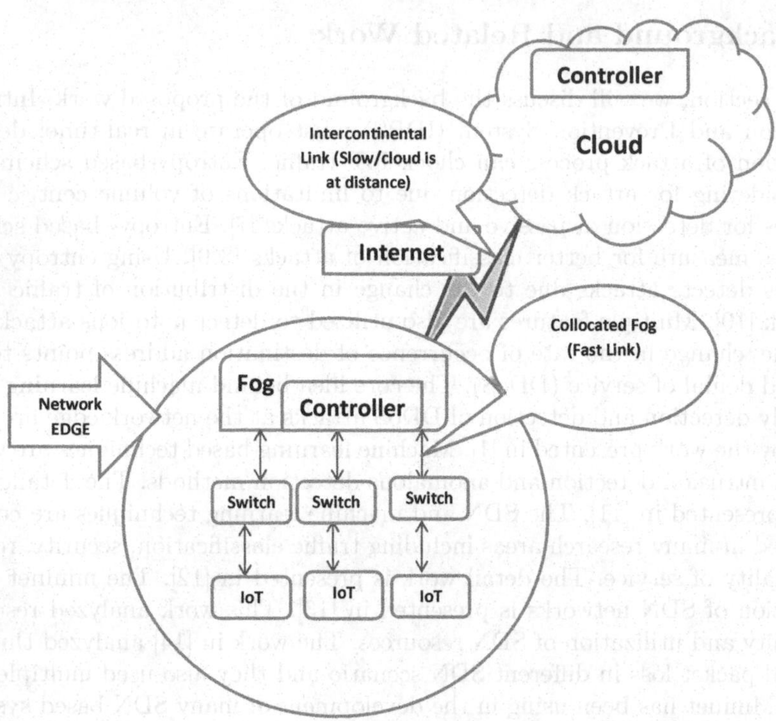

Fig. 1. Network architecture of cloud and collocated Fog

sections. In other words, attack detection is on cloud in the first arrangement and in second scenario attack detection is on the collocated fog node as already explained.

3.1 Anomaly/Attack Detection Methodology

The proposed scheme for ML-based anomaly detection is presented in this section. The idea of feature selection, ML classifier selection, training phase and prediction is motivated from the work in [1]. The anomaly detection offered in this work is the basic computation that we will carry out in this work. It combines the proposed work that this detection is carried out in the cloud or in collocated fog node at the edge of the network. The basic idea of anomaly detection used in this work is that there is a resource manager that assigns resources for labeling features after the selection of features from network traffic as shown in Fig. 2.

Recurrent Neural Network (RNN), Multi-Layer Perceptron (MLP) and Alternate Decision Tree (ADT) form the constituent building blocks of Entropy-based features with Triple Machine Learning Classifier Detection system (E3ML) [6] multi-classifier for detection and prevention of anomalies in IoT network as illustrated in Fig. 2. The idea behind detection protocol is to exploit three ML

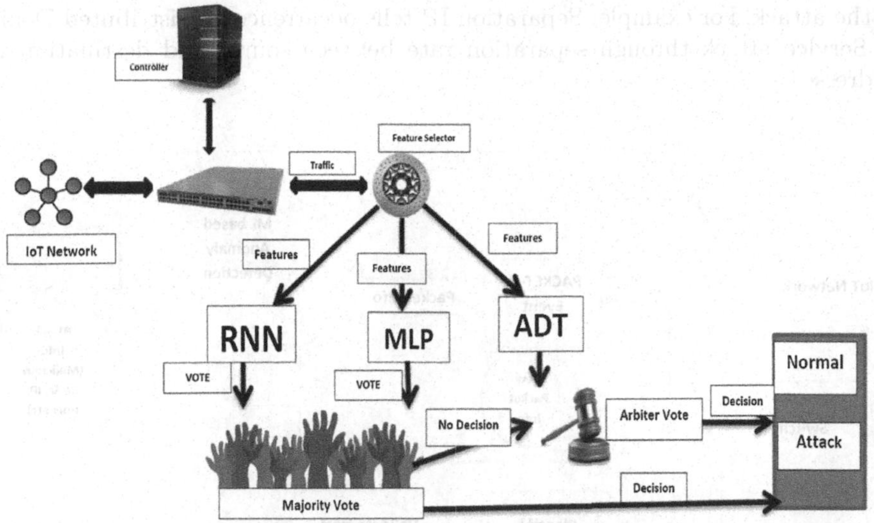

Fig. 2. ML classifier based Anomaly detection module(Multi-classifer System)

classifiers to boost the accuracy of detection of DDoS attacks. Between two standard ML classifiers (i.e. MLP and RNN), voting is carried out as illustrated in Fig. 2. Vote (attack or normal) is contributed by each classifier using its classification results. If attack and normal votes are equal third classifier (i.e. ADT) is introduced that is an arbiter. There is the number of processing units for processing of the data. After suitable processing, it produces labeled attributes. These labeled attributes are dispatched to the allocated processor running entropy calculation code. The code calculates the entropy of each attribute to produce a labeled feature required for traffic classification into normal and malicious categories. We have used a total of twenty (20) features, in contrast to six (06) features based classification model used by a majority of machine learning based intrusion detection systems. In addition to employing more number of features for intrusion detection, we classify traffic with Triple Machine Learning Classifier Detection system (E3CL).

In addition to six known features used by the majority of intrusion detection systems i-e. protocol, delta time, source and destination IP addresses, source and destination port addresses, we have considered another ten (10) independent features in addition to these commonly used features including source and destination MAC as well as network addresses, packet length, Differentiated Services Code Point (DSCP) value, TCP length, its window size and sequence number.

We have also used five (05) extended features constructed through independent features. These features include the rate of separation between source and destination IP, source and destination port, source and destination MAC, source and destination network and source TCP window size and destination TCP segment length, each of which is effective to detect the different version of the attack. For example, Separation IP tells occurrence of Distributed Denial of Service attack through separation rate between source and destination IP addresses.

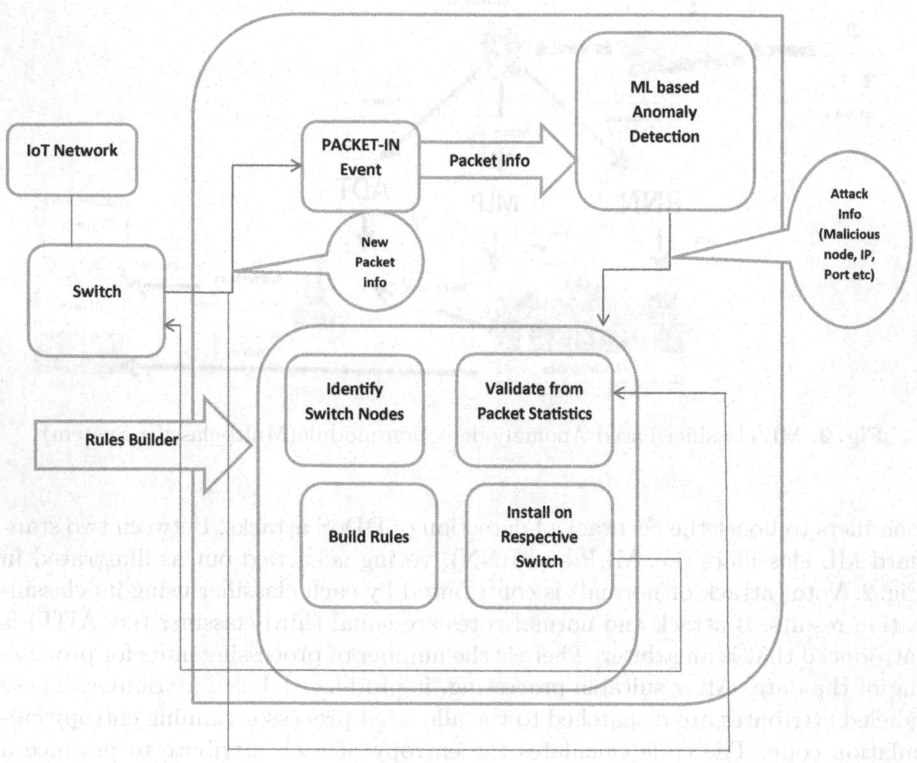

Fig. 3. The controller architecture

3.2 Inside the SDN Controller (Cloud and Fog)

The Fig. 3 shows the inside working of the controller with machine learning modules running in them. The machine learning based attack detection module is triggered with a PACKET-IN messages as shown in figure. The detection rules based on attack feedback and information (features) on which attack is calculated, RULE BUILDER is triggered. Switch inputs VALIDATE PACKET STATISTICS on which module are updated on respective switch that on the bases on packet statistics update and INSTALL RULES OF RESPECTIVE SWITCH. ML based IDPS is already discussed on which attack is detected.

3.3 Attack Mitigation Strategy with SDN Control

SDN has provided us ways to account for attack mitigation. SDN controller of an IoT network controls both in and out traffic flows across the IoT devices. Each controller preserves an access list that comprises of blacklist prefixes. Applicable rules are installed in respective flow tables of all switches so that switches can act as the sink for incoming traffic from blacklist prefixes.

4 Implementation and Experimentation

In this section, we will explain how we have set up our proposed work and how experiments are conducted. We have used the mininet emulation tool to evaluate the proposed framework employing different network topologies and links as shown in Fig. 1. We have used python based Ryu controller in our experiment. A tree topology is created with four(4) depth value and eight(8) fanout value in mininet. Random switches are associated with IoT network (Cooja simulated IoT nodes) using SDN-WISE [18,19].

Appropriate flow rules are installed to setup to verify traffic from malicious nodes. We have used UNSW-NB15 intrusion detection dataset [20] to verify our work. UNSW-NB15 consists of raw network packets in pcap format. They are created by IXIA PerfectStorm tool. Australian Centre for Cyber Security(ACCS) has generated this traffic. It consists of 100 GB traffic in a Pcap separated files. The dataset consists of nine types of attacks as discussed in [1].

The ML-based anomaly detection module is running in the controller are two cases, collocated or far-apart (fog vs cloud). Ryu controller instance is running over Virtual Machine (VM). Controller over each VM is connected to a mininet instance, emulating an area network that contains network switches and IoT devices as mininet hosts. As already discussed, we have evaluated our setup in three criteria. Packet delay as in case of cloud that is located far apart. The distant cloud on which attack detection module is running can take time to stop the attack as packets are delayed that can cause an attack to disseminate in the IoT network.

5 Results and Discussion

The results that we get from our proposed setup are shown in Figs. 4, 5 and 6. In these figures, the network evaluation criteria in terms of cloud and fog architecture are discussed. These evaluation criteria are packet delay in terms of ML-based anomaly detection running on cloud that is far apart versus the fog that is collocated and immediately acts to prevent any anomaly in the system. Second criteria are network throughput that is improved as fog computing layer is located near the IoT network and it helps in effective mitigation of attacks like DDoS that is started to originate in the IoT network. The third, evaluation criteria are network fairness. This criterion relates to varying the data rate and focus is networks packet loss.

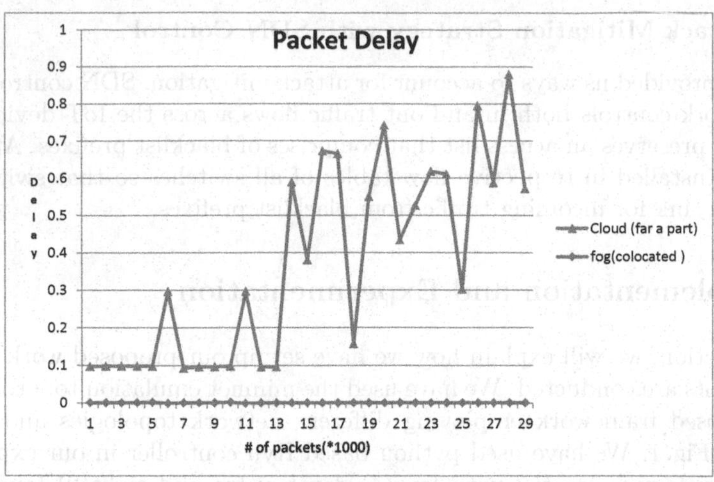

Fig. 4. Packet delay for effective attack detection (cloud vs fog)

Figure 4 shows the packet delay in terms of ML anomaly detection located at distance at cloud versus near (collocated fog) the IoT network. The x-axis shows the number of packets (multiple of 1000) and the y-axis shows the difference of time between sending and receiving of the packets. The cloud shows high packet delay thus more time for anomaly detection method to be implemented for the IoT network. Whereas, the collocated fog shows very less packet delay that will help the controller to analyze anomalous traffic with minimum delay and act as attack mitigation methodology to prevent DDoS and similar 9 attacks in the dataset as discussed earlier.

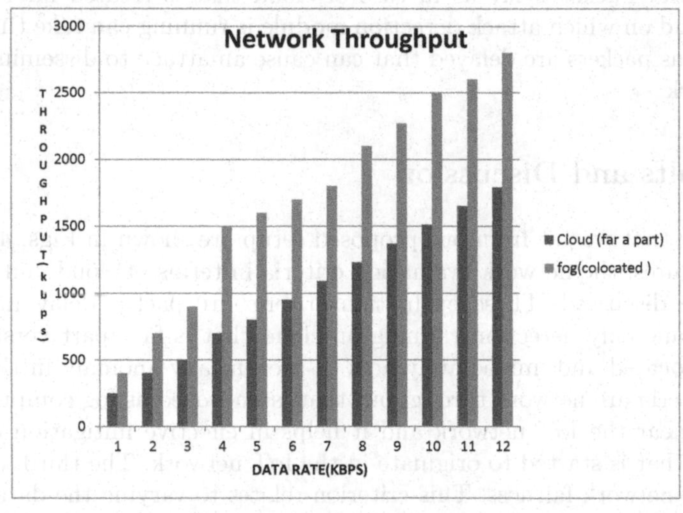

Fig. 5. Network throughput for effective attack detection (cloud vs fog)

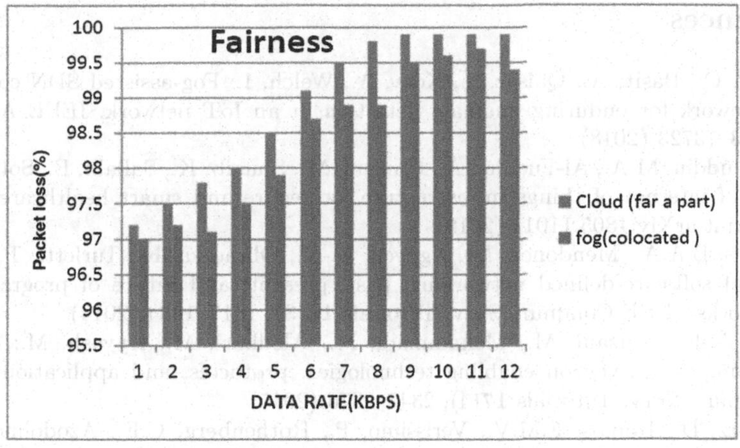

Fig. 6. Network fairness for effective attack detection (cloud vs fog)

The Fig. 5 illustrates the network throughput that is the second criteria on which proposed work is evaluated. The graph shown in this figure illustrates as data rates increase the network throughput also increases. The collocated fog shows better network throughput as compared to the cloud which is located at a distance. In the end, Fig. 6 has shown the fairness of the network against the data rate. The figure shows that amount of data loss in collocated fog is less compared to cloud arrangement. Hence the fairness of the fog arrangement is better than the ML-based anomaly detection module running in cloud infrastructure.

6 Conclusion

In this work, we have taken motivation that anomaly detection neither can be done in a cloud where analytical applications run nor in IoT device due to its limited computation capability. The Software Defined Networking (SDN) potentials better organization of network due to centralized control. In this paper, we proposed a software-defined machine learning (ML) based anomaly detection framework that provides network control in two scenarios, first is cloud Infrastructure, other in collocated fog infrastructure. We compare our work in the number of network parameters including delay in cloud against a collocated fog (processing) node; furthermore, we also evaluated both scenarios with respect to packet error rate, fairness and throughput. We conclude using our results and evaluation that in ML-based anomaly detection fog nodes provide better computational results in comparison with a cloud infrastructure. hence, fog or edge infrastructure provides better attack detection and mitigation system in terms of network arrangements against cloud infrastructure.

Acknowledgement. This work was supported in part by NUST, Ignite Project Xbits and Higher Education Commission, Pakistan.

References

1. Shafi, Q., Basit, A., Qaisar, S., Koay, A., Welch, I.: Fog-assisted SDN controlled framework for enduring anomaly detection in an IoT network. IEEE Access **6**, 73713–73723 (2018)
2. Salahuddin, M.A., Al-Fuqaha, A., Guizani, M., Shuaib, K., Sallabi, F.: Softwarization of internet of things infrastructure for secure and smart healthcare.: arXiv preprint arXiv:1805.11011 (2018)
3. Nunes, B.A.A., Mendonca, M., Nguyen, X.-N., Obraczka, K., Turletti, T.: A survey of software-defined networking: past, present, and future of programmable networks. IEEE Commun. Surv. Tutorials **16**(3), 1617–1634 (2014)
4. Ala, A.-F., Guizani, M., Mohammadi, M., Aledhari, M., Ayyash, M.: Internet of things: a survey on enabling technologies, protocols, and applications. IEEE Commun. Surv. Tutorials **17**(4), 2347–2376 (2015)
5. Kreutz, D., Ramos, F.M.V., Verissimo, P., Rothenberg, C.E., Azodolmolky, S., Uhlig, S.: Software-defined networking: a comprehensive survey. Proc. IEEE **103**(1), 14–76 (2015)
6. Koay, A., Chen, A., Welch, I., Seah, W.K.G.: A new multi classifier system using entropy-based features in DDoS attack detection. In: 2018 International Conference on Information Networking (ICOIN), pp. 162–167 (2018)
7. Bhuyan, M.H., Bhattacharyya, D.K., Kalita, J.K.: A multi-step outlier-based anomaly detection approach to network-wide traffic. Inf. Sci. **348**, 243–271 (2016)
8. Bawany, N.Z., Shamsi, J.A., Salah, K.: DDoS attack detection and mitigation using SDN: methods, practices, and solutions. Arab. J. Sci. Eng. **42**(2), 425–441 (2017)
9. Kamboj, P., Trivedi, M.C., Yadav, V.K., Singh, V.K.: Detection techniques of DDoS attacks: a survey. In: 2017 4th IEEE Uttar Pradesh Section International Conference on Electrical, Computer and Electronics (UPCON), pp. 675–679. IEEE (2017)
10. Bhuyan, M.H., Bhattacharyya, D.K., Kalita, J.K.: An empirical evaluation of information metrics for low-rate and high-rate DDoS attack detection. Pattern Recogn. Lett. **51**, 1–7 (2015)
11. Mishra, P., Varadharajan, V., Tupakula, U., Pilli, E.S.: A detailed investigation and analysis of using machine learning techniques for intrusion detection. IEEE Commun. Surv. Tutorials **21**, 686–728 (2018)
12. Xie, J., et al.: A survey of machine learning techniques applied to software defined networking (SDN): research issues and challenges. IEEE Commun. Surv. Tutorials **21**(1), 393–430 (2018)
13. Keti, F., Askar, S.: Emulation of software defined networks using mininet in different simulation environments. In: 2015 6th International Conference on Intelligent Systems, Modelling and Simulation, pp. 205–210. IEEE (2015)
14. Tantayakul, K., Dhaou, R., Paillassa, B., Panichpattanakul, W.: Experimental analysis in SDN open source environment. In: 2017 14th International Conference on Electrical Engineering/Electronics, Computer, Telecommunications and Information Technology (ECTI-CON), pp. 334–337. IEEE (2017)
15. Veena, S., Pal, C., Rustagi, R.P., Murthy, K.N.B.: A framework for implementing realistic custom network topology in Mininet. Int. J. Sci. Res. (IJSR) **7**, 1316–1323 (2014)
16. Kaur, K., Singh, J., Ghumman, N.S.: Mininet as software defined networking testing platform. In: International Conference on Communication, Computing & Systems (ICCCS), pp. 139–142 (2014)

17. De Oliveira, R.L.S., Schweitzer, C.M., Shinoda, A.A., Prete, L.R.: Using mininet for emulation and prototyping software-defined networks. In: 2014 IEEE Colombian Conference on Communications and Computing (COLCOM), pp. 1–6. IEEE (2014)
18. Galluccio, L., Milardo, S., Morabito, G., Palazzo, S.: SDN-WISE: design, prototyping and experimentation of a stateful SDN solution for Wireless Sensor networks. In: 2015 IEEE Conference on Computer Communications (INFOCOM), pp. 513–521. IEEE (2015)
19. Dunkels, A., Gronvall, B., Voigt, T.: Contiki-a lightweight and flexible operating system for tiny networked sensors. In: 29th annual IEEE international conference on local computer networks, pp. 455–462. IEEE (2004)
20. Moustafa, N., Slay, J.: UNSW-NB15: a comprehensive data set for network intrusion detection systems (UNSW-NB15 network data set). In: 2015 Military Communications and Information Systems Conference (MilCIS), pp. 1–6. IEEE (2015)
21. Mouradian, C., Naboulsi, D., Yangui, S., Glitho, R.H., Morrow, M.J., Polakos, P.A.: A comprehensive survey on fog computing: State-of-the-art and research challenges. IEEE Commun. Surve. Tutorials **20**(1), 416–464 (2018)

Quantum Chemical Modeling of Solids with Computers: From Plane Waves to Local Structures (QuaCheSol 2019)

Structure and Lattice Dynamics of $La_2Zr_2O_7$ Crystal: Ab Initio Calculation

V. A. Chernyshev(✉)

Ural Federal University, Mira St. 19, 620002 Ekaterinburg, Russia
vchern@inbox.ru

Abstract. Crystal structure and phonon spectrum of rare-earth zirconate $La_2Zr_2O_7$ as well as the whole row $R_2Zr_2O_7$ (R = La, Ce, Pr, Nd, Sm, Eu, Gd, Tb, Dy, Ho, Er, Tm, Yb, Lu) were studied within the framework of density functional theory and MO LKAO approach. The calculations were performed by using hybrid functionals that take into account both local and nonlocal (at the Hartree-Fock formalism) exchanges. Calculations were performed with the most used functionals B3LYP and PBE0. The calculations were also carried out with the functional PBESOL0. The fundamental vibration frequencies of $R_2Zr_2O_7$ were calculated. The calculations were performed in the CRYSTAL17 program designed to simulate periodic structures.

Keywords: Phonon spectrum · Ab initio · DFT · Hybrid functionals

1 Introduction

The interest to the study of rare earth zirconate $R_2Zr_2O_7$ (R is a rare earth ion) is due to the varies of their properties and diverse applications [1–6]. Lanthanum zirconate $R_2Zr_2O_7$ was experimentally investigated by methods of X-ray diffraction, Raman and IR spectroscopy [7–14]. The phonon spectra of other crystals from this series are much less studied [14, 15]. For most crystals the information about the experimental study of their IR and Raman spectra is absent in the research papers. Modeling of the lanthanium zirconate $La_2Zr_2O_7$ and some other crystals from the row were previously performed in the plane waves basis [16–18]. The band structure and elastic properties were calculated in the works [16–18], however the phonon spectrum was not studied. In the last few years the structural phase transitions in rare-earth zirconates were investigated by X-ray structural analysis and Raman spectroscopy [15, 19]. This is relevant to do an ab initio study of the crystal structure and IR and Raman spectra of whole row $R_2Zr_2O_7$ (R = La-Lu) within the framework of a unified approach. In this work the structure and dynamics of crystals $R_2Zr_2O_7$ (R = La-Lu) with the pyrochlore structure ($Fd\bar{3}m$) are investigated in the framework of the MO LCAO approach with hybrid DFT functionals.

S. Misra et al. (Eds.): ICCSA 2019, LNCS 11622, pp. 625–638, 2019.
https://doi.org/10.1007/978-3-030-24305-0_46

2 Calculations

Ab initio calculations were performed within the framework of the density functional theory (DFT) by using hybrid functionals which take into account both local and non-local (in the Hartree-Fock formalism) exchange. Calculations were performed with WC1LYP [20], HSE06 [21, 22], B3LYP [23], PBE0 [24], functionals which have been widely used at the last years [25], as well as with the PBESOL0 functional, which is incremented in the program CRYSTAL17 [26, 27]. By using the hybrid functionals that take into account both local and non-local (HF) exchanges, we can well describe the band structure, IR and Raman spectra, and elastic properties of compounds with an ion-covalent bond [20, 28]. Comparison of B3LYP, PBE0 and other functionals with CCSD calculations has been performed recently (128 functionals of different levels were tested) [29]. It was shown that PBE0 is characterized by a rather small error for functionals of its level relative to the CCSD calculation when reproducing electron density and other parameters [29]. By using the PBE0 hybrid functional we successfully described the structure and dynamics of the crystal lattice of rare-earth titanates with the pyrochlore structure $R_2Ti_2O_7$ (R – rare-earth ion) in our previous work [30]. The coordinates of the ions in the unit cell of zirconates $R_2Zr_2O_7$ with the pyrochlore structure ($Fd\bar{3}m$) are given in Table 1.

Table 1. Ion coordinates in the $R_2Zr_2O_7$ unit cell.

Ion	*x*	*y*	*z*	Wyckoff position
Zr	0	0	0	16*c*
R	1/2	1/2	1/2	16*d*
O1	*x*	1/8	1/8	48*f*
O2	3/8	3/8	3/8	8*b*

Oxygen is included in all structural units of this compound. It is located in two symmetrically nonequivalent positions. Therefore, the reproduction of the structure and properties will depend essentially on the oxygen basis. The basis of TZVP type was used in this work [31]. This basis available on the website of CRYSTAL code [32]. Zirconium basis [33] available on CRYSTAL website also. This basis was used by the authors of the CRYSTAL program to calculate the structure and IR spectrum of zirconium complexes with oxygen ligands [33]. Quasi-relativistic pseudopotentials ECPnMWB were used to describe the inner shells of rare-earth ions (ECP – "effective core potential"; n – the number of internal electrons replaced by a pseudopotential; WB – "quasi-relativistic") [34, 35]. Accordingly, for La n = 46, for Ce n = 47, etc. That is, n = Z-11, where Z is the number of the element in the periodic table. Thus, the inner shells of rare-earth ions were replaced by a pseudopotential on the 4f inclusive. TZVP type valence basis sets «ECP46MWB-II» were used to describe the outer shells, $5s^2 5p^6$, involved in the formation of a chemical bond [34, 36, 37]. These pseudopotentials and valence basis sets are available on the Stuttgart website [38]. Gaussian primitives with exponent values less than 0.1 were removed from the valence basis sets.

The last diffuse orbital of the f- type was also removed from the valence basis sets. The sequence of calculations was the follow. The optimization of the crystal structure was carried out first. After that the phonon spectrum (or the elastic constants) was calculated for the crystal structure corresponding to the minimum energy. The accuracy of self-consistently solving of the system of Kohn-Sham equations was set at 10^{-10} a.u. (TOLDEE = 10). The parameters "TOLINTEG", determining the accuracy of the calculation of the two-electron integrals were set equal to 8,8,8,8,16. The Monkhorst-Pack shrinking factor was taken to be 8. The phonon spectrum in the CRYSTAL program is calculated at the harmonic approximation. By calculating the Hessian matrix the first derivatives were calculated analytically, while the second derivatives were calculated numerically. The Born charges were used by calculations of the Raman and infrared intensities at CRYSTAL code [39]. Electric dipole properties were calculated by using a periodic Coupled-perturbed Hartree-Fock (CPHF) or Kohn-Sham (CPKS) approach [40–42]. Details of the calculation algorithms are considered in [43].

3 Results and Discussion

The crystal structure of $La_2Zr_2O_7$ was calculated with various hybrid functionals. The results are shown in Table 2. Hybrid functionals reproduce the crystal structure of lanthanum zirconate quite well. Functional HSE06 [21] gives quite a good result. Apparently, the separation of the exchange contribution into the short-range ("SR") and long-range ("LR") in HSE06 has been done successfully. This approximation saves the computer resources. The calculation of the crystal structure with the HSE06 functional requires 5 times less time than the calculation with the PBE0 functional. Such a reduction in computer costs only slightly worsens the discrepancy with the experiment (Table 2). The PBESOL0 functional differs from PBE0. Instead of the local exchange-correlation functional PBE it uses PBESOL [44]. The calculation with PBESOL0 functional underestimates the lattice constant. The discrepancy with the experiment at absolute value is comparable with the PBE0 calculation (Table 2). The B3LYP functional gives the maximum discrepancy with the experiment (Table 2), which may be associated with a smaller percentage of the HF exchange. The crystal structure for the all row $R_2Zr_2O_7$ (R = La-Lu) was calculated with the PBE0 functional, as well as with the PBESOL0 functional (Tables 3, 4 and 5). The calculation results are in good agreement with the experiment [2, 14, 45, 46]. The "Difference" column in Tables 3, 4 and 5 shows the change of the values at the La-Lu row. The information of the distances from rare-earth ion to ligands (Table 5) may be useful for crystal field calculation on the rare-earth ion.

According to calculations, the x coordinate increases slightly in the row La-Lu (Table 4). In the pyrochlore structure the rare-earth ion is surrounded by eight oxygen ions, two of which are at a certain distance and six are at another distance.

Table 2. The lattice constant, interionic distances (Å), x coordinate of oxygen O1 (relative units) at $La_2Zr_2O_7$. The percentage of HF-exchange is given in parenthesis after the name of the functional.

Hybrid functional	WC1LYP (16%)	HSE06 (25%)	B3LYP (20%)	PBE0 (25%)	PBESOL0 (25%)	Exp. [8]	Exp. [9]
Lattice constant	10.885	10.841	10.940	10.838	10.763	10.798 (3)	10.805
La–O1	2.65	2.64	2.67	2.64	2.62	2.63 (3)	–
La–O2	2.3567	2.3472	2.3685	2.3465	2.3303	2.3379 (9)	–
Zr-O1	2.124	2.116	2.132	2.115	2.103	2.105 (18)	–
La-Zr	3.8485	3.8330	3.8678	3.8318	3.8054	3.8178 (13)	–
x	0.333	0.333	0.332	0.333	0.333	–	0.332

Table 3. Lattice constant of $R_2Zr_2O_7$ (R = La-Lu), Å

R	PBE0	PBESOL0	Exp. [14]	Exp. [45]	Exp. [46]	Exp. [47]
La	10.8379	10.7633	10.805	10.7992 (1)		
Ce	10.7985	10.7234			10.7135 (1)	
Pr	10.7618	10.6872	10.715	10.7010 (1)		
Nd	10.7266	10.6526	10.678	10.6134 (1)		10.6611 (1)
Sm	10.6657	10.5896	10.594	10.5907 (1)		
Eu	10.6348	10.5589	10.554			
Gd	10.6092	10.5333	10.528	10.5341 (1)		
Tb	10.5818	10.5058	10.476			
Dy	10.5554	10.4792	10.450			
Ho	10.5304	10.4543	10.419			
Er	10.5060	10.4309	10.395			
Tm	10.4848	10.4102	10.368			
Yb	10.4623	10.3869	10.336			
Lu	10.4508	10.3763				
Difference	0.3871	0.3870	0.469			

The parameter ρ (Table 5), which characterizes the distortion of the oxygen environment of the rare-earth ion, according to [47], is equal to:

$$\rho = \frac{R-O2}{R-O1}$$

The closer ρ is to one, the less there is distortion. According to the calculations, the distortion decreases in the La-Lu series. The change of the R-O1 and R-O2 distances in the row is shown at Fig. 1. The results of the bandgap calculation are shown in Table 6. The calculations predict a straight (Γ-Γ) bandgap for the all row La-Lu. Note that the experimental bandgap value for a thin film of $La_2Zr_2O_7$ is 4.96–5.60 eV [48], which agrees with the calculations quite well. According to the calculations, the bandgap value decreases almost linearly in the La-Lu series.

Table 4. *x* coordinate of oxygen O1 (48*f*) at $R_2Zr_2O_7$ (R = La-Lu), relative units.

R	PBE0	PBESOL0	Exp.
La	0.3327	0.3332	0.332 [9]
Ce	0.3336	0.3342	
Pr	0.3345	0.3351	
Nd	0.3353	0.3359	0.3357 (2) [46]
Sm	0.3369	0.3375	
Eu	0.3376	0.3383	
Gd	0.3383	0.3390	
Tb	0.3390	0.3398	
Dy	0.3397	0.3404	
Ho	0.3404	0.3411	
Er	0.3411	0.3418	
Tm	0.3416	0.3424	
Yb	0.3422	0.3430	
Lu	0.3425	0.3433	
Difference	0.0098	0.0101	

Table 5. Interionic distances R-O at $R_2Zr_2O_7$ (R = La-Lu), Å. It is PBESOL0 calculation.

R	R-O2 × 2	R-O1 × 6	ρ
La	2.330	2.615	0.891
Ce	2.322	2.599	0.893
Pr	2.314	2.584	0.896
Nd	2.306	2.569	0.898
Sm	2.293	2.543	0.902
Eu	2.286	2.530	0.904
Gd	2.281	2.519	0.905
Tb	2.275	2.507	0.907
Dy	2.269	2.496	0.909
Ho	2.263	2.485	0.911
Er	2.258	2.475	0.913
Tm	2.254	2.466	0.914
Yb	2.249	2.456	0.916
Lu	2.247	2.451	0.917
Difference	0.083	0.064	0.026

Rare-earth zirconates $R_2Zr_2O_7$ (R = La-Lu) with pyrochlore structure have phonon modes at the Γ point:

$$\Gamma = A_{1g} + E_g + 2F_{1g} + 4F_{2g} + 3A_{2u} + 3E_u + 8F_{1u} + 4F_{2u}.$$

Here A_{1g}, E_g and $4F_{2g}$ are Raman active modes, $7F_{1u}$ are infrared active modes, 4F2u, 3Eu, 2F1 g, 3A2u are silent modes. The results of the calculation of phonon

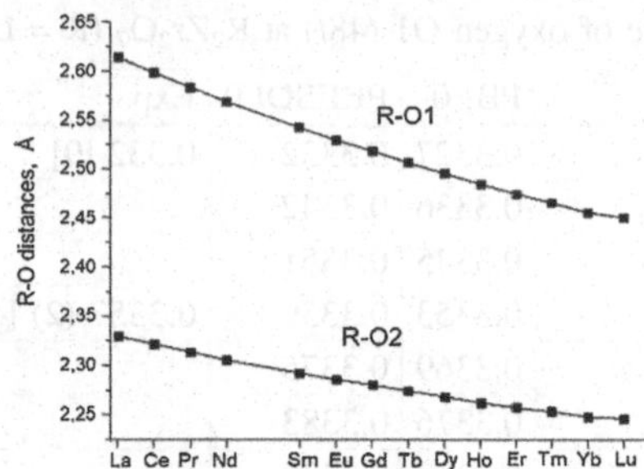

Fig. 1. The distances R-O at the row $R_2Zr_2O_7$ (R = La-Lu)

Table 6. Bandgap value (eV) at the row $R_2Zr_2O_7$ (R = La-Lu). It is PBE0 calculation.

La	Ce	Pr	Nd	Sm	Eu	Gd
6.19	6.11	6.01	5.96	5.79	5.71	5.64
Tb	Dy	Ho	Er	Tm	Yb	Lu
5.56	5.49	5.41	5.34	5.26	5.19	5.15

modes at the Γ point of $La_2Zr_2O_7$ are given in Table 7. Frequencies and types of the phonon modes were determined from the ab initio calculation. From the analysis of displacement vectors obtained from this ab initio calculations, the degree of participation of each ion in a particular mode is estimated. The ions that are shifted anyway significantly in the mode are listed in the column "Ion-participants". The "S" index is a strong shift ("Strong"), "W" is weak ("Weak"). We can distinguish modes in which only oxygen ions are involved. Only oxygen ions are involved in the infrared active mode F1u with a frequency of $\sim 245\ cm^{-1}$. O1 ions, located at 48*f* position, characterized by the x coordinate, participate mainly in this mode. O1 is also predominantly involved in the most intense Raman mode F_{2g} ($\sim 310\ cm^{-1}$). Only O1 ions are involved in the Raman Eg mode. According to calculations, this is the second most intense mode in the Raman spectrum (Table 7, Fig. 2). Only O1 ions also participate in the Raman modes A_{1g} and the high-frequency F_{2g}. Thus, the behavior of these modes gives information about the value of the x coordinate of the oxygen O1 under external influences on the crystal. The oxygen O2, located at 8*b* position, mainly participates in F_{2g} modes with frequencies of ~ 420 and $\sim 540\ cm^{-1}$. All ions are involved in IR active modes (F1u), but they participate in varying degrees. Zirconium and both O1 and O2 oxygens are involved in the most intense F1u mode with a frequency of $\sim 330\ cm^{-1}$, moreover, as oxygen O1 taking the most participation. At the low-frequency F1u mode ($\sim 100\ cm^{-1}$) all ions are involved, but mainly zirconium is involved. It may be noted that lanthanum and zirconium are significantly involved in silent modes. At an experimental work [12] the participation of the structural units La-O and ZrO_6 in the Raman modes with frequencies of 299 and 506 cm^{-1} ("stretching modes") was discussed. This is consistent with the fact that the calculation predicts a strong displacement of O1 oxygen in these modes and the participation of O2 oxygen (Table 7). The calculation results are also consistent with the experiment [13], where the intense IR modes 366 and 508 cm^{-1} were found, for which the calculation predicts a strong participation of O1 oxygen, i.e. change of Zr-O bond length. The results of modeling the Raman spectrum of the $La_2Zr_2O_7$ based on the calculated frequencies and intensities for the polycrystal are shown at Fig. 2. The Pseudo-Voigt functions with a damping factor of 8 cm^{-1} were used by modeling. The results agree well not only with the Raman spectrum measured at T = 298 K, but also with the spectrum measured at T = 1400 K. The results of the simulation of the IR spectrum are shown at Fig. 3. The presence of two peaks near to 350 and 500 cm^{-1} agrees well with the results of measuring the transmittance of the IR spectrum of $La_2Zr_2O_7$ [13].

Table 7. Frequencies (cm^{-1}) and types of phonon modes at the Γ point. The intensity of IR modes (km/mol) is given in parentheses. The abbreviations in the "R" (Raman) and "IR" columns: "A" is an active mode, "I" is inactive one.

Type	IR	R	Frequency, calculation		Frequency, experiment					Ions-participants
					[10] (IR)	[11] (IR)	[12] (R, IR)	[13] (IR)	[14] (IR)	
			PBE0	PBE SOL0						
F_{2u}	I	I	54	62						La^S, Zr^W, $O1^W$
E_u	I	I	96	99						La, Zr, O1
F_{1u}	A	I	101 (180)	105 (48)	101	104.8				La, Zr^S, O1, O2
F_{2u}	I	I	130	136						La, Zr^S, O1
F_{1u}	A	I	137 (1781)	142 (1589)	140	141.5				La^S, Zr, $O1^S$
E_u	I	I	146	154						La, Zr, $O1^S$
F_{1u}	A	I	202 (6812)	206 (6577)	176	166.8			215	La, Zr, $O1^S$
F_{1u}	I	I	245 (152)	249 (26)	244; 208	213.7			245	$O1^S$, O2
A_{2u}	A	I	250	259						La, Zr, O1
F_{1g}	I	I	256	264						$O1^S$
F_{2u}	I	I	281	287						Zr^W, $O1^S$
A_{2u}	I	I	301	306						La, Zr^S
F_{2g}	I	A	308	318			299			$O1^S$, O2
E_g	I	A	324	334						$O1^S$
F_{1u}	A	I	328 (16143)	341 (16244)	352	352.7		366		La^W, Zr, $O1^S$, O2
F_{1u}	A	I	383 (1.07)	396 (0.02)	412	411.9			370	La, O1, $O2^S$
A_{2u}	I	I	390	392						La^W, Zr^S, $O1^S$
E_u	I	I	393	400						La^W, Zr^W, $O1^S$
F_{2g}	I	A	413	421						O1, $O2^S$
F_{1u}	A	I	499 (2869)	508 (3354)	518	517.4	508	508	505	Zr^W, $O1^S$, O2
A_{1g}	I	A	505	510			506			$O1^S$
F_{2g}	I	A	535	545						O1, $O2^S$
F_{1g}	I	I	556.6	571						$O1^S$
F_{2u}	I	I	557.1	570						$O1^S$
F_{2g}	I	A	757	768						$O1^S$

Note. The "S" index is a strong shift ("Strong"), "W" is weak ("Weak") at the last column.

The results of the intensity calculation of the Raman modes for the polycrystal and single crystal $La_2Zr_2O_7$ are given in Tables 8 and 9 (PBE0 calculation).

Table 8. Raman modes intensity for polycrystalline sample $La_2Zr_2O_7$ (relative units). The intensity of the Raman modes was calculated for $\lambda = 488$ nm and T = 298 K.

Type	Frequency, cm^{-1}	I_{tot}	I_{par}	I_{perp}
F_{2g}	308	1000	571	429
E_g	325	219	125	94
F_{2g}	413	17	10	7
A_{1g}	506	45	45	0
F_{2g}	536	77	44	33
F_{2g}	758	27	15	12

Table 9. Raman modes intensity for single crystal $La_2Zr_2O_7$ (relative units). The intensity of the Raman modes was calculated for $\lambda = 488$ nm and T = 298 K.

Type	Frequency, cm^{-1}	I *xx*	I *xy*	I *xz*	I *yy*	I *yz*	I *zz*
F_{2g}	308	0	1000	1000	0	1000	0
E_g	325	438	0	0	438	0	438
F_{2g}	413	0	17	17	0	17	0
A_{1g}	506	63	0	0	63	0	63
F_{2g}	536	0	77	77	0	77	0
F_{2g}	758	0	27	27	0	27	0

The results of calculating the IR and Raman modes for the all row $R_2Zr_2O_7$ (R = La-Lu) are given in Tables 10, 11 and 12 as well as at Figs. 4 and 5. The frequencies of low-frequency F_{2g} modes slightly decrease in the La-Lu row. While the frequency of the high-frequency F_{2g} mode increases significantly (Table 10, Fig. 4). The frequencies of the IR modes in the La-Lu series vary considerably more than the frequencies of the Raman modes. The frequency of the low-frequency F1u mode decreases, while the frequencies of the high-frequency F1u modes increase (Table 11). The four most strongly varying infrared modes at the row are shown in Fig. 5. The calculation results are in good agreement with the available experimental data. The results of calculating the IR and Raman modes for the all row $R_2Zr_2O_7$ (R = La-Lu) are given in Tables 10, 11 and 12 as well as at Figs. 4 and 5. The frequencies of low-frequency F_{2g} modes slightly decrease in the La-Lu row. While the frequency of the high-frequency F_{2g} mode increases significantly (Table 10, Fig. 4). The frequencies of the IR modes in the La-Lu series vary considerably more than the frequencies of the Raman modes. The frequency of the low-frequency F1u mode decreases, while the frequencies of the high-frequency F1u modes increase (Table 11). The four most strongly varying infrared modes at the row are shown in Fig. 5. The calculation results are in good agreement with the available experimental data.

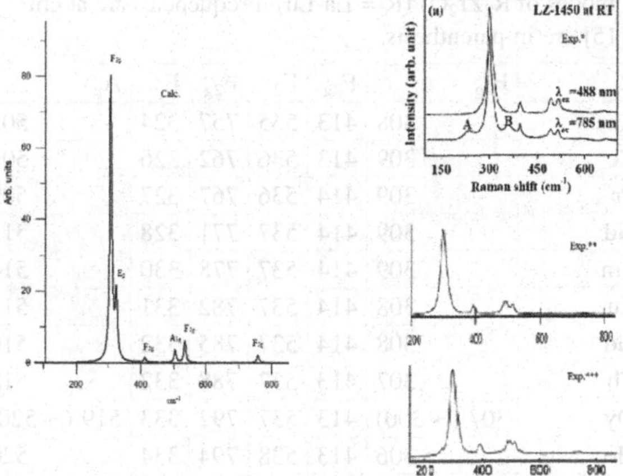

Fig. 2. Calculation results of the $La_2Zr_2O_7$ Raman spectrum (PBE0 calculation). The intensity of the Raman modes was calculated for λ = 488 nm and T = 298 K. At modeling the Raman spectrum based on the calculated frequencies and intensities for a polycrystal, the Pseudo-Voigt functions with a damping factor of 8 cm^{-1} were used. The sidebars show: Exp.* – is experiment [8], performed at λ = 488 nm as well as at λ = 785 nm and T = 298 K. Exp.** – is experiment [7], performed at λ = 488 nm and T = 298 K. Exp.***– is experiment [3], performed at λ = 532 nm and T = 1400 K.

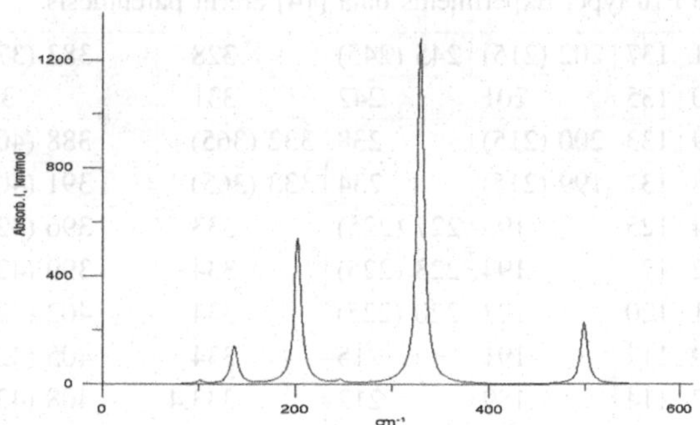

Fig. 3. Calculation results of the IR spectrum of $La_2Zr_2O_7$ (PBE0 calculation). All infrared modes are F_{1u} type.

The results of the calculation of the elastic constants and the bulk modulus are given in Table 13. The results are in good agreement with the calculations of the elastic constants in the plane-wave basis [16]. Experimental data by the elastic constants of $R_2Zr_2O_7$ (R = La-Lu) in the scientific publications could not be found.

Table 10. Raman modes of $R_2Zr_2O_7$ (R = La-Lu). Frequencies are at cm^{-1} (PBE0 calculation). Experiments data [15] are in parenthesis.

R	F_{2g}	F_{2g}	F_{2g}	F_{2g}	E_g	A_g
La	308	413	535	757	324	505
Ce	309	413	536	762	326	507
Pr	309	414	536	767	327	509
Nd	309	414	537	771	328	511
Sm	309	414	537	778	330	514
Eu	308	414	537	782	331	515
Gd	308	414	537	785	332	516
Tb	307	413	537	788	332	518
Dy	307 (~300)	413	537	792	333	519 (~520)
Ho	306	413	538	794	334	520
Er	305	412	538	797	335	521
Tm	304	412	538	800	335	522
Yb	304	411	538	803	336	523
Lu	303	411	539	804	336	524
Difference	6	3	4	67	12	19

Table 11. Infrared modes of $R_2Zr_2O_7$ (R = La-Lu). Frequencies are at cm^{-1} (PBE0 calculation). All modes are F1u type. Experiments data [14] are in parenthesis.

La	101	137	202 (215)	245 (245)	328	383 (370)	499 (505)
Ce	100	135	201	242	331	386	503
Pr	99	133	200 (215)	238	332 (365)	388 (400)	508 (530)
Nd	98	131	199 (215)	234	333 (365)	391 (400)	512 (525)
Sm	94	125	195	227 (225)	333	396 (420)	519 (530)
Eu	92	123	194	223 (225)	334	399 (420)	523 (525)
Gd	91	120	193	220 (225)	334	402 (420)	526 (510)
Tb	89	117	191	215	334	405 (420)	529 (500)
Dy	87	114	189	212	333.4	408 (420)	532
Ho	85	112	187	208	333	411 (420)	535
Er	82	109	186	205	332	413 (420)	538
Tm	81	107	184	201	333	416 (420)	541
Yb	77	103	181	198	332	418 (420)	543
Lu	75	102	180	195	332	420 (440,400)	544
Difference	26	35	22	50	4	37	45

Table 12. Silent modes at the row $R_2Zr_2O_7$ (R = La-Lu). Frequencies are in cm^{-1} (PBE0 calculation).

R	A_{2u}	A_{2u}	A_{2u}	E_u	E_u	E_u	F_{1g}	F_{1g}	F_{2u}	F_{2u}	F_{2u}	F_{2u}
La	250	301	390	96	146	393	256	557	54	131	281	557
Ce	248	302	391	95	141	396	256	562	53	131	283	565
Pr	245	303	391	94	138	399	254	568	52	130	285	572
Nd	242	305	392	93	133	402	253	573	51	130	287	578
Sm	231	306	392	89	125	407	251	580	48	129	292	589
Eu	227	308	393	87	122	409	249	585	47	128	294	595
Gd	222	309	393	85	119	412	248	588	46	128	297	600
Tb	218	310	394	83	115	414	247	591	45	128	299	604
Dy	213	312	394	80	113	416	245	595	43	127	301	609
Ho	210	313	395	77	111	419	244	599	42	127	304	614
Er	205	318	399	74	112	419	242	601	40	125	306	618
Tm	202	315	396	70	106	423	240	604	38	126	308	622
Yb	197	316	397	66	105	425	238	607	36	126	310	626
Lu	196	316	398	64	105	426	236	608	33	126	311	628
Difference	54	15	8	28	41	31	20	51	21	5	30	71

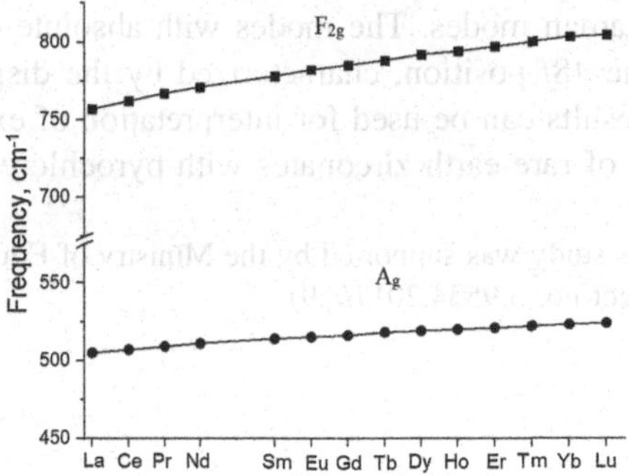

Fig. 4. The Raman modes at the row $R_2Zr_2O_7$ (R = La-Lu). The two most varying Raman modes at the row are shown.

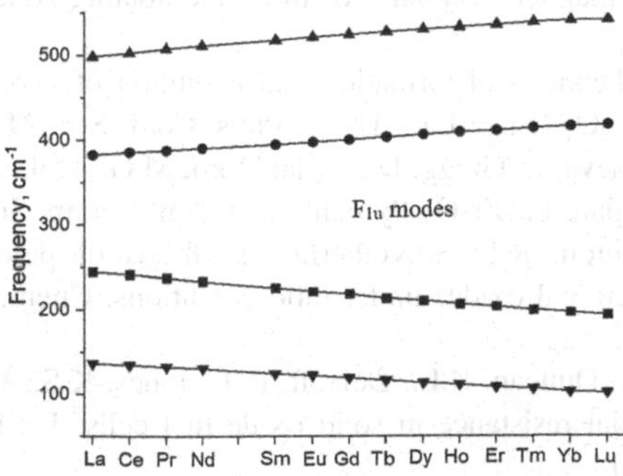

Fig. 5. The infrared modes at the row $R_2Zr_2O_7$ (R = La-Lu). The four most varying infrared modes at the row are shown.

Table 13. Elastic constants and bulk modulus of $R_2Zr_2O_7$ (GPa).

	$La_2Zr_2O_7$		$Gd_2Zr_2O_7$	$Yb_2Zr_2O_7$
	This work (PBE0)	VASP calculation (from work [16])	This work (PBE0)	This work (PBE0)
C_{11}	298.2	289.8	319.4	332.8
C_{12}	116.9	124.8	110.8	105.9
C_4	98.6	100.4	96.0	91.0
B	177.4	179.8	180.33	181.5

4 Conclusion

Ab initio calculation of all row the rare-earth zirconates $R_2Zr_2O_7$ (R = La-Lu) with the pyrochlore structure, carried out within the framework of the MO LCAO approach, with a hybrid DFT functionals that takes into account the contribution of the HF exchange. The calculations reproduce the crystal structure of these compounds in good agreement with the experiment. The calculation of the phonon spectrum of these compounds at the Γ point was carried out for the first time. From the analysis of displacement vectors obtained from this ab initio calculations, the degree of participation of each ion in a particular mode were estimated. It was shown that only oxygen ions are involved in Raman modes. The modes with absolute or predominant participation of oxygen at the 48*f* position, characterized by the displacement x, are determined. The obtained results can be used for interpretation of experimental data on the Raman and IR spectra of rare-earth zirconates with pyrochlore structure.

Acknowledgments. This study was supported by the Ministry of Education and Science of the Russian Federation (project no. 3.9534.2017/8.9).

References

1. Pokhrel, M., Alcoutlabi, M., Mao, Y.: Optical and X-ray induced luminescence from Eu3 + doped $La_2Zr_2O_7$ nanoparticles. J. Alloys Compd. **693**, 719–729 (2017)
2. Hatnean, M.C., Decorse, C., Lees, M.R., Petrenko, O.A., Balakrishnan, G.: Zirconate pyrochlore frustrated magnets: crystal growth by the floating zone technique. Crystals **6**(7), 79 (2016)
3. Popov, V.V., et al.: Features of formation and evolution of crystal and local structures in nanocrystalline $Ln_2Zr_2O_7$ (Ln = La - Tb). J. Phys: Conf. Ser. **941**(1), 012079 (2017)
4. Kong, L., Karatchevtseva, I., Gregg, D.J., Blackford, M.G., Holmes, R., Triani, G.: A novel chemical route to prepare $La_2Zr_2O_7$ Pyrochlore. J. Am. Ceram. Soc. **96**(3), 935–941 (2013)
5. Modeshia, D.R., Walton, R.I.: Solvothermal synthesis of perovskites and pyrochlores: crystallisation of functional oxides under mild conditions. Chem. Soc. Rev. **49**(11), 4303–4325 (2010)
6. Chen, A., Smith, J.R., Duncan, K.L., DeHoff, R.T., Jones, K.S., Wachsman, E.D.: Effect of $La_2Zr_2O_7$ on interfacial resistance in solid oxide fuel cells. J. Electrochem. Soc. **157**(11), B1624–B1628 (2010)

7. Shimamura, K., Arima, T., Idemitsu, K., Inagaki, Y.: Thermophysical properties of rare-earth-stabilized zirconia and zirconate pyrochlores as surrogates for actinide-doped zirconia. Int. J. Thermophysics. **28**(3), 1074–1084 (2007)
8. Paul, B., Singh, K., Jaron, T., Roy, A., Chowdhury, A.: Structural properties and the fluorite–pyrochlore phase transition in $La_2Zr_2O_7$: the role of oxygen to induce local disordered states. J. Alloys Compd. **686**(25), 130–136 (2016)
9. Subramanian, M., Aravamudan, G., Subba Rao, G.: Oxide pyrochlores - a review. Prog. Solid State Chem. **15**(2), 55–143 (1983)
10. Gundovin, N.V., Spiridonov, F.M., Komissarova, L.N., Petrov, K.I.: The vibrational spectra of zirconates and hafnates of rare-earth elements with pyrochlore structure. Zh. Neorg. Khim. **20**, 582–586 (1975)
11. Cheng, X., et al.: Infrared phonon modes and dielectric properties of $La_2Zr_2O_7$: Comparing thin film to bulk material. Phys. Stat. Sol. (b) 249(4), 854–857 (2011)
12. Tong, Y., Wang, Y., Yu, Z., Wang, X., Yang, X., Lu, L.: Preparation and characterization of pyrochlore $La_2Zr_2O_7$ nanocrystals by stearic acid method. Mater. Lett. **62**(6–7), 889–891 (2008)
13. Chen, D., Xu, R.: Hydrothermal synthesis and characterization of $La_2M_2O_7$ (M = Ti, Zr) powders. Mater. Res. Bull. **33**(3), 409–417 (1988)
14. Klee, W.E., Weitz, G.: Infrared spectra of ordered and disordered pyrochlore-type compounds in the series $RE_2Ti_2O_7$, $RE_2Zr_2O_7$ and $RE_2Hf_2O_7$. J. Inorg. Nucl. Chem. **31** (8), 2367–2372 (1969)
15. Rittman, D.R., et al.: Strain engineered pyrochlore at high pressure. Sci. Rep. **7**(1), 2236 (2017)
16. Guo, X., Zhang, J.: First principles study of thermodynamic properties of lanthanum zirconate. Mater. Today Proc. **1**, 25–34 (2014)
17. Feng, J., et al.: Electronic structure, mechanical properties and thermal conductivity of $Ln_2Zr_2O_7$ (Ln = La, Pr, Nd, Sm, Eu and Gd) pyrochlore. Acta Mater. **59**(4), 1742–1760 (2011)
18. Zhang, S., et al.: Impact of isovalent and aliovalent substitution on the mechanical and thermal properties of $Gd_2Zr_2O_7$. Sci. Rep. **7**(1), 6399 (2017)
19. Maram, P.S., Ushakov, S.V., Weber, R.J.K., Benmore, C.J., Navrotsky, A.: In situ diffraction from levitated solids under extreme conditions-structure and thermal expansion in the Eu_2O_3–ZrO_2 system. J. Am. Ceram. Soc. **98**(4), 1292–1299 (2015)
20. Pierre, M.L., Orlando, R., Maschio, L., Doll, K., Ugliengo, P., Dovesi, R.: Performance of six functionals (LDA, PBE, PBESOL, B3LYP, PBE0, and WC1LYP) in the simulation of vibrational and dielectric properties of crystalline compounds. The case of forsterite Mg_2SiO_4. J. Comp. Chem. **32**(9), 1775–1784 (2011)
21. Heyd, J., Scuseria, G.E., Ernzerhof, M.: Hybrid functionals based on a screened Coulomb potential. J. Chem. Phys. **118**(8), 8207–8215 (2003)
22. Benjamin, G.J., Thomas, M.H., Gustavo, E.S.: Screened hybrid density functionals for solid-state chemistry and physics. Phys. Chem. Chem. Phys. **11**(3), 443–454 (2009)
23. Becke, A.D.: Density functional thermochemistry. III. The role of exact exchange. J. Chem. Phys. **98**(7), 5648–5652 (1993)
24. Perdew, J.P., Ernzerhof, M., Burke, K.: Rationale for mixing exact exchange with density functional approximations. J. Chem. Phys. **105**(2), 9982–9985 (1996)
25. Burke, K.: Perspective on density functional theory. J. Chem. Phys. **136**(15), 150901 (2012)
26. Dovesi, R., et al.: 2018 CRYSTAL17 User's Manual. http://www.crystal.unito.it/Manuals/crystal17.pdf
27. Dovesi, R., et al.: Quantum-mechanical condensed matter simulations with CRYSTAL. Comput. Mol. Sci. **8**(4), e1360 (2018)
28. Evarestov, R.A., Bandura, A.V., Aleksandrov, V.E.: Calculations of the electronic structure of crystalline $SrZrO_3$ in the framework of the density-functional theory in the LCAO approximation. Phys. Solid State **47**(12), 2248–2256 (2005)

29. Medvedev, M.G., Bushmarinov, I.S., Sun, J., Perdew, J.P., Lyssenko, K.A.: Density functional theory is straying from the path toward the exact functional. Science **355**(6320), 49–52 (2017)
30. Chernyshev, V.A., Petrov, V.P., Nikiforov, A.E., Agzamova, P.A., Avram, N.M.: Elastic properties of rare earth pyrochlores $R_2Ti_2O_7$ (R = Gd, Tb, Dy, Ho, Er, Tm, Yb, Lu): Ab initio calculations. Opt. Mater. **72**, 565–570 (2017)
31. Peintinger, M.F., Oliveira, D.V., Bredow, T.: Consistent Gaussian basis sets of triple zeta valence with polarization quality for solid state calculations. J. Comp. Chem. **34**(6), 451–459 (2012)
32. CRYSTAL website. http://www.crystal.unito.it/index.php
33. Valenzano, L., et al.: Disclosing the complex structure of UiO-66 metal organic framework: a synergic combination of experiment and theory. Chem. Mater. **23**(7), 1700–1718 (2011)
34. Dolg, M., Stoll, H., Savin, A., Preuss, H.: Energy-adjusted pseudopotentials for the rare earth elements. Theor. Chim. Acta. **75**(3), 173–194 (1989)
35. Dolg, M., Stoll, H., Preuss, H.: A combination of quasirelativistic pseudopotential and ligand field calculations for lanthanoid compounds. Theor. Chim. Acta. **85**(6), 441–450 (1993)
36. Yang, J., Dolg, M.: Valence basis sets for lanthanide 4f-in-core pseudopotentials adapted for crystal orbital ab initio calculations. Theor. Chem. Acc. **113**(4), 212–224 (2005)
37. Weigand, A., Cao, X., Yang, J., Dolg, M.: Quasirelativistic f-in-core pseudopotentials and core-polarization potentials for trivalent actinides and lanthanides: molecular test for trifluorides. Theor. Chem. Acc. **126**(3–4), 117–127 (2009)
38. Energy-consistent Pseudopotentials of the Stuttgart. http://www.tc.uni-koeln.de/PP/clickpse.en.html
39. Maschio, L., Kirtman, B., Orlando, R., Rerat, M.: Ab initio analytical infrared intensities for periodic systems through a coupled perturbed Hartree-Fock/Kohn-Sham method. J. Chem. Phys. **137**(20), 204113 (2012)
40. Maschio, L., Kirtman, B., Rerat, M., Orlando, R., Dovesi, R.: Comment on "Ab initio analytical infrared intensities for periodic systems through a coupled perturbed Hartree-Fock/Kohn-Sham method" [J. Chem. Phys. 137, 204113 (2012)]. J. Chem. Phys. **139**, 164101 (2013)
41. Maschio, L., Kirtman, B., Rerat, M., Orlando, R., Dovesi, R.: Ab initio analytical Raman intensities for periodic systems through a coupled perturbed Hartree-Fock/Kohn-Sham method in an atomic orbital basis. II. Validation and comparison with experiments. J. Chem. Phys. **139**(16), 164102 (2013)
42. Orlando, R., Lacivita, V., Bast, R., Ruud, K.: Calculation of the first static hyperpolarizability tensor of three-dimensional periodic compounds with a local basis set: a comparison of LDA, PBE, PBE0, B3LYP, and HF results. J. Chem. Phys. **132**(24), 244106 (2010)
43. Dovesi, R., et al.: CRYSTAL14: a program for the ab initio investigation of crystalline solids. Int. J. Quant. Chem. **114**(19), 1287–1317 (2014)
44. Perdew, J.P., et al.: Restoring the density-gradient expansion for exchange in solids and surfaces. Phys. Rev. Lett. **100**(13), 136406 (2008)
45. Gao, B., et al.: Experimental signatures of a three-dimensional quantum spin liquid in effective spin-1/2 $Ce_2Zr_2O_7$ pyrochlore (2019). https://arxiv.org/abs/1901.10092
46. Xu, J., et al.: Magnetic structure and crystal-field states of the pyrochlore antiferromagnet $Nd_2Zr_2O_7$. Phys. Rev. B **92**(22), 224430 (2015)
47. Li, X., et al.: Long-range antiferromagnetic order in the frustrated XY pyrochlore antiferromagnet $Er_2Ge_2O_7$. Phys. Rev. B **89**(6), 064409 (2014)
48. Kaspar, T.C., et al.: Damage evolution of ion irradiated defected-fluorite $La_2Zr_2O_7$ epitaxial thin films. Act. Mater. **130**, 111–120 (2017)

CARTESIUS FORT - OBJECT FORTRAN Library for Chemistry and Materials Science

Andrei L. Tchougréeff[1,2,3](✉)

[1] A.N. Frumkin Institute of Physical Chemistry and Electrochemistry of RAS, Moscow, Russia

[2] Independent University of Moscow, Moscow, Russia

[3] Chair of Solid State and Quantum Chemistry, RWTH - Aachen University, Aachen, Germany

andrei.tchougreeff@ac.rwth-aachen.de

Abstract. Modeling of structure and properties of molecules and materials (crystals/solids) on the basis of their electronic structure is one of the most important consumers of computer resources (processor time, memory and storage). The known attempts to improve its efficiency reduce to massive parallelization. This approach ignores enormous diversity of types of structures and behaviors of molecules and materials. Moreover, this diversity is by no means reflected in the paradigm currently dominating the field of molecular/material modeling.

Much more efficient is, of course, a thorough analysis of the physical conditions occurring in different molecules/materials. On this way we could successfully build a series of efficient methods targeted upon specific classes of molecules/materials: inorganic ones with open *d*-shells and organic ones featuring local two-center bonds and developed conjugated π-systems (generalized chromophores).

The experience gained formulates as a new concept of semi-empirism: that is selecting the electronic wave function of a system under study as a product of the wave functions of the chromophores present in the system. This called for a new development: of a library of objects representing different types of chromophores to be freely combinable to represent an arbitrary molecule/material so that its respective parts (chromophores) are modeled by the most efficient method suitable for the specific type of the chromophore and taking into account the interactions between them. Apparently, the deep segmentation of the system achieved within the new concept of semi-empirism allows for the efficient parallelization and more efficient usage of the HPC software.

Keywords: New concept of semi-empirism · Polymorphic trees · Generalized chromophores · Cartesius fort library

T-platforms company (Russia) is acknowledged for support extended to the symposium "Quantum Chemical Modeling of Solids with Computers: from Plane Waves to Local Structures (QuaCheSol 2019)" in the frame of the "The 19th International Conference on Computational Science and its Applications (ICCSA 2019)".

S. Misra et al. (Eds.): ICCSA 2019, LNCS 11622, pp. 639–651, 2019.
https://doi.org/10.1007/978-3-030-24305-0_47

1 Motivation

1.1 Quantum Modeling Issues

Molecular or materials' modeling relying upon analysis of their electronic structure (quantum chemistry) is one of the largest consumers of the computer resources in terms of processor time, memory and storage. The reason for this is twofold: realistic models include large numbers of atoms to represent namely that system whose properties are modeled and it may be fairly large - hundreds to tens thousands of atoms - when it comes to processes in living matter or to technological (*e.g.* catalytic) processes. In the realm of materials' modeling the "size" of the realistic model is the number of atoms in the unit cell of the modeled crystal. In case of popular modeling objects like zeolites (Fig. 1 left) or metal-organic frameworks (MOF's - Fig. 1 right) it may reach hundreds or even thousands. These amounts determine the costs of modeling which for a system with open d-shells may scale as $O(N^7)$ where N is the number of atoms included in the model for standard modeling methods based on the wave functions. An alternative frequently portrayed as a "method of choice" for the materials (crystals/solid state) modeling - the DFT based methods - frequently face the convergence problems. In a recent study Ref. [1] more than 2600 published MOF structures had been processed by a DFT+D3 program the convergence has been reached in slightly more than in one third (!) of cases.

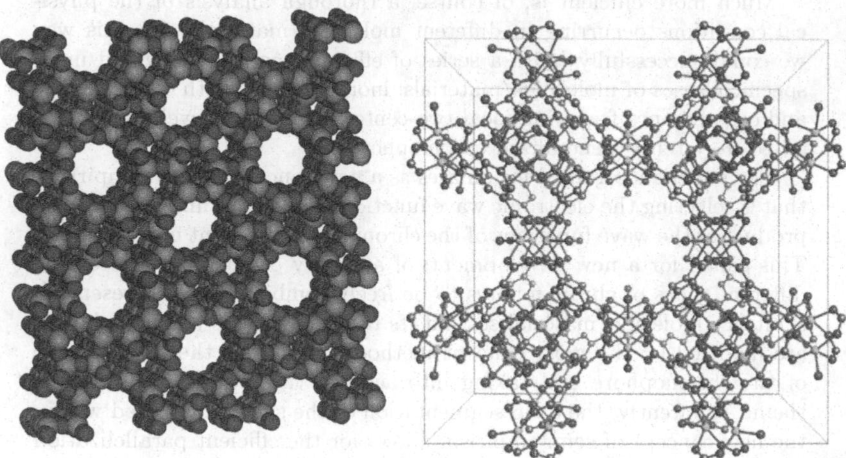

Fig. 1. Characteristic objects of materials modeling. Left: zeolite (ZSM-5); right: iron(II) containing MOF (Fe-BTC).

The DFT-based methods [2–4] (similar to one used in Ref. [1]) portray the electronic structure of, say, NiO as formed by Bloch states delocalized over the entire crystal and ascribe the observed anti-ferromagnetic ground state of this and other similar - very simple - crystals to opening of the gap in their one-electron spectrum [5]. This picture is *physically incorrect* (!): had it been true, NiO and other similar materials would have to become *metals* above respective Néel temperatures which is definitely not the case: they remain insulating and the values of the *local* momenta in the paramagnetic phase are almost the same as the saturation momenta in the anti-ferromagnetic one. The same was shown for "organic" analogs of transition metal oxides: simplest possible MOFs: transition metal carbodiimides of the general formula MNCN, M = Fe, Co, Ni [6,7]. Another fresh study [8] addressed a couple of rather simplistic Fe(II) complexes with use of a series of DFT functionals. It turned out that these functionals produce the energy differences between the ground high-spin and first excited low-spin states in the range from minus to plus 30 kcal/mol (more than 1 eV); *neither* of them was capable to give the correct *experimentally known* energy gap. The DMRG-CASPT2 method used in Ref. [8] for control does not help: in either case the ground state was incorrect.

The intrinsic complexity of the modeling problems either in molecular or in the materials' (solid state) contexts is aggravated by the paradigm dominating the field, which can be characterized as *naïve monism*. It represents a strong belief that the entire system must be modeled at the same, possibly most advanced level of theory. Practically it leads to the prohibitive computational costs mentioned above, but even these cost are spent in vain: the results are wrong (see [8] and references therein). It would be unfair to say that nothing is undertaken in the literature to avoid this. Attempts to take into account nonuniformity of molecular systems are known as hybrid quantum mechanics/molecular mechanics (force field) - QM/MM - methods which according to Ref. [9] "can be applied whenever one needs to model a localized electronic event in an active site (typically of the order of 100 atoms) that is influenced by an interacting larger environment". Obviously, 100 atoms is too much for a systematic application of $O(N^7)$ scaling methods.

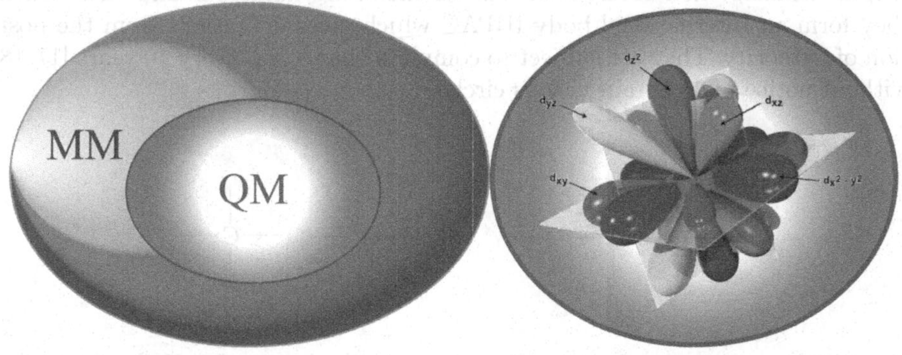

Fig. 2. Pictorial representation of the separation methods in the standard (hybrid) QM/MM methods (left) and in effective crystal field method (right)

The patterns of separation practiced in the standard QM/MM methods are, however, not fully consistent with quantum mechanics. The standard way is to set the quantum/classical boundary in the real space Fig. 2 (left) ignoring that bonds are broken by such boundary. A considerable list of *ad hoc* recipes to be used to handle the violation of quantum mechanics is given in Ref. [9] (see also references there), their critical analysis is given in Refs. [10–12].

1.2 Cheminformatics Issues

Representing chemistry objects in the computer codes is a cheminformatics problem [13]. It is usually addressed without explicit reference to electronic structure of molecules and materials. This approach runs into problems (inherited by the systems of computer coding of molecules and compounds [14,15]) which can be understood if one analyses the situation with the chemical nomenclature in general. While doing so one immediately recognizes that the situation drastically differs in "organic" and "inorganic" chemistry (the latter must be understood in a general sense: including coordination and organometallic chemistry). The "inorganic" realm (incidentally, including MOFs) is extremely diverse whereas "organic" realm is much more uniform, contains much smaller repertory of atoms. The "inorganic" realm contains kind of simplistic subset (basically taught in high school) where the compound can be fully characterized by its composition: KCl, H_2O etc. Switching to the "organic" realm changes the situation completely: even simple composition C_2H_6O does not characterize the thing completely: two different substances represented in Fig. 3 correspond to it. The very simple question arises: what in reality represent Fig. 3 (the structure formulae of organic chemistry)? What are these sticks? Everyone would say "what a stupid guy is him!" - these are bonds! But what are bonds? Here reigns a complete confusion: "The concept of bond appeared little by little in the mind of chemists from empirical observations. From the wavemechanical viewpoint it is not an observable."[16] - not bad, isn't it? So what do then they draw these stupid chemists? non-observable? The chemists are numerous and strike back: they form an International body IUPAC which gives definitions from the position of authority. They are subject to complete change *ca.* every 10 years [17,18] without notice and contain vicious circles.

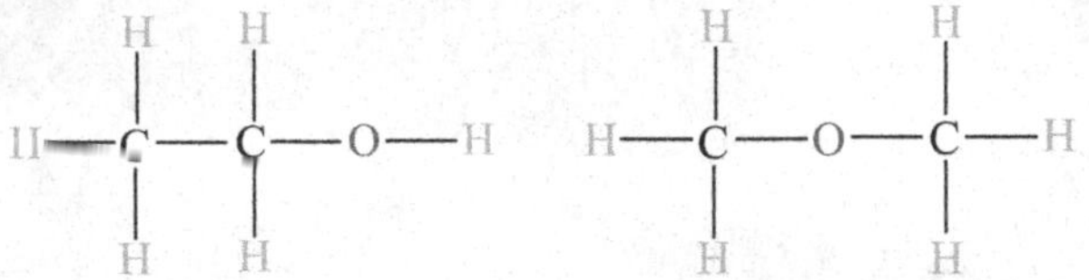

Fig. 3. Classical structure formulae of two isomers of archetypical C_2H_6O composition.

Amazingly the solution was known well before all this confusion had any chance to appear. Yet in 1900 Gordan (that one which is Clebsch-Gordan) and Alexejeff published a remarkable paper [19] entitled "Übereinstimmung der Formeln der Chemie und der Invariantentheorie" that is "coincidence of the formulae of Chemistry and Invariants Theory" where they could show that the pictures drawn by organic chemists are in one-to-one correspondence with functions of complex 2D vectors belonging to a special class called *invariants* (in contemporary terminology spin-invariant or spin-singlet). For more detailed discussion see Ref. [20]. Apparently it is nothing, but an abridged notation to the valence bond (VB) wave functions [21] depicted in Figs. 4 and 5.

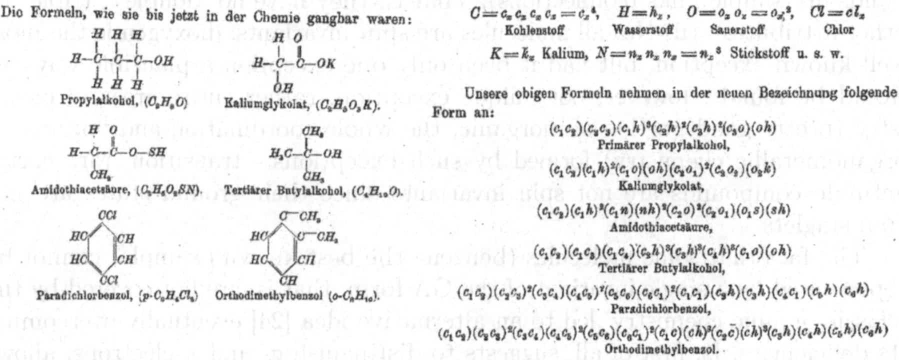

Fig. 4. First in the history pictorial representation of the isomorphism between structure formulae of organic chemistry and invariants of complex 2D-vectors.

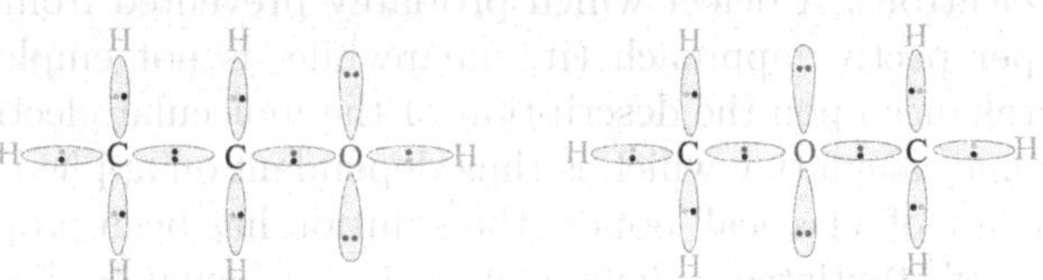

Fig. 5. Pictorial representation of the valence bond wave functions corresponding to classical structure formulae of two isomers of C_2H_6O.

The isomorphism between 'classic organic chemistry' and invariants means that everything which can be drawn according to the "rules of organic chemistry" is an invariant of the prescribed form and nothing else can be drawn (without breaking these rules). This predetermines either the enormous strength of the "normal" language of organic chemistry, but also its deficiencies. The most modern cheminformatics descendant of the 'classic organic chemistry' - InChI, "is able to handle almost 99% of the chemicals which scientists are concerned with every day" [22] at the same very time excludes entire areas of chemistry: "Organometallics, inorganics and other classes of compounds still present a significant challenge" [15]. Thus, the ambitious "eventual goal to extend InChI to cover all of chemistry", is effectively postponed. The reason is that "No widely accepted means of representing organometallic substances exists" [23], but why it is so? From the point of view of quantum theory of molecular electronic structure the exceptions are remarkable and characteristic: (i) Not all molecules have electronic structure of the form of invariants which GA meant - those which are formed of local electronic spins: there is benzene and other similar (aromatic, but not only) compounds, featuring "delocalized" 2D vectors (spins) of which the required invariants are formed. Of course, aromatic and other similar molecules are too ubiquitous, so that numerous workarounds have been developed to represent them. Nevertheless, the very classical model of bonding is too restrictive which when pushing it through like in InChI leads to information losses: "All bonds are simple links (connections). That is, they have no "double", "triple" or other attributes". (ii) Not all molecules are spin invariants: dioxygen is the most well known exception, but had it been only one exception a plausible way out would be found. However, not unique exception, rather entire areas of chemistry (pretty good portion of inorganic, the whole coordination and tentatively organometallic chemistry) formed by such exceptions - transition, rare earth, actinide compounds are not spin invariants since their ground states are not spin singlets.

The fact that some molecules (benzene the best known example) cannot be represented by a single invariant of the GA form, that is, are not covered by the 'classic organic chemistry' led to an alternative idea [24] eventually overcoming its deficiencies. It, first of all, suggests to distinguish σ- and π-electrons, allows multicenter bonds (inclusive what is called 'coordination' ones), eventually allowing, to describe, say, ferrocene more or less uniquely, as a system composed of 10 σ-C-H- and 10 σ-C-C-bonds supplied by a multicenter (in fact 11 centers) 'bond' formed by 18 electrons. A defect which probably prevented from a wider usage of this fairly perspective approach (it, meanwhile, is not employed in InChI) was its heavy reliance upon the description of the molecular electronic structure coming from some calculation which is thus dependent on applied computational method. As in case of 'classical' bonds, the solution has been proposed long ago. The physically substantiated indexing of molecules must be based on observable elements of their electronic structure. Such elements has been originally proposed in Ref. [25] where the name 'chromophore': a part of molecule giving color to it, has been coined. These are apparently observable (even visually). In organic realm the chromophores are usually rather large conjugated π-systems. The idea of observability of components of molecular electronic structure has been generalized to bonds [26] and can be further extended [10,20].

2 Proposed Solutions

Не в совокупности ищи единства, но более – в единообразии разделения. — К. Прутков.[1]

We see that the problems encountered either in modeling or in simply uniquely naming extremely diverse chemical species (molecules or materials) stem from attempt to squeeze this diversity in a monistic picture. In cases when the nonuniformity of physical conditions is recognized (QM/MM) the separation is described as one into "interesting" and "uninteresting" parts to be treated, respectively, at a "higher" (QM) and "lower" (MM) level methods and performs in the real space. Among other issues it leads to the necessity to make the QM part 'as large as possible'.

Any attempt of segmentation of the physical object on the basis of "interest/uninterest" is of course a solipsistic nonsense. The true basis of separation can be only the real localization of the lowest energy excitations in that or another part of the system. In variance with wide spread (mis)concept (setting boundaries in the real space) the true separation is to be performed in the Hilbert space, as it was clear yet to the inventor of such a separation [27] and reiterated in [20], that is the parts of the system are orthogonal subspaces of the orbital space of the molecule.

2.1 Preliminary Studies

In the realm of the molecules and materials with open d-shells we face a very unpleasant situation: the "method of choice" produces a wrong physical description of simplest representatives of the target class of compounds: the compounds of transition metals with some "organogenic" atoms. One can foresee that in other areas of molecular and materials' modeling it is not much better. What could be the way out? Our proposition is rather old-fashioned: instead of applying machine learning to the heaps of wrong "big data" obtained by inappropriate methods, to try to figure out the physical reasons of the failures and to take care of them. An alternative to mindless computation is, of course, a detailed analysis of physical conditions in different parts of the molecular system.

Transition Metal Complexes. A thorough analysis shows (and it can be expected in the systems of electrons subject to the *singular* - Coulomb potentials) that, in fact, the physical conditions in different parts of the objects which one might be willing to model are quite different. Yet in Ref. [28] we noticed that the ratio of the Coulomb interaction between electrons in the d-shells to the resonance interaction of these orbitals with other orbitals is much larger than say in π-system of benzene. Indeed, in the $[NiF_6]^{4-}$ anion the ratios of the one-center Coulomb repulsion parameters to the resonance integrals between Ni orbitals and F $2p$-orbitals are about 50 for $3d$-orbitals, about 1.5 for $4s$-orbitals, and about unity for $4p$-orbitals of the Ni atom [28] (analogously for other complexes).

[1] Not in totality seek for unity, rather in uniformity of separation—K. Prutkov.

Similar ratio for π-orbitals in benzene is about four. Harrison notes the similar situation in magnetic insulators and crystals with paramagnetic impurities [29]. In this case, when the Coulomb interaction turn out to be more significant than the interatomic interactions dominating the band structure calculations (the Coulomb-to-resonance ratio $\gg 1$), electrons in the crystal are to be described with use of local rather than delocalized Bloch states. The spectrum of the crystal (for example NiO) coincides with the band spectrum of the simple ionic crystal CaO complemented by the spectrum of d-shells split by the crystal field. This picture drastically differs from the ideas underlying the standard modeling methods [2–4].

In the case of transition metal complexes with open d-shells and the corresponding solids the clue is provided by the good old crystal field theory [30] proudly celebrating its 90-th anniversary this year. It produces the correct phenomenological description of the ground states and spectra by considering *only* the d-shells with fixed numbers of electrons split by the external field of the relevant symmetry. By this the problem of describing problematic transition metal compounds separates into two simpler ones: (i) to calculate the effective field induced by the environment upon the d-shell and (ii) to calculate the many-electronic (multi-reference) states of this shell with the fixed number of electrons. This approach fairly follows the main Cartesian idea: "Diviser chacune des difficultés afin de mieux les examiner et les résoudre" [31] and turns out extremely efficient: dozens of complexes has been calculated (see Fig. 6); none of them has manifested an incorrect ground state spin and symmetry, even highly problematic Fe(II) spin-active complexes could be successfully reproduced [34,35], including the relative energies of the spin-isomers with an unprecedented precision. Our approach allowed us to *reduce* as much as possible the sizes of the parts of the system (electronic groups) requiring application of numerically demanding methods. *E.g.*, singling out d^n-shells represented in Fig. 2 (right) fits the way of classification of transition metal complexes accepted in the compendium of their electronic spectra [32] where they are considered as chromophores. It eventually provides the way around the complications of the classical model of chemical structure and the representation problems related to it. For example, Fe(II) complexes (Fig. 6) are completely described by the list of σ-bonds, π-systems, complemented by the d^6-chromophore and by a chromofore for which a name of *close ligand shell* has been coined in Ref. [33]. This representation is eventually unique.

2.2 Formal Description

The example of transition metal complexes was extremely instructive in many respects: most important, it allowed us to break with the dominant paradigm of ostensible universality of the "unique" methods and to switch to object-targeted methods - those whose very structure is stipulated by that of the molecules/materials under consideration.

Reflecting the diversity of chemical (electronic) structures missing in *monistic* representations of electronic structure either in molecular/material modeling

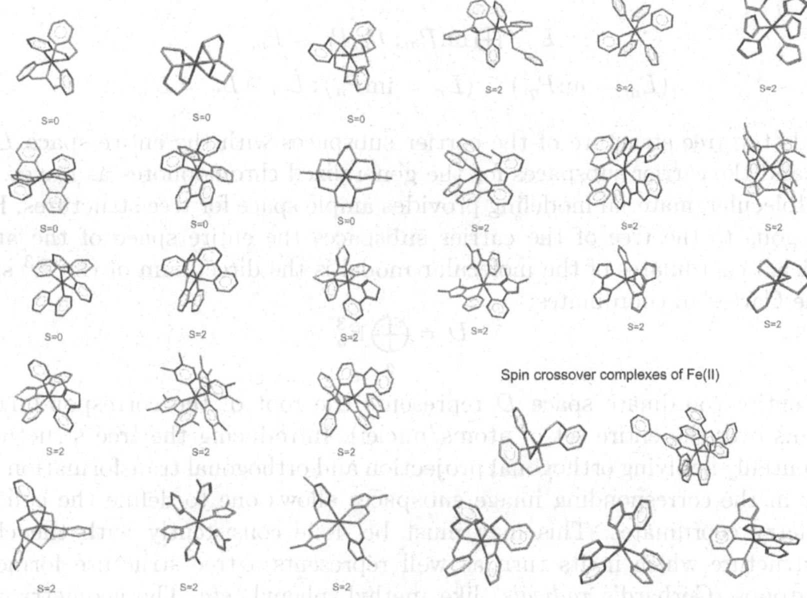

Fig. 6. A selection of Fe(II) compounds problematic for DFT and CASPT2 methods on the basis of effective crystal field theory. Green marks coincidence of the ground state spin with experiment, red - disagreement. For (experimentally) the spin-crossover complexes the respective (correct) ground state spins are reproduced for the respective geometries.

or in cheminformatics when achieved has a perspective to considerably improve the performance of both of them. The most abstract representation of the molecular (material) electronic structure through their observable parts (generalized chromophores) is given by the group function approximation:

$$\Psi_0 = \bigwedge_{m=1}^{M} \Psi_m \tag{1}$$

where $\wedge$ denotes the antisymmetrized product of the multipliers following it. The functions Ψ_m are the N_m-electron functions for respective chromophores built the carrier subspace L_m for the m-th chromophore. The carrier subspaces of the chromophores are orthogonal and formally express as follows:

$$\begin{aligned} L = \bigoplus_m L_m; \dim L_m \geq N_m \\ L_m \cap L_n = \{0\}, m \neq n; \end{aligned} \tag{2}$$

This alternatively expresses through projection operators:

$$\begin{aligned} \sum_m P_m = I; P_m P_n = \delta_{mn} P_m \\ L_m = \mathrm{im} P_m \end{aligned} \tag{3}$$

Releasing the condition Eq. (3) to

$$\begin{aligned} L = \bigoplus_m \mathrm{im} P_m ; P_m P_n = P_m \\ (L_m = \mathrm{im} P_m) \subseteq (L_n = \mathrm{im} P_n) ; L_m \cap L_n = L_m \end{aligned} \quad (4)$$

reveals the tree structure of the carrier subspaces with the entire space L as a root and the carrier subspaces for the generalized chromophores as leaves.

Molecular/material modeling provides ample space for tree structures. Fairly analogous to the tree of the carrier subspaces the entire space of the atomic (nuclear) coordinates of the molecular model is the direct sum of the $\mathbb{R}^3$ spaces of the Cartesian coordinates:

$$D = \bigoplus_a \mathbb{R}_a^3 \quad (5)$$

The entire coordinate space D represents the root of the corresponding tree (a runs over the entire set of atoms/nuclei). Introducing the tree structure by sequentially applying orthogonal projection and orthogonal transformation operators in the corresponding image subspaces allows one to define the collective geometry coordinates. This may/must be done consistently with the chemical structure which in its turn as well represents a tree structure formed by the groups (Gerhard's *radicals*) like methyl, phenyl, *etc.* The geometry variation/optimization is then possible in terms of such collective coordinates as the position of the center of mass of a *radical* and orientation of its inertia tensor principal axes relative to whatever other frame.

2.3 Implementation Details

With those ideas in mind we some time ago launched the development of a program library capable to cope with the problems described in previous Sections. It implements the results of the analysis of the structure of the hybrid methods of molecular/material modeling performed in Refs. [10, 34–36]. Presence of several tree like structures calls for a generic tool for representing them. With use of trees the molecular models structure in a natural way: following their chemical segmentation, allowing for the construction of the models in terms of molecular fragments (Gerhard's radicals). Basically, neither of the "big" languages (JAVA, C++, FORTRAN) intrinsically supports trees. However, the demand for them was fairly clear already many years ago. This demand enters into contradiction with the way the "big" languages are designed (uniformity of the components of "collective" data types). Nevertheless, within the latest years the development of the FORTRAN compilers [37] has advanced that much so that the many features available in the "high-level" languages (*e.g.* Python) can be implemented. Thus, it seemed to us that the amount of investment into developing of the missing collective data types in FORTRAN is smaller as compared to that required to rewrite in a "modern high-level language" the whole supply of the specific code relevant to molecular/material modeling (also with the account of the availability of more general mathematical software in the "big" languages) and we undertook some effort in this direction. Specifically, we developed a module POLYMORPHIC_TREE which allows an arbitrary content of the tree's node and provides basic functions of adding/deleting nodes/subtrees, addressing (getting and modifying) the node content by their identifier/name, traversing (recursively) the nodes/leaves, *etc.* This development eventually makes the features so far existent in the languages like Python available in FORTRAN making it "high-level" *per se*. This allowed us to profit from the available (previously developed) scientific FORTRAN code [38].

Analogously to *polymorphic trees* even simpler universally *polymorphic lists* and *pairs* had been implemented which eventually made available in FORTRAN another very useful abstract structure - dictionaries: lists of pairs (key, value[2]) both being pointers to universally polymorphic types (class(*)). Universally polymorphic lists/pairs allow to attach extensible lists of properties (attributes) to the nodes of a tree representing molecular structure. This solves the problem of multiple brands of atoms in the hybrid methods. By the brand of an atom we understand different incarnations of an atom of the same element differing by the way it enters in the model: extrema are e.g. Lennard-Jones and some quantum chemical (*ab initio* or valence approximation) atoms. Apparently the former has as attributes relevant Lennard-Jones parameters, the latter - the AO basis. Respectively the atom-based properties (charge distributions etc) when applicable are treated as universally polymorphic lists of attributes.

3 Current Implementations and Future Developments

Systematic development of a library requires significant resources which are normally not available in the context of the grant-based funding supporting projects with narrowly targeted outcome rather methodical development. Nevertheless, following certain programming discipline we could develop enough general and specific procedures and arragne them in the CARTESIUS FORT library. With help of it we could already successfully develop several targeted numeric tools:

- LIQUION - a tool for modeling thermodynamic properties of ionic liquids [39];
- ATOMS - a tool for developing atomic basis sets (solving direct Hartree-Fock and inverse spectrum fitting problems) [40];
- ADAMAS - a tool targeted on description of carbon allotropes which provides their crystalline structures, relative energies and elastic properties [41].

They are for the time being available through the NETLABORATORY system [42]. Further development on the basis of the CARTESIUS FORT library is foreseen.

[2] Values must be supplied by *metadata* including indication to the tensor type of the quantity - $\mathbb{R}$, $\mathbb{C}$, $\mathbb{H}$; rank; space to which the tensor belongs, basis in this space relative to which the quantity is given, units, and mode: whether the quantity is a parameter (input) or result of calculation (output).

Acknowledgments. Prof. Dr. I.V. Pletnev (Moscow) is acknowledged for valuable literature indications relative to InChI.

References

1. Nazarian, D., Camp, J.S., Chung, Y.G., Snurr, R.Q., Sholl, D.S.: Chem. Mater. **29**, 2521 (2017)
2. (a) Kresse, G., Hafner, J.: Phys. Rev. B 47 (1993) 558–561; (b) Kresse, G., Furthmüller, J.: Phys. Rev. B 54 (1996) 11169
3. Gonze, X., et al.: Comput. Phys. Commun. **180**, 2582 (2009)
4. Baroni, S., et al.: J. Phys. Condens. Matt. **29**, 465901 (2017)
5. Zaanen, J., Sawatzky, G.A., Allen, J.: Phys. Rev. Lett. **55**, 418 (1985)
6. Xiang, H., Dronskowski, R., Eck, B., Tchougréeff, A.L.: J. Phys. Chem. A **114**, 12345 (2010)
7. Tchougréeff, A.L., Dronskowski, R.: J. Phys. Chem. A **115**, 4547 (2011)
8. Phung, Q.M., Domingo, A., Pierloot, K.: Chem. Eur. J. **24**, 5183 (2018)
9. Thiel, W.: QM/MM methodology: fundamentals, scope, and limitations in multiscale simulation methods in molecular sciences. In: Grotendorst, J., Attig, N., Blügel, S., Marx, D. (eds.) Institute for Advanced Simulation, Forschungszentrum Jülich, NIC Series, vol. 42, p. 203 (2009)
10. Tchougréeff, A.L.: Hybrid Methods of Molecular Modeling. Springer, Netherlands (2008). https://doi.org/10.1007/978-1-4020-8189-7
11. Tchougréeff, A.L.: Khim. Fiz., 16 (1997) No 6, 62. [Chem. Phys. Reports, 16 (1997) 1035]
12. Tchougréeff, A.L.: Phys. Chem. Chem. Phys. **1**, 1051 (1999)
13. Gasteiger, J., Engel, T. (eds.) Chemoinformatics. Wiley-VCH Verlag GmbH & Co (2003)
14. Heller, S., McNaught, A., Stein, S., Tchekhovskoi, D., Pletnev, I.: J. Cheminform. **5**, 7 (2013)
15. Heller, S., McNaught, A., Pletnev, I., Stein, S., Tchekhovskoi, D.: J. Cheminform. **7**, 23 (2015)
16. Daudel, R.: In: Pullman, B., Parr, R. (eds.) The New World of Quantum Chemistry, vol. 2, p. 33. Springer, Netherlands (1976). https://doi.org/10.1007/978-94-010-1523-3
17. McNaught, A.D., Wilkinson, A.: Compendium of Chemical Terminology. The Gold Book, 2nd edn. Blackwell Science, Oxford (1997)
18. McNaught, A.D., Wilkinson, A.: Compendium of Chemical Terminology. The Gold Book, Version 2.3.3, 24 February 2014
19. Gordan, P., Alexejeff, V.G.: Z. Phys. Chem. 35, 610 (1900); Alexejeff, V.G.: Z. phys. Chem. 36, 740 (1901)
20. Tchougréeff, A.L.: Int. J. Quant. Chem. **116**, 137 (2016)
21. Shaik, S., Hiberty, P.C.: A Chemist's Guide to Valence Bond Theory. Wiley, Hoboken (2007)
22. Boucher, R., Heller, S., McNaught, A.: Chem. Int. **39**, 47 (2017)

23. "Ferrocene, for instance, may be drawn with the central iron atom connected to each of the two attached rings, to each of the atoms in the rings, to each of the bonds in the rings or not connected at all. The approach taken by InChI is to logically dissociate all atoms capable of forming coordination bonds (metals) and represent the structure as the individual, interconnected components along with the separated, unconnected metal atoms. For a large majority of organometallic compounds, this provides a unique InChI. If a bonded organometallic structure representation is desired, however, it may be specified by adding another series of layers to the InChI." S.E. Stein, S.R. Heller, D.V. Tchekhovskoi, I.V. Pletnev IUPAC International Chemical Identifier (InChI) InChI version 1, Software version 1.05 Technical Manual. Biomolecular Measurement Division. National Institute of Standards and Technology, Gaithersburg, Maryland, USA. However, this InChI does not necessarily represent adequately their electronic structure: a great advantage of the 'classical' structure
24. Bauerschmidt, S., Gasteiger, J.: J. Chem. Inf. Comput. Sci. **37**, 705 (1997)
25. Witt, O.N.: Ber. Deut. Chem. Ges. **9**, 522 (1876)
26. Ruedenberg, K.: Rev. Mod. Phys. **34**, 326 (1962)
27. Hückel, E.: Z. für Physik 60, 423 (1930); Hückel, E., Hückel, W.: Nature 129, 937 (1932); E. Hückel singled out π-systems; actually it was clear yet to Pauling and Rumer that in benzene it goes about the description of a collective state of six spins 1/2, but the relation of these spins namely to π-orbitals
28. Soudackov, A.V., Tchougréeff, A.L., Misurkin, I.A.: Theor. Chim. Acta **83**, 389 (1992)
29. Harrison, W.A.: Electronic Structure and the Properties of Solids. Freeman, San Francisco (1990)
30. Bethe, H.A.: Ann. Phys. **3**, 133 (1929)
31. Descartes, R.: Discours de la Méthode, J'ai Lu (2004). (original publication: Imprimerie Ian Meyre a Leyde, 1637)
32. Lever, A.B.P.: Inorganic Electronic Spectroscopy, 2nd edn. Elsevier, Oxford, Amsterdam, NY (1984)
33. Tchougréeff, A.L.: Int. J. Quant. Chem. **107**, 2519–2538 (2007)
34. Tchougréeff, A.L., Soudackov, A.V.: Russ. J. Phys. Chem. **88**, 1904 (2014)
35. Tchougréeff, A.L., Soudackov, A.V., van Leusen, J., Kögerler, P., Becker, K.-D., Dronskowski, R.: Int. J. Quant. Chem. **116**, 282 (2016)
36. Tchougréeff, A.L.: J. Struct. Chem. 48, S39 (2007). (in Russian); J. Struct. Chem. 48, S32 (2007). (in English)
37. Chapman, S.J.: Fortran 95/2003 for Scientists and Engineers, Third Edition The McGraw-Hill Companies, 2008; Intel & #x00AE;Fortran Language Reference. 2003–2005, Intel Corporation; Adams, J.C., Brainerd, W.S., Hendrickson, R.A., Maine, R.E., Martin, J.T., Smith, B.T.: The Fortran 2003 Handbook. The Complete Syntax, Features and Procedures. Springer Science+Business Media (2009)
38. Languages come and go, paradigms ripe and rot, the whole software business is a part of fashion industry now. But when you want your plane to fly, you still need to do the maths with your trusty Fortran. That's the beauty of the things that work; they don't have to change much. https://wordsandbuttons.online/fortran_is_still_a_thing.htm
39. Popov, I.V., Tchougréeff, A.L.: Comput. Theor. Chem. **1116**, 141 (2017)
40. Popov, I.V., Tchougréeff, A.L.: Theor. Chem. Acc. **138**, 9 (2019)
41. Popov, I.V., Slavin, V.V., Tchougréeff, A.L., Dronskowski, R.: Carbon (Submitted)
42. NetLaboratory system. https://netlab.cartesius.info/

Scientific Computing Infrastructure (SCI 2019)

Modern Approach to Creating University Learning Courses: Using Network Ideas for Creating a Hypertext (On Example of Courses on Physics and Concepts of Modern Science)

A. V. Barmasov[1,2](✉), A. M. Barmasova[2], E. N. Stankova[1], M. N. Bukina[1], D. A. Lisachenko[1], and S. O. Vysotskaya[1]

[1] St. Petersburg State University, 7-9, Universitetskaya Nab., St. Petersburg 199034, Russia
{a.barmasov, e.stankova}@spbu.ru, {mariabukina72, 123sony}@rambler.ru, da@fr.spb.ru

[2] St. Petersburg State Pediatric Medical University, 2, Litovskaya ul., St. Petersburg 194100, Russia
abarmasova@yandex.ru

Abstract. The total computerization of the last decades changes the structure of the information, the way of its use and the nature of human thinking. Science is rapidly developing, the inter- and trans-disciplinary links arise, and education becomes more intensive, but it also has its new problems. The way of thinking, the textbooks and education need to be adapted, combining the speed and flexibility with the stability and integrity of course units. In this situation, the digital educational information and the learning process itself acquire some hypertext (HT) features with its pro et contra which needs to be considered. We believe that a course should be built around a minimalist core, which contains all basic concepts, is closed and self-sufficient, and is surrounded by relatively independent HT-type structures with well-defined limits. We implement this concept based on our extensive teaching experience in a wide range of matters (physics, natural science, linguistics), at various levels and within different extents of courses.

Keywords: Computer technology · Hypertext · Teaching physics · General physics · Laboratory practicum · Virtual laboratories · E-lab · Computer mind · Clip thinking · Algorithmization in physics and language teaching

1 Introduction

As we know, the computer is not only a tool for all kinds of information processing, such as computing, search, representation, organization, etc., but it also affects the thinking style [1], although in different ways, depending on whether a person had studied programming and improved his thinking in the algorithmic direction, or just used a computer for entertainment. In the latter case, there will be mosaic thinking [1].

S. Misra et al. (Eds.): ICCSA 2019, LNCS 11622, pp. 655–666, 2019.
https://doi.org/10.1007/978-3-030-24305-0_48

In general, the computer age stimulated an increasing interest in hypertext (HT), its history and theory [2]. Furthermore, the computerization (and the progress as a whole) greatly influenced the technology and the quality of teaching and learning: (a) the diversity and the availability of textbooks increased, (b) the virtual learning technologies emerged, (c) the nature of thinking, perception, and comprehension changed.

We need to take it into account and try to get some benefit from it. This is the goal of our article: to give our understanding of specific problems and to suggest some techniques in order to improve the quality of teaching in three groups of matters where we have an extended convergent experience: (a) Physics for faculties of natural sciences [3–5], (b) Concepts of Modern Science (CMS) for students in humanities, (c) Foreign language for scientists [6–8].

HT has been extensively studied in linguistics, computer and cognitive studies [9]. In turn, we use this concept for a very practical purpose, as a theoretical basis for efficient high school courses. All the techniques described below were tested successfully in several St. Petersburg universities.

2 Modern Computer and Network Technologies Used in the Teaching of Physics at the Universities of St. Petersburg

In order to better understanding the HT meaning in education, we give a brief overview of our educative techniques and consider the role of digital techniques. It is not enough now to have only "printed course" [10–16]. This printed publication can and should be supplemented with advanced multimedia materials [17–19]. An imaginative visualization obtained by using multimedia materials is widely used also in order to bring the "theoretical" science in everyday life. The main feature of these courses is the degree of coverage of practical issues and their relevance. Among the main features of such courses is that a large amount of the background material allows using this knowledge during laboratory and practical studies, and links to Internet sites are provided where students can find additional and more detailed background information [11–15, 20, 21].

Blackboard Learn-Learning Management System (LMS Blackboard Learn) [22] and distance learning system – MOODLE (an acronym for Modular Object-Oriented Dynamic Learning Environment) [23] are used as platforms for creation, storing and presentation of various educational materials [21]. Almost the only important difference of these two systems is that Blackboard Learn is a fully commercial product; while MOODLE is open-source software using the "freemium" payment model (one gets the basic elements free of charge, but must pay for extra options). If one needs a powerful system and has the resources to pay for it, then Blackboard will be a good choice (e.g. the authors use it at St. Petersburg State University since 2012). If the budget is limited, but the ambitions are still high, MOODLE will be a good choice (e.g. Russian State Hydrometeorological University) [21].

Good results are obtained by conducting part of the lectures in the format of conferences, when students, after listening to another section of the general physics course, prepare reports on the basics of the physics of natural phenomena and processes occurring in living systems, based on materials prepared by their teachers [e.g. 17, 19, 21, 24–30].

Writing laboratory reports usually causes a lot of problems for university students. That is why a virtual group in a social network (vk.com/physlab) was created where students can find regularly updated information on the equipment in use, download needed brochures, textbooks, and tests, and get useful links and other necessary information. They also can contact their tutors by means of chat [34].

The authors have accumulated experience of teaching physics to medical students at St. Petersburg State University (Department of Medicine, Department of Dentistry and Medical Technologies), and at St. Petersburg State Pediatric Medical University, and have written several training manuals, taking into account this specificity [15, 16].

It is very important to give medical students basic knowledge, e.g. about telemedicine. The main purpose of telemedicine is the medical service of the remote patients who are far from the medical centres and have limited access to medical services. The telemedicine is based on modern technologies of transmitting and reproducing data that supports videoconferences and allows sending high-quality digital images at a distance in an effort to render more perfect reanimation aid, the fastest transportation of the patient and accelerated medical decisions. The telemedicine is impossible without experts having skills of working in remote locations. Medical school students can acquire such skills in the process of training within the grid segment, performing virtual labs and studying the educational materials in the remote access mode [21].

The infrastructure prototype of a distributed educational system developed by the authors can be viewed as a grid segment consisting of 5 sites located at St. Petersburg State University, St. Petersburg State Pediatric Medical University, Russian State Hydrometeorological University, St. Petersburg Mining University and St. Petersburg Electrotechnical University LETI. This Grid infrastructure could provide equal access to all kinds of resources for the students and lecturers in order to teach and study physics more efficiently [21].

The prototype of an informational infrastructure of a program instrumentation complex for carrying out a laboratory practicum on physics in a university should include: instrumental part for carrying out real physical experiments with the available equipment, program complex of virtual laboratories and a document management system, enabling students to learn the descriptions and to write reports on the laboratories and enabling professors to record student's results and to rate student's work appropriately [31–33]. Various scenarios for conducting classes in a virtual laboratory for both undergraduate students and masters, the ways of expanding the subject and technical capabilities of the virtual laboratory, methodical recommendations, and their possible technical solutions are offered in [33].

3 Theoretical Remarks

The Hypertext Notion. We understand the hypertext (HT) as a network with a text in its nodes, and we take into account the idea that the network representation of information is somewhat similar to the nature of the brain [9]. For our purposes, we will distinguish disciplinary, inter-disciplinary and trans-disciplinary courses, where inter-disciplinary means the junction between two or more different sciences, while the trans-disciplinary refers to a network structure itself as a whole, with the elements of particular sciences in its nodes. Close vicinity (physics and chemistry, biology and medicine for example) is not required, but on the contrary, all interconnections are possible [1]. We do not restrict ourselves to a linear sequence of pages in a typical textbook, but we use the networking ideas [1].

Nowadays the educational texts are often in free access, with very easy navigation, so the content of HT, its meaning and understanding depend on result from the actions of the reader [1]. Normally a student cannot do it well and should not do it himself. This is why the primary task of today's teaching is not to provide information (which can be easily googled out), but rather to analyze it, systematize and construct causal relationships. In other words, we need not raw information, but a product of its deep processing being a basis of progress in advanced countries. The essence of education is the creation of a high value added information product, but not a waste of primary information resources.

We do not intend to estimate the HT as "good or bad", but we consider it as a reality of our world and try to rebuild the educative process according to the new information environment and the new train of thought, where the problem is not to get the information, but to select, reorganize and understand it.

Consider some HT peculiarities and issues arising from the practical use of courses and textbooks on physics, contrasted to CMS.

Physics: Courses must be logical and consistent, with a minimum of sudden transitions to other topics, approaches, definitions or systems of units over the network, because the aim is to build a good understanding of nature: the students learn to understand and, more importantly, create logic links and conclusions. And a self-consistency of the course must be never lost at any level. No runaway is expected.

CMS: The main task is to interest humanist students in sciences; so many comparisons, analogies, and links should be revealed between different sciences in order to show their close relationship, while strict qualitative results and perfect logic links are not expected. However, the students are not suggested to create or reproduce these links. So the HT trajectory in the CMS course can be run in an unlimited number of ways and directions, depending on the demands and interest of students.

4 HT and Textbook Paradoxes

Consider from the HT point of view some paradoxes associated with modern digital textbooks, compared to the paper age.

A Textbook and a Person. HT is often characterized by a fast run away from a starting point [1]. This is also a case of some large paper textbooks, for example [10–16], with lots of references to other pages, chapters, and volumes, followed by other references, even in rather simple cases. In such books, it is often hard to learn a separate paragraph because it is hard to understand where it begins and stops and it contains too many references appearing stochastic for a novice reader. These books are not suitable for initial learning, but they can be rather an encyclopaedia for advanced studies.

Let us compare in terms of HT the interrelations of a textbook with an author, a teacher and a student.

Author: He (she) perfectly knows all the content and all the HT links in his book, fluently jumps between chapters and volumes in all simple and complicated cases, easily draws up links and analogies. Is sometimes unable to understand why students have problems when reading. The reason is that we can consider a physics textbook as written in some "foreign" language (formulas and logic) which is a kind of native language for the author. But we know that a native speaker is often unable to notice the problems in his own grammar [5].

Teacher: Is able to read and decode the HT of the author, but rarely follows it as a whole. Usually creates his own sequence from various sources

Student: Can easily be lost in a complex network structure of the textbook, jumps to other sources of information and is definitely lost.

What can a good teacher do for a real student? A good teacher may be considered as a "walking HT" who perfectly masters the material and all the interconnections feels the ambiance in the classroom and strictly follows the main trajectory, while making some improvisation when needed.

A Volume Paradox. Many textbooks have a similar thickness in spite of their level. About 300 pages in physics for a secondary school, the same for departments of biology or physics, a theoretical monograph and so on. In school textbooks, there are only a few formulas, but a lot of text, which is usually written for better understanding. However, note that five text pages need five times more efforts for understanding than only one page.

An Abundance Paradox. As our experience shows, a textbook longer than 100 pages is never read in its whole. Especially in the digital age where the choice of paper books is huge (in contrast to 40 years ago), and their electronic availability is unlimited. The knowledge risks becoming fragmented, mosaic and self-contradictory.

A Runaway Paradox. A runaway over hyperlinks in the age of the Internet, Google and Wikipedia can easily go to infinity. Consider the 5-volume course of physics [10] containing more than 3000 pages. In the paper age, the risk of runaway was noticeable but somewhat limited to these few volumes. Now there are no more limits, and we can quickly jump to other chapters, then to other textbooks, and fall in another system of assumptions and conclusions and finally in a different representation of the world. The runaway may become irreversible, with a kind of "phase transition": what will happen first, a correct understanding (of physics in our example) or a runaway to infinity. Maybe there are some kinds of attractors in such random travel, but one has to find a good one. We can compare this to the Mandelbrot set: it is very complex but invariant: a point from inside will not run away. Therefore, we can suggest a criterion for an educational HT: is it possible, in a real learning process, to stay within a few pages/paragraphs/chapters, and what is the average risk to run away too far, especially when only a small part of a course is to being studied.

Besides the runaway phenomenon, there also can be some points of the HT textbook with no entry. For example, inside long paragraphs, we can found some blocs whose importance is not restricted to this paragraph and which should constitute a separate paragraph referenced in the table of contents and is used in other paragraphs. Only a teacher (and not a student) can discover it and appreciate its importance.

All these paradoxes are not a hard problem for a teacher, but they usually overcome the student's abilities. Therefore, there is a great need for a brief, complete, consistent, clear course, which can be a kind of basis for an extended advanced course and can be adapted on the fly to any reality. This is just what we are doing. We believe that it can be an HT structure, and its basis can be a modular structure briefly described in [3].

Our team performs all kinds of lectures, seminars and practical works in disciplinary, multidisciplinary and transdisciplinary matters in the range from physics to linguistics for students in science and humanities in all combinations at different levels [3–8, 11–15, 21, 31, 34–43]. So the courses must be very flexible and adapted for a fast restructuring.

5 Modular Structure of Physics Course

Let us give our vision of a minimum core in the course of physic. It should be a simple but complete, self-consistent and relatively independent description of a relatively complete set of physical phenomena. All logical chains and main HT nodes should be well visible [3]: Assumptions – Basic descriptions – Mathematical developments – Applications. All the needed links are internal. All formulas are derived in a simple and clear way, without excessive maths. The external links to more detailed and complex calculations are given, but they are well marked and not mandatory. The mathematical apparatus is given in its most simple form, which can in principle describe a phenomenon under consideration. This core is entirely accessible for students, and the teacher (and an advanced student too) can make use of a system of links. Such HT is easy in use and always correct and self-consistent.

In addition to the thematic principle, logical links are established when different phenomena, usually separated by hundreds of pages, are considered together from a single viewpoint. For example, parallelism in electric and magnetic fields, or a uniform approach to a set of quantum barrier problems (potential well, tunnelling, reflection), or some grammatical aspects [3, 8, 44]. Thus, we create something that can be: (a) read and understood in a reasonable time, (b) studied without the use of other sources, (c) used as a level of knowledge, (d) used as a basis for further study.

Note a similarity to a heterogeneous crystallization or writing a complex program. One of the ways to write a long program is to write a short sketch, which already performs some basic functions required from the program as a whole. Then small changes are made gradually, some blocks and functions added, the program grows up, but at any moment remains well debugged and runnable. Similar ideas allow improving the teaching of foreign languages if we are looking for simple and operable knowledge [6, 8].

Our HT structured course of physics is under construction but we will give some examples.

The Heisenberg Uncertainty Relation. The core is made of classical wave packet and get a purely classical uncertainty relation (the wave packet width in frequency or energy and its length in space or time) $\Delta\omega \cdot \Delta\tau \geqslant \pi$ from the most simple evaluations: we consider a sum of 2 sine waves with close wave numbers (beating), where secondary school knowledge is quite sufficient. Then we declare that this is also the case of the de Broglie wave, where Planck constant appears linking maths to quantum mechanics. Any new idea appears only when it is really needed, and not before. Thus, we obtain a correct result, although with a different numerical factor. This is a typical feature of approximate calculations: a correct idea, a simple calculation, and a reasonably close numerical factor. If needed, one can use [45], where complicated maths is employed for the same subject. By the way, the authors of [45] note that the strictness can be illusory.

The Electronic Structure of Solids. Typically a Schrödinger equation (denote SE this node of HT) occurs in a physics course as a generalization for the de Broglie waves (BW node). Then a particle in a potential well (PW) is investigated using a SE solution. That is, first one goes from BW to SE (and not in the easiest way), and then returns back to the PW node, with an illusory rigour. So we at first complicate things and then simplify them back. To avoid that, we can start with the de Broglie wave in the potential well (go from BW right to PW without going through SE) and immediately obtain the energy spectrum. Then we generalize it to a finite depth of the well, go to a double well, generalize the wave to negative energies (tunnelling) and split the spectrum into sublevels. In a similar way, we consider the statistical physics: the barometric formula can be generalized directly to the Fermi-Dirac distribution and used in metals and semiconductors without going to the general and strict Gibbs theory. When this material will be well understood by the students (but not before), we can go to other HT nodes in the same course containing all the needed mathematics, Schrödinger equations, Gibbs distributions, thus exploring the next level of complexity (Fig. 1).

Our course is being gradually created, and in some time we plan to build a textbook in an electronic form, with selectable levels of complexity, where hyperlinks will be marked and will point to level-defined nodes while maintaining the consistency and integrity of the course.

Linguistics. Similar ideas (initial minimalism followed by added layers, hypertext, and mathematical formalism) can also be used in such cross-disciplinary matter as foreign languages for scientists. Many grammar elements may be given under a strict mathematical-like form. For example, the tenses of verbs can be expressed in terms of basic elements and their combinations [6, 8], a foreign language can be compared to quantum mechanics [5], a business letter be represented under the form of multiple embeddings [6], and a textbook itself can be built as a well fragmented HT-ready material [7].

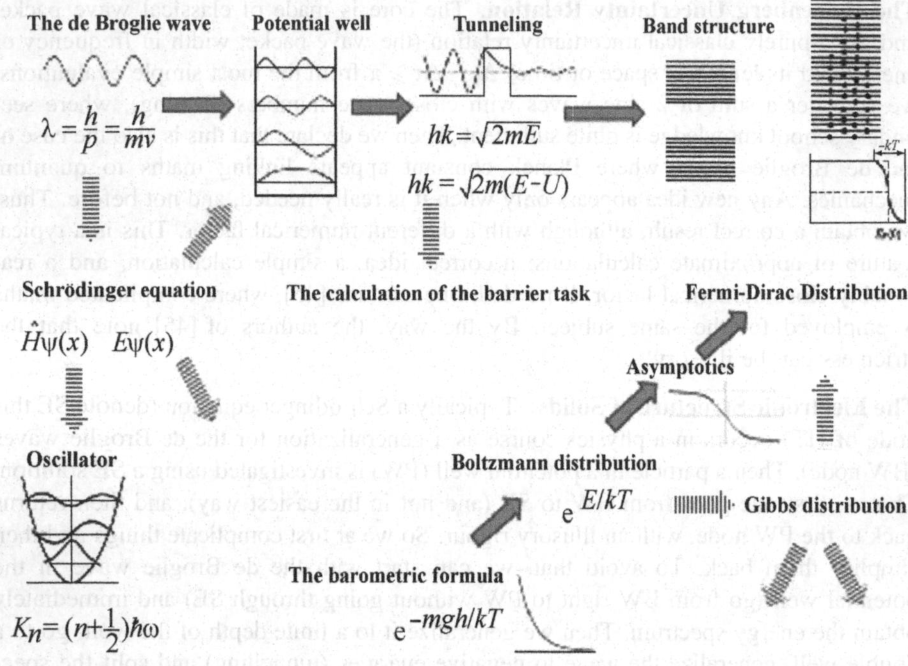

Fig. 1. The electronic structure of solids

6 Conclusions

The computer brings a new life in teaching, at least in three different senses: (1) it provides powerful tools, (2) it changes the teaching process, and (3) it changes the human mind. Everywhere there are pros and contras. Anyway, we all must adapt to a rapidly changing world, including in high school, and the educative techniques must also adapt to the total computerization. We have suggested here some approaches to such adaptation, based on a rigorous selection of primary elements and drawing up a multilevel set of links between them. The already obtained results make us believe that this approach is very promising.

Acknowledgment. This research was sponsored by the Russian Foundation for Basic Research under the projects: 16-04-00494 "Research of functioning of rhodopsin as the canonical representative of the class A receptors, which are the G-protein, by the methods of the local selective NMR, optical spectroscopy and numerical simulation", 16-07-01113 "Virtual supercomputer as a tool for solving complex problems", and 17-03-01372 "Investigation of energy conversion processes in nanoscale structures by vibrational spectroscopy, luminescence, and computer simulation".

References

1. Popova, A.V., Brylina, I.V.: Temporal aspects of education. Siberian J. Sci. **3**(18), 1–10 (2015). (in Russian)
2. Santopaolo, L.: From a gloss to a hypertext. Advantages and disadvantages of dynamic communication. In: Runov, S.A. (ed.) Russia and WTO: New Challenges and Perspectives: International Scientific and Practical Conference, pp. 367–375. Znanie, Novokuznetsk (2013)
3. Bukina, M.N., Barmasov, A.V., Lisachenko, D.A., Ivanov, A.S.: Modular design of general physics course for students in natural sciences. In: Modern Educational Technology in the Teaching Natural Sciences and the Humanities: Proceedings of the III International Scientific-Methodical Conference, 7–8 April 2016, pp. 814, 350–355. Mining University, St. Petersburg (2016). (in Russian)
4. Barmasov, A.V., Barmasova, A.M., Bukina, M.N., Zinkevich, E.R.: Modern trends in teaching of physics for medical students (Prepared for publication)
5. Lisachenko, D.A.: Quantum mechanics as a foreign language: interaction of educative methods. In: Innovative Educational Technologies: Proceedings of II International Scientific Conference (Kazan, May 2015), Kazan, Buk, pp. 189–192 (2015)
6. Lisachenko, D.A.: Teaching of foreign languages to students in science and engineering. In: Fokin, S.N. (ed.) Roman Collegium. Interdisciplinary Collection of Scientific Papers. St. Petersburg Economical University (2016)
7. Lisachenko, D.A.: French language. A view of a physicist, p. 198. Logos, St. Petersburg (2003)
8. Lisachenko, D.A.: Le français par la science: une langue étrangère enseignée par un scientifique aux scientifiques. Le français de spécialité. Enjeux culturels et linguistiques. Bertrand, O., Schaffner, I. (eds.), pp. 141–150. Editions de l'Ecole Polytechnique, Paris (2008). (in French)
9. Popov, E.A.: Approaches to the study of hypertext. Vestnik of Pushkin LSU **7**(1), 167–171 (2015). (in Russian)
10. Sivukhin, D.V.: The general course of physics. In. FIZMATLIT, Moscow, vol. 5 (2002–2005). (in Russian)
11. Barmasov, A.V., Kholmogorov, V.E.: Course of general physics for nature managers. Mechanics, Chirtsov, A.S. (ed.), p. 416. BHV-St. Petersburg, St. Petersburg (2008, 2012). (in Russian)
12. Barmasov, A.V. Kholmogorov, V.E.: Course of general physics for nature managers. Oscillations Waves, Bobrovsky, A.P. (ed.), p. 256. BHV-St. Petersburg, St. Petersburg (2009, 2012). (in Russian)
13. Barmasov, A.V. Kholmogorov, V.E.: Course of general physics for nature managers. Mol. Phys. Thermodyn., Bobrovsky, A.P. (ed.), p. 512. BHV-St. Petersburg, St. Petersburg (2009, 2012). (in Russian)
14. Barmasov, A.V. Kholmogorov, V.E.: Course of general physics for nature managers. Electricity, Bobrovsky, A.P. (ed.), p. 448. BHV-St. Petersburg, St. Petersburg (2010, 2013). (in Russian)
15. Barmasov, A.V., Barmasova, A.M., Struts, A.V., Yakovleva, T.Yu.: Dynamics of rigid body. Elements of the theory and the collection of tasks, p. 28. Publishing house of St. Petersburg State Pediatric Medical University, St. Petersburg (2012). (in Russian)
16. Barmasov, A.V., Barmasova, A.M., Struts, A.V., Yakovleva, T.Yu.: Processing of results of measurements of physical quantities, p. 92. Publishing house of St. Petersburg State Pediatric Medical University, St. Petersburg (2012). (in Russian)

17. Bukina, M.N., Barmasov, A.V., Ivanov, A.S.: Modern teaching methods for the teaching general physics and mathematical processing of results of measurements of physical quantities. In: Modern Educational Technology in the Teaching Natural Sciences and the Humanities: Proceedings of the International Scientific-Methodical Conference 27–29 May 2014, pp. 562, 408–414. Mining University, St. Petersburg (2014). (in Russian)
18. Bukina, M.N., Barmasov, A.V., Lisachenko, D.A., Ivanov, A.S.: Modern methods of teaching physics and the concepts of modern natural science. In: Proceedings of the II International Scientific-Methodical Conference on Modern Educational Technologies in Teaching Natural-Scientific and Humane Disciplines, 09–10 April 2015, pp. 732, 516–520. Mining University, St. Petersburg (2015). (in Russian)
19. Barmasova, A.M., Yakovleva, T.Yu., Barmasov, A.V., et al.: Multimedia lecture course on processing of results of measurements of physical quantities for students users. In: Spirin, G. G. (ed.) Abstracts of Scientific-Methodical Workshop on "The Physics in the Engineering Education System of the EurAsEC Member States" and The Meeting of Heads of Physics Departments of Technical Universities of Russia. The Scientific Seminar was Held from, 25–27 June 2007, p. 344, p. 42. Zhukovsky Air Force Engineering Academy, Moscow (2007). (in Russian)
20. Nordling, C.; Österman, J.: Physics Handbook for Science and Engineering. Authorized translation from the English language edition by Barmasov, A.V., p. 528. BHV-St. Petersburg, St. Petersburg (2011). (in Russian)
21. Stankova, E.N., Barmasov, A.V., Dyachenko, N.V., Bukina, M.N., Barmasova, A.M., Yakovleva, T.Yu.: The use of computer technology as a way to increase efficiency of teaching physics and other natural sciences. In: Gervasi, O., et al. (eds.) ICCSA 2016. LNCS, vol. 9789, pp. 581–594. Springer, Cham (2016). https://doi.org/10.1007/978-3-319-42089-9_41
22. Blackboard Learn. www.blackboard.com/platforms/learn/overview.aspx
23. Moodle. https://moodle.org
24. Barmasova, A.M., Barmasov, A.V., Skoblikova, A.L., et al.: Features of teaching general physics to the students-ecologists. In: The Problems of Theoretical and Applied Ecology, pp. 267, 15, 226–241. Publishing house RSHU, St. Petersburg (2005). (in Russian)
25. Barmasova, A.M., Barmasov, A.V., Bobrovsky, A.P., Yakovleva, T.Yu.: To the question about teaching general physics to the students-ecologists. In: Abstracts. Meeting of the Heads of Departments of Physics of Technical Universities in Russia. AVIAIZDAT, Moscow, pp. 46–48 (2006). (in Russian)
26. Barmasova, A.M., Yakovleva, T.Yu., Barmasov, A.V., et al.: An integrated approach to the teaching physics to students-nature managers. In: Spirin, G.G. (ed.) Abstracts of Scientific-Methodical Workshop on "The Physics in the Engineering Education System of the EurAsEC Member States" and the Meeting of Heads of Physics Departments of Technical Universities of Russia. The Scientific Seminar was Held from 25–27 June 2007, pp. 344, 40–41. Zhukovsky Air Force Engineering Academy, Moscow (2007). (in Russian)
27. Yakovleva, T.Yu., Barmasova, A.M., Barmasov, A.V.: Interdisciplinary connections in teaching General Physics to students of science and engineering. In: Spirin, G.G. (ed.) Abstracts of Scientific-Methodical Workshop on "The Physics in the System of Engineering and Pedagogical Education of the EurAsEC Member States". The scientific seminar was held in 2008, Moscow, pp. 364, 355–357. Zhukovsky Air Force Engineering Academy, Moscow (2008). (in Russian)
28. Bukina, M.N., Barmasov, A.V., Ivanov, A.S.: Some aspects of teaching physics in high school. In: VIII St. Petersburg Congress "Education, Science, Innovation in the Twenty-First Century". Collection of Works, 24–25 October 2014, pp. 414, 47–49. Mining University, St. Petersburg (2014). (in Russian)

29. Bukina, M.N., Barmasov, A.V., Ivanov, A.S.: Features of general physics teaching to students of natural science specialties in modern conditions. In: The Physics in the System of Modern Education (FSSO-2015): Proceedings of the XIII International Conference, St. Petersburg, 1–4 June 2015, vol. 2, pp. 393, 3–6 (2015). (in Russian)
30. Barmasov, A.V., Barmasova, A.M., Klikunova, K.A., Struts, A.V. Medical electronics. Physical methods in medicine. SPb: Publishing house of SPbGPMU (2019, Prepared for publication). (in Russian)
31. Dyachenko, N.V., Barmasov, A.V., Stankova, E.N., Struts, A.V., Barmasova, A.M., Yakovleva, T.Yu.: prototype of informational infrastructure of a program instrumentation complex for carrying out a laboratory practicum on physics in a university. In: Gervasi, O., Murgante, B., Misra, S., Borruso, G., Torre, C.M., Rocha, A.M.A.C., Taniar, D., Apduhan, B.O., Stankova, E., Cuzzocrea, A. (eds.) ICCSA 2017. LNCS, vol. 10408, pp. 412–427. Springer, Cham (2017). https://doi.org/10.1007/978-3-319-62404-4_30
32. Bobrovsky A.P., Dyachenko N.V., Barmasov A.V., et al.: Electronic lab for laboratory workshop on physics at the university. In: Istomin E.P. (ed.) Interuniversity collection of scientific works "Information Technologies and Systems: Management, Economics, Transport, Law", vol. 2, no. 20, pp. 150, 36–48. SPb: Andreevsky Publishing House LLC (2017). (in Russian)
33. Stankova, E.N., Dyachenko, N.V., Tibilova, G.S.: Virtual laboratories: prospects for the development of techniques and methods of work. In: Gervasi, O., et al. (eds.) ICCSA 2018. LNCS, vol. 10963, pp. 3–11. Springer, Cham (2018). https://doi.org/10.1007/978-3-319-95171-3_1
34. Lisachenko, D.A., Barmasov, A.V., Bukina, M.N., Stankova, E.N., Vysotskaya, S.O., Zarochentseva, E.P.: Best practices combining traditional and digital technologies in education. In: Gervasi, O., et al. (eds.) ICCSA 2017. LNCS, vol. 10408, pp. 483–494. Springer, Cham (2017). https://doi.org/10.1007/978-3-319-62404-4_36
35. Kholmogorov, V.Y., Barmasov, A.V.: The biosphere and physical factors. Electromagnetic fields and life. In: The Problems of Theoretical and Applied Ecology, RSHMU, St. Petersburg, pp. 267, 27–47 (2005). (in Russian)
36. Barmasov, A.V., Barmasova, A.M., Yakovleva, T.Yu.: The biosphere and the physical factors. Light pollution of the environment. In: Proceedings of the Russian State Hydrometeorological University, vol. 33, pp. 84–101 (2014). (in Russian)
37. Yakovleva, T.Yu., Barmasova, A.M., Barmasov, A.V.: The biosphere and the physical factors. Possible hazards of wide application of white LEDs. In: The World Science and Education in Contemporary Society: Collection of Scientific Works on Materials of the International Scientific-Practical Conference, 30 October 2014, Part III. OOO "AR-Consult", Moscow, pp. 42–50 (2014). (in Russian)
38. Barmasov, A.V., Barmasova, A.M., Yakovleva, T.Yu.: The biosphere and physical factors. The geomagnetic field. In: Modern Trends in the Development of Science and Technology, vol. 3–4, pp. 127–131 (2015). (in Russian)
39. Barmasov, A.V., Korotkov, V.I., Kholmogorov, V.Y.: Model photosynthetic system with charge transfer for transforming solar energy. Biophysics **39**(2), 227–231 (1994)
40. Struts, A.V., Barmasov, A.V., Brown, M.F.: Methods for studying photoreceptors and photoactive molecules in biological and model systems: rhodopsin as a canonical representative of the seven-transmembrane helix receptors. Bulletin of St. Petersburg University. Series 4. Physics, Chemistry, vol. 2, pp. 191–202 (2014). (in Russian)
41. Struts, A.V., Barmasov, A.V., Brown, M.F.: Spectral methods for study of the G-protein-coupled receptor rhodopsin. I. Vibrational and electronic spectroscopy. Opt. Spectrosc. **118** (5), 711–717 (2015)

42. Struts, A.V., Barmasov, A.V., Brown, M.F.: Spectral methods for study of the G-protein-coupled receptor rhodopsin. II. Magnetic resonance methods. Opt. Spectrosc. **120**(2), 286–293 (2016)
43. Bukina, M.N., Bakulev, V.M., Barmasov, A.V., et al.: Luminescence diagnostics of conformational changes of the Hsp70 protein in the course of thermal denaturation. Opt. Spectrosc. **118**(6), 899–901 (2015)
44. Lisachenko, D.A., Kuzmin, Yu.I., Sokolov, A.I., et al.: Quantum mechanics and statistical physics. Sokolov, A.I. (ed.), SPb: St. Petersburg Electrotechnical University LETI (1999)
45. Landau, L.D.; Lifshitz, E.M. (eds.): Quantum Mechanics Non-Relativistic Theory (Course of Theoretical Physics), 3rd edn., vol. 3, . Pergamon Press (1977)

Some Methods for Minimizing of d.c. Functions

L. Polyakova([✉]), V. Karelin, S. Myshkov, and E. Stankova

St. Petersburg State University, 7/9, Universitetskaya nab., St. Petersburg 199034, Russia
lnpol07@mail.ru, vkarelin@mail.ru, skmyshkov@mail.ru, e.stankova@spbu.ru
http://www.springer.com/gp/computer-science/lncs

Abstract. In the paper, we present algorithms for minimization of d.c. functions (difference of two convex functions) on the whole space R^n. Many nonconvex optimization problems can be described using these functions. D.c. functions are used in various applications especially in optimization, but the problem to characterize them is not trivial, due to the fact that these functions are not differentiable and certainly are not convex. The class of these functions is contained in the class of quasidifferentiable functions. Proposed algorithms are based on known necessary optimality conditions and d.c. duality. Convergence to inf-stationary points is established under fairly general natural assumptions.

Keywords: Convex function · Difference of convex functions (d.c. functions) · Subdifferential · Quasidifferentiable functions

1 Introduction

Nonsmooth optimization problems often arise in the applied fields of science. Nonconvex problems with nondifferentiable objective functions are interesting for researching. Therefore the development of theory and construction of numerical methods for solving nonsmooth problems optimization is a necessary object of research As it is well-known, functions represented as the difference of two convex functions (d.c. functions) form a linear space dense in the space of continuous functions. Hence the problem of d.c. programming forms an important class of optimization. It should be noted that algorithms of convex optimization are ineffective for the decision of nonsmooth optimization problems. But in the investigation of optimization properties of d.c. functions, of course, a well-developed apparatus of convex analysis is used. At present there exists a lot of papers devoted to the study of properties of the difference of convex functions which are the difference of two continuous convex functions (see, for example, [1–11]). The class of d.c. functions is a subclass of locally Lipschitz functions that is of interest both in analysis and optimization. An investigation of properties of such functions is, certainly, based on the fundamental knowledge and theorems

S. Misra et al. (Eds.): ICCSA 2019, LNCS 11622, pp. 667–677, 2019.
https://doi.org/10.1007/978-3-030-24305-0_49

of convex analysis as the class of convex functions is one of the most investigated among nonsmooth functions. A lot of real processes can be modeled with using the nondifferentiable optimization.

We will consider the following unconstrained nonsmooth optimization problem:

$$\min\{f_1(x) - f_2(x)\}, \quad x \in R^n,$$

where functions f_1, f_2 are convex on R^n.

1.1 Elementary Properties of Convex Sets and Convex Functions

The concepts of convex sets and convex functions are fundamental in Convex Analysis. Convex sets and convex functions are the main tool in theoretical studies in many subjects of nondifferentiable optimization. Formulate some definitions and statements [12,13].

A set $X \subset R^n$ is called convex, if for all $x_1 \in X$ and $x_2 \in X$ the following formula

$$\lambda x_1 + (1 - \lambda)x_2 \in X \quad \forall \lambda \in [0, 1] \subset R,$$

holds. A convex set of vectors is a set that contains all the points of any line segment joining two points of the set (see the next figure). Assume that the empty set $\emptyset$ is convex by definition. The sum of two convex sets $X_1, X_2 \subset R^n$ is called the set of

$$X = X_1 + X_2 = \{x_1 + x_2 \mid x_1 \in X_1, \quad x_2 \in X_2\}.$$

Sometimes the set $X = X_1 + X_2$ is called the algebraic sum of two convex sets X_1 and X_2 or the Minkowski sum. By writing $X_1 - X_2$ we will understand the set $X_1 + (-X_2)$. If a set $X \subset R^n$ is convex, then for $\alpha \in R$

$$\alpha X = \{y \in R^n \mid y = \alpha x, \ x \in X\}.$$

A set αX for $\alpha > 0$ is called the image set X with stretching or squeezing the space R^n in α times relative to the origin. Note some elementary properties of convex sets.

1. Let I be an arbitrary set of indices i, a set $X_i \subset R^n$ is convex for each index $i \in I$. Then $X = \bigcap_{i \in I} X_i$ is convex as well.
2. Let sets $X_1 \subset R^n$ and $X_2 \subset R^n$ be convex, then the algebraic sum $X_1 + X_2$ is also convex.

Let $f : R^n \to R \bigcup\{+\infty\} \bigcup\{-\infty\}$. The set dom $f = \{x \in R^n \mid f(x) < +\infty\}$ is called an effective domain of a convex function f. The set

$$\text{epi } f = \left\{ \begin{pmatrix} x \\ \mu \end{pmatrix} \in R^n \times R \mid f(x) \leq \mu \right\}$$

is called an epigraph of f. A function f is called convex if its epigraph is a convex set. A convex function f is said to be proper if its epigraph is non-empty and contains no vertical lines, i.e. if $f(x) < +\infty$ for at least one x and $f(x) > -\infty$ for all x. Further we will consider only proper convex functions. For proper convex functions it is possible to give another definition which equivalent to the above. A function $f : R^n \to R \cup \{+\infty\}$ is called convex if the following relations

$$f(\lambda_1 x_1 + \lambda_2 x_2) \le \lambda_1 f(x_1) + \lambda_2 f(x_2),\ \lambda_1, \lambda_2 \ge 0,\ \lambda_1 + \lambda_2 = 1,\ \forall x_1, x_2 \in R^n,$$

hold. The conjugate of a function f is

$$f^*(v) = \sup_{x \in R^n} \{\langle x, v\rangle - f(x)\},\ v \in R^n,$$

where $\langle x, v\rangle$ is the scalar product of two vectors x and v. A conjugate function f^* is closed and convex (even when f is not). If f is a closed proper convex function then f^* is also a closed proper convex function and the equality $f(x) = f^{**}(x)$ is true. A set

$$\partial f(x) = \{v \in R^n \mid f(z) - f(x) \le \langle v, z - x\rangle\ \forall z \in R^n\}$$

is called a subdifferential of the convex function f at x. Any $v \in \partial f(x)$ is called a subgradient of f. The subdifferential $\partial f(x)$ is a convex set. If a convex function is finite on R^n then its subdifferential is nonempty compact convex set. Let f be a convex function on R^n. For any $x \in R^n$ and any $g \in R^n$ we have

$$f'(x, g) = \sup_{v \in \partial f(x)} \langle v, g\rangle,$$

where $f'(x, g)$ is the directional derivative of f at x in the direction g.

1.2 Quasidifferentiable Functions

Let a function f be defined on R^n and be directionally differentiable at a point $x \in R^n$ and its directional derivative $f'(x, g)$ can be represented in the form

$$f'(x, g) = \lim_{\lambda \downarrow 0} \frac{f(x + \lambda g) - f(x)}{\lambda} = \max_{v \in \underline{\partial} f(x)} \langle v, g\rangle + \min_{w \in \overline{\partial} f(x)} \langle w, g\rangle,$$

where $\underline{\partial} f(x) \subset R^n$, $\overline{\partial} f(x) \subset R^n$ are convex compact sets in R^n. The function f is called a quasidifferentiable at a point $x \in R^n$. A pair of sets $\mathcal{D} f(x) = [\underline{\partial} f(x), \overline{\partial} f(x)]$ is called a quasidifferential of a quasidifferentiable function f at x. The set $\underline{\partial} f(x) \subset R^n$ is called a subdifferential of f at x, the set $\overline{\partial} f(x) \subset R^n$ is called a superdifferential of f at x.

The class of quasidifferentiable functions has been introduced by V.F. Demyanov and A.M. Rubinov [14,15]. Differentiable, convex, concave functions, the maximum functions are quasidifferentiable functions.

Let f_1, f_2 be finite convex functions on R^n and

$$f(x) = f_1(x) - f_2(x),\quad x \in R^n.$$

The function f is quasidifferentiable on R^n and $\mathcal{D} f(x) = [\partial f_1(x), -\partial f_2(x)]$ is its quasidifferential at a point $x \in R^n$, where $\partial f_i(x)$ are the subdifferentials of convex functions $f_i(x)$, $i = 1, 2$, at the point $x \in R^n$ in the sense of Convex Analysis.

Necessary Conditions for a Minimum of the Difference of Convex Functions. Consider an optimization problem: find

$$\inf_{x \in R^n} f(x).$$

The following necessary optimality conditions for the function f on R^n have been proven in [3].

Theorem 1. *For a point $x^* \in R^n$ to be a minimizer of the function f on R^n, it is necessary that*

$$\partial f_2(x^*) \subset \partial f_1(x^*). \tag{1}$$

For a point $x^* \in R^n$ to be a maximizer of the function f on R^n, it is necessary that

$$\partial f_1(x^*) \subset \partial f_2(x^*).$$

If the inclusion

$$\partial f_2(x^*) \subset int\, \partial f_1(x^*)$$

holds at the point $x^* \in R^n$ then this point is a strict local minimizer of the function f on R^n. If the inclusion

$$\partial f_1(x^*) \subset int\, \partial f_2(x^*)$$

is satisfied at the point $x^* \in R^n$ then this point is a strict local maximizer of the function f on R^n.

A point $x^* \in R^n$ satisfying inclusion Eq. (1) is called an inf-stationary point of the function f.

2 Minimization of d.c. Functions

Let f_1 and f_2 be finite convex functions on R^n. Consider the difference of these functions $f(x) = f_1(x) - f_2(x)$. Suppose that functions f_1, f_2 are strongly convex on R^n with strong convexity constant $m > 0$. Note that this assumption is not burdensome, since, if they are not strongly convex, then adding to each function $f_i (i = 1, 2)$, arbitrary strongly convex function on R^n , for example, $||x||^2$, we get the property we need.

Consider the optimization problem: find

$$\inf_{x \in R^n} f(x).$$

Since both functions f_1 and f_2 are strongly convex due to the properties of strongly convex functions, the function

$$f^o(v) = f_2^*(v) - f_1^*(v), \quad v \in R^n,$$

is continuously differentiable in R^n and

$$\inf_{x \in R^n} f(x) = \inf_{v \in R^n} f^o(v).$$

Thus, the problem of finding a global minimizer of the function f on R^n is equivalent to the problem of finding the global minimizer of continuously differentiable functions f^o on R^n.

Remind that if a convex function φ is defined and convex on R^n, then the decomposition

$$\varphi(x) = \sup_{z \in R^n} \{\varphi(z) + \langle w(z), x - z \rangle\} \tag{2}$$

holds, where $w(z)$ is a subgradient of φ at z. Therefore

$$f_2(x) = \sup_{z \in R^n} \{f_2(z) + \langle w(z), x - z \rangle\}, \quad w(z) \in \partial f_2(z),$$

We have

$$f(x) = f_1(x) - f_2(x) = f_1(x) - \sup_{z \in R^n} \{f_2(z) + \langle w(z), x - z \rangle\}$$

$$= \inf_{z \in R^n} \{f_1(x) - f_2(z) - \langle w(z), x - z \rangle\}.$$

Fix the point $z \in R^n$ and arbitrary subgradient $w(z) \in \partial f_2(z)$. Let

$$\psi(x, z) = f_1(x) - f_2(z) - \langle w(z), x - z \rangle.$$

Obviously, the function $\psi(x, z)$, as the function of the argument x is strongly convex on R^n with strong convexity constant $m > 0$ for each fixed $z \in R^n$ and $w(z) \in \partial f_2(z)$. Therefore, we have

$$\inf_{x \in R^n} f(x) = \inf_{x \in R^n} \inf_{z \in R^n} \psi(x, z) = \inf_{z \in R^n} \inf_{x \in R^n} \psi(x, z),$$

and for every $z \in R^n$ and $w(z) \in \partial f_2(z)$, by using Eq. (2), we have

$$f(x) \le \psi(x, z) = f_1(x) - f_2(z) - \langle w(z), x - z \rangle.$$

Note that

$$\inf_{x \in R^n} \psi(x, z) = \min_{x \in R^n} \psi(x, z) = \psi(\bar{x}(z), z),$$

moreover, the point $\bar{x}(z)$ is unique.

Choose an arbitrary point $x_0 \in R^n$ and an arbitrary subgradient $w(x_0) \in \partial f_2(x_0)$. Put

$$\varphi_0(x) = \psi(x, x_0) = f_1(x) - f_2(x_0) - \langle w(x_0), x - x_0 \rangle.$$

It is obvious that $f(x_0) = \varphi_0(x_0)$. Find

$$\min_{x \in R^n} \varphi_0(x) = \varphi_0(x_1) = \varphi_0(x_1(w_0)).$$

Due to the strong convexity of the function φ_0 and the uniqueness of the point x_1, we have

$$0 \in \partial \varphi_0(x_1) = \partial f_1(x_1) - w(x_0),$$

$$\psi(x, x_0) - \psi(x_1, x_0) \geq m||x - x_1||^2 \quad \forall x \in R^n.$$

Thus, $w(x_0) \in \partial f_1(x_1) \cap \partial f_2(x_0)$.

Consider two cases:

(a) If $w(x_0) \in \partial f_1(x_0)$, then $x_1 = x_0$.

(b) If $w(x_0) \notin \partial f_1(x_0)$, then $x_1 \neq x_0$.

As $w_0 \in \partial f_2(x_0), \quad w_0 \in \partial f_1(x_1), \quad$ then $x_0 = (f_2^*)'(w_0), \quad x_1 = (f_1^*)'(w_0)$. Hence the equality

$$x_0 - x_1 = (f_2^*)'(w_0) - (f_1^*)'(w_0) = (f^o)'(w_0)$$

holds. As

$$f_1(x_1) + f_1^*(w_0) = \langle x_1, w_0 \rangle, \quad f_2(x_0) + f_2^*(w_0) = \langle x_0, w_0 \rangle,$$

then

$$f^o(w_0) = f_2^*(w_0) - f_1^*(w_0) = f_1(x_1) - f_2(x_0) - \langle w_0, x_1 - x_0 \rangle = \psi(x_1, x_0). \quad (3)$$

But since

$$f_2(x_1) \geq f_2(x_0) + \langle w_0, x_1 - x_0 \rangle + m||x_1 - x_0||^2,$$

then

$$f^o(w_0) = f_2^*(w_0) - f_1^*(w_0) \geq f_1(x_1) - f_2(x_1) + m||x_1 - x_0||^2 = f(x_1) + m||x_1 - x_0||^2.$$

Therefore

$$f(x_1) \leq f^o(w_0) - m||x_1 - x_0||^2 \leq f(x_0) - 2m||x_1 - x_0||^2.$$

Remark 1. Note the fact that formula Eq. (3) is true for any continuous convex functions f_1 and f_2 and for each point x_1, which minimizes $\psi(x, x_0)$ on R^n when x_0 and $w_0 \in \partial f_2(x_0)$ are also fixed.

Thus, we can calculate the value of the difference of conjugate functions $f^o(v) = f_2^*(v) - f_1^*(v)$ at any point $v \in R^n$, although you need to know the point x_0, in which the vector is a subgradient of the function f_2.

Thus, if at k-th step the point x_k is not an inf - the stationary point of the function f on R^n, that is, $\partial f_2(x_k) \not\subset \partial f_1(x_k)$, then we can find the point x_{k+1} for which an inequality

$$f(x_{k+1}) \leq f^o(w_k) - m||x_{k+1} - x_k||^2 \leq f(x_k) - 2m||x_{k+1} - x_k||^2$$
$$= f(x_k) - 2m||(f^o)'(w_k)||^2,$$

holds, where $w_k \in \partial f_2(x_k), \quad w_k \notin \partial f_1(x_k)$. From these inequalities the next relations

$$f(x_{k+1}) \leq f(x_k) - 2m||x_{k+1} - x_k||^2, \quad f(x_{k+1}) \leq f(x_0) - 2m\sum_{i=0}^{k} ||x_{i+1} - x_i||^2,$$

$$f^o(w_k) \leq f(x_k) - m||x_{k+1} - x_k||^2, \quad f^o(w_k) \leq f(x_0) - m\sum_{i=0}^{k}||x_{i+1} - x_i||^2,$$

$$f^o(w_k) \leq f^o(w_{k-1}) - m(||x_{k+1} - x_k||^2 + ||x_k - x_{k-1}||^2)$$
$$= f^o(w_{k-1}) - m(||(f^o)'(w_k)||^2 + ||(f^o)'(w_{k-1}||^2).$$

follow. Describe the "principal" scheme of this relaxation algorithm for minimizing the function f on R^n.

2.1 Algorithm 1.

Step. 1. Take the arbitrary point $x_0 \in R^n$. If

$$\partial f_2(x_0) \subset \partial f_1(x_0),$$

then the point x_0 is inf - stationary point of the function f on R^n and the process is finished.

Step 2. Find a point $x_k \in R^n$, which is not an inf - stationary point of f on R^n. Then choose an arbitrary subgradient $w_k = w(x_k) \in \partial f_2(x_k)$. Put

$$\varphi_k(x) = \psi(x, x_k) = f_1(x) - f_2(x_k) - \langle w_k, x - x_k\rangle.$$

Find $\min\limits_{x \in R^n} \varphi_k(x) = \varphi_k(x_{k+1})$.

Step 3. If $\partial f_2(x_{k+1}) \subset \partial f_1(x_{k+1})$, then the process is finished, otherwise go to Step 2.

If a sequence $\{x_k\}$ is finite, then, by construction, the last received point is an inf - stationary point of the function f on R^n. Consider the case when the sequence $\{x_k\}$ is infinite.

Theorem 2. *If the series*

$$\sum_{i=0}^{\infty} ||x_{i+1} - x_i||^2 \tag{4}$$

diverges, then the function f is unbounded from below. If this series converges and the set

$$\mathcal{L} = \mathcal{L}(x_0) = \{x \in R^n \mid f(x) \leq f(x_0)\}$$

is limited then

$$(f^o)'(w_k) \to 0.$$

Proof. Consider the first case when series Eq. (4) diverges. Then we have

$$f(x_{k+1}) \leq f(x_k) - 2m||x_{k+1} - x_k||^2 \leq f(x_0) - 2m\sum_{i=0}^{k}||x_{i+1} - x_i||^2.$$

From this inequality it is easy to notice that, under our assumption on the divergence of series Eq. (4), the function f decreases infinitely on the sequence $\{x_k\}$. Let series Eq. (4) converge, then

$$||(f^o)'(w_k)|| = ||x_{k+1} - x_k|| \to 0 \quad \text{if} \quad k \to +\infty.$$

As the set $\mathcal{L}(x_0)$ is compact then the relations

$$f(x_k) \to \bar{f} > -\infty, \quad f^o(w_k) > \bar{f}$$

are true. Also by virtue of the construction the sequence $\{x_k\}$ is limited because $x_k \in \mathcal{L}(x_0)$. Therefore, the sequence of points $\{w_k\}$ is limited. Since the function f^o is continuously differentiable on R^n, then any limit point w^* of the sequence $\{w_k\}$ is a stationary point for the function f^o, that is, $(f^o)'(w^*) = 0$. The theorem is proved.

Remark 2. It is easy to see that for the convergence of the sequence $\{x_k\}$ series it is sufficient the convergence of a series $\sum\limits_{i=0}^{\infty} ||x_{i+1} - x_i|| < +\infty$.

Here is an example illustrating this algorithm for the difference of two quadratic forms with positive definite matrices.

Example 1. Consider the functions

$$f_1(x) = \frac{1}{2}\langle Ax, x\rangle + \langle c, x\rangle \quad f_2(x) = \frac{1}{2}\langle Bx, x\rangle, \quad x, c \in R^n,$$

where A and B are positive definite matrices.

It is obvious that the function f is smooth by R^n. Let the zero point $x_0 = 0$ be a starting point. If $c = 0$ then x_0 is the stationary point of the function f, otherwise we have $x_1 = \arg\min\limits_{x \in R^n} f_1(x) = -A^{-1}c$. Further put

$$\varphi_1(x) = f_1(x) - f_2(x_1) - \langle Bx_1, x - x_1\rangle, \; x_2 = -A^{-1}(c - Bx_1) = x_1 + A^{-1}Bx_1.$$

Similar to the previous cases we obtain

$$x_3 = -A^{-1}(c - Bx_2) = x_1 + A^{-1}B\,x_1 + \left(A^{-1}B\right)^2 x_1.$$

Let we find a point x_k, then

$$x_{k+1} = -A^{-1}(c - Bx_k) = x_1 + A^{-1}B\,x_1 + \cdots + \left(A^{-1}B\right)^k x_1 =$$

$$= \left[E + A^{-1}B + \cdots + \left(A^{-1}B\right)^k\right] x_1. \tag{5}$$

It is not difficult to notice that $||x_{k+1} - x_k|| = ||\left(A^{-1}B\right)^k x_1||$. Assume that all eigenvalues of the matrices $a^{-1}B$ are less than one, then the ratio is true

$$\sum_{i=0}^{\infty}\left(A^{-1}B\right)^i = \left(E - A^{-1}B\right)^{-1} =$$

$$= \left(A^{-1}A - A^{-1}B\right)^{-1} = \left(A^{-1}[A - B]\right)^{-1} = (A - B)^{-1}A.$$

If the sequence $\{x_k\}$ is infinite, then from Eq. (5) we have

$$x_k \to x^* = \sum_{i=0}^{\infty} \left(A^{-1}B\right)^i x_1 = (A-B)^{-1} Ax_1.$$

Let

$$f(x) = \bar{f}_1(x) - \bar{f}_2(x) = 1/2x_1^2 - 1/2x_2^2, \quad x = (x_1, x_2) \in R^2.$$

It is not difficult to see that the function f is unlimited from below.

Since functions $\bar{f}_1, \bar{f}_2$ are not strongly convex functions, then add to each of them a function $1/2\langle x, x\rangle$. Then $f(x) = f_1(x) - f_2(x)$, where

$$f_1(x) = 1/2\langle Ax, x\rangle, \ f_2(x) = 1/2\langle Bx, x\rangle, \ A = \begin{pmatrix} 2 & 0 \\ 0 & 1 \end{pmatrix} > 0, \quad B = \begin{pmatrix} 1 & 0 \\ 0 & 2 \end{pmatrix} > 0.$$

Case 1. Let $x_0 = (0,0) \in R^2$. Then we will not get out of the zero point, because $f_1'(x_0) = f_2'(x_0) = (0,0)$.

Case 2. Let $x_0 = (1,1) \in R^2$. Then

$$\varphi_1(x) = f_1(x) - f_2(x_0) - \langle Bx_0, x - x_0\rangle,$$

$$\varphi_1'(x) = Ax - Bx_0, \quad x_1 = A^{-1}Bx_0 = \begin{pmatrix} 0.5 & 0 \\ 0 & 2 \end{pmatrix} x_0.$$

And so on. On the k - step we find a point $x_k = \left(A^{-1}B\right)^k x_0$. Then

$$x_{k+1} - x_k = \left(A^{-1}B\right)^k \left(A^{-1}B - E\right) x_0 =$$

$$= \begin{pmatrix} (0.5)^k & 0 \\ 0 & 2^k \end{pmatrix} \begin{pmatrix} -0.5 & 0 \\ 0 & 1 \end{pmatrix} \begin{pmatrix} 1 \\ 1 \end{pmatrix} = \begin{pmatrix} (0.5)^k & 0 \\ 0 & 2^k \end{pmatrix} \begin{pmatrix} -0.5 \\ 1 \end{pmatrix} = \begin{pmatrix} -(0.5)^{k+1} \\ 2^k \end{pmatrix}.$$

Therefore, from a given starting point as a result of applying this of the algorithm, we obtain a sequence of points on which the function f is unbounded from below. Note that if we take a starting point $x_0 = (1,0) \in R^2$, then the resulting sequence of points $\{x_k\}$ tends to zero.

Example 2. Consider

$$f(x) = 5x^2 - |x| = 6x^2 - (|x| + x^2) = f_1(x) - f_2(x), \ x \in R.$$

Functions f_1, f_2 are strongly convex. The function f is unbounded from above, it has two global minimizers $x_1^* = -0.1, x_2^* = 0.1, \ f(x_1^*) = f(x_2^*) = -0.05$, and a local minimizer $x_0^* = 0$.

For every point $x_0 \in R$

$$f(x_0) = 6x^2 - (|x_0| + x^2) - \langle w(x_0), x - x_0\rangle,$$

where $w(x_0) \in \partial f_2(x_0), \ f_2(x) = |x| + x^2, \ x \in R$. Consider some variants of choosing subgradients at the point $x_0 = 0$.

1. Let $w(x_0) = 1$. At this case
$$\varphi_0(x) = 5x^2 - x, \ \min_{x \in R} f_0(x) = f_0(x_1), \ x_1 = 0.1,$$
Form function $\varphi_1(x) = 5x^2 - x = \varphi_0(x)$. Then $x_2 = x_1$
$$\partial f_1(x_1) = f_{\prime}^1(x_1) = 0.2, \quad \partial f_2(x_1) = f_{\prime}^2(x_1) = 0.2.$$
Therefore the point x_1 is an inf - stationary point for the function f.
2. Let $w(x_0) = -1$, then we give a point $\overline{x}_2 = -0.1$, which is an inf-stationary point for the function f.
3. Let $w(x_0) = 0$, then $\varphi_0(x) = 5x^2$ and $x_1 = 0$. Therefore the point x_0 is a q-stationary point for the function f.

If the sequence $\{x_k\}$ is finite, then, by construction, the last received point is an inf - stationary point of the function f on R^n. If the sequence $\{x_k\}$ is infinite, then the theorem similar to Theorem 2 holds. Unfortunately, under this choice of a subgradient w_k we also cannot claim that any limit point of the sequence $\{x_k\}$ is an inf-stationary point of the function f on R^n.

2.2 Algorithm 2

Step 1. Take the arbitrary point $x_0 \in R^n$. If the condition (1.2) holds then x_0 is an inf - stationary point of the function f and the process is finished.
Step 2. Let we find a point $x_k \in R^n$. If at the point x_k necessary condition (1.2) holds, then the point x_k - inf is a stationary point for the function f and the process is finished. Otherwise, choose an arbitrary subgradient $w(x_k)$ from the condition $w_k = w(x_k) \in \partial f_2(x_k) \backslash \partial f_1(x_k)$. Let
$$f_k(x) = \psi(x, x_k) = f_1(x) - f_2(x_k) - \langle w_k, x - x_k \rangle.$$
Find $\min_{x \in R^n} f_k(x) = f_k(x_{k+1})$. Herewith
$$f(x_{k+1}) \leq f(x_k) - m||x_{k+1} - x_k||^2.$$
If the sequence $\{x_k\}$ is finite, then by construction the last received point is an inf - stationary point of the function f on R^n. If the sequence $\{x_k\}$ is infinite, then the theorem similar to Theorem 2 holds. Unfortunately, under this choice of a subgradient w_k we also cannot claim that any limit point of the sequence $\{x_k\}$ is an inf - the stationary point of the function f on R^n.

3 Conclusion

The class of d.c. functions covers a broad family of nonconvex and often nondifferentiable functions. D.c. functions are widely used in many areas such as optimization, machine learning and statistics [16,17]. In the computational aspect the considered algorithm is significantly simplified in the case of minimizing of the difference of polyhedral functions, since in this case the quasidifferential of d.c. function consists of two polyhedra.

References

1. Hiriart-Urruty, J.-B.: From convex minimization to nonconvex minimization: necessary and sufficient conditions for global optimality. In: Clarke, F.N., Demyanov, V.F., Giannessi, F. (eds.) Nonsmooth Optimization and Related Topics. Ettore Majorana International Science Series, vol. 43, pp. 219–239. Springer, Boston (1989). https://doi.org/10.1007/978-1-4757-6019-4_13
2. Martínez-Legaz, J.-E., Volle, M.: Duality in D.C. programming: the case of several D.C. constraints. J. Math. Anal. Appl. **237**(2), 657–671 (1999). https://doi.org/10.1006/jmaa.1999.6496
3. Polyakova, L.N.: Necessary conditions for an extremum of quasidifferentiable functions. Vestnik St. Petersburg Univ. Math. **13**, 57–62 (1980). (In Russian)
4. Polyakova, L.: On global unconstrained minimization of the difference of polyhedral functions. J. Glob. Optim. **50**(2), 179–195 (2011). https://doi.org/10.1007/s10898-010-9589-6
5. Polyakova, L.N., Karelin, V.V.: On a continuous method for minimizing of nonsmooth functions. In: Petrosyan, L.A., Zhabko, A.P. (eds.) International Conference "Stability and Control Processes" in Memory of V.I. Zubov SCP 2015, pp. 338–341. IEEE (2015). https://doi.org/10.1109/SCP.2015.7342133
6. Stavroulakis, G.E., Polyakova, L.N.: Difference convex opitimization techniques in nonsmooth computational mechanics. Optim. Meth. Softw. **2**, 57–81 (1996). https://doi.org/10.1080/10556789608805644
7. Strekalovskij, A.S.: To a problem of a global extremum. Dokl. USSR Acad. Sci. **292**(5), 1062–1066 (1989). (In Russian)
8. Tao, P.D., Hoai An, L.T.: Convex analysis approaches to DC programming: theory, algorithms and applications. Acta Math. Vietnam. **22**(1), 289–355 (1997)
9. Thoai, N.V.: A modified version of Tuy's method for solving D.C. programming problems. Optimization **19**(5), 665–674 (1988)
10. Törn, A., Žilinskas, A. (eds.): Global Optimization. LNCS, vol. 350. Springer, Heidelberg (1989). https://doi.org/10.1007/3-540-50871-6
11. Tuy, H.: Global minimization of a difference of two convex functions. Math. Program. Study **30**, 150–182 (1983)
12. Leichtweiß, K.: Konvexe Mengen. Hochschultext, 1st edn. Springer-Verlag, Berlin (1980)
13. Rockafellar, R.T.: Convex Analysis. Princeton University Press, Princeton (1970)
14. Demyanov, V.F., Rubinov, A.M.: Quasidifferential Calculus. Optimization Software Inc. Publications Division, New-York (1986)
15. Demyanov, V.F., Stavroulakis, G.E., Polyakova, L.N., Panagiotopoulos, P.D.: Quasidifferentiability and Nonsmooth Modelling in Mechanics Engineering and Economics. Kluwer Academic, Dordrecht (1996)
16. Stankova, E.N., Balakshiy, A.V., Petrov, D.A., Shorov, A.V., Korkhov, V.V.: Using technologies of OLAP and machine learning for validation of the numerical models of convective clouds. In: Gervasi, O., et al. (eds.) ICCSA 2016. LNCS, vol. 9788, pp. 463–472. Springer, Cham (2016). https://doi.org/10.1007/978-3-319-42111-7_36
17. Stankova, E.N., Ismailova, E.T., Grechko, I.A.: Algorithm for processing the results of cloud convection simulation using the methods of machine learning. In: Gervasi, O., et al. (eds.) ICCSA 2018. LNCS, vol. 10963, pp. 149–159. Springer, Cham (2018). https://doi.org/10.1007/978-3-319-95171-3_13

Industrial Fisheye Image Segmentation Using Neural Networks

A. Beloshapko[1(✉)], V. Korkhov[1], C. Knoll[2], and U. Iben[2]

[1] Saint-Petersburg State University, 7/9 Universitetskaya nab., St. Petersburg 199034, Russia
beloshapko-alexey@rambler.ru, v.korkhov@spbu.ru

[2] Robert Bosch GmbH, Robert-Bosch-Campus 1, 71272 Renningen, Germany
{Christian.Knoll,Uwe.Iben}@de.bosch.com

Abstract. Fisheye cameras have recently became very popular in computer vision applications due to their wide field of view. In addition to a better overview of the surrounding area, they enable to capture objects at extremely close ranges. These advantages come at a cost of strong image distortion, which cannot be removed completely maintaining image continuity. This complicates the use of traditional computer vision algorithms, which expect a single image as an input. This paper presents a performance evaluation of neural network algorithms for object detection and segmentation on fisheye camera images. Three approaches are evaluated: semantic image segmentation with Fully Convolutional Network (FCN) [13], a fully convolutional approach to instance segmentation with U-Net [18] and a region-based approach to instance segmentation with Mask R-CNN [10]. All of these networks successfully solved the task. However, as they were designed to different purposes, each of them has its own strengths and shortcomings. These three approaches are used to perform euro container image segmentation task. An image dataset was created in order to train and evaluate these algorithms. Huge part of this dataset was generated artificially, which simplified the task of ground truth labeling. The power of neural networks enable for fast and reliable image segmentation. As to our knowledge, this is the first neural networks application for euro container fisheye image detection and segmentation.

Keywords: Fisheye cameras · Euro container detection · Image semantic segmentation · Image instance segmentation · FCN · Mask R-CNN · U-Net

1 Introduction

Warehouse automation is an area with a huge potential. The use of robots that handle euro containers can both improve workplace ergonomics and safety, as well as reduce operational expenses. One major problem that has to be solved is the development of an automatic box picking and carrying system, which uses optical devices to detect, localize and track boxes using optical cameras as

S. Misra et al. (Eds.): ICCSA 2019, LNCS 11622, pp. 678–690, 2019.
https://doi.org/10.1007/978-3-030-24305-0_50

sensors. Thus, there is a need for a reliable real-time box detection algorithm that will process images from cameras and locate objects of interest on them. Despite that, there are classical computer vision algorithms that are capable to detect objects of known shapes or properties; they are not robust enough to the appearance change or occlusion. The same applies to euro container objects. Introduction of a new type of a container may require the algorithm manual fine-tuning or even its complete reimplementation.

On the other hand, machine learning approaches offer a flexibility to tune the algorithm automatically when new object types become available. Use of machine learning based algorithm can make system setup much faster and more intuitive. The most promising type of machine learning algorithm is a convolutional neural network.

In this paper, we evaluate performance of three neural network-based approaches applied to the task of euro container image detection and segmentation. One of the methods does image semantic segmentation, while the other two perform image instance segmentation.

Semantic segmentation algorithm assigns a class label to each pixel on the image. Thus, an object can be detected as a continuous blob of pixels of the same class label. However, this approach cannot distinguish between different objects of the same class. This can give misleading results in case when more than one box is present on the same image. Instance segmentation algorithms additionally perform object detection, which enable to distinguish between multiple objects captured on the same image.

In this paper, we use Fully Convolutional Network (FCN) as a basis for semantic segmentation algorithm. Though some newer approaches exist (like DeepLab, [4], PSPNet [28]), it still outperforms many others in terms of speed (see [27]). U-Net and Mask R-CNN networks are evaluated to solve the instance segmentation task.

2 Related Work

There are several approaches to object detection in warehouse environment. In [14] Faster R-CNN neural network [17] is used for pallet detection on 2D range images. Master thesis of [21] describes an implementation of box detection and segmentation algorithm based on Point Cloud Library. Neither of them uses images acquired with fisheye camera, and thus impose a distance limitation on a system. Also, a typical object of interest of [21] has a relatively simple shape (a rectangular box with planar sides). These assumptions are violated in case of euro containers.

Fisheye cameras are a very popular choice in automotive applications, as they enable to capture the whole surrounding area with four cameras only. Autonomous driving task may benefit of urban scenes image segmentation. Authors of [19] developed a neural network algorithms applied to urban scenes fisheye image segmentation. Authors of [8] introduced Overlapping Pyramid Pooling and zooming image augmentation technique to train an OPP-net to perform fisheye image segmentation of traffic scenes. These works are similar to ours because camera calibration is not assumed. In [7] a novel approach with deformable convolutions was used to solve a similar task. Deformable convolutions are meant to compensate for severe image distortion, but they has to be trained at each pixel location. We have shown that in the task of euro pallets image segmentation this feature is not strictly required.

There are several works related to fisheye image processing with neural networks. The work of [16] presents a fairly simple neural network architecture for robot navigation using a single fisheye camera. Works of [23] and [5] present approaches to spherical image processing with neural networks. These works require a calibrated camera, which imposes an additional limitation on the algorithm application.

As to our knowledge, this paper present a first attempt to use fisheye camera for object detection and segmentation in warehouses. We are not going to use any specialized network for fisheye image segmentation to avoid the need of camera calibration. Instead, we focus on using neural network algorithms that are initially designed to handle images captured with commonly used narrow-angle cameras.

There is a plenty of neural networks designed to handle object image segmentation. They fall into two distinct groups: neural networks for image semantic segmentation and neural networks for instance segmentation.

FCN is one of the simplest and most effective networks for image semantic segmentation. It uses a backbone classification network to create a coarse image segmentation map, and then iteratively upscales the result and refines it with skip-connections. SegNet network [1] improves this approach by introducing non-linear upsampling. Work of [26] introduced dilated convolutions to image segmentation neural network. Dilated convolutions replaced pooling layers typical to image classification network to enable dense multi-scale feature computation. In the work [3] this architecture was further developed by adding Fully Connected CRFs to refine the final segmentation result. PSPNet [28] used pyramid pooling to iteratively refine the segmentation mask, starting from high-level context and combining the intermediate result with lower-level features. The authors of [4] combined ideas of dilated convolutions, residual blocks and spatial pooling in a single network DeepLab v3. This network showed a great performance improvement over the original FCN network.

Instance segmentation neural networks additionally enable to distinguish between object instances of the same class. Most of them are region-based, that is, they use an object detection network like Faster R-CNN [17] to separate different object instances. One of the most notable implementation is the Mask R-CNN [10] which is based on Faster R-CNN object detection network and provides one additional output for dense image segmentation. The latest version of this network uses pyramid pooling as well. Some improvement was shown by the latest MaskLab [2] network, which is also built on top of the Faster R-CNN architecture, but also generates direction map, which enables to further separate objects from each other. Other region-based neural network architectures include SharpMask [15], OMN [9], RNN for Semantic Instance Segmentation [20].

On the other hand, there are several existing approaches that do not rely on a pre-generated object regions. U-Net [18] improves the idea of a Fully Convolutional Network with a more general skip-connection type and a weighted loss function that improves segmentation accuracy near image edges. Thus, distinct objects appear separated with a thin boundary. TernausNetV2 [11] adopts this idea to satellite imagery. Authors of [25] suggested to augment FCN architecture with the MaskSplitter strategy that penalize the loss when more than one object correspond to a single mask region (and vice versa).

The biggest challenge of the task of euro container image segmentation is to distinguish between an actual container and the industrial environment on the highest semantic scale. Both environment and the object of interest lack of visual features, contain a lot of parallel straight lines. In most of the cases, the object of interest is well aligned with the environment, which makes it hard to extract. Fisheye camera distortion introduces additional difficulty to the task.

We aim to overcome these problems with the use of neural networks, which can learn high-level features in an automatic manner. However, care should be taken in order to avoid model overfitting. Usually, this is done through either enhancement of the training dataset or restriction of the model structure.

Our target is to fulfill the following requirements:

- High box detection rate (≥99%) and high segmentation accuracy (≥0.95 IoU metric value)
- Fast inference (less than 1s per image on a GPU)
- Low memory consumption during training (11 GB or less)

We assume that objects of interest have a nearly-rectangular shape. Given these requirements, we have decided to avoid dilated convolutions and extensive pyramid pooling as they raise memory consumption during training. Also, CRF and RNN strategies could potentially violate the fast inference requirement. Thus, we evaluate three network architectures that are lightweight, fast and accurate:

- FCN for image semantic segmentation
- Mask-RCNN as a region-based instance segmentation network
- U-Net as a fully-convolutional instance segmentation network

3 Methods

3.1 Classification Neural Network

Each of the networks for image segmentation uses a classification network for image pre-processing. A typical classification network like AlexNet [12], VGG [22], or GoogLeNet [24] consist of two parts, e.g. Fig. 1. First part consists of blocks of convolutional layers followed by pooling layers. This block is connected to an input image. Convolutional layers compute feature maps of the image while pooling layers reduce spatial dimensionality. Second part of a network consists of a stack of fully connected layers. It takes the last feature map from the lower part and process it to generate a classification hypothesis. The input of such a classification network is an image, and the output is usually a vector of scores for each of image classes.

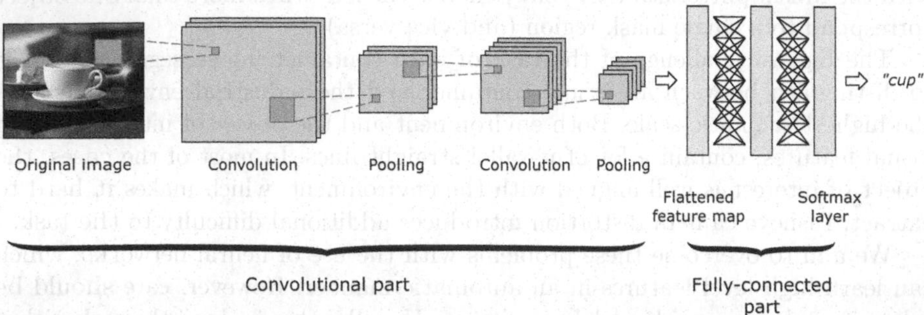

Fig. 1. Structure of a simple classification network which does cup image classification. This network consists of two convolution layers followed by spatial pooling, then two fully-connected layers and a softmax block. Blue rectangles represent 2D image feature maps, while green ones represent 1D layer activation (Color figure online)

3.2 Fully Convolutional Network

The Fully Convolutional Network [13] idea is fairly simple. First, consider a classification network that takes a small part of an image as an input and generates a score that a particular object is present on this image patch. A convolution of an input image with a classification network would generate a score map, e.g. Fig. 2.

This can be achieved by turning a classification network into a fully-convolutional one. Fully-connected layers of a classification network can be represented with convolutional layers with large kernel size.

FCN uses such a network to generate a raw image segmentation. Then, it additionally performs intelligent score map upsampling. It does a raw score map upsampling with a bilinear interpolation and combines upscaled map with a feature map generated by the classifier, e.g. Fig. 3 for an example. This operation is meant to propagate low-scale details to the upsampled score map and is repeated several times to achieve the same score map resolution as of the input image.

We use VGG-19 as a classification network to implement the FCN. The number of classes is reduced to two (object of interest and the background). The classification network weights are pre-trained on the imagenet [6] dataset.

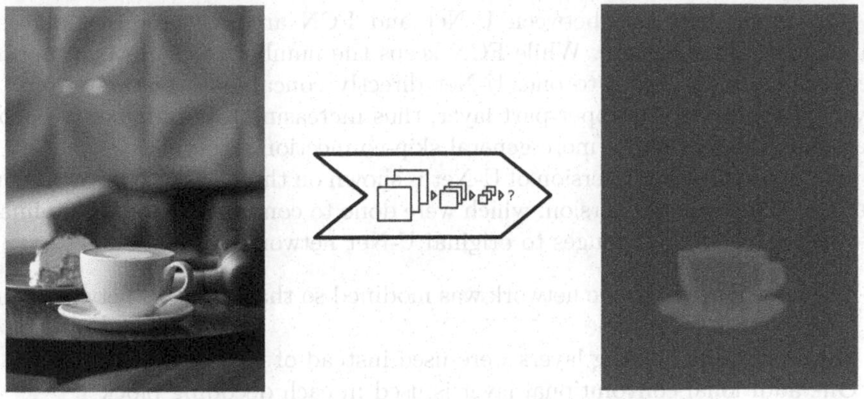

Fig. 2. Image convolution with a classification network generates a score "heatmap". Higher values (red) mean higher probability that an object of interest occupies this particular pixel. (Color figure online)

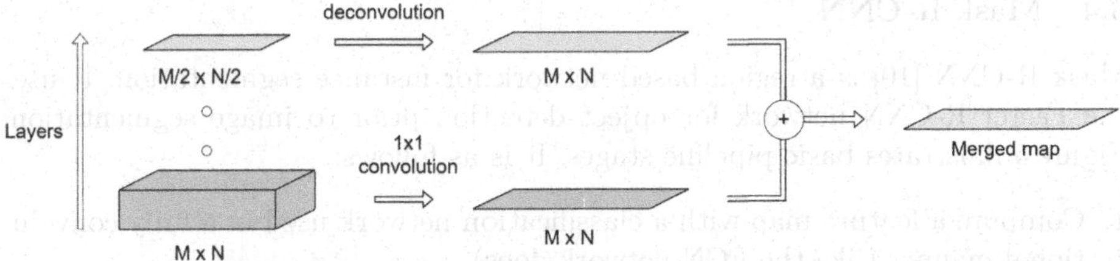

Fig. 3. A scheme of FCN skip-connection. When upsampling the raw score map, a classifier-generated feature maps are used to enhance localization. First, a low-level feature layer is convolved with a kernel of shape $[1 \times 1 \times \text{channels}]$ to reduce the number of channels to 1. The score map being upsampled is deconvolved with 2×2 deconvolution kernel. Finally, these score maps are combined elementwise. The resulting score map has double resolution while being more detailed than the original one.

3.3 U-Net

U-Net network architecture is very similar to the FCN one. A classification network is used in a fully convolutional manner to generate intermediate feature maps. The subsequent part performs an iterative upsampling combined with feature concatenation.

The main difference between U-Net and FCN architectures is a different skip-connection structure. While FCN keeps the number of channels of upsampled feature maps equal to one, U-Net directly concatenate features from the lower-part layer to the upper-part layer, thus increasing total number of output channels. This leads to a more general skip-connection structure.

The structure of our version of U-Net is shown on the Fig. 4. There are several changes to the original version, which were done to compensate for higher image resolution. The main changes to original U-Net network structure are:

- The encoder part of the network was modified so that VGG-19 network could be used as a backbone
- Total of 5 max pooling layers were used instead of 4
- One additional convolutional layer is used in each decoding block
- A pretrained VGG-19 network was used to initialize encoder weights
- Batch normalization layer was inserted after each non-initialized convolutional layer

3.4 Mask R-CNN

Mask R-CNN [10] is a region based network for instance segmentation. It uses the Faster R-CNN network for object detection prior to image segmentation. Figure 5 illustrates basic pipeline stages. It is as follows:

1. Compute a feature map with a classification network used in a fully convolutional manner (like the FCN network does)
2. Generate bounding box proposals. This is done via Faster-RCNN pipeline. First, a predefined set of anchor boxes are tested against "objectness" metric. Then, bounding box proposals are refined.
3. Perform classification and segmentation of each image patch defined by a bounding box proposals.

The result of this procedure is a set of classified and segmented image patches. These patches can possibly overlap while belonging to the same class. Thus, the network tries to distinguish between different instances of a single object class.

We used a Mask-RCNN implementation with Feature Pyramid Network integrated. The input to the FPN is downsampled to the size of 56×56 pixels (this technique is called "minimask"). This is done to limit memory consumption during training. The ResNet-101 was used as a classification backbone.

Table 1 summarises differences between these 3 networks.

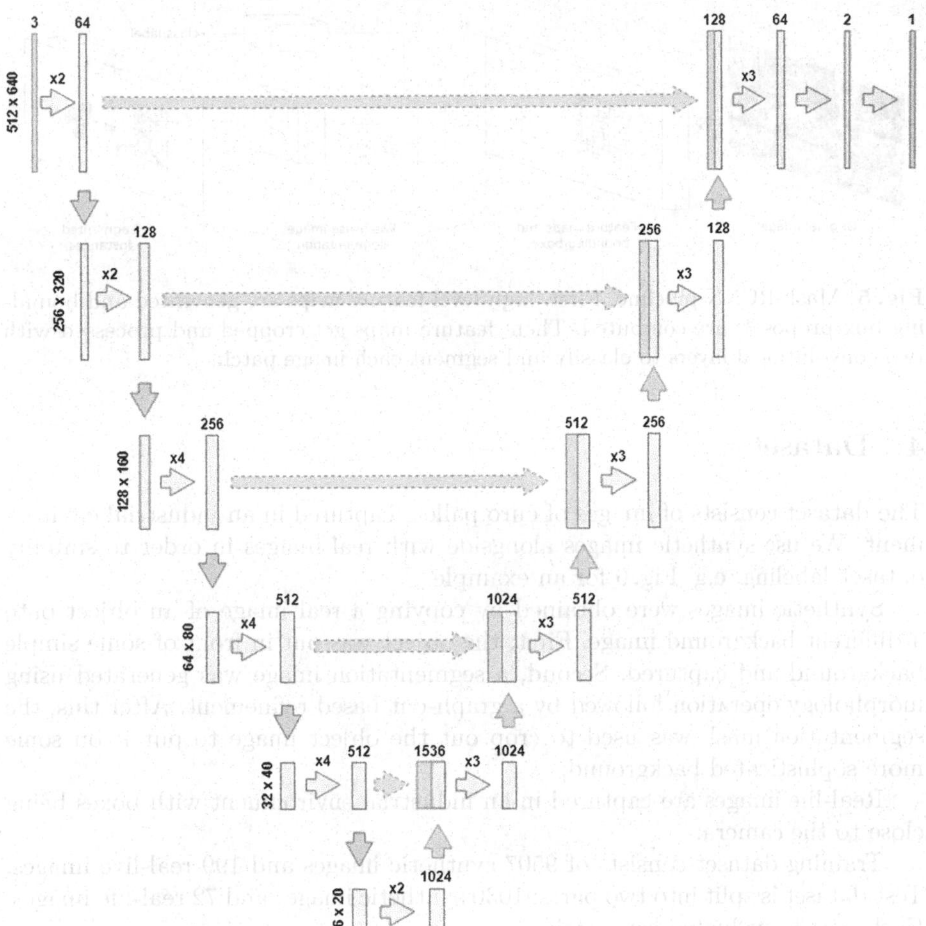

Fig. 4. A scheme of U-Net used in this paper. An input frame is a 3-channel image with resolution of 640 × 512 pixels. Red arrows depict downsampling procedure with the stride of 2, green arrows do 2 × 2 deconvolution. Gray arrows perform 3 × 3 convolution multiple times. Blue lines represent feature map concatenation (U-Net skip-connection). (Color figure online)

Table 1. Feature comparison of the three neural network architectures

Feature	FCN	U-Net	Mask R-CNN
Image segmentation	Yes	Yes	Yes
Object detection	No	Yes	Yes
Overlapping objects detection	No	No	Yes
Pixel-to-pixel segmentation	Yes	Yes	No (with minimask feature enabled)

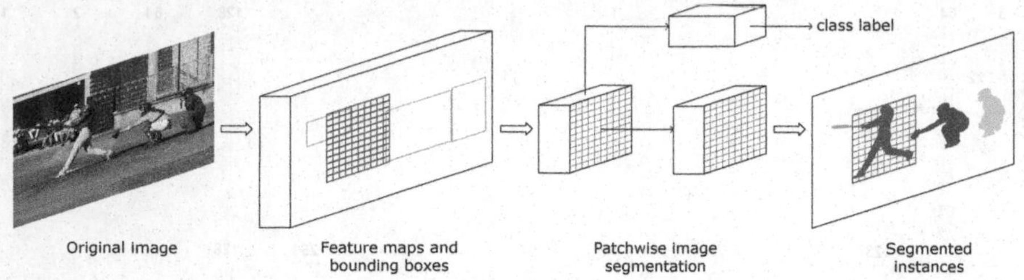

Fig. 5. Mask-RCNN pipeline. First, high-level feature maps are generated and bounding box proposals are computed. Then, feature maps get cropped and processed with two convolutional layers to classify and segment each image patch.

4 Dataset

The dataset consists of images of euro pallets captured in an industrial environment. We use synthetic images alongside with real images in order to simplify dataset labeling, e.g. Fig. 6 for an example.

Synthetic images were obtained by copying a real image of an object onto a different background image. First, the object was put in front of some simple background and captured. Second, a segmentation image was generated using morphology operation followed by a graph-cut based refinement. After this, the segmentation mask was used to crop out the object image to put it on some more sophisticated background.

Real-life images are captured in an industrial environment with boxes being close to the camera.

Training dataset consists of 9507 synthetic images and 199 real-live images. Test dataset is split into two parts: 1030 synthetic images and 72 real-life images. Each part is evaluated separately.

5 Experiments

The networks were trained on a machine with 4 Nvidia GeForce 1080 Ti GPUs. The input images have size of 512 × 640 pixels. It took around one day to fully train the FCN network while U-Net and Mask-RCNN took 3 days to train.

The accuracy of image segmentation was evaluated with the IoU metric. Assume that A represents the ground-truth entity of pixels that belong to box region, and B is the pixel entity predicted with a neural network. The IoU metric is calculated with the following formulae:

$$IoU = \frac{|A \cap B|}{|A \cup B|}$$

Fig. 6. An example of artificial and real-live test images

Thus, this metric captures how well the ground-truth and the predicted region overlap with each other. The metric is normalized to be in the range from 0 to 1, where higher is better.

In Table 2 you can see averaged IoU metric calculated over both synthetic and real-life parts of the test image set.

Table 2. Intersection over union score of the trained models evaluated on synthetic and real-life part of the test dataset

IoU	FCN	U-Net	Mask R-CNN
Synthetic images (1030)	0.9898	0.9921	0.9785
Real-life images (72)	0.9739	0.9544	0.9731

FCN and Mask R-CNN show comparable accuracy. The U-Net network shows better results on synthetic dataset, but performs poorly on real-life images. This might indicate overfitting of the U-Net network.

Figure 7 shows some cases of test images processing with these three networks.

Table 3 shows average processing time for each of the networks. FCN shows the best performance with processing more than 10 frames per second. Mask-RCNN is able to process around 5–6 frames per second. U-Net has the longest processing time.

Table 3. Average processing time for each of the networks

Time, seconds	FCN	U-Net	Mask R-CNN
Real-life images (72)	0.08785	0.31466	0.170926

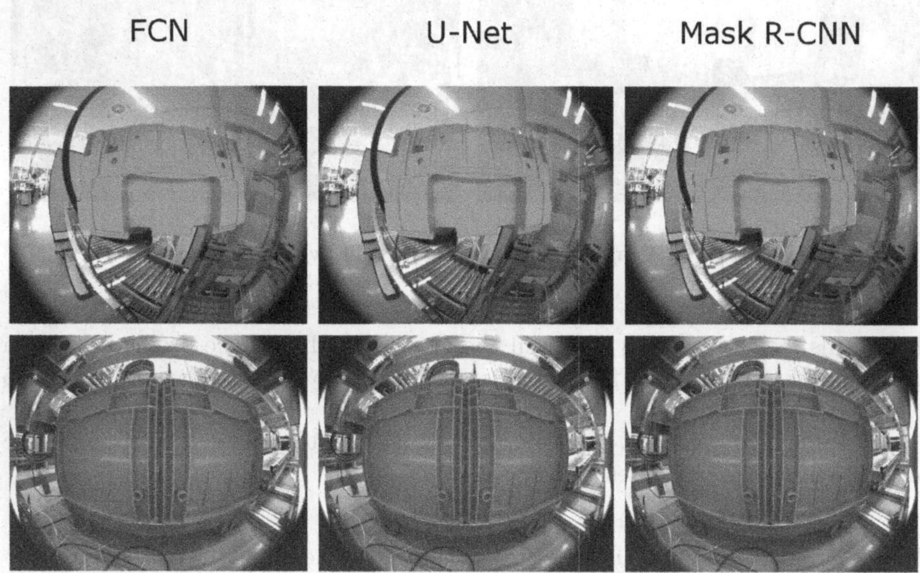

Fig. 7. Some examples of images processed with the trained models. Red area is an estimated box region. Upper row of images were obtained through processing an artificial image, while lower row contains processed real-life images. (Color figure online)

6 Discussion

All the networks reach the desired accuracy. FCN provides both best accuracy and computation time, but lacks of object detection capabilities. Mask-RCNN is twice slower than FCN and has slightly lower segmentation accuracy, but enables for object detection. U-Net based on VGG-19 has the worst performance.

Given that, it is better to use Mask-RCNN when object detection is required, and to use FCN for pure semantic segmentation tasks. U-Net architecture could be further improved to approach the accuracy of FCN network by changing its hyperparameters or by choosing a different backbone network.

7 Conclusion

All of the networks (FCN, Mask R-CNN and U-Net) reach the required performance and are able to handle fisheye image segmentation directly without any rectification. FCN provide box image segmentation of an excellent quality. Mask R-CNN can be used to additionally distinguish between several box instances. U-Net has to be further constrained to reach the performance of Mask R-CNN neural network.

Acknowledgments. This work is supported by the German-Russian Interdisciplinary Science Center (G-RISC) funded by the German Federal Foreign Office via the German Academic Exchange Service (DAAD).

References

1. Badrinarayanan, V., Kendall, A., Cipolla, R.: Segnet: a deep convolutional encoder-decoder architecture for image segmentation. CoRR abs/1511.00561 (2015). http://arxiv.org/abs/1511.00561
2. Chen, L., Hermans, A., Papandreou, G., Schroff, F., Wang, P., Adam, H.: Masklab: instance segmentation by refining object detection with semantic and direction features. CoRR abs/1712.04837 (2017). http://arxiv.org/abs/1712.04837
3. Chen, L., Papandreou, G., Kokkinos, I., Murphy, K., Yuille, A.L.: Deeplab: semantic image segmentation with deep convolutional nets, atrous convolution, and fully connected CRFS. CoRR abs/1606.00915 (2016). http://arxiv.org/abs/1606.00915
4. Chen, L., Papandreou, G., Schroff, F., Adam, H.: Rethinking atrous convolution for semantic image segmentation. CoRR abs/1706.05587 (2017). http://arxiv.org/abs/1706.05587
5. Coors, B., Condurache, A.P., Geiger, A.: Spherenet: learning spherical representations for detection and classification in omnidirectional images. In: European Conference on Computer Vision (ECCV), September 2018. http://www.cvlibs.net/publications/Coors2018ECCV.pdf
6. Deng, J., Dong, W., Socher, R., Li, L.J., Li, K., Fei-Fei, L.: ImageNet: a large-scale hierarchical image database. In: CVPR 2009 (2009)
7. Deng, L., Yang, M., Li, H., Li, T., Hu, B., Wang, C.: Restricted deformable convolution based road scene semantic segmentation using surround view cameras. CoRR abs/1801.00708 (2018). http://arxiv.org/abs/1801.00708
8. Deng, L., Yang, M., Qian, Y., Wang, C., Wang, B.: CNN-based semantic segmentation for urban traffic scenes using fisheye camera, pp. 231–236, June 2017. https://doi.org/10.1109/IVS.2017.7995725, https://www.researchgate.net/publication/318805934_CNN_based_semantic_segmentation_for_urban_traffic_scenes_using_fisheye_camera
9. Hayder, Z., He, X., Salzmann, M.: Shape-aware instance segmentation. CoRR abs/1612.03129 (2016). http://arxiv.org/abs/1612.03129
10. He, K., Gkioxari, G., Dollár, P., Girshick, R.B.: Mask R-CNN. CoRR abs/1703.06870 (2017). http://arxiv.org/abs/1703.06870
11. Iglovikov, V.I., Seferbekov, S.S., Buslaev, A.V., Shvets, A.: Ternausnetv2: fully convolutional network for instance segmentation. CoRR abs/1806.00844 (2018). http://arxiv.org/abs/1806.00844

12. Krizhevsky, A., Sutskever, I., Hinton, G.E.: Imagenet classification with deep convolutional neural networks. In: Pereira, F., Burges, C.J.C., Bottou, L., Weinberger, K.Q. (eds.) Advances in Neural Information Processing Systems, vol. 25, pp. 1097–1105. Curran Associates Inc., New York (2012). http://papers.nips.cc/paper/4824-imagenet-classification-with-deep-convolutional-neural-networks.pdf
13. Long, J., Shelhamer, E., Darrell, T.: Fully convolutional networks for semantic segmentation. CoRR abs/1411.4038 (2014). http://arxiv.org/abs/1411.4038
14. Mohamed, I.S., Capitanelli, A., Mastrogiovanni, F., Rovetta, S., Zaccaria, R.: Detection, localisation and tracking of pallets using machine learning techniques and 2D range data. CoRR abs/1803.11254 (2018). http://arxiv.org/abs/1803.11254
15. Pinheiro, P.H.O., Lin, T., Collobert, R., Dollár, P.: Learning to refine object segments. CoRR abs/1603.08695 (2016). http://arxiv.org/abs/1603.08695
16. Ran, L., Zhang, Y., Zhang, Q., Yang, T.: Convolutional neural network-based robot navigation using uncalibrated spherical images. Sensors **17**, 1341 (2017)
17. Ren, S., He, K., Girshick, R.B., Sun, J.: Faster R-CNN: towards real-time object detection with region proposal networks. CoRR abs/1506.01497 (2015). http://arxiv.org/abs/1506.01497
18. Ronneberger, O., Fischer, P., Brox, T.: U-net: convolutional networks for biomedical image segmentation. CoRR abs/1505.04597 (2015). http://arxiv.org/abs/1505.04597
19. Saez, A., Bergasa, L., Romeral, E., Guillén, M., Barea, R., Sanz, R.: CNN-based fisheye image real-time semantic segmentation, pp. 1039–1044, June 2018. https://doi.org/10.1109/IVS.2018.8500456
20. Salvador, A., Bellver, M., Baradad, M., Marqués, F., Torres, J., Giró i Nieto, X.: Recurrent neural networks for semantic instance segmentation. CoRR abs/1712.00617 (2017). http://arxiv.org/abs/1712.00617
21. Shipitko, O.: 3D pose estimation algorithm for intelligent box picking of warehouse automation robot (2018). https://www.researchgate.net/publication/325780223_3D_pose_estimation_algorithm_for_intelligent_box_picking_of_warehouse_automation_robot
22. Simonyan, K., Zisserman, A.: Very deep convolutional networks for large-scale image recognition. CoRR abs/1409.1556 (2014). http://arxiv.org/abs/1409.1556
23. Su, Y., Grauman, K.: Flat2sphere: learning spherical convolution for fast features from 360° imagery. CoRR abs/1708.00919 (2017). https://arxiv.org/pdf/1708.00919.pdf
24. Szegedy, C., et al.: Going deeper with convolutions. CoRR abs/1409.4842 (2014). http://arxiv.org/abs/1409.4842
25. Ter-Sarkisov, A., Ross, R.J., Kelleher, J.D., Earley, B., Keane, M.: Beef cattle instance segmentation using fully convolutional neural network. CoRR abs/1807.01972 (2018). http://arxiv.org/abs/1807.01972
26. Yu, F., Koltun, V.: Multi-scale context aggregation by dilated convolutions. CoRR abs/1511.07122 (2015). http://arxiv.org/abs/1511.07122
27. Zhao, H., Qi, X., Shen, X., Shi, J., Jia, J.: ICNet for real-time semantic segmentation on high-resolution images. In: Ferrari, V., Hebert, M., Sminchisescu, C., Weiss, Y. (eds.) ECCV 2018. LNCS, vol. 11207, pp. 418–434. Springer, Cham (2018). https://doi.org/10.1007/978-3-030-01219-9_25
28. Zhao, H., Shi, J., Qi, X., Wang, X., Jia, J.: Pyramid scene parsing network. CoRR abs/1612.01105 (2016). http://arxiv.org/abs/1612.01105

Parameter Estimation Problems in Markov Random Processes

Vladimir Karelin(✉), Alexander Fominyh, Stanislav Myshkov, and Lyudmila Polyakova

St. Petersburg State University,
7/9 Universitetskaya nab., St. Petersburg 199034, Russia
vkarelin@mail.ru, alexfomster@mail.ru, skmyshkov@mail.ru, lnpol07@mail.ru
http://www.springer.com/gp/computer-science/lncs

Abstract. Problems of convergence and stability of Bayesian estimates in the identification of stochastic control systems are considered. The informational measure of the mismatch between the estimated distribution and the estimate is the main apparatus for establishing the fact of convergence. The choice of a priori distribution of parameters is not always obvious. The Kullback-Leibler information number is taken as such measure. The convergence of the estimates of the transition function of the process to the non-stationary transition function is established in this paper. The problem of synthesis of optimal strategies for dynamic systems in which there is no part of the main information needed for constructing the optimal control is also considered. It is assumed that the system contains at least one unknown parameter belonging to some parameter space. Therefore, the class of control systems considered in the article is the class of parametric adaptive systems.

Keywords: Bayesian probability theory · Parameter estimation · Kullback-Leibler information number

1 Introduction

Recently in connection with the presentation of increasingly higher requirements to control processes in various fields of technology there appeared a need in the management of such objects for which not only there is no adequate mathematical model but sometimes even general qualitative research is little studied. An emerging approach for new control problems is based on the idea of adapting a control system to the properties of particular objects to which it refers is known in advance.

Let the process $x_t \in X \subset R^m$ be observed. It is assumed that the conditional distribution $P_t(x_{t+1}|x^t, \theta)$ depends on a parameter $\theta \in \Theta$ the value of which is not known, but is constant throughout the experiment. This situation occurs, for example, when

$$x_{t+1} = f(x_t, \theta, \eta_t),$$

S. Misra et al. (Eds.): ICCSA 2019, LNCS 11622, pp. 691–701, 2019.
https://doi.org/10.1007/978-3-030-24305-0_51

where $\eta_t, t = 1,...$ is a sequence of independent identically distributed random variables and η_t does not depend on $x_t \in X \subset R^m$.

In mathematical statistics there are many methods for parameter estimation. For example, the minimax approach [1], where statistical decisions are evaluated according to the "worst" possible values of θ or the Bayesian approach in which for an unknown parameter θ some distribution $\nu(d\theta)$ called a priori distribution is defined on $(\Theta, \mathcal{F})$.

In the paper we consider the Bayesian approach. Further we assume that $P_\theta(dx_t|x^t) = P_t(dx_t|x^t, \theta)$. Let $\nu(d\theta)$ belong to some family $\aleph$.

Assume that the family $\aleph$ is dominated by a measure $n(d\theta)$. A density $\nu(d\theta)$ with respect to $n(d\theta)$ is denoted by $\nu(d\theta)$. Suppose that $\varphi(\theta)$ is some measurable function of a parameter θ.

Definition 1. *The function $\nu_t(\theta|x^t)$ is called a posteriori distribution density of θ.*

Definition 2. *The value*

$$\bar{\varphi}(x^t) = \int_{\Theta} \varphi(\theta)\nu_t(\theta|x^t)n(d\theta)$$

is called the Bayesian estimate of the function $\varphi(\theta)$,

where

$$\nu_t(\theta|x^t) = \frac{P_\theta(x^t)\nu_0(\theta)}{\int_{\Theta} P_\theta(x^t)\nu_0(\theta)n(d\theta)}. \tag{1}$$

We study the Bayesian estimation for the transition function $P_\theta(dx_t|x^t)$. The process x_t defined by a transition function $P_\theta(dx_t|x^t)$ can be interpreted as a partially observed controlled Markov process in phase space $\Theta \times X$ with a transition function for $\theta : \theta_t = \theta_{t+1}$. Let us use the well-known construction for constructing an auxiliary model of the process with complete information. As phase space we consider the space $\{X, \aleph\}$, where $\aleph$ is a distribution space on Θ. It is a Borel space. It follows from the fact that a set of probabilistic measures on the Borel space is a Borel space. Define a transition function in the space $\{x, \aleph\}$

$$P(x_{t+1}|x_t, \nu_t) = \int_{\Theta} P(x_{t+1}|x_t)\nu_t n(d\theta)$$

where the distribution density ν_{t+1} is determined by formula Eq. (1),

$$\nu_t(\theta) = \frac{P_\theta(x_{t+1}|x_t)}{\int_{\Theta} P_\theta(x_{t+1}|x_t, \nu_0(\theta))}.$$

To specify a process we define an initial distribution $P_1(x_1)$ and a priori density $\nu_1(\theta) = \nu_1/dn$.

In this paper closed control systems are considered. Let us consider a linear difference equation of order n

$$x_{t+1} = \sum_{k=0}^{n-1} \alpha_k x_{t-k} + \sum_{k=0}^{m} \beta_k u_{t-k} + f_{t+1}, \tag{2}$$

where α_k, β_k are constant coefficients; f_t is an independent sequence of Gaussian quantities with zero mean and a variance σ^2, u_t is a control, $\beta_0 \neq 0$. Assume that coefficients α_k are unknown. Denote

$$w_t = \sum_{k=0}^{m} \beta_k u_{t-k}, \quad \theta^T = (\alpha_0, \alpha_1, ..., \alpha_{n-1}).$$

Then

$$x_{t+1} = \theta^T z_t + w_t + f_{t+1}, \tag{3}$$

where $z_t^T = (x_t, x_{t-1}, ..., x_{t-n+1})$. The transient function of process $P_\theta(x_{t+1}|z_t, w_t)$ defined by Eq. (3) has the form

$$P_\theta(x_{t+1}|z_t, w_t) = F(x_{t+1} - \theta^T z_t - w_t),$$

where $F(\cdot)$ is a distribution density of a random variable f_t.

2 Problem Statements

In real situations a transition function of the controlled Markov process depends on an unknown parameter. Generally speaking, for control purposes the knowledge of this parameter θ is not necessary, but the proximity of the distribution estimate to the true distribution is desirable. In order to formulate the concept of proximity of distribution functions we introduce a definition [2].

Definition 3. *A set of subsets A_i of a space Y is called a partition of the space Y if all subsets A_i are disjoint and their union equals Y.*

Then the proximity of two distribution functions P_1, P_2 is understood in the sense of a metric which can be determined by the following relation [3]

$$\rho(P_1; P_2) = \sup \sum_i |P_1(A_i) - P_2(A_i)|,$$

where sup is taken over all finite partitions of the space Y. Thus we can talk about the metric space of the distributions P. Assume that the distribution $P(dy|x, \theta)$ is dominated by the measure $m(dy)$. The distribution density $P(\cdot|x, \theta)$ with respect to $m(dy)$ is denoted by $P(y|x, \theta)$. Assume also that θ is given by σ-algebra F, i.e. (Θ, F) is a measurable space. Define a problem of statistical identification of the distribution law $P(dy|x, \theta)$, that is, it is necessary to construct such a sequence of estimates $P_t(dy|x^t)$, that if $t \to \infty$ then

$$P_t(dy|x^t) \to P(dy|x_t, \theta)$$

in some fixed sense (in probability, with probability 1, etc).

The main apparatus in establishing of convergence is an information measure of a mismatch between the estimated distribution and evaluation. Let $P_1(y)$ and $P_2(y)$ be two distribution densities on a measurable space Y with respect to a positive measure $m(dy)$.

Definition 4. *The value*

$$I(P_1(y), P_2(y)) = \int_Y \left[\ln \frac{P_1(y)}{P_2(y)}\right] P_1(y)m(dy) \tag{4}$$

is called the Kullback-Leibler information number.

The value of I is not a metric (since it is not a symmetric function of P_1 and P_2, but it has some properties that can be used as a measure of mismatch between the distribution of $P_2(y)$ and its estimate of $P_1(y)$. If integral Eq. (4) exists, then $I(P_1(g), P_2(g)) \geq 0$. Herewith $I(P_1(g), P_2(g)) = 0$ if and only if $P_1 = P_2$ is almost everywhere. The following inequality [4]

$$I(P_1(y), P_2(y)) \geq \frac{1}{8}\left[\int_Y |P_1(y) - P_2(y)|m(dy)\right]^2$$

holds. Thus, it is possible to estimate the metric ρ from above by value $\sqrt{8I}$ i.e. $I \to 0$ is enough to show that $\rho \to 0$.

For the family of normal distributions another property holds. Let $P_0(x)$ be an arbitrary distribution in R^n centered at a with a covariance matrix V. Consider a family of normal distributions Q in R^n, $q_0(x)$ is the normal distribution with the same center at a and the covariance matrix V.

Theorem 1. *For every $q(x) \in Q$ the following inequality*

$$I(P_0, q_0) \leq I(P_0, q)$$

holds. The equality is achieved if and only if $q \equiv q_0$.

3 The Bayesian Approach for Solving the Problem

Consider the Bayesian approach to estimating the parameters of the conditional distribution. Let the process x_t be observed. It is assumed that the conditional distribution $P(dx_{t+1}|x_t, \theta)$ depends on a parameter $\theta \in \Theta$, for which its value is unknown but is constant throughout the experiment. Furthermore we assume that

$$P_\theta(x_{t+1}|x^t) = P(x_{t+1}|x^t, \theta).$$

The problem of this section is to study the Bayesian estimation for the transition function $P_\theta(x_{t+1}|x^t)$. A process x_t defined by $P_\theta(x_{t+1}|x^t)$ can be interpreted as a partially observed, controlled Markov process in phase space $\Theta \times x$.

Let us use the well-known construction for building an auxiliary model of the process with full information. We consider a space $\{X, N\}$ as a phase space where N is the space of distributions on Θ. Define a transition function in the space $\{X, N\}$

$$P(x_{t+1}|x_t, \nu_t) = \int\limits_{\Theta} P_\theta(x_{t+1}|x_t)\nu_t(\theta)n(d\theta). \tag{5}$$

Definition 5. *A function $\nu_t(\theta)$ is called a posteriori distribution density of the parameter θ if it is defined by the formula*

$$\nu_{t+1}(\theta) = \nu_t(\theta)\frac{P_\theta(x_{t+1}|x_t)}{P(x_{t+1}|x_t, \nu_t)}.$$

The initial distribution and a priori distribution density $\nu_1(\theta) = d\nu_1/dn$ are also defined. Note some properties of a sequence $\nu_t(\theta)$. Let $v(\theta)$ be an arbitrary function for which there is an integral

$$\xi_t = \int\limits_{\Theta} v(\theta)\nu_t(\theta)n(d\theta)$$

and at the same time the ratio

$$E(\xi_{t+1}|x_t, \nu_t) = \xi_t, \tag{6}$$

is true, that is, the sequence ξ_t is a martingale (with respect to $\{x_t, \nu_t\}$). Since

$$\xi_{t+1} = \int\limits_{\Theta} v(\theta)\nu_t(\theta)\frac{P_\theta(x_{t+1}|x_t)}{P(x_{t+1}|x_t, \nu_t)}n(d\theta),$$

then

$$\int\limits_X \xi_{t+1}P(x_{t+1}|x_t, \nu_t)m(dx_{t+1}) = \int\limits_X m(dx_{t+1})\int\limits_{\Theta} v(\theta)\nu_t(\theta)P_\theta(x_{t+1}|x_t)n(d\theta) =$$

$$= \int\limits_{\Theta} n(d\theta)v(\theta)\nu_t(\theta)\int\limits_X P_\theta(x_{t+1}|x_t)m(dx_{t+1}) = \int\limits_{\Theta} v(\theta)\nu_t(\theta)n(d\theta).$$

Let

$$\sigma_t^2 = \int\limits_{\Theta} |v(\theta) - \xi_t|^2\nu_t(\theta)n(d\theta).$$

The next equality

$$E(\sigma_{t+1}^2|x_t, \nu_t) = \sigma_t^2 - E\{(\xi_{t+1} - \xi_t)^2|x_t, \nu_t\}$$

holds. Thus, the sequence σ_t^2 is a supermartingale. Let Θ be a linear set in R^n, $\bar{\theta}_t$ be the mean vectors θ with a distribution density $\nu_t(\theta)$, S_t be a correlation matrix. Then

$$E(\bar{\theta}_{t+1}|x_t, \nu_t) = \bar{\theta}_t; \quad E\{S_{t+1}|x_t, \nu_t\} \le S_t.$$

To verify the last inequality, let $\varphi(\theta) = c^T\theta$, where c^T is a constant vector. Then $\sigma_t^2 = c^T S_t c$ and for any vector c the inequality

$$E\left\{c^T S_{t+1} c | x_t, \nu_t\right\} \leq c^T S_t c$$

holds. From Eq. (6) we have

$$E(\xi_{t+1} - \zeta_t)^2 = E\sigma_t^2 - E\sigma_{t+1}^2.$$

As a consequence of the above calculations the inequality

$$E\sum(\xi_{T+1} - \xi_T)^2 < \Sigma_1^2$$

follows. In particular, for $\xi_t = C^T\theta$ we have

$$E\left\{\sum_{T=1}^{\infty} c^T \|\bar{\theta}_{T+1} - \bar{\theta}_T\|^2\right\} < \Sigma_1^2.$$

Since the vector c is arbitrary, then

$$E\left\{\sum_{T=1}^{\infty} \|\bar{\theta}_{T+1} - \bar{\theta}_T\|^2\right\} < \Sigma_1^2.$$

Consider asymptotic properties of the sequence ν_t. Define a transition process function $\{x_t, \lambda_t\}$ by relations

$$P(x_{t+1}|x_t, \lambda_t) = \int_{\Theta} P_\theta(x_{t+1}|x_t)\lambda_t(\theta)n(d\theta), \tag{7}$$

$$\lambda_{t+1}(\theta) = \lambda_t(\theta)\frac{P_\theta(x_{t+1}|x_t)}{P(x_{t+1}|x_t, \lambda_t)}. \tag{8}$$

It is assumed that x_t is observed but the distribution $\lambda_t(\theta)$ is unknown. As an evaluation function $\lambda_t(\theta)$, we select the distribution $\nu_t(\theta)$ determined by the next recurrence relation

$$\nu_{t+1}(\theta) = \nu_t(\theta)\frac{P_\theta(x_{t+1}|x_t)}{P(x_{t+1}|x_t, \nu_t)}$$

with an arbitrary initial value of $\nu_1(\theta)$. Our task is to establish that for $T \to \infty$ the transition function $P(x_{t+1}|x_t, \nu_t)$ becomes close to "true" $P(x_{t+1}|x_t, \lambda_t)$.

Theorem 2. *Let $\{x_t, \lambda_t\}$ be the Markov process defined by Eqs. (7) and (8). Then the following inequality*

$$E\left(\sum_{t=1}^{\infty} I_t\right) \leq \int_{\Theta} \ln\left[\frac{\lambda_1(\theta)}{\nu_1(\theta)}\right] \lambda_1(\theta)n(d\theta) \tag{9}$$

holds where $I_t = I(P(\cdot|x_t), \lambda_t), P(\cdot|x_t, \nu_t))$.

Corollary 1. *The next statements*

$$\sum_{t=1}^{\infty} I_t \leq +\infty; \ \lim_{t\to\infty} I_t = 0$$

are true with probability 1.

A distribution $\lambda_1(\theta)$ is arbitrary. For example, as $\lambda_1(\theta)$ we can take any distribution concentrated in an arbitrarily small neighbourhood u_0 of the point θ_0. Then all distributions $\lambda_1(\theta)$ are concentrated in this neighbourhood.

The process $\{x_t, \lambda_t\}$ can be interpreted as follows: θ_t is a random variable with a distribution $\lambda_1(\theta)$, x_{t+1} is a random variable with a conditional distribution $P_\theta(x_{t+1}|x_t)$ and $\theta_t \in u_0$ for all $t \geq 1$. Thus, the process x_t can be interpreted as the process for which a transient function is determined by a parameter subject to "small" perturbations. Thus, the convergence of the estimation of the transition function to a nonstationary transition function $P_\theta(x_{t+1}|x_t)$ is established. If the set Θ is finite, then the neighborhood of the point θ_I coincides with the point θ_I (you can choose the discrete topology). In this case, integral relations take the form of finite or infinite sums and the functions $\nu_T(\theta)$ turn into probabilistic sequences $\nu_t(i), i = 1, 2, \ldots$. Ratio Eq. (9) takes the form

$$E\left(\sum_{t=1}^{\infty} I_t\right) \leq -\ln \nu_1(i_0),$$

where i_0 is the number of the transition function defined by the process x_t;

$$I_t = I(P_{i_0}; P_t), \ P_t = \sum_{t=1}^{\infty} P_i(x_{t+1}|x_t)\nu_t(i).$$

The question is whether the distribution ν_t converging to the distribution δ focused on the true parameter θ_0 remains generally open. It is easy to give an example when it is not true.

In the described approach it is assumed that the true distribution $P_0(y|x^t)$ belongs to the class of hypotheses P.

Obviously, the wider the class P is, the more computationally expensive is. Assume that the following conditions take place:

1. $\exists v_0 \in \Theta : v_0 = \left\{\Theta \,|\, E\left\{\ln \frac{P_0}{P_\theta}\right\} < +\infty\right\}$;
2. $a = \inf\limits_{\theta \in v_\epsilon} E\left\{\ln \frac{P_0}{P_\theta}\right\}$; $\delta > 0$; $\exists v_\delta \subset v_0$; $E\left\{\sup\limits_{\theta \in v_\delta} I(P_0; P_\theta) < a + \delta\right\}$,

   $\theta \in v_\delta$, $\left|\ln \frac{P_0}{P_\theta}\right|^2 < c < +\infty$, $\int\limits_{v_\delta} \nu_0(\theta)\, n(d\theta) > 0$;
3. $\ln P_\theta$ has finite the mathematical expectation and the dispersion.

Denote

$$l(\theta, x_t) = \int\limits_Y [\ln P_\theta(y|x_t)]\, P_0(y|x_t) m(dy).$$

Example 1. Give an example illustrating the introduced conditions. Let

$$y_t = \theta^T x_t + f_t,$$

where x_t, y_t are observed vectors; x_t is an independent random vector; f_t is an unobservable sequence of random variables. The "true" hypothesis $P(y|x_t, \theta)$ has the form

$$P(y|x_t, \theta) = \varphi\left(y_t - \theta^T x_t\right),$$

where φ is the density f. If the density f is unknown and if the family of normal distributions is taken as hypotheses, then condition 2 means that vectors x_t have finite fourth moments.

Theorem 3. *If $\varphi(\theta_0) > \varphi(\theta_1)$, then for any N the relation*

$$P\left\{\frac{\nu_t(\theta_0)}{\nu_t(\theta_1)} > N\right\} \to 1, \text{ if } t \to \infty,$$

holds

Theorem 4. *If $\theta \notin v_\delta$ then $\nu_t(\theta) \to 0$ in probability if $t \to \infty$.*

Now back to Eq. (3). The Bayesian construction defined by formulas Eqs. (5), (6) and associated to the family of transition functions $P_\theta(\cdot|z_t, w_t)$ has the form

$$P(x_{t+1}|\nu_t, z_t, w_t) = \int\limits_{\Theta} F(x_{t+1} - \theta^T z_t - w_t)\nu_t(\theta) n(d\theta),$$

$$\nu_{t+1}(\theta) = \nu_t(\theta)\frac{F(x_{t+1} - \theta^T z_t - w_t)}{P(x_{t+1}|\nu_t, z_t, w_t)}.$$

Let $\nu_t(\theta)$ be the density of a normal random vector with an average value of θ_t and a correlation matrix S_t:

$$\nu_t(\theta) = \Gamma_t \exp\left\{-\frac{1}{2}(\bar{\theta}_t - \theta_t)^T S_t^{-1}(\bar{\theta}_t - \theta_t)\right\}.$$

Then $\nu_{t+1}(\theta)$ is the density of the normal vector with the correlation matrix S_{t+1} and the average value of θ_{t+1} while the following recurrence relations analogous to the relations of the discrete Kalman filter

$$S_{t+1}^{-1} = S_t^{-1} + \frac{1}{\sigma_f^2} z_t z_t^T,$$

$$\theta_{t+1} = S_{t+1}[S_t^{-1}\theta_t + \frac{1}{\sigma_f^2}(x_{t+1} - w_t)z_1]. \tag{10}$$

are valid. From relation Eq. (10) it follows that in the case of the Gaussian quantities f_t a posteriori distribution densities $\nu_t(\theta)$ have an interesting property. Namely their correlation matrices are monotonically decreasing $S_{t+1} \leq S_t$.

Denote by $z_t^T = (x_t, x_{t-1}, ..., x_{t-n})$ the phase vector of equation Eq. (2), then this equation can be rewritten as follows

$$z_{t+1} = Az_t + b(\theta^T z_t + \sum_{k=0}^{m} \beta_k u_{t-k} + f_{t+1}), \tag{11}$$

where

$$A = \begin{pmatrix} 00...00 \\ 10...00 \\ \cdots \\ 00...01 \end{pmatrix}, \quad b = \begin{pmatrix} 1 \\ \vdots \\ 0 \end{pmatrix}.$$

Let $V(z)$ be an arbitrary quadratic form of a vector z. Calculate the conditional expectation $E\{V(z_{t+1})|z_t, \nu_t, u_t\}$. As the consequence of the above, to calculate the conditional distribution of the vector z_{t+1} in the Bayesian construction defined by relations Eqs. (5) and (6), in formula Eq. (11) we should consider θ as a random vector with the distribution $\nu_t(\theta)$. Therefore

$$E\{V(z_{t+1})|z_t\} = V(b)Ef_{t+1}^2 + \int_{\Theta} V\left(Az_t + b\left(\theta^T z_t + \sum_{k=0}^{m} \beta^k u\right)\right) \nu_t(\theta)d\theta =$$

$$= V(b)Ef_{t+1}^2 + V\left(Az_t + b\left(\theta^T z_t + \sum_{k=0}^{m} \beta^k u_{t-k}\right)\right) + V(b)\int_{\Theta} |(\theta - \theta_t)^T z_t|^2 \nu_t(\theta)d\theta,$$

where

$$\theta_t = \int_{\Theta} \theta \nu_t(\theta)d\theta. \tag{12}$$

It is obvious that

$$\int_{\Theta} |(\theta - \theta_t)^T z_t|^2 \nu_t(\theta)d\theta = z_t^T S_t z_t,$$

where

$$S_t = \int_{\Theta} (\theta - \theta_t) * (\theta - \theta_t)^T \nu_t(\theta)d\theta.$$

Finally write

$$E\{V(z_{t+1})|x^t\} = qd^2 + qz_t^T S_t z_t + V\left(Az_t + b\left(\theta_t^T z_t + \sum_{k=0}^{m} \beta^k u_{t-k}\right)\right). \tag{13}$$

Let the quadratic form $V(z)$ have the form

$$V(z_t) = nx_t^2 + (n-1)x_{t-1}^2 + ... + x_{t-n+1}^2.$$

Then

$$V(Az_t + bv) + z_t^2 = V(z) + nv^2;\ V(b) = n.$$

Relation Eq. (13) can be rewritten as

$$E(V(z_{t+1})|x^t) + (z_t^2 - qz_t^T S_t z_t) = n\left(d^2 + |\theta_t^T z_t + \sum_{k=0}^{m} \beta^k u_{t-k}\right) + V(z_t).$$

Theorem 5. *The strategy* $\sum_{k=0}^{m} \beta_k u_{t-k} = -\theta_t^T z_t$ *minimizes the value*

$$J_T = E_\nu \left\{ \sum_{t=0}^{T-1} z_t^T (I - S_T n) z_t + V(z_T) \right\}$$

at each T. *Herewith*

$$\inf_u J_T = nTd^2 + V(z_0).$$

Corollary 2. *Let for some* t *the inequality* $I - qS_T > \epsilon_0 I$ *be satisfied. Then there exists* ρ, $0 < \rho < 1$, *for which the inequality*

$$E\{V(z_{t+1})|z_t, \nu_t\} \le \rho V(z_t) + nd^2$$

holds.

Corollary 3. *Let* $\lambda(\theta)$ *be a priori density for which the inequality* $\lambda(\theta) \le C\gamma(\theta)$ *holds. Then the following inequality*

$$E_\lambda \left(\sum_{t}^{T} z_t^2 \right) \le CE_\nu \left(\sum_{t}^{T} z_t^2 \right)$$

holds.

Theorem 6. *Let*

$$\sum_{k=0}^{m} \beta_k u_{t-k} = -\theta_t^T z_t,$$

where θ_t *is defined by Eq. (12),* $\nu_t(\theta)$ *be a sequence of a posteriori distributions corresponding to the normal a priori distribution* $\nu_t(\theta)$ *and* $nS_1 < I$. *Let* $\lambda(\theta)$ *be the density of distribution concentrated at a bounded domain and satisfying the inequality* $\lambda(\theta) < C\gamma(\theta)$. *Then*

$$E\{z_t^2\} \le const, \quad E\{u_t^2\} \le const.$$

Remark 1. Let us explain the meaning of the statements of this theorem. The process $(x_t; \nu_t)$ defined by the transition function $P(x_{t+1}|z_t, \nu_t, u_t)$ can be interpreted as the process defined by the equation

$$x_{t+1} = \theta_t^T z_t + \sum_{k=0}^{m} \beta^k u_{t-k} + f_{t+1},$$

where θ_t is a random vector with a distribution $\lambda_t(\theta)$. Since the carrier distributions of $\lambda_t(\theta)$ are centered in the neighbourhood of the point θ_0, then for all t the inequality $|\theta_t - \theta_0| < \epsilon$ holds.

Thus, the theorem states that the strategy stabilizes the trajectory of equation Eq. (11) with a "small" random perturbation of the vector coefficients of equation Eq. (11). Also we can definitely hope that this strategy stabilizes the trajectory and for the equation with the unperturbed parameter vector $\theta_t \equiv \theta_0$.

4 Conclusion

The problem of convergence and stability of the Bayesian parameter estimation of the linear stochastic control system is considered. The problem of synthesis of optimal strategies for dynamic systems in which there is no part of the basic information necessary for the construction of optimal control is formulated. The optimal strategy which stabilizes the trajectory of a linear stochastic control system with a "small" random perturbation of the coefficient vector is obtained. The Bayesian parameter estimation is widely used in many areas such as medicine, biology and economics and many others [2,5–9].

References

1. Demyanov, V.F., Karelin, V.V.: On a minimax approach to the problem of identification of dynamic systems in the presence of uncertainty. In: Oettli, W., Pallaschke, D. (eds.) Advances in Optimization Proceedings of 6th French-German Colloquium of Optimization. Lecture Notes in Economics and Mathematical Systems, pp. 515–518. Springer, Heidelberg (1991). https://doi.org/10.1007/978-3-642-51682-5
2. Lipcer, R.S., Sirjaev, A.N.: Statistics of Random Processes: I General Theory. Springer Science & Business Media, Heidelberg (2013). https://doi.org/10.1007/978-3-662-13043-8
3. Aoki, M.: Optimization of Stochastic Systems. Academic Press, New York (1967)
4. Karelin, V.V.: Adaptive optimal strategies in controlled markov processes. In: Oettli, W., Pallaschke, D. (eds.) Advances in Optimization Proceedings of 6th French-German Colloquium of Optimization, FRG. Lecture Notes in Economics and Mathematical Systems, pp. 518–525. Springer, Heidelberg (1991)
5. Liang, H., Wu, H.: Parameter estimation for differential equation models using a framework of measurement error in regression models. J. Am. Stat. Assoc. **103**(484), 1570–1583 (2008). https://doi.org/10.1198/016214508000000797
6. Mariño, I.P., Zaikin, A., Miguez, J.: A comparison of monte carlo-based bayesian parameter estimation methods for stochastic models of genetic networks. PLoS One **12**(8), e0182015 (2017). https://doi.org/10.1371/journal.pone.0182015
7. Prendes, J., Chabert, M., Pascal, F., Giros, A., Tourneret, J.-Y.: A bayesian nonparametric model coupled with a markov random field for change detection in heterogeneous remote sensing images. SIAM J. Imaging Sci. **9**(4), 1889–1921 (2016). https://doi.org/10.1137/15M1047908
8. Schindler, M.R., Phillips, D.R.: Bayesian methods for parameter estimation in effective field theories. Ann. Phys. **324**(3), 682–708 (2009). https://doi.org/10.1016/j.aop.2008.09.003
9. Shaby, B., Ruppert, D.: Tapered covariance: bayesian estimation and asymptotics. J. Comput. Graph. Statist. **21**(2), 433–452 (2012). https://doi.org/10.1080/10618600.2012.680819

Boosting HPC Applications in the Cloud Through JIT Traffic-Aware Path Provisioning

Guilherme R. Pretto[1], Bruno L. Dalmazo[1(✉)], Jonatas A. Marques[1], Zhongke Wu[2], Xingce Wang[2], Vladimir Korkhov[3,4], Philippe O. A. Navaux[1], and Luciano P. Gaspary[1]

[1] Federal University of Rio Grande do Sul, Porto Alegre, Brazil
{grpretto,bldalmazo,jamarques,navaux,paschoal}@inf.ufrgs.br

[2] Beijing Normal University, Beijing, China
{zwu,wangxingce}@bnu.edu.cn

[3] Saint Petersburg State University, Saint Petersburg, Russia

[4] Plekhanov Russian University of Economics, Moscow, Russia
v.korkhov@spbu.ru

Abstract. Data centers, clusters and grids have historically supported High-Performance Computing (HPC) applications. Due to the high capital and operational expenditures associated with such infrastructures, in recent past, we have witnessed consistent efforts to run HPC applications in the cloud. The potential advantages of this shift include higher scalability and lower costs. If on the one hand, app instantiation – through customized Virtual Machines (VMs) – is a well-solved issue, on the other, the network still represents a significant bottleneck. When switching HPC applications to be executed on the cloud, we lose control of where VMs will be positioned and of the paths that will be traversed for processes to communicate with one another. To alleviate this problem, and taking advantage of new advances in programmable networks, we propose a mechanism for dynamic, just-in-time path provisioning in cloud infrastructures. It continuously monitors the network conditions and, given the current communication patterns of the application, systematically (re)programs paths to avoid uncongested links and reduce end-to-end delays. The proposed mechanism achieves a speedup of up to 44.24% regarding application runtime when compared to the traditional shortest-path, static approach.

Keywords: HPC applications · Cloud infrastructures · Link usage-aware path provisioning

1 Introduction

Handling massive amounts of data is commonplace for most modern scientific, engineering, and business applications. As these applications need to target

S. Misra et al. (Eds.): ICCSA 2019, LNCS 11622, pp. 702–716, 2019.
https://doi.org/10.1007/978-3-030-24305-0_52

big data-related challenges, while delivering expected results promptly, they frequently pose large computing power requirements. In this context, High-Performance Computing (HPC) becomes a key factor for speeding up data processing. To this end, HPC solutions have traditionally taken advantage of cluster, grid and data center infrastructures for running applications having those computing power requirements [6]. More recently, we have witnessed consistent efforts to run HPC applications in the cloud. The pay-per-use cost model makes cloud computing a promising environment for HPC, which can be provided with instant availability and flexible scaling of resources (*i.e.*, elasticity).

Although the allocation of virtual machines in the cloud (for HPC application execution) has been extensively studied, the inter-process communication rates still represent the main performance bottleneck [10]. In addition to the possibility of virtual machines to be deployed physically far from each other into the cloud, the provisioned paths are typically static and based on shortest paths (potentially traversing congested, high delay links). The dynamic nature of communication patterns observed in most HPC applications makes these limitations even more prominent. In summary, subjecting HPC flows to high network latencies is *still* one of the leading open research challenges that cloud environments have to cope with to be able to offer a suitable infrastructure for HPC.

Previous studies [3,6,13,15,18] have assessed the feasibility of using public clouds for HPC. Their findings suggest that clouds were not designed for running tightly coupled HPC applications. The main limitation is the poor network performance resulting from I/O virtualization overhead, processor sharing, and usage of commodity interconnection technologies. Lee *et al.* [9] and Faizian *et al.* [4] have identified limitations of network technologies used by cloud infrastructures, namely the use of simplistic routing schemes, which may result in degraded communication performance. To overcome this limitation, they have proposed routing mechanisms that avoid congested paths, which however are computed priorly to the execution of an HPC application and therefore can cope neither with network traffic fluctuation nor with varying communication patterns.

In this paper, we advance the state-of-the-art by proposing a novel mechanism for dynamic, just-in-time path provisioning in cloud infrastructures. It monitors cloud infrastructure links and keeps track of their utilization. Taking advantage of new advances in programmable networks, the proposed mechanism dynamically computes and programs the best paths (*i.e.*, shortest uncongested paths) between processes according to their momentaneous communication needs. In addition to the mechanism, another equally important contribution is the formalization of a *Link Usage-Aware Routing* (LUAR) strategy, which plays a crucial role in reducing end-to-end communication delays. To prove the concept and technical feasibility, we have evaluated our solution using the experimental setup of a realistic cloud infrastructure with different levels of background traffic and multiple instances of the NAS Parallel Benchmarks [2].

The remainder of the paper is organized as follows. In Sect. 2, we cover some of the most prominent related work. In Sect. 3, we describe the overarching conceptual solution and its main components. In Sect. 4, we present the evaluation and discuss the obtained results. In Sect. 5, we conclude the paper with some final remarks and prospective directions for future research.

2 Related Work

Several feasibility studies about using public clouds for HPC point out the network communication overheads as a significant barrier. Other investigations propose strategies to reduce these overheads. Two classes of solutions stand out: those resorting on topologies that attempt to maximize connectivity between nodes and those that explore resource and/or network management. Given the nature of our proposed approach, next, we revisit work on the general problem of executing HPC applications in the cloud and recent proposals that apply Software-Defined Networks (SDNs) as a crucial component to configure efficient inter-process communication paths.

Gupta *et al.* [6] investigate network bottlenecks in commercial cloud infrastructures and propose new mechanisms to improve the performance experienced by HPC applications. Essentially, they employ lightweight virtualization and grant Virtual Machines (VMs) native access to physical network interfaces. Despite the overhead reduction in average turnaround time (up to 2x) and throughput (up to 6x), the authors recognize that their proposal may not be enough to improve the performance of HPC applications. Similarly, Ramakrishnan *et al.* [14] claim that virtualization of network resources accounts for the main performance issue, being responsible for at least 60% delay and throughput degradation if compared with typical local cluster and supercomputer options.

Mauch *et al.* [11] introduce an approach to use InfiniBand in a private virtualized environment. It allows for an individual network configuration to operate with QoS mechanisms. Similarly, Alsmadi *et al.* [1] propose a method for logically slicing the network and isolating applications from one another. While the former is based on a complex architecture that requires interfacing with several APIs and protocols to configure the network, the latter cannot handle path reallocation in case of a switch or link failure. Moreover, both proposals deploy static paths that cannot change during application execution.

Motivated by the fact that InfiniBand is increasingly available in commercial clouds, Lee *et al.* [9] address one of its central weakness for HPC, namely the employment of simple routing schemes such as *destination-mod-k* routing. The authors propose an enhancement to InfiniBand, incorporating OpenFlow-style SDN capability to provision uncongested paths. While the proposal is a cornerstone towards the employment of programmable networks to speed up HPC applications in the cloud, it fails by requiring routes to be determined before the execution of an application. It, therefore, wastes a valuable opportunity to adapt the network to meet fluctuating application communication demands.

Along the same lines as the work by Lee *et al.*, Faizian *et al.* [4] include SDN-related functionality to Dragonfly networks and propose a set of routing schemes to achieve the performance required by HPC applications. One limitation of this work is the lack of a mechanism for accurate traffic demand estimation, making it difficult to make optimal global decisions. Another limitation is that even when several paths are available, only two (*i.e.*, a primary and a backup) are considered for forwarding a packet. A final shortcoming is that these paths are provisioned upon application instantiation and cannot change.

3 The Proposed Path Provisioning Approach

As a relevant research step further in comparison with the related work, we propose a mechanism based on SDN for *just-in-time path selection and provisioning* in cloud infrastructures. It continuously monitors the network conditions and, given the current communication patterns of an HPC application, systematically (re)programs paths to avoid congested links and reduce end-to-end delays. The proposed approach is *complementary* to the VM placement and instantiation process, which we assume will be taken care of by a third party resource management system such as OpenStack [17] or OpenNebula [12].

Figure 1 introduces the basis of our solution, highlighting its main conceptual components and their interactions. In the following subsections, we describe them in detail, starting with (*i*) the SDN-based Path Provisioning Controller, then (*ii*) illustrating a working example, and finally (*iii*) presenting the accompanying proposed routing strategy.

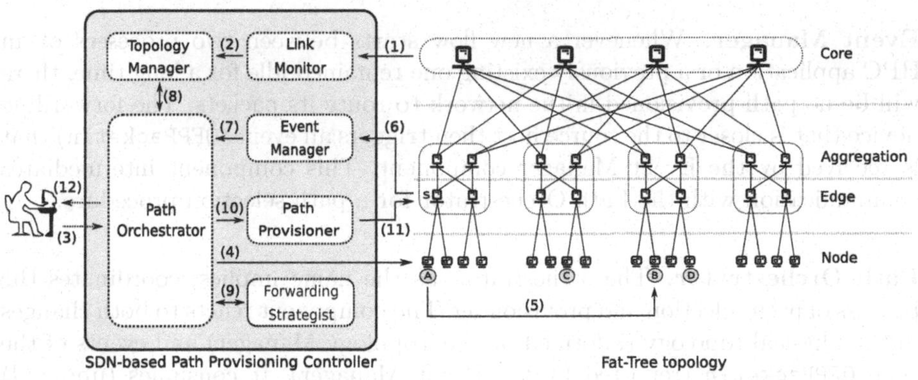

Fig. 1. Components of the proposed solution and their interactions

3.1 SDN-Based Path Provisioning Controller

The SDN-based Path Provisioning Controller consists of six components: *Link Monitor*, *Topology Manager*, *Event Manager*, *Path Orchestrator*, *Forwarding Strategist*, and *Path Provisioner*. Next we summarize the role of each of these components.

Link Monitor. This component plays a vital role in periodically gathering traffic statistics from the forwarding devices. Assuming the infrastructure is OpenFlow-enabled, this information can be obtained via `OFPPortStatsRequest` requests. The infrastructure operator must tune the frequency of this process. Highly frequent requests favor accuracy while sparsed ones favor low intrusiveness. After each round of information collection, the Link Monitor calculates the amount of traffic that traversed each link and derives its average utilization. This information is calculated according to Eq. 1 and sent to the Topology Manager component.

$$LkUsage_i(t, t-1) = LkCapacity_i - \frac{[tx + rx\_bytes](t) - [tx + rx\_bytes](t-1)}{\Delta(t, t-1)} \quad (1)$$

Topology Manager. It maintains updated information about the topology of the cloud network infrastructure in the form of an *annotated graph.* Forwarding devices (*e.g.*, OpenFlow switches) are abstracted as vertices while physical links are represented as edges. The average utilization of each link, measured by the Link Monitor, is used to denote the edge weight. The reader should keep in mind that (*i*) the representation of the topology might be updated in response to changes in the infrastructure (*e.g.*, due to a link failure – event `OFPErrorMsg`) and (*ii*) the weights are updated regularly in response to periodic link usage measurements carried out by the Link Monitor.

Event Manager. Whenever a new flow starts between two processes of an HPC application or a previously existing one remained idle for a long time, there will be no path provisioned in the network to route its packets. The forwarding device that is closer to the source host then triggers an event (`OFPPacketIn`) that is received by the Event Manager component. This component intermediates communication with the Path Orchestrator for a path selection procedure.

Path Orchestrator. The orchestrator, as the name implies, coordinates the process of path selection and provisioning. The component reacts to both changes in the physical topology (informed by the Topology Manager) and events of the type `OFPPacketIn` (reported by the Event Manager). It consumes (updated) information made available by these components, invokes the Forwarding Strategist for the determination of a path and resorts to the Path Provisioner for its deployment. The Path Orchestrator is also responsible for interfacing with the human network operator (*e.g*, to receive configuration commands and send him/her notifications about the path provisioning process).

Forwarding Strategist. The Forwarding Strategist can implement different approaches for determining a path between a source and a destination (HPC application) process. It uses an updated view of the annotated graph and location information of the processes to be "interconnected". The problem addressed by this component is then of a *graph-based path finding* one. As a proof of concept, in this paper, we propose a *Link Usage-Aware Routing* strategy, which favors shortest and uncongested paths. It is described in detail in Subsect. 3.3.

Path Provisioner. This component is responsible for performing the actual deployment of end-to-end paths on the network infrastructure. This process unfolds in the invocation of a coordinated set of `OFPFlowMod` commands to install forwarding rules on the devices that (are calculated to) compose the paths. The duration of these rules is determined by the operator, who can favor either path freshness/efficiency or stability/reuse.

3.2 A Working Example

To illustrate how the described components interact, we introduce now a working example. Initially, recall that the Link Monitor is expected to be continuously monitoring the traffic to consolidate statistics from the cloud network infrastructure (Flow 1 in Fig. 1). The gathered information (*tx_bytes* and *rx_bytes*) is sent to and stored by the Topology Manager (Flow 2).

The process of deploying an HPC application consists of (*i*) instantiating and configuring the VMs (with any off-the-shelf resource management system), as well as (*ii*) requesting our proposed SDN-based Path Provisioning Controller (via the Path Orchestrator component) to manage the path provisioning process (Flow 3). Should the third-party resource management system expose an API that can be used to control the resource provisioning life-cycle, then it is possible to integrate (*i*) and (*ii*) to have the whole application deployment/execution process dealt with by the SDN-based Path Provisioning Controller (3 and 4).

Consider the situation in which an HPC application has been deployed and that the process running on node A needs to communicate with the process on node B (5). When the first packet from A reaches its closest forwarding device (*s* in the figure), the device will not know how to route it further and will send an `OFPPacketIn` event to the Event Manager (6). This component will then pass the event to the Path Orchestrator (7).

At this point, the Path Orchestrator consults the Topology Manager to receive updated information about the current topology and the utilization of the links (8). Next, it invokes the Forwarding Strategist to determine an optimized route to connect processes running on A and B (9). Finally, it requests the Path Provisioner (10) to deploy the forwarding rules on the network devices (11). From this moment on, the packet that triggered the event is reintroduced by the controller into the network, and the remaining flow packets will be transmitted through the configured route.

The process above is executed for each new application communication flow (or when the physical topology changes). To avoid frequent communications with (and interventions from) the external controller, the operator can resort to two system parametrization options. The first is setting up a higher value for the `idle_timeout` associated with the flow rules configured on the forwarding devices. The consequence will be that provisioned paths will be kept active for more extended periods (assuming that short inter-process *no* communication periods will be succeeded by new message exchanges). The second option is *proactively* provisioning paths for which there exists a single possible route, or that will be undoubtedly necessary along the execution of a whole application (*e.g.*, master/worker communication channels). An in-depth analysis of the additional performance gains (*i.e.*, in application runtime) reached with these configuration options are out of the scope of this work and are left as future work.

3.3 Link Usage-Aware Routing (LUAR)

In this subsection, we propose and formalize our strategy – called *Link Usage-Aware Routing* (LUAR) – designed to efficiently compute the best path from a source to a destination point in a cloud network topology. LUAR is one of the possible approaches to be implemented by the Forwarding Strategist. It considers the best path to be the shortest, least utilized, currently available path. In the future, we plan to investigate other algorithms and approaches to this task.

Algorithm 1 shows the pseudo-code of LUAR. The algorithm has five input parameters: a set V of nodes in the topology graph; a vector of adjacency lists E, where $E(v)$ lists the nodes connected to node v; a link utilization matrix U, where $U(v, u)$ indicates the utilization of the link that connects node v to u; and the source and destination nodes s and t. The algorithm can be logically divided into two blocks. Next, we detail each block.

The first block (Lines 1–12) is an adaptation of the Breadth-First Search (BFS) algorithm extended to record, for every node, its possible predecessors in any of the shortest paths starting from the source. The algorithm maintains two main data structures in Block 1, Predecessors and Seen, that indicate, respectively, the possible predecessors for each node v and the first level in which they were seen during the search. These structures are initialized with *nil* values for every node in the graph (Line 2). In Line 3, we set Predecessors(s) of source node s to an empty list (since it has no predecessors) and Seen(s) to level 0 (since the search will start from it). The algorithm also maintains three auxiliary variables l, N and C (Lines 4 and 6), where l indicates the current level of the search, N is the set of nodes to explore in the next level, and C is the set of nodes being explored in the current level.

Lines 5–12 contain the main repeat loop of Block 1. Every iteration of the outermost loop represents the exploration of a level in the graph. Each iteration starts by updating C to be what was previously N and resetting N to an empty set (Line 6). The algorithm then checks, for each node v currently in C (Line 7), if any of its adjacent nodes $u \in E(v)$ has not been visited (Line 9). In the positive case (Line 10), the Predecessor(u) is initialized to a list containing only the node currently being explored (*i.e.*, v), u is added to the set N of nodes to explore in the next level and is also marked as to have been seen in next level $l+1$. Otherwise, LUAR checks if node u has already been seen in the next level (Line 11), in which case it simply appends v to the list of predecessors of u. This procedure is repeated until all nodes in the graph have been visited, *i.e.*, no item

Algorithm 1. Compute the shortest, least utilized, currently available path from source s to destination t.

Input: V, E, U, s, t

```
1: ▷ Block 1: Generate predecessor tree for the graph starting from node s.
2: Predecessors(v) ← nil, ∀v ∈ V;  Seen(v) ← nil, ∀v ∈ V
3: Predecessors(s) ← EmptyArrayList();  Seen(s) ← 0
4: l ← 0; N ← {s}
5: while N ≠ ∅ do
6:   C ← N; N ← ∅
7:   for v ∈ C do
8:     for u ∈ E(v) do
9:       if Seen(u) = nil then
10:        Predecessors(u) ← ArrayList([v]); N ← N ∪ {u}; Seen(u) ← l+1
11:      else if Seen(u) = l + 1 then Append(Predecessors(u), v)
12:  l ← l + 1
13: ▷ Block 2: Compose the shortest paths and find the least utilized one.
14: W ← ArrayList([(t, 0, 0)]); ρ_best ← nil; au_best ← ∞
15: while Length(W) > 0 do
16:   v, i, au ← Last(W)
17:   if v = s and au < au_min then
18:     ρ_best ← Reversed(List({FirstItem(w): w ∈ W}))
19:     au_best ← au
20:   if i < Length(Predecessors(v)) then
21:     Append(W, (Predecessors(v)_i, 0, au + U(Predecessors(v)_i, v)))
22:   else
23:     RemoveLast(W)
24:     if Length(W) > 0 then
25:       SecondItem(Last(W)) ← SecondItem(Last(W)) +1
```

Output: ρ_{best}

is added to N during an outermost iteration (Line 5). In the end of Block 1, data structure Predecessors has been populated with the predecessors of all nodes in the shortest paths starting from node s.

Block 2 (Lines 13–31) is a modified version of the non-recursive Depth-First Search (DFS) algorithm. The search is started from the destination node t and targets source node s (*i.e.*, a reverse search) and the Predecessors data structure (populated in Block 1) is used instead of the original adjacency list. Along with the search, LUAR records the path being traversed and its aggregate utilization.

The path is recorded using an array list W of triples (v, i, au_{cur}), where v is a node, i is index of the next predecessor to explore for v, and au is the current aggregate utilization in the path ending on node v (Line 4). Block 2 also maintains two auxiliary variables (Line 14): the best path ρ_{best} found in the search (initialized as nil); and the aggregate utilization au_{best} of this best path (initialized as ∞).

Lines 15–25 contain the main loop of Block 2. Each iteration starts by loading the last triple from W into variables v, i, and au (Line 16). Line 17 checks whether the current node v is the source node s and the current aggregate path utilization au is smaller than the best known value au_{best}. In case both conditions are true, LUAR builds the current path by creating a list from the nodes listed in W, which are the first items of each triple (Line 18), and updates the best known path ρ_{best} to be it. Line 19 also updates the minimum known aggregate utilization au_{best} to be the current one au. Regardless of the previous conditions, if there is predecessors that should still be explored for node v (Line 20), a new triple is added to W containing the next predecessor of v to be explored and adding up the utilization from the predecessor to v to the current aggregate utilization (Lines 21). Otherwise, LUAR removes the last triple from W, and if W does not become empty, it increments by one the index of the next predecessor to explore from the last triple. This process is repeated until all of the shortest paths from source node s to destination node t have been analyzed. At the end of the algorithm, variable ρ_{best} is returned and indicates the shortest, least utilized, currently available path.

The worst-case complexity of LUAR is given by $\mathcal{O}(n + m)$, where n is the number of nodes and m refers to the number of links in the topology, since both of the adapted algorithms (BFS and DFS) have complexity $\mathcal{O}(n + m)$ and are executed sequentially in our algorithm. Therefore, LUAR runs in polynomial linear time to the number of devices and links in the network and is suited to quickly compute the best path to route traffic from two processes of an HPC application.

4 Evaluation

In this section, we evaluate the proposed solution aiming at assessing application execution speedup under varying conditions. We start by detailing the experimental setup. Next, we characterize the workloads employed. Finally, we present and discuss the results obtained with the SDN-based Path Provisioning Controller (with LUAR).

4.1 Experimental Setup

We implemented the cloud infrastructure with Mininet [8]. Hosts were instantiated as full-fledged lightweight Linux VM instances. The network infrastructure was comprised of Open vSwitch version 2.0.2 switches (that support OpenFlow version 1.3) and links of 1 Gbps. The SDN-based Path Provisioning Controller was implemented as an application that runs on top of Ryu [16]. This experimental environment was deployed on a 3.4 GHz, 64-bit quad-core Intel (i7-8550U) processor, with 16 GB of RAM and running Ubuntu 18.04 LTS.

The right-most side of Fig. 1 illustrates a simplified version of the cloud network topology used in the experiments. It is a *fat-tree* that, as usual, is organized in three hierarchical layers: *edge*, *aggregation*, and *core*. In our topology, 32 hosts ($h1 \dots h32$) were attached to edge switches. In the aggregation layer, we instantiated 16 switches, while in the core, 4 (totaling 20: $s1 \dots s20$). The switches in the aggregation layer were organized in 4 PoDs (Points of Delivery).

Throughout the evaluation, two distinct scenarios were considered: one named *Dense*, in which the VMs allocated to execute an HPC application were randomly provisioned within the same PoD, and one entitled *Sparse*, meaning the VMs were spread across multiple PoDs. The workloads to which the experiments were submitted are described in the next Subsect. 4.2. We compared the results obtained using LUAR with those observed with more traditional forwarding strategies, namely *Shortest Path* and *Random*. The metric employed for the comparison was *application runtime*. Each experiment was repeated 30 times. Results have a confidence level of 90%.

4.2 Workloads

Regarding the HPC application used to carry out the experiments, we employed the NAS Parallel Benchmarks (NPB) version 3.3 [2]. The benchmarks are designed to support the performance evaluation of HPC infrastructure and systems. They are derived from computational fluid dynamics and consist of five kernels and three compact applications. The choice for NPB was due to, in addition to encompassing a wide range of HPC application profiles, it is regarded as a reference and is extensively employed for performance evaluation in the literature.

We selected six representative NPB applications, whose communication patterns are illustrated in Fig. 2 (considering their instantiation with four nodes). Thick edges denote intensive communication demands, while thin ones represent the opposite. Observe that in BT all nodes exchange data with one another, but at low amounts. Similarly to BT, in EP data exchange is also low, but not all nodes communicate directly (*e.g.*, 2 and 3 in the example). The LU and MG applications take the form of a ring-based topology, with massive information exchange. Finally, CG and SP comprise an initial data distribution step, followed by data-intensive communication between half of the process pairs.

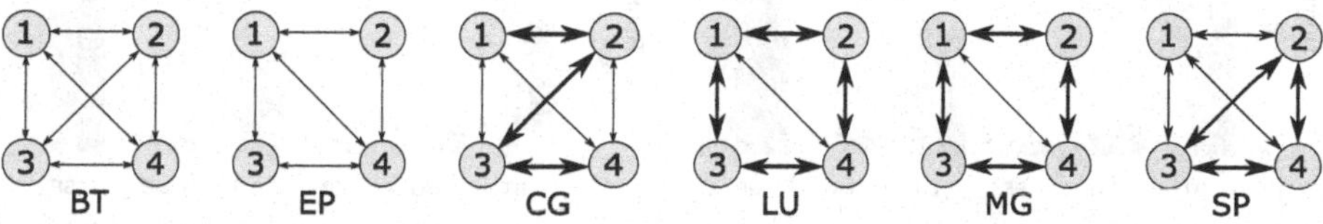

Fig. 2. Communication patterns of six NPB applications

According to recent data center measurements [5], a large portion of data center traffic is carried by a small fraction of long-lived, voluminous flows (called *elephant* flows). Similarly, Joy *et al.* [7] report that nine out of ten flows transfer less than 1 MB of data (*mice* flows), while 90% of the total bytes transferred belongs to flows larger than 100 MB (*i.e.*, elephant).

In line with the studies mentioned above, we emulated a realistic traffic workload composed of mice and elephant flows. Each experiment had a duration of 15 min and was composed of two states: *warmup* (1–3 min) and *steady* (4–15 min) states. During the former, the number of ongoing background flows increased gradually until reaching the desired level of resource competition. During the latter, whenever a background flow ended, a new one was started to maintain the expected overall concurrence level. To create such a new flow, we randomly selected a pair of *producer* and *consumer* processes, and determined its duration to be of up to 4 min (respecting the proportion of 9/10 mice and 1/10 elephant flows). It was also during the steady state that we instantiated the HPC application, *i.e.*, one of the NAS benchmarks shown in Fig. 2, complying with either the Dense or the Sparse scenario.

4.3 Results

We now present and discuss the results obtained starting with the Sparse scenario, followed by the Dense one. Figure 3 summarizes the application performance when the VMs (and, as a consequence, the HPC application processes)

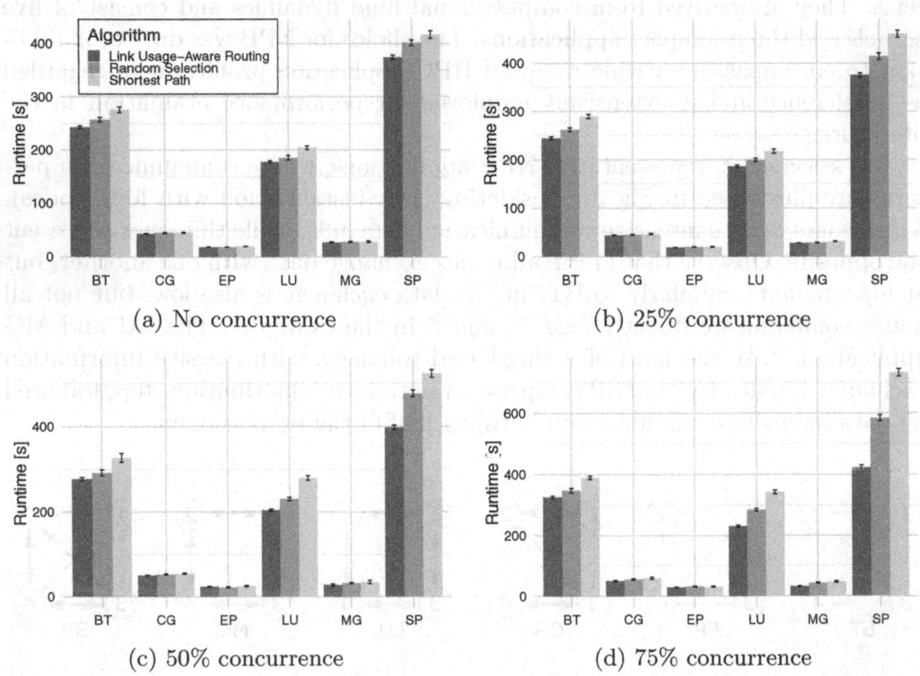

Fig. 3. Application performance observed for the Sparse scenario

are spread across multiple PoDs. Notice that larger applications tend to take more advantage of our proposed approach. The application runtime observed for BT, LU, and SP is, on average, 22.86 s lower (8.79% speedup) than what is achieved with Shortest Path and Random. The gains of LUAR for CG, EP, and MG are more modest, being of nearly 1-second runtime improvement.

Another important angle from which to analyze the results is the performance gains as a function of the concurrency level. The higher the contention of the cloud network, the higher the advantage and the value of employing LUAR. On average, it outperforms Shortest Path by 8.61% in (a – no concurrence), 11.23% in (b), 17.82% in (c), and 31.35% in (d – 75% concurrence). Taking both the size of an application and the level of concurrence into consideration simultaneously, we observe that the shortest application, EP, exhibits nearly constant 8% runtime improvement with LUAR (against Shortest Path) regardless of concurrency level. Conversely, the largest application, SP, presents consistently increasing gains of 9.87% (a), 20.23% (b), 26.61% (c), and 44.24% (d).

We move now to the scenario in which the VMs (and the HPC application processes) are allocated on hosts of a single PoD. This scenario is expected to be more common, but with fewer opportunities to speed up application performance through just-in-time traffic-aware path provisioning. Figure 4 shows the results. Despite the reduction of path diversity on the network edge for the Dense scenario, LUAR beats its counterparts. For example, SP executes 24.36% faster than when using Shortest Path under the condition of 50% concurrency.

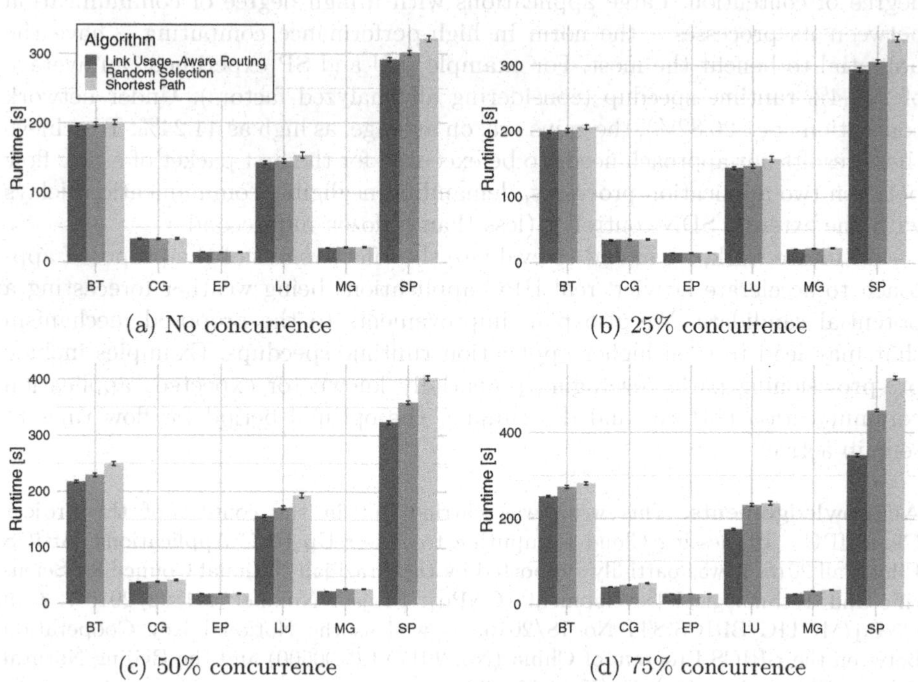

Fig. 4. Application performance observed for the Dense scenario

Other applications are too short-lived to take full advantage of LUAR but still run faster. This is the case of CG, which took 34.12 s to complete with Shortest Path and 33.20 s with LUAR (2.7% faster).

Finally, it is worth analyzing the performance observed with Random. The reason is that this strategy mimics load balancing, which is currently used by state-of-the-art cloud infrastructures. Although its results are better than the Shortest Path, it performs consistently worse, *i.e.*, for all applications and concurrency levels, than LUAR. Our gains range, on average, from 2.23% to 17.47% for the Dense scenario (and from 4.51% to 19.1% for the Sparse one). These results underscore that deciding paths dynamically and with accurate knowledge of network traffic has the potential to allow better routing decisions.

5 Final Considerations and Future Work

In this paper, we proposed a mechanism for *dynamic* path provisioning in cloud network infrastructures. It keeps track of *link utilization* and deploys *shortest, least utilized paths* to "interconnect" the processes of a running HPC application. The mechanism unfolds into *two main research contributions*: (*i*) an SDN-centric path provisioning architecture and (*ii*) a link usage-aware routing strategy.

The results suggest that the proposed solution is promising. LUAR performs particularly well under challenging, yet ordinary circumstances such as when VMs are dispersed across the infrastructure, and the network exhibits some degree of contention. Large applications with a high degree of communication between its processes – the norm in high-performance computing – have the potential to benefit the most. For example, LU and SP experiment an average of 23.14% runtime speedup (considering all analyzed factors). Under network contention (*i.e.*, 26.82%), the gains are, on average, as high as 44.24%. To achieve these results our approach needs to be executed for the first packet of a new flow between two application processes, demanding negligible communication delays with the external SDN controller (less than a dozen milliseconds).

As future work, we intend to evaluate the effectiveness of the proposed approach to accelerate heavier, real HPC applications being weather forecasting a potential candidate. We also plan improvements to the proposed mechanism that may lead to even higher application runtime speedups. Examples include pre-provisioning paths leveraging potentially known (or expected) application communication patterns and determining the optimal period for flow rules to remain active.

Acknowledgements. This work was carried out in the context of the project CloudHPC – Harnessing Cloud Computing to Power Up HPC Applications, BRICS Pilot Call 2016. It was partially supported by the Brazilian National Council for Scientific and Technological Development (CNPq), Project Number 441892/2016-7, Call CNPq/MCTIC/BRICS-STI No 18/2016, as well as the National Key Cooperation between the BRICS Program of China (No. 2017YE0100500) and the Beijing Natural Science Foundation of China (No. 4172033).

References

1. Alsmadi, I., Khamaiseh, S., Xu, D.: Network parallelization in HPC clusters. In: International Conference on Computational Science and Computational Intelligence (CSCI 2016), pp. 584–589, December 2016. https://doi.org/10.1109/CSCI.2016.0116
2. Bailey, D.H.: NAS parallel benchmarks. In: Padua, D. (eds) Encyclopedia of Parallel Computing, pp. 1254–1259. Springer, Boston (2011). https://doi.org/10.1007/978-0-387-09766-4
3. Evangelinos, C., Hill, C.N.: Cloud computing for parallel scientific HPC applications: feasibility of running coupled atmosphere-ocean climate models on amazon's EC2. In: The 1st Workshop on Cloud Computing and its Applications (CCA) (2008)
4. Faizian, P., Mollah, M.A., Tong, Z., Yuan, X., Lang, M.: A comparative study of SDN and adaptive routing on dragonfly networks. In: Proceedings of the International Conference for High Performance Computing, Networking, Storage and Analysis, p. 51. ACM (2017)
5. Guo, Z., Liu, R., Xu, Y., Gushchin, A., Walid, A., Chao, H.J.: STAR: preventing flow-table overflow in software-defined networks. Comput. Netw. **125**, 15–25 (2017)
6. Gupta, A., et al.: Evaluating and improving the performance and scheduling of HPC applications in cloud. IEEE Trans. Cloud Comput. **4**(3), 307–321 (2016). https://doi.org/10.1109/TCC.2014.2339858
7. Joy, S., Nayak, A.: Improving flow completion time for short flows in datacenter networks. In: IFIP/IEEE International Symposium on Integrated Network Management (IM 2015), pp. 700–705, May 2015. https://doi.org/10.1109/INM.2015.7140358
8. Lantz, B., Heller, B., McKeown, N.: A network in a laptop: rapid prototyping for software-defined networks. In: Proceedings of the 9th ACM SIGCOMM Workshop on Hot Topics in Networks, p. 19. ACM (2010)
9. Lee, J., Tong, Z., Achalkar, K., Yuan, X., Lang, M.: Enhancing infiniband with openflow-style SDN capability. In: Proceedings of the International Conference for High Performance Computing, Networking, Storage and Analysis SC 2016, pp. 36:1–36:12. IEEE Press, Piscataway (2016). http://dl.acm.org/citation.cfm?id=3014904.3014953
10. Li, C., Zhang, J., Luo, Y.: Real-time scheduling based on optimized topology and communication traffic in distributed real-time computation platform of storm. J. Netw. Comput. Appl. **87**, 100–115 (2017)
11. Mauch, V., Kunze, M., Hillenbrand, M.: High performance cloud computing. Future Gener. Comput. Syst. **29**(6), 1408–1416 (2013)
12. Milojičić, D., Llorente, I.M., Montero, R.S.: Opennebula: a cloud management tool. IEEE Internet Comput. **15**(2), 11–14 (2011)
13. Netto, M.A.S., Calheiros, R.N., Rodrigues, E.R., Cunha, R.L.F., Buyya, R.: HPC cloud for scientific and business applications: taxonomy, vision, and research challenges. ACM Comput. Surv. **51**(1), 8:1–8:29 (2018). https://doi.org/10.1145/3150224
14. Ramakrishnan, L., Canon, R.S., Muriki, K., Sakrejda, I., Wright, N.J.: Evaluating interconnect and virtualization performance for high performance computing. ACM SIGMETRICS Perform. Eval. Rev. **40**(2), 55–60 (2012)

15. Roloff, E., Diener, M., Diaz Carreño, E., Gaspary, L.P., Navaux, P.O.A.: Leveraging cloud heterogeneity for cost-efficient execution of parallel applications. In: Rivera, F.F., Pena, T.F., Cabaleiro, J.C. (eds.) Euro-Par 2017. LNCS, vol. 10417, pp. 399–411. Springer, Cham (2017). https://doi.org/10.1007/978-3-319-64203-1_29
16. RYU: Ryu, a component-based software defined networking framework (2019). http://osrg.github.io/ryu/. Accessed 26 Jan 2019
17. Sefraoui, O., Aissaoui, M., Eleuldj, M.: Openstack: toward an open-source solution for cloud computing. Int. J. Comput. Appl. **55**(3), 38–42 (2012)
18. Walker, E.: Benchmarking amazon EC2 for high-performance scientific computing. Login: Mag. USENIX & SAGE **33**(5), 18–23 (2008)

Virtual Testbed: Ship Motion Simulation for Personal Workstations

Alexander Degtyarev, Vasily Khramushin, Ivan Gankevich(✉), Ivan Petriakov, Anton Gavrikov, and Artemii Grigorev

Saint Petersburg State University, Saint Petersburg, Russia
{a.degtyarev,v.khramushin,i.gankevich}@spbu.ru,
{st049350,st047437,st016177}@student.spbu.ru
https://spbu.ru/

Abstract. Virtual testbed is a computer programme that simulates ocean waves, ship motions and compartment flooding. One feature of this programme is that it visualises physical phenomena frame by frame as the simulation progresses. The aim of the studies reported here was to assess how much performance can be gained using graphical accelerators compared to ordinary processors when repeating the same computations in a loop. We rewrote programme's hot spots in OpenCL to able to execute them on a graphical accelerator and benchmarked their performance with a number of real-world ship models. The analysis of the results showed that data copying in and out of accelerator's main memory has major impact on performance when done in a loop, and the best performance is achieved when copying in and out is done outside the loop (when data copying inside the loop involves accelerator's main memory only). This result comes in line with how distributed computations are performed on a set of cluster nodes, and suggests using similar approaches for single heterogeneous node with a graphical accelerator.

Keywords: Wavy surface · Pressure field · Pressure force · Ship · Wetted surface · OpenCL · GPGPU

1 Introduction

Simulation of ship motion in ocean waves is done in several computer programmes [9,11,12] that differ in what physical phenomena they simulate (manoeuvring in waves, compartment flooding, regular and irregular waves, wind, real-time simulation or batch processing etc.) and application area (scientific studies, education or entertainment). These programmes are virtual analogues of ship model basins that are used to simulate characteristics and behaviour of ship in a particular sea conditions. The advantage of using virtual ship model basin over a physical one is that experiments are performed in real scale (with real-sized ships and ocean waves) and on a computer without the need to access high-technological facility.

S. Misra et al. (Eds.): ICCSA 2019, LNCS 11622, pp. 717–728, 2019.
https://doi.org/10.1007/978-3-030-24305-0_53

Although, all numerical experiments are performed on a computer, one computer is not powerful enough to perform them fast. Often, this problem is solved by using a cluster of computer nodes or a supercomputer; however, a supercomputer or a cluster is another high-technological facility that a researcher have to gain access to. In that case virtual ship model basin has little advantage over a physical one: the research is slowed down by official documents' approvals and time-sharing of computing resources.

One way of removing this barrier is to use graphical accelerator to speed up computations. In that case simulation can be performed on a regular workstation that has a dedicated graphics card. Most of the researchers use GPU to make visualisation in real-time, but it is rarely used for speeding up simulation parts, let alone the whole programme. In [2] the authors use GPU to speed up computation of free surface motion inside a tank. In [14] the authors rewrite their simulation code using Fast Fourier transforms and propose to use GPU to gain more performance. In [6] the authors use GPU to simulate ocean waves. Nevertheless, the most efficient way of using GPU is to use it for both computation and visualisation: it allows to minimise data copying between CPU and GPU memory and use mathematical models, data structures and numerical methods that are tailored to graphical accelerators.

The present research proposes a numerical method for computing velocity potentials and wave pressures on a graphical accelerator, briefly explains other methods in the programme, and presents benchmarks for asynchronous visualisation and simulation.

2 Methods

Virtual testbed is a computer programme that simulates ocean waves, ship motions and compartment flooding. One feature that distinguishes it with respect to existing proposals is the use of graphical accelerators to speed up computations and real-time visualisation that was made possible by these accelerators.

The programme consists of the following modules: `vessel` reads ship hull model from an input file, `gui` draws current state of the virtual world and `core` computes each step of the simulation. The `core` module consists of components that are linked together in a pipeline, in which output of one component is the input of another one. The computation is carried out in parallel to visualisation, and synchronisation occurs after each simulation step. It makes graphical user interface responsive even when workstation is not powerful enough to compute in real-time.

Inside `core` module the following components are present: wavy surface generator, velocity potential solver, pressure force solver. Each component in the `core` module is interchangeable, which means that different wavy surface generators can be used with the same velocity potential solver. Once initialised, these components are executed in a loop in which each iteration computes the next time step of the simulation. Although, iterations of the loop are sequential, each component is internally parallel, i.e. each component uses OpenMP or OpenCL to perform computations on each processor or graphical core. In other words, Virtual testbed follows BSP model [13] for organising parallel computations, in which a programme consists of sequential steps each of which is internally parallel (Fig. 1).

2.1 Wavy Surface Generation

There are three models that are used for wavy surface generation in Virtual testbed: autoregressive moving average model (ARMA), Stokes wave, and plane sine/cosine wave. It is not beneficial in terms of performance to execute ARMA model on a graphical accelerator [5]: its algorithm does not use transcendental mathematical functions, has nonlinear memory access pattern and complex information dependencies. It is much more efficient (even without serious optimisations) to execute it on a processor. In contrast, the other two wave models are embarrassingly parallel and easy to rewrite in OpenCL.

Each wave model outputs three-dimensional (one temporal and two spatial dimensions) field of wavy surface elevation, and ARMA model post-processes this field using the following algorithm. First, autocovariance function (ACF) is estimated from the input field using Wiener—Khinchin theorem. Then ACF is used to build autocovariance matrix and determine autoregressive model coefficients. Finally, the coefficients are used to generate new wavy surface elevation field.

The resulting field is stochastic, but has the same integral characteristics as the original one. In particular, probability distribution function of wavy surface elevation, wave height, length and period are preserved. Using ARMA model for post-processing has several advantages.

- It makes wavy surface aperiodic (its period equals period of pseudo-random number generator, which can be considered infinite for all practical applications) which allows to perform statistical studies using Virtual testbed.
- It is much faster to generate wavy surface with this model than with the original model, because ARMA model involves only multiplications and additions rather than transcendental mathematical functions.
- This model allows to use any wavy surface as the input (not only plane and Stokes waves). Frequency-directional spectrum of a particular ocean region can be used instead.

This paper gives only a short description of the model, please refer to [4,5] for in-depth study.

To summarise, wavy surface generator produces wavy surface elevation field using one of the models described above. For ARMA model it is impractical to generate it using graphical accelerator, and for other models it is to trivial to discuss. This field is an input for velocity potential solver.

2.2 Velocity Potential Computation

Since wavy surface generator produces discretely given elevation field we may not use formula from linear wave theory to compute velocity potential; instead, we derived a formula for arbitrary surface for inviscid incompressible fluid:

$$\phi(x,y,z,t) = \mathcal{F}^{-1}_{x,y}\left\{ \frac{\cosh\left(2\pi|\boldsymbol{k}|(z+h)\right)}{2\pi|\boldsymbol{k}|} \frac{\mathcal{F}_{u,v}\{f(x,y,t)\}}{\mathcal{F}_{u,v}\{\mathcal{D}_3\left(x,y,\zeta\left(x,y\right)\right)\}} \right\}, \tag{1}$$

where

$$\begin{aligned}
f(x,y,t) &= \zeta_t(x,y,t) / \left(i f_1(x,y) + i f_2(x,y) - f_3(x,y) \right), \\
f_1(x,y) &= \zeta_x / \sqrt{1+\zeta_x^2+\zeta_y^2} - \zeta_x, \qquad \mathcal{F}_{u,v}\{\mathcal{D}_3\left(x,y,z\right)\} = \cosh\left(2\pi|\boldsymbol{k}|z\right), \\
f_2(x,y) &= \zeta_y / \sqrt{1+\zeta_x^2+\zeta_y^2} - \zeta_y, \qquad |\boldsymbol{k}| = \sqrt{u^2+v^2}, \\
f_3(x,y) &= 1 / \sqrt{1+\zeta_x^2+\zeta_y^2}.
\end{aligned}$$

Here $\boldsymbol{k}$ is wave number, ζ — wavy surface elevation, h — water depth, $\mathcal{F}$ — Fourier transform, ϕ — velocity potential. The formula is derived as a solution for continuity equation with kinematic boundary condition

$$\begin{aligned}
&\nabla^2\phi = 0, \\
&\phi_t + \frac{1}{2}|\boldsymbol{v}|^2 + g\zeta = -\frac{p}{\rho}, && \text{at} z = \zeta(x,y,t), \\
&D\zeta = \nabla\phi \cdot \boldsymbol{n}, && \text{at} z = \zeta(x,y,t),
\end{aligned} \tag{2}$$

without assumptions of linear wave theory (wave length is much larger than wave height). Hence it can be used for arbitrary-amplitude ocean waves. Here the first equation is continuity equation, the second is dynamic boundary condition, and the last one is kinematic boundary condition; p — pressure, ρ — fluid density, $\boldsymbol{v} = (\phi_x, \phi_y, \phi_z)$ — velocity vector, g — acceleration of gravity, and D — substantial (Lagrange) derivative. Since we solve for ϕ, dynamic boundary condition becomes explicit formula for pressure and is used to compute pressure force acting on a ship hull (see Sect. 2.3).

Integral in (1) converges when summation goes over a range of wave numbers that are actually present in discretely given wavy surface. This range is determined numerically by finding crests and troughs for each spatial dimension of the wavy surface with polynomial interpolation and using these values to determine wave length. For small-amplitude waves this approach gives the same values of velocity potential field as direct application of the formula from linear wave theory.

Formula (1) is particularly suitable for computation on a graphical accelerator: it contains transcendental mathematical functions (complex exponents) that help offset slow global memory loads and stores, it is explicit which makes it easy to compute in parallel, and it is written using Fourier transforms that are efficient to compute on a graphical accelerator [15].

This paper gives only a short description of the method, please refer to [4,5] for in-depth study.

2.3 Pressure Force Computation

There are three stages of pressure force computation: determining wetted surface of a ship hull, computing wave pressure field under wavy surface, and computing pressure force acting on a ship hull.

In order to determine wetted surface, ship hull is decomposed into triangular panels (faces) that approximate its geometry. Then for each panel the algorithm determines its position relative to wavy surface. If it is fully submerged, it is considered wetted; if it is partially submerged, the algorithm computes intersection points using bisection method and wavy surface interpolation, and slices the part of the panel which is above the wavy surface (for simplicity the slice is assumed to be straight line, as is the case for sufficiently small panels). Wave pressure at any point under wavy surface is computed using dynamic boundary condition from (2) as an explicit formula. Then the pressure is interpolated in the centre of each panel to compute pressure force acting on a ship hull.

It is straightforward to rewrite pressure computation for a graphical accelerator as its algorithm reduces to looping over a large collection of panels and performing the same calculations for each of them; however, dynamic boundary condition contains temporal and spatial derivatives that have to be computed. Although, computing derivatives on a processor is fast, copying the results to accelerator's main memory proved to be inefficient as there are four arrays (one for each dimension) that need to be allocated and transferred. Simply rewriting code for OpenCL proved to be even more inefficient due to irregular memory access pattern for different array dimensions. So, we resorted to implementing the algorithm described in [10], that stores intermediate results in the local memory of the accelerator. Using this algorithm allowed us to store arrays of derivatives entirely in graphical accelerator's main memory and eliminate data transfer altogether.

2.4 Translational and Angular Ship Motion Computation

In order to compute ship position, translational velocity, angular displacement and angular velocity for each time step we solve equations of translational and angular motion (adapted from [9]) using pressure force computed for each panel:

$$\dot{\boldsymbol{v}} = \frac{\boldsymbol{F}}{m} + g\boldsymbol{\tau} - \boldsymbol{\Omega} \times \boldsymbol{v} - \lambda \boldsymbol{v}, \qquad \dot{\boldsymbol{h}} = \boldsymbol{G} - \boldsymbol{\Omega} \times \boldsymbol{h}, \qquad \boldsymbol{h} = \mathcal{I} \cdot \boldsymbol{\Omega}.$$

Here $\boldsymbol{\tau} = (-\sin\theta, \cos\theta\sin\phi, -\cos\theta\cos\phi)$ is a vector that transforms g into body-fixed coordinate system, $\boldsymbol{v}$—translational velocity vector, g—gravitational acceleration, $\boldsymbol{\Omega}$—angular velocity vector, $\boldsymbol{F}$—vector of external forces, m—ship mass, λ—damping coefficient, h—angular momentum, $\boldsymbol{G}$—the moment of external forces, and $\mathcal{I}$—inertia matrix.

We compute total force $\boldsymbol{F}$ and momentum $\boldsymbol{G}$ acting on a ship hull by adding forces acting on each panel. Then we solve the system of equations using numerical Runge-Kutta-Fehlberg method [8]. The vector of values determined by the method consists of all components of the following vectors: ship position, translational velocity, angular displacement and angular velocity (twelve variables in total). Since we are not interested in angular momentum, we use inertia matrix to obtain it from angular velocity and inverse inertia matrix to convert it back. Twelve vector components are too few to efficiently execute this method on a graphical accelerator and there is no other way of making iterative method parallel, so we execute it on a processor.

3 Results

3.1 Test Setup

Virtual testbed performance was benchmarked in a number of tests. Since we use both OpenMP and OpenCL technologies for parallel computing, we wanted to know how performance scales with the number of processor cores and with and without graphical accelerator.

Graphical accelerators are divided into two broad categories: for general purpose computations and for visualisation. Accelerators from the first category typically have more double precision arithmetic units and accelerators from the second category are typically optimised for single precision. The ratio of single to double precision performance can be as high as 32. Virtual testbed produces correct results for both single and double precision, but OpenCL version supports only single precision, and graphical accelerators that we used have higher single precision performance (Table 1). So we choose single precision in all benchmarks.

Table 1. Hardware configurations for benchmarks. For all benchmarks we used GCC version 8.1.1 compiler and optimisation flags `-O3 -march=native`.

Node	CPU	GPU	GPU GFLOPS	
			Single	Double
Storm	Intel Q9550	Radeon R7 360	1613	101
GPUlab	AMD FX-8370	NVIDIA GTX1060	4375	137
Capybara	Intel E5-2630 v4	NVIDIA P5000	8873	277

Double precision was used only for computing autoregressive model coefficients, because round-off and truncation numerical errors make covariance matrices (from which coefficients are computed) non-positive definite. These matrices typically have very large condition numbers, and linear system which they represent cannot be solved by Gaussian elimination or *LDLT* Cholesky decomposition, as these methods are numerically unstable (at least in our programme).

Since Virtual testbed does both visualisation and computation in real-time, we measured performance of each stage of the main loop (Fig. 1) synchronously with the parameters that affect it. To assess computational performance we measured execution time of each stage in microseconds (wall clock time) together with the number of wetted panels, and wavy surface size. To assess visualisation performance we measured the execution time of each visualisation frame (one iteration of the visualisation main loop) and execution time of computational frame (one iteration of the computational loop), from which it is easy to compute the usual frames-per-second metric. The tests were run for one minute and were forcibly stopped after the time ran out. Wall clock time was measured as a median across all simulation steps (or visualisation frames).

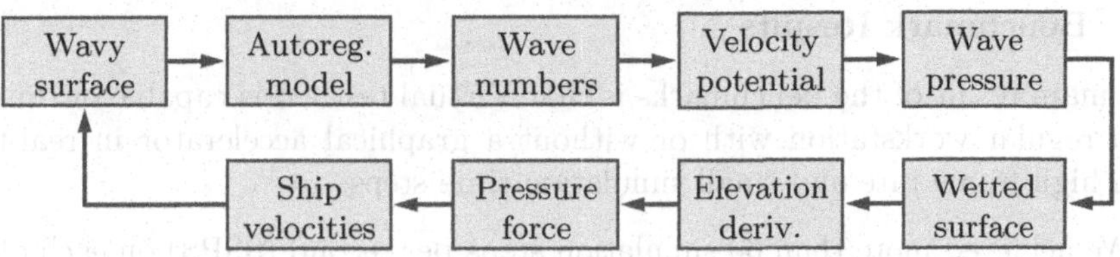

Fig. 1. Virtual testbed main loop.

We ran all tests on each node for increasing number of processor cores and with and without graphical accelerator. The code was compiled with maximum optimisation level including processor-specific optimisations which enabled auto-vectorisation for further performance improvements.

We ran all tests for each of the three ship hull models: Aurora cruiser, MICW (a hull with reduced moments of inertia for the current waterline) and a sphere. The first two models represent real-world ships with known characteristics and we took them from Vessel database [1] registered by our university which is managed by Hull programme [7]. Parameters of these ship models are listed in Table 2, three-dimensional models are shown in Fig. 2. Sphere was used as a geometric shape wetted surface area of which is close to constant under impact of ocean waves.

We ran all tests for each workstation from Table 1 to investigate if there is a difference in performance between ordinary workstation and a computer for visualisation. Storm is a regular workstation with mediocre processor and graphical accelerator, GPUlab is a slightly more powerful workstation, and Capybara has the most powerful processor and professional graphical accelerator optimised for visualisation.

Table 2. Parameters of ship models that were used in the benchmarks.

	Aurora	MICW	Sphere
Length, m	126.5	260	100
Beam, m	16.8	32	100
Depth, m	14.5	31	100
No. of panels	29306	10912	5120

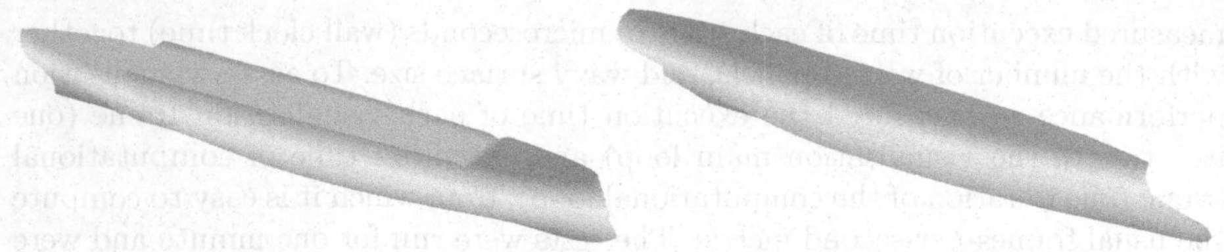

Fig. 2. Aurora and MICW three-dimensional ship hull models.

3.2 Benchmark Results

The main result of the benchmarks is that Virtual testbed is capable of running on a regular workstation with or without a graphical accelerator in real-time with high frame rate and small simulation time steps.

- We achieved more than 60 simulation steps per second (SSPS) on each of the workstations. SSPS is the same metric as frames per second in Visualisation, but for simulation. For Storm and GPUlab the most performant programme version was the one for graphical accelerator and for Capybara the most performant version was the one for the processor (Table 3).
- The most performant node is GPUlab with 104 simulation steps per second. Performance of Capybara is higher than of Storm, but it uses powerful server-grade processor to achieve it.
- Computational speedup for increasing number of parallel OpenMP threads is far from linear: we achieved only fourfold speedup for ten threads (Fig. 3).
- Although, GPUlab's processor has higher frequency, even one core of Capybara's processor achieves slightly higher performance.
- The least powerful workstation (Storm) has the largest positive difference between graphical accelerator and processor performance (Fig. 4). The most powerful workstation (Capybara) has comparable but negative difference.
- Usage of graphical accelerator increases time needed to synchronise simulation step with the visualisation frame (*exchange* stage in Fig. 4).

4 Discussion

Although, graphical accelerator gives noticeable performance increase only for the least powerful workstation, we considered only the simplest simulation scenario (ship motions induced by a plane Stokes wave) in the benchmarks: The problem that we solve is too small to saturate graphical accelerator cores. We tried to eliminate expensive data copying operations between host and graphical accelerator memory, where possible, but we need to simulate more physical phenomena and at a larger scale (ships with large number of panels, large number of compartments, wind simulation etc.) to verify that performance gap increases for powerful workstations. On the bright side, even if a computer does not have powerful graphical accelerator (e.g. a laptop with integrated graphics), it still can run Virtual testbed with acceptable performance.

Table 3. Best median performance for each workstation and each ship hull. Here t is simulation step computation time, m—no. of simulation steps per second (SSPS), and n—the number of OpenMP threads, CL—OpenCL, MP—OpenMP.

Node	Sphere				Aurora				MICW			
	t, ms	m	n	ver.	t, ms	m	n	ver.	t, ms	m	n	ver.
Storm	16	64	1	CL	14	72	1	CL	29	34	1	CL
GPUlab	10	104	1	CL	9	112	1	CL	18	55	1	CL
Capybara	12	85	10	MP	15	66	10	MP	19	51	10	MP

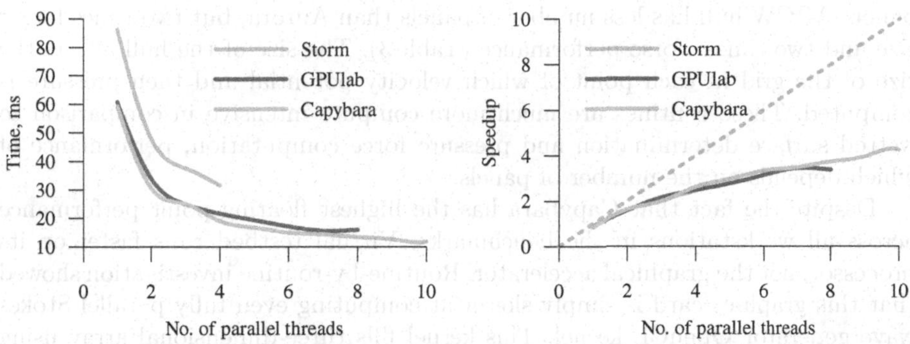

Fig. 3. Median simulation step computation time for different number of parallel threads (sphere).

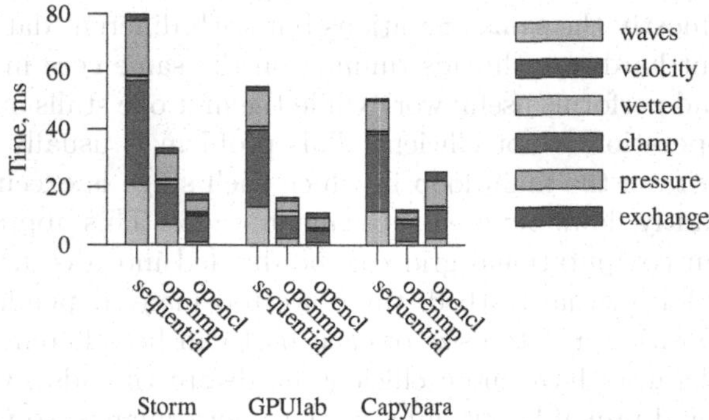

Fig. 4. Median computation time for each main loop stage, each node and sequential, OpenMP and OpenCL versions (sphere).

Large SSPS is needed neither for smooth visualisation, nor for accurate simulation; however, it gives performance reserve for further increase in detail and scale of simulated physical phenomena. We manually limit simulation time step to a minimum of 1/30 of the second to prevent floating-point numerical errors due to small time steps. Also, we limit maximum time step to have wave frequency greater or equal to Nyquist frequency for precise partial time derivatives computation.

Real-time simulation is essential not only for educational purposes, but also for on-board intelligent systems. These systems analyse data coming from a multitude of sensors the ship equips, calculate probability of occurrence of a particular dangerous situation (e.g. large roll angle) and try to prevent it by notifying ship's crew and an operator on the coast. This is one of the directions of future work.

Overall performance depends on the size of the ship rather than the number of panels. MICW hull has less number of panels than Aurora, but two times larger size and two times worse performance (Table 3). The size of the hull affects the size of the grid in each point of which velocity potential and then pressure is computed. These routines are much more compute intensive in comparison to wetted surface determination and pressure force computation, performance of which depends on the number of panels.

Despite the fact that Capybara has the highest floating-point performance across all workstations in the benchmarks, Virtual testbed runs faster on its processor, not the graphical accelerator. Routine-by-routine investigation showed that this graphics card is simply slower at computing even fully parallel Stokes wave generator OpenCL kernel. This kernel fills three-dimensional array using explicit formula for the wave profile, it has linear memory access pattern and no information dependencies between array elements. It seems, that P5000 is not optimised for general purpose computations. We did not conduct visualisation benchmarks, so we do not know if it is more efficient in that case.

Although, Capybara's processor has 20 hardware threads (2 threads per core), OpenMP performance does not scale beyond 10 threads. Parallel threads in our code do mostly the same operations but with different data, so switching between different hardware threads running on the same core in the hope that the second thread performs useful work while the first one stalls on input/output or load/store operation is not efficient. This problem is usually solved by creating a pipeline from the main loop in which each stage is executed in parallel and data constantly flows between subsequent stages. This approach is easy to implement when computational grid can be divided into distinct parts, which is not the case for Virtual testbed: there are too many dependencies between parts and the position and the size of each part can be different in each stage. Graphical accelerators have more efficient hardware threads switching which, and pipeline would probably not improve their performance, so we did not take this approach.

Our approach for performing computations on a heterogeneous node (a node with both a processor and a graphical accelerator) is similar to the approach followed by the authors of Spark distributed data processing framework [16]. In this framework data is first loaded into the main memory of each cluster node and then processed in a loop. Each iteration of this loop runs by all nodes in parallel and synchronisation occurs at the end of each iteration. This is in contrast to MapReduce framework [3] where after each iteration the data is written to stable storage and then read back into the main memory to continue processing. Not interacting with slow stable storage on every iteration allows Spark to achieve an order of magnitude higher performance than Hadoop (open-source version of MapReduce) on iterative algorithms.

For a heterogeneous node an analogue of stable storage, read/writes to which is much slower than accesses to the main memory, is graphical accelerator memory. To minimise interaction with this memory, we do not read intermediate results of our computations from it, but reuse arrays that already reside there. (As a concrete example, we do not copy pressure field from a graphical accelerator, only the forces for each panel.) This allows us to eliminate expensive data transfer between CPU and GPU memory. In early versions of our programme this copying slowed down simulation significantly.

Although, heterogeneous node is not a cluster, efficient programme architecture for such a node is similar to distributed data processing systems: we process data only on those device main memory of which contains the data and we never transfer intermediate computation results between devices. To implement this principle the whole iteration of the programme's main loop have to be executed either on a processor or a graphical accelerator. Given the time constraints, future maintenance burden and programme's code size, it was difficult to fully follow this approach, but we came to a reasonable approximation of it. We still have functions (*clamp* stage in Fig. 4 that reduces the size of the computational grid to the points nearby the ship) in Virtual testbed that work with intermediate results on a processor, but the amount of data that is copied to and from a graphical accelerator is relatively small.

5 Conclusion

We showed that ship motion simulation can be performed on a regular workstation with or without graphical accelerator. Our programme includes only minimal number of mathematical models that allow ship motions calculation, but has performance reserve for inclusion of additional models. We plan to implement rudder and propeller, compartment flooding and fire, wind and trochoidal waves simulation. Apart from that, the main direction of future research is creation of on-board intelligent system that would include Virtual testbed as an integral part for simulating and predicting physical phenomena.

Acknowledgements. Research work is supported by Saint Petersburg State University (grant no. 26520170 and 39417213).

References

1. Bogdanov, A., Khramushin, V.: Vessel: blueprints for the analysis of hydrostatic characteristics, stability and propulsion of the ship (2015). http://www1.fips.ru/fips_servl/fips_servlet?DB=EVM&DocNumber=2015621368&TypeFile=html. (in Russian)
2. Cercos-Pita, J.L., Bulian, G., Pérez-Rojas, L., Francescutto, A.: Coupled simulation of nonlinear ship motions and a free surface tank. Ocean Eng. **120**, 281–288 (2016). https://doi.org/10.1016/j.oceaneng.2016.03.015
3. Dean, J., Ghemawat, S.: MapReduce: simplified data processing on large clusters. Commun. ACM **51**(1), 107–113 (2008). https://doi.org/10.1145/1327452.1327492
4. Gankevich, I.: Simulation modelling of irregular waves for marine object dynamics programmes. Ph.D. thesis, Saint Petersburg State University, Saint Petersburg, Russia, June 2018
5. Gankevich, I., Degtyarev, A.: Simulation of standing and propagating sea waves with three-dimensional ARMA model. In: Velarde, M.G., Tarakanov, R.Y., Marchenko, A.V. (eds.) The Ocean in Motion. SO, pp. 249–278. Springer, Cham (2018). https://doi.org/10.1007/978-3-319-71934-4_18
6. Keeler, T., Bridson, R.: Ocean waves animation using boundary integral equations and explicit mesh tracking. In: Proceedings of the ACM SIGGRAPH/Eurographics Symposium on Computer Animation, SCA 2014, pp. 11–19. Eurographics Association, Aire-la-Ville (2014). http://dl.acm.org/citation.cfm?id=2849517.2849520
7. Khramushin, V.: Analytic ship hull shape construction, wave resistance calculations, theoretical blueprint feature curve calculations, and ship stability diagrams (2010). http://www1.fips.ru/fips_servl/fips_servlet?DB=EVM&DocNumber=2010615849&TypeFile=html. (in Russian)
8. Mathews, J.H., Fink, K.D.: Numerical Methods Using MATLAB, 4th edn. Pearson Prentice Hall, London (2004)
9. Matusiak, J.: Dynamics of a Rigid Ship. No. 11/2013 in SCIENCE + TECHNOLOGY, Aalto University; Aalto-yliopisto (2013). http://urn.fi/URN:ISBN:978-952-60-5205-2
10. Micikevicius, P.: 3D finite difference computation on GPUs using CUDA. In: Proceedings of 2nd Workshop on General Purpose Processing on Graphics Processing Units, GPGPU-2, pp. 79–84. ACM, New York (2009). https://doi.org/10.1145/1513895.1513905
11. Shin, Y., et al.: Nonlinear time domain simulation technology for seakeeping and wave-load analysis for modern ship design. Trans. Soc. Naval Architects Marine Engineers **111**, 557–583 (2003). Authors' closure
12. Ueng, S.K., Lin, D., Liu, C.H.: A ship motion simulation system. Virtual Reality **12**(1), 65–76 (2008). https://doi.org/10.1007/s10055-008-0088-8
13. Valiant, L.G.: A bridging model for parallel computation. Commun. ACM **33**(8), 103–111 (1990). https://doi.org/10.1145/79173.79181
14. Varela, J.M., Soares, C.G.: Interactive simulation of ship motions in random seas based on real wave spectra. In: Proceedings of the International Conference on Computer Graphics Theory and Applications, pp. 235–244 (2011)
15. Volkov, V., Kazian, B.: Fitting FFT onto the G80 architecture. Technical report 6, University of California, Berkeley, May 2008
16. Zaharia, M., et al.: Apache spark: a unified engine for big data processing. Commun. ACM **59**(11), 56–65 (2016). https://doi.org/10.1145/2934664

Vessel: Efficient Plain Text File Format for Ship Hull Geometry

Alexander Degtyarev, Ivan Gankevich(✉), Anton Gavrikov, Artemii Grigorev, Vasily Khramushin, and Ivan Petriakov

Saint Petersburg State University, Saint Petersburg, Russia
{a.degtyarev,i.gankevich,v.khramushin}@spbu.ru,
{st047437,st016177,st049350}@student.spbu.ru
http://www.shipdesign.ru/

Abstract. Initially, digital geometric model of a ship hull is assumed to maintain continuity in solving traditional ship theory problems, ship hydromechanics and seakeeping in severe storm waves. In the research reported here we consider using a table of plaza ordinates (transversal projection of frames) supplemented with a description of sterns as a means of describing digital geometric model. This description, which we call Vessel (VSL) format, allows for later addition of compartments, appendages and superstructures. These more complicated ship structures and their characteristics (e.g. ship compartments and superstructures are characterised by template-based modelling) are added to initial ship hull model in separate files from the working directory of a particular experiment. We show how this model is converted into three-dimensional triangular mesh suitable for ship motion simulations. VSL format is generally more efficient than industry standard IGES format and is distinguished by the simplicity and capability of editing by hand.

Keywords: Ship lines · Ship blueprint · Ship theory · Ship design · Ship hydromechanics · Storm seakeeping · Coons surface · Hermite spline · VSL · IGES

1 Introduction

Initial geometric model of a ship hull is close to traditional hull blueprints which are naturally rendered as a table of plaza ordinates in ship theory. Such a model quite reliably characterises ship hull lines and above-water ship hull parts, while preserving continuity in hydrostatic and hydrodynamic calculations in ship theory and hydromechanics. This is important for verification of newly created numerical experiments with a multitude of historical series of ship calculations, model basin experiments and sea trials. Obvious advantage of this digital format is that it is relatively simple and has compact data layout, with the data prepared and refined as plain text strings representing stern and frame coordinate sequences. We call this format Vessel (or VSL for short).

S. Misra et al. (Eds.): ICCSA 2019, LNCS 11622, pp. 729–739, 2019.
https://doi.org/10.1007/978-3-030-24305-0_54

Numerous variants of ship hulls were systematically collected in VSL format in Saint Petersburg State University in Vessel database [3]. The database is maintained with the help of Hull software suite [5] which allows for editing ship hull coordinates and calculates certain hydrostatic characteristics. In this paper we describe VSL format, compare and contrast its efficiency and performance with industry standard IGES format, and outline advantages and disadvantages of using plain text for creating and editing ship hull geometry by hand.

2 Methods

2.1 Vessel Format

Formalised description of ship hull geometry is done using plain text data which include ship name, hull dimensions, and successive description of aft, main (table of plaza ordinates) and bow sections. When digital ship hull model is first added to Vessel database the following design characteristics are specified in the comments: displacement, wetted surface area, hull volume ratio coefficient, date and time of file creation. The diagram of a VSL file is presented in Table 1, projections and three-dimensional model of Aurora cruiser are presented in Figs. 8 and 9.

Table 1. VSL file format diagram.

<table>
<tr><td colspan="3">1. Technical vessel description (lines starting with // or ; are comments)</td></tr>
<tr><td colspan="3">2. Format magic number (30) and hull model name in angle brackets <...></td></tr>
<tr><td colspan="3">3. The number of frames and middle frame number</td></tr>
<tr><td colspan="3">4. Hull dimensions (length, beam, draft)</td></tr>
<tr><td>The number of points on a curve</td><td colspan="2">5. $X(z)$ — sternpost contour abscissas as a function of applicates</td></tr>
<tr><td></td><td colspan="2">6. $Y(z)$ — transom width ordinates as a function of applicates</td></tr>
<tr><td></td><td>Frame abscissas</td><td>7. $Y(z)$ — frame curves as functions of applicates of general hull line</td></tr>
<tr><td></td><td colspan="2">8. $Y(z)$ — bulbous bow width ordinates as a function of applicates</td></tr>
<tr><td></td><td colspan="2">9. $X(z)$ — stern contour abscissas as a function of applicates</td></tr>
<tr><td colspan="3">10. Design characteristics (displacement, wetted surface, volume ratio coefficient)</td></tr>
</table>

Ship hull is divided into three sections (Fig. 1): aft, main and bow sections. Main section consists of frames each of which is defined by a collection of points lying in transverse plane. Smooth curve that goes though all of these points is created by cubic Hermite spline interpolation. Each frame may not have the same number of points (but usually do), and there are no additional points between endpoints of subsequent frames in longitudinal plane. Aft and bow sections consist of frames in transverse plane and a curve in longitudinal plane that defines the shape of the ship hull in this plane. This curve go through (usually) all frames and defines intermediate points between endpoints of subsequent frames. If it does not go between some frames, then there are no intermediate points between them. Curves are not closed and define only left part of the ship hull, the full ship hull model is created by mirroring each point of the curve with respect to longitudinal axis and connect corresponding curve endpoints by straight lines.

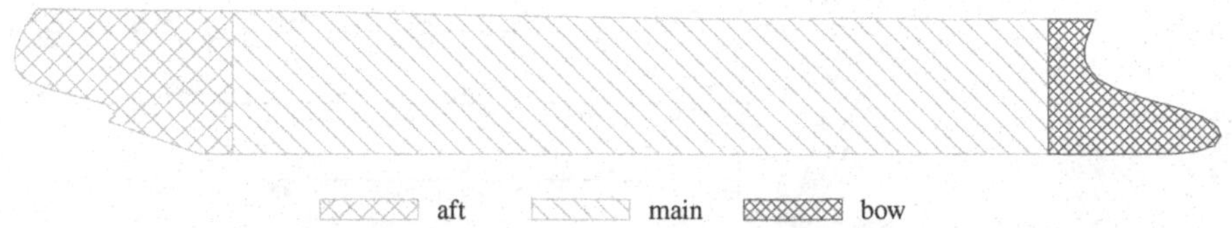

Fig. 1. Three sections of a ship hull as defined by VSL format.

In accordance with initial purpose of a digital ship hull model, Hull programme makes basic calculations of certain characteristics of a ship hull, curved elements and ship stability diagrams by fixing the centre of gravity with respect to general line, centre of buoyancy, metacentre or current waterline (Fig. 2). The programme also performs wave resistance calculations for arbitrary travel speeds taking into account radiation intensity and interference of ship waves with respect to waterline as a function of Froude number.

2.2 Hydrostatic Calculations for Historic, Traditional and Contemporary Ship Hulls

As an illustrative example of simulating seakeeping ship characteristics we consider ship stability diagrams for contemporary and historical ships, and for a ship that is purposely optimised for improved seakeeping in storm waves.

Figure 3 shows that Aurora cruiser ship hull has excellent seakeeping characteristics in severe storm waves conditions, which guarantee safe small oscillations and smoothness of roll by reducing metacentric height — initial ship hull stability. Additional positive stability appears for large roll angles and arbitrary heaving.

More complicated usage scenario of computational model is optimisation of ship lines to achieve certain form of wave resistance curve (Fig. 4). In the calculations we build radiation intensity and ship waves interferences along the current waterline. By changing ship lines we reduce resistivity extrema for relative speeds (on Froude) on the order of 0.3 and 0.5 without sacrificing propulsion for minimum wave formation for speeds 0.4 and 0.2.

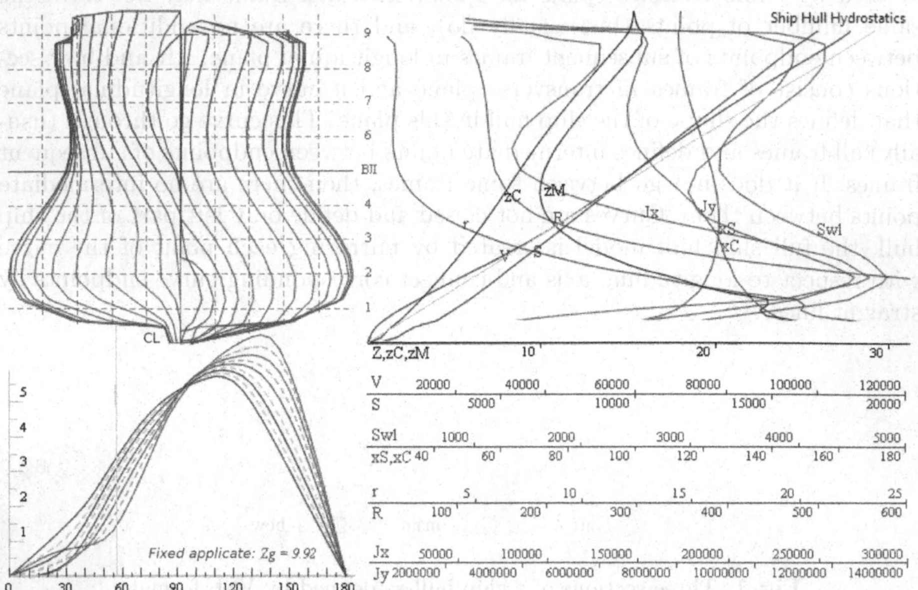

Fig. 2. Ship stability calculations for a ship with small moments of inertia for the area of the current waterline (MICW-85). For a design draught roll moments are small up to 30° wave slope, and stability increases in response to any change in draught.

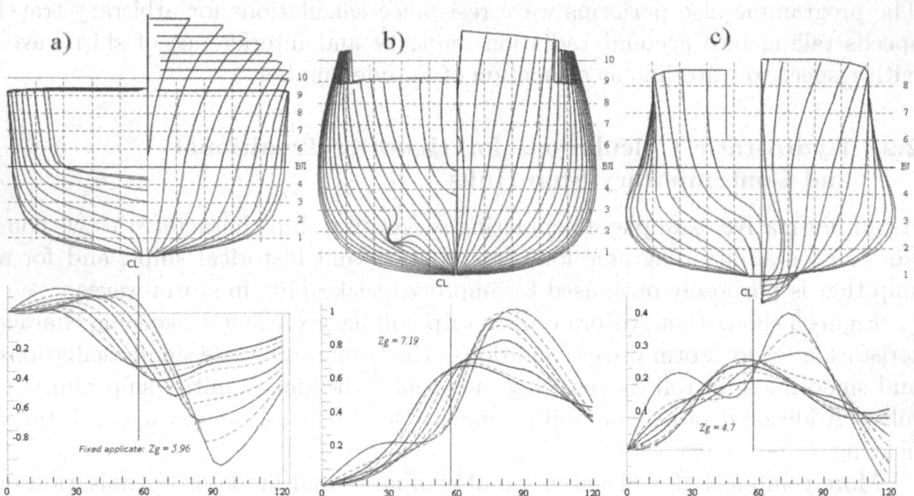

Fig. 3. Transversal projection of a ship hull (top), static ship stability diagrams for a fixed centre of gravity Z_g and metacentric height equal to 1% of a beam for contemporary (a), historical (b) and improved storm seakeeping (c) ships.

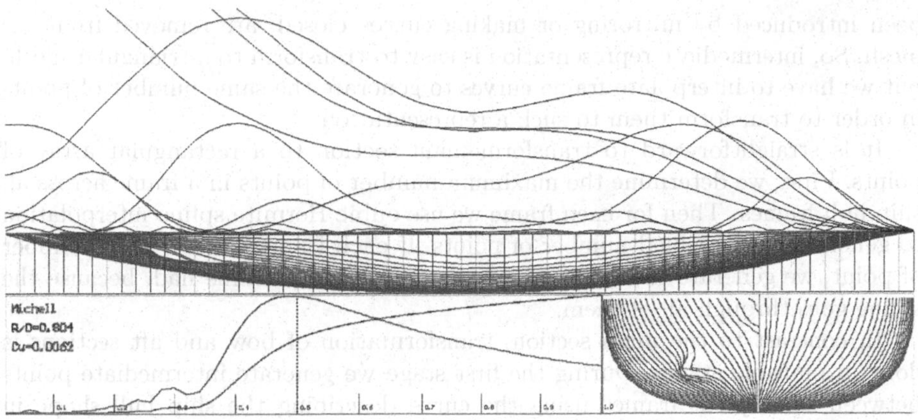

Fig. 4. Wave resistance, radiation intensity and ship waves intensity along the ship hull.

2.3 Triangulation of a Ship Hull Given by a Collection of Curves

In the original programme [5] that visualises ship lines and calculates hydrostatic characteristics, ship hull is described by a collection of curves; however, for a programme that simulates ship dynamics in rough sea this description is not convenient. A better representation would be a collection of triangles (a *triangular mesh*) that approximates analytic ship hull geometry. At the centre of each triangle pressure force induced by ocean waves is applied, and then these forces are used to calculate ship motion. Triangles is a better representation because they

- do not require recomputation every frame (like analytic curves),
- have simple formula for area (which is needed for pressure force calculation), and
- the same representation is used internally by graphical accelerators that visualise simulation frames.

In the following paragraphs we describe how analytically given ship hull is transformed into a fully connected collection of triangles.

Ship hull is transformed from analytic to discrete form by using *intermediate representation* — two-dimensional rectangular array of points, which makes it easy to obtain triangular mesh. Each ship hull section is transformed to such an array, and then these arrays are concatenated. Each row of the resulting array represents a frame, and each frame is an array of points of this frame. Since the array have to be rectangular, the number of points equal the maximum number of points among all original frames in VSL file. After that, endpoints are added to make curves closed, and the whole array is mirrored with respect to longitudinal axis. Then each rectangular patch of the resulting array is divided into two triangles to obtain triangular mesh. Duplicate vertices and faces, that may have been introduced by mirroring or making curves closed, are removed from the mesh. So, intermediate representation is easy to transform to a triangular mesh, but we have to interpolate frame curves to generate the same number of points in order to transform them to such a representation.

It is straightforward to transform main section to a rectangular array of points. First, we determine the maximum number of points in a frame across all ship hull frames. Then for each frame we use cubic Hermite spline interpolation to generate the specified number of points. If each frame has the same number of point, we generate the same points that the original frame had, because the spline goes through all of them.

In contrast to the main section, transformation of bow and aft sections is done in multiple stages. During the first stage we generate intermediate points between subsequent frames using the curve describing the ship hull shape in longitudinal plane. For that purpose we create a polygon in longitudinal plane that consists of all points of this curve, all points of the frame that is the closest to the curve endpoints, but does not cross the curve, and all endpoints of the frames that are between this frame and the curve (it happens when first and last endpoint of the curve are close to different frames). Frame points that lie outside this polygon are removed. Polygon points that lie between subsequent frames become intermediate points. At this stage we decompose a bow/aft section into a collection of "rectangular" patches vertical sides of which are curves created from subsequent frames and horizontal sides of which are curves created from intermediate points (Fig. 5).

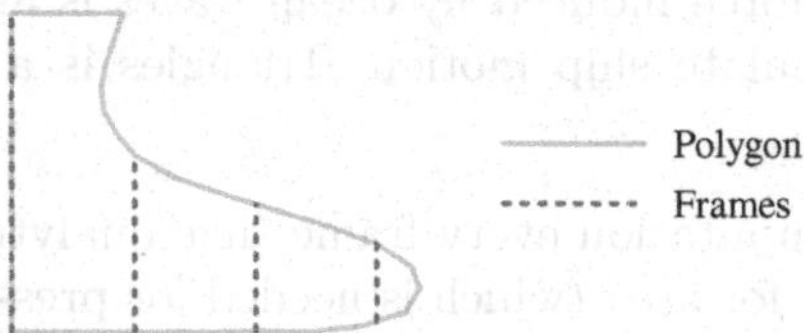

Fig. 5. Longitudinal slice of bow section of a ship hull that shows horizontal curves with large curvature.

A patch that is defined by four curves is called Coons patch [4]. Coons patch is a parametric surface $S(u,v)$ between four curves $c_0(u)$, $c_1(u)$, $d_0(v)$, $d_1(v)$:

$$\begin{aligned}
&S(u,v) = C_1(u,v) + C_2(u,v) - C_3(u,v),\\
&C_1(u,v) = v'c_0(u) + vc_1(u), \quad v' = 1 - v,\\
&C_2(u,v) = u'd_0(v) + ud_1(v), \quad u' = 1 - u,\\
&C_3(u,v) = c_0(0)u'v' + c_0(1)uv' + c_1(0)u'v + c_1(1)uv,\\
&c_0(0) = d_0(0), \quad c_0(1) = d_1(0), \quad c_1(0) = d_0(1), \quad c_1(1) = d_1(1).
\end{aligned}$$

Here C_1 is linear interpolation between points c_0 and c_1, C_2 is linear interpolation between points d_0 and d_1, and C_3 is bilinear interpolation between corner points of the patch. C_1 and C_2 are ruled surfaces — surfaces between two curves, that are generated by interpolating corresponding curve points. Bicubic interpolation can be used instead of bilinear to get the same derivative when joining multiple Coons patches together, but for a grid of interior points linear interpolation is enough.

Using these formulae we generate a grid of interior points between curves of each bow/aft patch during the second stage. Our first approach was to use one Coons patch for each subsequent pair of frames, but we have found that some ship hulls have horizontal curves with large curvatures which cause linear interpolation to produce cusps on the resulting surface (Fig. 6). We solved this problem by using multiple smaller Coons patches that were arranged vertically for each subsequent pair of frames. This approach removes the cusps, but the vertical size of the patch have to be small enough to reduce the effect of the large curvature of the horizontal curve. After generating grids of intermediate points with Coons patches for each subsequent frame, we concatenate them to obtain rectangular array for bow/aft sections.

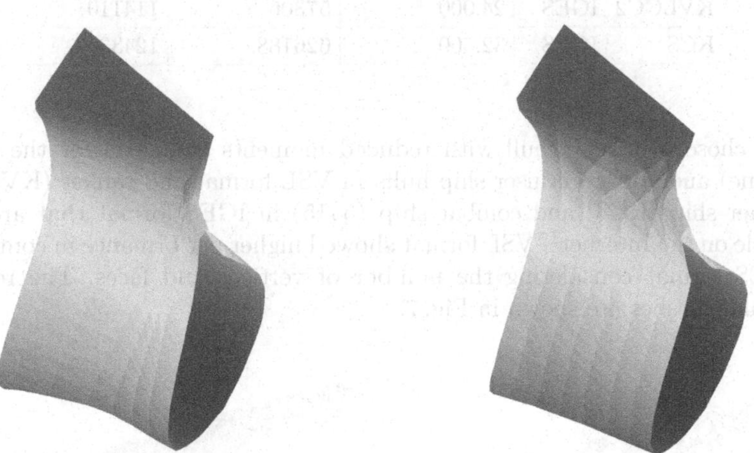

Fig. 6. Part of the bow section of the ship hull. The section with single Coons patch spanning the whole frame (left). The section with multiple smaller Coons patches arranged vertically (right).

After transforming each section of the ship hull into a rectangular array and concatenating them, we obtain an array of dimensions $m \times n$. We then use two-dimensional cubic Hermite spline interpolation to generate a grid of $(2m-1) \times (2n-1)$ points. Additional points increase surface smoothness and provide better approximation for the original ship hull. Finally, we transform the resulting grid into a triangular mesh to obtain three-dimensional discrete ship hull model, which is ready for the use in ship motion simulation and visualisation.

3 Results

To prove VSL viability for using it as an alternative to another format that uses analytic curves called IGES [7], we measured triangulation performance and measured how many vertices and faces are generated when analytic curves and surfaces are transformed into them. We do not have the same ship hulls in both formats, so we resorted to measuring performance relative to vertex and face count. To work with IGES format we use OpenCASCADE library [6]. Benchmark results are presented in Table 2.

Table 2. VSL performance in comparison to IGES for different ship hulls.

Ship	Format	Import time, s	No. of vertices	No. of faces
MICW	VSL	0.019	5457	10912
Aurora	VSL	0.054	14653	29306
5415	IGES	1.300	21088	41841
KVLCC2	IGES	24.000	57306	114110
KCS	IGES	32.500	626188	1243307

We chose MICW (a hull with reduced moments of inertia for the current waterline) and Aurora cruiser ship hulls in VSL format and tanker (KVLCC2), container ship (KCS) and combat ship (5415) in IGES format that are freely available on the Internet[1]. VSL format showed higher performance in comparison to IGES format considering the number of vertices and faces. The resulting triangular meshes are shown in Fig. 7.

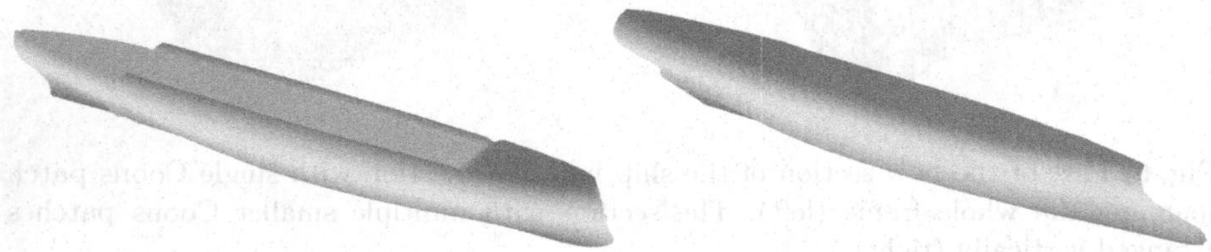

Fig. 7. Final Aurora and MICW three-dimensional triangular meshes.

4 Discussion

4.1 Advantages

Faster Triangulation. Faster triangulation is advantageous for performing ship motion simulations on a regular workstation. These machines are usually not

[1] https://simman2014.dk/ship-data/.

very powerful and do not have a lot of memory for complicated mesh pre-processing. IGES importer uses multiple threads for triangulation, whereas VSL does everything in one thread. Yet, it achieves higher performance on a regular workstation.

Ease of Editing. Most of the VSL files from Vessel database were written by hand. Points for frames were generated in a drawing programme by using legacy blueprints as an overlay and approximating curve projections by points. Then points were exported in plain text format and subsequently converted to VSL format by hand. Thus, there is no need in complicated and expensive CAD programme to produce Vessel files.

Compatibility with Legacy Blueprints. Legacy ship hull blueprints were mostly done by drawing projections of ship lines on a paper, and VSL incorporates longitudinal projections for bow and aft and transversal projection for the main section. It is easy to convert legacy blueprint to VSL file by overlaying frame points on the drawing. It is also easy for people who used to legacy blueprints to reason about ship hull characteristics.

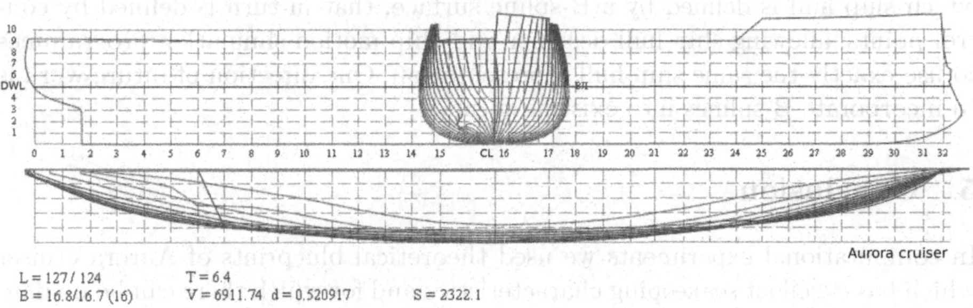

Fig. 8. Aurora cruiser digital model.

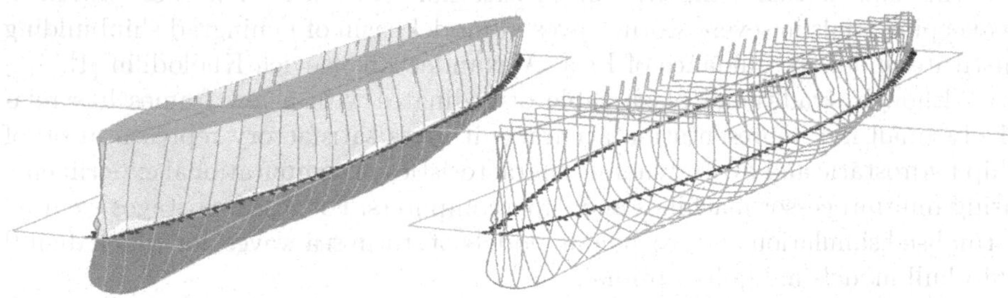

Fig. 9. Aurora cruiser hull is prepared for a numerical ship hydromechanics experiment. Although, the number of frame points in the main section is relatively small, it allows for smooth approximation of hull surface with the desired accuracy.

4.2 Disadvantages

The main disadvantage of VSL format is that a triangular mesh generated from it approximates ship hull surface only with a certain accuracy, but cannot represent it exactly. This is due to the fact that we choose the same number of points for each frame to be able to create rectangular array of all points and convert it to a mesh. Obvious solution to this problem is to use non-rectangular array, but it does not come without disadvantages. Non-rectangular array complicates triangle generation as we need to compute intermediate points for smaller patches, and it would be more difficult to make the resulting surface as smooth as the original, especially at intersections of frames with different number of points.

A simpler approach is to use rectangular array as the original ship hull representation, not an intermediate one. In that case each array element represents a geometric vertex and in addition the type of spline surface that represents ship hull surface *exactly* is specified in the file. That way it is easy to create triangular mesh that would be an exact representation of the original analytic surface when the number of grid points tends to infinity, and the resulting surface would be as smooth as the original one with all derivatives and surface normals computed using analytic representation. Similar approach is followed by FastShip [2] in which ship hull is defined by a B-spline surface, that in turn is defined by control points, allowing ship hull designer and ship motion simulation programmes to use exactly the same ship hull representation. One direction of future work is to incorporate B-splines into existing format.

5 Conclusion

In computational experiments we used theoretical blueprints of Aurora cruiser which has excellent seakeeping characteristics and for which there can be no dangerous situations in severe storm waves. We presented the more complicated geometric ship hull form which is optimised for storm seakeeping. This ship hull has relatively small moments of inertia for the area of the current waterline (MICW). For this hull mutual compensation of external force excitations was proved in seakeeping trials in severe storm waves in model basin of Leningrad shipbuilding institute under the guidance of Prof. Alexander Nikolaevich Kholodilin [1].

Although, traditional plaza table of ordinates with a few frames has relatively small hull representation accuracy, it gives satisfactory representation of ship hydrostatic and hydrodynamic characteristics in computational experiments using multiprocessor machines and supercomputers. For research stages we used formalised simulation and trochoidal models of storm sea waves, for which digital ship hull models are quite optimal.

We described efficient plain text format for three-dimensional ship hull geometry called VSL. This format uses longitudinal and transversal projections of ship lines given in analytic form. This format is easy to write by hand and easy to use for converting legacy ship hull blueprints into digital form. We demonstrated efficiency and viability of this format in comparison to IGES. Although, there are more precise alternatives for storing ship hull geometry, and VSL format gives only approximate representation of the original ship hull, it is distinguished by the simplicity and efficiency.

Acknowledgements. Research work is supported by Saint Petersburg State University (grant no. 26520170 and 39417213).

References

1. Search studies of ship seakeeping in storm waves, 3 edn. Lambert Academic Publishing (2018). (in Russian)
2. Alion Science Inc.: FastShip: basic ship design (2019). http://www.proteusengineering.com/fastship.htm
3. Bogdanov, A., Khramushin, V.: Vessel: blueprints for the analysis of hydrostatic characteristics, stability and propulsion of the ship (2015). http://www1.fips.ru/fips_servl/fips_servlet?DB=EVM&DocNumber=2015621368&TypeFile=html. (in Russian)
4. Coons, S.A.: Surfaces for computer-aided design of space forms. Technical report, Massachusetts Institute of Technology (1967)
5. Khramushin, V.: Analytic ship hull shape construction, wave resistance calculations, theoretical blueprint feature curve calculations, and ship stability diagrams (2010). http://www1.fips.ru/fips_servl/fips_servlet?DB=EVM&DocNumber=2010615849&TypeFile=html. (in Russian)
6. Open Cascade SAS: Open CASCADE technology, 3D modeling & numerical simulation (2019). https://www.opencascade.com/
7. Smith, B.M., Wellington, J.: IGES, a key interface specification for CAD/CALM systems integration. In: Computer-Aided Geometry Modeling, pp. 279–319 (1983)

Fair Resource Allocation for Running HPC Workloads Simultaneously

Ruslan Kuchumov(✉) and Vladimir Korkhov(✉)

Saint Petersburg State University,
7/9 Universitetskaya nab., St. Petersburg 199034, Russia
kuchumovri@gmail.com, v.korkhov@spbu.ru

Abstract. In high performance computing (HPC) job schedulers usually divide resources of computing nodes into slots. Each slot can be assigned to execute only a single job from the queue. In some cases, jobs do not fully utilize all available resources from the slot which leads to internal fragmentation, wasted resources and to an increase of queue wait time. In this paper, we propose fair resource allocation strategies that can be applied in job schedulers for resource allocation. We cover such resources as CPU time, residential memory and network bandwidth.

Keywords: High performance computing · Scheduling · Fair resource allocation

1 Introduction

In high performance computing (HPC) field job schedulers are widely used for maintaining queues of jobs created by different users and assigning nodes of the computing cluster to execute these jobs. Usually, at any moment one computing node is assigned for execution of a single job. Sometimes, nodes are divided into slots (for example, one slot per CPU core) and a slot is assigned to a single job. It leads to better utilization of computing nodes and to an increase of throughput of a cluster, as multiple jobs can be executed simultaneously.

But nevertheless, with this approach some computing nodes or slots may not be fully utilized. For example, CPU time of a slot may not be consumed fully, when the jobs it is executing are io- or network-intensive. Underutilized slots are not schedulable, they can not be reclaimed by the scheduler and the resources they have occupied become idle for some portion of job make-span. Right next to an under-utilized slot there may be an over-utilized one that can benefit from these idle resources.

The wasted resources of a node or a slot in some cases may be significant and expensive. For example, when performing HPC in a public cloud, it would lead to greater prices of job computations as users are charged for these idle resources as well. Thus, using the strategy of assigning a single slot to a job is not ideal.

By assigning a single computing node to execute multiple jobs it would be possible to decrease the amounts of idle resources compared to aforementioned

S. Misra et al. (Eds.): ICCSA 2019, LNCS 11622, pp. 740–751, 2019.
https://doi.org/10.1007/978-3-030-24305-0_55

strategy with slots. Furthermore, more jobs can be executed at the same time as node resources may be utilized more efficiently. All that would lead to decrease of job wait time in the queue and higher throughput of the cluster.

In order to achieve that, it would not be enough to execute multiple jobs simultaneously, as fair resource allocation between jobs must be provided. For example, one job may spawn more processes than the other, so on average it would receive more CPU time as the scheduler of operating system distributes it evenly.

In this paper we continue our earlier research [1–3] and cover fair resource allocation strategies for the resources such as CPU time, main memory and network bandwidth. These strategies guarantee jobs an equal shares of each resource and also allow jobs to exceed their shares at the expense of under-utilized shares of other jobs (which can later be reclaimed back).

2 CPU Time

Linux kernel scheduler by default uses Completely Fair Scheduling (CFS) strategy to equally distribute CPU time among threads and processes [4]. By default it treats all the tasks (e.g. threads and processes) the same way without considering their position in hierarchy. Because of that, when one job creates more child processes than the other, it would get on average more CPU time.

CFS scheduling strategy is based on the concept of virtual time. Each scheduler task in the queue has virtual time which equals to the weighted CPU time the task has spent executing on CPU. It is weighted so that the more the weight that task has, the slower its virtual time flows.

Runqueues are represented by red-black tree sorted by virtual time. It allows to quickly find the next task which would be executed on the CPU. CFS scheduler always picks the task with lowest virtual time and executes it for certain period of time without preemption. This time period (called slice) equals to the scheduling period proportionally divided between all the weights of tasks in the queue.

Each logical CPU core has its own runqueue. Each CPU is included in a scheduling group, which are, in turn, included in scheduling domains. Scheduling groups form non-intersecting sets of CPUs. Task balancing within a domain occurs between the groups. Each group has a load value which is defined as load of all the runqueues it includes, and when these loads are becoming out of balance the tasks are migrated. Scheduling domains may have hierarchical structure. The scheduler traverses this structure and periodically performs the same balancing procedure as for groups.

CFS scheduling strategy is also hierarchical. Each task is represented by a scheduling entity which can either be a leaf task (process, thread or tasklet) or a task group with another CFS queue. In case of non-leaf runqueue, the CPU time would be equally distributed between both tasks and task groups.

By creating control groups it is possible to define a hierarchy inside of CFS scheduler. In case we create a control group for each job, nest it in the same parent control group and assign equal weights to each cgroup we would be able to distribute CPU time equally, at first, between job and then between processes within an job.

To demonstrate that, we have placated two CPU-intensive benchmarks into two separate control groups. The benchmark instance in the first control group spawn $N = 4$ CPU-intensive threads and the time the instance in the second control group spawns $M = 2$ threads. In our test-bed we had 4 CPU cores, which yield $C = 4$ units of CPU-time.

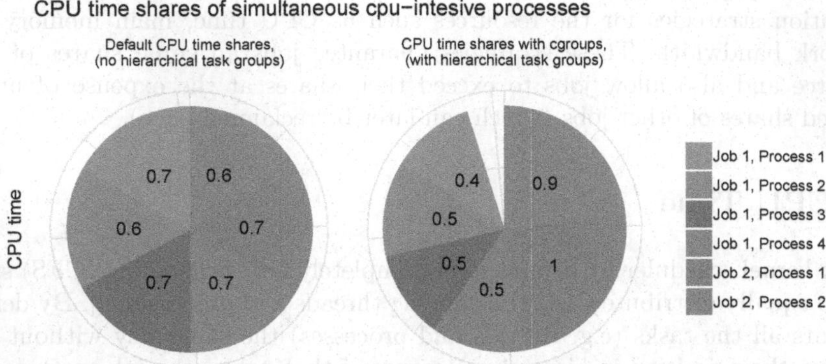

Fig. 1. Comparison of CPU shares with and without task groups. Left chart shows equal CPU time distribution between jobs processes. After placing jobs into separate control groups, CPU time was distributed fairly, at first, between groups and then between processes within groups.

Figure 1 shows that without placing these benchmark instances into control group, reported CPU-time was distributed evenly and was equal to $0.6 \approx C/(N+M)$ for each thread. After defining control groups, CPU time was distributed evenly between the groups and after that within a group. CPU-time ratio in this case was equal to $0.5 \approx C/2N$ and $1 \approx C/2M$ for the first and the second group respectively.

3 Memory

For equally distributing memory between jobs we had also used control groups since it is the standard way of limiting the usage of both swap and residential memory.

At any point in time, given the number of running jobs we may equally divide all available memory among them, but the problems would arise when one of the memory of one of control groups would grow and would reach its limit. There are several possible scenarios:

- Other groups have spare memory. In this case, it is better to rent their space instead of, for example, using swap or freezing the group. But, we have to

guarantee that, when these groups start to grow, they would have higher priority and would be able to reclaim memory pages back.
- Other groups do not have spare memory. In this case, more radical actions should be taken, since the system is running out of memory. Some unused memory pages can be migrated from residential memory to the swap without affecting the job. It would allow to shrink residential memory consumption. After the point when shrinking residential memory shares is no longer possible, a victim job must be chosen that would be almost completely displaced to swap or frozen.

3.1 Using Memory Pages from Other Groups

It is possible to guarantee the amount of residential memory that would not be reclaimed by other groups by setting the low boundary ('memory.low') limit. If we divide the total available memory by the number of groups and set it as the low boundary, then when this share is underutilized by job, all of its pages would stay in memory. At the same time, others may claim the free space. Even when the job starts to reclaim pages back (below the low limit), the pages would stay in memory, while the pages of other job may be displaced to the swap.

For example, two jobs have low limit of 100 MB. We had limited the total amount of residential memory available to both jobs to 200 MB by setting root's control group high and max memory limit to this value. The first one (job1) grows by 20 MB regularly, while the other one (job2) takes 75 MB constantly.

As the result (Fig. 2), job2 always stays in memory (at 75 MB), job1 reclaimed some of the space from job1 ($100 - 75 = 25$ MB), and when this space also becomes full (because of the root limit of 200 MB) it starts to use swap.

3.2 Reclaiming Memory Pages

The next case is when underutilized group starts to reclaim its space and becomes over-utilized. The group that was using the space of the fist group must now "find" another space to claim.

In the next example both groups have low limit set to 100 MB and root's high limit is 200 MB again. The first group (job1) constantly uses 160 MB, while the second group (job2) periodically grows to 200 MB by 20 MB. The first group is over-utilized and take more space in RES memory than its low limit; the second group starts to grow, reclaims its pages, and becomes over-utilized as well.

As the result (Fig. 3), the pages of the first group has moved to swap when the pages from the second group has reclaimed their space. When both groups have reached their limit of 100 MB and the second group has continued to grow, it started to use swap.

Shrinking Residential Memory Usage. When the memory is distributed tightly, and some tasks start to grow, it is necessary to move some page to swap. Memory stall information that is introduced in recent kernel patches (pressure

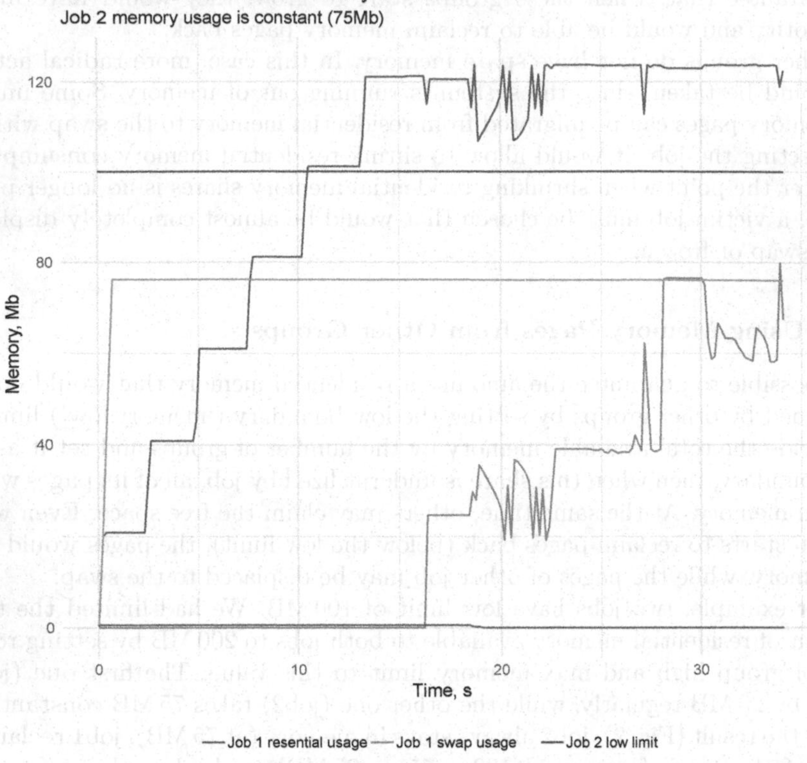

Fig. 2. Memory distribution between two jobs within confined space (200 Mb). Each job has a low memory limit of 100 Mb. Memory usage of Job 2 is constant (75 Mb) and memory usage of Job 1 grows by 20 Mb every 2 s. It can be noticed, that Job 1 claims unused memory of job 1 after 10 s and after that it starts to use swap.

stall information, PSI) may help to choose the victim group. By migrating unused pages it is possible to shrink residential memory usage causing the minimal effect to the job.

Recent upstream patches to the Linux Kernel (4.20) introduce pressure stall information (PSI) per control group. For the memory resource it presents the amount of time each task in control group has spent performing memory operations. Among these operations are, for example, memory page locking and waiting on the lock, page disk writebacks, memory compaction (by kcompactd and before page allocations). This time is averaged among all CPUs runqueus and weighed by non-idle runqueue time. Similar information is defined for disk I/O, CPU time.

In our case, PSI value would allow to tell by how much the job is affected by moving its pages to the swap. In case when the pages that are accessed frequently are required to move to the swap, memory thrashing would begin and PSI values

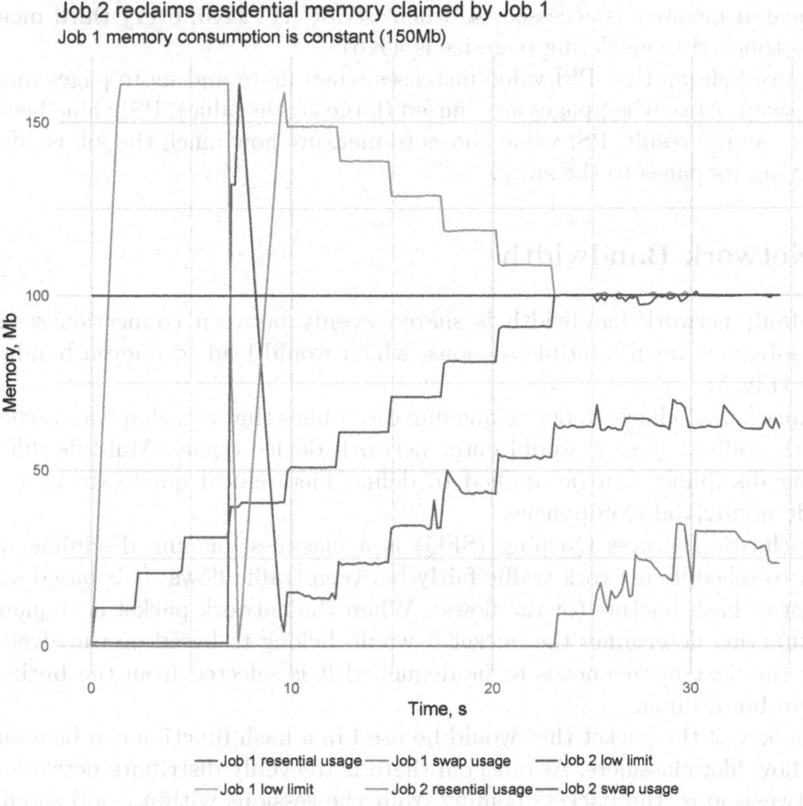

Fig. 3. Memory distribution between two jobs within confined space (200 Mb). Each job has a low memory limit of 100 Mb. Memory usage of Job 2 is constant (150 Mb) and it has partially claimed the share of Job 1 (by 50 Mb). Memory usage of Job 1 grows by 20 Mb every 2 s. It can be noticed, that Job 1 gradually reclaims its memory shares causing memory pages of Job 2 to migrate to swap. At 22nd second both jobs reach their low limits, and after this point Job 2 has no other space to grow besides swap.

would rise. So, by gradually moving pages to swap until PSI value starts to rise, it is possible to shrink group without interfering with job.

In the following example (Fig. 4), the first job (job1) requires 200 MB, but its low limit is restricted to 100 MB. As the time goes by, low boundary is gradually decreased causing page migration to the swap. Similar to the previous experiments, the second job (not shown) constantly uses the rest of the memory (100 MB). Nominal and real memory shares show specified and observed residential memory share ($RES/(RES + SWAP)$) of the each job. The third line in the plot shows pressure of the first job. The ratio of unused pages is controlled by stride (1 Kb, 8 Kb and 12 Kb) parameter which means that every 'stride' byte of allocated memory is accessed, so when 'stride' is 12 Kb, every third memory page is touched (considering pagesize is 4 Kb).

Figure 4 shows that PSI value increases when more and more pages migrate to the swap. Also, when pages are unused (large stride value), PSI value becomes smaller. As the result, PSI value allows to measure how much the job is affected by moving its pages to the swap.

4 Network Bandwidth

By default network bandwidth is shared evenly between connection sessions. Some jobs may open multiple sessions, which would lead to uneven bandwidth shares (Fig. 5).

Linux kernel allows to define queuing disciplines that can shape and schedule network traffic before it would enter network device queue. Multiple different queuing disciplines can be applied to define hierarchical queue structure and provide non-trivial QoS policies.

Stochastic Fairness Queuing (SFQ) is a classless queuing discipline which allows to schedule network traffic fairly between traffic flows. It is based on the concept of hash buckets (or the flows). When the network packet is enqueued a hash function determines the bucket it would belong to based on the given key. When the next packet needs to be dequeued it is selected from the buckets in round-robin fashion.

The key of the packet that would be used in a hash function can be assigned using flow filer classifiers. As our goal there is to evenly distribute network traffic between jobs, the packets coming from the sessions within a job should be scheduled to the same bucket and packets coming from different jobs should be scheduled to different buckets.

Since we have already used control groups for fair CPU time and memory allocations it is worth to continue using them for networking as well. Linux kernel firewall (iptables) allows to define netfilter rules to mark packets that are coming from the threads and processes within a specific control groups. By using Linux traffic control flow classifier to define flows based on the packet mark, or, in the other words, to use packet mark as key in bucket hash function, it is possible to schedule multiple flows coming from the same job into a single hash bucket. This would allow us to evenly distribute bandwidth among different jobs.

Since SFQ does not shape the traffic, its effect would be noticeable only when the maximum throughput of the data link is reached. In our case, it would mean that one job may take all available bandwidth when the other jobs do not require it, but when all jobs require network access, it would be shared evenly.

In our experiments demonstrating the feasibility of this concept we have used two hosts with Gigabit Ethernet NIC connected together with a patch cord. We had used iperf benchmark to measure interconnect speed in different conditions. iperf benchmark has reported us a baseline bandwidth of 900 Mbit/s with a single running client and no other processes using these NICs.

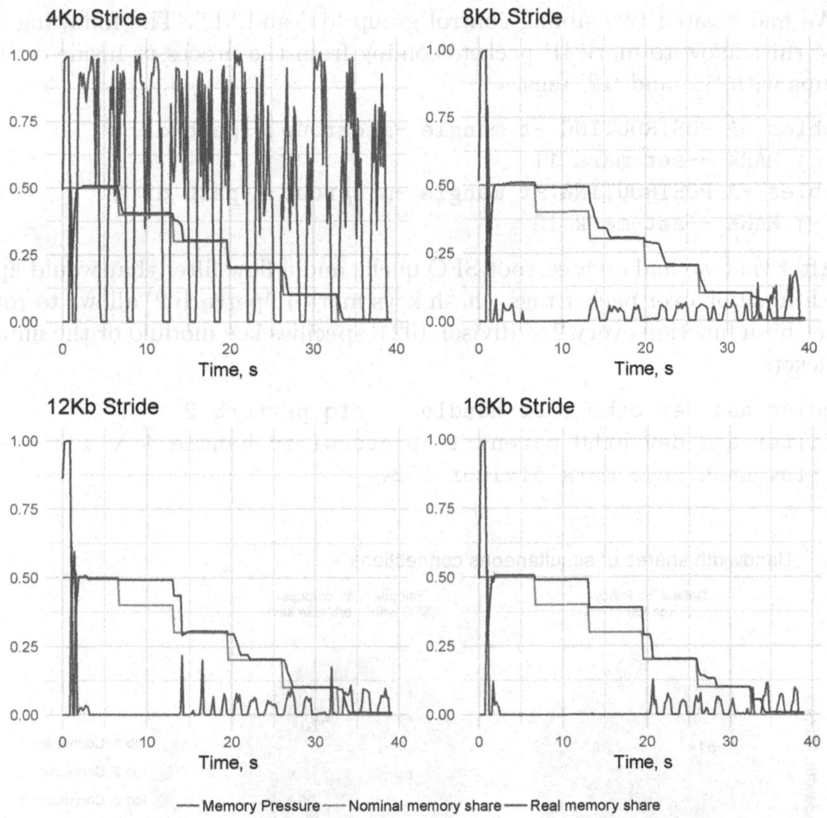

Fig. 4. Memory pressure value for different shares of residential and swap memory and for different page access patterns. It can be noticed that, when every page is accessed (4 Kb stride) the memory pressure is high regardless the number of pages in residential memory. When the number of accessed pages is significantly lower, the pressure decreases. More pages can be moved to swap without causing any noticeable changes in pressure, for example, when the stride is 16 Kb, memory pressure starts to rise only when 25% of pages are left in the residential memory.

To demonstrate even bandwidth distribution between connection session with default queueing policy (codel) we had started 3 iperf client instances simultaneously. As the result, bandwidth of 314, 312 and 380 Mbit/s was reported, which is approximately equal to the third of a baseline bandwidth.

To simulate jobs with uneven number of network connection, we had placed three iperf instances in two control groups. As the result, the first control group had a single connection session, while the second control group had two connection session. After creating SFQ queuing policy and flow specifier for the traffic coming from these control groups, the first connection should get 1/2 and the second and the third should get 1/4 of the baseline bandwidth.

We had created two sibling control group 'd1' and 'd2'. The following 'iptables' rules allow to mark IP packets coming from the processes inside of these cgroups with '11' and '12' tags.

```
iptables -A POSTROUTING -t mangle -m cgroup --path d1 \
    -j MARK --set-mark 11
iptables -A POSTROUTING -t mangle -m cgroup --path d2 \
    -j MARK --set-mark 12
```

After that we had created root SFQ queue and a flow filter that would apply a hash function over packet tags ('hash keys mark'). 'perturb 2' allows to rotate bucket hash function every 2 s. 'divisor 1024' specifies key modulo or the number of buckets.

```
tc qdisc add dev eth0 root handle 1: sfq perturb 2
tc filter add dev eth0 parent 1: protocol ip handle 1 \
    flow hash keys mark divisor 1024
```

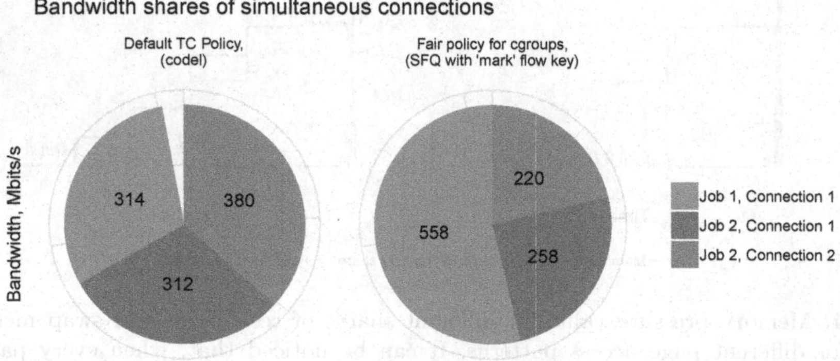

Fig. 5. Comparison of network bandwidth shares with and without fair policy. Left chart shows equal bandwidth distribution between connection sessions. After placing jobs into separate control groups, marking groups outgoing traffic and creating flow classifier for packets marks, the network bandwidth was distributed fairly, at first, between control groups and then between connection sessions within groups.

As the result (Fig. 5), the bandwidth is shared evenly across two jobs, as expected. The first job with a single connection received a half of a bandwidth (578 Mbits/s), and the second job received another half of a bandwidth for two connections (258 and 220 Mbits/s)

5 Related Works

Some batch schedulers such as SLURM [5] and Son of a Grid Engine [6] allow to oversubscribe CPU cores in some way. They achieve that by allowing administrators to specify load threshold under which oversubscription may occur. The fairness of CPU time distribution between jobs is left out of scope in these cases.

On the other hand, the majority of schedulers allow to launch multiple jobs in a single node at the same time by dividing them between CPU cores. Since the total amount of memory required by all of the jobs running simultaneously may exceed all available memory of the node, memory over-subscription may occur. In order to handle this situation, some schedulers, e.g. Maui [7], offload some of the pages to the swap memory up to the specified over-commit factor. Another strategy utilized by LSF [8] scheduler, where jobs can be preempted or suspended to free residential memory for higher priority jobs. Similar to CPU time resource, the fairness of memory distribution is not covered in these solutions.

The problems of unfair resource allocation of HPC schedulers were covered from both technological and users perspectives in [9] and in the works linked therein.

For CPU time distribution the paper [10] states the problem of unfair CPU time distribution in the Linux Kernel scheduler. It is caused by the processes that have more child processes than the others. The proposed solution in this paper is scheduler modification.

The usage of Linux control groups for enforcing the limits on residential memory shares is a commonly known practice. Similar approaches for migration of pages to swap based on memory pressure values are used for virtual machines [11]. For virtual machines, memory pressure value is provided by hypervisors and it is specific to it. But, in this paper, to achieve our goals we are using standard capabilities provided by the recent updates in the Linux Kernel, such as process stall information (PSI).

6 Conclusion and Future Work

In this paper we have proposed resource allocation strategies that can be applied to HPC workloads. By grouping resource consumers into separate control groups it is possible to provide fair resource shares between groups regardless on the number of resource consumers in each group.

We have covered the resources such as CPU time, memory and network bandwidth. These strategies guarantee jobs equal shares of each resource and also allow jobs to exceed their shares at the expense of under-utilized shares of other jobs (which can later be reclaimed back).

CPU time is shared evenly by using abilities of Linux Kernel CFS scheduler, which allows to create hierarchical structure of processes and the groups of processes. CPU time is distributed evenly between groups and processes that belong to the same parent. By creating a task group (control group) for each job it is possible to distribute CPU time evenly.

To control memory page allocations we have used control groups, which allow to define guaranteed limit of residential memory for each job. When a job exceeds this limit, it can utilize spare memory of other jobs that have not reached it. Later, when these under-utilized jobs start to grow, they can reclaim their pages. We have also showed that it is possible to migrate unused memory pages to swap without causing any effect by using memory pressure as a feedback.

Network bandwidth is also shared fairly between control groups by using SFQ traffic control queuing policy. Each packet that is coming from connections within a control group is marked and then this mark is used to map traffic flows within SFQ queue. SFQ allows us to schedule traffic of multiple flows and to achieve fair distribution regardless the number of sessions within each group.

HPC workloads have a high demand on these resources and they usually define the cost of the computational cluster. Job schedulers that are commonly used right now for HPC workloads simply divide available resources of a computing node between jobs and do not allow any job to exceed available resource shares. This strategy leads to fragmentation problems and, in turn, to wasted resources.

When moving HPC workloads to the cloud, where users are billed for the resources they use, the cost of this fragmentation may be significant. In this case, using HPC schedulers would not be the best solution. Moreover, some workloads may have different resource demands, e.g. some jobs can be cpu-intensive, some network-intensive and others may require only accelerators, since each node may have all of these resources, these jobs can be executed simultaneously without interference.

In the future, based on the results of this paper, we are going to propose a different kind of an HPC scheduler, which would not be based on discrete slots but rather on continuous resource shares. This, in turn, would allow us not only to decrease resource fragmentation, but also to decrease job wait time in the queue.

References

1. Kuchumov, R., Petrunin, V., Korkhov, V., Balashov, N., Kutovskiy, N., Sokolov, I.: Design and implementation of a service for cloud HPC computations. In: Gervasi, O., et al. (eds.) ICCSA 2018. LNCS, vol. 10963, pp. 103–112. Springer, Cham (2018). https://doi.org/10.1007/978-3-319-95171-3_9
2. Kuchumov, R.I., Korkhov, V.V.: Design and implementation of a service for performing HPC computations in cloud environment. In: CEUR Workshop Proceedings, vol. 2267, pp. 233–236 (2018)
3. Korkhov, V., Kobyshev, S., Degtyarev, A., Bogdanov, A.: Light-weight cloud-based virtual computing infrastructure for distributed applications and hadoop clusters. In: Gervasi, O., et al. (eds.) ICCSA 2017. LNCS, vol. 10408, pp. 399–411. Springer, Cham (2017). https://doi.org/10.1007/978-3-319-62404-4_29
4. Wong, C.S., Tan, I.K.T., Kumari, R.D., Lam, J.W., Fun, W.: Fairness and interactive performance of o(1) and CFS Linux kernel schedulers. In: International Symposium on Information Technology, vol. 4, pp. 1–8. IEEE, August 2008
5. Yoo, A.B., Jette, M.A., Grondona, M.: SLURM: simple Linux utility for resource management. In: Feitelson, D., Rudolph, L., Schwiegelshohn, U. (eds.) JSSPP 2003. LNCS, vol. 2862, pp. 44–60. Springer, Heidelberg (2003). https://doi.org/10.1007/10968987_3
6. SGE, Son of Grid Engine. https://arc.liv.ac.uk/trac/SGE. Accessed 07 May 2019
7. Maui: 5.2 Node Allocation, Page Redirection. http://docs.adaptivecomputing.com/maui/5.2nodeallocation.php. Accessed 07 May 2019

8. LSF: Fairshare Scheduling. https://www.bsc.es/support/LSF/9.1.2/lsf_admin/index.htm?chap_fairshare_lsf_admin.html~main. Accessed 07 May 2019
9. Sedighi, A., Deng, Y., Zhang, P.: Fariness of task scheduling in high performance computing environments. Scalable Comput. Pract. Experience **15**(3), 271–288 (2014)
10. Wong, C.S., Tan, I., Kumari, R.D., Wey, F.: Towards achieving fairness in the Linux scheduler. ACM SIGOPS Operat. Syst. Rev. **42**(5), 34–43 (2008)
11. Waldspurger, C.A.: Memory resource management in VMware ESX server. ACM SIGOPS Oper. Syst. Rev. **36**(SI), 181–194 (2002)

Automated Creation of Unique Editable Textures for Three-Dimensional Models of Archaeological Artefacts

Oleg Iakushkin(✉), Egor Budlov, Alexei Uteshev, and Valery Grishkin

Saint-Petersburg University, 7/9 Universitetskaya nab., St. Petersburg 199034, Russia
o.yakushkin@spbu.ru

Abstract. The article is devoted to the description of the algorithm for obtaining a complete model from a colourless model of a stone and its prototype image with a material that allows you to manually make changes for greater detalization. Since it is often necessary to make some manual changes in the tasks of modelling archaeological objects, which necessarily requires special skills in working with complex software, as well as considerable time costs, the task was to implement an algorithm that facilitates this process. First, using an image of the object, PBR maps are created. After that, the UV map of the object is formed, and at the end, a unique PBR texture of the object is created. The algorithm was tested on a number of colourless models of stones and various images. At the output, we get an object wrapped in a texture obtained from the original image. Also, an extension for professional free software was created, allowing to make any additional changes in its texture if needed and get the desired result for the minimum number of user actions.

Keywords: Modelling · Archaeology · Photogrammetry · Object reconstruction

1 Introduction

One of the most important tasks of 3D-modelling is the creation of three-dimensional models of artefacts, taking into account their size, materials and shape [16]. In addition to single items, an actual task is the reconstruction of monuments and buildings [3]. In this process, high accuracy is absolutely necessary to make these objects look natural. This way we can easily ensure access to cultural heritage objects, including those carefully protected, to a wide range of users [13,14]. Creating such models shows us to solve two main problems of preserving unique artefacts:

- interaction with an electronic object does not damage it, while the original object can deteriorate even from light and climatic conditions of local exposure;

A. Uteshev—This research was partially supported by Russian Foundation for Basic Research grant (project no. 17-29-04288).

S. Misra et al. (Eds.): ICCSA 2019, LNCS 11622, pp. 752–760, 2019.
https://doi.org/10.1007/978-3-030-24305-0_56

- scientists from all around the world can conduct their research without direct contact with the artifact [2,4,12].

Some other opportunities offered by digital three-dimensional copies can be noted such as:

- demonstration of elements of scientific collections with the possibility of examining objects from all sides [19];
- visualization of artefacts in context of reconstruction of the historical scene [11,17];
- placement of an unlimited number of items in the limited space of the museum;
- the possibility of forming various expositions and stands, modelling and animation of events;
- making hard copies of any museum objects and their distribution, including in the form of souvenirs [1].

As a result of archaeological research, an array of information and documentation about the state of cultural and historical monuments is formed. To carry out reconstruction and research of objects in the context of archaeology, tools of automated modelling are necessary [7]. However, the data which you can work with is often very limited, and the process itself is very laborious and time-consuming. Some developments in this field are reconstructing:

- stones from pairs of sketches;
- walls from recreated stones with user's instructions [8];
- surfaces from video taken with a camera from above;
- continuous textures from pictures [9].

Modern technologies allow us to recreate the texture of the image, but it is often necessary to make any changes manually. Therefore, special skills to work with complex software are necessary. In this work, we set a goal to facilitate the task of 3D-modelling of archaeological finds and provide artists with the opportunity to influence the final result of the textures of objects obtained earlier in an automated way.

2 Problem Definition

Let us consider the situation when we have a prepared colourless model of a stone and its real image. The problem is to solve the problem of obtaining a 3D-model of a stone, visually as close as possible to its prototype. In addition to form, it becomes particularly important to solve the problem of obtaining realistic Physically-Based Rendering (PBR) textures [18] in which the artist could make changes.

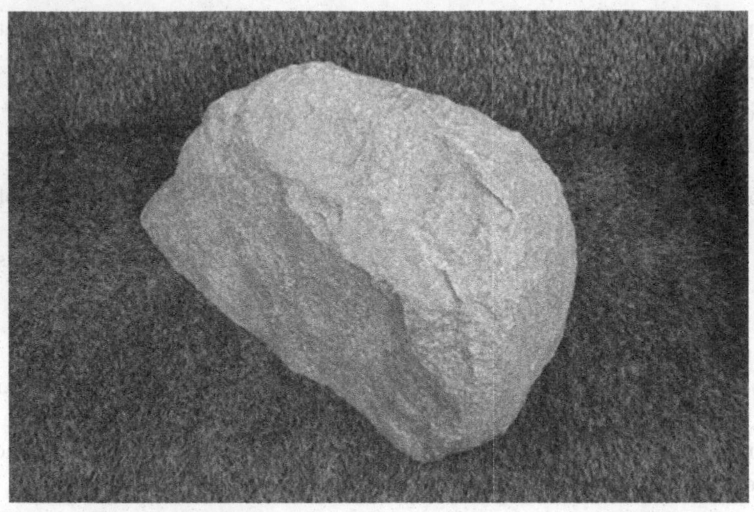

Fig. 1. Input image

3 Solution Method

For input, the algorithm receives a colourless model of the object and one two-dimensional image of its prototype - a photo or a drawing (Fig. 1).

The algorithm can be divided into four steps:

I. Creating a scalable PBR material from the image.
II. Forming a UV map of an object sweep to represent it on a surface.
III. Making a PBR texture specific to the current object.
IV. Exporting the resulting object to Unity.

The first stage is performed with Python 'scikit-image' library using the 'bitmap2material' algorithm. At the output we obtain the following images (Fig. 2):

Now we can proceed to the procedure of creating a UV map of an object sweep. We will execute the algorithm in Blender 3D-editor [5,6,15], one of the most popular, rapidly developing software for modelling nowadays. To begin with, we need to load the object and change its size in order to display it correctly in the editor. After that, we can begin the process of creating a UV-scan.

The following method allows us to create a 2D image from a 3D mesh that almost completely retains crucial characteristics of the object, such as shape, size and connectivity [10]:

1. Cluster faces of the object into groups using their normal vectors as basis. It should be noted that we do not consider how these faces are connected.
2. Compute average normal vector for each group. After that, derive the orthogonal projection to convert 3D faces into 2D plane. Weighting coefficients proportional to their sizes are used to average the normal vectors. Therefore,

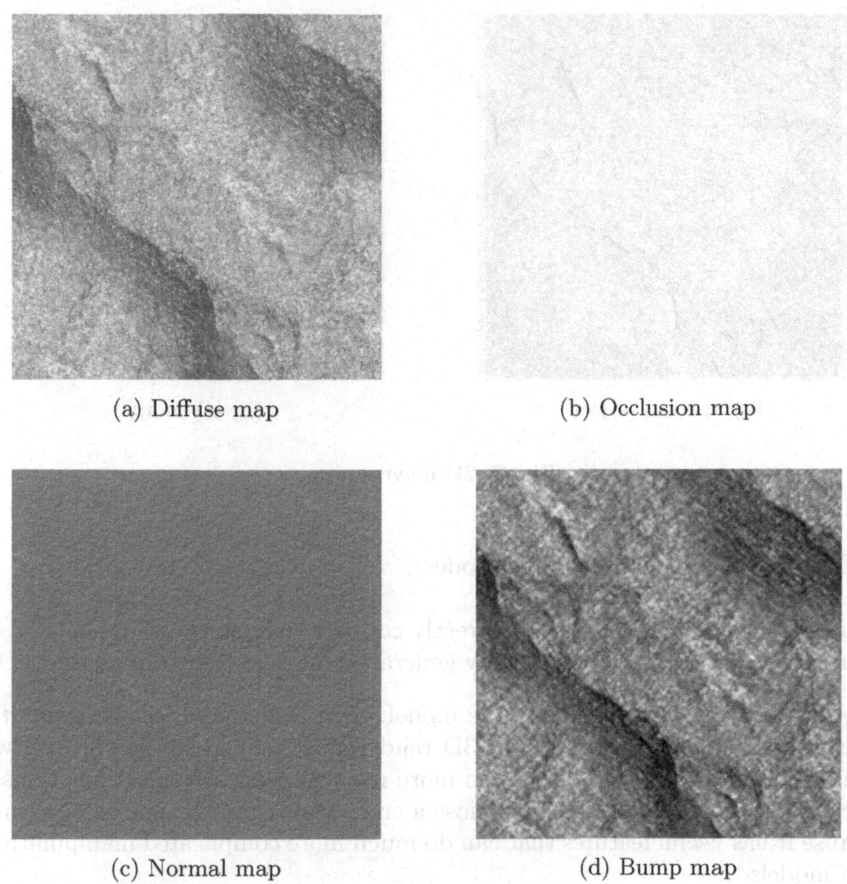

(a) Diffuse map (b) Occlusion map

(c) Normal map (d) Bump map

Fig. 2. Generated PBR maps

vectors of larger faces are prioritized. This way we can transform polygons from 3D to 2D and mostly preserve their size and shape.

3. Merge every cluster's neighbouring member faces to created 2D islands.
4. Place generated islands to a rectangular area. It should be done as compactly as possible in order to obtain a correct UV unwrapping of the object. In this case 'UV' means two-dimensional coordinate system.

Figure 3 illustrates the result of UV unwrapping of imported object using Blender smart UV project. Here "Unwrapping" means transformation from a 3D mesh surface to a 2D rectangular map. "UV" is referred to as texture coordinates of the surface texture.

The third stage - the creation of the material. It can be divided into several steps:

1. Create material for the object;

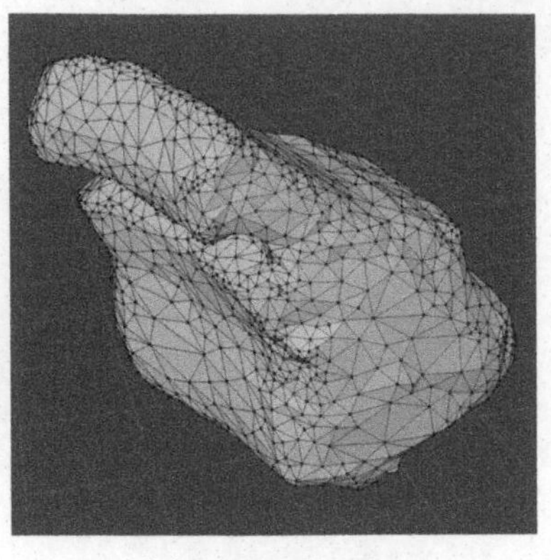

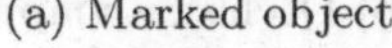

(a) Marked object

(b) UV map

Fig. 3. 2D unwrapping

2. Enable use of graphic schemes (nodes);
3. Create a texture map;
4. Load the generated maps and correctly connect them in the diagram (Fig. 4). In this stage, we will need already generated maps obtained in phase I.

And the last step - exporting the model. Now that the object is ready, it is time to transfer it into some other 3D renderer (Fig. 5). If we do this, we will be able to make our model look even more natural using advanced functions of other applications. In our case, we chose a cross-platform real-time engine Unity because it has useful features that can do much more complicated manipulations with models.

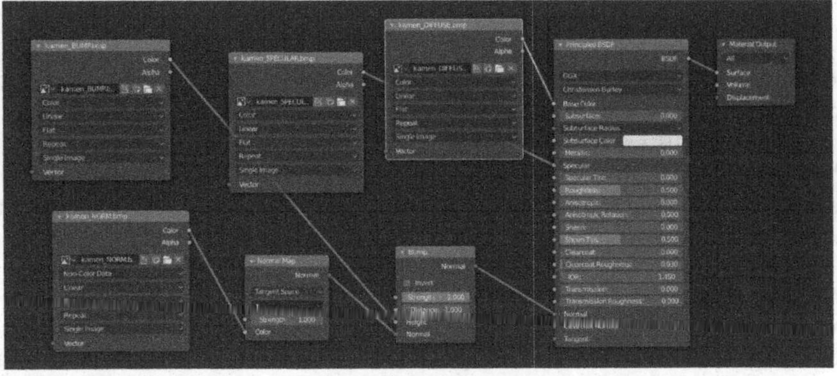

Fig. 4. Node graph

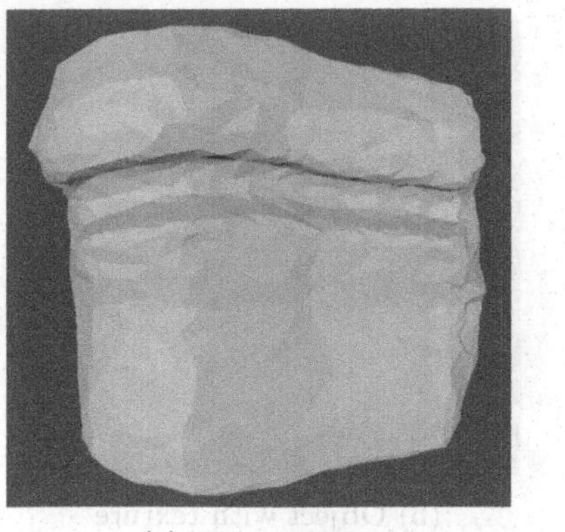

(a) Clean object

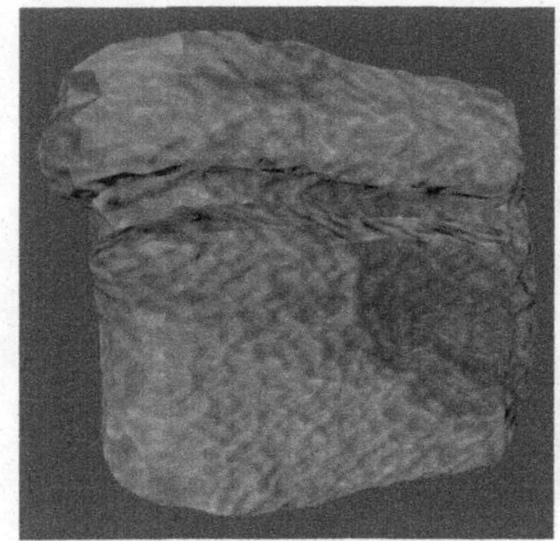

(b) Object with texture

Fig. 5. Model exported to Unity 3D

4 Experiments

The algorithm was tested on a number of colourless models of stones and various images (Figs. 6, 7, 8 and 9). As a result, we get an object wrapped in a texture obtained from the original image. In this case, it is possible to make any artistic changes in this texture if needed.

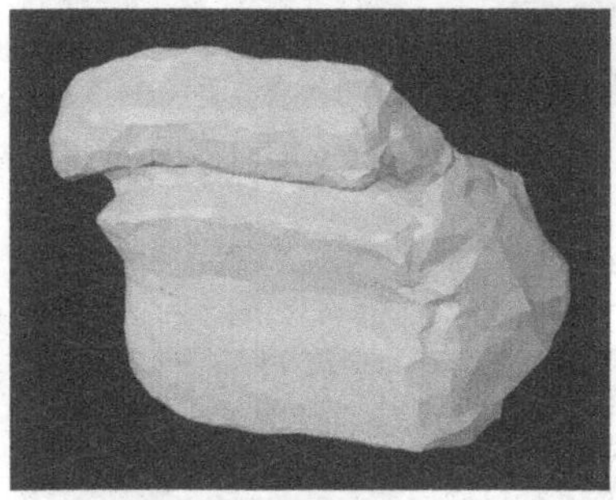

(a) Clean object

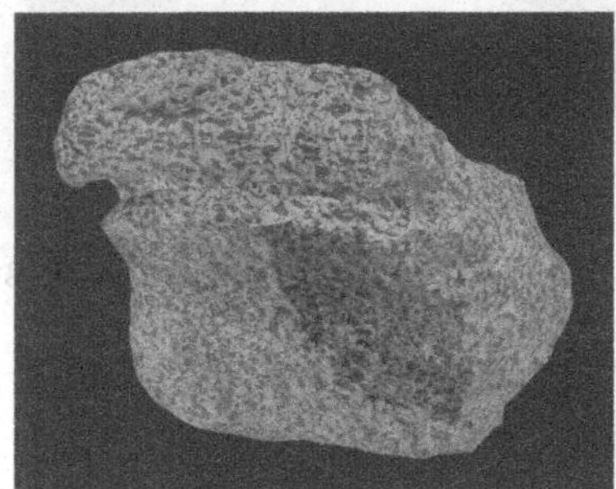

(b) Object with texture

Fig. 6. Stone

The execution time of the algorithm for different models:

1. Actual stone model: 0.3 s.
2. Standard Blender cube: 0.1 s.
3. Standard Blender sphere: 0.1 s.
4. Subdivisioned Blender sphere: 3.1 s.
5. Bunny model: 1.3 s.

(a) Clean object (b) Object with texture

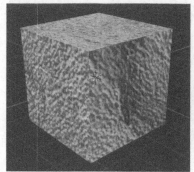

Fig. 7. Cube

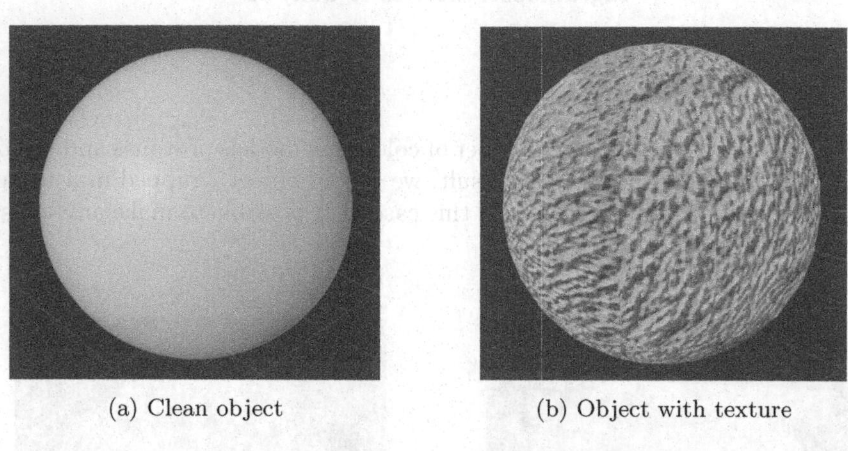

(a) Clean object (b) Object with texture

Fig. 8. Sphere

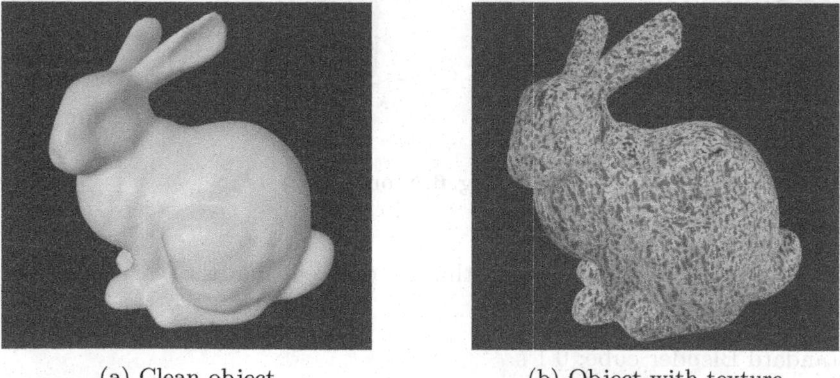

(a) Clean object (b) Object with texture

Fig. 9. Bunny

5 Conclusion

An algorithm was presented that allows obtaining a model with material from a colourless model of a stone and its prototype image, which allows manual changes to be made for detail. An extension has been created for professional software Blender that allows you to get the desired result for the minimum number of user actions. The implementation of the algorithm showed good results in terms of execution time and the quality of the object received at the output. In the future, it is planned to integrate the program into the web-service format and use tools for automatic texture styling.

Acknowledgments. This research was partially supported by the Russian Foundation for Basic Research grant (project no. 17-29-04288). The authors would like to acknowledge the Reviewers for the valuable recommendations that helped in the improvement of this paper.

References

1. Anastasiadou, C., Vettese, S.: "From souvenirs to 3D printed souvenirs". Exploring the capabilities of additive manufacturing technologies in (re)-framing tourist souvenirs. Tourism Manag. **71**, 428–442 (2019)
2. López, B., et al.: 3D modelling in archaeology: the application of structure from motion methods to the study of the megalithic necropolis of Panoria. J. Archaeol. Sci. Rep. **10**, 495–506 (2016)
3. El-Hakim, S., et al.: Detailed 3D modelling of castles. Int. J. Archit. Comput. **5**(2), 199–220 (2007)
4. Eve, S.: Augmenting phenomenology: using augmented reality to aid archaeological phenomenology in the landscape. J. Archaeol. Method Theory **19**, 582–600 (2012)
5. Hess, R.: The Essential Blender: Guide to 3D Creation with the Open Source Suite Blender. No Starch Press, San Francisco (2007)
6. Hess, R.: Blender Foundations: The Essential Guide to Learning Blender 2.5. Focal Press (2013)
7. Iakushkin, O., Fatkina, A., Plaksin, V., Sedova, O., Degtyarev, A., Uteshev, A.: Reconstruction of stone walls in form of polygonal meshes from archaeological studies. In: Gervasi, O., et al. (eds.) ICCSA 2018. LNCS, vol. 10963, pp. 136–148. Springer, Cham (2018). https://doi.org/10.1007/978-3-319-95171-3_12
8. Iakushkin, O., Selivanov, D., Tazieva, L., Fatkina, A., Grishkin, V., Uteshev, A.: 3D reconstruction of landscape models and archaeological objects based on photo and video materials. In: Gervasi, O., et al. (eds.) ICCSA 2018. LNCS, vol. 10963, pp. 160–169. Springer, Cham (2018). https://doi.org/10.1007/978-3-319-95171-3_14
9. Iakushkin, O.O., Malevanniy, D.M., Degtyarev, A.B., Selivanov, D.A., Fatkina, A.I.: Texture generation for archaeological reconstructions. In: Proceedings of the VIII International Conference Distributed Computing and Grid-Technologies in Science and Education, pp. 462–466 (2018)
10. Julius, W.: Developing a process for automating UV mapping and polygon reduction (2016)
11. Kersten, T., Pardo, C.A., Lindstaedt, M.: 3D acquisition, modelling and visualization of north German castles by digital architectural photogrammetry. In: Proceedings of ISPRS XXth Congress, pp. 126–131 (2004)

12. Krokos, M., Dykes, T., Hassan, A., Croton, D., Gheller, C.: Interactive 3D visualization for theoretical virtual observatories. Mon. Not. R. Astron. Soc. **477**(2), 1495–1507 (2018). https://doi.org/10.1093/mnras/sty855
13. Liarokapis, F., Kouřil, P., Agrafiotis, P., Demesticha, S., Chmelík, J., Skarlatos, D.: 3D modelling and mapping for virtual exploration of underwater archaeology assets. ISPRS Int. Arch. Photogrammetry Remote Sens. Spat. Inf. Sci. **XLII-2/W3**, 425–431 (2017)
14. Marques, L., et al.: Cultural heritage 3D modelling and visualisation within an augmented reality environment, based on geographic information technologies and mobile platforms. ACE Archit. City Environ. **11**, 117–136 (2017)
15. Matsuyama, T., Nobuhara, S., Takai, T., Tung, T.: 3D Video and Its Applications. Springer, London (2012). https://doi.org/10.1007/978-1-4471-4120-4
16. Remondino, F., Campana, S.: 3D recording and modelling in archaeology and cultural heritage. BAR Int. Ser. **2598**, 111–127 (2014)
17. Remondino, F., El-Hakim, S., Girardi, S., Rizzi, A., Benedetti, S., Gonzo, L.: 3D virtual reconstruction and visualization of complex architectures-the 3D-ARCH project. Int. Arch. Photogrammetry Remote Sens. Spat. Inf. Sci. **38**(5/W10) (2009)
18. Sairiala, J., et al.: PBR workflows in cycles render engine: PBR workflows for realistic rendering in cycles render engine (2015)
19. Scopigno, R., et al.: 3D models for cultural heritage: beyond plain visualization. Computer **7**, 48–55 (2011)

The Architecture of the Robot-Finder Based on SLAM and Neural Network

Iakushkin Oleg(✉), Ruslan Sevostyanov, Alexander Degtyarev, Egor Krasilnikov, Maria Mingazova, Alexey Rusakov, Olesya Kondratieva, and Andrey Bobryshev

Saint-Petersburg University, 7/9 Universitetskaya nab., St. Petersburg 199034, Russia
o.yakushkin@spbu.ru

Abstract. The task of this paper is to find lost or frozen people in the wood. That takes accurate exploration of a large space with a minimum time duration. This work is dedicated to the architecture part of the assigned task.

We give an architecture for robot-finder capable to find a human being in the wood or in the snow area. For us, the robot is blending of two elements, which we can develop independently. That are a wheeled platform and an operating module. In this task, we look at the second one. During that way we assume that the first one is developed, therefore the robot is driving upon the airbag or wheeled platform.

Our solution to this task is architecture and algorithm. These two are made for and directed to learn robot follow the map and detect human being alongside. We use computer vision, neural network and GPS technologies. In the end, we have a theoretical basis for developing robot-finder.

1 Introduction

In our thought, the robot is final equipment which capable and aimed to complete the task provided by a human being. The robot includes in itself required equipment and program.

In this paper, we solve the problem dedicated to missing human. Young and old can lost in the wood or in unknown areas without an opportunity to find a way back. This is the reason why we create a robot-finder to be competent to help search and rescue teams.

The task of this robot is to find a human being in the bounded area for a finite period of time. It must be sustained for the environment condition and work autonomously. We assume to use our robot in the unknown, dynamically changed terrain. Also, we consider obstacles avoiding in an aggressive environment such as animals.

This research was partially supported by Russian Foundation for Basic Research grant (project no. 17-29-04288) and by SPbU (Saint Petersburg State University) grant no. AAAAA18-118071790047-9 (id: 28612502).

S. Misra et al. (Eds.): ICCSA 2019, LNCS 11622, pp. 761–771, 2019.
https://doi.org/10.1007/978-3-030-24305-0_57

At the finish of this paper, we will provide a theoretical basis for a robot that can find a human being and deliver water or medicines.

1.1 Functional Subsystems and Their Tasks

To give a proper solution we work on the five subsystems. They belong to the main controller. The controller process an intermediate results from these subsystems. It can be a microcontroller or computer. The subsystems that are needed for full functionality robot are provided in the Table 1 below.

Table 1. Robot-finder subsystems

Subsystem	Task
SLAM algorithm	Control logical moving by changing local route
Neural network	Detect human in a visible area
Wheeled platform/airbag	Perform physical moving
GSM-modem	Send information
GPS-tracker	Give global coordinates

2 Related Works

There were many explorations about robots moving in the unknown hazards and dynamically changed areas. Classification of the existing approaches was given in [15]. Mathematical model of the maneuvering between moving obstacles was given in [4,7,14]. In the [5] authors gave a motion algorithm for self-driving on the bumpy road using ultrasonic sensor and gyroscope. In the [9] fuzzy neural network for obstacle avoiding is provided.

For the navigation task, there were suggested several different approaches. First is completed library for perceiving the environment using mesh estimation [10]. Second is capable to detect obstacles using a neural network that accept RGB image [9]. The third solution uses accurate stereo-vision technology [2,3]. Fourth suggest using sensors to estimate the distance to the object [6,8]. Fifth paper [12] describes a navigation algorithm. Its authors give a clear algorithm for obstacle avoidance. All these approaches take a different amount of resources and give different benefits.

The third part of our robot that takes the proper solution is architecture. In the paper [1] 2d navigating system architecture is suggested. There are the odometry and location information let compute proper robot velocity. An interesting approach is also presented in [1,11], where sensors are placed on the board, information flows from which are processed by the computing module. These works have affected to our robot. But there is still no out of the box solution that can solve our problem. In particular, there is no complete obstacle avoidance algorithm.

Our decision is to use computer vision libraries with open-source code. These packages are using depth map data. This choice was accepted because of our needs in free and reusable solutions. This library builds an analysis-friendly field that shows the location of the obstacle polygon. It gives the distance to the obstacle and its form. It helps to accurately estimate the environment in the robot sight. The benefit of this library in comparison to others is open-source. Thanks to it we are able to support real-time processing of incoming data from the camera.

3 Task

Our main task was to build robot-finder architecture using open-source and the cheapest software and hardware. Therefore we've learned technologies in chosen areas, compare them and choose the most proper. Besides architecture, we purpose motion algorithm. This algorithm requires an only RGB-d camera, network adapter, and microcontroller or small computer. It is possible because we introduce sufficient math model.

3.1 Mathematical Model and Task

Let robot's world model is an unchangeable environment with the only dynamic robot. The motion is performing iteratively, where one iteration includes sufficient actions in Fig. 1. For the easiness we can let that world is 2d.

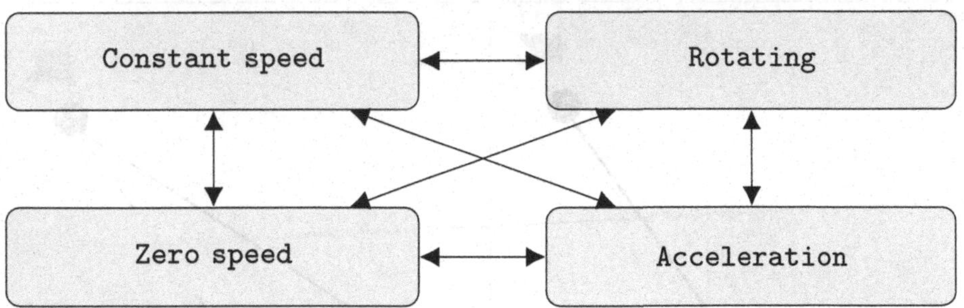

Fig. 1. Robot states.

The robot can be in four states:

- Constant speed
- Acceleration
- Rotating
- Zero speed

The robot includes in itself compute module which gives final commands to motion platform API. We claim that every state is the result of previous states. Therefore the motion model is: robot moves forward in bounded coordinate system, follows a closed graph which vertices are GPS-coordinates. There is a finite number of these vertices. These assumptions allow us to reduce task from moving along the graph to moving along the edge.

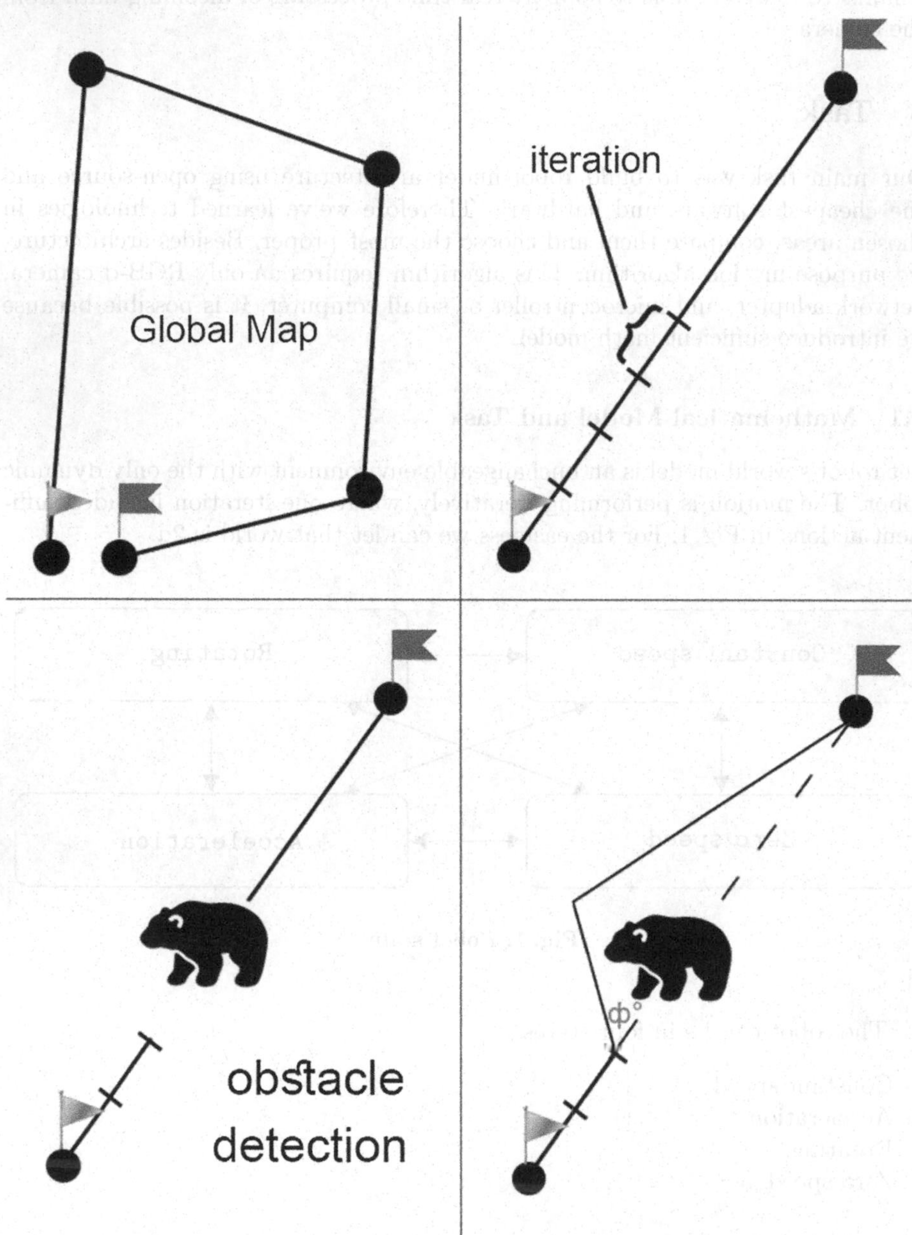

Fig. 2. Changing local route according to the obstacle.

The robot drives straight ahead iteratively in Sect. 4.2. On every iteration, the robot scans terrain to detect human and obstacles. We assume that the algorithm can't handle the situation when it bumps into an animal. It is because of ambiguous behavior. Therefore we can formulate subtask: change the local route according to the new circumstances in Fig. 2. Let us have several parameters:

- Orientation (O)
- Obstacle parameters (Π)
- Target (P)
- Rotating angle (Φ)

Hence we have a formula:

$$\widetilde{\Phi} = \min \Phi(O, \Pi, P) \tag{1}$$

Here Φ is function of three arguments. Minimization is conducted for all possible rotating angles:

$$\Phi \in [O - \frac{\pi}{2}, O + \frac{\pi}{2}]. \tag{2}$$

After minimization and rotating we compute orientation again and proceed iterative algorithm. If the robot detects human being, he goes back to the base station follows the shortest way in Fig. 3.

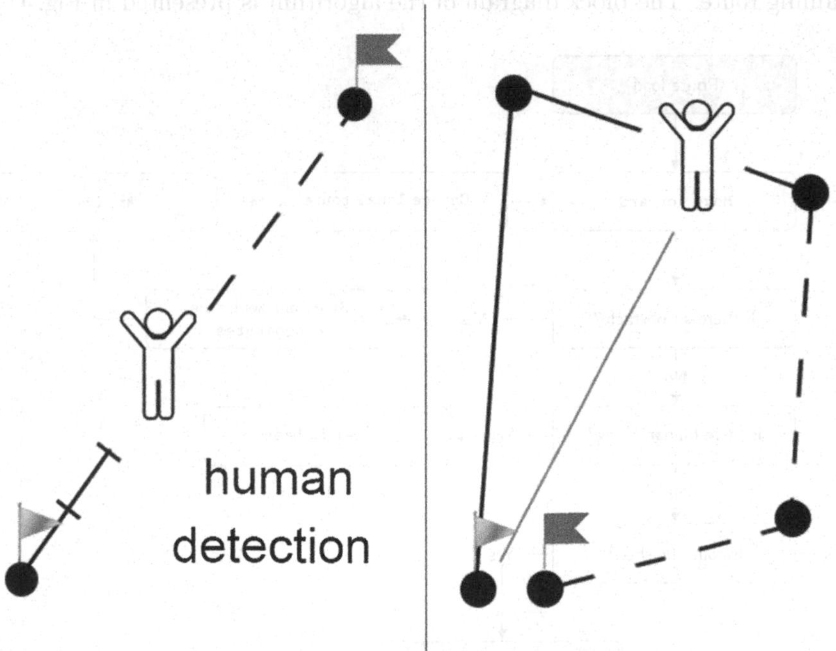

Fig. 3. Changing route after human detected.

4 Positioning Algorithm

Autonomous vehicles require an accurate obstacle detection mechanism for correct navigation in unmonitored environments. During developing the positioning algorithm, the need for its flexibility in the conditions of an uneven road and the possibility of obstacles were taken into account. The basis is the SLAM (simultaneous localization and mapping) method. This approach allows to simultaneously follow the global route and build a local route in accordance with the circumstances of the movement.

To implement this algorithm, we devise a local model of robot behavior. It lies in the fact that the robot recognizes the nearest obstacles and circles them with a minimum deviation from the specified trajectory.

4.1 The Efficiency Criterion of the Iterative Algorithm

For search work in rough terrain, we have developed an algorithm for an effective search for a person. The performance criteria include two conditions:

- The robot must follow the specified route as close as possible.
- In most cases, the robot should recognize a person who was met on the way.

It is worth saying that it is a possible situation when the robot revealed not a lost person, but just a passer-by. In this case, after sending the data to the server, the robot operator sends the task of finding a person again on the remaining route. The block diagram of the algorithm is presented in Fig. 4

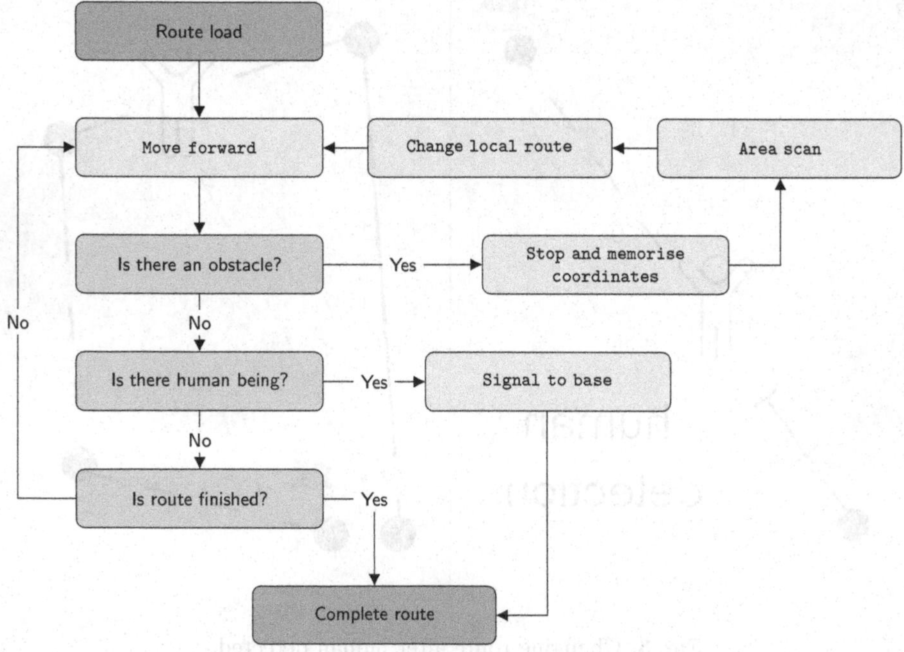

Fig. 4. Iterative algorithm.

4.2 Description of the Iterative Algorithm

The robot starts moving from a given point and executes its program iteratively in an infinite loop. During one iteration, the robot scans the obstacles in its path. To do this, it uses a special program based on the OpenCV library, which receives a frame from the RGB-Depth camera. On the basis of the frame, its parameters are calculated: the presence, size, and location of obstacles. Considering the data, the robot changes the route. Based on the orientation and the modified route, the robot decides to move on or stop and make a turn (see Sect. 3.1 Mathematical model and task).

After detecting obstacles, the robot proceeds to detect the person in sight (see Sect. 5.2). The neural network gives an answer about detecting a person or that nobody is detected. In this article, we do not consider meeting with animals and their potential threat to the algorithm operation. This is also stipulated in the task model (see Sect. 3.1). Based on the answer about the presence of a person, the robot either approaches it and checks who it is, and then helps it by explaining the shortest path out of the forest, or continues to move, returning to navigation tasks. If the robot did not find the person, he completes the route, passing it completely.

It should be said that the task is not intended to rotate the camera in order to more likely to detect a person. This approach, however, can be implemented in the following studies.

5 Architecture (System Design)

5.1 Hardware and Software

The diagram in Fig. 5 shows the system architecture.

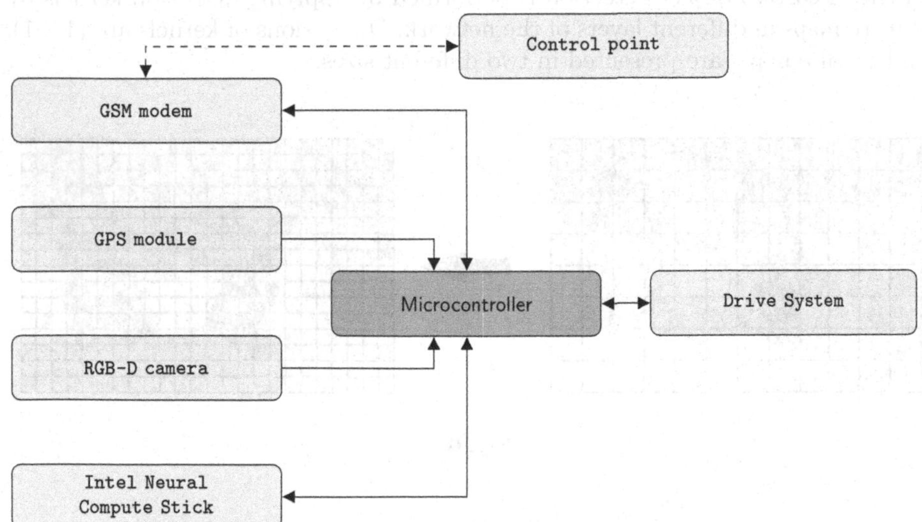

Fig. 5. The architecture of the prototype system architecture.

The robot is controlled by two microcontrollers. One of them combines a set of sensors consisting of a GSM modem, a GPS module, an RGB-Depth camera, and a coprocessor. We use two microcontrollers as an intermediate layer connecting the individual components into a single system. One of them controls the movement, passing commands through the API of the platform to go in a given direction or to stop. The second microcontroller is responsible for choosing one or another command.

It collects environmental information from the sensors, organizes the processing of the received data, and sends the final result of the calculations to another microcontroller as an instruction about changing, continuing the motion path or stopping. Data about the current situation come from the GPS module and RGBD camera. GPS provides the world coordinates of the robot. The RGB-Depth camera sends pictures of the surrounding space to the 2D RGB board and builds a 3D map in the form of a cloud of points [13]. Data from these sensors are needed to solve the issue of navigation.

Communication with the remote control point is carried out using a GSM modem. Using this communication channel, the robot first receives the coordinates of the terrain in which it is necessary to search for a person, and then sends back the search results or notification of the return. The task of pattern recognition is solved by a coprocessor connected to the microcontroller board using a trained neural network.

5.2 Convolutional Neural Network for Human Detection

We use the tiny YOLOv3 for searching for a person in sight of the robot. This algorithm is a fully convolutional neural network. The extractor of this network is DarkNet, which highlights the area in the image, where objects are further detected and classified. Then 53 layers are superimposed on top of the extractor. In tiny YOLOv3 object detection is performed by applying detection kernels to feature maps in different layers of the network. Dimensions of kernels are (1×1) and feature maps are presented in two different sizes.

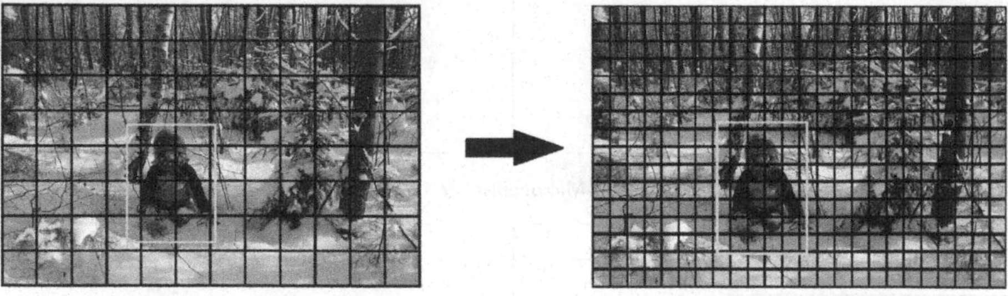

Fig. 6.

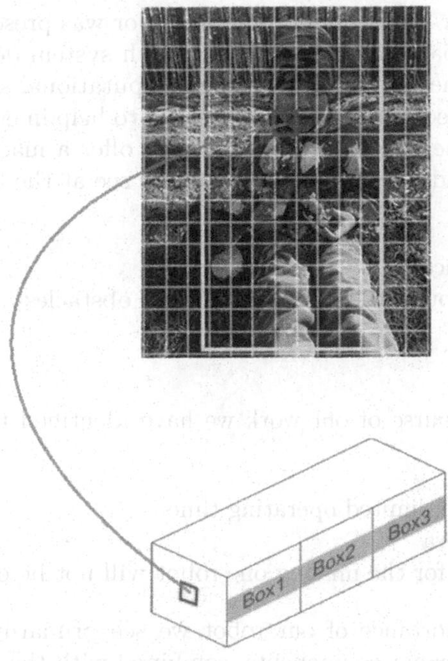

Fig. 7.

This is necessary for detecting small objects more often in Figs. 6 and 7 because the robot has to find a person, who got into an emergency, as quickly as possible. As soon as the robot detects a person, he will be provided with help. Tiny YOLO v3 makes a prediction at two scales which are precisely defined by reducing the size of the input image by 32 and 16 times respectively.

This approach is more resource-intensive and decreases the speed of the algorithm and also allows significantly reduce the number of undetected objects. This is because features maps analysis occurs in different layers of the network which allows detecting objects at different scales of image. Therefore it is possible to detect a person at a greater distance from the robot.

The robot scans the area during the motion, makes RGB-d photo in sight of the camera and transmits RGB image to the neural network processing. Further received image scales and neural network detects objects (humans) in it. If the human is found, the robot will start to approach him and send a GPS signal. It tries to come as close as possible and compare object on RGB image with the point cloud, received from the camera. After that, the robot stops near the person, send detection signal and, if it is possible, photo to headquarters.

6 Conclusions

In this article, we presented the algorithm and architecture of the robot-rescuer. By analyzing the existing research, we came to the conclusion that solutions can be optimized. Our algorithm of robot behavior was presented on this publications base. SLAM-based algorithms joined with system design, based on two microcontrollers, connecting sensors at one computational space. It was shown above that the proposed design has the potential to help in emergency situations of loss of people in the forest. In the article, we offer a machine that currently has no analogs. The advantages of our model we see at the following points:

- Cheapnest
- Practical significance
- Ability to move around the area with a lot of obstacles
- Compactness
- Autonomy of work

However, in the course of our work we have identified the following disadvantages:

- Energy dependence, limited operating time
- Using a fixed camera
- For a quick search for the missing one robot will not be enough

The practical importance of our robot we see primarily in cost reducing, through the use of cheaper components, combined with the optimization of the algorithm. Secondly, our robot not that big, so it able to pass through small obstructions. With the introduction of this technology in areas where it is expensive or dangerous to search for missing people, it is possible to improve the situation, due to the timely response of rescue robots that do not need rest.

Future research in this area is important, as it will help to optimize the work of rescue services and save human lives. Applications of such machines can be very diverse. One of these cases may be patrolling the borders of countries, states, cities. We believe that this direction has great prospects in improving the quality of life. Thus, our plans for future research are to expand the limits of applicability thanks to a massive wheeled platform that will be able to move over rough terrain. It is also planned to develop an algorithm for detecting obstacles on the basis of the presented mathematical model. Computer vision technologies and patterns will be used for this purpose.

Acknowledgments. This research was partially supported by the Russian Foundation for Basic Research grant (project no. 17-29-04288) and by SPbU (Saint Petersburg State University) grant no. AAAAA18-118071790047-9 (id: 28612502). The authors would like to acknowledge the Reviewers for the valuable recommendations that helped in the improvement of this paper.

References

1. Ball, D., et al.: Vision-based obstacle detection and navigation for an agricultural robot. J. Field Robot. **33**(8), 1107–1130 (2016). https://doi.org/10.1002/rob.21644, https://onlinelibrary.wiley.com/doi/abs/10.1002/rob.21644

2. Brand, C., Schuster, M.J., Hirschmüller, H., Suppa, M.: Stereo-vision based obstacle mapping for indoor/outdoor SLAM. In: 2014 IEEE/RSJ International Conference on Intelligent Robots and Systems, pp. 1846–1853, September 2014. https://doi.org/10.1109/IROS.2014.6942805
3. Brand, C., Schuster, M.J., Hirschmüller, H., Suppa, M.: Submap matching for stereo-vision based indoor/outdoor SLAM. In: 2015 IEEE/RSJ International Conference on Intelligent Robots and Systems (IROS), pp. 5670–5677, September 2015. https://doi.org/10.1109/IROS.2015.7354182
4. Cui, M., Sun, D., Liu, W., Zhao, M., Liao, X.: Adaptive tracking and obstacle avoidance control for mobile robots with unknown sliding. Int. J. Adv. Rob. Syst. **9**(5), 171 (2012). https://doi.org/10.5772/52077
5. Evstigneev, M., Litvinov, Y., Mazulina, V., Chashchina, M.: Algorithm for mobile robot cross country motion. Nauchno-Tekhnicheskii Vestnik Informatsionnykh Tekhnologii, Mekhaniki i Optiki **17**(3), 393 (2017)
6. Fabrizio, F., De Luca, A.: Real-time computation of distance to dynamic obstacles with multiple depth sensors. IEEE Robot. Autom. Lett. **2**(1), 56–63 (2017). https://doi.org/10.1109/LRA.2016.2535859
7. Ferreira, A., Pereira, F.G., Vassallo, R.F., Bastos Filho, T.F., Sarcinelli Filho, M.: An approach to avoid obstacles in mobile robot navigation: the tangential escape. Sba: Controle & Automação Sociedade Brasileira de Automatica **19**, 395–405 (2008). http://www.scielo.br/scielo.php?script=sci_arttext&pid=S0103-17592008000400003&nrm=iso
8. Hernández-Aceituno, J., Arnay, R., Toledo, J., Acosta, L.: Using kinect on an autonomous vehicle for outdoors obstacle detection. IEEE Sens. J. **16**(10), 3603–3610 (2016). https://doi.org/10.1109/JSEN.2016.2531122
9. Kim, C., Chwa, D.: Obstacle avoidance method for wheeled mobile robots using interval type-2 fuzzy neural network. IEEE Trans. Fuzzy Syst. **23**(3), 677–687 (2015). https://doi.org/10.1109/TFUZZ.2014.2321771
10. Leishman, R.C., McLain, T.W., Beard, R.W.: Relative navigation approach for vision-based aerial GPS-denied navigation. J. Intell. Rob. Syst. **74**(1), 97–111 (2014). https://doi.org/10.1007/s10846-013-9914-7
11. Moniruzzaman, M., Zishan, M.S.R., Rahman, S., Mahmud, S., Shaha, A.: Design and implementation of urban search and rescue robot. Int. J. Eng. Manufact. **8**(2), 12 (2018)
12. Mouad, M., Adouane, L., Khadraoui, D., Martinet, P.: Mobile robot navigation and obstacles avoidance based on planning and re-planning algorithm. IFAC Proc. **45**(22), 622–628 (2012)
13. Mur-Artal, R., Tardós, J.D.: ORB-SLAM2: an open-source slam system for monocular, stereo, and RGB-D cameras. IEEE Trans. Rob. **33**(5), 1255–1262 (2017). https://doi.org/10.1109/TRO.2017.2705103
14. Savkin, A.V., Wang, C.: Seeking a path through the crowd: Robot navigation in unknown dynamic environments with moving obstacles based on an integrated environment representation. Robotic. Auton. Syst. **62**(10), 1568 – 1580 (2014). https://doi.org/10.1016/j.robot.2014.05.006, http://www.sciencedirect.com/science/article/pii/S0921889014000955
15. Subhan, M., Bhide, A.: SSGB COE: study of unmanned vehicle (robot) for coal mines. Int. J. Innovative Res. Adv. Eng. (IJIRAE) **1**(10), 116–120 (2014)

Position Tracking in 3D Space Based on a Data of a Single Camera

Iakushkin Oleg(✉), Ruslan Sevostyanov, Alexander Degtyarev, P. E. Karpiy, E. G. Kuzevanova, A. A. Kitaeva, and S. A. Sergiev

Saint-Petesburg State University, Saint Petersburg, Russia
o.yakushkin@spbu.ru, st054717@student.spbu.ru

Abstract. A high cost of equipment that solves the problem of tracking the position and direction of users in real time is one of factors that negatively affect the speed of development of the augmented reality industry. The urgency of this problem is a premise for the development of a financially available tracking system. In this research, we propose a software and hardware architecture of a system that solves three-dimensional tracking problems in a closed space and postures classification using neural network models. Distinctive feature of our system is the feasibility in borders of strictly limited computing power and the absence of any sensors placed on monitored objects. After setting the boundaries of the active area, all the necessary input data is provided by a static camera without an infrared filter. As an example of the implementation of a resource-limited solution, we present the assembly of this solution on a Raspberry Pi version 3 single board computer equipped with the Intel Neural Stick version 2 co-processor and a Raspberry version 2 NoIR camera. The first section of the article describes technical characteristics of the equipment used in the study. The second part is dedicated to the solution algorithm and its brief description. Further, in the third stage, the ways of data collection, necessary for a correct assessment of position, direction and posture are illustrated. The fourth, final section presents the results, discussion and possible directions for further work.

Keywords: Software · Optical flow · Augmented reality · Internet of things

1 Introduction

Owing to the growth of computing components capabilities of the Internet of Things, artificial intelligence allows us to solve more non-strictly formalized tasks in the field of computer vision: for example, face recognition [1] and image classification [2]. Such solutions are used in various fields: medicine [3], ecology [4], industry [5], entertainment [6].

Supported by Russian Foundation for Basic Research, grant number 17-29-04288.

S. Misra et al. (Eds.): ICCSA 2019, LNCS 11622, pp. 772–781, 2019.
https://doi.org/10.1007/978-3-030-24305-0_58

The task of tracking is a special interest of [7]. The program proposed by the authors processes video frames and provides the position of objects regarding the surface on which the objects are located. Determining the position of an object possessing several degrees of freedom is called positional tracking. It is widely used in the field of virtual reality [8].

For example, tracking a person's position in space can be used in video games for positioning characters in augmented reality. However, most of the solutions proposed in literature are proprietary, technically complex, expensive, and use large computational powers.

The solution described in the work [9] requires the use of sensors fixed directly on each user's head and legs, which causes additional inconvenience, as well as the direct dependence of the cost of the final set of equipment on the number of players involved in the gameplay.

The solution [10], built on the basis of a convolutional network, is an assessment of posture using several cameras, which implies the use of equipment whose computing power will be sufficient for parallel processing of images from two cameras using a neural network. The essence of the method is that an RGB network processes images taken from the cameras as input data, and the output of the relative rotation and displacement as output data.

Another solution [11] is trained to assess of the current pose based on the previous postures. These scores are then appropriately combined with the output of a visual tracking system using a linear Kalman filter to ensure reliable final posture assessment. Application of such a solution for our purposes is hindered by the cost of devices capable to process images from the camera by the neural network and the subsequent application of the Kalman filter.

The high cost of equipment that solves the problem of positional tracking is one of the factors that negatively affect the speed of development of the virtual reality industry [12]. An obvious solution to this problem is to develop software that can track coordinates in real time, calculate directions, and classify users'postures on low-power systems.

The proposed task can be characterized from different sides and highlight additional aspects for further development. One of them is the problem of restoring the scene [13]. Described in the paper approach is based on the extraction of objects from the database of three-dimensional figures so that the coordinates of the object to be modeled can be determined. Owing to this approach, it is possible to replace real two-dimensional shapes with objects found in the base of three-dimensional shapes. It is necessary at the final stage when visualization occurs so that the administrator has an idea of what is happening with the player and what environment surrounds them. In the most elementary case, a set of points of three-dimensional space can be used as input data.

Also in the section of actual questions for this article, we consider object recognition [14] as the process of teaching the machine to answer the question whether the image or video contains some specific detail, a special feature. The input data for the system is the flow of images from one constant position as well as user records: their names, color of clothes, height and width of shoulders.

Tracking results are transmitted to a remote device for visualization. We have chosen the Outside-in approach, which implies the presence of a fixed observer, in this case a single camera. Similar results can be achieved by restoring original objects [15]; however, modeling using a 3D laser scanner is a very laborious process, often accompanied by an original object shape.

The characteristic feature of our solution is that it does not require large computing power which is why it can be deployed on cheap equipment.

1.1 Motivation and Value

There are many different applications of computer vision and its implementations. They, as a rule, require high performance from the equipment used, specific knowledge from the user in the field of this equipment and its applicability, and, as a result, large financial costs.

Taking it into account, it becomes clear that there is a need for development of a prototype that solves the problem of positional tracking, which would be relatively cheap, easy to install, maintain/replace components, easy to use and available for everyone to buy (Fig. 1).

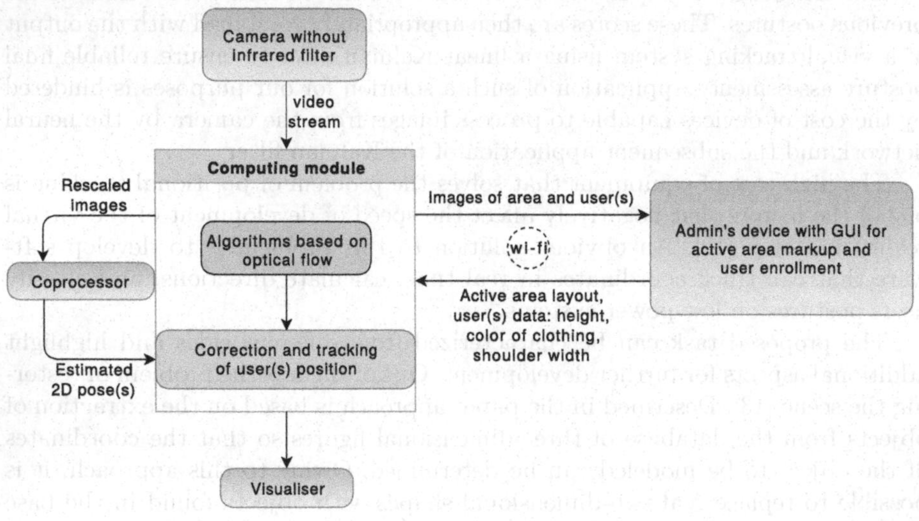

Fig. 1. Description of the interaction between the hardware

2 Existing Software and Algorithms

It was decided to use the OpenPose neural network to initially determine the player's posture from the camera's image. OpenPose is a convolutional neural network that jointly determines the position of the head, torso, arms, legs using key points and displays it in a picture or video in real time. 18 key points are assigned to the spine and legs, 21 for each arm, 70 for the head [17]. To work correctly, OpenPose requires Python3, tensorflow 1.4.1+, protobuf, python3-tk. After the initial position of people is determined by the OpenPose network, players will be tracked using the open source OpenCV library containing computer vision processing algorithms.

The task of analyzing the position of objects and the direction of their movement in real time in one form or another is reduced to analyzing the position of these objects on separate successive frames. In the minimal scheme of our project, we plan to analyze the video signal on the Raspberry Pi 3 Model B module, which is directly connected to the camera. The data from the module is transmitted in separate frames to the administrator's device, where the user can set the camera's view area for analysis, which then returns to the Raspberry module. The video signal, along with data on the size and position of the analysis area, is transmitted to the neural network enhanced by the Intel Compute Stick, which returns the approximate coordinates of the objects. The processed data is then transmitted to the main output device, which may be the same or different from the administrative device, and become available to the user.

It is worth noting that limiting the computational capabilities of Raspberry may require subsequent modification of the scheme of our project. Moreover, the scaling of the proposed solution for a wide range of users is noticeably limited by the need to use additional hardware modules. For this reason, we will consider the possibility of transmitting the primary video signal to the user's device with the possibility of analyzing the video signal on the same device or the subsequent sending of the compressed image to the RP module. Note that the modification of the minimum scheme of the project with the exception of the RP module will separate the camera and the analyzing device, and exclude all external modules except for the motion sensor itself. Thus, the implementation of the project in the future can be reduced to a software component.

In our task, the relevance of the data to a high degree depends not only on the speed of the program analysis, but also on the quality of information transmission from the sensor to the analyzing element to the user's device. In particular, the use of the body position analysis system, which is the ultimate goal of our work, for a wide range of users inevitably affects the interaction task, which in turn imposes additional requirements on the choice of information storage and transmission format.

In the minimal scheme of the project, the main question is the choice of the format of transmitting symbolic information obtained from the analysis of the video signal by a neural network. Among the existing alternatives for the transmission and storage of structured data, we can mention such options as JSON, MessagePack, ProtocolBuffers. Nowadays the generally accepted standard for transferring information from application to application is JSON. Thus, the solution of the problem of compatibility with third-party applications of visualization developers is facilitated by the choice of this format. MessagePack, in its turn, is fully compatible with JSON, but allows to win in data storage efficiency. By saving traffic, it is possible to transfer more data for the same period of time.

Note that the use of the ProtocolBuffers binary format can somewhat speed up the data formatting process, which is an important limitation with the continuous transfer of processed information. However, the processed data on the positions of the bodies and the directions of their movement can be compactly presented in textual form, and the expected amounts of memory required for storing and transmitting this information are small. Thus, compatibility and simplicity of debugging turn out to be more important criteria for choosing the format of data transfer. Summing up this observation with the reasoning above, we conclude that the optimal solution in our project is MessagePack. Speaking about the possibility of direct transmission of the video signal to the administrator's device with subsequent analysis that would not involve additional external systems, we need to analyze the possible options for data transmission protocols.

Currently, the most common and widely supported real-time video transmission and processing protocols are HLS and RTMP. The HLS protocol is built on splitting the video signal up to a sequence of small HTTP-based download files. In its turn, the RTMP protocol is based on the TCP and allows to maintain a continuous connection with low latency in video transmission. Recently, HLS has continuously been strengthening its position in the market and providing more than half of the views of all videos from the analysis [18] (Fig. 2), leaving a quarter of all views on RTMP. Thus, these two protocols are the most natural possible candidates for implementing our system for recognizing the position and direction of motion of objects in a video signal.

Usage of the most common HLS protocol has several undoubted advantages: higher degree of compatibility, a high degree of relevance, active support and updating of protocol versions, and so on. However, the main reason for the popularity of HLS is its compatibility with standard web services and content distribution services, which allows the developers to scale the broadcast simultaneously to multiple users. This protocol is also more convenient for working with modern mobile devices and provides the ability to adapt the signal to the state of the user's connection. However, the considered problem of analyzing the position of objects and the direction of their movement in real-time video is more sensitive to the delay in signal transmission and does not imply a continuous wide broadcast of the video signal itself to many users. Thus, the very structure of the HLS protocol, based on the transfer of small but finite files containing segments of the transmitted signal, makes it less suitable for our project.

3 Preparation

The image of the room and in particular the plane on which the users will be located is transmitted from the camera. Through RTMP, an image is transmitted to a remote device, on which the administrator will designate the boundaries of the plane by setting its four corners on the received image and entering the metric parameters of the space where users are to be searched for.

Specifying the characteristics of the space (in our case, the length and width of the plane) is necessary in order to determine the position of the camera relative to the plane. Using OpenCV library, the allocated space is projected as a quadrilateral onto the camera plane, transforming the perspective. Thus, there is a one-to-one correspondence between the points of the initial image of the space and the rectangular coordinate system specially introduced for this space. Perspective transformation occurs using a square matrix M of dimension 3.

Assuming that each participant has a T-shirt with sufficiently distinguishable colors from each other to uniquely identify each user and assign them a personal number, which is used later to distinguish the participants. The tracking process is preceded by a preparatory stage in which the shoulders of any of the participants are parallel to the camera plane. The procedure is necessary in order to assign each participant a unique ID. In order to do this, the positions of the 2 edge points on the shoulders, as well as the point between them, are estimated. Next, the average color of these points is calculated and assigned to the player that is currently being identified. After that, the administrator enters the player's shoulder width.

4 Recognition Stage

Raspberry Pi NoIR Camera transfers the image to the Raspberry Pi. Next, the Raspberry Pi through the Intel Neural Compute Stick, which is necessary for deploying a neural network on low-power equipment and speeding up calculations, returns the processed frame with defined and marked human limbs. Initially, the neural network highlights the points of the user's nose, neck, shoulders, elbows, wrists, hips, knees, ankles, feet, ears, and eyes. To solve the problem, it was necessary to choose a method for determining the pose of the object in the image. This can be done in one of several ways, depending on the choice of methodology.

The first, analytical, method requires to know the points on the object and the points on the plane as soon as a set of such points has been identified. This allows to restore the pose with the help of equations linking the known points. But all the required points for solving equations are not always known, or the systems are too cumbersome to solve.

Another method for solving our problem is to use neural networks, the weights of which can also be obtained in various ways. We settled on choosing OpenPose - a pre-trained neural network. When choosing a solution method, energy efficiency and low productivity of the proposed computing equipment were taken into account.

From the obtained marked position of a person, one can determine their position in space as follows: the position of two human feet is averaged, and using the position of the obtained point on the image and the parameters obtained earlier for the perspective transformation (data on the size of the area where the person is located and the transformation matrix M) coordinates of the point are determined, which is the average position of a person in a rectangular coordinate system associated with the area.

To determine the angle of rotation of the body, we use information about the width of the shoulders of this person, the positions of their legs and the midpoint between the shoulders. The average position of the user on the floor is the average of the coordinates of the feet. Then, using the calculated midpoints, we find the projection of the shoulder points onto the floor plane.

Calculating the distance between the points of the projections, we estimate the width of the shoulders. By comparing this result with the ground-truth width of the shoulders, it is possible to estimate the angle of the shoulders relative to the floor plane and correct the coordinates of the projections.

Further, having built a perpendicular to the line connecting the projections of the shoulder points, we obtain a line along which the intended view is directed. True direction can be obtained from information about the direction of the head relative to the camera plane, which can be determined using the OpenPose library: in the case of head pointing towards the camera, the library has the ability to determine the coordinates of the person's nose in the image, if the head is directed back to the camera there is no such possibility. There are two ways to determine a person's posture. The first approach is to estimate the angle between the thighs and the shin, indicating the smallest bend angle in the knees, at which the player is considered to be in a standing position. This method has two main problems that we encountered in this work: first, the available angle is calculated with a certain error and at positions close to the boundary ones, it can give distorted information about the player's actual pose; secondly, if the player is positioned in such a way that when they bend their knees, they move in a plane perpendicular to the plane of the camera matrix, the camera will not be able to distinguish the player's position in the sense of squat according to the specified evaluation criterion. The second approach is to estimate the distance from the center point between the shoulders to the floor, which can be calculated by knowing the position of the player (midpoint of the legs) and the distance from the camera to the player. In the second approach, a posture is considered to be in a sitting position, in which the shoulders of a person are at a smaller distance from the floor than a value equal to the product of a person's height by a factor chosen in advance.

5 Results

A successful connection of all technical devices with the highest possible performance was made. There were problems with installing software on the Raspberry Pi for the correct operation of the Intel Neural Compute Stick due to the fact that the native operating system of the board does not appear in the list of compatible operating systems.

The neural network was optimized so that it gave only the data necessary for the project, and not the full set of key points. Original ways of determining a person's pose from the available data were proposed. The frame frequency of the network, together with Optical Flow, has been improved compared with the operation of a neural network without optical flow at least 1.7 times.

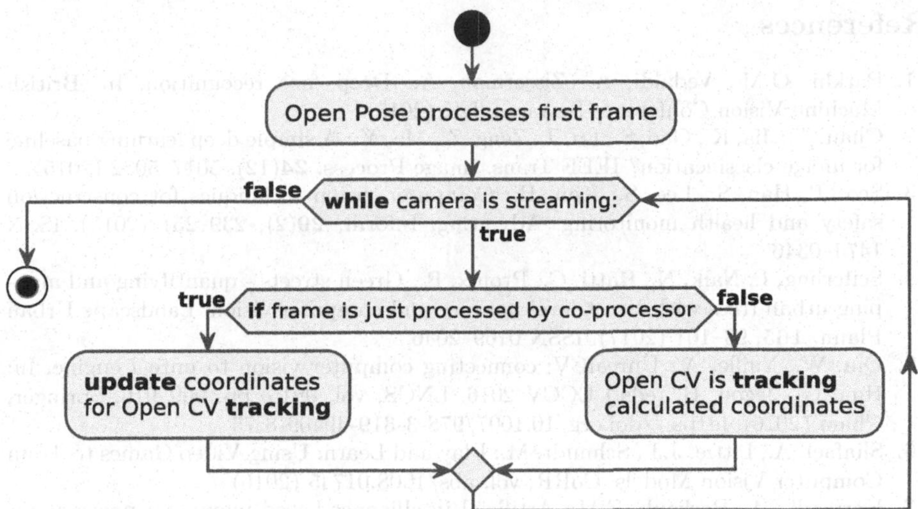

Fig. 2. Schematic description of the process of increasing the tracking frequency

6 Prospects

It is possible to increase the number of coprocessors that accelerate the network performance on the Raspberry Pi. With an increase in computing power, frames will be processed faster, which means that the information provided to the final device will have greater accuracy.

There is a need to increase the number of sensors in order to obtain more information about the object, that is, to more accurately determine the position of a person in space and the direction of the player. It makes sense to convert points from a 2D format to a 3D format [19], to help the system understand how a point appears from different points of view. Since all technical elements are easily replaceable, it is possible to try out several different combinations and determine the optimal configuration. Certainly, it is necessary to try to improve the quality of the image by technical means, as an option, using the super-resolution method [20].

In the long term there is the possibility of developing an application on the target device, more convenient for the side developer, who will be able to use the results obtained by working for their own purposes, for example, to calculate the trajectory of the character in a VR-game.

Acknowledgments. This research was partially supported by the Russian Foundation for Basic Research grants (projects no. 17-29-04288). The authors would like to acknowledge the Reviewers for the valuable recommendations that helped in the improvement of this paper.

References

1. Parkhi, O.M., Vedaldi, A., Zisserman, A.: Deep face recognition. In: British Machine Vision Conference Swansea, UK (2015)
2. Chan, T., Jia, K., Gao, S., Lu, J., Zeng, Z., Ma, Y.: A simple deep learning baseline for image classification? IEEE Trans. Image Process. **24**(12), 5017–5032 (2015)
3. Seo, J., Han, S., Lee, S., Kim, H.: Computer vision techniques for construction safety and health monitoring. Adv. Eng. Inform. **29**(2), 239–251 (2015). ISSN 1474–0346
4. Seiferling, I., Naik, N., Ratti, C., Proulx, R.: Green streets - quantifying and mapping urban trees with street-level imagery and computer vision. Landscape Urban Plann. **165**, 93–101 (2017). ISSN 0169–2046
5. Qiu, W., Yuille, A.: UnrealCV: connecting computer vision to unreal engine. In: Hua, G., Jégou, H. (eds.) ECCV 2016. LNCS, vol. 9915, pp. 909–916. Springer, Cham (2016). https://doi.org/10.1007/978-3-319-49409-8_75
6. Shafaei, A., Little, J.J., Schmidt, M.: Play and Learn: Using Video Games to Train Computer Vision Models. CoRR, vol. abs/1608.01745 (2016)
7. Kermadi, M., Berkouk, E.M.: Artificial intelligence-based maximum power point tracking controllers for photovoltaic systems: comparative study. Renew. Sustain. Energy Rev. **69**, 369–386 (2017). ISSN 1364–0321
8. Thies, J., Zollhöfer, M., Stamminger, M., Theobalt, C., Nießner, M.: FaceVR: Real-Time Facial Reenactment and Eye Gaze Control in Virtual Reality. CoRR, vol.abs/1610.03151
9. Zank, M., Nescher, T., Kunz, A.: Tracking human locomotion by relative positional feet tracking. In: IEEE Virtual Reality, pp. 317–318, Arles (2015). https://doi.org/10.1109/VR.2015.7223423
10. Melekhov, I., Ylioinas, J., Kannala, J., Rahtu, E.: Relative camera pose estimation using convolutional neural networks. In: Blanc-Talon, J., Penne, R., Philips, W., Popescu, D., Scheunders, P. (eds.) ACIVS 2017. LNCS, vol. 10617, pp. 675–687. Springer, Cham (2017). https://doi.org/10.1007/978-3-319-70353-4_57
11. Rambach, J.R., Tewari, A., Pagani, A., Stricker, D.: Learning to fuse: a deep learning approach to visual-inertial camera pose estimation. In: 2016 IEEE International Symposium on Mixed and Augmented Reality (ISMAR), pp. 71–76 (2016)
12. Avila, L., Bailey, M.: Virtual reality for the masses. IEEE Comput. Graph. Appl. **34**(05), 103–104 (2014). https://doi.org/10.1109/MCG.2014.103
13. Li, Y., Dai, A., Guibas, L., Nießner, M.: Database-assisted object retrieval for real-time 3D reconstruction. Comput. Graph. Forum **34**(2), 435–446 (2015). https://doi.org/10.1111/cgf.12573
14. Sawyer, R., Smith, A., Rowe, J., Azevedo, R., Lester, J.: Models in game-based learning with facial expression recognition. In: Proceedings of the 25th Conference on User Modeling, Adaptation and Personalization, pp. 192–201, New York, NY, USA (2017)
15. Ruchti, P., Steder, B., Ruhnke, M, Burgard, W.: Localization on OpenStreetMap data using a 3D laser scanner. In: 2015 IEEE International Conference on Robotics and Automation (ICRA), pp. 5260–5265, Seattle, WA (2015). https://doi.org/10.1109/ICRA.2015.7139932
16. Sajjad, M., et al.: Raspberry Pi assisted face recognition framework for enhanced law-enforcement services in smart cities. Future Gener. Comput. Syst. (2017)
17. Cao, Z., Hidalgo, G., Simon, T., Wei, S.-E., Sheikh, Y.: OpenPose: Realtime Multi-Person 2D Pose Estimation using Part Affinity Fields. CoRR, vol. abs/1812.08008 (2018)

18. State of streaming protocols (2018). https://blog.wmspanel.com/2018/12/state-of-streaming-protocols-2018-summary.html. Accessed 24 Dec 2018
19. Pavllo, D., Feichtenhofer, C., Grangier, D., Auli, M.: 3D human pose estimation in video with temporal convolutions and semi-supervised training. CoRR, vol. abs/1811.11742 (2018)
20. Shi, W., et al.: Real-time single image and video super-resolution using an efficient sub-pixel convolutional neural network. In: the IEEE Conference on Computer Vision and Pattern Recognition (CVPR), pp. 1874–1883 (2016)

Controlled Remote Usage of Private Shared Resources via Docker and NoVNC

Daniil Malevanniy(✉), Olga Sedova, and Oleg Iakushkin

Saint-Petersburg State University, 7/9 Universitetskaya nab., St. Petersburg 199034, Russia

rukmarr@gmail.com, o.yakushkin@spbu.ru

Abstract. Shared usage of computational power in scientific projects is often associated with organizational problems, since different users may need different software environments, and used resources may have no public access. The usage of the majority of existing environment managers is often not suitable for inexperienced users participating in such projects, as well as access to shared resources only through public gateways. This paper describes a method of organizing public remote access to an isolated working environment on shared resources based on containerization technology and a system for the remote call of console applications via the web interface. Combined usage of these systems allows inexperienced users to use shared computational resources with full effectivity.

Keywords: Remote access · Shared resources · Containerization

1 Introduction

The need for computing resources in scientific projects can be high even in areas far from Computer Science. Depending on the scale of the project, it may require the use of a GRID network or voluntary computing [1], or it will be limited to just leasing resources in cloud services. But, in any case, there is a need to provide end users with access to the shared resources used. This raises several problems.

Despite the fact that Linux was originally created as a multi-user operating system, the free use of one machine by several users is associated with certain inconveniences. The possibility of uncontrolled changes to the working environment by users, in particular, installing new software or changing versions of an existing one, can break the workflow of other users, but on the other hand, when the administrator controls the environment, users are often limited in their choice of software used.

In addition, it should be borne in mind that in research projects, despite their possible complexity, users who do not have extensive experience with Linux

This research was partially supported by Russian Foundation for Basic Research grant (project no. 17-29-04288).

S. Misra et al. (Eds.): ICCSA 2019, LNCS 11622, pp. 782–791, 2019.
https://doi.org/10.1007/978-3-030-24305-0_59

and the command-line interfaces can participate. However, a large proportion of software used in such projects is available only in Linux-like environments and in the form of console applications [10–12].

Other problems may include strict firewall policies regarding incoming connections and the absence of the public IP address of the private machines of educational institutions acting as computational resources. This greatly complicates access to such resources for users, especially untrained.

This paper describes a possible solution to the problems described above. The created system provides users with two interfaces: a full system GUI and a simplified web-interface for launching console programs. The working environments of each user are isolated from one another, and there is no restriction to user permissions in them. In addition, we describe how to provide public access to the work environment in the case when it deployed on private resources.

2 Approach

The goal of this work is to implement a system for remote use of shared resources, which, on the one hand, will allow experienced users to fully manage their work environment, and on the other hand, will provide their less advanced colleagues with a convenient interface for working with console applications.

Also, in order to ensure the safety and efficiency of data storage, the system should provide centralized file storage located on a separate machine, containing both public and private user files. Access to this repository should be possible from both available interfaces.

Another important requirement for the system is the ability to work with several host machines, including those located behind the firewall in private networks. At the same time, the way for a user to access their work environment should not depend on the machine on which it is deployed.

For the administrator, the system should provide control over users and their work environments and at the same time automate the process of adding new hosts or users to the system.

3 Results

To isolate users and give them full control over their working environment, the Docker containerization platform is used [2]. When working in the Docker container, the user has no restrictions but works in isolation from other users. This allows them to fully control their environment, without side-effects in the other ones.

However, the only user interface of most Docker images is a virtual terminal, which is unsuitable for use by an untrained user. To access the graphical interface of the system, the TigerVNC vncserver [3] is used, which provides remote access to the virtual display running inside the container. On the client side, the NoVNC JavaScript library [4] is used, allowing users to connect to the VNC server in a browser window with WebSocket protocol (Fig. 1).

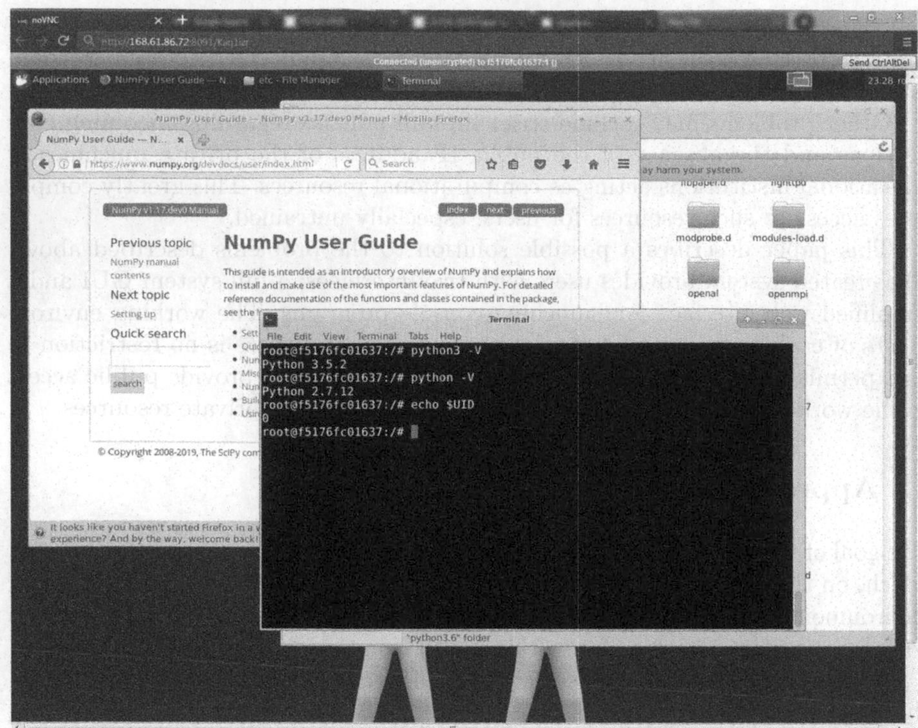

Fig. 1. System GUI, provided by NoVNC library in the browser window

If users of the system need to work with console programs, using the graphical interface of the system does not make the workflow easier. To provide inexperienced users with a convenient interface in such cases, a system was developed that generates a web-interface with the same functionality as the console program, based on a command line template and implemented as a web server running in a user container. To organize the execution of programs, the Celery task queue is used. Tasks sent to it by the user interface can be performed both in their containers, where they completely control the environment or on other nodes.

If manipulating large data is necessary when working on shared resources, it may be inconvenient to store it in a container. To organize the central storage of user data, a file system was created on the basis of the libfuse library, using Celery tasks to manipulate files located on a separate machine. Using Celery allows not only to mount the file system in a container but also to integrate it into the web interface, used to run console commands, which further simplifies the use of the system by users of different levels of experience.

To use both the system GUI provided by VNC server working in the container and the simplified web interface, public access to certain container TCP ports is required. In our case, the publication of ports on the servers used for

Fig. 2. Task definition, describing template for console program execution and web-interface, generated for this task

container hosting was prohibited, and the servers themselves were operating in the private network. When working with computing resources closed from external connections, often the only way to provide public access to TCP ports is reverse tunneling. This technique uses outbound connections to transfer data in the opposite direction and requires fine-tuning of the firewall to intercept (Fig. 2).

To organize the operation of reverse tunnels, the "Fast Reverse Proxy" [5] was used, which provides the client and server parts necessary for the organization of the TCP-over-TCP reverse tunnels. It allows you to open and control in detail the external access to services deployed on private resources that are closed by the firewall.

However, each tunnel requires a separate port on a public machine, which degrades the scalability of the system because of the need to create a separate set of tunnels for the services of each user. Another technique, reverse proxy, can be used to solve this problem. It is used to provide access to several web services under the guise of one, working, on the one hand, as a server responding to client requests, and, on the other, as a client, sending proxied requests to services (Figs. 3, 4, 5 and 6).

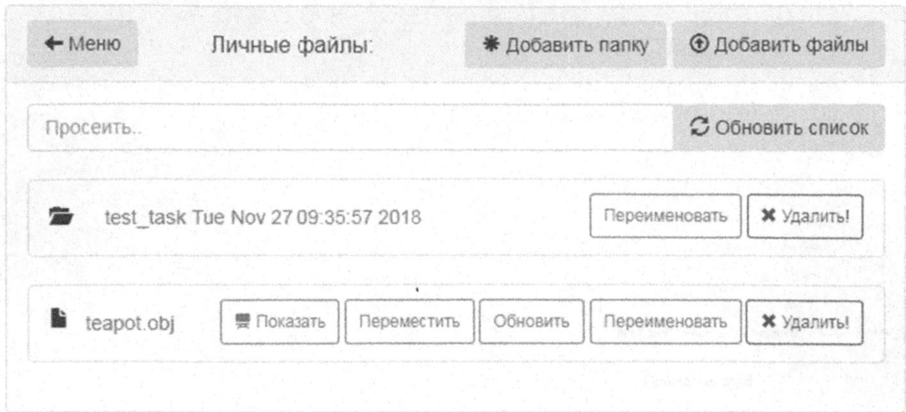

Fig. 3. Overview of a folder located in the shared storage in the web interface

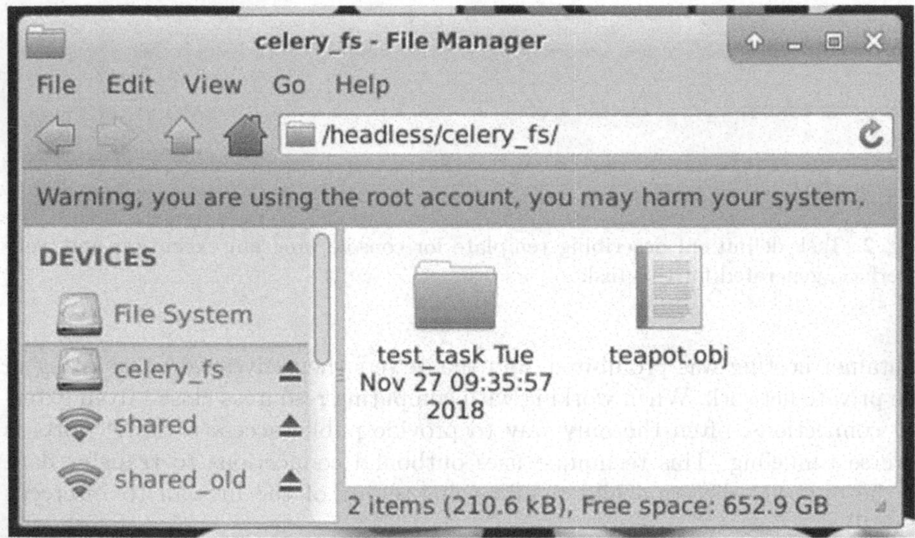

Fig. 4. Overview of the same folder in GUI

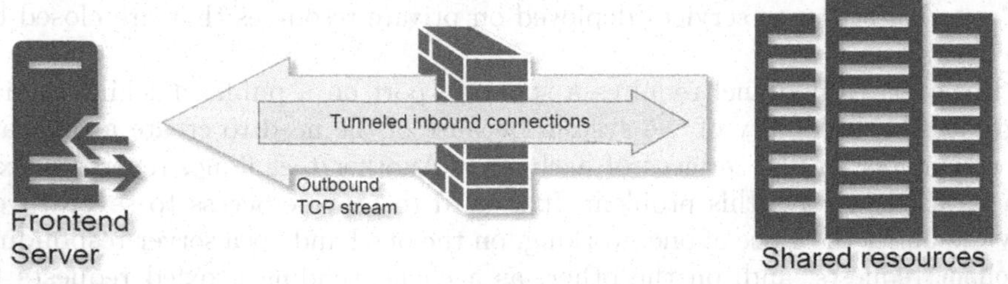

Fig. 5. Reverse tunnel workflow diagram

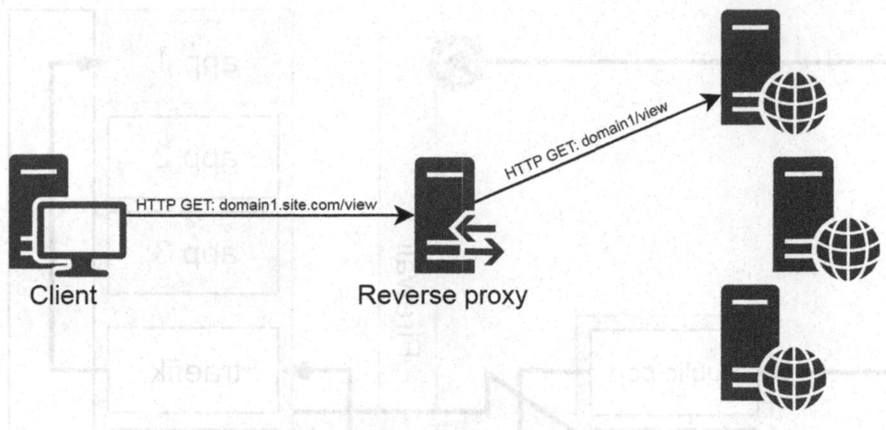

Fig. 6. Reverse proxy workflow diagram

Traefik [6] was chosen as the reverse proxy server. It allows its users to redirect HTTP and HTTPS requests and WebSocket connections based on their HTTP headers and supports the dynamic redefinition of request routing logic. To minimize the number of TCP ports required for the operation of services through a reverse tunnel, slightly different use of this technology is needed. Instead of redirecting to other machines, the reverse proxy will serve as an entry point for all requests passing through the reverse tunnel and redirect them to services running on the same machine through a loopback interface unregulated by the firewall.

Thus, connection to containers running on private host machines is possible through a single public server. However, access to each of the hosts is open through separate public TCP port of the corresponding FRP tunnel. To unify access to containers running on different machines, these public ports are hidden beside a single reverse proxy Traefik, operating according to the scheme described earlier. This allows users to access their work environment from a single URL, regardless of exact deployment location.

It is easy to see that manual control of all components of the system of such complexity would take an unreasonably long time. To automate this process, an admin panel and a system for sending configurations to system nodes were implemented. In order to simplify the user authorization logic, users are divided into groups defining the containers they use and the tasks available in the web interface. The admin panel, deployed on a public site, allows administrators to manage groups, user containers, add or remove system nodes. The broadcasting system starts and stops the containers on nodes and updates the logic of the routing of Traefik requests if it is necessary (Fig. 7).

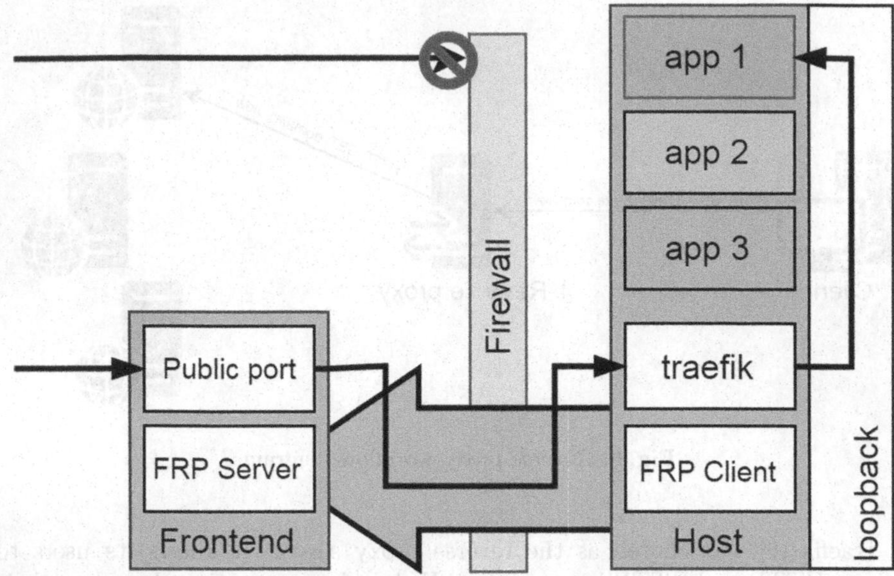

Fig. 7. Publishing system diagram

4 Evaluation

The described system of remote access to shared resources is based on a combination of several technologies: containerization using Docker, remote execution of tasks through Celery and bypassing firewalls using reverse tunneling. The advantages and disadvantages of the constructed solution arise from the features of these technologies and the method of their use in the system.

As an example, the combination of reverse proxy and reverse tunneling affects the speed of message transmission between the client and the server, compared to the use of a separate tunnel for each server, but allows more efficient use of available TCP ports on a public machine and thereby improves the scalability of the system.

The use of containerization technology reduces the overhead required to isolate the user environment, compared to virtual machines. Choosing Docker as a containerization platform allows usage of an extensive library of Docker images for container creation, but limits the ability of users to work with the kernel [7] and further slows down message transfer between the client and the server working in the container [8] (Fig. 8).

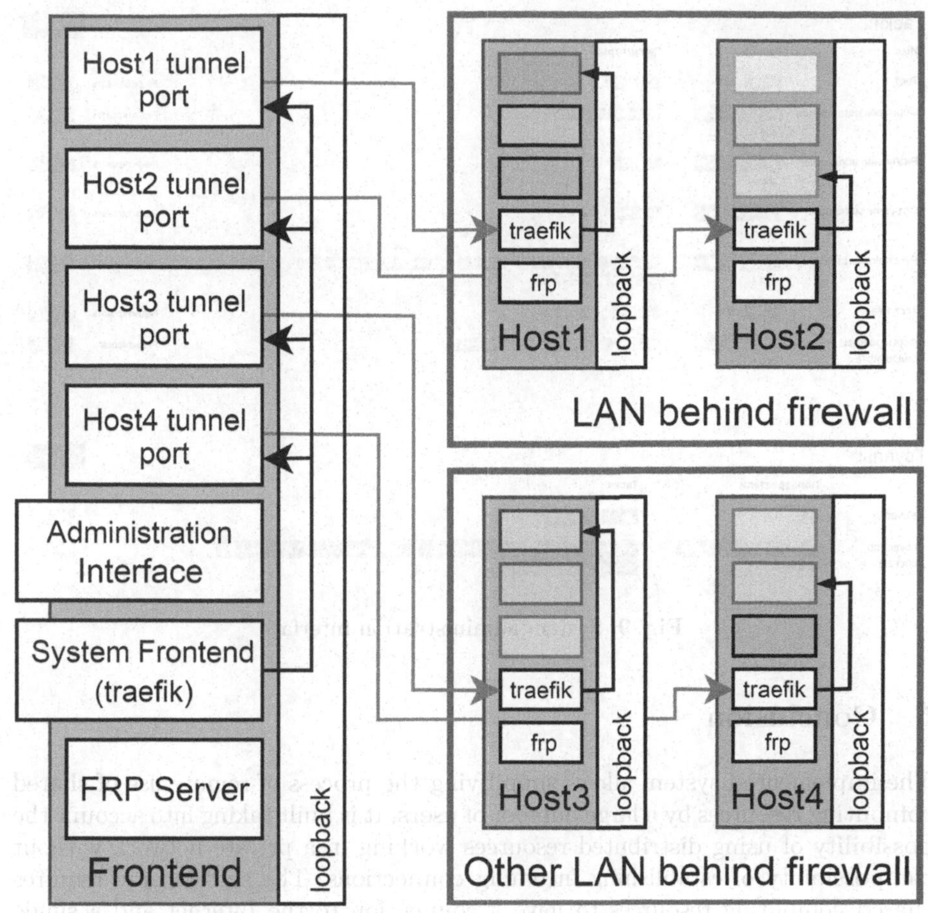

Fig. 8. Complete system structure overview

The usage of the Celery task queue to organize work with console applications allows users to choose execution environment but affects performance compared to the direct invocation of applications by the web server that provides the user interface. On the other hand, this difference is not noticeable in comparison with the total running time of the majority of applications. In addition, Celery makes it easier to monitor user activity, allows administrators to control access to task queues, and provides the opportunity for the future development of the system for remote execution of applications (Fig. 9).

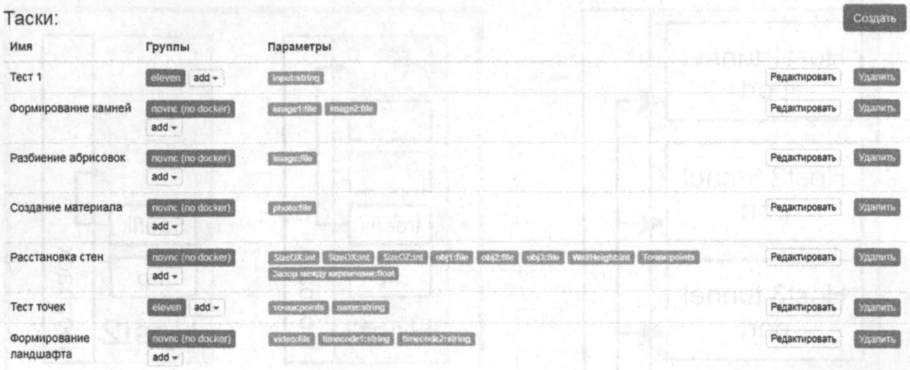

Fig. 9. System administration interface

5 Conclusion

The implemented system allows simplifying the process of remote use of shared computing resources by a large number of users. It is built taking into account the possibility of using distributed resources working in a private network without the possibility of establishing incoming connections. The system only requires shared computing resources to have a connection to the Internet and a single node with a public IP address.

Further development of the system can be associated with the use of alternative containerization platforms. Due to security risks, Docker usage may not be allowed on high-performance computing resources used in research projects. As an alternative containerization platform, Singularity is the most popular choice [9]. However, the use of network software in Singularity is inconvenient, since it does not manage container networks. Overcoming these difficulties and adapting the system to use Singularity can be the next step in its development.

Regardless of the choice of containerization platform used, both Docker and Singularity allow you to limit computing resources, such as the percentage of CPU or RAM available to applications running in the container. Integrating the management of these constraints into the administration interface would allow centralized control of users' resource usage. This feature may appear with future system updates.

Other system changes may be related to the publication system. In particular, the separation of host machines into private and public, without tunneling in the second case, will improve the speed of connection with services running on public machines.

Usage of this system in research projects makes remote use of shared resources easier for end users. For experienced users, direct use of the system GUI is possible, and for those less familiar with the console, a web interface that implements the functionality of a predefined set of console applications. Simplification of the workflow increases the efficiency of the use of computing resources in scientific projects.

Acknowledgments. This research was partially supported by the Russian Foundation for Basic Research grants (projects no. 17-29-04288). The authors would like to acknowledge the Reviewers for the valuable recommendations that helped in the improvement of this paper.

References

1. Anderson, D.P., Cobb, J., Korpela, E., Lebofsky, M., Werthimer, D.: SETI@ home: an experiment in public-resource computing. Commun. ACM **45**(11), 56–61 (2002)
2. Merkel, D.: Docker: lightweight linux containers for consistent development and deployment. Linux J. **2014**(239), 2 (2014)
3. TigerVNC vncserver (2019). https://tigervnc.org/doc/vncserver.html
4. Martin, J., Mannehed, S., Astrand, P., Ross, S.: noVNC: HTML5 VNC Client (2015)
5. fatedier/frp: A fast reverse proxy to help you expose a local server behind a NAT or firewall to the internet (2019). https://github.com/fatedier/frp
6. Traefik: The cloud native edge router (2019). https://traefik.io/
7. Bui, T.: Analysis of docker security. arXiv preprint arXiv:1501.02967 (2015)
8. Felter, W., et al.: An updated performance comparison of virtual machines and linux containers. In: 2015 IEEE International Symposium on Performance Analysis of Systems and Software (ISPASS). IEEE (2015)
9. Kurtzer, G.M., Sochat, V., Bauer, M.W.: Singularity: scientific containers for mobility of compute. PLoS ONE **12**(5), e0177459 (2017)
10. Iakushkin, O.O., Malevanniy, D.M., Degtyarev, A.B., Selivanov, D.A., Fatkina, A.I.: Texture generation for archaeological reconstructions (2018)
11. Iakushkin, O., Selivanov, D., Tazieva, L., Fatkina, A., Grishkin, V., Uteshev, A.: 3D reconstruction of landscape models and archaeological objects based on photo and video materials. In: Gervasi, O., et al. (eds.) ICCSA 2018. LNCS, vol. 10963, pp. 160–169. Springer, Cham (2018). https://doi.org/10.1007/978-3-319-95171-3_14
12. Iakushkin, O., Fatkina, A., Plaksin, V., Sedova, O., Degtyarev, A., Uteshev, A.: Reconstruction of stone walls in form of polygonal meshes from archaeological studies. In: Gervasi, O., et al. (eds.) ICCSA 2018. LNCS, vol. 10963, pp. 136–148. Springer, Cham (2018). https://doi.org/10.1007/978-3-319-95171-3_12

Use of Digital Technology for the Attribution of Paintings

N. L. Shchegoleva[1,2] and Y. A. Vaulina[3(✉)]

[1] Saint Petersburg State University, 7/9 Universitetskayanab., St. Petersburg 199034, Russia
n.shchegoleva@spbu.ru
[2] Plekhanov Russian University of Economics, Stremyannylane, 36, Moscow 117997, Russia
[3] Saint Petersburg Electrotechnical University "LETI", ul.Professora Popova 5, 197376 St. Petersburg, Russian Federation
yanchik_vau@mail.ru

Abstract. Modern attribution of art works depends on the expert experience. This implies some subjectivity of his assessments. Recently for making a more informed decision digital image processing techniques have been used. Therefore, the study of the methods for obtaining additional information about the painting, which cannot be obtained using existing methods, is an important task.

The joint use of several features extraction methods will allow increase the effectiveness of its analysis. The application developed by the authors based on using of several methods (HOG, DCT, frequency analysis of color, color moments, color histograms, LBP, Gabor filter, GLCM, Hough transform) and allows making an assumption about belonging artwork to a particular art school, style or direction. The results obtained are confirmed by historical data about his teacher and where the artist studied, and who of the masters had the greatest influence on him.

Keywords: Attribution of paintings · Digital attribution · HOG · DCT · Frequency analysis of color · Color moments · Color histograms · LBP · Gabor filter · GLCM · Hough transform · Application for attribution

1 Introduction

Attribution of painting – the identification of authorship or belonging painting to an art school based on comprehensive scientific examination. Today it is one of the important research areas of artworks. The attribution is based on the finding out material evidence that allowed accept the expert opinion as indisputable. Such evidence is the author's signature, the presence of the date or monogram of the artist, etc. Unfortunately, on many paintings artist autographs are absent at all. On others these autographs are poorly visible to the naked eye, as they consist of the letters remains that are strongly worn and covered with varnish layers. This is due to the change of paintings over time associated with the influence of the environment, adverse storage conditions and the consequences of illiterate paintings restoration.

S. Misra et al. (Eds.): ICCSA 2019, LNCS 11622, pp. 792–801, 2019.
https://doi.org/10.1007/978-3-030-24305-0_60

Therefore, experts opinion is the main "method" of attribution, which is based on the its experience, the presence of his penetrating gaze, deep and detailed knowledge about artist and his contemporaries, the conditions in which the picture was created, expert knowledge of the features of brush strokes and the choice of colors by the artist. That is why this method will always include some subjectivity and, therefore, the opinion of different specialists may differ, despite their acceptance by the international community of experts.

2 Modern Attribution Methods

In recent years new physical and chemical methods of evaluating paintings such as ultraviolet fluorescence, infrared reflectography, stereomicroscopy, radiography and etc. have been proposed as additional tools supporting the work of experts in order to make a more justified decision. Dendrochronology and radiocarbon dating are used to study wood panels and paint layers, allowing determining the age of the artworks. For example, radiography can reveal the presence of another image under the painting, which can shed light on its origin or find out about the artist intentions and how his original plan has changed.

Surface analysis of paints is determining the proportion of a certain lead isotope in the paint compared to the expected content allows you to determine the date of writing the picture. Since the painting uses pigments, which are similar in color but differ in composition and crystal structure, the methods of microchemical analysis are used to determine this. However, despite the presence of a wide arsenal and potential of modern research methods, they are not always effective enough for attribution even in combination with art expertise.

3 Application of Computer Image Processing Methods for Attribution

Constantly growing capabilities of digital devices (processors work more and more quickly, computers, scanners and cameras increase resolution, data storages are getting bigger and etc.) generated a desire to use these tools for the study of collections of digitized works of art, whose volume has increased significantly over the last few years. Significant advances in the field of digital image processing, machine learning and artificial intelligence led to the fact that the world of art began to consider the use of computers in the artworks analysis at least as a trial step or the first stage in determining whether the picture is forgery or not.

This became the basis for the active stylometry development– the examination of authorship and the artworks style via statistical and numerical methods. Stylometry is based on the assumption that there are certain differences in the styles of different artists, as well as the characteristic movements of the artist's hand when drawing. Therefore, the characteristics that reflect these habits can be considered as features for determining the authorship of paintings. The methods of stylometry are far from perfect, but over the last few years there have been quite a lot of interesting works deals with the determination of authorship which based on mathematical description of the unique artist style. This allows distinguishing his work from other authors or detecting a forgery and to determine the artistic reception used by the artist and his original idea. Some method allow us to identify whether the restoration and assess its quality.

The application of existing digital technologies can form a new understanding and new methods of art research, develop tools that will enable the computer to make aesthetic judgments on a semantic level, such as defining a style and genre of a picture based not only on the measure of similarity, but also on understanding art, and also taking into account the historical interpretation of the events depicted in the picture. Of particular note are the works associated with the study of aesthetics using computer vision methods [1]. Do not forget that the constant growth in quantity of digitized art works collections requires the development of multimedia systems for archiving and retrieving all sorts of information from this colossal amount of data.

Accordingly, the problem of researching digital image processing methods that could provide additional information about the artworks, which cannot be obtained using existing methods of studying painting, is currently topical.

For image processing today a large number of methods have been proposed that allow extract of textural, color, spectral, structural, statistical features for image analysis. Some methods have also been used to process the paintings of artists. The most widely used methods are color histograms [2, 3] and color moments [6].

Estimating the pixel frequency of different colors helps to get important information about the painting - to determine the colors that the artist loves and the most likely color scheme that he uses in his paintings.

Calculation of the histogram in different color spaces, such as RGB, HSV, CYK, etc. allows you to get the colors distribution in the painting and estimate the "amount" of a certain color in the painting. Unfortunately, analyzing the histograms of color, we cannot estimate the details of the paintings, describing the orientation, shape of objects, textures. In addition, histograms are largely dependent on lighting and are influenced by various kinds of noise.

Another frequently used method is the Histogram of Oriented Gradients [2, 4, 5]. Typically, these descriptors are used to define the edges or corners of an object. It is in these places that the gradient values change significantly.

Well-known methods such as discrete cosine transform (DCT) [7, 14], Fourier transform [2, 14], wavelet transform [1, 8–13], Gabor filters [7], hidden Markov models [12, 15, 16] have found application in this area.

Local Binary Patterns (LBP) [2] are used to evaluate the texture of an image, which is important for the study of an artist's brushstroke and helps to determine its style.

However, most of the published works do not explain the criterion for the selection of paintings and their authors for analysis, and there is also no justification for the choice of processing methods.

This allows us to conclude that the methods are determined purely empirically and based on the experience of researchers or the presence of already implemented processing methods. In our opinion, the joint use of several methods of feature extraction from paintings will allow to increase the effectiveness of the analysis, since more data is objectively used: the space of image representations is expanded and a greater number of hypotheses are considered, reducing the risk of a wrong decision.

4 Application for the Attribution of Paintings

The application for automatic attribution has been developed and allows using the following methods: histogram of oriented gradients, discrete cosine transform, frequency analysis of color, color moments, color histograms, local binary patterns, Gabor filter, Gray-Level Co-Occurrence Matrix (GLCM) and Hough transform.

Table 1. Description of the digital art collection.

Artist	Painting school	Painting direction	Genre
Ivan Aivazovsky	Cimmerian Art School	R	M
Konstantin Bogaevsky	Mir Iskusstva (World of Art), Cimmerian Art School, Union of Russian Artists	S	L
Alexey Bogolyubov	Peredvizhniki (Society for Traveling Art Exhibitions)	R, Re	M, C
Karl Bryullov	Imperial Academy of Arts, Saint Petersburg, Russia	N, R	L
Konstantin Makovsky	Peredvizhniki (Society for Traveling Art Exhibitions)	Ac, R, Re	H, P
Edvard Munch	Berlin Secession, Degenerate art	S, E	G
Wassily Kandinsky	Blue Rose, Der Blaue Reiter (The Blue Rider), Bauhaus, Degenerate art, Der Sturm	E, Ab	A
Amedeo Modigliani	École de Paris, La Ruche	E	N
Arthur Segal	Der Blaue Reiter (The Blue Rider), Die Brücke (The Bridge)	E, D	F
Boris Grigoriev		E	
Claude Monet		I	
Edouard Manet		Re, I	
Valentin Serov	Peredvizhniki (Society for Traveling Art Exhibitions)	Re, I	P
Henri Matisse	École de Paris, Les Fauves	I, PI	
Arkhip Kuindzhi	Peredvizhniki (Society for Traveling Art Exhibitions)	Re, I	L
Theodore Rousseau	Barbizon school	Re	L
Alexey Venetsianov		Re	
Boris Kustodiev	Mir Iskusstva (World of Art), AKhRR (Association of Artists of Revolutionary Russia), Union of Russian Artists	Re, AN	
Ilya Repin	Peredvizhniki (Society for Traveling Art Exhibitions)	Re	
Ivan Shishkin	Peredvizhniki (Society for Traveling Art Exhibitions)	Re	L

The Table 1 describes the digital collection of paintings used in the experiments. The following notation is used in the Table 1: for genre M – Marina, L – Landscape, C – Cityscape, H – Historical painting, P – Portrait, G – Genre painting, A – Abstraction, N – Nude painting (nu), F – Figurative painting; for painting direction: R – Romanticism, S – Symbolism, Re – Realism, N – Neoclassicism, E – Expressionism, I – Impressionism, PI – Post-Impressionism, AN – Art Nouveau, Ac – Academic Art, Ab – Abstract Art, D – Dadaism.

The developed application allows you to perform an analysis of paintings on the similarity with the works of other artists and the artist's belonging to a particular style, movement, genre by using extracted features. Informative visualization simplifies the work of an expert in the study of a work of art, when hypotheses are put forward (for example, whether a picture is fake or not, which direction the picture belongs to, etc.) and allows flexible selection of specific features to substantiate his conclusion.

The Fig. 1 shows the result of images classification using the features extraction method selected by an expert for set of images. To do this, the following metrics are calculated: the number of neighbors for the most accurate classification by the k-nearest neighbors method, the prediction accuracy with this number of neighbors, the report on the quality of the classification (prediction accuracy, recall, F-measure), the error matrix, image feature mapping into two-dimensional space which is performed by the t-SNE method.

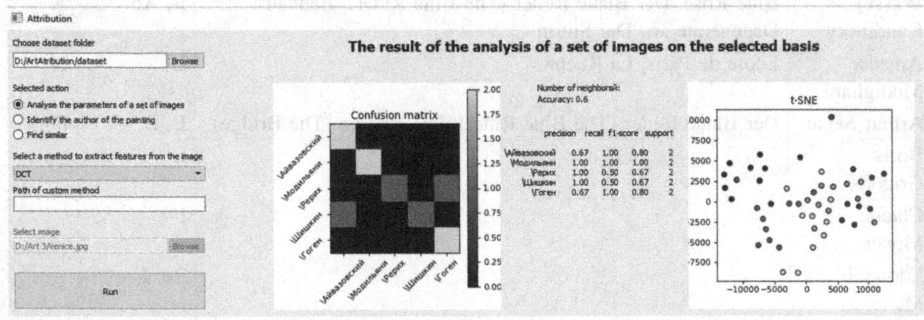

Fig. 1. An example of defining the parameters of a set of images of paintings.

The user is given the opportunity to determine the author of the painting on based on the chosen features of him. The application displays the name of the intended author and three images that are closest to the given, with the visualization of the selected features, as well as the distance between them and the original image in multidimensional space (see Figs. 2, 3).

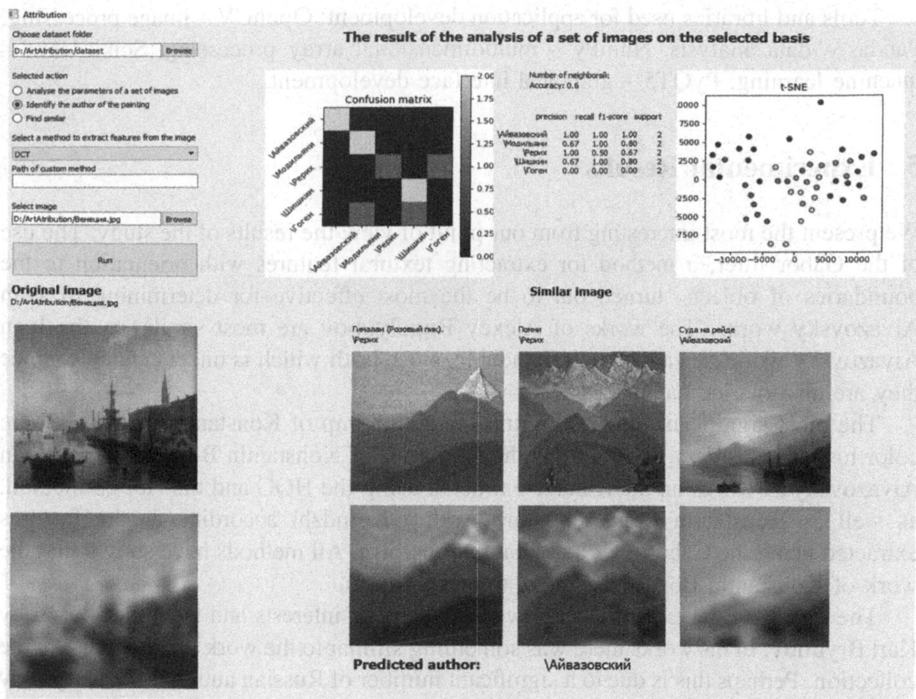

Fig. 2. The definition of the author of the picture based on the methods chosen by the user.

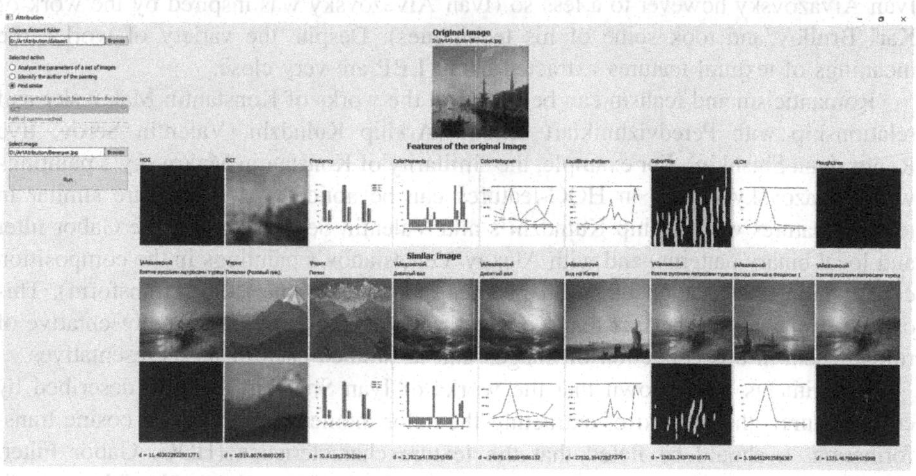

Fig. 3. The definition of the author of the picture on the basis of all the features of the extraction of characteristics implemented in the application.

Tools and libraries used for application development: OpenCV – image processing, Pandas – data analysis, NumPy – multidimensional array processing, Scikit-learn – machine learning, PyQT5 – graphical interface development.

5 Experimental Results

We present the most interesting from our point of view the results of the study. The use of the Gabor filter, a method for extracting textural features with orientation to the boundaries of objects, turned out to be the most effective for determining of Ivan Aivazovsky works. The works of Alexey Bogolyubov are most similar to the Ivan Aivazovsky works, which is understandable, since both which is understandable, since they are also marine painters.

The most significant for determining the authorship of Konstantin Bogaevsky are color histograms. Very interesting is the similarity of Konstantin Bogaevsky and Ivan Aivazovskyart works on the features extracted using the HOG and the Hough method, as well as Konstantin Bogaevsky and Arkhip Kuindzhi according to the features extracted using the Gabor filter and Hough transform. All methods have shown that the work of Konstantin Bogaevsky refers to romanticism.

The results of the experiment showed a variety of interests and techniques used by Karl Bryullov. In his works there was something similar to the work of each artist in the collection. Perhaps this is due to a significant number of Russian authors. Karl Bryullov influenced not only the creativity of each of them as a colleague, mentor or inspirer, but also the entire Academy of Arts as he used his own new teaching methods.

Karl Bryullov's works can be attributed to the romanticism and realism movement. The values of HOG-features and features extracted by the Hough transform are close to Ivan Aivazovsky however to a less so (Ivan Aivazovsky was inspired by the work of Karl Brullov and took some of his techniques). Despite the variety of works, the meanings of textural features extracted using LBP are very close.

Romanticism and realism can be traced in the works of Konstantin Makovsky and relationship with Peredvizhnikiart school (Arkhip Kuindzhi, Valentin Serov, Ilya Repin, Ivan Shishkin). For example, the similarity of Konstantin Makovsky's paintings with Aivazovsky's work in HOG-features can be noticed. Also they are similar in texture features with Arkhip Kuindzhi's and Valentin Serov's works (the Gabor filter and local binary patterns) and with Alexey Venetsianov's paintings in the composition construction (the location of the main lines identified by the Hough transform). This can be explained by the fact that Konstantin Makovsky is the latest representative of romanticism in this collection of images and he studied each of its representatives.

Experiments have shown that the works of Ivan Shishkin are best described by color features: the method of extracting the color moments and discrete cosine transformation. It should be noted that the texture characteristics (HOG, Gabor Filter, Hough transform) of the Ivan Shishkin works are similar to the work of Ivan Aivazovsky, but the texture features poorly describe the Ivan Shishkin's works because of the due to the extremely detailed portrayal of landscapes.

For the works of Boris Kustodiev it was not possible to identify the features that uniquely characterize his work. However, it was found that his paintings clearly belong to the realism direction. His used colors are close to Valentin Serov, Edouard Manet and Claude Monet.

Ilya Repin's paintings were extremely diverse. It was not possible to distinguish from the features analyzed in the experiment those that most clearly describe his work. However, there is a similarity with artists of romanticism (to a greater extent) and realism movement. The influence of Ivan Aivazovsky and Alexey Venetsianov, that is typically for the artists of realism (HOG and Hough transform), should also be noted.

According to the results of the experiment, Theodore Rousseau's work is at the junction of romanticism and realism. DCT features are characteristic of his artworks. According to the texture features based on the Gabor filter, the paintings are close to Ivan Aivazovsky and Arkhip Kuindzhi.

Realism and romanticism brightly expressed in the paintings of Arkhip Kuindzhi. The paintings of this author are well characterized by features obtained by methods describing the structure and texture of the image (DCT, Local binary patterns, Gabor Filter), as well as methods reflecting the color distribution (moments of color and color histogram). Very interesting is the similarity of Arkhip Kuindzhi and Aivazovsky on the values of the features extracted with the help of HOG and Hough transform. This indicates that both authors painted color transitions and guide lines in a similar way. Note that the Arkhip Kuindzhi began his studies at the Ivan Aivazovsky's studio.

According to the results of the experiment, it was not possible to identify signs features of Valentin Serov. He was the closest to romanticism and realism. Textures used by Serov are similar to Munch's textures (LBP). It is interesting that the portrait of Ilya Repin in style close to Ilya Repin's artworks.

None of the features presented in the experiment fully characterize Claude Monet. In a sense, the work of this artist can be evaluated by color characteristics: color moments and histograms of color.

The diversity and versatility of Edouard Manet's works did not allow revealing the features characterizing the author. Also, according to the results of the experiment, it is impossible to determine which movement the artist belongs to.

Thus, the study results of the digital images collection showed that Aivazovsky stile plays a very important role for the artists of romanticism. The similarity with it can be estimated belonging to the works of painting to this area. For realists clearly traced the dependence on the Venetsianov works, manifested in the use of straight lines identified by the Hough method. The works of expressionists have similar values of the features obtained by color frequency analysis.

6 Conclusion

The article shows that the problem of developing new approaches to the study of art works, which could provide additional information about the paintings, which cannot be obtained using existing traditional methods of studying painting, is currently topical.

One of the possible ways to solve this problem is the use of computer image processing methods for automatic assessment of the paintings features, which will help to give more reasonable conclusions about the authenticity, authorship or stylistic qualities of painting.

Experiments have shown that on the basis of image processing methods it is possible to make an assumption about the belonging of a painting to a certain art school, style, movement. This conclusion is confirmed by historical data on who taught him and where the artist studied, and who of the masters had the greatest influence on him.

The most promising for solving the problem of attribution is the use of color moments method, histograms and local binary patterns. However, do not discard other features, as they complement the description of the picture. It is necessary to emphasize the great importance of the images set contents and its role in the analysis of works.

The application does not give a clear answer to the question of whether a particular author or direction belongs to the picture, but gives reason for reflection and justification for the study of art works by art historians and experts in a certain direction.

References

1. Saleh, B., Elgammal, A.: Large-scale Classification of Fine-Art Paintings: Learning The Right Metric on The Right Feature. arXiv:1505.00855v1 [cs.CV], 5 May 2015
2. Nemade, R., et al.: Detection of forgery in art paintings using machine learning. Int. J. Innovative Res. Sci. Eng. Technol. **6**(5) (2017)
3. Floreaa, C., Giesekeb, F.: Artistic movement recognition by consensus of boosted SVM based experts. J. Vis. Commun. Image Rep. **56**, 220–233 (2018)
4. Brachmann, A., Redies, C.: Computational and experimental approaches to visual aesthetics. Front. Comput. Neurosci. **11**, 102 (2017). https://doi.org/10.3389/fncom.2017.00102
5. Dalal, N., Triggs, B.: Histograms of oriented gradients for human detection. In: International Conference on Computer Vision & Pattern Recognition, vol. 2, pp. 886–893, June 2005
6. Huang, Z.-C., Chan, P.P.K., Ng, W.W.Y., Yeung, D.S.: Content-based image retrieval using color moment and Gabor texture feature. In: 2010 International Conference on Machine Learning and Cybernetics (2010). https://doi.org/10.1109/icmlc.2010.5580566
7. Albadarneh, I.A., Ahmad, A.: Machine learning based oil painting authentication and features extraction. IJCSNS Int. J. Comput. Sci. Netw. Secur. **17**(1), 8 (2017)
8. Hughes, J.M., Mao, D., Rockmore, D.N., Wang, Y., Wu, Q.: Empirical mode decomposition analysis for visual stylometry. IEEE Trans. Pattern Anal. Mach. Intell. **34**, 2147–2157 (2012)
9. Johnson, C.R., et al.: Imageprocessing for artist identification. IEEE Signal Process. Mag. **25**, 37–48 (2008)
10. Lyu, S., Rockmore, D., Farid, H.: A digital technique for art authentication. Proc. Nat. Acad. Sci. U.S.A. **101**, 17006–17010 (2004)
11. Qi, H., Taeb, A., Hughes, S.M.: Visual stylometry using background selection and wavelet-HMT-based Fisher information distances for attribution and dating of impressionist paintings. Sig. Process. **93**, 541–553 (2013)
12. Jafarpour, S., Polatkan, G., Brevdo, E., Hughes, S., Brasoveanu, A., Daubechies, I.: Stylistic analysis of paintings using wavelets and machine learning. In: 17th European Signal Processing Conference, 24–28 August 2009. ISBN: 978-161-7388-76-7
13. Tan, W.R., Chany, C.S., Aguirre, H.E., Tanaka, K.: Cecin'est pas une pipe: a deep convolutional network for fine-art paintings classification. In: 2016 IEEE International Conference on Image Processing (ICIP) (2016). https://doi.org/10.1109/icip.2016.7533051

14. Kukharev, G., Kamenskaya, E., Matveev, Y., Shchegoleva, N.: Methods of facial images processing and recognition in biometrics, p. 388. Politechnika Publisher, Saint-Peterburg (2013). ISBN: 978-5-73251-028-7. [In Russian]
15. Polatkan, G., Jafarpour, S., Brasoveanu, A., Hughes, S., Daubechies, I.: Detection of forgery in paintings using supervised learning. In: 16th IEEE International Conference on Image (2009). https://doi.org/10.1109/icip.2009.5413338
16. Jacobsen, C.R., Nielsen, M.: Stylometry of paintings using hidden Markov modelling of contourlet transforms. Sig. Process. **93**(3), 579–591 (2013). https://doi.org/10.1016/j.sigpro.2012.09.0

Using Boosted k-Nearest Neighbour Algorithm for Numerical Forecasting of Dangerous Convective Phenomena

E. N. Stankova(✉) and E. V. Khvatkov

Saint-Petersburg State University,
7-9 Universitetskaya nab., St. Petersburg 199034, Russia
e.stankova@spbu.ru, e.hvatkov@gmail.com

Abstract. The authors propose a boosted k-nearest neighbour algorithm for numerical forecasting of dangerous convective phenomena. The algorithm is applied for processing the output data of the numerical cloud model. The results show that boosted algorithm is able to predict the very fact of convective phenomena occurrence with the high accuracy, but it is not so good in distinguishing the specific type of convective phenomena. Comparison with the k-NN algorithm without boosting shows that boosting resulted in better accuracy of forecasting.

Keywords: Machine learning · Naive bayes classifier · Boosted k-nearest neighbour algorithm · AdaBoost algorithm · Support-vector machine model · Numerical model of convective cloud · Weather forecasting · Thunderstorm forecasting

1 Introduction

Constant anthropogenic influence on the atmosphere is resulted in global warming, which in turn leads to an increase in the intensity of convective processes. An increase in temperature and an increase in air humidity are two facts that together lead to the intensification of active convection in the atmosphere, which entails an increase in thunderstorm activity, in the number of heavy showers, tornadoes and other dangerous convective phenomena that have a tremendous destructive effect such as forest fires or flood waters. Therefore, the problem of timely prediction of dangerous convective phenomena is one of the most relevant and practically important areas of research.

The development of convection is determined by the physics of the complex interaction of dynamic, microphysical and electrical processes occurring in the cloud. Computer modeling is the most successful instrument for cloud research allowing to provide detailed investigation of variable specificity of convective clouds caused by high vertical velocities within the cloud and its surroundings without expensive field experiments. Computer research is based on numerical simulation, the result of which is a large amount of data that needs to be analyzed using modern methods of data analysis and processing.

S. Misra et al. (Eds.): ICCSA 2019, LNCS 11622, pp. 802–811, 2019.
https://doi.org/10.1007/978-3-030-24305-0_61

As a rule, modern models of convective clouds do not contain a block describing electrical processes due to complexity of the block realization and the large amount of required computing resources. In this regard, it seems relevant to investigate the possibility of forecasting the probability of such a dangerous convective phenomenon as a thunderstorm, only by the values of dynamic and microphysical parameters calculated in the process of modeling.

At present, machine learning seems to be the most adequate tool for such kind of research. The concept of machine learning implies processing the large amounts of data and identification various interrelations and patterns for the restoration of dependencies by empirical data.

The use of machine learning methods in meteorology is twofold. On the one hand, "pure" machine learning models are being developed, where certain atmospheric parameters are predicted on the basis of observational data obtained at meteorological stations, weather centers, etc. On the other hand, machine learning methods are used to verify models by establishing relationships between model forecasts and the actual meteorological situation. Both approaches were described in detail in our previous works [1–4] where we analyze the achievements of Microsoft [5], Yandex [6], and IBM [7] companies in the field of application of information technologies for weather forecasting.

Last year Yandex company used machine learning algorithms for the implementation of nowcasting technology, which is a technology of a short-term hyperlocal precipitation forecast [8].

Our previous works concerned the usage of machine learning technology both for validation of one and half dimensional numerical model of a convective cloud [1, 4] and for the operational forecast of dangerous convective phenomena using the verified model [2, 3]. Three methods of machine learning were used: Support Vector Machine (SVM), Logistic Regression (LR) and Ridge Regression (RR), providing rather high value of accuracy, up to 98%. But these methods, especially SVM, are rather expensive for training and have a lot of meta parameters for tuning. So now we decide to use k-Nearest Neighbour algorithm [9] which is, in opposite, cheap for training, but may be subject to retraining. We use AdaBoost algorithm [10] in conjunction with k-nearest neighbour algorithm (boosted k-NN) to avoid this drawback. Some preliminary results are presented in the present paper.

2 Data Selected for Research

Integrated information system [11–13] was applied for gathering of specific meteorological data used as the model input parameters. 480 radiosonde soundings were collected in the place and at the time when dangerous convective phenomena were observed, including 220 soundings for thunderstorms, 174 ones for heavy rains and 86 soundings for light rains. 196 soundings were collected in the cases when no dangerous convective phenomena were observed.

Aone and a half dimensional, time-dependent model with a detailed description of microphysical processes of convective cloud [14–18] was used to carry out numerical calculations. The model allows one to obtain dynamic and microphysical characteristics of a convective cloud with a high degree of reliability without large computational costs. Model calculations were provided in automated regime in order to process series of input soundings at a time.

The output data of the model were grouped in sets, each of the set included 12 cloud parameters and the variable that described the type of dangerous convective phenomenon.Calculated cloud parameters were as follows:

- the vertical component of the velocity,
- radial component of the velocity,
- pressure,
- air density,
- ambient temperature,
- temperature excess in the cloud,
- relative humidity,
- vertical height of the cloud,
- mixing ratio of water vapour,
- mixing ratio of aerosol particles,
- mixing ratio of water drops,
- mixing ratio of ice particles,

It is necessary to divide the available data into training and test samples. Separation is performed randomly for each experiment in order to simulate the randomness of the nature of the occurrence of dangerous convective phenomena. Each parameter set is considered by the algorithm as a point in a 12-dimensional space.

3 Usage of k-Nearest Neighbour Algorithm

K-Nearest Neighbors algorithm (k-NN) is a lazy classifier. This means that in the process of learning it does not use new data, but only stores training data. It begins the classification only when new unmarked data appears.

Through the training sample, the algorithm remembered the coordinates of each set and the type (class) of the phenomenon. Each considered set of parameters from a test sample was matched by k neighbors from the training sample, provided that the sum of the Euclidean distances to them was minimal. The value of k was set manually, or the forecast accuracy was calculated for all values of k from k_O to k_n in order to determine the value of k_i at which the accuracy will be maximum. The Euclidean distance was expressed by the following formula:

$$D_E = \sqrt{\sum_{i}^{n} (x_i - y_i)^2},$$

where n is the number of parameters.

The considering set of parameters that characterized one of the types of a dangerous convective phenomenon was ranked as the class with the highest number of votes resulted from the neighbors voting. In the case of even number of classes, the value of k was set to odd to improve the accuracy of the algorithm, because of an error appearing in the case of equality of votesfor even k.

As it was noted above, K-NN algorithm is cheap during training, but it can be expensive during classification, and, although it is usually very accurate, it can be subject to retraining.

Applying the k-NN method, we decided to improve it using the AdaBoost algorithm [10]. AdaBoost is sensitive to data noise and outliers, but it is less susceptible to retraining compared to other machine learning algorithms. AdaBoost was not used in the classic version, but was adapted to work with a strong classifier by using the operations of creating a committee of classifiers and weighted evaluation of a data set [19].

4 Usage of AdaBoost Algorithm

Unlike the lazy classifier, which begins the classification only when new unlabeled data appears, the active classifier creates a classification model in the learning process. When new data is entered, such a classifier adds data to the classification model. AdaBoost is an active classifier because it builds an ensemble classification.

This algorithm can be used in combination with several classification algorithms to improve their efficiency. The algorithm strengthens the classifiers, combining them into a "committee". AdaBoost is adaptive in the sense that each next classifier committee is built on objects that have been incorrectly classified by previous committees. AdaBoost is sensitive to data noise and outliers. However, it is less prone to retraining compared to other machine learning algorithms.

AdaBoost and weighted k-NN algorithms were implemented so that both of them complemented each other. AdaBoost was launched on the training set, creating weak classifiers for k-NN algorithm. Then the later ranin the feature space. Afterwards AdaBoost was used to improve classification accuracy and to prevent retraining by editing datasets provided by the weighted k-NN algorithm and thus improved the quality of training data. This joint algorithm (boosted k-NN) achieved significantly better classification accuracy than AdaBoost and kNN, used separately [20].

The detailed description of the joint algorithm is described below [21].

There is a sample G, which consists of n data sets (n = 676) that represent the output parameters of the model X and the type of phenomenon Y.

Array X is the d-size vector of cloud characteristics x_i, $(i = 1, \ldots, d)$, d is equal to 12.

Array$Y$ is the vector of available classes y_i, $(i = 1, \ldots, J)$. J equals to 4 and represents the type of phenomenon (no phenomena, light rain, heavy rain, thunderstorm).

The sample G was divided into 2 parts G_t and G_v, $G_t$was the subset which was used for building classifiers, G_v was the one for validating the obtained results. The division of the complete set of G into G_t and G_v was carried out by randomly mixing the initial data set for each iteration of learning.

At the first stage, a set of weak classifiers was built.

The size of characteristic subset was chosen equal to f, where $f < d$. The more was the value of f, the stronger the classifier turned out. The best results were observed when f was equal to$d/2$. We formed a set of randomly selected subsets of characteristics of size n. So each new data set G_f contained n subsets of the size f.

G_f was used as a training sample for weak classifiers. We got m training samples: G_{f1}, G_{f2},.., G_{fm}, where m is the number of weak classifiers (m = 12).

At the second stage fusion of classifier committee was performed.

1. Using the Gt sample, the accuracy of each weak classifier was calculated.
2. Classifiers were ranked according to the accuracy of the result, in descending order, using the same set of characteristics
3. The committee was formed from l most accurate classifiers. Best results were obtained when l was equal to 4.
4. To estimate the accuracy, the Brier score function (1) was used, showing the efficiency of the classifier forecast [22]:

$$BS = \frac{1}{N}\sum_{t=1}^{N}(f_t - o_t)^2 \quad (1)$$

where f_t is the forecast probability, o_t is the outcome (0 or 1).

At the third stage the final decision was made on the type of convective phenomenon (forecast formation).

A weight, initially equal to 1/n, was assigned to each set of the training data. The most accurate weak classifier was the first to forecast. Next, the less accurate classifier worked, and it increased the weight of the data set under consideration in the case if its forecast differed from the one of the previous classifier. Otherwise it decreased the weight of the data set. Thus, each subsequent classifier spent more resources on processing data with the greater weight, and, accordingly, received more accurate results. Data that were classified uniquely required less cost. This saved computing resources, and the entire data set was processed faster.

A diagram describing the decision-making process by an ensemble of 3 classifiers is presented in Fig. 1.

5 Results

Three types of numerical studies were conducted.

The first concerned the determination of the accuracy of forecasting a specific type of convective phenomenon from four classes: no phenomena, light rain, heavy rain, thunderstorm. The calculation results showed that the boosted k-NN determined the type of the phenomenon with an accuracy that varied from 82% to 84% on average.

The accuracy of the k-NN algorithm without using Adaboost turned out to be significantly lower and varied from 42–61% on average.

The second type of numerical study concerned whether the phenomenon took place or not, without defining the type of it. The calculation results showed that the boosted k-NN algorithm determined the phenomenon occurrence with a high accuracy, achieving the value of 98%.

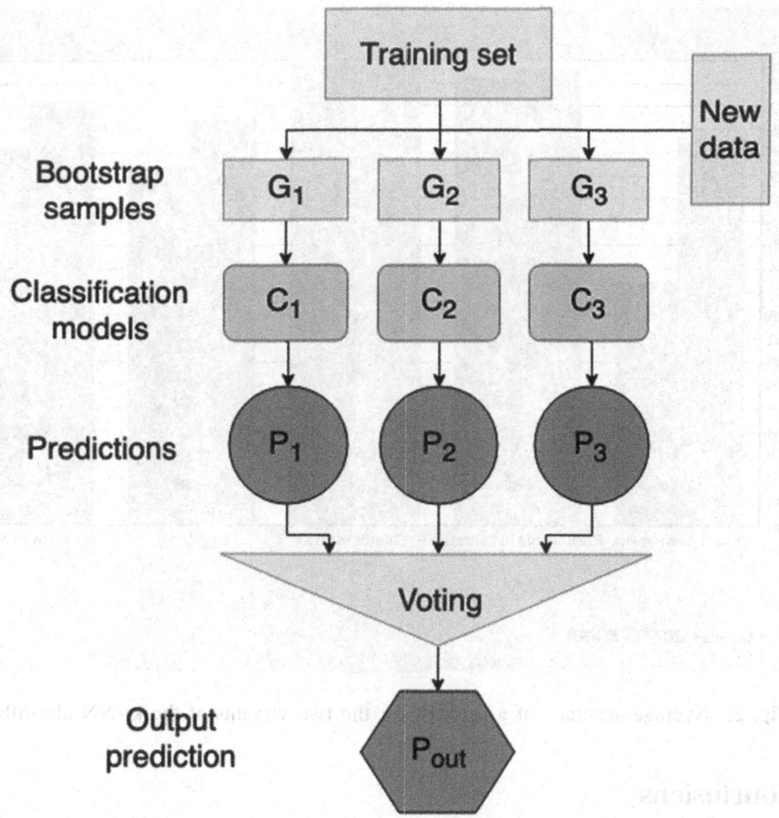

Fig. 1. Diagram describing the decision-making process by an ensemble of 3 classifiers

The accuracy of the k-NN algorithm without using Adaboost appeared to be less precise, but also high, achieving 96%.

The third research investigated the accuracy of the forecast of phenomenon occurrence, when the data set contained only pairs of classes: no phenomena and a light rain, no phenomena and a heavy rain, no phenomena and a thunderstorm.In this case boosted k-NN showed the highest accuracy in case of a thunderstorm (99%) and sufficiently lower accuracy for a light rain (86–89%) and for a heavy rain (88–92%).

The accuracy of the k-NN algorithm without using Adaboost was the same in case of a thunderstorm and lower for the other pairs 72–83% and 77–86% for a light and heavy rain correspondingly.

Figure 2 shows a comparative chart of the average accuracy of a forecast for the two variants of the k-NN algorithm.

All the calculations were provided using the open source library Scikit-learn [23]. It is written in the Python programming language and allows one to use a broad variety of machine learning algorithms. BSD (Berkeley Software Distribution) is a license distributer. Commercial use of the product is also allowed.

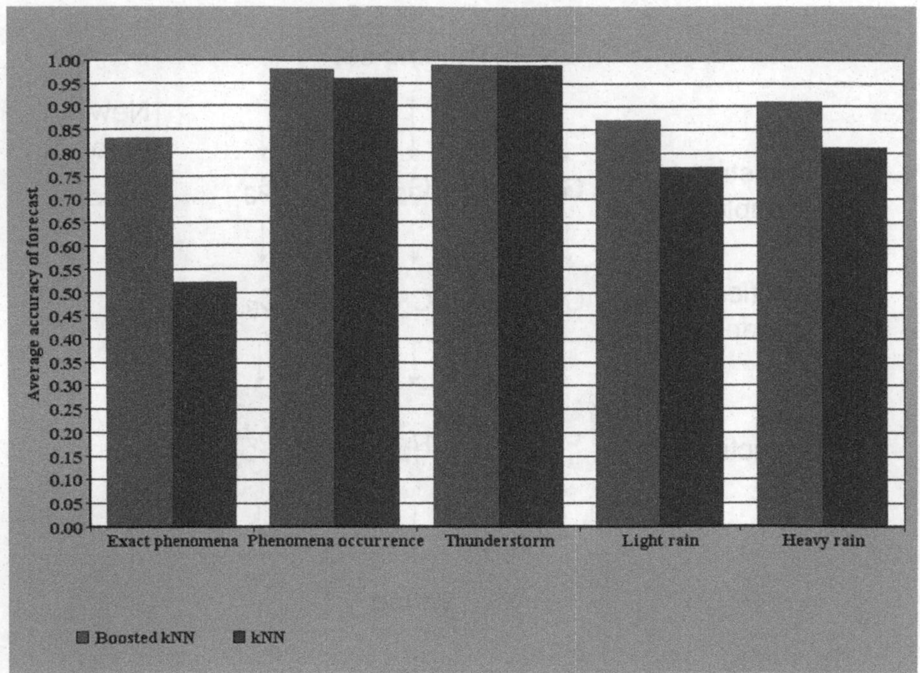

Fig. 2. Average accuracy of a forecast for the two variants of the k -NN algorithm

6 Conclusions

The boosted k-nearest neighbour algorithm was applied for processing the output data of the numerical cloud model for forecasting of convective phenomena (a thunderstorm, a heavy rain and a light rain). Boosting algorithm applied for k-nearest neighbour classifier was described in details.

The data set comprised 12 calculated dynamical and microphysical cloud characteristics and the parameter, describing the type of the phenomenon. Cloud characteristics were taken at the mature stage of evolution of the simulated cloud at a moment when the cloud achieved the maximum value of its upper boundary height and at the height corresponded to the maximum value of the mixing ratio of cloud drops.

Integrated information system [11–13] was applied for gathering of specific meteorological data used as the model input parameters. 480 radiosonde soundings were collected in the place and at the time when dangerous convective phenomena were observed, including 220 soundings for thunderstorms, 174 ones for heavy rains and 86 soundings for light rains. 196 soundings were collected in the cases when no dangerous convective phenomena were observed.

Three types of numerical studies were conducted with the aim to find out the cases when the processing of the cloud output data gave the highest values of forecast accuracy.

The first study tested the ability of the algorithm to distinguish the exact type of the phenomenon between four classes: no phenomena, a light rain, a heavy rain, and a thunderstorm. The second type of numerical study concerned whether the phenomenon took place or not, without defining the type of it. The third study investigated the accuracy of the forecast of phenomenon occurrence, when the data set contained only pairs of classes: no phenomena and a light rain, no phenomena and a heavy rain, no phenomena and a thunderstorm.

The research results showed that the highest accuracy of forecast (99%) was achieved in the third case when the pair no phenomena and a thunderstorm was considered. The lowest forecast accuracy (82 to 84%) was achieved in the first case study.

It can be noted in general that boosted k-NN algorithm was able to predict the very fact of convective phenomena occurrence with the high accuracy, but it was not so good in distinguishing the specific type of phenomena. It is planned to test the performance of the algorithm on a larger volume of input data obtained in different geographic regions.

Boosted k-NN algorithm provided better or equal results of forecast accuracy in all three cases in comparison with k-NN without boosting. The results obtained in the third case study for heavy and light rain are the only exception, where boosted k-NN algorithm provided significantly better classification accuracy.

In future we plan to include numerical cloud model and the block, processing the model output with the help of machine learning algorithms to the integrated information system [11–13] for providing the full cycle of forecasting of dangerous convective phenomena by joint system.

We plan that our improved and modified system should become a block of the Virtual private supercomputer [24, 25] and will be composed using the ideas presented in [26, 27]. The final aim is to enable users with the elaborated tool for individual forecast of the dangerous convective phenomena.

References

1. Stankova, E.N., Balakshiy, A.V., Petrov, D.A., Shorov, A.V., Korkhov, V.V.: Using technologies of OLAP and machine learning for validation of the numerical models of convective clouds. In: Gervasi, O., et al. (eds.) ICCSA 2016. LNCS, vol. 9788, pp. 463–472. Springer, Cham (2016). https://doi.org/10.1007/978-3-319-42111-7_36
2. Stankova, E.N., Grechko, I.A., Kachalkina, Y.N., Khvatkov, E.V.: Hybrid approach combining model-based method with the technology of machine learning for forecasting of dangerous weather phenomena. In: Gervasi, O., et al. (eds.) ICCSA 2017. LNCS, vol. 10408, pp. 495–504. Springer, Cham (2017). https://doi.org/10.1007/978-3-319-62404-4_37
3. Stankova, E.N., Ismailova, E.T., Grechko, I.A.: Algorithm for processing the results of cloud convection simulation using the methods of machine learning. In: Gervasi, O., et al. (eds.) ICCSA 2018. LNCS, vol. 10963, pp. 149–159. Springer, Cham (2018). https://doi.org/10.1007/978-3-319-95171-3_13
4. Stankova, E.N., Balakshiy, A.V., Petrov, D.A., Korkhov, V.V.: OLAP technology and machine learning as the tools for validation of the numerical models of convective clouds. Int. J. Bus. Intell. Data Min. **14**(1/2), 254–266 (2019)

5. Grover, A., Kapoor, A., Horvitz, E.: A deep hybrid model for weather forecasting research (2015). https://microsoft.com/en-us/um/people/horvitz/weather_hybrid_representation.pdf. Accessed 13 Aug 2016
6. Meteum technology. https://yandex.ru/pogoda/meteum. Accessed 17 Jan 2017. (in Russian)
7. The Weather Company Launches 'Deep Thunder' - the World's Most Advanced Hyper-Local Weather Forecasting Model for Businesses. https://www-03.ibm.com/press/us/en/pressrelease/49954.wss. Accessed 15 June 2016
8. How we perform a short-term forecast of precipitation. Lecture in Yandex. https://habr.com/ru/company/yandex/blog/328158/. Accessed 17 Jan 2017. (in Russian)
9. Fukunaga, K., Hostetler, L.: k-nearest-neighbor estimation. IEEE Trans. Inf. Theory **21**(3), 285–293 (1975)
10. Zhang, T.: Statistical behavior and consistency of classification methods based on convex risk minimization. Ann. Stat. **32**(1), 56–85 (2004)
11. Petrov, D.A., Stankova, E.N.: Use of consolidation technology for meteorological data processing. In: Murgante, B., et al. (eds.) ICCSA 2014. LNCS, vol. 8579, pp. 440–451. Springer, Cham (2014). https://doi.org/10.1007/978-3-319-09144-0_30
12. Petrov, D.A., Stankova, E.N.: Integrated information system for verification of the models of convective clouds. In: Gervasi, O., et al. (eds.) ICCSA 2015. LNCS, vol. 9158, pp. 321–330. Springer, Cham (2015). https://doi.org/10.1007/978-3-319-21410-8_25
13. Stankova, E.N., Petrov, D.A.: Complex information system for organization of the input data of models of convective clouds. Vestnik of Saint-Petersburg University. Series 10. Applied Mathematics. Computer Science. Control Processes. no 3, pp. 83–95 (2015). (in Russian)
14. Raba, N., Stankova, E.: Research of influence of compensating descending flow on cloud's life cycle by means of 1.5-dimensional model with 2 cylinders. In: Proceedings of MGO, vol. 559, pp. 192–209 (2009). (in Russian)
15. Raba, N., Stankova, E., Ampilova, N.: On investigation of parallelization effectiveness with the help of multi-core processors. Procedia Comput. Sci. **1**(1), 2757–2762 (2010)
16. Raba, N., Stankova, E.: On the possibilities of multi-core processor use for real-time forecast of dangerous convective phenomena. In: Taniar, D., Gervasi, O., Murgante, B., Pardede, E., Apduhan, B.O. (eds.) ICCSA 2010. LNCS, vol. 6017, pp. 130–138. Springer, Heidelberg (2010). https://doi.org/10.1007/978-3-642-12165-4_11
17. Raba, N.O., Stankova, E.N.: On the problem of numerical modeling of dangerous convective phenomena: possibilities of real-time forecast with the help of multi-core processors. In: Murgante, B., Gervasi, O., Iglesias, A., Taniar, D., Apduhan, B.O. (eds.) ICCSA 2011. LNCS, vol. 6786, pp. 633–642. Springer, Heidelberg (2011). https://doi.org/10.1007/978-3-642-21934-4_51
18. Raba, N.O., Stankova, E.N.: On the effectiveness of using the GPU for numerical solution of stochastic collection equation. In: Murgante, B., et al. (eds.) ICCSA 2013. LNCS, vol. 7975, pp. 248–258. Springer, Heidelberg (2013). https://doi.org/10.1007/978-3-642-39640-3_18
19. La, L., Guo, Q., Yang, D., Cao, Q.: Multiclass boosting with adaptive group-based kNN and its application in text categorization. Math. Probl. Eng. **2012**, 24 (2012)
20. Yang, J.M., Yu, P.T., Kuo, B.C.: A nonparametric feature extraction and its application to nearest neighbor classification for hyperspectral image data. IEEE Trans. Geosci. Remote Sens. **3**, 1279–1293 (2010)
21. Gul, A., et al.: Ensemble of a subset of kNN classifiers. Adv. Data Anal. Classif. **12**(4), 827 (2018)
22. Brier, G.W.: Verification of forecasts expressed in terms of probability (PDF). Mon. Weather Rev. **78**, 1–3 (1950)
23. Scikit-learn. Machine Learning in Python. http://scikit-learn.org/

24. Bogdanov, A., Degtyarev, A., Korkhov, V., Gaiduchok, V., Gankevich, I.: Virtual supercomputer as basis of scientific computing. In: Clary, T.S. (eds.) Horizons in Computer Science Research, vol. 11, pp. 159–198, Nova Science Publishers (2015). ISBN: 978-1-63482-499-6
25. Korkhov, V., Krefting, D., Kukla, T., Terstyanszky, G.Z., Caan, M., Olabarriaga, S.D.: Exploring workflow interoperability tools for neuroimaging data analysis. In: WORKS'11 - Proceedings of the 6th Workshop on Workflows in Support of Large-Scale Science, Co-located with SC 2011, pp. 87–96 (2011). https://doi.org/10.1145/2110497.2110508
26. Kulabukhova, N., Bogdanov, A., Degtyarev, A.: Problem-solving environment for beam dynamics analysis in particle accelerators. In: Gervasi, O., et al. (eds.) Computational Science and Its Applications – ICCSA 2017. Lecture Notes in Computer Science, vol. 10408, pp. 473–482. Springer, Cham (2017)
27. Kulabukhova, N., Andrianov, S.N., Bogdanov, A., Degtyarev, A.: Simulation of space charge dynamics in high intensive beams on hybrid systems. In: Gervasi, O., et al. (eds.) ICCSA 2016. LNCS, vol. 9786, pp. 284–295. Springer, Cham (2016). https://doi.org/10.1007/978-3-319-42085-1_22

Development Tools for Heterogeneous Computing

Victor Smirnov(✉) and Nikita Storublevtcev(✉)

St. Petersburg State University, 7/9 Universitetskaya Nab,
St. Petersburg 199034, Russia
ariox41@gmail.com, 100.rub@mail.ru

Abstract. The problem of porting various applications to parallel computing accelerators, such as GPU and FPGA, is becoming ever more relevant. Such accelerators can significantly improve the performance and energy efficiency of applications.

In this paper, modern development tools focused on heterogeneous computing are reviewed. Particular attention is paid to the opportunities they provide for the porting of applications to different platforms with various architectures, and issues of application performance and reliability.

In particular, this article describes SYCL, a new standard for heterogeneous programming for C++, and presents the test results of one of its implementations -ComputeCpp.

ComputeCpp test results on the NVIDIA video card demonstrate the correctness of its implementation, but ComputeCpp performance was noticeably lower than CUDA. Given that ComputeCpp is in a beta state, there is hope that its performance will increase in the future, which will allow SYCL to become a real competitor to OpenCL in the development of portable applications for parallel accelerators.

Keywords: Parallel computing · GPGPU · Heterogeneous computing

1 Introduction

Currently, parallel data processing accelerators such as GPUs and FPGAs are increasingly being used to solve various computational problems. In many cases, they can improve the performance and energy efficiency of applications, and in some areas they allow to use of previously difficult-to-implement approaches, such as machine learning on mobile platforms. In this regard, the need to develop new applications for accelerators and to transfer old one's increases.

Developing an application for such accelerators requires the use of specialized and often new algorithms and development tools. The need to use specialized algorithms can be considered an inevitable evil, but questions arise about development tools. Although there is already a fairly stable ecosystem for heterogeneous computing: CUDA for NVIDIA graphics cards, HCC for AMD and OpenCL as a portable solution, portability between different platforms is still a problem. The quality of OpenCL

S. Misra et al. (Eds.): ICCSA 2019, LNCS 11622, pp. 812–824, 2019.
https://doi.org/10.1007/978-3-030-24305-0_62

support varies for different platforms, but generally leaves much to be desired, and other solutions are non-portable.

In addition, there are more and more devices specializes for parallel data processing. Many processors contain embedded graphics cores (this is especially true for mobile platforms), there are processors with a large number of discrete cores that can also be effectively used for parallel data processing, and new GPUs and FPGAs are being developed.

Thus, the problem of choosing development tools suitable for specific computing platforms is becoming ever more relevant, and the need for portable application development tools that allow for truly heterogeneous computing is increasing.

2 Development Tools for Heterogeneous Programming

Due to the constant increase in the diversity of accelerators, development tools must, to one degree or another, ensure the portability of applications between devices. This can manifest itself in two forms: either an already compiled program is launched on different platforms without recompiling, or the program is compiled from one source code for different platforms. The second method also includes compiling platform-dependent fragments into dynamic libraries for different platforms with the subsequent selection of the appropriate fragment for a particular platform.

Porting without recompilation requires a unified intermediate language, and porting with recompilation requires a unified high-level API.

2.1 Portable Intermediate Representation

By the end of the 2000s, the LLVM ecosystem reached a stable state [1]. LLVM is based on the idea that some program translation stages are independent of a programming language or platform, which means that they can be processed by one tool. LLVM provides the middle layers of a complete compiler system, taking intermediate representation (IR) code from a compiler and emitting an optimized IR. This new IR can then be converted and linked into machine-dependent assembly language code for a target platform. It also provides various tools to facilitate the compiler development. The development of this ecosystem has led to the creation of a clang compiler for C and C++ languages, virtual machines for various executable languages, and the emergence of many other tools.

Heterogeneous computing development tools developers could not ignore this approach, and in 2011 the Standard Portable Intermediate Representation (SPIR), an intermediate representation language based on LLVM IR, was released as an optional part of OpenCL 1.2 [2]. It was assumed that the development tools would generate a SPIR code independent of the platform, and the graphic cards drivers and other devices would consume it, transforming it into their own representation. This would make it relatively easy to create compilers in SPIR based on existing implementations in the LLVM ecosystem, since the differences between SPIR and LLVM IR are not too big. In particular, it would be possible to compile OpenCL in SPIR, which would remove OpenCL support from drivers, bringing it to the level of regular libraries.

However, in practice, NVIDIA developers did not provide SPIR support at all, and AMD developers removed SPIR support from drivers for most graphic cards in 2018. As the result, only Intel provides good support for SPIR. Most likely, the refusal to support SPIR was due to the fact that it does not always allow to take into account the features of specific architectures of video cards due to the LLVM IR heritage.

In 2015, the standard SPIR-V was released as a part of the Vulkan ecosystem [2]. It was originally developed taking into account the features of the architecture of high-parallel accelerators, and, perhaps, the developers of such accelerators in the future will provide its full support. However, at the moment they provide only a limited subset of SPIR-V for graphic shaders.

Despite the problems, an ecosystem is still forming around SPIR. The Portable Computing Language (POCL) project provides open OpenCL drivers with SPIR support for CPUs and NVIDIA (experimentally), and there are projects that generate SPIR.

It is also worth noting that NVIDIA has its own open standard for intermediate representation - PTX. It can be used only for NVIDIA GPUs, but serves the same purpose - it allows to transfer applications between different accelerators from NVIDIA.

Thus, the idea of an intermediate representation of programs for accelerators is being developed, but in practice, the ability to compile the same program for different platforms is more important than portability of an already compiled program. From this point of view, standards providing a high-level APIare more interesting.

2.2 High Level API

The most portable API is still OpenCL. Although the degree of support varies for different platforms and many platforms still do not support OpenCL 2.0, it is difficult to find a platform oriented at accelerating parallel data processing but not supporting OpenCL at all. In the case of mobile platforms (especially on Android), there are essentially no portable OpenCL alternatives.

Despite the good portability, OpenCL has many disadvantages. For example, because of the compilation at runtime, the device driver must contain an almost complete C compiler, and the source code of the kernels is open. The kernel works in its own context, even if it runs on a host, which requires unnecessary copying of data from the host into this context. Computing kernels have to be written in a special language that is a subset of C. It creates potential vulnerabilities in data transfer between the host and the device that are not detected by static analyzers. It also means that compiler cannot perform context-sensitive optimization. Apple even declaredOpenCL deprecated in IoS 12 [3].

Many developers prefer to use NVIDIA CUDA. CUDA is free of many of the drawbacks of OpenCL, in particular, it supports the use of C++ (including C++ 17) in the kernels and does not separate the kernel code from the host code, which allows data transfer to be typesafe. The question of comparing the performance of CUDA and OpenCLkernels remains open in general, but cuBLAS (linear algebra library as part of CUDA) outperforms both user made implementations on OpenCL and CUDA, which is also an argument in favor of CUDA [4].

But the choice of CUDA over time can lead to complications: the computing accelerators ecosystem is evolving, new hardware solutions are emerging, and switching to other platforms may become a necessity. For large projects, this can be a really serious problem.

An interesting solution is offered by the ROCm project: it contains a HIP – tool that allows you to semi-automatically convert CUDA code into portable C++ code and compile this portable C++ for AMD and NVIDIA, or you can write initially portable applications. At the moment this tool is only applicable for NVIDIA and AMD, although the idea can be implemented for other platforms [5]. For projects designed for long-term support, standardized APIs originally designed as portable are more interesting.

Such API can be provided by the Parallelism project in the C++ standardization framework. Its idea is that the interfaces provided by the standard C++ library for algorithms are already well suited for parallel algorithms, an example of which is Boost. Compute and other similar libraries. So this interface can be extended for automatic parallelization [6]. The CPU-oriented part of this project is already included in the C++ 17 standard, and there is a potential for expanding the approach to the GPUs and other devices [7]. The main problem here is that the level of abstraction is too high to allow you to manually optimize the code for specific devices. Even the choice of the device is actually inaccessible to the user, the compiler chooses it. But thanks to this project, the C++ memory model is now expanding towards greater support for parallel algorithms, including for accelerators.

A beter compromise option is the SYCL standard - a heterogeneous-oriented API for C++, released in 2014.

2.3 SYCL

SYCL is a high-level heterogeneous programming standard that provides OpenCL abstractions for C++ [6, 8]. One of the main goals of SYCL is to increase the reliability of applications and ensure the portability of applications between different devices. Unlike OpenCL, the code for the host and the accelerator is not separated in the SYCL, which allows you to fully use the C++ type system to ensure secure data transfer between devices, as well as to minimize the overhead in the case of running the computing kernel on the host. In addition, SYCL provides interfaces based on the ideas of modern C++ and the capabilities of C++ 11, which also improves the reliability of programs. In most cases, the resource leak problem no longer arises or can be resolved relatively easily.

The lack of separation of host and accelerator code has other consequences. First of all, the possibilities for optimization are increase: the SYCL compiler has access to the full context of the program, which allows it to perform high-level optimizations, for example, to delete unused code. This approach also makes it much easier to develop tools for SYCL. In a simple case, the program on the SYCL can be compiled by a conventional C++ compiler for the CPU, which allows you to debug it using conventional means.

To run on the accelerator, the program must be compiled by two compilers: the first one finds and compiles the compute kernels, and the second one compiles the host code and creates an intermediate layer that selects the desired kernel implementation for a particular device. Ideally, one compiled program can contain compiled kernels for CPU, NVIDIA, AMD, and other devices. Or, it can contain a single intermediate view code, such as SPIR.

Compiling kernels for accelerators still needs a separate compiler, but it is relatively easy to implement based on existing tools. Clang is already able to compile C++ into an abstract syntax tree, and the interpretation of this tree is quite a doable task (in comparison opposed to developing a full-featured C++ compiler).

Since this standard, at first glance, has advantages over CUDA and OpenCL, it was chosen for more detailed analysis.

2.4 SYCL Implementations

There are already several implementations of SYCL: ComputeCpp, triSYCL, hipSYCL, sycl-gtx (non-standard macros required), clang (effort announced by Intel on 2019/01/11) [9]. Most of them are based on the LLVM ecosystem and the Clang compiler, but the implementation details and readiness of the implementations are various.

The most "advanced" can be called trySYCL – in fact it is a platform for experiments with the specification of SYCL [10]. This is a fully open source project that can be used to compile the SYCL program for the CPU and, theoretically, for SPIR – compatible accelerators. There are also relatively successful attempts to use it for FPGA [11]. In practice, the deployment of all the necessary tools is a non-trivial task, and in general, the project is more interesting for those who want to participate in the development of the SYCL ecosystem.

The most stable project is ComputeCpp [12]. In the fall of 2018, its developers were the first to declare full support for the SYCL 1.2 specification, providing tools for compiling the SYCL in SPIR and experimental support for SPIR-V. In addition, ComputeCpp allows you to translate SYCL to PTX, which allows you to use it for NVIDIA graphics cards. Support for PTXis not yet complete, but most of the functions are already working. When using old drivers, you can also use AMD graphics cards, but new drivers do not support SPIR for most platforms, and older drivers require older Linux kernels.

The prospects for using ComputeCpp for mobile platforms are also interesting. ComputeCpp already provides development tools for ARM, but so far only for Linux. Perhaps in the future there will be support for Android. ComputeCpp also provides support for R-Car H3 (computer systems for cars).

The main disadvantage of ComputeCpp is closed source code, but it does not impose restrictions on commercial use.

Another promising implementation is HipSycl [9]. This implementation is based on the already mentioned HIP tool, which allows you to compile code for both NVIDIA and AMD. In essence, this is just a library that implements SYCL over an existing API This is an open source project and is available for commercial use, but at the moment there is no compliance with the SYCL specification, in particular, there is no support for profiling. But in general, it is already operational.

2.5 Other Approaches

All the previously mentioned solutions are focused on C and C++. For the most part, this is due to historical reasons, as well as the desire to optimize programs for accelerators. Nevertheless, development tools that are entirely focused on other languages are being developed.

There are many solutions for .NET, most of which are based on translating C# code into CUDA code on the fly. For example, Aleagpu [13] and Hybridizer [14]. There are similar solutions for Java and other languages. There are experimental projects for translating various languages to SPIR-V [15], for example, SpirvNet for .NET. This can lead to a fragmentation of the ecosystem of computing on accelerators, as has happened with other areas.

Evaluating the effectiveness of using different languages for computing on GPU is beyond the scope of this article, but Rust language is worth mentioning separately [16]. For long-term calculations, the possibility of errors in the program becomes a big problem. In the case of accelerators, this is complicated by inability to handle errors directly in the kernel code, which leads to asynchronous errors on the host side. Such errors are difficult to handle, and often they cannot be fixed without emergency termination of the program. Thus, the issue of finding errors during compilation becomes particularly important.

The C++ type system often allows you to find errors at compile time, which distinguishes it from other languages. But the C++ type system is too complex and contains many problems caused by backward compatibility. Rust uses similar approach, but it was originally designed to find the maximum number of errors during compilation, and it lacks many of the problems inherent in C++. At the same time, it allows to implement zero-cost abstractions as well as C++. All this makes Rust a good candidate for computing in general and for heterogeneous programming in particular.

The advantages of the Rust type system can be seen now, but the GPU computing ecosystem for Rust is in a very early stage of development.

3 SYCL Health and Performance Testing

When it comes to acceleration due to data parallelization, the first thing that comes to mind is the matrix-matrix multiplication and the matrix-vector multiplication operations. These operations were implemented for testing. These operations are convenient for testing, since the results obtained can be compared with the results of CUDA testing in [17].

Since on small data volumes the cost of data transmission to the accelerator exceeds the benefit from acceleration, a set of 64 pairs of matrices of the same size was used for testing. Such a set of 2048 $\times$ 2048 matrices of double precision numbers takes up 4 GB of memory, and another 2 GB is needed to store the result.

To test performance, several classic approaches to accelerating matrix multiplication on graphics cards were implemented. These approaches can be divided into two groups: management of the computation process by the host (optimization of data transfer between the host and the device) and calculations (optimization of data transmission within the device).

Also for comparison, Eigen is one of the best libraries of linear algebra for the central processor, and similar tests for CUDA are used.

3.1 Ways to Manage the Process of Computing

The following approaches to managing the calculation process have been implemented:

Simple Loop. A simple loop on a set of matrices, at each iteration, a pair of source matrices is transmitted to the device, processed on it, and the result is transmitted to the host. All tasks are performed sequentially. Obviously, for small matrices overhead must be greater than for large ones.

One-In One-Out. All source matrices are written to one large buffer, the result is also written to one buffer, the computational kernels are started asynchronously and can be executed in parallel. Overhead costs should be less dependent on the size of the matrices, but in practice the use of this approach is rarely possible.

One-In Many-Out. The original matrices are also recorded in one buffer, which is transferred to the accelerator once, but the computational kernel is started and the data is transferred to the host sequentially for each pair of initial matrices (the kernels are executed sequentially). This allows the program to perform calculations and transmit to the host the results of previous calculations in parallel.

Auto Transfer Simple Loop. Similar to Simple Loop, but instead of explicit data transfer, SYCL data automatic control was used. In this case, only the total operation time is measured, since SYCL does not measure data transfer times separately with automatic control.

3.2 Ways to Optimize Computational Kernels

Computational kernels are implemented for the operation of matrix multiplication and matrix multiplication by a vector.

Simple Kernel. The classic loop used to multiply matrices by the CPU. The only optimization is to change the traversal order so as to streamline the memory access.

Local Memory Kernel. Classic block algorithm taken from CUDA documentation [18]. At each step, two fragments of the original matrices are placed in the local memory of the working group (shared memory in terms of CUDA), the intermediate result is calculated and also placed in the local memory. In the case of multiplication by a vector, the local memory is not needed for the left matrix. The block size was calculated automatically based on accelerator characteristics.

Private Memory Kernel. It is similar to Local Memory Kernel, but the intermediate result is placed directly into private (register) memory.

3.3 Platform for Testing

The following hardware configuration was used:
CPU: Intel (R) Xeon (R) E5440 @ 2.83 GHz, 64bit, 8 cores
GPU: GeForce GTX 1060 6 GB
max compute units: 10
max work group size: 1024
local memory size: 48 K
CUDA 9.2.106

3.4 Test Results

It was possible to use only one implementation - ComputeCPP. HipSycl failed to install on target machine. Despite the presence of the Docker image, the distributed HipSycl components turned out to be sensitive to the version of the operating system. Theoretically, HipSycl can be compiled from source files, but it has many dependencies, and their resolution was impossible in our conditions.

Test results are visualized in the form of graphs of the dependence of the execution time on the matrix size (N), and the execution time is divided by the number of elements in the left matrix (N ^ 2). The time scale is logarithmic, the lower the better. The size of the left matrix varied from 1 × 1 to 2048 × 2048.

To begin with, let's compare different implementations of computing kernels with a simple data transfer strategy on device for matrix and matrix multiplication(see Fig. 1) and matrix and vector multiplication (see Fig. 2).

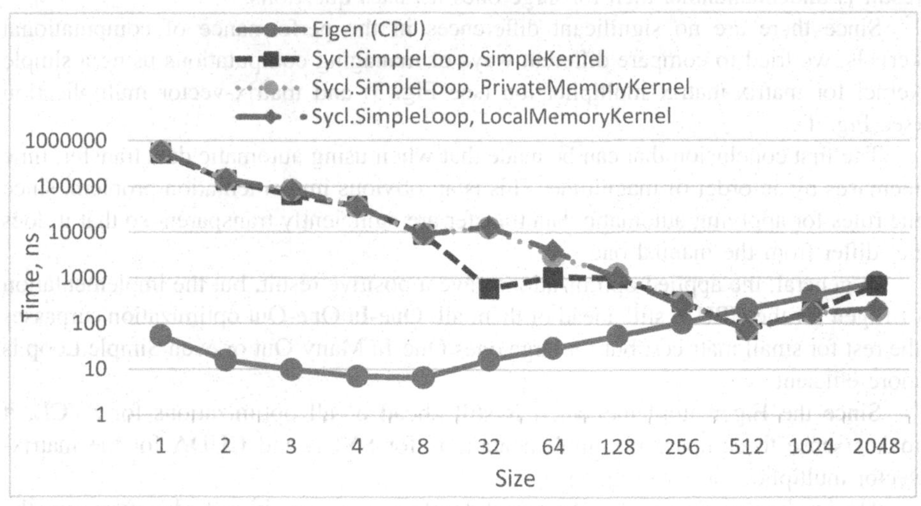

Fig. 1. Test results of a simple data transfer strategy for matrix-matrix multiplication

Surprisingly, none of the optimization yielded a significant performance increase compared with the implementation on the CPU, and the naive implementation on the

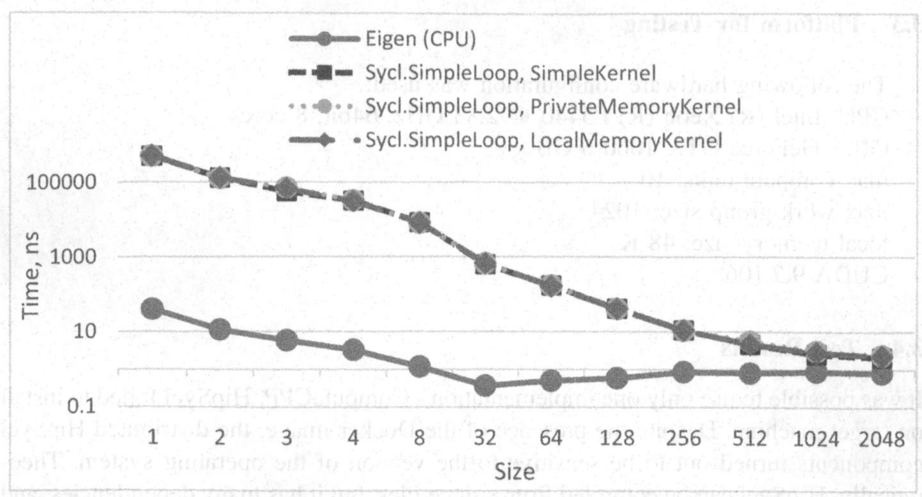

Fig. 2. Test results of a simple data transfer strategy for matrix-vector multiplication

SYCL turned out to be noticeably faster for 32×32 and 64×64 matrices, which coincides with the restriction on the size of the working group. The optimizer was good enough to compete with typical manual optimizations, but did not provide good overall performance.

What is even more surprising, it was not possible to obtain a significant superiority over the implementation on the CPU, even for large matrices. If for small matrices this result is understandable, then for large ones it raises questions.

Since there are no significant differences in the performance of computational kernels, we tried to compare different ways of managing computations using a simple kernel for matrix-matrix multiplication (see Fig. 3) and matrix-vector multiplication (see Fig. 4).

The first conclusion that can be made that when using automatic data transfer, time increases by an order of magnitude. This is an obvious implementation problem, since the rules for applying automatic data transfer are sufficiently transparent so that it does not differ from the manual one.

In general, the applied optimizations gave a positive result, but the implementation of Eigen for the CPU is still ahead of them all. One-In One-Out optimization surpasses the rest for small matrices, but for large ones One-In Many-Out or even Simple Loop is more efficient.

Since the Eigen implementation is still ahead of all optimizations for SYCL, it makes sense to compare the implementations for SYCL and CUDA for the matrix-vector multiplication (see Fig. 5).

The implementation for CUDA also did not receive a significant advantage over the implementation of Eigen for the CPU, which can be explained by the active use of SIMD - instructions in the implementation of Eigen and a relatively weak graphics card, but compared to SYCL this implementation is 1–3 orders of magnitude faster.

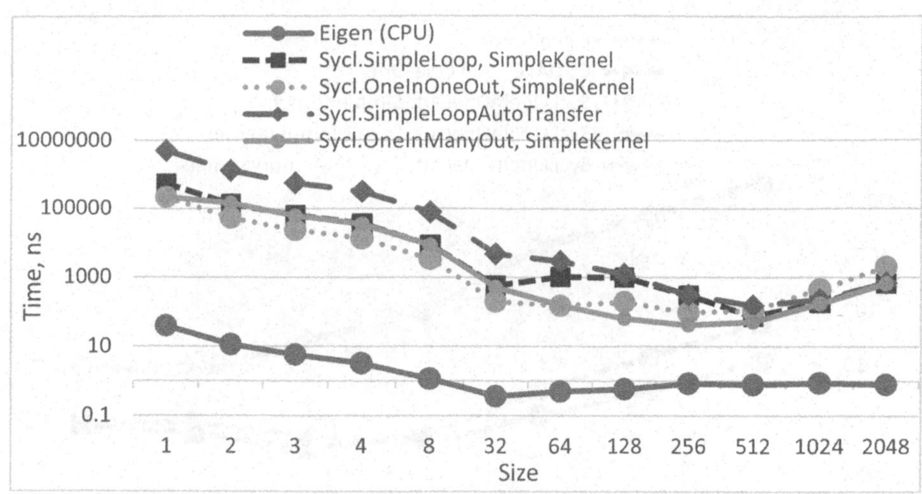

Fig. 3. Test results with different data transfer strategies for matrix-matrix multiplication

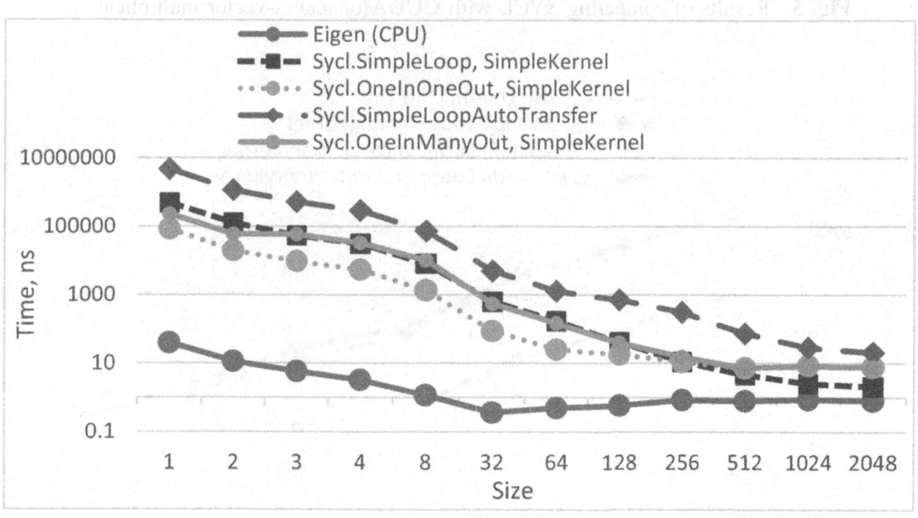

Fig. 4. Test results with different data transfer strategies for matrix-vector multiplication

To localize the problem, an independent comparison was made between the calculation time(see Fig. 6) and the data transfer time(see Fig. 7).

The data transfer time for SYCL is higher by 3–4 orders of magnitude, and the kernel execution time is only one order of magnitude. The low performance of the kernel is quite understandable, since the developers have added support for PTX only recently. But it is difficult to explain such high costs of data transfer. The implementation should simply call the functions supplied by the driver, and there should be no additional costs.

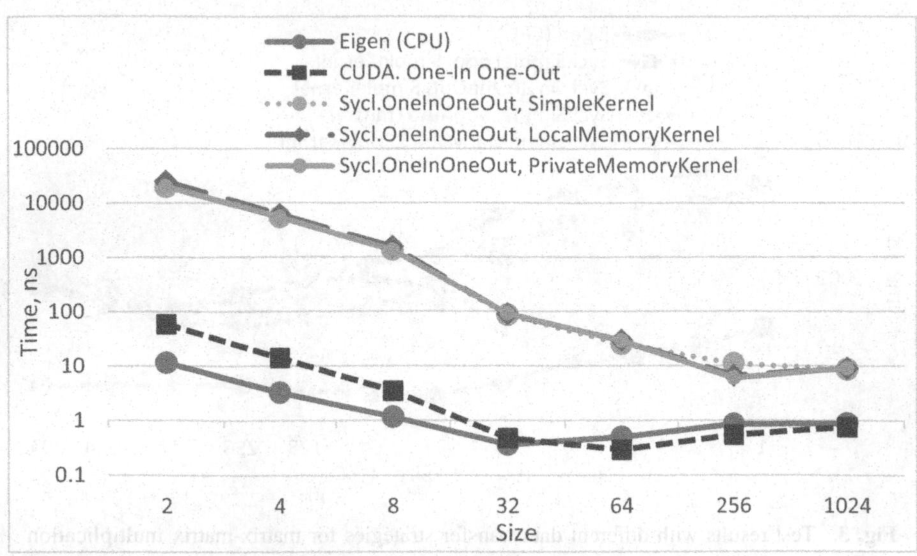

Fig. 5. Results of comparing SYCL with CUDAfor matrix-vector multiplication

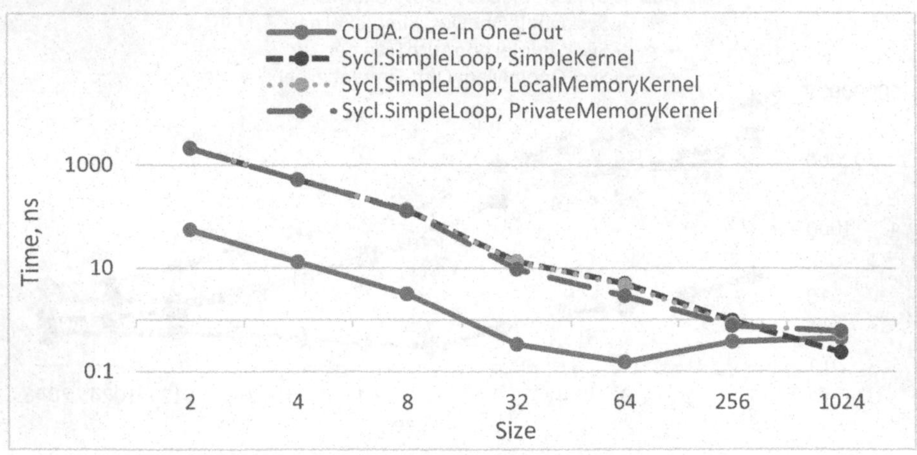

Fig. 6. Calculation time

3.5 Recommendations for Choosing Development Tools for Parallel Computing Accelerators

As shown by the test results, the ComputeCPP implementation does not yet provide sufficient performance for SYCL, at least on NVIDIA graphics cards. The HipSYCL implementation has not been tested, but in any case it does not fully comply with the specification.

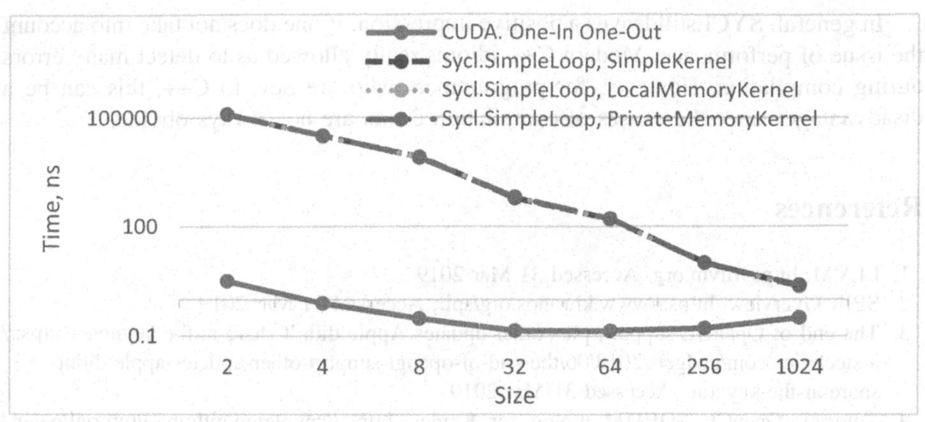

Fig. 7. Transfer Time

Thus, at the moment, the main development tools for heterogeneous computing are still CUDA and OpenCL. However, the development of SYCL is fast, and for long-term projects it makes sense to consider the possibility of switching to SYCL, especially since all these tools are based on similar abstractions.

In some cases, tools for languages other than C and C++ may also be useful. But since they usually translate the code into CUDA or OpenCL, they do not provide significant advantages, apart from the ability to preserve the homogeneity of the development ecosystem.

In addition, one should not discount calculations on the central processor - in many cases, proper use of SIMD instructions (or libraries using them) allows to achieve good performance, which is especially noticeable against the background of reducing data transfer costs.

4 Conclusion

In this paper, we considered promising development tools for portable programs for parallel computing accelerators, in particular, the new standard for heterogeneous programming SYCL and its main implementations.

The ComputeCpp implementation for SYCL has been tested. The results show that this implementation works correctly, but still does not provide sufficient performance for practical use, at least for NVIDIA graphics cards. However, given that this implementation is a beta version, and NVIDIA support was added quite recently, there is hope for rapid changes for the better.

The implementation of HipSycl has not been tested due to installation difficulties, but it looks more suitable for practical use at present. Since it does not compile the source code on its own, but simply wraps the CUDA and HCC implementations into a single interface, there is no reason for a serious decrease in performance compared to the original tools. However, this still requires verification.

In general, SYCLstill leaves a positive impression, if one does not take into account the issue of performance. Modern C++ idioms really allowed as to detect many errors during compilation. However, for programmers who are new to C++, this can be a disadvantage, since the causes of compilation errors are not always obvious.

References

1. LLVM. https://llvm.org. Accessed 31 Mar 2019
2. SPIR Overview. https://www.khronos.org/spir. Accessed 31 Mar 2019
3. The end of OpenGL support, plus other updates Apple didn't share at the keynote. https://arstechnica.com/gadgets/2018/06/the-end-of-opengl-support-other-updates-apple-didnt-share-at-the-keynote. Accessed 31 Mar 2019
4. Tutorial: OpenCL SGEMM tuning for Kepler. https://cnugteren.github.io/tutorial/pages/page1.html. Accessed 31 Mar 2019
5. ROCm project page. https://github.com/RadeonOpenCompute/ROCm. Accessed 31 Mar 2019
6. Keryell, R., Reyes, R., Howes, L.: Khronos SYCL for OpenCL. In: Proceedings of the 3rd International Workshop on OpenCL – IWOCL 2015 (2015). https://doi.org/10.1145/2791321.2791345
7. Parallel Algorithms for Better Performance. https://devblogs.microsoft.com/cppblog/using-c17-parallel-algorithms-for-better-performance. Accessed 31 Mar 2019
8. SYCL. https://www.khronos.org/sycl. Accessed 31 Mar 2019
9. hipSYCL project page. https://github.com/illuhad/hipSYCL. Accessed 31 Mar 2019
10. triSYCL project page. https://github.com/triSYCL/triSYCL. Accessed 31 Mar 2019
11. Keryell, R., Yu, L.Y.: Early experiments using SYCL single-source modern C++ on Xilinx FPGA. In: Proceedings of the International Workshop on OpenCL – IWOCL 2018 (2018). https://doi.org/10.1145/3204919.3204937
12. Codeplay: ComputeCpp. https://www.codeplay.com/products/computecpp. Accessed 31 Mar 2019
13. Alea GPU. http://www.aleagpu.com/release/3_0_3/doc/introduction.html. Accessed 31 Mar 2019
14. Hybridizer. http://www.altimesh.com. Accessed 31 Mar 2019
15. SpirNet project page. https://github.com/Philip-Trettner/SpirvNet. Accessed 31 Mar 2019
16. Rust (programming language). https://en.wikipedia.org/wiki/Rust_(programming_language). Accessed 31 Mar 2019
17. Storublevtcev, N., Korkhov, V., Beloshapko, A., Bogdanov, A.: Application Porting Optimization on Heterogeneous Systems. In: Gervasi, O., et al. (eds.) ICCSA 2018. LNCS, vol. 10963, pp. 25–40. Springer, Cham (2018). https://doi.org/10.1007/978-3-319-95171-3_3
18. CUDA C Best Practices Guide. https://docs.nvidia.com/cuda/cuda-c-best-practices-guide/index.html#shared-memory. Accessed 31 Mar 2019

Localization of Text in Photorealistic Images

Grishkin Valery[(✉)], Ebral Alexander, and Iakushkin Oleg

Saint-Petersburg State University, St.Petersburg 199034, Russia
v.grishkin@spbu.ru

Abstract. Detection and localization of text in photorealistic images is a difficult, and not yet completely solved, problem. We propose the approach to solving this problem based on the method of semantic image segmentation. In this interpretation, text characters are treated as objects to be segmented. In this paper proposes the network architecture for text localization, describes the procedure for the formation of the training set, and considers the algorithm for pre-processing images, reducing the amount of processed data and simplifying the segmentation of the object "background". The network architecture is a modification of well-known DeepLabv3 network and takes into account the specifics of images of text characters. The proposed method is able to determine the location of text characters in the images with acceptable accuracy. Experimental results of assessing the quality of text localization by the IoU criterion (Intersection over Union) showed that the obtained accuracy is sufficient for further text recognition.

Keywords: Text localization · Semantic segmentation · Convolution neural network

1 Introduction

Photorealistic images containing text information comprise a large part of the multimedia content presented on the Internet. These include real photos and videos, in which there are titres, pictures with inscriptions, signs, ads, etc. Automatic detection and reading of text from photorealistic images is an important part of systems such as machine translation based in images, video indexing, robot control, internal navigation, autonomous driving, and other systems that process visual information.

For high-quality recognition of text placed over natural images of the scene, it is necessary to separate the text from a rather complex background, in other words, to segment the image. Normally, the problem of text recognition of a scene is solved in two stages—the stage of detection and localization of text and the stage of textual content recognition [1–3]. There are two approaches to localizing and reading text from photorealistic images.

In the first approach, heuristic features such as HOG [4], MSERs [5], wavelet features [6] or Stroke Width transforms [7] are used to localize text areas. Text recognition is carried out at the second stage using a sliding window and one

S. Misra et al. (Eds.): ICCSA 2019, LNCS 11622, pp. 825–834, 2019.
https://doi.org/10.1007/978-3-030-24305-0_63

of classifiers such as SVM [8] or k-Nearest Neighbor [4,9]. This approach shows good results, but is based on heuristics and requires fine tuning of a large number of parameters depending on the properties of the processed images.

The second approach is based on the localization of text areas using deep neural networks. The paper [1] describes a text detection model that uses a fully convolutional deep neural network to identify text areas. Then the images of the identified areas of the text are passed on to the input of other deep neural networks that perform text recognition. A known system [3] detects text using a convolutional network within a sliding window, which is represented in several resolutions. Character-by-character text recognition is performed in a small window that slides over the identified text area using a CNN-based classifier. In a large number of papers on this topic, various modifications of convolutional neural networks are used, both for localization and for text recognition. In these works, the result of localization are the parameters of the rectangles that limit the text areas. In other words, the result of localization is a set of bounding boxes. At present, works have appeared in which systems are proposed that simultaneously detect and recognize text in images of natural scenes [10,11]. These systems successively localize the boundaries of the text areas and immediately recognize the text content of the found areas.

In this paper, we also use a deep convolutional neural network to localize the text. Unlike traditional text localization methods, we suggest using the semantic segmentation method. This method allows achieving high-quality segmentation of various objects on a complex background [12,13]. The methods of semantic segmentation are good in localizing objects representing closed and sufficiently large areas of the image. However, text characters in most cases consist of relatively thin lines and occupy a small area. Therefore, it is not possible to use neural networks designed for segmentation of large objects directly for text localization. However, it is possible to modify the architecture of well-proven deep convolutional neural networks for working with images containing text characters.

2 Convolution Neural Network for Text Localization

Quality of segmentation of objects is estimated by criterion of IoU (Intersection over Union). Currently, the DeepLabV3 neural network [14] shows the best segmentation results. For this network, IoU criterion reaches 77% on the PASCAL VOC 2012 data set [15]. Therefore, we chose architecture of this network as the basis for developing a new network for symbol segmentation.

2.1 Network Topology

Figure 1 shows the proposed topology of network for text localization. This topology is similar to the topology of DeepLabv3 network. It contains sequential convolutional layers with average pooling. Network output unit performs atrous spatial pyramid pooling (ASPP).

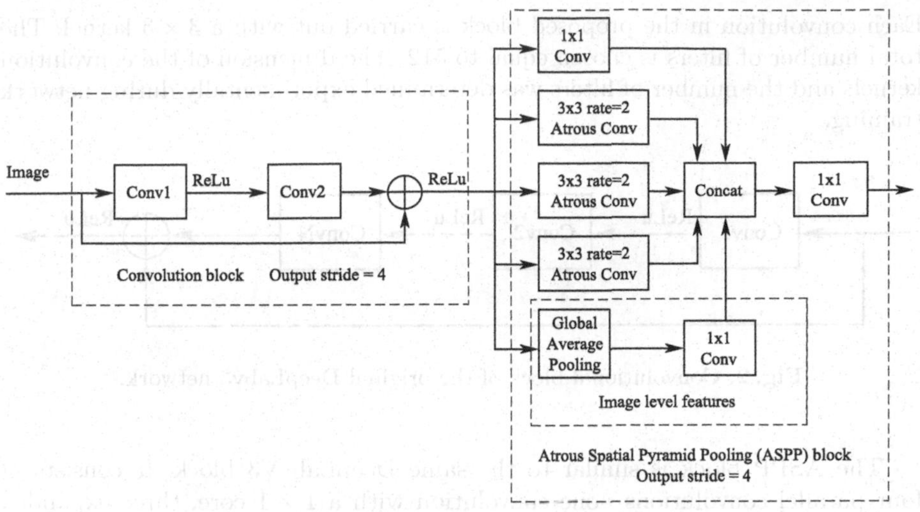

Fig. 1. Topology of network for text localization.

The ASPP block uses several parallel layers of extended convolutions with different spatial steps (atrous rate) between convolution weights. These expanded convolutions allow you to increase the perceptual field without reducing the spatial dimension. This block also calculates image level features. These low-level features are obtained by processing the output of the convolutional block using global average pooling. The result of the pooling is then processed by convolution 1×1. Output features of all five branches are combined and passed through a 1×1 convolution. The resulting image at the output of the ASP block is the segmentation mask.

Convolution of the original DeepLabv3 network is configured so that output stride i.e. the value of the ratio of the resolution of the input image to the resolution of the output image equals 16. This approach is not valid for text segmentation because the geometric structure of text symbols is not preserved. Considering these differences, as well as the fact that the text symbols are of a simpler geometric structure than the objects of the PASCAL VOC 2012 dataset, we suggest reducing the output stride to 4.

Each convolutional block of the original DeepLabv3 network contains two image paths: a short and a long one - through several consecutive convolutions. This allows us not to lose the data that turned into zero at convolutions. This property is useful for presenting text, since the loss of part of the fine lines that make up the text can affect the overall quality of segmentation. Usually for segmentation of complex objects of many classes several blocks of the structure shown in Fig. 2 are used. To ensure the output stride value of 4, we suggest using only one block of this type. The proposed block contains only two consecutive convolutions, to the outputs of which the activation function ReLu is applied, followed by averaging pooling with a 4×4 window and a shift parameter of two.

Each convolution in the proposed block is carried out with a 3 × 3 kernel. The total number of filters is chosen equal to 512. The dimension of the convolution kernels and the number of filters was determined experimentally during network training.

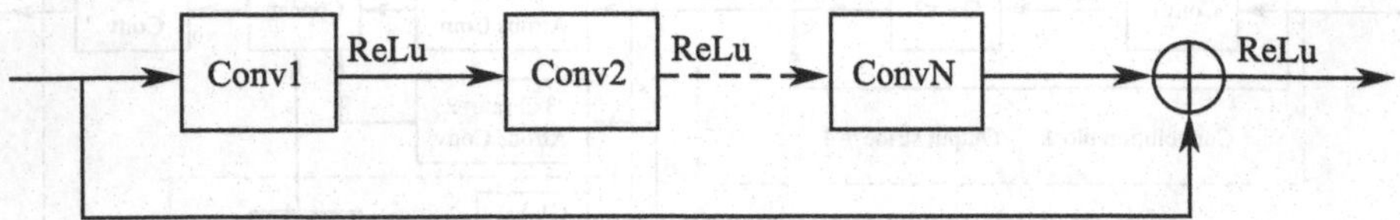

Fig. 2. Convolutional block of the original DeepLabv3 network.

The ASPP block is similar to the same DeepLab V3 block. It consists of four parallel convolutions—one convolution with a 1 × 1 core, three expanded convolutions with a 3 × 3 core, and has an image level features calculation unit. The difference is that for extended convolutions, the spatial steps between the convolution weights have been reduced. We chose the following values of atrous rates—2,4, and 6, while in the original network their values were—6,12, and 18. We apply triple reduction in rate because the text consists of relatively thin lines. Note that convolution with a 3 × 3 kernel and a maximum rate of six covers a line width of 15 pixels, which seems sufficient for text localization. Like in the original network, we combine the resulting feature maps and pass them through convolution 1 × 1.

2.2 Dataset

To train the proposed network, a pre-marked dataset of photorealistic images containing text is required. Specialized datasets, such as ICDAR2013 [16], SVT [17] or similar, are commonly used to develop and test text detection and recognition systems. However, these sets have no areas marked in the image that contain only text symbols. In addition, there are no Cyrillic characters in all these data sets. Currently, only one public dataset is known that is suitable for the subject area—Chars74K [18]. However, the quantity and quality of images, as well as annotations of the text in them, are quite low.

Thus, to apply the semantic segmentation method for text detection, we created our own dataset. This set is generated on the basis of a set of a sufficiently large number of existing fonts, which take into account various options for displaying characters of a given alphabet. When generating a set, we formed the text, which was then superimposed, with a certain level of transparency, in the photorealistic image. The text itself can be of any size, color, and angle of inclination, displayed in one or several fonts, and located anywhere in the image.

The text overlay algorithm to the original image is as follows: we divide the image into 4 blocks and superimpose the pre-formed text with the specified transparency to each image block. The position and orientation of the text in the block is randomly selected.

To generate text, we used lower case letters of the Cyrillic alphabet, numbers, and common punctuation marks ('.', ',', ';', '-', ':', '!')—49 characters overall. The text generation algorithm randomly selects characters from this alphabet and then forms a long string of several words. The length of each word is chosen randomly from the range of lengths of Russian words. The number of words in a long string is chosen randomly in the range of 1 to 40. The text block in each image is printed with one of 30 standard TrueType fonts. The font type and its size and color are all selected randomly. It should be noted that the text color is ensured to differ from the background in brightness. If a word in a long string is outside the block, it is truncated, and the new text line of the block begins with the next word.

As background images, 5000 photorealistic images that do not contain text are used. Usually text symbols shade the background and differ from it in brightness. The Fig. 3 an example of the generated image for our data set.

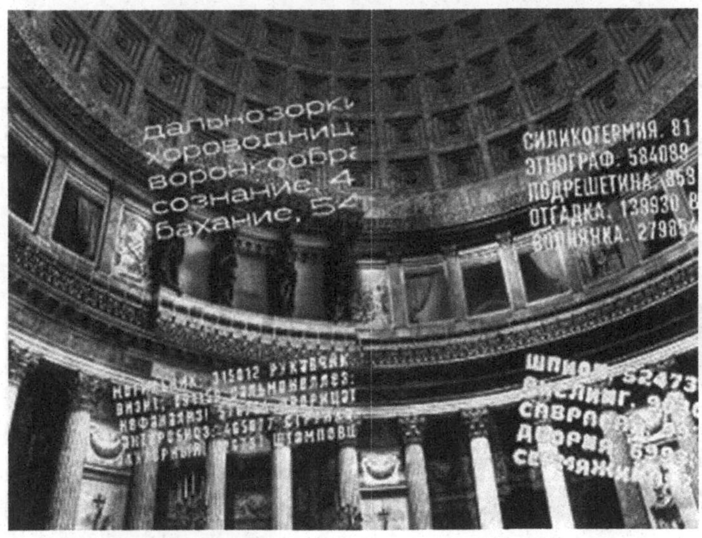

Fig. 3. An example of the generated image.

Together with the text overlay procedure, two masks are also created. These masks are used to markup the generated dataset. The first mask is a binary image of white text on a black background. The second mask is a grayscale image of the same text, where the brightness of the symbol corresponds to the position of the symbol in the alphabet. We use the first mask for binary segmentation between the text and the background, and the other mask for multi-class segmentation of character type vs. background.

2.3 Preprocessing

The main purpose of the preprocessing is to try to reduce the variability of the background and highlight areas in the image whose brightness is different from the background.

Before serving to the input of the neural network, we convert the original color image to grayscale. Then, using the Canny operator on this halftone image, we search for the boundaries of the brightness differences. Since the text is different in brightness from the background, this allows highlighting the borders of the characters. At the same time, all other rather sharp differences in brightness in the halftone image are also highlighted. The generated binary image of all boundaries is processed using the morphological dilation operation. Then, element-wise multiplication of the resulting binary mask by a halftone image is performed. This processing allows for filtering out most of the background, keeping just information about the brightness near the borders, which simplifies the task of separating the background borders from the text borders. Figure 4 shows the structure of the preprocessing algorithm. Figure 5 shows an example of image processing using the proposed algorithm.

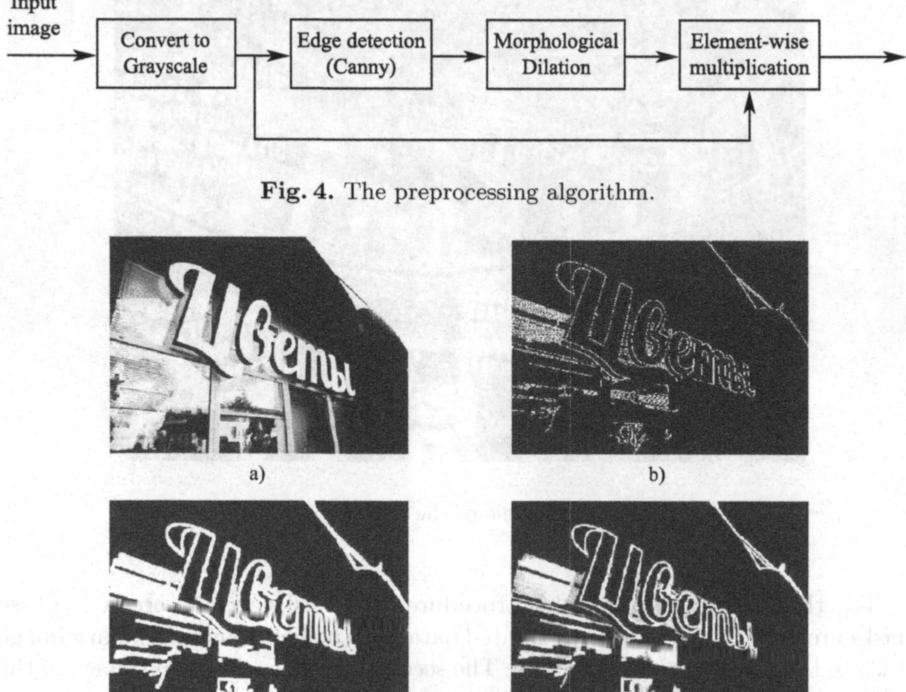

Fig. 4. The preprocessing algorithm.

Fig. 5. The preprocessing stages: (a) the original image; (b) the mask of borders; (c) the mask of borders after morphological dilation; (d) the result of element-wise multiplication.

The proposed preprocessing algorithm simplifies the segmentation of the "background" class, which is usually diverse and therefore requires large computational costs for network training. Segmentation of a background consisting of zero-brightness pixels requires less computation.

3 Experimental Results

The proposed neural network is implemented in Python using the TensorFlow machine learning library for the GPU platform. Software for generating the necessary dataset is also implemented in the Python language. We trained our network model using 4000 training images and evaluated it against 1000 verification images from the generated dataset. The localization quality is evaluated by the metric IoU (Intersection over Union).

We explored two approaches to the segmentation of images containing text. In the first approach, the network was trained to recognize two classes—background and text. In the second approach, the network was trained to recognize 50 classes: 49 characters and background.

When training networks, we used the batch normalization procedure, and cross-entropy as a function of losses. The following condition serves as the criterion for stopping the training:

$$\mathrm{IoU}_i - \mathrm{IoU}_{i-1000} < 0.01,$$

where IoU_i the average metric value obtained during training, i is the current iteration number.

For binary segmentation (background vs. text), the learning rate was chosen experimentally and amounted to $5 \cdot 10^{-3}$. A larger coefficient led to a drop in accuracy, and a smaller one—to an increase in the training time, but at the same time, the accuracy did not increase.

For multi-class segmentation (background vs. symbols), it was found out that the learning rate used for binary classification is too high. Therefore, the new coefficient was taken an order of magnitude less, which increased the training time, but at the same time, the growth of the metric was more stable. The remaining parameters of training did not change.

Figure 6 shows the process of training the network for segmentation of the background vs. the text, while Fig. 7 shows training process for segmentation of background vs. symbols. All of these charts show the change of the IoU metric value during network training.

For binary segmentation, the maximum value of the metric over the training set for the background was 94.8%, while the value of the same metric for the text was 58.6%, with average of 76.7%. For multi-class segmentation, the average maximum value of the metric was much less and amounted to 47.6%.

Figures 8 and 9 show the results of binary and multi-class segmentation for the image shown in Fig. 5, respectively. Segmentation was performed using the proposed trained neural networks. Note that in the case of background vs. symbols segmentation, the accuracy drops significantly. However, both approaches can be combined and used to clarify the results of each other.

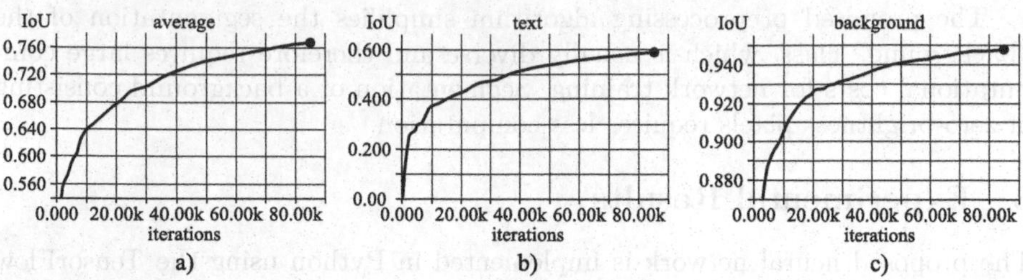

Fig. 6. Background vs. text segmentation. Changing IoU metrics during training: (a) the average value of the metric; (b) metric value for the text class; (c) metric value for the background class.

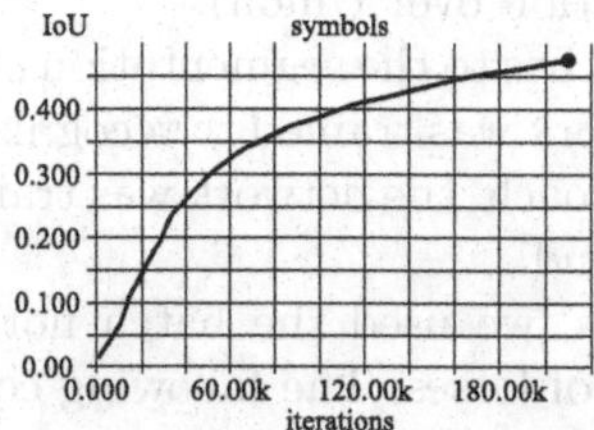

Fig. 7. Background vs. symbols segmentation. Changing average IoU metrics during training.

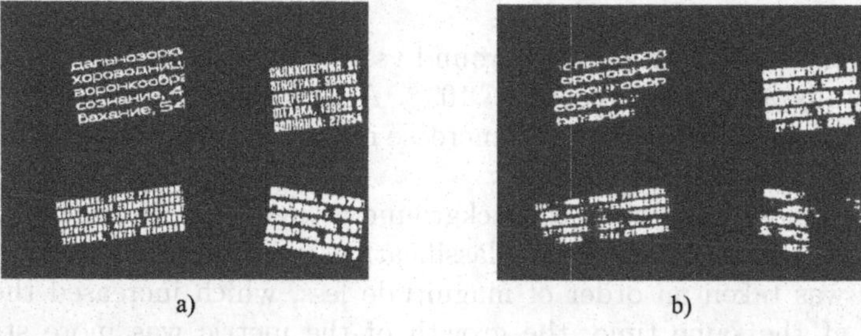

Fig. 8. An example Background vs. text segmentation: (a) real mask; (b) predicted mask.

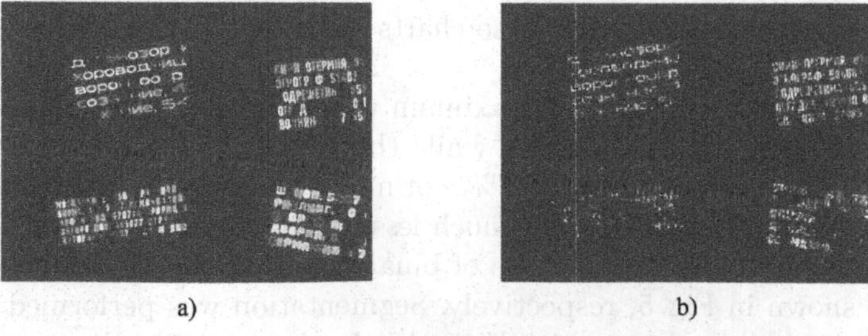

Fig. 9. An example Background vs. symbols segmentation: (a) real mask; (b) predicted mask.

4 Conclusion

In this paper, we applied the semantic segmentation method to detect and localize text in photorealistic images. Deep neural networks that implement this method are designed to localize and recognize large objects in an image, but cannot be used for text segmentation. Therefore, we propose a modification of the well-known network DeepLabV3, which showed good results of semantic segmentation. Unlike the original network, our modified neural network keeps the geometric structure of text characters into the feature maps. To reduce the computational cost of network training, we also propose the image preprocessing algorithm that simplifies background segmentation.

Known datasets that are used for both semantic segmentation and text detection are not suitable for semantic segmentation of text characters. Thus, to apply the semantic segmentation method for text localization, we created our own dataset.

The proposed neural network is implemented using the TensorFlow machine learning library with support for GPU computing. The quality of the localization of the text characters and the background is evaluated experimentally by the metric IoU. With the validation data set, the value of this criterion reaches 78%, which is sufficient for further processing of the segmented image using OCR systems.

Acknowledgment. The authors acknowledge Saint-Petersburg State University for a research grant 39417687.

References

1. Gupta, A., Vedaldi, A., Zisserman, A.: Synthetic data for text localisation in natural images. In: 2016 IEEE Conference on Computer Vision and Pattern Recognition (CVPR), pp. 2315–2324. IEEE, Las Vegas, NV (2016). https://doi.org/10.1109/CVPR.2016.254
2. Liao, M., Shi, B., Bai, X., Wang, X., Liu, W.: TextBoxes: A fast text detector with a single deep neural network. In: 31st AAAI Conference on Artificial Intelligence, pp. 4161–4167. AAAI, San Francisco (2017)
3. Jaderberg, M., Simonyan, K., Vedaldi, A., Zisserman A.: Reading text in the wild with convolutional neural networks. Int. J. Comput. Vis. **116**(1), 1–20 (2016). https://doi.org/10.1007/s11263-015-0823-z
4. Wang, K., Babenko, B., Belongie, S.: End-to-end scene text recognition. In: 2011 International Conference on Computer Vision, pp. 1457–1464. IEEE, Barcelona, Spain (2011). https://doi.org/10.1109/ICCV.2011.6126402
5. Neumann, L., Matas, J.: A method for text localization and recognition in real-world images. In: Kimmel, R., Klette, R., Sugimoto, A. (eds.) ACCV 2010. LNCS, vol. 6494, pp. 770–783. Springer, Heidelberg (2011). https://doi.org/10.1007/978-3-642-19318-7_60
6. Grishkin, V.: Document image segmentation based on wavelet features. In: 2015 Computer Science and Information Technologies (CSIT), pp. 82–84. IEEE, Yerevan, Armenia (2015). https://doi.org/10.1109/CSITechnol.2015.7358255

7. Epshtein, B., Ofek, E., Wexler, Y.: Detecting text in natural scenes with stroke width transform. In: 2010 IEEE Computer Society Conference on Computer Vision and Pattern Recognition, pp. 2963–2970. IEEE, San Francisco, CA (2010). https://doi.org/10.1109/CVPR.2010.5540041
8. Yao, C., Bai, X., Shi, B., Liu, W.: Strokelets: A learned multi-scale representation for scene text recognition. In: 2014 IEEE Conference on Computer Vision and Pattern Recognition, pp. 4042–4049. IEEE, Columbus, OH (2014). https://doi.org/10.1109/CVPR.2014.515
9. Wang, K., Belongie, S.: Word spotting in the wild. In: Daniilidis, K., Maragos, P., Paragios, N. (eds.) ECCV 2010. LNCS, vol. 6311, pp. 591–604. Springer, Heidelberg (2010). https://doi.org/10.1007/978-3-642-15549-9_43
10. Bartz, C., Yang, H., Meinel, C.: STN-OCR: A single neural network for text detection and text recognition. https://arxiv.org/abs/1707.08831. Accessed 20 Mar 2019
11. Busta, M., Neumann, L., Matas, J.: Deep TextSpotter: An end-to-end trainable scene text localization and recognition framework. In: 2017 IEEE International Conference on Computer Vision (ICCV), pp. 2223–2231. IEEE, Venice, Italy (2017). https://doi.org/10.1109/ICCV.2017.242
12. Chen, L., Barron, J.T., Papandreou, G., Murphy, K., Yuille, A.L.: Semantic image segmentation with task-specific edge detection using CNNs and a discriminatively trained domain transform. In: 2016 IEEE Conference on Computer Vision and Pattern Recognition (CVPR), pp. 4545–4554. IEEE, Las Vegas, NV (2016). https://doi.org/10.1109/CVPR.2016.492
13. Chen, L., Papandreou, G., Kokkinos, I., Murphy, K., Yuille, A.L.: Semantic image segmentation with deep convolutional nets and fully connected CRFs. https://arxiv.org/abs/1412.7062. Accessed 10 Mar 2019
14. Chen, L., Papandreou, G., Schroff, F., Adam, H.: Rethinking atrous convolution for semantic image segmentation. https://arxiv.org/abs/1706.05587. Accessed 20 Mar 2019
15. Pascal VOC data set mirror. https://pjreddie.com/projects/pascal-voc-dataset-mirror/. Accessed 27 Feb 2019
16. Karatzas, D. et al.: ICDAR 2013 robust reading competition. In: 2013 12th International Conference on Document Analysis and Recognition, pp. 1484–1493. IEEE, Washington, DC (2013). https://doi.org/10.1109/ICDAR.2013.221
17. The Street View Text Dataset (SVT). http://tc11.cvc.uab.es/datasets/SVT_1. Accessed 3 Mar 2019
18. The Chars74K dataset. http://www.ee.surrey.ac.uk/CVSSP/demos/chars74k/. Accessed 10 Feb 2019

Author Index

Printed in the United States
By Bookmasters